W9-ANG-241

American Jewish Year Book

The American Jewish Committee acknowledges with appreciation the foresight and wisdom of the founders of the Jewish Publication Society (of America) in the creation of the AMERICAN JEWISH YEAR BOOK in 1899, a work committed to providing a continuous record of developments in the U.S. and world Jewish communities. For over a century JPS has occupied a special place in American Jewish life, publishing and disseminating important, enduring works of scholarship and general interest on Jewish subjects.

The American Jewish Committee assumed responsibility for the compilation and editing of the YEAR BOOK in 1908. The Society served as its publisher until 1949; from 1950 through 1993, the Committee and the Society were co-publishers. In 1994 the Committee became the sole publisher of the YEAR BOOK.

American

Jewish

Year Book 2002

VOLUME 102

Editors

DAVID SINGER

LAWRENCE GROSSMAN

THE AMERICAN JEWISH COMMITTEE

NEW YORK

ISBN 0-87495-117-8

Library of Congress Catalogue Number: 99-4040

PRINTED IN THE UNITED STATES OF AMERICA
BY MAPLE-VAIL BOOK MANUFACTURING GROUP, BINGHAMTON, N.Y.

Preface

Volume 102 of the AMERICAN JEWISH YEAR BOOK covers the events of the year 2001. The first of three specially commissioned articles, Marilyn Henry's "Fifty Years of Holocaust Compensation" presents a coherent picture of the complicated process of securing some financial redress for Nazi depredations against the Jews. But, as Harris O. Schoenberg shows in "Demonization in Durban: The World Conference Against Racism," even as the blatant racial anti-Semitism of the Nazi era fades into history, anti-Israel bias, a more subtle form of Jew-hatred, seems to have taken its place. The third special article, "Census of U.S. Synagogues, 2001," by Jim Schwartz, Jeffrey Scheckner, and Laurence Kotler-Berkowitz, sounds a happier note. The first such census since 1936, it provides telling evidence of a diverse and dynamic American Judaism.

For Jews, 2001 was a year of momentous events, and all of them are covered in the YEAR BOOK's regular articles about Jewish life in the United States, Israel, and other countries around the world. Two related themes that surface in virtually all of these articles are the widespread impact of ongoing violence between Palestinians and Israelis, and the threat of international terrorism—especially in light of the horrific events of September 11, 2001.

Updated estimates of Jewish population are provided for the United States and for the world. Carefully compiled directories of national Jewish organizations, periodicals, and federations and welfare funds, as well as obituaries and religious calendars, round out the 2002 AMERICAN JEWISH YEAR BOOK.

We gratefully acknowledge the indispensable role played by Denise Rowe, our administrative assistant, in preparing the directories and the index, and the assistance of our colleagues, Cyma M. Horowitz and Michele Anish, of the American Jewish Committee's Blaustein Library.

THE EDITORS

Contributors

TOBY AXELROD: Correspondent, Jewish Telegraphic Agency and *Jewish Chronicle* (London); Berlin, Germany.

SERGIO DELLAPERGOLA: Professor and head, Division of Jewish Demography and Statistics, Avraham Harman Institute of Contemporary Jewry, Hebrew University of Jerusalem, Israel.

RICHARD T. FOLTIN: Legislative director and counsel, Office of Government and International Affairs, American Jewish Committee.

ELISE FRIEDMANN: Correspondent, Jewish Telegraphic Agency; Amsterdam, Holland.

THOMAS GERGELY: Professor, French literature, and director, Institute of Jewish Studies, Free University of Brussels, Belgium.

ZVI GITELMAN: Professor, political science, and Preston R. Tisch Professor of Judaic Studies, University of Michigan.

LAWRENCE GROSSMAN: Editor, AMERICAN JEWISH YEAR BOOK; associate director of research, American Jewish Committee.

RUTH ELLEN GRUBER: European-based American journalist and author, specialist in contemporary Jewish affairs; Morre, Italy.

GEORGE E. GRUEN: Adjunct professor, international affairs, Middle East Institute and School of International and Public Affairs, Columbia University.

MARILYN HENRY: Contributing editor, *ARTnews*; long-time reporter on Holocaust compensation issues, *The Jerusalem Post*.

LIONEL E. KOCHAN: Historian; Wolfson College, Oxford, England.

MIRIAM L. KOCHAN: Free-lance journalist and translator; Oxford, England.

LAURENCE KOTLER-BERKOWITZ: Senior project director, United Jewish Communities.

COLIN L. RUBENSTEIN: Executive director, Australia/Israel and Jewish Affairs Council; honorary associate, Monash University, Melbourne, Australia.

JEFFREY SCHECKNER: Research consultant, United Jewish Communities; administrator, North American Jewish Data Bank, City University of New York.

GEORGES SCHNEK: President, Jewish Museum of Belgium; former president, Jewish Central Consistory of Belgium; emeritus professor, biochemistry, Free University of Brussels, Belgium.

HARRIS O. SCHOENBERG: Founder and chairman, UN Caucus of Jewish NGOs; president emeritus, Center for UN Reform Education.

JIM SCHWARTZ: Research director, United Jewish Communities; director, North American Jewish Data Bank, City University of New York.

MILTON SHAIN: Professor, Hebrew and Jewish studies, and director, Kaplan Centre for Jewish Studies and Research, University of Cape Town, South Africa.

HANAN SHER: Senior editor, *The Jerusalem Report;* Jerusalem, Israel.

MURRAY GORDON SILBERMAN: Adjunct professor, Austrian Diplomatic Academy, Vienna, Austria.

BRIGITTE SION: Secretary general, CICAD, the Committee Against Anti-Semitism and Defamation; Geneva, Switzerland.

MEIR WAINTRATER: Editor in chief, *L'Arche,* the French Jewish monthly, Paris, France.

HAROLD M. WALLER: Professor, political science, McGill University; director, Canadian Centre for Jewish Community Studies, Montreal, Canada.

Contents

OTHER COUNTRIES

DIRECTORIES, LISTS, AND OBITUARIES

Special Articles

Fifty Years of Holocaust Compensation

By Marilyn Henry

At the close of the 20th century, a dramatic juncture of legal, political, moral, and economic pressures culminated in agreements that led to the greatest amounts of compensation for victims of Nazi persecution since the original German compensation programs of the 1950s. They came with demands and pleas to "secure a measure of justice" for the surviving victims. "For these victims, the approach of a new millennium takes on a uniquely poignant significance. We must not enter a new millennium—when the issues of today will begin to become ancient history—without completing the work before us," said Stuart Eizenstat, undersecretary of state and the Clinton administration's point man on restitution. "We must not enter a new century without completing the unfinished business of this century. We have a collective responsibility to leave this century having spared no effort to establish the truth and to do justice."[1]

There seemed to be no shortage of efforts. In the late 1990s, there was an unprecedented series of interrelated and often competing negotiations, audits, class-action lawsuits, and international commissions. They entangled governments, courts, lawyers, survivors' organizations, historians, nongovernmental organizations, agencies and institutions in a dozen countries, members of Congress, and national, state, and local regulators and public finance officers. There was a flurry of announcements, beginning in August 1998, that Nazi victims—primarily Jews—were expected to receive billions of dollars in settlements of claims from German, Austrian, Swiss, and French governments and enterprises.

As was the case in the 1950s, the demand for compensation in the 1990s raised awkward moral and material issues. The notion

---

[1]Closing Plenary Statement, London Conference on Nazi Gold, Dec. 4, 1997, http://www.stategov/www/policy__remarks/971204__eizen__nazigold.html.

that damages demand redress is universal, and the idea that perpetrators should not profit from murder is rooted in the Bible, the prophet Elijah challenging King Ahab: "Hast thou killed and also taken possession?"[2] But if life is priceless and the losses are incalculable, what amount of compensation, if any, is proper? If payments are, to some extent, symbolic gestures, what precisely are they gestures of? For the victims, restitution is a form of recognition of suffering; for the perpetrator, it is a settlement of claims.[3] In the original compensation talks, Jews had worried that payments would be confused with the expiation of the perpetrators. Two generations later, facing the German sentiment *"Gnade der späten"* (the "clemency" of postwar birth), they were concerned that the perpetrators' heirs and successors would refuse to acknowledge their moral debt for Nazi-era crimes.

In the 1950s, the circumstances were unprecedented—the Holocaust was a catastrophe of unimaginable horror and loss—and so were the demands. The insistence that direct compensation be paid to individual surviving victims, and to a state that did not exist at the time of the atrocities, was revolutionary. The compensation was intended primarily for one group of victims—Jews. And the arrangement itself was novel: A voluntary association of Jewish organizations—the Conference on Jewish Material Claims Against Germany (often called, simply, the Claims Conference)—negotiated with a sovereign state, West Germany.

"Holocaust compensation" is an unwieldy shorthand for a multifaceted array of payments and activities stemming from the material claims of World War II:

1. The payments to Nazi victims are known as indemnification, which is compensation for specific personal losses or damages. The original German indemnification program provided one-time settlements as well as monthly payments, known as pensions, for a variety of persecution-related damages, including harm to a victim's health or loss of professional opportunity.

2. Reparations are payments in money or materials from one nation to another for damages inflicted. Thus reparations generally

---

[2]I Kings 21:19.

[3]See Elazar Barkan, *The Guilt of Nations: Restitution and Negotiating Historical Injustices* (New York, 2000).

refer to the war-related debts of a defeated aggressor nation, and may entail a punitive element, as well.

3. Restitution is the return or recovery of identifiable assets, including machinery, real estate, business enterprises, and cultural properties that are restored to the original owners—nations, communities, institutions or individuals. (There were parallel claims for compensation in lieu of restitution for assets that could not be restored.) For Nazi-era properties, international Jewish organizations lodged claims after the war only against Germany and Austria for properties that were looted, confiscated, and "Aryanized." Restitution in Western Europe was a domestic matter; the states in the Soviet bloc did not believe in restitution. Since the collapse of communism, there have been claims to recover Jewish properties in Central and Eastern Europe. These have been fraught with legal and economic difficulties because Nazi-era claims compete with communist-era claims.

The language of compensation, in both the vernacular and legal meanings, fails to convey the uniqueness of the circumstances and the claims. The German term *Wiedergutmachung* is anathema to the Jewish community because it means "to make whole." Israel originally used the word "reparations" for its claim against Germany, but that term was unsuitable; the State of Israel technically could not seek reparations because it did not exist until after World War II, the event in which the damages were inflicted. Israel subsequently used the Hebrew term *shilumim* to refer to the goods that West Germany provided, in lieu of cash, under the 1952 Luxembourg Agreements.

The Holocaust has been called a compilation of crimes, and the redress has been spotty. Germany has paid some DM 100 billion in compensation. It is a substantial sum, but clouds the fact that tens of thousands of Nazi victims received only minimal payments, or were excluded from compensation programs altogether. The restitution of properties proceeded fairly successfully in Germany (first in West Germany, and, after the 1990 reunification, in the former East Germany), but abysmally in Central and Eastern Europe. And the plunder of cultural properties, which got significant attention from the Allied authorities right after the war, practically disappeared from view until its sudden reemergence at the end of the century.

ESTABLISHING THE PRINCIPLE

The first declaration of war by Nazi Germany was against the Jewish people, and it took a special form. Chaim Weizmann, then president of the Jewish Agency, told the Allies in 1945:

> Its aim was not conquest and enslavement, but the complete physical extermination of the Jews, the utter destruction of their spiritual and religious heritage, and the confiscation of all their material possessions. In executing their declaration of war, Germany and her associates murdered some six million Jews, destroyed all Jewish communal institutions wherever their authority extended, stole all the Jewish treasures of art and learning, and seized all Jewish property, public and private, on which they could lay their hands.[4]

Nazi Germany relentlessly expropriated the assets of German Jews through numerous measures after the enactment of the 1935 Nuremberg Laws, which lent a veneer of legality to the thefts of German and Austrian Jewish properties: special discriminatory taxes, blocked accounts, the "Aryanization" of property, and outright confiscations. In addition, Nazi restrictions and boycotts of Jewish businesses and the ejection of Jews from professions forced Jews to liquidate their possessions under duress, often at only a fraction of their value. Jews able to flee Germany before deportations began in 1941 were forced to pay a heavy "emigration" tax (*Reichsfluchtsteuer*). Jews also were compelled to pay the *Judenvermögensabgabe,* or JUVA, a property tax the Germans initiated after Kristallnacht in 1938, contending that, having "provoked" the outrage of the German people, the Jews had to pay for the damages.

Across Europe, the Nazis plundered the assets of the Jewish populations, communities, and institutions, as well as the assets—particularly the gold reserves—of the occupied nations. With the defeat of Hitler, all had restitution claims.[5] Restitution and reparations are matters for governments. Traditionally, governments

---

[4]Weizmann letter to the Allied Powers, Sept. 20, 1945, in Israel Ministry of Foreign Affairs, *Documents Relating to the Agreement between the Government of Israel and the Government of the Federal Republic of Germany* (Jerusalem, 1953), p. 10.

[5]In their January 1943 London Declaration, known officially as the "Inter-Allied Declaration Against Acts of Dispossession Committed in Territories Under Enemy Occupation or Control," the Allies warned that they "reserved the right" not to recognize property transfers in Axis-occupied territories, whether the transfers appeared to be legal, voluntary, or the result of looting. The declaration, however, was vague about the disposition of the confiscated property.

make claims against each other, on behalf of themselves and their citizens. When the Allies recovered certain identifiable assets after World War II, they restituted them to the countries of origin.[6] It was then that nation's responsibility to locate and return the property to the rightful owner. Materials subject to restitution included cultural properties, securities, and agricultural, industrial, and transportation equipment.[7]

International law was inadequate to address the unique circumstances confronting the Jewish victims. Weizmann said that Hitler's war against the Jews created a three-fold problem—of reparation, rehabilitation, and restitution. He demanded indemnification and compensation from Germany. He also called for heirless Jewish property to be turned over to the Jewish Agency, since that body was the official representative of the Jews and bore the cost of resettling Jewish refugees in Palestine.

The measures to aid and benefit Jewish victims of Nazi persecution were first established by the multilateral postwar reparations agreements and later by the Allied authorities in the Western zones in Germany. However, these measures were intertwined with, and subordinate to, the Allies' priorities of reconstructing Europe and preventing the spread of communism.

When the Allied governments attempted to recover assets that had been plundered by the Nazis, they focused on the theft of the gold reserves of the central banks of Nazi-occupied Europe, not on private property. Throughout the war, Germany had acquired gold as she occupied territory. In addition to gold from the occupied countries' national reserves, gold, silver, and valuables of all kinds were amassed through the systematic dispossession of private businesses and individuals, and in particular of the Jewish communities in Germany and elsewhere. In April 1945, the British Ministry of Economic Warfare and the Bank of England set the value of gold looted since 1939 at $545–$550 million. But this estimate was based primarily on information regarding government-

---

[6]Gold was treated separately, its restitution conducted by the Tripartite Gold Commission, established by the U.S., Britain, and France in 1946.

[7]*Plunder and Restitution: Findings and Recommendations of the Presidential Advisory Commission on Holocaust Assets in the United States* (Washington, D.C., Dec. 2000). The commission said it found no evidence that the United States monitored the recipient countries' compliance with their expected restitution responsibilities.

owned gold rather than private gold, and therefore understated the true total.[8]

The Allies kept their distance from the question of individual property claims. They said it was impossible to make individual restitution or satisfy individual claims except for very specific items whose origin was incontestable. Not only would the validity of claims be difficult to prove, the Allies reasoned, but the number of claims would likely be overwhelming.

Further, the Allies were confronted with millions of displaced people. Their primary concern was to be relieved of the burden of refugees, not to restore refugees' property rights. Special arrangements clearly had to be made for what the postwar governments called "non-repatriable refugees." These were stateless, destitute Jews, refugees from Germany, Austria, and other Nazi-occupied areas, as well as the survivors of concentration camps. They could not use the traditional mechanism to pursue their claims; they were unable or unwilling to make restitution claims through their former governments.

The Paris Agreement

When the Allies met at the end of 1945 to discuss reparations from Germany, they dealt with two sources of aid for refugees—funds derived from German assets, and the recovery of Jewish properties. Under the terms of Article 8 of the 1945 Paris Reparations Agreement, 18 nations agreed to allocate a total of $25 million for those "who suffered heavily at the hands of the Nazis and now stand in dire need of aid to promote their rehabilitation but will be unable to claim the assistance of any government receiving reparation from Germany."[9] The funds were to come from German assets in

---

[8]Foreign & Commonwealth Office General Services Command, History Notes No. 11, *Nazi Gold: Information from the British Archives* (London, Sept. 1996, rev. ed. Jan. 1997). This amount included some $223 million of Belgian gold and $193 million from Holland. According to historian Arthur L. Smith, in *Hitler's Gold: The Story of Nazi War Loot* (New York, 1989), Germany looted some $621 million in gold from the central banks of Europe.

[9]Those eligible were defined as "nationals or former nationals" of Nazi-occupied countries who had been incarcerated in Nazi concentration camps or camps erected by regimes "sympathetic to the National Socialists." In addition, refugees from Nazi Germany or Austria could obtain aid if they were unable to return to those countries "within a reasonable time because of prevailing conditions." Victims living in Germany and Austria were eligible for assistance "in exceptional cases in which it is reasonable on grounds of humanity

neutral states. Survivors would be assisted based on their needs, not on the size of their losses; and all needy survivors would be eligible for assistance, not only those from Germany. It was expected that $11 million would come from Switzerland and $14 million from Sweden, both neutral states that had traded with Germany.[10]

In addition, the Allies designated two other sources of funds for refugee assistance: nonmonetary gold found in Germany, and heirless property found in neutral countries. Although part of the Paris agreement, they were not "reparations," since, unlike German external assets, these properties once belonged to the victims themselves. There were untold assets that had belonged to people who had no living heirs. Nonmonetary gold referred to the Nazi war loot that the Allies recovered in Germany, but whose individual ownership could not be determined. The single most-valuable cache, uncovered in a cavern at the Merkers mine, contained jewelry, cigarette cases, silverware—and gold teeth that clearly had been taken from murdered inmates of concentration camps.[11]

Under the Paris accord, the neutral governments were to identify and forward the $25 million and the heirless assets to the Inter-Government Committee on Refugees, which later became the International Refugee Organization (IRO). In turn, the IRO was to allocate the funds to designated field agencies—in this case, the Jewish Agency and the American Jewish Joint Distribution Committee (JDC). Ninety percent of the $25 million and of the nonmonetary gold, and 95 percent of the heirless property was to be used to rehabilitate and resettle Jews. The remainder was to assist non-Jewish victims. This ratio reflected the reality that the overwhelming majority of those persecuted on political, racial or religious grounds were Jewish, and that the recovered funds were overwhelmingly Jewish in origin.

---

to assist such persons to emigrate and providing they emigrate to other countries within a reasonable period."

[10]Seymour J. Rubin and Abba P. Schwartz, "Refugees and Reparations," *Law and Contemporary Problems* 16, no. 3, Summer 1951, pp. 379–94. With the decision in Paris, the Allies linked their financing for refugee resettlement to the formidable political issue of how they would gain access to German property that was outside of Germany. The Allies' access to German assets located in Switzerland became part of a broader dispute between the Allies and Bern over Switzerland's relations with Germany and its obligations to restore Nazi-looted gold and to cede private German assets to the Allies.

[11]*Plunder and Restitution,* p. 98.

The restitution of identifiable property began in the German *Länder* (states) under the Occupation governments, although the measures taken in Bavaria, Baden-Württemberg, and Greater Hesse in the Western zone were independent of the Occupation authorities. The Allies began to pay serious attention to restitution after a limited program was initiated in Thuringia in the Soviet zone. In 1946, U.S. officials began to work on restitution laws with German representatives, but they were unable to orchestrate a restitution policy that had the support of the other Allies or the *Länder,* and that would cover all of Germany. There were disagreements over who would benefit from restitution and what properties would be eligible for recovery. German officials wanted to limit restitution to Nazi-seized property that was in public hands after the war. Jewish groups, however, with the support of the U.S., wanted to include private property. They also sought a legal presumption in the restitution measures that properties transferred after the Nuremberg Laws were not voluntary, but forced.[12]

There were also disputes over the use of heirless assets. Jewish groups maintained that a successor organization should use them for the rehabilitation and resettlement of Jews, but the British feared that Jewish organizations would use them to fund immigration into British Mandatory Palestine.[13] The Soviet Union, for its part, argued that heirless assets belonged to the state.

General Lucius Clay, the American military governor, acted unilaterally to break the impasse. In November 1947, he promulgated Military Government Law 59, entitled "Restitution of Identifiable Property." The law, limited to the American zone, was intended to "effect to the largest extent possible the speedy restitution of identifiable property . . . to persons who were wrongfully deprived of such property within the period from 30 January 1933 to 8 May 1945 for reasons of race, religion, nationality, ideology, or political opposition to National Socialism." By the deadline set for fil-

---

[12]The Jewish organizations were the American Jewish Committee, the American Jewish Conference, the Jewish Agency, the Joint Distribution Committee, and the World Jewish Congress.

[13]See Nehemiah Robinson, *Indemnification and Reparation, Jewish Aspects* (New York, 1944). For evidence that the Palestine issue was far more important to the British than the problem of displaced persons see Ronald W. Zweig, "Restitution and the Problem of Jewish Displaced Persons in Anglo-American Relations, 1944–48," *American Jewish History* 78, Sept. 1988, pp. 54–78.

ing claims—December 31, 1948—property worth close to $250 million in the American zone was restored to former owners, who lived in 60 countries throughout the world.[14]

In 1947, Jewish groups formed the Jewish Restitution Successor Organization (JRSO) to claim heirless property and the assets of dissolved Jewish organizations and communities.[15] On the basis of legal theories developed by Jacob and Nehemiah Robinson—Lithuanian-born brothers who were the intellectual force behind the push for reparations—the Jewish groups persuaded the U.S. political and military authorities to accept the principle that Jewish property in the American zone should be restituted to the survivors or their heirs. As for heirless property, which, under customary inheritance law, escheats to the state, the Jewish groups also won a victory: properties that had become heirless as a result of Nazi persecution, together with properties belonging to dissolved Jewish communities, were to be transferred to a Jewish trust organization that would use the proceeds for the relief and rehabilitation of the victims.[16]

However, the JRSO was not designated as the successor organization in the American zone until the summer of 1948, just a few months before the claims deadline at the end of the year. Benjamin B. Ferencz, a former Nuremberg prosecutor, was hired to run the JRSO in August 1948. "We had about three months, four months, in which to find staff, find funding, train staff, locate the property, submit the claims," he later recounted. Investigators were dispatched to every real-estate registry in Germany with instructions to make note of any property transferred since 1933 that listed a Jewish name. "About the day of the filing deadline, we loaded all the claims into a U.S. army ambulance, which I had requisitioned somewhere, and drove it up the claims center and filed, I think it

[14]Benjamin B. Ferencz, "Restitution to Nazi Victims—A Milestone in International Morality," in Harry Schneiderman, ed., *Two Generations in Perspective* (New York, 1957), p. 302.

[15]The JRSO operated only in the U.S. zone. Similar agencies subsequently were named as successor organizations in the British and French zones, but the JRSO enjoyed an especially advantageous position because the American authorities were more sympathetic than its allies to Jewish claims.

[16]Others had developed similar restitution proposals, among them Sir Herbert Emerson, director of the Inter-Governmental Committee on Refugees, and Dr. Siegfried Moses of the Association of Central European Immigrants in Palestine.

was 173,000 claims for 173,000 pieces of property in the American zone of Germany," he recalled.[17]

Property claims in postwar Germany entailed navigating a morass of military, civilian, Allied, and *Länder* rules and regulations. Each claim had to be negotiated with the current German possessor, or adjudicated by German administrative agencies and courts. "These proceedings, touching the private pocket-nerve of persons long in possession, encountered bitter opposition and hostility," Ferencz noted. The process was slow, and the JRSO later used bulk settlements with the *Länder* to collect cash to aid survivors.[18] All told, it recovered more than DM 220 million.[19]

AGREEMENTS WITH GERMANY AND AUSTRIA

Indemnification laws also were established in some of the *Länder* under the Occupation authorities, but they "differed considerably and none of them was satisfactory," according to Nehemiah Robinson.[20] The most comprehensive and uniform laws were those in the *Länder* in the American zone, promulgated in August 1949, shortly before the Federal Republic of Germany (FRG) was founded. But even these were insufficient. "We had a rather inferior German law, which had been passed by the state of Bavaria, under pressure from the American government, to provide compensation for false imprisonment, the time spent in the concentration camps," according to Ferencz.[21] The original compensation for deprivation of liberty (*Schaden an Freiheit*), based on the earnings, at that time, of a lower-class laborer, was a one-time payment of DM 150 per month of internment—or DM 5 a day. In the British zone, compensation was provided to former residents of Germany, primarily for the loss of liberty, but no such measures were enacted in the French zone. When the Western Allies and West

---

[17]Transcript of interview with Benjamin B. Ferencz, Oct. 21, 1994, U.S. Holocaust Memorial Museum Oral History Library.

[18]Ferencz, "Restitution to Nazi Victims," p. 302.

[19]Saul B. Kagan and Ernest H. Weisman, *Report on the Operations of the Jewish Restitution Successor Organization, 1947–1972* (New York, 1975), p. 4.

[20]Nehemiah Robinson, *Ten Years of German Indemnification* (New York, 1964), p. 22.

[21]Transcript of interview with Benjamin B. Ferencz, Apr. 1971, Hebrew University of Jerusalem Oral History Library.

Germany drafted agreements in 1952 toward ending the occupation, the FRG agreed to enact a uniform federal compensation law that was at least as favorable as that in the American zone.

In the interim, the new State of Israel had sent a diplomatic note to the four occupying powers—the United States, Great Britain, France, and the Soviet Union—seeking compensation from Germany. "When the victorious Allies at the end of the war allocated the reparations due from Germany, the Jewish people had as yet no *locus standi* [legal standing] in the community of sovereign nations," Israel, then three years old, pointed out in its note of March 12, 1951. "As a result, the claims, though morally perhaps stronger than those of any other people that had suffered at the hands of the Nazis, went by default. The time has come to rectify this omission." Between 1939 and 1950, nearly 380,000 Jews had come to Israel as refugees from, or survivors of, the Nazi-conquered territories. "Israel has made itself responsible for the absorption and rehabilitation of the survivors of that catastrophe," the note said. "The State of Israel regards itself as entitled to claim reparations from Germany by way of indemnity to the Jewish people." It asked for $1.5 billion, which it calculated as the cost of resettling the Jewish immigrants from the Nazi-occupied countries. However, Israel cautioned, "No indemnity, however large, can make good the loss of human life and cultural values or atone for the suffering and agonies of the men, women and children put to death by every inhuman device."[22] The Soviet Union simply ignored the Israeli note, and the Western Allies suggested that Israel deal directly with Germany, which left the nearly bankrupt Israel with little choice.

At the same time, there were overtures back and forth between the first chancellor of the FRG, Konrad Adenauer, and Jewish groups concerning redress for Nazi crimes.[23] They culminated in Adenauer's 1951 speech, entitled "Attitude Toward Jews," delivered

---

[22]Israel Ministry of Foreign Affairs, *Documents Relating to the Agreement Between Israel and Germany,* pp. 20–24.

[23]Adenauer was said to be motivated by religious and moral convictions, as well as by his government's self-interest, because the West—primarily the Americans—expected the FRG's "reconciliation" with the Jews. The chancellor's first gesture toward the Jews came in a November 1949 interview with the German Jewish paper *Allgemeine Wochenzeitung der Juden in Deutschland.* The chancellor offered DM 10 million to Israel as "an immediate sign of Germany's determination to redress the wrongs done to the Jews throughout the world." Israel did not respond, but the World Jewish Congress issued a statement say-

in the German Parliament on September 27—Rosh Hashanah eve. Adenauer said that Germany was responsible for material compensation and restitution to Jewish victims of Nazism.

> The federal government and with it the vast majority of the German people are conscious of the immeasurable suffering that was brought to bear on the Jews in Germany and in occupied territories during the period of National Socialism. The great majority of the German people abhorred the crimes committed against the Jews, and had no part in them. During the time of National Socialism, there were many Germans who, risking their own lives for religious reasons, obeying the commands of their conscience, and feeling ashamed that the good name of Germany should be trodden upon, were prepared to help their Jewish compatriots. But unspeakable crimes were perpetrated in the name of the German people, which impose upon them the obligation to make moral and material amends, both as regards the individual damage which Jews have suffered and as regards Jewish property for which there are no longer individual claimants .... The Federal Government is prepared, jointly with representatives of Jewry and the State of Israel, which has admitted so many homeless Jewish refugees, to bring about a solution of the material reparation problem, in order to facilitate the way to a spiritual purging of unheard-of suffering.[24]

Nahum Goldmann, longtime president of the World Jewish Congress, noted the significance of Adenauer's initiative:

> What was truly revolutionary was the fact that the new Germany was to make global restitution to the Jewish people as a whole to help it secure a new life and establish new institutions in the devastated communities of Europe. According to international law, the Jewish people was not at war with Germany, since only sovereign states can wage war. To ask reparations for this people was as audacious as it was ethically justified.[25]

---

ing that "the German state and people must acknowledge their solemn obligation to redress the wrongs inflicted on the Jewish people and to make such reparations as would enable the survivors to rebuild their lives in Israel and elsewhere in freedom and security."

[24]Although Adenauer deserves much credit for the compensation program, it was proposed originally in Germany by Kurt Schumacher, the head of the opposition Social Democratic Party. Further, German compensation for Jewish victims lagged behind benefits and services for former Nazi functionaries, and had less public support. According to a survey of German public opinion conducted by U.S. Occupation authorities, in December 1951, compensation for Jews was supported by 68 percent of the population. It trailed far behind support for German war widows and orphans (96 percent); people who suffered damage by bombing (93 percent); and "refugees and expellees," meaning ethnic Germans who had been expelled, primarily from the Sudetenland (90 percent).

[25]Nahum Goldmann, *The Autobiography of Nahum Goldmann: Sixty Years of Jewish Life* (New York, 1969), p. 251.

The Claims Conference

One month after Adenauer's declaration, representatives of 23 voluntary Jewish organizations from the West and the State of Israel, substantially the same groups that made up the JRSO, met in New York for a "conference on Jewish material claims against Germany."[26] The conference was convened by Goldmann.

"Israeli Foreign Minister Moshe Sharett (Shertok) approached me with the suggestion that as chairman of the Jewish Agency for Palestine, I should invite the leading Jewish organizations of the United States, the British Commonwealth, and France to a conference to support Israel's demands and create a body to execute them," Goldmann wrote in his autobiography. "I did so because I realized that Israel would not be able to negotiate with Germany alone and that a body as representative as possible of all Jews, whose authority both the Jewish public and the German Federal Republic could respect, would be required."[27] The participants decided to create the Conference on Jewish Material Claims against Germany (Claims Conference), to endorse Israel's claims, and to present additional ones on behalf of Jews outside Israel. The organizations agreed to negotiate with West Germany only about material claims—compensation and restitution—not moral claims.[28] Goldmann, who had excellent relations with Adenauer, was elected president, a position he would hold until his death in 1982. Jacob Blaustein of the American Jewish Committee, who had extraordi-

---

[26]The current membership of the Claims Conference remains essentially the same as the original founding membership, though one founding member, the Synagogue Council of America, is defunct, the Jewish War Veterans of the U.S.A withdrew in 1953, and survivor organizations—the American Gathering/Federation of Jewish Holocaust Survivors and the Center of Organizations of Holocaust Survivors in Israel—did not join until 1988. There is no specific representation of Jews from Central and Eastern Europe. The members are: Agudath Israel World Organization; Alliance Israëlite Universelle; American Jewish Committee; American Jewish Congress; American Jewish Joint Distribution Committee (JDC); Anglo-Jewish Association; B'nai B'rith International; Board of Deputies of British Jews; Canadian Jewish Congress; Central British Fund for World Jewish Relief; Conseil Représentatif des Institutions Juives de France (CRIF); Council of Jews from Germany; Delegación de Asociaciones Israelitas Argentinas (DAIA); Executive Council of Australian Jewry; Jewish Agency for Israel; Jewish Labor Committee; South African Jewish Board of Deputies; World Jewish Congress; World Union for Progressive Judaism (joined 1957); and Zentralrat der Juden in Deutschland.

[27]Goldmann, *Autobiography,* p. 255.

[28]For a detailed account, see Nana Sagi, *German Reparations: A History of the Negotiations* (Jerusalem, 1980).

nary access to key figures in the American government, was elected senior vice president.

The Claims Conference membership represented a broad spectrum of Diaspora Jewish life. "This was the first time where 23 Jewish organizations of divergent geographical and ideological coloration sat around one table for one objective that did not exist before," said Saul Kagan, who was the long-time director of the Claims Conference until his retirement in 1998. "There were people whose entire past public Jewish record was a record of public antagonism," he said, referring, for example, to the tensions between the World Jewish Congress and the American Jewish Committee, and those between the ultra-Orthodox Agudath Israel and the Reform movement's World Union for Progressive Judaism. "Even in the worst Nazi period there wasn't that type of a structural joining of forces and hands together."[29]

In January 1952, after stormy protests and emotional debates over whether it was acceptable to negotiate with West Germany, the Knesset, Israel's parliament, voted 61-50 to accept Chancellor Adenauer's invitation. "The debate raged in the whole Jewish world and the Jewish press, the main opposition coming from the two extremes of the political spectrum, the right-wing Herut-Revisionists, and the Left, i.e., Mapam and the communists, but also from large circles of religious Jewry, Mizrachi and Agudath Israel," according to S.J. Roth of the Institute of Jewish Affairs. "In fact, the split over this great moral issue stretched across all Jewish parties and communities."[30]

There were those who passionately opposed negotiations with the Germans, arguing that such talks were immoral and that any payment received would be "blood money." The conference countered that it would be immoral to allow Germany to enrich itself with Jewish property. There was nothing moral in relieving the perpetrator of the obligation to pay for injuries, Kagan said. "The concept was that whatever will come out of these negotiations is not going to be German philanthropy or charity or goodwill, but

---

[29]Transcript of interview with Saul Kagan, Dec. 10, 1971, American Jewish Committee Oral History Library, housed at the Dorot Jewish Division, New York Public Library.

[30]S.J. Roth, "West German Recompense for Nazi Wrongs: 30 Years of the Luxembourg Agreement," research report of the Institute of Jewish Affairs, in association with the World Jewish Congress, London, Nov. 1982, p. 19.

it will be in payment of legally established and legally anchored claims and demands."[31]

The Jewish-German negotiations opened in The Hague, under heavy security, on March 21, 1952. There were two parallel, coordinated sets of talks—one between the FRG and Israel, and the other between the FRG and the Claims Conference. "The Claims Conference is, in a sense, the trustee for a broad collective interest, acting on behalf of hundreds of thousands of survivors," Kagan said.[32]

In its opening statement, the Claims Conference delegation supported the claims of Israel "in respect of rehabilitation in Israel of victims of Nazi persecution." The Israeli claims bore no relationship to the Jewish material losses in Germany. The Claims Conference, in contrast, pursued compensation for individual victims for damages resulting from Nazi persecution, and a "global payment" for relief and rehabilitation of Nazi victims. Like the 1951 Israeli note, its demands came with a strong caveat. "We are ready to negotiate on certain claims of a material nature. But we want to make clear from the beginning that there can be no negotiation on moral claims," the Claims Conference said in its opening statement. It sought a uniform measure to cover all of the FRG that would also expand the scope of compensation for the surviving victims. As for claims for which there were no living owners or heirs: "The millions who have perished are, together with their survivors, the ones whose rights are at stake here. Though they are absent, their assets must not be abandoned. Germany should not retain any benefit from the thoroughness of the Nazi extermination program," the Claims Conference delegation said. It called for heirless and unclaimed Jewish property to accrue to Jewish organizations caring for the survivors.[33]

The negotiations, which began under tense conditions, were arduous. They almost collapsed when the German government offered Israel some $300 million, less than one-third of the Israeli

[31]Kagan interview, American Jewish Committee Oral History Library. These differences often led to confrontations, and some New York hotels, wanting to avoid turmoil, would not allow the Claims Conference to rent space for meetings.

[32]Saul Kagan, "Morality and Pragmatism: A Participant's Response," remarks at symposium, "*Shilumim* in the 1950s," Deutsches Haus of Columbia University, New York, Mar. 15, 1991.

[33]Claims Conference Delegation Statement at opening of negotiations with West Ger-

demand. The Israeli delegation broke off the talks, and the two principal German negotiators, Franz Boehm and Otto Küster, resigned to protest the unwillingness of their government to fulfill its promises. It required Adenauer's intervention to break the deadlock and meet the Israeli claim.

It was more difficult to reach an agreement on the global payment to the Claims Conference. The Germans objected to the conference's insistence on $500 million, based on an estimate of heirless assets; the Germans contended that the payment to Israel would discharge this obligation. They also said that the Claims Conference was not a representative body from a "legal point of view," and therefore the FRG could not undertake to make a global payment to it.[34] Goldmann refused to budge, saying it was immoral for Germany to retain Jewish property. Goldmann also reminded the German delegation that Adenauer, in his declaration, had invited representatives of the Jewish people to negotiate; there was no point in negotiating if the Germans decided from the start not to provide anything to the representatives of world Jewry. Further, Jewish organizations had spent millions of dollars on the relief and resettlement of Nazi victims living outside of Israel. To continue the welfare work and to reconstruct the institutions the Nazis destroyed, he argued, new sums had to be mobilized, and it was Germany's duty to help.[35]

Although the U.S. government was not a party to the talks, High Commissioner John J. McCloy quietly insisted that West Germany make restitution, even as others on the American side worried that forcing the FRG to undertake such a financial commitment would increase its dependence on American aid. McCloy reminded Chancellor Adenauer that the reconciliation of West Germany with the Jewish people was "so significant" for Germany's international position.[36]

---

many, Mar. 21, 1952, Claims Conference file no. 14597, Central Archives for the History of the Jewish People, Jerusalem.

[34]Sagi, *German Reparations,* pp. 143–44.

[35]Goldmann, *Autobiography,* p. 269.

[36]McCloy was convinced that German fulfillment of Jewish claims would help rehabilitate Germany's image among the American public and thus help pave the way for its acceptance as a credible American ally. See Thomas Alan Schwartz, *America's Germany: John J. McCloy and the Federal Republic of Germany* (Cambridge, Mass., 1991).

The Luxembourg Agreements

The Hague negotiations led to the Luxembourg Agreements of September 10, 1952. Under these, West Germany was to pay Israel DM 3 billion in goods and services over the course of more than a decade, to go toward the costs of absorbing refugees. The German agreements with the Claims Conference were "protocols"—so named because a voluntary organization could not sign a treaty with a sovereign state. Under Protocol I, West Germany was obliged to enact federal legislation providing direct compensation and restitution for individual victims of Nazi persecution. Under Protocol II, West Germany agreed to provide DM 450 million to the Claims Conference to aid Jewish organizations for the relief, rehabilitation, and resettlement of Jewish victims who lived outside of Israel. The payment was in recognition of uncompensated Jewish losses.[37]

Protocol I ultimately led West Germany to pay more than DM 100 billion in compensation. At the turn of the century, some 100,000 Nazi victims were still receiving monthly pensions, valued collectively at DM 1.2 billion a year, and the average monthly payment was about DM 1,000.[38] Although the FRG initially saw its responsibility as limited to compensation to its former citizens, the Claims Conference negotiated terms that added two other important groups of beneficiaries: stateless people and refugees living in the West.[39] Between 1953 and 1965, the West German government enacted three laws that established the basis for compensation for "victims of National Socialist persecution."[40] Under these

[37]West Germany's payments reflected two-thirds of Germany's obligation, as determined by these negotiations. East Germany would theoretically be responsible for the remaining one-third. However, the latter did not view itself as a successor state of the Nazi regime, and refused to pay compensation. Its liabilities for Nazi-era damages were not resolved until after the 1990 reunification of Germany, as described below.

[38]"State payments made by the Federal Republic of Germany in the area of indemnification," Jan. 2000, http://www.germanemb.org.il/messages/318.htm. The actual numbers of claimants from the period was not known, because individuals submitted multiple claims under different categories, such as deprivation of liberty, loss of property, and damage to health. As of 2000, about 40 percent of those receiving compensation lived in Israel, 20 percent in Germany, and 40 percent in other countries.

[39]Under German law, "stateless persons" referred primarily to Holocaust survivors who were in displaced-persons camps after World War II. "Refugees" were those who emigrated or who were deported from an area that was German on December 31, 1937.

[40]The word "victims" is significant, indicating a wider group than "survivors," since the latter could conceivably be limited to survivors of camps and ghettos.

laws, which were known as the *Bundesentschädigungsgesetze* (B.E.G.), individuals could file multiple claims for a variety of damages caused by Nazi persecution.[41] Some damages—such as deprivation of liberty—were compensated for with one-time payments. Others—primarily involving damage to health—resulted in monthly annuities called pensions.[42] Between October 1953 and December 1987, more than 4.3 million claims were submitted, and almost half, 2,014 million, approved.[43]

None of the compensation measures that would follow later neared the value of the pensions created by the German legislation under Protocol I. For Nahum Goldmann, however,

> more important than the financial significance of the Luxembourg Agreement is its moral significance. It established a precedent. Here for the first time a mighty nation had declared itself ready to make partial restitution for the wrong it had done a weaker people, and it had done this in response to an ethical imperative and the pressure of public opinion and out of its respect for moral law, not because of the force of a victor's military power. This agreement is one of the few great victories for moral principles in modern times.[44]

The indemnification laws were open-ended; West Germany did not set a ceiling on what it would pay or on the number of claimants it would try to satisfy, so long as they met the eligibility requirements. Compensation was not uniform, and there were "historic anomalies" in which victims who endured the same persecution received widely disparate treatment under the German laws. Compensation depended on prewar citizenship, the location and duration of incarceration, the extent and nature of the damages suffered, and assorted other criteria, including where the survivor lived after the war.[45] For four decades, compensation was limited

---

41The B.E.G. is referred to by its initials, and is not pronounced "beg."

42Early in the compensation program, victims faced traumatic medical examinations by German or German-approved physicians to establish that their injuries were related to persecution and that they therefore were eligible for pensions for damage to health. There is evidence that victims abandoned claims rather than submit to the exams, and that physicians were exceptionally rigid before affirming that injuries were related to persecution.

43http://www.germanemb.org.il/messages/318.htm.

44Goldmann, *Autobiography,* p. 276.

45Country of origin made a significant difference. Former German citizens, for instance, were entitled to pensions for damage to professional advancement. A German lawyer and a Polish lawyer who each survived the same concentration camp and emigrated to the U.S.

to victims living in the West; there were no benefits available to those behind the Iron Curtain.

There was a separate procedure for citizens of Western European nations who returned to their home countries after the war. They were not eligible for direct payments from West Germany. Instead, Bonn negotiated a series of bilateral agreements with 11 Western European states in the 1950s and 1960s, whereby the FRG made payments to each state with the understanding that that state would, in turn, provide compensation to the Nazi victims among its population.

Adenauer's commitment to compensation encountered political and administrative resistance in Germany, including from members of his own political party, the Christian Democratic Union (CDU). This was apparent from the outset. The Bundestag vote to ratify the Luxembourg Agreements was 238-34, with 86 abstentions. It was the opposition Social Democratic Party that voted unanimously in favor of the agreements, while 39 members of Adenauer's CDU abstained.[46]

The implementation of the laws was widely criticized by the Claims Conference and by German parliamentarians for being too rigid. "In no other area of law are the administration and courts so narrow-minded, sometimes heartless, so petty, or do they act in such a hairsplitting and quibbling fashion," complained Adolph Arndt of the Social Democratic Party in 1955. "Thus, a task whose generous fulfillment should move an entire people has fallen to the ink blotters and pen pushers."[47] The laws' novelty and intricacy added to the difficulty in implementation. "There is hardly any major provision of the law which, in one way or another, did not become controversial," said Nehemiah Robinson. Within the first decade of the indemnification laws, the German Supreme Court was called upon to render almost 2,000 decisions.[48]

---

after the Holocaust would be entitled to compensation for deprivation of liberty; but while the German lawyer also would be entitled to a lifelong pension for damage to his professional advancement, the Polish lawyer would not. The rationale was that the FRG had a greater responsibility to its former citizens.

[46]*New York Times,* Mar. 19, 1953.

[47]Christian Pross, *Paying for the Past: The Struggle Over Reparations for Surviving Victims of the Nazi Terror* (Baltimore, 1998), p. 46.

[48]Robinson, *Ten Years of German Indemnification,* p. 35. Many of the improvements in compensation resulted from lawsuits brought on behalf of Nazi victims by the United Restitution Organization, a legal-aid society supported by the Claims Conference.

Later Compensation Agreements

Subsequently, Germany enacted other compensation programs, but they were not as broad as the original law and did not carry the same legal rights. Instead of basing eligibility on the extent of persecution or the damages suffered, the new programs were predicated on the victims proving "hardship."

The first of these, the so-called Hardship Fund, came into effect under a 1980 agreement between the Claims Conference and the FRG. It dealt with the many Holocaust victims among the Jews who were able to leave the Soviet Union beginning in 1965. Once they arrived in the West, their Nazi-era experiences made them eligible for the German B.E.G. program. By that time, however, the deadlines for application had long passed. West Germany was unwilling to reopen the filing period for these victims. Instead, it agreed to finance this new Hardship Fund for victims who had not been able to obtain compensation earlier. It provides one-time payments of DM 5,000.

This fund changed the fundamental nature of the Claims Conference. Its original mission had been to negotiate for benefits for Nazi victims that would be provided under German legislation and administered by German agencies. The new fund, in contrast, was administered by the Claims Conference, which thus became an operating agency responsible for processing and approving (or disapproving) applications for compensation. By the end of 2000, more than 238,000 victims had received a one-time payment from this fund.[49]

Yet another fund for Jewish victims of Nazi persecution was created in conjunction with the 1990 reunification of Germany, and it was based on the premise that the former East Germany had not paid its share of compensation as a successor state to Nazi Germany. After intervention by the American government, German foreign minister Hans-Dietrich Genscher pledged that Germany would "seek, shortly after unification, to provide expeditious and satisfactory resolution of claims of Jewish victims of the Nazi regime against the German Democratic Republic."[50] That resolu-

---

[49]Claims Conference, *Annual Report 2000*, p. 17. The fund was only for Jewish victims. In 1981, West Germany created a fund of DM 100 million for hardship payments to non-Jewish victims who had previously been unable to receive compensation.

[50]President George H.W. Bush, statement accompanying submission of "2+4 Agreement"

tion came under Article II of the September 1990 "Agreement on the Enactment and Interpretation of the Unification Treaty," known informally as the "2+4 Agreement" (referring to the two Germanys and the four postwar Occupation powers).

Under Article II, Germany agreed to establish a fund for victims who had received little or no compensation previously. Known as the "Article II Fund," it is administered by the Claims Conference and provides monthly pensions of DM 500. These payments, however, were not a matter of right. Instead, victims had to prove "hardship," and the income of the applicant was taken into account as one of many factors determining eligibility. Like the Hardship Fund, it was available only to victims living in the West. Unlike B.E.G. pensions, it did not provide for cost-of-living adjustments. As of the end of 2000, more than 53,000 Jewish victims were receiving Article II pensions.[51]

Reunification also prompted Germany to negotiate bilateral agreements in the early 1990s with Poland, Belarus, the Russian Federation, and Ukraine. In the new political environment after the fall of the Berlin Wall, Germany provided a total of DM 1.5 billion for "Reconciliation Funds" in those states to compensate victims of Nazi persecution, both Jews and non-Jews.[52] These funds paid an average of DM 1,000 to each victim, primarily former forced laborers. "It is not that Jews are excluded from getting money," Kagan said. "But when you add the forced laborers, the fund is diluted, the per-capita claims are minimal."[53] That created another anomaly based on geography: Had the Jewish victim gone to the West, he would have been eligible for DM 5,000 from the Hardship Fund.

Even after these programs were launched, German compensation was still oriented to the West. By 1995, 50 years after the end of World War II, Nazi victims in Central and Eastern Europe remained ineligible for the German compensation programs. In the

---

to U.S. Senate, Sept. 25, 1990, included in *101st Congress, 2 Sess., Senate, Treaty Document 101-20.*

[51]Claims Conference, *Annual Report 2000,* p. 19.

[52]In 1997, a German-Czech agreement was reached under which Germany provided DM 140 million to finance projects to benefit Nazi victims.

[53]*Jerusalem Post,* Feb. 25, 1996. There were other complaints. For instance, given the long-term Soviet occupation of the Baltic nations, the Latvian Jewish victims resented being steered to Moscow for compensation. These victims contended they were twice injured: as Jews and as Latvians.

1950s, the FRG had refused to pay compensation to Nazi victims in the Eastern bloc, arguing that it did not have diplomatic relations with those states, and, in the era of cold-war politics, it was unwilling to make payments that would infuse cash into the communist world. By 1995, Germany simply was unwilling to undertake any new Nazi-era compensation commitments.

It was, however, compelled to act, amid publicity, beginning in 1996, that it was providing monthly disability pensions to Latvian veterans of the Waffen SS, but not to their victims.[54] Among the most powerful inducements for Germany to alter its policy was a dramatic May 1997 newspaper advertisement published by the American Jewish Committee in several American and international publications. It featured a photograph of a former Nazi officer alongside one of a Holocaust survivor. "Guess which one receives a pension from the German government," said the text of the ad. "If you guessed the survivor, you're wrong." In August, the AJC published another ad, displaying an "open letter" to German chancellor Helmut Kohl signed by 82 American senators who said it was "distressing" that Kohl's government "refused to provide any meaningful compensation to this forgotten group of Holocaust survivors." Under that pressure, Germany and the Claims Conference reached an agreement on a new fund for Jewish Nazi victims in Central and Eastern Europe. The fund, which commenced payments in 1998, had a lower rate of compensation than the others—DM 250 per month—and, like the Article II Fund, was based on the victims' "hardship."[55]

Property Restitution

The restitution of identifiable property in Germany, based on laws that had been developed in the occupation zones, was covered in Protocol I of the Luxembourg Agreements, and again, decades later, under the "2+4 Agreement."

The restitution legislation envisioned under Protocol I was not enacted for five years. Under the Federal Restitution Law (*Bun-*

---

[54]Ibid.

[55]Claims Conference, *Annual Report 2000,* p. 20. In 2000, more than 15,000 Jewish victims in Central and Eastern Europe received these monthly payments.

desrückerstattungsgesetz) of 1957, Nazi victims were eligible for compensation (in lieu of restitution) for a variety of assets—including bank accounts, securities, and household furnishings—that had been confiscated by Nazi authorities. The compensation paid did not bear a direct relationship to the value of the plundered assets. The law included stringent burdens of proof and, as in the case of indemnification claims, there is evidence that the legal requirements prompted victims to abandon claims for restitution in the belief that their applications were futile. West Germany paid some DM 3.9 billion for restitution claims, most of which were settled by 1987.[56]

With reunification, Germany again enacted restitution measures. These were concerned primarily with the reprivatization of property in the former East Germany that had been nationalized by the communist government. In a harbinger of what would come in Central and Eastern Europe, restitution of property was simply one aspect of a larger effort to overhaul and Westernize the economy and political system in the former communist nations. Nazi-era property claims competed against those of owners whose properties had been confiscated by the communist regimes. The 1990 restitution law, called the Act on the Regulation of Unclarified Property Questions, did not address the rights of Nazi victims, but dealt solely with acts of confiscation that occurred between 1949 and 1990. The law was changed, after the intervention of the Claims Conference, to include a presumption in favor of Nazi victims whose property was confiscated between 1933 and 1945.[57] The deadline for filing claims was tight—December 1992.

As had happened earlier in the American zone, when the JRSO became eligible to file property claims, a "successor organization" was given the right to claim unclaimed and heirless properties in the former East Germany. In this case it was the Claims Conference, which subsequently found itself fighting over the rights to properties against heirs who had missed the filing deadline. The Claims Conference subsequently developed a Goodwill Fund to share the proceeds of the properties with these heirs; as of 2000, the fund had paid out DM 136 million. The other proceeds, again

---

[56]http://www.germanemb.org.il/messages/318.htm.

[57]Claims Conference, *Annual Report 2000,* p. 21.

using the model developed by the JRSO, were used primarily for social services for survivors.[58]

The Case of Austria

Nazi victims from Austria found themselves in a unique position. Germany refused to provide compensation to them, contending that Austria was a successor state to the Nazis, and therefore Austria should pay. The birthplace of Hitler and Eichmann had welcomed Nazi troops with a wild reception in the 1938 Anschluss. "The only injuries the German soldiers received on entering Vienna was from the stems of the flowers that were enthusiastically thrown at them as they marched by," French ambassador Robert Coulondre wrote in his memoirs.[59] However, Austria refused to see itself as a Nazi successor state, and in this it had help from the Allies. In the 1943 Moscow Declaration, the Allies had anointed Austria as "the first free country to fall a victim to Hitlerite aggression."[60] Armed with the declaration, Austria refused to pay compensation. Its argument was that, as the first victim, it should be entitled to receive compensation, not required to pay it.

Austria's stand drew criticism at the time. "Whatever the validity of these arguments, there is one point that would seem to take precedence over all others, and this is that the issue is not primarily a legal one, and in view of the sum involved not even one of economics, but first and foremost a moral one," the *New York Times* said in a 1953 editorial. "Since the anti-Jewish atrocities were perpetrated not only by German but also by Austrian Nazis, it would seem that the Austrian government would act in its own best interest if it did its utmost to settle the issue in conformity with the conscience of the Western World, to which it belongs."[61]

In fact, the Austrians, until the turn of the 21st century, over-

---

[58]Ibid., pp. 22–23. The Goodwill Fund itself became a bone of contention, and in the late 1990s the Claims Conference was obliged to raise the proportion it shared with heirs.

[59]Robert Coulondre, *Von Moskau nach Berlin 1936–1939* (Bonn, 1950), p. 257.

[60]*Österreichische aussenpolitische Dokumentation, Sonderdruck: Österreichische Massnahmen zur Restitution und Entschädigung von Opfern des Nationalsozialismus* (Vienna, 2002), p. 7. The declaration was issued by the foreign ministers of the United States (Cordell Hull), the Soviet Union (Vyacheslav Molotov), and Great Britain (Anthony Eden).

[61]*New York Times*, Dec. 21, 1953.

looked the second paragraph of the Moscow Declaration, which stated: "Austria is reminded, however, that she has a responsibility, which she cannot evade, for participation in the war at the side of Hitlerite Germany, and that in the final settlement account will inevitably be taken of her own contribution to her liberation."

Austria paid only modest compensation to Nazi victims, and the government portrayed it as a charitable gesture, not an obligation. The payments were financed, in part, by DM 102 million that West Germany paid to Austria under the terms of their 1961 Bad Kreuznach Treaty, which settled their Nazi-era claims.[62] In lieu of a compensation program akin to the German B.E.G., Austria gave preferential treatment to Austrian-born Nazi victims, allowing them to participate in the national social-insurance pension program even if they were too young at the time of the Anschluss to have worked in Austria. These "social security" pensions became the primary means through which Austria compensated Jewish Nazi victims who reached retirement age. The Austrian government acknowledged that the pensions were not quite restitution. However, it said, "In many respects [the pension program] nevertheless contains important elements of restitution and compensation (preferential treatment) for victims of National Socialism with respect to pension rights."[63]

It would take years before Austria was finally jolted into examining its Nazi-era history. In a 1991 parliamentary debate, Jörg Haider, the leader of the right-wing Freedom Party who was also the governor of the province of Carinthia, praised the Nazis: "They had a sound employment policy in the Third Reich, which is more than your government in Vienna has managed," Haider told a Socialist member. Austrian chancellor Franz Vranitzky responded: "We must not forget that there were not a few Austrians who, in the name of this [Nazi] regime brought great suffering to others, who took part in the persecutions and crimes. We own up to all facts of our history and to the deeds of all parts of our people. As we take credit for the good, we must apologize for the

---

[62]Boris Sapir, "Austria," AJYB 1962, Vol. 63, pp. 362–63.

[63]Office of the Special Envoy for Restitution Issues Ernst Sucharipa, "Survey of Past Austrian Measures of Restitution, Compensation and Social Welfare for Victims of National Socialism," Oct. 2000, http://www.nationalfonds.parliament.gv.at/aef/deutsch/aufgPastMeasures.htm.

evil."[64] But it was not for another ten years, until January 2001—and after Austrian banks had been sued in the U.S.—that Austria, the U.S., and the Claims Conference would reach an agreement for expanded compensation and restitution measures for Austrian Jewish victims of Nazi persecution.

SWISS GOLD AND SLAVE LABOR

There was a new wave of interest in Holocaust compensation at the end of the century. In the final moments of the Clinton administration, in 2000, there was a race to conclude agreements with Austria and France on the restitution of Nazi-looted assets. Those came six months after an agreement with Germany to establish a Foundation for Remembrance, Responsibility, and the Future that was intended to be the "exclusive remedy" for all outstanding Nazi-era claims against the German government and German industry.

The roots of the new focus on compensation can be traced to 1995 and the events commemorating the 50th anniversary of the end of World War II. In Switzerland, President Kaspar Villiger apologized for his nation's treatment of the Jews during the Nazi era. At that time, Switzerland had instituted the distinctive "J" stamp on the passports of Jews, and had turned away more Jewish refugees than it had admitted. "Was the boat really full? Would Switzerland have been threatened with destruction if she had been considerably more open toward victims of persecution than she was? Did anti-Semitism in our country also play a part in this issue?" Villiger asked in a speech to the Swiss Federal Assembly on May 7, 1995. "Did we always do all that was humanly possible for the victims of persecution and those who had been deprived of their rights? . . . We made a wrong choice in the far too narrowly interpreted interest of our country. The Federal Council [the Swiss cabinet] deeply regrets this and apologizes for it in the knowledge that such a refusal is inexcusable in the final analysis."

A month later, a *Wall Street Journal* story revealed the daunting problems victims faced in attempting to recover Holocaust-era ac-

---

[64] *New York Times,* July 19, 1991.

counts in Swiss banks. Since the end of World War II, these banks "have cast a dismissive blanket of silence over the question of what they did with accounts opened by Jews and others who were then persecuted, and often murdered, by the Nazis," wrote reporter Peter Gumbel in "Secret Legacies: Heirs of Nazis' Victims Challenge Swiss Banks On Wartime Deposits."[65] That story opened a Pandora's box that led to class-action lawsuits, congressional hearings, historical commissions, and international inquiries into the fate of Holocaust-era assets, and settlements valued at billions of dollars.

Gumbel reported that the Swiss Bankers Association planned to establish a centralized, independent office to handle claims for accounts that had been sent to Switzerland to avoid Nazi confiscation. The World Jewish Congress soon met with Swiss government and banking officials to discuss the procedures for handling the dormant and unclaimed accounts. "Nobody really knows the exact amount that is being held in the Swiss banks or what has happened to the money. I have figures that range from tens of millions of dollars to billions of dollars, if you take into account currency fluctuations and accrued interest," said Israel Singer, secretary general of the World Jewish Congress.[66]

That claims process might have been the end of it. In February 1996, however, the bankers association released a survey indicating that the dormant accounts deposited in Swiss banks by foreign clients before 1945 were valued at $32.75 million. The chief executive of the largest Swiss bank, Robert Studer of Union Bank of Switzerland, said his bank had found the equivalent of $8.9 million, adding, "I think I can say in this case that the original amounts were peanuts."[67]

The association report incensed the WJC, which thought that the process had been one-sided and had not been transparent. The WJC turned to U.S. Senator Alfonse D'Amato, a New York Republican. "You have to figure out what kind of a lever to use if you have to move a very heavy rock. And it occurred to Israel Singer and myself that maybe that lever was the chairman of the Senate

---

[65] *Wall Street Journal,* June 21, 1995.
[66] Reuters, June 22, 1995.
[67] Ibid., Feb. 23, 1996.

Banking Committee, Alfonse D'Amato," recalled Edgar Bronfman, the WJC chairman.[68]

From that moment, events moved at a dizzying pace. In April 1996, D'Amato convened the first of what would ultimately be more than a dozen congressional hearings on the fate of Jewish Holocaust-era assets in Europe and held by European institutions. At the same time, D'Amato and the World Jewish Congress each began to release documents from the Safe Haven files in the U.S. National Archives. Operation Safe Haven had been a broad U.S. wartime intelligence operation to identify and track the flow of Nazi assets in neutral countries in order to deprive Nazis of resources for any possible resurgence after the war. The release of the Safe Haven documents was intended to bolster claims for dormant Jewish bank accounts; instead, they diverted the focus to a broad review of Switzerland's relations with Nazi Germany.[69]

This was no longer a controversy between the Swiss bankers and the WJC, a nongovernmental organization. Holocaust restitution had some muscular political backers. D'Amato threw the weight of his powerful committee behind the issue. And Bronfman, a leading fund-raiser for the Democratic Party, mobilized other political support—the White House. The Clinton administration began to show a serious interest in the dormant Swiss accounts after Bronfman "buttonholed Hillary back in 1996, and said I had to see him the next day . . . because the time for redress was running out," President Clinton recounted. "And I did as he said."[70]

The congressional hearings and the documents generated wide publicity, putting moral, economic, and political pressure on Switzerland, which depended on American markets for its powerful banking industry. In congressional hearings in 1996, Swiss of-

---

[68]*Los Angeles Times,* Apr. 13, 1997.

[69]The documents appeared to have been released for their effect, without any historical analysis or attempt to confirm the material or its significance. Some appeared to be profoundly damaging to Switzerland and its banks. Others were curiosities, such as the September 1996 media reports of a U.S. intelligence document indicating that Hitler's royalties from *Mein Kampf* may have been deposited in a Swiss bank account belonging to his publisher. When released to the media, the documents usually were declared "newly declassified," which added a sense of urgency, if not mystery, to the contents. However, much of the material had been declassified two decades earlier, but had failed to attract interest or attention.

[70]Clinton remarks delivered at the World Jewish Congress "Partners in History" dinner, New York, Sept. 11, 2000, distributed by the White House press office.

ficials and bankers pledged to resolve the accounts. "At the end of the day, not one penny that could have belonged to victims of the Holocaust will be held by Swiss banks," said Hans Baer, chairman of Bank Julius Baer and a member of the executive board of the Swiss Bankers Association.[71] In short order, the WJC, the World Jewish Restitution Organization, and the Swiss Bankers Association signed an agreement establishing an independent committee of Jewish and Swiss delegates to supervise a "forensic" audit of dormant accounts in Swiss banks. Paul Volcker, formerly chairman of the U.S. Federal Reserve, was named chairman of the committee soon afterward. The Swiss Parliament began to draft legislation to enable a "critical legal and historical review" of the scope and fate of Jewish assets that were received in Switzerland during World War II. The measure led to the creation of an international panel of historians to review Swiss wartime activity; bank-secrecy laws were modified to facilitate the inquiry.

More actors became involved in the fall of 1996, but they were not focused on individual assets. The British Foreign Office, for instance, released a report based on material in its archives saying that Switzerland turned over to the Allies only a small part of the Nazi gold it had bought during World War II. The U.S. State Department said it would conduct a "thorough and immediate study of the retrieval and disbursement of Nazi assets after the Second World War."

For individual victims, the key event was the October 1996 filing of a class-action lawsuit, in U.S. District Court in New York, against the dominant Swiss commercial banks, seeking $20 billion in damages and a full accounting of the deposits made by the survivors and their families. A second lawsuit was filed weeks later.[72] Once its banks were sued, the Swiss government became actively engaged. That elevated the matter to the diplomatic level, and an additional set of actors, with different interests, styles, and constraints, emerged and attempted to command the issue.[73]

---

[71]Baer made his remarks at the April 23, 1996, hearing of the D'Amato committee, at which he also rued the paradox of the flawed results of a 1962 search of Swiss banks for dormant accounts. "On the one hand, we are being asked to explain why there are any assets left at all, and on the other hand, we are being asked why there are so little assets left."

[72]Reuters, Oct. 24, 1996.

[73]Swiss officials, unschooled in American political style and initially naive about the significance of the issue in the U.S., made a series of blunders. On December 31, 1996, Jean-

Impact of the Eizenstat Reports

In the meantime, the U.S. historical inquiries also seemed to raise the stakes—again, not in a manner that directly aided victims. In two reports, published in 1997 and 1998, the U.S. examined the massive plundering by the Nazis of gold and other assets from conquered nations and individual victims. It was "no rogue operation," said Stuart Eizenstat, then the undersecretary of commerce, who led the 11-agency task force that produced the reports. "It was systematic, intentional, and essential to the financing of the German war machine, and they used neutral countries as banking and financial facilitators."

The 1997 report "documents one of the greatest thefts by a government in recorded history—the confiscation by Nazi Germany of an estimated $580 million of central bank gold, which would be worth about $5.6 billion in today's values, along with indeterminate amounts of other assets from individual victims of Nazi atrocities during World War II," said Eizenstat in a briefing, on May 8, at the release of the report. It was entitled "U.S. and Allied Efforts to Recover and Restore Gold and Other Assets Stolen or Hidden by Germany during World War II (Preliminary Study)."[74] Most of the looted gold, which Germany used to pay for its wartime imports, went to Switzerland. The report also found that despite postwar agreements with the Allies, Switzerland had resisted parting with Nazi-looted gold. Under the Washington Agreement of 1946, Switzerland agreed to turn over to the Allies some $58 million, which was far less than the $185–$289 million in looted gold that the U.S. estimated was in Swiss national accounts. The Swiss were "even less forthcoming" in providing the Allies with a nego-

---

Pascal Delamuraz, finishing his one-year rotation as Swiss president, said in a newspaper interview that demands for a $250-million fund to compensate Jews who lost assets in the Holocaust "amounts to being blackmailed and held to ransom." Delamuraz later said he had been misunderstood, but his retraction failed to placate Jewish groups, who then raised the prospect of a boycott of Swiss banks. The Swiss ambassador to the U.S., Carlo Jagmetti, was compelled to resign in January 1997 after a blunt cable to Bern was leaked to the media. "In light of the main goal, for once it is good advice for us to do things differently than what we are used to and to release the necessary means without bargaining, which gives a poor impression to the outside," he said in his cable. "Once again: We are faced with a war which Switzerland must conduct and win abroad and at home. Most of the opponents cannot be trusted."

[74]http://www.state.gov/www/regions/eur/970507eizenstat.html.

tiated share of the German assets in Switzerland, badly needed at the time both for the economic reconstruction of Europe and for refugee relief.

These new relevations raised serious moral issues. "In the unique circumstances of World War II, neutrality collided with morality. Too often being neutral provided a pretext for avoiding moral considerations," Eizenstat said. The Americans noted that while many of Switzerland's actions benefited the Allies, "without question, Switzerland and other neutral nations benefited from their trade and financial dealings with the Germans and helped prolong the war effort."[75]

The second report, released on June 2, 1998, looked at Germany's links with the other neutrals: Argentina, Portugal, Spain, Sweden, and Turkey. The report, entitled "U.S. and Allied Wartime and Postwar Relations and Negotiations With Argentina, Portugal, Spain, Sweden, and Turkey on Looted Gold and German External Assets and U.S. Concerns About the Fate of the Wartime Ustasha Treasury," essentially completed the 1997 report. "By illuminating the trade as well as the financing side of the equation, our two reports together provide a seamless web, a comprehensive and integrated view of the important part the wartime neutrals cumulatively played in the structure of the German war economy," Eizenstat said. Although the transactions between Nazi Germany and the neutrals were legal for much of the period, trade continued "in many cases well past the point where, from the Allied perspective at the time, there appeared to be a genuine threat of German attack."[76]

Eizenstat cautioned that the reports should not be seen as "finger-pointing." "I really view this as a sort of cleansing process for all of us—the Axis, the neutrals, the Allies—about the worst events and hidden events, particularly with respect to the confiscation of assets, that occurred in this century—a century we're about to leave," he said. "I think it's important before we do, and

---

[75]Ibid.

[76]http://www.state.gov/www/policy__remarks/1998/980602__eizenstat__nazigld.html. He noted that different factors shaped these nations' neutrality, including traditional avoidance of entanglements in European wars, fear of Nazi invasion or reprisal, and a desire to profit from the trade. Although the 1998 report concentrated on financial and trade matters, Eizenstat noted that these nations provided refuge to more than 250,000 Jews.

as we prepare for the next, that we be a little more just, a little more sensitive and that we have a clear understanding."[77]

In May 1997, Britain's foreign secretary, Robin Cook, announced that London would host an international conference on Nazi gold. It was the first of four extraordinary forums that elevated the question of restitution to the highest levels of governments. The London Conference, in December 1997, drew delegations of ranking officials and historians from 41 countries, the Vatican, and six nongovernmental organizations (NGOs). It was intended to provide a forum for discussion, not to apportion blame.

The conference focused on the facts relating to looted gold; a review of efforts to reimburse countries through the Tripartite Gold Commission and to compensate individual Nazi victims; and consideration of the possibility of providing additional funds for claimant countries or individuals.[78] The claimant nations had received, on average, about 60 percent of their claims. By 1997, the gold commission was ready to shut down, and had some $60 million in so-called "residual gold" in its coffers. In light of the new attention given to the losses of Nazi victims, the commission's triad—Britain, the U.S., and France—proposed that the residuals be used to aid survivors, and seven nations at the London conference agreed to do so.[79]

If national governments were interested in Nazi gold, victims of Nazi persecution had more personal concerns, including what had

[77]Ibid.

[78]The term "Nazi gold" is often used as shorthand for assets that the Nazis looted. In this context it refers primarily to the gold the Nazis took from the national treasuries of occupied countries.

[79]*Jerusalem Post,* Sept. 14, 1997. The residual gold financed the so-called "Nazi Persecutees' Relief Fund." The fund was flexible; donor countries could choose how their funds would be allocated. Nongovernmental organizations were eligible to receive money if they would use it to assist needy victims of Nazi persecution, or for relevant educational projects. The initial pledges were from Argentina, Austria, Britain, Croatia, Greece, and Luxembourg. The U.S., although not a claimant nation, also made a pledge. The gold conference opened two weeks after the first payments were distributed from a separate Swiss "humanitarian fund." Overseen by a board of Swiss and Jewish delegates, the Swiss private-sector fund was established in February 1997 as a goodwill gesture to aid needy Nazi victims. The first recipients were from the small survivor community in Riga, Latvia, whose members—like those elsewhere in Central and Eastern Europe—had not been eligible for compensation under earlier German programs. Riva Sefere, who survived a Nazi labor camp, received the first check. It was for $400. "What I really need is a washing machine, because all my life I had to do the washing by hand," she told reporters. "Unfortunately, this sum isn't even enough for a washing machine." *Los Angeles Times,* Nov. 19, 1997.

happened to their bank accounts, insurance policies, securities, and artworks. Some of these were on the agenda the following year, in December 1998, when the U.S. State Department, in conjunction with the U.S. Holocaust Memorial Museum, convened the Washington Conference on Holocaust-Era Assets. Like the London Conference, Washington drew prestigious delegations from 44 countries and 13 NGOs. And, like the 1997 conference, it was not a venue for governmental decision-making. The conference was intended "to forge an international consensus on how governments and other entities can cooperate to redress grave injustices that remain from the Holocaust era, especially issues relating to art and insurance, communally owned property by religious groups—Catholic, Jewish, Protestant—and other assets," said Eizenstat on November 24.[80]

By this time, however, the issue was no longer solely a matter of establishing a solid historical record or of restoring looted assets. While governments were writing historical reports and convening international conferences, class-action lawsuits, "monitoring groups," and commissions had become independent venues for recovering assets. Public finance officers imposed—or threatened to impose—sanctions against European businesses until they resolved Nazi-era claims.[81] Five months after the 1996 lawsuits against the Swiss banks, Holocaust survivors and heirs filed a class-action lawsuit against seven European insurers, charging that the companies failed to honor insurance policies purchased by Nazi victims before the war. Class-action suits were filed in U.S. federal courts in 1998 against German banks and businesses, contending that the companies profited from the "Aryanization" of Jewish property and failed to pay compensation for slave labor used during the Nazi era.[82]

Governments continued to express concern for Nazi victims, but they were equally, if not more, anxious about the effect of the lawsuits and sanctions on open markets and diplomatic relations.[83]

---

[80]http://fcit.coedu.usf.edu/holocaust/resource/assets/holocaust.htm.

[81]*Jerusalem Post,* Oct. 12, 1997.

[82]For an overview of the litigation, see Michael J. Bazyler, "The Holocaust Restitution Movement in Contemporary Perspective," *Berkeley Journal of International Law* 20, no. 1, 2002, pp. 11–44.

[83]Eizenstat implicitly made this point in his July 22, 1998, testimony to the Senate Banking, Housing and Urban Affairs Committee (http://www.senate.gov/~banking/98_07

These were not theoretical concerns. Businesses that operated in the U.S. were vulnerable to state and local regulatory pressures. The New York State Banking Department, for instance, had a long reach, supervising more than 190 foreign banks that maintained agencies or branches in the state. Months before the 1998 settlement of the Swiss banks case, the department had recommended that federal authorities disapprove the planned merger of UBS and Swiss Bank Corporation. The banks' "seemingly inattentive regard for the depositors who fell victim to the Holocaust, or their heirs, who have never received funds to which they are entitled, raises regulatory questions about the character and fitness of these banks' privilege to maintain operations in the United States," said Elizabeth McCaul, the superintendent of banks.[84] In turn, Swiss officials suggested that they would take retaliatory "countermeasures" against American companies if sanctions were imposed on their banks.[85] (Nor were these concerns limited to business and diplomatic matters. As will be noted below, American museums warned that litigation on the ownership of Nazi-looted art threatened international cultural exchanges and undercut confidence in the world art market.)

The Nazi victims and their heirs, whose claims had been largely ignored during the cold war, now found those claims complicated by political debates on economic and foreign policy. The pursuit of compensation and restitution through litigation and regulatory measures could hurt bilateral relations. Eizenstat, for instance, repeatedly took American state and local finance officials to task for threatening to impose sanctions on European enterprises. "We also have a responsibility to safeguard the preeminence of the United States as the most open financial market in the world," Eizenstat told D'Amato's Senate committee. And, he admonished, "Mr. Chairman, I get paid to make judgments about how our ac-

---

hrg/072298/witness/eizenst.htm). Survivors and foreign relations seemed to be on an equal footing when he said: "The U.S. Government continues to have important interests in seeing this matter resolved both in order to obtain prompt justice for aging Holocaust survivors and in order to maintain positive relations with Switzerland."

[84]McCaul letter to Alan Greenspan, Mar. 19, 1998, provided to the author by the New York State Banking Department. The merger was subsequently completed, creating the world's second-largest bank.

[85]Reuters, Mar. 19, 1998.

tions affect foreign countries. I can assure you that far from helping Holocaust survivors achieve a just and fair settlement, sanctions will delay and retard the process—making it more difficult for us to get a measure of justice for Holocaust survivors."[86]

In addition to warning American officials, Eizenstat also appealed to Europeans to resolve Holocaust claims. "It appears to us in the United States that the consequences of the public debate can be destructive, bearing the seeds of future political conflicts, unless we, the international community, try together to find cooperative and constructive ways to address this subject," he said. "Unresolved Nazi-era insurance issues, for instance, risk acrimony affecting the foundation of our business relations."[87]

Confronting History

Restitution propelled important Holocaust scholarship, as at least 18 nations created national commissions to study their war-era history. There were extraordinary educational initiatives, such as the Task Force for International Cooperation on Holocaust Education, Remembrance and Research, the first intergovernmental effort to promote Holocaust education around the world. The third international conference on the Holocaust, held in Stockholm in January 2000, focused on education and remembrance.

The historical inquiries carried out in different countries did not have uniform mandates or composition—some included Jewish communal participation, others not. Nor did the inquiries necessarily presuppose that restitution would be the end result.

The Swiss commission, headed by Swiss historian Jean-François Bergier, spent five years studying all facets of Swiss wartime trade with Nazi Germany. The commission—made up of historians from Switzerland, Israel, the United States, and Poland—established that Switzerland had been an indispensable supplier of foreign exchange to Germany, had amassed at least $1.25 billion in German assets by the end of the war, and had engaged in postwar economic deals that violated agreements with the Allies.

---

[86]http://www.senate.gov/banking/98__07hrg/072298/witness/eizenst.htm.

[87]Opening Statement, Washington Conference on Holocaust-Era Assets; Organizing Seminar, June 30, 1998, http:www.ushmmm.org/assets/eizen.htm.

"The question which arises is not whether Switzerland should or could have maintained its business contacts and foreign trade with the warring powers in the first place, but rather how far these activities went: In other words, where the line should be drawn between unavoidable concessions and intentional collaboration," the Bergier report said.[88] It found that, in general, Swiss companies played a "significant role" in preparing German industry for the war, that Swiss exporters found a profitable market in Germany, and that Swiss subsidiaries employed forced labor and, in some cases, prisoners from concentration camps.

Swiss business interests stood in a "triangular relationship" with the Swiss government and Germany before the end of 1937, when German rearmament and the expropriation of Jewish property intensified, the report said. "Swiss authorities had no doubts about the illegality of the measures taken in Germany. However, as a result of Germany's strengthened position, the Swiss business community sensed a growing pressure to conform to German behavior and with few exceptions accommodated itself," even though such accommodation violated Swiss legal principles. Specifically, this meant "the neglect of the interests of those banking and insurance clients who were persecuted by the Nazis," and even "pressure on Swiss newspapers not to antagonize German commercial partners or political bodies through critical commentary." While one rationalization for these policies was the hope that "a more prosperous Germany would be a more peaceful and friendlier Germany than an isolated one," the report found that "more important, however, were business and commercial interests, upon which both the business world and the authorities agreed."[89]

The Bergier report also confirmed earlier research on the "draconian measures" that Switzerland had used to limit the influx of refugees, saying that "in terms of humanitarian aid and asylum where its refugee policy was concerned, neutral Switzerland not only failed to live up to its own standards, but also violated fundamental humanitarian principles."[90]

However, none of these findings led to restitution measures. The

---

[88]*Switzerland, National Socialism and the Second World War, Final Report, the Independent Commission of Experts, Switzerland* (Zurich, 2002), p. 497.

[89]Ibid., p. 504.

[90]Ibid., p. 499.

settlement of the lawsuits against the Swiss banks was reached in 1998, preceding the Bergier report by several years.

The Netherlands, in 1997, established committees to examine the postwar restoration of bank accounts, insurance policies, art, stocks, and securities that had belonged to Dutch Jews. The reports criticized the government's bureaucratic approach to postwar restitution. According to Prime Minister Wim Kok, the investigators found that the "restitution of legal rights in the impoverished postwar Netherlands was basically correct from a legal and formal point of view, but at the same time their reports identify and criticize a number of shortcomings: the length of the process, the cumbersome and inflexible procedures and, above all, the chilly reception and lack of understanding that awaited those returning from the camps"—adding, "a situation that was without any doubt not unique to the Netherlands."[91]

In 2001, the Dutch government, banks, insurers and the Bourse tacitly acknowledged that they had profited from the deaths and deportations of the Jews, and paid some 764 million guilders, primarily in the form of individual one-time payments to all Jews who were in the Netherlands during World War II (see below, pp. 369–70).[92]

France made funds available in conjunction with the findings of the government-sponsored commission led by Jean Mattéoli, a member of the World War II resistance (see AJYB 2001, pp. 334–36). That panel reported in April 2000 on the Nazi and Vichy measures that despoiled the 330,000 Jews in France between 1940 and 1944. The losses were significant: The Nazis or the Vichy government froze 86,000 Jewish-owned bank accounts and safe-deposit boxes, confiscated 50,000 Jewish companies or properties, and seized 100,000 Jewish-owned artworks and the contents of 38,000 Jewish apartments. The commission found that the French government often did this work more zealously than the Nazis. But

---

[91]http://www.holocaustforum.gov.se/conference/official_documents/messages/kok.htm.

[92]The payments of 14,000 Dutch guilders ($6,000) were for Jews born before May 8, 1945, and who were in the Netherlands for any amount of time between May 10, 1940 (the invasion of Holland) and the end of the war, and who were still alive on May 8, 1945. The funds, which were expected to be paid to an estimated 35,000 victims and some heirs, were distributed by a new foundation known as Maror. That name has a dual meaning: it is an acronym for the Dutch words referring to responsibility for looting and the restoration of rights; in Hebrew, it refers to the bitter herb used during the ritual Passover Seder.

it also reported that some 90 percent of the assets had been restored after the war. "Two things struck us in particular. One was the scale of the despoilment, which was much greater than we originally thought," said historian Claire Andrieu. "The other was the scale of the restitution after the liberation. The Republic really did do its duty."[93]

The commission estimated that Jewish-owned assets worth some $205 million were still in French custody, and recommended that those funds be used for a Remembrance Foundation, and the government established this in December 2000. France also set up a special compensation program for orphans whose parents were victims of anti-Semitic persecution.[94]

Slave and Forced Labor

Compensation, however, was not generally driven by international conferences or historical commissions. More often it was propelled by specific events—primarily lawsuits, sanctions, and, in the case of Austria, by domestic political turmoil. The lawsuit against the Swiss banks, which reached a $1.25-billion settlement in August 1998,[95] was followed by a steady stream of other suits targeting European governments and enterprises. In 1998 and 1999, some 50 lawsuits were filed against more than 100 German and Austrian companies for the use of slave labor during World War II.

The Nazis and German industry exploited millions of slave and forced laborers to build war materiel, dig tunnels, harvest crops, and perform other life-threatening labor under subhuman condi-

---

[93]*Los Angeles Times,* Apr. 18, 2000.

[94]"Agreement between the Government of France and the Government of the United States of America Concerning Payments for Certain Losses Suffered During World War II," French embassy press release, Washington, D.C., Jan. 18, 2001.

[95]The Swiss settlement set aside $800 million to cover claims for Swiss bank accounts. Other funds were for slave and forced laborers for Nazi-era companies that hid their assets in Swiss banks, and for refugees fleeing the Nazis who were ejected or turned away from Switzerland. Among those who originally were supposed to benefit were people whose assets had been looted. However, because of costs associated with claims for specific looted assets and the likelihood that the per-capita payments would be low, the court instead ruled that the funds assigned to this class should be used for the neediest elderly Nazi victims, primarily in the form of food packages, medical assistance, and emergency cash grants.

tions during World War II. Although non-Jews also were coerced into labor, the Jews worked under the imminent threat of death. The Nazis understood Jewish slave labor as *Vernichtung durch Arbeit* (destruction through work), part of their extermination plan.

The B.E.G. recognized slave labor as persecution, but provided no specific compensation. In the 1950s and 1960s, after a lawsuit brought in a German court by Auschwitz survivor Norbert Wollheim against the I.G. Farben firm, a handful of companies—out of the thousands that had exploited slave labor—reached agreements with the Claims Conference to provide compensation to the surviving workers of their particular enterprises. Agreements with the companies—Farben, Krupp, Siemens, AEG-Telefunken, and Rheinmetall—totaled some DM 52 million, and provided modest compensation to 14,878 survivors in 42 countries.[96] The agreements differed in their terms and levels of compensation. What they had in common was that all were "voluntary"—none of the companies accepted legal responsibility for their use of slave labor. As the German courts had issued no final ruling on corporate liability for slave labor, it was virtually impossible to extract compensation for laborers from enterprises that ignored the demand or refused to pay, from those that had been run by the Nazi government or the SS, or from private companies that had gone out of business after the war.

After prodding by the Claims Conference, Daimler-Benz in 1988 made a payment of DM 10 million, but the company refused to provide compensation to individual victims. Instead, the funds were distributed to organizations that provided support for "former forced workers in need." The same condition applied four years later, when Volkswagen provided the Claims Conference with DM 2.5 million for institutional programs that aided Holocaust survivors.[97]

In 1998, under threats of legal action in Germany and lawsuits in the U.S., both Volkswagen and Siemens announced that they

---

[96]For a detailed discussion of slave labor and the early agreements on compensation, see Benjamin B. Ferencz, *Less Than Slaves: Jewish Forced Labor and the Quest for Compensation* (Cambridge, Mass., 1979). There also was an agreement in principle with Dynamit Nobel, but it was not honored until the company was sold, some 20 years later, to Deutsche Bank.

[97]Claims Conference, *Annual Report 1996,* pp. 36–37.

each would establish a DM 20 million "humanitarian" fund for Nazi-era slave laborers. Victims who labored for those companies during the Nazi era were to receive DM 10,000 each. Volkswagen had another incentive for paying compensation: It was an election year in Germany, and the Social Democratic Party candidate for chancellor, Gerhard Schröder, was then the minister-president of Lower Saxony, and that state owned 20 percent of the automaker.

Shortly after Schröder became chancellor, the federal government and German industry announced plans for the creation of a "Remembrance, Responsibility and the Future" fund, which would provide "humanitarian" compensation to former laborers. The fund was designed to address the "moral responsibility of German firms with regard to such issues as forced laborers, 'Aryanization,' and other injustices during the Nazi regime." After 16 months of negotiations, an agreement was reached in July 2000 for the German government and industry to pay a total of DM 10 billion for slave-labor compensation and assorted restitution programs, on condition that the U.S. ensure "legal peace"—an end to further lawsuits for Nazi-era claims.

One million surviving victims were expected to benefit from the fund, which was to provide DM 15,000 to each former "slave laborer," and DM 5,000 to each "forced laborer." Under the agreement's definitions, slave laborers were those who had been inmates of concentration camps or similar facilities; forced laborers were those who were forced to live and work under less harsh conditions. There were Jews and non-Jews in both categories.[98]

ALLOCATIONS

In the decades since the Shoah, there have been literally millions of individual and collective claims for compensation and restitution. The collective claims—primarily against Germany, German industry, and Austria—have yielded hundreds of millions of Deutsche marks that changed the Jewish landscape in Israel and postwar Europe.

The funds that went from Germany to Israel in the 1950s and

---

[98]"Joint Statement on occasion of the final plenary meeting concluding international talks on the preparation of the Foundation, 'Remembrance, Responsibility and the Future,' " http://www.usembassy.de/policy/holocaust/jointstatement.htm.

1960s were not intended as direct benefits for Nazi victims, but to aid the new state in the absorption of refugees. The funds to aid Holocaust survivors, on the other hand, were those obtained by the Jewish Restitution Successor Organization and, later, by the Claims Conference. More than $353 million and another DM 515 million were obtained through numerous collective claims over the course of 50-plus years, and used to finance relief, rehabilitation, and resettlement, to reconstruct postwar Jewish communities in Europe, and for research, education, and documentation of the Shoah. Though impressive, the sums do not represent the totality of the Jewish material losses.

The collective sums were negotiated and obtained in three distinct periods: from 1947 through 1965; in the 1980s; and after 1995. They came either from government and industry, or from the recovery of heirless and unclaimed Jewish properties. In the 1950s and 1960s the funds were spent primarily in Europe, where they financed a wide variety of services, ranging from kindergartens to old-age homes.[99] At the end of the 20th century, the overwhelming majority of the funds were used in Israel and the former Soviet Union (FSU), almost entirely for social-welfare programs and capital projects to aid elderly victims of the Nazis.[100]

1947–1965

Between 1947 and 1972, the JRSO collected DM 222.3 million through the recovery of heirless and unclaimed Jewish properties in West Germany and bulk settlements of property and financial claims. The funds were not used for direct payments to individuals. Instead, most was allocated to the Jewish Agency for Israel and to the JDC to expand their relief and resettlement activities. In 1956, the JRSO established an allocations formula whereby the Jewish Agency received 56.95 percent; the JDC, 28.05 percent; the Council of Jews from Germany, 11 percent; and religious projects in Israel (synagogues, yeshivahs, and seminaries), 4 percent.[101]

---

[99]Claims Conference, *Twenty Years Later: Activities of the Conference on Jewish Material Claims Against Germany, 1952–1972* (New York, 1973), pp. 14–15.

[100]Claims Conference, *Annual Report 1996*, p. 27.

[101]Kagan and Weisman, *Report on the Operations of the Jewish Restitution Successor Organization,* p. 37. In the years between 1947 and 1972, the organization spent 6.4 percent of its receipts on administrative expenses.

The Jewish Agency got more than DM 114 million, which it used to finance prefabricated homes (*ma'abarot*), agricultural machinery, and construction equipment, as well as immigration and absorption services in Israel. The funds to the JDC—DM 56 million—were used at the Foehrenwald DP camp and for institutional care of the elderly and handicapped, including the Malben institutions in Israel that provided special services to aged and disabled immigrants.[102]

The 1952 Luxembourg Agreements vastly increased the amount of money available—but from a very different source. While the JRSO distributed funds it had acquired from recovering properties that had belonged to murdered Jews and destroyed Jewish communities, the Luxembourg Agreements generated payments from the West German government.

The State of Israel received DM 3 billion from West Germany, delivered in the form of goods and services over the course of a dozen years. The funds established the basic industrial and economic foundations of the state. Thirty percent of the German payments went directly to Britain to buy crude oil for Israel. The rest were in capital and consumer goods, making German products—like the ubiquitous Mercedes taxis—common in the Israeli market. Some 1,400 initiatives in assorted branches of Israeli industry received equipment and machinery with funds generated by the Luxembourg Agreements. German funds built transport, power, and communications facilities, the Israeli merchant fleet, and the port at Ashdod. Israeli agriculture was mechanized and modernized with German equipment and services, including a water-diversion project that expanded the cultivation of the Negev. The improvements were so extensive that local agriculture was able to supply all domestic needs except for cereals.[103]

Under Protocol II, West Germany pledged to provide the Claims Conference, via Israel, with DM 450 million over a dozen years. Those funds were used for the relief and resettlement of Jewish victims, and to rebuild Jewish communities in Europe and Jewish cul-

---

[102]Foehrenwald, near Munich, was one of the largest Jewish DP centers in the American zone, and it was the last of 66 camps to close. Foehrenwald functioned until 1957 as a home for Jewish survivors, many of them severely ill, who were unable or unwilling to emigrate.

[103]Sagi, *German Reparations,* pp. 197–98.

tural life, according to "the urgency of the need" as determined by the Claims Conference.[104]

When the funds first became available, the Claims Conference was overrun with applications from Jewish communities and institutions across the continent, and the requests far exceeded the amounts on hand. There also were appeals from individual Nazi victims. "We received countless letters from individuals to the effect that 'There are so many survivors and so much money; when the money is divided up, my share is $1,400. Please send me a check,' " Saul Kagan recalled.[105]

The funds were directed to existing agencies, primarily the JDC, the preeminent provider of relief, transit, social, and medical services to Jews in Europe, which received about $7.5 million a year.[106] Those funds were directed to programs in the countries that had been occupied by the Nazis, even though thousands of victims had left Europe. The Claims Conference financed cash assistance, medical care, vocational training, housing grants, and educational and religious assistance.[107] "Not only had individual members of the European communities suffered, but the whole structure of their institutions and services had been destroyed," said Kagan. "The conference felt it should try to make the kind of contribution to their total reconstruction that would rebuild their basic framework as well as meeting immediate relief needs."[108] By 1965, France—with two-thirds of Western Europe's postwar Jewish population—was the largest single beneficiary of Claims Conference aid. But there was scarcely any community of any size in Western Europe that had been occupied by the Nazis that did not have at least one capital project financed by the Claims Conference. There were 480 capital projects in 29 countries—primarily in Western

[104]For a detailed analysis of the Claims Conference's use of German funds until 1965, see Ronald W. Zweig, *German Reparations and the Jewish World: A History of the Claims Conference*, 2nd ed. (London, 2001).

[105]Saul Kagan, "The Claims Conference and the Communities," *Exchange* 22 (1965), p. 13.

[106]The JDC was both a key member of the Claims Conference and an applicant for large sums from it, and this caused friction at times.

[107]In addition to aiding Nazi victims, in the 1960s the Claims Conference initiated a program to provide modest assistance to needy "righteous" non-Jews who had saved Jewish lives at the risk of their own. From its inception through 2000, the program helped 784 people, with total payments amounting to $2.4 million. See its *Annual Report 2000*, p. 39.

[108]Kagan, "The Claims Conference and the Communities," p. 13.

Europe—including 150 schools, 107 community and youth centers, 65 religious institutions, 56 homes for the aged, and 12 medical institutions.[109]

"The transformation in Jewish life that took place in western and central Europe, in the course of the years 1954–64, is all but incredible," the Claims Conference said:

> In 1953, the Jewish communities on the European continent, the bearers of historical traditions centuries old, were on the verge of destitution in many instances. Sacked and plundered at Nazi hands, their communal leaders, rabbis, teachers and other officials mostly murdered or driven off to overseas lands, their surviving members impoverished, their possessions accumulated in the course of centuries looted, their communal institutions razed or reduced to ruin, the prospect that they would ever flourish again within our own lifetimes seemed all but visionary.[110]

Overall, nearly half the original funds held by the Claims Conference—some $48 million—was used for a then-secret welfare program with the vague name of "relief in transit." Under German law, Nazi victims were not eligible for compensation unless they were in the West. Likewise, the Claims Conference was barred from overtly using Protocol II funds for projects behind the Iron Curtain. In 1954, with an allocation of $1 million, it began financing "relief in transit," spiriting cash and material goods to Jews in Central and Eastern Europe. By 1964, some 200,000 people had been assisted in this way.

The cultural and educational programs attempted to train a cadre of communal leaders for European Jewry. "The shortages of trained personnel—rabbis, teachers, social workers, administrators—were as serious for the continuity of communal life as this shortage of funds, and attracting the younger generation to Jewish life was a vital facet in building for the future," Kagan said.[111] The cultural program was pluralistic, recognizing the right of groups to their particular cultural, spiritual, ideological, and religious beliefs.

Some 13,000 people each year attended Jewish primary, secondary, and supplementary schools, yeshivahs, seminaries, teachers colleges, and adult-education programs financed by the Claims

---

[109] Claims Conference, *Twenty Years Later,* p. 15.

[110] Ibid., pp. 10–11.

[111] Kagan, "The Claims Conference and the Communities," pp. 18–19.

Conference. Special funds were established to aid refugee rabbis as well as displaced former leaders of Jewish communities. About 1,800 victims participated in fellowship programs for Jewish scholars, artists, and writers. Among them was Nathan Rappaport, whose *Wall of Remembrance,* a bronze sculpture commemorating the Warsaw Ghetto uprising, is prominently displayed at Yad Vashem. Another fellow was André Schwarz-Bart, whose novel, *The Last of the Just,* won the French literary prize Prix Goncourt in 1959. With aid from the Claims Conference in its first dozen years, victims of the Nazis produced more than 400 books written in a dozen languages, including general and religious literature, children's stories, Jewish social studies, and textbooks.

Funds were also set aside to salvage cultural treasures, primarily through the YIVO Institute for Jewish Research in New York, the Centre de Documentation Juive in Paris, and the Wiener Library in London. The Claims Conference, also committed to documenting what was then known as the "Jewish Catastrophe" (the word Holocaust was not yet in vogue), gave an important allocation to help found Yad Vashem in Jerusalem.[112]

In its early years, the Claims Conference allocated some $19.4 million, 20 percent of its funds, for cultural and educational programs in 30 countries. It expected to close after it had distributed the funds from Protocol II, and the bitter issue it faced in 1964 was how to use its last $15 million. The JDC wanted it used for relief, but Nahum Goldmann, the forceful and charismatic president of the Claims Conference, insisted that the funds be used for culture. "*Tzdoke* [charity] is a very dangerous thing with Jews; billions have been wasted on that. But what maintained a people is cultural life, and not hospitals," he said. "If I had all 100,000 intellectuals buried in Auschwitz, I would rebuild the Jewish people. But if you go on and spend it for relief, then everything will become meaningless."[113]

In the end, the Claims Conference decided that one-third of its remaining funds would be used for relief, and two-thirds (roughly $10 million) would go to create a "cultural trust"—the Memorial Foundation for Jewish Culture, which still exists today.

---

[112]Yad Vashem was built by a partnership of the Claims Conference, the Jewish Agency, and the State of Israel.

[113]Quoted in Zweig, *German Reparations and the Jewish World,* p. 183.

Since 1980

Fifteen years after winding down Protocol II, the Claims Conference entered its second phase, administering payments to individual victims and making institutional grants. In 1980, the Claims Conference and West Germany reached agreement on the creation of the Hardship Fund (see above). It provided one-time payments of DM 5,000 each to Nazi victims who arrived in the West after 1965. The fund also set aside 5 percent of the total (some DM 63 million) for grants to institutions that provided shelter and social services to needy survivors. These funds, however, came with restrictions: West Germany did not permit allocations to institutions in the Soviet orbit. Between 1981 and 1993 (when the Hardship Fund programs were consolidated with another program), the Claims Conference made institutional grants under the fund to 166 programs in 16 countries, but primarily in Israel. There also were some limited funds made available through a 1988 agreement with Daimler Benz, which provided DM 10 million for grants to institutions that provided shelter or home care to survivors. And in 1991, Austria provided $23.5 million for projects to aid Austrian-born victims.

The largest pool of funds for institutions that aided survivors became available in 1995, and this marked the beginning of the third stage of allocations. These were the funds generated, after German reunification, from the Claims Conference's recovery and sale of unclaimed and heirless Jewish properties in the former East Germany. From 1995 through 2000, the Claims Conference, as the "successor organization," distributed more than $400 million from the funds generated by these sales. In 2000 alone, it allocated $81.86 million to projects in 26 countries.[114]

Unlike the funds from German sources, there were no restrictions on how these new funds could be used. Thus, for the first time in decades, money was available for aid to Central and Eastern Europe—particularly in the regions of the FSU that had been occupied by the Nazis. Nazi victims there had not benefited from the German compensation programs and were living in extreme poverty in states that lacked social safety nets for their most vul-

---

[114]Claims Conference, *Annual Report 2000,* p. 23.

nerable members. Once again, the Claims Conference worked with the JDC, this time as its conduit to the East, establishing regional *hesed* (welfare) centers for survivors. "We have a holy responsibility to use the money from people who did not survive for the benefit of those who did," Rabbi Israel Miller, president of the Claims Conference, said at the 1996 inauguration of the center in Kiev.[115] In the period between 1995 and 2000, the Claims Conference allocated $122 million to projects in the FSU.[116]

Twenty percent of the funds were designated for research, education, and documentation of the Shoah, the first time in some 30 years that substantial funds had been available for these purposes. In the first few years, the Claims Conference's primary use for these funds was capital construction and renovation projects for "established" institutions engaged in Holocaust education and documentation, and the primary beneficiary was Yad Vashem. Money has also been used to collect and preserve documents and archival materials, and to fund teacher-training and educational programs, including the "March of the Living," which takes Jewish teenagers from around the world to sites of Nazi atrocities, followed by a visit to Israel.

The research, education, and documentation funds have stirred some controversy. Many among the survivors argue that, while education is important, the funds belong to the victims, and all available moneys should be used to assist them. Other critics oppose the preferential treatment given to established institutions, such as Yad Vashem and the U.S. Holocaust Memorial Museum in Washington. The Claims Conference is partial to these institutions because of the wide impact and influence they command. The critics contend, however, that such institutions can easily attract money from alternate sources, while newer programs compete for very modest grants, or go begging. There also are ideological disputes about the breadth of Holocaust education—whether it should be limited to the 1933–45 period, or cover Jewish life before and after the Shoah as well, and if it should be targeted toward Jewish or non-Jewish publics.

Israel is the largest beneficiary of Claims Conference funds. Be-

---

[115]*Jerusalem Post,* Nov. 7, 1996.

[116]Claims Conference, *Annual Report 2000,* p. 27.

tween 1995 and 2000, Israeli institutions and projects received $213.8 million.[117] This priority reflects both the fact that the largest number of survivors are there, and also the moral assumption that funds from the Claims Conference should help develop resources that will be of long-term benefit to the state. The money certainly has made a dramatic impact on the provision of geriatric care in Israel, contributing to the construction and renovation of more than 3,000 geriatric and nursing beds, sheltered living, and day-care centers for seniors. Even in this instance, however, there were clashes over whether it was more important to build facilities or to support home care. The latter is provided through the Foundation for the Benefit of Holocaust Survivors, financed by the Claims Conference, which supplements home-care services provided by Israeli agencies and also makes one-time grants to needy survivors to buy items not covered by Israel's national health program, such as dentures, hearing aids, and orthopedic shoes.

Some survivors living outside of Israel complain that they do not have the same services and benefits as the Israelis. However, programs such as the foundation are particularly well suited to Israel because of the small size of the country. Further, regions in the U.S. that are home to large numbers of survivors, such as metropolitan New York, often have publicly financed social-service and medical programs.

Allocations via the Claims Conference successor organization are expected to continue at least until 2010. In addition, new sources of funding for services to survivors were due to become available in 2002, more than 60 years after the war. These are from "humanitarian funds"[118] associated primarily with settlements of slave labor, insurance, and "Aryanization" claims against the German and Austrian governments, and the industries of the two countries. The funds, which could total more than $400 million, are to be distributed by the Claims Conference, which was chosen for this role because it is the traditional agency administering Holocaust-related compensation.

---

[117]Ibid.

[118]"Humanitarian," which implies charity, is a misnomer, since the funds are a substitute for global payments to cover heirless assets.

RESTITUTION

Shimshon Klueger was the last Jew living in an Upper Silesian city in Poland. It wasn't much of a life. A former Belzer Hassid, Klueger was a tormented recluse who lived in a hovel. Townsfolk and visitors would leave food and money in a wooden bowl outside his door. Klueger died in June 2000, at the age of 72. He was buried by a minyan of foreign visitors he had never met—students from the Ramaz School in New York and the director of the Morasha Heritage seminars.

Klueger was the last Jew in Oswieçim, whose Jewish community had been founded in the 16th century and whose name became forever infamous for the death camp built astride the town—Auschwitz. The death camp is synonymous with the extermination of Jewish life in Europe. Klueger's burial itself was a powerful symbol. "I was helping perform a Jewish ritual that will never again be performed in this city," said Michael Berl of Jerusalem, the director of Morasha, which organizes Holocaust educational programs. "There will never be another Jewish burial in Oswieçim. It means that the door is closed on this town—finished. Another door in the history of Polish Jewry has been slammed shut."[119]

The end of Klueger's life coincided with the reopening of the last surviving synagogue in Oswieçim, Chevra Lomdei Mishnayot. Used as a carpet warehouse under the communist regime, the synagogue building was returned to the Jewish community of Bielsko-Biale early in 1998, the first edifice restored to the Jews under Poland's legislation on the restitution of communal property. The community transferred ownership of the building to the Auschwitz Jewish Center Foundation in New York, which renovated it as a religious and cultural facility. "Our goal is to recreate a permanent structure symbolizing Jewish life in a place that, for too many years, has only represented Jewish death," said Fred Schwartz, a New York philanthropist and businessman who led the foundation.[120] The site reopened in 2000.

In Central and Eastern Europe, property restitution was akin to the situation in reunified Germany—the recovery of Nazi-confiscated properties in the former East Germany occurred amid

[119]*Jerusalem Post,* June 18, 2000.
[120]Ibid., June 16, 1998.

the reprivatization and modernization of the society and its institutions. However, unlike Germany, whose western *Länder* had a prior history of restitution and compensation for the damages of the Nazi era, the Eastern European states were novices in the technical and practical aspects of restitution. Morever, they were concerned with communist, not Nazi, expropriations, and thus, as was the case in the former East Germany, restitution of confiscated properties of the Nazi era was a marginal concern.

Like Chevra Lomdei Mishnayot, there are tens of thousands of other Jewish communal properties across Central and Eastern Europe—synagogues, cemeteries, yeshivahs, clubs, and *mikvaot* (ritual baths)—as well as an untold numbers of private houses, farms, and businesses that were confiscated and plundered during the period of Nazi rule, and then nationalized by the communist regimes that followed. These sites were both tragic monuments to the millennium of Jewish life, culture, and tradition that had found its home in Europe, as well as the potential building-blocks to begin to resurrect that life decades after the Holocaust. With the collapse of communism came the possibility to reclaim them.[121]

At the end of the 20th century and more than a decade after the fall of the Berlin Wall, there were some opportunities to recover properties in Central and Eastern Europe, especially as archival materials increasingly become available to document specific losses. But the prospects that at first seemed broad have proven disappointing. Property-restitution laws, where they exist, are limited, and, in most cases, filing deadlines for property claims have passed.

At stake in Central and Eastern Europe were three different types of Jewish properties that had been "stolen" twice—confiscated by the Nazis, then expropriated by the communists. There were public or communal properties, including cemeteries, synagogues, and schools; private properties with recognized heirs; and heirless or "abandoned" private properties. Restitution of these properties entailed different economic, political, and social costs, making some more or less "attractive" for governments to retain.[122]

---

[121]On attempts, mostly unsuccessful, to recover properties of deported Jews in Western Europe, see Nehemiah Robinson, *Spoliation and Remedial Action* (New York, 1962). In 1946, Greece became the first European country to pass property-restitution measures: the state waived its right to inherit heirless properties, and they were turned over to the Greek Jewish community.

[122]The prospect of recovering "heirless private property" in Central and Eastern Europe

From the outset, a variety of factors unique to each state complicated the recovery of Jewish property, which was never more than a marginal aspect of a broader reprivatization plan to transform the Central and Eastern European economies. Within the Jewish community, complications arose from the acrimony between the survivor communities and the new centers of Jewish life in Israel and the U.S. They battled over who was the legitimate heir of the communities that were destroyed in the Holocaust, who should negotiate with the governments for restitution, how much and which property to pursue, and how to use the proceeds. Collectively, these factors militated against the restitution of both public and private Jewish properties. (Virtually no Jewish organizations or international advocacy groups paid sustained attention to individual rights to private property; the claimants were left to their own devices and compelled to rely on private lawyers to pursue claims.)

For more than five years, beginning in 1995, the United States was the most powerful and steadfast proponent of property restitution in Central and Eastern Europe. The effort was led by Stuart Eizenstat, who supplemented the moral argument with appeals to these nations' aspirations to join the economic and military alliances of the West. Eizenstat suggested that progress in restitution would be a consideration for states in the East seeking to join NATO and the European Union (EU). Property rights were a measure of these nations' commitment to values of the West. He said:

> The basic principle that wrongfully expropriated property should be restituted (or compensation paid) applies to them all, and their implementation of this principle is a measure of the extent to which they have successfully adopted democratic institutions, the rule of law with respect to property rights, and market-economy practices. As these governments seek to join Western economic and political organizations, and to integrate their economies more closely with ours, we do expect them to adopt the highest international standards in their treatment of property.[123]

For its part, the EU has said it would welcome property restitution measures but would not impose them. With specific regard to

---

remains only theoretical. In the absence of the formation of a special Jewish successor organization, no one is legally entitled to claim it.

[123]Testimony before the Commission on Security and Cooperation in Europe, Washington, Mar. 25, 1999, http://www.restitution.org/us/eizenstat.399.htm.

Poland, "the European Commission is fully aware that this issue is both from the legal and the fiscal point of view a very sensitive one and mainly one of Poland's internal policy," said an EU official. "Within the European Union, the division of competencies (or powers) is such that the creation of schemes for restitution of property falls within the competence of member state countries rather than at the level of the European Union itself."[124]

In raising the moral argument for restitution, Eizenstat stressed the importance of returning property because religious groups, which had been barred from practicing their religion by decades of repression, were trying to reestablish their roots. These were the "double victims" of both fascism and communism. They needed the properties to generate income and develop institutions in order to flourish. "They need to have places to pray, places where the kids can be educated, communal facilities to use," Eizenstat said.[125]

Local Resistance

But Central and Eastern European governments, even those that were sympathetic to Jewish claims, had practical and ideological incentives to limit their measures to the reprivatization of communist-era properties.[126] For one thing, the communist-era claims were easier to manage. There was no doubt about the previous government's responsibility for expropriation, and no overlapping or conflicting claims rooted in different historical events. Further, national borders were stable behind the Iron Curtain. That was not the case in the Nazi era. Eastern Galicia, for example, was in Poland before the war and in Ukraine afterward; which postwar government should be liable for property claims there? Ideologically, too, governments have preferred to confine themselves to dealing with communist confiscations. In regard to Nazi confiscations, the people of these countries often see themselves as victims, and therefore reject responsibility for Nazi actions, including the plunder of property.

---

[124]Correspondence dated Mar. 14, 2001, on file with the author.

[125]Briefing on Washington Conference on Holocaust-Era Assets, Nov. 24, 1998, http://fcit.coedu.usf.edu/holocaust/resource/assets/holocaus.htm.

[126]For an overview, see Marilyn Henry, *The Restitution of Jewish Property in Central and Eastern Europe,* American Jewish Committee International Perspectives no. 40 (New York, 1997).

The postcommunist governments' willingness to deal with the restitution of Jewish assets depended on several historical factors: the degree of local support for and collaboration with the Nazis, the size of the prewar Jewish population and its legal and social position, the extent of its wealth, and to whom it was lost. There were also other factors affecting restitution that had to do with the new post-1990 reality: the pace of national economic and legal reforms, the financial stability of the state, the relationship of the current Jewish communities to the postcommunist governments and their place in the postwar society, and the economic hardship and social turmoil that religious communities' claims would stir.

Jewish property restitution is unpopular in societies with a tradition of violent anti-Semitism, since the governments fear that restitution measures would revive these sentiments. Restitution is also a delicate issue in regions where national borders had shifted, and large segments of the population had been transferred, or experienced considerable losses from the war and Nazi occupation. Emerging Eastern European democracies feared that these populations, bearing the scars and memories of trauma, would resent being asked to make good on Jewish property claims when they had not been compensated for their own losses.

In Poland alone, where some 3 million Jews were murdered by the Nazis, there were an estimated 5,000 communal properties and an unknown number of private properties that had once belonged to Jews. The costs of compensation for the properties and the potential social upheaval involved in displacing the occupants of once-Jewish sites militated against a law governing the return of private property. After more than a dozen attempts to pass a reprivatization restitution law since 1989, Poland, at the end of the 20th century, had the dubious distinction of being the only postcommunist country in Europe without one.

In March 2001, President Aleksander Kwasniewski vetoed legislation that would have compensated individuals for property seized during the Nazi and communist eras. "First of all, [the legislation] strikes against Poles' basic interest, which is creation of the best possible conditions for economic growth," said Kwasniewski, a former communist. His veto was in line with the public mood. With the unemployment rate above 15 percent in the spring of 2001, some 60 percent of the population thought restitution would harm the economy, according to a published poll. Furthermore, less than half the population—48 percent—thought that restitution of confiscated property was "morally correct," even though many Poles themselves would benefit from it.[127] In addition, the proposed legislation was considered flawed because it would have limited its provisions to Polish citizens.

The restitution laws, where they exist in Central and Eastern Europe, cover different types of property, are controlled by different levels of government, and impose different conditions on claimants. In many cases, national restitution laws are confounded by the fact that much of the property is controlled by provincial or municipal authorities that balk at the measures. In these decentralized post-Soviet days, national governments, even when they have the official authority, often lack the will to impose restitution measures on their reluctant provinces. In addition, many of the laws are limited to properties remaining in public hands, long after many valuable properties have passed into the market economies.[128]

Restitution measures are often further limited in terms of who can recover properties and which properties are eligible for return. The broad definition of Jewish communal property includes anything that was owned by the community, the *kehillah*. However, some countries divide this category into "religious" and "secular" property, and their restitution measures provide only for the return of "religious" property. This narrow interpretation includes such obvious properties as synagogues and cemeteries, but excludes hospitals, social facilities, and old-age homes. Similarly, some national laws name the officially recognized "religious" community as the sole eligible claimant, barring Jewish social or fraternal associations from recovering their assets.

The "local" nature of the laws, however rational in appearance, create enormous problems for individual Jewish claimants. These often include citizenship requirements, which in effect discriminate against the majority of Jews trying to recover property, who live abroad. Such requirements also do not take into account that the original loss of citizenship that resulted in leaving the country was

---

[127] *Jerusalem Post,* Mar. 23, 2001.

[128] In the overwhelming majority of instances, restitution concerns the recovery of existing property. Usually left out of the equation is compensation in lieu of restitution in in-

unlikely to have been voluntary, and thus the restriction further penalizes people for having been persecuted.[129]

Intra-Jewish Coordination

There is a corollary to the citizenship requirement when it comes to communal property. The laws assign to the local Jewish communities the right to recover property. This excludes Jewish organizations and *landsmanschaften* (organizations of Jews who came from the same European communities) abroad. Fifty years after the Holocaust, the Jewish world had changed dramatically. There are fewer than 2 million Jews in Europe—less than the number who lived in Poland before the war. After the murder of 6 million, the heart of the Jewish world is no longer in Europe; it beats elsewhere. With its birth in 1948, the State of Israel claimed to be that heart, while millions of Jews live in the United States.

American and Israeli organizations joined forces in 1992 to form the World Jewish Restitution Organization (WJRO) to pursue Jewish property claims in Central and Eastern Europe.[130] They contended that the European Jewish communities were too feeble or timid to successfully negotiate with their governments, did not have the capacity to absorb the properties, and were too small to be the legitimate heirs of the millions of Jews who died. This had a subtext, as well: property had became a proxy measure for attitudes about the viability of Jewish life in Eastern Europe, and for whether "world Jewry" could come to terms with the Jews of Eastern and Central Europe. Many simply viewed Europe as a grave-

---

stances in which the site no longer exists, because of war-era destruction or postwar abuse and neglect, or removal for postwar land development.

[129]It is widely believed that these citizenship requirements are tinged with anti-Semitism. However, it seems equally likely that rather than intentionally discriminating against the Jews, the criteria are designed to give preferential treatment to local populations over "outsiders," because the locals, who are domestic voters, should be rewarded for having endured communist deprivations. In the case of Poland, there also is anecdotal evidence that a citizenship requirement was meant to exclude any benefits for "Polonia," the Polish diaspora, which includes a large contingent of Polish army veterans who refused to return to Soviet-occupied Poland after World War II.

[130]The founding members of the WJRO were the Claims Conference, the World Jewish Congress, the Jewish Agency, the JDC, B'nai B'rith, Agudath Israel, the World Zionist Organization, the American Gathering/Federation of Jewish Holocaust Survivors, and the Center of Organizations of Holocaust Survivors in Israel.

yard and denied the authenticity and the rights of the surviving Jewish communities. Jewish leaders in Central and Eastern Europe vehemently disagreed.

That the Jewish communities in these countries were weak was certainly true, but after a decade in postcommunist societies, none had disappeared. Instead, to varying degrees, they were beginning to mature. "The Holocaust and decades of communist oppression—often with its own special form of anti-Semitism—led many to conclude that immigration to the West or aliyah to Israel were the only real choices for those few Jews remaining," said Rabbi Andrew Baker, director of international Jewish affairs for the American Jewish Committee. "In the past decade Jewish communal life has again taken root. Synagogues have been rebuilt and Jewish schools have opened. Special links have been established with the State of Israel. Rabbis and teachers as well as material assistance have come from abroad, while at the same time a new generation of local leaders has also emerged."[131]

The WJRO tried to assert its role by noting that the surviving property owners and their descendants were not in Europe. "There are more than 1.5 million Jews of Polish origin or descent, Holocaust survivors and their heirs, living elsewhere in the world," the WJRO's Naphtali Lavie told the Polish prime minister in 1997. "They are the people to whom compensation should be made."[132]

A way to include the Jewish organizations abroad was for the local Jewish communities to form foundations or partnerships with them, through which they would jointly file claims, and recover and administer properties. In theory, this provided the Jews abroad

---

[131]American Jewish Committee, *Anti-Semitism, Holocaust Memory, Property Restitution, and Related Issues Confronting the Jewish Communities of Central and Eastern Europe: A Status Report* (Washington, D.C., 2002), p. 1.

[132]*Jerusalem Post,* Mar. 5, 1997. Only months later, however, at a particularly tense moment, he seemed to shift position and advocate for the local community. Frustrated with the pace of restitution, Lavie threatened that the WJRO might work against the admission of Poland, Romania, and the Czech Republic into NATO "until these countries return all the property to their local Jewish communities," according to the June 5, 1997, edition of the Polish daily newspaper *Rzeczpospolita.* "It is difficult to imagine that countries that do not respect private property, the rights of ethnic and religious minorities, could be integrated into European structures and western civilization." He later retreated, but not before he had irritated the American government and exacerbated tensions with the Jewish communities in Warsaw, Bucharest, and Prague, over what they saw as interference in their nations' foreign relations.

with a significant voice in the process. In exchange, such an arrangement could provide the local Jewish community with legal and financial assistance, and technical expertise.[133] This system seemed to work in Romania and Hungary, where the WJRO and the local Jewish communities created foundations to oversee restitution of communal property. The Hungarian initiative was especially noteworthy because it established a fund that provided stipends to victims of the Nazis. However, these foundations were not without flaws, one of which was that they sometimes underestimated the value of the properties.

The attempt to create a foundation could also become the focus for acrimonious intra-Jewish disputes, as happened in Poland. For about two years, relations between the WJRO and the local Union of Jewish Religious Communities in Poland deteriorated over this issue, and Henry Clarke, a State Department official with the rank of ambassador, had to be called in to mediate, without much success.[134] This was a battle with practical consequences: As the two Jewish groups clashed, the deadline for filing claims was nearing. An agreement on a joint approach was not achieved until there was only one year remaining in the original five-year claims period. Although the local community filed property claims without the WJRO's assistance in the early stages of the claims period, it seemed likely that an untold number of properties would be left unclaimed at the deadline because the two sides had been distracted arguing over who would control property that had not yet been claimed. Another potential long-term consequence was that such battles would leave the local communities vulnerable by exposing the lack of international Jewish commitment—real or presumed—to their stability and success.

[133]At the 1998 conference on Holocaust-era assets, Eizenstat encouraged the establishment of "foundations jointly managed by local communities and international groups to aid in the preparation of claims and to administer restituted property, where these are needed to assist the local communities. Such foundations enable international groups to share the burdens, and potentially some of the benefits, of the restituted property."

[134]Antagonism between local and international Jewry was not confined to Central and Eastern Europe. At a meeting of the World Jewish Congress in November 1996, Henri Hajdenberg, the president of CRIF, the umbrella group of French Jewish secular organizations, warned that he would oppose "Jews from America or from Israel coming in and speaking to our government," insisting that outsiders did not understand the local situation.

Practical Problems

No one knows for sure the scope of European Jewry's assets before the Holocaust, and how much Jewish property was stolen, spoiled, destroyed, and lost during the Nazi rampage. The long-used figure was one derived before the end of World War II by Nehemiah Robinson. Using a sophisticated matrix and prewar exchange rates, he estimated Jewish wealth at $8 billion.[135] A half-century later, economist Helen B. Junz studied Jewish prewar assets in Austria, France, Germany, Hungary, the Netherlands, and Poland, countries that together had an estimated Jewish population of 5 million—more than three-quarters of European Jewry outside the Soviet Union—before the Holocaust. Junz estimated that the Jewish communities in these six countries had prewar assets valued (in 1938 dollars) at some $12 billion.[136]

The lack of clarity has created a profound hardship for individual claimants, who have faced an onerous process of identifying and documenting plundered Jewish property. Other factors compound the difficulties: the passage of more than 50 years, inadequate records, and the near certainty of multiple property transfers, guaranteeing that there will be competing and overlapping claims of ownership. Furthermore, the recovery of Nazi-era Jewish property depends on the existence of clear laws, fair regulatory agencies, functioning judicial systems, and the authorities' will to enforce legal decisions.

The early days of postcommunist restitution and reprivatization proceeded amid the chaos of other economic and legal reforms, often resulting in confusion about the applicability or interpretation of laws—where they existed. The courts were often overbur-

---

[135]Robinson, *Indemnification and Reparations, Jewish Aspects,* p. 83.

[136]Helen B. Junz, *Report on the Pre-War Wealth Position of the Jewish Population in Nazi-Occupied Countries, Germany and Austria, Annex to Report on Dormant Accounts of Victims of Nazi Persecution in Swiss Banks, Independent Committee of Eminent Persons* (Bern, 1999). The Independent Committee of Eminent Persons, also known as the Volcker Committee, was established in 1996 to conduct a forensic audit of Holocaust-era accounts in Swiss banks. The committee engaged Junz to conduct a baseline study of prewar European Jewish wealth in order to estimate the potential amounts available for "transfer to, or already lodged in, a safe haven destination." It is noteworthy that until the Volcker Committee, there had been no concerted postwar effort to identify the scope of Jewish assets and losses in Europe, outside of Germany and Austria (which had been undertaken after the war by the JRSO and the Claims Conference).

dened, and inexperienced in the fledgling Westernization of their institutions. There were occasions when the courts operated with dueling systems of law—the entrenched Soviet-era versions and the underdeveloped Western ones. And if the courts were unreliable, their judgments were not necessarily enforceable. In Bulgaria, for instance, nearly a decade after Sofia's Jewish community first won a 1992 court ruling to recover its stake in a hotel—prime real estate in the heart of the capital—the government has consistently failed to enforce the ruling. The legal battle over the hotel, which stands on the site of a former Jewish school that was destroyed in World War II by American bombs, was paradoxical, in light of Bulgaria's pride in being the first Eastern European state to have enacted a postcommunist restitution law. To compound the conundrum, the site was partly privatized after the court ruling, compelling the Jewish community to battle on two fronts: against the government and against the new "owners."[137]

Costs associated with property restitution posed a significant problem, and there is anecdotal evidence that Jewish claims were abandoned because the expense of recovering the property was simply too high. Many restitution laws place severe financial burdens on the successful claimant, including liability for back taxes and liens. In other instances, the property may be unencumbered by debt, but the community or individual cannot afford the rehabilitation, maintenance, and preservation costs. This often is the case where small communities find themselves guardians of properties that require care, but that do not generate the income to sustain themselves.

Another significant cost is compensation to the current occupant for improvements he or she made to the facility, or simply to ease what would otherwise be an eviction. Central and Eastern European governments—as well as the U.S.—have expressed great concern for the rights of current occupants. Two generations after the war, it is common that property would have been transferred several times. It had been "Aryanized" by the Nazis through confiscation or sales that are presumed to have been under duress. The property was later nationalized by the communists, and may have changed hands since the fall of the Berlin Wall. Jewish claims, while morally defensible, are thus extremely awkward, since they

[137] *Jerusalem Post,* July 30, 2000.

are against current occupants who may be innocent of any theft. Often, restoring Jewish property is viewed as correcting one injustice with another.

While costs have discouraged many individuals from pursuing their properties, they pose a special dilemma for cash-strapped Jewish communities. The properties that the governments are most eager to return and for which Jews abroad clamor, are the most religiously significant—and the most expensive to protect and preserve—cemeteries.

There are between 5,000 and 10,000 Jewish cemeteries and mass-burial sites in Europe, and this number refers only to those that have been identified or presumed to exist, according to Samuel Gruber, director of the Jewish Heritage Research Center and president of the International Survey of Jewish Monuments. But cemeteries are not the local communities' immediate priority. They are a distracting burden without any tangible benefit. "Our priorities are with the Holocaust survivors, the living generation," said Tomas Kraus, head of the Czech Jewish community, echoing a sentiment heard across Central and Eastern Europe. "Take care of them, and then we can talk about heritage."[138]

Some claims, however, are driven by emotion and nostalgia. There have been instances in which tiny communities, motivated in part by a desire to regain symbols of their past, have sought to recover prominent sites they cannot afford to rehabilitate and do not have the members to fill. In Poland, the local Jewish community claimed Yeshivat Chachmei Lublin. "The yeshivah is a monument to the Jewish past and we want to preserve it," said Helena Datner, an official of the community. But she added: "What do people want to do with Yeshivat Chachmei Lublin?"[139]

It often appears that the properties that are most accessible to the Jewish communities of Central and Eastern Europe are precisely the ones that drain resources. In theory, one way of preserving Jewish sites and generating funds is to recover properties that would be useful for "Jewish tourism." There has been a flowering of interest in European "Judaica" in the decade since the collapse of communism. The "European Day of Jewish Culture," a

---

[138]Ibid.

[139]Ibid., May 11, 2000.

continental "open house" of cultural events in dozens of Jewish communities, draws tens of thousands of people, and quickly was established as an annual event. This is what author Ruth Ellen Gruber has called the "Judaizing terrain," in which monuments, museums, concerts, and cafés conjure up a rich Jewish tradition and a "virtual Jewish world" in places with few Jews.

However, this prospect raises an additional and entirely new set of concerns, including whether communities are interested in properties that they may not use themselves, whether gaining title to the sites that are suitable for tourism requires assistance from outsiders, whether such aid is likely, and whether the local community and the government will support such intervention. More important, would such efforts fairly and authentically reflect Jewish life and culture?[140]

CULTURAL PROPERTY

On January 30, 2002, the president of Israel, Moshe Katzav, was at Ben-Gurion International Airport to greet the arrival of Torah scrolls, as the scrolls, along with hundreds of Jewish holy books, arrived in Israel on a special El Al flight from Vilnius, Lithuania.[141] After six decades, the sacred items were reunited with the People of the Book. This Judaica had been confiscated by the Nazis, then kept under wraps in Soviet-ruled Lithuania. It was only in October 2000, on the eve of an international conference on Nazi-looted cultural property, that independent Lithuania's parliament voted to release the scrolls to Jewish groups and synagogues outside the country. Lithuanian officials did not know what a Torah scroll was and had no conception of the different Jewish holy books, let alone their sacred significance to the Jewish people. Yet many Lithuanians had believed that these items were part of their national patrimony, and they did not want to part with them.

The scrolls are highly symbolic in the long struggle to recover Nazi-looted cultural property. For years, their survival had been

---

[140]Ruth Ellen Gruber has explored these and other issues regarding postwar European Jewish culture in *Upon the Doorposts of Thy House: Jewish Life in East-Central Europe, Yesterday and Today* (New York, 1994), and *Virtually Jewish: Reinventing Jewish Culture in Europe* (Berkeley, 2002).

[141]*Ha'aretz*, Jan. 31, 2002.

unknown to the Jewish community. When their existence was publicly revealed, they were difficult to extricate from Lithuanian control, and, finally, Jews bickered over who was entitled to them. Their fate mirrors that of an untold number of other Jewish cultural properties that were despoiled and damaged in the Nazi and communist eras—artworks subsequently held by governments, museums or private collectors, and Jewish books and ceremonial objects that wound up in the permanent custodial care of non-Jewish institutions.

Hitler looted Europe of its treasures. But, because of the Nazis' different motives for the cultural plunder, the treasures faced different fates. European art appealed to Hitler's greed; it was coveted either for its aesthetic significance or its market value—art could be sold to finance the German war machine. Judaica was anathema; it was to be destroyed, with only a remnant to be saved as a relic of a despised race. Entire art collections, archives, and libraries were despoiled.

In Central and Eastern Europe, it is not clear how many items survived the Nazi era because it is not known what was captured afterwards by Soviet troops and carted off as booty. Among the Jewish cultural materials that have been recovered, the most remarkable are in Prague. After the war, there were 15,000 Jews in the city out of a prewar population of more than 300,000. Unable to care for its Jewish Museum, the surviving community ceded the museum to the communist government in 1949. In 1994, the government returned the museum to the Jewish community.[142]

The recovery of cultural properties is subject to legal, moral, economic, and political problems that are far more entangled than those hampering the recovery of real estate and other types of Nazi-looted assets. For one thing, artworks and artifacts travel. Through public exhibitions and the private art market, they cross borders in which different and often conflicting legal codes govern ownership and concepts of theft. Also, the objects themselves are far more intimate than other kinds of assets. Cultural property, in a sense, embodies a personal history that reflects its creator and owner. To the individual, the objects often represent the last link

[142]Ruth E. Gruber, "Head of Prague Jewish Museum yearns for an 'active' institution,'" Jewish Telegraphic Agency Daily News Bulletin, Dec. 17, 1995.

to families that were annihilated by the Nazis. To a community, they represent a proud legacy created and nurtured by its members over generations. Jewish cultural, religious, and intellectual traditions—and the objects that embody them—collectively represent the soul of the Jewish people. The theft of cultural objects is not simply a robbery, but the theft of identity, and the effort to recover them is a crusade to restore memory and salvage a heritage.

That salvage work began shortly after the beginning of World War II, with the relocation of the YIVO Institute for Jewish Research, established in Vilna (Vilnius, then in Poland) in 1925, to New York in 1940. Then, prominent scholars in the U.S., led by Professor Salo Baron of Columbia University—supplied with information gleaned from refugees and other sources—began the task of trying to inventory the Judaica and other cultural properties that had to be salvaged from Europe. They founded Jewish Cultural Reconstruction (JCR) in 1947 as a "cultural agent" of the JRSO, which recognized the JCR as trustee for heirless cultural properties.[143]

There were vast quantities of them. The U.S. military in Germany and Austria found extraordinary hoards of Nazi loot in deserted SS headquarters and government agencies, salt mines, concentration camps, castles, and corporate offices, and on intercepted trains. In September 1948, the U.S. military occupation authorities estimated that U.S. forces had found some 1,500 repositories of art and cultural objects—containing some 10.7 million objects worth an estimated $5 billion—in Germany alone.[144]

The plundered property was assembled at collection points in Germany. At one time, the JCR depot at Offenbach had a half-million books, 8,000 ceremonial objects, and 1,024 Torah scrolls. "Our first goal was to restore them to the rightful owners, but usually you couldn't tell," recalled Benjamin Ferencz.[145] JCR, representing constituencies in the U.S. and Mandatory Palestine, developed a distribution formula—resented in Europe at the

[143]The founders were essentially the same as those who founded the JRSO, with one significant addition: The Hebrew University was among the JCR founders. The president of the JCR was Professor Baron; Hannah Arendt served as executive secretary.

[144]*Plunder and Restitution,* p. 97. This source provides an overview of the collection points and the activities of Jewish Cultural Reconstruction.

[145]Transcript of Ferencz interview, Oct. 21, 1994, U.S. Holocaust Memorial Museum Oral History Library.

time—that would aid in the reconstruction of Jewish life, which, at that moment, was seen as being possible only outside the continent. The surviving European communities would receive objects limited to "the prospective religious and cultural needs of the community and its capacity to retain, to care for, and to use them for the religious and cultural purposes for which they were intended." Of the rest, 40 percent of the books were sent to Israel and another 40 percent to American Jewish institutions. The remainder was divided among Jewish communities outside Europe.[146] (Rare books were treated differently, and their distribution was not confined to Jewish institutions. In recognition of the American government's aid to JCR, the Judaic departments of non-Jewish institutions were also recipients, including the Library of Congress, the New York Public Library, and Harvard, Yale, and Columbia universities.) The distribution was completed in 1952. In addition to the books, scrolls, and Judaica, "a total of 700 works of Jewish art, which had been seized by the Gestapo, were sent to enrich the new museums of Israel," Ferencz said. "The temples had been destroyed, but these symbols of a great tradition would be seeds of the regeneration of Jewish life."[147]

Who Owns It?

In general, JCR was widely credited for a thoughtful and practical policy that was of enormous benefit to the postwar centers of Jewish life. Five decades later, however, a more-confident European Jewry began to assert its rights. The venue was Vilnius, which, in October 2000, hosted the last of four annual international conferences focusing on Nazi-era looted assets (the first three had been held in London, Washington, and Stockholm). The Vilnius conference was devoted to the question of cultural property. "Our Jewish community of Europe is not negotiable," said Rabbi Aba Dunner, secretary general of the Conference of European Rabbis. "We want our history here. We want those Jewish communities to build themselves up with their own history, with their pride."[148]

---

[146]Michael J. Kurtz, "Resolving a Dilemma: The Inheritance of Jewish Property," *Cardozo Law Review* 20, no. 2, Dec. 1998, p. 643.

[147]Ferencz, "Restitution to Nazi Victims," p. 303.

[148]http://www.vilniusforum.lt/proceedings/d/rabbi_aba_dunner_en.htm.

It was a sentiment expressed the year before in the Council of Europe, where Emanuelis Zingeris, a member of the Lithuanian delegation to the Parliamentary Assembly, had been the rapporteur for Assembly Resolution 1205 on "Looted Jewish Cultural Property."[149] It said that the restitution of cultural property "to its original owners or their heirs (individuals, institutions or communities) or countries is a significant way of enabling the reconstitution of the place of Jewish culture in Europe itself."[150]

This raised the tricky issue that emerged at the conference in Vilnius. Much of the heirless and unclaimed Jewish cultural property had been distributed by JCR, a Jewish organization, to Jewish institutions around the world. In the interim, however, "communities and museums, which had been written off as never again to exist, have taken on new lives," said Tom Freudenheim, the director of the Gilbert Collection in London and the former director of YIVO. At the end of the century, there were Jewish museums in Berlin, Frankfurt, Vienna, Vilnius, and other cities the Nazis had looted, but their art and artifacts had been dispersed. "Material formerly belonging to Jewish institutions in those cities now sits in New York, Los Angeles, Jerusalem, and elsewhere," Freudenheim said. And he asked:

> Is today's Jewish museum in Frankfurt somehow less deserving of works that are documented to have belonged to the prewar Jewish museum of Frankfurt? Does the Israel Museum have higher legal or moral rights to works documented to have belonged to the Jewish community museum in Berlin, when today there are two Jewish museums in Berlin? Indeed, did the Israel Museum have the legal right to sell on the open market works it had been given after the war "on behalf of the Jewish people" as part of the conventional deaccession process that most museums engage in?[151]

The Israeli delegation, led by Colette Avital, chair of the Knesset committee on war-era assets in Israel, made a moral claim to heirless property. Holocaust-era art, books, paintings, sculpture, and Judaica should be returned to their rightful owners or heirs, said Avital. But if these properties were heirless, "it should be es-

---

[149]Zingeris also was a primary organizer of the Vilnius Forum.

[150]Council of Europe, Parliamentary Assembly, Resolution 1205, adopted by the Standing Committee, acting on behalf of the Assembly, Nov. 4, 1999.

[151]http://www.vilniusforum.lt/proceedings/d/tom_freudenheim_en.htm.

tablished that the Jewish people and its representatives will become the natural heirs, both in their right to claim, and in their right to ultimately own that property."[152]

The Vilnius conference was not a forum for decision-making. Nonetheless, it concluded with a declaration, adopted by officials from 37 countries, asking all governments "to undertake every reasonable effort to achieve the restitution of cultural assets looted during the Holocaust era." It did not take a position on the contentious issue of who had the right to heirless Jewish cultural property, noting simply the "urgent need to work on ways to achieve a just and fair solution to the issue of Nazi-looted art and cultural property where owners, or heirs of former Jewish owners, individuals or legal persons, cannot be identified."[153]

In truth, the phrase "Jewish cultural property" is ambiguous. While Torah scrolls, Hebraica, and Judaica are obvious, Jewish "art" is less clear. The definition in the 1999 Parliamentary Assembly resolution is broad. It states that an "essential part of the Nazi plan to eradicate the Jews was the destruction of the Jewish cultural heritage," defined as "movable and immovable property, created, collected or owned by Jews in Europe." There is a difference, however, between "Jewish" and Jewish-owned" art, and a question of how restituted heirless Jewish-owned art should be used. Some say it should be auctioned, and the proceeds used to aid survivors. Others believe it should be exhibited and its history recounted, to serve as a tool in Holocaust education. But some Jewish museums are not interested in displaying the recovered art if the artists were not Jewish, and, even if they were, their work would not necessarily be exhibited in these institutions. Thus while the restitution is to be applauded, and legally the object would be "Jewish property," an item may not be valuable as a "Jewish" artifact. For instance, one of the most celebrated recoveries at century's end was the restoration of a Nazi-looted painting to the heirs of Viennese collector Philip von Gomperz. The painting is a small devotional image by the German Renaissance artist Lucas Cranach the Elder, entitled *Madonna and Child in a Landscape*.[154]

---

[152]http://www.vilniusforum.lt/proceedings/session/colette_avital_en.htm.

[153]http://www.vilniusforum.lt/media/declaration.htm.

[154]Much of the celebration concerned the heirs' generosity under the terms of the settlement in 2000. The painting had been a bequest, in 1984, to the North Carolina Museum

There are numerous instances in which heirless, formerly Jewish-owned art is considered part of the "national heritage" of the country where the Nazi victims once lived. Although Lithuania's former claim to the Torah scrolls as its patrimony strained credulity, the principle is real. The French, for instance, claim Camille Pissarro, a member of the founding group of 19th-century French Impressionists, as part of their cultural heritage. For Colette Avital, however, he is a Jewish painter, his works "a testimony of Jewish creativity, spirituality and talent."

There is not much incentive for European nations to part with Nazi-era cultural property, and a state may have a number of reasons to resist restitution and claim the art for itself. The artists and the art may truly express, and be associated with, that specific place or national culture.[155] The works may have a decades-long history as vital ingredients in the "permanent" exhibitions of prominent museums, and restitution would create a profound loss both for the museum and the public it serves.[156] Four Vienna museums in 1999, for instance, had to relinquish more than 200 Old Master and 19th-century paintings that were restituted to Bettina Looram-Rothschild, the daughter of Alphonse and Clarice Rothschild. Several years later, in 2002, there were continuing legal battles between Austria and the heir of industrialist Ferdinand Bloch-Bauer over six important Gustav Klimt paintings in the Belvedere, the Austrian national gallery. The surviving heir argues that the paintings, valued at $150 million, were seized twice—by the Nazis in 1938, and again when the Austrian government refused to return them to Bloch-Bauer's heirs after World War II. The legal issues in the case are murky, but it is clear that if Austria returned the paintings to the heir, the Belvedere would lose some of its most

---

of Art in Raleigh. Although the museum was alarmed to learn that a prized possession had been confiscated by the Gestapo in 1940, it returned the Cranach to the heirs. The museum then offered to buy the painting, but its acquisition budget of $600,000 was only half the painting's appraised value. In appreciation of the museum's no-fuss return, the heirs accepted $600,000 for the painting, which was returned to Raleigh.

[155]This, of course, does not preclude a museum from trying to reach a settlement with the rightful owner and paying compensation for the object.

[156]For an outstanding review of private versus collective rights to a variety of cultural properties, including art, scientific and historical documents, and the Dead Sea Scrolls, see Joseph L. Sax, *Playing Darts with a Rembrandt: Public and Private Rights in Cultural Treasures* (Ann Arbor, 1999).

prized possessions, including two famous paintings of Viennese beauty Adele Bloch-Bauer.

After the war, it was the policy of the victorious powers to repatriate artworks to the national government of the object's country of origin, and the recipient government was responsible for locating the rightful owner. However, the United States did not monitor the recipient countries' compliance, and there was little public discussion of the repatriation efforts until a December 1984 article in *ARTnews* magazine, "A Legacy of Shame: Nazi Art Loot in Austria." It revealed that a cache of art that had been stolen from Viennese Jews was turned over to the Austrian government in 1955. Austria did not make a strenuous effort to find the heirs. Instead, it placed the artworks in its museums or stored them in a 14th-century monastery in Mauerbach, some 30 miles from Vienna.

The article prompted the Austrian government to undertake a new effort to locate heirs, and, a decade later, it turned over to the Jewish community of Vienna the residual unclaimed articles. There were some 8,000 items—paintings, books, tapestries, textiles and carpets, furniture, coins, and arms and armor. They were sold in an emotional, two-day auction in October 1996 that raised $14.5 million for Holocaust victims.[157]

The extraordinary publicity generated by the Mauerbach auction (coupled with the publication of Lynn Nicholas's book *The Rape of Europa: The Fate of Europe's Treasures in the Third Reich and the Second World War,* and attention to Holocaust-era assets generated by class-action lawsuits against the Swiss banks) stimulated interest in how other nations had handled Nazi-looted art. The situation in Austria was not unique. The Netherlands in 2001 tacitly acknowledged problems in the restoration of repatriated artwork to Dutch victims. The government's Art Property Foundation, known as the Stichting Nederlandsch Kunstbezit (SNK), had been responsible between 1945 and 1952 for the recovery and restitution of works of art. At the turn of the century, however, about 4,000 items—including some 1,600 paintings—remained in the state-administered Nederlands Kunstbezit collection. It appears that the government used the postwar repatriation program to stock its national museums. "The SNK acted in [prominent]

[157]Reuters, Oct. 31, 1996.

cases as a kind of art requisition bureau for the state," said Dr. Gerard Aalders, a researcher at the Netherlands Institute of War Documentation in Amsterdam and the author of *The Art of Cloaking Ownership.*[158]

The Shulz Fragments

In January 1995, the Bard Graduate Center for Studies in the Decorative Arts, in New York, convened an impressive symposium of officials, historians, curators, and lawyers from two dozen countries to discuss problems with the repatriation of World War II-era cultural property. It was called "The Spoils of War."[159] At that time, it was customary to refer to the art stolen during the war as "trophy art," and it was perceived, in general terms, as "spoils of war." Jewish claims were a stepchild in the discussion.[160] Soon after, the new international focus on Jewish material losses changed the frame of reference, and it became common to refer to "Nazi-looted" or "Holocaust" art.

If the old terminology had marginalized Jewish claims, the new vernacular masked the fact that nations themselves still focus on their substantial war-related art losses, of which Jewish or Nazi-looted art may be only a fraction. For instance, as part of its campaign to deal with Nazi-looted art, Germany, in April 2000, launched a Web site listing some 2,000 works of art of dubious origin that were held in public institutions. The works are generally known as the "Linz list," referring to a collection that Hitler planned for an art museum near his Austrian hometown. Michael Naumann, the minister of culture, estimated that only 10 percent of the 2,000 paintings were looted from Jews.[161] In addition, many governments and cultural institutions are searching for their own

---

[158]*ARTnews,* Sept. 2001.

[159]The proceedings were published: Elizabeth Simpson, ed., *The Spoils of War—World War II and its Aftermath: The Loss, Reappearance and Recovery of Cultural Property* (New York, 1997).

[160]At the Bard symposium, for example, there were dozens of presentations by government and museum officials representing Austria, Belarus, France, Germany, Hungary, the Netherlands, Poland, Russia, Ukraine, and the United States. There was only one presentation dealing exclusively with Judaica, by Vivian Mann of the Jewish Museum in New York.

[161]*Jerusalem Post,* Apr. 21, 2000.

wartime cultural losses, not for the loot in their possession. Germany, for instance, has outstanding claims for the hundreds of thousands of objects that were seized by the Soviets as "compensation" for war damages. The Russians, willing to restore Nazi-looted art to individual Jews, are not so inclined with the German government.

In May 2001, Yad Vashem "acquired" the fragments of murals of fairy-tale figures that had been painted on the walls of a Nazi officer's house in Drohobycz by Bruno Schulz, a Polish artist and writer who was murdered on the streets of that city on November 19, 1942. The decaying fragments had been discovered in February 2001 by German documentary filmmaker Benjamin Geissler, in a room being used as a pantry in what had become a private flat. The "acquisition," in one fell swoop, set off a multifaceted debate on a host of legal, moral, and ideological issues that divided Jewish communities, institutions, governments, artists, and preservationists. These overlapping issues included how to define Jewish cultural property, who has the rights to artifacts, whether Holocaust-era artifacts differ from others, how cultural property should be preserved and used, and what public purpose preservation serves.

Yad Vashem insisted it had a "moral right" to the remnants of Schulz's work, which were painted in the room of the children of SS officer Feliks Landau. "As Bruno Schulz was a Jewish artist forced to illustrate the walls of the home of a German SS officer with his sketches as a Jewish prisoner during the Holocaust, and killed by an SS officer purely because he was a Jew, the correct and most suitable place to house the drawings he sketched during the Holocaust is Yad Vashem, the Holocaust Martyrs' and Heroes' Remembrance Authority in Jerusalem," it said in a statement. Yad Vashem also argued that it had gotten the approval of local officials, but the latter disputed that account.

What Yad Vashem called a rescue, others called a robbery. "Bruno Schulz is one of the key figures of Polish literature in the 20th century," said Konstanty Gebert of Warsaw, the founding editor of the Polish Jewish magazine *Midrazs.* "I can hardly begin to describe how much outrage and how much pain we feel," Gebert said in New York, at a forum in July 2001 sponsored by the American Jewish Committee and the National Foundation for Jewish

Culture. "We feel robbed. We feel something, a living part of our heritage, has been smuggled away."[162]

Given the shifts in postwar borders, the Polish city where Schulz worked and was murdered is now in Ukraine. Ukrainian national law bars the export of antiquities and pre-1945 cultural objects without a permit. But it was not clear whether the fragments qualify as cultural property, whether national or local authorities had the right to determine their disposition, or whether indeed the fragments are considered Ukrainian. Looked at from a different perspective, the fragments may have been the legal property of Nikolai Kaluzhny, who, some 60 years later, owned the flat.

Within the Jewish world, moral issues hover over the legal ones. Yad Vashem's claim to a moral right has its supporters, both because it is a documentation-commemoration center and because it is in Jerusalem. Schulz "lived as a Jew and died as a Jew. I see no more appropriate repository," said Melvin James Bukiet, a New York novelist who is a member of Yad Vashem's board. But local communities argue that they have the moral right to their communal patrimony. They take umbrage at the implication that they are unwilling or unable to preserve their cultural property, as well as with the presumption that Israel represents the Jews. The idea that the fragments belong in Israel "invalidates us—not just the small Jewish communities in Ukraine and Poland, but also the Diaspora," said Gebert.[163]

During the cold war, there had been the sense of an urgent need to rescue Jewish heritage sites in Central and Eastern Europe, quickly and often surreptitiously. That was no longer the case, said Samuel Gruber. It was quite the reverse, he felt, and he feared that Yad Vashem's act could have "a destructive effect on hundreds of other Jewish sites throughout the world. It sets back recent progress in preservation of Jewish monuments and Holocaust sites in Central and Eastern Europe, where local involvement and legal protections are still evolving." Yad Vashem's claim of a "moral

---

[162]Schulz's stories were originally published in the 1930s in Poland. They were reissued in Poland after the war, and have since been translated into several languages. The two books so far published in English are *Street of Crocodiles* (1992) and *Sanatorium Under the Sign of the Hourglass* (1997).

[163]The debate at the forum was reported in the *New York Times,* July 18, 2001.

right" to remove Holocaust artifacts is a "kind of false reasoning" that could be used by anyone "to justify plundering cultural heritage," he wrote. "Whose moral right should prevail, particularly in postcommunist Europe, where local Jewish communities are attempting to reassert their identity?"[164]

There were other nagging questions: Were the fragments "Jewish art," or art painted by a Jew? Were they art, or were they the product of slave labor, or both? Yad Vashem said that it would preserve the work for generations, and so it "may be viewed by the millions of tourists from all over the world who visit Yad Vashem each year." There is no doubt that millions more people would view the fragments in Yad Vashem than at some restored site in Drohobycz. And yet many argue that sites must be preserved at the source, where they serve as an important historical marker and educational tool in a locality's confrontation with its past. Under Yad Vashem's logic, all evidence of Jewish life in Europe could be removed, piece by piece, and its history erased.

The "Bondi Schiele" and Other Artworks

The museum world was shaken early in 1998 when the heirs of a Jewish art dealer from Vienna appealed to New York's Museum of Modern Art to detain an Egon Schiele painting that was part of an exhibit on loan from Austria's government-financed Leopold Foundation. The painting, *Portrait of Wally,* was due to leave the U.S. when the exhibition closed, and the heirs of Lea Bondi Jaray were urgently trying to keep the painting in the country. They contended that it had been confiscated from the dealer, who was unable to recover it and who was never compensated for the loss. "We earnestly request that you do not return the painting to the jurisdiction of the 'lenders' until the matter of true ownership has been clarified," the heirs said in a letter to MOMA.[165] The museum, expressing sympathy, said it was contractually obligated to release the painting. It also feared that any detention would disrupt the orderly conduct of other international exhibitions.

The controversy created a predicament for Ronald S. Lauder,

---

[164]Op-ed in *New York Times,* July 3, 2001.

[165]*New York Times*, Jan. 1, 1998.

which also was a dilemma for the organized Jewish community. The businessman-philanthropist was the museum's chairman. He also was the chairman of the World Jewish Congress's Commission on Art Recovery, an entity newly created to assist claimants seeking Nazi-looted art. When the commission was announced, the incoming director, art historian Constance Lowenthal, said, "We will try to recover art wherever we find it."[166] Jewish organizations, however, never advocated for Nazi-looted art with the energy they devoted to Holocaust-era bank accounts, insurance policies, or real estate.[167]

A legal battle over the Schiele began in January 1998, when the Manhattan district attorney, Robert Morgenthau, seized the painting until its ownership could be determined. When state courts subsequently ruled that Morgenthau had exceeded his authority and was obliged to release *Wally,* the federal government detained the painting. At the end of 2001, the case was still pending in U.S. District Court in Manhattan.

Morgenthau's seizure led Austria's minister for education and cultural affairs, Elisabeth Gehrer, to establish a Commission for Provenance Research, whose work in 1998 served as the basis for legislation to restitute property that, more than a half-century after its "Aryanization," remained under state control, or that had been extorted in the course of export proceedings after 1945. That paved the way for new art restitution, such as that to the Rothschild family, which had been coerced into donating the majority of its art to the state after the war in exchange for the right to "export" the remaining objects.[168]

---

[166]Ibid., Nov. 29, 1997.

[167]In the subsequent legal skirmishes over *Wally,* Jewish organizations were conspicuous by their silence. While a number of nongovernmental organizations had set up entities to deal with Nazi-looted art, they concentrated on collating existing information from multiple sources and creating databases. They did not see themselves as aggressive agencies assisting individual claimants seeking specific objects. The only authoritative body conducting such work, at no cost to the claimant, was the Holocaust Claims Processing Office, established in 1997 in the New York State Banking Department.

[168]The heirs auctioned the recovered items and divided the proceeds. The sale, in London in July 1999, broke the record for European auctions, bringing in $90 million, more than twice the presale estimated value of the objects. Along with Old Masters, the family sold the *Rothschild Prayerbook,* a 16th-century illuminated manuscript that fetched a record-breaking $13.3 million.

In Europe, governments and museums, prompted in part by fear that objects on loan in the U.S. might be seized as stolen property, began to establish mechanisms to examine the provenance of works held by public institutions. The museum community in the U.S. also began such review. "The hunt for Nazi loot has turned into the greatest treasure hunt in history," said Lord Greville Janner of the London-based Holocaust Educational Trust. "We don't know where it will end."[169]

In 1998, at the Washington Conference on Holocaust-Era Assets, delegations from 44 countries adopted the so-called "Washington Principles." These were non-binding guidelines that aimed to restore Nazi-looted art. They called for the opening of archives to facilitate research, a central registry, public announcements of unrestituted works, alternative dispute-resolution strategies for resolving ownership questions, and a "just and fair solution" for looted works whose owners cannot be identified. "The art world will never be the same in the way it deals with Nazi-confiscated art. From now on, the sale, purchase, exchange, and display of art from this period will be addressed with greater sensitivity and a higher international standard of responsibility," said Stuart Eizenstat. "This is a major achievement which will reverberate through our museums, galleries, auction houses, and in the homes and hearts of those families who may now have the chance to have returned what is rightfully theirs. This will also lead to the removal of uncertainty in the world art market and facilitate commercial and cultural exchange."[170]

The Washington principles were "moral commitments," said Ambassador J.D. Bindenagel, who organized the conference. "How they are applied is up to governments, individual auction houses, galleries, and museums."[171] Although not binding, the principles had an impact. They encouraged nations to examine the history of the war-era cultural property they had acquired, or supported efforts already under way, in a manner that was not threatening to individual nations or institutions. "There is a value to the international arena, where each country is undertaking a task, each in

[169]Reuters, Nov. 17, 1998.

[170]Eizenstat's concluding statement, Dec. 3, 1998, http://fcit.coedu.usf.edu/holocaust/resource/assets/concl2.htm.

[171]*ARTnews,* May 1999.

its own way, instead of being isolated, or with the finger-pointing as was originally the case with Switzerland," said one French official. "Our review is the French answer to a problem that is not only French."[172]

The Washington principles recognized that countries must "act within the context of their own laws." The call for "resolution strategies" and "just and fair" solutions is vague, in part, because cultural property has special characteristics that set it uniquely apart. Modern-day claims—whether they are pursued by individuals, communities, institutions, or nations—are efforts to recover specific and identifiable items that have to be tracked one by one, and that are subject not only to international conventions on cultural property, but also to national, civil and criminal legal codes that vary by jurisdiction and are open to different legal interpretations. Different jurisdictions have various rules governing such key elements of restitution claims as "good faith" purchases and statutes of limitation.

Individuals have turned to civil courts for redress, but the process is taxing, time-consuming, and expensive. For instance, when the heirs of Friedrich Gutmann filed a lawsuit in 1996 to recover a single painting plundered from the family's art collection, they faced uncontrollable costs to document and litigate the claim, and resorted to placing an ad in the *Forward,* a weekly Jewish newspaper based in New York, seeking donations for a "legal defense fund."[173] Given the original size and subsequent dispersal of the Gutmann collection, the heirs, in their quest, had to hire researchers to scour archives, libraries, and galleries around the globe, and engage legal services in three different cities and translators for documents in five different languages. The costs of litigation are "astonishing," said Thomas Kline of Washington, an attorney who represented the Gutmann heirs. "I am almost at the point where I would say that if the art is worth less than $3 million, give up."[174]

For the individual claimant, the major hurdle to recovering art is simply locating the object. Prewar collections did not survive in-

[172]Interview with author, Apr. 25, 2001.

[173]The painting at the center of the 1996 lawsuit was Edgar Degas's *Landscape with Smokestacks,* which, at the time, was owned by a Chicago art collector.

[174]*Jerusalem Post,* Apr. 3, 1998.

tact. They were dispersed during the Nazi era through confiscations and forced sales. In the decades since the war, objects have moved through commercial and cultural exchanges, and many plundered works have quietly reentered the legitimate art trade and museum world, gradually acquiring what appeared to be authoritative provenance. They can suddenly emerge, startling both the claimant and the current possessor.

Consider the tale of two paintings that were separated, sold, and seized during the Nazi era from the collection of Ismar Littmann of Breslau, who committed suicide in 1934 in the face of the Nazi persecution. *Seated Nude on Blue Cushion,* a 1927 painting by the German artist Karl Hofer, was seized by the Gestapo in 1935, only days before it was to be sold at a "Jew auction." The Gestapo turned the painting over to the National Gallery in Berlin, then seized it again in 1937 for the Munich exhibition of "degenerate art." To earn foreign exchange, the Nazis put the painting on the market, where it was bought by a Norwegian collector in 1941. Almost 60 years later, in 1999, it was consigned to a London art dealer, when it was claimed by Littmann's Israeli daughter, who by that time was in her 80s. Another item from the Littmann collection, Lovis Corinth's *Portrait of Charlotte Corinth,* was sold in 1935 at a "Jew auction" and changed hands several times before it was acquired by a Berlin dealer in 1940. Over time, it changed hands at least three more times before arriving at the Hamburger Landesbank, as collateral for a loan. The bank put the painting up for auction in November 2000 when the borrower defaulted. Littmann's daughter recovered both paintings in November 2001, with the assistance of the New York State Banking Department's Holocaust Claims Processing Office, after exhaustive research to track the paintings' distinctive paths over six decades and a number of countries.[175]

HAS JUSTICE BEEN DONE?

There is much talk, more than 50 years after the end of the Shoah, about "doing justice" for Nazi victims. Shortly after the end of World War II, "doing justice" meant ensuring that victims were

---

[175] *ARTnews,* Feb. 2002.

compensated for the material damages they suffered from persecution, and that they could recover the properties, bank accounts, art, and artifacts that were taken from them. By that standard, there has been a measure of justice. In 2000, nearly 100,000 Nazi victims were still receiving a check each month of about DM 1,000 from Germany, payments based on agreements that were negotiated in The Hague in 1952. Of course, despite the duration and the amount of the payments, they cannot compensate for the loss or relieve the suffering. Nor did the original German programs address all facets of material losses—either for all groups of Nazi victims, or for assets outside of Germany.

At the beginning of a new century, it was still not clear who should determine what measure of justice is sufficient, what form it should take, and which vehicle is appropriate. There were "monetary" and "nonmonetary" forms of justice, and these were of varying degrees of relevance and importance to the extraordinary number of actors who had become involved in these issues.

The most visible of the actors was the peripatetic Stuart Eizenstat, who represented the American government's interests between 1995 and 2001. There also were the Claims Conference, the World Jewish Restitution Organization, and the World Jewish Congress; American state insurance commissioners and local finance officials; as well as government officials from Germany, Austria, France, Israel, and Central and Eastern Europe—not to mention the class-action lawyers representing victims.[176] They represented different agendas, many of them adversarial. All were swimming in uncharted seas. Restitution and compensation claims had legal, diplomatic, economic, historical, moral, and political dimensions, and these claims were being pursued through courts, commissions, legislation, and regulation. The discordant approaches often threatened to derail each other and delay any resolution—in part because each of the varied approaches had its own requirements, advocates, and constituencies.

"We know there are survivors in need, and they deserve to be

---

[176]Because of overlapping memberships and common interests between the Claims Conference, the WJRO, and the WJC, it was often unclear which organization assumed which role in the various proceedings. In the summer of 2002, Israel Singer, the new president of the Claims Conference and also cochairman of the WJRO, called for a formal merger between the two. He had just stepped down as secretary general of the WJC.

helped now," said Andrew Baker of the AJC. "Everyone agrees with this statement, but it appears to be the beginning and not the end of problems and controversy, as help is delayed and as organizations and lawyers and governments vie with each other to be the conduit for this aid."[177]

Where claims could be consolidated,[178] no particular potential "conduit" was universally beneficial for the victims. Each had merits and disadvantages. The issue of the Swiss banks, for example, seemed suited to a legal settlement because it was concerned primarily with recovering a specific type of asset from private institutions for a specific group—the bank accounts of particular depositors. However, in the slave-labor cases, the German foundation, which was a creation of both legal and diplomatic initiatives, appeared to be superior to a court settlement.[179] The foundation would provide benefits to many more former slave and forced laborers than would have been covered by a court judgment against the companies being sued, especially since the claimants including workers from Nazi-era public enterprises and from now-defunct businesses. It also would benefit Nazi-era agricultural workers who had no company to sue.[180]

Efforts to develop the appropriate venue led to some proceedings

---

[177]Plenary session on Nazi-confiscated communal property, *Proceedings of the Washington Conference on Holocaust-Era Assets* (Washington, D.C., Dec. 1998), p. 704.

[178]This refers to instances in which the claimants or the assets themselves have something in common—such as slave and forced laborers, or insurance policies and banks accounts.

[179]It is not clear that any of the cases against German industry for war-era slave labor compensation would have prevailed in U.S. courts. In September 1999, in the first ruling in the recent spate of American class-action lawsuits, the U.S. District Court in Newark, New Jersey, dismissed the cases against two companies, Degussa and Siemens. The federal judge, Dickinson Debevoise, said that he was bound to defer to the postwar treaties governing reparations claims, and that his court "does not have the power to engage in such remediation."

[180]The processes themselves have different virtues and drawbacks. The Swiss settlement was subject to formal procedural rules governing all class-action lawsuits filed in American federal courts. Those rules guarantee a substantial amount of transparency in the process, provide opportunities for the potential beneficiaries to comment on the settlement terms, and appear to be a bulwark against political pressure. However, these rules also significantly lengthen the amount of time between a settlement and the actual distribution of the funds. The demographics of the claimants also extended the time involved in the Swiss case: legal materials had to be translated into dozens of languages and sent to potential claimants who lived in dozens of countries. The German foundation could distribute funds at an accelerated pace, but it is not governed by established rules. Instead, it is run by a board representing victims, nine governments, and German industry, and they must thrash out competing interests.

that, in retrospect, were bizarre, and, for all the good intentions, appeared to harm survivors' interests. In August 1998, for instance, American insurance regulators scuttled a proposed settlement in which the Italian insurer Assicurazioni Generali agreed to pay some $100 million to settle a class-action lawsuit filed in an American court. Deborah Senn, then the Washington State insurance commissioner, said that survivors' and heirs' claims for Generali policies could easily be worth more than $1 billion. "We cannot allow individual insurance carriers to cap their liability unfairly," Senn said.[181] The commissioners argued that they had a special role, not only because of their regulatory powers, but because insurance policies were legally binding contractual arrangements that had to be scrupulously honored. The implication was that a settlement negotiated through a court was inadequate to the task. At the time, there was considerable pressure for Generali—and other European insurers—to join the International Commission of Holocaust-era Insurance Claims, a consortium of insurers, American state regulators, and Jewish organizations that was formed in 1998 to resolve the claims. Generali joined the commission, which was chaired by Lawrence Eagleburger, a former secretary of state. Two years later, the commission approved a settlement of Holocaust-related insurance claims against Generali—for $100 million, the amount the company had been prepared to pay two years earlier.[182]

The settlements reached between 1998 and January 2001 generated more than $6.5 billion, most of which was to be allocated directly to individual Jewish and non-Jewish victims of Nazi persecution. However, many of the wrenching claims were in limbo or went unresolved. Communal and private properties in Central and Eastern Europe, as well as Nazi-looted cultural property and art, were assets that had to be pursued one by one, often by individuals.

Whether the German and Swiss settlements provided "justice"—symbolic or otherwise—is essentially a question for the individual victims. The "survivors" are not a monolithic group. They have disagreed ideologically about whether it is appropriate to pursue com-

---

[181]Press release from Commissioner Senn's office, Aug. 17, 1998.

[182]*Jerusalem Post,* Nov. 17, 2000. Eagleburger's commission faced fire on multiple fronts. For instance, it was attacked at a November 2001 hearing of the House Committee on Government Reform over its expenses; in its first three years, the commission had spent $40 million in administrative costs but recovered less than half that in Holocaust-era policies.

pensation, the strategies of the pursuit, and the justness of the agreements. The German foundation's payment of DM 15,000 (about $7,500) to each surviving former slave laborer, for instance, was intended to be a "dignified" sum. For some recipients this could have been true. However, as Eli Rosenbaum, director of the Justice Department's Office of Special Investigations, noted, it did not seem quite so dignified when compared to certain class-action awards for other kinds of crimes in the United States. He referred specifically to a $45.7-million settlement in 1994 against an American restaurant chain, Denny's, which was accused of refusing service to, or otherwise discriminating against, minority customers. "If a person of color in this country is not seated at a Denny's restaurant, he or she will get a lot more than $7,500," Rosenbaum said.[183]

With all the attention focused on Holocaust claims, there also was public hand-wringing that the "last word" on the Holocaust would be about money, not memory. That certainly seemed to be the case. There were occasions when the murder of 6 million Jews appeared to be relegated to the shadows. The relief was almost palpable when the third of the international conferences on the Holocaust, convened in Stockholm on January 26–28, 2000, had as its theme Holocaust education and remembrance. "We have been dealing heavily with restitution of assets, trying to bring some measure of justice to surviving victims in everything from communal property to art to Swiss bank accounts to German slave and forced labor and insurance. These are all important and we are making progress in each of those areas," Stuart Eizenstat said. "The significance of this historically important conference is that it begins, as we enter a new century, to move us away from what is important and immediate—money and assets—to what is enduring and lasting—memory and education. Financial restitution, while critical, cannot be the last word on the Holocaust. This conference assures [that] education, remembrance, and research will be."[184]

However, while a number of nations have issued apologies for their war-era activities, there were perils in how the 46 governments represented in Stockholm chose to convey their history.[185] In their

---

[183]"Symposium: Holocaust Restitution: Reconciling Moral Imperatives with Legal Initiatives and Diplomacy," *Fordham International Law Journal* 25, 2001, p. 193.

[184]Eizenstat's remarks at the closing press conference, http://www.usembassy.it/file2000_01/alia/a0013109.htm.

[185]An interesting review of this topic that preceded the recent wave of litigation is Judith Miller, *One, By One, By One: Facing the Holocaust* (New York, 1990).

presentations, both Latvia and Lithuania deflected attention away from their local populations. "Through an aggressive campaign of racist, anti-Jewish propaganda, the Nazi German regime succeeded in recruiting local collaborators to carry out some of the worst crimes ever committed on Latvian citizens," said Vaira Vike-Freiberga, the president of Latvia. Lithuania's prime minister, Andrius Kubilius, went even further in exculpating his nation, saying: "The Jewish community, remarkable for its culture and intellectual achievements, was almost totally wiped out in Lithuania during World War II. So far, no one can explain why this happened in Lithuania, a country with no anti-Semitism throughout its recorded history."[186] Given the niceties of diplomacy, both statements went unchallenged.

The end of the cold war has been credited for the surge in efforts to recover Jewish assets. After the fall of the Berlin Wall and the collapse of communism, Central and Eastern European nations rushed to try to reverse the effects of decades of communist rule. Their legal and economic reforms appeared to create the opportunity to recover properties that had been plundered decades earlier. There also were other factors at work. The massive declassification of documents and the opening of archives made it possible to research the fate of people and properties. The stream of commemorations and ceremonies marking the 50th anniversary of war-era events provided occasions for national introspection, as did the advent of the millennium. In the U.S., public awareness and interest in the Shoah was heightened by the phenomenal popularity of two cultural events in 1993: the opening of the U.S. Holocaust Memorial Museum and the film *Schindler's List*.

And there was the moral imperative of the victims themselves. After struggling privately to rebuild their lives and families after the war, many had reached old age in dire need of financial aid and specialized welfare and medical assistance. Demographic studies conducted in the 1990s also revealed that the number of surviving Jewish victims was substantially higher than anyone had anticipated, with estimates ranging as high as 935,000.[187] The need was

---

[186] *Jerusalem Post,* Jan. 28, 2000.

[187] This estimate uses the broadest definition of a Nazi victim: a Jew who lived in a country under Nazi occupation or under a regime of Nazi collaborators, as well as those who fled from a Nazi-occupied country. See In re Holocaust Victims Assets Litigation (Swiss banks settlement), CV 96-4849(ERK)(MDG), Special Master's Proposed Plan of Allocation and Distribution of Settlement Proceeds, Sept. 11, 2000, Vol, I, Annex C.

especially acute among the "double victims" in the former Soviet Union and Central and Eastern Europe, who had been excluded until 1998 from the German compensation programs.

In the demands for redress a half-century after the war, there also was a tendency to accompany the "legal" demand for the restoration of what had belonged to the victims with a "moral" demand for the public acknowledgment of war-era guilt. But events showed this was not so simple. It became known in 1997, at the height of the controversy over the Swiss banks, that the successor institution to the Anglo-Palestine Bank had more than 10,000 dormant accounts. These were the so-called "minimum" prewar deposits of £1,000 that European Jews made in order to acquire an entry permit to Mandatory Palestine. The successor bank was Bank Leumi, which admitted in 2000 that it held dormant accounts that are believed to have belonged to Holocaust victims. Another Israeli institution, the Jewish National Fund, had parcels of land that may have belonged to Nazi victims. The dormant and unclaimed assets in Israel—primarily land and bank accounts—were valued at as much as 25 billion shekels, according to Colette Avital.[188]

Fifty years of efforts to achieve justice for the victims of Nazi persecution have had limited success. Collectively, these efforts form a haphazard system in which some survivors of similar fates received some compensation for their damages once; some got compensation twice—once in the 1950s and again at the end of the century; and others will get virtually nothing. The recovery of properties shows even more meager results. The frenetic activity of the last decade, with its few important settlements, likely signals the end of this search for justice, however inadequate it may be, in what the noted legal scholar Irwin Cotler has called "thefticide," the greatest mass theft on the occasion of the greatest mass murder in history.[189]

---

[188]*Jerusalem Post,* Nov. 9, 2001. The bank accounts were first brought to light by Israeli historian Yossi Katz in his 1997 book, *Forgotten Assets,* which has not yet been translated from Hebrew into English.

[189]Irwin Cotler, "The Holocaust, Thefticide and Restitution: A Legal Perspective," *Cardozo Law Review* 20, no. 2, Dec. 1998, pp. 601–23.

Demonization in Durban: The World Conference Against Racism

By Harris O. Schoenberg

In late summer 2001, a coalition of Arab and Islamic countries and their allies, along with many nongovernmental human rights organizations (NGOs), used the UN World Conference Against Racism, Racial Discrimination, Xenophobia, and Related Intolerance (WCAR), held in Durban, South Africa, to demonize Israel. Powerful voices at the conference sought to brand Israel as a racist state, casting doubt on whether there was a place for it in the community of nations. This perspective found its way, explicitly or by implication, into official conference documents. The message of Durban could easily be construed to justify violence against Israel and its citizens of the kind that the Palestinians had reignited a year earlier in the so-called "second intifada," including suicide bombings. Similar justifications for terrorism would be heard again soon after the conference, in the wake of the horrific events of September 11.

Genesis of the Conference

No century in recorded history has witnessed genocide on a scale comparable to the 20th. The creation of the United Nations after World War II seemed to usher in a new era when such disregard for human life and dignity would not be permitted.

In a search for a new world vision for the fight against group hatred, the UN has convened a series of world conferences on racism and related phenomena. The first two took place in 1978 and 1983, and a major theme of both was dismantling the apartheid system of racial segregation in South Africa. The third conference, scheduled to begin on August 31, 2001, was set for Durban, South Africa, in order to underscore the victory of the South African people—with the substantial help of the UN—over apartheid. Its declared purposes were to increase the level of awareness of the horrors of racism, review existing standards, and formulate concrete recommendations that would be applicable around the world.[1] In addition to a conference of governmental representatives, there would be a number of parallel meetings in Durban, the most important of them a forum of nongovernmental human rights organizations, or NGOs.

Two major regional groups at the UN came with their own specific political agendas for the WCAR. The first were the African states. The second were the Muslim/Arab states, organized in the Arab League and the Organization of the Islamic Conference (OIC).

The Africans were interested in securing reparations for the slavery practiced in previous centuries in Western countries; slavery in other parts of the world, outside the West—including contemporary manifestations of the phenomenon in Islamic countries—was not on their agenda. Since 1996, the principal supporters of the initiative had demanded an admission that slavery had been a crime against humanity, which required some form of redress from the West. The payment, according to these African states, was not to go to the descendents of the African slaves living across the Atlantic, who were perceived as well-off compared to most Africans. Rather, it would provide debt relief and increased economic aid for African development.

The Muslim and Arab NGOs sought to revive the Zionism-equals-racism libel that the UN General Assembly had adopted on November 10, 1975, but which it later repealed overwhelmingly, 111 to 25, on December 16, 1991,[2] and to add a new action component. They wanted to make use of the South African venue to resurrect the anti-apartheid coalition of third-world states, and use it this time against Israel. The new multiracial South Africa symbolized a successful UN struggle against racism, and Israel was now to be singled out as the next embodiment of that evil, and, like the old apartheid regime in South Africa, one that the international community was obligated to dismantle. Destroying Israel, not merely condemning certain of its policies, was the goal. As UN High Commissioner for Human Rights Mary Robinson, secretary general of the WCAR, warned, "the reopening of the

---

[1]UN General Assembly Resolution 52/111 of Dec. 12, 1997.

[2]This resolution was one of only two ever to have been repealed by the General Assembly in its first 55 years.

specific debate that Zionism is racism . . . has been used in the historical context to challenge the very existence of the State of Israel itself."[3]

Several factors facilitated this agenda. Ongoing bloodshed in the Middle East, initiated in late-September 2000 by the Palestinian Authority after it turned down the offer of a Palestinian state worked out by Israel and the U.S. at Camp David, induced a mind-set of confrontation in the Arab and Islamic worlds. The violence also generated slanted media images of Israelis as oppressors and Palestinians as innocent victims, so that in those parts of the world where ignorance or naïveté about the Middle East were common, the identification of Zionism with racism and apartheid seemed reasonable. Furthermore, Israel—widely considered a beachhead of the West and especially the United States—became a vicarious target for anti-American, anti-colonial, and anti-globalization sentiment in the developing world. Thus, anger at U.S. "unilateralism" and at its perceived refusal to discuss reparations for the slavery it practiced centuries ago had anti-Israel repercussions.

Cuba, for its part, encouraged the African and the Muslim/Arab groups to press their grievances, thereby hoping to further its own goal of solidifying a coalition of the economically underdeveloped nations of the "South," and isolating and condemning the industrialized "North."

Another important factor was the failure of most, though certainly not all, of the NGOs to resist the exploitation of the conference for anti-Israel purposes. To some extent this may have reflected a simple desire to go along with the vocal majority of the "developing world," or an aversion to the policies of Israeli prime minister Ariel Sharon. But the problem had deeper roots. A number of leading NGOs had been slow to adapt to a post-cold-war world in which some of the greatest challenges to human rights have come not from governments, but from terrorists, war lords, criminal organizations, and other nongovernmental actors. Such respected human rights organizations as Amnesty International and Human Rights Watch never fully grasped that the anti-Israel forces in Durban did not want to *change* the policies of Israel but

[3]Letter from Mary Robinson to Raji Sourani, Aug. 3, 2001, http://www.pchrgaza.org/test/mary__r2__en.htm.

to *eliminate* Israel as a Jewish state, and in that sense advocated the suppression of the human rights of Jews.[4]

Making the task of the Israel-haters easier was their already established tradition of using the UN's human-rights apparatus against Israel. The UN Commission on Human Rights annually adopted five anti-Israel resolutions. The first two UN world conferences on women's rights—in Mexico City (1975) and Copenhagen (1980)—explicitly called Zionism a form of racism, even though this was a political issue that had nothing to do with the purpose of these conferences. Likewise, the first UN conference against racism, in 1978, condemned Zionism as racism, and the second, in 1983, called Israeli policies racist.

Another factor contributing to the debacle in Durban was the equivocal role of the WCAR secretary general, UN High Commissioner for Human Rights Mary Robinson.[5] When she first took up her position at the UN, Mrs. Robinson had received high marks for seeking to mainstream human rights into all areas of UN activity and promoting the idea that every UN professional should have some training in human rights. It soon became evident, however, that to deter or deflect attacks from governments opposed to a strong human-rights agenda she placed great emphasis on the economic and social "rights" championed by the developing world, and on political "balance." These goals frequently took priority over tackling the most egregious violations of human rights wherever they occurred, and led her to coddle some governments known for their abuses.

To mollify the Arab/Islamic bloc, she voiced criticism of Israeli policies. Thus, after Arab rioters threw stones and shot at Israeli soldiers on the 50th anniversary of the State of Israel in May 1998, High Commissioner Robinson condemned Israel for not permitting the right of "peaceful assembly." When 20 NGOs wrote to her expressing their concern about this breakdown in the credibility of her supposedly nonpolitical office, she did not respond. Later that same year, the Swiss government, as the depositary of the Fourth Geneva Convention on the Protection of Civilians in Time of War,

---

[4]David Matas, "Civil Society Smashes Up," http://www.bnaibrith.ca/institute/articles/dm020107.html.

[5]On the Office of the High Commissioner, see Harris O. Schoenberg, *Enhancing and Advancing Human Rights: An Essay on Improving UN Human Rights Instruments, Mechanisms, and Procedures* (Wayne, N.J., 1999), pp. 16–21.

called a meeting of experts for October 27–29 in Geneva to discuss the establishment of general principles for the convention's application. To prevent the politicization of international humanitarian law, the rules of the meeting permitted no mention of specific situations. Nevertheless, High Commissioner Robinson's representative denounced Israel and recommended the adoption of sanctions against it, and when the chairperson called this out of order, the representative defended his actions. Mrs. Robinson later stated that she stood by the words of her representative. Another indication of Mrs. Robinson's eagerness to win the confidence of the Arab/Muslim bloc was her hiring of a Palestinian Arab woman with a long record of activism in the Palestinian cause to serve as a high-level adviser, replacing the highest-level American citizen serving in the commissioner's office.

Preparations

When Secretary General Kofi Annan chose High Commissioner Robinson to run the WCAR, she at first resisted, and then accepted the task with great reluctance, perhaps anticipating problems. The UN General Assembly determined that the WCAR be preceded by four regional conferences, and Mrs. Robinson made positive contributions to the first three, organizing meetings of experts to add depth to the deliberations and pressing governments to confront the impact of racial discrimination on the political, economic, and social development of their countries. These conferences took place in Strasbourg, France, October 11–13, 2000 (Europe); Santiago, Chile, December 5–7, 2000 (the Americas); and Dakar, Senegal, January 22–24, 2001 (Africa). The documents they generated focused on ways to combat the evils of racism, xenophobia, slavery, Islamophobia, and anti-Semitism, with no indication of the assault on Israel that was to come.

The Clinton administration, opposed in principle to costly UN conferences outside of UN headquarters and well aware of the bad experiences the U.S. had had with previous UN conferences on racism, went along, albeit unenthusiastically, and established a task force to lay the groundwork for American participation. When President Clinton left office on January 20, 2001, the first three regional meetings to prepare for the WCAR had already taken place.

The incoming Bush administration was briefed about the plans for the conference in January. High Commissioner Robinson visited Washington on February 8, and Secretary of State Colin Powell told her he supported the idea. A State Department spokesman explained to reporters that Powell had a "personal as well as professional interest" in the event.[6]

The fourth and final regional preparatory meeting, the one for the UN's Asian region, was scheduled for Tehran on February 19–21, 2001. Iran, the host government, did not recognize Israel and indeed favored its elimination, and the ongoing intifada ensured an anti-Israel atmosphere at the heavily Arab and Muslim Asian meeting. Iran barred the Israeli delegation, as well as the Baha'i International Community and Kurdish NGOs. It effectively excluded non-Israeli Jewish NGOs as well: it granted their people visas—negotiated through High Commissioner Robinson—but too late for transportation to be arranged. The Organization of the Islamic Conference (OIC), which quickly took control of the Tehran meeting, even kept Australia and New Zealand from participating, presumably fearing any Western voice in the proceedings. The day the conference opened, the Iranian government placed an article in the *Tehran Times* denying the Holocaust. The Declaration and Plan of Action that emerged in Tehran (it was actually negotiated beforehand, though the anti-Israel portion was strengthened in Tehran) singled out Israel for its alleged "ethnic cleansing of the Arab population of historic Palestine," described as "a new kind of apartheid, a crime against humanity." Zionism, the text stated, was "based on racial superiority."[7]

High Commissioner Robinson offered no appeal for tolerance, respect, or understanding of non-Muslims in the Middle East, nor did she mention the Taliban's destruction of sacred Buddhist artifacts in Afghanistan. Though an avowed champion of women's rights, she did not call for elevating the status of women in Islamic society, and she reportedly even told the women who were there representing NGOs that they should wear veils or head scarves in conformity with local law. Mrs. Robinson did criticize some points in the Tehran document, but said nothing about the singling out

---

[6]Tom Lantos, "The Durban Debacle: An Insider's View of the UN World Conference Against Racism," *Fletcher Forum of World Affairs* 26, Spring 2002, p. 38.

[7]UN Document A/CONF.189/PC.2/9, the Report of the Asian Preparatory Meeting, February 19–21, 2001.

of Israel for condemnation. Later, she ascribed the anti-Israel language to "the situation in the Palestinian occupied territories . . . ." In what Congressman Tom Lantos (D., Cal.)—a founding member of the Congressional Human Rights Caucus and a member of the U.S. delegation to the WCAR—called "a baffling statement to the press" upon the conclusion of the Tehran meeting, High Commssioner Robinson characterized it as a "productive dialogue" and congratulated the delegates. "From that moment," Lantos noted, "the conference began to take a dangerous trajectory that became ever more difficult to correct."[8]

At another preparatory meeting, held May 21–June 1 in Geneva, with all governments and regions in attendance to coordinate the four sets of regional recommendations and make them into one document, Mrs. Robinson presented a draft, in the name of the UN Secretariat, which omitted the abusive Tehran language. The Arab and Muslim states rejected her version and secured the "bracketed" (tentative; proposed but not agreed) inclusion of the Tehran language about Israel and Zionism. In addition, they perverted the language of the conference document by adding proposals insisting that Israeli policies be described as anti-Semitic, since Arabs were, they said, Semites. They also proposed that references to the Holocaust be put in the plural so as to include what Israel was allegedly doing to the Palestinians.[9]

At this point, Secretary of State Powell told High Commissioner Robinson that the U.S. would not participate in the Durban conference if the condemnation of Israel remained in the document, pointing out that no state was supposed to be singled out, and that the Arab conflict with Israel was political, not racial. Another problem the U.S. had with the text was the proposed "apology" that the West was to make for slavery, adopted from the document approved at the African regional meeting in Dakar. Such an apology might subject the U.S. and other countries to pay compensation. Powell said that while the U.S. was prepared to express regrets, there could be no apology.[10]

With no agreement reached, another, truly "final," preparatory

---

[8]Lantos, "Durban Debacle," p. 36.

[9]Ibid., p. 37. Mrs. Robinson's draft clearly would have had a better chance of passage had she arranged for South Africa, the chair, to propose it.

[10]Ibid., p. 40.

meeting was needed to iron out these issues, and it convened in Geneva on July 30. In her remarks at the opening session, High Commissioner Robinson said that references to Zionism as a form of racism were not only inappropriate, but could threaten the success of the Durban conference. Raji Sourani, director of the Palestinian Center for Human Rights, responded in a letter that he was "shocked and dismayed" that this issue was off the table since "Zionism as a racist doctrine is not a problem of the past, rather it continues to prevail today as a major obstacle . . . ."[11] That same view was reflected in a "non-paper" prepared and circulated by the OIC that restored some of the most anti-Israel language of the Tehran document.

Congressman Lantos, who was part of the U.S. delegation in Geneva, believes that a developing consensus on how to handle the slavery issue came close to unifying the Western and African representatives in opposition to the anti-Israel language. However, he notes, Mary Robinson took a different tack and encouraged others to do so as well. At a crucial moment on August 9, she made a carefully prepared speech—the text was circulated to the delegates beforehand—proposing the inclusion of both "the historical wounds of anti-Semitism and of the Holocaust on the one hand, and . . . the accumulated wounds of displacement and military occupation on the other." While insisting that the final document denounce anti-Semitism and not reopen the charge that Zionism was a form of racism, she endorsed and legitimized the inclusion of "Palestinian suffering" in the conference document, although it was silent on any other cases of such "suffering" elsewhere in the world. Mrs. Robinson also undercut the U.S. strategy of resolving all disputes over language before Durban, and declared, in the same speech, that the major issues could be debated at the WCAR. The projected compromise over slavery broke down as well, and this issue too would haunt the Durban conference.[12]

David A. Harris, executive director of the American Jewish Committee, wrote to Mrs. Robinson that her insistence on a section about the Middle East in the WCAR document was "deeply troubling." The issue, he wrote, "is simply not germane to a con-

---

[11]Letter of Raji Sourani to Mary Robinson, Aug. 1, 2001, http://www.pchrgaza.org/test/mary__r2__en.htm.

[12]Lantos, "Durban Debacle," pp. 43–44.

ference on racism and the appropriate means to combat racism." Harris also protested her equation of anti-Semitism and the Holocaust, on the one hand, and displacement and military occupation, on the other. The Holocaust, he reminded her, was "the most monstrous genocidal act of human history." Rather than resist efforts, alongside the United States, to keep out extraneous issues, Mrs. Robinson was prolonging and exacerbating the agenda dispute, he stated.[13]

Several NGOs, Jewish and non-Jewish, warned about the possible revival of Zionism=racism at Durban. Major Jewish organizations, as well as the UN Caucus of Jewish NGOs and the Center for UN Reform Education, emphasized the harm that a new condemnation of Zionism would have on the Jewish people and Israel. The U.S. branch of the United Nations Association, the NGO dedicated to promoting the role of the UN, held a high-level briefing at UN headquarters, pointing out that such an attack on Israel would damage the UN and its programs by endangering U.S. engagement in its work. Amnesty International and Human Rights Watch, while avoiding the substantive issues, also opposed raising Zionism=racism since that would bring up "ideologies," and these should not be considered at a conference on human rights.

In late August, Secretary Powell, dissatisfied with the Geneva meeting's insistence on keeping the Middle East on the WCAR agenda, decided not to go himself to Durban, but to send a small group of State Department negotiators.[14] Jewish organizations were divided over whether to attend. On the one hand, they were reluctant to lend legitimacy to what was now likely to be a disaster, and yet, on the other hand, it was possible that their presence could limit the damage. Among the Jewish NGOs that sent representatives were the Jacob Blaustein Institute for the Advancement of Human Rights of the American Jewish Committee, the Anti-Defamation League, B'nai B'rith International, Hadassah, the International Council of Jewish Women, the Jewish Council for Public Affairs (JCPA), UN Watch, the Simon Wiesenthal Center, and the World Union of Jewish Students. These groups formed a Jewish Caucus at the NGO Forum in Durban.

---

[13]Letter of from David A. Harris to Mary Robinson, Aug. 9, 2001, *New York Times,* Aug. 17, p. A18.

[14]*New York Times,* Aug. 28, 2001, p. A6.

Delegitimizing Israel and the Jewish People

Apart from the actual UN conference of member states, there were also several parallel meetings planned for Durban—of youth, of victims, of political and other distinguished personalities—that were expected to broaden the impact of the conference. The one that attracted the most publicity was the NGO Forum.

NGOs are voluntary associations of citizens working on human-rights issues—in this instance, on practical measures to combat racism. However, many of the NGOs at Durban were not independent voluntary associations of citizens. Some were organized by their governments, and were thus actually GONGOs—government-organized NGOs, often led by professional agitators. For example, the Iraqi government sent its GONGOs to combat both the U.S. and Israel. Cubans sent theirs to fight for the transfer of wealth from the developed world to the developing world and to help the Palestinians agitate against Israel and the Jewish people.

A key role would be played by SANGOCO, the South African National NGO Coalition, which the UN chose to organize and host the NGO Forum, and which dominated its International Steering Committee. SANGOCO had been founded in 1995 by people associated with the African National Congress (ANC), which, in turn, had a long and close association—political, financial, and military—with the PLO.[15]

The reason that many governments had set up their own NGOs was that a good number of UN member-states wanted above all to prevent the exposure of harsh truths about themselves that might come out at the meetings. There was "a lot of nervousness" about the conference, since almost every participating country had something to hide.[16] Some examples were the plight of migrant workers and Gypsies in Europe, Dalits in India, and slaves in contemporary North Africa and South Asia. South Africa, the host nation, worried that its failure, ten years after the end of apartheid, to provide minimal amenities for its people—relative safety from

---

[15]See Arye Oded, *Africa, the PLO, and Israel* (Jerusalem, 1990), Policy Studies of the Leonard Davis Institute for International Relations of the Hebrew University of Jerusalem 37, pp. 23–25.

[16]*New York Times,* Mar. 4, 2001, p. A12.

violent crime, decent housing, adequate education and health care, safe drinking water, and jobs—might prove embarrassing.[17]

A coalition of four groups transformed the NGO Forum from a conference with a global thrust into one whose overriding objective was "to brand one country and one people as uniquely, transcendently evil."[18]

The first consisted of Palestinians NGOs—among them the Palestinian Center for Human Rights (PCHR), and LAW: The Palestinian Society for the Protection of Human Rights and the Environment.

The second consisted of Arab and Muslim activists, among them established organizations such as the Cairo-based Arab Lawyers Union. While many of these activists were officially accredited to the NGO Forum, there were also ordinary Muslim South Africans, who participated in the proceedings as well as in demonstrations against Israel.

The third group, in this postcommunist era, were the people who addressed each other as "comrade," insisted that the "liberal bourgeois" model of human rights was inappropriate,[19] said they were for the redistribution of wealth, admired Marxism, and wildly cheered Fidel Castro. This militantly secularist camp of leftists was, on the surface, ideologically distant from the Arab and Islamic militants. Nevertheless, as Catherine A. Fitzpatrick, executive director of the International League for Human Rights, explains, the "aggressive anti-Western Marxist-based ideologies" of Cuba and its radical allies in Africa and other parts of the developing world "make them actually profoundly conservative in a funny way in terms of rejecting modernity . . . ."[20] After all, Cuba and the Soviet Union had initiated the Zionism=racism libel of 1975. Similarly, in Durban as at the preparatory meetings before it, the Cuban

---

[17]A million jobs had reportedly been lost since the end of apartheid. A survey conducted in 2001 by the South African Institute of Race Relations found that South Africans ranked racism as the country's ninth biggest problem, with the amenities mentioned in the text considered more important. Peter Beinart, "Going South," *New Republic,* Sept. 17, 2001, p. 8.

[18]Charles Krauthammer, "Disgrace in Durban," *Weekly Standard,* Sept. 17, 2001, p. 15.

[19]See, for example, Cuba's contribution to the report by the UN Commission on Human Rights' Special Rapporteur on Racism, Racial Discrimination and Xenophobia, in UN Document E/CN.4/2001/21 of Feb. 6, 2001.

[20]Catherine Fitzpatrick, "Durban/Dur-dom" [Durban/ Madhouse], unpublished manuscript, p. 23. Many South Africans at the conference were reportedly attracted to the Islamo-leftist rhetoric, especially since they believed that Muammar Qaddafi, Yasir Arafat, and

pupils of the old USSR were in the vanguard of the onslaught against the United States, Israel, and the Jewish people, even sending some governmental delegates into the NGO Forum to reinforce the Arab and Muslim cadres.

These groups prevailed at the NGO Forum because they were allowed to do so by the large international human rights NGOs—particularly Human Rights Watch, Amnesty International, and, most shamelessly, the Paris-based International Federation of Human Rights (FIDH)—and by the equivocations of High Commissioner Mary Robinson.

The Nongovernmental Meetings

On August 7, as the final Geneva meeting drew to a close, several representatives of NGOs spoke with Mrs. Robinson regarding their concerns about the Durban NGO Forum, which, like the intergovernmental meetings, was preparing a comprehensive document for adoption. They cited "the disrespect, disenfranchisement and hostility" against Jewish representatives in the preparations for the NGO part of the Durban conference, and that "the climate was getting worse." Mrs. Robinson said that she was troubled by their report. She promised to use her good offices to address the language in the NGO document and also "the non-inclusive and secretive nature of the [NGO] drafting process," even though "political considerations" required the inclusion of language about the situation in the Middle East in the governmental conference document.[21]

The Durban proceedings began on August 26 with a day-and-a-half "youth summit" for students. The rationale for this was that young people are particularly vulnerable to becoming victims of racial discrimination, or to experiencing the feelings of alienation that may cause them to discriminate against others. Ironically, the youth meeting itself proved the point, and set the scene for what followed: some 200 participants received free T-shirts that carried the official logo of the conference along with a slogan identifying Israel as an evil "apartheid" state. Over the course of the next

---

Fidel Castro had supported them in their liberation struggle. See Michael Hamlyn, "Banners, Beatings and Boycotts," *Jerusalem Report,* Feb. 11, 2002, pp. 34–35.

[21]Lantos, "Durban Debacle," p. 43.

week, the Jewish students tried to distribute a T-shirt reading "Fight Racism, Not Jews," followed by a quote from the Rev. Martin Luther King, Jr., declaring that when people criticize Zionism, they mean Jews. Mercia Andrews, president of SANGOCO, tried to stop its distribution. A delegation from the World Union of Jewish Students participated in the proceedings of the "youth summit" until its proposal for an end to violence and a peaceful resolution of the Arab-Israeli conflict was rejected and its representatives were refused permission to speak.

The NGO Forum opened on August 28.[22] On the great stage at Kingsmead Stadium in Durban, a performance by Zulu dancers welcomed the participants. Already at that performance there were harbingers of things to come. Opposite the dancers were huge printed banners screaming out: "STOP THE MASSACRE OF THE PALESTINIANS" and "RACISM = . . . ISRAELI RULE." At the registration desk, a representative of the organizing committee wore the anti-Israel T-shirt with the official conference logo that had been distributed at the Youth Summit. At the opening ceremony, Mercia Andrews appeared on stage with a Palestinian kaffiyeh around her neck and announced, to considerable applause, that the forum would deal with "the Israeli occupation of Palestine." She did not refer to any examples of actual racial discrimination that the conference had been called to address.

Meetings of the NGOs took place in large white tents that were set up on the Kingsmead cricket field, and "the atmosphere was folksy and vibrant, with posters advertising a wide range of people's struggles worldwide." But the Jewish participants were to experience a different reality. "Hatred for Israel has become almost a folk idea," noted a South African Jewish journalist who was there, "shared in brotherhood among different people who feel themselves oppressed in one way or another." [23] One particularly popular flyer that was handed out showed a photograph of Adolf Hitler asking the question, "What if I had won?" Below the photo, the page was divided in half. On one side were the good things—no Israel and no Palestinian bloodshed—and on the other was the

---

[22]Matas, "Civil Society Smashes Up," is a vivid eyewitness account of the NGO Forum by the representative of B'nai Brith Canada. Much of the description that follows is derived from it.

[23]Geoff Sifrin quoted in New York *Jewish Week,* Aug. 31, 2001, p. 30.

one bad thing—Hitler would not have permitted the production of the Volkswagen Beetle. On September 9, upon the conclusion of the conference, the *Sunday Times,* a South African newspaper, reported that 20,000 copies of this flyer had been printed and distributed by Yousef Deedat of the Islamic Propagation Centre, who claimed to be an associate of Osama bin Laden and was on the payroll of the bin Laden family.

On August 31—the day that the governmental conference got under way while the NGO Forum was still in session—thousands were bused in from Cape Town for a march that combined the grievances of the Landless People's Movement together with the cause of the Palestinians. One journalist remarked: "Here were South Africans of color—undisputed symbols of a just and triumphant cause—marching with their anti-imperialist, anti-globalization, antiracist supporters in loud denunciation of the next international pariah: The Jewish State."[24] But it was not Israel alone that was under attack. The marchers ended up at the Durban Jewish Club, making clear that, in their minds, Jews and the State of Israel were one. Built in 1931 down the road from the Kingsmead cricket grounds, it was the only place where the Jewish participants thought they could meet and enjoy kosher meals together. Instead, it was closed as a safety precaution, and surrounded by South African riot police.

Nearby, in the exhibition tent set up for the distribution of antiracist literature, that most notorious of anti-Semitic tracts, the *Protocols of the Elders of Zion,* was for sale. Arab groups brought huge boxes there, full of banners and posters. They also provided free kaffiyeh scarves and T-shirts. One of the latter portrayed the Palestinian boy, Muhammad al-Dura, who had been caught in a crossfire and killed at the outset of the new intifada in 2000, and others proclaiming that "Israel Is an Apartheid State" and "Zionism Is Racism."

There were even Jews who gave aid and comfort to the haters of Israel. A number of left-wing Israeli Jewish groups that agreed with conference organizers that Israel practiced apartheid sent people to Durban to say so. At the other end of the Jewish ideological spectrum, three men from the ultra-Orthodox anti-Zionist Neturei

---

[24]Stuart Schoffman, "Deconstructing Durban," *Jerusalem Report,* Oct. 8, 2001, p. 36.

Karta, wearing black coats and sidelocks, arrived in Durban to proclaim to the media that "Zionism is the antithesis of Judaism." One carried a large red-bordered placard that read, "Authentic RABBIS have always opposed Zionism," and although he represented no legitimate NGO, his photo was reproduced on the front page of SANGOCO's Internet site, with the caption: "Delegates having their say . . . ."[25]

Elsewhere on the grounds of the NGO Forum, representatives of the Arab Lawyers Union displayed posters and distributed pamphlets filled with grotesque caricatures of hook-nosed Jews depicted as Nazis, spearing Arab children. The Jews dripped blood from their fangs, and missiles bulged from their eyes. Nearby, pots of money were depicted strewn on the ground.[26] UN Watch complained to the forum's International Steering Committee and asked it to recall the credentials of the Arab Lawyers Union, but the request was refused with the explanation that the material was not racist but "political," and therefore constituted no problem.[27] High Commissioner Robinson denounced this blatant anti-Semitism in no uncertain terms, and identified herself with the Jews under attack, saying, "I am a Jew . . . because these victims are hurting."[28] But she did not call for the Arab Lawyers Union to be ousted from the conference.

The Arabs and their friends dominated many of the "caucuses" and "commissions" that conducted the NGO sessions. One session run by the Palestinians had the title "The Palestinians and the New Apartheid." The session on the environment and racism was run by a Palestinian, as was the one on hate crimes, where Israel's existence was itself defined as a "hate crime." The Jewish Caucus, made up of the Jewish NGOs, had arranged for a session on anti-Semitism as a form of racial discrimination and intolerance, but it was disrupted by Arabs and their allies. The Jewish Caucus then called a press conference, but it too was broken up by hostile demonstrators, forcing "the abandonment of what had been hoped

---

[25]See http://www.racism.org.za/intro.html.

[26]See Michael J. Jordan, "Jewish delegates to U.N. forum enduring a circus of Jew baiting," JTA [Jewish Telegraphic Agency], Daily Electronic Edition, Sept. 4, 2001.

[27]Janine Zacharia in *Jerusalem Post,* Internet Edition, Aug. 31, 2001.

[28]Gay McDougall, "The World Conference Against Racism: Through a Wider Lens," *Fletcher Forum of World Affairs* 26, Summer/Fall 2002, p. 145.

would be a rare opportunity for Jewish voices to be heard." A workshop on the subject of Holocaust denial, which had been on the formal program of the NGO Forum, had to be canceled on the advice of security officers.[29]

The NGO Declaration and Action Program

The vote on a "declaration," a set of resolutions emerging from the NGO Forum, was scheduled for Saturday, September 1, and Jewish delegates asked that it be held after sundown so that Sabbath observers might participate. Even though the Jewish Caucus had a natural concern about how the declaration would handle the issues of anti-Semitism and anti-Zionism, a concern that made them, at the very least, interested parties, the steering committee turned down their request. But the dispute turned out to be academic: translations of the draft document were not ready on time, and the voting had to be postponed until after the official closing session, when the Jewish Sabbath had already concluded. As the Jewish participants returned to the forum on Saturday night, the closing session was still on; Fidel Castro was in the middle of a two-hour-long tirade, mostly directed against the United States. This dictator was wildly cheered.

After Castro finished, the proposed declaration was to come up for a vote. Under the agreed-upon rules of procedure for framing the declaration, each "victim group" had the right to define its own experience and describe the nature of its victimization. Thus the anti-Israel coalition of NGOs had proposed language that labeled Israel a "racist apartheid state," revived the equation of Zionism and racism, recommended sanctions against Israel, and demanded an end to the "ongoing Israeli systematic perpetration of racist crimes, acts of genocide and ethnic cleansing." For its part, the Jewish Caucus had submitted a section on anti-Semitism whose "Paragraph 14" denounced attacks on synagogues and Jews anywhere in the world that were motivated by anti-Zionism that had spilled over into anti-Semitic acts and violence. However, the World Council of Churches, speaking for the Ecumenical Caucus and act-

---

[29]Jeremy Jones, "Durban Daze," *The Review* (Australia/Israel and Jewish Affairs Council), Oct. 2001, pp. 32, 21.

ing at the request of the Palestinian NGOs, proposed the deletion of Paragraph 14.

The chair refused to allow debate or discussion on the issue, and, despite a procedural protest by the representative of the Jewish Caucus, the delegates went ahead and voted to drop the paragraph. Thus the Jews became the only official "victim caucus" at the NGO Forum to have the language it presented challenged and eliminated, and it was done in a way that has aptly been described as "intimidating and undemocratic."[30]

The Jews then walked out, chanting "Shame! Shame! Shame!" to the taunts of the assembled, and the Palestinians called back: "Free, free Palestine."[31] Many of the Jews felt personally threatened, and their non-Jewish friends feared for their safety. "I was frankly frightened," recalled Catherine Fitzpatrick of the International League for Human Rights. "I have never [before] been in a situation, at home or in any foreign country, where I literally felt I had to cover Jewish colleagues with my body, and watch out lest they be physically attacked."[32] To their credit, the Central and East European NGOs also left the hall in protest; they returned later hoping to vote against the entire declaration, but no vote was taken at the time. Later, the West Europeans and the Roma (Gypsies) walked out as well, one of the latter taking the microphone before leaving to explain that they could not approve the hate language in the declaration. Three other caucuses—Cultural Diversity, South Asia, and Peace—also distanced themselves from the declaration.

With the Jewish participants absent, the Palestinian and other Arab NGOs appropriated the victimization of the Jewish people by adding "anti-Arab racism" to the definition of anti-Semitism.[33] In the middle of the night, a rump session of some 100–200 people—out of 7,000 official participants—took it upon themselves to approve the declaration. But the anti-Israel and anti-Jewish forces were not yet satisfied. Ronald Eissens of the Magenta

---

[30]McDougall, "World Conference Against Racism," p. 134.

[31]Yair Sheleg in *Ha'aretz,* Internet English Edition, Sept. 28, 2001.

[32]Fitzpatrick, "Durban/Dur-dom," p. 21.

[33]In his address to the governmental conference, read by Ambassador Mordechai Yedid, Israel's deputy foreign minister, Michael Melchior, commented that efforts to eradicate the plain meaning of the word were not only anti-Semitic, they were anti-semantic.

Foundation, a Dutch NGO, describes what happened two days later:[34]

> On the evening of September 3 members of the Palestinian Caucus together with a few members of the ISC [International Steering Committee] and SANGOCO invaded the office where the drafting committee was working hard to incorporate all amendments and new paragraphs that resulted from the Declaration adoption meeting on September 1. They demanded from the drafters that some paragraphs be changed and some put into another section (for example, the paragraphs on anti-Semitism should be moved to the section on Palestine since anti-Semitism was, "in fact," against "Semites," which are Arab people).[35]
>
> The drafters asked them to leave several times since their presence was illegal. No one, not even ISC members, were allowed to enter the drafting room. This did not help. The invaders shouted, screamed and intimidated the drafters. Recounted one drafter: "They shouted that we were all Jewlovers since we did not want to make any changes. We told them they were trying to corrupt the process and that they should get out. They did not listen. The ISC members who were present gave them full support." Drafters were personally threatened. Bizarre remarks were made: "You look Jewish. Now we understand why you do not want to change anything in the draft!" The invaders left only when they managed to grab some diskettes.

In the end, the official NGO document did not include the statement on anti-Semitism in the section on Palestine, but maintained it as a separate section. However it did add to it that "Arabs as a Semitic people have also suffered from alternative forms of anti-Semitism, manifesting itself as anti-Arab discrimination and for those Arabs who are Muslim, also as Islamophobia." Under the rubric of "colonialism and foreign occupation," the declaration denounced Israel's "brand of racism and apartheid and other racist crimes against humanity" as well as "ethnic cleansing" in the territories, identified the denial of the Palestinians' "right of return to their homes of origin" as racist, and asserted the right of the Palestinians "to resist such occupation by any means provided under international law." These sentiments appeared again under the "Palestinians and Palestine" item, which also accused Israel of "genocide," called for an end to its "racist crimes," and charged that

---

[34]http://www.icare.to (Internet Centre Anti-Racism Europe), Oct. 8, 2001.

[35]The section in which a paragraph was placed was crucial, since, according to the rules, it determined which group had the right to decide on the wording in that paragraph.

Israeli policies particularly targeted women and children. In its "action program," the NGO document recommended the dismantling of all Jewish settlements in the territories, the trial of Israeli nationals before an international war-crimes tribunal, and "the launch of an international anti-Israeli-Apartheid movement" that would "impose a policy of complete and total isolation of Israel . . . the full cessation of all links (diplomatic, economic, social, aid, military cooperation and training) . . . ."[36]

A joint statement prepared by 77 of the roughly 3,000 NGOs in attendance strongly criticized the process by which the declaration and program of action were adopted. It specifically noted that the language of the chapter on "Palestinians and Palestine" and "the deliberate distortion of language" involved in describing the Palestinians as victims of anti-Semitism were "extremely intolerant, disrespectful and contrary to the very spirit of the World Conference . . . ."[37] A black member of the American Congress who was present, Representative Sheila Jackson Lee (D., Tex.), noted that the Arab conflict with Israel is "a political land-based conflict that is not grounded in racism. The berating of the Jewish people fills the conference with unnecessary hatred." Barbara Arnwine, executive director of the Lawyers Committee for Civil Rights Under Law, resigned from the International Steering Committee in protest, declaring that the process had been corrupted.[38]

Nevertheless, some of the most prestigious NGOs vacillated in their comments about the anti-Israel declaration. An official of Human Rights Watch agreed that the language was "intemperate" and that "the use of the word genocide is not appropriate," but added that Israel "commits serious abuses, including extrajudicial executions, torture, and arbitrary arrests." Amnesty International, for its part, declined to endorse the declaration but did not repudiate it either, due to "the contentious and complex nature of some of the problems." Felice Gaer, director of the Jacob Blaustein Institute for the Advancement of Human Rights, commented: "The human rights movement is, above all, about speaking out. The tepid, after-the-fact remarks about the unquestionably hate-filled language and spreading of hate propaganda is an extraordinary

---

[36]http://www.racism.org.za/delaration.html.

[37]Jones, "Durban Daze," p. 21.

[38]McDougall, "World Conference Against Racism," p. 149, n. 50.

disappointment."[39] Even for some NGOs that unequivocally rejected the defamation of Zionism and Israel, the matter was hardly a high priority: Michael Posner of the Lawyers Committee for Human Rights, for example, told a press conference, "it's time to move on."[40]

The Governmental Conference

As noted above, the draft resolution for the governmental meeting of the WCAR, adopted in Geneva in August, mentioned only one political conflict in the world, that in the Middle East, and condemned only one country by name, Israel. As a result, Secretary of State Powell decided not to go to Durban. Instead, he sent a small U.S. delegation to the governmental conference, led by Ambassador Michael Southwick, the deputy assistant secretary of state for international organization affairs, a senior diplomat with considerable experience. Recognizing that it was politically impossible to remove the reference to the Middle East, the Americans in Durban worked behind the scenes with the Norwegian and Canadian delegations on crafting "essentially generic language expressing concern about the conflict in the Middle East without veiled criticism of Israel."[41]

Meanwhile, on August 31, the opening day of the governmental conference, the Rev. Jesse Jackson arrived and announced that Palestinian Authority president Yasir Arafat had committed himself to reject the equation of Zionism with racism, and to support language deploring the Holocaust and condemning anti-Semitism. Jackson said he had this commitment in writing from Nabil Sha'ath, a member of the Palestinian cabinet. That same day, however, Arafat delivered a speech asserting that Israel engaged in "racist practices." In a blistering attack on Israel, the Palestinian leader said:

> Palestine is tormented by racial discrimination, occupation, aggression, and settlements . . . . The bloody tragedy . . . is a racist, colo-

---

[39]Michael J. Jordan, "Faced with hostility at U.N. forum, Jewish activists seek to place blame," JTA Daily Electronic Edition, Sept. 5, 2001. In fact, an Amnesty International press release handed out during the NGO Forum cited examples of violations of human rights around the world, but mentioned only Israel by name.

[40]Ina Friedman, "Here We Go Again," *Jerusalem Report,* Apr. 8, 2002, p. 24.

[41]Lantos, "Durban Debacle," p. 45.

> nialist conspiracy of aggression, forced eviction, usurpation of land, and infringement upon the Christian and Islamic holy places . . . . They have stolen our water. They have made refugees of many of our people. . . . This brutality, this arrogance is moved by a supremacist mentality that practices racial discrimination, that adopts ethnic cleansing . . . and that protects the daily attacks carried out by the settlers against our people.[42]

Even though an understanding had been reached at the Geneva preparatory meetings not to push, in Durban, for a denunciation of Zionism, the Syrian and Egyptian delegations advocated the position Arafat took in his tirade. Syria's foreign minister, Farouq a-Shara, railed against "racist" Israel, which, he charged, started by massacring children, and ended up "hunting children." Representing one of the most brutal regimes in the world, Shara had the effrontery to say that "many contemporary historians have registered with admiration, not shorn of surprise, the human and religious diversity in Syria, as many of the oppressed people found a generous and secure haven there." Egypt's new foreign minister, Ahmed Maher, was equally vitriolic. Other Arab delegates, including Maher's predecessor, Amr Moussa, now serving as secretary general of the Arab League, vigorously resisted any compromise language that would have avoided demonizing the State of Israel.[43]

And High Commissioner Robinson went along. During the NGO Forum, Robinson had denounced expressions of anti-Semitism, and then refused to convey the NGO declaration to the governmental conference, saying, "It's sad for me that for the first time I can't recommend to delegates that they pay close attention to the NGO declaration.[44] But she was publicly committed to the specific mention of the "plight of the Palestinians" in the WCAR declaration, and, on September 2, she told Ambassador Southwick of the U.S. that the American threat to leave the meeting if the WCAR document singled out Israel for criticism was "warped, strange, and undemocratic."[45]

On September 3, when it was clear that the governmental con-

---

[42]Full text in "Transcript of Arafat's WCAR Speech," http://sf.indymedia.org/2001/09/103664_comment.php.

[43]Lantos, "Durban Debacle," pp. 47–48.

[44]McDougall, "World Conference Against Racism," p. 145.

[45]Lantos, "Durban Debacle," p. 47.

ference would condemn Israel, Secretary Powell instructed the American delegation to come home. He declared it unacceptable to fight racism by drafting statements containing "hateful language," by suggesting that "apartheid exists in Israel," and by singling out only one country in the world, Israel, for censure and abuse. Powell himself came in for some criticism for his principled stand. Among the critics were Jesse Jackson and former president Jimmy Carter.[46]

After the Americans announced their withdrawal, the Israeli delegation followed suit. Before leaving, Israeli ambassador Mordechai Yedid spoke words that were to have been delivered by Deputy Foreign Minister Michael Melchior, who did not attend:

> It might have been hoped that this first conference of the 21st century would have taken up the challenge of, if not eradicating racism, at least disarming it. But instead, humanity is being sacrificed to a political agenda . . . . A group of states for whom the terms "racism," "discrimination," and even "human rights" simply do not appear in their domestic lexicon, have hijacked this conference and plunged us into even greater depths.[47]

The U.S. withdrawal and other embarrassing media reports coming out of Durban apparently stiffened the resistance of Australia, Canada, Guatemala, Latvia, Peru, and the European Union. After difficult and intense negotiations that forced the conference into overtime, agreement was reached by Belgium—acting on behalf of the European Union and, more broadly, the Western democracies—and South Africa, on behalf of the anti-Israel forces,[48] on a declaration and program for action. It did not mention Zionism and had no negative references to Israel. It did, however, single out "the plight of the Palestinian people under foreign occupation" and recognized their right to an independent state, as well as "the right to security for all states in the region, including Israel." The text also enshrined "the right of refugees to return voluntarily to their homes and properties in dignity and safety," urging "all states to facilitate such return." That an unlimited Palestinian "right of

---

[46]Carter's view was somewhat surprising, since, in 1978, he had prevented the U.S. ambassador to the UN, Andrew Young, from participating in the first UN conference on racism for the very same reason that Powell called the U.S. delegation home in 2001.

[47]Full text reproduced in *Jerusalem Post,* Internet Edition, Sept. 3, 2001.

[48]They included Iraq, Syria, Iran, Libya, Algeria, Tunisia, Pakistan, Nigeria, and Cuba.

return" might threaten Israel's "right to security" was not addressed. There was no reference to terrorist attacks on Israelis. Other paragraphs condemned anti-Semitism along with Islamophobia, and asserted that "the Holocaust must never be forgotten."

At the last minute, Syria, supported by Pakistan, sought to sabotage the compromise by insisting on an open vote on three paragraphs from the earlier anti-Israel draft that the negotiators had agreed to drop, asserting that Israel's policies in the territories were manifestations of racism. This was voted down on a procedural motion offered by Brazil, 51 to 38. The Arab and Muslim states, South Africa, Barbados, Trinidad and Tobago, and Saint Vincent and the Grenadines voted against the Brazilian motion. A compromise was also reached on the other divisive issue, responsibility for slavery: the conference acknowledged that slavery and the slave trade were crimes against humanity, and expressed regret for both slavery and colonialism. Although the statement asserted that an economic-assistance package should be offered to Africa, the European Union countries stressed that they were making no financial commitments.[49]

The Aftermath

High Commissioner Robinson and her defenders believe that Durban, despite its acknowledged shortcomings, was an overall success. Among the positive accomplishments, they list the empowerment of victim groups that had never before had a forum to express their grievances; the Western acknowledgement of regret for slavery and its consequences; and the pledges of the governments to take practical steps toward the elimination of racial discrimination. Gay McDougall, executive director of the Washington-based International Human Rights Law Group and one of the preeminent figures in mobilizing support for the WCAR, writes: "This is the time to champion these renewed commitments, not to belittle them by declaring that the WCAR was a failure." McDougall argues that those who felt shortchanged at Durban, such as Jews, "cannot let their own agendas undermine the advances gained by so many other groups." A "distorted focus"

---

[49]*New York Times,* Sept. 9, p. A1.

on the role of the Israel/Palestinian issue at the conference, in her words, "misses the proverbial forest for the trees." As for claims that the conference, especially the NGO Forum, was permeated with an anti-Israel and anti-Jewish atmosphere, McDougall doubts that the vast majority of the people who were there experienced any such thing.[50]

Even leaving aside the Israel-related matters, however, the document produced by the governmental conference came as a great disappointment to many of those sincerely committed to human rights. They point out that, amid all the political posturing, racial minorities with serious grievances were not mentioned at all—the Dalits (Untouchables) in India, for example. Ironically, India had been the first country to raise the issue of South African apartheid in a UN context back in 1946. In Durban and at the preparatory conferences leading up to it, however, India adamantly opposed consideration of the plight of the Dalits, which, it claimed, was a "domestic social problem," or a religious and not a racial issue, and was already the subject of remedial action. India succeeded in removing the issue from discussion. Similarly, "indigenous peoples" that had hoped for some progress found out, in the WCAR document, that anything mentioned about them was legally subordinate to the overriding principle adopted in Durban asserting that the term "indigenous peoples . . . cannot be construed as having any implications as to rights under international law."[51]

The Jewish world was not of one mind about the governmental conference's significance. The document did include the first affirmation of Holocaust memorialization and the first denunciation of anti-Semitism ever to emerge from a UN world conference. The Israeli Foreign Ministry expressed "satisfaction" that the governmental meeting had neither revived the old equation of Zionism with racism nor identified the Jewish national movement with apartheid. But, on the negative side, it noted that the conference had singled out the "Palestinian plight" and the plight of no other people in a UN document ostensibly dealing with racism, and, furthermore, that it had given international recognition—for the first time—to refugees' "right of return." Both could become ominous

---

[50]McDougall, "World Conference Against Racism," pp. 133–49, quotes on pp. 147, 133.

[51]*International Herald Tribune,* Internet Edition, Sept. 4, 2001. The Aboriginal Caucus walked out upon the adoption of this language.

precedents for further attempts at the diplomatic isolation of Israel. The NGO Forum, in contrast, had no redeeming features for Jews, and its inflammatory delegitimization of Israel could be read to justify the terrorism of "oppressed" Palestinians against Israelis on the essentially racist basis that the Jewish state—and no other—was fair game.[52]

The conference ended on September 8. Three days later, Muslim hijackers flew two planes into the World Trade Center in New York and another into the Pentagon in Washington, while a fourth plane, apparently targeting the White House or the Capitol, crashed in Pennsylvania. More than 3,000 Americans were killed.

The temporal proximity between Durban and September 11 has not gone unnoticed. Anne F. Bayefsky, a Canadian expert on international law who attended the NGO Forum as a representative of the International Association of Jewish Lawyers and Jurists, believes that the juxtaposition "was as close in substance as it was in time." Under the cover of the rhetoric of human rights, Durban had declared that terrorism against certain types of people was acceptable. The lesson, writes Bayefsky, is clear: "The linkage between racial hatred and terrorism is a phenomenon which democracies ignore at their peril."[53] Arch Puddington perceives another strand connecting the WCAR to September 11. Those Arabs, Muslims, and leftists who impugned Israel and Zionism in Durban were also lashing out at the United States—the only government beside Israel to leave in protest when Israel's policies were singled out for criticism—and at liberal democracy as a way of life. These were precisely the targets of Osama bin Laden and militant Islam: the U.S. and its Western values, and the Jewish state perceived as their outpost in the Middle East.[54]

Given the widespread demonization of Israel and its American ally that was manifest in Durban, it was little wonder that Palestinians danced in the streets to celebrate the carnage of September 11. Many Muslims and Arabs around the world casually

---

[52]"The Conclusion of the Durban Conference: Comments by Israeli Leaders and Officials," Sept. 9, 2001, http://www.mfa.gov.il/mfa/go.asp?MFAHOkgvO; Eric Silver, "Off With the Gloves," *Jerusalem Report,* Oct. 8, 2001, p. 34.

[53]Anne F. Bayefsky, "Terrorism and Racism: The Aftermath of Durban," *Jerusalem Viewpoints* 468, Dec. 16, 2002, p. 1.

[54]Arch Puddington, "The Wages of Durban," *Commentary*, Nov. 2001, pp. 29–34.

blamed "the Jews" for the attacks. The "proofs" were wild allegations that 4,000 Jews who worked at the World Trade Center supposedly stayed home that day, Jews sold their shares in United and American airlines beforehand, and a "Jewish" film crew had been ready to record the World Trade Center tragedy.[55] In other bastions of anti-Americanism and anti-Westernism—including leftist circles in the West itself—there was a sense that even though fundamentalist Muslims had committed the crime, somehow the U.S. deserved it. While deploring the loss of life and disassociating themselves from the act, many suggested that perhaps a more "evenhanded" American policy in the Middle East would assuage the anger of a beleaguered Islam.[56] In many countries, the identification of Israel as the party somehow responsible for international terrorism helped spark attacks on Jews and Jewish institutions.[57] On college campuses in the U.S., where pro-third-world sentiment was fashionable, there were calls for divestment from Israeli firms and companies doing business in Israel. This campaign was explicitly modeled on the one that had been waged against South African apartheid.[58]

Just a few weeks after September 11, the UN General Assembly met in New York to conduct a special debate on international terrorism. Arab and Muslim representatives pledged their support for the war on terror, but, in the spirit of Durban, insisted that Palestinian violence against Israelis was not terrorism. As the Syrian representative put it, there was "a clear distinction between terrorism, which is a criminal act and an unlawful form of warfare, and armed resistance to . . . racism and foreign occupation, which is a legitimate struggle." On October 8, four days after these re-

---

[55]More than four months after the attacks and despite the publication of clear evidence of who was responsible for them, columnist Thomas Friedman found the idea of a Jewish conspiracy still prevalent in the Arab world. See Friedman, "Run, Osama, Run," *New York Times,* Jan. 23, 2002, p. A19. A Gallup poll released in late February 2002 showed that the overwhelming view in Muslim countries was that Muslims did not perpetrate the attacks. This perception has been confirmed by later polls, as noted in "The Big Lie," which aired on CBS on Sept. 4, 2002, transcript available at http://www.cbsnews.com/stories/2002/09/04/6011/main520768.shtml.

[56]Bayefsky, "Terrorism and Racism," p. 2.

[57]For details, consult the articles in this volume on individual countries.

[58]Plans were discussed even while the WCAR was still in session. See Julie Wiener, "College students call on schools to divest holdings in 'racist' Israel," JTA Daily Electronic Edition, Sept. 5, 2001.

marks were delivered, the General Assembly elected Syria to membership on the Security Council.[59] At several subsequent UN gatherings held in Geneva, Israeli policies were repeatedly singled out as uniquely evil, for example at the meeting of the High Contracting Parties of the Fourth Geneva Convention in December 2001, and at the annual session of the UN Commission on Human Rights in March 2002.[60]

The significance of the UN's role was underscored in October 2001, by the award of the Nobel Peace Prize to the UN and its secretary general, Kofi Annan. Many in the Jewish community—still traumatized by Durban and the UN's overall pro-Palestinian tilt—found this sign of recognition hard to comprehend. "The prize is a reminder to those who dismiss or underestimate the significance of the UN," commented Malcolm Hoenlein, executive vice chairman of the Conference of Presidents of Major American Jewish Organizations. "It is a reminder of why we should continue to focus on it and some of the dangerous trends there we have witnessed of late."[61] Adding to the problem is the systemic bias against Israel at the UN—Israel, for example, is the only state excluded from full membership in any of the five regional groups, and thus cannot serve on the Security Council or most other UN bodies.[62]

In the end, as Congressman Lantos argues, it is the United States that "must challenge our Middle Eastern allies to move away from their promotion of popular resentment towards Jews, Americans, and the West." Lantos warns:

> The UN World Conference on Racism provided the world with a glimpse into the abyss of international hate, discrimination, and indeed, racism. The terrorist attacks on September 11 demonstrated the evil such hate can spawn. If we are to prevail in our war against terrorism, we must take to heart the lessons of Durban.[63]

---

[59]Bayefsky, "Terrorism and Racism," p. 4.

[60]Friedman, "Here We Go Again," pp. 22–26.

[61]Michael J. Jordan, "While world honors U.N. with Nobel, Israel and Jewish leaders are leery," JTA Daily Electronic Edition, Oct. 17, 2001.

[62]Israel has recently been granted temporary inclusion in WEOG (West Europe and Others Group), still a far cry from equal status in the UN.

[63]Lantos, "Durban Debacle, pp. 51–52.

Census of U.S. Synagogues, 2001

By Jim Schwartz, Jeffrey Scheckner, and Laurence Kotler-Berkowitz

The synagogue is the most prevalent and arguably the most important institution in American Jewish life. One measure of its significance is that more Jews belong to a synagogue than to any other Jewish organization. The synagogue is classically depicted as the site for prayer, study, and communal gathering. Less frequently mentioned are other reasons for affiliation with a synagogue, such as companionship, communal identification, children's education, transacting business, gathering news, and exchanging gossip. The significance of the synagogue for Jews who belong may vary from essential to minimal. It also may be important for many Jews who do not attend as a reference point for positive or negative Jewish memories, a focus for accepting or rejecting Jewish identity, or other reasons.

Historically, the primary source of information regarding the number of U.S. synagogues was the decennial Census of Religious Bodies conducted between 1850 and 1936.[1] According to the data collected, there were 37 "congregations" in 1850, increasing to 3,728 by 1936. But the number of "edifices"—a category that may better approximate the definition of a modern synagogue—was lower. For example, in 1916 there were 1,901 congregations but only 866 edifices (see table 1).

However, the Jewish data from these censuses, as one scholar noted, "are very defective from the point of view of comprehen-

---

Note: The authors gratefully acknowledge the assistance of Deborah Bursztyn of the United Jewish Communities in preparing many of the tables that appear in this article and Michele Anish of the Blaustein Library of the American Jewish Committee for providing bibliographic sources. The authors thank United Jewish Communities for supporting this research as part of its mandate in serving the Jewish community.

[1]Uriah Zvi Engelman, "Jewish Statistics in the U.S. Census of Religious Bodies (1850–1936)," *Jewish Social Studies* 9, Apr. 1947, pp. 127–174. See also H. S. Linfield, "The Communal Organization of the Jews in the United States, 1927," AJYB 1929–30, Vol. 31, pp. 107–18.

siveness, completeness, and accuracy,"[2] and therefore should be used with caution. To the best of our knowledge there has been no attempt to enumerate the number of synagogues since the 1936 Census of Religious Bodies.[3]

This article reports on a 2001 census of U.S. synagogues, providing the number of synagogues at the national, regional, state, county, and metropolitan levels, as well as categorizing them by denomination within geographic divisions. Our data are about synagogues, not individual Jews; the denomination with which a Jew identifies is not necessarily the denomination of the synagogue(s) s/he attends, belongs to, or financially supports.

Definition of a Synagogue

A typical dictionary definition of a synagogue is "a Jewish community meeting for religious observances or instruction; the building or assembly place used by Jewish communities for this purpose" (Webster). This definition, however, is not specific enough to distinguish a synagogue from other forms of Jewish assembly, such as a minyan (a quorum of ten Jews for praying) or a *havurah* (often a gathering for prayer that is less formal than a synagogue). We consider five factors to be essential to the definition of a "synagogue":

1. Religious: Primary purpose is Jewish prayer.
2. Physical: A permanent location for such prayer.
3. Time: Regularly scheduled Jewish religious services, even if infrequent.
4. Leadership: Ordained (rabbi and/or cantor) and/or lay.
5. Psychological: Members'[4] perception of the entity as a synagogue.

---

[2]Engelman, "Jewish Statistics," p. 127.

[3]There was one additional U.S.-government-sponsored study of religion, in 1957, but it explored religion at the individual level and did not deal with the church/synagogue dimension. See Bureau of the Census, Current Population Reports, Population Characteristics, *Religion Reported by the Civilian Population of the United States: March 1957,* Series P-20, No. 79, Feb. 2, 1958; and Samuel A. Mueller and Angela V. Lane, "Tabulations from the 1957 Current Population Survey of Religion: A Contribution to the Demography of American Religion," *Journal for the Scientific Study of Religion* 11, Mar. 1972, pp. 76–98.

[4]The term "member" is used in a generic sense and may have different meanings in different synagogues. The overwhelming majority of synagogues have a membership fee, but not all.

When a group of Jews first begins holding religious services infrequently, or in an informal setting such as a living room, meeting room or other facility that is not perceived as a permanent location, their entity has not reached the point of qualifying as a synagogue. This is the case with many minyanim and *havurot,* some of which function independently and others that are within the structure of a synagogue.

Factors that are not essential to the definition of a synagogue but are often associated with it are:

1. Ownership of a building. The vast majority of synagogue buildings are owned by their congregations. However, some synagogues are located in rented or donated facilities.[5]
2. Legal status, such as incorporation or development of bylaws identifying the entity as a synagogue.
3. Membership in a denominational association and adherence to the rules and standards of that group.

We exclude Christian (e.g. Jews for Jesus, Hebrew Christians) and other groups that may use the word "synagogue" in describing their houses of worship, for their primary purpose is not Jewish prayer as defined by the mainstream Jewish community.

Methodology

The enumeration and identification of synagogues required the acquisition of lists from all Jewish denominations and organizations known to represent or to be associated with synagogues. Most encompassing were the lists prepared by the four major Jewish denominations:

1. Conservative—United Synagogue of Conservative Judaism (USCJ)
2. Orthodox—Agudath Israel; Chabad/Lubavitch[6]; Union of Orthodox Jewish Congregations of America (OU); Young Israel

---

[5]There are some Orthodox rabbis who own their synagogue buildings.

[6]Chabad is the Hebrew acronym referring to Lubavitch Hassidim. We use the terms interchangeably in this article.

3. Reconstructionist—Jewish Reconstructionist Federation (JRF)
4. Reform—Union of American Hebrew Congregations (UAHC)

Lists were also acquired from other organizations representing or associated with synagogues:

5. Gay/Lesbian—World Congress of Gay and Lesbian Jewish Organizations (WCGLJO)
6. Humanistic—Society for Humanistic Judaism
7. Sephardi—American Sephardi Federation
8. Traditional—Union for Traditional Judaism (UTJ)

Most of the denominations and organizations noted above suggested utilizing their Web sites for their most complete and accurate synagogue lists. Each list was scrutinized for specific synagogue indicators. These included the use of the words "synagogue" or "temple" in the name, noting the name of an officiating rabbi and/or cantor, and publishing the times at which services were conducted.

However, two of the lists, WCGLJO and Chabad, contained so many entries indicating the presence of non-synagogues that they required particularly careful review. The WCGLJO had more than 50 U.S. members, but upon review, only 19 qualified as synagogues.

A rabbi actively involved in national Chabad affairs provided a list of approximately 470 facilities. To confirm that the facilities on that list were synagogues, we called at least one in each area to confirm whether it and other Chabad facilities in close proximity met our criteria. We determined that about 120 of the units functioned primarily as education or outreach centers, youth centers, administrative offices, or schools, or else were university-based and served mainly college students. These Chabad centers did not have regularly scheduled services, or in some other way did not meet the criteria for being a synagogue.[7]

To augment the information obtained from the organizations,

---

[7]Given the rapid expansion of Chabad centers over the last decade it is possible that some of these non-synagogues will become synagogues. Our impression is that the number of Chabad synagogues is growing at a faster pace than the number of any other synagogue

we acquired synagogue lists from all Jewish federations whose catchment areas have a Jewish population of 10,000 or more, and cross-referenced them with other lists. As many catchment areas extend well beyond metropolitan boundaries and some even cover entire states, many local communities with fewer than 10,000 Jews are included in this process. These federation directories probably cover more than 90 percent of the American Jewish population.

Further, we used the 2001 listing of local Jewish populations appearing in the *American Jewish Year Book* to ensure that we did not overlook the presence of any synagogue in all communities with a known Jewish population of at least 100. This involved double-checking contact information for synagogues appearing in the United Jewish Communities' files and cross-checking with a Jewish travel guide, plus a keyword search on the Internet for the presence of synagogues that might not appear in other lists that we obtained.

Several areas are known to have a large concentration of Orthodox Jews, including a substantial number of Hassidim—Brooklyn, Manhattan, and Queens in New York City; Rockland County and Kiryas Joel (Orange County) in New York State; and Lakewood in New Jersey. In these areas we made additional efforts at gathering synagogue names. We cross-referenced the local telephone directory yellow pages with other lists we had of these communities. In addition, lists were acquired from local rabbis and other community leaders so as to locate smaller, independent, and nonaffiliated entities that might meet the criteria for being synagogues.

Our search—using name, location, denomination, and other relevant descriptor information—is, we believe, the most extensive effort ever conducted to enumerate U.S. synagogues. However, our data may contain errors due to such factors as the voluntary nature of synagogue identification and the unreliability of lists.

---

organization. This may largely be due to the Chabad strategy of sending young couples to areas previously not serviced by Chabad, with the goal of raising sufficient funds and other support within a relatively short period of time so as to become self-sustaining. While a synagogue may be described as Chabad, the actual number of members and attendees in such synagogues who consider themselves to be Chabad is often very small.

Total U.S. Synagogues by Denomination

The total number of synagogues in the United States in 2001 was 3,727 (see table 2). The denomination with the largest number of synagogues was Orthodox (40 percent), followed by Reform (26 percent), and Conservative (23 percent). All other denominations and forms of synagogue identification have 3 percent or less of the synagogues: Reconstructionist (3 percent), Sephardi (3 percent), Traditional (1 percent), Humanistic (1 percent), Gay/Lesbian (0.5 percent), and Jewish Renewal (0.4 percent). All but four of the Sephardi synagogues also identify themselves as Orthodox. Four percent of synagogues intentionally do not identify with any specific denomination, probably for a variety of reasons, including a desire to appeal to a broad range of members. One percent of the synagogues provided no denominational identification.

Formal affiliation with a denominational association does not necessarily follow from denominational identification. There may be fiscal, ideological, theological, political, geographic, and other reasons for some synagogues not to formally join the synagogue association of the denomination with which they identify. Among the 976 synagogues that consider themselves Reform, 90 percent belong to that movement's association, the Union of American Hebrew Congregations. Of the 865 synagogues identifying as Conservative, 79 percent are members of the Conservative movement's association, the United Synagogue of Conservative Judaism. All 99 Reconstructionist synagogues are members of the Jewish Reconstructionist Federation.

The Orthodox sector, unlike the other denominations, has several different synagogue groups. Of the 1,501 Orthodox synagogues, 352 identify as Orthodox Union (24 percent). In addition, OU officials maintain that since they have different levels of association, the number of synagogues in some sense affiliated with the organization is much larger than the number of formal members. Lubavitch has nearly as many members as the Orthodox Union, 346 (23 percent). The third largest Orthodox synagogue group is Young Israel, with 150 members (10 percent). Agudath Israel, with 55 members (4 percent), is the fourth largest Orthodox synagogue group. Like their counterparts at the OU, Agudath Israel leaders state that a good number of Orthodox synagogues that are not actual members are nevertheless aligned with it. There is duplicate membership among all four of these groups. Among Orthodox Union synagogues, 56 are also members of another group, among Young Israel 35, among Lubavitch six, and among Agudath Israel five.

Over a third of all Orthodox synagogues (36 percent) appear to function independently. These 542 synagogues apparently are not members of any of the groups mentioned above, although many sympathize or identify with at least one of them. Based on their names and location we believe that many in this group are among the most traditional segments of the Jewish community, both Hassidic and non-Hassidic. The Hassidic groups include Satmar, Ger, Bobov, Vishnitz, Bratslav, Skver, and Boston, none of which practice the Lubavitch philosophy of actively proselytizing among Jews. Some of these independent synagogues tend to have relatively few members, and prefer the Yiddish term *shtieblach* (small prayer houses) to characterize their synagogues.

Forty-six synagogues use the word "traditional" to describe themselves. The Union for Traditional Judaism (UTJ), originally an offshoot of the Conservative movement, claims to represent a philosophy and does not define itself as a denomination. Nevertheless, two traditional synagogues reported UTJ membership without connections to any other denominational group. Another use of the identifier "traditional" is for a synagogue with an Orthodox-style service but without a physical divider separating men and women. Of the 19 synagogues identifying as gay and lesbian, seven are members of the UAHC, one of the JRF, and the remaining 11 are independent.

U.S. Synagogues by Metropolitan Area

The 50 metropolitan areas with the largest Jewish populations contain 3,075 synagogues, amounting to 82 percent of all U.S. synagogues (see table 3). The plurality of those synagogues is Orthodox (46 percent), more than a fifth are Conservative (24 percent) and Reform (21 percent), 3 percent Reconstructionist, and 7 percent some other type.

The metropolitan area with the greatest number of synagogues, by far and away, is New York-Northern New Jersey-Long Island, with a third (33 percent) of all synagogues.[8] Six other areas contain 3 percent or more of all synagogues. The area with the second largest number of synagogues is Los Angeles-Riverside-Orange County (7 percent), followed by Boston-Worcester-Lawrence (5 percent), Chicago-Gary-Kenosha (4 percent), Philadelphia-Wilmington-Atlantic City (4 percent), Miami-Ft. Lauderdale (4 percent), and San Francisco-Oakland-San Jose (3 percent). These seven communities, the only ones with over 100 synagogues, account for well over half (58 percent) of all the synagogues in the country.

Three other communities have over 50 synagogues: Washington, D.C. (65), Baltimore (56), and Detroit-Ann Arbor (51). Two more have over 40, Cleveland-Akron (48) and West Palm Beach-Boca Raton (45). Sixteen additional communities have 20 or more synagogues, and nine more have 10–19 synagogues. In total, there are ten or more synagogues in 37 metropolitan areas. Three-quarters of all the synagogues are within the 26 metros with the largest Jewish populations.

The New York metro area, which contains 1,233 synagogues, dominates not only in the total number, but also in the number for all four major denominations. Relative to their national levels, the Orthodox are overrepresented in the New York area (57 percent) and the Conservative are in their proper proportion (24 percent), while the Reform (14 percent) and Reconstructionist (l percent) are underrepresented.

In addition to New York, other areas where Orthodox synagogues are well represented are Los Angeles (128 synagogues), Miami (67), Boston (53), Chicago (53), Philadelphia (37), Baltimore (35), and San Francisco (35). Eleven other communities have at least ten Orthodox synagogues. There are eight metropolitan areas in which at least half of all the synagogues are Orthodox: Memphis (67 percent), Baltimore (62 percent), New York (57 percent), Syracuse (57 percent), Springfield, MA (54 percent), Miami (52 percent), Los Angeles (50 percent), and Columbus, OH (50 percent). The fact that three of these areas are the nation's largest Jewish population centers, along with the data noted above,

[8]Full names of metropolitan areas are listed for the first mention. Thereafter, only the first city in a metropolitan area is noted.

demonstrates the disproportionate concentration of Orthodox synagogues in major urban centers.

The greatest number of Conservative synagogues is in the New York metro area (295), with other major centers being Los Angeles (49), Philadelphia (49), Boston (37), Miami (33), and Chicago (30). Five other communities have at least ten Conservative synagogues.

Reform synagogues are most prevalent in New York (175), with other major concentrations in Los Angeles (57), Chicago (41), Boston (34), and Philadelphia (32). Eleven other communities have at least ten Reform synagogues.

The two metropolitan areas where Reconstructionist synagogues are best represented are New York (15) and Philadelphia (13). Proportionately, Reconstructionism is strongest in Philadelphia (9 percent), at least partly owing to the presence of the Reconstructionist Rabbinical College in that community.

Altogether, there is at least one Orthodox, Conservative, and Reform synagogue in every one of the top 50 metros. A Reconstructionist synagogue exists in each of the top 16 metros, and 32 of the top 50.

Of the "other" types of synagogues, the 120 Sephardi synagogues are especially concentrated in the New York metropolitan area (64 synagogues). Within the New York area the counties having the greatest number of Sephardi synagogues are Kings (Brooklyn) 24, Queens 13, Monmouth, NJ 9, Nassau 4, and New York (Manhattan) 4. The two other metro areas with the greatest number of Sephardi synagogues are Los Angeles (10) and Miami (10).

The 46 "traditional" synagogues are most represented in Chicago (14), New York (9), and Philadelphia (5). The only communities with at least two Humanistic synagogues are New York (7), Los Angeles (4), and San Francisco (2). Two or more Jewish Renewal synagogues exist only in San Francisco (5) and Los Angeles (2). Synagogues without denominational affiliation are especially present in Boston (43), New York (16), and San Francisco (11).

Groups within Orthodoxy

Because Orthodox synagogues predominate and there are several divisions within Orthodoxy, it requires separate attention (see table 4).

The 708 Orthodox synagogues in the New York area are nearly

half (47 percent) of all Orthodox synagogues. Three-quarters of all Orthodox synagogues are in the top ten metros and 94 percent in the top 50. The dominant type of known, affiliated Orthodox synagogue in the New York area belongs to the Orthodox Union (25 percent; 22 percent are members of the OU only and not some other group). However, an even larger group (44 percent) has no known synagogue association. About a tenth of the New York Orthodox synagogues are Young Israel (11 percent; 9 percent are members only of Young Israel and not some other group) and Lubavitch (10 percent), while 5 percent are Agudath Israel.

There are at least ten nonaffiliated Orthodox synagogues in each of nine metropolitan areas. In addition to the 310 in the New York area, the greatest numbers are in Los Angeles (41), Baltimore (22), Miami (21), Chicago (19), Boston (17), and San Francisco (17). Lubavitch has ten or more synagogues in seven communities. Its greatest penetration is in the New York (69) and Los Angeles (54) areas. Other communities with at least ten Lubavitch synagogues are Miami (23), Boston (17), Philadelphia (13), Chicago (12), and San Francisco (10). Aside from New York, with 176 synagogues, the Orthodox Union has at least ten synagogues in four communities: Chicago (17), Los Angeles (12), Boston (12), and Washington, D.C. (10).

Of the 150 Young Israel synagogues, over half (81) are in the New York area. The only other metro area with at least ten Young Israel synagogues is Miami (10). Over half of the Orthodox Sephardi congregations are in the New York metro area (51 are non-OU and 10 are OU). Two other communities, Los Angeles and Miami, each have ten Sephardi synagogues (all non-OU). The only metro area with a large number of Agudath Israel synagogues is New York (38).

Metro vs. Non-Metro Concentration

While 82 percent of all U.S. synagogues are in the 50 largest metropolitan areas, the Orthodox are even more heavily concentrated in those areas (94 percent). Among the individual Orthodox groups, Chabad, with its outreach programs, has the lowest percentage in the top 50 metros (87 percent). In contrast, 84 percent of Conservative, 65 percent of Reform, and 81 percent of Reconstructionist synagogues are in the 50 metropolitan areas with the largest Jewish populations. Conversely, many more Reform synagogues are located outside the major metros than is the case for the other denominations, both in absolute numbers (339) and relative terms (35 percent). There are 141 Conservative synagogues outside the 50 major metros (16 percent), 93 Orthodox (6 percent), 19 Reconstructionist (19 percent), and 60 "other" synagogues (21 percent).

U.S. Synagogues by Regions, States, and Counties

Table 5 provides details on the number of synagogues by denomination within states, as well as for all counties containing at least five synagogues.

There are synagogues in all 50 states. The state with the greatest number of synagogues is New York (995), followed by California (425), New Jersey (331), Florida (263), and Massachusetts (201). These five states also have the largest Jewish populations, with one exception—Pennsylvania's 197 synagogues rank it slightly below Massachusetts, even though its Jewish population is a bit larger (282,000 vs. 275,000).[9] Three more states have more than 100 synagogues: Illinois (161), Ohio (114), and Maryland (107). Another 14 states have at least 20 synagogues, five of them with 50–99, six with 30–49, and three with 20–29. In contrast, over half of the states (27) and the District of Columbia have fewer than 20 synagogues—ten states below 10, another ten states and Washington, D.C., having 10–14, and seven with 15–19. North Dakota, Idaho, and Wyoming have the fewest synagogues, with only two each.

Only in New York State are Orthodox synagogues a majority of all synagogues (60 percent). In ten additional states—regionally diverse and with Jewish populations ranging from small to substantial—Orthodox synagogues constitute a plurality. In order of the Orthodox plurality, these are Maryland (49 percent), Rhode Island (47 percent), New Jersey (43 percent), California (43 percent), Ohio (39 percent), Florida (37 percent), Michigan (35 percent), Colorado (32 percent), Massachusetts (32 percent), and Oregon (27 percent).

[9]Population estimates are taken from Jim Schwartz and Jeffrey Scheckner, "Jewish Population in the United States, 2001," pp. 247–74 in this volume. That article reports a compilation of estimates provided by local communities.

Reform synagogues dominate in small communities and rural areas, especially in the South. In five states, 90 percent or more of all synagogues are Reform: Arkansas, Idaho, Mississippi, North Dakota, and Wyoming. Furthermore, in 16 states 50–89 percent of the synagogues are Reform: Alabama, Alaska, Hawaii, Indiana, Iowa, Kentucky, Louisiana, Missouri, Montana, New Hampshire, North Carolina, Oklahoma, South Carolina, South Dakota, Utah, and West Virginia.

Conservative synagogues do not constitute a majority in any state. However, the plurality of synagogues in Connecticut (33 synagogues=38 percent) and Pennsylvania (65 synagogues=33 percent) are Conservative.

Aggregating the data to the regional level, the Northeast contains half of all U.S. synagogues (1,865=50 percent), the South has a fifth (744=20 percent), and the West (613=16 percent) and the Midwest (505=14 percent) less than a fifth each.

There are 3,066 counties in the U.S.[10] Of these, 24 have 30 or more synagogues, 47 have 10–29, 47 have 5–9, 167 have 2–4, 335 have only one, and 2,446 have none (see table 6). In other words, the most prevalent Jewish institution does not exist in 80 percent of U.S. counties, and only 4 percent of all counties have at least five synagogues.

The counties with the largest number of synagogues are in the large metropolitan areas, with five of the top ten in the New York area (see table 7). Cumulatively, these ten counties account for a third (33 percent) of all U.S. synagogues.

With the exception of Westchester and Broward counties, Orthodox synagogues dominate in these ten counties. The proportion of Orthodox synagogues is highest in Kings County (Brooklyn), at 86 percent. Ocean County, NJ, which includes the community of Lakewood, is second (83 percent), and Baltimore City third (81 percent). In addition to Kings County, three other New York City counties rank in the top ten: Bronx (73 percent), Queens (68 percent), and New York—Manhattan (67 percent). Other counties where more than 65 percent of all synagogues are Orthodox are Sullivan (Catskill Mountain area), NY (70 percent), Dade

---

[10]National Association of Counties, Washington, D.C., http://www.naco.org/counties/general, 2002.

(Miami), FL (69 percent), Shelby (Memphis), TN (67 percent), and Rockland (Monsey-Spring Valley), NY (66 percent).

Turning again to table 5, counties with fewer than five synagogues are collapsed into the category "all other counties," with an indication of their number. (See table 8 below for counties with one to four synagogues.) Eighteen states (Alaska, Arkansas, Hawaii, Idaho, Iowa, Maine, Mississippi, Montana, New Hampshire, New Mexico, North Dakota, Oklahoma, South Carolina, South Dakota, Utah, Vermont, West Virginia, and Wyoming) do not have even one county with as many as five synagogues. There is not one state in which all counties have at least five synagogues.

Synagogue Density

The concentration of synagogues may be measured by the number of synagogues per 1,000 Jewish population. Tables 3 and 5 provide this data for the 50 top metros, the 50 states, and the District of Columbia. The ten metropolitan areas with the highest ratios are medium-size communities, eight of them in the Northeast and Midwest: Providence-Fall River-Warwick (1.4), Albany-Schenectady-Troy (1.0), Buffalo-Niagara Falls (1.0), Cincinnati (1.0), Milwaukee-Racine (1.0), Springfield (MA) (1.0), Norfolk-Virginia Beach-Newport News (1.0), Pittsburgh (0.9), Hartford (0.8), and Austin (0.8). None of these communities ranks higher than 23 (Pittsburgh) in total Jewish population. We hypothesize that the high synagogue densities in these communities, particularly those in the Northeast and Midwest, reflect the length of Jewish settlement, the more traditional Jews who tend to live there, and the priority given to institution-building and affiliation in moderate-sized communities as a way of sustaining social connections among Jews.

Conversely, the ten communities with the lowest synagogue densities are in the South and West: Las Vegas (0.2), West Palm Beach (0.3), Portland-Salem (OR-WA) (0.3), Phoenix-Mesa (0.3), Los Angeles (0.4), Miami (0.4), Washington, D.C. (0.4), Atlanta (0.4), San Diego (0.4), and Sacramento-Yolo (0.4). Most of the communities with low ratios have posted significant Jewish population growth in recent decades, and, with two exceptions (Portland and Sacramento) are now among the top 17 metros. This suggests that the number of synagogues commencing operations has not kept pace with the growth in Jewish population. Another factor possibly contributing to the low ratio of synagogues to Jewish population is that new areas of growth attract relatively less traditional Jews, who have less desire to support and be connected to Jewish institutions. Among the largest Jewish population centers in this category (Los Angeles, Miami, West Palm Beach, Washington, D.C.), low synagogue density may reflect reduced pressure on Jews to affiliate with and support synagogues in order to develop social ties to other Jews.

The states with the highest ratios tend to be rural and to have relatively small and declining Jewish populations: South Dakota (10.0), Mississippi (9.3), Montana (7.5), Arkansas (5.9), Wyoming (5.0), West Virginia (4.8), North Dakota (4.4), Iowa (2.6), Vermont (2.4), Alabama (2.0), and Oklahoma (2.0). We hypothesize that this is a residual effect of Jewish settlement—many of the synagogues in these areas were established in the last half of the 19th and first half of the 20th centuries. These communities went into decline due to the passing of the founders and the movement of their children and grandchildren to larger urban areas, and many of the synagogues remain more as a testament to earlier generations than as thriving institutions.

The five states with the lowest ratios are in the South and West: Nevada (0.3), Florida (0.4), California (0.4), Arizona (0.5), and Oregon (0.5). As with the metro areas with low synagogue concentrations, each of these states experienced significant Jewish population growth in recent decades. This also suggests either that population growth precedes institutional development, or that the Jews moving to these areas are less inclined to build and support synagogues.

Discussion

In conclusion, we wish to highlight three findings.

First, American Jews are primarily an urban population, and consequently their synagogues are located primarily in urban areas. A remarkably high 50 percent of American Jews live in the top three metropolitan areas, and 94 percent in the top 50. Their synagogues are almost as concentrated, with 43 percent in the top three metros and 82 percent in the top 50.

One factor that helps explain the smaller proportion of synagogues than Jewish population in the largest metros is Jewish mobility. American Jewish population was more dispersed among smaller communities during the 19th and first half of the 20th centuries than it would later become, and the primary physical expression of those communities was the synagogue building. As Jews moved up the socioeconomic ladder, they and their children migrated to more populated areas, leaving a declining and often less affluent population.[11] Many of the synagogues that they built remained.

Second, Orthodox synagogues are highly overrepresented relative to the Orthodox population. Though less than 10 percent of American Jews are estimated to be Orthodox,[12] the Orthodox synagogues represent 40 percent of all U.S. synagogues.

Several factors might account for this. Orthodox Jews tend to have a greater population concentration than other Jews, and this provides a social structure that encourages development of and participation in the Orthodox synagogue. A major reason for this concentration is the desire to be within walking distance of a synagogue on Shabbat, when other forms of transportation are prohibited. That social structure also creates a demand for other communal services, such as Jewish schools, kosher butchers, and ritual baths (*mikvaot*).

In addition, a higher proportion of Orthodox Jews attend and "use" their synagogues, at least for traditional religious purposes, than is the case among other Jews, and they do so for a greater proportion of their lives, thus increasing the demand for synagogues. In contrast, many non-Orthodox Jews who attend services do so less frequently and tend to affiliate with a synagogue for fewer years, most commonly the period prior to a child's bar/bat mitzvah. Additionally, the need for synagogues among the non-

---

[11]For examples, see Ira M. Sheskin, "The Dixie Diaspora: The 'Loss' of the Small Southern Jewish Community," *Southeastern Geographer* 40, May 2000, pp. 52–74; Lee Shai Weissbach, "East European Immigrants and the Image of Jews in the Small-Town South," *American Jewish History* 85, Sept. 1997, esp. pp. 260–61; and Lee Shai Weissbach, "Small Town Jewish Life and the Pennsylvania Pattern," *Western Pennsylvania History* 83, Spring 2000, esp. p. 45.

[12]Barry A. Kosmin, et al., *Highlights of the CJF 1990 National Jewish Population Survey* (New York: Council of Jewish Federations, 1991), p. 33; Ira Sheskin, *How Jewish Communities Differ: Variations in the Findings of Local Jewish Population Studies* (New York: North American Jewish Data Bank, 2001), pp. 71–76.

Orthodox declines even further to the extent that non-Orthodox Jews have fewer children than the Orthodox, and tend to intermarry more as well, both factors limiting the number of Jewish children.

Furthermore, anecdotal information suggests that the average membership size of Orthodox synagogues is smaller than membership in Reform and Conservative synagogues, the two denominations with which the greatest number of American Jews identify.[13] Also, the Orthodox community is divided internally in ways that Conservative and Reform Jews are not, and those internal divisions may take institutional form in the creation and maintenance of more synagogues.

The third significant finding is the relationship between Jewish population and two important characteristics of synagogues—total number and density. Not surprisingly, the correlation between Jewish population size and absolute number of synagogues is remarkably high and statistically significant at both the metropolitan (r=.99, p=.00) and state (r=.98, p=.00) levels. The greater the number of Jews who reside in a geographic area, the greater the number of synagogues in that area as well.

Less intuitively, Jewish population size appears to have a weak inverse relationship to synagogue density across all 50 metros (r=.14, p=.35) and the 50 states (r=–.23, p=.11). These correlations must be interpreted cautiously because they do not reach conventional levels of statistical significance. As a general pattern, though, they suggest that the larger the number of Jews in a geographic area, the lower the concentration of synagogues, as measured by the number of synagogues per 1,000 Jews. As noted above, several factors may explain this, including differences between small and large Jewish communities in the pressures and incentives to affiliate with a synagogue, historic and contemporary mobility patterns, and the time lag between shifting populations and institutional decline or development.

[13]Kosmin, et al., *Highlights,* p. 33; Sheskin, *How Jewish Communities Differ,* pp. 71–76.

TABLE 1. NUMBER OF CONGREGATIONS AND EDIFICES REPORTED IN U.S. CENSUS OF RELIGIOUS BODIES*

Year	Number of Congregations	Number of Edifices
1850	37	Not provided
1860	77	Not provided
1870	189	152
1875–78	270	Not provided
1890	533	301
1906	1769	821
1916	1901	866
1926	3118	1782
1936	3728	2851

*The numbers are culled from Engelman, "Jewish Statistics," cited in note 1 in the text. Census for 1875–78 was conducted by two major Jewish organizations of that time, and not an agency of the U.S. government.

TABLE 2. U.S. SYNAGOGUES BY DENOMINATION

	Total	% of Total U.S. Synagogues	% within Denomination
Total Orthodox	**1,501**	**40.3**	**100.0**
Total Orthodox Union (OU)	352	9.4	23.5
Orthodox Union*	296	7.9	19.7
Orthodox Union and Agudath Israel	3	0.1	0.2
Orthodox Union and Lubavitch	4	0.1	0.3
Orthodox Union and Young Israel	33	0.9	2.2
Sephardi OU	16	0.4	1.1
Total Lubavitch/Chabad	346	9.3	23.1
Lubavitch/Chabad*	340	9.1	22.7
Lubavitch/Chabad and Orthodox Union	4	0.1	0.3
Lubavitch/Chabad and Young Israel	2	0.1	0.1
Total Young Israel	150	4.0	10.0
Young Israel*	115	3.1	7.7
Young Israel and Lubavitch	2	0.1	0.1
Young Israel and Orthodox Union	33	0.9	2.2
Total Agudath Israel	55	1.5	3.7
Agudath Israel*	50	1.3	3.3
Agudath Israel and Orthodox Union	3	0.1	0.2
Sephardi Agudath Israel	2	0.1	0.1

TABLE 2.—*(Continued)*

	Total	% of Total U.S. Synagogues	% within Denomination
Sephardi Other Orthodox	98	2.6	6.5
Other Orthodox	542	14.5	36.1
Total Reform	**976**	**26.2**	**100.0**
Reform-UAHC	875	23.5	89.7
Gay/Lesbian-UAHC	7	0.2	0.7
Reform-non-UAHC	94	2.5	9.6
Total Conservative	**865**	**23.2**	**100.0**
Conservative-USCJ	684	18.4	79.1
Conservative-non-USCJ	181	4.9	20.9
Total Reconstructionist	**99**	**2.7**	**100.0**
Reconstructionist-JRF	98	2.6	99.0
Gay/Lesbian-Reconstructionist-JRF	1	0.0	1.0
Total Sephardi	**120**	**3.2**	**100.0**
Sephardi OU	16	0.4	13.3
Sephardi Agudath Israel	2	0.1	1.7
Sephardi other orthodox	98	2.6	81.7
Sephardi-non-orthodox	4	0.1	3.3
Total Traditional	**46**	**1.2**	**100.0**
Union for Traditional Judaism	2	0.1	4.3
Traditional-non-UTJ	44	1.2	95.7
Humanistic	**32**	**0.9**	
Total Gay/Lesbian	**19**	**0.5**	**100.0**
Gay/Lesbian-no denomination	11	0.3	57.9
Gay/Lesbian-Reconstructionist	1	0.0	5.3
Gay/Lesbian-UAHC	7	0.2	36.8
Jewish Renewal	**14**	**0.4**	
No Denomination noted	142	3.8	
Other/Not Known	37	1.0	

Total number of U.S. synagogues = 3,727

*No duplicate membership

TABLE 3. U.S. SYNAGOGUES IN 50 METROPOLITAN AREAS WITH LARGEST JEWISH POPULATIONS, 2001

	Total	Orthodox	Conservative	Reform	Reconstructionist	Other*	Jewish Population	Synagogues per 1,000 Jewish Pop.	Synagogues % of Total	Synagogues Cumulative %
1. New York-No. NJ-Long Island, NY-NJ-CT-PA	1,233	708	295	175	15	40	2,051,000	0.60	33.1	33.1
2. Los Angeles-Riverside-Orange County, CA	254	128	49	57	4	16	668,000	0.38	6.8	39.9
3. Miami-Ft. Lauderdale, FL	129	67	33	20	3	6	331,000	0.39	3.5	43.4
4. Philadelphia-Wilmington-Atl. City, PA-NJ-DE-MD	141	37	49	32	13	10	285,000	0.49	3.8	47.1
5. Chicago-Gary-Kenosha, IL-IN-WI	144	53	30	41	3	17	265,000	0.54	3.9	51.0
6. Boston-Worcester-Lawrence, MA-NH-ME-CT	174	53	37	34	5	45	254,000	0.69	4.7	55.7
7. San Francisco-Oakland-San Jose, CA	103	35	19	27	2	20	218,000	0.47	2.8	58.4
8. W. Palm Beach -Boca Raton, FL	45	14	19	10	1	1	167,000	0.27	1.2	59.6
9. Washington, DC-MD-VA-WV	65	18	19	15	5	8	166,000	0.39	1.7	61.4
10. Baltimore, MD	56	35	9	8	3	1	106,000	0.53	1.5	62.9
11. Detroit-Ann Arbor, MI	51	24	9	11	3	4	103,000	0.50	1.4	64.3
12. Cleveland-Akron, OH	48	23	8	13	1	3	86,000	0.56	1.3	65.5
13. Atlanta, GA	34	12	4	10	2	6	86,000	0.40	0.9	66.5
14. Las Vegas, NV-AZ	19	7	2	7	1	2	75,000	0.25	0.5	67.0
15. San Diego, CA	29	13	7	7	1	1	70,000	0.41	0.8	67.7
16. Denver-Boulder-Greeley, CO	30	11	5	7	1	6	67,000	0.45	0.8	68.6

TABLE 3.—*(Continued)*

	Total	Orthodox	Conser-vative	Reform	Reconstruc-tionist	Other*	Jewish Population	Synagogues per 1,000 Jewish Pop.	Synagogues % of Total	Synagogues Cumulative %
17. Phoenix-Mesa, AZ	20	6	5	7		2	60,000	0.33	0.5	69.1
18. St. Louis, MO-IL	24	8	3	10	1	2	54,500	0.44	0.6	69.7
19. Dallas-Ft. Worth, TX	24	9	4	9		2	50,000	0.48	0.6	70.4
20. Houston-Galveston-Brazoria, TX	26	6	5	11	1	3	45,500	0.57	0.7	71.1
21. Tampa-St. Petersburg-Clearwater, FL	24	4	6	11		3	45,000	0.53	0.6	71.7
22. Minneapolis-St. Paul, MN-WI	22	6	7	4	1	4	40,500	0.54	0.6	72.3
23. Pittsburgh, PA	36	10	12	8	1	5	40,500	0.89	1.0	73.3
24. Seattle-Tacoma-Bremerton, WA	28	10	4	11	1	2	40,000	0.70	0.8	74.0
25. Hartford, CT	28	9	12	6		1	33,500	0.84	0.8	74.8
26. Portland-Salem, OR-WA	9	3	1	2	2	1	27,000	0.33	0.2	75.0
27. Cincinnati, OH-KY-IN	24	10	5	5	1	3	24,000	1.00	0.6	75.7
28. Rochester, NY	15	5	4	5		1	23,000	0.65	0.4	76.1
29. Columbus, OH	12	6	1	5			22,000	0.55	0.3	76.4
30. Sacramento-Yolo, CA	9	2	1	5	1		21,500	0.42	0.2	76.6
31. Milwaukee-Racine, WI	21	7	4	7	1	2	21,000	1.00	0.6	77.2
32. Orlando, FL	15	3	5	6	1		21,000	0.71	0.4	77.6
33. Tucson, AZ	12	2	3	5	1	1	20,000	0.60	0.3	77.9
34. Kansas City, MO-KS	9	3	2	3		1	19,000	0.47	0.2	78.2
35. Albany-Schenectady-Troy, NY	20	6	6	6		2	19,000	1.05	0.5	78.7
36. Buffalo-Niagara Falls, NY	19	8	5	5	1		18,500	1.03	0.5	79.2
37. Providence-Fall River-Warwick, RI-MA	24	11	9	4			17,000	1.41	0.6	79.8
38. Sarasota-Bradenton, FL	7	1	1	4		1	15,500	0.45	0.2	80.0
39. Austin, TX	11	3	2	2	1	3	13,500	0.81	0.3	80.3

TABLE 3.—*(Continued)*

	Total	Orthodox	Conser-vative	Reform	Reconstruc-tionist	Other*	Jewish Population	Synagogues per 1,000 Jewish Pop.	Synagogues % of Total	Synagogues Cumulative %
40. Norfolk-Virginia Beach-Newport News, VA-NC	13	3	6	4			13,500	0.96	0.3	80.7
41. Springfield, MA	13	7	3	2		1	13,000	1.00	0.3	81.0
42. New Orleans, LA	9	4	1	4			13,000	0.69	0.2	81.3
43. Richmond-Petersburg, VA	8	3	3	2			13,000	0.62	0.2	81.5
44. San Antonio, TX	5	2	1	1	1		11,000	0.45	0.1	81.6
45. Indianapolis, IN	6	2	2	1	1		10,000	0.60	0.2	81.8
46. Syracuse, NY	7	4	2	1			9,500	0.74	0.2	82.0
47. Charlotte-Gastonia-Rock Hill, NC-SC	5	1	1	2	1		9,000	0.56	0.1	82.1
48. Louisville, KY-IN	5	1	2		2		8,500	0.59	0.1	82.2
49. Memphis, TN-AR-MS	6	4	1	1			8,500	0.71	0.2	82.4
50. Ft. Myers-Cape Coral, FL	4	1	1		2		8,000	0.50	0.1	82.5
Total—top 50 Metro areas	3,075	1,408	724	637	80	226	5,806,500	0.53	82.5	82.5
Percent of 50 Metros	100.0	45.8	23.5	20.7	2.6	7.3				
Percent of U.S. Total	82.5	93.8	83.7	65.2	80.8	79.0	94.3			
Total—remainder of U.S.	652	93	141	339	19	60	348,500	1.9	17.5	100.0
Percent of remainder of U.S.	100.0	14.3	21.6	52.0	2.9	9.2				
Percent of U.S. Total	17.5	6.2	16.3	34.7	19.2	21.0	5.7			
U.S. Total	3,727	1,501	865	976	99	286	6,155,000			
Percent of U.S. Total	100.0	40.3	23.2	26.2	2.7	7.7				

*Other denominations/groups include Traditional (45), Humanistic (27), Jewish Renewal (14), Gay/Lesbian non-UAHC/non-Reconstructionist (11), Sephardi non-Orthodox (2), no denomination noted (120), and other (7)

TABLE 4. U.S. ORTHODOX SYNAGOGUES IN 50 METROPOLITAN AREAS WITH LARGEST JEWISH POPULATIONS, 2001

	Total	Lubavitch	Orthodox Union	Young Israel**	OU/Young Israel	Sephardi Non-OU	Agudath Israel	Other Orthodox	Orthodox Synagogues % of Total	Orthodox Synagogues Cumulative %
1. New York-No. NJ-Long Island, NY-NJ-CT-PA	708	69	159	64	17	51	38	310	47.2	47.2
2. Los Angeles-Riverside-Orange County, CA	128	54	11	8	1	10	3	41	8.5	55.7
3. Miami-Ft. Lauderdale, FL	67	23	3	7	3	10		21	4.5	60.2
4. Philadelphia-Wilmington-Atl. City, PA-NJ-DE-MD	37	13	5	5		3		11	2.5	62.6
5. Chicago-Gary-Kenosha, IL-IN-WI	53	12	15	2	2	1	2	19	3.5	66.2
6. Boston-Worcester-Lawrence, MA-NH-ME-CT	53	17	10	4	2	2	1	17	3.5	69.7
7. San Francisco-Oakland-San Jose, CA	35	10	4	1		3		17	2.3	72.0
8. W. Palm Beach-Boca Raton, FL	14	7	4	1		1		1	0.9	73.0
9. Washington, DC-MD-VA-WV	18	5	9	2	1			1	1.2	74.2
10. Baltimore, MD	35	3	5			2	3	22	2.3	76.5
11. Detroit-Ann Arbor, MI	24	6		2	1	2	1	12	1.6	78.1
12. Cleveland-Akron, OH	23	6	4	2		1	1	9	1.5	79.6
13. Atlanta, GA	12	4	1	1		2		4	0.8	80.4
14. Las Vegas, NV-AZ	7	3	1	1				2	0.5	80.9
15. San Diego, CA	13	7	2	1				3	0.9	81.7
16. Denver-Boulder-Greeley, CO	11	2	2				1	6	0.7	82.5
17. Phoenix-Mesa, AZ	6	4	1	1					0.4	82.9
18. St. Louis, MO-IL	8	1	1	1			1	4	0.5	83.4

TABLE 4.—*(Continued)*

	Total	Lubavitch	Orthodox Union	Young Israel**	OU/Young Israel	Sephardi Non-OU	Agudath Israel	Other Orthodox	Orthodox Synagogues % of Total	Orthodox Synagogues Cumulative %
19. Dallas-Ft. Worth, TX	9	2	1	1		1	1	3	0.6	84.0
20. Houston-Galveston-Brazoria, TX	6	2	1	1		1		1	0.4	84.4
21. Tampa-St. Petersburg-Clearwater, FL	4	1		2				1	0.3	84.7
22. Minneapolis-St. Paul, MN-WI	6	3	1	1				1	0.4	85.1
23. Pittsburgh, PA	10	2	4	1			1	2	0.7	85.7
24. Seattle-Tacoma-Bremerton, WA	10	3	5			1		1	0.7	86.4
25. Hartford, CT	9	2	4	1	1			1	0.6	87.0
26. Portland-Salem, OR-WA	3	1	1			1			0.2	87.2
27. Cincinnati, OH-KY-IN	10	4	3			1		2	0.7	87.9
28. Rochester, NY	5	1	2			1		1	0.3	88.2
29. Columbus, OH	6	1	3	1				1	0.4	88.6
30. Sacramento-Yolo, CA	2	1	1						0.1	88.7
31. Milwaukee-Racine, WI	7	3				1		3	0.5	89.2
32. Orlando, FL	3	2						1	0.2	89.4
33. Tucson, AZ	2			1				1	0.1	89.5
34. Kansas City, MO-KS	3		1	1				1	0.2	89.7
35. Albany-Schenectady-Troy, NY	6	2	4						0.4	90.1
36. Buffalo-Niagara Falls, NY	8	2	2	1	1			2	0.5	90.7
37. Providence-Fall River-Warwick, RI-MA	11	2	5	1		1		2	0.7	91.4
38. Sarasota-Bradenton, FL	1	1							0.1	91.5
39. Austin, TX	3	1						2	0.2	91.7

TABLE 4.—*(Continued)*

	Total	Lubavitch	Orthodox Union	Young Israel**	OU/Young Israel	Sephardi Non-OU	Agudath Israel	Other Orthodox	Orthodox Synagogues % of Total	Orthodox Synagogues Cumulative %
40. Norfolk-Virginia Beach-Newport News, VA-NC	3	1	2						0.2	91.9
41. Springfield, MA	7	3	3					1	0.5	92.3
42. New Orleans, LA	4	3	1						0.3	92.6
43. Richmond-Petersburg, VA	3	1	1		1	0.2	92.8			
44. San Antonio, TX	2	1	1						0.1	92.9
45. Indianapolis, IN	2		1			1			0.1	93.1
46. Syracuse, NY	4	1	1	1					0.3	93.3
47. Charlotte-Gastonia-Rock Hill, NC-SC	1	1							0.1	93.4
48. Louisville, KY-IN	1	1							0.1	93.5
49. Memphis, TN-AR-MS	4	1	2					1	0.3	93.7
50. Ft. Myers-Cape Coral, FL	1	1							0.1	93.8
Total—top 50 Metro areas	1,408	296	287	116	30	98	53	528	93.8	93.8
Percent of 50 Metros	100.0	21.0	20.4	8.2	2.1	7.0	3.8	37.5		
Percent of U.S. Total	93.8	87.1	90.1	99.1	90.9	100.0	96.4	97.4		
Total—remainder of U.S.	93	44	29	1	3		2	14	6.2	100.0
Percent of remainder of U.S.	100.0	47.3	31.2	1.1	3.2		2.1	15.0		
Percent of U.S. Total	6.2	12.9	9.9	0.9	9.1	—	3.6	2.6		
U.S. Total	1,501	340	316	117	33	98	55	542		
Percent of U.S. Total	100.0	22.7	21.1	7.8	2.2	6.5	3.7	36.1		

*Orthodox Union includes 16 Sephardi synagogues in the following communities: 7 in Kings County (NYC), NY, 2 in Cook County (Chicago), IL, 2 in King County (Seattle), WA, and one each in Bergen, NJ, Essex, NJ (both counties in NYC metro), Montgomery County (Washington DC metro), MD, Philadelphia, PA, and Queens County (NYC), NY. In addition, three OU synagogues are also members of Agudath Israel: Pittsburgh, PA, Savannah, GA, and Scranton, PA. To avoid duplication they are listed only in the Agudath Israel column. Four synagogues are members of both OU and Lubavitch: Nashville, TN, Raleigh, NC, Reading, PA, and Youngstown, OH. To avoid duplication they are listed only in the OU column.

**Two synagogues are members of both Young Israel and Lubavitch: Palm Harbor, FL, and Tucson, AZ. To avoid duplication they are listed only in the Young Israel column.

TABLE 5. U.S. SYNAGOGUES BY DENOMINATION WITHIN STATES AND COUNTIES, 2001*

	Total	Orthodox	Conservative	Reform	Reconstructionist	Other***	State Jewish Population§	Synagogues per 1,000 Jewish Population
ALABAMA								
Jefferson	5	2	1	1	1			
All other counties (9)**	13		3	9		1		
Total	18	2	4	10	1	1	9,000	2.00
ALASKA								
All other counties (3)**	5	1		3		1		
Total	5	1		3		1	3,400	1.47
ARIZONA								
Maricopa	20	6	5	7		2		
Pima	12	2	3	5	1	1		
All other counties (6)**	6			5		1		
Total	38	8	8	17	1	4	81,500	0.47
ARKANSAS								
All other counties (9)**	10	1		9				
Total	10	1		9			1,700	5.88
CALIFORNIA								
Alameda	8	1	2	5				
Contra Costa	15	2	3	6		4		
Los Angeles	202	114	35	38	3	12		
Marin	5	1		1		3		
Orange	28	6	6	11	1	4		
Riverside	11	4	4	3				
Sacramento	7	2	1	3	1			
San Bernardino	7	1	3	3				
San Diego	29	13	7	7	1	1		
San Francisco	36	23	4	5		4		
San Mateo	7		3	2		2		
Santa Clara	17	7	3	5	1	1		
Sonoma	7		2	2	1	2		
Ventura	6	3	1	2				
All other counties (24)**	40	4	7	18		11		
Total	425	181	81	111	8	44	999,000	0.43

TABLE 5.—*(Continued)*

	Total	Orthodox	Conservative	Reform	Reconstructionist	Other***	State Jewish Population§	Synagogues per 1,000 Jewish Population
COLORADO								
Boulder	6	1	2	2		1		
Denver	17	8	2	3	1	3		
All other counties (10)**	18	4	2	6	1	5		
Total	41	13	6	11	2	9	73,000	0.56
CONNECTICUT								
Fairfield	28	8	9	8		3		
Hartford	25	8	10	6		1		
New Haven	19	6	8	5				
New London	7	4	2	1				
All other counties (4)**	8	2	4	2				
Total	87	28	33	22		4	111,000	0.78
DELAWARE								
New Castle	6	2	1	1	1	1		
All other counties (1)**	1		1					
Total	7	2	2	1	1	1	13,500	0.52
DISTRICT OF COLUMBIA								
District of Columbia	11	3	2	3		3		
Total	11	3	2	3		3	25,500	0.43
FLORIDA								
Broward	59	19	20	12	2	6		
Dade	70	48	13	8	1			
Duval	5	2	2	1				
Hillsborough	10	3	2	4		1		
Orange	9	3	2	3	1			
Palm Beach	45	14	19	10	1	1		
Pinellas	12	1	3	6		2		
Sarasota	5	1	1	2		1		
All other counties (26)**	48	6	14	26	1	1		
Total	263	97	76	72	6	12	620,000	0.42

TABLE 5.—*(Continued)*

	Total	Orthodox	Conservative	Reform	Reconstructionist	Other***	State Jewish Population§	Synagogues per 1,000 Jewish Population
GEORGIA								
Fulton	26	10	3	6	2	4		
All other counties (16)**	26	3	5	14		4		
Total	52	13	8	20	3	8	93,500	0.56
HAWAII								
All other counties (2)**	4	1	1	2				
Total	4	1	1	2			7,000	0.57
IDAHO								
All other counties (2)**	2			2				
Total	2			2			1,100	1.82
ILLINOIS								
Cook	117	50	23	28	3	13		
Lake	15	3	4	6		2		
All other counties (22)**	29	1	7	18		3		
Total	161	54	34	52	3	18	270,000	0.60
INDIANA								
Marion	6	2	2	1	1			
All other counties (14)**	21	1	5	15				
Total	27	3	7	16	1		17,500	1.54
IOWA								
All other counties (11)**	16	3	5	8				
Total	16	3	5	8			6,100	2.62
KANSAS								
Johnson	6	3	1	1		1		
All other counties (4)**	4			2		2		
Total	10	3	1	3		3	14,000	0.71
KENTUCKY								
Jefferson	5	1	2	2				
All other counties (4)**	6		2	4				
Total	11	1	4	6			11,500	0.96

TABLE 5.—*(Continued)*

	Total	Orthodox	Conservative	Reform	Reconstructionist	Other***	State Jewish Population§	Synagogues per 1,000 Jewish Population
LOUISIANA								
Orleans	6	3		3				
All other counties (9)**	11	1	2	8				
Total	17	4	2	11			16,000	1.06
MAINE								
All other counties (5)**	10	3	3	3		1		
Total	10	3	3	3		1	9,300	1.08
MARYLAND								
Baltimore	19	11	4	3	1			
Baltimore City	27	22	2	1	1	1		
Howard	5	1	1	2	1			
Montgomery	36	15	10	5	2	4		
Prince Georges	9	1	4	1	2	1		
All other counties (8)**	11	2	3	5		1		
Total	107	52	24	17	7	7	213,000	0.50
MASSACHUSETTS								
Barnstable	5	1	1	3				
Berkshire	6	1	1	3	1			
Bristol	5	2	3					
Essex	29	5	9	5	2	8		
Hampden	10	6	2	1		1		
Middlesex	51	14	9	14	2	12		
Norfolk	41	13	12	8		8		
Plymouth	8	3	1	1	1	2		
Suffolk	22	13	1	1		7		
Worcester	18	5	2	3		8		
All other counties (4)**	6	1	2	2		1		
Total	201	64	43	41	6	47	275,000	0.73

TABLE 5.—*(Continued)*

	Total	Orthodox	Conservative	Reform	Reconstructionist	Other***	State Jewish Population§	Synagogues per 1,000 Jewish Population
MICHIGAN								
Oakland	35	21	5	6	1	2		
Washtenaw	5	2	1	1	1			
All other counties (19)**	31	2	7	16	2	4		
Total	71	25	13	23	4	6	110,000	0.65
MINNESOTA								
Hennepin	14	3	4	3	1	3		
Ramsey	7	3	2	1		1		
All other counties (3)**	4	1	1	2				
Total	25	7	7	6	1	4	42,000	0.60
MISSISSIPPI								
All other counties (14)**	14	1		13				
Total	14	1	13		1,500	9.33		
MISSOURI								
St. Louis	20	8	3	7		2		
All other counties (10)**	13		1	11	1			
Total	33	8	4	18	1	2	62,500	0.53
MONTANA								
All other counties (6)**	6			4		2		
Total	6			4		2	800	7.50
NEBRASKA								
Douglas	5	2	1	1	1			
All other counties (1)**	2		1	1				
Total	7	2	2	2	1		7,000	1.00

TABLE 5.—*(Continued)*

	Total	Orthodox	Conservative	Reform	Reconstructionist	Other***	State Jewish Population§	Synagogues per 1,000 Jewish Population
NEVADA								
Clark	18	7	2	6	1	2		
All other counties (2)**	5	1	1	3				
Total	23	8	3	9	1	2	77,000	0.30
NEW HAMPSHIRE								
All other counties (7)**	12		4	6		2		
Total	12		4	6		2	10,000	1.20
NEW JERSEY								
Atlantic	12	4	4	2	1	1		
Bergen	66	28	22	12	1	3		
Burlington	5	3	1	1				
Camden	13	3	5	4	1			
Essex	31	13	11	5	1	1		
Hudson	9	4	3	2				
Mercer	16	7	4	2		3		
Middlesex	27	11	12	3		1		
Monmouth	42	25	9	5		3		
Morris	19	5	8	4	1	1		
Ocean	35	29	4	2				
Passaic	16	6	6	3		1		
Somerset	9	1	4	2	2			
Union	16	6	6	4				
All other counties (5)**	15	1	6	4	3	1		
Total	331	143	107	55	10	16	485,000	0.68
NEW MEXICO								
All other counties (5)**	10	3	1	4		2		
Total	10	3	1	4		2	11,500	0.87

TABLE 5.—*(Continued)*

	Total	Orthodox	Conservative	Reform	Reconstructionist	Other***	State Jewish Population§	Synagogues per 1,000 Jewish Population
NEW YORK								
Albany	8	3	2	2		1		
Bronx	44	32	7	3		2		
Erie	16	8	3	4	1			
Kings	256	219	21	11		5		
Monroe	14	5	4	4		1		
Nassau	141	57	45	34	2	3		
New York	102	68	15	13	2	4		
Onondaga	6	4	1	1				
Orange	9	1	5	3				
Queens	159	108	40	7		4		
Richmond	18	11	6	1				
Rockland	44	29	9	6				
Suffolk	48	16	18	12	1	1		
Sullivan	10	7	1	2				
Tompkins	5	2	1	1		1		
Ulster	7	2	1	2	2			
Westchester	62	16	18	22	3	3		
All other counties (27)**	46	7	18	17		4		
Total	995	595	215	145	11	29	1,657,000	0.60
NORTH CAROLINA								
Durham	6	2	1	1	1	1		
Wake	5	2	1	2				
All other counties (16)**	23	1	5	15	1	1		
Total	34	5	7	18	2	2	26,500	1.28
NORTH DAKOTA								
All other counties (2)**	2			2				
Total	2			2			450	4.44

TABLE 5.—*(Continued)*

	Total	Orthodox	Conservative	Reform	Reconstructionist	Other***	State Jewish Population§	Synagogues per 1,000 Jewish Population
OHIO								
Cuyahoga	39	22	5	8	1	3		
Franklin	11	6	1	4				
Hamilton	21	9	4	4	1	3		
Montgomery	5	2	1	2				
All other counties (24)**	38	6	9	20	1	2		
Total	114	45	20	38	3	8	149,000	0.77
OKLAHOMA								
All other counties (6)**			10	2	2	6		
Total	10	2	2	6			5,000	2.00
OREGON								
Multnomah	6	3	1	1	1			
All other counties (8)**	9	1	1	2	2	3		
Total	15	4	2	3	3	3	32,000	0.47
PENNSYLVANIA								
Allegheny	29	10	8	6	1	4		
Bucks	16	3	4	5	4			
Dauphin	5	2	2	1				
Delaware	9	6	2	1				
Luzerne	6	2	2	2				
Montgomery	28	8	10	8	1	1		
Philadelphia	44	16	12	7	3	6		
All other counties (33)**	60	8	21	23	4	4		
Total	197	49	65	54	14	15	282,000	0.70
RHODE ISLAND								
Providence	12	7	3	2				
All other counties (3)**	7	2	3	2				
Total	19	9	6	4			16,000	1.19

TABLE 5.—*(Continued)*

	Total	Orthodox	Conservative	Reform	Reconstructionist	Other***	State Jewish Population§	Synagogues per 1,000 Jewish Population
SOUTH CAROLINA								
All other counties (10)**	15	2	4	9				
Total	15	2	4	9			11,500	1.30
SOUTH DAKOTA								
All other counties (3)**	3		1	2				
Total	3		1	2			300	10.00
TENNESSEE								
Shelby	6	4	1	1				
All other counties (8)**	13	2	3	7		1		
Total	19	6	4	8		1	18,000	1.06
TEXAS								
Bexar	5	2	1	1	1			
Dallas	17	8	2	5		2		
Harris	21	6	5	8	1	1		
Travis	11	3	2	2	1	3		
All other counties (27)**	38	2	6	25		5		
Total	92	21	16	41	3	11	131,000	0.70
UTAH								
All other counties (3)**	6	1	1	3	1			
Total	6	1	1	3	1		4,500	1.33
VERMONT								
All other counties (8)**	13	1	2	3	1	6		
Total	13	1	2	3	1	6	5,500	2.36

TABLE 5.—*(Continued)*

	Total	Orthodox	Conservative	Reform	Reconstructionist	Other***	State Jewish Population§	Synagogues per 1,000 Jewish Population
VIRGINIA								
Fairfax	8	2	2	2		2		
Richmond (city)	7	3	2	2				
All other counties (23)**	38	5	12	18	1	2		
Total	53	10	16	22	1	4	66,000	0.80
WASHINGTON								
King	21	10	3	7	1			
All other counties (11)**	15		4	7	1	3		
Total	36	10	7	14	1	4	43,000	0.84
WEST VIRGINIA								
All other counties (11)**	11		2	9				
Total	11		2	9			2,300	4.78
WISCONSIN								
Dane	5	1	1	1	1	1		
Milwaukee	16	6	4	5	1			
All other counties (12)**	15	1	4	7		3		
Total	36	8	9	13	2	4	28,000	1.29
WYOMING								
All other counties (2)**			2	2				
Total	2			2			400	5.00
Total United States	**3,727**	**1,501**	**865**	**976**	**99**	**286**	**6,155,000**	**0.61**

*Counties with at least 5 synagogues
**Number of counties with 1-4 synagogues
***Other include Traditional (46), Humanistic (32), Jewish Renewal (14), Gay/Lesbian non UAHC/non-Reconstructionist (11), Sephardi-non-Orthodox (4), no denomination noted (142), and other (37)
§Details may not add to total because of rounding

TABLE 6. NUMBER OF COUNTIES AT SYNAGOGUE LEVEL

Number of Synagogues	Number of Counties Containing Synagogues at Noted Level
100+	6
50–99	5
30–49	13
20–29	16
15–19	17
10–14	14
9	6
8	4
7	8
6	12
5	17
	29
3	44
2	94
1	335
None	2,446
Total	3,066

TABLE 7. COUNTIES WITH LARGEST NUMBER OF SYNAGOGUES

County	Number of Synagogues
1. Kings (Brooklyn), NY	256
2. Los Angeles, CA	202
3. Queens, NY	159
4. Nassau, NY	141
5. Cook, IL	117
6. New York (Manhattan), NY	102
7. Dade, FL	70
8. Bergen, NJ	66
9. Westchester, NY	62
10. Broward, FL	59
Total	1,234

TABLE 8. COUNTIES WITH FEWER THAN FIVE SYNAGOGUES, 2001

Note–Counties listed are those with one to four synagogues. Unless otherwise noted each county has only one synagogue.

ALABAMA
Calhoun
Dallas
Etowah
Houston
Madison 2
Mobile 2
Montgomery 3
Tuscaloosa
Walker

ALASKA
Anchorage 3
Fairbanks North Star
Juneau

ARIZONA
Cochise
Coconino
LaPaz
Mohave
Yavapai
Yuma

ARKANSAS
Craighead
Desha
Garland
Jefferson
Mississippi
Phillips
Pulaski 2
Sebastian
Washington

CALIFORNIA
Alpine
Amador
Butte
Fresno 3
Humboldt
Imperial
Kern 2
Mendocino
Merced
Monterey 3
Napa
Nevada 2
Placer
San Joaquin
San Luis Obispo 2
Santa Barbara 4
Santa Cruz 4
Shasta
Solano 3
Stanislaus
Tuolomne
Tulare
Yolo
Yuba 2

COLORADO
Adams 2
Arapahoe 3
Eagle
El Paso 4
Jefferson 2
Larimer
Mesa
Pitkin 2
Pueblo
Routt

CONNECTICUT
Litchfield 3
Middlesex
Tolland 2
Windham 2

DELAWARE
Kent

FLORIDA
Alachua 3
Bay
Brevard 2
Charlotte 2
Citrus
Collier 2
Escambia
Hernando
Highlands
Indian River 2
Lake 2
Lee 4
Leon 3
Manatee 2
Marion
Martin 2
Monroe 2
Okaloosa
Osceola
Pasco
Polk 2
Santa Rosa
Seminole 3
St. Johns
St. Lucie 2
Volusia 4

GEORGIA
Bibb 2
Chatham 3
Clarke
Clay 2
Cobb 4
Decatur
Dougherty
Fayette
Floyd
Glynn
Gwinnett 2
Lowndes
Muscogee 2
Richmond 2
Rockdale
Whitfield

HAWAII
Honolulu 3
Maui

IDAHO
Ada
Custer

ILLINOIS
Adams 2
Champaign
Coles
Dekalb
DuPage
Kane 2
Kankakee
Knox
LaSalle
Macon
Madison
Marion
McHenry 2
McLean
Peoria 3
Rock Island
Sangamon 2
Vermillion
Whiteside
Will
Williamson
Winnebago 2

INDIANA
Allen 2
Bartholomew
Delaware
Grant
Howard
La Porte 2
Lake 3
Monroe
St. Joseph 3
Tippecanoe 2
Vanderburgh
Vigo
Warrick
Wayne

IOWA
Alamakee
Black Hawk
Des Moines 2
Dubuque
Johnson 2
Linn
Polk 3
Scott
Story
Wapello
Woodbury 2

KANSAS
Douglas
Riley

TABLE 8.—*(Continued)*

Sedgwick
Shawnee

KENTUCKY
Daviess
Fayette 3
McCracken
Warren

LOUISIANA
Caddo
Calcasieu
E. Baton Rouge
Iberia
Jefferson 2
Ouachita
Rapides 2
St. Tammany
W. Baton Rouge

MAINE
Androscoggin
Cumberland 4
Kennebec
Knox
Penobscot 3

MARYLAND
Allegany
Anne Arundel 3
Carroll
Frederick
Harford
Washington
Wicomico
Worcester 2

MASSACHUSETTS
Dukes
Franklin
Hampshire 3
Nantucket

MICHIGAN
Alpena
Bay
Berrien
Emmet
Genesee 3
Grand Traverse 2
Houghton
Ingham 2
Isabella
Jackson
Kalamazoo 2
Kent 3
Macomb 2
Marquette
Monroe 2
Muskegon
Saginaw
Van Buren
Wayne 4

MINNESOTA
Dakota
Olmsted 2
St. Louis

MISSISSIPPI
Adams
Bolivar
Claiborne
Coahoma
Forrest
Harrison
Hinds
Holmes
Lauderdale
Lee
Leflore
Lowdnes
Warren
Washington

MISSOURI
Boone
Buchanan
Cole
Greene
Jackson 3
Jasper
Miller
Pettis
St. Charles
St. Louis (city) 2

MONTANA
Cascade
Flathead
Gallatin
Missoula
Silver Bow
Yellowstone

NEBRASKA
Lancaster 2

NEVADA
Douglas
Washoe 4

NEW HAMPSHIRE
Belknap
Cheshire 2
Grafton 2
Hillsborough 4
Merrimack
Rockingham
Strafford

NEW JERSEY
Cape May
Cumberland 4
Hunterdon 4
Sussex 4
Warren 2

NEW MEXICO
Bernalillo 4
Colfax
Dona Ana
Los Alamos
Santa Fe 3

NEW YORK
Broome 3
Cattaraugus
Cayuga
Chatauqua
Chemung 2
Clinton
Columbia
Cortland
Delaware 2
Dutchess 4
Fulton
Greene
Herkimer
Jefferson
Montgomery
Niagara 3
Oneida 3
Ontario
Otsego
Putnam 2
Rensselaer 3
Saratoga 4
Schenectady 4
St. Lawrence
Steuben
Warren

NORTH CAROLINA
Buncombe 2
Catawba
Craven
Cumberland
Edgecombe
Forsyth
Gaston
Guilford 3
Halifax
Henderson
Iredell
Lenoir
Mecklenburg 4
New Hanover 2
Pitt
Wayne

NORTH DAKOTA
Cass
Grand Forks

OHIO
Allen
Ashtabula
Athens
Butler 2
Clark
Columbiana
Darke
Erie
Jefferson
Lake
Licking
Lorain 3
Lucas 4
Mahoning 4
Marion
Montgomery 4
Muskingam
Richland
Ross
Scioto
Stark 3

TABLE 8.—*(Continued)*

Summit 4
Trumbull
Warren
Wayne

OKLAHOMA
Carter
Kay
Muskogee
Oklahoma 3
Pontotoc
Tulsa 3

OREGON
Benton
Clackamas
Deschutes
Jackson
Klamath
Lane 2
Marion
Washington

PENNSYLVANIA
Adams
Beaver 2
Berks 4
Blair 2
Butler
Cambria
Centre 2
Chester 3
Clearfield
Clinton
Cumberland 2
Erie 2
Fayette 2
Franklin
Indiana
Lackawanna 3
Lancaster 3
Lawrence
Lebanon
Lehigh 4
Lycoming
McKean
Mercer
Monroe
Northampton 4
Northumberland
Pike
Schuylkill 3
Venango
Washington
Wayne
Westmoreland 3
York 2

RHODE ISLAND
Bristol 2
Kent 2
Newport 3

SOUTH CAROLINA
Aiken
Beaufort 2
Charleston 3
Florence
Georgetown
Greenville 2
Horry
Richland 2
Spartanburg
Sumter

SOUTH DAKOTA
Brown
Minnehaha
Pennington

TENNESSEE
Anderson
Davidson 4
Hamilton 2
Haywood
Knox 2
Madison
Marion
Sullivan

TEXAS
Bowie
Brazoria
Brazos
Cameron 2
Collin 3
Denton
Ector 2
El Paso 2
Fayette 2
Fort Bend
Galveston 2
Grayson
Gregg
Hidalgo
Jefferson
Lubbock
McLennan 2
Montgomery
Nueces
Potter
Smith 2
Tarrant 3
Taylor
Victoria
Webb
Wharton
Wichita

UTAH
Salt Lake 4
Summit
Weber

VERMONT
Bennington 3
Caledonia
Chittenden 3
LaMoille
Rutland
Washington
Windham 2
Windsor

VIRGINIA
Alexandria (city) 3
Arlington 2
Charlottesville (city) 2
Danville (city)
Fairfax (city) 2
Falls Church (city)
Fredericksburg (city)
Hampton (city)
Harrisonburg (city)
Loudon 2
Lynchburg (city)
Martinsville (city)
Montgomery
Newport News (city) 2
Norfolk (city) 4
Petersburg (city)
Portsmouth (city) 2
Prince William
Roanoke (city) 2
Stafford
Staunton (city)
Virginia Beach (city) 4
Winchester (city)

WASHINGTON
Benton
Clallam
Clark
Grays Harbor
Kitsap 2
Pierce 2
Snohomish
Spokane
Thurston 2
Whatcom 2
Yakima

WEST VIRGINIA
Berkeley
Cabell
Harrison
Kanawha
Mercer
Mingo
Monongahela
Ohio
Raleigh

TABLE 8.—*(Continued)*

Wayne
Wood

WISCONSIN
Eau Claire
Green
Kenosha
La Crosse
Marathon
Outagamie
Ozaukee 2
Racine
Rock
Sheboygan
Waukesha 2
Winnebago 2

WYOMING
Albany
Natrona

Review of the Year

UNITED STATES

United States

National Affairs

MEMORY HAD TO REACH BACK to the 1930s and 1940s for a period when Jews seemed to be so under assault on a global basis as in 2001, and in which the larger American society—indeed, civilization itself—seemed faced with such an immediate mortal threat. Months of mounting anti-Semitism abroad—granted legitimacy in international institutions through a campaign of isolation and delegitimization directed at Israel—was followed by the September 11 assault on America. The attacks on the World Trade Center and the Pentagon that day provided American Jews with the cold comfort that Americans would now understand what Israelis had been going through since the outbreak of Palestinian violence a year earlier.

There were also other matters on the national scene for Jews to address: preserving religious liberty, responding to a rise in domestic anti-Semitic hate incidents, and building a relationship with a new president.

THE POLITICAL ARENA

The Bush Administration Takes Shape

As George W. Bush organized his administration before inauguration day, it became evident that his highly diverse cabinet would include ethnic minorities (two African Americans and an Arab American) and women in proportions not heretofore associated with the Republican Party—but no Jews. Ira Forman, executive director of the National Jewish Democratic Council, expressed concern at the implications of a cabinet without a single Jewish member, commenting, "Either their circle of friends doesn't include Jews or the Jews just didn't get picked. I think it's the former." Representatives of other Jewish organizations cautioned, however, against reading too much into the cabinet choices. "The Jewish community has graduated beyond the point where, at every election, we have to hold a stopwatch and count how many people cross the finish line," commented Jason Isaacson, director of government and international affairs for the American Jewish Committee. Others noted that several Jews had played prominent roles in the Bush campaign, and that they and other prominent Jewish Republicans would hold key posts, albeit not cabinet seats, in the new administration. Thus, Ari Fleischer was named White House press secretary, Joshua Bolten deputy chief of staff for public policy, and Paul Wolfowitz deputy secretary of defense.

Virtually no concern was heard in the Jewish community about the selection of Senator Spencer Abraham (R., Mich.), an Eastern Orthodox Christian of Lebanese ancestry, as energy secretary. In addition to his bona fides as a leader in promoting fair immigration policies, Abraham, while serving in the Senate, had proved accessible to the Jewish community. Furthermore, notwithstanding the fact that there was three times the number of Arabs in Michigan as Jews, local Jewish leaders considered his record on Israel-related matters as good. "You would think that on Middle East issues, there would be problems," said David Gad-Harf, executive director of the Jewish Community Council of Metropolitan Detroit, "but we were able to work with him on issues that were supportive of the peace process."

A number of Jewish organizations were less sanguine about the nomination of another just-defeated senator, John Ashcroft (R., Mo.), as attorney general, questioning Ashcroft's ability to separate his religious beliefs and his official responsibilities. These concerns were strengthened when, during the run-up to confirmation hearings, reports surfaced of a speech that Ashcroft, then a senator, had given in 1999 at the controversial Bob Jones University, at which he said, "Because we have understood that our source is eternal, America has been different. We have no king but Jesus." The Anti-Defamation League issued a statement calling on Ashcroft to "assure the American people that his personal religious beliefs will not dictate how he will carry out his duties." The National Council of Jewish Women and Jewish Women International went further, opposing confirmation based on the nominee's positions on such hot-button issues as civil rights, abortion, and gun control.

Ashcroft did have some supporters in the Jewish community. The Republican Jewish Coalition termed the attacks on Ashcroft "character assassination." Jewish staffers for Ashcroft, both past and present, attested that their boss had been considerate of and accommodating to their faith, and had never sought to impose his own on them. Agudath Israel of America said that Ashcroft had shown respect for all people, whatever their religion or race, and its director of public affairs—Rabbi Avi Shafran—suggested that his references to Jesus were similar to a Jew's invocation of "God." Senator Orrin Hatch (R., Utah), in fact, commented that many of those critical of Ashcroft had not been as critical of Joseph Lieberman's references to his Jewish faith during the Connecticut senator's failed campaign as the Democratic nominee for vice president in 2000. Mark Pelavin, associate director of the Religious Action Center of Reform Judaism, countered that Lieberman, before his nomination, had had a long record of commitment to religious pluralism and religious liberty. Ashcroft's supporters noted that their man espoused those principles as well; in a speech delivered a year before his remarks at Bob Jones University, long before his cabinet nomination, Ashcroft had stated, "We must embrace the power of faith, but we must never confuse politics and piety. For me, may I say that it is against my religion to impose my religion."

With the early Bush administration falling into place, the Jewish community tended to focus its attention on Ari Fleischer, who, in his role as press secretary, would present the perspective of the president on a daily basis. The official spokesman for the incoming administration was personable, young (40), a proudly self-identified Jew—and a highly eligible bachelor. Even as he stressed that he would not mingle his religion and his political responsibilities, Fleischer made no secret that he was a "relatively observant, basically Reform" Jew who looked to the ethics of Judaism for guidance in carrying out his responsibilities. In an interview with the Jewish Telegraphic Agency he stated: "The Jewish religion teaches people to be responsible, to be open-minded and to care about others. And I hope that people see that in me as I do my job."

By midyear, President Bush had in place his Middle East policy team. William Burns, a former ambassador to Jordan, was the new assistant secretary of state for Near Eastern affairs, and some wondered whether the breadth of his responsibilities for the entire region would give him enough time for the Arab-Israeli conflict. Daniel Kurtzer, an Orthodox Jew and the outgoing ambassador to Egypt, replaced Martin Indyk as ambassador to Israel. The Zionist Organization of America and other hard-line Jewish groups attacked the choice because of Kurtzer's support for territorial compromise and the evacuation of certain settlements, but the Jewish mainstream backed the appointment, and he was easily confirmed.

Congress Takes Shape

The 107th Congress convened in January with the previous Republican majorities reduced in both houses. The Senate, split 50-50 as a result of the 2000 election, remained under Republican control only by virtue of Vice President Richard Cheney's tie-splitting vote. Indeed, during the period between the swearing-in of the 107th Congress on January 3 and the new vice president's inauguration on January 20, it was Senate Democratic leader Tom Daschle (D., S. Dak.) who, by virtue of Vice President Al Gore's incumbency, wielded the majority leader's gavel.

As a result of Republican caucus rules limiting chairs of House committees and subcommittees to three terms holding a particular office, Rep. Benjamin Gilman (R., N.Y.) was compelled to step down from his post as chairman of the House International Relations Committee. A new Middle East subcommittee was created within the committee, however, with Rep. Gilman at its head, leaving the long-time strong supporter of Israel in a continuing leadership role with respect to the Jewish community's most paramount issue.

Replacing Gilman at the helm of the International Relations Committee was Rep. Henry Hyde (R., Ill.), who was, in turn, obligated to hand over chairmanship of the House Judiciary Committee. Although often on the opposite side from much of the organized Jewish community on issues coming before Judiciary, Hyde was widely respected even among adversaries as a fair and capable chairman. With a strong record on Israel, Hyde was expected to be an ally of the Jewish community in his new role. His replacement at Judiciary was Rep. James Sensenbrenner (R., Wis.), whose conservative voting record on church-state issues and other matters suggested that much of the Jewish community would be at odds with him on a number of core concerns. In another significant development resulting from term limits, Rep. Sonny Callahan (R., Ala.) was replaced by Jim Kolbe (R., Ariz.) as head of the House Appropriations Committee's subcommittee on foreign relations, a body with significant responsibility for determining the amount of U.S. aid to Israel. While Democratic House ranking members were not subject to term limits, the ranking position on the International Relations Committee saw a change as a result of the defeat of Sam Gedjenson (D., Conn.) in the 2000 election. His replacement was Rep. Tom Lantos (D., Cal.), the only Holocaust survivor serving in Congress.

From the beginning of the session, Congress-watchers focused on the possibility that a single Republican senator's disability or demise could cause a seismic shift to Democratic control of the Senate, but few expected a senior Republican member to leave the party. When Vermont Senator Jim Jeffords did just that on May 24—declaring himself an Independent—the shift gave the Democrats a 50-49-1 majority and handed the majority leader's gavel back to Tom Daschle. Jewish leaders were quick to note that strong bipartisan support for Israel meant that the change would have little impact on that core area of concern, though there was likely to be a difference on the domestic front. Initiatives opposed by much of the community, such as charitable choice, would have more trouble moving forward, while other agenda items, such as hate-crimes legislation, would get more attention, at least in the Senate.

Far less surprising was the announcement on August 22 that Jesse Helms (R., N.C.), long-time chairman and ranking member of the Senate Foreign Relations Committee, would be retiring from the Senate when his term ended at the close of 2002. In his early years as senator, Helms had consistently opposed aid to Israel, and was a harsh critic of Israel's 1982 invasion of Lebanon. But only a few years later, following a 1985 trip to Israel, the senator's perspective shifted, ultimately leading him to defend Israel against what he regarded as undue pressure by the first President Bush and, later, President Clinton. Thus the retirement of Helms meant the loss of an important ally of the Jewish state. To be sure, many in the Jewish community never did become reconciled to Helms because of his outspoken identification with very conservative positions on a raft of social-policy issues, such as school prayer and abortion.

New York Mayoral Election

As Election Day 2001 approached, New York City turned its attention to a race that had gained in importance since September 11. Who would, or could, replace Mayor Rudy Giuliani, who, through stunning displays of heroism, empathy, and strength, had all but carried the city on his shoulders as it recovered from the worst day in its history? One thing was certain: the results of the primaries ensured that the next mayor would be Jewish. In the end, late on the evening of November 7, the city discovered that it had elected Republican Michael Bloomberg—a hugely wealthy businessman who had been a lifelong Democrat until he switched his registration the year before to prepare to run for office—over Democrat Mark Green.

Many credited Bloomberg's win to the value New Yorkers placed on his financial acumen at a time of economic uncertainty, although others noted that Green, in the course of an aggressive campaign to secure the Democratic nomination, had alienated many minority voters, and that Bloomberg had the benefit of a Giuliani endorsement. It was also apparent that the nominally Republican Bloomberg's socially liberal and fiscally conservative views were the kind of mix that had proven a winning combination for his predecessor.

Fighting Terrorism

Enacted in 1996 for an initial period of five years, the Iran-Libya Sanctions Act (ILSA) provided for sanctions—subject to presidential waiver—on any foreign entities investing in either of the two countries' energy sector. The purpose was to limit the resources available to these rogue nations to support terrorism and pursue weapons of mass destruction. Faced with the law's expiration on August 1, 2001, supporters of the bill sought a five-year extension. The Bush administration favored a two-year extension, but in the face of overwhelming support in Congress for the longer period, it ceased lobbying on the issue. In the end, the House of Representatives passed a five-year extension for ILSA on July 26 by a vote of 409-6, after the Senate passed its parallel bill 96-2 on July 25. President Bush signed the bill into law on August 3.

For the first eight months of the year, it seemed almost inevitable that Congress would act on the Secret Evidence Repeal Act (SERA). As originally introduced in the 106th Congress, this bill would have imposed a categorical ban on the use of classified information in deportation proceedings, even in cases of an alien alleged to have been involved in terrorism, unless that information were subject to discovery and examination on the same basis as any other evidence. While the version of SERA introduced in the 107th Congress (H.R.1266) was somewhat modified, a number of Jewish organizations—the American Jewish Committee and the Anti-Defamation League, in particular—believed that the bill still gave too little regard to crucial national security concerns. The Religious Action Center of Reform Judaism, on the other hand, endorsed the revised SERA as a protection for due process that adequately addressed earlier concerns. The House Judiciary Committee was scheduled to mark up the new SERA on September 26, but the events of September 11 changed the political landscape, stalling action on SERA.

September 11 and its Aftermath

On the sun-splashed morning of September 11, the United States was attacked with stunning ferocity as homicidal hijackers took control of and crashed four commercial airliners, and succeeded in flying three of the aircraft into the twin towers of the World Trade Center and the Pentagon, killing thousands. American Jews, already psychologically battered by the ongoing terrorist attacks against Jews in Israel, were as shocked as other Americans at the massive attack on home soil.

Immediately after the attacks, Jewish congregations across the nation came together—some as early as the evening of September 11—for prayer services and recitation of Psalms. The Jewish agencies responded with angry condemnations of the attacks and assurances to President Bush that he had their support in the battle against terrorism. Jewish institutions began to consider whether the security arrangements they had in place for their own facilities were adequate.

Although speculation that Saudi billionaire Osama bin Laden was responsible immediately came to the fore, Jewish leaders followed the lead of the American government in avoiding ascribing the attacks to any individual or organization until more information was available. Nevertheless, two contending themes as to how the American response to the attacks might play out immediately arose. On the one hand, it was thought, September 11 would help Americans understand as never before Israel's motivations in responding to terrorism. On the other hand, however, if it turned out that the terrorists' actions were somehow linked to the Middle East, Americans might question their nation's support for Israel, which could be viewed as the "reason" for September 11.

By the end of the week, the administration had identified bin Laden as the chief suspect and was beginning to gather together a broad-based coalition in support of a war to root out terrorism, beginning with the Al Qaeda terrorist network that bin Laden headed from his redoubt in Taliban-controlled Afghanistan. For Jewish leaders, the burgeoning coalition quickly gave rise to a new set of concerns, reminiscent of the dilemma that the community had faced when the first President Bush organized a similar coalition to wage the Gulf War. Overwhelmingly supportive of Bush *fils* in his war effort as it had been of Bush *père* in his, the community nevertheless watched with alarm as the administration courted countries that were themselves supporters of terrorism. Furthermore, the administration declined to treat Yasir Arafat and the terrorist groups operating out of Palestinian territory as the equivalent of the Taliban and bin Laden, and initially would not include Hamas and Hezballah among the suspected Islamic terrorist groups whose assets were to be frozen.

Some Jewish leaders feared that the desire to broaden the coalition would lead the administration to pressure Israel to negotiate with the Palestinians even while the latter's terrorism campaign continued unabated, and that the administration might go so far as to pressure Israel to make substantive concessions that would endanger its security. In fact, within two weeks of September 11, enormous pressure was placed on Prime Minister Sharon of Israel to allow Foreign Minister Shimon Peres to meet with Arafat. However, Jewish organizations muted their protests out of a combination of patriotic desire to support the president, fear that dissent at a crucial and sensitive time would diminish influence with the White House and support from the public at large, and appreciation for the record of support for Israel that the administration had already demonstrated during its short time in office.

On October 7, the U.S. commenced its strikes against Afghanistan. With an administration now actually engaged in combat—and encouraged by a seeming reconciliation between the president and Prime Minister Sharon on the issue of American pressure on Israel, as well as behind-the-scenes promises that Hamas, Hezballah, and other similar anti-Israel terrorist groups would soon make the list of targeted terrorist organizations—Jewish leaders quickly moved, once again, to state their strong support for the war against terrorism.

As November began, assurances from the American administration that the battle against terrorism would not disregard the terrorist assaults against Israel bore fruit. The Justice Department included a Palestinian organization associated with Hezballah and the Martyrs of Al-Aqsa Brigades among 46 groups named as "terrorist organizations," whose members would be precluded from entering the United States and whose funds could be frozen. The naming of the Al-Aqsa group was particularly noteworthy, since it had been linked to Arafat's own Fatah. The Justice Department's action was praised by AIPAC, which hailed Attorney General Ashcroft for "clearly recognizing that terrorism against both Americans and Israelis must be countered." Others expressed surprise that certain other groups, particularly Hamas, were not on the list, but expressed the hope that this would come soon.

One month later, the administration signaled once again that the war on terrorism would target groups carrying out attacks against Israel. Following weekend suicide bombings in Jerusalem and Haifa for which Hamas took credit, the Treasury Department announced on December

4 that the assets of three charitable organization with alleged links to Hamas, including the Texas-based Holy Land Foundation for Relief and Development, would be frozen. The Holy Land Foundation was accused of directly transferring its funds to offices of charity groups in Palestinian-controlled areas that had links to, or were controlled by, Hamas. The president himself announced the action, saying that contributions to the foundation were "used by Hamas to support schools and indoctrinate children to grow up into suicide bombers." Jewish groups and lawmakers that had long called for government action against the foundation commended the administration's action, while Muslim and Arab groups condemned it as not based on any evidence and as a violation of due process.

A key issue raised by the September 11 attacks was how to strike the appropriate balance between due process and an open society, on the one hand, and effective law enforcement to prevent acts of terrorism, on the other. On September 19, Attorney General Ashcroft sent up to Capitol Hill the administration's proposal for omnibus antiterrorism legislation. Citing the pressing threat of possible further terrorist acts, he called for Congress to pass the measure by the end of the week. Many Democrats and more than a few Republicans, including Senator Arlen Specter (R., Pa.) and Representative Bob Barr (R., Ga.), called for a more deliberative examination of the sweeping additional law enforcement authority sought by the administration. They noted that much of the new law-enforcement authority included in the bill had been called for by the Justice Department in prior years, without success.

On the same day that this legislative package arrived on Capitol Hill, the American Civil Liberties Union (ACLU) released a letter, signed by over 100 ethnic, religious, and public-interest groups of various ideological stripes, urging that care be taken not to sacrifice civil liberties in order to protect national security. Although the letter did not specifically address the legislation, it was not long before the ACLU and a number of the letter's signatories began to speak out against the Ashcroft bill and other initiatives that they found problematic.

It was widely noted that Jewish groups were all but absent from the ACLU letter. Breaking with coalition partners with whom they had often agreed, in the past, on civil-liberties issues, Jewish groups now largely supported the administration's push for speedy legislative action. As the bill was molded by the legislative process, the Jewish organizations tended to favor the initiative's provisions, even while recognizing that there was room for improvement on specifics. Thus, in a statement issued on October 18, as the process of reconciling the House and Senate bills was under way, the American Jewish Committee applauded the quick action of Congress in response to the threat posed by a "ruthless and implacable foe." Noting that the bill's drafters sought to deal with a set of significant and serious civil liberties concerns, AJCommittee stated, "We are confident Congress will monitor implementation of the bill, as will AJC and other concerned Americans, to ensure that our civil liberties are protected and to amend the bill as necessary to assure that the balance between national security and civil liberties is properly maintained." The Religious Action Center of Reform Judaism struck a more guarded note, expressing "strong support" for most of the bill's provisions, but cautioning that several of them "would severely imperil fundamental civil liberties." (Before year's end, it would state similar concerns about some of the law-enforcement and regulatory steps taken by the administration in response to September 11.)

Senate and House leaders worked together with administration officials to reconcile differences between the Senate and House bills. In this process of informal negotiation, a number changes were made that addressed some, although by no means all, of the concerns that had been raised on civil liberties and due process. In the end, the two versions were reconciled not by formal conference, but by introduction in the House of a new bill, H.R.3162, which incorporated agreed-upon changes. It passed in the House by 537-66 on October 24 and in the Senate by 98-1 the next day. Senator Russell Feingold (D., Wis.), a Jewish member, cast the sole dissenting vote in the Senate, motivated by civil-liberties concerns. A number of the "no" votes in the House were also cast by Jewish members and for the same reason, including a difficult but principled "no" vote by Rep. Jerrold Nadler (D., N.Y.), who represented the district where the World Trade Center was located.

Although the antiterrorism package did not pass within the few days called for by Attorney General Ashcroft, nor, when enacted, did it include all of the powers he had requested, Congress moved from first consideration to final passage in what might well have been record time for such sweeping legislation.

On October 26, President Bush signed into law H.R.3162, the Uniting and Strengthening of America by Providing Appropriate Tools Required to Intercept and Obstruct Terrorism (USA-PATRIOT) Act. The enactment expanded law enforcement surveillance authority, with particular attention to the challenges presented by technological change as well as the ability of authorities to share information. It also imposed stronger penalties on those who engage in terrorism, or harbor or finance terrorists, eliminated the statute of limitations for certain terrorism offenses, and provided additional support to border patrol and customs officials. Additionally, the USA-PATRIOT Act allowed authorities to detain for seven days non-citizens whom the attorney general had reason to believe posed a threat to national security. Such detention orders, however, were reviewable by any federal district court—not, as originally requested by the administration, only the District of Columbia district court. The law also included money-laundering provisions that had initially been passed only by the Senate, and "sunset" provisions based on the initial House version, whereby certain of the sections expanding electronic and foreign intelligence-gathering surveillance authority would expire after four years.

Durban Conference

The September 11 attacks all but pushed out of communal consciousness the so-called UN World Conference Against Racism, held in Durban, South Africa, from August 31 through September 8. American Jewish leaders understood long before the conference met that it was likely to be little more than a concerted effort to attack and delegitimize Israel, resurrect the "Zionism is Racism" libel, and accuse Israel of "genocide" against the Palestinians. Longer term, it was feared, Durban could very well legitimize a global war against the Jews by making blatant anti-Semitism acceptable under the thinnest of veneers.

This perception of the upcoming conference, however, stood in stark contrast to the hopes held by the African-American community, traditional political allies of the Jews on many issues. To be sure, leaders of that community tended to agree that it was unfair to single out Israel for blame and that Zionism was not a form of racism, and they resented the Arab bloc's single-minded anti-Israel campaign for diverting attention from the rest of the conference's agenda. Yet, African-American and allied civil-rights groups nevertheless hoped to see the conference serve as a platform for addressing the legacy of slavery, possibly including some form of reparations. The scene was set for potential black-Jewish conflict.

As August 31 approached, the strain in black-Jewish relations increasingly focused on whether Colin Powell, America's first black secretary of state, would attend the conference. Throughout the preparatory meetings preceding Durban, the Bush administration fought to keep anti-Semitic and anti-Israel provisions out of the conference documents. In fact, the administration warned that if those provisions were on the agenda Secretary Powell might send a lower-level delegation in his stead, or the United States might boycott the conference altogether. Adding its voice, the U.S. House of Representatives, on July 26, adopted a resolution sponsored by Representative Lantos condemning the inclusion of anti-Israel language in the conference agenda.

A low-level American presence or none at all would certainly undermine the credibility of the conference, and, conversely, the presence of America's African-American secretary of state would be seen as a boon to the prestige of the proceedings. But these very considerations were what impelled civil-rights groups to insist that Powell should attend, regardless of the outcome on the anti-Israel wording. Some asserted, as well, that the administration was using the Israel issue as a mere smokescreen to avoid having to deal with the slavery issue in the context of an international forum. Moreover, civil-rights leaders maintained that a high-level presence would mean more influence for the United States over the final result of the conference, and thus a better likelihood that anti-Israel language could be excluded.

Wary of being blamed should Powell pull out and the conference collapse—and, in any event, not of one mind as to the best course regarding Powell's attendance—Jewish groups initially kept their counsel on this issue. As the date of the conference neared, however, and it became more obvious that the conference would single out Israel for criticism in a world filled with far more significant offenders, Jewish organizations began to speak out. Virtually all of them praised the administration for its role in trying to fend off the attacks on Israel, but they differed on strategy for the conference. The Religious Action Center of Reform Judaism wrote to Secretary Powell on August 16 urging his attendance "as long as the possibility exists that the noxious language might be removed, or modified in a way which would make it acceptable." The Anti-Defamation League and the American Jewish Committee, in contrast, called on the U.S. to boycott the conference. B'nai B'rith International suggested that if Powell did not attend, at least a lower-level delegation should be sent so as not to "leave the battlefield defenseless"; that delegation would have the option of walking out in protest if necessary.

There were reports of growing anger among some black politicians and within the civil-rights community about American Jewry's "single-mindedness"—one common complaint was that the Lantos resolution had failed even to mention the need to deal in some fashion with the legacy of slavery. In response, the New York-based Foundation for Ethnic Understanding and the World Jewish Congress organized a letter, dated July 31 and signed by 28 prominent Jewish and black members of Congress, that condemned the anti-Israel language but also stated: "We . . . support the efforts of African American leaders to raise and address important issues surrounding the historic tragedy of slavery and the resulting efforts to seek reparations." The letter did not take a position on reparations or even on whether Durban was the appropriate forum to address slavery and reparations.

With the conference about to commence, and after a statement by President Bush that "we will have no representative there so long as they . . . continue to say Zionism is racism," Secretary Powell announced on August 27 that he would not attend, leaving open the option of sending a low-level delegation. The State Department's spokesman said that the decision was based on "a whole series of references to one particular government, to one particular country, and to its policies as being racist." Israel and Jewish groups praised the administration and said that they too would either boycott or have only a limited presence at the event. B'nai B'rith president Richard Heideman stated, "Sending Secretary Powell dignifies the conference. By refusing to send Powell, the statement is being made very clear that the United States disapproves of the language of the conference and disapproves of the environment of hate that is surrounding the conference." In sharp contrast, the rest of the civil-rights community condemned Powell's decision, and the Leadership Conference on Civil Rights, notwithstanding the significant number of Jewish organizations that belonged to it, issued a statement to that effect.

The atmosphere in Durban made the conference a virtual hate festival directed against Jews and Israel, especially the declaration produced by nongovernmental organizations (NGOs) there (see above, pp. 100–04). Several representatives of American civil-rights organizations took pains to distance themselves from what they termed the "fervently rhetorical attacks" on Israel. Wade Henderson, executive director of the Leadership Conference on Civil Rights, said that much of the NGO declaration was valid, but he termed "totally unacceptable" the portion that "clearly crosses the line into elements of anti-Semitism." Karen Narasaki, president and executive director of the National Asian Pacific American Legal Consortium, who served at the NGO conference as head of the Asian and Asian Descendents Caucus, went so far as to apologize for having inadvertently cast a vote for the motion that caused the Jewish delegation walk out, a mistake that she attributed to the chaotic nature of the proceedings. Reva Price, Washington representative of the Jewish Council for Public Affairs, expressed appreciation for these remarks, saying, "The heartfelt emotion and understanding of our issues is very gratifying. It's tragic that the issues that they've come to talk about in Durban have not gotten the same attention as the Middle East and Israel."

Soviet Jewry, Refugees, and Immigration

Measures to provide fairer treatment of immigrants, many of them supported by the organized Jewish community, were put on hold following September 11. Instead, lawmakers pushed proposals to tighten security at the nation's borders and to improve the tracking of foreigners so as to protect the nation from terrorists. On October 29, President Bush issued an executive order directing the attorney general to establish a task force aimed at closing the immigration-related loopholes that allowed a number of the 19 September-11 hijackers to enter the country legally. The USA-PATRIOT Act, signed by President Bush in October (described above), while less sweeping in the detention authority it afforded than the measure first proposed by the administration, still allowed non-citizens who won deportation cases to be detained if the attorney general considered them a threat. (The Enhanced Border Security and Visa Reform Act also had major implications for immigration policy, but, though passed by the House of Representatives just before Congress recessed, it was still awaiting action in the Senate as the year ended.)

In addition to these detention provisions, the USA-PATRIOT Act beefed up resources for border control; provided the Immigration and Naturalization Service (INS) and the State Department access to FBI criminal records; required INS and the State Department to adopt a standard technology that would allow for verification of the identity of persons applying for U.S. visas or seeking to enter the country; added new grounds of inadmissibility for aliens deemed to be representatives of foreign terrorist organizations or groups that publicly endorsed terrorist acts; made fund-raising, material support, or solicitation for membership in a terrorist organization a deportable offense; and directed the INS to implement fully the provisions of the 1996 immigration reform law, including an integrated entry-and-exit data system and a visa-monitoring program for foreign students. The law also provided a variety of special protections for immigrants directly affected by the September 11 attacks, including the extension of filing or reentry deadlines, and humanitarian relief for spouses and children of September 11 victims.

Refugee admissions and processing of refugee visa applications were frozen after September 11, profoundly affecting many people seeking to enter the U.S., including Jews from the former Soviet Union (FSU). On November 13, a number of Jewish organizations jointly wrote to President Bush urging that "the Department of Justice and Immigration and Naturalization Service . . . work with the State Department to initiate expeditious and creative approaches to ensure that our nation's commitment to refugee protection and resettlement does not become another casualty of terrorism." On November 21, the State Department issued a statement committing the administration to resume admission of up to 70,000 refugees during fiscal year 2002. At year's end, however, the flow of refugees remained at a trickle.

In the wake of September 11 and the moratorium on refugee admissions, movement on the Refugee Protection Act (RPA) initiative was put on hold. The RPA was designed to limit the application of the expedited review procedures established by the 1996 immigration law, under which an asylum seeker's claims of persecution could be subject to a one-time review by a low-level INS employee at the point of entry. Critics pointed out a number of problems: possible inconsistencies between INS officers in the conduct of interviews, poor translations that could lead to erroneous decisions and inaccurate records, and lack of access to counsel and independent agencies monitoring for abuse and ill treatment. The RPA would limit the use of the expedited procedure to instances of immigration emergencies, and would prohibit its use altogether against aliens fleeing from countries that engage in serious human-rights violations. Prior to September 11, HIAS (the Hebrew Immigrant Aid Society), in coalition with other Jewish and pro-immigrant organizations, had been working to increase the number of Senate cosponsors for RPA, and, at the same time, had been seeking to introduce a bipartisan House companion measure to the Senate bill (S.1311) introduced on August 2 by Senators Sam Brownback (R., Kan.) and Patrick Leahy (D., Ver.).

As in previous years, the conference report on the Labor/HHS/Education spending measure, adopted by both the House and Senate, included the Specter Amendment (formerly known as the Lautenberg Amendment). This provision, as extended, provided for expedited treatment through September 30, 2002, of applications for refugee status by Jews, evangelical Christians, and other religious minorities in the FSU.

At the same time, Congress considered repeal of the Jackson-Vanik Amendment, a 1974 provision imposing trade sanctions on what was, then, the Soviet Union, for failing to allow its citizens to emigrate freely. In the eyes of the U.S. and of Russian Jews, the amendment had played a crucial role in inducing the USSR to let tens of thousands of Jews emigrate. Jackson-Vanik continued in effect after the fall of communism, though some of the successor republics had been "graduated" from its provisions because of improved conditions for religious minorities. In mid-November, while Russian president Vladimir Putin was in the U.S., President Bush—possibly as an inducement to Russia to play a leading role in the antiterror coalition—said he would seek an end to Jackson-Vanik. Russian Jews, viewing Putin as a friend, liked the idea, but American Jews, worried by reports of ongoing anti-Semitism in Russia, were ambivalent. The National Conference on Soviet Jewry (NCSJ) backed a proposal by Representative Lantos to accede to the administration's wishes only if Russia committed itself to allow free Jewish emigration and took steps to ensure religious liberty.

Shortly before it recessed for the year, the Senate debated, but put off action on, a farm bill sponsored by Senator Tom Harkin (D., Iowa), chairman of the Senate Agriculture, Nutrition, and Forestry Committee, which, among other things, would have restored such benefits as food stamps, Medicaid, and Temporary Assistance for Needy Families (TANF) to certain legal immigrants, immigrant children, and refugees. These had seen their eligibility for benefits drastically cut in 1996, with only some of those benefits restored in the intervening years.

Congress and U.S.-Israel Relations

On December 19, the House adopted a conference report on a foreign-aid bill (H.R. 2506) by 357-66, and the Senate following suit the next day by unanimous consent. The measure included $2.04 billion in military aid to Israel and $720 million in financial assistance. While the aid to Israel was in keeping with past practice, Israel's supporters saw this approval and the votes leading up to it as a welcome indication that Congress would continue to stand by Israel even as the U.S. was engaged in its own war against terror.

However, the final appropriations bill did not include a section initially passed by the House aimed at penalizing the Palestinian Authority (PA) for its continuing use of violence. Subject to presidential waiver, that section would have closed the Palestinian information office in the United States, designated the PLO and its constituent groups foreign terrorist organizations, and restricted U.S. assistance to the West Bank and Gaza. Based on the Middle East Peace Commitments Act of 2001 (H.R.1795/S.1409)—introduced in the House in May by Representatives Gary Ackerman (D., N.Y.), Benjamin Gilman (R., N.Y.), and Tom Lantos (D., Cal.), and in the Senate in September by Senators Mitch McConnell (R., Ky.) and Dianne Feinstein (D., Cal.)—these provisions had been incorporated into appropriations bills pending in both houses. After the September 11 attacks, however, the administration urged the elimination of these provisions since they might hamper efforts to sustain the international coalition against terrorism.

The conference report as adopted did include modified language providing for more limited sanctions should the president find that the Palestinians had not "substantially complied" with their commitments. The sanctions included downgrading the PLO office in Washington, designating the PLO-affiliated organizations Fatah, Force 17, and Tanzim as foreign terror organizations, and eliminating all non-humanitarian aid. But the final bill did not require the president to issue a report on Palestinian compliance, and afforded him waiver authority. The conference report also included a provision withholding $8 million in U.S. assistance from the International Committee of the Red Cross (ICRC) should the president determine that Israel's Magen David Adom "is being denied participation in the activities of the ICRC and the Red Crescent."

There was no movement, however, on a supplemental request to Congress for an additional aid package for Israel worth $750 million. Originally suggested during the Clinton administration in November 2000, the package would have included $250 million for the withdrawal of Israeli forces from Lebanon and an additional $200 million in military assistance. Egypt would have received $225 million in military assistance, and Jordan $25 million for border security and $50 million in economic assistance. The 106th Congress took no action on this, and while the Bush administration initially expressed interest, a supplemental budget request released on June 1, 2001, did not include it.

On November 16, 89 senators wrote to President Bush urging him not to restrain Israel from responding to Palestinian terrorism. They said: "the American people would never excuse us for not going after the terrorists with all our strength and might. Yet that is what some have demanded of the Israeli government after every terrorist incident they suffer. No matter what the provocation, we urge restraint." The letter, prepared and circulated by Senators Kit Bond (R., Mo.) and Charles Schumer (D., N.Y.), also praised President Bush for taking "the correct course" by not meeting with Yasir Arafat while the violence continued.

In a similar vein, on December 5, the House of Representatives passed (384-11) H.Con.Res.280, introduced by Representative Lantos, which expressed solidarity with Israel in the fight against terrorism. The resolution specifically condemned the terrorist attacks of December 1–2 that resulted in 26 deaths and the wounding of at least 175 within 14 hours. Furthermore, it urged the president to take any and all necessary steps to ensure that the Palestinian Authority carried out its responsibilities to halt terrorism, including, if necessary, suspending all relations with Arafat and the Palestinian Authority.

In perhaps the least surprising foreign policy development of 2001, the administration announced in mid-June that it was exercising its waiver authority under the Jerusalem Embassy Act of 1995 to postpone moving the U.S. embassy in Israel from Tel Aviv to Jerusalem. Jewish groups were philosophical about the decision, which, while it followed in the path well trod by President Clinton before him, flew in the face of President Bush's campaign promise to begin the process of moving the embassy as soon as he took office.

Pollard, and Pardons

The continued advocacy of his champions notwithstanding, convicted spy Jonathan Pollard was not among the beneficiaries of a raft of last-minute pardons granted by President Clinton just before he left office. Despite widespread hope among his supporters that the departing president might see fit to grant Pollard a pardon, or at least clemency, as a way to boost Israeli prime minister Ehud Barak's diminishing chances for reelection, continuing strong opposition from the American intelligence community prevailed once again. As President Bush took office, Pollard was expected to renew his battle in the courts to set aside his guilty verdict and receive a new trial. In February, Pollard wrote to Ariel Sharon, just elected prime minister of Israel, urging that he request Bush to grant him a pardon. Little was expected to come of this, and little did.

If the theory behind leaving Pollard off the list was that the outgoing president would thereby avoid controversy, it was not to be. The controversies associated with certain of the pardons and related clemencies that Clinton signed as he left office had to do both with the circumstance of his actions—an astounding 140 were signed on the morning of inauguration day by a chief executive who was, by all reports, operating under severe sleep deprivation—and the beneficiaries. It quickly emerged that the two most controversial were connected to the Jewish community.

The president commuted the sentences of several men from the New York Hassidic community of New Square who had been convicted of fraud and embezzlement. Some questioned whether this was a payback for that community's unexpectedly strong (indeed, almost unanimous) vote for the president's wife, Hillary Rodham Clinton, in her successful run for the U.S. Senate in 2000.

There was also the president's last-minute pardon of fugitive financier Marc Rich, who had fled the United States for Switzerland following a 1983 indictment on racketeering and tax evasion. Advocates for Rich claimed that he had been the victim of overly zealous prosecutors. But the overwhelming weight of opinion was that Rich could only have obtained the extraordinary boon of a pardon even while he remained a fugitive from justice through his wealth and special connections—in particular, an ex-wife who was a formidable Democratic fund-raiser. As the controversy gained momentum, it emerged that Israeli and American Jewish leaders at the highest levels—including Israeli prime minister Ehud Barak, Anti-Defamation League national director Abraham Foxman, and U.S. Holocaust Memorial Museum Council chairman Rabbi Irving Greenberg—had weighed in with President Clinton to urge clemency for Rich. After fleeing to Switzerland, Rich had become a major benefactor of Jewish institutions and charities around the world.

In mid-February, Rabbi Eric Yoffie, president of the Union of American Hebrew Congregations, asserted that the joining of so many leaders in the campaign for Rich had "undermined our community's moral fabric." Others speculated that the campaign on behalf of Rich had afforded President Clinton the opportunity to view a pardon for Rich as a trade-off for not pardoning Pollard. Bill Clinton himself weighed into the debate in a February 17 op-ed piece in the *New York Times*. Clinton defended the Rich pardon partly on the grounds that Israeli and American Jewish officials wanted it. This claim led a number of American Jewish leaders to complain that Clinton was exaggerating their impact on the now-discredited pardon, and virtually accused him of scapegoating the Jewish community.

By late February, reports emerged that Manhattan U.S. Attorney Mary Jo White was investigating whether either the Rich or the New Square clemencies were the product of illicit deals. On March 19, a day on which he also discussed his involvement in the Rich pardon with investigators for the House Committee on Government Reform, Abraham Foxman issued a letter saying that he may have erred in backing Rich. Notwithstanding Rich's substantial contributions to Jewish institutions (which another ADL official confirmed included donations to that organization), Foxman now said that he had subsequently come to question "whether a person's good deeds should overcome other aspects of his behavior."

President Bush and the Jewish Community

As the year began, some American Jews faced the incoming administration with a degree of trepidation. Less than 20 percent of American Jews had voted for George W. Bush in the 2000 election. The Jewish community recalled its confrontations with the first President Bush over matters affecting Israel. And it knew from the start that the incoming administration differed strongly with the bulk of the Jewish community on issues of domestic policy such as church-state separation and abortion. Yet, before the year was half over, Jews had a far warmer relationship with the new president than anyone had expected.

As the conflict between Israel and the Palestinians heated up early in the year and supporters of Israel felt increasingly isolated on the world stage, the president clearly showed that he blamed the Palestinians for the escalation of the violence. If any one fact could symbolize this, it was Bush's White House invitation to Prime Minister Sharon soon after the latter's election, even as the president declined to invite Yasir Arafat, who had been to the White House often during the Clinton years.

In early May, at his first formal appearance before a Jewish organization since his election, President Bush spoke warmly of Israel at the annual dinner of the American Jewish Committee, sharing the dais with Mexican president Vincente Fox, Israeli foreign minister Shimon Peres, and German foreign minister Joschka Fischer. Then, on May 31, there was a "working dinner" at the White House, where the president and senior administration officials met with Israeli president Moshe Katzav and a group of top American Jewish leaders for what some of the latter would later term an "extraordinary" discussion about Israel and the Middle East. Far from a routine "grin and grip," by all reports it was a candid and wide-ranging conversation. Abraham Foxman noted that Bush "had a very hands-on knowledge of the area, its problems and challenges." Jack Rosen, president of the American Jewish Congress, asserted, "I walked away from that evening feeling this is a president who knows right from wrong and good guys from bad guys." Also at the meeting were representatives of the American Jewish Committee, the Conference of Presidents of Major American Jewish Organizations, the Republican Jewish Coalition, the United Jewish Communities, and others.

These warm feelings, a grace note in an otherwise bleak year, were reinforced when President Bush again hosted Jewish leaders on December 10. This was, as far as anyone could recall, the first Hanukkah party ever held at the White House—complete with latkes and jelly doughnuts, all kosher. In public comments before the festivities and during private conversation at the event, the president allied himself with the Israeli position. This was soon after horrendous suicide bombings in Jerusalem and Haifa, and Bush clearly placed the onus on Arafat to do more to stop the violence. His statements were welcome, as well, because they eased relations that had become somewhat strained when, after September 11, some Jewish leaders felt that the administration seemed to be unfairly pressuring Israel in an effort to placate Arab countries into joining the coalition against terror.

ANTI-SEMITISM AND EXTREMISM

Assessing Anti-Semitism

The Anti-Defamation League's annual audit of anti-Semitic incidents, released in late March, reported that there were 1,606 such incidents directed at individuals and institutions in the United States during 2000, an increase of some 4 percent from 1999. The ADL audit attributed the increase to a targeting of Jews in the wake of the new round of Israeli-Palestinian violence that erupted in late September 2000. The rise was not evenly distributed around the country: New York saw a startling increase of 50 percent, while anti-Semitism on college campuses rose by 15 percent, ending a five-year decline in campus incidents.

The FBI's national hate-crimes statistics report for 2000, issued late in 2001, indicated that Jews and Jewish institutions were the target of choice in religion-bias crimes, as in previous years. Based on data received from 11,690 law-enforcement agencies, the FBI found that religion-bias crimes constituted 18.3 percent of all hate crimes, and, of these, about three-quarters (1,109 incidents) were against Jews and Jewish institutions.

Acts of Violence and Hate Speech

The new year was not even an hour old when an apparent arson occurred at Temple Emanu-El in Reno, Nevada, a synagogue that had been firebombed some 13 months earlier by five skinheads. The latest conflagration, set off by a flammable liquid, damaged the front entrance and entryway of the synagogue, and was quickly extinguished.

Anti-Israel demonstrations, often incorporating what Jewish students and organizations perceived as anti-Semitic messages, became common on college campuses throughout 2001. At times, the anti-Semitic content was overt. In late March, Jewish students at the State University at Binghamton, in upstate New York, were confronted with 23 swastikas drawn with a felt-tip marker on various buildings around campus. The swastikas, which followed on incidents of anti-Semitic vandalism the previous year, were quickly cleaned up, and the university president reaffirmed an offer, originally made in 2000, of a $5,000 reward for information leading to a conviction.

An old case of hate violence was brought to a close in 2001. In late January, Buford Furrow, the white supremacist who had gone on a shooting spree in August 1999 during which he wounded five at a Los Angeles Jewish community center and killed a Filipino American mail carrier (see AJYB 2001, p. 171), entered a plea of guilty. In his plea bargain with federal prosecutors, Furrow agreed to a life sentence without possibility of parole, thereby avoiding the possibility of a death sentence. Prosecutors cited Burrow's severe psychiatric problems as a significant factor in their decision to accept the plea. In statements made after his arrest in 1999, Furrow had characterized his attack on the JCC as "a wake-up call to America to kill Jews," and, according to prosecutors at that time, he killed the mailman because he was "angered at the sight of a nonwhite federal employee." The sentence was imposed in federal district court in late March, with U.S. District Judge Nora Manella commenting that Furrow's actions "were a reminder that bigotry is alive."

On November 30, another case of anti-Jewish violence was brought to a close, as brothers Benjamin and James Williams received lengthy prison sentences in U.S. district court, following guilty pleas for their role in the 1999 firebombings of three Sacramento synagogues. In court, Rabbi Brad Bloom of congregation B'nai Israel, the most severely damaged of the synagogues, told the self-described anti-Semites and white supremacists that "ironically" they had "strengthened the determination of the entire community to make no room for bigotry." The Williams brothers still faced trials in state court for killing a homosexual couple two weeks after the synagogue arsons.

On December 12, there came a reminder that Jews, too, were capable of plotting to commit hate crimes, when federal authorities in Los Angeles announced the arrest of Irv Rubin, chairman of the Jewish Defense League (JDL), and Earl Krugel, a JDL member. The two were charged with conspiring to blow up the King Fahd Mosque and the offices of the Muslim Public Affairs Council, both in Los Angeles. Also allegedly targeted were the Orange County offices of an Arab-American congressman,

Darrell Issa (R., Cal.). Jewish organizations and leaders immediately condemned the alleged plot. Founded by the late Rabbi Meir Kahane in 1968, the JDL had developed a reputation for using violence and intimidation to respond to anti-Semitism, although the organization had been inactive in recent years. Rubin's lawyer denied the charges, terming the arrests an "overreaction" triggered by the events of September 11.

In early May, eBay, the leading Internet auction site, announced that, effective May 17, it would no longer allow its facilities to be used for the sale of Nazi memorabilia. This was a reversal of eBay's previous position that items more than 50 years old were to be considered "historical" and therefore exempt from the company's ban on hate artifacts. The eBay action brought it into conformance with European practice, and was praised by the Simon Wiesenthal Center and other Jewish groups, while others raised concerns about free speech.

Discrimination

On June 11, a jury sitting in federal district court in Orlando, Florida, handed down a $100,000 verdict on a religious-discrimination claim brought against the BellSouth telephone company by former employee Jeffrey Bander, an Orthodox Jew. Bander said that he had been subject to harassment by his supervisor after he became Orthodox following his son's death—such as being told to shave his beard and stop wearing his yarmulke, and anti-Semitic remarks. Although the jury rejected those charges, it found that BellSouth had fired Bander in February 1999 in retaliation for his filing of complaints with the company and the federal government. BellSouth denied discrimination or retaliatory motives, claimed that Bander had been fired for cause, and said it would appeal. Jewish advocacy groups pointed to the case as showing the need for Congress to act on the Workplace Religious Freedom Act, legislation that would strengthen employers' obligation to accommodate the religious practices of employees.

Another high-profile claim of discrimination came to light in late October, when Major Shawn Pine, a reserve officer in the army, alleged that anti-Semitism lay behind the decision to strip him of his security clearance—and, therefore, his command of an intelligence unit—because of his ties to Israel. "When they see a Jew, they see Jonathan Pollard," Pine commented. The army denied any invidious motivation and asserted that its action reflected the implementation of a new policy whereby anyone with dual citizenship was denied top clearance.

INTERGROUP RELATIONS

Black-Jewish Relations

Following on the heels of the strain in black-Jewish relations caused by America's downgraded participation in the Durban conference against racism (see above, pp. 164–65), a new focus of controversy appeared. The Rev. Al Sharpton, a New York-area African-American activist widely regarded in the Jewish community as a rabble-rouser and, at best, a borderline anti-Semite, traveled to Israel in October. This was a fence-mending mission in anticipation of an expected run for the Democratic presidential nomination. In advance of the trip, Rabbi Marc Schneier, president of the Foundation for Ethnic Understanding, and Rabbi Shmuel Boteach, author of the best-selling book *Kosher Sex,* announced that they would accompany Sharpton. Schneier, one of the few Jewish leaders who had been willing to meet with Nation of Islam leader Louis Farrakhan, applauded Sharpton's decision to visit Israel, calling it "a significant step in the strengthening of black-Jewish relations in New York and throughout the country." Sharpton, for his part, announced that he would not be meeting with Palestinian officials since he was "not trying to mediate the Middle East situation." The theme of the trip was, instead, to understand how Israel was coping with terror and build bridges to the Jewish community. Several Jewish leaders expressed reservations, however, even as they welcomed Sharpton's action. "This trip to Israel appears to be a step in the right direction," said Michael Miller, executive vice president of the Jewish Community Relations Council of New York, "but an expression of genuine remorse for his past misdeeds will be a more accurate measure of his relationship to the Jewish community of New York."

As it turned out, the trip did not perform the healing function that its organizers had anticipated. Once it became clear that Sharpton was to meet with Arafat after all—albeit with the encouragement and assistance of Israeli officials who wanted Sharpton to send a message to stop the violence—Schneier decided not to go. "If I were looking to reconcile with the Jewish community, my first overture would not be sitting down with Yasir Arafat," Schneier commented, adding that Sharpton's session with Arafat meant that he would have no time to meet with victims of the June 1 bombing of the Tel Aviv Dolphinarium. Boteach, for his part, did accompany Sharpton to Israel but not to the Arafat meeting, and insisted that the trip as a whole, which included visits to Yad Vashem and an Ethiopian immigrant-absorption center, and meetings with Israeli officials and other terror victims, was a success. Boteach called on the Jewish community to be "gracious" to Sharpton, recognizing that he had come "all this way at a very dangerous time" to meet "with civilians and victims of terror."

Whatever the intergroup tensions, there certainly remained leaders in both the black and Jewish communities who continued to work to maintain the historic relationship. A survey of black and Jewish views, released by the Foundation for Ethnic Understanding in August, confirmed an overall sense that this was a relationship that could use improvement—but also a shared desire for such improvement and cooperation. In one striking finding, 74 percent of Jews in New York (73 percent elsewhere in the country) thought that Jews and blacks should work in partnership on civil rights, a view shared by 87 percent of New York blacks (and 77 percent elsewhere).

Latino-Jewish Relations

The 2000 census had shown that the burgeoning American Latino community was likely to grow in numbers and political influence in coming years. It was, therefore, hardly surprising that B'nai B'rith International and New American Alliance, an organization of Latino business leaders, joined together to organize a national Jewish-Latino "summit" in early March. Attended by representatives of an array of Jewish and Latino organizations, the meeting sought to identify common priorities and develop cooperative strategies to pursue them. Among the key issues the participants discussed were the portrayal of Jews and Latinos in the media, the quality of public education, support for Israel and increased aid for Latin American nations, and the economic empowerment of minority communities. The conference also saw release of a new survey commissioned by the Foundation for Ethnic Understanding that identified areas of agreement and disagreement between the two communities: there was strong support among both Jews and Latinos for tougher antidiscrimination laws, but substantial disagreement over bilingual education, supported overwhelmingly by Latinos but opposed by nearly a third of Jews. Nevertheless, as Dina Siegel Vann, B'nai B'rith director for Latin American affairs, observed, Jewish organizations for the most part supported bilingual education.

Catholic-Jewish Relations

Although Jewish leaders remained as quick as ever to praise the ever-more-frail Pope John Paul II for his historical role in creating a new and warmer relationship between the Catholic and Jewish communities, that relationship seemed more strained in 2001 than in preceding years.

In early May, Pope John Paul II visited Damascus where he was greeted by Bashar al-Assad, the young president of Syria. Assad chose the occasion to launch into an anti-Semitic diatribe in which he resuscitated the accusation that Jews killed Jesus, threw in for good measure a charge that Jews had tried to kill Mohammed, and called on Christians and Muslims to unite against the Jews. While American Jewish leaders saw obscene expressions of Jew-hatred as par for the course among the Syrian leadership, they could not help but express their disappointment that a pontiff who had stressed Jewish-Christian reconciliation sat by and said nothing in response to Assad's attacks. Linking this silence to charges that the Vatican had been silent in the face of the Nazi extermination of the Jews, Rabbi A. James Rudin, senior interreligious adviser to the American Jewish Committee, commented: "If there's one thing we've learned from the 1930s, it's that words—especially the words of leaders—have consequences. And these words should not go unchecked or uncriticized." Some Jewish leaders worried that the Vatican might have decided to mend relations with the Muslim world by acquiescing in the expressions of anti-Semitism coming from its leaders, even at the risk of implicitly granting legitimacy to those expressions.

Church spokesmen rejected this analysis. Eugene Fisher, director of Catholic-Jewish relations for the U.S. Conference of Catholic Bishops, asserted that the Vatican had clearly rejected the idea that the Jews were to blame for the death of Jesus, "and nothing Mr. Assad says will change the mind of the pope or of one billion Catholics." But Seymour Reich, chairman of the International Jewish Committee for Interreligious Consultations (IJCIC), expressed disappointment that the pope had not found a diplomatic way to express his displeasure with Assad's words, even if only after returning to Rome. In Reich's view, reliance on knowledge of current Catholic doctrine was not a sufficient substitute for public repudiation of bigotry.

One of the longest running irritants in Jewish-Vatican relations exploded in an exchange of charges and countercharges after an interfaith panel of historians created to review the role of Pope Pius XII during the

Holocaust era disbanded because it was denied access to all of the Vatican's pertinent wartime records (see AJYB 2001, p. 181, and below, p. 389). The Vatican-approved group of Catholic and Jewish scholars had been put together as a way of dealing with the substantial tensions that had emerged as Pope John Paul moved toward beatification of, and ultimately sainthood for, the wartime pontiff who, many Jews believed, did little or nothing to stop the Nazi Holocaust. When the Vatican, citing "technical reasons," declined to provide access to more than 11 volumes of archives—and those only through 1923—the panel wrote on July 20 to the Vatican's Commission for Religious Relations with the Jews, saying that "we cannot see a way forward at present to the final report you request, and believe we must suspend our work."

Seymour Reich released the scholars' letter to the public, and noted his own "deep disappointment" in "the lack of positive response" from "a good pope." Far less diplomatic was Elan Steinberg, executive director of the World Jewish Congress, an IJCIC member organization, who called the failure to provide more complete access to the archives a "cover-up." Upon the public release of the scholars' letter, the Catholic members of the panel issued a statement assuring the Vatican that they did not agree with Reich and that they had not signed the letter with any intent of protesting Vatican policy.

Matters heated up even further after Cardinal Walter Kasper, who was now in charge of the Vatican's relations with Jews, issued a communiqué on August 24 accusing the Jewish members of the panel of "indiscretion" through "polemical remarks to the press" that made it impossible for the research to continue. The Jewish scholars responded with a statement on September 4, charging that "the Jewish members of the group of scholars have been singled out for blame," and that the appropriate way out of this "impasse" was for the Vatican to heed the scholars' call for additional documentation. With no sign that any access to more documents would be forthcoming, two of the panel's Jewish scholars announced several weeks later their resignation from the group. One of them, Robert Wistrich of the Hebrew University of Jerusalem, told the World Jewish Congress at its annual meeting in Jerusalem that the turn of events had brought Catholic-Jewish relations to their lowest ebb since the 1960s. Other observers, though, suggested that the matter, inflammatory as it was, constituted just one part of a complex and multifaceted relationship between the two religions.

Notably, soon after the imbroglio over his visit to Syria, the pope took the occasion of a June visit to Ukraine to make a pilgrimage, in the company of the chief rabbi, to Babi Yar, where the Nazis had killed thousands of Jews in September 1941 (see below, p. 383).

Muslim-Jewish Relations

Muslim-Jewish relations, uneasy even at the zenith of the Israeli-Palestinian peace process, seemed to metastasize as, first, that process continued to unravel, and, second, people purporting to act in the name of Islam subjected the U.S. to savage terrorist attacks.

The difficulties of dialogue between Muslims and Jews were underscored after the American Jewish Committee, in May, released a pair of books published under the joint heading *Children of Abraham,* one explaining the Muslim faith to Jews, and the other explaining the Jewish faith to Muslims. The book on Judaism, authored by Rabbi Reuven Firestone of Hebrew Union College, attracted little attention. But the companion volume, written by Khalid Duran, drew a sharp denunciation from the Washington-based Council on American-Islamic Relations (CAIR) even before the book was issued and before CAIR could have read the volume. Duran, a leading academic analyst of Islam in the modern world, was controversial in the Muslim community because of his ongoing criticism of, as he saw it, the domination of Islamic institutions by theological radicals—a critique that found voice in the book. After its publication, Arab newspapers condemned Duran for spreading "anti-Muslim propaganda," and, in June, Sheikh Abd-al-Mun'im Abu Zant, a Muslim cleric from Jordan, issued a *fatwa* to "shed the blood" of the author. While this was later "clarified" as a call to investigate Duran, the author treated the edict as a death threat, and went into hiding for an extended period. Unapologetic about AJC's publication of a work that had been reviewed and approved by Islamic scholars before its release and that received a number of excellent reviews, AJC acting executive director Shula Bahat asserted that the uproar exposed the very problem of Muslim extremism that Duran was describing.

Following the September 11 attacks, Jewish groups were quick to stress that individuals and groups should not be held responsible for acts carried out by others simply because they were members of the same ethnic group or faith. Furthermore, Jewish leaders condemned the rash of hate incidents that followed September 11 in which persons of Middle East "appearance" and Islamic institutions were attacked or vandalized. Nevertheless, in many—but not all—cities with large Jewish, Muslim, and

Arab populations, relations became strained, particularly when Muslim leaders who condemned the September 11 attacks declined to criticize terrorism generally, or used September 11 as a platform to make anti-Jewish or anti-Israel statements.

In Los Angeles, a Jewish-Muslim dialogue that was already on shaky ground because of hard feelings on both sides over the violence in Israel seemed about to dissolve following September 11. A prominent Muslim participant in the dialogue, Salam Al-Marayati, executive director of the Muslim Public Affairs Council, asserted on a radio program on the day of the attacks that Israel should be a suspect—this, even while Jewish leaders were scrupulously avoiding casting blame on any country or organization until the facts were in. A subsequent "clarification" by Al-Marayati, in which he claimed that his remarks had been taken out of context, only made things worse. Rabbi John Rosove of Temple Israel, whose view was widespread in the Jewish community, termed Al-Marayati's statements "so offensive and provocative that I am in crisis as to whether I am going to stay in the dialogue." At the same time, area Muslims expressed their own grievance over a posting on the Simon Wiesenthal Center Web site of a photo of West Bank Palestinians cheering news of the September 11 attacks. The Muslims complained that this was "fanning the flames of ethnic and religious hatred."

A contentious sideshow to the deteriorating Muslim-Jewish relationship was a series of dueling estimates of the number of Muslims in America. In late April, CAIR, along with several other Muslim organizations, claimed that there were some 7 million U.S. Muslims, on the premise that for every one of the 2 million Muslims said to be affiliated with a mosque, there were 3.5 million additional Muslims. Earlier in the year, an estimate released by the Georgetown University Center for Muslim-Christian Understanding had found the Muslim population at 4–6 million, and steadily increasing. What seemed indisputable was the conclusion voiced by John Zogby, president and CEO of the Zogby International polling agency, that American Muslims would soon outnumber an American Jewish population that was shrinking due to assimilation and a low birthrate.

Some Jewish observers, however, suggested that the political implications of the CAIR study were not clear, noting that 33 percent of mosque members were of South Asian origin and 30 percent were black, while only some 25 percent were of Arab background. Martin Raffel, associate director of the Jewish Council for Public Affairs (JCPA), said: "The critical question here is to distinguish between the growing American

Muslim community on the one hand and certain anti-Israel Arab and Muslim organizations that have been seeking to make political inroads in Washington and in communities around the United States." Another point was made by David Gad-Harf, executive director of the Jewish Community Council of Metropolitan Detroit, that Muslims had reached out to Jews in his community in the recognition that, whatever disagreements they had on the Middle East, there were "concrete opportunities to work together" on matters affecting the needs of religious minorities.

In October, with the estimates of 6–7 million American Muslims gaining increased acceptance in the wake of September 11, two unrelated studies appeared that raised doubts about these numbers. Tom Smith, a highly respected scholar at the National Opinion Research Center (NORC) at the University of Chicago, proposed that the figure was far smaller, between 1.9 and 2.8 million. Smith cited a number of factors accounting for the earlier overestimate, including the tendency for groups to exaggerate their numbers and the faulty assumption that an immigrant population that has come from a particular country is likely to mirror the religious composition of that country. Smith analyzed several population surveys and found that between 0.2 and 0.6 percent of households had at least one Muslim adult. He then adjusted for a likely low Muslim participation in the survey because of the large number of immigrant Muslims who had limited English skills, and estimated that Muslims made up about 0.7 percent of the adult population.

Another study released the same week, carried out by the City University of New York, generated an even lower estimate. Using random telephone dialing to reach homes and ask those over 18 to describe their religious identification, the researchers came up with about 1.1 million adult American Muslims. Egon Mayer, one of the authors of the study, noted that although, under this analysis, there were more than twice as many Jews as Muslims living in the U.S., the Muslim population had more than doubled in the last decade while the number of Jews had declined.

Ibrahim Hooper of CAIR immediately denounced the Smith survey, sponsored as it was by the American Jewish Committee (which he described as part of "the extremist wing of the pro-Israel lobby"), calling it a "desperate attempt to discount the role of American Muslims." AJC, however, denied any political motivation. Terming Hooper's "vile language" to be "not a very thoughtful response to a scholarly study," David Harris, the AJC's executive director, noted: "We had every reason to believe that [the 7-million figure] was way off because all the data suggested it. . . . Here was an attempt to invent a figure and then make it stick." Harris added that "population figures in the U.S. have societal, cultural and political implications."

CHURCH AND STATE

Charitable Choice

"Charitable choice" was the central church-state issue of 2001. This term was shorthand for a particular approach to expanding government funding of social services provided by faith-based institutions, and loosening restrictions on the use of those funds. President Bush, who had made charitable choice a priority while he served as governor of Texas, turned his attention to its national implementation almost as soon as his election to the presidency was confirmed in December 2000. Shortly after his inauguration, in accordance with plans finalized during the transition, Bush issued an executive order establishing the White House Office of Faith-Based and Community Initiatives under Dr. John DiIulio of the University of Pennsylvania. A companion executive order directed cabinet departments to prepare reports reviewing, and proposing modifications of, existing regulations and policies that presented "barriers" to the involvement of faith-based groups in government-funded programs.

Most of the organized Jewish community opposed charitable choice on the grounds that it would open the door to proselytization of beneficiaries, engender conflict among religious groups competing for public funds, and allow discrimination on the basis of religion in the hiring of federally funded service providers. The Anti-Defamation League focused, as well, on the potential of charitable choice to open the door to government funding of hate groups, such as the Nation of Islam. Orthodox groups, however, were strongly on the other side, championing charitable choice as a means to promote a system of social services that treated religious organizations and their potential beneficiaries more equitably.

To the surprise of the administration, it was not long before some on the right joined the left in raising concerns about charitable choice, leading to reports in March that the White House was holding off on introducing its own legislation on the matter. Early on, however, DiIulio, pointing to the review of existing regulations and policies under way, stated that much of what the administration wanted to accomplish might be done without legislation. In Congress, Senator Rick Santorum (R.,

Pa.) delayed the introduction of a comprehensive measure, choosing instead to introduce on March 21, together with Senator Joseph Lieberman (D., Conn.), a bipartisan bill creating new tax-deduction incentives for expanded charitable giving. This measure drew broad support from the Jewish community, including many who opposed charitable choice.

Supporters of charitable choice moved forward, however, in the House of Representatives. On March 29, Representatives J.C. Watts (R., Okla.) and Tony Hall (D., Ohio) introduced H.R.7, the Community Solutions Act, which combined the noncontroversial tax incentives of the Santorum-Lieberman bill with measures that applied charitable choice to a host of additional federal programs.

Bills including charitable choice provisions had been enacted at least four times, beginning with the welfare reform law of 1996. Remarkably enough, however, prior to 2001, there had never been a congressional hearing on the pros and cons of this approach. Now, the House of Representatives made up for lost time, holding several hearings from April through June in the Judiciary, Government Reform, and Ways and Means committees. In the Senate, the Judiciary Committee held a hearing on June 6, even as the committee gavel was being transferred from Senator Orrin Hatch (R., Utah) to Senator Patrick Leahy (D., Ver.) as a result of the Democrats' sudden accession to majority status (see above, p. 157). Jewish organizations were well represented at these hearings on both sides, as the Religious Action Center of Reform Judaism, the American Jewish Committee, the Orthodox Union, and Agudath Israel were among those testifying.

On June 28, the charitable choice provisions of H.R.7 were marked up in a hotly debated all-day session of the House Judiciary Committee. The bill was reported out of committee in a 20-5 party-line vote—realizing that Republicans had the votes to report the bill out of committee, most Democrats had left for their districts earlier that evening. On July 11, the House Ways and Means Committee held a mark-up on the tax provisions of H.R.7 and reported the bill out of committee 23-16, also a party-line vote. Despite objections from some moderate Republican House members that the bill would override local and state antidiscrimination laws, H.R.7 passed by 233-198 in the House of Representatives on July 19. The House also rejected, by 195-234, a motion to recommit the bill to the Judiciary Committee with instructions to add language stating that federally funded religious service providers could not discriminate on the basis of religion, and that none of the bill's provisions superceded state or local civil-rights laws. The motion would have essentially shelved the bill. It failed in large part because the concerns of most moderate Republicans were placated by a colloquy on the House floor in which Representative Watts promised to address those concerns when the bill was considered in conference with the Senate. With that, the focus on expansion of charitable choice shifted to the Senate, where Senators Lieberman and Santorum were expected to introduce a separate and scaled-down bill in the fall.

A report prepared under the direction of DiIulio, *Unlevel Playing Field: Barriers to Faith-Based and Community Organizations' Participation in Federal Social Service Programs,* that summarized the review of existing regulations and policies undertaken at the direction of the president, was released by the White House on August 16. The report found significant barriers to the provision of government-funded social services by faith-based organizations, including restrictions on which types of religious organizations and which religious activities might receive funding, as well as cumbersome government regulations and requirements. However, the administration also determined that there were insufficient data to determine precisely which organizations received federal funds, since those funds were mainly disbursed through block grants to the states, which in turn distributed the funds. On August 17, DiIulio announced his intention to resign from his senior White House post as soon as his replacement and a transition team were in place.

Also on August 17, the Pew Forum on Religion and the Brookings Institution cosponsored a "rapid-response" session to analyze the DiIulio document. There, Richard Foltin, the American Jewish Committee's legislative director and counsel, praised the report insofar as it encouraged regulatory reforms that would enable small community-based organizations to provide social services in partnership with government. However, Foltin criticized the report's implicit call for an expansion of government funding to faith-based organizations in the absence of data on the implementation of the charitable-choice provisions enacted in 1996. Others at the session were critical of the report because the administration failed to define the term "faith-based organization," and thus it remained unclear which organizations the administration believed should receive federal funds.

Like so many other matters on the public agenda, the push for charitable choice was temporarily diverted by the events of September 11. Returning to the fray on November 7, President Bush wrote to Senate leaders, urging them to move forward on several provisions of his faith-based initiative. The president noted that Americans had contributed generously to groups offering assistance related to the terror attacks, but expressed concern that other charities might suffer a drop-off in donations. Citing the House's action in July on H.R.7, he called on Congress to enact, before the end of the year, an "armies of compassion" bill that would enable federal money to flow to religious charitable organizations. Following the analysis presented in the *Unlevel Playing Field* report, Bush urged removal of "unneeded barriers to government support for faith-based groups," "equal treatment of faith-based charities," and "technical assistance and capacity building for faith-based groups." He also called, in his letter, for allowing tax deductions for charitable contributions made by those who did not itemize their tax deductions, an approach, as noted above, widely popular in the Jewish community because it would encourage charitable donations without raising the church-state problems posed by charitable choice.

Prior to the year-end recess, Senators Lieberman and Santorum had planned to introduce their own compromise "armies of compassion" legislation that would include those elements of H.R.7 they viewed as uncontroversial, while leaving other aspects of charitable choice for later. By all reports, the White House had indicated its support for such a measure even though it did not include the president's entire faith-based initiative package, if Congress moved to enact the legislation in 2001. A draft bill circulated in November included provisions allowing non-itemizers to take charitable contributions; created a special fund that would distribute federal money to the private sector to improve social-service programs; and provided technical assistance for religious charities to compete for federal funding. The Lieberman-Santorum bill also included language intended to provide religious organizations with "equal treatment"—allowing them to receive federal funds for the provision of social services even while they maintained the religious character of their boards and charters, and displayed religious icons and symbols on their premises. However it omitted the provisions of H.R.7 that barred "discrimination" in government contracting on the basis of the religious character of an organization and that specifically exempted funded organizations from prohibitions on employment discrimination on the basis of religion, even with respect to the government-funded programs.

Progress on the Lieberman-Santorum initiative stalled, with no bill introduced by year's end, when Congress was unable to resolve differences concerning pending economic stimulus proposals, since the amount of the tax deduction for non-itemizers could not be determined until the size of the stimulus package was finalized. In any event, a number of Jewish organizations viewed its "equal-treatment" provisions as problematic, although an improvement on H.R.7.

With a grant from the Pew Charitable Trusts, the American Jewish Committee, in partnership with the Feinstein Center of American Jewish History at Temple University, released a report in February titled *In Good Faith: A Dialogue on Government Funding of Faith-Based Social Services.* This was the culmination of a two-year study that brought together advocates of both sides of the charitable-choice debate to explore the possibility of attaining a mutually acceptable consensus. The report reaffirmed the groups' differences of opinion, but also identified common ground on appropriate types of nonfinancial cooperation between government and religious institutions, and on nongovernment community support for religious groups.

Education

In 2000, for the first time, Congress failed to reauthorize regular funding for programs under the Elementary and Secondary Education Act (ESEA), which, passed in 1965, authorizing massive federal aid to public schools. Instead, the lawmakers ended up funding ESEA programs on a temporary basis in the year-end omnibus-spending package as the 106th Congress concluded its work. The task of giving the programs a longer lease on life—within the context of broad educational reforms called for by the newly elected President Bush—was left to the 107th Congress.

True to his campaign pledge to put education at the top of the agenda, President Bush introduced his plan, at least in broad strokes, soon after his inauguration. Among its key provisions were the development of measures to increase school accountability, annual academic assessments for reading and math, allowing students in failing schools to use Title I funds to transfer to higher-performing public or private schools, and the use of federal funds to improve teacher quality. While there was bipartisan support for the need to address school accountability and teacher quality, there remained substantial disagreement about how to accomplish these goals.

Reflecting its desire to move forward on this issue on a bipartisan basis, the administration quickly signaled that vouchers would not be an essential component of the final package. Both houses of Congress, accordingly, produced education packages that increased funding and provided for alternative approaches to accountability, but did not include vouchers. S.1, the Better Education for Students and Teachers Act, which passed the Senate on March 8, included language supported by many Jewish organizations reauthorizing funding for educational programs that combated hate crimes. H.R.1, the No Child Left Behind Act, passed in the House of Representatives on June 14, did not fund such programs. Instead, it included provisions, opposed by many of those same Jewish organizations, allowing a school district to use up to 20 percent of federal administrative funds to defend against lawsuits over religious expression, and that conditioned federal funding on a district's written certification that "no policy of the agency prevents or otherwise denies participation in constitutionally protected prayer in public schools." Many Jewish groups, and allied groups, viewed these provisions as likely to hamper the efforts of school officials to avoid practices that blurred church-state separation.

Following lengthy negotiation, the House voted 381-14 on December 13 to adopt a conference report reauthorizing the ESEA for six years, and the Senate following suit by 87-10 on December 18. The omnibus bill provided additional federal spending for poor and disadvantaged students, and also included provisions designed to increase school accountability that President Bush had long championed: states were required to give math and reading tests to all students from third through eighth grades; before any steps were taken against them, failing schools could receive money and technical help to improve; and children in the worst schools could, at public expense, get private tutors and attend after-school programs, or transfer to a different public school.

The act did not include any reference to the vouchers programs that were part of the administration's original proposal, it did, however, provide funding for antibias education, and made the civil rights laws applicable to any private programs it funded. The law also empowered the Department of Education to issue a "guidance" on when prayer is permissible in public schools, violation of which could lead to a cut-off of federal funds to the school district involved, and included provisions for funding after-school programs offered by private organizations, apparently including pervasively religious organizations such as houses of worship and religious schools.

Whatever Congress did on the vouchers front in 2001 was overshadowed by the sense that the constitutional landscape on this matter was about to change forever. As it opened its 2001–02 term, the U.S. Supreme Court announced that it would hear the appeal from a federal court-of-appeals decision that struck down Cleveland's vouchers program as an unconstitutional establishment of religion. Argument was set for 2002.

Efforts to obtain the Supreme Court's blessing for public displays of the Ten Commandments came to naught. In late May, the high court declined to consider an appeal from a federal appellate court ruling that the town of Elkhart, Indiana, impermissibly promoted "religious ideals" through its 40-year-old practice of maintaining a six-foot monument inscribed with the Ten Commandments. In an unusual written statement in support of the decision not to hear the case, Justice John Paul Stevens, responding to Chief Justice William Rehnquist's dissent, noted that the Elkhart display was not comparable to the marble frieze in the Supreme Court's own courtroom depicting Moses with the Ten Commandments, since, in the latter case, Moses appeared with other historical lawgivers such as Mohammed and Confucius.

The Supreme Court was more favorably inclined to a lawsuit brought by a Christian youth group that maintained that its free-speech rights had been violated when New York State public-school officials declined to allow the club to meet after school hours at a public elementary school. In the case of *Good News Club v. Milford Central School,* in a decision hailed by the Orthodox community and decried by most of the rest of the Jewish community, the court ruled 6-3, in June, that the club sought "nothing more than to be treated neutrally and given access to speak about the same topics as are other groups." Much of the disagreement between the Jewish groups turned not on the neutrality principle—previous decisions had consistently held that religious groups must be treated the same as other groups when the public is afforded access to school premises after hours—but on the facts of the case. The bulk of the Jewish groups raised particular alarm that the club in question was meeting immediately after school, thereby conveying the impression that the club was "official."

HOLOCAUST-RELATED MATTERS

Reparations

Early in the year, Stuart Eizenstat, the outgoing deputy treasury secretary and the U.S. official chiefly charged with seeking reparations for Holocaust survivors, expressed concern that the reparations issue was, to the best of his knowledge, not "on the radar screen of the incoming administration." Among other matters left uncompleted as Mr. Eizenstat prepared to move on were finalizing funding for the approximately $395 million that Austria had agreed to pay to some 15,000 former slave and forced laborers, and a $300-million minimum that that nation had promised as property restitution.

The new Bush administration did move forward, naming Ambassador James Bindenagel to be special envoy for Holocaust issues, with Deputy Secretary of State Richard Armitage also given responsibility in this area. Bindenagel had previously worked with Eizenstat in negotiating an agreement with Germany to obtain restitution for forced laborers. In addition to moving forward to implement those comprehensive restitution agreements already signed and addressing other outstanding issues, Bindenagel also sought to follow up on Eizenstat's work in advancing projects of education and research relating to the Holocaust. "We want memory to have priority, not money," he said.

On January 16, the Presidential Advisory Commission on Holocaust Assets in the United States, established by President Clinton in 1998, issued a 250-page report reviewing the history of how U.S. government officials had dealt with assets found in the United States that belonged to Holocaust victims. The commission concluded that the government had in certain instances made "extraordinary efforts" to return property to victims or their heirs, but had also made mistakes that resulted in some victims never receiving restitution. Among these mistakes was entrusting property intended for restitution to officials or organizations of countries where the victims lived, rather than to the victims themselves. In some cases this meant that the restituted property never reached its intended destination.

The commission also considered ways to facilitate research that would assist in the identification of stolen property such as gold and artworks, and to reach agreement with New York banks and the Library of Congress on how to facilitate the identification of Holocaust-era assets that they might have. As part of its final report, the commission recommended that its work be continued by a foundation funded both by the federal government and private sources. Jewish organizations praised the report, Roman Kent, chairman of the American Gathering of Jewish Holocaust Survivors, commenting, "Our government had the guts to say what happened and how we behaved."

As the year began, it seemed that the $5.2-billion fund created by the German government and German businesses in February 1999 would soon begin payments to compensate individuals who had been dragooned into slave and forced labor during the war years. An agreement made in 2000 stipulated that such payments would foreclose further lawsuits.

Early in the year, however, Judge Shirley Wohl Kram declined to dismiss class-action suits that were pending against Germany and German businesses in federal court in New York. Then, on May 10, Judge Kram dismissed the cases. But German officials claimed that that they could still not certify that payments from the fund would afford "legal closure" because the order incorporated "assumptions and conditions" that the fund cover, as well, claims arising in Austria. Representatives of the forced laborers, however, maintained that dismissal of the claims was sufficient to afford the desired closure, and they charged, as stated in a letter from Lothar Evans, director of the German-based Federation for Information and Support for the Survivors of Nazi Persecution, that "industry would like to get more time, and the best way is to pretend that the cases are not closed." Advocates for the laborers noted that, as German officials debated whether they had sufficient protection from further legal action, the elderly potential beneficiaries of the fund were dying every day.

The issue seemed resolved on May 17, when a U.S. appellate court ruled that Judge Kram had exceeded her authority in purporting to bring Austrian claims under the fund. This led Kram to dismiss one of the few remaining cases within days, and she accompanied the dismissal with the comment, "It is my hope that payments begin immediately." German chancellor Gerhard Schröder and a number of the German firms that had contributed to the fund understood the court order as opening the door to payment. But a spokesman for the German Industry Foundation, representing the bulk of contributing firms, said that it was still awaiting the conclusion of other pending cases, including one in California.

These last uncertainties notwithstanding, officials of the Claims Conference announced on June 19 that distribution to the first 10,000 slave laborers had gone out. Ultimately, it was expected that payments would be made to as many as a million former slave and forced laborers, of whom some 16,000 were believed to be Jewish. Slave laborers, who had been expected to be worked to death, were to receive up to $7,000 apiece, while forced laborers were to receive up to $2,200. By no means did the commencement of payments bring an end to controversy. Roman Kent lashed out at the German government for delaying matters for so many years, and at the 51 lawyers for the survivors who were dividing some $52 million in legal fees among themselves. Even though, as a percentage of the settlement fund, the fees were far below those customarily paid in contingency cases, some of the payments to attorneys stood in stark contrast to the amounts to be received by surviving slave and forced laborers. One of the attorneys, for instance, estimated that he would, in effect, be receiving a payment of $3,000 a day, even though he had originally taken the case never expecting to be paid.

On June 7, President Bush signed into law a bill that included the provisions of the Holocaust Victims Tax Fairness Act, introduced in the Senate by Senators Peter Fitzgerald (R., Pa.) and Charles Schumer (D., N.Y.), and in the House by Representative Jerrold Nadler (D., N.Y.). The new law exempted victims of the Holocaust and their heirs from paying taxes on Holocaust-related compensation and restitution payments, and stated that Holocaust survivors and their families receiving such payments remained eligible for federal or federally assisted need-based programs. The bill also established the initial tax basis of property returned to Holocaust victims or their heirs at the fair-market value of the property on the date of recovery, so that Holocaust survivors who received in-kind restitution did not have to pay capital-gains tax if they immediately sold the property.

Nazi War Criminals

In June, after seven days of trial, the long-running case of John Demjanjuk was submitted for determination by U.S. District Judge Paul R. Matia, sitting in Cleveland. Attorneys for the Justice Department's Office of Special Investigations (OSI) argued that the 81-year-old Cleveland resident should be stripped of his U.S. citizenship because, in seeking entry into the United States after World War II, he had lied about his role during the Holocaust. OSI had alleged, in a complaint filed in May 1999, that the Ukrainian-born Demjanjuk had served as a guard at the Sobibor extermination camp and the Majdanek and Flossenburg concentration camps, and as a member of the SS-run "Trawniki" unit that participated in the Nazi campaign of genocide. At year's end, Judge Matia had not yet issued his ruling in the case.

An earlier decades-long effort to deport Demjanjuk, based on allegations that he was the infamous Nazi war criminal known as Ivan the Terrible, seemed to have come to an end in February 1998, when Judge Matia restored the American citizenship that had been stripped from Demjanjuk in 1981. Judge Matia's action at that time followed an appellate decision that the Justice Department had knowingly withheld information in 1981 that Demjanjuk could have used in his defense. It followed, as well, a determination by the Israeli Supreme Court in 1993 that it had not been shown beyond a reasonable doubt at trial that Demjanjuk was Ivan the Terrible, the allegation that had been the basis of his deportation to, and trial in, Israel. But in restoring Demjanjuk's citizenship, Judge Matia had left the door open for the Justice Department to file new denaturalization and deportation proceedings. The OSI took up this invitation in filing its 1999 complaint.

The OSI continued its mission of identifying and moving to deport Nazi war criminals who came to the United States after World War II under false pretenses, even as the passage of time inexorably reduced the number of such criminals. In March, the OSI moved in federal court to deport Missouri resident Michael Negele, 80, who had already been stripped of his citizenship for his role as a guard at the Sachsenhausen concentration camp and in the Theresienstadt ghetto. That same month, following the action of an appellate court upholding a deportation order, the U.S. deported Juozas Naujalis for his role as part of a World War II Lithuanian battalion that killed more than 11,000 people in Lithuania and Belarus.

Even as the OSI continued to pursue Nazi war criminals, the CIA made available nearly 100,000 pages of newly declassified documents that revealed the extent to which American intelligence officials had employed Nazis as informants after the war in an effort to gather information about the Soviet Union. The information was released on April 27 on the basis of the 1998 Nazi War Crimes Disclosure Act. Although historians cautioned that the material required further analysis, the documents made it clear that not only had Nazis been on the U.S. payroll, but that some benefited from the sale of stolen Jewish property. Other Nazis, it appeared, were retained by the Soviets to spy on the United States. "These documents show that the real winners of the cold war were Nazi war criminals," commented OSI director Eli Rosenbaum.

RICHARD T. FOLTIN

The United States, Israel, and the Middle East

THE FIRST TWO MONTHS of 2001 brought leadership changes both in Washington and Jerusalem. On January 20, George W. Bush, a Republican, was inaugurated as president to succeed Democrat Bill Clinton. The new president, who had little background in international affairs, was expected to concentrate on domestic matters and leave foreign policy to his more experienced advisers—most notably Secretary of State Colin Powell, National Security Adviser Condoleezza Rice, and Vice President Richard Cheney.

Even while the Bush team was beginning to examine its Middle East options, there was a dramatic political shift in Israel. On February 6, Ariel Sharon of the Likud decisively defeated Ehud Barak and proceeded to set up a government of national unity. Sharon was committed to ending Palestinian violence and bringing peace and security to an Israeli public deeply disillusioned by the failure of the previous year's intensive peace efforts and traumatized by the growing number of suicide attacks against Israeli civilian targets.

On the face of it, the new Israeli government was an unwieldy coalition. Sharon gave the two top cabinet portfolios to the Labor Party: Shimon Peres, the venerable and comparatively dovish former prime minister, became foreign minister, and Binyamin Ben-Eliezer, a more hawkish Laborite, was given the Ministry of Defense. If the prominence of Labor in the government created pressures from the left of the political spectrum, Sharon also had to address the demands voiced by ministers of the parties of the right, as well as their supporters among the settlers living in communities in the West Bank—biblical Judea and Samaria—and Gaza. They wanted harsher measures to uproot the unending terrorist threat to their lives.

It was Yasir Arafat, president of the Palestinian Authority, who kept Israel's coalition government intact through the year. The mounting evidence that he was unwilling or unable to live up to his promises to stop the violence had a devastating effect on the morale of what had been the Israeli peace camp. It caused many former doves to question their basic assumption that the Oslo peace process would lead to a benign Palestinian state prepared to live side-by-side with a sovereign Jewish state.

In Washington as well, both in Congress and the administration, there was growing disenchantment with Arafat's leadership and increasing questioning of whether he sought genuine peace with Israel. One tangible sign of this disillusionment was that in contrast to the Clinton era, when Arafat was the most frequent official foreign visitor to the White House, President Bush gave him the cold shoulder and refused to reward him with an official invitation to the White House in 2001.

Although there were growing signs of the 72-year-old Arafat's increasing physical frailty, he had not designated a successor and continued his traditional policy of maneuvering among the contending groups of his supporters. These constituencies had somewhat different priorities. The older PLO leadership, which represented the refugees of the 1948 war, most of whom still lived in neighboring Arab countries or in squalid camps in the West Bank and Gaza, gave the highest priority to gaining the refugees' "right of return"—preferably to their original homes in Israel. In contrast, those middle-class and professional Palestinians already living in their own homes in the disputed territories cared far more about ending the Israeli occupation and creating a viable Palestinian state. They tended to be highly critical of the mismanagement, corruption, and lack of democracy that characterized the PA under Arafat's authoritarian rule.

There was also growing evidence, confirmed by some of Arafat's own supporters, that Sharon's inopportune visit to the Temple Mount in September 2000 was only the spark that helped set off a conflagration long in the planning. Indeed, there was much evidence that Arafat himself had at least approved, if he did not directly order, the policy of violent confrontations after the failure of Camp David. Ambassador Dennis Ross, Clinton's special Middle East peace envoy, suggested that Arafat had resorted to violence so that "fissures would grow within Israeli society, or that a worsening of the situation would bring international intervention that either imposed a solution or enabled him to maneuver more freely."

The policy had the opposite effect. It alienated the United States, strengthened the hard-liners in Israel, and resulted by the end of the year in the Israeli Defense Force's destruction of key elements of the Palestinian Authority infrastructure, growing unemployment and poverty in the Palestinian communities, and severe restrictions on Arafat's freedom of movement in Ramallah.

Although Arafat failed in 2001 to win official American support for an imposed settlement on his terms, he did succeed in further radicalizing the Palestinian masses and winning the support of "the street" throughout much of the Arab world, thanks to the proliferation of cable and satellite television channels, most notably the Qatar-based al-Jazeera, which provided viewers with a constant barrage of one-sided coverage of the confrontations between Palestinian militants and Israeli troops, focusing on the suffering of the Palestinian people. The message was particularly effective after the events of September 11.

Clinton's Final Push

At the end of 2000 and the beginning of 2001, President Clinton made one last, unsuccessful effort to achieve a negotiated solution of the Palestinian-Israeli conflict. Later, the Americans involved in the negotiations would almost unanimously place the blame for their failure squarely on the shoulders of Yasir Arafat.

Ambassador Dennis Ross, the president's special Middle East peace-process coordinator, recounted what happened in a televised interview with Brit Hume and Fred Barnes on Fox News (Apr. 21, 2002). According to Ross, after the Camp David summit collapsed at the end of July 2000, Arafat immediately came back to the Americans and said, "We need to have another summit," to which, according to Ross, the president in effect replied, "We just shot our wad. We got a no from you." To demonstrate his seriousness, Arafat agreed to set up a private channel between his people and the Israelis, which Ross said he joined at the end of August. "And there were serious discussions that went on, and we were poised to present our ideas at the end of September, which is when the intifada erupted. He knew we were poised to present the ideas. His own people were telling him they looked good." As for the event that allegedly ignited the intifada, the U.S. thought it had gotten assurances from the Palestinians that as long as Sharon did not actually enter the mosque on the Temple Mount, his visit would pass without incident.

Early in December 2000, after private channels for communication between the Israelis and the Palestinians had finally been reestablished, both parties once again asked the Clinton administration to present its ideas for a settlement, which it did at a meeting on December 23. Fred Barnes asked Ross about Arafat's response, noting that "Palestinian officials say to this day that Arafat said yes." Ross replied that he was present in the Oval Office when Arafat came to meet with the president on January 2. He recalled that the Palestinian leader "said yes, and then he added reservations that basically meant he rejected every single one of the things he was supposed to give."

When Brit Hume inquired about the concessions the president had asked Arafat to make, Ross responded:

> He was supposed to give, on Jerusalem, the idea that there would be, for the Israelis, sovereignty over the Western Wall, which would cover the areas that are of religious significance to Israel. He rejected that. He rejected the idea on the refugees. He said we need a whole new formula, as if what we had presented was non-existent. He rejected the basic ideas on security. He wouldn't even countenance the idea that the Israelis would be able to operate in Palestinian airspace. . . . So every single one of the ideas that was asked of him he rejected.

Ross denounced as "completely untrue" the Palestinian contention that all Clinton had offered the Palestinians were isolated cantons. In fact, under the U.S. proposal Israel would totally withdraw from the Gaza Strip and all of the Palestinians' West Bank territory would be contiguous. To connect Gaza with the West Bank, Ross said, "there would have been an elevated highway, an elevated railroad, to ensure that there would be not just safe passage for the Palestinians, but free passage." Ross had the clear impression that Arafat's lieutenants "understood this was the best they were ever going to get. They wanted him to accept it. He was not prepared to accept it." He noted that there was one point of disagreement between Barak and Clinton—when the Israelis would relinquish their control over the Jordan Valley area bordering Jordan. Barak had encountered serious opposition within Israel over giving up this strategic asset.

When Hume asked Ross to explain what he believed was the reason that Arafat, in effect, said no, the veteran U.S. negotiator responded:

> Because fundamentally I do not believe he can end the conflict. We had one critical clause in this agreement, and that clause was, "this is the end of the conflict." Arafat's whole life has been governed by struggle and a cause. Everything he has done as leader of the Palestinians is to always leave his options open, never close a door. He was being asked here, you've got to close the door. For him to end the conflict is to end himself.

Although the Palestinian Authority made a written copy of the president's proposals, Ross noted, "to this day, the Palestinians have not presented to their own people what was available."

In late January 2001, senior Israeli and Palestinian negotiators met for six days of intense discussions at the Sinai resort of Taba, on the Egyptian-Israeli border, and apparently made some progress in dealing with the refugee problem and several other issues. At the conclusion of the talks on January 27, they issued an optimistic joint statement noting "the positive atmosphere" that had pervaded the discussions, asserting that they "have never been closer to reaching an agreement," and expressing "our shared belief that the remaining gaps could be bridged with the resumption of negotiations following the Israeli elections." The Likud opposition in Israel dismissed the statement as a desperate ploy by the supporters of Barak, who had fallen far behind Sharon in the opinion polls, to portray the prime minister as a successful negotiator. (For more details, see below, pp. 525–26.)

The joint statement issued at Taba noted that "the two sides took into account the ideas suggested by President Clinton together with their respective qualifications and reservations." The president had publicly set forth his ideas in a major speech two weeks earlier, on January 7, at a gala dinner of the Israel Policy Forum (IPF) in New York's Waldorf Astoria Hotel. He outlined the lessons he said he had learned over the past eight years in the elusive quest for peace. Clinton rejected the view that the Arab-Israel conflict could afford a period of benign neglect by the United States. Using a medical analogy, he compared it to an abscessed tooth, which, if neglected will "just infect the whole rest of your mouth." Clinton chastised the extremists on both sides. The escalating violence of the previous months, he said, "confirms the need to prepare both publics for the requirements of peace, not to condition people for the so-called glory of further conflict." The Palestinian side would have to end the culture of violence "that, since Oslo, has not gone unchecked." Young children were still being educated to believe in confrontation with Israel, and "multiple militia-like groups carry and use weapons with impunity." The Israelis, for their part, should reconsider "the settlement enterprise and building bypass roads in the heart of what they already know will one day be part of a Palestinian state." Restoring confidence, he added, meant enabling Palestinians "to lead a normal existence, and not be subject to daily, often humiliating reminders that they lack basic freedom and control over their lives."

Clinton told the IPF leaders that both the Israeli and Palestinian leaders had asked him to present his own ideas. He called these "parameters" that he believed should guide further efforts toward a comprehensive peace, and noted that Barak and Arafat had accepted them, although with reservations. There would be a "sovereign, viable, Palestinian state that accommodates Israel's security requirements and the demographic realities," that would include Gaza and the vast majority of the West Bank. Blocs of Jewish settlements would be incorporated into Israel, with the goal of maximizing the number of settlers in Israel while minimizing the land annexed, so that Palestine would "be a geographically contiguous state." He added that the land annexed to Israel should include as few Palestinians as possible, and that to make the agreement durable there would have to be "some territorial swaps and other arrangements." To guarantee Israel's security, Clinton would rely on "an international presence in Palestine to provide border security along the Jordan Valley and to monitor implementation for the final agreement."

All Palestinian refugees, according to the Clinton parameters, would have the right to live in the new Palestinian state. Those who wanted to reside in other countries could do so "consistent with those countries' sovereign decisions"—and that, he noted, "includes Israel," and so Israel would not be expected to acknowledge an unlimited Palestinian "right of return." Clinton called for the refugees to be compensated for their losses and "assistance in building new lives," and pledged that the United States would take the lead in raising the necessary money.

Turning to the status of Jerusalem, which Clinton acknowledged as probably the most emotional and sensitive of all the issues, the president said that it should be "an open and undivided city, with assured freedom of access and worship for all. It should encompass the internationally recognized capitals of two states, Israel and Palestine." Without going into further geographic details, he declared that "what is Arab should be Palestinian," while "what is Jewish should be Israeli. That would give rise to a Jewish Jerusalem, larger and more vibrant than any in history." As for what was holy to both religions, that "requires a special care to meet the needs of all." Indirectly responding to Arafat's denial of any Jewish rights in the area of the Temple Mount, Clinton spoke of "the area holy to the Jewish people, an area which for 2,000 years, as I had said at Camp David, has been the focus of Jewish yearning."

Finally, Clinton insisted that any agreement would "have to mark the decision to end the conflict, for neither side can afford to make these painful compromises, only to be subjected to further demands."

Two New Administrations

With the end of the Taba talks, the onset of the Bush administration, and Ariel Sharon's election, Clinton's ideas had no official standing and were not binding on any of the parties. On January 13, a week before leaving office, Clinton made clear that "President-elect Bush is in no way, shape or form bound by the positions I've taken." On February 8, two days after the Sharon victory over Barak, the Bush administration declared that "the ideas and parameters that were discussed in the last few months were President Clinton's parameters, and therefore, when he left office, they were no longer a U.S. proposal or a presidential proposal." Outgoing Israeli prime minister Ehud Barak, too, noted that his negotiations with the Palestinians "do not place Israel's new government under any obligations."

The first item on President Bush's Palestinian-Israeli agenda was to stop the violence. Secretary-of-State-designate Colin Powell, testifying before the Senate Foreign Relations Committee at his confirmation hearings on January 17, placed the onus on the Palestinian Authority. He said that the administration's first step would be to call on Chairman Arafat to put an end to the violence against Israelis, "and only then can we see what the next step in this process is going to be." The Bush administration, he added, whose Middle East policy would be "based on unshakable support for the security of Israel," planned to wait until after the Israeli elections on February 6 before considering additional moves. Implying that the new president would follow a less intrusive, hands-on approach than Clinton had, Powell stressed that the Bush policy would be based on "a hard-headed recognition that the parties themselves must make the peace."

Donald Rumsfeld, Bush's choice as secretary of defense, told the Senate committee, at his confirmation hearing on January 11, that he would oppose any U.S. attempt to force a solution on the Israelis and Palestinians, since an imposed solution would not "stick." Any agreement "has to make sense on the ground," he said, noting that Israel was a "very small" state and therefore the Israelis "cannot make many mistakes about what they give up." Rumsfeld, who had served as defense secretary during the Ford administration, was a strong proponent of missile defense systems, an area in which the U.S. and Israel had long cooperated and that would be further enhanced during 2001.

Following Sharon's landslide victory over Barak, Bush called to congratulate the winner, saying he looked forward to working with him, "especially with regard to advancing peace and stability in the region." The new president had already met Sharon in 1998, when the former general guided then-Governor Bush on a helicopter tour of Israel and the West Bank. When Sharon pointed out to his American guest that, according to the 1949 armistice demarcation lines, pre-1967 Israel was highly vulnerable to military attack since at one point the country was only nine miles wide, Bush jokingly remarked that in Texas there were some driveways longer than that.

Congress echoed the pro-Israel sentiment. The Republican and Democratic leaders of both the House and the Senate sent Sharon a letter of congratulations on his victory, assuring him that the American commitment to Israel's security was "unshakeable." Saying that they looked forward to working with him, the leaders underscored, in their letter, that "the special relationship between our two countries is both the foundation for a more stable region and the only basis on which true and lasting peace in the region can be built." Similarly, the House, on February 13, overwhelmingly (401-1) passed a resolution congratulating Sharon and restating the American commitment to a secure peace for Israel. The resolution also demanded that Arafat act to end the violence, which had by then escalated to the use of mortars and other banned weapons.

In his victory speech, Sharon said that one of his top priorities would be to bolster Israel's relations with the United States. Knowing of the concern both in Israel and Washington that his expected hard-line policies could hurt the prospects for peace and complicate American relations with the Arab world, Sharon offered reassurance. Following Knesset approval of his coalition government by a vote of 72-21, Sharon announced that if the Palestinian Authority stopped using violence and lived up to its "basic commitment" to fight terrorism and incitement against Israel, the new government would examine "ideas for advancing a dialogue and easing the distress of the Palestinian people." He also acknowledged that "we know peace entails painful concessions on both sides." Sharon said, as well, that his government aimed to reach peace with Syria and Lebanon and to strengthen relations with Egypt and Jordan. On March 12, Israel began to ease economic and travel restrictions on four West Bank cities.

Prime Minister Sharon rejected the underlying assumption of the Clinton approach—the belief that an immediate and comprehensive end of the Arab-Israel conflict was possible. He advocated instead a gradual process that started with achieving a cease-fire and long-term armistice, followed by an extended interim agreement. Although Sharon said that he accepted in principle the idea of a Palestinian state living peacefully alongside Israel, he contended that a final peace agreement would have to wait until democratic governments genuinely committed to peace with Israel developed among the Palestinians and in neighboring belligerent Arab states, notably Syria. And in response to the priorities of his right-wing coalition partners and the settler movement, Sharon pledged not to remove any Israeli settlements during his term.

Sharon developed these themes when he came to Washington in mid-March. Addressing the policy conference of AIPAC (American Israel Public Affairs Committee), the preeminent pro-Israel lobby, Sharon declared that he had come "to deepen and strengthen the special relationship between our peoples" by developing a close relationship with President Bush and his administration, while also working to "enhance our ties with both houses of Congress and with the American people as a whole." All Israelis, he asserted, sought peace, "but Israel needs peace with security, a peace that will last for generations." Acknowledging that the Arab-Israeli peace process had reached a stalemate, he said this was because the "forces of instability feel they are gaining momentum." Among the disturbing and destabilizing developments in the region, he listed the following: "Syria is looking east to its ties with a resurgent Iraq and Iran instead of better relations with the West. The Palestinians are waving the flags of Iraq and Hezballah. Yasir Arafat and the Palestinian Authority are returning to their belief that they can defeat Israel by means of armed struggle."

These trends could be reversed, he said, and the foundations of peace and stability established, but it would take a long time. What was required meanwhile were "strong democracies determined to protect themselves." He also promised to "make every effort" to reach an agreement with the Palestinians, in two stages. The first, which Israel had already begun to implement, were immediate steps to ease restrictions and improve the economic situation of the Palestinian population. For the second stage, he proposed "a new, more realistic approach of nonbelligerency and a long-term interim agreement" that would include international cooperation to provide the Palestinians "a better economic future." Time was also needed, he stressed, "to make sure that incitement and hatred are removed from Palestinian media and from school textbooks, and the children are taught the language of peace so that we can achieve real reconciliation and a true end to the conflict."

Secretary Powell also addressed the AIPAC conference and reassured his audience that the special relationship between the two "fellow democracies is and will remain rock solid." The United States and Israel were united "in an unconditional bond that is both deep and wide; one based on history, on values and on principle." Acknowledging the regional threats that Sharon had outlined, Secretary Powell went on to declare: "We recognize that Israel lives in a very dangerous neighborhood, so we will look for ways to strengthen and expand our valuable strategic cooperation with Israel so that we can help preserve Israel's qualitative military edge." As one example, he cited the ongoing U.S.-Israeli collaboration in missile defense. Although Powell underscored that "we believe that a secure Israel within internationally recognized borders remains a cornerstone of the United States' foreign policy," left unsaid was the considerable gap between what Sharon envisaged as viable borders and the traditional State Department preference for the pre-Six-Day-War armistice lines, with only mutually agreed-upon adjustments or "minor rectifications" to achieve more defensible frontiers. Powell did not even bring up two other potentially divisive issues: the future of the settlements and the timetable for reaching a political agreement.

Senator Joseph I. Lieberman (D., Conn.), who had been Al Gore's vice-presidential running mate in 2000, told the AIPAC conference that history would judge Arafat harshly for not accepting "the breathtaking terms of the peace offered by Ehud Barak at Camp David." He said he agreed with Prime Minister Sharon that "there can be no negotiating while Israelis are being attacked." As for the pressures being exerted on Washington to distance itself from the Sharon government, Lieberman declared: "I would say to those who believe that they can weaken Israel by promoting a split with America, you are harboring illusions. You will no more separate America from Israel than you will separate America from NATO. The Israeli-American alliance may be less formal, but it is no less real, because it is built on the strongest and most enduring foundation, . . . shared values, shared moral values." Recent public opinion polls, he noted, found that the American people supported ties with Israel "because they understand that Israel is a fellow democracy and is a most consistent and constant friend of the United States."

American Backing for Israel

As violence continued and there appeared to be no end to the intifada, Washington's friends and allies in Europe and the Arab world escalated their demands on the Bush administration. They wanted the Americans to convince Sharon to agree to their interpretation of UN Security Council Resolution 242 of 1967, which envisaged a virtually complete Israeli withdrawal to the 1967 lines, and the creation of a Palestinian state in the vacated territory.

In striking contrast, solid majorities in Congress urged the president to reassess U.S. relations with the Palestinians. On April 6, 87 senators and 189 members of the House wrote the president suggesting that the reassessment include such questions as whether Palestinian groups involved in violence should be designated as foreign terrorist organizations, whether the PLO office in Washington should be closed and Arafat barred from the White House, and whether U.S. financial aid to the Palestinians was in fact being used for humanitarian purposes. The president was receptive to these expressions of concern. At a press conference on March 29, Bush declared: "The signal I am sending to the Palestinians is stop the violence, and I cannot make it any more clear," adding: "And I hope that Chairman Arafat hears it loud and clear." In congressional testimony that same day, Assistant Secretary of State for Near East Affairs Edward Walker charged that Arafat had not heeded the American calls to stop the violence.

On March 30, the State Department submitted to Congress its semiannual report on PA compliance with the terms of the Oslo Accords, and it documented numerous Palestinian violations of post-Oslo agreements with Israel. The Palestinians had reneged on their pledge not to use violence; failed to confiscate illegal weapons and protect Jewish holy sites (such as Joseph's Tomb in Shechem [Nablus] and Rachel's Tomb on the road to Bethlehem); released known terrorists from Palestinian jails; and continued to incite the Palestinian public, including children, to resort to violence. While blaming the leaders of the Tanzim militia affiliated with Arafat's own Fatah faction of the PLO and members of the PA's security forces for the violence, the State Department report stopped short of directly implicating the PA leadership, saying that the role of Arafat and his key aides in initiating and directing the violence was not clear.

On May 21, Secretary of State Powell said that the United States backed the recommendations contained in the report of the Mitchell Committee that had examined the outbreak of Palestinian-Israeli hostilities in the fall of 2000 (see AJYB 2001, p. 218). Powell urged an immediate and unconditional end to the violence and resumption of security cooperation between the Israeli and Palestinian authorities. These steps, he said, should be followed by a cooling-off period and confidence-building measures aimed at leading the sides back to the negotiating table. He noted that the committee report, prepared by an international panel of distinguished statesmen chaired by George Mitchell, the former senator from Maine, had stressed "the need for the Palestinians to make an all-out effort to enforce a complete cessation of violence." Acknowledging that the report had also called upon Israel to freeze its settlement activity, he stressed that this came later in the timetable of required actions. "Senator Mitchell and the other committee members put the settlement issue in the context of confidence-building measures," Powell noted. "It is not linked in any way to his earlier call for an immediate cessation of hostilities." Prime Minister Sharon also endorsed the Mitchell recommendations, saying, "I propose to our neighbors to work together for an immediate cease-fire and I hope the Palestinians will answer the call positively. Then we can begin carrying out the outlines of the Mitchell report."

The Bush administration repeatedly called upon Chairman Arafat to condemn all attacks on Israeli civilians, arrest known sponsors and perpetrators of terrorist acts, and make a 100-percent effort to stop the violence. While conceding that Arafat might not be 100-percent successful, especially in monitoring the activities of groups that were not under his control, administration officials and members of Congress grew increasingly impatient and disillusioned with him. They complained that even when Arafat occasionally ordered arrests of some Palestinian terrorists, the PA jails, with Arafat's knowledge, practiced a revolving-door policy, quietly releasing suspects soon after ostentatiously arresting them.

Lingering hopes that Arafat might move seriously against terrorism were finally dashed after the suicide bombing on June 1 at the Dolphinarium night club in Tel Aviv that killed more than 20 Israeli teenagers, mostly recent immigrants from the former Soviet Union, and wounded many more. Sharon deferred an immediate military response, in effect giving Arafat one last chance to clamp down on the violent Palestinian elements. Bowing to mounting U.S. and international pressure, Arafat, on June 2—for the first time since the outbreak of violence in September—called for an unconditional cease-fire. However, as Secretary Powell noted at the time, "the Israelis don't just want statements; they want to see something happen on the ground." Moreover, on June 6 Arafat said that he was committed to enforcing the cease-fire only in the territories under his control, not in Israel itself or in the territories controlled by Israel.

Congress Acts

By midyear, when it was clear that the PA was not curbing the continuing campaign of attacks on Israeli soldiers and civilians, Congress stepped up its efforts to hold the PA accountable. On July 24, the House overwhelmingly passed legislation authorizing the president to impose sanctions on the Palestinian Authority if he was unable to certify that the PA was meeting its commitments to combat terrorism and end incitement. William Burns, who had recently been designated to succeed Walker as assistant secretary of state for Near East affairs, testified before Congress on July 26 that the United States was carefully reviewing whether Palestinian groups should be put on the terrorist list. Such action was provided for in the fiscal year 2002 foreign-aid bill passed by the House, the Senate legislation authorizing funding for the State Department, and a free-standing bill known as the Middle East Peace Commitments Act (MEPCA), introduced by Reps. Gary Ackerman (D., N.Y.), Benjamin Gilman (R., N.Y.), and Tom Lantos (D., Cal.).

Burns testified that there was no question that "there are individuals who belong to those [PA-affiliated] organizations, Force 17 and Tanzim in particular, who have been involved in acts of violence against Israelis." He assured the indignant members of the Middle East subcommittee of the House International Relations Committee that the State Department was "very seriously reviewing" this evidence as "we look at the possible designation of particular groups as foreign terrorist organizations." Burns agreed that Arafat was not doing enough to rein in violence. In addition, he stressed, "more needs to be done to curb incitement," which, he pointed out, "has had a poisonous effect, not just over the last ten months, but for years before that as well."

While threatening to cut off American aid to the Palestinian Authority, the House of Representatives on July 24, by a vote of 381-46, approved the foreign-aid bill for fiscal year 2002. This earmarked $2.04 billion in military assistance and $720 million in economic assistance for Israel. These allocations reflected the fourth year of a ten-year program to gradually shift American help from primarily economic to defense-related aid. This arrangement had been formalized on January 19, 2001, in a memorandum of understanding signed by Israeli ambassador David Ivry and Assistant Secretary Walker, which stated that the U.S. and Israel "agree on the importance of restructuring annual U.S. bilateral assistance to Israel in a way that strengthens the security relationship between our two countries and recognizes the strong economic progress that has been achieved over the past decades."

Under the agreed timetable, economic aid would diminish by $120 million annually until totally phased out in 2008. Meanwhile, military assistance would increase $60 million annually, reaching $2.4 billion in 2008. Israeli officials pointed out that at the end of the ten-year period the total U.S. aid package would have dropped from $3 billion annually to $2.4 billion. Significantly, it would provide Israel with more funds to purchase American-made military equipment. Since, under the agreement, Israel was required to spend nearly 75 percent of the military assistance money in the United States, this also provided employment opportunities for American workers and additional revenues for companies in the defense sector.

In November, a House-Senate conference committee reconciled differences in the two chambers' versions of the foreign aid bill in regard to the amount for Israel. The bill also included a number of items unique to Israel's aid, including early disbursal—a provision allowing Israel to receive its aid in a lump-sum payment at the beginning of the fiscal year—and offshore procurement, which allowed Israel to spend a portion of the military aid in Israel. The bill also provided Israel with $60 million to resettle refugees. The final version of the bill passed Congress at the end of the year by a vote of 387-66 in the House and by unanimous consent in the Senate. The overall aid figures allocated for Israel were the same as had been approved by the House in July. However, the law contained two new pro-Israel provisions included at the initiative of Rep. Jim Kolbe (R., Ariz.), chairman of the House Appropriations Foreign Operations Subcommittee, Rep. Nita Lowy (D., N.Y.), the committee's ranking member, and Sen. Mitch McConnell (R., Ky.), ranking member of the Senate Appropriations Foreign Operations Subcommittee.

One of the provisions recommended sanctions against the Palestinian Authority if the president determined that it had failed to meet its commitments to fight terrorism. The other stipulated that $8 million in U.S. assistance pledged for the headquarters of the International Committee of the Red Cross (ICRC) be withheld unless the president determined that Israel's Magen David Adom (Red Shield of David) was no longer being denied participation on an equal basis in the International Red Cross and Red Crescent Movement. The ICRC had long rejected the Israeli request, supported by the American Red Cross, to recognize the Israeli symbol.

Military cooperation between the U.S. and Israel was also reflected in the defense-spending bill for fiscal 2002. This provided a total of $214.5 million for nine jointly developed high-tech projects that would help the two countries deal more effectively with terrorism and other new threats. The allocations included $131.7 million for the Arrow antimissile program; $13 million for the Tactical High Energy Laser; $25 million for the Litening Targeting Pod; and $20 million for Bradley Fighting Vehicle Reactive Armor.

American Patriot missile units were dispatched to Israel in February 2001 for the largest-ever combined training exercise with the IDF. This was a time of increased regional tension and renewed signs of Iraqi belligerence that led to new U.S. and British missile strikes against Iraqi radar and communications sites (see below, p. 215). The two-week military drill, code-named "Juniper Cobra," was conducted to test the interoperability of Israel's missile defense systems, such as the newly deployed Arrow battery, with similar U.S. military hardware that might be stationed in or near Israel in a future regional crisis.

According to Charles Perkins, AIPAC's senior military analyst, these war games represented a major milestone in the 20-year history of formal U.S.-Israeli strategic cooperation. The USS *Porter,* a navy Aegis cruiser capable of detecting and intercepting hostile missiles, was deployed off Israel's Mediterranean coastline and practiced coordinating its operations with the Israel missile defense network. Mindful of the Scud missile barrages that Saddam Hussein hurled against Israel ten years earlier during the 1991 Gulf War, the American-Israeli defense maneuvers were intended both to reassure the Israeli public that it could count on effective American support, and also to send a powerful message to potential regional adversaries such as Iran, Iraq, and Syria.

The U.S.-Turkey-Israel Connection

As Washington and Jerusalem sought to confront the growing threats posed by the rogue states in the region, they found a useful ally in Ankara. Although Turkey's population of some 67 million was 99-percent Muslim and there was considerable popular sympathy for the Palestinians, the country's political leadership strictly followed the secularist principles established by Mustafa Kemal Atatürk, the founder of the modern Turkish republic after World War I. Non-Arab and pro-Western Turkey was the only NATO member that also belonged to the Organization of the Islamic Conference. Eager to maintain good relations with both Israel and the Palestinian Authority and concerned that the escalating Palestinian-Israeli violence would further destabilize the region, Ankara tried to use its diplomatic contacts to defuse the situation. Thus, former Turkish president Süleyman Demirel had been selected as one of the five members of the Mitchell Committee that had been set up to look into the causes of the violence that had erupted the previous September and to suggest ways of stopping the intifada and resuming political negotiations (see above, p. 204).

The influential Turkish military establishment, which saw itself as the guardian of Atatürk's secularist principles, regarded democratic, pro-American Israel as a natural ally against regimes that espoused the export of Islamic fundamentalism, or neighboring states that harbored hostile intentions toward Turkey. This strategic cooperation, which began to be formalized in 1996, when Turkey awarded a $630-million contract to Israel to upgrade its U.S.-supplied military aircraft and also agreed on a program of joint training of Turkish and Israeli pilots, reached new heights during 2001.

On January 17, a small flotilla of Turkish, American, and Israeli frigates pulled out of Haifa and, guided from above by a U.S. Navy PC-3 Orion patrol plane, responded to a prearranged distress call. The operation, called "Reliant Mermaid III," was the third annual joint search-and-rescue naval exercise by the navies of the three countries. Originally scheduled for the previous November, the exercise was put off. This encouraged speculation that the Turks were considering canceling it altogether, in line with the actions of Qatar, Bahrain, Tunisia, and Morocco, which suspended their low-level ties with Israel, and the actions of Egypt and Jordan, which also scaled back their joint activities with Israel in the weeks after the outbreak of Palestinian-Israeli violence. Consequently, there was relief in Israel when the two-month postponement of the exercise with Turkey was attributed to "technical problems."

The growing strategic alliance reached new heights in mid-June, when jet fighters of the three countries began two weeks of joint aerial training exercises in the skies over southern Turkey. Dubbed "Anatolian Eagle," this major operation marked the first time the three militaries had come together for such mock combat drills. The units of the three air forces focused on joint operations and command procedures, taking advantage of the similar American-made planes in their respective air forces, to prepare for the possibility of combined missions during future regional crises. Besides honing their skills in simulated air-to-air duels, the participating aircraft also staged mock attacks on ground-based air-defense missile sites and engaged in midair refueling exercises to extend the operational range of the combat aircraft. The exercises were conducted in an area covering some 7,600 square miles near the Turkish city of Konya. While Ankara played down the political significance of the joint maneuvers with Israel and the U.S., insisting that they were not directed against any third party, they were clearly intended to send a deterrent message to hostile neighbors.

During the year, Turkey and Israel also reached an agreement in principle for Israel to purchase a minimum of 50 million cubic meters of water annually from Turkey's Manavgat River, some 50 miles east of Antalya on the Mediterranean coast. While initially meeting only some 2.5 percent of Israel's total water needs, it would help ease the effects of a three-year drought that had made it difficult for Israel to meet its commitment to supply water to Jordan under its 1994 peace treaty. By the end of 2001, the Turkish and Israeli negotiators had not yet reached agreement on price and other terms of the contract. The Palestinian Authority also expressed interest in obtaining Turkish water to alleviate its desperate shortage, especially in the Gaza Strip, where overpumping of wells near the coast resulted in seawater intrusion into the aquifer and raised the salinity of the drinking water. The PA was hoping for international subsidies to pay for the water imports. For his part, Prime Minister Sharon revived the idea he had first floated years earlier for a multibillion-dollar desalination project that would meet the needs of Israelis, Palestinians, and Jordanians.

Terrorism and the Iranian Connection

In his testimony on February 7 before the Senate Select Committee on Intelligence, CIA director George Tenet warned that the terrorist threat to Israel and to other participants in the Middle East peace negotiations had increased since the outbreak of Palestinian-Israeli violence. "Palestinian rejectionists, including Hamas and the Palestinian Islamic Jihad, have stepped up violent attacks against Israeli interests since October. The terrorist threat to U.S. interests because of our friendship with Israel has also increased." But, he pointed out, America's connection to Israel was not the only factor motivating anti-American acts. "At the same time, Islamic militancy is expanding and the worldwide pool of potential recruits for terrorist networks is growing. In Central Asia, the Middle East and South Asia, Islamic terrorist organizations are attracting new recruits, including under the banner of anti-Americanism."

Turning to other potential threats to U.S. interests, Tenet noted that "Iran has one of the largest and most capable ballistic missile programs in the Middle East." While both Iran and Iraq were likely to develop intercontinental ballistic missiles (ICBMs) capable of striking the United States "in the next few years," the immediate threat to U.S. interests and forces in the Middle East came from short-range and medium-range ballistic missiles (MRBMs). The proliferation of MRBMs, driven largely, though not exclusively, by sales from North Korea, "is altering strategic balances in the Middle East and Asia." These missiles included Iran's Shahab-3.

Tenet singled out "the catalytic role that foreign assistance has played" in advancing the missile and weapons-of-mass-destruction (WMD) capabilities of Iran and Libya. He singled out Russia's cash-starved defense and nuclear industries as potential sellers of missile components and

WMD related technologies. "Indeed, the transfer of ballistic missile technology from Russia to Iran was substantial last year," and the CIA had concluded that this would continue to help Iran accelerate its efforts to become self-sufficient in missile production. Moreover, Russia remained a key supplier for a variety of Iranian civilian nuclear programs, which could be used to advance Tehran's clandestine nuclear weapons programs. In addition, Russian entities were a significant source of dual-use biotechnology and chemicals production technology and equipment. Iran was not the only regional state seeking Russian help in developing WMD capabilities. Turning to Iran's hostile neighbor, Iraq, Tenet declared that "our most serious concern with Saddam Hussein must be the likelihood that he will seek renewed WMD capability."

"It's a reality that Iran remains one of the principal supporters of Hamas and Hezballah," Rep. Henry Hyde (R., Ill.) declared in a speech in mid-March. He noted that despite the reports about deep divisions within Iran between hard-liners and reformers, the so-called moderates also supported the anti-Israeli Islamic groups and joined in openly calling for Israel's destruction. "These acts of state-sponsored terror are aimed not only against Israel," he told the AIPAC meeting in Washington, "but also against the U.S., as occurred in the Khobar Towers bombing." FBI director Louis Freeh confirmed to an investigative reporter for the *New Yorker* in early 2001 that the agency had provided the Bush administration evidence that senior Iranian intelligence officials had been involved in planning the 1996 Khobar Towers attack in which 19 American servicemen were killed. Because of recent efforts at rapprochement between Saudi Arabia and Iran, the Saudis had failed to fully cooperate with the U.S. investigation. Hyde called for concerted action, together with America's European allies, to inhibit Iran's offensive weapons capacity and to tighten the sanctions designed to restrict dual-technology exports to Iran.

In April, Congress began considering legislation to extend the Iran-Libya Sanctions Act, which was due to expire in August. The law, originally passed in 1996, gave the president the authority to impose sanctions on foreign companies investing significant sums in Iran's and Libya's oil and gas sectors. U.S. oil companies were not happy with the law, since it gave foreign companies a competitive advantage. Some officials in the State Department and a number of Middle East experts favored extending the law for only two years, as a signal to the reformers in Tehran that the U.S. was open to the development of positive relations. In response to a reporter's question in mid-April, President Bush said, "I have no intentions as of this moment [of] taking sanctions off countries like Iran and Libya." In March, Bush had renewed a 1995 executive order barring American companies from doing business with Iran. Explaining his decision, the president said: "The actions and policies of the government of Iran continue to threaten the national security, foreign policy, and economy of the United States."

If there was need to prove the accuracy of the president's characterization of Iran's hostile intent, on April 24 and 25 Tehran officially hosted a major international conference in support of the Palestinian armed struggle against Israel. Senior Iranian officials, including Supreme Leader Ayatollah Ali Khamenei and President Mohammed Khatami, representatives from more than 30 Arab and Islamic countries, and leaders of several terrorist groups attended the conference. They accused the Zionists of collaborating with the Nazis and greatly exaggerating the numbers killed in the Holocaust, vilified Israel as racist, attacked the American-sponsored peace process, and denounced the United States as an oppressor. Typical was the speech by Sheikh Hassan Nasrallah, the leader of Hezballah. He began by thanking Iran for its position on Palestine, "an issue that accepts no bargaining or discussion," and for Iran's "continuous support for Palestine, Lebanon, Syria and the Arabs against the Zionist danger, and for assuming all the burdens of their clear and brave position on the issue of Israel's existence in our region." He then exhorted the assembled Arab and Islamic delegates: "We all have an extraordinary historic opportunity to finish off the entire cancerous Zionist project. The Palestinian people's resistance is the vanguard of jihad and resistance in defense of the entire nation."

The State Department condemned the vitriolic rhetoric voiced at the Tehran conference as "outrageous and deplorable." The State Department's annual *Global Patterns of Terrorism* report, issued on May 30, criticized Iran's top leaders for demonstrating "unrelenting hostility to Israel" in their speeches. "Despite the victory for moderates in Iran's [parliamentary] elections in February [2000], aggressive countermeasures by hard-line conservatives have blocked most reform efforts," the report asserted. It further declared that "Iran remained the most active state sponsor of terrorism in 2000. Its Revolutionary Guard Corps and Ministry of Intelligence and Security continued to be involved in the planning and the execution of terrorist acts and continued to support a variety of groups that use terrorism to pursue their goals." In addition to providing full support to anti-Israeli terrorist groups, Iran also provided a somewhat lower level of support—including funding, training, and logistics assistance—to Islamic and other extremist groups in the Persian Gulf, Turkey and Central Asia, and Africa, the report said.

Mohammed Khatami was reelected president of Iran overwhelmingly on June 8. While this reflected wide support for reform and liberalization in domestic affairs, especially among the younger generation, it heralded no substantial change in Iran's official policy of hostility to Israel. Khatami, at the pro-Palestinian conference in Tehran, had harshly attacked Zionism and Israel, saying that the Jewish state had distorted the religious values of Judaism, was "founded on the fallacious concepts of superiority, transgressing human rights," and was "a parasite in the heart of the Muslim world."

Despite strong opposition from oil companies and others in the American business community, Congress overwhelmingly passed legislation extending the Iran-Libya Sanctions Act for an additional five years. The Senate did so on July 24 by a vote of 96-2, and the House followed two days later, 409-6. The Bush administration was also active in enforcing the Iran Nonproliferation Act, which Congress had passed unanimously the previous year to prevent the transfer of sensitive technology to Iran (see AJYB 2001, p. 222). In July 2001 it was reported that, under the act's provisions, the Bush administration had suspended the licenses of U.S. companies that had been involved in regulated trade with China's Yongli Chemicals and Technology Import and Export Corp. and North Korea's Changgwang Sinyong Corp. These two major companies had also been sanctioned by the Clinton administration for transferring chemical weapons components and exporting missile-related technology to Iran.

September 11 and the Iraqi Connection

On September 11, 19 suicide bombers affiliated with the Al Qaeda terrorist organization, headed by Saudi dissident Osama bin Laden, hijacked four U.S. commercial airliners and crashed two of them into the Twin Towers of the World Trade Center in New York, causing the buildings to collapse, and a third plane into the Pentagon in Washington, resulting in severe damage to one side of the Defense Department's headquarters. The fourth plane, which, according to later information, was reportedly intended to destroy the White House, crashed in a field in Pennsylvania, apparently following a struggle by some passengers with the hijackers. The coordinated terrorist attack resulted in more than 3,000 deaths, the highest domestic toll in a single day in U.S. history. The events horrified the nation, caused major economic disruptions, and profoundly changed the administration's priorities.

The president made it clear that the United States was now engaged in a global war on terrorism, and that all nations would have to choose between becoming America's allies in this struggle or being branded as enemies. Since 15 of the 19 suicide bombers were Saudi nationals, there also began a reassessment of the U.S. relationship with Saudi Arabia, which had been funding fundamentalist Islamic religious schools throughout the Arab world, in Pakistan and Afghanistan, and among the Muslim immigrant communities in Western Europe. When it emerged that most of the plane hijackers came from middle-class backgrounds and possessed some professional skills, many wondered what had made them so dissatisfied with their society and future prospects that they had turned to militant Islamic teachers for guidance. It was these preachers and bin Laden's agents in the Al Qaeda training camps who indoctrinated them with a homicidal hatred of the United States.

As evidence mounted that the Al Qaeda network had managed to establish terrorist cells in dozens of countries, it became clear that the assault on the United States was only the latest and most spectacular success in Osama bin Laden's worldwide terrorist campaign. In February 1998, bin Laden had announced the establishment of the "World Islamic Front for Jihad against the Jews and the Crusaders." In essence, he said then, he was fighting to overthrow the corrupt and godless Saudi ruling family, remove the American military presence from the holy soil of Arabia, and end the suffering of the Iraqi and Palestinian peoples, victims of American sanctions and U.S.-armed Israeli occupiers, respectively.

Some Middle East analysts and social psychologists saw deeper roots for bin Laden's animosity toward American Christians and Jews: The United States represented the leading modern Western power, whose material wealth and seductive popular culture threatened to undermine bin Laden's fundamentalist version of Wahhabi Islamic society and values. At the same time, the military, economic, and scientific success of the tiny State of Israel, with its mere five million Jews in contrast to the hundreds of millions of Arabs and Muslims, was a constant reminder of how low the Arab world had sunk from its days of glory in the decades following the rise of Islam. Bin Laden portrayed Israel's success in defeating the combined Arab armies and its continued occupation of Arab lands as a constant source of shame and humiliation for the Muslim world.

The first target of the American counterattack was the Taliban regime in Afghanistan, which shared bin Laden's version of fundamentalist Islam and had provided safe haven and training facilities to Al Qaeda. Once the Taliban had been ousted from power and the Al Qaeda forces in Afghanistan were disrupted and dispersed, the United States turned its attention to other terrorist-supporting regimes.

Persistent rumors circulated in Washington that Iraq would be the next target. Indeed, action against Iraq had been taken earlier in the year. On February 15, the United States and Britain had sent two dozen high-tech aircraft with smart missiles to destroy Iraqi radar installations and antiaircraft sites near Baghdad. Administration officials said the show of force was necessary to reduce the risk to pilots who were patrolling the southern no-fly zone. Apparently in an attempt to test the resolve of the new president, Iraq had, during January, fired more surface-to-air missiles at U.S. and British patrols than in all of the previous year.

But while this American riposte signaled determination to preserve the status quo, it did not answer the broader long-term policy question of how to deal with the threat to American interests posed by Iraq's regional ambitions. While berating the international community for the sanctions that allegedly kept food and medicine from reaching the impoverished Iraqi people, during 2001 Saddam lavishly awarded $10,000 to each family of a "martyred" Palestinian suicide bomber and to other Palestinians who had lost homes as a result of Israeli military action. (This figure was raised to $25,000 in early 2002.) Such largesse appealed not only to the Palestinians but also to other Muslims in the Arab world who were disenchanted with their own rulers and saw Saddam Hussein as a hero. As a consequence, pro-Western Arab rulers, feeling themselves increasingly vulnerable to criticism for their close ties to the U.S., intensified their appeals to Washington to distance itself from the policies of Israeli prime minister Sharon and to take a more active role in resolving the Israeli-Palestinian conflict.

The Bush administration and many members of Congress were becoming increasingly alarmed by credible reports from Iraqi defectors and other intelligence sources that the brutal regime of Saddam Hussein was making progress in its clandestine program to develop weapons of mass destruction. Among those publicly urging a swift campaign to overthrow Saddam was former CIA director R. James Woolsey. He cited with approval the evidence meticulously assembled by Laurie Milroie in her book, *Study of Revenge: Saddam Hussein's Unfinished War Against Amer-*

ica, that Iraqi agents had been involved in the first attack on the World Trade Center in 1993.

Iraqi relations with Al Qaeda continued after 1993. *Washington Post* editor and columnist Jim Hoagland and *New York Times* columnist William Safire reported in October 2001 on a series of meetings between bin Laden and high Iraqi intelligence officials going back at least to 1994, while bin Laden was still in Sudan, and continuing with a meeting in Baghdad in 1998 between bin Laden's second-in-command, Ayman al-Zawahiri, and Saddam's vice president, Taha Yasin Ramadan. According to intelligence sources cited by Safire (Oct. 22), during 2000, foreign "Islamicists" were given training in assassination and simulated plane hijacking at a base in the Salman Pak suburb of Baghdad. Safire added that operational cooperation between Al Qaeda and the Iraqi authorities had already been agreed upon in April 1998, when a high-level Al Qaeda delegation went to Baghdad ostensibly to celebrate Saddam Hussein's birthday, and met with the president's influential son Uday. They formally established a joint force consisting of some of Al Qaeda's fiercest "Afghan Arab" fighters and covert combatants in an Iraqi intelligence unit.

This cooperation continued in 2001, when bin Laden reportedly supplied some 400 "Afghan Arabs" to Saddam to launch guerrilla attacks against officials in the autonomous Kurdish-administered area in Iraq's northern no-fly zone. During the year, fighters of the Patriotic Union of Kurdistan (PUK), one of the two leading Kurdish groups in northern Iraq, reported seeing members of the Iraqi Republican Guards training these Al Qaeda supporters in a remote mountainous enclave in northern Iraq near the Iranian border. Louis Meixler of the Associated Press reported that five members of the group trained by Al Qaeda were killed and ten captured after they tried to kill Barhan Salih, prime minister of the PUK-controlled region in Kurdistan, shortly after Salih had met with visiting U.S. officials to coordinate policy against Saddam Hussein.

There was even circumstantial evidence linking Iraq directly with the September 11 terrorists. Czech intelligence sources revealed that, back in April 2001, Mohamed Atta, who directed the terrorist group that crashed American Airlines Flight 11 into one of the Twin Towers of the World Trade Center, had met with Ahmed Khalil Ibrahim Samir al-Ani, an Iraqi consular official in Prague who was also an officer in the Iraqi foreign intelligence service. It was only after September 11 that the Czechs realized Atta may have gone to Prague to receive money from the Iraqi official to finance the anti-American terrorist campaign. While acknowledging that "no indisputable smoking gun may ever be found," Safire concluded that it was "absurd to claim—in the face of what we already know—that Iraq is not an active collaborator with, harborer of, and source of sophisticated training and unconventional weaponry for bin Laden's world terror network."

Whether directly linked to September 11 or not, Saddam Hussein was seen by the Bush administration as a major threat in his own right. There had been no UN weapons inspectors in the country since December 1998. Saddam had, in the past, attempted to build an atomic bomb (which was set back by the Israeli raid on the Osirak reactor in June 1981), and had used chemical weapons against Iranian civilian targets during the seven-year Iraq-Iran war (1980–1987) and against his own Kurdish citizens in 1988. Moreover, the Iraqi attempt to assassinate former president George H. W. Bush during his visit to Kuwait in April 1993 added a personal reason for his son, the current President Bush, to oust the regime and complete the unfinished business of the Gulf War of 1991. Among those making the argument for regime change in Iraq now were some of the same key foreign-policy advisers who had served in the administration of the president's father.

For the U.S. to take decisive action against Saddam it would clearly need the support of other states in the Middle East. Ideally, this would be a broad coalition similar to the one the senior President Bush had successfully mobilized in support of the liberation of Kuwait from Iraqi occupation in 1991. At a minimum, U. S. defense planners believed that American forces would need the active support of nearby countries such as Saudi Arabia, Kuwait, and Turkey, plus at least the tacit backing of most of the members of the Arab League. Bush's advisers were divided over the effectiveness of Iraqi opposition groups in exile and potentially helpful Kurdish and Shi'ite elements within Iraq itself.

There was agreement among President Bush's advisers that any successful move against the Iraqi dictator would require many months of careful planning. Therefore, it would probably have to be deferred until after the situation in Afghanistan was stabilized and the remaining Al Qaeda terrorist groups in Afghanistan and Pakistan had been eliminated. Also, in order to establish the legal groundwork for a military campaign, the U.S. would first have to go through the diplomatic motions of demanding, through the UN, that Baghdad agree to a return of international inspectors with unfettered ability to search for unauthorized weapons throughout Iraq. Consequently, the United States did not undertake any major military action against Iraq during 2001.

War on Terrorism

President Bush met with key foreign leaders and dispatched Vice President Cheney, Defense Secretary Rumsfeld, and Secretary of State Powell on a series of missions to countries in Europe, the Middle East, and Central Asia. Though America's objective in the Arab League states was the forthcoming confrontation with Iraq, their Arab interlocutors stressed the need, first, to deal with the growing violence between Israelis and Palestinians. Pro-Western regimes in the region were facing massive demonstrations in support of the Palestinians, endangering the stability of their own governments, as bin Laden, like Saddam Hussein, portrayed himself as a true champion of the Palestinian cause.

Calls mounted in the Arab world for the U.S. to adopt a more evenhanded posture and to exert pressure on Sharon. This ran counter to prevailing sentiment in Congress, where it was often noted that Israel had immediately condemned the September 11 attacks on the United States and that Israel had long been a valuable strategic ally in the fight against terrorism. This contrasted with televised pictures of some Palestinians rejoicing at the news of the damage inflicted upon the American superpower, which they regarded as the principal backer of their Israeli enemy.

Most Arab governments—Iraq was the notable exception—had also expressed sympathy with the United States over the attacks on innocent civilians. However, many sought to explain, if not fully justify, the anti-American strikes as the natural consequence of Arab anger and frustration at the material and political support that Washington continued to provide to Israel, and the failure of the Americans to press Israel to withdraw from the territories and end the suffering of the Palestinians. A few former State Department officials and others joined in claiming that excessive U.S. support for Israel was the main reason for the attacks.

Yet a review of earlier anti-American terrorist attacks by Al Qaeda did not support this thesis. The two attacks against American military installations in Saudi Arabia in 1995—a bombing in Riyadh that killed five American soldiers and the massive truck bomb of the U.S. troop barracks at Al Khobar towers in Saudi Arabia that killed 19—the simultaneous bombings in 1998 of the U.S. embassies in Kenya and Tanzania that killed 224, and the attack in October 2000 on the USS *Cole* in the Yemeni port of Aden that killed 17 sailors and wounded 39, had nothing to do with the Arab-Israel conflict or the plight of the Palestinians.

With the administration's launching of an intensified war on international terrorism following September 11, calls mounted in Congress for the U.S. to impose sanctions on the PLO and other militant Palestinian groups. On November 2, the State Department announced that it had added to the list of outlawed terrorist groups the Islamist militant Hamas, Islamic Jihad, and Lebanese Hezballah, as well as the secular Popular Front for the Liberation of Palestine, which had resumed anti-Israel terrorism, including the assassination in October of Rehavam Ze'evi, Israel's minister of tourism, in his room at a Jerusalem hotel.

At the end of November, 89 members of the Senate sent a letter to President Bush urging him not to restrain Israel from responding forcefully to Palestinian terrorism. The bipartisan letter, authored by Senators Christopher Bond (R., Mo.) and Charles Schumer (D., N.Y.), drew a parallel between "the terrorism that Israel has been subjected to since its birth" and September 11, and urged that the same standard be adopted for judging the American and Israeli responses. "The American people would never excuse us for not going after the terrorists with all our strength and might," the senators wrote, "yet that is what some have demanded of the Israeli government after every terrorist incident they suffer. No matter what the provocation, they urge restraint." The senators voiced their "full support" for the president in the war against terrorism. They also expressed strong backing for Israel, referring to the Jewish state as "our one reliable and democratic ally in the entire Middle East," and "our close ally in the fight against terrorism." The letter went on to praise Bush for following "the correct course" by refusing to meet personally with Arafat. (The president had publicly snubbed Arafat when they were both at the UN in New York in September.)

Israel's traditional support in Congress and the American administration was greatly bolstered by the enthusiasm of the conservative wing of Bush's own Republican Party. Not only did these conservatives see Israel as an important strategic ally in the war against terrorism, but many who were evangelical Christians—among whose ranks President Bush included himself—considered the Jewish state to be a fulfillment of the Bible's prophecies and a harbinger of the second coming of Jesus.

On November 19, Secretary of State Powell outlined the administration's vision for Palestinian-Israeli peace in a speech at the University of Louisville. (Prepared originally for delivery at the UN General Assembly in September, it had had to be postponed because of September 11.) Powell reiterated the U.S. commitment to the eventual establishment of a state of Palestine living in peace alongside Israel. He also called on Israel to ease the living conditions of the Palestinians and to embark on a series of confidence-building measures, including a halt to settlement expansion. At the same time, Powell made it clear that "the key to peace is in the hands of the Palestinians, who must make every effort to bring all acts of terror against Israelis to a complete halt." He pointedly noted that "the intifada is now mired in the quicksand of self-defeating violence and terror directed against Israel," and stressed that "no national aspiration, no remembered wrong can ever justify the deliberate murder of the innocent." He also called for an end to anti-Israeli incitement in Palestinian schools and in the Palestinian and Arab-world media. He added that the members of the Arab League should also take positive measures to encourage negotiations and prepare their people for peace with Israel.

The Powell speech was accompanied by practical steps to revive the stalemated peace process. The administration announced it was sending two key officials to the region. General Anthony Zinni, recently retired from the Marine Corps, was appointed special envoy to work with the parties to reestablish security cooperation and seek to implement the Tenet cease-fire plan (see AJYB 2001, p. 217). He would be accompanied by William Burns, assistant secretary of state for Near Eastern Affairs, who would concentrate on the diplomatic efforts to begin implementation of the Mitchell Committee recommendations.

However, neither was able to report substantial progress before year's end. Indeed, the practical difficulties facing the Zinni mission were dramatically illustrated shortly after the general's arrival in Israel. While flying in a helicopter with Prime Minister Sharon, they arrived in Afula, a town in northern Israel, just minutes after a terrorist attack in which two Israelis were killed and dozens injured. Israeli defense officials later pointed out to General Zinni that the perpetrators came into Israel proper from West Bank territory controlled by Arafat's security forces.

Secretary Powell had opened the Middle East section of his Louisville address with a comment on American-Israeli relations. "The United States has an enduring and ironclad commitment to Israel's security," he declared, and emphasized once again that the relationship between the United States and Israel "is based on the broadest conception of American national interest, in which our two nations are bound forever together by common democratic values and traditions."

GEORGE E. GRUEN

Jewish Communal Affairs

American Jews and Israel

As THE YEAR BEGAN, Israel prepared for an election on February 6 pitting the incumbent prime minister, Ehud Barak of the Labor-led coalition, against Likud candidate Ariel Sharon. With Barak's peace plans apparently dashed by the failure of the Camp David talks in the summer of 2000 and the onset of a bloody new intifada that entered its fourth month in January 2001, Barak nevertheless kept negotiations going with the Palestinians in the hope of a last-minute deal. But the Israeli opposition was not idle, scheduling a massive demonstration for January 8 in Jerusalem. While officially nonpartisan, the event was called to protest the idea, allegedly being contemplated by government negotiators, of giving the Palestinians some form of sovereignty over parts of the city, including—so it was rumored—the Temple Mount.

Natan Sharansky, well-known in the U.S. from his days as a Soviet refusenik and now working for the Sharon campaign, came to the U.S., and met on January 3 with the Conference of Presidents of Major American Jewish Organizations—the high-profile umbrella body for American Jewry on issues related to Israel—to ask it to endorse the demonstration and participate in it. A number of the conference's constituent organizations objected to involvement in what they saw as a matter of internal Israeli politics, and the lack of consensus meant that the conference could take no official action. Nevertheless, Ronald Lauder, the conference chairman, attended the Jerusalem demonstration and was a featured speaker. Noting that he spoke only in his individual capacity, Lauder nevertheless claimed that he was "representing millions of Jews throughout the world" in opposing the division of Jerusalem. Reporting the story, the Israeli press described Lauder not simply as an individual Jew, but as chairman of the conference or as an "American Jewish leader."

About a dozen of the 54 member organizations of the Conference of Presidents—echoed by Labor leaders in Israel—expressed outrage that Lauder had, in effect, used the aura of his leadership position to take sides in an Israeli election. A spokeswoman for Lauder commented that he "is deeply concerned about the peace and security of Israel, and surely no one would seriously suggest he be muzzled on a vital issue he has cared about his entire life. In fact, remaining silent would be a greater cause for criticism." Upon his return to the U.S., Lauder spoke at another rally against dividing Jerusalem, this one at New York's City Hall.

The Conference of Presidents met on January 31 and overwhelmingly approved new limitations on the prerogatives of its chairman, who, from now on, "in public remarks, should reflect policies already determined through the conference consensus," and "should refrain from speaking in his/her individual capacity, or in the capacity of volunteer or professional head of a member or other organization on issues related to the conference agenda." Backing for this resolution came even from organizations that supported Lauder's stand on the unity of Jerusalem, since they too recognized that an unfettered chairman, no matter what his ideological bent, endangered the effectiveness of the conference.

A side effect of the Jerusalem demonstration and Lauder's participation was the revelation of fissures within American Jewry over the future of the city. Nobel laureate Elie Wiesel, writing in the *New York Times* (Jan. 24) argued that "the holiest of cities" was so vital to "the Jewish soul" that it should not even be discussed in negotiations for at least 20 years. But in a letter responding to Wiesel (Jan. 26), Rabbi Charles Kroloff, president of the Central Conference of American Rabbis (CCAR, the organization of Reform rabbis) argued for sharing the city since it "has become a central symbol for Arabs." And while Arthur Hertzberg, a Conservative rabbi and academic, felt that a "deal" on Jerusalem could be "the best hope that we have for an historic breakthrough," Rabbi Haskel Lookstein, who was Orthodox, insisted that holding on to the entire city "is what we mean by our pledge not to forget Jerusalem" (New York *Jewish Week,* Jan. 12, 26).

The Lauder incident also sparked the first of several controversies that the Reform movement would have with Israeli officials over the course of the year. The most outspoken critic of Lauder's participation in the Jerusalem demonstration was Rabbi Eric Yoffie, president of the Union of American Hebrew Congregations (UAHC), the organization of Reform synagogues. Asked about Yoffie's objections, Ehud Olmert, the mayor of Jerusalem and one of the primary sponsors of the demonstration, told a reporter that Reform Judaism was "an insignificant minority that is meaningless when it comes to Jerusalem." Yoffie countered that Olmert seemed to be ignorant of the fact that American Reform was "by far the largest group of any organized body of Jews on this continent," to which Olmert responded that Yoffie should stick to religion, since, "if you are in politics, then we are in a different ball game and we can talk in a different way" (*Forward,* Jan. 19).

After Sharon defeated Barak overwhelmingly on February 6, the *New York Times* reported that American Jewish liberals, who were pro-Labor, felt that it was the Palestinians, by rejecting the Barak peace offer and launching the intifada, who had elected Sharon. Rabbi Yoffie told the *Times* reporter that his normally liberal Reform constituents felt "enormous anger" at Yasir Arafat. Yoffie nevertheless announced that the Reform movement would speak out against the new government if Sharon expanded West Bank settlements or did anything else to undermine chances for peace. Commenting on Sharon's belligerent image in the U.S., Malcolm Hoenlein, executive vice president of the Conference of Presidents, said: "There is a lot of demonization of Sharon, particularly in the media. The American Jewish community will work with him."

Ronald Lauder, meanwhile, buoyed by Sharon's victory, indicated that he did not feel bound by the recent Conference of Presidents resolution limiting the public expression of his personal political opinions. Saying that he was encouraged by the new prime minister's pledge not to divide Jerusalem, Lauder asserted that he would not hesitate to criticize Sharon if he went back on that promise.

With a new Israeli government in place, Israel and the organized American Jewish community put into operation a high-powered media campaign to counter Palestinian claims that Israel was a brutal aggressor. The Israeli foreign ministry hired Howard Rubinstein Associates, a major New York public-relations firm, to place Israeli spokespeople on TV news shows and to provide media professionals with material giving Israel's perspective on the news. In a separate project to bolster American Jewish enthusiasm for Israel that had started months before the election, the Conference of Presidents, the American Jewish Committee, the Anti-Defamation League, and other Jewish bodies worked with a team of American consultants and pollsters who conducted focus groups around the country. Some who were privy to the early findings reported widespread apathy among younger American Jews about Israel, and ignorance of some of the basic facts about the Jewish state.

The national Jewish groups also commissioned a survey of the attitudes of American Jews and the broader American public about the Middle East conflict, and the results, released in March, had a calming effect on an anxious pro-Israel community. Asked if their view was closer to that of Israel or that of the Palestinians, 51 percent of the sample of Americans identified with the Israeli position and just 11 percent with the Palestinian (among Jews, the breakdown was 83 to 2). The Palestinians were considered "more at fault" for the situation by 42 percent of the Americans, 14 percent blamed the Israelis, and 30 put the onus on both equally (among Jews, 70 percent blamed the Palestinians, 5 percent the Israelis, and 16 percent both). Yet, media images of the intifada had made an impact: 54 percent of the Americans surveyed (37 percent of the Jews) believed that Israel overreacted in shooting at Palestinian stone-throwers.

It was against the backdrop of these poll numbers that Ariel Sharon arrived in Washington, in mid-March, for his first meeting as prime minister with President Bush and congressional leaders. By all accounts, things went well, Sharon's moderate demeanor and restrained words doing much to belie his hard-line reputation. Sharon also addressed the policy conference of AIPAC (American Israel Public Affairs Committee), the key pro-Israel lobby, along with Secretary of State Colin Powell. Sharon said that Jerusalem would remain united under Israeli sovereignty and that Israel would not "negotiate under the threat of violence," but drew a distinction between terrorists and their supporters, on the one hand, and the bulk of the Palestinian people, on the other, who, he felt, wanted peace. The most controversial words at the AIPAC conference came from Elie Wiesel, who castigated anyone "who uses their Jewishness as a context to attack or condemn Israel." Though Wiesel did not specify whom he had in mind, the audience assumed that he was referring to American Jewish pro-peace groups that publicly criticized Israeli policy in putting down the intifada.

The United Jewish Communities (UJC), the umbrella organization of the local Jewish federations, under criticism for failing to pull off any mass national pro-Israel event since the onset of the intifada the previous September, launched an "Israel Now Initiative" aimed at "repositioning Israel in the hearts and minds of North American Jewry." A closed-door meeting of federation heads in April resulted in a decision to stage rallies in New York City and Los Angeles on June 3, when Prime Minister Sharon was next expected in the U.S. This immediately brought complaints from the people planning the annual New York City Salute to Israel Parade, scheduled for May 20, who feared that the UJC activities just two weeks later would hurt support for the parade. As it turned out, Sharon postponed his visit till the end of June. The UJC plan for rallies was shelved until the fall, and the events of September 11 would turn this into an indefinite postponement.

Frustrated at the cancellation of the rallies and at the vacuum of Jewish leadership that they felt it demonstrated, a number of New York congregations, led by Rabbi Avi Weiss, went ahead with their own pro-Israel rally at the Israeli mission to the UN on June 3. Weiss explained the rationale: "Let's just get people into the street. I just don't think we can wait four months." The rally drew some 10,000 people, and one of the speakers was Rudy Giuliani, the city's mayor.

Another key component of the UJC's Israel solidarity plan, worked out in the spring, was a massive program of visits to Israel by American Jews that would, it was hoped, reenergize the American Jewish-Israeli bond. These trips would build upon the Birthright Israel initiative, launched by a small group of philanthropists in late 1998, that had already provided the "Israel experience" for hundreds of Jewish college students, free of charge (see AJYB 2000, pp. 212–13; 2001, pp. 227–28). Early in the year, federations were gearing up for a large increase in applicants for Birthright Israel, and, in April, Rabbi Sheldon Zimmerman, who had recently resigned as president of Hebrew Union College (HUC), was appointed Birthright Israel's executive vice president.

But an already uneasy security situation in Israel deteriorated rapidly, beginning with the May 18 suicide bombing at a Netanya shopping mall that killed five, and one began to hear, more and more, of American Jews canceling their plans to visit. Then, on June 1, came the atrocity at the Tel Aviv Dophinarium disco, where 21 were killed and some 120 injured. The next day, Rabbi Eric Yoffie announced, in the name of the UAHC, that all of the Reform movement's summer youth trips to Israel for 2001 were canceled. "Our religious and Zionist commitments run deep and are well known to all," Yoffie explained, "but this movement never uses other people's children to make a political or ideological point."

This decision proved controversial. Knesset member Tommy Lapid, whose anticlerical views usually aligned him politically with Reform, compared the cancellation to "a rabbi announcing that the synagogue will be closed for Yom Kippur on account of the High Holidays" (*Forward*, June 15). The Reform movement in Israel expressed deep resentment, fearing that the move would only reinforce the common Israeli stereotype that Reform did not sympathize with Zionism—a perception encouraged as well, Reform Israelis said, by the movement's meager financial support for its congregations in Israel. Charles Bronfman, chairman of the UJC and one of the founders of Birthright Israel, declared: "I would hope that all trips continue! The terrorists must be taught that we are no chicken kind of people." Rabbi Yoffie explained that many youngsters had dropped out of the programs already, and that families of those remaining were insisting on "security provisions that we felt we could not in good conscience provide." He said he was "bewildered by the intensity and vitriol of the response."

The heated controversy over the cancellation of the Reform program drew attention away from significant statements about the Middle East situation that Yoffie enunciated at the same time. Acknowledging that the generally dovish Reform movement had "been wrong about Palestinian intentions," he publicly condemned Yasir Arafat and his followers for supporting terror and encouraging anti-Semitism. At the same time, Yoffie called on Israel to freeze settlement construction in the territories. "Occupation involves acts of degradation and cruelty," Yoffie said, "and Israel's occupation has been no different." Critics questioned why, if Arafat had now proven himself to be an unrepentant terrorist, he should be rewarded with an Israeli settlement freeze.

Also in early June, Rabbi Haskel Lookstein spearheaded a protest movement against the way the *New York Times* reported the news from Israel. Pointing out numerous instances of what he considered anti-Israel and pro-Palestinian bias, Lookstein proposed that "every reader who is fed up" should suspend his or her subscription, and not buy the paper on the newsstand, from Rosh Hashanah through Yom Kippur (New York *Jewish Week,* June 15). Several weeks later, at Lookstein's request, the executive editor of the *Times* met with him about the matter. The editor acknowledged that several of the rabbi's complaints about specific articles were valid, but he attributed inaccuracies in the paper's coverage to simple "mistakes" rather than to bias. Lookstein, for his part, was gratified that "someone is listening" at the *Times,* but said that his ten-day boycott plan was still in effect.

As American Jewish sentiment shifted increasingly rightward with the continuation of Palestinian violence, organized American Jewry experienced some discomfort when the Bush administration did not seem to see things in the same light. To be sure, the Zionist Organization of America was virtually alone within the Jewish community when it called, in July, for cutting off all U.S. aid to the Palestinian Authority until the violence stopped. But in August, AIPAC publicly called on the American government to cease its "even-handed" criticism of both sides, and instead issue a public condemnation of Yasir Arafat.

September 11 only heightened Jewish anxieties. The American administration announced its plan to create an international coalition against terror, a step that was surely, in theory, in Israel's interest. In practice, however, it raised the possibility of pressure on Israel to make diplomatic concessions so as to induce the Palestinians and the Arab nations to join the U.S.-led venture, and from Israel's perspective, these putative partners in antiterrorism were themselves sources of terror. For many American Jewish leaders, another unfortunate aspect of the situation was the need to cancel the long-delayed national pro-Israel demonstration that the UJC had planned for September 23 in New York City. Both security considerations and a reluctance to press Israel's case at a time of America's national mourning made the cancellation unavoidable.

In the weeks after September 11, reports circulated that the administration was going to affirm support for the establishment of a Palestinian state, and on October 2 the president himself confirmed this, stating as a condition that such a state must recognize Israel's right to exist. AIPAC immediately criticized the plan, which, it said, would "reward, rather than punish, those that harbor and support terrorism." Mortimer Zuckerman, the new chairman of the Conference of Presidents, described the policy initiative as "very short-sighted and erroneous," since it would send the message that "if you attack America, you'll get something." However, some 50 other American Jews signed a letter to the president, prepared by the Israel Policy Forum, endorsing his policies against terror and for Middle East peace; among the signatories were several who held prominent positions in the American Jewish community. On October 4, Prime Minister Sharon called on the U.S. not to "appease the Arabs at our expense" and invoked the memory of the appeasement of Hitler in 1938. The administration immediately termed his remarks "unacceptable," and Sharon withdrew the comparison.

On October 30, Edgar Bronfman, president of the World Jewish Congress, attracted headlines with a speech in Jerusalem calling on Israel to "put the moral high ground back where it belongs." It could do so, he felt, by stopping military operations against the Palestinians and simply drawing a line of separation between Israel and the Palestinian areas, even if that meant dismantling settlements.

Several public-opinion polls conducted toward the end of the year—*Newsweek,* Harris, Gallup, and Zogby International—indicated that, whatever its geopolitical ramifications, the events of September 11 had increased pro-Israel feeling in the U.S. and depressed even further the already negative opinion that Americans had of the Palestinians. And before the year ended, the administration too moved toward a more unambiguously pro-Israel stance. On December 13, two days after Israel severed all contact with Yasir Arafat, President Bush told a delegation of top Jewish leaders—invited to the White House to celebrate Hanukkah—that Arafat was to blame for the violence.

Throughout the year, however, the Jewish community was haunted by the sense that it was losing the battle in one crucial arena—the college campus. Reports from many parts of the country indicated that Palestinian and other Arab/Muslim students were knowledgeable about Middle East issues, committed to their cause, and well organized. In contrast, despite efforts by Hillel and other Jewish organizations to mobilize pro-Israel sentiment, many Jewish students appeared to be ignorant and apathetic, and some even espoused the Palestinian viewpoint. To some extent, this was one part of a much larger problem: the erosion of distinctive Jewish identity.

Keeping Jews Jewish

The widespread perception that many young Jews did not feel very Jewish had been agitating the community for some time, and research findings released in the fall seemed to justify a sense of foreboding. "Jews Turning from Judaism" was the somewhat sensational headline in the New York *Jewish Week* (Nov. 2), reporting on the American Jewish Identity Survey, the work of sociologists Egon Mayer, Barry Kosmin, and Ariella Keysar. They found that the number of Jews who identified with a religion other than Judaism had more than doubled in one decade: while 625,000 individuals who were of Jewish parentage or ethnicity espoused other religions in 1990, the number was now 1.4 million. Furthermore, another 1.4 million said they were secular or had no religion. Comparison with members of other religions yielded additional startling information: only 15 percent of American adults described themselves as secular, but 72 percent of people of Jewish background did, including 42 percent of those who said they were Jewish by religion.

It was surely serendipitous that, soon after release of the study, Dennis Ross, the Clinton administration's Middle East envoy, was appointed to head a new campaign to strengthen Jewish identity worldwide, sponsored by the Jewish Agency for Israel. In the U.S., while the numbers cited by the three sociologists were new, the problem was not, and several strategies were already in place aimed at promoting Judaism.

One approach was liturgical innovation aimed at young adults. At Sinai Temple, a Conservative congregation in Los Angeles, for example, Rabbi David Wolpe's monthly "Friday Night Live" drew 2,000 Jews, most of them unmarried, by providing an abbreviated prayer service, guitar and keyboard music that "inspires clapping and cheering," and a "spiritually uplifting" speech by the rabbi (*Forward,* Jan. 19). In communities where the local rabbi was not as forthcoming, young adults often broke away from the established synagogue to form their own informal prayer groups, opting for an eclectic mélange of practices associated with different denominations that, they felt, enhanced spirituality.

Some Jews seemed to resonate to Buddhist-style meditation in Jewish guise—minutes of silent contemplation followed by the utterance of words from the Hebrew prayers. "Meditation," reported the New York *Jewish Week* (Feb. 2), "is rapidly moving from the margins of Jewish life into the heart of the mainstream." Such practices were proliferating in congregations and at schools, Jewish community centers, retreats, and private gatherings, often under the influence of the Jewish Renewal movement. Proponents noted that now, unlike the situation in years past, Jews of a meditative bent did not have to face an either/or choice between synagogue and ashram, but could practice a truly Jewish form of mysticism.

Beyond the sphere of Jewish worship, innovative Jewish voices sought to prove to young Jews that Jewishness was relevant to their secular lives. The leading exponent of this approach was Rabbi Irwin Kula, president of the National Jewish Center for Learning and Leadership (CLAL). Building on research that showed that "being Jewish" was important to most American Jews even as Judaism was becoming less important in their daily lives, Kula convened a two-day conference in mid-January for some 50 leading figures in science, business, culture, and religion. The aim was to find ways—"markers" was Kula's term—to make unaffiliated Jews "understand that many of their most basic acts are informed by their Jewish heritage." The search for such markers, he noted, should be done with a "non-judgmental attitude" (*Forward,* Feb. 16).

A good example of finding Jewish meaning in a secular calling was provided by Shawn Green, the slugging outfielder and cleanup hitter for the Los Angeles Dodgers. Green announced that he would not play on September 26, Yom Kippur eve, even though his team was locked in a close pennant race. Green was doing this, he said, "partly as a representative of the Jewish community, and as far as my being a role model in sports for Jewish kids." His manager, a Catholic, had no complaints, saying, "This is about family and religion, and I'm not one to stand in the way of that" (*New York Times,* Sept. 9).

Whether a Jewish marker could be found in every endeavor was put to the test by the November issue of *Playboy.* "Miss November" was a 20-year-old Jewish woman, Lindsey Vuolo; the magazine printed pictures taken at her bat mitzvah, along with more recent and more revealing photos. Makor, the popular singles mecca on Manhattan's Upper West Side, hosted a dialogue on December 19 between Vuolo and Rabbi Shmuel Boteach. The rabbi, whose book, *Kosher Sex,* had been excerpted in an earlier issue of *Playboy,* argued that posing nude was against Jewish values. However, another rabbi, Bradley Hirschfeld, vice president of CLAL, felt that posing for *Playboy* could be interpreted as a positive Jewish marker. He told the popular Internet site beliefnet.com that "a beautiful Jewish body that's actually being fantasized over by millions of men" was "a real step forward" for American Jews.

The seemingly inexorable proliferation of Jewish-Gentile marriage and the growing acceptance of its inevitability continued in 2001, but not without one energetic attempt to buck the trend.

The high level of acceptability that intermarriage had achieved among American Jews—about half believing that opposition to such marriages was racist—had been amply documented in the American Jewish Committee's Annual Survey of American Jewish Opinion 2000 (see AJYB 2001, pp. 226–27). The American Jewish Identity Survey, using the same methodology employed by the 1990 National Jewish Population Survey, found an over-50-percent intermarriage rate for American Jews over the 1990–2001 period. It also showed that the proportion of Jews married to non-Jews had risen from 28 percent to 37 percent over that time, and that 80 percent of single Jews living with someone had a non-Jewish partner.

The number of books published in 2001 on the subject of mixed-married families was another way to gauge the extent of the phenomenon and also the degree of fascination with it. There were, to begin with, *The Half-Jewish Book: A Celebration, Suddenly Jewish: Jews Raised as Gentiles Discover their Jewish Roots,* and *The Interfaith Family Guidebook: Practical Advice for Jewish and Christian Partners.* For readers of an academic bent, there was *Common Prayers: Faith, Family, and a Christian's Journey Through the Jewish Year,* in which the eminent Harvard theologian Harvey Cox described what it was like to be married to a Jewish woman, raise a Jewish son, and celebrate Jewish holidays, even while remaining a Christian. Perhaps the most surprising publication on the topic was *Building the Faith: A Book of Inclusion for Dual-Faith Families,* a pamphlet put out by the Federation of Jewish Men's Clubs—an arm of the Conservative movement, which itself maintained strict policies against intermarriage.

Yet another straw in the wind was the palpable relaxation of the old Jewish tension over the "December Dilemma." Whereas Jews had historically felt great discomfort about public manifestations of Christmas in America society since they made Jews feel less than fully American, the perceived secularization of the holiday, along with the growing number of Jewish-Christian households, had minimized the problem. Even Jewish children celebrating Christmas in such homes, one researcher told the *Forward* (Dec. 21), "don't see it as a dilution of their Judaism . . . but see it as obeying the commandment to honor one's parents."

An attempt at a counter-movement began on February 20, when a coalition of some 25 rabbis, communal leaders, and academicians convened at the headquarters of the American Jewish Committee. The group issued a statement reasserting the traditional norm that Jews should marry Jews, pledged to work to "shape the communal climate" in line with that standard, and advocated conversion efforts when intermarriage did take place. Predictably, the new coalition drew expressions of scorn from some who viewed intermarriage as unstoppable and who believed that talk of conversion alienated the non-Jewish partner. Sociologist Egon Mayer, founding director of the Jewish Outreach Institute, called the initiative "ludicrous" and "comical." Edmund Case, who ran an Internet site for mixed-religion families, complained that implying that intermarriage is bad "will only exacerbate the rejecting experience and feeling of lack of welcome that many interfaith families identify as obstacles to their Jewish affiliation."

The debate soon precipitated a battle of research findings. Much of the intellectual force behind the efforts of the anti-intermarriage coalition came from the conclusions contained in *Jewish and Something Else,* a report prepared for the American Jewish Committee by Prof. Sylvia Barack Fishman of Brandeis University. Based on quantitative data and extensive work with focus groups, Fishman found that parental expectations for their children to marry Jews often did have the desired effect, suggesting that intermarriage was hardly inevitable. Also, Fishman discovered that it was very rare for children in mixed-religion households—even where they were nominally being raised as Jews—to have an unambiguous Jewish identification.

Edmund Case countered that Fishman, a member of the nascent anti-intermarriage coalition, had allowed her bias against mixed-religion families to distort her findings, a charge that she vehemently denied. The Jewish Outreach Institute, which operated on the premise that widespread intermarriage was inevitable and that the Jewish community could only accommodate itself to the phenomenon, published its own study of the attitudes of the intermarried. It indicated that programs of outreach to them were often successful in increasing Jewish awareness and participation. The questionnaire did not ask about attitudes toward conversion of the non-Jewish partner.

9/11 and American Jewry

The terrorist acts of September 11—two hijacked planes flown into the World Trade Center in New York, another into the Pentagon in Washington, and a fourth crashing in Pennsylvania—killed more than 3,000 people. These surprise attacks traumatized all Americans, but the impact on Jews had two unique aspects. First, Osama bin Laden's Muslim terrorists represented the same ideology that lay behind the Palestinian intifada that had killed hundreds of Israelis over the previous year. And second, Jews were not randomly distributed across the U.S. An overwhelmingly urban people, almost 1.5 million of them—some 32 percent of all American Jews—lived in the New York area, the prime target of the atrocity. Indeed, one of the first ambulances to reach the site of the Twin Towers was from Hatzolah (Hebrew for "rescue"), the Orthodox emergency medical service.

In the immediate aftermath, synagogues held special prayer services and Jewish schools struggled to address their students' sudden feelings of vulnerability. Rabbis and therapists spoke of having to counsel Holocaust survivors who suffered from flashbacks of that earlier exercise in inhumanity. As the High Holidays approached, the rabbis strove to strike the appropriate note in their sermons, and synagogues and other Jewish institutions worked feverishly to beef up security, fearing further attacks, this time aimed specifically at Jews. Simhat Torah, the holiday marking the annual completion of the reading of the entire Torah, celebrated in many Jewish neighborhoods with dancing in the streets, came out this year on October 9–10; the dancing was moved indoors due to safety concerns. Meanwhile, families of Jews who were missing lived in Jewish limbo, unable to sit shivah (the traditional seven-day mourning period) and come to terms with their loss until proof of death was forthcoming (Orthodox rabbis approved the use of DNA evidence). At a November 5 conference for rabbis held at Yeshiva University in New York, Rabbi Tzvi Weinreb, the incoming president of the Union of Orthodox Jewish Congregations (OU) and a professional psychologist, pointed out that conventional forms of therapy were insufficient in this case. He advised his colleagues to help people "recognize there is evil in the world. Real evil" (*New York Times,* Nov. 18).

The Jewish community also experienced a significant upsurge in open manifestations of American patriotism, as the stark recognition of Islamic terrorism as the common enemy brought to consciousness the previously taken-for-granted affinity between Jewishness and Americanism. Significantly, there were no attempts to tally up the number of Jewish victims as a separate and distinct category. In November, the American Jewish Committee issued a "Thanksgiving Haggadah" that melded Jewish tradition with the quintessential American holiday; it included the question, "Why is this Thanksgiving different from all others?" American patriotism was notable even in ultra-Orthodox neighborhoods of New York, places where Jews had sought to keep apart from American cultural influences, doing without TV and reading no secular literature. Now, hundreds of American flags could be seen affixed to the houses and stores of these Jews, just as in other parts of the city.

Jewish philanthropy was deeply affected by September 11. A number of national and New York Jewish organizations immediately established special funds to help the victims and their families, and a month after the attacks an estimated $4 million had been collected. But this created complications for the regular fund-raising campaigns of these groups. UJA-Federation of New York sought to surmount the problem through a fund that would help all victims of terror, and thus support programs in Israel as well as cover 9/11 aid, though this did not sit well with some donors. Another difficulty confronting the charities that used mass mailings was that many people refused to open letters from addresses they did not recognize, for fear of anthrax infection. There was also considerable controversy over whether it was ethical for Jewish fund-raising appeals to exploit fears of terrorist attacks.

Denominational Life

Strife and Cooperation

A period of several years of public civility between Orthodox and non-Orthodox American Jews was broken with the publication of the February issue of *Moment* magazine. In it, Rabbi Avi Shafran, director of public affairs for the Orthodox organization Agudath Israel of America, had a message for "sincere and dedicated Conservative Jews"—"Their movement is a failure." While careful to acknowledge that Orthodoxy too had its faults, Shafran pointed to changes within Conservative Judaism—he specifically mentioned the ordination of women and the growing acceptance of homosexuality—that, he felt, effectively detached the movement from Halakhah, the Jewish legal tradition. Conservative Judaism, therefore, could no longer fulfill its original aim, "to inspire Jews to Jewish observance." Shafran claimed that that was why only 29 percent of Conservative Jews bought kosher meat, just 15 percent considered themselves Sabbath observers, and, according to data collected by the Conservative movement, a majority of its youth saw nothing wrong with marriage to a non-Jew.

Conservative leaders were outraged, especially since Shafran himself had often taken issue with critiques of his own brand of Judaism and called them "Orthodox-bashing." The major Conservative organizations issued a joint statement describing Shafran's article as "shameful" and his viewpoint that of "fundamentalists." Not challenging Shafran's data on halakhic laxity and instead attributing the movement's difficulties with Jewish law to "an honest struggle," the Conservative statement pointed to other areas of Jewish life where the movement could claim greater success: "synagogue affiliation, communal involvement, Jewish study, and social action." Shafran also received criticism of a tactical nature from within his own right-wing Orthodox constituency: many complained that while the positive exposure of non-Orthodox Jews to Jewish observance could win Orthodoxy many new adherents, attacks like that of Shafran on non-Orthodox movements only generated animosity. For his part, Shafran expressed just one regret about the article—that he had allowed the editors of *Moment* to change his suggested title, "Time to Come Home," to the far more incendiary "The Conservative Lie."

The tables were turned in the fall, when Orthodoxy complained that it was being maligned. In the days following September 11, with registration under way for elections to the 2002 World Zionist Congress (WZC), Rabbi Uri Regev, a prominent leader of Reform Judaism in Israel, addressed the Anshe Chesed Fairmount Temple in Cleveland. According to a report in the Cleveland *Jewish News* (Oct. 12), he urged his audience to register with Arza, the World Union of Reform Judaism, for the WZC elections, and thus strengthen religious pluralism in the Jewish state and break the Orthodox monopoly. The reporter described Regev as drawing "a chilling parallel between Islamic and Israeli religious extremists." He said, "if we don't learn from the September 11 loss of human lives, we haven't learned anything." Orthodox leaders vehemently rejected the implied comparison of Muslim fundamentalism to Orthodox Judaism. Avi Shafran, for one, argued that, unlike the Islamic haters, Orthodox Jews "love all Jews." Regev responded that he had not suggested any equivalence between Muslim and Jewish fundamentalism, but only noted the dangers of incendiary rhetoric within any religion. The reporter who wrote the story admitted that she had embellished her account of Regev's remarks, but this did not mollify his outraged critics.

Despite the doctrinal and political barriers that still evidently divided Orthodox from non-Orthodox, an interdenominational forum on Jewish law entitled "The Contemporary Study of Halakhah: Methods and Meaning," held to mark the 125th anniversary of Hebrew Union College (HUC), the Reform seminary, took place peacefully in New York on March 18–20. At the forum, Orthodox rabbis from Yeshiva University appeared on scholarly panels together with their Conservative and Reform counterparts. While the sectarian Orthodox of Agudath Israel did not participate, their spokesman, the same Avi Shafran, said he was encouraged "to read that the Reform movement recognizes Halakhah and its study as vital to the perpetuation of Jewish life."

One specific interdenominational clash of a local nature—sports competition between Jewish high schools in the New York metropolitan area—reached a resolution of sorts. Concerned that allowing non-Orthodox schools into the existing Orthodox yeshivah league might lend legitimacy to their interpretations of Judaism, a majority of yeshivah principals voted, on February 5, to bar the three Solomon Schechter high schools—affiliated with the Conservative movement—from participation. In May, however, stung by the negative publicity their ban had evoked, the principals reversed themselves and welcomed the Schechter schools on condition that there would be no cheerleaders and that "female athletes wear pants that extend below the knees and T-shirts as opposed to tank-tops" (*Forward,* May 25). Furthermore, in league meetings the Conservative schools would not have a vote on any matters of a religious nature.

Orthodox Judaism

It was clear, in 2001, that for all of its attempts to achieve isolation from cultural trends it considered destructive, American Orthodoxy could not completely escape them.

Women's issues received considerable attention. At the beginning of the year, the OU and the Rabbinical Council of America (RCA)—respectively the primary lay and rabbinic Modern Orthodox bodies—announced approval of new guidelines to streamline and standardize rabbinical court procedure in handling Jewish divorces. The aim was to make it more difficult for men—who, under Jewish law, had the power to withhold such divorces, preventing their former wives from remarrying—to use extortion and blackmail in such cases.

In May, Sharona Margolin Halickman, 27, was appointed "spiritual mentor" at the Hebrew Institute of Riverdale, an Orthodox synagogue in New York City. While not functioning officially as a rabbi, Halickman, who had been one of the two first Orthodox female "congregational interns" (see AJYB 2001, p. 240), would be teaching, counseling, and delivering sermons. This was believed to be the highest-level synagogue position ever attained by a woman in Orthodox Judaism.

Another barrier to women's participation in Orthodox life was shattered in the fall, when Rabbi David Silber, dean of the Drisha Institute, a school of advanced Jewish studies for women in New York City, had women lead certain parts of the prayers and be called up to the Torah at the Orthodox High Holy Day services that the school sponsored. Although there were rabbis who felt that Jewish law theoretically sanctioned such practices, they had never before been implemented by the Orthodox in the U.S.

In May, two separate conferences for Jewish women took place in New York City, each drawing several hundred participants. The meeting of the Jewish Orthodox Feminist Alliance (JOFA) focused on how Jewish feminist mothers could help their daughters negotiate gender issues in Judaism. Meanwhile, a group of more traditional Orthodox women who did not consider themselves feminists—brought together by the Jewish Renaissance Center—discussed the tensions between running an observant home and the pressures of the workplace. This concern was a clear indication that American socioeconomic trends were affecting even the most insular bastions of Orthodoxy, as the *New York Times* noted earlier in the year (Jan. 4) in an article headlined, "Working World Grows for Orthodox Women: New Field and Strict Judaism Coexist."

Another sign that Orthodox Jews were not immune from societal trends was the large and growing phenomenon of unmarried Orthodox adults. A daylong conference on the subject held in Queens, New York, on November 18 drew an overflow crowd of singles and their worried parents to discuss what was, from the standpoint of Jewish tradition if not from the perspective of contemporary American mores, a "problem." Rabbi Yoel Schonfeld, the host of the conference, declared: "The singles situation has reached crisis proportions. Young women and men are just not getting married at the rates they should be."

Even the longstanding traditional taboo on homosexuality, rooted in the Bible, came under question. In October, a new film, *Trembling Before God,* opened in New York City. It depicted the lives of gay and lesbian Orthodox Jews, sensitively portraying their guilt and anguish about violating a cardinal principle of Jewish law while also showing their abiding commitment to live traditional Jewish lives and be part of the Orthodox community. Several local Orthodox rabbis were so moved by the film that they arranged for screenings at their synagogues, followed by discussions. Not all sectors of Orthodoxy, however, were prepared to reassess traditional views about homosexuality. In March, the National Council of Young Israel, an important network of Orthodox synagogues, honored "Dr. Laura" Schlesinger, a convert to Judaism and a politically conservative media personality, despite protests from many who were appalled by her public description of homosexuality as "deviant" and a "biological error."

The phenomenon of young Orthodox "dropouts," teenage boys and girls who stopped attending school and became involved in petty crimes and drug use (see AJYB 2000, p. 224), was getting more attention. The winter issue of *Viewpoint,* the organ of the National Council of Young Israel, featured a "Family and Teen Resource Guide" for help with a host of problems—"behavioral and learning disorders, anorexia, bulimia, kids thrown out of yeshivahs, kids using drugs, abusing alcohol, teens disaffected from their religious upbringing, kids on the street." The editor noted, "one can hardly pick up a Jewish publication without reading a myriad of articles on the topic." The *Forward* (Aug. 17) reported that in the previous 18 months "at least a dozen new drug and crime prevention programs were launched for Orthodox teens in the New York City area alone." The *Jewish Sentinel,* a New York newspaper, devoted a cover story (Mar. 23–29) to "Dope Yomi: Drug Abuse Rises among Orthodox Teens"—a play on *daf yomi,* the "daily page" of Talmud study.

The second biennial conference of Edah, the movement seeking to revitalize Modern Orthodoxy, took place February 18–19 in New York City, with some 1,200 in attendance. The theme was "The Quest for Holiness." In contrast to the tensions surrounding the first conference in 1999, which came under heavy fire from more insular sectors of the Orthodox community (see AJYB 2000, pp. 225–26), this year's conference drew little notice outside its own constituency. Edah now boasted its own Web site and scholarly journal, and two of its leaders, Rabbis Saul Berman and Avi Weiss, had founded a new Modern Orthodox rabbinical school, Chovevei Torah, that drew students from both Yeshiva University and the Conservative movement's Jewish Theological Seminary.

In March, Dr. Norman Lamm, 73, announced that he was stepping down as president of Yeshiva University, the flagship educational institution of Modern Orthodoxy, after 25 years. "I didn't want to be carried out feet first," he told the *New York Times* (Mar. 14). Taking over an institution that was on the verge of bankruptcy in 1976, Lamm had transformed Yeshiva into a thriving university with a large and constantly growing student body. He set his retirement for August 2002, giving the university more than a year to search for a successor. Almost immediately, however, observers warned that the serious erosion of Modern Orthodoxy in recent years might make it difficult to locate qualified candidates who were both erudite Talmudists and seasoned academicians, and that administrative responsibilities might have to be divided. Lamm, aware of the problem, gave a public address in November in which he cautioned against splitting the leadership of the institution in two, one rabbinic and the other academic.

At the start of 2001, the OU was still reeling from the findings of a special commission that investigated charges of physical and emotional abuse allegedly committed over the course of three decades by Rabbi Baruch Lanner, a long-time outreach worker for its National Conference of Synagogue Youth (NCSY). The commission substantiated many of the allegations and also found that other people associated with NCSY and OU had known about the abuse and ignored it. The overall findings were contained in a 54-page document that was made public in December 2000, while a longer, 331-page report that went into considerable detail was seen only by top OU officers (see AJYB 2001, p. 241).

On January 19, 2001, Rabbi Raphael Butler resigned as executive vice president of the OU. Before assuming that post Butler had headed NCSY from 1981 to 1989, and had thus been Lanner's long-time supervisor. Butler explained his resignation as an attempt "to prevent the divisiveness and rancor that threaten the mission of the OU." Sources close to the situation indicated that pressure from the RCA, the rabbinic body closely aligned with the OU, induced Butler to leave. In September, Rabbi Tzvi Weinreb, a pulpit rabbi and psychotherapist from Baltimore, was named to replace him. Meanwhile, a grand jury in Monmouth County, New Jersey, handed down a criminal indictment against Rabbi Lanner for alleged abuse committed while he was principal of a day school there.

On June 16–17, thousands visited the grave, in Queens, New York, of Rabbi Menachem Schneerson, the late rebbe of the Chabad-Lubavitch Hassidim, to mark the seventh anniversary of his death. Despite the continuing lack of any successor to the childless rebbe, the movement was accelerating its outreach work; it claimed a 40-percent increase in the number of Chabad institutions worldwide since their leader's passing.

In Orthodox circles outside Lubavitch there was mounting alarm over reports that many in the sect viewed the late rebbe as the messiah who would soon be resurrected, and that some even identified him as God. Nevertheless, there was considerable reluctance about raising the issue in public. The first to overcome this inhibition had been David Berger, a rabbi and Jewish historian at Brooklyn College, who convinced the RCA to issue a denunciation of such messianism in 1996 (see AJYB 1997, p. 198). In 2001, Berger published a book, *The Rebbe, the Messiah, and the Scandal of Orthodox Indifference,* that set out the evidence that great numbers of Lubavitchers were messianists; pointed out the allegedly heretical implications of such a view; denounced the passivity of mainstream Orthodoxy about the situation; noted the use that Christian proselytizers were already making of the doctrine of a resurrected messiah; and urged practical steps to isolate the messianists from the Jewish community. Berger's book drew criticism, however, from defenders of Lubavitch—some charging that he had wildly exaggerated the number of messianists in the movement, others citing Jewish sources that, they argued, spoke of a messiah who would indeed rise from the dead.

Conservative Judaism

In his annual spring "state-of-the movement" address, delivered in Jacksonville, Florida, Chancellor Ismar Schorsch of the Jewish Theological Seminary claimed that Conservative Judaism was largely responsible for the renaissance of Jewish education in America. He stressed the large number of Conservative-led day schools on the elementary and secondary levels—both those officially affiliated with the movement and "community" institutions largely supported and attended by Conservative Jews—adult-education programs, and early-childhood education.

Early in the year, the Ratner Center for the Study of Conservative Judaism published *Four Up,* the findings of a study it commissioned on Jewish high-school students whose parents were affiliated with Conservative congregations. A unique feature of the report was that it was longitudinal, following the paths of the same young people whose Jewish identity had been studied in 1995, at bar/bat mitzvah age. Only half of the respondents had continued their Jewish education in their high-school years, and, overall, the teenagers were less observant and attended synagogue less regularly than when previously surveyed. Nevertheless, an impressive 43 percent said they hoped to become more observant in the future. Those teenagers who attended day school, Hebrew high school or Jewish summer camp, and those belonging to Jewish youth movements, tended to view being Jewish as more important to their lives than those without such involvements.

In late January, Conservative women rabbis—there were over 120 of them—held their first group meeting since 1994. It was closed to outsiders and the press. According to accounts given by some participants afterwards, the rabbis discussed such matters of mutual concern as their sense of isolation in the rabbinate and remnants of opposition to egalitarianism in the movement. The latter included their perception that they were paid less than their male colleagues and that congregations were reluctant to grant maternity leave, and the movement's refusal, on grounds of Jewish law, to grant women rabbis the authority to sign and witness Jewish legal documents, such as divorce decrees.

A major breakthrough for Conservative women occurred in February, when Judy Yudoff, of St. Paul, Minnesota, was elected president of the United Synagogue of Conservative Judaism, the movement's lay body. Yudoff thus became the first woman, volunteer or professional, to head either the lay or rabbinic arm of Conservative Judaism.

In late summer, the Conservative movement found itself in a nasty wrangle over Israeli policy toward the Palestinians. More than 30 Conservative rabbis in Israel, including some top leaders of Masorti Judaism (the Israeli Conservative movement), belonged to Rabbis for Human Rights, a dovish interdenominational group that publicized what it viewed as human-rights violations of the Israeli government. Ten other Masorti rabbis in Israel, led by Rabbi Avraham Feder, publicly called on them to sever that affiliation, arguing that the human-rights body was "bringing comfort and aid to the enemy" and "betraying and undercutting Israel's harsh and terrible struggle."

A new Bible commentary, *Etz Hayim*—the first to be officially commissioned by the Conservative movement and the first to embody its ideology—was published in the fall, and Conservative synagogues across the country ordered thousands of copies. The volume contained three sections, each edited by noted scholars and writers: an exposition of the literal meaning; a compendium of moral insights on the text drawn from the Talmud, midrash, and later commentators; and an explanation of how contemporary Conservative authorities have applied the Bible to current issues. Other features of *Etz Hayim* were a modern English translation, a heavy feminist influence, and acceptance of the findings of academic scholarship on the Bible. *Etz Hayim* drew criticism on two fronts. The Orthodox, predictably, cited its use of biblical criticism as proof that Conservative Judaism had severed all ties to tradition. At the same time, some non-Orthodox readers with a spiritual bent, complaining of scholarly overkill, doubted that a volume so academic would deepen the Jewish lives of many rank-and-file Conservative Jews.

Reform Judaism

Reform Judaism filled two top leadership positions in 2001: Rabbi David Ellenson was named president of Hebrew Union College (HUC), the movement's seminary and graduate school, and Rabbi Uri Regev became executive director of the World Union for Progressive Judaism (WUPJ), the global network of Reform synagogues based in Jerusalem. Ellenson, a long-time professor at HUC and an expert in the history of Jewish law and theology, had been raised as a traditional Jew and had close ties with leaders of the other movements, leading many observers to predict that his appointment would improve interdenominational relations. Regev, in contrast, who was appointed to head the WUPJ in December, had not long before been quoted in the press as comparing the fundamentalism of the Israeli Orthodox establishment to that of the Muslim perpetrators of September 11, though he claimed that his comments had been misinterpreted (see above, p. 234). The *Forward* reported (Dec. 7) that "Rabbi Regev is likely to continue to find himself in the middle of the pluralism tug of war between Reform and Orthodox."

In 2001, Reform became the first Jewish religious movement to implement a strategy to deal with Jewish population mobility. With an estimated 10,000 Reform Jews moving to new locations each year and clear evidence of very low Jewish affiliation rates for those who are new to a community, the movement's new "Synagogue Match" program provided a Web site for anyone to enter a new address and other personal information, and receive a list of three Reform synagogues within 25 miles of his or her new home. In addition, the three synagogues would be notified about that individual.

In 2000, the Reform movement had officially endorsed rabbinic officiation at same-sex unions (see AJYB 2001, pp. 236–37). Consistent with this position as well as with its overall posture of support for gay rights, on January 5, 2001, the Joint Commission on Social Action of Reform Judaism responded to a Supreme Court ruling allowing the Boy Scouts of America to exclude gays by urging synagogues to stop sponsoring Boy Scout troops, and calling on individual Reform Jews to remove their children from the Boy Scouts. Several Reform rabbis, including Rabbi Paul Menitoff, executive vice president of the movement's Central Conference of American Rabbis (CCAR) had already turned in their Eagle Scout badges in protest.

Reform's leading role in championing the equality of homosexuals was underlined as well by the publication of *Lesbian Rabbis: The First Generation,* a collection of reminiscences by 18 of these rabbis, the great majority of them Reform. The book made clear that the proportion of lesbians within the female rabbinate was markedly higher than within the general female population. Rabbi Eric Yoffie, president of the UAHC, commented, "the publication of the book per se is not dramatic news. . . . The fundamental issue here was a decision of our movement many years ago to work to achieve acceptance of gay and lesbian Jews in our midst."

Considerably more controversial was a decision by the Reform Rodeph Sholom elementary day school in New York City to cancel Mother's Day programs because the activities might harm the "emotional well-being" of students who were part of "different family make-ups." The *New York Post* cover story was "School Kills Mother's Day," and, on the "Tonight Show," host Jay Leno ridiculed the decision. Rabbi Robert Levine of Rodeph Sholom explained the school's policy: "children who, for whatever reason, have no mother should not have to sit in class while cards are being made for the mothers of others."

The interest in Jewish ritual that had been growing within Reform found expression in new voluntary guidelines for conversion, developed over the previous four years, which were overwhelmingly approved at the CCAR convention in June. Rabbis were urged to recommend to candidates the traditional elements of conversion that Reform had discarded in the 19th century—circumcision for men (drawing a symbolic drop of blood for those already circumcised), examination of the convert by a three-rabbi panel, and ritual immersion in a *mikveh.* The CCAR also recommended that rabbis have prospective converts pledge to join a synagogue, maintain a Jewish home, and raise future children as Jews.

At the same time, the CCAR's Responsa Committee, which issued Jewish legal opinions for the movement on an advisory basis, decided that intermarried Jews might serve as teachers in Reform Hebrew schools. This conflicted with the view of the Conservative movement, which barred the practice. While the Conservatives did not want their children coming into contact with religious role models who did not embody the traditional Jewish commitment to endogamy, the Reform committee, acknowledging a shortage of qualified educators, declared that a teacher's "Jewish depth and family life" was more important than the religious identification of his or her spouse. "Mixed marriages," it stated, "*may* be evidence that an individual is not the sort of Jew we want as a religious-school teacher, and then again it may not. Each case must be judged on its own merits."

Organizations and Institutions

Conference of Presidents

The choice of a new chairman for the Conference of Presidents—the most visible American Jewish umbrella body—was heavily influence by the controversy at the beginning of the year over the personal involvement of the outgoing chairman, Ronald Lauder, in Israeli politics (see above, pp. 221–22). The more dovish constituent organizations of the conference did not want to choose another Likud sympathizer who might circumvent the new rules restricting the chairman's freedom of political expression and make statements that went beyond the conference consensus. The leading contender, Mortimer Zuckerman, honorary president of the America-Israel Friendship League, was suspect on this score since, as publisher of the *New York Daily News* and *U.S. News & World Report,* he had never been shy about expressing his personal opinions on the Middle East, and they seemed very close to the position of the current right-of-center Israeli government. Another problem that had been raised about a Zuckerman chairmanship in earlier years—his wife was not Jewish—had apparently been solved by the breakup of the marriage.

On April 19, the conference's seven-member nominating committee approved Zuckerman (six voted for him, the seventh abstained). The four Reform groups that belonged to the 54-member conference announced their opposition on the grounds that Zuckerman said he would not stop writing editorials in his own name. On May 4, the Reform faction circulated a letter to the other member organizations detailing its objections, but on May 23, the full conference elected Zuckerman with only six votes against him—and those six then blocked a motion to make the choice unanimous. Rabbi Eric Yoffie, the UAHC president and Zuckerman's most vocal critic, said that he would be monitoring the new chairman's statements carefully.

United Jewish Communities

The two-year-old United Jewish Communities (UJC), product of a merger between the Council of Jewish Federations, the United Jewish Appeal, and the United Israel Appeal, still seemed plagued by a lack of focus and low morale. Charles Bronfman, stepping down as founding chairman in November, urged the UJC to bring younger people into leadership positions, work more closely with private family foundations, and adopt a democratic system of decision-making without worrying about alienating big givers. The new chairman was James Tisch, previously the president of New York UJA-Federation. Tisch was president and CEO of Loews Corporation, which owned the Lorillard Tobacco Company, and he was chosen over the objections of anti-smoking activists. Replacing Stephen Solender as UJC president and CEO in June was Stephen Hoffman, who had been president of the Jewish Community Federation of Cleveland.

Holocaust Museum

Controversy had long plagued the U.S. Holocaust Memorial Museum in Washington, D.C., as ideological battles raged over how "Jewish" the federally sponsored museum should be, and personality conflicts led to turf wars (see AJYB 1999, pp. 195–96; 2000, pp. 217–18). Now, with the incoming Bush administration noncommittal about whether it would renominate Rabbi Irving Greenberg—a Clinton appointee—as museum chairman, the sparks began flying again. Journalist Ira Stoll, in a *Wall Street Journal* op-ed (Dec. 29, 2000), cited statements Greenberg had made in an address to the General Assembly of the United Jewish Communities the previous November that seemed to suggest that some Israeli soldiers may not always have acted with proper restraint in responding to the new Palestinian intifada. Greenberg's exact words were: "it is entirely possible in my judgment that they overreacted, and in that overreaction killed people unnecessarily." Greenberg believed that this constituted "a serious violation of the Jewish ethic of power."

In Stoll's eyes, such an assertion marked Greenberg as a leftist critic of Israel, and Morton Klein, president of the Zionist Organization of America (ZOA), immediately called on Greenberg for a retraction. Greenberg, for his part, said that his talk to the General Assembly had been a ringing endorsement of Israeli policy and that Stoll had taken one phrase out of context. Greenberg called the charge against him "the equivalent of a forgery, a complete misrepresentation of what I said." And Greenberg believed there was more to the story, telling the New York *Jewish Week* (Jan. 12): "The people who have been attacking the museum needed a new angle. Pinning this image as a left-wing anti-Zionist on me would be the capstone of their indictment against the museum."

Given Greenberg's long record of support for Israel, this tempest would have subsided quickly had a new and even more embarrassing charge not surfaced in February: Greenberg was one of the prominent Jews who had written to President Clinton requesting a pardon for fugitive financier Marc Rich, a pardon granted on January 20, Clinton's last day in office. Worse, Greenberg's letter, dated December 11, 2000, had been on museum stationery. Greenberg explained that he believed that Rich deserved the pardon because of his extensive philanthropic works, but acknowledged that it had been a mistake to use museum stationery for correspondence unrelated to the museum, and he apologized.

The controversy simmered, with Greenberg's critics adding the pardon to the earlier remarks about Israel to suggest a pattern of politicizing the museum, and Greenberg's supporters arguing that the most the man was guilty of was naïveté. Rumors flew that all the old, unresolved conflicts over the museum were fueling the fight: Greenberg had detractors who perceived him as an ineffective manager and as having a too parochially "Jewish" vision for the museum. In early April, a letter was hand-delivered to Greenberg at a Detroit airport. Signed by 17 current and former members of the museum's council, it charged that Greenberg's letter in support of Rich had caused serious damage to the museum, and that only his resignation could put matters right. In a counter-letter, 35 of the 65 members of the council urged Greenberg to stay on the job.

Two weeks later, the two sides declared a truce. The museum council unanimously passed a resolution calling it a "mistake" for Greenberg to have written the letter on museum stationery, accepting an apology offered by Greenberg, and pledging to work together under the rabbi's leadership. On April 18, Greenberg and the council hosted President Bush at the museum, and the next day the president delivered a moving address at the U.S. Capitol in commemoration of Yom Hashoah (Holocaust Memorial Day). Bush was still not saying whether he would appoint a new museum chairman.

Anti-Defamation League

Abraham Foxman, the long-time national director of the Anti-Defamation League (ADL) and one of the most prominent and powerful American Jewish leaders, was also tarred by the Rich pardon, and his role in it proved to be far more central than that of Greenberg. Rich had known Foxman for years, claimed to hail from the same East European town, and had donated large sums of money to the ADL. By Foxman's own admission, he not only wrote Clinton to pardon Rich, but it was he who had first suggested the "pardon strategy" to Rich's associates in February 2000. Foxman denied, however, that Rich's donations had "bought" his support (*Forward,* Mar. 30). There were calls for Foxman's resignation, including one from *New York Times* columnist William Safire, who accused the ADL head of "ethical blindness." But Foxman, acknowledging that helping Rich had "probably" been a mistake, refused to step down.

Toward the end of the year, Foxman made headlines again. On December 22, he summoned David Lehrer, the ADL's highly regarded Los Angeles regional director, to New York headquarters, and fired him. Jewish leaders on the West Coast who had worked with Lehrer over the years expressed shock at the move. Foxman gave no explanation, but some observers suggested that the dismissal represented an attempt to maintain tight central control over the organization's regional directors.

American Jewish Congress

The American Jewish Congress, historically the most left-leaning and activist of the Jewish defense organizations, moved closer to the center of the political spectrum in 2001. "The great causes, injustices, and threats that drove previous generations to organize and speak out are largely absent from our society today," said AJCongress president Jack Rosen in October. The organization, he explained, would henceforth deal with "modern concerns" that emanate "from the values Jews embrace today." Several staff changes were made, with political moderates and conservatives replacing old-line liberals. Two important local chapters refused to accommodate to the shifts and seceded, amalgamating with other like-minded Jews in their communities to form independent, left-leaning groups: In Boston they called themselves the Jewish Alliance for Law & Social Action, and in Philadelphia, the Progressive Zionist Alliance. Two years before, in 1999, a similar split had occurred in Los Angeles, leading to the formation of the Progressive Jewish Alliance there.

World Jewish Congress

In December, the World Jewish Congress (WJC), which had become preeminent on issues having to do with Holocaust compensation, underwent a significant leadership shakeup. Israel Singer, the secretary general, said he would be stepping down, as would Elan Steinberg, the executive director. The new secretary general was Avi Beker, an Israeli, and he would run the organization from there. Edgar Bronfman, the billionaire philanthropist who was WJC president and footed the bill for 15–20 percent of its budget, was rumored to be contemplating retirement within the next two years. Bronfman indicated that he saw the erosion of Jewish identity as the greatest threat to the Jewish future, leading some to speculate that the WJC might shift its focus in that direction.

Lawrence Grossman

Jewish Population in the United States, 2001

BASED ON LOCAL COMMUNITY counts—the method for identifying and enumerating Jewish population that serves as the basis of this report—the estimated size of the American Jewish community in 2001 was approximately 6.1 million. This was over half a million more than the 5.5 million "core" Jewish population estimated in the Council of Jewish Federations' 1990 National Jewish Population Survey (NJPS).[1] The NJPS 2000–01, conducted from August 2000 to August 2001, will provide a new national estimate (see below).

The difference between the national and aggregated local figures may be explained by the passage of time, varying definitions of "Jewishness," disparate sample sources (lists, distinctive Jewish names, random digit dialing, etc.), and the lack of uniform methodology for local demographic research.

Analysis of the 1990 NJPS and other sources suggested that the population grew slightly during the late 1980s as the number of Jewish births exceeded the number of Jewish deaths. Extrapolation from the age structure, however, suggests that births and deaths were in balance by the late 1990s, creating a situation of zero population growth. It was only Jewish immigration into the U.S., particularly from the former Soviet Union, that provided growth in numbers.

The 1990 NJPS used a scientifically selected sample to project a total number of Jews in the United States as a whole, but could not provide accurate information on the state and local levels. Therefore, as in past years, this article contains local population estimates provided by knowledgeable local informants, and these serve as the basis for calculation of state and regional population counts.

Leaders at the approximately 200 Jewish federations that are part of the new philanthropic entity United Jewish Communities provided estimates of the Jewish population in their communities, the largest Jewish population centers. However, their service areas vary in size and thus may represent quite different geographic divisions: several towns, one county, or an aggregate of several counties. In some cases we have subdivided fed-

1. See Barry A. Kosmin et al., *Highlights of the CJF 1990 National Jewish Population Survey* (New York, Council of Jewish Federations, 1991).

eration areas to reflect more natural geographic boundaries or preferred U.S. Census definitions of metropolitan areas.

Local rabbis and other informed Jewish communal leaders provided estimates from small communities without federations. A form requesting the current population estimate was mailed to leaders of 57 such communities that had not provided an update in more than five years, and 34 replied. Five other requests were returned with indications that the synagogue, whose leader had previously provided an estimate, had either closed in recent years, moved without leaving a forwarding address, or could otherwise not be found. For communities that did not provide a current estimate, figures have either been retained from past years or extrapolations were made from the older data. The estimates requested from informants were for the resident Jewish population, including those in private households and in institutional settings. Informants were asked to exclude non-Jewish family members from the total.

The state, regional, and metropolitan totals shown in Appendix tables 1–3 were derived by summing the local estimates shown in table 4, including communities of less than 100, and then rounding to the nearest hundred or thousand, depending on the size of the estimate.

Because population estimation is not an exact science, the reader should be aware that in cases where a figure differs from last year's, the increase or decrease did not occur suddenly, but occurred over a period of time and has just now been substantiated. Recently completed local demographic studies are the primary sources for altering previously reported Jewish population figures in larger communities. The results of such studies should be understood as either an updated calculation of gradual demographic change or the correction of faulty older estimates.

In determining Jewish population, communities count both affiliated and nonaffiliated residents who are "core" Jews, as defined in NJPS 1990. This definition includes born Jews who report adherence to Judaism, Jews by choice, and born Jews without a current religion ("secular Jews"). A common method for estimating the population is to multiply the estimated number of households containing at least one self-defined Jew by the average number of self-defined Jewish persons per household. As stated above, informants were asked to exclude non-Jews living in Jewish households—primarily the non-Jewish spouses and non-Jewish children—from the 2001 estimates they provided which are reported below.

Only persons residing in a community for the majority of the year were included in local counts. In many Sunbelt and resort communities, the population increases during the winter months, but these part-year residents were not included in these estimates. However, demographer Ira Sheskin notes that if we were to include residents who are present for at least three months per year, four Southeast Florida communities would increase as follows: Boca Raton-Delray Beach 30,000 (32 percent), Broward County 21,000 (10 percent), Miami-Dade County 11,000 (9 percent), and Palm Beach County (excluding Boca Raton-Delray Beach) 21,000 (20 percent). Many other Sunbelt communities, resort areas throughout the country, college towns, and communities with seasonally affected industries also become home to more Jews for part of the year, but there are no accurate data for such communities.

Local Population Changes

The community reporting the largest numeric increase in 2001 was Ocean County, New Jersey, up 17,500 to 29,000. This 152-percent increase mainly reflected the relatively large and growing Orthodox community in the municipality of Lakewood, whose numbers were not fully reported in previous years. Columbus, Ohio, had the largest gain documented by a recent Jewish population study, a 41-percent increase from 15,600 to 22,000. The only other gain of at least 4,000 reported was in the primarily Satmar Hasidic village of Kiryas Joel in Orange County, New York. The 4,000 increase (27 percent) brought the county total to 19,000.

The largest percentage gain (328 percent) was in the Antelope Valley area in the northernmost part of Los Angeles County, California. The increase from 700 to 3,000 reflected general population growth as well as a new estimate of Jews, which had not been updated in many years.

Other places reporting increases of at least 1,000 were Long Beach, California; Fort Collins, Colorado; Westport, Connecticut; Bangor, Maine; and Houston, Texas. More modest increases were reported in San Luis Obispo, California; Greenwich, Connecticut; Athens, Georgia; Ocean City, Maryland; Pittsfield-Berkshire County, Massachusetts; Santa Fe, New Mexico; Chapel Hill-Durham and Hickory, North Carolina; Bend, Oregon; Charleston, South Carolina; and Madison, Wisconsin.

The largest numeric decline reported for any community was 8,000 in the Norfolk-Virginia Beach area of Virginia. A new demographic study in that community indicated that the previous Jewish population estimate of 19,000, which had not been changed in many years, was much too high. The next largest decline was 6,000 in Miami-Dade County, Florida, a 5-percent drop, reflecting losses mainly in Miami Beach. Baltimore's decline of 3,100 to 91,400 was discovered in its recently completed demographic study. The decrease of 2,000 in Sarasota, Florida, was a correction of a faulty older estimate that had included all part-year residents. Three other communities had decreases of at least 1,000: Buffalo, New York; Akron, Ohio; and Richmond, Virginia. More modest declines were reported in Columbus, Georgia; Alexandria, Louisiana; Quad Cities, Illinois and Iowa; Terre Haute, Indiana; Wichita, Kansas; Taunton, Massachusetts; Omaha, Nebraska; North Hudson County, New Jersey; Binghamton, New York; Fargo, North Dakota; Youngstown, Ohio; Wilkes-Barre, Pennsylvania; and Burlington, Vermont.

The community of Paducah, Kentucky, previously included in Southern Illinois, is listed separately for the first time, as are Easton, Maryland, and Ketchum, Idaho.

Data on Metropolitan Areas

In addition to detailed population figures by community, region, and state, information is provided for 50 metropolitan areas, rank-ordered by Jewish population (table 3). Included in this table are the Jewish percentage of each metropolitan area, its share of the U.S. Jewish population, and the cumulative share of the total Jewish population for communities up to that ranking.

In 1999, the United States Statistical Policy Office revised the definitions of many metropolitan regions and changed some names. Further, several Consolidated Metropolitan Statistical Areas (CMSAs) were designated as MSAs, and a few MSAs became CMSAs. Since 1998, when this analysis last appeared in the AJYB, the significant definitional changes relevant to this analysis were the inclusion of New Haven-Meriden, Connecticut, in the New York-Northern New Jersey-Long Island CMSA, the addition of Atlantic City to the Philadelphia-Wilmington-Atlantic City CMSA, and the incorporation of Worcester into the Boston-Worcester-Lawrence CMSA. The Statistical Policy Office also combined Baltimore and Washington, D.C., into one CMSA. However, because the Jewish communities in these two areas function independently and both have large Jewish populations—over 100,000—they are noted individually in the table.

The rankings of most metropolitan regions are similar to those of 1998, though in that year only the top 40 metros were listed. Significant shifts in ranking occurred for Portland-Salem (from 40 to 26), Milwaukee-Racine (from 25 to 31), Norfolk-Virginia Beach-Newport News (from 32 to 40) and Buffalo-Niagara Falls (from 27 to 36). Columbus, Ohio, which would have been ranked 41 in 1998, is now 29. The only other community now appearing in the top 40 that was not listed in that group in 1998 is Austin, ranked 39. Prior to 1998, the table on metropolitan areas was presented in the 1995 AYJB. The most important change from that year until this report is that Las Vegas, then ranked 31, is now 14.

A central finding of the 2001 data was the continuing concentration of American Jews within a few metropolitan areas, a pattern quite different from that of the American population as a whole. One-third of the nation's Jews lived in the New York-Northern New Jersey-Long Island metropolitan region, which encompassed parts of four states. Yet despite this demographic dominance, the region's proportion of the Jewish population dramatically declined from conditions half a century earlier: in 1955, over half of U.S. Jews lived in the New York metropolitan region. The second largest Jewish population center in 2001 was the Los Angeles-Riverside-Orange County area, home to 11 percent of American Jews. Another 5 percent lived in the third largest Jewish community, Miami-Fort Lauderdale, Florida. Cumulatively, half of all U.S. Jews resided in these top three metropolitan areas, three-quarters lived in 11 communities, 90 percent in 31 communities, and 94 percent in the top 50. In striking contrast, only 17 percent of the U.S. total population lived in the three top metropolitan areas, and 50 percent in the 39 largest metros.

The fact that the number of communities comprising 90 percent of U.S. Jewry declined from 36 in 1998 to 31 in 2001 reflected primarily definitional changes and not greater concentration of the population. First, as noted above, two metro areas were absorbed into larger metros, and, second, the geographic coverage of several additional metros was enlarged.

The Jewish proportion of the total 2001 population in particular locales was noteworthy. The metropolitan area with the highest percentage of Jews remained West Palm Beach-Boca Raton, at 15 percent. New York-Northern New Jersey-Long Island and Miami-Fort Lauderdale were the only other metropolitan areas with a Jewish population density greater than 8 percent. In only four other areas—Las Vegas, Philadelphia-Wilmington-Atlantic City, Boston-Worcester-Lawrence, and Los Angeles-Riverside-Orange County—were Jews more than 4 percent of the population.

NJPS 2000–01

Recognizing a need for current data, United Jewish Communities (UJC) sponsored a new National Jewish Population Survey (NJPS) that was the most comprehensive and sophisticated study ever conducted of

American Jews. So that the results should be representative of all American Jews, respondents were selected using random-digit-dialing techniques and a complex screening process. Interviews were conducted between August 2000 and August 2001. The questionnaire and overall study design were developed by the UJC Research Department in close collaboration with its National Technical Advisory Committee (NTAC), a distinguished group of 20 academicians and federation professionals with expertise in demography, sociology, religion, geography, economics, education, and other relevant disciplines.

The UJC Research Department worked closely with local federation planning, campaign, marketing, and other departments, as well as with the newly formed UJC "pillars," its lay leadership, in preparing the NJPS questionnaire. Interviewing was to have begun in early 2000, but was postponed until the second half of the year in order to give the pillars sufficient opportunity for input. Meetings were held with these groups, Jewish religious denominations, other major Jewish organizations, and other constituencies. The NJPS Board of Trustees provided the financial resources for conducting this effort, and the Federation Professional Advisory Committee provided guidance on issues of relevance to the federation system. The NJPS Steering Committee, comprised of the chairs of all the committees involved in the NJPS, set policy for the study. All of the aforementioned groups provided significant input to the development of the questionnaire. Focus groups were conducted to improve the introductory part of the interview and cognitively test the phrasing of questions. The questionnaire was extensively pretested for length, the most appropriate language, and correct skip patterns.

The NJPS 2000–01 respondents were adults 18 and older residing in the 50 United States. Nearly 4,500 people completed the Jewish questionnaire, and interviews were conducted with more than 650 people with Jewish backgrounds but who do not consider themselves Jewish. The sample was stratified by census region, metropolitan/non-metropolitan area, and then by zip code within each region. Areas of higher-density Jewish population were sampled at a higher rate than other areas so as to increase the pace of interviewing and reduce costs, with results weighted to ensure accurate projectability to the Jewish population.

The first UJC report of the findings was scheduled for fall 2002, with major presentations at the UJC General Assembly in November. NJPS 2000–01 will become the definitive source of data on the Jewish community during the first decade of the century. The information will help UJC, Jewish federations, denominations, and other organizations in the

Jewish community conduct communal planning, policy-making, resource development, Jewish education, scholarly research, and many other necessary functions.

Among the multitude of topics explored in NJPS 2000–01 are Jewish population size, socioeconomic characteristics, family structure, fertility, marital history, intermarriage, Jewish identification, religious practices, Jewish education, synagogue affiliation, philanthropic behavior, and relationship to Israel. UJC and others will underwrite a broad range of analyses based on NJPS results to guide the planning and policy-making of the Jewish community. NJPS 2000–01 is expected to deliver the critical data and analyses necessary for strengthening and enriching Jewish life in North America in the 21st century.

JIM SCHWARTZ
JEFFREY SCHECKNER

APPENDIX

TABLE 1. JEWISH POPULATION IN THE UNITED STATES, 2001

State	Estimated Jewish Population	Total Population*	Estimated Jewish Percent of Total
Alabama	9,000	4,451,000	0.2
Alaska	3,400	628,000	0.5
Arizona	81,500	5,165,000	1.6
Arkansas	1,700	2,678,000	0.1
California	999,000	34,000,000	2.9
Colorado	73,000	4,323,000	1.7
Connecticut	111,000	3,410,000	3.2
Delaware	13,500	786,000	1.7
Dist. of Columbia	25,500	571,000	4.5
Florida	620,000	16,054,000	3.9
Georgia	93,500	8,230,000	1.1
Hawaii	7,000	1,212,000	0.6
Idaho	1,100	1,299,000	0.1
Illinois	270,000	12,436,000	2.2
Indiana	17,500	6,090,000	0.3
Iowa	6,100	2,928,000	0.2
Kansas	14,000	2,692,000	0.5
Kentucky	11,500	4,047,000	0.3
Louisiana	16,000	4,470,000	0.4
Maine	9,300	1,277,000	0.7
Maryland	213,000	5,311,000	4.0
Massachusetts	275,000	6,357,000	4.3
Michigan	110,000	9,952,000	1.1
Minnesota	42,000	4,931,000	0.9
Mississippi	1,500	2,849,000	0.1
Missouri	62,500	5,603,000	1.1
Montana	800	903,000	0.1
Nebraska	7,000	1,713,000	0.4
Nevada	77,000	2,019,000	3.8
New Hampshire	10,000	1,240,000	0.8
New Jersey	485,000	8,429,000	5.7

State	Estimated Jewish Population	Total Population*	Estimated Jewish Percent of Total
New Mexico	11,500	1,821,000	0.6
New York	1,657,000	18,990,000	8.7
North Carolina	26,500	8,077,000	0.3
North Dakota	450	641,000	0.1
Ohio	149,000	11,360,000	1.3
Oklahoma	5,000	3,453,000	0.1
Oregon	32,000	3,429,000	0.9
Pennsylvania	282,000	12,283,000	2.3
Rhode Island	16,000	1,050,000	1.5
South Carolina	11,500	4,023,000	0.3
South Dakota	300	756,000	(z)
Tennessee	18,000	5,702,000	0.3
Texas	131,000	20,947,000	0.6
Utah	4,500	2,242,000	0.2
Vermont	5,500	610,000	0.9
Virginia	66,000	7,104,000	0.9
Washington	43,000	5,908,000	0.7
West Virginia	2,300	1,808,000	0.1
Wisconsin	28,000	5,372,000	0.5
Wyoming	400	494,000	0.1
U.S. TOTAL	**6,155,000	282,125,000	2.2

N.B. Details may not add to totals because of rounding.
* Resident population, April 1, 2001 (*Source:* U.S. Bureau of the Census, Population Division).
** Exclusive of Puerto Rico and the Virgin Islands which previously reported Jewish populations of 1,500 and 350, respectively.
(z) Figure is less than 0.1 and rounds to 0.

TABLE 2. DISTRIBUTION OF U.S. JEWISH POPULATION BY REGIONS, 2001

Region	Total Population	Percent Distribution	Estimated Jewish Population	Percent Distribution
Northeast	53,645,000	19.0	2,850,000	46.3
Middle Atlantic	39,701,000	14.1	2,424,000	39.3
New England	13,944,000	4.9	426,000	6.9
Midwest	64,473,000	22.9	706,000	11.4
East North Central	45,210,000	16.0	574,000	9.3
West North Central	19,263,000	6.8	132,000	2.1
South	100,562,000	35.7	1,265,000	20.6
East South Central	17,050,000	6.0	40,000	0.6
South Atlantic	51,964,000	18.4	1,071,000	17.4
West South Central	31,548,000	11.1	154,000	2.5
West	63,445,000	22.5	1,334,000	21.7
Mountain	18,267,000	6.5	250,000	4.1
Pacific	45,178,000	16.0	1,084,000	17.6
TOTALS	282,125,000	100.0	6,155,000	100.0

N.B. Details may not add to totals because of rounding.

TABLE 3. RANK-ORDERED METROPOLITAN STATISTICAL AREAS, BY JEWISH POPULATION, 2001

Metro Area	Estimated Jewish Population	Jewish % of Total Population	% Share of U.S. Jewish Population	Cumulative % Share of Jewish Population
1. New York-Northern NJ-Long Island, NY-NJ-CT-PA*	2,051,000	9.7	33.3	33.3
2. Los Angles-Riverside-Orange County, CA*	668,000	4.1	10.9	44.2
3. Miami-Ft. Lauderdale,FL*	331,000	8.5	5.4	49.6
4. Philadelphia-Wilmington-Atlantic City, PA-NJ-DE-MD*	285,000	4.6	4.6	54.2
5. Chicago-Gary-Kenosha, IL-IN-WI*	265,000	2.9	4.3	58.5
6. Boston-Worcester-Lawrence, MA-NH-ME-CT*	254,000	4.4	4.1	62.6
7. San Francisco-Oakland-San Jose, CA*	218,000	3.1	3.6	66.2
8. West Palm Beach-Boca Raton, FL	167,000	14.8	2.7	68.9
9. Washington, DC-MD-VA-WV	166,000	3.4	2.7	71.6
10. Baltimore, MD	106,000	3.9	1.7	73.3
11. Detroit-Ann Arbor, MI*	103,000	1.9	1.7	75.0
12. Cleveland-Akron, OH*	86,000	2.9	1.4	76.4
13. Atlanta, GA	86,000	2.1	1.4	77.8
14. Las Vegas, NV-AZ	75,000	4.8	1.2	79.0
15. San Diego, CA	70,000	2.5	1.1	80.1
16. Denver-Boulder-Greeley, CO*	67,000	2.3	1.1	81.2
17. Phoenix-Mesa, AZ	60,000	1.8	1.0	82.2
18. St. Louis, MO-IL	54,500	2.1	.9	83.1
19. Dallas-Ft. Worth, TX*	50,000	1.0	.8	83.9
20. Houston-Galveston-Brazoria, TX*	45,500	1.0	.7	84.6
21. Tampa-St. Petersburg-Clearwater, FL	45,000	1.9	.7	85.4
22. Minneapolis-St. Paul, MN-WI	40,500	1.4	.7	86.0

Metro Area	Estimated Jewish Population	Jewish % of Total Population	% Share of U.S. Jewish Population	Cumulative % Share of Jewish Population
23. Pittsburgh, PA	40,500	1.7	.7	86.7
24. Seattle-Tacoma-Bremerton, WA*	40,000	1.1	.6	87.3
25. Hartford, CT	33,500	2.8	.5	87.9
26. Portland-Salem, OR-WA*	27,000	1.2	.4	88.3
27. Cincinnati, OH-KY-IN*	24,000	1.2	.4	88.7
28. Rochester, NY	23,000	2.1	.4	89.1
29. Columbus, OH	22,000	1.4	.4	89.4
30. Sacramento-Yolo, CA*	21,500	1.2	.3	89.8
31. Milwaukee-Racine, WI*	21,000	1.2	.3	90.1
32. Orlando, FL	21,000	1.3	.3	90.5
33. Tucson, AZ	20,000	2.4	.3	90.8
34. Albany-Schenectady-Troy, NY	19,000	2.2	.3	91.1
35. Kansas City, MO-KS	19,000	1.1	.3	91.4
36. Buffalo-Niagara Falls, NY	18,500	1.6	.3	91.7
37. Providence-Fall River-Warwick, RI-MA	17,000	1.4	.3	92.0
38. Sarasota-Bradenton, FL	15,500	2.6	.3	92.2
39. Austin, TX	13,500	1.1	.2	92.4
40. Norfolk-Virginia Beach-Newport News, VA-NC	13,500	0.9	.2	92.7
41. Springfield, MA	13,000	2.2	.2	92.9
42. New Orleans, LA	13,000	1.0	.2	93.1
43. Richmond-Petersburg, VA	13,000	1.3	.2	93.3
44. San Antonio, TX	11,000	0.7	.2	93.5
45. Indianapolis, IN	10,000	0.6	.2	93.6
46. Syracuse, NY	9,500	1.3	.2	93.8
47. Charlotte-Gastonia-Rock Hill, NC-SC	9,000	0.6	.1	93.9
48. Louisville, KY-IN	8,500	0.8	.1	94.1
49. Memphis, TN-AR-MS	8,500	0.7	.1	94.2
50. Ft. Myers-Cape Coral, FL	8,000	1.8	.1	94.3

Designations for the metropolitan areas are in accordance with the United States Statistical Policy Office, Office of Management and Budget, Bulletin Number 99-04 and established June 30, 1999. All areas are Metropolitan Statistical Areas (MSA) except those designated with an asterisk (*), which are Consolidated Metropolitan Statistical Areas (CMSA). The one exception to this rule is the Washington-Baltimore CMSA, which is separated.
N.B.: Details may not add to totals because of rounding.

TABLE 3. COMMUNITIES WITH JEWISH POPULATIONS OF 100 OR MORE, 2001 (ESTIMATED)

State and City	Jewish Population
ALABAMA	
*Birmingham	5,300
Dothan	100
Huntsville	750
**Mobile	1,100
**Montgomery	1,200
Tuscaloosa	300
Other places	250
ALASKA	
*Anchorage	2,300
*Fairbanks	540
Juneau	285
Kenai Peninsula	200
Ketchikan (incl. in Juneau)	
Other places	100
ARIZONA	
Cochise County	350
*Flagstaff	500
Lake Havasu City	200
*Phoenix	60,000
Prescott	300
Sierra Vista (incl. in Cochise County)	
*Tucson	20,000
Yuma	150
Other places	100
ARKANSAS	
Fayetteville	175
Hot Springs	150
**Little Rock	1,100
Other places	250
CALIFORNIA	
Antelope Valley	3,000
Aptos (incl. in Santa Cruz)	
Bakersfield-Kern County	1,600
Berkeley (incl. in Contra Costa County, under S.F. Bay Area)	
Carmel (incl. in Monterey Peninsula)	
*Chico	750
Corona (incl. in Riverside area)	
*Eureka	1,000
Fairfield	800
Fontana (incl. in San Bernardino)	
*Fresno	2,300
Lancaster (incl. in Antelope Valley)	
Long Beach[N]	18,000
Los Angeles area[N]	519,000
*Mendocino County	600
*Merced County	190
*Modesto	500
Monterey Peninsula	2,300
Moreno Valley (incl. in Riverside)	
Murrieta Hot Springs	550
*Napa County	1,000
Oakland (incl. in Alameda County, under S.F. Bay Area)	
Ontario (incl. in San Gabriel and Pomona Valleys)	
Orange County[N]	60,000
Oroville (incl. in Chico)	
Palmdale (incl. in Antelope Valley)	
Palm Springs[N]	17,000
Palo Alto (incl. in South Peninsula, under S.F. Bay Area)	
Paradise (incl. in Chico)	
Pasadena (incl. in L.A. area)	
Paso Robles (incl. in San Luis Obispo)	
Petaluma (incl. in Sonoma County, under S.F. Bay Area)	
Pomona Valley[N] (incl. in San Gabriel and Pomona Valleys)	
*Redding area	150
Redwood Valley (incl. in Mendocino County)	
Riverside area	2,000
Sacramento[N]	21,300
Salinas	1,000
San Bernardino area	3,000
*San Diego	70,000

[N]See Notes below. *Includes entire county. **Includes all of two counties. ***Figure not updated for at least five years.

State and City	Jewish Population
San Francisco Bay Area[N]	210,000
Alameda County	32,500
Contra Costa County	22,000
Marin County	18,500
N. Peninsula	24,500
San Francisco	49,500
San Jose	33,000
Sonoma County	9,000
S. Peninsula	21,000
San Gabriel and Pomona Valleys[N]	30,000
*San Jose (listed under S.F. Bay Area)	
*San Luis Obispo	2,000
*Santa Barbara	7,000
*Santa Cruz	6,000
Santa Maria	500
Santa Monica (incl. in Los Angeles area)	
Santa Rosa (incl. in Sonoma County, under S.F. Bay Area)	
Sonoma County (listed under S.F. Bay Area)	
*South Lake Tahoe	150
Stockton	850
Sun City	200
Tulare and Kings counties	350
Ukiah (incl. in Mendocino Co.)	
Vallejo area	900
*Ventura County[N]	15,000
Visalia (incl. in Tulare and Kings counties)	
Other places	200
COLORADO	
Aspen	750
Boulder (incl. in Denver)	
Breckenridge (incl. in Vail)	
Colorado Springs	1,500
Denver[N]	66,700
Eagle (incl. in Vail)	
Evergreen (incl. in Denver)	
*Fort Collins	1,000
*Grand Junction	320
Greeley (incl. in Fort Collins)	
Loveland (incl. in Fort Collins)	
Pueblo[N]	425
Steamboat Springs	250
***Telluride	125
**Vail	650
Other places	200
CONNECTICUT	
Bridgeport[N]	13,000
Bristol (incl. in Hartford)	
Cheshire (incl. in Waterbury)	
***Colchester	300
Danbury[N]	3,200
***Danielson	100
Darien (incl. in Stamford)	
Greenwich	4,200
Hartford[N]	32,200
Hebron (incl. in Colchester)	
Lebanon (incl. in Colchester)	
Lower Middlesex County[N]	1,600
Manchester (incl. in Hartford)	
Meriden (incl. in New Haven)	
Middletown	1,200
New Britain (incl. in Hartford)	
New Canaan (incl. in Stamford)	
New Haven[N]	24,300
New London[N]	3,850
New Milford (incl. in Waterbury)	
Newtown (incl. in Danbury)	
Norwalk (incl. in Westport)	
Norwich (incl. in New London)	
Rockville (incl. in Hartford)	
Shelton (incl. in Bridgeport)	
Southington (incl. in Hartford)	
Stamford	9,200
Storrs (incl. in Willimantic)	
Torrington area	580
Wallingford (incl. in New Haven)	
Waterbury[N]	4,500
Westport[N]	11,400
Willimantic area	700
Other places	250
DELAWARE	
Dover (incl. in Kent and Sussex counties totals)	
Kent and Sussex counties	1,600
Newark area	4,300
Wilmington area	7,600

State and City	Jewish Population
DISTRICT OF COLUMBIA	
Washington D.C.[N]	25,500
FLORIDA	
Arcadia (incl. in Fort Myers)	
Boca Raton-Delray Beach (listed under Southeast Fla.)	
Brevard County	5,000
Broward County (listed under Southeast Fla.)	
***Crystal River	100
**Daytona Beach	2,500
Fort Lauderdale (incl. in Broward County, under Southeast Fla.)	
**Fort Myers	8,000
Fort Pierce	1,060
Gainesville	2,200
Hollywood-S. Broward County (incl in Broward County, under Southeast Fla.)	
**Jacksonville	7,300
Key West	650
***Lakeland	1,000
*Miami-Dade County (listed under Southeast Fla.)	
Naples-Collier County	4,200
New Port Richey (incl. in Pasco County)	
Ocala-Marion County	500
Orlando[N]	21,000
Palm Beach County (listed under Southeast Fla.)	
Pasco County	1,000
**Pensacola	975
Pinellas County	24,200
**Port Charlotte-Punta Gorda (incl. in Fort Myers	
**Sarasota	15,500
Southeast Florida	498,000
Boca Raton-Delray Beach	93,000
Broward County	213,000
Miami-Dade County	118,000
Palm Beach County (excl. Boca Raton-Delray Beach)	74,000
*St. Petersburg-Clearwater (incl. in Pinellas County)	
Stuart-Port St. Lucie[N]	4,300
Tallahassee	2,200
*Tampa	20,000
Venice (incl. in Sarasota)	
*Vero Beach	400
***Winter Haven	300
Other places	100
GEORGIA	
Albany area	200
Athens	600
Atlanta Metro Area	85,900
Augusta[N]	1,300
Brunswick	120
**Columbus	750
**Dalton	125
Macon	1,000
*Savannah	3,000
**Valdosta	100
Other places	250
HAWAII	
Hilo	280
Honolulu (incl. all of Oahu)	6,400
Kauai	100
Maui	210
IDAHO	
**Boise	800
Ketchum	100
Lewiston (incl. in Moscow)	
Moscow	100
Other places	100
ILLINOIS	
Aurora area	750
Bloomington-Normal	500
Carbondale (incl. in S. Ill.)	
*Champaign-Urbana	1,400
Chicago Metro Area[N]	261,000
**Danville	100
*Decatur	130
DeKalb	180
East St. Louis (incl. in S. Ill.)	
Elgin[N]	500
Freeport (incl. in Rockford)	
*Joliet	210
Kankakee	100
Moline (incl. in Quad Cities)	
*Peoria	800
Quad Cities-Ill. portion	400
Quincy	100
Rock Island (incl. in Quad Cities)	
Rockford[N]	1,100

State and City	Jewish Population
Southern Illinois[N]	500
*Springfield	1,090
Waukegan	300
Other places	250
INDIANA	
Bloomington	1,000
Elkhart (incl. in S. Bend)	
Evansville	400
**Fort Wayne	900
**Gary-Northwest Indiana	2,000
**Indianapolis	10,000
**Lafayette	550
*Michigan City	300
Muncie	120
South Bend[N]	1,850
*Terre Haute	200
Other places	200
IOWA	
Ames (incl. in Des Moines)	
Cedar Rapids	420
Council Bluffs	150
*Davenport (incl. in Quad Cities)	
*Des Moines	2,800
*Iowa City	1,300
Postville	150
Quad Cities-Iowa portion	500
**Sioux City	400
*Waterloo	170
Other places	250
KANSAS	
Kansas City area-Kansas portion[N]	12,000
Lawrence	200
***Manhattan	425
*Topeka	400
Wichita[N]	1,100
Other places	100
KENTUCKY	
Covington-Newport area	500
Lexington[N]	2,000
*Louisville	8,700
Paducah	150
Other places	150
LOUISIANA	
Alexandria[N]	350
Baton Rouge[N]	1,600
Lafayette (incl. in S. Central La.)	
Lake Charles area	200
Monroe (incl. in Shreveport)	
**New Orleans	13,000
**Shreveport	815
***South Central La.[N]	250
Other places	150
MAINE	
***Augusta	140
Bangor	3,000
Biddeford-Saco (incl. in S. Maine)	
Brunswick-Bath (incl. in S. Maine)	
Lewiston-Auburn	500
Portland (incl. in S. Maine)	
***Rockland area	300
Southern Maine[N]	6,000
***Waterville	225
Other places	150
MARYLAND	
Annapolis area	3,000
**Baltimore	91,400
Columbia (incl. in Howard County)	
Cumberland	275
*Easton	100
*Frederick	1,200
*Hagerstown	325
*Harford County	1,200
*Howard County	10,000
Montgomery and Prince Georges counties	104,500
Ocean City	200
Salisbury	400
Silver Spring (incl. in Montgomery County)	
Other places	250
MASSACHUSETTS	
Amherst area	1,300
Andover[N]	2,850
Athol area (incl. in N. Worcester County)	
Attleboro area	700
Beverly (incl. in North Shore, under Boston Metro Region)	
Boston Metro Region[N]	227,300
Boston	21,000
Brockton-South Central	31,500
Brookline	20,300
Framingham	19,700
Near West	35,800
Newton	27,700
North Central	22,900
Northeast	7,700
North Shore	18,600
Northwest	13,600
Southeast	8,500
Brockton (listed under Boston Metro Region)	

State and City	Jewish Population
Brookline (listed under Boston Metro Region)	
Cape Cod-Barnstable County	3,250
Clinton (incl. in Worcester-Central Worcester County)	
Fall River area	1,100
Falmouth (incl. in Cape Cod)	
Fitchburg (incl. in N. Worcester County)	
Framingham (listed under Boston Metro Region)	
Gardner (incl. in N. Worcester County)	
Gloucester (incl. N. Shore, listed under Boston Metro Region)	
Great Barrington (incl. in Pittsfield)	
*Greenfield	1,100
Haverhill	800
Holyoke	600
*Hyannis (incl. in Cape Cod)	
Lawrence (incl. in Andover)	
Leominster (incl. in N. Worcester County)	
Lowell area	2,000
Lynn (incl. in N. Shore, listed under Boston Metro Region)	
*Martha's Vineyard	300
New Bedford[N]	2,600
Newburyport	280
Newton (listed under Boston Metro Region)	
North Adams (incl. in N. Berkshire County)	
North Berkshire County	400
North Worcester County	1,500
Northampton	1,200
Peabody (incl. in N. Shore, listed under Boston Metro Region)	
Pittsfield-Berkshire County	4,000
Plymouth area	1,000
Provincetown (incl. in Cape Cod)	
Salem (incl. in N. Shore, listed under Boston Metro Region)	
Southbridge (incl. in S. Worcester County)	
South Worcester County	500
Springfield[N]	10,000
Taunton area	1,000
Webster (incl. in S. Worcester County)	
Worcester-Central Worcester County	11,000
Other places	150
MICHIGAN	
*Ann Arbor	7,000
Bay City	150
Benton Harbor area	240
**Detroit Metro Area	94,000
*Flint	1,500
*Grand Rapids	1,850
**Jackson	200
*Kalamazoo	1,500
Lansing area	2,100
Midland	120
Mt. Clemens (incl. in Detroit)	
Mt. Pleasant[N]	130
*Muskegon	210
*Saginaw	115
Traverse City	200
Other places	350
MINNESOTA	
**Duluth	485
*Minneapolis	31,500
Rochester	550
**St. Paul	9,200
Other places	150
MISSISSIPPI	
Biloxi-Gulfport	250
**Greenville	120
**Hattiesburg	130
**Jackson	550
Other places	450
MISSOURI	
Columbia	400
Joplin	100
Kansas City area-Missouri portion[N]	7,100
*St. Joseph	265
**St. Louis	54,000
Springfield	300
Other places	100
MONTANA	
*Billings	300
Butte	100
Helena (incl. in Butte)	
*Kalispell	150
Missoula	200
Other places	100
NEBRASKA	
Grand Island-Hastings (incl. in Lincoln)	

State and City	Jewish Population
Lincoln	700
**Omaha	6,100
Other places	50
NEVADA	
Carson City (incl. in Reno)	
*Las Vegas	75,000
**Reno	2,100
Sparks (incl. in Reno)	
NEW HAMPSHIRE	
Bethlehem	200
Concord	500
Dover area	600
Exeter (incl. in Portsmouth)	
Franconia (incl. in Bethlehem)	
***Hanover-Lebanon	600
***Keene	300
**Laconia	270
Littleton (incl. in Bethlehem)	
Manchester area	4,000
Nashua area	2,000
Portsmouth area	1,250
Rochester (incl. in Dover)	
Salem	150
Other places	100
NEW JERSEY	
Asbury Park (incl. in Monmouth County)	
**Atlantic City (incl. Atlantic and Cape May counties)	15,800
Bayonne (listed under Hudson County)	
Bergen County (also incl. in Northeastern N.J.)	83,700
Bridgeton	110
Bridgewater (incl. in Somerset County)	
Camden (incl. in Cherry Hill-S. N.J.)	
Cherry Hill-Southern N.J.[N]	49,000
Edison (incl. in Middlesex County)	
Elizabeth (incl. in Union County)	
Englewood (incl. in Bergen County)	
Essex County (also incl. in Northeastern N.J.)[N]	76,200
East Essex	10,800
Livingston	12,600
North Essex	15,600
South Essex	20,300
West Orange-Orange	16,900
*Flemington	1,500
Freehold (incl. in Monmouth County)	
Gloucester (incl. in Cherry Hill-S. N.J.)	
Hoboken (listed under Hudson County)	
Hudson County (also incl. in Northeastern N.J.)	11,800
Bayonne	1,600
Hoboken	1,400
Jersey City	6,000
North Hudson County[N]	2,800
Jersey City (listed under Hudson County)	
Lakewood (incl. in Ocean County)	
Livingston (listed under Essex County)	
Middlesex County (also incl. in Northeastern N.J.)[N]	45,000
Monmouth County (also incl. in Northeastern N.J.)	65,000
Morris County (also incl. in Northeastern N.J.)	33,500
Morristown (incl. in Morris County)	
Mt. Holly (incl. in Cherry Hill-S. N.J.)	
New Brunswick (incl. in Middlesex County)	
Newark (incl. in Essex County)	
Northeastern N.J.[N]	417,000
Ocean County (also incl. in Northeastern N.J.)	29,000
Passaic County (also incl. in Northeastern N.J.)	17,000
Passaic-Clifton (incl. in Passaic County)	
Paterson (incl. in Passaic County)	
Perth Amboy (incl. in Middlesex County)	
Phillipsburg (incl. in Warren County)	
Plainfield (incl. in Union County)	
Princeton area	3,000
Somerset County (also incl. in Northeastern N.J.)	11,000
Somerville (incl. in Somerset County)	

State and City	Jewish Population
Sussex County (also incl. in Northeastern N.J.)	4,100
Toms River (incl. in Ocean County)	
Trenton[N]	6,000
Union County (also incl. in Northeastern N.J.)	30,000
Vineland[N]	1,890
Warren County	400
Wayne (incl. in Passaic County)	
Wildwood	330
Willingboro (incl. in Cherry Hill-S. N.J.)	
Other places	200
NEW MEXICO	
*Albuquerque	7,500
Las Cruces	600
Las Vegas (incl. in Santa Fe)	
***Los Alamos	250
Rio Rancho (incl. in Albuquerque)	
Santa Fe	2,500
***Taos	300
Other places	100
NEW YORK	
*Albany	12,000
Amenia (incl. in Poughkeepsie-Dutchess County)	
Amsterdam	100
*Auburn	115
Beacon (incl. in Poughkeepsie-Dutchess County)	
*Binghamton (incl. all Broome County)	2,400
Brewster (incl. in Putnam County)	
*Buffalo	18,500
Canandaigua (incl. in Geneva)	
Catskill	200
Corning (incl. in Elmira)	
*Cortland	150
Ellenville	1,600
Elmira[N]	950
Fleischmanns	100
Geneva area	300
Glens Falls[N]	800
*Gloversville	300
*Herkimer	130
Highland Falls (incl. in Orange County)	
*Hudson	500
*Ithaca area	2,000
Jamestown	100
Kingston[N]	4,300
Kiryas Joel (incl. in Orange County)	
Lake George (incl. in Glens Falls)	
Liberty (incl. in Sullivan County)	
Middletown (incl. in Orange County)	
Monroe (incl. in Orange County)	
Monticello (incl. in Sullivan County)	
Newark (incl. in Geneva total)	
Newburgh (incl. in Orange County)	
New Paltz (incl. in Kingston)	
New York Metro Area[N]	1,450,000
Bronx	83,700
Brooklyn	379,000
Manhattan	314,500
Queens	238,000
Staten Island	33,700
Nassau County	207,000
Suffolk County	100,000
Westchester County	94,000
Niagara Falls	150
Olean	100
**Oneonta	300
Orange County	19,000
Pawling (incl. in Poughkeepsie-Dutchess County)	
Plattsburg	250
Port Jervis (incl. in Orange County)	
Potsdam	200
*Poughkeepsie-Dutchess County	3,600
Putnam County	1,000
**Rochester	22,500
Rockland County	90,000
Rome	100
Saratoga Springs	600
**Schenectady	5,200
Seneca Falls (incl. in Geneva)	
South Fallsburg (incl. in Sullivan County)	
***Sullivan County	7,425
Syracuse[N]	9,000
Troy area	800
Utica[N]	1,100
Walden (incl. in Orange County)	
Watertown	100
Woodstock (incl. in Kingston)	
Other places	600

State and City	Jewish Population
NORTH CAROLINA	
Asheville[N]	1,300
**Chapel Hill-Durham	4,600
Charlotte[N]	8,500
Elizabethtown (incl. in Wilmington)	
*Fayetteville	300
Gastonia	210
*Greensboro	2,500
Greenville	240
*Hendersonville	250
**Hickory	260
High Point (incl. in Greensboro)	
Jacksonville (incl. in Wilmington)	
Raleigh-Wake County	6,000
Whiteville (incl. in Wilmington)	
Wilmington area	1,200
Winston-Salem	485
Other places	450
NORTH DAKOTA	
Fargo	200
Grand Forks	130
Other places	100
OHIO	
**Akron	4,000
***Athens	100
Bowling Green (incl. in Toledo)	
Butler County	900
**Canton	1,450
Cincinnati[N]	22,500
Cleveland[N]	81,500
*Columbus	22,000
**Dayton	5,000
Elyria	155
Fremont (incl. in Sandusky)	
Hamilton (incl. in Butler County)	
Kent (incl. in Akron)	
*Lima	180
***Lorain	600
Mansfield	150
Marion[N]	125
Middletown (incl. in Butler County)	
New Philadelphia (incl. in Canton)	
Norwalk (incl. in Sandusky)	
Oberlin (incl. in Elyria)	
Oxford (incl. in Butler County)	
**Sandusky	105
Springfield	200
*Steubenville	115
Toledo[N]	5,900
Warren (incl. in Youngstown)	
Wooster	175
Youngstown[N]	3,200
*Zanesville	100
Other places	350
OKLAHOMA	
Norman (incl. in Oklahoma City)	
**Oklahoma City	2,300
*Tulsa	2,650
Other places	100
OREGON	
Ashland (incl. in Medford)	
Bend	500
Corvallis	500
Eugene	3,250
Grants Pass (incl. in Medford)	
**Medford	1,000
Portland[N]	25,500
**Salem	1,000
Other places	100
PENNSYLVANIA	
Allentown (incl. in Lehigh Valley)	
*Altoona	575
Ambridge (incl. in Pittsburgh)	
Beaver Falls (incl. in Upper Beaver County)	
Bethlehem (incl. in Lehigh Valley)	
Bucks County (listed under Philadelphia area)	
*Butler	250
**Chambersburg	150
Chester (incl. in Delaware County, listed under Phila. area)	
Chester County (listed under Phila. area)	
Coatesville (incl. in Chester County, listed under Phila. area)	
Easton (incl. in Lehigh Valley)	
*Erie	850
Farrell (incl. in Sharon)	
Greensburg (incl. in Pittsburgh)	
**Harrisburg	7,000
Hazleton area	300
Honesdale (incl. in Wayne County)	
Jeannette (incl. in Pittsburgh)	
**Johnstown	275
Lancaster area	3,000
*Lebanon	350

State and City	Jewish Population
Lehigh Valley	8,500
Lewisburg (incl. in Sunbury)	
Lock Haven (incl. in Williamsport)	
McKeesport (incl. in Pittsburgh)	
New Castle	200
Norristown (incl. in Montgomery County, listed under Phila. area)	
**Oil City	100
Oxford-Kennett Square (incl. in Chester County, listed under Phila. area)	
Philadelphia area[N]	206,000
Bucks County	34,800
Chester County	10,100
Delaware County	15,700
Montgomery County	58,900
Philadelphia	86,600
Phoenixville (incl. in Chester County, listed under Phila. area)	
***Pike County	300
Pittsburgh[N]	40,000
Pottstown	650
Pottsville	120
*Reading	2,200
*Scranton	3,100
Shamokin (incl. in Sunbury)	
Sharon	300
State College	700
Stroudsburg	600
Sunbury[N]	200
Tamaqua (incl. in Hazleton)	
Uniontown area	150
Upper Beaver County	180
Washington (incl. in Pittsburgh)	
***Wayne County	500
Waynesburg (incl. in Pittsburgh)	
West Chester (incl. in Chester County, listed under Phila. area)	
Wilkes-Barre[N]	3,000
**Williamsport	225
York	1,800
Other places	900
RHODE ISLAND	
Cranston (incl. in Providence)	
Kingston (incl. in Washington County)	
Newport-Middletown	700
Providence area	14,200
Washington County	1,200
Westerly (incl. in Washington County)	
SOUTH CAROLINA	
*Charleston	5,500
**Columbia	2,750
Florence area	220
Georgetown (incl. in Myrtle Beach)	
Greenville	1,200
Kingstree (incl. in Sumter)	
**Myrtle Beach	475
Rock Hill	100
*Spartanburg	500
Sumter[N]	140
York (incl. in Rock Hill)	
Other places	450
SOUTH DAKOTA	
Sioux Falls	195
Other places	100
TENNESSEE	
Chattanooga	1,450
Knoxville	1,800
Memphis	8,500
Nashville	6,000
Oak Ridge	250
Other places	200
TEXAS	
Amarillo[N]	200
*Austin	13,500
***Baytown	300
Beaumont	500
*Brownsville	450
***College Station-Bryan	400
*Corpus Christi	1,400
**Dallas	45,000
El Paso	5,000
*Fort Worth	5,000
Galveston	450
Harlingen (incl. in Brownsville)	
**Houston[N]	45,000
Laredo	130
Longview	100
*Lubbock	230
*McAllen[N]	500
Midland-Odessa	200
Port Arthur	100
*San Antonio	11,000
South Padre Island (incl. in Brownsville)	

State and City	Jewish Population
Tyler	400
Waco[N]	300
Wichita Falls	260
Other places	600
UTAH	
Ogden	150
*Salt Lake City	4,200
Other places	50
VERMONT	
Bennington area	500
***Brattleboro	350
**Burlington	2,500
Manchester area	325
Montpelier-Barre	550
Newport (incl. in St. Johnsbury)	
Rutland	625
**St. Johnsbury	140
Stowe	150
***Woodstock	270
Other places	100
VIRGINIA	
Alexandria (incl. in N. Virginia)	
Arlington (incl. in N. Virginia)	
Blacksburg	175
Charlottesville	1,500
Chesapeake (incl. in Portsmouth)	
Colonial Heights (incl. in Petersburg)	
Danville area	100
Fairfax County (incl. in N. Virginia)	
Fredericksburg[N]	500
Hampton (incl. in Newport News)	
Harrisonburg (incl. in Staunton)	
Lexington (incl. in Staunton)	
Lynchburg area	275
**Martinsville	100
Newport News-Hampton[N]	2,400
Norfolk-Virginia Beach	11,000
Northern Virginia	35,100
Petersburg area	350
Portsmouth-Suffolk (incl. in Norfolk)	
Radford (incl. in Blacksburg)	
Richmond[N]	12,500
Roanoke	900
Staunton[N]	370
Williamsburg (incl. in Newport News)	
Winchester[N]	270
Other places	150
WASHINGTON	
Bellingham	525
Ellensburg (incl. in Yakima)	
Longview-Kelso (incl. in Vancouver)	
*Olympia	560
***Port Angeles	100
*Seattle[N]	37,200
Spokane	1,500
*Tacoma	2,000
Tri Cities[N]	300
Vancouver	600
**Yakima	150
Other places	350
WEST VIRGINIA	
***Bluefield-Princeton	200
*Charleston	975
Clarksburg	110
Huntington[N]	250
Morgantown	200
***Parkersburg	110
**Wheeling	290
Other places	200
WISCONSIN	
Appleton area	100
Beloit	120
Fond du Lac (incl. in Oshkosh)	
Green Bay	500
Janesville (incl. in Beloit)	
*Kenosha	300
La Crosse	100
*Madison	5,000
Milwaukee[N]	21,000
Oshkosh area	170
*Racine	200
Sheboygan	140
Waukesha (incl. in Milwaukee)	
Wausau[N]	300
Other places	300
WYOMING	
Casper	100
Cheyenne	230
Laramie (incl. in Cheyenne)	
Other places	50

Notes

CALIFORNIA

Long Beach—includes in L.A. County: Long Beach, Signal Hill, Cerritos, Lakewood, Rossmoor and Hawaiian Gardens.Also includes in Orange County: Los Alamitos, Cypress, Seal Beach, and Huntington Harbor.

Los Angeles—includes most of Los Angeles County, but excludes those places listed above that are part of the Long Beach area and also excludes the eastern portion that is listed below as part of San Gabriel and Pomona Valleys. Also includes eastern edge of Ventura County.

Orange County—includes most of Orange County, but excludes towns in northern portion that are included in Long Beach.

Palm Springs—includes Palm Springs, Desert Hot Springs, Cathedral City, Palm Desert, and Rancho Mirage.

San Gabriel and Pomona Valleys—includes in Los Angeles County: Alhambra, Altadena, Arcadia, Azusa, Baldwin Park, Bellflower, Bell Gardens, Chapman Woods, Charter Oak, Claremont, Commerce, Covina, Diamond Bar, Downey, Duarte, East Los Angeles, East Pasadena, East San Gabriel, El Monte, Glendora, Hacienda Heights, La Canada Flintridge, La Habra Heights, La Mirada, La Puente, La Verne, Los Nietos, Monrovia, Montebello, Monterey Park, Norwalk, Pico Rivera, Paramount, Pasadena, Pomona, Rosemead, Rowland Heights, San Dimas, San Gabriel, San Marino, Santa Fe Springs, Sierra Madre, South El Monte, South Pasadena, South San Gabriel, South San Jose Hills, South Whittier, Temple City, Walnut, West Covina, West Puente Valley, West Whittier, Whittier, and Valinda. Also includes in San Bernardino County: Alta Loma, Chino, Chino Hills, Mira Loma, Montclair, Ontario, Rancho Cucamonga, and Upland.

Sacramento—includes Yolo, Placer, El Dorado, and Sacramento counties.

San Francisco Bay area—North Peninsula includes northern San Mateo County. South Peninsula includes southern San Mateo County and towns of Palo Alto and Los Altos in Santa Clara County. San Jose includes remainder of Santa Clara County.

COLORADO

Denver—includes Adams, Arapahoe, Boulder, Denver, and Jefferson counties.

Pueblo—includes all of Pueblo County east to Lamar, west and south to Trinidad.

CONNECTICUT

Bridgeport—includes Monroe, Easton, Trumbull, Fairfield, Bridgeport, Shelton and Stratford.

Danbury—includes Danbury, Bethel, New Fairfield, Brookfield, Sherman, Newtown, Redding, and Ridgefield.

Hartford—includes all of Hartford County and Vernon, Rockville, Somers, Stafford Springs in New Haven County and Ellington and Tolland in Tolland County.

Lower Middlesex County—includes Branford, Guilford, Madison, Clinton, Westbrook, Old Saybrook, Old Lyme, Durham, and Killingworth.

New Haven—includes New Haven, East Haven, Guilford, Branford, Madison, North Haven, Hamden, West Haven, Milford, Orange, Woodbridge, Bethany, Derby, Ansonia, Quinnipiac, Meriden, Seymour, and Wallingford.

New London—includes central and southern New London County. Also includes part of Middlesex County and part of Windham County.

Waterbury—includes Bethlehem, Cheshire, Litchfield, Morris, Middlebury, Southbury, Naugatuck, Prospect, Plymouth, Roxbury, Southbury, Southington, Thomaston, Torrington, Washington, Watertown, Waterbury, Oakville, Woodbury, Wolcott, Oxford, and other towns in Litchfield County and northern New Haven County.

Westport—includes Norwalk, Weston, Westport, East Norwalk, Wilton, and Georgetown.

DISTRICT OF COLUMBIA

Washington, D.C.—For a total of the Washington, D.C. metropolitan area, include Montgomery and Prince Georges counties in Maryland, and northern Virginia.

FLORIDA

Orlando—includes all of Orange and Seminole counties, southern Volusia County, and northern Osceola County.

Stuart-Port St. Lucie—includes all of Martin County and southern St. Lucie County.

GEORGIA

Augusta—includes Burke, Columbia, and Richmond counties.

ILLINOIS

Chicago—includes all of Cook and DuPage counties and a portion of Lake County.

Elgin—includes northern Kane County and southern McHenry County.

Rockford—includes Winnebago, Boone, and Stephenson counties.

Southern Illinois—includes lower portion of Illinois below Carlinville.

INDIANA

South Bend—includes St. Joseph and Elkhart counties.

KANSAS

Kansas City—includes Johnson and Wyandotte counties. For a total of the Kansas City metropolitan area, include Missouri portion.

Wichita—includes Sedgwick County and towns of Salina, Dodge City, Great Bend, Liberal, Russell, and Hays.

KENTUCKY

Lexington—includes Fayette, Bourbon, Scott, Clark, Woodford, Madison, Pulaski, and Jessamine counties.

LOUISIANA

Alexandria—includes towns in Allen, Grant, Rapides, and Vernon parishes.

Baton Rouge—includes E. Baton Rouge, Ascension, Livingston, St. Landry, Iberville, Pointe Coupee, and W. Baton Rouge parishes.

South Central—includes Abbeville, Lafayette, New Iberia, Crowley, Opelousas, Houma, Morgan City, Thibodaux, and Franklin.

MAINE

Southern Maine—includes York, Cumberland, and Sagadahoc counties.

MASSACHUSETTS

Andover—includes Andover, N. Andover, Boxford, Lawrence, Methuen, Tewksbury, and Dracut.

Boston Metropolitan region—Brockton-South Central includes Avon, Bridgewater, Brockton, Canton, East Bridgewater, Easton. Foxborough, Halifax, Randolph, Sharon, Stoughton, West Bridgewater, Whitman, and Wrentham. Framingham area includes Acton, Bellingham, Boxborough, Framingham, Franklin, Holliston, Hopkinton, Hudson, Marlborough, Maynard, Medfield, Medway, Milford, Millis, Southborough, and Stow. Northeast includes Chelsea, Everett, Malden, Medford, Revere, and Winthrop. North Central includes Arlington, Belmont, Cambridge, Somerville, Waltham, and Watertown. Northwest includes Bedford, Burlington, Carlisle, Concord, Lexington, Lincoln, Melrose, North Reading, Reading, Stoneham, Wakefield, Wilmington, Winchester, and Woburn. North Shore includes Lynn, Saugus, Nahant, Swampscott, Lynnfield, Peabody, Salem, Marblehead, Beverly, Danvers, Middleton, Wenham, Topsfield, Hamilton, Manchester, Ipswich, Essex, Gloucester, and Rockport. Near West includes Ashland, Dedham, Dover, Natick, Needham, Norfolk, Norwood, Sherborn, Sudbury, Walpole, Wayland, Wellesley, Weston, and Westwood. Southeast includes Abington, Braintree, Cohasset, Duxbury, Hanover, Hanson, Hingham, Holbrook, Hull, Kingston, Marshfield, Milton, Norwell, Pembroke, Quincy, Rockland, Scituate, and Weymouth.

New Bedford—includes New Bedford, Dartmouth, Fairhaven, and Mattapoisett.

Springfield—includes Springfield, Longmeadow, E. Longmeadow, Hampden, Wilbraham, Agawam, and W. Springfield.

MICHIGAN

Mt. Pleasant—includes towns in Isabella, Mecosta, Gladwin, and Gratiot counties.

MISSOURI

Kansas City—For a total of the Kansas City metropolitan area, include the Kansas portion.

NEW HAMPSHIRE

Laconia—includes Laconia, Plymouth, Meredith, Conway, and Franklin.

NEW JERSEY

Cherry Hill-Southern N.J.—includes Camden, Burlington, and Gloucester counties.

Essex County-East Essex—includes Belleville, Bloomfield, East Orange, Irvington, Newark and Nutley in Essex County, and Kearney in Hudson County. North Essex includes Caldwell, Cedar Grove, Essex Fells, Fairfield, Glen Ridge, Montclair, North Caldwell, Roseland, Verona, and West Caldwell. South Essex includes Maplewood, Millburn, Short Hills and South Orange in Essex County, and Springfield in Union County.

Middlesex County—includes in Somerset County: Kendall Park, Somerset, and Franklin; in Mercer County, Hightstown; and all of Middlesex County.

Northeastern N.J.—includes Bergen, Essex, Hudson, Hunterdon, Mercer, Middlesex, Monmouth, Morris, Ocean, Passaic, Somerset, Sussex, Union, and Warren counties.

North Hudson County—includes Guttenberg, Hudson Heights, North Bergen, North Hudson, Secaucus, Union City, Weehawken, West New York, and Woodcliff.

Somerset County—includes most of Somerset County and a portion of Hunterdon County.

Trenton—includes most of Mercer County.

Union County—includes all of Union County except Springfield. Also includes a few towns in adjacent areas of Somerset and Middlesex counties.

Vineland—includes most of Cumberland County and towns in neighboring counties adjacent to Vineland.

NEW YORK

Elmira—includes Chemung, Tioga, and Schuyler counties.

Glens Falls—includes Warren and Washington counties, lower Essex County, and upper Saratoga County.

Kingston—includes eastern half of Ulster County.

New York Metropolitan area—includes the five boroughs of New York City, Westchester, Nassau, and Suffolk counties. For a total Jewish population of the New York metropolitan region, include Fairfield and New Haven counties, Connecticut; Rockland, Putnam, and Orange counties, New York; Northeastern New Jersey, and Pike County, Pennsylvania.

Syracuse—includes Onondaga County, western Madison County, and most of Oswego County.

Utica—southeastern third of Oneida County.

NORTH CAROLINA

Asheville—includes Buncombe, Haywood, and Madison counties.

Charlotte—includes Mecklenburg County. For a total of the Charlotte area, include Rock Hill, South Carolina.

OHIO

Cincinnati—includes Hamilton and Butler counties.For a total of the Cincinnati area, include the Covington-Newport area of Kentucky.

Cleveland—includes all of Cuyahoga County and portions of Lake, Geauga, Portage, and Summit counties. For a metropolitan total, also include Elyria, Lorain, and Akron.

Toledo—includes Fulton, Lucas, and Wood counties.

Youngstown—includes Mahoning and Trumbull counties.

PENNSYLVANIA

Philadelphia—For total Jewish population of the Philadelphia metropolitan region, include the Cherry Hill-Southern N.J., Princeton, and Trenton areas of New Jersey, and the Wilmington and Newark areas of Delaware.

Pittsburgh—includes all of Allegheny County and adjacent portions of Washington, Westmoreland, and Beaver counties.

Sunbury—includes Shamokin, Lewisburg, Milton, Selinsgrove, and Sunbury.

Wilkes-Barre—includes all of Luzerne County except southern portion, which is included in the Hazleton total.

SOUTH CAROLINA

Sumter—includes towns in Sumter, Lee, Clarendon, and Williamsburg counties.

TEXAS

Amarillo—includes Canyon, Childress, Borger, Dumas, Memphis, Pampa, Vega, and Hereford in Texas, and Portales, New Mexico.

Houston—includes Harris, Montgomery, and Fort Bend counties, and parts of Brazoria and Galveston counties.

McAllen—includes Edinburg, Harlingen, McAllen, Mission, Pharr, Rio Grande City, San Juan, and Weslaco.

Waco—includes McLennan, Coryell, Bell, Falls, Hamilton, and Hill counties.

VIRGINIA

Fredericksburg—includes towns in Spotsylvania, Stafford, King George, and Orange counties.

Newport News—includes Newport News, Hampton, Williamsburg, James City, York County, and Poquoson City.

Richmond—includes Richmond City, Henrico County, and Chesterfield County.

Staunton—includes towns in Augusta, Page, Shenandoah, Rockingham, Bath, and Highland Counties.

Winchester—includes towns in Winchester, Frederick, Clarke, and Warren counties.

WASHINTON

Seattle—includes King County and adjacent portions of Snohomish and Kitsap counties.

Tri Cities—includes Pasco, Richland, and Kennewick.

WISCONSIN

Milwaukee—includes Milwaukee County, eastern Waukesha County, and southern Ozaukee County.

Wausau—includes Stevens Point, Marshfield, Antigo, and Rhinelander.

Review of the Year

OTHER COUNTRIES

Canada

National Affairs

SEPTEMBER 11 HAD A PROFOUND IMPACT on Canada. First, several dozen Canadian citizens died in the terrorist attacks. Second, Canada's economy, already weakening earlier in the year, teetered close to recession as interest rates dropped and the unemployment rate rose to around 8 percent by the end of 2001. The Canadian dollar declined by about 6 percent relative to its U.S. counterpart, hitting record lows. Third, the threat of further terrorist incidents led to calls for tighter security that produced new legislation.

About a month after the terrorist attacks in New York and Washington, the government introduced a package of antiterrorism bills that defined "terrorist" groups and activities, criminalized the collection of money for terrorism, eased the rules governing surveillance of suspected terrorists, provided for preventive arrest of terrorist suspects, and codified tougher penalties for hate crimes. Canadian Jewish Congress (CJC) president Keith Landy supported the bill, citing the mood of Jews across the country in the aftermath of September 11. In contrast, a representative of the Canadian Islamic Congress denounced the legislation as "obscene," adding, "you might as well delete the constitution from our landscape." The bills passed in December.

In fact there had been warnings about terrorism well before September. CJC, in February, urged the government to take many of the actions that were, in fact, implemented after September 11. CJC reiterated its concerns after the convictions, in two separate trials in the United States, of Arab terrorists who had lived in Montreal, Ahmed Ressam and Mokhtar Haouari. At his trial, Ressam testified that before setting his sights on the Los Angeles International Airport he had considered setting off a bomb in a neighborhood of "Israeli interest," which was subsequently identified as a part of the Montreal suburb of Outremont where many Hassidim lived. In July, Keith Landy declared: "We don't want a major terrorist incident to be the clarion call. As a Jewish community and as

Jewish Canadians we call upon our government to make a strong commitment to opposing terrorism at every turn."

After September 11, two Egyptians with alleged ties to the al-Jihad group were arrested in Toronto. Another man, Nabil Al-Maralh, who used to live in Toronto, was arrested in Chicago in connection with the hijackings. A Moroccan man who had continued to live in Montreal for three years after the government had rejected his claim for refugee status, Said Atmani, was put on trial in France. He was charged with being a key aide to Fateh Kamel, an Algerian-born Canadian who had earlier been convicted in Paris for assisting terrorists. The French also claimed that Atmani had worked for Osama bin Laden.

Sensibilities of Canadian Arabs became an issue. The Canadian Museum of Civilization in Ottawa had scheduled an Arab-Canadian art exhibit for October that included a video with extreme anti-Israel material. After September 11, the exhibit was postponed indefinitely. But Prime Minister Jean Chrétien, responding to the Arab community, intervened to insure that it opened on schedule. CJC president Landy complained to the chair of the board of the museum. Landy found it unacceptable to allow "one of our national institutions to be used as a vehicle to promote the kind of hatred which is at the root of the attack against the U.S. in the first place, as well as the ugly situation in our own country."

In August, the Federal Court of Appeal in Ottawa ruled in favor of Andrew Liebmann. He had been a reserve lieutenant in the navy during the period of the Gulf War in 1991 and had sued after being barred from an important assignment in the Persian Gulf because he was Jewish. Though Liebmann had originally lost at trial, he was vindicated on appeal when the court agreed that he had suffered discrimination because he was Jewish. The decision, commented CJC Ontario Region chair Ed Morgan, endorsed the principle that "Canadian Forces cannot pander to the prejudices of foreign countries."

In October, Ontario premier Mike Harris announced his retirement. In an assessment of his nearly two terms in office, Landy praised him for introducing a tax credit that assisted parents of day school children, while others in the Jewish community criticized him for his conservative social policies.

Karen Leibovici and Stephen Mandel were elected to the Edmonton city council in October.

The new Quebec premier, Bernard Landry, continued to reach out to Jews, despite the Jewish community's overwhelming rejection of the secessionist option that defined his Parti Québécois. In a speech to Jewish leaders marking Israel Independence Day, Premier Landry asked his auditors to reconsider their devotion to the federalist cause and to be more open-minded about possible Quebec sovereignty. Drawing parallels between Quebec and Israel as a way to connect with his Jewish audience, he expressed the hope that "many of you, and more and more of you, will participate in that dream of ours," Quebec as a nation.

Residents of the suburban Montreal towns of Côte Saint-Luc and Hampstead—both with substantial Jewish majorities—were dismayed in June when the Quebec commission assigned to redraw riding (district) boundaries recommended that the riding of D'Arcy McGee, which included the two towns, be eliminated and its population be absorbed into adjoining districts. D'Arcy McGee regularly elected a Jewish member of the National Assembly, currently Lawrence Bergman, and it was rare for any other riding to elect a Jew. Thus, this redistricting threatened to put an end to almost a century of at least one Jew serving in the legislature. Bergman termed it "vandalism of the worst nature" and lamented the potential loss of community representation in Quebec City. CJC Quebec Region chair Joseph Gabay accused the commission of "targeting minorities." Community pressure on the commission paid off. In December, in its final report, the commission decided to leave the riding intact.

The Quebec government forced a merger of Montreal with the 27 suburban municipalities that shared the island of Montreal. The new "megacity" came into existence at the end of the year. Elections for mayor, city councilors, and borough councilors were held in November. Among the 103 councilors elected: Saulie Zajdel, Michael Applebaum, Marvin Rotrand, Robert Libman, Dida Berku, Howard Zingboim, Irving Grundman, Karin Marks, Anthony Housefather, and Maurice Cohen. Libman was named to the executive committee.

Israel and the Middle East

Canada's voting record in the UN continued to be a source of tension between the government and the community as Canada's membership on the Security Council during 1999–2000 brought it under intensified Jewish scrutiny. While the government saw itself as pursuing a balanced and even-handed policy in the Middle East, Jews saw it as tilting toward the Arab side, especially on the Palestinian issue.

In April, the annual meeting of the UN Commission on Human Rights in Geneva passed a number of resolutions considered hostile to Israel. Canada abstained on a resolution regarding the Palestinian right to self-determination on the grounds that it ignored the process of direct negotiations. Canada abstained as well on three resolutions alleging Israeli human-rights violations, and on two involving Syrian and Lebanese aspects of Israeli policy. It did vote in favor of a motion condemning Israel's settlement activities in the territories, but on the other hand it voted against a resolution that was perceived as opening the way to a revival of the "Zionism is racism" canard. Canada-Israel Committee (CIC) executive director Rob Ritter was generally pleased that Canada had not supported the bulk of the resolutions.

The December meeting of the UN General Assembly provided a forum for 19 resolutions unfriendly to Israel. Canada voted in favor of most of them—including one sharply critical of alleged Israeli interference with the delivery of humanitarian supplies to the Palestinians—and abstained on the others. The organized Jewish community, which would have applauded Canada's adoption of the U.S. position supporting Israel even on just some of the resolutions, was not hopeful of any new direction in the Canadian approach. The CIC's David Goldberg observed that "they may be consistently wrong, but there's no change in policy."

Also in December, at a meeting of the signatories to the Geneva conventions, Canada supported a resolution that essentially charged Israel with serious violations of the rules of war, in connection with its treatment of civilians in the territories. Opposition leader Stockwell Day accused the prime minister of having authorized that vote himself. Whether Jean Chrétien or officials in the Department of Foreign Affairs were responsible, the prime minister did try to finesse the matter by stating that Canada had objected to some of the text in question. Nevertheless, Day accused him of moving Canada away from its traditional neutral stance. "It's a very disturbing pattern of duplicity on the part of the Canadian government. There isn't even a pretense of balance," said Day. In response, Deputy Prime Minister Herb Gray told the House of Commons that, aside from the United States, there was no country "that stands up in a more forthright and balanced way for Israel." MP Irwin Cotler criticized the government for allowing the meeting to take place because it resulted in "undermining the very regime of international humanitarian law." The CIC denounced the final declaration, and CJC's Keith Landy called it "a morally outrageous document" that would incite hatred of Israel, "making Canada's footnote to the contrary irrelevant."

When the question of electing Syria to a two-year term on the Security Council came up, Canada would not reveal its secret vote, though it was widely believed that Canada voted in favor despite calls from Jewish organizations to vote against.

Considerable dispute surrounded Canadian policy with regard to the World Conference Against Racism, Racial Discrimination, Xenophobia and Related Intolerance held in Durban, South Africa, in September. Although the Jewish community urged the government not to participate because the conference was likely to became a forum for Israel-bashing and anti-Semitism, Canada was represented there, albeit by a low-level cabinet minister. MP Irwin Cotler was a member of the delegation. During the August preparatory meetings, Canada did try to dissuade the Arab countries from pursuing a "Zionism is racism" resolution. Karen Mock, national director of B'nai Brith's League for Human Rights, led a delegation of representatives of Jewish nongovernmental organizations (NGOs) at a meeting with Mary Robinson, the United Nations High Commissioner for Human Rights, but the group was unable to convince Robinson to redirect the agenda.

Canada did not follow the example of the U.S. and Israel in boycotting the conference or walking out, the government arguing that it might ameliorate the attacks on Israel and Jews by being there. Canadian Jewish representatives to the NGO forum, held in late August before the conference itself began, complained about the oppressive and discriminatory atmosphere. As CJC president Landy put it, "you just have to walk in there as a Jew and you feel extremely threatened." After the conference ended, Landy described it "as an unmitigated failure and a complete fiasco." The Canadian delegation distanced itself from what it termed the "irresponsible" declaration and expressed its "strongest objections" to inclusion of anything to do with the Palestinian-Israel conflict in the final document. Canada's ambassador to the UN, Paul Heinbecker, noted that his delegation "registers its strongest objections and dissociates itself integrally from all text in this document directly or indirectly relating to the situation in the Middle East."

Irwin Cotler, in a Montreal speech in November, criticized the award of the Nobel Peace Prize to the United Nations and to Secretary General Kofi Annan. Their selection, he charged, conferred legitimacy on the "festival of hate" that had singled out Israel and Jews for international opprobrium. In recounting his experiences in Durban, Cotler stressed the pervasive anti-Semitism. He noted that, by remaining until the end of the conference, when the declaration was adopted by consensus, Canada made itself a party to it, despite the subsequent attempt to dissociate itself. However he did praise his fellow members of the Canadian delegation for their strong efforts to remove offending language. Cotler also lamented the inattention of Israel and the rest of the Jewish world to the impending conference until the summer, whereas the Palestinians had been working for their cause for three years.

A number of policy issues related to the Middle East arose during the year, and they often put Minister of Foreign Affairs John Manley at the center of controversy. Rumors surfaced in January that Canada had made a secret offer to take in thousands of Palestinian refugees in the context of a peace settlement. Palestinian leaders were outraged because they feared that such action would undermine their claim to a right of return. Manley confirmed that Canada was ready to take in refugees, and noted that, as chair of the Refugee Working Group, Canada had a particular interest in the matter. Visiting Israel in May as part of a trip to the region, Manley publicly called for an end to the construction of settlements in the territories, a view that Prime Minister Ariel Sharon rejected. The two also clashed on the proper response to an Egyptian-Jordanian initiative. Upon his return to Canada, Manley announced Canada's support for the Mitchell Report proposed by the U.S., saying, "it closely mirrors our own policies."

Israel Asper, whose CanWest Global Communications Corp. had become a major media presence, pulled no punches in his evaluation of Canadian foreign policy at a dinner in his honor in Toronto in June. He denounced Canada's "shameful and wrong-headed policy on Israel," asserting that "it is not too late to regain our honor and integrity." He criticized Manley by name, and the foreign secretary responded with an article in the *National Post* in July that termed the criticism "unfortunate, untrue, and harmful," adding that strong support for Israel "has been at the core of Canada's . . . policy since 1947. . . ."

Manley created a great rift between the government and the Jewish community with comments in a newspaper interview in October, just before he left on another trip to the Middle East. He suggested a distinction between the terrorism that the U.S. suffered on September 11 and that which Israel faced on a regular basis, saying: "Whatever else you might say about September 11, I'm not aware it was a claim for some kind of territory on Manhattan Island. These are very different situations." Hit by a storm of criticism, Manley explained, in a letter to the editor of the *Canadian Jewish News,* that he rejected the notion that "terrorist attacks against Israel could be more acceptable than the recent terrorist attacks against the United States." The basis for distinguishing the two cases, he explained, was that there was a peace process going on in the Middle East. At a panel discussion in Montreal, the new CIC executive director, Shimon Fogel, pointed out that Manley had taken a strong stand against terrorism in his talks with Arab leaders. In remarks made in December, Manley lamented the increasing violence involving Israel and the Palestinians. Although he called on Palestinian chairman Yasir Arafat to end the uprising and dismantle the terrorist networks, the CIC nevertheless took him to task for not being more forceful in putting his demands to the Palestinians.

Opposition leader Stockwell Day came out squarely on Israel's side. In a speech to the CJC national plenary assembly in May, Day delighted the delegates when he blamed the violence on the Palestinians. Day drew a moral distinction between "an accidental injury or death of bystanders who are tragically caught in the crossfire of violence, and the deliberate murder of innocent people in a premeditated act of terrorism." He sharply criticized Canadian foreign policy as being based on "groupthink" rather than facts, and blasted Canada's UN voting record for supporting "blatantly anti-Israel resolutions." Spokespeople for the Canadian Arab community were outraged, threatening legal action for alleged incitement against Arabs and called for Day's resignation.

Responding to pressure from the Jewish community and others, the government decided in December to widen its official list of terrorist groups to include the entire Hamas structure. As a result, any funds belonging to Hamas or associated organizations, such as the Holy Land Fund and the Al Aqsa Bank, would be frozen if found in a Canadian financial institution. Previously, charitable operations of the group were considered acceptable.

Léger Marketing conducted a poll of Canadians in December to ascertain their views on the Israel-Palestinian conflict. The major finding was that 26 percent held Arafat responsible for the surge of violence, 12 percent blamed Sharon, 24 percent assigned blame equally, and 38 percent had no answer. As for general sympathies in the conflict, 21 percent favored Israel, 11 percent favored the Palestinians, 45 percent favored neither, and the rest had no opinion.

An old terrorist case, dating from 1988, continued to work its way through the legal process. Mahmoud Mohammad Issa Mohammad, who had been convicted in Greece for his part in a Popular Front for the Liberation of Palestine attack on a plane at the Athens airport in 1968, had been seeking permanent residence status in Canada for years. Canada, however, had been trying to deport him because of his terrorist background. In November, the Immigration and Refugee Board dismissed his appeal on the grounds that his continued presence in Canada would be "a mockery of Canadian legislation." Mohammad indicated that he would appeal further in the courts.

Anti-Semitism and Racism

The controversy over the alleged anti-Semitism of Quebec nationalist Yves Michaud was a contributing factor in the surprise decision of Premier Lucien Bouchard to resign in January. Michaud, while seeking the Parti Québécois (PQ) nomination for a vacant legislative seat in Montreal in 2000, had made several hostile remarks on radio and television about Jews who opposed an independent Quebec, and spoke slightingly about the Holocaust. Bouchard, the party leader, denounced him, eliciting praise from Jewish organizations. Allan Adel, for example, Quebec Region chair of B'nai Brith Canada (BBC), spoke of the premier's "great leadership and courage." For the Jews of Quebec, Bouchard's rejection of Michaud's intolerance marked an important milestone: a separatist leader was on record affirming that Jews were full citizens regardless of their position on the independence issue (see AJYB 2001, p. 288).

In his resignation announcement, Bouchard demonstrated his distaste for the issues raised by Michaud, stating that he had "no appetite" for debates over which groups tended to oppose secession or over the Holocaust. "The Holocaust," he declared, "was the supreme crime, a systematic attempt to eliminate people. . . . We should not hold it against the Jewish people for being traumatized by this." Bouchard also defended the National Assembly for its vote to condemn Michaud. BBC Quebec director Robert Libman termed the remarks "the most articulate and passionate defense of the Jewish community I have ever heard from a Quebec leader, PQ or Liberal." The CIC Quebec chair, Thomas Hecht, observed that the Michaud affair demonstrated that "Quebec has changed significantly. It is a much more open society. . . . The old ethnocentric chauvinism is no longer mainstream or forms the consensus."

In a letter to Bouchard, Michaud argued that he was no anti-Semite, pointing out that he had lived harmoniously for 37 years in a Jewish neighborhood and acknowledging the "unique and incomparable character" of the Nazi attempt to wipe out the Jews. Michaud nevertheless renewed his attack on B'nai Brith for having the temerity to challenge the Quebec nationalists. Some 150 of Michaud's supporters, including a former Quebec premier and two members of Parliament, signed an advertisement that appeared in the newspaper *Le Devoir* in January condemning the 2000 National Assembly motion that censured Michaud, and calling it an attack on "the freedom of expression of Quebecers."

In an address in March to the Stockholm International Forum on Combating Intolerance, MP Cotler, who headed the Canadian delegation, called for the development of a new international legal strategy to deal with the incitement of group hatred that would include measures to fight the hate transmitted over the Internet. He proposed an international legal commission to launch such efforts.

B'nai Brith Canada expressed ongoing concern about a rising tide of hate crimes and anti-Semitic incidents that was clearly tied to the new round of Palestinian violence that began in late 2000 (see AJYB 2001, pp. 288–89). September 11, 2001 brought even more incidents in its wake—anti-Semitic graffiti, bomb threats, synagogue and cemetery desecrations, and verbal and written abuse. Of the 286 anti-Semitic incidents audited by B'nai Brith Canada for 2001, 35 percent occurred during September and October. In Toronto, 41 percent of the year's incidents were concentrated in those two months, including the spray painting of graffiti against Jews and for Osama bin Laden on the walls of Shaar Shalom Synagogue in the suburb of Thornhill, and a rash of anti-Semitic graffiti at Ryerson University.

After many years of legal tangles with the authorities, Holocaust denier and anti-Semite Ernst Zundel left Canada in March and settled in the United States. Keith Landy, then the Ontario Region chair of CJC, expressed his satisfaction: "The many years of efforts, of hounding Zundel, have finally paid off." Landy concluded that Canadian extremists had "lost their champion."

The Doug Collins case, in which the Human Rights Tribunal of British Columbia ruled against the journalist in 1999 for promoting hatred of Jews (see AJYB 2000, p. 271), appeared in the news again, this time on appeal. Another tribunal upheld the constitutionality of the judgment that Collins's newspaper columns fomented hatred or contempt of Jews, holding that the provincial human-rights code was compatible with the federal Charter of Rights and Freedom. Collins also lost in the Supreme Court of Canada, where his appeal on jurisdictional grounds was denied in August.

In the New Brunswick Court of Appeal in May, cartoonist Josh Beutel succeeded in overturning a 1998 judgment for $7,500 against him for a cartoon that depicted anti-Semitic former teacher Malcolm Ross as a Nazi (see AJYB 2001, p. 289). The court found Beutel's cartoon to be fair comment on the views expressed by Ross in two books, and also agreed with the lower court that "Ross is a racist and anti-Semite." Beutel, awarded court costs of $5,000 from Ross, praised the decision as a victory for free expression.

Al-Moustakbal, an Arabic language newspaper in Montreal, published two articles that CJC characterized as inflammatory attacks on Jews. The editor, however, claimed that the articles referred to Israel and not Jews, even though the writer had employed classic anti-Semitic stereotypes. She said that she had demanded that Elias Bittar, the freelance journalist who wrote the offensive pieces, write another article to clear up the confusion: "I asked him to write and explain. It's a form of apologizing."

Eustace Mullins, a West Virginia author accused of anti-Semitism, was dropped from the program of the Total Health 2001 show, which was held in Toronto in March. His invitation was withdrawn after pressure from CJC, which demonstrated that Mullins promoted notions of Jewish conspiracies. David Icke of Great Britain, similarly known for his advocacy of bizarre conspiracy theories involving Jews, suffered the cancellation of a scheduled lecture at a Unitarian church in Toronto in June. In addition, both Mullins and Icke had also been booked to appear on a Canadian speaking tour, but the former withdrew after adverse publicity. Icke appeared without Mullins at a seminar in Montreal in June that was closed to the press, but two talks scheduled for Toronto had to be canceled when the owners of the planned venues backed out of their agreements.

Nazi War Criminals

In the annual report of the War Crimes Section of the Justice Department, issued in July, the government reported that no new cases had been launched over the preceding year, largely due to the paucity of evidence that would be admissible in court. Some 1,600 files had been examined since 1986, when war crimes prosecutions began. Currently, there were 85 active files from the Nazi period, with 147 preliminary investigations underway in other prospective cases. In 1998 the government had promised to launch 14 new cases by 2001, but fell far short, with only a handful filed.

Since 1995, when the strategy changed from criminal prosecution to citizenship revocation and deportation, the government had initiated 17 cases. Of these, five were successful (two of the defendants died after losing their cases and the other three were contesting denaturalization), three defendants won in court and preserved their citizenship, six died before proceedings could be completed, two cases are still in court, and one had been completed but not yet decided. Two other accused war criminals departed Canada voluntarily. A particularly egregious example of delay was the case of Vladimir Katriuk. Even though a Federal Court judge found in 1999 that he had entered Canada illegally, the government had yet to denaturalize him. On the other hand, Serge Kisluk, subject of a similar finding in 1999, did lose his citizenship in 2000. He died in June 2001 while awaiting a deportation hearing.

Terry Beitner, director of the War Crimes Section, addressed the executive of the CJC Ontario Region in September, trying to explain his group's slow progress. "We only go after those people who we say were war criminals," said Beitner, and the decision of whom to pursue reflected a policy judgment based on evidence of criminal responsibility. Beitner noted that the department had committed resources to enable him to pursue cases, and said that new legal actions would be filed in the near future. He concluded: "We'll see the fruits of those efforts shortly."

It was revealed in December that the federal government has paid $1.7 million to cover the legal fees of defendants in the three cases it had lost, those of Eduards Podins, Peteris Vitols, and Johann Dueck.

Andrew Telegdi, an MP from the Kitchener area of Ontario, where there were many residents of German descent, caused a stir when he sharply criticized the process of denaturalizing alleged Nazi war criminals. Since it was the cabinet that made the final decision to revoke citizenship, and naturalized citizens who obtained their citizenship fraudulently did not have the right to appeal to higher courts, Telegdi considered the Canadian process comparable to totalitarian abuse. After a public outcry, he was forced to apologize in the House of Commons in May, and he told his colleagues of his loathing for Hitler's regime.

In a public speech in June, New York investigator Steve Rambam, who had identified a number of alleged Nazi war criminals living in Canada, argued that the slow pace of action on these cases was due both to the government's fear of antagonizing certain ethnic groups in the country and to passivity on the part of the Jewish community. Rambam asserted that at least 500 of the 1,000 war criminals originally admitted to Canada after the war were still alive. He observed that "Canada has become an old-age home for Nazi war criminals. The lesson is that if you killed Jews, you have nothing to fear living here." In September, Rambam and the CJC announced that they would cooperate on several cases of alleged war criminals.

In 2000, a Federal Court judge found that Helmut Oberlander had misrepresented his background—membership in Einsatzkommando 10A—when he obtained citizenship. In 2001, the German-Canadian Congress accused Citizenship and Immigration Minister Elinor Caplan of seeking "revenge" rather than justice; Paul Tuerr, vice president of its Toronto chapter, went so far as to suggest that the Jewish community had special access to government officials. Incoming CJC president Landy lamented that "some leaders of the German-Canadian community are trying to turn this into an ethnic conflict." After agreeing in May to hear from Oberlander, the cabinet announced in August that he would lose his citizenship. Appeals were anticipated that would delay deportation, possibly for years.

Wasyl Odynsky, a former guard at the Trawniki SS camp who entered Canada in 1949, faced a Federal Court proceeding on how he had obtained citizenship. The judge ruled in March that he had lied about his wartime activities, but did not find any evidence that he had "participated personally in any incident involving the mistreatment of prisoners." The matter then went to the cabinet for a decision on revocation of Odynsky's citizenship.

The trial of Walter Obodzinski, scheduled to begin in July, was put off because the defense team launched an appeal on procedural grounds related to his health. Until such time as the Supreme Court of Canada would decide whether the case might proceed notwithstanding his ill health, the matter was in abeyance. Meanwhile the trial of Jacob Fast began in November, despite his lawyer's claims that he could not represent Fast properly because of the defendant's Alzheimer's disease. The government alleged that Fast served as an auxiliary member of the German security police in Ukraine between 1941 and 1944, participated in "the arrest and mistreatment of prisoners," and lied about his past when immigrating to Canada in 1947.

A Federal Court judge ruled in September that Michael Baumgartner, an SS man and a guard at concentration camps, would have been ineligible for entry to Canada had he told the truth about his background when he entered the country in 1953. This decision paved the way for the cabinet to denaturalize him.

The government filed a case against Michael Seifert in November, accusing him of personal involvement in war crimes in Italy in 1944–45 and of lying about his past during his immigration process in 1951. Seifert was an SS guard who, according to the government, participated in "the beatings, the torture and the killing of prisoners in the camp and in the [camp's] isolation cells." He was convicted in absentia in Italy in 2000 for killing 11 prisoners. His lawyer, Douglas Christie, claimed that Seifert had been a prisoner during the period in question, and that Minister Caplan was motivated by "Jewish animosity" and bias.

Holocaust-Related Matters

In January, CJC and the Canadian Museums Association agreed to try to locate artworks stolen from Jews during the Holocaust that might be in Canada. Among the museums that had identified works with uncertain provenances were the National Gallery, the Art Gallery of Ontario, and the Montreal Museum of Fine Arts. Ian Lumsden, executive director of the Beaverbrook Art Gallery in Fredericton, New Brunswick, created a furor when he suggested, in an interview in December, that "the greater good of mankind might have been served inadvertently" by the Nazi confiscations, since "if some of these works had been left in homes in Amsterdam and God knows where, they'd have been bombed and the works might have been destroyed. That would be much more heinous than actually having these things surface in major collections. . . ." He quickly apologized.

In connection with the processing of claims of Holocaust survivors, CJC and the Jewish Holocaust Survivors of Canada charged that Canadian Jewish survivors were not receiving proportional institutional support from the Conference on Jewish Material Claims Against Germany. Michael Rosenberg, president of the Holocaust Survivors, stated that "we must ensure that Canadian Jewish organizations show no complacency in seeking institutional funds to support Holocaust survivors and long-term education on the Holocaust."

In June, the federal government designated January 17 as Wallenberg Day, to be commemorated annually in honor of Canada's only honorary citizen, Raoul Wallenberg, the Swedish diplomat who had saved thousands of Jews in wartime Hungary. The Canadian Heritage Ministry would prepare an educational program for all Canadian schools to mark the day. In remarks in the House of Commons, MP Cotler praised the initiative to recognize "the best of humanitarian intervention" and to demonstrate "that one person can confront radical evil, prevail and transform history."

In October, a photography exhibit at the Koffler Centre of the Arts at the Bathurst Jewish Community Centre in Toronto told the heroic story of journalist Varian Fry, who helped save many Jews in France in 1940–41.

That same month, Vision TV showed two documentaries in connection with Holocaust Education Week: "Out of the Fire," directed by Shelley Saywell, and "Rendezvous," directed by Dominique Darmon. Both were about survivors returning to visit the villages where they once lived.

Prof. Gary Evans, a University of Ottawa film historian, spoke in Montreal in December about Holocaust films. In particular, he reviewed the National Film Board projects and television programs on the Holocaust that had appeared, going as far back as the war years. He criticized filmmakers for "looking for meaning instead of presenting the reality" and urged them to use the testimony of survivors as the basis for scripts. Often, he pointed out, Canadian films downplayed the tragedy of the Jews during the Holocaust period, but he believed that the situation was improving.

JEWISH COMMUNITY

Demography

In the hope of reversing a long-term demographic decline, the Winnipeg Jewish community launched its Grow Winnipeg plan. Despite the substantial growth of the Jewish population in the country as a whole over the previous 40 years, the number of Jews in Winnipeg had dropped from 19,000 in 1960 to about 14,000, of whom a quarter were senior citizens. Grow Winnipeg sought to boost the Jewish population to 18,000 by 2010 by attracting immigrants from Argentina, the former Soviet Union, South Africa, and elsewhere, luring back former residents, and finding employment for young Winnipeg Jews so as to keep them from moving. Bob Freedman, executive director of the Jewish Federation of Winnipeg/Combined Jewish Appeal—the source of funding for the project—warned: "if we don't take a proactive approach, we will continue to slide backwards."

Montreal's Federation/Combined Jewish Appeal conducted a survey of Russian immigrants who arrived during the 1990s. Some 198 families were located and interviewed, nearly all of them still living in Montreal. Over half of the respondents were working in the same field as they had in the former Soviet Union, but nearly 45 percent reported difficulty finding work or considered themselves to be underemployed. Only about a sixth belonged to a synagogue or other Jewish group. Nearly 82 percent said that they were optimistic about their lives in Canada.

Communal Affairs

The Canadian Jewish Congress held its 26th triennial plenary in May in Toronto, with nearly 1,000 registered delegates in attendance. Sessions dealt with funding religious schools, advocacy strategies, Holocaust restitution, child poverty, student issues, the Middle East and Jerusalem, the media, and anti-Semitism. Keith Landy was elected president by acclamation and Irving Abella was elected honorary president.

Two controversial organizational suggestions were made during the year. First, there was a proposal to integrate much of the work of the Jewish Immigrant Aid Services within the UJA Federation of Greater Toronto, but opponents warned that this might hamper the effectiveness of JIAS. Also, Rabbi Gunther Plaut, the community's elder statesman, addressed the competition between CJC and B'nai Brith Canada in a *Canadian Jewish News* column in May. He expressed concern about the competition and occasional conflict that occasionally "goes off the rails and produces quite embarrassing situations." Arguing that "we are too small a number in Canada to fritter our energy away with useless antagonisms," Plaut wondered, "when will we come to our senses?"

In the immediate aftermath of the September 11 terrorist attacks, the community went on the alert, fearful of possible violence but with no specific evidence about any threat within Canada. The government supplied added security for Israeli diplomatic missions, and police forces stepped up their protection of community institutions. Some community events were postponed or canceled. In October several Jewish organizations in Toronto, Ottawa, Windsor, and Montreal received letters containing a white, powdery substance that resembled, but turned out not to be, anthrax. At least two contained threats against Jews.

In Toronto the Bloor JCC was completely renovated, at a cost of some $10 million, and then renamed the Miles S. Nadal Bloor JCC. Community officials saw it as a key to revitalizing the downtown Jewish community, home to about 20,000 Jews. The effort was part of the federation's Jewish Toronto Tomorrow community-wide infrastructure improvement plan, in which the federation matches private gifts. The federation also decided to shift its spending in light of the situation in Israel. The Jewish Agency for Israel was to receive more money, reversing a trend of several years toward greater emphasis on local needs. Montreal's federation budget for local needs increased by nearly 11 percent due to record fundraising.

The merger between the Jewish Hospital of Hope and the Jewish Nursing Home, two Montreal institutions, led to a lawsuit over control of several million dollars. The Jewish Eldercare Centre, the product of the merger, contended that the JHH Foundation was not releasing income from its endowment or from its new fund-raising to the new entity.

Another Montreal merger, this one involving two synagogues, also ignited a legal battle. Russian Jewish worshipers at Congregation Anshei Ozeroff objected to a merger with Adath Israel Poale Zedek Synagogue, and charged that the leadership of their synagogue had brought about the merger over their resistance. But the doors of the synagogue were locked in October, leaving its largely Russian congregants with few suitable alternatives.

In Toronto, Leon Edery was convicted of income tax violations for issuing false tax receipts for charitable donations in the names of three different synagogues. He was fined and sentenced to a year of house arrest.

Israel-Related Matters

Three Toronto rabbis, John Moscowitz, Moshe Shulman, and Baruch Frydman-Kohl, organized the Israel Now Consortium in July to mobilize support for Israel through education, rallies, and missions to Israel. Its first project was an Israel Solidarity Rally for Freedom, which attracted about 3,000 people to the Beth Tzedec Synagogue in December. Among the speakers were MP Irwin Cotler, Minister of Defense Art Eggleton, Israeli cabinet minister Dan Meridor, and Consul General Meir Romem. Eggleton declared that "Canada and Canadians must stand firmly with Israel."

Montreal's Jewish community set up a Strategic Action Committee in November to combat attempts to undermine Israel's legitimacy. This joint project of the federation, CIC, and CJC focused on synagogues, campus activities, providing information, monitoring the media, and public affairs. CIC Quebec chair Thomas Hecht stressed the need "to have an engaged community in the media struggle of deciding whether Israel is the victim or the 'victimizer.' " Two rallies were held in Montreal to protest Palestinian terrorist attacks in Israel, the first in August, just after the Sbarro pizzeria bombing in Jerusalem, and the second in December, after large-scale terrorist bombings in Haifa and Jerusalem.

Under the leadership of Rabbi Chaim Steinmetz, a delegation of 15 rabbis from Montreal, Toronto, Ottawa, and Kingston sought to combat the impression that the Jewish community was not deeply involved in Israel's plight. The delegation traveled to Ottawa in May, where it met with members of both houses of Parliament. The rabbis, who were welcomed by the Canada-Israel Friendship Group, told the assembled parliamentarians that Canadian Jews strongly supported Israel and rejected any notion of moral equivalence between Palestinians and Israelis. They also met with senior foreign-affairs officials and representatives of the various political parties.

Toronto artist Michaele Jordana and her partner Douglas Pringle launched a pro-Israel Web site called Project One Soul. The combination of stunning visual imagery and pointed commentaries enabled visitors to the site to comprehend how terror affected Israelis.

Rabbi John Moscowitz criticized his own Reform movement for canceling summer youth trips to Israel, a decision he described as "a large blow to Israel, and a victory for Palestinian terrorists." Other Reform rabbis, however, such as Steven Garten of Ottawa, expressed sympathy for the dilemma faced by the trip organizers, who could not confidently guarantee the safety of the participants.

The situation on many university campuses, where Arab students energetically organized against Israel, was a source of deep concern. The crisis led Jewish student activists to gather at a retreat in the Laurentian Mountains north of Montreal, in January, to organize a national advocacy structure to combat the anti-Israel propaganda.

The atmosphere at Montreal's Concordia University was probably the most hostile in the country. Large numbers of Arab students and a well-organized and very active organization called Solidarity for Palestinian Human Rights made Jewish students feel uncomfortable and even intimidated. In April, Concordia students passed by referendum a resolution, "Palestinian Human Rights," that called upon the government to consider cutting political and economic ties with Israel. Only about 1,400 of the 20,000 eligible students actually bothered to vote, and the resolution passed by a thin margin. The student union, under the control of pro-Palestinian elements, put out a student handbook, entitled *Uprising,* replete with anti-Israel material and blatantly promoting the Palestinian cause. The handbook, financed from student fee revenue, was distributed free to all students. Adverse publicity hurt the university's fund-raising efforts, especially since many of its benefactors were Jewish. Rector Frederick Lowy tried to mollify donors by pointing out that the student union was legally independent and not under the administration's control. He deplored the handbook's contents, calling many of its statements "inflammatory and possibly libelous." The radical element was ousted in new student union elections in December, but the election was nullified on a technicality and the situation on campus remained in limbo.

There were also anti-Israel activities at Toronto's York University, including anti-Israel articles in the student newspaper, graffiti, and an "anti-racism" rally in November with pictures and posters that were offensive to pro-Israel students.

An attempt, in January, to craft a statement acceptable to a broad consensus of Jewish community leaders and academics proved to be divisive. Over 150 prominent Jews did sign a declaration supporting Israeli sovereignty over an undivided Jerusalem, which appeared in local and community newspapers. But a number of those asked to sign declined. Some were reluctant to appear to be committing their organizations, others did not want to be seen as taking sides in the Israeli election campaign then underway, and yet others argued that an Israeli government might not choose to adhere to the positions taken in the statement. University of Toronto Jewish history professor Derek Penslar, commenting on the lack of unity, observed that "Jerusalem is a symptom of a much larger and deeper problem, of a rift within each Jewish community."

In July, Canada's Jews sent a smaller-than-planned team to Israel to compete in the Maccabiah, because of the threat of terrorism there. Canadian athletes won two gold medals, ten silvers, and 18 bronze medals. Maccabi Canada president Roy Salomon pointed out that "there was a level of emotionalism that we have never seen before."

Religion

Toronto was the site of several important events and initiatives. The Conservative movement's Rabbinical Assembly held its annual convention there in June. One highlight was a session devoted to rabbinic leadership that featured a panel of Orthodox, Conservative, and Reform rabbis. The Canadian Council for Reform Judaism joined with several other faith groups in organizing an "End Child Poverty" fast in Toronto in September. Rabbi Larry Englander of Solel Congregation declared that "as we fasted on Yom Kippur, we not only made the statement that we were fasting for forgiveness for our sins, but for the collective sin of allowing our children to starve."A group in Toronto announced plans to establish a virtual synagogue on the Internet, to be known as myShul, that would offer several kinds of synagogue experiences online. One of the backers, Martin Hoffmitz, said that the site "will encourage people to build their own spiritual space at a level that is comfortable for them." Toronto rabbis arranged an "interdenominational Jewish service of memorial and hope" for the victims of the September 11 terrorist attacks. Several hundred people attended the event, which was held at a local synagogue.

Rabbi Elyse Goldstein, president of the Toronto Board of Rabbis, said, "we weep at the perversion of God's holy name, and through these tears we bring this message: Though there are madmen in this world, the world is not mad."

Education

Ontario was the only province that did not provide public funding for Jewish schools, a situation that Jews deeply resented, especially since Catholic schools were constitutionally guaranteed such funding. For 17 years Jewish community organizations had pursued legal and political avenues to rectify this inequality, but without success. In March, all 42 Jewish day schools in Toronto, Ottawa, Hamilton, London, and Kitchener jointly founded the Ontario Association of Jewish Day Schools, which was to coordinate advocacy and lobbying activities.

The first major breakthrough—an unanticipated one—occurred in May, when the provincial government of Progressive Conservative Premier Mike Harris announced that it would introduce an income-tax credit to help parents who were paying tuition to private schools. The credit would be worth a maximum of $700 per child in 2002, increasing annually until it reached $3,500 per child in 2006. Jews welcomed the news enthusiastically, but outside the community feelings were mixed. Backers of the public-school system, fearing that it would lose students, expressed opposition, and even some who favored tax credits for families sending their children to faith-based schools felt that the proposed legislation went too far by including private schools that did not have a religious orientation. Dalton McGuinty, the leader of the Liberal Party, announced his opposition. At the legislative hearings on the plan, spokespeople for the Jewish community were fulsome in their praise. Rabbi David Shochet, speaking for the Toronto Board of Rabbis, described the plan as a "bold initiative," which would begin "to eliminate the discrimination that characterizes the current system." The bill passed in June as part of the budget, with the Liberals and New Democrats opposed.

At the beginning of the year, unionized teachers at six Jewish day schools in Montreal engaged in work-to-rule tactics in a dispute with the school administrations over how to allocate a $1-million retroactive salary adjustment received from the Quebec government. The parties settled in January when the schools agreed to abide by the same principles as those used in the public sector.

Several universities benefited from community largesse directed toward their Jewish studies programs. The Diamond Foundation gave $1 million to the University of British Columbia, to be matched by UBC, for a chair in Jewish law and ethics. At the University of Toronto, Andrea and Charles Bronfman established a chair in Israeli studies, and Prof. Emanuel Adler, a political scientist from the Hebrew University of Jerusalem, was named as the initial chairholder. At Montreal's McGill University, Leanor Segal donated $1 million to create a chair in Jewish studies. There were also plans for an Institute for Jewish Education at McGill, which already had a program for training Jewish studies teachers. Prof. Gershon Hundert, chair of Jewish studies, predicted that "the institute will make McGill one of North America's leading centers for the preparation of teachers in Jewish studies."

Montreal's Torah and Vocational Institute (TAV), serving ultra-Orthodox Jews, launched a lawsuit in March against the Université du Québec à Montréal for $8.1 million in damages because UQAM terminated its contract with TAV in 2000. The two institutions had originally agreed that TAV students would receive university credit for their programs through UQAM. But faculty opposition at UQAM over separation of the sexes, the particularistic nature of TAV, and the fact that English was the major language of instruction, induced the administration to renege on its agreement only one year into its three-year commitment.

Community and Intergroup Relations

Efforts at improving interreligious relations were a prominent feature of community life. In February, priests and rabbis got together at Beth Tzedec Synagogue in Toronto for a day of study to address the problem of difficult texts associated with the Easter and Passover seasons. The Toronto Board of Rabbis and the Roman Catholic Archdiocese of Toronto cosponsored the event. Among the speakers, Rev. Thomas Rosica said that anti-Jewish teaching "is no longer authentic Christian proclamation today" and that the Jewish covenant with God is "theologically intact."

The University of Toronto was the site of a meeting, in October, devoted to Jewish-Catholic dialogue. The main speakers, Edward Cardinal Cassidy, who had been the Vatican official responsible for relations with Jews, and David Novak, a professor of Jewish studies at the university, addressed developments since the Second Vatican Council and prospects for the future.

The need for Jewish-Muslim communication was obvious after September 11. The Muslim-Jewish Dialogue of Montreal, a group consisting of both laypeople and clergy, had been meeting for three years. After the terrorist attacks it issued its first public statement, deploring and condemning the deeds and affirming that "Islam is a religion of peace and not a religion of violence." Another group, the Canadian Association of Jews and Muslims, rallied at Toronto's city hall on September 15 in support of mutual respect, the sanctity of life, and coexistence.

Despite attempts at dialogue, interfaith tensions surfaced on matters relating to Israel. The Middle East Working Group, an offshoot of the Canadian Council of Churches, produced a document in January calling for "peace with justice in the Middle East." While early drafts, according to the group's Jewish interlocutors, were quite antagonistic toward Israel, the final version was more evenhanded. CJC's national director of community relations, Manuel Prutschi, noted that the Catholic Church played a key role in moderating the statement. In August, the *Anglican Journal,* that church's national newspaper, featured an article that blamed Israel for the conflict with the Palestinians and compared Israel to South Africa of the apartheid era. Rabbi Reuven Bulka and Keith Landy, on behalf of CJC, expressed their "deep disappointment and dismay" to the Anglican primate in Canada.

In an incident involving public schools, a district organization of the union for Toronto high school teachers reprinted in its own newsletter an article from a leftist magazine that was hostile toward Israel, and recommended the article to its members as a resource in geography and history classes. According to editor Doug Little, "we view America, and Israel as its agent, as the prime oppressor in this case in the Middle East." But after a wave of protests, the union president backed away, declaring that "it's not an appropriate lesson plan," and the chair of the Toronto district school board repudiated the article as unbalanced.

Conflict over the recitation of the Lord's Prayer in public institutions arose during the year. In January, a lawsuit was filed in the Ontario Superior Court of Justice asking to end recitation of the prayer at each session of the legislature on the ground that it unconstitutionally promoted Christianity. In June, the Ontario Court of Appeal held that the provincial Human Rights Commission could not order the speaker of the legislature to desist from reciting the prayer, since the legislature was immune from intervention in its internal affairs. The question of whether regular recitation of the prayer should continue also came up in the legislature of Nova Scotia in April; members of that body were generally opposed to any change.

In the Montreal area, efforts to find land for new Chabad synagogues finally bore fruit in the predominantly Jewish suburbs of Côte St. Luc and Hampstead. In January, after three years of controversy and intense opposition from residents of several neighborhoods, the Côte St. Luc city council approved the necessary zoning change to permit the construction of a synagogue and community center. Another Chabad group took Hampstead to court in March in order to obtain permission to build on its chosen site, which was very close to the only Reconstructionist synagogue in the Montreal area. The town had said that it would not allow two synagogues on the same street. Now, however, in a quick turnaround to avoid a trial, the council reversed itself and granted permission for the building.

Celine Forget, a member of the Outremont city council, challenged her own colleagues in court, arguing that they had improperly allowed a Hassidic congregation, Amour Pour Israël, to modify an existing building and turn it into a synagogue. But a Superior Court judge dismissed her action and found that the council had acted in the public interest. Forget, who had a long history of clashing with the Hassidim in this predominantly French town, lost another case against a different group of Hassidim in October. She had accused Congregation Toldos Yacov Yosef of creating a nuisance because the sounds of prayer were disruptive to the public. The judge found in favor of the synagogue, noting that it had not had any problem with neighbors until Forget moved there in 1995.

The film *Keepers of the Faith: Canadian Chasidim,* directed by Ian McLaren, was a Chabad project funded in part by the federal government. Its depiction of the Lubavitch community provided insight into the history, traditions, and routines of its adherents and highlighted the lives of several prominent members, while also giving some attention to other Hassidic groups. The film was shown on television in both French and English versions.

Culture

Arnold Bennett's film about the life of A.M. Klein, *The Messiah from Montreal,* premiered in October at the Saidye Bronfman Centre in Montreal. Al Waxman narrated the tragic story of the brilliant poet and writer whose productivity was stilled by depression. Many of Klein's poems were recited and dramatized in the film.

The disaster of the *Struma,* a ship carrying Jewish refugees from Romania to Palestine that sank in the Black Sea under mysterious circumstances in 1942 with the loss of 778 lives, was recounted in a documentary film by Simcha Jacobovici. *The Struma* premiered at the Toronto International Film Festival in September. The filmmaker's investigation into the mystery of who sank the ship led him to conclude that it was a Soviet submarine.

Other films that appeared during the year included David Kaufman's *The New Klezmorim,* filmed at KlezKanada in 1998, and *Je Me Souviens* by Eric Scott, which recounted the story of Esther Delisle and her efforts to expose the historical record of anti-Semitism in Quebec society. The Toronto Jewish Film Festival in April included the premiere of Robert Cohen's story of a folk-music group, *The Travellers: This Land is Your Land.* Other films exhibited there were Coleman Romalis's *Emma Goldman: The Anarchist Guest* and Nikila Cole's *Wanderings: Postcards from the Diaspora.*

Leonard Pearl accompanied and interviewed over 100 Canadian Birthright Israel participants in 2000 and 2001. Then he, Rena Godfrey, and Isaac Szpindel made the film *Birthright Israel,* which premiered in November at the Toronto Centre for the Arts. Also in November, Cinémathèque Ontario presented a retrospective of the films of Amos Gitai.

The Koffler Gallery in Toronto hosted an exhibit of photographs by Jill Culiner in March. Entitled "La Mémoire Effacée," it juxtaposed battlefield photos from the two world wars and from concentration camps with contemporary shots of the same land as well as the sites of some former Jewish communities in Eastern Europe.

The Jewish Heritage Society of Western Canada held a conference in Winnipeg in September on Jewish Radicalism in Winnipeg, 1905–1960, recalling the days when the city's North End was a hotbed of socialism and other leftist movements.

The new Institut de la culture sépharade was inaugurated in Montreal in November. Judah Castiel, its prime mover and first president, described its goal as preserving and promoting the historic and cultural heritage of Sephardic Jews. The joint backers of the institute were the Canadian Sephardic Federation and the Communauté Sépharade du Québec.

Publications

Canada lost one of its greatest writers with the death of Mordecai Richler. Despite the ambivalence that many Jews felt toward one of their own who did not always depict them or their religion in the kindest terms, his literary achievements were a source of pride. Richler was acclaimed internationally for his novels, which included *The Apprenticeship of Duddy Kravitz, Barney's Version, St. Urbain's Horsemen,* and *Solomon Gursky Was Here.*

Morton Weinfeld brought together a wealth of social scientific data in *Like Everyone Else . . . But Different: The Paradoxical Success of Canadian Jews.* Examining religious practices, attitudes, anti-Semitism, and socioeconomic status, Weinfeld concluded, "Jewish life in Canada today is as good as it has been anywhere since the Golden Age of Spain." Since Jews participated in all aspects of Canadian society while maintaining an active Jewish life, he suggested, the community had good reason to be optimistic.

From Immigration to Integration: The Canadian Jewish Experience, edited by Ruth Klein and Frank Dimant, was a collection of essays by academics—mainly historians and social scientists—about the community's past, the struggle for equal rights, relationships with Israel, and future challenges. A complementary reference work, *Jews and Judaism in Canada: A Bibliography of Works Published Since 1965,* compiled by Michael Brown, Richard Menkis, Benjamin Schlesinger, and Stuart Schoenfeld, included over 1,600 entries.

Other books on Canadian Jewry and Canada included *The First Century of Jewish Life in Edmonton and Northern Alberta, 1893–1993: The First and Second Generations* edited by Uri Rosenzweig; *Montreal of Yesterday* by Israel Medres, published in Yiddish in 1947 and now translated by Vivian Felsen; *Through the Eyes of the Eagle: The Early Montreal Yiddish Press, 1907–1916* edited by Pierre Anctil; William Weintraub's *Getting Started: A Memoir of the 1950s; René Lévesque et la communauté juive* by Victor Teboul; *Où va le Québec?* by Ghila Sroka; *A Concise History of Canadian Architecture* by Harold Kalman; and *Hidden Canada* by Norman Ravvin. Two books were published about a noted singer and poet: *Leonard Cohen* by David Sheppard, and *The Song of Leonard Cohen: Portrait of a Poet, a Friendship, and a Film* by Harry Rasky.

Rabbi Erwin Schild published an account of his life in Germany before and during World War II in *The Very Narrow Bridge: A Memoir of an Uncertain Passage.* Kurt Jonassohn and Mervin Butovsky coedited a series called *Memoirs of Holocaust Survivors in Canada.* Historian Régine Robin wrote *Berlin chantiers: Essai sur les passés fragiles,* a reflection on Berlin and Jewish memory.

Historian Gil Troy wrote *Why I Am a Zionist: Israel, Jewish Identity and the Challenges of Today.* Although realistic about the Jewish state, Troy presented an unapologetic Zionist position, citing historical facts to make the case for Israel. Julien Bauer's *Le système politique israélien,* a more academic presentation, explained Israel's often impenetrable political process.

Fixing God's Torah: The Accuracy of the Biblical Text and Rabbinic Law by B. Barry Levy focused on how rabbis through the ages dealt with questions about the spelling of the traditional Torah text. *The Lay People in Palestine from Augustus to Hadrian: A Prosopographic Study* by Claude Cohen Matlofsky examined the daily lives of ordinary residents of the land of Israel between 40 B.C.E. and 135 C.E. Rabbi Elyse Goldstein edited *The Women's Torah Commentary,* containing essays on each of the Torah portions from a woman's perspective. In *Et Hazamir,* Dina Sabbah examined a number of pieces of Sephardic liturgical music. Joseph Lévy, Josué Elkouby, and Marc Éliany compiled the *Dictionnaire biographique du monde juif sépharade et méditerranéen.*

Books of poetry included *The Song That Never Died: The Poetry of Mordecai Gebirtig,* translated by Simcha Simchovitch and coedited by him and Raymond Souster; and *Carbon Filter, Light Industry* by Seymour Mayne. Among the novels published were *Clara's War* by Kathy Kacer, *Une Juive en Nouvelle-France* by Pierre Lasry, and *L'Empire de Kalman l'infirme,* a translation by Pierre Anctil of Yehuda Elberg's novel. Adam Gopnik published *Paris to the Moon,* essays about his experiences and observations in the French capital, while Leonard J. Cohen wrote *Serpent in the Bosom: The Rise and Fall of Slobodan Milosevic.*

The annual Jewish Book Awards ceremony was held in June at the Leah Posluns Theater in Toronto. Among the winners were *Typing: A Life in 26 Keys* by Matt Cohen, *That's What I Am* by Al Waxman, *Long Shadows* by Erna Paris, *The Possibility of Dreaming on a Night Without Stars* by Michael Kaufman, *Delayed Impact* by Franklin Bialystock, *Remember Me* by Irene Watts, *Art and Tradition* by Dorion Liebgott, *Apples of Gold in Settings of Silver* by Barry Dov Walfish, *Montreal of Yesterday* translated by Vivian Felsen, *My Bones Don't Rest in Auschwitz* by Gitel Donath, *The Law of Return* by Karen Shenfield, *Unauthorized Entry* by Howard Margolian, and *The Holocaust's Ghost* edited by F.C. De Coste and Bernard Schwartz.

Personalia

A number of Jews were appointed to the Order of Canada. Companions: Jack Diamond and Mordecai Richler. Officers: Mark Greenberg and Mark Wainberg. Members: Judy Feld Carr, Murray Frum, Norbert

Rubin Morgenstern, Mona Winberg, J. Joel Wolfe, Clara Balinsky, Marjorie Bronfman, Eric Maldoff, Rabbi Erwin Schild, and Herbert Siblin. Rabbi Israel Sirota received the Citation for Citizenship.

David Young was appointed attorney general of Ontario, and Mark Freiman was named deputy attorney general. Anne Golden was appointed president of the Conference Board of Canada, Chaviva Hosek as president of the Canadian Institute for Advanced Research, Jacques Bensimon as chair of the National Film Board, and Karen Mock as executive director of the Canadian Race Relations Foundation. Avrum Gotlieb became president of the American Society for Investigative Pathology, Harvey Weingarden was named president of the University of Calgary, Bernard Langer was elected president of the Royal College of Physicians and Surgeons of Canada, and David Mock was appointed dean of dentistry at the University of Toronto. Régine Robin won the literary prize of the city of Montreal, while professors Norbert Morgenstern and Ronald Melzack won Killam Prizes for distinguished lifetime academic achievement, and architecture professor Avi Friedman won the Southam Newspapers Manning Award of Distinction.

Appointments and elections within the Jewish community included Stanley Hartt as chairman of the board of Israel Bonds; Keith Landy as CJC president and Dorothy Zalcman Howard as chair of its national executive; Shimon Fogel as executive director of the Canada-Israel Committee; Rochelle Wilner as president of B'nai Brith Canada; Sandy Posluns as president of JNF Canada; Myer Bick as president of the Jewish General Hospital Foundation; Joseph Gabay as chair of CJC Quebec Region, Ed Morgan as chair of its Ontario Region, and Nisson Goldman as chair of its Pacific Region; Steven Cummings as president of Federation CJA in Montreal; Leslie Wilder as president of JIAS Canada; Barry Steinfeld as president of the Canadian Council of JCCs and YM/YWHAs; Ralph Shedletsky as chair of the board and Allan Reitzes as president of UJA Federation in Toronto; and Gerry Fisher as executive director of Hamilton's UJA Federation.

Members of the community who died this year included actor Al Waxman, in January, aged 65; Ben Lappin, community official and professor of social work, in January, aged 86; Irving (Yitz) Feldman, lay leader in education, kashrut supervision, and religion, in January aged 68; Rabbi Zelig Wolkenstein, executive director of the Latner Jewish Public Library, in February, aged 55; psychotherapist and community activist Rebbetzin Phylllis Weinberg, in February, aged 73; multifaceted composer Milton Barnes, in February, aged 69; UN diplomat and crusader for nuclear disarmament William Epstein, in March, aged 88; longtime community professional Irwin Gold, in March, aged 82; master piano teacher, composer, and author Boris Berlin, in March, aged 93; jazz musician Moe Koffman, in March, aged 72; comedian Jackie Kahane, in April, aged 79; artist Aba Bayefsky, in May, aged 78; developer, philanthropist, and community leader Maxwell Cummings, in May, aged 103; Rebbetzin Naomi Bulka, in May, aged 55; Cantor Henry Zimmerman, in June, aged 91; A.L. Stein, a lawyer who won a landmark civil liberties case against a Quebec premier, in June, aged 93; retired Senator Sidney Buckwold, in June, aged 84; eminent writer Mordecai Richler, in July, aged 70; community leader and builder Gordon Brown, in July, aged 92; academic and Yiddishist Arthur Lermer, in July, aged 92; human-rights and civil-liberties lawyer Irving Himel, who fought restrictive covenants, in July, aged 86; *Canadian Jewish News* founder Meyer Nurenberger, in August, aged 90; artist Louis Muhlstock, in August, aged 97; film producer and patron of the arts Sandra Kolber, in September, aged 67; community leader and fund-raiser Morley Cohen, in September, aged 84; former newspaper publisher Max Wollock, in September, aged 84; Reconstructionist and community leader Rabbi Lavy Becker, in October, aged 95; real estate developer and philanthropist André Aisenstadt, in October, aged 104; former Hadassah-WIZO president Patricia Alpert, in October, aged 70; Rebbetzin Judy Taub, in November, aged 54; and Philip Simon, community leader, in December, aged 79.

HAROLD M. WALLER

Western Europe

Great Britain

National Affairs

IN JANUARY, Peter Mandelson, Prime Minister Tony Blair's friend and political mentor, resigned for the second time, again because he concealed his dealings with a wealthy man. Despite predictions of trouble for a Labor government facing an imminent election, the party and the government emerged virtually unscathed.

Chancellor Gordon Brown's budget, presented in March, which proposed modest tax cuts and increased spending for such purposes as the National Health Service, public transportation, and education, created a favorable atmosphere: the chancellor earned higher approval ratings than any of his postwar predecessors, and half the electorate thought Labor the party most able to cope with economic difficulties (the opposition Conservatives scored only 31 percent on the economy).

The general election, held in May, confimed this assessment. Labor once again won overwhelmingly, with 413 seats against 166 for the Conservatives and 52 for the Liberal Democrats. Despite its victory, Labor was not as popular as the bare election results suggested, as the two leading opposition parties attracted 50 percent of the votes cast, as against 40.8 percent for Labor. Only the vagaries of the voting system secured Labor its large overall majority of seats. An immediate result of the election was the resignation of Tory leader William Hague, precipitating an election for new party leadership that brought the relatively unknown Iain Duncan Smith to office as head of the opposition. At the end of the year neither the new Conservative leader nor his shadow cabinet had made much of an impact.

Labor received credit for the performance of the economy. Inflation hovered around the targeted level of 2.5 percent; interest rates were down to 4 percent; and consumption was up. Economic growth was forecast at

2.25 percent—the lowest since the government took office, but still the highest among the Group of Seven. This success, however, only reinforced the government's persistent dilemma over setting the date for a referendum on entry into the single-currency system. Labor itself was divided on the matter, and the electorate was hostile.

Israel and the Middle East

Great Britain remained committed to the Middle East peace process. In February, after President George Bush took office in the U.S. and Prime Minister Ariel Sharon in Israel, a Downing Street spokeman said that Prime Minister Blair was ready to work with all concerned parties. In October, Foreign Secretary Jack Straw spoke against any separate British or European initiative, insisting that it was essential for the European Union to work closely with Washington.

As violence escalated in the Middle East, Britain urged the Palestinians to do everything possible to halt extremism and curb violence, Israel to refrain from escalating matters and to keep its response to Palestinian attacks proportionate, and both sides to exercise restraint. But as the year wore on, and especially in September and October, British condemnation of Israeli retaliation grew harsher. By year's end, however, the British had veered back again to follow the American lead, placing most of the blame for the situation on the Palestinians.

In April, Foreign Secretary Robin Cook called on Israelis and Palestinians to resume security cooperation: the Israeli government should ease restrictions on the occupied territories, "which only fuel bitterness and resentment." That same month Cook endorsed U.S. criticism of Israel's response to Palestinian mortar fire from Gaza. Whitehall understood Israel's anger, Cook told Israeli foreign minister Shimon Peres, but was "disappointed and concerned" about the demolition of Palestinian homes and the departure from Sharon's initial determination to hit only military installations. Then in May, Blair and Cook expressed concern at Israel's use of F-16 aircraft to hit back at the Palestinians for a suicide bombing in Netanya, and also called on the Palestinians to stop such violence. The situation, said Blair in a radio interview, was "more worrying than for some years."

The July appointments of Jack Straw as foreign secretary, Ben Bradshaw as Middle East minister, and Phyllis Starkey—chair of the all-party British-Palestinian parliamentary group—as parliamentary private secretary heralded a harder line toward Israel. In July, Straw accused

Israel of acting "provocatively" by destroying Palestinian homes in Jerusalem and Rafah in Gaza. He disappointed Israelis by failing to mention, at the same time, Palestinian violations of the cease-fire, though Straw did agree that month to a three-day mission by Blair's special envoy Lord Levy to impress on Israeli and Palestinian leaders the need to do everything possible to consolidate the cease-fire. Also in July, Bradshaw described Israel's missile attack on Nablus, which killed six senior Hamas members and two boys, as "wrong and illegal under international law." Britain, he went on, could not accept "targeted assassination of Palestinian militants." Returning from a Middle East fact-finding mission in August, Bradshaw said that Israel must stop insisting on a total cessation of violence before agreeing to negotiations, and suggested that Britain would seriously consider contributing personnel to an international observer force. Condemning the suicide bomb that killed 15 Israelis in the crowded Sbarro pizzeria in Jerusalem the same month, Bradshaw angered Israelis and British Jews with his comment that the tragedy underlined "the futility of the course on which the parties were headed." "It is witheringly pathetic," Israeli embassy spokesman D.J. Schneeweiss told the *Jewish Chronicle,* "that the Foreign Office cannot bring itself in public to acknowledge who are the perpetrators, who the victims."

In August, too, Straw described Israel's incursion into the West Bank village of Beit Jala, from which Palestinian gunmen bombarded Jerusalem's Gilo neighborhood, as "excessive, disproportionate, and threatening to stoke the cycle of violence." He demanded an immediate Israeli withdrawal. At the same time, Straw called on Israel to freeze all settlements, including the "natural growth" of existing settlements. In September, after Israeli tanks rolled into Jenin and Jericho on the West Bank following the shooting of an Israeli woman, Britain demanded that Israel withdraw its forces.

Following the events of September 11, Straw acknowledged that Israel was suffering the "most terrible terrorism" by extremist groups, and Blair called on the Muslim and Arab world to make "defeating this barbarism" a common cause. It was, he said, more important than ever to keep the Middle East peace process alive. However, the Iranian press quoted Straw, visiting there at the time, as suggesting that Israeli policy toward the Palestinians helped breed terrorism, and this angered Israelis. When Straw arrived in Israel, Prime Minister Sharon canceled a scheduled meeting with him, and only Blair's intervention made Sharon change his mind. Plans for a state dinner in Straw's honor, hosted by Foreign Minister Peres, were dropped. In Great Britain, Labor Friends of Israel (LFI) called for an urgent meeting with Straw over the apparent "shift in policy"; "it seems the Arabists are in full control of the Foreign Office," an LFI spokesman commented.

Blair quickly assumed a pivotal role in organizing the war against terrorism. He held largely fruitless discussions in Damascus, where he urged Syria's president Bashar al-Assad to cease supporting terrorist groups, before proceeding to Saudi Arabia and Israel. Meanwhile, Foreign Minister Straw said that the violence in Israel and the territories had the effect of weakening Islamic support for the battle against Osama bin Laden and the Taliban. In answer to questions in the House of Commons, he demanded "a 100 percent effort" from Arafat to halt violence by Palestinian militants, while calling on Israel to halt its West Bank incursions, stop '"extrajudicial killings," and "exercise proper respect for human rights."

Jewish political and communal figures voiced concern that British Jewry and Israel could become isolated as the government courted British Muslims to ensure their support for the Afghanistan war. However, a ten-member delegation of leading Jews that met with Blair in Downing Street was completely satisfied with the prime minister's assurance that his government remained supportive of both Israeli and Jewish community concerns. But certain elements outside the government took a "blame Israel" stand. Two influential newspapers, the *Guardian* and the *Evening Standard,* gave considerable space to critics of the Jewish state. In October, the Leicester National Union of Teachers distributed leaflets calling for a boycott of Israeli goods. Then, during Christmas shopping season, Selfridges, a top department store, bowed to demonstrators from the Boycott Israeli Goods campaign and stopped selling products manufactured in the West Bank, the Golan, and Gaza, purportedly so as to prevent anti-Israel leafleting and picketing from inconveniencing customers. The store reversed course and allowed the sales of such items again, with an apology, on January 2, 2002.

In October, Straw in the House of Commons and Blair at the Labor Party's conference reiterated Britain's commitment to an independent "viable Palestinian state" living peacefully alongside Israel. Blair told Yasir Arafat in London that month that the murder of Israeli cabinet minister Rehavam Ze'evi "refocuses the need to get the peace process moving again." The theme was reiterated at the Lord Mayor's banquet in London's Guildhall in November, where Blair said that after the Palestinian Authority acted against suspected terrorists and Israel withdrew from areas ceded to Palestinian control under previous accords, the international community should resume "proper negotiations" toward a

Palestinian state side-by-side with a State of Israel that was accepted fully by its Arab neighbors.

By the end of the year, British policy had come full circle. Blair and Straw joined President Bush in condemning the suicide bombings in Jerusalem and Haifa, barely criticizing Israeli retaliation. Straw reported to the Commons that he had told Arafat it was "imperative" for the Palestinian Authority to take action against people connected with organizations like Hamas and Islamic Jihad, which claimed responsibility for the attacks. Arafat, he said, should not just arrest and release them, but detain them securely.

In December, Blair said that ties between Britain and Iran would not progress unless Iran ceased supporting terrorism. Officials in Tehran called his remarks "irresponsible" and registered an official protest to the British embassy. Also in December, Britain's ambassador in Lebanon called on Hezballah to halt its terrorist activities.

The British Jewish community was hardly monolithic in its support of Israel. On November 1, a predominantly Jewish audience in London, assembled under the banner of "Just Peace," applauded the remarks of pro-Palestinian speakers, among them actress Vanessa Redgrave and the Palestinian envoy to Great Britain. In December, Rabbi David Goldberg of St. John's Wood Liberal Synagogue joined Christian and Muslim colleagues in a public letter accusing Israel of practicing a system that "resembles apartheid."

Anti-Semitism and Racism

The number of reported anti-Semitic incidents rose steeply, from 270 in 1999 to 405 in 2000, according to the Community Security Trust (CST) annual report published in January 2001. While most of the cases involved abusive behavior and damage to property, 51 were physical attacks, including two attempted murders. The figures were "clearly worrying," said CST spokesman Mike Whine, who suggested that they represented a spillover effect of the Israel-Palestinian conflict. As in 1999, about 30 percent of the incidents took place in Manchester.

The CST report noted a drop in cases of distribution of anti-Semitic literature, reflecting both the death of Lady Birdwood, a leading publisher of such material, as well as the success of legal prosecutions. In March 2001, more than 100 people suspected of hate crimes were arrested in dawn raids across London as part of the metropolitan police's "march against hate" initiative. Muslims picketed Brent Town Hall in April, when

Chief Rabbi Jonathan Sacks was conducting a celebration of Israeli Independence Day there; police refused to take action when called to the scene, saying, "they'll go away in an hour." In October, the director of public prosecutions decided not to press charges against five men arrested a year earlier for allegedly distributing anti-Semitic literature in Stamford Hill, North London. When the Board of Deputies of British Jews asked the attorney general for an explanation, the Crown Prosecution Service (CPS) responded that the material was unlikely to cause civil unrest since it was distributed only in one neighborhood and targeted only the Jewish community. In December, the Board of Deputies condemned the CPS's failure to enforce the laws against race hatred, vice president Henry Greenwood charging: "There were clear cases of incitement to racial hatred investigated by the police but not prosecuted."

In a spring by-election for the local council in Newham, East London, the extreme right-wing British National Party (BNP) gained 17 percent of the vote on a low turnout, pushing the Conservatives into third place. Prior to the general election in June, the leaders of Britain's five main political parties signed a pledge to keep racism out of their campaigns. The BNP and the National Front (NF), which had not signed the pledge, contested 42 seats and won a total 50,211 votes—3.34 percent of the poll, their highest percentage since 1974. To use the previous national election as a basis for comparison, in 1997, though fighting twice as many constituencies, they had together polled only 49,750 votes.

A particularly sensitive area was Oldham (Lancashire). In March, police banned a planned NF demonstration there after protests by the Black/Jewish Forum and Oldham Action Against Racism; then in June, Asian and white groups clashed in serious riots. BNP chairman Nick Griffin, candidate for Oldham West and Royton, received 6,552 votes, or 16 percent, beating out the Liberal Democrat for third place. The successful Labor candidate, Minister of the Environment Michael Meacher, called for an independent investigation into the BNP's high vote. In Ilford South, pro-Israel Labor MP Mike Gapes retained his seat, but police had to be called twice on election day when groups of youths menaced his supporters. After the election, Special Branch detectives investigated the role of Islamic extremists in organizing the anti-Gapes activities. An electoral commission was formed in September to investigate a claim that the BNP received illegal funds from the American Friends of BNP.

According to the provisions of antiterrorism legislation adopted in February, British-based organizations that incited and supported terrorism abroad were liable to prosecution. The government, said Foreign Secretary Straw, was determined to insure that Great Britain was "not used as a base for the perpetration and planning of terrorism overseas." A draft list of 21 terrorist groups the Home Office wanted to ban, subject to parliamentary approval, included Islamic Jihad, the military wing of Hezballah, the Armed Islamic Group, and the Abu Nidal organization. Straw cautioned that although these organizations had Islamic or Palestinian connections, the list should not be construed as an attack on the Muslim community.

In February, the Oxford Union, the famed debating society, voted 190-186 "that Israel's problems are of its own making." In May, pressure from dons and students persuaded the union to cancel an invitation to Holocaust denier David Irving, who was scheduled to participate in a debate on freedom of speech. There was more bad news for Irving in July, when three Appeal Court judges rejected his appeal against the verdict of his failed libel action against historian Deborah Lipstadt and her book *Denying the Holocaust* (see AJYB 2001, p. 310).

During the summer, the Board of Deputies spearheaded an extensive campaign to prevent the UN's Durban conference on racism from becoming a platform for attacking Israel and Zionism (see above, pp. 85–111). Chief Rabbi Sacks participated in London talks organized by Jordan's Prince Hassan aimed at amending the conference's draft declaration. "If it goes ahead in its present form," said Sacks—who did not attend the conference because of "grave concern" about language relating to Israel—"it will injure the fight against racism and damage the moral authority of the UN."

In October, Home Secretary David Blunkett stated that the government would seek permission to appeal a High Court decision to lift the ban on U.S. black separatist Louis Farrakhan, leader of the Nation of Islam, who had been refused entry to Britain since 1986 because of his outspoken attacks on Jews and other groups.

That same month, Blunkett announced new measures for asylum seekers, including phasing out the controversial system whereby the newcomers received benefits in the form of vouchers for the purchase of specific items, rather than cash. He advocated building new facilities for accommodating the newcomers, and giving them lessons in English and citizenship. In December, Edie Friedman, director of the Jewish Council for Racial Equality, welcomed new legislation in the area of race relations that required public authorities to monitor the ethnic background of employees and to publish detailed programs for achieving racial equality on their staffs.

On September 23, more than 2,000 people gathered at a mass rally in the Theatre Royal, Drury Lane, in central London, organized by most of the major Jewish communal bodies to show solidarity with the United States and Israel in the wake of September 11. Expressions of horror and condolence came from virtually all sectors of British society. The Muslim Council of Britain condemned the attacks, and the principal of the Muslim College stood together with the chief rabbi and Christian leaders on the steps of Lambeth Palace, where the archbishop of Canterbury read a joint statement of outrage.

As early as July, Scotland Yard's head of special operations had warned the Jewish community that it faced threats both from far-right groups and Islamic fundamentalists, particularly young Muslim radicals, and after September 11 the authorities treated a series of assaults in London and Manchester as racist attacks. The CST reported 39 anti-Jewish incidents in September alone, 50 percent more than in September 2000. In October, swastikas were daubed on 65 gravestones in the Birmingham Jewish cemetery, and "C18," the abbreviation of the name of a neo-Nazi group, was written on the wall of the cemetery prayer hall. Four Jewish institutions had to be evacuated due to anthrax hoaxes.

The Union of Jewish Students campaign officer reported increased anti-Israel activity on campuses. The government instructed the police to conduct a "wide-ranging" investigation into the activities of the anti-Israel and anti-Western organization Al-Muhajiroun and its London-based leader Sheikh Omar Bakri Mohammed; the National Union of Students, in pursuance of its "no platform for racism" policy, had already banned the group from campuses in March. On November 4, Chief Rabbi Sacks publicly warned that Islamic extremists could very well reawaken the kind of anti-Semitism that led to the Holocaust. Both he and the Board of Deputies refused to sign a pledge of tolerance to mark Islam Awareness Week, and two rabbis who did sign the pledge later regretted it when the sponsoring organization, the Islamic Society of Britain, was discovered to have distributed anti-Israel leaflets. In December, the Charity Commission was looking into the activities of eight charities suspected of having terrorist links.

Legislation introducing a range of new policies to combat terrorism, including allowing the government to detain suspected terrorists without trial, became law in December after the House of Lords forced the government to drop a clause extending the law on inciting racial hatred to include religious hatred as well.

Holocaust-Related Matters

Almost 2,000 people attended Britain's main Holocaust Memorial Day event at Westminster's Central Hall in January. They included Prince Charles, leaders of the three main political parties, Holocaust survivors, prominent clergy, diplomats, and representatives of the Jewish and general communities. The Muslim Council of Britain turned down an invitation to attend because of what it called "genocide" in Israel and the Palestinian territories. In February, the extremist Muslim group Al-Muhajiroun issued a statement claiming that Holocaust Memorial Day was part of a Zionist campaign "to ensure the myth of the Holocaust was kept alive."

In July, the Heritage Lottery Fund awarded non-Jewish brothers, Drs. James and Stephen Smith, a grant of £314,000 to help meet the growing demand for the educational services of their Beth Shalom Holocaust Center.

There were a number of developments in regard to Holocaust-era looted artworks. In January, the Department of Culture's spoliation advisory panel recommended that the government pay £125,000 to compensate a London family for the painting *View of Hampton Court* by Jan Griffier the Elder. Sold for a pittance by a women hiding from the Nazis, it was later brought to Britain and had been displayed at the Tate Gallery since 1961. In April, drawings by Max Klinger taken by the Nazis from the family of a German Jewish art collector brought his heirs more than £360,000 at a Sotheby's auction. And through the efforts of the World Jewish Congress Commission for Art Recovery, the Kirstein collection was reclaimed from a Leipzig museum. Art collector and painter Gustav Kirstein died in Germany in 1934, his wife committed suicide when the Nazis would not let her leave the country in 1939, and his daughters fled to Great Britain.

Home Office minister Barbara Roche informed the House of Commons in January that the metropolitan police were investigating claims that Ukrainian members of the Galitzian Waffen-SS division, involved in the murder of thousands of Jews and others in Eastern Europe, were living in Britain. In March, Home Secretary Jack Straw released to Scotland Yard the individual records of these men, waiving the usual 100-year confidentiality rule.

Anton Gecas, an 85-year-old Edinburgh guest-house owner and alleged Nazi war criminal, died in a Scottish hospital in September. Back in March, the Lithuanian government had handed the British embassy in Vilnius a warrant for Gecas's extradition to face genocide charges, and in July the Scottish authorities issued a warrant for his arrest. But Gecas suffered a stroke in May, and by August was already gravely ill

JEWISH COMMUNITY

Demography

The number of marriages under Jewish religious auspices declined from 1,017 in 1999 to 907 in 2000, according to statistics issued by the community research unit of the Board of Deputies. The Sephardi and Liberal sectors registered small gains, but Orthodox marriages were down by 57 and Reform by 40. The number of gittin (religious divorces) completed in 2000 rose to 268 from 259 in 1999.

Statistics based on figures for circumcision showed Jewish births in 1999 at 2,509, down from 2,673 in 1998, while burials and cremations under Jewish religious auspices rose from 3,772 in 1999 to 3,791 in 2000. Seven out of ten burials and cremations in 2000 were in Greater London, and three-quarters were Orthodox.

The religious courts of the Reform Synagogue of Great Britain (RSGB) reported accepting 112 proselytes in 2001 as compared with 97 in 2000.

Communal Affairs

Jewish Care, Anglo-Jewry's largest social-services organization, announced plans in February to set up support groups for families of young Jews with drug or alcohol problems. This was in response to a report, based on 1994 British addiction figures, that estimated some 14,000 Jewish addicts in Great Britain. Previously it had been assumed that the Jewish community was immune to such problems. In April, Jewish Care added a twelfth residential home for the elderly, Rosetrees, with 55 beds.

In March, the Heritage Lottery Fund granted Norwood-Ravenswood, the largest Jewish family-services organization, more than £15,000 to help preserve historic records dating back over three centuries. In August, Norwood-Ravenswood was selected over eight other voluntary adoption services to run a new adoption register for England and Wales, designed to match adoptees with suitable parents. Norwood-Ravenswood was "flexible and dynamic in its approach," said Health Minister Jacqui Smith, and was therefore "the most cost-effective and efficient organization to run the register for us."

Ignoring protests and rejecting an offer of £150,000 from an anonymous donor, the Board of Deputies offered for auction a manuscript suppressed for nearly a century for fear of sparking anti-Semitism: "Human Sacrifice among the Sephardim or Eastern Jews," completed in 1877 by Sir Richard Burton, orientalist, explorer, and diplomat. But it failed to meet the £150,000 reserve price at Christie's July auction, and it was subsequently sold to an unidentified buyer.

In October, with the rent on its Holborn premises having quadrupled, the Board of Deputies bought new premises, a Georgian house in London's Bloomsbury Square, once home to Benjamin Disraeli's father.

Religion

The year ended unhappily for the United Synagogue (US) when the trial of three US cemetery employees accused of conspiring to defraud it of some £1.7 million collapsed in November. Judge George Bathurst-Norman told the jury at Southwark Crown Court, South London, that the US had "shown an approach to the prosecution of its former employees so casual as to offend the very name of justice," citing the US's alleged failure to provide certain documents. The accused, along with seven other individuals, were charged with submitting false or inflated invoices purporting to cover the cost of goods and services at Waltham Abbey and East Ham cemeteries between December 1994 and October 1998. The alleged fraud was discovered after a financial review by the accounting firm of PricewaterhouseCoopers revealed that the cost of running Waltham Abbey in 1997 was seven times higher than that of the larger Bushey cemetery. While in April 2001, before the trial, the Charity Commission said it was satisfied that the US had set up the tighter financial controls the accountants recommended to prevent such losses, in December the commission decided on a further investigation focusing on Judge Bathurst-Norman's comments. In December, too, former Waltham Abbey cemetery attendant Paul Nathan, found not guilty on the direction of the judge, stated that he was suing the US for racial discrimination, malicious process, malicious prosecution, and intimidation.

The year 2001 had seemed to promise better things for the US. In March, the sale of returned books stolen from the Bet Din library by former *dayan* (religious judge) Rabbi Casriel Kaplin netted the US some £75,000. Buyers included the library of Leo Baeck College, which, in October, held an exhibition of rare volumes acquired from the Bet Din. Sales of books and other assets over the previous five years enabled the US to solve its decade-long pension dispute by paying £2.55 million into the pension plan prior to winding it up, an arrangements which the High Court approved in March. "We have removed an albatross from around our necks," US president Peter Sheldon told the *Jewish Chronicle.* In July, Sheldon reported steady progress toward eliminating a "crippling deficit," but a major campaign was launched in November to raise funds to support core US activities, including educational and welfare services that could not be funded from membership fees alone. That same month the US launched a "Kehillah Community" project, with a £500,000 budget, for young people in Wembley.

In February, US bylaws were changed to allow women to serve as vice chairs and financial representatives of synagogues, so long as men remained the majority on the executive. In May, 36-year-old Rabbi Yonason Abraham was appointed a full *dayan* on the London Bet Din. In July, Rabbi Saul Zneimer became chief executive of the US. In September, Hammersmith and West Kensington synagogue, founded more than a century before, closed due to rapidly falling membership. In November, the US announced that a new community in Shenley, Hertfordshire, would become its 65th congregation in January 2002.

Activity on behalf of *agunot,* women whose husbands refused to give them religious divorces, continued throughout the year. In January, the Federation of Zionist Youth launched a campaign to raise the profile of this issue, which, it said, "bothers Jewish youth." Indicating that some progress had been made, in June the Agunah Campaign wound down its support group, Agunot Anonymous, since many of the women in the group had managed to obtain their religious divorces. In July, the Jewish Marriage Council launched "Get Information Advice," an educational pilot project to complement its existing advisory service. The same month, a demonstration, organized by the Agunah Campaign and endorsed by the Bet Din, took place outside the Golders Green home of a man who had denied his wife a Jewish divorce for more than 40 years. Parliamentary activity continued as well. Although a private member's bill permitting judges to withhold a civil divorce in the absence of a religious divorce was blocked in the House of Commons in February, a new bill to the same effect proposed in July raised hopes when it passed the committee stage of the House of Commons in November.

Alan Finlay, the new president of the Federation of Synagogues—which is more strictly Orthodox than the US—announced in June that three new synagogues had joined over the previous two years, including Beth Midrash Netzach Israel in Golders Green, North-West London, the federation's first Sephardi constituent member. Bevis Marks, Britain's oldest surviving synagogue, celebrated its tercentenary in July with an exhibition at the Jewish Museum about Sephardi Jewry. In October, archaeologists discovered a 13th-century *mikveh* (ritual bath) in the City of London.

Britain's Masorti movement (similar to Conservative Judaism in America) had nine congregations and 2,700 adult members in 2001, according to official estimates. In April, the oldest and most traditional Masorti congregation, the New London Synagogue, introduced alternative High Holy Day services with mixed seating and a greater role for women. In September, Edgware's Kol Nefesh community, which broke away from Edgware Masorti in April 2000 so as to enhance the participation of women in the service, appointed its first part-time rabbi.

In August, Leo Baeck College, the seminary of Progressive Judaism, announced that new rabbinical students receiving scholarships would be asked to commit themselves to work for five years in the movement. This rule was apparently triggered by the decision of two recent graduates to take positions with Masorti congregations.

In January, the Reform Synagogues of Great Britain (RSGB), running a serious deficit, made cuts in its cultural program "Living Judaism," which was aimed at boosting the profile of Reform and increasing participation in synagogue life. In April, however, the movement launched its first national adult-education project, "A Community of Learners." In June, Rabbi Jacqueline Tabbick became RSGB's first woman vice president. In October, the chief rabbi recommended the appointment of Rabbi Dr. Albert Friedlander as the first Progressive Jewish president of the Council of Christians and Jews, which had five Christian and one Jewish president.

Education

The government showed considerable interest in Jewish day schools. In March, Education Secretary David Blunkett expressed government support for Jewish schools, noting that since Labor came to power five of the schools had become state-aided. In May, in the run-up to the general election, both Labor and the Conservatives pledged support for state-aided Jewish schools. "Our recent proposals for the reform of secondary education emphasized the proven benefits of faith-based schools," Prime Minister Blair told the *Jewish Chronicle*. However in December, a Home Office-sponsored report on the summer race riots in Bradford and Oldham suggested that religiously affiliated schools posed "a significant problem" in already divided communities. Jewish educators and the government both rejected its recommendation that 25 percent of places in these schools be offered to children of different faiths.

Within the community, two publications studied the phenomenon of burgeoning enrollments at Jewish day schools at a time of declining Jewish population—51 percent of Anglo-Jewry's children aged 5–17 attended such schools in 1999, as compared to 30 percent in 1992. In July, the Institute for Jewish Policy Research (JPR) published *The Future of Jewish Schooling in the United Kingdom: A strategic assessment of faith-based provision of primary and secondary school education* by Oliver Valins, Barry Kosmin, and Jacqueline Goldberg, the fourth part of JPR's "Long-Term Planning for British Jewry" project. In October, the Board of Deputies Community Research Unit produced *Jewish Education at the Crossroads* by Rona Hart, Marlena Schmool, and Frances Cohen.

In March, the United Jewish Israel Appeal (UJIA) published *The Next Horizon,* a three-year plan for Jewish renewal in Britain, including suggestions for helping young people save toward the cost of trips to Israel, scholarships for students taking degrees in Jewish studies, developing arts and cultural programs, and education for lay leadership. In all, the report set more than 100 practical targets. "Whereas Jewish Continuity [UJIA's predecessor] had focused on the crisis of assimilation when it was launched eight years ago," said UJIA renewal department chairman Michael Goldstein, "there is now an 'upbeat culture' in British Jewry. We're tabling a challenge, not trumpeting a crisis."

In May, UJIA announced plans to contribute "substantial funds" toward expanding the scope of Leo Baeck College, which would move beyond the training of rabbis to offer teaching and other professional training for Progressive Judaism, as well as adult education, degree studies, and synagogue consultancies. In October, in a first step toward such expansion, Leo Baeck merged with its Centre for Jewish Education to form LBC-CJE, with Rabbi Jonathan Magonet as principal. In October, eight students enrolled for Britain's first M.A. in Jewish education, a two-year part-time course run by LBC-CJE, sponsored by UJIA, and validated by the University of North London.

In November, UJIA's chief executive, Jonathan Kestenbaum, reported an increase in donations in 2000 that yielded an income of nearly £14 million, £550,000 above 1999. Spending on Anglo-Jewish youth and education rose to £4.3 million in 2000 from £4.1 million in 1999, while spending in Israel—mainly to support new immigrants—rose to £7.1 million in 2000 from £6.9 million in 1999.

In April, Balliol College, Oxford, established a program of lectures in memory of Leonard Stein, author of the standard work on the Balfour Declaration. In May, JPR in London and the Alliance Israélite Universelle in Paris jointly formed the European Association for Jewish Culture to promote Jewish art and culture. In June, it was announced that, through its partnership with the London School of Jewish Studies (formerly Jews' College) the London University's School of Oriental and African Studies (SOAS) would launch an M.A. in Israeli and Jewish studies. In June too, Dr. Jonathan Webber was appointed to a UN Educational, Scientific and Cultural Organization (UNESCO) chair at Birmingham University with responsibility for building a new center for Jewish studies, focusing primarily on contemporary Jewry. In September, the Association for Jewish Refugees announced its sponsorship of a research post at Manchester University's Center for Jewish Studies that would study the impact of refugees on Manchester. In December, Sir Martin Gilbert gave his inaugural address as president of the new Center for Israeli Studies launched at University College, London.

Overseas Aid

In January, London-based UK Jewish Aid and International Development (UKJAID) launched a relief fund for victims of the earthquake in India and worked closely with the American Jewish Joint Distribution Committee (JDC) to ensure supplies went where most needed. In April, it was reported that UKJAID was largely funding a water purification plant in Boene, Mozambique.

Work for East European Jewry continued. In January, the Jewish Chernobyl Children's Committee launched a fund to provide medicine and medical equipment for people still suffering from the 1986 Chernobyl nuclear disaster. In May, the Jewish charity One-to-One held a Jewish heritage walk through Lithuania, which helped raise some £4,000 for impoverished Jewish communities, with most of the money going to Vilnius.

Local British communities pursued individual projects. South London's Catford and Bromley Synagogue ladies' society sent clothing through World Jewish Relief (WJR) to Tbilisi, Georgia. In September, a group from Hampstead Garden Suburb, North London, delivered a Torah scroll to the Jewish community of Lviv (formerly Lvov) in Ukraine; in November, members of Radlett and Bushey Reform Synagogue visited their twin congregation in Grodno, Belarus. In October, WJR sent a medical mission to the Jewish community of Minsk, Belarus, to provide eye surgery.

In March, at a House of Commons rally of pro-Israel parliamentarians, a 4,000-signature petition calling for the release of Iranian Jews and Muslims imprisoned on charges of spying for Israel and the United States was presented to Foreign Office minister Brian Watson.

In May, the families of four of the Israelis captured by Hezballah met with Foreign Secretary Robin Cook in London as part of an international campaign for their release. The Foreign Office and an all-party parliamentary group were reportedly putting pressure on Syria, Lebanon, and the Red Cross to discover where they were held. In July, United Synagogue president Peter Sheldon launched a cross-community initiative to highlight the plight of eight Israelis held by Hezballah.

Publications

The 2001 Jewish Quarterly-Wingate literary prizes were awarded to Mona Yahia for her first novel *When the Grey Beetles Took Over Baghdad,* and to Mark Rosman for *The Past in Hiding,* based on the experiences of Holocaust survivor Marianne Ellenbogen.

The first Jewish Chronicle Festival of Jewish Arts and Culture opened in November, funded largely by the Kessler Foundation, a charitable trust established by former *Jewish Chronicle* proprietor and chairman David Kessler. The monthlong festival, which aimed to raise the profile of Jewish culture in Britain, offered an extensive program built on the existing Jewish music and film festivals, Jewish book week, and the exhibits at London's Jewish Museum.

Jewish Renaissance, a quarterly dedicated to arts and culture, was launched in October.

Works of autobiography and biography published during the year included *Uncle Tungsten: Memories of a Chemical Boyhood* by Oliver Sacks; *Goodbye, Twentieth Century: An Autobiography* by Danny Abse, who also published *Encounters,* a collection of nine poems; *The Manager* by

Richard Burns, an autobiography in verse; *Who Are You Mr. Grymek,* the memoirs of Natan Gross; *Where Do You Come From?* by Carl F. Flesch, about being a refugee in Britain; *Ritual Slaughter: Growing up Jewish in America* by Liberal rabbi Sidney Brichto, who also published *The Genius of Paul,* a new translation of the apostle's letters; *Ted Hughes: The Life of a Poet* by Elaine Feinstein; *The Lost Messiah* by John Freely; *A Double Thread* by literary critic John Gross; *A Life,* literary critic Gabriel Josipovici's biography of his mother, poet and translator Sacha Rabinovitch; *Mark Rothko, 1903–1970* by Diane Waldman; *The Chasing Shadows* by Rabbi Hugo Gryn; *Freud Ego,* Clement Freud's autobiography; and *Beside Myself* by Antony Sher.

Books on religious subjects included *Radical Then, Radical Now* by Chief Rabbi Jonathan Sacks; Joanna Weinberg's translation of a classic 16th-century Italian-Jewish work, *Meor Einayim* by Azariah de Rossi, an investigation into aspects of Jewish history including the calendar; *Jewish Philosophy Reader,* edited by Daniel Frank, Oliver Leaman, and Charles Manekin; *For Heaven's Sake* by Chief Rabbi Cyril Harris of South Africa; and *From Autumn to Summer,* a collection of pieces by Rabbi Dr. Jonathan Magonet originally broadcast on German radio.

Studies of local history were *The "Jewish" Schools of Leeds 1880–1930* by Murray Friedman, and a pocket-sized history of Bevis Marks Synagogue by Sharman Kadish, published by English Heritage to mark the synagogue's 300th anniversary.

Collections of essays included *Feeding Frenzy,* short pieces by Will Self, who also published *Self Abuse,* a memoir; and *Snake Oil and Other Preoccupations* by journalist John Diamond.

Works of fiction were *Our Weddings* by Dorit Rabinyan; *The Red Tent* by Anita Diamant, a fictionalized version of the story of Dinah; *Distant Music* by Lee Langley; *The Secret* by Eva Hoffman; *Wolfy and the Strudelbakers* by Zvi Jagendorf; *Clerical Errors* by Alan Isler; *The Procedure* by Harry Mulisch; *Milwaukee* by Bernice Rubens; *The Wild* by Esther Freud; *The Bay of Angels* by Anita Brookner; *The Nose* by Elena Lappin; *Wittgenstein's Poker* by David Edmonds and John Eidinow—a mixture of fiction and philosophy; and *Ashes and Other Stories* by Naomi Shepherd.

Two books of literary criticism were *Post-War Jewish Fiction: Ambivalence, Self-Explanation and Transatlantic Connections* by David Brauner, and *Writers and Their Work: Muriel Spark* by Bryan Cheyette.

The Holocaust continued to yield a quantity of publications, including *The Battle for Auschwitz: Catholic-Jewish Relations under Strain* by

Emma Klein; *Unshed Tears* by Edith Hofman, a fictionalized autobiography of a camp survivor; *Encyclopaedia of the Holocaust* edited by Robert Rozett and Shmuel Spector; *Into the Light,* 34 short stories and poems written by 14 Holocaust survivors; *The Holocaust on Trial* by D.D. Guttenplan, describing the David Irving trial; *Legacies of Dachau: The Uses and Abuses of a Concentration Camp, 1933–2001* by Harold Marcuse; *An Englishman in Auschwitz* by Leon Greenman; *My Child is Back* by Ursula Pawel; *The Uncharted Voyage* by Gitta Ogg; *Eventful Journeys: The Story of Leah and Sigo Weber,* as told to Elizabeth Winkler; *A Life Sentence of Memories* by Issy Hahn; *My Lucky Star* by Zdenka Fantlova; *The Inextinguishable Symphony: A True Story of Music and Love in Nazi Germany* by Martin Goldsmith; and a three-volume publication, *Remembering for the Future,* with John K. Roth and Elisabeth Maxwell as editors-in-chief.

Publications about World War II included *Into the Arms of Strangers* by Mark Jonathan Harris and Deborah Oppenheimer, a book accompanying the film by the same name about the Kindertransport; *Hitler's Loss: What Britain and America Gained from Europe's Cultural Exiles* by Tom Ambrose; and *The Avengers: A Jewish War Story* by Rich Cohen.

Poetry published during the year included *The Phantom Lane* by Lottie Kramer; *Insisting on Yellow: New and Selected Poems* by Myra Schneider, who also, along with Dilys Wood, edited *Parents: An Anthology of Poems by Women Writers; Femenismo* by Joanne Limburg; *POP!,* an anthology edited by Michael Horovitz and Inge Elsa Laird; *Passionate Renewal: Jewish Poetry in Britain since 1945* edited by Peter Lawson; and *Russian Poet, Soviet Jew* by Maxim D. Shrayer, about Eduard Bagritskii.

Two books concerning art were *Idolizing Pictures* by Anthony Julius and *Legacies of Silence: The Visual Arts and Holocaust Memory* by Glen Sujo, written to accompany an exhibition at the Imperial War Museum.

Books about Israel and the Middle East included *Holy Land Unholy War, Israelis and Palestinians* by Anton La Guardia; *The Sabra: The Creation of the New Jew* by Oz Almog; *Divided Jerusalem: The Struggle for the Holy City* by Bernard Wasserstein; *House of Windows: Portraits from a Jerusalem Neighbourhood* by Adina Hoffman; and *Ethiopian Jewish Immigrants: The Homeland Postponed* by Tanya Schwarz.

Crypto-Judaism and the Spanish Inquisition by Michael Alpert was a work of general history, while *The Forgotten Millions,* edited by Malka Hillel Shulewitz, dealt with Jews who had to leave their homes in Arab lands.

Personalia

Honors conferred on British Jews in 2001 included a peerage for retiring MP Robert Sheldon, Labor Party stalwart, in the dissolution of Parliament honors list, while Sir Claus Moser, chancellor of Keele University and of Israel's Open University, was one of 15 newly chosen peers. Ruth Deech, chair of the Human Fertilization and Embryology Authority, law don, and St. Anne's College principal, was appointed a pro-vice-chancellor of Oxford University.

Prominent British Jews who died in 2001 included Alfred Cohen, artist, in Kings Lynn, Norfolk, in January, aged 80; Nat Basso, for 36 years chairman, British Boxing Board of Control, in January, aged 84; Sir Denys Lasdun, architect, in London, in January, aged 86; Fay Pomerance, artist, in Bristol, in January, aged 88; Jeffrey Green, lawyer and communal figure, in Zermatt, Switzerland, in January, aged 67; Leo Marks, code-breaker and filmmaker, in London, in January, aged 80; Ilse Wolff, publisher and Wiener Library personality, in London, in January, aged 92; Irwin Bellow, Lord Bellwin, Leeds businessman and politician, in Leeds, in February, aged 78; John Diamond, journalist, in London, in March, aged 47; Rabbi Shammai Zahn, founder of Sunderland Talmudical College, in Sunderland, in March, aged 80; Rabbi Joseph Shaw, Palmers Green and Southgate Synagogue minister, in London, in March, aged 78; Michael Leifer, pioneer of Southeast Asian academic studies in Britain, in London, in March, aged 67; Alexander Flinder, architect and pioneer of underwater archaeology, in London, in March, aged 80; William Rawlinson, jurist and European law expert, in London, in March, aged 84; David Nathan, *Jewish Chronicle* deputy editor 1978–1991 and theater critic for 28 years, in London, in March, aged 74; Nathan Science, grand old man of Newcastle Jewry, in Newcastle upon Tyne, in April, aged 90; George Willman, United Synagogue chief executive, in London, in April, aged 60; Professor Julius Carlebach, Jewish scholar and sociologist, in Brighton, in April, aged 78; Abner Cohen, social anthropologist, in Oxford, in May, aged 79; Alan Symons, author, in Trieste, in May, aged 72; Sir Sidney Hamburger, acknowledged leader of Manchester Jewry, in Salford, in June, aged 86; Ray Rosenberg, man of the theater, in Birmingham, in June, aged 48; William Margolis, agricultural economist, in London, in June, aged 87; Sonia Glasman, founding member of the Colchester, Essex, Jewish community, in Colchester, in June, aged 91; Ansel Harris, UKJAID chairman, in London, in July, aged 75; Irene Bloomfield, founding member and first clinical director of the Raphael Center, in London, in July, aged 82; Tom Phillips, who ran the Jewish Board of Guardians for 21 years, in London, in July, aged 96; Emmanuel Fisher, musician and conductor of London's Jewish male choir for 21 years, in Poole, Dorset, in July, aged 80; David Massel, Board of Deputies administrator for 35 years, in London, in July, aged 74; Stephanie Barnett, chair, Jewish Women's Aid, in Welwyn Garden City, in August, aged 58; Lord Paul Hamlyn, publisher and philanthropist, in London, in August, aged 75; Elana Rosenblatt, cofounder of the outreach organization Aish UK, in London, in August, aged 30; Larry Adler, internationally renowned harmonica player, in London, in August, aged 87; Greta Hyman, first woman organizing secretary of the Union of Liberal and Progressive Synagogues (ULPS), in London, in August, aged 88; Max Kochmann, mainstay of German-Jewish institutions, in London, in September, aged 80; Harold Feigen, founding member of the Licensed Taxi Drivers' Association, in London, in October, aged 81; Jack Rothstein, violinist, in London, in November, aged 75; Raphael Sommer, internationally known cellist, in Tel Aviv, in November, aged 64; Professor Sir Ernst Gombrich, art historian, in London, in November, aged 92; Morris Lederman, Federation of Synagogues president 1951–1989, in London, in December, aged 93; Tommy Gould, Britain's only World War II recipient of the Victoria Cross who was Jewish, in Peterborough, in December, aged 86.

MIRIAM & LIONEL KOCHAN

France

National Affairs

AS FAR BACK AS 2000, France had already fallen under the shadow of the presidential election scheduled for 2002, which was to pit the incumbent, Jacques Chirac, of the political right, against the Socialist prime minister, Lionel Jospin. During 2001, anticipation of this event reached fever pitch. Everything done—or not done—by both men related directly to their positions in the upcoming election. Under the French system, the president retains a limited role, while the prime minister, as head of government, controls the policy of the country, and thus the preelection mania was particularly evident in Jospin's case.

Jospin and his friends had become convinced that the presidential election would be decided on the record: that is, according to the results of past actions rather than any plan for the future. His record was not bad, especially with respect to the economy, as France had seen a reduction in unemployment and a smooth transition into the European Union. Thus, the Socialist leaders reasoned that their best strategy was to show their achievements in their best light and refrain from undertaking any new initiatives that might risk dividing the left majority or give fodder for criticism from the right. In concrete terms, this translated into an almost complete freeze on all government action. The social measures that the leftist majority was taking credit for had already been implemented, most notably the highly controversial 35-hour work week. The sole substantive innovation undertaken in 2001 was a constitutional change: the presidential term was reduced from seven years to five.

The Jospin government also passed a law changing the sequence of the 2002 elections, scheduling the presidential election just before the legislative election, and not, as a straightforward application of the calendar would have dictated, immediately after. With this change, Jospin hoped to accomplish two things. First, he hoped that the Communist Party and the Greens—the Socialists' often troublesome allies—would feel constrained to rally behind the main left-wing candidate, namely himself. Second, he counted on a dynamic in which success would breed success: after being elected president (which the polls predicted), he would obtain a parliamentary majority to support his platform.

For his part, Chirac was counting on being reelected, paradoxically, as a new man on the scene. Although he had been president since 1995, he had hardly participated in major decisions since 1997, when the National Assembly came under the control of a left-wing majority. Chirac was forced to leave the bulk of the political action to Jospin, while he concentrated on his responsibility as guarantor of state institutions and his joint responsibility for foreign affairs and national defense—largely symbolic functions. This unequal power sharing, the source of so much frustration for the right and its leader since 1997, would suddenly become, during an election, a source of strength. Chirac could claim his part in common successes, notably at the European level, while denouncing the "mistakes of the Socialist government."

As the electoral deadline of spring 2002 approached, this face-off between left and right increasingly monopolized political debate. Chirac and Jospin avoided getting involved personally so as to maintain their images as statesmen, but all around them it was the only issue, as each side focused on the weaknesses of the other. The press was called on extensively to echo the themes deemed most helpful. This process did not contribute to raising the moral standard of political life in France.

Chirac's weakness lay in his past role as party leader. When he was mayor of Paris, he transformed that position into a power base for himself and his party, the Rally for the Republic (RPR). According to evidence from various sources that came to light in recent years, Chirac's friends had used illegal financing methods, especially kickbacks on contracts with a variety of firms that were handled through the mayor's office. Nothing about these revelations was really surprising, especially given the context of the time during which these events occurred. However, some of the testimony related directly to Chirac himself, who, although denying having been aware of these practices, chose to hide behind his presidential status and refused to answer questions posed by judges investigating the matter. The president's entourage accused the Socialists of manipulating the justice system for political gain. The controversy bounced back and forth, occupying all of 2001.

Jospin had his weaknesses too, which his adversaries did not hesitate to exploit. As with Chirac, there were questions concerning his past. Newspaper articles and books revealed what had been whispered for years without ever being proved: Jospin had for a number of years been a Trotskyite "mole" within the Socialist Party. If it had been only a matter of youthful activism, the prime minister would not have stood out from a good number of other politically engaged people of his generation. But his involvement had been clandestine, and had continued over the years. To make matters worse, Jospin had always denied the allegations, claiming that people were confusing him with his brother, a leader in the same Trotskyite organization. Only in the wake of mounting proof did he finally concede the truth, and his image suffered significant damage. No one actually suspected him of still being a follower of Trotskyism. Indeed, it appeared certain that although he had initially joined the Socialist Party under orders from his Trotskyite leaders, Jospin had been gradually converted to social-democratic values. Nevertheless, the accusations of lying that Jospin's supporters had hurled at Chirac were turned against the prime minister.

Another weakness on Jospin's side became clear during the course of the year. It can be summed up in a word that had become one of the key terms in French public life: insecurity. The phenomenon itself was not new. For years, people had complained about the rise in violence and theft, and had called on elected officials to take steps to ensure security in the streets and cities. But exploitation of the problem by the far right, which laid the blame squarely on North African immigrants, had often led political leaders to treat the issue as racist fantasy. In 2001 it became clear, however, that the problem was real and that denial was unacceptable to a growing proportion of voters—especially since the most disadvantaged social groups suffered the most from the situation.

The attacks of September 11 on the U.S. reinforced this change in attitude. Some translated the legitimacy of resolute action against terrorism, as exemplified by the behavior of the United States, to the French situation, even though the social and ideological background was completely different. Attacks against French Jews, which had increased since the onset of the Palestinian intifada in September 2000 and then eased off during the first half of 2001, returned stronger than ever after September 11, further convincing many French non-Jews that tolerance was no longer in fashion. The French police were doing their part on the ground, but there was no firm message coming from the highest political levels. On this subject, Jospin was hostage to the dogmatic position taken by his political allies in Communist and Green circles, and largely accepted within his own Socialist Party: nothing must be said that could be interpreted as an accusation against the residents of "difficult neighborhoods," generally immigrants and children of immigrants. In this way, fear of playing into the hands of the far right led to a lack of political action that itself would eventually play into the hands of the far right.

Meanwhile, the far right, led by Jean-Marie Le Pen, president of the National Front (FN), attracted popular support without having to invest any effort. All the factors noted here played in its favor. The theme of insecurity, which had been its hobbyhorse for years, gradually slipped out of the moral ghetto where it had been kept for fear of its racist origins. The revelations about Jospin's Trotskyite past and Chirac's political financing seemed to echo the far right's old slogans denouncing the communist threat on the one hand and democratic corruption on the other. In essence, five years of cohabitation between a right-wing president and a left-wing prime minister (coming soon after two two-year periods, 1986–88 and 1993–95, when left-wing president François Mitterrand had cohabitated with right-wing prime ministers Jacques Chirac and Édouard Balladur) had convinced many citizens that the right and the left did not differ much from each other, and that if one really wanted to change "the system," one should vote elsewhere.

Would Jean-Marie Le Pen, who, according to polls taken since the preceding election, had barely 15 percent of the vote, have any real chance of success? It seemed highly unlikely. But the internal split that had occurred in the National Front when Le Pen's second-in-command, Bruno Mégret, quit the party to form the National Republican Movement (MNR), had not proven fatal. Quite the contrary: although Mégret, like the Italian neofascists, sought to put together a large right-wing bloc including nationalist elements, he brought with him to the MNR the strongest ideologues, whose ideas, reminiscent of the pagan enthusiasms of some of the early Nazis, were the most disturbing to public opinion.

As a result, the National Front developed a less odious, more populist image after the split. The fascist, racist, and anti-Semitic tendencies that remained firmly established at the party's core were no longer exposed for all to see. The majority of Le Pen sympathizers, like the majority of potential FN voters, were not motivated by a desire to do away with democracy or persecute minorities, but by the sense that their voices were not heard by people in power, a desire to protest the lack of security, a reflexive fear for their identity in the face of open borders, and resistance to the new European framework, symbolized by the abandonment of the French franc and its replacement by the euro on December 31, 2001. On all of these points, Jean-Marie Le Pen was able to run an extremely low-cost campaign: By their words, the other candidates—and occasionally the newspapers—did his work for him.

Another political force also began to emerge over the course of 2001. Bringing together various forms of dissatisfaction with the current system, but situating itself—at least in appearance—at the exact opposite end of the spectrum from the far right, a new extreme left began to carve out a place for itself. A checkered mix of unrepentant Trotskyites, Christian supporters of the Third World, communists in search of an alternative, activists from the antiglobalization movement, and environmentalists of various stripes, this new far left appealed both to those who felt let down by the traditional left and to young people looking for political involvement. Many came together to support the Palestinian cause without any knowledge of Middle Eastern realities, in blind solidarity with those presented as the ultimate victims in today's world. Heading this coalition were cynics and fanatics, manipulators and the pure of heart. The new far left offered a message of generosity, but because—in the absence of galvanizing issues—the Israeli-Palestinian conflict played an increasingly important role on its agenda, it was susceptible to anti-Semitic rhetoric of the basest kind. This was not a strictly French phenomenon, and much of the literature making the rounds in these circles had been translated from English.

In an overview of French politics in 2001, one particular group needs to be mentioned: the Arab-Muslim community. This term actually describes an entity with shifting boundaries. Of the roughly 3–5 million Muslims living in France, about 2 million had French citizenship. In the absence of actual census data (collecting information based on religion or ethnic origin is illegal), these figures were far from exact, but the trends were clear. The Arab-Muslim community represented a growing force. Although not yet heavily involved on the political scene, this group certainly represented a reservoir of votes, and possibly of activism, for future elections. It might take another decade before this group realized its potential, but at that point it would represent close to 10 percent of the electorate, enough to tip the balance in elections.

In France in 2001, the main issues for this group were the social injustices of which they were victims and recognition of their particular cultural and religious identity. International politics also heavily influenced their agenda. Although black Africans made up a large proportion of the group, the tone was set primarily by people with origins in North Africa—especially Algeria and Morocco—for whom the Palestinian cause struck a strong chord. The political class in France took note. The Communist Party, which had suffered electoral setbacks for years and feared losing its last municipal bastions, threw itself into a militant pro-Palestinian stance designed to rally the Arab-Muslim community. But the communists were not the only ones setting their sights in that direction (see "The 'Boniface Affair'" below).

Israel and the Middle East

At the beginning of 2001, President Clinton's proposals for resolving the Israeli-Palestinian conflict greatly interested the French people and provoked considerable debate within the Jewish community. While the daily *Le Monde* called on Yasir Arafat to accept Clinton's proposals, a petition circulating among Jews called on Ehud Barak not to divide Jerusalem. These issues, however, quickly disappeared from the agenda in the face of a breakdown in negotiations, a resurgence of violence, and the election of Ariel Sharon as prime minister of Israel. French public opinion had turned increasingly anti-Israel after September 30, 2000, when France 2, the public television station, broadcast images of the death of a 12-year-old boy who was caught with his father in a gun battle between Israelis and Palestinians at an intersection in Netzarim. With the breakdown of peace talks, anti-Israeli feeling spread with remarkable speed to every corner of French society.

In April 2001, the French public learned that, in a school in Boulogne-Billancourt, near Paris, students were given the following as part of an English test: "Change the following sentences to passive voice: (1) The Palestinian Imad family had buried Wael. (2) Israeli soldiers shot him in the head. (3) His friends took him to hospital immediately. (4) Teenagers' deaths keep Doctor Abdel Masri busy every night. (5) Israeli soldiers will again kill Palestinian children." When challenged by parents at the school, the teacher replied that she found nothing inappropriate in the exam questions, noting, "These were excerpts from the American press." This was no doubt an extreme case, but it illustrated the demonization of Israel, notably through images of slain Palestinian children.

There was a subtext to the anti-Israel frenzy. For many in France, denunciation of Israel may well have constituted a largely unconscious way of escaping a sense of guilt related to the memory of the Holocaust. Coming after a period marked by public acts of repentance toward the Jews (President Chirac in 1995, France's bishops in 1997), high-profile trials of French collaborators with the Nazis (Paul Touvier followed by Maurice Papon), and revelations about the confiscation of Jewish goods under the Vichy regime (see "Restitution" below), denunciation of the Jewish state seemed to "prove" that yesterday's victims could be today's persecutors. As a result, no one was completely innocent—another way of saying that no one was completely guilty.

The Jews, however, were far from being totally isolated. Proof came with the state visit of Syrian president Bashar al-Assad on June 25–26, 2001. This was just after Pope John Paul II's visit to Syria, during which Assad attacked Israel using overtly anti-Semitic language. In addition, the recent trial of Aloïs Brunner (see "Holocaust-Related Matters" below) reminded the French of how Brunner had enjoyed Syrian hospitality for decades. In sum, there were a host of reasons not to welcome the Syrian president. Nevertheless, both Jacques Chirac and Lionel Jospin received Assad with all the honors reserved for a head of state. The new Socialist mayor of Paris, Bertrand Delanoë, took a different approach. Required by protocol to receive President Assad at City Hall, Delanoë kept the formalities to a strict minimum, receiving his visitor from the top of the large staircase instead of making the polite gesture of coming down to meet him. In his remarks to the guests, the mayor condemned anti-Semitism and terrorism in the strongest terms. To reinforce the message even more, some city council members held up signs saying, "Assad is an anti-Semite." At the same time, a demonstration organized by CRIF, the Representative Council of Jewish Institutions of France (Conseil Représentatif des Institutions Juives de France) brought out 8,000 people in Paris to protest the Syrian president's visit; similar demonstrations also took place in other parts of the country, notably Lyon, Nice, Marseille, and Strasbourg.

A few days later, on July 5 and 6, Ariel Sharon visited Paris. During his brief stay, the Israeli prime minister also met with Jacques Chirac and Lionel Jospin, as well as a substantial delegation from CRIF. A demonstration against Sharon's visit drew very few people.

In November 2001, the French polling company Sofres published the results of a survey tracking "French opinion on the Israeli-Palestinian conflict." The survey, commissioned by the Israeli embassy in France, was conducted September 10–14, but Sofres did not detect any significant connection between the survey results and the events that occurred in the United States at that time.

On the whole, the analysts at Sofres found "a slightly more pro-Israeli than pro-Palestinian sentiment in public opinion." The predominant feeling, however, seemed to be indifference. Thus, when asked, "In the conflict between Israel and the Palestinians, with whom do you sympathize more?" 26 percent said Israel, 19 percent said the Palestinians, 11 percent responded "both the same," 35 percent chose "neither one," and 9 percent had no opinion. In another question, people were asked if they felt "sympathy or no sympathy" for each country listed; 44 percent said they had sympathy for Israel and 43 percent did not (13 percent had no opinion). The "sympathy index" for Israel (the difference between those for and those against) was thus +1. The same index was strongly negative for "Palestine"—32 percent for and 55 percent against, yielding a difference of –23. By way of comparison, the sympathy index was +60 for the United States, +44 for Egypt, and +14 for Russia; the most negative indices were for Syria (–38) and Iran (–62).

A sympathy index for selected individuals was calculated in the same way. Ariel Sharon had a strongly negative index (–43, made up of 18 percent who sympathized compared with 61 percent who did not), worse even than that of Palestinian Authority president Yasir Arafat (–37, from 25 percent for and 62 percent against). But the Israeli foreign minister, Shimon Peres, had a strong +22, while American president George Bush proved clearly unpopular at –17, and Russian president Vladimir Putin was even more unpopular at –26.

Regarding the basis of the conflict, 83 percent of the French public thought that the region should have "an Israeli state and a Palestinian state" (3 percent said "only an Israeli state" and 1 percent said "only a Palestinian state"). People surveyed had the impression that, in the conflict between the Israelis and the Palestinians, the French government had acted more favorably towards Israel (34 percent, compared to 13 percent who judged it more favorable to the Palestinians, while the rest thought it was neutral or had no opinion). However, a large majority (61 percent) considered French policy "balanced," with only 12 percent stating that the government supported Israel too much and 6 percent that it supported the Palestinians too much.

The "Boniface Affair"

In April 2001, French academic Pascal Boniface, director of the Institute of International and Strategic Relations (IRIS), sent an internal memo to the leaders of the Socialist Party. Titled "The Middle East, Socialists, International Fairness, Electoral Effectiveness," the note recommended a change in the French government's attitude toward Israel. After condemning Israeli policy with respect to the Palestinians, Boniface accused "the Jewish community" of "cashing in on its electoral clout to allow the Israeli government to act with impunity."

This was a very serious accusation. In French political culture, it is considered unacceptable for a minority (ethnic, religious, or other) to try to influence government policy (internal or international) that relates to national sovereignty. Furthermore, anyone who knew anything about the Jewish community in France was aware that this accusation was baseless. The electoral weight of French Jews was less than 1 percent, and they had no lever, financial or otherwise, that would allow them to influence the country's policies in any significant way.

Oddly, after criticizing the Jews for pro-Israeli activity, Boniface advocated a strategy cast in the same mold, except this time in favor of Israel's adversaries. "I am struck," he wrote in his note, "by the number of young *beurs* [a recent expression, referring to French of ethnic Arab origin], of French Muslims of all ages, who describe themselves as leftists but who, because of the situation in the Middle East, do not want to vote for Jospin in the presidential election. An unbalanced approach to the Middle East— and of course, according to them, once again to the disadvantage of the Arabs—confirms their feeling that the Socialist family does not take the Arab-Muslim community into consideration or even rejects it." As a result, Boniface explained to the Socialist leaders that their party must "abandon a position that, in trying to find balance between the Israeli government and the Palestinians, becomes, because of the reality, more and more abnormal." According to him, such a change in France's foreign policy would improve Lionel Jospin's chances of winning the upcoming election. Finally, he posed a rhetorical question: "Is supporting Sharon worth losing in 2002?"

Boniface did have one thing right: Palestinian supporters and those who, more generally, identified as "Arab-Muslims," found Jacques Chirac closer to their views than Lionel Jospin. Two images summed up the situation. During his last trip to Israel in 2001, Chirac was openly angry with his Israeli bodyguards, whom he suspected of wanting to keep him from making physical contact with Palestinians in the streets of Jerusalem. This unpleasantness caused a minor diplomatic incident. In contrast, Jospin, on his subsequent trip to Israel, called the Lebanese Hezballah a "terrorist" group. These words, which earned an immediate rebuke from President Chirac, made him a target for stone-throwing the next day during a visit to a Palestinian university. Quite likely because of this difference in perception, a high proportion of "Arab-Muslims," given a choice between the right and the Socialist Party, would vote for the right. Nevertheless, the boorish tone in which Boniface called on his Socialist friends for a policy change, and the explicit connection that he made with "electoral effectiveness"—that is, the relative political weight of the two communities in France—was very disturbing.

Pascal Boniface's note, distributed in April 2001 to a small number of Socialist leaders, did not stay secret for long. However, because of the particularly sensitive nature of the subject, none of the people privy to its contents, including some Jews, was willing to publicize it. At a time of unprecedented violent anti-Jewish attacks perpetrated by the group Boniface called "the Arab-Muslim community," it was important to avoid adding oil to this fire. As it turned out, the author of the note himself brought the matter to the public's attention. In an article called "Letter to an Israeli Friend" published in *Le Monde* on August 4, he repeated the first part of his note, denouncing the Israeli government's policy toward the Palestinians ("unjust, if not odious") and warned the Jewish community in France that by supporting this policy it risked "isolating itself."

Israel's ambassador to France, Élie Barnavi, immediately responded in the same newspaper, emphasizing that the "honeyed" tone Boniface used in the article contrasted with the more virulent style that he had employed for internal use. In his reply to Barnavi published in late August, Boniface pleaded his good intentions ("Must I repeat that, for me, Israel's right to exist in peace and security, within pre-1967 recognized borders, is absolute?") but acknowledged the existence of the internal memo, thus bringing it into the public sphere.

Under the title "Doctor Pascal and Mister Boniface," the Jewish monthly *L'Arche* later published an article (Nov. 2001) protesting the "double discourse" involved in associating a critique of Israeli policy (certainly legitimate) with a discriminatory (and therefore illegitimate) charge directed at French Jews. This *L'Arche* article reproduced the part of the original memo that had not been printed in *Le Monde,* in which the author recommended a change in government policy for the sake of electoral gain. In its next issue, *L'Arche* published a response from Boniface. After defending himself against the reproach that he had issued an accusation against the Jews, he wrote, "I believe that everyone should question whether it is normal that the Middle East should be the only subject about which many leaders do not dare to speak their minds publicly for fear of the reactions that their words might unleash." Opposite this letter, *L'Arche* published a letter from Serge Weinberg, chair of the board of the institute where Boniface served as director, in which he personally vouched for Boniface's "constant commitment against racism and anti-Semitism."

Beyond its personal implications and the light it shed on the factors influencing France's Middle East policy, the "Boniface affair" demonstrated something about the self-image of Jews in France. While a small number of Jews, generally with no ties to the Jewish community, condemned Israel in particularly strong terms, the most widespread sentiment among French Jews was that charges against the State of Israel were roughly equivalent to charges against the Jews themselves, at a time when anti-Jewish attacks were stronger than ever.

Anti-Semitism and Racism

On January 12, 2001, the Palestinian journalist Raymonda Hawa-Tawill (whose daughter, Souha Arafat, was married to the president of the Palestinian Authority), spoke live on the public radio station France Culture, attacking the "racism of the Jews of France" and the "influence of the Jewish lobby." This incident highlighted a fact that had become entrenched in French political reality: the predominance of the Middle Eastern factor in anti-Jewish attacks. While there were only sporadic incidents of far-right anti-Semitism, and Jean-Marie Le Pen spared no effort to make people forget his "slips of the tongue" of years past, Arab sources incited hostility toward Jews. A Paris-based radio station, Radio-Orient, was sued after it broadcast, live from Mecca, an Arabic-language sermon containing violently anti-Semitic passages in October 2000. The trial took place on May 30, 2001, and on June 27 the court fined the people in charge of Radio-Orient and ordered them to issue a correction in French and Arabic. The conviction was not appealed.

In early November 2001, a pamphlet entitled *Le sionisme, image véritable du diable sur terre* (Zionism, the True Image of the Devil on Earth) was distributed in Paris-area mosques. According to the pamphlet, "From America, [the Jews] have infiltrated other countries in every possible way. They have created a racist system, Zionism, which has shown their true diabolical face. They lit the fire of the Second World War in Europe and divided the peoples of that continent. They have done the same thing for the Muslim peoples." Readers of the pamphlet also learned that genocide was a Jewish invention, that Jews were the real perpetrators of the September 11 attacks, and similar notions. Such ideas appeared to be widespread among Muslims, and some Muslim authorities in France called on their coreligionists not to fall into the trap of anti-Semitism.

It was not only a question of literature. The year 2000 was marked by an unprecedented eruption of anti-Jewish violence in France (see AJYB

2001, p. 325). Ranging from minor local incidents of aggression to the burning of synagogues and Jewish schools, this violence was carried out almost exclusively by "Arab-Muslims." Perpetrators arrested by the police usually had a history of petty delinquency, and there was no evidence linking them to Islamist groups or other networks. The violence appeared to involve mostly an exacerbation of neighborhood conflicts against a background of identification with the Palestinian struggle. It let up in early 2001, primarily because of the deterrent effect of arrests. But the violence never stopped completely, and it gained strength again immediately after September 11.

While the total number of attacks in 2001 did not break the record that had been set in 2000, anti-Semitism appeared to have become more deeply entrenched in the "Arab-Muslim" population, with an "ideological" message picking up where the spontaneous reaction that coincided with the early weeks of the intifada left off. By all indications, the French public was broadly aware of this phenomenon and disapproved of the anti-Jewish violence. Thus, in the Sofres survey commissioned by the Israeli embassy (see "Israel and the Middle East" above), respondents were asked to react to "attacks on synagogues in France." Offered a choice between two responses, 78 percent chose, "It's scandalous, the government should punish the guilty parties very severely," while only 10 percent preferred, "If Jews in France didn't support Israel so much, these attacks wouldn't have happened."

Welcoming Prime Minister Lionel Jospin at the annual CRIF dinner on December 1, CRIF president Roger Cukierman gave a very strong speech criticizing the demonization of the State of Israel, noting its effects on the physical security of some Jews and on the peace of mind of most of them. However, even though the prime minister had been considered a friend of the Jews and of Israel, he avoided saying anything too clear on the subject in a preelection period. He devoted his speech primarily to the lessons learned from the study of the plundering of Jewish property during the Second World War, and the need to pass on the memory of the Holocaust.

Holocaust-Related Matters

In early 2001, American writer Norman Finkelstein's book *The Holocaust Industry* was published in France under the title *L'Industrie de l'Holocauste*. This book, which accused Jewish organizations of extorting funds from Swiss banks and explained the attention devoted to the

Holocaust in recent years as a result of coordinated maneuvers by American imperialism and the Zionist state, had initially appeared in translation on the Internet site of the French Holocaust deniers. Éric Hazan and Rony Brauman arranged for the publication of a new translation by a small far-left publishing house. Finkelstein's book was welcomed in anti-Zionist circles, where it confirmed longstanding conspiracy theories. But it was the subject of a scathing editorial in *Le Monde* on February 16, which said that "the rhetoric employed here is close to that of Holocaust denial." The paper explained its decision to pay attention to the book by noting the need to be "on guard against the misleading alibis of a new anti-Semitism" (see "The Assault on Holocaust Memory," AJYB 2001, pp. 3–20).

In February and March, a major exhibition, *Mémoires des camps, photographies des camps de concentration et d'extermination nazis (1933–1999)* (Memories of the Camps: Photographs of Nazi Concentration and Extermination Camps, 1933–1999), was held in Paris. It consisted of photographs taken in the camps during the Nazi regime, at the time of liberation, and in the decades that followed. Filmmaker Claude Lanzmann (who made the film *Shoah*) strongly criticized the exhibition, accusing it of perpetuating the confusion between concentration camps and extermination camps, mixing photographs of victims with those of perpetrators without distinguishing between them, and wallowing in an aestheticism that was indecent in light of the context. The exhibition's commissioner, Clément Chéroux, defended it, saying that his objective was to provide "not a history of the camps but a history of photography of the camps." Chéroux also noted that to avoid any tendency toward aestheticism he had made sure that a "cultural mediator" would be available on site to accompany visitors and explain the significance of the images.

On March 2, 2001, the trial in absentia of Aloïs Brunner, a Nazi war criminal who was responsible for the murder of 120,000 Jews in Austria, Germany, Greece, Slovakia, and France, took place in Paris. In 1943–44, Brunner was head of the camp at Drancy near Paris from which tens of thousands of Jews were sent to Auschwitz. Brunner, who fled to Syria after the war where successive leaders of that country protected him, did not respond to the call of French justice. The court sentenced him to life in prison.

Also in early 2001, plans were announced for an international conference on "historical revisionism"—that is, Holocaust denial. Cosponsored by an American organization, the Institute for Historical Review, and a Swiss organization, Vérité et Justice (Truth and Justice), whose director had taken refuge in Iran, the conference was supposed to take place in Beirut. In *Le Monde* on March 16, a group of Arab intellectuals published a forceful protest along with a call to cancel the conference. The Lebanese government finally yielded to international pressure and prevented the conference from convening. A lively controversy erupted in the Arab world, some saying that the signers of the *Le Monde* protest had made a pact with Zionism. One of the signers of the protest, the Palestinian-American Columbia University professor Edward Said, made it known that his signature had been extorted from him, and that, in the name of freedom of expression, he never would have supported a call to cancel the conference.

In 2001, lawyers for Maurice Papon continued a campaign, begun the year before, to free their client. Papon, who was a sub-prefect in Bordeaux under the German occupation and then had a brilliant administrative and political career in postwar France, had been sentenced to ten years in prison for "complicity in crimes against humanity." His lawyers, citing his advanced age (over 90) and poor health, had launched proceedings in the European Court of Human Rights, demanding that it censure France for "inhuman and degrading treatment." In January 2001, the appeal to free Papon received the unexpected support of a leading French Jew, Robert Badinter, who, as minister of justice in a previous government, had sponsored legislation abolishing capital punishment. "People say, 'crime against humanity,' " Badinter declared. "I say there is a time when the humanity has to prevail over the crime." Another well-known Jew expressed similar views: Gilles Bernheim, chief rabbi of the Synagogue de la Victoire in Paris, argued in a regional newspaper that Papon's *"déchéance"*—his physical deterioration as well as the obsolescence of what he symbolically represented—made it pointless to keep him incarcerated.

There was strong reaction to these statements within the Jewish community. Lawyer and historian Serge Klarsfeld, one of the originators of the legal action against Papon, came out against any clemency. The chief rabbi of France, Joseph Sitruk, argued that Papon's early release was not justified since he had "tried to escape justice for 18 years" and "had never repented" of his actions. Rabbi Bernheim said he would not express himself further on the subject because he feared that his position would be misinterpreted—especially since it appeared that Papon's lawyers had tried to make people believe that Bernheim and Papon had exchanged correspondence, which was untrue. Finally, on June 8, 2001, the European Court of Human Rights rejected the request for Papon's early release. A request for mercy presented to President Chirac was no more successful.

At the end of 2001, Papon was still in prison, where, it was noted, he was better treated than the elderly Jews he had interned 60 years earlier.

Restitution

The FMS, the Foundation for the Remembrance of the Holocaust (Fondation pour la Mémoire de la Shoah), started operation at the beginning of 2001. The foundation had been officially established on December 26, 2000, by a decree of the French government, following research into the plundering of the property of French Jews during the German occupation. A study commission appointed by the government in 1997 had presented a detailed report in April 2000 (see AJYB 2001, p. 334). It noted that restitution had been made for the vast majority of the plundered goods after the war, but a certain amount had remained heirless under government management, and in public and private financial institutions. The commission had recommended that the current cumulative value of these goods be assigned to a foundation, and the government implemented this recommendation by establishing the FMS.

The FMS began its work with a figure of the first rank as its president—Simone Veil, former cabinet minister and former president of the European Parliament, who herself had been deported to Auschwitz—and an endowment of 393 million euros, which made it the best-endowed foundation in France. Legally established as a private foundation but recognized by the government, it was run by a board of 25 members: ten representatives of France's Jewish institutions, eight representatives of public agencies, and seven "qualified figures" coopted by the other board members (the initial "qualified figures" were Christine Albanel, Claude Lanzmann, Samuel Pisar, Israel Singer, Saul Friedländer, Simone Veil, and Elie Wiesel). Income from the endowment, estimated at 14 million euros a year, was to be used to support activities in a number of predetermined areas: the history of anti-Semitic persecution and the Holocaust, education and transmission, commemoration and communication, solidarity with former victims and the Righteous Gentiles, and development of Jewish culture.

The French government also continued to deal with the other problems that had appeared during the study of the plundering of French Jewry, such as compensation for individuals, pensions for Jewish orphans, claims against banks and insurance companies, tracking looted paintings and objets d'art, and French government activities to remember the Holocaust. These efforts were coordinated by civil servants in the prime minister's office and the Ministry of Foreign Affairs, working in close cooperation with other government departments and with French and international Jewish organizations. These civil servants felt—with considerable justification, in the opinion of French Jews—that their government had done everything possible to assume France's debt, both moral and material. In private conversations, the French officials expressed their irritation at seeing their country become the object of accusations in international bodies, often from nationals of countries that, it seemed to them, had not put forth a comparable effort to come to grips with their own past.

JEWISH COMMUNITY

Communal Affairs

In January 2001, Zvi Ammar took office as president of the Marseille Consistory. Ammar had been elected in December 1999, but the result was challenged and the dispute was taken to the courts, so that it took 13 months for the legitimacy of the new officers to be recognized. To make up for the long wait, Ammar's inauguration was a festive occasion, with the chief rabbi of France in attendance along with all the regional authorities: the mayor of Marseille, the president of the regional council, the prefect, and others. This event served as the kickoff for the year 2001, an election year in the Jewish community.

The calmest election was the one to choose a new president of CRIF to succeed lawyer Henri Hajdenberg, who, after serving two three-year terms, was not allowed to run for a third. There were two candidates, banker Roger Cukierman and chartered accountant Roger Benarrosh. Since there was no fundamental difference between their platforms, the campaign was based primarily on personal relationships. On May 13, Cukierman was elected by 84 votes to 71.

Two other elections also took place without incident: Edwige Elkaim was elected president of B'nai Brith of France on June 24, and Patrick Klugman was elected president of the Union of Jewish Students of France on July 1.

By contrast, the election for chief rabbi of France took place only after a controversy that spilled over into the public arena. The statutes of the Central Consistory provided for the chief rabbi to be named by an electoral college in which rabbis could make up only 10 percent of the membership. In November 2000, a rabbinic congress presented a proposal to revise the statutes that would have led to a substantial increase in the proportion of rabbis in the electoral college. The incumbent chief rabbi, Joseph Sitruk, supported this proposal. However, the Paris Consistory was firmly opposed, and for a while events teetered on the edge of crisis.

In the end, the election took place on June 17 under the existing statutes. Sitruk was reelected for a third seven-year term, with 179 votes to 82 for his only opponent, the chief rabbi of Nice, Marc Bensoussan. Meanwhile, on May 30, the chief rabbi of Paris, David Messas, was also reelected, receiving all 43 votes cast even though he faced an opponent. The final election of the year within religious Judaism took place on November 25, and involved the leadership of the Paris Consistory. Moïse Cohen was reelected president, and a notable feature of the new leadership team was the presence of seven women. The "feminization" of the Consistory, which had begun with the previous election, was now an established fact.

On December 5, Chief Rabbi Sitruk suffered a stroke while speaking at a wedding. His treatment required a lengthy hospital stay.

Religion

The most notable event of the year in the area of religion concerned a subject that had long provided nourishment (in all senses of the word) for the ongoing saga of French Judaism: kashrut. In France, in the absence of rich endowments for synagogues and generous donors for organizations, the main source of income for religious Judaism was a tax on kosher meat. As a result, conflicts about kashrut quickly turned into existential questions. Another peculiarity of the French situation was that warnings relating to meat quality (mad cow disease, foot-and-mouth disease) thus affected not only the supply of safe meat and continued consumption by the general public, but, because of the tax, the very survival of Jewish institutions. Supervising kashrut, then, involved significant responsibility.

In theory, at least, the Paris Consistory had a virtual monopoly on the certification of kosher meat, which it exercised through its Bet Din (see AJYB 2001, p. 338). In practice, peaceful-coexistence agreements had been established, for example with the Lubavitch movement, which imported meat from Argentina under its own kosher label with the approval of the Consistory. But when Emsellem, one of the three major suppliers of kosher meat, announced its intention to import kosher meat from Uruguay, this represented a casus belli. All the necessary guarantees of kashrut were provided, and the slaughtering was being carried out in

Uruguay by Israeli ritual slaughterers under the supervision of the chief rabbinate of Israel. But the Paris Bet Din—supported by the chief rabbi of Paris, David Messas, and the president of the Paris Consistory, Moïse Cohen—balked at providing its label, on the grounds that it would be turned into nothing more than a rubber stamp.

At this point, the Central Consistory entered the fray and offered to provide its own kosher label to Emsellem for the Uruguayan meat. At the Paris Consistory, people saw red. Emsellem made it clear that meat imported in this way would be sold only through a special distribution network and not in stores bearing the Paris Bet Din symbol, but it was no use. The Paris Consistory accused the president of the Central Consistory, Jean Kahn, and Chief Rabbi Sitruk of paving the way for the introduction of a "Central" kosher label that would compete with the Bet Din's label.

From Rabbi Sitruk's corner came denials that the chief rabbi had been directly involved in the certification of Uruguayan meat. It was acknowledged, however, that he had given his approval in principle, and that the idea of a kosher "super-label" under the authority of the Central Consistory was under study. The reply from Jean Kahn was that if the Paris Consistory did not want competition for its kosher label, it should begin by paying the back dues it owed to the Central Consistory. While in theory the Central Consistory was the "head office" for all the regional consistories, in fact it was financially dependent on the Paris Consistory, and disputes over payments between the two bodies had been common coin for some time.

To avoid a crisis, the Paris Consistory reversed its previous decision and agreed to place its kosher label on the meat imported from Uruguay, even though it had been slaughtered without Bet Din supervision. It was doing this, it said, "in an exceptional manner, because of the supply problems that threaten to harm Jews who eat kosher in France." And so, at the last minute, the Central Consistory's kosher label on the Uruguayan meat was replaced by the Paris Consistory's label. But the underlying problems remained, and eventual resumption of the kosher-meat wars was a virtual certainty.

Publications

Among the books of Jewish interest published in France in 2001 were: Liliane Atlan's *Petites bibles pour mauvais temps* (Small Bibles for Bad Times); Henry Raczymow's *L'homme qui tua René Bousquet* (The Man

Who Killed René Bousquet); Henri Lewi's *Isaac Bashevis Singer. La génération du déluge* (Isaac Bashevis Singer: The Generation of the Flood); Évelyne Dress's *Les tournesols de Jérusalem* (The Sunflowers of Jerusalem); Madeleine Kahn's *L'écharde* (The Splinter); Albert Grunberg's *Journal d'un coiffeur juif à Paris sous l'Occupation* (Journal of a Jewish Hairdresser in Paris Under the Occupation); Lysette Hassine-Mamane's *Le Piyyut de David Hassine* (David Hassine's Piyyut); *Le brûlement du Talmud à Paris (1242–1244)* (The Burning of the Talmud in Paris, 1242–1244), edited by Gilbert Dahan; Henri Meschonnic's *L'utopie du Juif* (The Jew's Utopia); Laurent Rucker's *Staline, Israël et les Juifs* (Stalin, Israel and the Jews); *Le judéo-christianisme dans tous ses états* (Judeo-Christianity in All Its Aspects), edited by Simon C. Mimouni; François Blanchetière's *Enquête sur les racines juives du mouvement chrétien (30–135)* (Inquiry into the Jewish Roots of the Christian Movement, 30–135); Eliette Abécassis's *Le trésor du temple* (The Temple's Treasure); Rabbi Pauline Bebe's *Isha. Dictionnaire des femmes et du judaïsme* (Isha: Dictionary of Women and Judaism); Georges Nataf's *Les sources païennes de l'antisémitisme* (The Pagan Sources of Anti-Semitism); Gérard Israël's *Jérusalem, la sainte* (Jerusalem, the Holy); Michaël Prazan and Tristan Mendès France's *La Maladie n° 9* (Illness No. 9); Édouard Valdman's *La Blessure* (The Wound); Cyrille Fleischman's *Un slow des années 50* (A Fifties Slow Dance); Gérard Silvain's *Sépharades et Juifs d'ailleurs* (Sephardim and Jews From Elsewhere); Michel Gurfinkiel's *La cuisson du homard* (Cooking Lobster); Marc-André Charguéraud's *Silences meurtriers. Les Alliés, les Neutres et l'Holocauste, 1940–1945* (Murderous Silences: The Allies, the Neutrals and the Holocaust, 1940–45); Paul Webster's *Le crime de Pétain* (Pétain's Crime); Laurent Joly's *Xavier Vallat. Du nationalisme chrétien à l'antisémitisme d'État* (Xavier Vallat: From Christian Nationalism to State Anti-Semitism); Patrick Petit-Ohayon's *L'éveilleur des esprits* (The One Who Roused Spirits); Sarah Taïeb-Carlen's *Les Juifs d'Afrique du Nord* (The Jews of North Africa); Dominique Laury's *Les chaises du Luxembourg* (The Chairs of Luxembourg); Gilles Rozier's *Moïse fiction* (Moses Fiction); Pierre Hazan's *La guerre des Six Jours* (The Six-Day War); and Serge Klarsfeld's *La Shoah en France* (The Holocaust in France).

Personalia

On January 15, 2001, an esplanade in the 15th arrondissement of Paris was given the name of Max Guedj, belatedly honoring one of France's most glorious fighters in World War II. Born in 1913 in Sousse, Tunisia, to a Jewish family of French nationality, Max Guedj grew up in Casablanca, Morocco. The son of a lawyer, he obtained a doctor of laws degree before working in his father's office. But the war changed the course of his life: in September 1940, he secretly went to London, where he was one of the first to join the Royal Air Force. He took part in many battles and stood out for his courage and operational skill. Wing Commander Max Guedj was killed in action on January 15, 1945.

Among Jewish figures who died in 2001, two names stood out: Gilbert Trigano, founder of Club Méditerranée, who died in early February at the age of 80, and Charles Liché, the "rabbi of the deportees," who died in July, also at the age of 80.

Professor Ady Steg, president of the Alliance Israélite Universelle, received the insignia of a grand officer of the Legion of Honor from President Jacques Chirac at the Élysée Palace on February 26. He marked the occasion with a speech that received considerable attention and was widely quoted: while speaking of his homage and gratitude to France, he criticized the "perverse development" of a "delegitimization" of the State of Israel.

On May 15, it was the turn of Jean Kahn, president of the Central Consistory, to receive the insignia of a grand officer of the Legion of Honor from President Chirac at the Élysée Palace.

Meïr Rosenne, former Israeli ambassador to France, was promoted to the rank of commander of the Legion of Honor. Chief Rabbi Sitruk, Professor Haïm Zafrani, Bernard Kanovitch, Joseph Roubache, and Jean Meyer were promoted to the rank of officer of the Legion of Honor. Chief Rabbi Michel Guggenheim, Professor André Kaspi, Professor Michel Revel (Israel), Nadine de Rothschild, Annette Wieviorka, Michel Zaoui, Patrick Gaubert, David Fuchs, and Richard Prasquier were named knights of the Legion of Honor.

MEIR WAINTRATER

Belgium

National Affairs

BELGIUM HAD A POPULATION of 10.3 million in 2001, with an annual growth rate of 0.2 percent. Its population density of 336 inhabitants per square kilometer made it one of the most densely populated countries in Europe. The fertility index was low, only 1.61 children per woman of childbearing age. The long life expectancy (78 years) and the consequent aging of the population were characteristic of an industrialized country with extensive modern hospital facilities and health care.

The two major groups in Belgium were the Flemings, who spoke Dutch and various Dutch dialects, and the Walloons, who spoke French, Picard, and Walloon dialects. Flanders corresponds to the northern half of the country and Wallonia to the southern half. The populations of the eastern cantons of Eupen and Malmedy, near the German border, were German-speaking.

Achieving independence in 1830, the country developed its current federal structure quite recently as a result of reforms passed in 1970, 1980, 1988/89, and 1993. Article 1 of the Belgian constitution now stated (for the first time), "Belgium is a Federal State composed of communities and regions." Policy decisions were no longer made entirely by the central government but rather by a variety of bodies that wielded independent powers in the specific areas assigned to them.

The distribution of powers followed two major axes, the first connected to language and culture, and the second to geography and economic aspirations. "Communities" denoted groups united by language and cultural ties: the Dutch Community, the French-speaking Community (which was renamed the "Wallonia-Brussels Community"), and the German-speaking Community. Dutch, French, and German were all official languages. The three "Regions" of the country were roughly comparable to the states in the U.S., though they also enjoyed some degree of economic autonomy. They were the Flemish Region, Brussels-Capital Region, and Walloon Region. The country was also subdivided into ten provinces and 589 municipalities.

The federal government retained powers in many areas, such as foreign affairs (including relations with NATO and the European Union), national defense, justice, finance, social security, and large parts of public health and domestic affairs (through the Department of the Interior). The Communities and Regions were nevertheless empowered to establish relations with foreign states in matters over which they had jurisdiction.

Federal legislative power was in the hands of a Parliament composed of two chambers, the House of Representatives and Senate. Proposed legislation had to be approved by both chambers and signed by the king's ministers (the cabinet had to contain an equal number of French- and Dutch-speaking ministers). While the House of Representatives was elected by universal suffrage, virtually the entire Senate was chosen by a complicated system of proportional representation for the different Communities.

The elections of 1999 marked an upheaval in Belgian political life as voters demonstrated their dissatisfaction with scandals and corruption cases over the years; the depredations of organized crime; the apparently lax handling of the case of Marc Dutroux, who, in 1996, kidnapped, raped, and killed several young girls and adolescents; and the long time it took for the ministries of health and agriculture to bring the "mad cow" epidemic under control.

Since then, Belgium was governed by a so-called "rainbow majority" composed of the two traditional large secular parties, Socialists (PS) and Liberals (VLD), and the recently founded Ecolo, a green party made up of defectors from the Communist Party (itself now practically nonexistent) and left-wing Christians.

On the regional and local levels in Flanders, Wallonia, and Brussels, power was in the hands of similar alliances of "greens" (Ecolo), "reds" (Socialists), and "blues" (Liberals). In Flanders, the government also included a party created on a Flemish-language platform, the Volksunie. As was the case on the national level, the two Christian parties—the CVP in Flanders and the PSC in Wallonia and Brussels—were in the opposition. What is more, the PSC underwent a partial split with the birth of the MCC (Mouvement du Changement Citoyen, or Civic Change Movement), which has joined forces with the FDF (Front des Francophones) and Liberal Party to form a united political front in some local election districts.

The far-right National Front, which had practically disappeared in Wallonia and Brussels, enjoyed a new lease on life in Flanders, especially Antwerp Province, under the banner of the Vlaamse Blok, a Flemish nationalist party. This party, itself a radical offshoot of the Volksunie that was in the Flemish government, made spectacular gains, winning 10 percent of the vote in 1999, and 15 seats in the House of Representatives. Indeed, in towns such as Antwerp and Mechelen, up to 20 percent of the voters supported the Flemish far right. While this trend certainly reflected a xenophobic reaction to rising immigration, it also indicated heightened concern about personal safety, especially a rise in the number of attacks on elderly people.

Belgium—whose capital Brussels was the headquarters of the European Commission, the administrative heart of the European Union—occupied the presidency of the EU during the second half of 2001, when the exceptional events surrounding September 11 took place. Under Belgium's presidency, the EU prepared for the introduction of the "euro," intended to replace the national currencies of 12 of the 15 member states (Great Britain, Denmark, and Sweden remained outside the Euro Zone for the time being).

The Middle East and Anti-Semitism

Israel's image in Europe, Belgium in particular, deteriorated in the 1980s, and the downturn accelerated after the outbreak of the second intifada in September 2000. This often spilled over into antagonism toward Jews, and the word "Judeophobia" was sometimes used to describe the atmosphere.

Over the course of 2001 the overwhelming majority of the media hounded Israel, sometimes in vulgar fashion. Both the press and the electronic media tended to ignore the broader context of events in the Middle East, displaying scenes of violence and Palestinian suffering that could readily lead to one-sided and partial judgments. This was due not just to anti-Semitism in Europe and Belgium, but also to the phenomenon of schadenfreude, the enjoyment of others' moral distress: the Jew, a constant victim throughout history, had now allegedly become a bloodthirsty oppressor. Emphasizing the flaws of Jews more than those of other people—a form of anti-Semitism—was encouraged in Belgium by the Arabic press and virulent sermons in mosques and Muslim schools. In contrast to France, however, actual anti-Semitic incidents were infrequent in Belgium (see below).

A task force created by the Jewish community published a "blue paper" reporting on the anti-Semitic and anti-Israel remarks that appeared in the Belgian press. It singled out *Le Soir,* one of the major French dailies, for its consistent pro-Palestinian bias, such as comparing the West Bank to the Nazi camps and the Gaza Strip to the Warsaw Ghetto. The "blue paper" found that even respectable, mainstream journalists—both Flemish and French-speaking—who denounced anti-Semitic incidents, would, in the same article or section, equate Ariel Sharon with Saddam Hussein, or Israel's defensive actions with the September 11 attacks. An example was *De Standaard,* considered one of the kingdom's two or three best papers, which barely differed in this respect from the sensationalistic *P Magazine,* a mass-circulation Antwerp weekly that published articles calling Sharon a criminal and accused Jews of genocide.

Equally frightening, politicians on both the left and the right—and not just the extremists—mouthed similar anti-Israel sentiments. Many in the Jewish community feared that the lessons of Auschwitz had been forgotten and that raw anti-Semitism was about to explode again.

In June, suits were filed in Brussels against Ariel Sharon for allegedly allowing the massacres in the Sabra and Shatila refugee camps in 1982, when Lebanese Christian militias allied with Israel killed some 800 Palestinians. Belgium had enacted a law in 1993 giving Belgian courts jurisdiction over war crimes committed anywhere in the world, and just a few weeks before the Sharon case came up Belgian courts had convicted four Rwandans under that law. A spokesman for the Ministry of Foreign Affairs commented that the suits against Sharon caused "diplomatic embarrassment" for Belgium, making it more difficult for the country to play an evenhanded role in the Middle East. The Belgian attorney that Israel hired to handle the case argued that Belgian courts had no jurisdiction. As the year ended it was considered highly unlikely that the case would ever come to trial.

The Terrorist Threat

Pro-Palestinian terrorism became a problem for Western Europe in the 1980s. Belgium—the capital of Europe and seat of the European Commission and Parliament—was a prime target, as was its Jewish community. There were two attacks against Jews in Antwerp in 1981 and another in 1982. In 1988, the chairman of the Coordinating Committee of Belgium's Jewish Organizations (CCOJB), Dr. Jo Wybran, an outstanding researcher in the field of immunology, was mysteriously assassinated coming out of his hospital. The murderer was never found.

In 2001, the Jewish community continued to benefit from a collaborative relationship with the police and gendarmerie (paramilitary federal police) that had been in place for over two decades to provide heightened surveillance for the country's Jewish institutions and their buildings.

These law-enforcement officials worked in tandem with the Jewish community's own security service, set up by the Central Consistory, which had a staff of paid professionals assisted by several dozen young volunteers trained in self-defense and antiterrorism tactics. As the Israeli-Palestinian situation deteriorated with the breakdown of the Camp David talks in 2000, the Belgian Jewish community beefed up its security service.

In 2001, graffiti were scrawled on synagogues, the National Memorial to the Jewish Martyrs of Belgium, and Jewish schools. A number of pro-Palestinian demonstrations resulted in the looting of downtown stores owned by Jews, but each time the police took control of the situation and damage was kept to a minimum.

The private Jewish security service was reinforced once again following September 11, and the government gave synagogues and the buildings of certain important Jewish institutions special antiterrorist protection such as that afforded the embassies of Israel and the U.S. Largely due to the two-tiered protection provided by the police and the security service, the day-to-day functioning of the community and its institutions was not affected. The only significant post-September-11 incident occurred in December, when some Orthodox Jews, including Albert Guigui, chief rabbi of Brussels, were attacked and roughed up by young men of Moroccan descent.

Investigations of the international networks of Islamic extremists revealed that Brussels was a true terrorist hub, harboring organizations that maintained contact with networks close to Al Qaeda and Osama bin Laden. The few suspects who were actually arrested were young Belgians of Turkish or Moroccan descent who adhered to fundamentalist Islam.

Holocaust Restitution

The 1995 commemoration of the 50th anniversary of the country's liberation and the end of the war triggered a new awareness of the Holocaust. It also coincided with the opening of government archives that had remained closed for 50 years under the laws governing the declassification of official documents.

Belgium voluntarily contributed the equivalent of $1 million to the compensation fund set up in the aftermath of the conference on gold stolen by the Nazis that took place in London in December 1997. This sum was subsequently paid out to the Jewish community and divided between the country's two Jewish museums, the Jewish Museum in Brussels and the Museum of the Deportation and Resistance in Mechelen. The

Belgian Jewish community and the Belgian government participated in several subsequent international conferences on the Holocaust.

On July 6, 1997 the Belgian government, following the precedent set by France and the Netherlands, created a National Study Commission to determine what happened to Jewish-owned assets during the Holocaust era. It was chaired first by Jean Godeaux, a former governor of the National Bank of Belgium, and then by Lucien Buysse, a former grand marshal of the king's court (and thus is often referred to as the Buysse Commission). It consisted of five senior civil servants representing government ministries; representatives of the country's war victims; a retired judge; two historians; and four representatives of Belgium's Jewish organizations—Professor Georges Schnek, then president of the Central Consistory; Elie Ringer, representing the Forum of Antwerp's Jewish Institutions; Henig Apfelbaum, president of Antwerp's Central Administration of Jewish Welfare Organizations; and David Susskind, former president of the Coordinating Committee of Belgium's Jewish Organizations. In 1999, the government provided the commission with a research staff.

The final report, submitted in July 2001, detailed the role played by the country's banks, insurance companies, and government officials in the disposal of the assets, and the approximate worth of what was taken by each sector. This document was expected to serve as a basis for restitution claims.

To implement the final report, the government proposed a bill providing for the restitution of the stolen assets to the victims and their heirs in the Jewish community. It called for the creation of a new commission to examine the validity of all submitted claims and the conditions for returning assets or paying out compensation. A portion of the sums collected from banks, insurance companies, and the Belgian state would go toward the creation of a foundation managed jointly by representatives of the country's Jewish institutions and government appointees. The foundation was to use the interest generated by its endowment to finance social, cultural, and educational projects of Belgium's Jewish community.

This legislation was debated in the House and Senate and adopted in November 2001. All parties within Prime Minister Guy Verhofstadt's coalition government supported it. The exact amount of the endowment was not yet known, but the Belgian Jewish community's National Commission for Restitution was already meeting regularly in preparation for the foundation's creation, and negotiating with banks, insurance companies, and government bodies.

Some of the experts working for the Buysse Commission intended eventually to turn their attention to tracking down missing cultural assets such as artworks. These, unlike bank deposits, insurance policies, and property nationalized by the government, would require a global hunt.

According to a law passed in December 1998, Jews living in Belgium during World War II who were not Belgian nationals could henceforth claim the status of political prisoners, a designation with moral but not financial implications. The Jewish community had earlier secured government recognition of this status for hidden children, hidden adults, and the orphans of deportees. In 2001, however, the community demanded compensation for the Jewish orphans as well as for other children and adults who lived in hiding during the war. The number of surviving Jews who had lived in Belgium at some time between 1940 and 1945 was not expected to exceed 5,000, including 300 deportees and 3,000 hidden children (1,800 of them orphaned). France and the Netherlands already provided such compensation.

JEWISH COMMUNITY

Demography

The Jewish population of Belgium was estimated at around 31,700, somewhat lower than the number found in the 1974 survey conducted by the National Center of Jewish Studies under its director, Professor Willy Bok. While the fall of the Berlin wall and the collapse of the communist regimes stimulated Jewish immigration from the East, this influx was more than offset by the emigration of young people to North America and Israel and by the low birthrate. The rate of intermarriage was estimated at around 50 percent.

As Jewish activities came increasingly to be concentrated in the large urban centers of Brussels and Antwerp, each home to about 15,000 Jews, smaller Jewish communities such as those of Liège and Charleroi grew smaller. The community was rapidly aging overall, though more so in Brussels than in Antwerp, where the large Orthodox presence included many young families.

The Consistory

The Belgian constitution guarantees freedom of religion and provides for government financial support to all recognized faiths. Even before Belgian independence in 1830, when the country was under the control of Napoleonic France, Jewish communities were organized under the consistorial system that had been established for French Jews in 1808. That framework, the Jewish Central Consistory of Belgium, comprised 16 communities in 2001, two of them Sephardi (one in Brussels, the other in Antwerp) and the rest Ashkenazi. The latest communities to gain official recognition were that of Waterloo, which brought together all of the Jews in the southern part of Walloon Brabant Province (CIWABS), and the flourishing community in Knokke, on the Belgian coast, in Western Flanders Province. Consistorial policy was set by an assembly whose 40 delegates were elected democratically by their respective communities.

The Central Consistory was the uncontested religious and moral authority of Belgian Jewry, and not only because it was the oldest Jewish institution in the country. By encompassing all of Belgium it brought together in one federation all Jewish communities despite their varied ideological currents—from Orthodoxy to moderate religious liberalism—and thus included the vast majority of the Jewish population. The Central Consistory also personified the model of Jewish integration into modern Western society; when it celebrated its 175th and 190th anniversaries with pomp and circumstance, the kingdom's highest authorities were there. As the representative institution of Judaism in Belgium, it engaged in dialogue with other religions. It now also helps sponsor projects to help integrate recently arrived religious minorities, notably Muslims.

The Consistory's activities in the area of education were vital for the internal strength of the community. Two of its appointees, rabbis who held the title of "religious inspectors," supervised the teaching of Jewish religion to Jewish students in the nation's public schools. These classes were voluntary. Approximately 60 percent of public-school children from Jewish families in Brussels and 30 percent in Antwerp attended them. In addition, the Central Consistory largely funded, either directly or indirectly, the three large Jewish schools in Brussels (attended by some 2,000 children) and all of the Jewish schools in Antwerp (attended by some 5,000 children).

Besides its role, mentioned above, in arranging security for Jewish institutions, the Consistory was behind the creation of two Jewish museums, the Deportation and Resistance Museum in Mechelen and the Jewish Museum of Belgium in Brussels. The Consistory also acquired a building, conveniently located near the main campus of Brussels Free University (ULB), to house the Union of Jewish Students of Belgium (UEJB) and the European Jewish Students' Union. It also joined with the

CCOJB and FJO (respectively the French-speaking and Flemish coordinating committees of Jewish organizations) in arranging the special commemoration of important events. Like the representative institutions of all the recognized faiths, the Consistory was given radio and television slots for broadcasts in French and Dutch.

Under the presidency of Baron Jean Bloch (1978–82) the Consistory set up an academic council, consisting of the chief rabbi and a prestigious group of Jewish university professors, to consider new issues raised by scientific and medical advances. Professor Georges Schnek was the Consistory's president from 1982 until October 2000, when Professor Julien Klener took the post. Klener was the first person from a Flemish Jewish family to head that body.

Religion

The last official chief rabbi of Belgium retired in 1980. To help fill the rabbinical vacuum, the Consistory prevailed upon the Justice Ministry in 1996 to create the position of regional chief rabbi. In 2001 there were four such governmentally recognized rabbis, two in Brussels—one for the general community and the other for the strictly Orthodox—and two in Antwerp, one for each of the main Orthodox communities. In addition, Rabbi Albert Guigui, rabbi of the Brussels general community since 1983 and thus one of the regional rabbis, was appointed rabbinic advisor to the Consistory, making him, in effect, a de facto chief rabbi.

Brussels

The Great Synagogue, built in 1878, was the center of religious life for the Jewish Community of Brussels (JCB). Recognized by the government as a national historic landmark, the synagogue was also the site for major communal ceremonies. Even though it was Orthodox, it had traditionally featured organ music on Sabbath and holidays, as well as a mixed male-female choir. Albert Guigi, however, the present rabbi, eliminated both practices, arguing the need to bring the JCB into line with other Orthodox Jewish communities.

Rabbi Israël Chaikin, the other "regional rabbi" in Brussels, led the Orthodox communities of the boroughs of Saint Gilles and Schaerbeek, and presided over Beth Israel Synagogue. In addition, the Maale community had become attractive to a number of young Jewish academics who were sympathetic to the Orthodox tradition. The Sephardi Synagogue of Brussels was noted for taking the initiative in meeting with Muslims. In 1999, the Sephardi chief rabbi of Israel came to Brussels to install Rabbi Chalom Benizri as the city's Sephardi chief rabbi.

The borough of Forest had the greatest concentration of Orthodox Jews. There were two relatively new *shtieblach* (prayer rooms) run by Orthodox Sephardi Jews, one sponsored by Chabad. An ultramodern *mikveh* (ritual bath) was located in this borough, installed in the headquarters of the Brussels Bet Din (religious court), which supervised it. There was also a Sephardi Community Center set up primarily for educating Jewish children living in the area.

The Liberal Jewish community in Brussels, whose synagogue, Beth Hillel, was also in Forest, grew gradually after World War II at the initiative of a group of American Jews, and most of the current officers were formerly affiliated with the Great Synagogue in the city. Though the Ministry of Justice recognized this community, thus putting it on a par with the Orthodox communities, it was not accredited by the Consistory. Nevertheless, its activities that were not of a religious nature were represented within the Coordinating Committee of Belgian Jewish Organizations (CCOJB).

Antwerp

Three Antwerp communities were represented within the Consistory, all labeled "Orthodox." The largest was Shomre Hadass, which supervised important religious activities as well as the Tachkemoni School. Machsike Hadass was a federation of all the city's Hassidic groups and considered itself more strictly Orthodox than Shomre Hadass. It had its own kashrut certification system. The "Portuguese" community, smaller that the other two, was supported by many Sephardi Jews.

Jewish Education

An extremely high percentage of Belgian Jewish children attended Jewish schools (the ratio in Antwerp outstripped that in Brussels), and it was probably the highest of any European Jewish community. In addition, as noted above, Belgian law guaranteed children of Jewish families in the public schools the right to attend religion classes that were provided by the Consistory.

Brussels had three Jewish schools attended by more than 2,000 children. The Maimonides Athenaeum, the most religiously traditional of the three, had a large nursery school, a primary school, and a secondary school. The Ganenou Athenaeum, which had grown exponentially over the previous few years, had started primarily to service the children of Israelis living in the country. It now had a secondary school offering excellent preparation for university study. The third and newest school, Beth Aviv, consisted of a nursery school and a primary school. While Jewish studies were taught in all three, Maimonides had the most intensive Jewish program.

In Antwerp more than 3,000 children attend the city's two main Jewish schools, Tachkemoni and Yesode Hatora. The latter was for the children of Orthodox families only, and boys and girls were taught separately. Both institutions had secondary schools, and Yesode Hatora also had a program for training future elementary-school teachers. Yavne, a third large Jewish school in Antwerp, was run by Modern Orthodox Jews, and included the teaching of Zionism. The Hassidic Jews of the Belz and Satmar movements had their own schools in Antwerp, attended by nearly 800 kindergarten and primary-school pupils. The Jewish community also supported Tikvatenu, a school and center for children with mental and physical disabilities servicing more than 100 children.

There was an Orthodox yeshivah in the Brussels borough of Forest that had been functioning for over 20 years. In Antwerp there were two such yeshivahs, attended primarily by Hassidic youths, as well as a weekly *kolel* (intensive seminar) that brought together erudite adult scholars for the study of Jewish texts.

The Jewish Studies Institute (originally known as the Martin Buber Institute), the first school of its kind to be established in Europe, operated under the auspices of Brussels Free University (ULB), and some of its academic courses were eventually recognized as part of the regular curriculum of the university. Besides the regular two-year curriculum leading to a degree, the institute held seminars on Jewish topics for secondary-school teachers and summer classes in Yiddish. The institute's Dutch section, originally located at the ULB's sister institution, the Vrije Universiteit Brussel (VUB), was moved to Antwerp's university center (Instituut voor Joodse Studies at the UIA) and was expected to become gradually more independent from the Brussels section.

In addition, almost all of the Belgian universities had programs in Jewish studies.

Communal Institutions

The Coordinating Committee of Belgian Jewish Organizations (CCOJB) had 41 affiliates in 2001. It was recognized, along with the Central Consistory, as a representative voice for Belgium's Jewish community in dealings of a political nature with Belgian and foreign official bodies, such as, for example, on the question of Holocaust restitution.

Most of Antwerp's Jewish institutions, however, stayed out of the CCOJB and founded the Forum der Joodse Organisaties (Forum of Jewish Organizations) in 1994 to represent Dutch-speaking Jews to the authorities of the Flemish Community. Both it and the CCOJB participated in the Central Consistory.

In the area of social welfare, the Brussels-based Centrale des Oeuvres Sociales Juives (Central Administration of Jewish Welfare Organizations) was primarily a fund-raising body, much like the federation system in the U.S. The money raised went to the Jewish Social Service (equivalent to Jewish family and children's services in the U.S. and open to all, regardless of religion), an old people's home, the three Jewish schools in Brussels, two cultural centers, an athletic center, summer camps, and an education loan fund, all of which also sought to raise money on their own. The Central Administration published a cultural magazine, *La Centrale*.

A similar coordinating role in Antwerp, where bad economic conditions and the 1996 collapse of the Fischer Bank had greatly increased the number of people needing assistance, was played by the Central Beheer van Joodse Weldadigheid en Maatscheppelijk Hulpbetton (Central Administration for Social Welfare Organizations). Its most recent achievement was the creation of the Queen Elisabeth Residence, consisting of studio apartments for elderly persons who want to continue to live relatively independent lives.

The *Belgisch Israëlitisch Weekblad* (BIW) was the only regular Jewish newspaper in the country. A weekly, it was published in Antwerp by Louis Davids, who was also the head of an association to promote the Flemish language in the Jewish community. The paper reported on Jewish life in Antwerp and avidly defended Israel.

The Cercle Ben Gurion (Ben-Gurion Circle) was founded in 1977 by socialist Zionists in Brussels to counteract anti-Israel propaganda. Among its activities were a youth center with seminars, festivals, tournaments, Hebrew and Bible classes, Sabbath dinners, and trips. In 1987, it began publishing a monthly on Jewish issues. Most important, the circle created the first Jewish community radio station in Europe, Radio Judaica, on March 11, 1980, and it quickly became a force to reckon with in Belgium and elsewhere in Europe. It broadcast on matters of interest to the Jewish community, providing a forum for the expression of diverse points of view, round the clock Sunday through Friday. In a sense, Radio Judaica became the voice of Belgium's Jewish community.

A number of other pro-Israel organizations operated in Belgium. The Centre d'Information et de Documentation (Center for Information and Documentation, or CID), created in the aftermath of the Yom Kippur War, promoted understanding of Israel and its security concerns, especially in the media. Since the start of the second intifada, Solidarité avec Israël (Solidarity with Israel) had collected funds for Israeli projects. L'Aide médicale à Israël, an association of doctors and members of the allied paramedical professions, created in 1967 and now working under the aegis of Solidarité avec Israël, raised money for Israel's hospitals and health-care projects. There were also groups allied with specific Israeli educational and social institutions, and with the different Israeli political parties. Finally, the Maccabis, the country's oldest Jewish athletic association, organized in a Brussels section and an Antwerp section, promoted sports in the Jewish community and participated regularly in the international Maccabiahs in Israel.

The Jewish Secular Community Center (CCLJ), founded by former communists, was the most important voice of secular Judaism, and its headquarters was one of the most active meeting places for Brussels Jewry. The CCLJ organized lectures, colloquia, and seminars on ethnic, historical, and cultural topics outside the traditional religious structure, as well as Yiddish and Hebrew courses. Its members tended to be political leftists, favoring a negotiated peace in the Middle East and the creation of a Palestinian State. The CCLJ prepared children for a "secular bar mitzvah" at age 13 and published the magazine *Regards,* the most widely read Jewish magazine in the community.

The Union of Jewish Progressives of Belgium (Union des Progressistes Juifs de Belgique, or UPJB) was situated even farther to the left than the CCLJ and had a much smaller following, most of whom belong to the Ecolo and Socialist parties. The organization was not only pro-Palestinian, but openly supportive of the PLO. Like the CCLJ, it sponsored activities centered on Jewish history and culture, and the Yiddish language. Its monthly, *Points Critiques* (Critical Points), and its quarterly, *Entre Points Critiques* (Between Critical Points), had very limited circulation. The Jewish community of Belgium excluded the UPJB from federative institutions such as the CCOJB.

L'Union des Etudiants Juifs de Belgique (UEJB, Jewish Students' Union of Belgium) was created in the wake of World War II to bring the Jewish students of the entire country under one organizational structure. Most of the current leaders of the community had been active in the UEJB when they were students. In 2001 it had several hundred members from the country's main universities, and constituted a chapter of the World Union of Jewish Students.

The Conseil des Femmes Juives (Jewish Women's Council), an affiliate of the International Council of Jewish Women, defended the rights of Jewish women, particularly in regard to the problem of the *agunot* (women whose husbands refused to give them a Jewish divorce).

The Jewish Museum of Belgium, initiated by leaders of the Consistory in 1980 to display the art and history of the Belgian Jewish community, teach visitors something about the Jewish religion, and demonstrate the Jewish contribution to Belgian life, was now run by a nonprofit organization, Pro Museo Judaico. The museum was expected to move very soon to a beautiful building in the Sablon museum district in Brussels that the government offered to the Jewish community.

The Fondation de la Mémoire Contemporaine (Contemporary Memory Foundation), created in 1994, collected documentation, including oral histories, on the role Jews have played in Belgian life. It published an annual, *Cahiers de la Mémoire Contemporaine*.

Holocaust Commemoration

There were several organizations dedicated to memorializing the Holocaust. The Belgian Union of Jewish Deportees (Union Belge des Déportés Juifs et Filles et Fils de la Déportation/Verenigen van Joodse Weggevoerden in België, Dochters en Zonen der Deportatie) was created upon the country's liberation from Nazi rule by former deportees and survivors of concentration and death camps. It held yearly pilgrimages to Auschwitz, recorded the testimony of survivors, and arranged with school principals for these survivors to speak to students and teachers about their experiences. The organization's new name, Belgian Union of Jewish Deportees and Daughters and Sons of Deportees, reflected the decision to include the second generation in its activities.

The union provided the inspiration for the creation of the National

Memorial for Belgium's Jewish Martyrs in 1970, with the names of the deportees engraved on its stone walls, and the Jewish Museum of the Deportation and Resistance, officially inaugurated by the king in 1995. This museum was located on the very site in Mechelen where more than 25,000 men, women, and children were herded and deported, under unspeakable conditions, to suffering and death (only 2,335 returned). While depicting some aspects of Jewish life in Belgium before World War II, the museum focused on the Nazi era and stressed the role of Jews in the Belgian resistance.

The Auschwitz Foundation organized annual study trips to Auschwitz, maintained a center for study and documentation with a specialized library of more than 7,000 volumes, provided study kits in Flemish and French, and sponsored an essay contest as well as an annual prize for doctoral dissertations on the Holocaust. As an officially recognized body, it had standing to bring legal action against Holocaust deniers.

Interreligious Relations

Christians

The Central Consistory remained deeply involved in relations with Belgian Christians, especially the Roman Catholic Church, which claimed the allegiance of some 90 percent of the population. The Consistorial Commission for Pluralistic Relations had conducted these activities for more than a quarter-century.

There was another organization, Organe de Concertation entre Juifs et Chrétiens (OCJB), a consensus-building body for Jews and Christians. It promoted regular "summit meetings" among Protestants, Catholics, and Jews to review issues facing them, especially on educational matters and on major international events. An ongoing aim of the Belgian Jewish community was to ensure that schoolbooks did not include negative Christian stereotypes about Jews. The OCJB worked with the International Jewish Committee on Interreligious Consultations (IJCIC) in Europe and globally to carry on dialogue between Jews and Christians.

Jewish-Catholic dialogue groups existed in the main cities of Belgium where Jews lived. Seminars, colloquia, and other meetings were held regularly in a climate of mutual respect. The Brussels chapter of B'nai B'rith also organized a number of Jewish-Christian dialogue groups in coordination with the Consistory.

Muslims

After World War II, Belgium brought in immigrant workers from North Africa and Turkey to work in its mines, steel mills, and other heavy industries. By 2001 there were close to 450,000 practicing Muslims in the country, making Islam Belgium's second religion. Two-thirds of this group were of Moroccan descent; the remaining third were primarily Turkish nationals, but also some Algerians, Tunisians, Pakistanis, Albanians, and others.

There were some 300 mosques in Belgium. Although the government recognized Islam as an official religion, it did not consider the mosques to be official "houses of worship" under the law. However, it was expected that this would change for about 50 of them in 2002. The Executive of Muslims of Belgium (EMB), the Muslim equivalent of the Central Consistory of the Jews, was created in 1998. It was the official representative, to the government and to the Jewish community, of all those claiming the Islamic faith, with the right to recognize mosques and certify the credentials of imams and religious teachers. There was also a Federation of Unions of Mosques, made up of eight associations of mosques totaling 140 individual mosques in Belgium. It represented only North African, mostly Moroccan, mosques. There was a separate federation of Kurdish and Turkish mosques.

Relations between the Muslim and Jewish communities and institutions were generally proper and peaceful. Personal relations between the rabbis (who were often themselves of Moroccan descent and spoke Arabic fluently) and the imams were courteous. One or another imam at the Great Mosque of Brussels had received representatives of the Jewish community on several occasions, just as Jewish leaders received representatives of the EMB at the Consistory. However, in some Brussels neighborhoods, Muslim immigrants living near certain synagogues sometimes hampered ingress and egress. Each time an incident occurred, such as the attack on Rabbi Guigui in December 2001, the president of the Consistory and the president of the Muslim Executive issued a statement calling for calm and mutual respect.

Personalia

King Baudouin elevated Georges Schnek, emeritus professor at ULB, former Consistory president, and president of the Jewish Museum of Belgium, to the rank of baron in July.

Important Belgian Jews who passed away in 2001 were: Ruth Sosnowski, Brussels businesswoman, former president of B'nai Brith, and member of B'nai Brith Europe's presidium, October; Rabbi Marc Kahlenberg of Brussels, October; Chief Rabbi Chaïm Kreiswirth of the Machsike Hadass community, Antwerp, December. (Salomon Klagsbald, diamond merchant and president of Machsike Hadass, had passed away in September 2000.)

GEORGES SCHNEK
THOMAS GERGELY

The Netherlands

National Affairs

THE NETHERLANDS REMAINED THE MOST densely populated country in Europe. Though its population reached 16 million at the beginning of the year, the rate of population growth was down slightly because of a reduction in immigration. An estimated 38,000 asylum-seekers entered the country during 2001 as compared to 43,000 in 2000, and a new immigration law, passed at the end of 2000, requiring quick decisions in such cases ensured the prompt expulsion of many who were turned down. Meanwhile, there were still thousands of would-be immigrants whose cases were already in the pipeline before the new law was passed, and their applications proceeded under the old, more cumbersome, procedure. The minister of justice, however, was determined to resolve these cases expeditiously, and thus many more were expelled than in previous years. Over the course of 2001 it became increasingly more acceptable to object to the presence of immigrants "with different customs"—that is, non-Western ones—a trend that intensified after September 11.

The tragic events of that day deeply affected the Netherlands. Many ordinary Dutch citizens, horrified by the attacks on innocent Americans, attended memorial ceremonies for the victims that were held throughout the country. The largest such event took place on the Dam, the main square of Amsterdam and the spot where national events commemorating the victims of World War II were regularly held. At noon on September 12 the whole of Amsterdam fell still for three minutes of silence (one more than the customary two minutes observed for the wartime dead). Cars and buses stood in the streets while workers in shops, offices, and factories stopped working and stood together in little groups. Other Dutch towns witnessed similar scenes. Prime Minister Willem Kok, together with all the cabinet ministers and their deputies, walked on foot from the houses of Parliament to the American embassy where a large crowd had gathered and the gates were covered with flowers. Kok placed a wreath and observed the three minutes of silence there.

Most Islamic organizations in the country denounced the acts of terror, but in the town of Ede, Moroccan youngsters celebrated in the streets. The attack itself and reports of what happened in Ede heightened an already existing mistrust of Muslims. Some mosques were vandalized, others had anti-Muslim slogans painted on them, and Muslims wearing traditional dress reported being threatened when walking down the street.

The Jewish community was also affected. Dutch Jews, with many ties to Israel, identified easily with the victims in New York and their families. Several Jewish institutions, including the only two Jewish day schools in Amsterdam, closed the day after the attack. While the national media explained this as an act of solidarity, in fact these Jewish institutions had been warned that it was unsafe to open their doors that day. A number of Jewish organizations wrote an open letter of protest against the Islamophobia that surfaced in the days after the attack. Meanwhile, verbal abuse by Muslim youths of "visible Jews" became more frequent, while local police were unwilling to act, for fear of escalating tensions and "further stigmatizing" the Muslim community.

On the national political scene, the Netherlands started to move towards the elections of May 2002. After a period of relative stability the major parties were coming under pressure both internally and through the rise of a new right-wing populist party. The government coalition, made up of Labor (PvdA), Conservative Liberals (VVD), and the small center-left Democrats 1966 (D'66), had begun its tenure in August 1998 under the leadership of Prime Minister Kok (PvdA). In August 2001, with elections less than a year away, Kok announced his resignation as leader of the PvdA after 15 years at its helm. He would remain in office as prime minister, he said, but would not lead his party in the elections. His successor, Ad Melkert, was much less popular than Kok, and some party members tried to sabotage his candidacy by leaking scandals about him. In September, Marnix van Rij, leader of the Christian Democrats, the largest opposition party, followed Kok's example, unexpectedly announcing his resignation as party chairman. After some infighting, Jan Peter Balkenende emerged as his replacement.

Meanwhile a new party appeared, "Livable Netherlands," headed by Pim Fortuyn. Seeking to cash in on the popularity of several local parties that went by the same name, it advocated such right-wing populist measures as greatly reducing the number of "bureaucrats," making government services such as the police force "work harder rather than pouring ever more money into them," freeing up prison cell space by locking up drug smugglers in large cages containing more than a hundred at a time, and forcing immigrants to pay for obligatory courses on assimilation into Dutch culture for spouses they imported from their countries of origin. Fortuyn particularly objected to Muslims, and that was clearly the group he had in mind when he claimed that Holland was much too tolerant towards intolerant cultures. This fitted nicely with post-September 11 popular anger at Islam and resentment at the apparent reluctance of the police to do anything effective about abusive Muslim youngsters. The new party—which included a well-known Jew, David Pinto, within its ranks—performed well in opinion polls and by the end of the year it had the allegiance of an estimated 13 percent of the electorate. More than half of these had previously voted for the VVD. Pollsters predicted that the current coalition would lose its majority in the next election.

The Dutch economy slowed significantly in 2001 due to weaknesses in the international economic situation. The growth rate was only 1 percent as compared to as much as 4 percent in recent years. The main cause of this drop was a decline in exports. The economic blow was cushioned somewhat by increased public spending, which was made possible because the government was paying out less for social security and unemployment payments; the latter, however, though still going down, declined at a slower rate than in 2000. Employment growth was negative, in sharp contrast to the growth rate of nearly 3 percent in previous years. Unemployment among immigrants was down somewhat from 2000, but it remained much higher than in the general population.

Israel and the Middle East

When Israel's new ambassador, Eitan Margalit, quietly presented his credentials just days after September 11, he referred to the "special relationships" between the two countries. While his assessment may have been true in regard to parts of the population, official Dutch-Israeli relationships in 2001 were far from "special." The Netherlands maintained a high level of economic and political support for the Palestinian Authority, both unilaterally and through the European Union, and there was much criticism of Israeli policies.

Politicians reacted to the many Palestinian terror attacks during the year in a painstakingly "evenhanded" way. Foreign Minister Jozias van Aartsen and, with just a few notable exceptions, members of Parliament, generally took the line that "of course it is a terrible thing when civilians are killed on both sides," always adding that "of course Israel's occupation of the territories causes understandable Palestinian rage." Some, particularly in the left-wing Green Party, blamed Israel outright for Palestinian terror. This became especially grating after the attack on the Sbarro pizzeria in Jerusalem on August 9, which left the Jewish community in Holland feeling particularly bereaved by wiping out five of its members—both parents and three of the smaller children of the much-loved Schijveschuurder family. Even after settling in Israel, they had kept up close contacts with Dutch family and friends. As the Dutch Jewish community mourned the victims and raised funds to aid the five surviving orphans, one country after another sent condolences to the Israeli government—except Holland. The foreign minister only did so belatedly, and, it is said, after pressure from "a friendly" member of Israel's Knesset.

September 11 brought a slight change, as the shock appeared to make the Dutch in general, including some politicians, more empathetic toward civilians struck by terrorism. One MP from the D'66 party who still walked the tightrope of evenhandedness even after Sbarro, wholeheartedly condemned the December 1–2 attacks in Jerusalem and Haifa, though he was still unprepared to denounce Arafat himself. Even while the Dutch showed more sympathy than usual for Israel after September 11, public opinion, paradoxically, also tended to agree with many of the local imams, who blamed "Israel's aggression against the Palestinian people" for the attacks in New York. When the EU demanded the dismantling of Hamas and Islamic Jihad, Foreign Minister Van Aartsen criticized the EU statement as too harsh and suggested that Israel should "find its way to negotiations as well." Economically, the attacks had a devastating effect on the travel industry, and tourism to the Middle East, to Israel in particular, ground to a virtual standstill. Even at the end of the year traffic to Israel remained largely confined to people traveling to family occasions, and a small number of vacationers headed for Eilat.

Fear that unrest in the region might endanger their investments induced some Dutch firms and the government to cut back on economic relations with the Palestinians. Several projects that were in their initial stages—a new police academy, a training program for Palestinian Authority policemen, and the construction of a port in Gaza—were suspended in May, and the Gaza port plan was canceled in September. Debates on whether to demand financial compensation from Israel for damage to structures that had already been put up were still going on at the end of the year, just as they were in the EU in regard to projects that had been funded collectively by the member states.

Israeli security sources charged that tens of millions of dollars donated to the Palestinian Authority—presumably including funds from the roughly $15 million that Holland budgeted for direct aid to the PA—were going into Yasir Arafat's personal account and were being used to buy weapons. Eveline Herfkens, the minister for overseas development, was questioned about it in Parliament on November 19. Ten days later she responded that all EU support to the PA was paid into a separate account monitored by the International Monetary Fund and "cannot possibly be used to buy weapons." The issue of anti-Semitism in Palestinian schoolbooks was a very sensitive one for the Dutch government since not only did an unknown amount of direct Dutch aid to the PA go toward their publication, but Holland was also an important contributor to the $17.5 million that the EU provided specifically to produce these books. The first editions of the texts, published in 1998 and found to contain blatantly anti-Semitic statements, gave special thanks to Holland for contributing to their publication. After some pressure from the EU, the PA had promised to remove anti-Semitic content from future editions. However the Center for Monitoring the Impact of Peace and other experts claimed that the new 2001 editions still contained offensive passages. After some pointed questioning by members of Parliament, the Dutch government promised on July 12 to review the texts, and repeated the promise in September. Though this review was to take a mere "few weeks," nothing had been done as the year ended.

At the "anti-racism" conference in Durban, South Africa, which began in late August and quickly turned into an anti-Israel forum, members of the Dutch government delegation disagreed among themselves over whether to follow the lead of the U.S. and Israel and walk out, a dilemma made all the more difficult by the strong desire to develop a common EU position. In the end, all the EU states remained, and the closing statement refrained from naming Israel. Only five Dutch organizations refused to sign the closing statement of the nongovernmental organizations (NGOs) that ran parallel to the main proceedings in Durban, South Africa; the statement equated Zionism with racism. Afterwards, some delegates claimed they were unaware of the vote on this statement and had never seen the text. Representatives of Dutch NGOs confirmed this, saying: "The NGO conference was total chaos; there was no list of participating NGOs, it was unknown how many participated, and delegates were unaware which issues were voted where and when." (See above, pp. 96–104.)

The Dutch Jewish community's relations with Israel were not smooth sailing either. The group calling itself "A Different Jewish Voice," founded in 2000 (see AJYB 2001, p. 344), published a full-page ad in the Israeli daily *Ha'aretz* (June 8) telling Israel to "Stop the bloodshed. Stop the occupation. The intifada is the result of 34 years of occupation." This greatly enraged the 10,000-strong community of Dutch-born Jews living in Israel, and strained relations between Israel and Dutch Jewry. In Holland, A Different Jewish Voice placed similar newspaper ads and sponsored meetings on the Middle East conflict that drew large audiences of fervent supporters as well as adversaries.

Then, in September, a new group organized, calling itself the Anti-Racism-Zionist Initiative (ARZI). According to its spokesman, media personality Ralph Inbar, this was a movement "against hate, prejudice, and the falsification of history, and for support to a democratic Israel and the Palestinian right to a state." Unlike A Different Jewish Voice, which claimed that only its posture of opposition could generate a strong critique of its policy in the territories and that other Jewish groups were no more than apologists for the occupation, ARZI sought to stake out a middle ground by criticizing the occupation but at the same time supporting Israel. In December, CIDI, the Center for Information and Documentation on Israel, a pro-Israel organization, also appeared ready to criticize the Jewish state when it sent an open letter to Sharon asking him to review his veto on Yasir Arafat's Christmas visit to Bethlehem.

The question of Dutch participation in the 16th Maccabiah games in Jerusalem was a painful episode that dragged on for months. After much discussion, Maccabi Netherlands announced in May that "for security reasons" it would not send a delegation, and forbade individual sportsmen to participate under the Dutch flag. Holland was to be the only country without representation. At the opening ceremony on July 15, however, one single Dutchman showed up and was paraded around the arena behind two Israeli beauties carrying the Dutch flag, while the announcer broadcast in Hebrew and English that this was Charles Nenner, "the only Dutchman who came to support Israel in spite of everything." This was followed by a physical confrontation between board members of Maccabi Netherlands who were present at the opening (they called it "some pushing and shoving"), and Nenner (he called it "a beating"). Discussions continued in Holland long after the games were over, and Maccabi Netherlands eventually admitted that "it would have been better to send a delegation."

Anti-Semitism and Extremism

There were several disturbing anti-Semitic incidents in 2001, starting with a dramatic series of graveyard desecrations around May 4, the Dutch

Remembrance Day for the victims of World War II, and May 5, Liberation Day.

The week before, Jews from the community of Breda went to the Jewish cemetery of Dorst for their annual remembrance ceremony. On arrival they discovered swastikas and anti-Semitic slogans on more than 70 gravestones. Police reasoned that this must have been planned, since the cemetery was hard to find, the number of desecrated gravestones was large, and the wall around the graveyard had been destroyed, apparently to facilitate a quick getaway. The media covered the incident extensively, particularly when Prime Minister Kok denounced it in his opening speech to the International Remembrance Conference, hosted by the city of Amsterdam on May 2.

The next day, May 3, the CIDI published its yearly report on anti-Semitic incidents for the year 2000. For the first time in years, there had been a rise both in the number of incidents and their severity. (While the report for 2001 was not yet released at the end of the year, Haddassa Hirschfeld, the compiler, believed that the numbers for 2001 would be even higher.)

Two days after that, on May 5, Holland's Liberation Day, seven gravestones in the little Jewish cemetery of Zaltbommel were covered with swastikas and anti-Semitic slogans. Nanny Peerenboom, the mayor (and one of Holland's few Jewish mayors) seriously considered keeping the incident from the press for fear of copycat attacks. Instead, she organized a meeting at the graveyard: "I will not be ruled by fear," she said. Members of Parliament and representatives of the Jewish community who arrived for the meeting were greeted by yet another set of desecrations: swastikas had appeared all over the town of Zaltbommel. A police unit assigned to investigate concluded that these were indeed copycat incidents, and things quieted down. At the end of June three arrests were made, and all the suspects confessed to the desecrations in Dorst. The three were members of the Stormfront, a tiny splinter group that had broken away from the extreme right-wing Nederlandse Volks Unie party.

Despite the rising number of such incidents, experts agreed that organized racism was still negligible in the Netherlands. Extreme right-wing parties were estimated to have a mere 650 members, with a hard core of about 60 activists.

Another category of anti-Semitic incidents was the work of unorganized groups of bored youngsters—often, but not always, of Moroccan descent. Jewish inhabitants of ethnically mixed neighborhoods were often the targets of verbal abuse, which usually went unreported. Even small Jewish children learned to take it in stride. Occasionally, however, verbal abuse escalated into outright harassment. In one case, congregants of a synagogue in Amsterdam had to remain inside the building until a group of aggressive youngsters outside had been dispersed by Jewish security personnel.

In November things got worse: six youngsters started shouting at three elderly Jews leaving a synagogue in a mixed Amsterdam neighborhood, and then threw stones. They shouted in Arabic, but the drift was clear enough from words such as "Palestinian," "Bin Laden," and "Jews." The three phoned the police, but nobody came. When they went to the local station house they were told that the station was understaffed and could not even take their statements. Later, they took the incident to the press, and even this did not produce a reaction from the police. Local authorities, including Job Cohen, the Jewish mayor of Amsterdam, promised initiatives to improve Muslim-Jewish relations in the neighborhood, but there was no follow-up.

Racism on the Internet was on the rise. Though less physically threatening and easier to avoid than outright confrontation, it was particularly insidious because the perpetrators could hide their identity. In January, a local court in Apeldoorn fined an unnamed Dutchman nearly $600 for racism and anti-Semitism on the Internet. This was the first such conviction of an individual; the only other conviction, in 2000, was of an extreme right-wing party.

Holocaust Restitution

Many of the international and national restitution schemes that were set in motion in 2000 continued into 2001. In most cases, the process of restitution itself had become a routine matter.

The German fund for slave laborers was ready to start payments in 2001, and applications had to be submitted to the Claims Conference in Germany by August 11. The Jewish Social Welfare Board was flooded with requests for help from concentration camp survivors. One official described complaints from those who had come up against "unheard-of chaos, incompetence, lack of understanding and inability to implement a policy that did justice to the Claims Conference's real solidarity with victims of war."

The Ekkart Commission continued its investigations into the provenance of some 4,000 works of art currently in Dutch museums (see AJYB 2001, p. 348). Its second report, released in January, covered some 460 paintings. It stated that the ownership of some was unclear, as was the role of the Foundation for Dutch Art Collection, which was supposed to have restored art recovered from Germany to the rightful owners after World War II. In July the Dutch Parliament, the Central Jewish Organization (CJO, which represented Dutch Jewry on restitution issues), the World Jewish Congress in New York, and commission chairman Rudi Ekkart all criticized the Dutch minister of arts for not following the Ekkart recommendations on the reopening of claims. In the end the government went along, announcing that any sales by Dutch Jews to non-Jews after May 1940 would be considered forced sales unless proven otherwise, and that former owners could once again present claims that had been rejected in the 1950s.

For most Dutch survivors, the main event of the year was the distribution of individual restitution monies put up by the government, banks, insurance companies, and the stock exchange in 2000 (see AJYB 2001, pp. 347–48). About $235 million was available, but no one knew how many legitimate claimants there were. The main reason for the uncertainty was a fear of registration. An unusually high number of Dutch Jews had perished during the war, more, both in absolute numbers (100,000) and on a percentage basis (75 percent), than in any other occupied country in Western Europe. One reason for this high death rate was that the community had been so well organized that its registration lists made it easy for the Germans to find and deport Jews; after the war, therefore, many shied away from anything resembling registration, and thus there were survivors unknown to the community. Adding to the uncertainty was the fact that there had not been a demographic survey of Dutch Jewry in 35 years.

The Maror Foundation, which had the responsibility of distributing the funds, estimated that there were some 50,000 Dutch survivors of the Holocaust, each of whom would receive $5,500 from the fund. In those cases where a survivor died after the war, the money would go to the surviving spouse or be divided among the children. Since so many of the survivors were elderly, the "Maror money" was to be dispensed as quickly as possible. To determine who qualified, the foundation sent out a fairly simple form, and the information supplied on it was entered into a computer and matched up with various databases to determine if the applicant was indeed a Jewish survivor who had lived in Holland during the

Holocaust. Many applicants received their money promptly and painlessly after sending in this form. Complications arose, however, when the information on the form did not match the databases. Then, a second, much more intrusive form had to completed, and many found it upsetting. In some cases, one sibling received money immediately, while another child of the same parents was sent the infamous "pink form" and had to submit extra evidence.

Nevertheless, when the deadline for individual claims came, on December 31, most survivors or their children had received their money, or at least a decision. At the end of the year, with just 900 forms still to be processed, about 26,000 claims had been satisfied, far fewer than the anticipated 50,000 claimants. Clearly, not all survivors or their families had been reached. The next step for the foundation was to calculate how much of the money remained unclaimed. From 10 to 20 percent of that, depending on how much was unclaimed, would be distributed to Jewish institutions for communal purposes. Whatever was left thereafter would go to individuals who qualified in a "second round."

One side effect of the recognition of communal ignorance about the number of survivors was that the Foundation for Jewish Social Work (JMW) was able to get individuals and organizations to cooperate on a demographic study—or, as some elderly survivors described it, "Jew counting." It was carried out in conjunction with the Netherlands Interdisciplinary Demographic Institute (NIDI). A preliminary report was published in 2000, and the final report in October 2001 (see below, p. 000). Since it included questions about Jewish affiliation and attitudes, the results were expected to be useful in drawing up a plan for the next stage of the distribution of restitution money, to the "Jewish infrastructure" that served Jewish needs and helped guarantee Jewish continuity.

The data showed that the religious congregations could hardly claim to represent the community: only about 26 percent of all Jews belonged to a synagogue. This finding encouraged other Jewish institutions to assert claims to the money, and they formed a new umbrella organization, Platform Infrastructure Netherlands (PIN). As the new group picked up steam, the religious bodies joined as well, and by the end of the year PIN was the largest Jewish umbrella organization ever seen in Holland. Still, it did not include the large percentage of Jews who were unaffiliated, and the committee formed to draw up a plan for the distribution of the communal money sought to make allowances for future organizations, particularly those catering to the unaffiliated.

JEWISH COMMUNITY

Demography

The full results of the new demographic survey of the Jews in the Netherlands—the first in 35 years—were published in October, and they did not bode well for the future of the community. Based on a sample of 1,036 respondents, it estimated the Jewish population of the country at 44,000, or .275 percent of the total Dutch population of 16 million. The previous survey, done in 1966, found roughly the same number of Jews, but the data showed that the current community had maintained its numbers only because of Russian and Israeli immigration.

Fully 30 percent of the community in 2001 was not Jewish according to Halakhah, traditional Jewish law, because they were children of Jewish fathers and non-Jewish mothers. (Among the bona fide Jews, 24 percent had non-Jewish fathers.) And intermarriage was accelerating. Among younger married Jews, 76 percent of men and 68 percent of women had intermarried. Even of the roughly 46 percent who had two Jewish parents, fully half were themselves intermarried.

Another factor contributing to demographic pessimism was the low birthrate. First-time Jewish mothers in the Netherlands were, on average, 35 years old—seven years older than their non-Jewish counterparts—though religiously observant Jews tended to have children at a younger age. A third of all Jewish women born since 1955 had not had children by the time they reached the age of 40, and were therefore unlikely ever to have children, with the percentage of childless rising as more women reached that age each year. Women of the postwar generation who did start a family had, on average, 1.5 children, below the national average of 1.9 children per woman.

Over two-thirds of Dutch Jews were still unmarried at age 30, more than twice the rate among the general population. In some age brackets, the Jewish divorce rate was double the national average. (Those with two Jewish parents and/or a Jewish spouse showed lower divorce rates.) The percentage of Jewish family units consisting of couples with children fell from 44 percent in 1966 to 28 percent in 2001. Only about half of the Jewish over-35 group lived with a partner and children, as opposed to 61 percent among the general Dutch population. While only 23 percent of people under age 35 in the general population lived alone, 44 percent of Jews that age did.

Communal Affairs

The "Portuguese" Sephardi Congregation of The Hague discontinued its activities due to lack of members. The national Sephardi community, with less than 500 members, was now reduced to the "main" congregation in Amsterdam and a "secondary minyan" in nearby Amstelveen. The latter was the more viable of the two, with a growing number of young families and a lively program. Most of the congregants were of North African origin, only a few were paying members, and most were unfamiliar with the customs that Jewish immigrants from Portugal had brought to Amsterdam in the 17th century. These customs still reigned in the Esnoga, the historic Portuguese synagogue of Amsterdam, where a dwindling congregation staggered under the enormous costs of maintaining the monumental building. Sam Behar resigned as chairman of the Portuguese community of Amsterdam in May, just two months after being chosen for the office. "Problems within the community affected his health so badly that he received doctor's orders to resign," said Behar's successor, Rudi Cortissos.

Membership in the Ashkenazi Jewish community of Amsterdam had remained constant for years at just under 2,900, but since there had been many more deaths than births, this was achieved by attracting new members. One project aimed at keeping membership up was offering those Jews in Ijar, the Jewish student union, free membership for one year, and then a special student membership for about $10 a year.

When the Jewish community of Amsterdam held elections for its board in March, the eligibility of women for membership in that body was a prominent issue. The results of the election kept the ruling coalition basically intact, but months passed before the formation of a new board. Meanwhile, Amsterdam seemed likely to remain the only Jewish community in the Netherlands that banned women from its board.

In other communal news, Motti Rosenzweig, the only kosher slaughterer in the whole of Holland, resigned and went back to Israel. Kosher meat prices immediately skyrocketed as the community had to fly a *shohet* (ritual slaughterer) in from Israel. The Jewish community of Arnhem raised several million dollars for the restoration of its 147-year-old synagogue. The Dutch government contributed generously, as did the province, the town of Arnhem, and individual sponsors. The building was due to reopen in 2003.

Publications

For a country with a small Jewish community, a remarkable number of "Jewish" books were published.

There were several works on World War II and its aftermath. Historian Martin Bossenbroek wrote *De Meelstreep* (The Line Drawn with Flour), the first in a projected series of works investigating Dutch attitudes toward postwar returnees. The Dutch government had commissioned SOTO, an institute employing a group of mostly young historians, to research the topic. Bossenbroek's book described the experiences of a wide range of returnees, from former concentration camp inmates to Dutchmen returning from (forced or unforced) labor in Germany, and concluded that while the reception of returnees may appear callous in hindsight, in the context of postwar Holland it was not. Other historians—notably Professor Ies Lipschitz, a specialist in postwar restitution of properties robbed from Jews—criticized his conclusions. A second volume in the series, *Mensenheugenis* (Living Memory), contained actual testimonies of returnees, edited by Hinke Piersma. Three more books were planned for 2002 and 2003.

Gerard Aalders of the National Institute for Wartime Documentation published *Berooid: De beroofde joden en het Nederlandse restitutiebeleid sinds 1945* (Destitute: Jews Robbed during the War and the Dutch Restitution Policies after 1945), presenting his view on the restitution process. Historian Dienke Hondius chronicled the story of the Jewish High School, which opened in 1941 when the Nazis barred Jewish students from Dutch schools, until 1943 when most of the pupils had been deported. The book was based on interviews with surviving students and teachers, and the publisher, Vassallucci, organized a reunion for the official release of the book, *Absent: Herinneringen aan het Joods Lyceum Amsterdam 1941–1943* (Absent: Memories of the Jewish High School Amsterdam, 1941–43).

Piet Klein, one of Holland's top economic historians, published a most unusual work, *Kaddisj voor Isaac Roet* (Kaddish for Isaac Roet). Klein worked for the National Institute of Wartime Documentation before becoming head researcher for one of the government commissions investigating postwar restitution policies. He resigned after a few months, shocked by the cold and bureaucratic attitude toward survivors that he uncovered, and especially by what he learned happened to Isaac Roet, an inventor of working-class origin who perished.

Journalist Daphne Meijer wrote *Onbekende kinderen: De laatste trein uit Westerbork* (Unknown Children: The Last Train from Westerbork), the story of 50 Jewish toddlers who were caught without their parents and deported on the last train from Holland to Theresienstadt in 1944. Many were too young to know their own names; they were registered as "group of unknown children." Those who survived were later placed with Dutch foster parents. Meijer spent years tracking them down and documenting their stories. Several had since kept in touch and become each other's "family."

Several Dutch translations of modern Israeli authors appeared in 2001, thanks largely to the small publishing house Vassallucci, which had made these works so popular in Holland that Dutch translations outnumbered those in English. Vassallucci also published translations of the great Yiddish authors.

Four Jewish academics resigned from the supervisory board of a new Dutch translation of the Bible in protest of a decision to translate the four-letter name of God as LORD. This left the 51-member board with only three Jews.

Personalia

Fred Ensel, who, among many other activities, was vice chairman of the Maror Foundation for the distribution of restitution monies, was named by Queen Beatrix to the National Committee May 4 and 5. This committee organizes National Remembrance Day (for all victims of World War II, May 4) and National Liberation Day (May 5).

Rob van der Heijden, the Jewish mayor of the seaside town of Zandvoort, became chairman of the Maror Foundation.

The Liberal rabbi Awraham Soetendorp was elected president of the European division of the World Union for Progressive Judaism.

G. Philip Mok (Gerrie) discontinued his weekly column in the Dutch Jewish weekly *Nieuw Israelitisch Weekblad* (NIW) after more than 30 years, at the request of the paper's new editor. Mok had made both friends and enemies with his forceful writings on Israel from a very right-wing point of view. Some readers canceled their subscriptions in protest of the move, while others wrote thank-you notes to the editor.

Author Ida Vos received two awards in 2001—the Sidney Taylor Book Award from the American Union of Jewish Libraries for *The Key is Lost,* a translation of her children's book *De sleutel is gebroken,* and Das Rote Tuch, a German award for books criticizing authoritarianism and neo-fascism, in recognition of all of her work.

Gerrit Zalm, the Dutch minister of finance, received the Scopus Award of the Hebrew University in Jerusalem for his "commitment in resolving restitution issues."

The death of Henriette Boas, 89, was commemorated in all of the Dutch dailies and in the *Jerusalem Post,* where she was a correspondent for years. Blessed with an independent mind and a cast-iron memory for the tiniest detail, this exceedingly frail historian was the scourge of any journalist who got his facts wrong, and bravely attacked views she considered off the mark. She continued to write—among other things, the entry on the Netherlands in the *American Jewish Year Book*—even when she was old and ill.

Other prominent Jews who died in 2001: Berry Biedermann, 49, just after resigning as secretary of the Amsterdam Jewish community for health reasons, leaving two young children; Annetje Fels-Kupferschmidt, 87, founding mother (in 1956), chairman, and honorary chairman of the Dutch Auschwitz Committee, whose activism gained recognition and financial support for Dutch victims of war, and who was at the forefront of the struggle against neofascism, racism, and anti-Semitism; Bob Levisson, nearly 88, an active member of the Liberal Jewish Congregation in The Hague and who, in 1974, founded and headed the Center for Information and Documentation on Israel to counter EU-style "evenhandedness" then surfacing in the Netherlands under Arab economic pressure; Ab Rijksman, 82, the last living memory of the poorest Jewish neighborhood in Amsterdam, who built up a new life from scratch after his return from Auschwitz, and supported many others; Daan Stibbe, chairman of the Jewish Community of Zwolle and major fundraiser for the restoration of Zwolle's decrepit century-old synagogue; Otto Treuman, whose top quality graphic work gave face to many of Holland's Jewish organizations, and who also designed logos for KLM, El Al, and other major businesses; Sophie (Fieps) van Emde, 94, one of the founding mothers and later chairman of WIZO Netherlands, honorary life member of World WIZO, and first female chairman of the Dutch Zionist Union; and Louis van Veen, 96, former clerk of the district court of Amsterdam, secretary and mainstay of the Gerard Dou synagogue, dubbed the "Van Veen synagogue" after him.

ELISE FRIEDMANN

Italy and the Vatican

National Affairs

A CENTER-RIGHT ALLIANCE headed by billionaire media tycoon Silvio Berlusconi swept to power in the general elections in May, ousting the previous center-left government. Berlusconi took office as prime minister in June at the head of Italy's 59th government since 1945. The cabinet included his own business-oriented Forza Italia party as well as the National Alliance (AN), which had its roots in neofascism, and the once separatist Northern League, which was known for its anti-immigrant policies.

The government came under fire soon after taking office for the way security forces handled the violence that marred the Group of Eight summit in Genoa in July. The government deployed 20,000 police and paramilitary carabinieri, but they proved unable to quell violent antiglobalization demonstrations. Police shot dead a 23-year-old demonstrator and were accused of brutality against other protestors. The riots caused millions of dollars of damage to Genoa.

Italian Jews were divided over the new government. On the one hand, Berlusconi's administration was expected to be the most pro-Israel Italian government in years. But many Jews not only distrusted the Northern League, some of whose members had close ties with Jörg Haider's Freedom Party in Austria, but also had particular qualms about the National Alliance, whose leader, Gianfranco Fini, was now deputy prime minister.

Fini had tried over the previous few years to distance himself from his party's fascist roots and make the AN a mainstream rightist party, but many Italian Jews, including Amos Luzzatto, president of the Union of Italian Jewish Communities, remained skeptical. In June, as part of his ongoing effort to ease Jewish fears, Fini made his first visit to the only World War II Nazi death camp in Italy, La Risiera di San Sabba near Trieste, now a memorial to the Shoah, where he laid a wreath.

Israel apparently no longer shared these concerns about Fini and his party. In the fall, Foreign Minister Shimon Peres and Ehud Gol, who had just replaced Yehuda Millo as Israel's ambassador to Rome, indicated that Israel was willing to set aside longstanding objections and allow Fini to visit the Jewish state. Such a visit was considered likely to go a long way toward legitimizing the AN's transition. In local elections at the end of May, Franca Eckert Coen, a former director of Rome's Il Pitigliani JCC, was elected to the Rome city council and was given responsibility for multiethnic affairs. In the same elections, Guido Mussolini, 64, grandson of Italy's wartime fascist dictator Benito Mussolini, ran for mayor of Rome as the candidate of the far-right fringe Forza Nuova movement, but received little electoral support.

Italian reaction to the September 11 attacks and the subsequent air strikes in Afghanistan revealed a mix of ambivalence, division, and insecurity in the face of new global and domestic challenges. Italy pledged troops, ships, and fighter jets, and Berlusconi sought to present himself as the responsible leader of a country fully committed to America's war on terrorism. But the prime minister was forced to engage in extensive damage control after asserting, in September, that Western civilization was superior to Islam. Anti-immigrant sentiment, particularly directed against the growing population of Muslim immigrants, mushroomed after September 11, especially after the U.S. described Milan's Islamic cultural center and mosque as "the main station house in Europe" for the Al Qaeda terrorist network.

Italian public opinion sympathized with the Americans as victims of terrorism, but many opposed the Afghan war and feared its effects. Much of the skepticism about the war grew out of Italy's differences, over the years, with the U.S. on Middle East policy and its attempts to strengthen links with Iran and Libya, countries that Washington considered "rogue states." An angry article by journalist Oriana Fallaci became a catalyst for debate. She lambasted Italians for their ambivalence toward the U.S. and their lack of ideals and moral principles. She warned that the current war was one of religion and culture in which Muslim immigrants represented a "secret invasion."

In November, Rome was the site of two huge rival demonstrations. Tens of thousands attended a pro-America rally led by Berlusconi and his party, while at the same time a similar number of people protested against the Afghan war.

Israel and the Middle East

The continuing Israel-Palestinian conflict and other Middle East tensions were a major focus of Italy's foreign policy throughout the year, both before and after the September 11 terrorist attacks.

Indeed, the threat of terrorism, often linked to the Middle East, hung over Italy even prior to September 11. In January, the U.S. embassy in Rome was shut down without warning for three days following what officials called a "very specific" terrorist threat. In April, a bomb damaged the building that housed an institute for Italian-American relations. That same month, in a raid coordinated with police forces elsewhere in Europe and in the United States, police in Milan arrested five suspected members of an Islamic guerrilla group believed linked to Osama bin Laden. In August, Italian police deactivated a rudimentary bomb near the U.S. consulate in Florence; close to the device police found an anti-imperialist and anti-Zionist leaflet that contained slogans backing the new Palestinian intifada.

Italy attempted to play the role of mediator in the Middle East. Both government policy and public sentiment favored the formation of an independent Palestinian state so long as Israel's security was guaranteed. Senior Italian officials made numerous trips to the Middle East and elsewhere in the Muslim world, both before and after Berlusconi's government came to power. In February, before the national elections, Prime Minister Giuliano Amato visited Iran to show support for Mohammed Khatami, the reformist president, and to foster trade. That same week, a large, high-ranking Italian trade delegation also visited Iran.

Italian leaders held meetings in Rome throughout the year with Middle East leaders, including Prime Minister Ariel Sharon and Foreign Minister Shimon Peres of Israel, President Yasir Arafat of the Palestinian Authority, and President Hosni Mubarak of Egypt. During a 24-hour visit to Rome in July, Sharon characterized the atmosphere as the warmest he had experienced in a recent round of foreign trips. He said he "found a government that is friendly and a prime minister who is much more than a friend toward Israel." During a one-day visit to Rome in October, Arafat won a promise from Berlusconi that Italy would back a major economic assistance package for a future independent Palestinian state. Berlusconi referred to this as a "Marshall plan for Palestine," modeled on the U.S. aid program that helped rebuild Europe after World War II. He reiterated this idea in late November during a meeting with a B'nai B'rith International delegation headed by the organization's president, Richard D. Heideman, and again in December at a meeting with Peres.

Italian public opinion was highly critical of Israel's tough military policy against the Palestinians, and Italian Jews expressed alarm and concern throughout the year at what they perceived as a sharp anti-Israel and anti-Jewish bias in the print and broadcast media, including state-run television. Jewish monitors, making use of Web sites set up for the purpose, analyzed the media's performance and denounced instances of inaccuracy, misinformation, and prejudice regarding Israel. Jews feared that anti-Israel bias could foster anti-Semitism.

In particular, two high-profile cases ignited intense debate. One was the broadcast of a talk show on September 28 over the state-run television RAI. The guests, chosen by host Michele Santoro, a leftist journalist, were vehemently anti-Israel. In response, Leone Paserman, president of the Rome Jewish community, wrote a toughly worded letter to RAI's president accusing Santoro of anti-Semitism and calling for his dismissal. He noted that Santoro appeared to be contributing to the creation of a climate of opinion that would allow Palestinian terrorists to think that "Italy was a suitable country in which to carry out their criminal terrorist attacks." While some Jewish leaders in Rome applauded Paserman's letter, others sharply criticized it as "excessive, impulsive and unwise."

Another inflammatory media case was ignited in October, when *La Stampa* newspaper prominently featured an opinion piece by commentator Barbara Spinelli calling on the Jewish world to issue a collective mea culpa to "the peoples or individuals" who had paid in "blood or exile" so that Israel could exist. Spinelli charged that neither Israel nor the Jewish people as a whole had yet recognized how profoundly the world situation had changed as a result of the attacks of September 11. She accused Jews of acting as if they were the only people who had the divine right to "live in absolute freedom while the other mortals struggle forward under the harsh regime of necessity." Spinelli called on Jews in the Diaspora—many of whom, she said, "live a double and contradictory loyalty, toward Israel and toward the states to which they belong and in which they vote"—to make public penance and press Israel to end its occupation of Palestinian territory. Jews in the West, she said, should line up with the West, rather than with Israel, choosing "electoral links" over "blood links."

Italian Jewish leaders reacted immediately. They suggested that Spinelli's attribution of the policies of the Israeli state to the Jewish people as a whole betrayed her ignorance of Judaism, Jewish history, and the relationship between Israel and the Jewish Diaspora, and smacked of anti-Semitism as well. But many Jews were quite upset and disappointed at how few non-Jewish voices publicly supported their protests against this article.

On February 8, Jewish arbor day (the 15th day of the Hebrew month of Shevat), the Jewish National Fund joined with the Rome municipal authorities in planting 100 trees in a section of historic woodland in an area on the coast near Rome that had been devastated by forest fires in 2000. Taking part in the ceremony were Italy's agriculture minister, the Israeli ambassador, Italian Jewish leaders, and 200 pupils from the Jewish day school.

Vatican-Mideast Relations

Throughout the year, Pope John Paul II repeatedly called for peace in the Middle East and a return to the negotiating table, denounced terrorism, and expressed concern over the situation of Christians in the Holy Land. The tone was set on New Year's Day, when the pope announced that he had sent personal messages to Israeli and Palestinian authorities asking them to "continue along the path of dialogue in order to reach a much-desired peace, which is the essential foundation for fruitful coexistence among all people on earth." Two weeks later, in a "state of the world" address, the pope said that "Israelis and Palestinians can only think of their future together, and each party must respect the rights and traditions of the other." He spoke of "the persistence of injustice, the contempt for international law, the marginalization of Holy Places and the requirements of the Christian communities." Appearing more critical of the Israelis than the Palestinians, he said it was "time to return to the principles of international legality," listing these as the inadmissibility of the acquisition of territory by force, the right to self-determination, and respect for UN resolutions.

As the year wore on, the pope repeated such sentiments with increasing urgency. In May, he sent two senior envoys to Jerusalem to try to broker a cease-fire and the resumption of peace talks, and during the year he also met at the Vatican with a number of officials from the Middle East, including Egyptian president Mubarak and Yasir Arafat.

Also in May, the pope made a historic but controversial three-day visit to Syria. He had three goals in mind: to walk in the footsteps of the Apostle Paul, to improve the Vatican's ties with Islam, and to plead for Middle East peace. He ended up outraging Jews worldwide by refusing to rebut the anti-Semitic and anti-Israeli rhetoric that emanated from his hosts. In his public welcome to the pope, President Bashar al-Assad said that Israelis "attack sacred Christian and Muslim places in Palestine. . . . They try to kill the principle of religions in the same mentality in which they betrayed Jesus Christ and in the same way they tried to kill the Prophet Mohammed." The next day, Syria's grand mufti, Sheikh Ahmad

Kiftaro, asked "the Catholic Church all over the world, with His Holiness the Pope at its head, and all the Christian governments of the West, to stand in support of justice and put pressure on Israel by every means to curb its atrocious aggression." He added, "This is the least Christianity, as proof of its allegiance to Jesus Christ, can offer the world."

World attention focused on the words of the Syrian president. Israeli president Moshe Katzav called Assad an "anti-Semite and racist" for his comments. A U.S. State Department spokesman called the remarks "as regrettable as they are unacceptable," and a long list of Jewish organizations outside Italy sharply criticized the pope for not having responded. The Union of Italian Jewish Communities (UCEI) reacted with "pain and concern" to what happened in Syria. In a toughly worded statement that avoided mentioning the pope's silence, the UCEI warned Italians to "be on guard against the renewed attempt to make Jews the scapegoat for everything and everyone."

(Assad later told French television that his remarks had been misinterpreted. He said he respected Judaism. "I did not talk about racism. I talked about the principles of the three divine religions, that they call for justice, peace, love, and other basic principles. I tried to compare what is happening now in Palestine and what happened during the days of Jesus Christ and Prophet Mohammed.")

The pope focused even more sharply on the Middle East after September 11, repeatedly denouncing terrorism and condemning warfare conducted in the name of religion. A month-long synod of Roman Catholic bishops held at the Vatican in October expressed its "deepest sympathy" for the victims of the September 11 attacks. A closing statement strongly condemned all forms of terrorism, saying that nothing could justify it, although, it added, "some endemic evils, when they are too long ignored, can produce despair in entire populations." On December 11, exactly three months after the attacks, the pope released his annual message for the church's World Peace Day, which is marked on January 1. The theme was "no peace without justice, no justice without forgiveness." While self-defense against terror was legitimate, the pope noted, perpetrators should be "correctly identified," and entire nations, ethnic groups or religions must not be blamed. He also said that the global crisis prompted "a more intense call" for a resolution to the Arab-Israeli conflict.

The pontiff summoned Catholic religious leaders from the Middle East to the Vatican on December 13 to discuss the future of Christians in the Holy Land. In his opening speech to the group, he criticized both

Palestinians and Israelis for "disfiguring" the Holy Land with extremist violence. After the meeting, the Vatican issued a statement repeating its call for peace in the region that would include "security for Israel, the birth of a state for the Palestinian people, the evacuation from occupied territories, an internationally guaranteed special statute for the most sacred parts of Jerusalem, and a fair solution for Palestinian refugees." The statement also touched upon another issue that had vexed Vatican relations with Israel for several years, Israel's authorization of the construction of a mosque in Nazareth, next to the Basilica of the Annunciation. Such a move, the Vatican now stated, could be seen as "provocative" and displaying a "grave lack of respect for the feelings of Christians and for a place of prayer rich in profound significance for their faith"(see below, pp. 588–89).

Holocaust-Related Developments

Italy marked its first official Holocaust memorial day on January 27, 2001, with high-profile ceremonies, broadcasts, performances, and other public events throughout the country. There was special emphasis on educational programs, since recent surveys had shown that many Italians, particularly young people, were ignorant of Italy's wartime role in the Holocaust. A poll conducted by an Italian television network in connection with the commemoration showed that *none* of the 442 viewers interviewed knew the meaning of the word "Shoah," a term frequently used in Italy to denote the Holocaust. Nicolo Mancino, speaker of the Italian Senate, told one audience, "with the passing of time, the worry is becoming strong that a veil of forgetfulness may fall on what happened regarding European racism and the Holocaust." A theme often heard at the commemorations was the need to speak out against contemporary evils and atrocities. Luciano Violante, president of the Chamber of Deputies, spoke to students in Agrigento. Describing the slaughter in the Soviet gulags, in Africa, and in Cambodia, he said, "You have to know how to say no when you are asked to do something that is against democracy, against freedom, against civil and moral values."

Other events commemorating the Shoah took place at different times over the course of the year. In March, government and religious leaders took part in the annual commemoration of the mass execution of 335 men and boys at the Ardeatine Caves south of Rome, which the Germans carried out on March 24, 1944, in reprisal for the partisan slaying of 33 German soldiers. Some 75 of the Ardeatine Caves victims were Jews. The site of the massacre is now Italy's main monument to victims of the Nazis and fascists. In October, a series of events organized by the city of Rome and Jewish communal organizations marked the 58th anniversary of the Nazi deportation of Jews from Rome during World War II. Events included interfaith ceremonies, a theater performance, a public roundtable on aspects of Holocaust restitution, and a presentation of educational work about the Shoah.

In May, after more than two years of work, a government commission looking into Holocaust-era compensation claims issued a 540-page report urging compensation to Jews for the seizure of assets during the fascist regime up to the end of World War II. Originally commissioned by former prime minister Massimo D'Alema, the report noted that while Italy had already made some payments to survivors, these were insufficient. It recommended setting up a government commission on restitution and compensation claims that would "quickly compensate individual victims of seizures and thefts carried out between 1938 and 1945 during the persecution of the Jews." It also suggested the creation of a second commission that would take steps to maintain an awareness of the history of the fascist period and perpetuate the memory of its victims.

During an official visit to Ukraine in June that had interreligious reconciliation as one of its themes, the pope paid homage to the tens of thousands of victims shot dead by the Nazis and thrown into a ravine at Babi Yar, near Kiev. With Yaakov Bleich, Kiev's chief rabbi, standing at his side at the monument on the spot where the Nazis killed as many as 150,000 Jews and 50,000 others over the course of two years, the pope bowed his head and prayed in silence for five minutes. He then recited the Catholic *de profundis* prayer, as a wreath of red, white, and yellow flowers was placed on the monument. During a meeting with Ukrainian religious leaders he said that Babi Yar was "one of the most atrocious of the many crimes" of the 20th century, adding that the Jewish people "suffered injustices and persecutions for having remained faithful to the religion of their ancestors." Jews found the Babi Yar commemoration particularly significant since it was the pope's first participation in such a ceremony since his controversial trip to Syria.

Two initiatives surfaced during the year for the creation of Holocaust museums. In June, Italy's new government appointed a committee to explore the idea of establishing such a museum in the northern city of Ferrara, which had played an important role in Italian Jewish history. Ferrara already had a Jewish museum run by the small Jewish community still living in the town. In the fall, the Milan Jewish community, along with the Children of the Shoah Association and Milan's Center for Contemporary Jewish Documentation (CDEC), announced plans to establish a Holocaust museum in that city. In December, CDEC sponsored Holocaust-education events in Milan. On December 2–3, there was a seminar on the teaching of the Holocaust. On December 12, an educational CD-ROM called "Destination Auschwitz"—produced with funding from the European Commission—was released just prior to a conference on Holocaust transit camps.

Anti-Semitism and Racism

As noted above, Italian Jews worried throughout the year about anti-Israel and anti-Semitic bias in the mass media and its impact on public opinion. Concern deepened after the September 11 attacks, as anti-Semitic articles and cartoons appeared in the press. At one point the newspaper *La Repubblica* allowed the text of the *Protocols of the Elders of Zion* to be posted on one of its online discussion forums dedicated to the war in Afghanistan. It was removed in October, following a complaint from the Simon Wiesenthal Center.

There were episodes of racial intolerance throughout 2001, mostly the work of skinheads and militant soccer fans. There were anti-Semitic slogans scrawled on walls, and one reported incident of anti-Semitic violence: on November 3, unknown persons attempted to set fire to the entrance of the synagogue in Siena. The fire, quickly extinguished, did little damage.

In February, police conducted a dawn raid in the town of Merano, near the border with Austria, and arrested 13 suspected members of the international neo-Nazi skinhead group "Blood and Honor." The arrests were the fruit of an undercover operation that had lasted nearly a year. Police confiscated large amounts of Nazi material including banners, publications, and other racist propaganda. Those arrested were charged with violating a 1993 law banning the incitement of racial hatred. In April, on the 56th anniversary of liberation from fascist rule, neofascists and leftists clashed in Milan and Rome. In Rome, police used tear gas to prevent leftist protesters from attacking a group of neofascists commemorating Italian soldiers who died during World War II. In June, about 200 skinheads and others demonstrated against a gay pride march, and some tried to force police barricades. In August, neofascist material was found at the homes of suspects in the bombing of a Venice courthouse. In the autumn, a Rome court convicted Francesco Ciapanno, editor of a monthly photographic magazine, of defamation and inciting racial hatred for publishing vehemently anti-Semitic articles. He was sentenced to 13 months in prison.

In May, sports authorities penalized the Rome soccer team Lazio because some of its fans unfurled a huge banner with a racist and anti-Semitic slogan during a match with arch-rival Roma. In recent years militant Lazio fans had frequently come under fire for using similar objectionable slogans against opposing teams. In September, hoping to promote intergroup harmony, Lazio took part in a three-way tournament in Rome, called the "Shalom Cup," along with Maccabi Haifa of Israel and Asec Mimosas of Ivory Coast. The tourney was marred by one disruption—a banner reading "Against Zionist racism for a true peace, Intifada until victory" was briefly unfurled in the stands. In another attempt to combat soccer hooliganism, a roundtable conference was held in Florence in the fall on the topic of sports and racism.

Another troubling trend was the ongoing fascination with, and nostalgia for, the fascist regime of Benito Mussolini. This took various forms, ranging from the sale of Mussolini memorabilia—including videos, books, and even a calendar—to attempts to name streets after him and other fascist figures. Mussolini's hometown, Predappio, was an attraction for right-wing extremists and other nostalgic fascists. In the late spring, some young men began standing vigil at Mussolini's tomb there. Dressed in black cloaks, they told reporters that they were members of a newly formed Benito Mussolini Honor Guard. Their action drew a sharp reprimand from Predappio's mayor. At Rome fashion shows in July, Italian designer Francesco Barbaro's use of the swastika motif in his latest clothing and accessories came in for heavy criticism. One British fashion writer called it a "sick attempt to court publicity on the back of millions of people's deaths." In the fall, protests forced the right-wing mayor of Tremestieri Etneo, a small Sicilian town, to withdraw his plan to name a local street for Mussolini.

JEWISH COMMUNITY

Demography

About 26,000 Jews were officially registered as members of Italian Jewish communities, but the actual number of Jews in the country was believed to be between 30,000 and 40,000. Three-quarters of Italy's Jews lived in two cities where there was a full infrastructure for an active Jewish life: Rome, with about 15,000 Jews, and Milan, with about 10,000. The rest of the country's Jews were scattered in a score of other towns and cities—mostly in northern and central Italy—with few local Jewish resources, in communities ranging from a handful of Jews to a thousand or so people. About half of Italy's Jews were native born, and the other half were immigrants who had come over the past few decades. Between one-third and one-half of Rome's Jews were members of families that had emigrated from Libya following the Six-Day War of 1967. The Milan Jewish community included recent arrivals from more than two dozen countries. The largest contingent was Iranian, with most of the others coming from other Muslim states, and many maintained the traditions of their hometowns.

Communal Affairs

Orthodoxy was still the only officially recognized form of Judaism in Italy, encompassing three ritual traditions: Sephardi, Ashkenazi, and Italian, the latter a local rite that evolved from the Jewish community that lived in the country before the destruction of the Second Temple. Chabad-Lubavitch maintained its strong presence, particularly in Rome, Milan, and Venice, where the movement ran a yeshivah. Most Italian Jews, however, were not strictly observant, and even most of the observant Italian-born Jews were highly acculturated, with a strong Italian as well as Jewish identity. On the other hand, many of the Jewish immigrants from Muslim countries were very observant.

Preliminary results of a demographic survey of the Rome Jewish community were released in 2001. Conducted in 1996–98 under the direction of Professor Eugenio Sonnino of La Sapienza University in Rome, the survey studied a representative sample of 815 people. The respondents were highly educated, one-third of them having a university degree. Most owned their own homes and worked in the commercial sector. The data showed a strong sense of Jewish identity—most respondents said they observed the Sabbath and major holidays, and about half said they kept kosher. Younger people were more observant then the middle-aged generation. Nevertheless, there was widespread acceptance of intermarriage. Only 4 percent said it was essential for the non-Jewish partner to convert, 22 percent said it would be better to avoid mixed marriage, and just 10 percent—including some who were themselves intermarried—said such marriages were unacceptable.

The year saw an increase in Jewish "lifestyle infrastructure" in some places, including an expansion of kosher facilities in Rome. Several new kosher restaurants operated in the old ghetto, and a cheese manufacturer in Caserta announced in November that it would begin producing kosher mozzarella.

While Reform and Conservative streams did not officially exist in Italy, an independent liberal Jewish association called Lev Chadash was formally established in Milan in the spring. Many if not most of its members were gentiles seeking to convert to Judaism, or others who were not Jewish according to Halakhah. In July this group officially affiliated with the World Union for Progressive Judaism. Lev Chadash had no rabbi and was not accepted as a member of the Union of Italian Jewish Communities. It received support, however, from the St. John's Wood Liberal Synagogue in London, whose senior rabbi, David Goldberg, made regular visits to Milan to lead services and give lectures. In the summer, the London synagogue loaned a 250-year-old Torah scroll to Lev Chadash, which used it for the first time on Yom Kippur. At the end of the year another small liberal Jewish group was organized in Florence.

The Rome Jewish community went through an important rite of passage in 2001. In a surprise move, Elio Toaff retired as the community's chief rabbi after holding the job—Italian Jewry's most prominent religious position—for 50 years. (Italy has no national chief rabbi.) Later that month, officials of Rome awarded Toaff, 86, the city's highest honor, "honorary citizen"—the equivalent of receiving the keys to the city—at an emotional ceremony attended by President Ciampi, Rome's mayor, and other dignitaries. In November, Dr. Riccardo Di Segni, 52, was chosen to succeed Toaff. Di Segni had served as director of Italy's Rabbinical College since 1999. A medical doctor as well as a rabbi, he was chief radiologist at a major Rome hospital and said he intended to keep his medical job.

Italian Jews had a well-organized though financially troubled infrastructure of schools (including the Rabbinical College), clubs, associations, youth organizations, and other services. The women's organization ADEI-WIZO was active nationwide, sponsoring bazaars, lectures, meetings, and other social, cultural, and fund-raising events. Jewish community and culture centers in Milan and Rome also provided a full schedule of programs. A large Italian delegation attended the General Assembly of the European Council of Jewish Communities that was held in Madrid in May. Cobi Benatoff, from Milan, was president of the council. Italian Jewish leaders also took part in other international events, such as the World Jewish Congress meeting in Jerusalem in November. In August, more than 400 young Jews from all over Europe met in northern Italy for the annual weeklong European Union of Jewish Students Summer University.

Given their traditionally strong links with Israel, Italian Jews followed the continuing conflict between Israel and the Palestinians with extreme concern. Jews were very worried by the negative portrayal of Israel in the mass media and the pro-Palestinian stance of many political parties and public figures. With the support of organizations such as the Italy-Israel Association (most of whose members are not Jewish), they staged several pro-Israel solidarity rallies. In December, Prime Minister Berlusconi, Mayor Walter Veltroni of Rome, and other senior officials joined hundreds of Rome Jews at the city's main synagogue in a solidarity vigil for the victims of terrorist attacks in Israel. Earlier that same day, city officials turned off the lights of the Campidoglio city hall for 15 minutes and observed a minute of silence at noon.

Nevertheless, there were divisions within the Jewish community over Israel's policies, and these tended to be linked to broader political loyalties. This was demonstrated most dramatically in the furor over an opinion piece that appeared in the Rome Jewish monthly *Shalom,* entitled "Stop the Madness," that criticized Israel's policy. The writer was Giorgio Gomel, a well-known left-wing Jewish peace activist who was also a member of the board of the Rome Jewish community. In early June, soon after the article appeared, Gomel was accosted by other Jews who shouted insults, called him a "friend of Arafat," and tried to physically attack him as he walked toward the Israeli embassy to attend a vigil in support of Israel. Jewish community leaders condemned what was done to Gomel, but the incident prompted debate: a subsequent issue of *Shalom* contained a number of letters to the editor, some denying and others endorsing Gomel's right to express public criticism of Israel.

Jewish-Catholic Relations

Official interactions between the two faiths were marked by several milestone events. Despite tensions and even acrimony over several issues regarding the Shoah, overall relations were generally positive.

In late February, Cardinal Edward I. Cassidy, 76, retired after more than a decade as president of the Commission for Religious Relations with the Jews. His successor was Cardinal Walter Kasper, a German theologian. One of Kasper's first official functions, at the beginning of May, was to attend a meeting in New York of the International Catholic-Jewish Liaison Committee, which consisted of the Vatican commission and its primary formal partner in Vatican-Jewish dialogue, the International Jewish Committee on Interreligious Consultations (IJCIC).

That meeting resulted in a joint statement that, among other things, dealt with the commission of Catholic and Jewish scholars set up by the Liaison Committee in 1999 to examine the role of the Vatican and Pope Pius XII in World War II. The scholars had asked, in October 2000, for full access to the Holy See's secret wartime archives so as to resolve questions that still remained after the examination of documents previously released by the Vatican (see AJYB 2001, p. 362). The new joint statement appeared to endorse this request, saying: "While the opening of the Vatican archives will not definitely put this matter to rest, opening the archives will help remove the aura of suspicion and will contribute to a more mature level of understanding." Nonetheless, Kasper, in a letter dated June 21, informed the commission of scholars that the archives dated after 1923 were not accessible for "technical reasons." Church officials explained that the Vatican had only two archivists to catalog the documents, and that the material would be released as it became ready. In July, the commission of scholars suspended its work because it had been denied access to the archives. Relations between the Vatican and Jews deteriorated sharply over this issue, and there were acrimonious accusations on both sides.

IJCIC chairman Seymour Reich distributed a statement expressing "deep disappointment" with the Vatican and made public what he said the historians had conveyed in a letter to Kasper when they decided to suspend their work. Elan Steinberg, executive director of the World Jewish Congress, accused the Vatican of a "cover-up." But Cardinal William Keeler of Baltimore, the senior American Catholic involved in Vatican-Jewish dialogue, charged that Reich had misrepresented the content of the historians' letter to Kasper.

In early August, Rev. Peter Gumpel, a German Jesuit who had been gathering material to support the beatification of Pius XII, denounced a "violent attack" and "defamatory campaign"conducted against the memory of the wartime pope. He said that Jewish scholars on the panel had leaked "distorted and tendentious"information to the media and "publicly spread the suspicion"that the Vatican was trying to hide documents that could embarrass it. He defended Pius XII and said that the archives would be opened "as soon as possible." Kasper issued a similar statement two weeks later, saying that the wish for access to the archives was "understandable and legitimate" and that the Holy See would grant access "as soon as the reorganizing and cataloging work is concluded."

In November, however, two of the three Jewish scholars resigned from the commission, making it unlikely that the group would resume its work. Kasper, for his part, made it known that he would look for other scholars to continue the research.

Despite the apparent impasse over access to the secret archives, Vatican-Jewish dialogue proceeded in other areas. Kasper made clear that he wanted to identify areas on which Jews and Catholics could find common ground, and that he sought closer contacts with Israeli Jews. In November, during a visit to Jerusalem at the invitation of the Israeli government and with the blessing of the chief rabbinate, he laid out his priorities in a major policy speech on Jewish-Christian relations. He said, "We may not and we cannot forget the horrors of the Holocaust; we must remember them as a warning for the future." But, he added, "our dialogue should not be merely past oriented, but future oriented. . . . Our dialogue should more and more become a contribution for the solution of today's and tomorrow's spiritual and ethical problems and challenges."

In his address, Kasper dwelt at some length on "Dabru Emet" (Hebrew for "Speak the Truth"), a Jewish theological statement on Christians and Christianity formulated by a group of Jewish scholars and published in September 2000 (see AJYB 2001, pp. 182–83). He, as well as other senior Catholic officials, pointed to this document as a basis for future discussions with world Jewry. Signed by scores of Jewish scholars and rabbis, "Dabru Emet" listed eight points where Jews and Christians found common ground and upon which they might build further dialogue. It also called on Jews to relinquish their fear and mistrust of Christianity and "learn about the efforts of Christians to honor Judaism."

(Some prominent Jews had refused to sign the document because they felt it insufficiently emphasized Christianity's connection to the Holocaust. It said, "Without the long history of Christian anti-Judaism and Christian violence against Jews, Nazi ideology could not have taken hold nor could it have been carried out. Too many Christians participated in, or were sympathetic to, Nazi atrocities against Jews. Other Christians did not protest sufficiently against these atrocities." But, it said, "Nazism was not a Christian phenomenon," and "Nazism itself was not an inevitable outcome of Christianity.")

Shortly after his trip to Israel, Kasper attended a meeting at Sacred Heart University in Fairfield, Connecticut, where Catholic and Jewish scholars discussed theological issues. This was the second meeting of

Kasper's Vatican commission with a new Jewish group, the Rabbinic Committee for Interreligious Dialogue, which had been set up as a partner for interreligious discussion of theological issues. (Opposition from IJCIC's Orthodox members prevented that body from engaging in such discussions.)

In Italy, numerous interfaith events took place during the year. On October 11, Chief Rabbi Toaff of Rome joined with a Roman Catholic cardinal, the imam of Rome's main mosque, a Protestant minister, and an Orthodox priest for an interfaith ceremony commemorating the victims of the terror attacks in the United States. Prayers were recited in Hebrew, Arabic, and English, and the representatives of the various faiths stood together and lit candles. The service took place at the Basilica of St. John Lateran in Rome, and was attended by numerous dignitaries including Italy's president.

Three days later, on the evening of October 14, more than 1,000 people staged a candlelit procession through downtown Rome calling for world peace, an end to international terrorism, and remembrance of the Shoah. The silent march, culminating in a ceremony at the main synagogue, was the first of several events marking the 58th anniversary of the deportation of Jews from Rome, which occurred on October 16, 1943. It was organized jointly by the Catholic Sant'Egidio community and the Rome Jewish community. Participants included Toaff, Kasper, and the mayor of Rome. Later that night, hundreds of people, including Vatican, Jewish, and political VIPs, crowded the Basilica of Santa Maria degli Angeli e dei Martiri for a performance of the "Holocaust Requiem" by English composer Ronald Senator, an interfaith oratorio commemorating the 1.5 million children killed in the Shoah. This was the first time the oratorio was performed in a Roman Catholic church. Cardinal Keeler, who was the titular bishop of the basilica, told the audience that the performance aimed at building spiritual bridges between Christians and Jews.

Culture

As an indication of the priority that Jewish leaders gave to the promotion of Jewish culture, the Union of Italian Jewish Communities set up a new Department of Education and Culture, and, in the summer, appointed Rabbi Roberto Della Rocca, formerly the rabbi of Venice, as its director.

Italy was one of four countries with small Jewish populations chosen by the London-based Institute for Jewish Policy Research (JPR) for a "mapping of Jewish culture" survey. This was an attempt to chart all Jewish cultural events in Italy, Sweden, Belgium, and Poland during the twelve-month period from May 2000 through April 2001. Preliminary results, made public in July, indicated a total of more than 700 events in the four countries, including 99 individual events and 13 Jewish cultural festivals in Italy.

There were numerous Jewish cultural events throughout the year, some organized by Jewish communities, some by the Israeli embassy, some by private organizations or civic and state bodies, and some by a combination of sponsors.

Annual Jewish festivals included the summer festival of klezmer music in Ancona, the Nessiah music festival in Pisa in October, and the Pitigliano Jewish film festival in southern Tuscany in November. Numerous concerts of Jewish music took place, ranging from liturgical music to klezmer. In January, four cantors from Central European synagogues gave a concert of liturgical music in the synagogue of Trieste, in order to raise funds for the construction of a synagogue in Zagreb, Croatia. At the end of May, Florence was the site of a series of concerts by international performers of Yiddish, Sephardic, and Israeli Jewish music. Sponsoring this series were the Milan-based Yuval Center for the Study of Jewish Music, the Hebrew University of Jerusalem, the Florence Jewish community, and the Israeli embassy. In October, the second European festival of Jewish choirs took place in Milan, with participants from France, England, Israel, and Italy.

Several notable theatrical productions were mounted during the year. The European premiere of *Possession,* a play by Israeli author A.B. Yehoshua, took place in Rome in February. Coinciding with the play's run, an exhibition of photographs, "Encounters in Jerusalem: People and the Divine," was shown in the foyer of the theater. Another major production was the musical play *Saccarina* (Saccharine), set in the Lodz ghetto and wartime Rome, which was performed in several cities and also broadcast on radio. Singer/actor Moni Ovadia, Italy's most prominent Jewish theatrical personality, toured with a new production, *Yosl Rakover Talks to God.*

There were also exhibitions, in several cities, of artwork by Jewish artists and on Jewish themes. The Tikkun bookstore in Milan was a leading venue for exhibits, readings, and other Jewish-themed cultural events. Meanwhile, work progressed slowly—for lack of funds—on the expansion and modernization of the Jewish museum in Rome.

Numerous conferences, seminars, and academic meetings on Jewish themes took place. In February, there was a full-day conference at the State University in Milan on the significance of the jubilee year in Jewish tradition. At the same institution, Professor Alfredo Mordechai Rabello of the Hebrew University of Jerusalem taught a seminar course on Jewish and Israeli law in February and March, cosponsored by the university's law department and the Goren Goldstein Judaica Center. This was the first course in Jewish law to be offered at an Italian university. In March, there was a conference in Rome on the Yiddish theater and klezmer music. In May, a three-day conference on Jewish cultural heritage in Italy took place in Ravenna, organized by the University of Bologna and sponsored by a number of institutions, including the Israeli embassy, Israeli universities, and the Italian Jewish community. Among the topics discussed were plans to catalog centuries-old manuscripts held in the Jewish Bibliographic Center in Rome, and the possibility of restoring the city's Jewish catacombs. The year saw various initiatives toward restoring or repairing Jewish heritage sites, including the Jewish cemetery in Pesaro on the Adriatic. In November, an international conference and exhibit of illuminated Jewish manuscripts took place in Parma to mark the publication of a new catalog of Jewish manuscripts in the city's Palatina Library.

A number of films with Jewish themes made news. *Concorrenza Sleale* (Unfair Competition), by Italian director Ettore Scola and starring French actor Gerard Depardieu, was released in 2001. Set in Rome in 1938, the year that the fascist regime imposed strict anti-Semitic legislation, it told the story of these laws' effects on two neighboring families, one Jewish and one Catholic. *Eden,* a film by Israeli director Amos Gitai that was based on a novel by Arthur Miller, competed for the Golden Lion at the summer Venice Film Festival. *La Vita e' Bella* (Life is Beautiful), Roberto Benigni's Academy Award-winning film about the Holocaust, had its premiere showing on Italian television in October and grabbed a record share of the viewing audience. More than 16 million Italians—more than half of all viewers—watched it. In Rome, meanwhile, Greek director Constantin Costa-Gavras was shooting part of a new film on Pope Pius XII's role during the Shoah.

As usual, numerous books on Jewish topics or by Jewish authors were published, and there were book launches, readings, roundtables, and other literary events throughout the year. The political journal *Limes* devoted its first issue of 2001 to the theme of "Israel/Palestine: the Narrow Land," with 19 in-depth articles by well-known writers on aspects of the continuing conflict. In May, five noted Israeli authors—David Grossman, Meir Shalev, Etgar Keret, Batya Gur, and Dorit Rabinyan—came to Italy. They took part in a "week of Israeli literature" that coincided with the fifth annual Sefer Jewish book fair in Milan. The group also gave presentations in Rome, Bologna, and Turin. The Italian translation of *Barney's Version,* by the Canadian writer Mordecai Richler, became a surprise best-seller and a literary sensation in Italy. Giuliano Ferrara, editor of the newspaper *Il Foglio,* even modeled a daily column on protagonist Barney Panofsky's politically incorrect mode of sounding off about his adversaries. Richler's death was mourned with lengthy obituaries in leading newspapers. In October, the historic Jewish publishing house and bookstore Salomone Belforte in Livorno, founded in 1834 and closed at the onset of World War II, marked its rebirth with a conference and art exhibit on Sephardic culture in the Mediterranean area.

Italy and Italians participated enthusiastically in the European Day of Jewish Culture on September 2. Held under the patronage of the president and the Ministry of Culture of Italy, there were events in 36 towns and cities, drawing a total of about 50,000 visitors. Sites on display included a number of Italy's 70 magnificent synagogues, many of them no longer in use. Italy's undersecretary for culture, Vittorio Sgarbi, and other senior officials took part in an official ceremony in Bologna. Though only about 200 Jews lived in the city, hundreds of people lined up to visit the Jewish museum and synagogue, tour the medieval ghetto, sample Jewish culinary specialties, or leaf through books displayed at an open-air Jewish book fair. Sgarbi said: "Even without being born Jewish or being of the Jewish religion, we all are or have been Jews in virtue of the dialogue that Jewish civilization has had with Italian civilization, interrupted only in moments of ferocity and barbarism."

There were signs, however, that Italian attitudes toward the intifada and the September 11 attacks may have had a negative impact on participation in Jewish cultural events. At a number of conferences and roundtables, there was palpable tension between pro-Israel and pro-Palestinian participants. A bomb threat disrupted a performance by Moni Ovadia. The annual Pitigliano Jewish film festival in southern Tuscany had to be moved to a nearby town because of security concerns. There were also reports that a number of concerts of Jewish music had been canceled, including some by the Rome-based Jewish musician Adriano Mordenti.

Personalia

In February, Raimondo Di Neris—known as "Uncle Raimondo"—a Holocaust survivor and prominent figure in the Rome Jewish community, died. Also in February, Roberto Jarach was elected the new president of the Milan Jewish community. He succeeded Emanuele Fiano, who resigned after three years as president to run for local office. Jewish publisher Mario Lattes died at the end of December, aged 78.

In March, in separate ceremonies, the late Giuseppina Gusmano of Casale Monferrato, and the late Antonio Mani and Bortola Bertoli of Lavenone, near Brescia, were recognized by Yad Vashem as "Righteous among the Nations" for saving Jews during the Holocaust.

Scientist Rita Levi Montalcini, 92, who fled prewar Italy to escape fascist anti-Semitism and went on to win a Nobel Prize for medicine in 1986, was, in August, named a Life Senator for honoring Italy with her scientific and social work. She thus became only the second woman to receive this title, one of the highest honors bestowed by Italy. In December, author Lia Levi was awarded two literary prizes: the Moravia Prize for her novel *L'albero della magnolia* (The Magnolia Tree), and the Grinzane Cavour Prize for *Che cos'è l'antisemitismo? Per favore rispondete,* a book on anti-Semitism written for young people.

RUTH ELLEN GRUBER

Switzerland

National Affairs

THE YEAR WAS ONE OF CRISIS and self-doubt for Switzerland. Swissair, the national airline that had been a paradigm of Swiss quality and a source of pride, filed for bankruptcy after September 11. Two tragedies weakened people's sense of security: a fire in the Gothard tunnel caused 11 deaths; and a psychotic killer emptied his rifle in the parliament of the canton of Zug killing 15, including members of the local government. And finally, the World Economic Forum announced it would host its 32nd annual meeting in New York City rather than the usual place, the ski resort of Davos.

Early in the year, Swiss voters showed they still preferred political isolation when, in a referendum on joining the European Union, 76 percent voted against membership. In light of the war on terrorism after September 11, Switzerland took steps to alter its banking secrecy laws so as to prevent Swiss banks from being used for money laundering and the financing of terror.

Israel and the Middle East

Swiss sentiment about the situation in the Middle East, whether expressed in the media, by politicians, or in everyday conversations with ordinary people, was overwhelmingly pro-Palestinian. Statements apparently meant to criticize specific Israeli policies often slipped into blanket condemnations of the Jewish state, showing no understanding of the broader context and no compassion for Israeli victims of terrorism. At times, anti-Semitism reared its head: "Jews" were accused of oppressing Palestinians, parallels were drawn between Gaza and the Warsaw Ghetto, and anti-Semitic incidents were explained away by blaming them on the behavior of Jews.

There were many public demonstrations in support of the Palestinian cause where one could read placards denouncing "the massacre of the Palestinian people" or "Israel's apartheid policy," and proclaiming Israel's share of responsibility for the September 11 attacks. Even the far-left demonstrations against the World Trade Organization and the World

Economic Forum—both symbolizing globalization and headquartered in Geneva—were tinged with anti-Semitism.

Pointing out Israel's flaws in public debate and letters-to-the-editor served an important psychological function for many Swiss. After Switzerland was criticized over issues of justice and morality in connection with its handling of Holocaust victims' assets in Swiss banks, the Middle East situation provided an opportunity to attack Israel on similar moral grounds for what it was supposedly doing to Palestinians. And in some circles the same reasoning was applied to America after September 11. One could hear Swiss saying that, having criticized Switzerland for its behavior during World War II, the U.S. had now gotten its comeuppance for the arrogant way it treated the rest of the world and its unconditional support of Israel.

The crisis in the Middle East triggered diplomatic tension between Israel and Switzerland that was not eased by the visit of Swiss foreign minister Joseph Deiss to Israel and the Palestinian territories in March. A particular point of controversy was the agreement of Switzerland, repository of the Geneva Conventions, to host a special session of the "high contracting parties" to examine Israel's alleged violations of the Fourth Convention—which dealt with treatment of civilian populations—in the territories. The session took place in December behind closed doors and without debate; the conclusion condemning Israel had been written in advance. Israel and the United States boycotted the conference.

The International Committee of the Red Cross (ICRC), based in Switzerland, showed hostility toward Israel. In May, the Red Cross delegate to Israel, René Kosirnik, stated publicly that "population transfer or installation by an occupying power in occupied territories is considered illegal and is a major violation. Formally, it is a major violation, but in principle it is equivalent to war crimes." After U.S. Representative Eliot Engel (D., N.Y.) protested, ICRC president Jakob Kellenberger apologized and said that the reference was "inappropriate and will not be repeated." But later in the year Paul Grossrieder, the ICRC director, accused Israel of violating humanitarian law, particularly in its treatment of members of the Popular Front for the Liberation of Palestine; Grossrieder was unsure whether they were "civilians" or "militants." He also sought to justify the continuing exclusion of the Magen David Adom, the State of Israel's equivalent of the Red Cross, from the international Red Cross movement.

The "special" treatment of Israel within the international organizations headquartered in Geneva, which had gone on for years, continued. This was particularly blatant at the UN Commission for Human Rights, where Israel was the only country entered as a "special item" on the agenda, while all other countries (including human-rights violators such as Libya, Algeria, China, Syria, and Saudi Arabia) were examined globally, as one entity. With the U.S. voted off the commission for 2002, the situation for Israel was likely to worsen.

At the UN World Conference Against Racism held in Durban, the Swiss delegation kept a very low profile. It considered "unacceptable" some of the phrasing about Israel in the final resolution, but did not get involved in the working groups dealing with "difficult questions." The Forum Against Racism, a national federation of Swiss NGOs, attended the parallel NGO Forum at Durban. It stated its "satisfaction with the final documents" and considered the "NGO declaration and action program as an indispensable base to pursue [our] work." It did not comment on the anti-Israel and anti-Semitic elements in the document (see above, pp. 100–04).

Swiss Jews tried to keep a low profile in the public debate about the Middle East. But the media repeatedly questioned them about their support for Israel, often blaming them, after each Israeli act of retaliation against the Palestinians, for not criticizing or at least distancing themselves from Israeli policies. Swiss Muslims were never asked for their opinions after Palestinian suicide attacks or calls for jihad against Jews.

Anti-Semitism and Extremism

The Swiss parliament refused to lift the immunity of one of its members from Zurich, Christoph Blocher (Swiss People's Party), who had been sued for a 1997 speech in which he said that, with Jews, "it's always a matter of money." The protection afforded by his parliamentary immunity would make it impossible to convict him of violating the antiracism law.

After a local Christian Democratic politician from Solothurn publicly accused Jews of being behind the events of September 11, the party expelled him.

On the popular level, the upsurge in anti-Semitism triggered by the onset of Palestinian violence in late 2000 intensified, as seen in leaflets, slogans, and banners at pro-Palestinian street rallies, and in the media. In a few cases, those responsible for such statements were reprimanded or even fired from their jobs. A number of anonymous anti-Semitic tracts, posters, and stickers turned up in schools and mailboxes, or were found glued onto street poles. Some of these went so far as to blame Jews for the cost of health insurance and Swissair's bankruptcy.

Abraham Grünbaum, an Israeli rabbi visiting Switzerland, was killed during the night of June 7 on a Zurich street. No one claimed responsibility and no clues were found.

Far-right groups found a new lease on life in the wake of the Palestinian intifada and September 11, both of which gave them the opportunity to revive anti-Semitic conspiracy theories. One such group was Vérité & Justice (Truth and Justice) based in Châtel-Saint-Denis near Fribourg. It reprinted old anti-Semitic books, such as *The International Jew* that had originally been published by Henry Ford, and propagandized for Holocaust denial. Affiliated with the Institute for Historical Review in California, Vérité & Justice was one of the organizers of a Holocaust-denial conference scheduled for March in Beirut, but the Lebanese government banned the event. The organization's leaders were Jürgen Graf, Philippe Brennenstuhl, and René-Louis Berclaz. Graf fled to Iran in 2000 after being sentenced to a 15-month prison term for racial incitement, and the other two were expected to go on trial for the same crime in 2002.

Gaston-Armand Amaudruz, whose monthly *Courrier du Continent* spewed racism and anti-Semitism, had received a one-year jail sentence under the racism law in 2001, which was subsequently cut back to three months. In 2001 the Federal Court rejected his appeal, and Amaudruz would begin serving his sentence in 2002.

Another far-right Swiss publication was the bulletin put out by the Amis de Robert Brasillach, which was headed by Geneva lawyer Pascal Junod, an activist who also ran three other similar groups: Thulé, Cercle Proudhon, and Synergies Européennes. Junod regularly invited extremists who had been convicted of racism in France, such as Guillaume Faye and Roger Garaudy, to address audiences in Switzerland.

Geneviève Aubry, a former member of parliament, published *L'Atout,* which frequently used anti-Semitic and anti-American rhetoric to argue for a neutral and independent Switzerland. In Basel, Ernst Indlekofer distributed *Recht und Freiheit* (Right and Freedom) along with a French version, *Droit et Liberté,* charging that the UN was dominated by Jews and Masons. Far-right views were also spread by Claude and Mariette Paschoud's *Le Pamphlet,* distributed from Lausanne, and Max Wahl's *Notizen.* Extremists in Valais saw their Web site, romandit.ch, closed down by the Swiss authorities because of homophobic statements made on the site before a gay pride parade in July. Jeunesse Nationaliste Suisse et Européenne (Swiss and European Nationalist Youth), which had published a monthly electronic newsletter on a French Canadian Web site, stopped its activity at the end of the year.

Federal police estimated that there were about 1,000 skinheads in Switzerland and that they held some 60 gatherings around the country during the year. At many of these events, which attracted sympathizers from all over Europe, racist books, videos, CDs, uniforms, and flags were on sale. To avoid prosecution under the laws against public manifestations of racism, the organizers called these gatherings "private." Skinheads were now recruiting younger people (even 12–13-year-olds), and were increasingly likely to carry guns. A former skinhead, Marcel von Allmen, 19, was whipped to death in 2001 after he broke the skinhead law of silence and described some of his group's activities. Another far-right extremist, Marcel Strebel, cofounder of the Patriotic Front, was killed in a private fight.

A key link between far-right circles and Islamic extremists—a relationship both highlighted and enhanced by the September 11 events—was Ahmed Huber. He was a Swiss Holocaust denier converted to Islam who worked for Al-Taqwa, a company in Lugano suspected of financing the attacks on the U.S. The offices of Al-Taqwa, which had changed its name to the Nada Management Organization, were searched by police after September 11. In November, Huber organized a meeting in Lucerne "against world Zionist domination and the American Satan," and lectured before Roger Wüthrich's neopagan Avalon group. To be sure, the far-right extremists shared little in common with Muslims beyond their common enemies, Jews and Americans, but they did express admiration for the attacks and aspired to divide the world between the swastika in the West and the crescent in the East. Wüthrich declared that "Muslims are the far-right's only allies." Racist Internet sites that had previously targeted Arabs or Muslims stopped doing so.

Ironically, Jews and Muslims found themselves on the same side against the extreme rightists at the end of 2001, when a national debate broke out over ritual slaughter. Earlier in the year, the government decided to lift the ban on ritual slaughter that had been in effect since 1873 and which had forced Jews and Muslims to import kosher or halal meat. But the liberalizing move aroused emotional opposition, including charges that Jews and/or Muslims, who, it was argued, only lived in the country as "guests," were "barbaric" and followed "archaic principles" that they sought to "impose" on Switzerland. Samuel Debrot, president of the Vaud section of the Society for the Protection of Animals, declared that Jews and Muslims should "become vegetarian or leave the country." Another opponent of ritual slaughter was Erwin Kessler, president of Verein gegen Tierfabrik (Association against Animal Factories). A far-right figure who maintained close contact with Holocaust deniers, Kessler had already been convicted of racial incitement for comparing Jewish kosher slaughter with Nazi treatment of Jews. He was given a nine-month suspended jail sentence, which he appealed. The anti-ritual-slaughter camp launched a petition campaign in the hope of collecting enough signatures to put the issue to a popular referendum. This would take place in 2003 at the earliest.

Outside the Jewish community there was little reaction to anti-Semitism. The great majority of political, social, religious, and public-policy organizations, whether they took the Palestinian side or kept their distance from the Middle East conflict, were silent about anti-Jewish manifestations. Programs for teaching tolerance in the schools depended almost entirely on funding from local NGOs, religious communities, and individuals. The Department of Foreign Affairs, which had been allocated 10 million Swiss francs (about $6 million) to combat racial discrimination, had not yet chosen how to spend the money as the year ended.

Holocaust-Related Matters

With the publication of 12 new studies by the historical commission headed by Prof. Jean-François Bergier, the national debate about Switzerland's role during World War II seemed to be drawing to an end. These studies examined financial aspects of Switzerland's relations with Nazi Germany (for example, Swiss holdings in I.G. Farben, the export of electricity to Germany, and secret banking operations), as well as legal questions and other issues (looting of artworks, asylum policies). The public at large generally reacted to these publications with indifference. The final report of the commission was due in March 2002.

The Special Fund for needy Holocaust victims, headed by Rolf Bloch, distributed 298 million Swiss francs ($175 million) to beneficiaries around the world—Jews, political prisoners, Gypsies, homosexuals, handicapped people, Christians of Jewish descent, Jehovah's Witnesses, and Gentiles who had helped save Jews. The fund was to cease operations in May 2002.

The global settlement reached in 1998 between Swiss banks and the filers of class-action suits had still not brought an effective distribution of money to heirs of Holocaust victims who had held Swiss bank accounts. A third list of holders of dormant accounts was published containing the names of about 21,000 people "with a possible link to victims of Nazism." This brought the total of names to 33,000. Brooklyn Federal Court in the U.S. ordered a new examination of 580,000 applications by Holocaust survivors or their heirs.

The Swiss Solidarity Foundation, proposed in 1997, was intended to use 7 billion Swiss francs (more than $4 billion) from the national gold reserves for humanitarian projects. The various political parties differed among themselves about how to use the money, but they did agree to lower the amount to one-third of the original sum. A referendum on the actual creation of the foundation was scheduled for 2002.

Two Swiss religious bodies issued studies about their activities during the Holocaust. The one produced by the Reformed Evangelical Church pointed to the excessive caution, if not indifference, of its leaders at the time, and denounced manifestations of anti-Semitism by some of them. It also paid tribute to several individuals who helped refugees. The study sponsored by the Roman Catholic Central Conference concluded that Swiss Catholics never explicitly condemned National Socialism or the persecution of Jews, and, despite the aid that certain individual Catholics gave Jews, Catholic authorities never protested the treatment of Jews seeking refuge in Switzerland.

Eight Swiss citizens were honored as "Righteous among the Nations" by Yad Vashem in Jerusalem, bringing the total number of Swiss designees to 49.

JEWISH COMMUNITY

The 2001 census showed an increase of 5.9 percent in the Swiss population, mostly due to immigration. But the number of Jews in Switzerland remained at about 17,500, mostly in urban areas. The Muslim population was now at 310,000, or 4.5 percent of the population.

Historian Jacques Picard, a specialist in the history of 20th-century Swiss Jews, was named the first professor to hold the chair in Jewish studies at the University of Basel.

Gerhart Riegner, former secretary general of the World Jewish Congress, died in Geneva at the age of 90. One of the first to receive information about the Nazi plan to exterminate the Jews in World War II, he attempted to alert the Allies and world Jewry. Reigner, trained as a lawyer, spent his life fighting anti-Semitism and defending human rights.

Two books of Jewish interest were published in 2001: *Documents about*

Refugees 1930–1950, a summary of what was available in Swiss archives; and *The Righteous of Switzerland: Heroes of the Holocaust* by Meir Wagner, stories of 37 Swiss men and women who saved Jews during World War II.

An old ring dating back to the 3rd century was found on the archaeological site of Augusta Raurica, between the cantons of Basel-Land and Argau. This bronze piece, engraved with images of four Jewish ritual objects—a menorah, a shofar, a *lulav,* and an *etrog*—was now the oldest testimony to the Jewish presence in Switzerland. Previously, the oldest Jewish remnants were graves and documents from the 13th century.

BRIGITTE SION

Central and Eastern Europe

Germany

National Affairs

GERMAN POLITICS IN 2001, especially in the second half of the year, were largely geared toward the national elections to be held in 2002, though the unexpected events of September 11 made previous political assumptions highly uncertain.

In November, Prime Minister Gerhard Schröder (Social Democratic Party, SPD) accepted the resignation of his foreign affairs advisor, Michael Steiner, who had embarrassed the government by demanding caviar and insulting senior German soldiers during a delayed flight to Germany via Moscow. He was replaced by Dieter Kastrup, Germany's ambassador to the UN since 1998. Kastrup previously served in embassies in Brazil, Iran, and the U.S., and was appointed ambassador to Italy in 1994. Steiner had already been pressured to quit his post in May after he was blamed for leaking a private communiqué supposedly suggesting that Libyan leader Muammar Qaddafi had admitted Libyan involvement in the 1988 Lockerbie airliner bombing and the 1986 bomb attack on a West Berlin night club in which several U.S. servicemen died. The government denied that Qaddafi said any such thing to Steiner.

The election of the ultraconservative judge Ronald Schill as Hamburg's minister of interior in late September sent a chill down the spines of those concerned about extremism in mainstream German politics. Schill, who won more than 19 percent of the vote on a law-and-order platform in a city with a high crime rate, was known as the "merciless judge" for his tendency to hand down severe verdicts in minor cases. Creating his own "Party of a State-Led Offensive," he built alliances with the conservative Christian Democratic Union (CDU) and the liberal Free Democratic Party, sidelining the SPD in Hamburg for the first time since the end of World War II. Schill appeared ready to go national. Already the number two person in the CDU in Rostock (former East Germany), Michael Necke, 28, had defected and joined the new party. Necke said the CDU no longer spoke to younger people. Schill's party was expected to run in elections in the former East German state of Saxony-Anhalt in April, 2002.

Local politics in Germany's capital took a few interesting twists in the fall of 2001. Berlin's longtime conservative mayor, Eberhard Diepgen of the CDU, lost his post over revelations that the city's finances were in ruin. He was replaced by Klaus Wowereit of the SPD, who announced, before the election, that he was gay. In another remarkable political shift, the reformed communist party, the Party of Democratic Socialism (PDS), won enough votes in the Berlin state election to become a partner in the new coalition government there. PDS chief Gregor Gysi, who was Jewish, became minister of economics for the state, which covered the area including and immediately surrounding Berlin.

Immigration

Germany progressed slowly toward enactment of a law, first suggested by the coalition government in 1998, to streamline regulations for asylum seekers, facilitate the integration of foreigners, and develop a method of determining who might enter the country in order to work. There were some seven million noncitizens living in Germany on a long-term basis—nearly 9 percent of the country's entire population of 82 million. The great majority, nearly six million, came from European countries (mostly Turkey, Italy, Greece, and former Yugoslavia). The next largest groups were Asians, Africans, North and South Americans, and Australians. An estimated 200,000 were arriving each year.

Conservatives and the extreme right had long blamed unemployment and crime on "foreigners." In broader terms, the right resisted redefining Germany as a multicultural society. But there was also an emerging consensus among other groups—industry, labor unions, and churches—on the need for an immigration law. Discussion began in earnest in the summer of 2000, after a wave of right-wing extremist attacks on foreigners. At that time, Interior Minister Otto Schily created an independent commission on immigration policy headed by Rita Süssmuth (CDU), former president of the Bundestag (lower house of Parliament), and including Paul Spiegel, president of the Central Council of Jews in Germany (CCJG).

No law was enacted in 2001 since agreement could not be achieved between those favoring a fixed immigration quota—the political right—and those, primarily on the left, who preferred flexible guidelines that might be adjusted on humanitarian grounds. It appeared likely that immigration would be an issue in the 2002 elections. It was unclear whether an eventual immigration law for Germany would affect the status of future Jewish refugees or immigrants from the former Soviet Union. Under existing law such Jews enjoyed a special status not shared by most other refugees (aside from "ethnic Germans," who were automatically repatriated). Since 1991 Germany had allowed 5,000 Jews per year to emigrate from the former Soviet Union in order to help rebuild Germany's destroyed Jewish community.

September 11

The terrorist attacks on American targets on September 11 affected German politics both domestically and internationally. By the end of the year it was clear that Germany was prepared to be a committed partner with the U.S. in the fight against terrorism.

After the attacks, Chancellor Schröder pledged Germany's "unlimited solidarity" with the United States. That solidarity withstood a Bundestag vote of no confidence in November over the question of whether German troops could take part in the war in Afghanistan: the SPD-Green Party coalition government narrowly survived. According to the German constitution, every military deployment had to be approved by the Bundestag. Foreign Minister Joschka Fischer, leader of the traditionally pacifist Greens, had threatened to resign if his party failed to support deployment of German troops in Afghanistan. This was just the fourth time since World War II that Germany held a vote of confidence, and this vote was the biggest test for the Red-Green coalition since its formation in October of 1998.

At the end of the year, Schröder and Fischer were reelected to head their respective parties in the national elections scheduled for September 2002. Polls indicated that a serious challenge to the coalition might be in the offing from Edmund Stoiber of the Christian Social Union (CSU), the Bavarian sister party of the Christian Democratic Union (CDU) of former chancellor Helmut Kohl. Stoiber was the governor of Bavaria. A slowing German economy was causing considerable voter dissatisfaction with the government: the deficit was growing and unemployment had risen to 10.4 percent (in his 1998 campaign, Schröder had promised to cut unemployment to 3.5 percent by 2002). Though Schröder received public approval for his leadership after the September 11 attacks, critics said he seemed to have lost control of the "new middle," or the center majority, to which he had appealed successfully in 1998.

It remained to be seen, however, whether the CDU had recovered sufficiently from the slush-fund scandal that rocked the party in 1999–2000. Former chancellor Kohl was no longer making negative headlines for the party, and the CDU was trying to create a positive, forward-looking image. Down to nearly the last minute, CDU party head Angela Merkel was considered the favorite to lead the party. But after opinion polls showed that Merkel would garner only 19 percent of the vote against 68 percent for Schröder, Stoiber, who polled 35 percent against the chancellor's 41 percent, was chosen instead.

Germany's response to the events of September 11 included numerous pro-American demonstrations, including a gathering of more than 200,000 in the capital on September 14, where President Johannes Rau and the newly appointed U.S. ambassador to Germany, Dan Coats, spoke. Both Chancellor Schröder and Foreign Minister Fischer visited New York City's "Ground Zero" in the fall.

Ambassador Coats, in his first official speech on U.S.-German relations, said the debate about whether or not America was "drifting away from Europe" had ended on September 11. He listed what he considered the highest priorities for German-American cooperation: law enforcement and the fight against terrorism; NATO expansion; Balkan peacekeeping; missile defense; economic cooperation; environmental protection; labor and social affairs; and fighting Internet crime.

Popular sentiment, sympathetic to the United States immediately after September 11, turned sour when it came to the war in Afghanistan, which began with bombings on October 7. While antiwar protests came nowhere near matching the size of the earlier pro-American demonstrations, their anti-American tone was very sharp. They attracted both left- and right-wing extremists angered by American "imperialism"—and its supposed Jewish connections.

Some prominent intellectuals also expressed anti-American sentiments as the war against Afghanistan continued. The writer and Nobel Laureate Günter Grass, for example, said he identified with "American writers like Norman Mailer, who after [the attacks on] New York said 'We have to ask ourselves why Arab terrorists hate us so much.'" This prompted Interior Minister Schily to describe the anti-Americanism within certain German intellectual circles as "really terrible." Schily in turn was lambasted by, among others, the German philosopher Peter Sloterdijk, who compared Schily to a modern-day German version of U.S. Senator Joseph McCarthy.

One result of the terror attacks was the cancellation of a planned October mission to Berlin by the New York-based United Jewish Communities, the merged entity of what had been the United Jewish Appeal and the Conference of Jewish Federations. It was to have been the first official trip to Germany by this major American Jewish umbrella organization. The mission was rescheduled for October 2002. (Other Jewish groups that visited earlier in the year were B'nai B'rith USA, the Conference of Presidents of Major American Jewish Organizations, the North American Boards of Rabbis [NABOR], and the World Union for Progressive Judaism.)

According to the Federal Office for the Protection of the Constitution, some 30,000 Islamic extremists had made Germany their home in 2000. When it became known that three of the four pilots in the terror attacks had been living in Hamburg until shortly before carrying out their deadly plans, German security forces searched the country and made several arrests. In October, Germany cracked down on politically suspect Muslim clubs, while issuing a public reminder that only a small minority of Muslims living in Germany belonged to such clubs.

Nevertheless, as in the United States, supporters of civil liberties in Germany condemned this crackdown and other attempts to limit freedom in the name of security. The Green Party, in fact, pressured its government coalition partner, the SPD, to preserve laws that protected individuals from unlawful arrest or from being expelled from Germany without due process. Such German sensitivity to civil liberties reflected the nation's vivid memory of the abuse of police powers under Nazi and communist rule.

One law that did pass, in November, criminalized membership in and support of terrorist organizations abroad, and allowed the banning of religious groups that abused their legal protection and tax advantages by harboring terrorists or promoting extremism. Interior Minister Schily first enforced the law in December when he banned the 1,100-member Islamic State, a group based in Cologne with 19 affiliates around the country, which was reportedly linked to Osama bin Laden. The leader of Islamic State, Turkish-born Muhammed Metin Kaplan, then serving a four-year sentence in Germany for incitement to kill a rival, had called for the overthrow of non-Islamic governments.

In late November, after the U.S.-led coalition had succeeded in driving the Taliban from power, Germany hosted a conference of leaders of

Afghan ethnic and political groups in Bonn, where plans were made for an interim government. Germany was a natural choice for the conference, given its relatively large Afghan population (some 100,000 refugees and students) and its traditional commitment to "nation building" based on its own post-World War II rejuvenation through the Marshall Plan. Some viewed the decision to hold the meeting in Germany as a chance to raise the country's international profile, especially in light of the fact that Berlin had been rejected as a site for a Middle East peace conference earlier in the year.

Another development that raised Germany's international profile was the election in November of General Harald Kujat as chairman of NATO's military committee, to take effect in June 2002.

Germany's relatively large population and great economic strength ensured that it would have the greatest number of seats in the European Parliament and play a key role within the European Union, especially with the expected expansion of the EU to include countries in Eastern Europe. Both Prime Minister Schröder and Foreign Minister Fischer supported an American-style elected president rather than a rotating EU presidency.

Israel and the Middle East

Germany's long-standing close relationship with Israel, built on its recognition of guilt and responsibility, was sorely tested during a year of unending violence in the Middle East.

History was made on the first day of 2001 when Israel sent its new ambassador, Shimon Stein, to the newly reestablished capital, Berlin. Stein not only had the unenviable task of representing his country to one of its most important supporters during an exceptionally difficult time in Israel's history, but he also followed a very popular ambassador, Avi Primor, who, in pre-intifada days, often criticized his own government—in fluent German—and was a darling of the country's official, intellectual, and media circles. Stein quickly cemented strong connections with the government, and consistently challenged unfair criticism of Israel.

The official opening of the new Israeli embassy in Berlin in May was a major public event that drew 2,000 guests and featured a live klezmer band and kosher hors d'oeuvres. Shimon Peres, on his first official visit to Germany as Israel's new foreign minister, offered a prayer for peace in the Middle East and for the victims of the Holocaust. Peres called the embassy "not only a House of Israel, but also a house representing all those driven out of their homes" by the Nazis. (The embassy was built on land purchased in 1928 by a Jewish businessman, Hermann Schöndorf, who was forced to emigrate in 1934, a year after the Nazis came to power.) The new building was faced with Jerusalem stone and consisted of six segments, a reminder of the six million Jews murdered in the Holocaust. It was designed by Israeli architect Orit Willenberg-Giladi and built by Hochtief, Germany's second-largest construction firm. German press reports made much of the fact that the company had also built Hitler's Berlin bunker.

During his visit to Germany, Peres met with both Schröder and Fischer, and took part in a congress of European Social Democrats, where he faced tough questioning on Israel's settlement policy.

In July, only two months later, Germany welcomed Syrian president Bashar al-Assad for a state visit to Berlin. Assad had meetings with the chancellor, the president, the foreign minister, and others. German Jewish leaders were incensed at the dignified treatment given Assad, who, during a visit to Spain earlier in the year, had said that "the racism of the Israelis [was reminiscent] of National Socialism" and, during the May 2001 visit of the pope to Syria, had declared that Jews wanted to "destroy the basis of all religions, just as they betrayed Jesus and just as they tried to kill the Prophet Mohammed." Michel Friedman, vice president of the Central Council of Jews in Germany (CCJG), said it was "unbearable" to see political leaders "who are actively anti-Semitic, racist and defamatory against Jews" treated like any other leaders. Reportedly, Foreign Minister Fischer had used the occasion of his meeting with Assad to suggest that the Syrian rethink his approach to Israel and Jews.

Meanwhile, Jürgen Möllemann, a vice president of the liberal Free Democratic Party, said it was high time that more Arab leaders were invited to Germany. Möllemann, who was also head of the German-Arab Society, said that if Schröder could meet with Ariel Sharon, who, in his opinion, was a greater threat to the peace process, then he could certainly meet with Assad. Möllemann's anti-Israel views surfaced several more times during the year, and drew criticism from the government and the CCJG. Michel Friedman said that "if Möllemann has not grasped" the fact that Israel had a right to defend itself against "brutal, hate-filled and cowardly assassins of this world," then he "disqualifies himself from being taken seriously in politics."

Israeli embassy spokesman Yuval Fuchs called Foreign Minister Fischer "one of the greatest friends of Israel in Europe." Fischer played an active role in trying to broker an end to violence, maintaining good relations with both Israel and many Arab countries, and insisting on the need for American participation in any peace talks. In late October Fischer visited Pakistan, followed by trips to Tehran, Riyadh, and Tel Aviv. Particularly in Iran, Fischer emphasized Germany's unbending support for Israel's right to exist. He came under criticism there for his statements to the Bundestag in which he had condemned Hezballah and Islamic Jihad as terror organizations. In Israel, Fischer tried unsuccessfully to convince Prime Minister Sharon to withdraw troops from several Palestinian cities, and to pressure Yasir Arafat to extradite the murderers of Israeli tourism minister Rehavam Ze'evi.

In September, Fischer stood up for Israel at the UN's World Conference Against Racism in South Africa, from which both Israel and the United States withdrew in protest. Responding to comments by UN secretary general Kofi Annan, who related Israel's treatment of Palestinians today to the Nazi genocide against the Jews, Fischer said Germany "cannot accept the trivialization, relativization or even denial of the Holocaust, and it will resolutely counter any such attempts." Fischer called the Holocaust "the 20th century's most terrible crime" and said its memory "will have a lasting influence on German politics."

After some 3,000 nongovernmental organizations (NGOs) at the conference signed a nonbinding declaration condemning Israel as a "racist, apartheid state" and accusing Israel of war crimes, Fischer warned that the conference was in danger of failure. Several major German NGOs, including the pro-immigration lobby PRO ASYL, publicly condemned the resolution for its anti-Semitic and anti-Israel rhetoric. (While in South Africa, Fischer also met privately with Arafat and Italian foreign minister Renato Ruggiero to discuss the possibility of talks in Italy between Arafat and Peres.) Following the conference, diplomat Michael Gerdts, who headed the German delegation, said he was extremely pleased with the changed language in the final resolution, which did not mention Israel by name. He said this was the result of European cooperation.

While Germany had little success in moderating the generally pro-Palestinian stance of the European Union, German representatives took the lead in challenging EU funding of virulently anti-Semitic, anti-Israel Palestinian schoolbooks. In August 2001, CDU members Amin Laschet, a member of the EU legislative body and Germany's representative to its economics committee, joined with Elmar Brok, head of the EU Parliament's foreign policy committee, to publicize texts funded indirectly by the EU that described Jews as "treacherous and disloyal," suggested that

Zionism benefited from persecutions and the Holocaust, called "martyrdom in the struggle against Israel" the highest goal for young Muslims, and left the State of Israel off the maps.

In November, they and other pro-Israel members of the EU Parliament, including the prominent French lawyer François Zimeray, succeeded in attaching a rider to an EU budget line of 45 million euros earmarked for promoting the peace process. It stated that EU money was "for projects that support peace, understanding, reconciliation, and a decrease of hate," and could not be used for Palestinian textbooks that contained anti-Semitic material or incited hatred. Passage of the amendment was said to have been facilitated by intense lobbying on the part of Israel's mission to the EU in Brussels.

Popular sympathies in Germany, however, seemed to have shifted in favor of the Palestinians, the notion gaining credibility that they were victims of persecution by the former victims of the Nazis—a position rejected by the government. At year's end, politicians across the spectrum said they were under pressure from constituents to halt the sale of weapons to Israel. As Germany prepared for elections in 2002, it appeared that the Middle East could play a major role.

The Media

Upon his election as president of the Berlin Jewish Community in May, Dr. Alexander Brenner devoted his first public remarks to the negative image of Israel in the German media, which, he said, "has awakened bad memories." "Every Jew already hears in his head the next step: instead of 'Don't buy from Jews,' it is 'Don't buy from Israelis,' " he told the *Berliner Zeitung,* referring to the 1933 Nazi boycotts of Jewish businesses in Germany. "Jews can stand on their heads—it won't get rid of anti-Semitism. I see the discussion about Israel as a vent for latent anti-Semitism in this country."

Throughout 2001, German media reports on the Middle East reflected a distinctly pro-Palestinian, anti-Sharon bent. Thus Rudolf Augstein, for example, publisher of *Der Spiegel,* suggested in his magazine (Dec. 17) a comparison between Ariel Sharon and Adolf Hitler. According to Richard Chaim Schneider, an award-winning German-Jewish documentary director, "For most Germans, Sharon is an ideal lightning rod, because most of them consider him a war criminal, like Hitler." Schneider, who organized a panel discussion on German media and Israel in Munich in the summer of 2001, noted a clear "development in Germany to compare the atrocities of the Israeli defense forces with the deeds of the Nazis, as a way to be liberated from guilt." Lars Rensmann, a political scientist at the Free University in Berlin who specialized in anti-Semitism, anti-Zionism, and right-wing extremism, said his research confirmed the growing popularity of linking Zionism to Nazism.

Of special concern, since it emanated from the German mainstream, was a series of articles in the highly respected conservative daily *Frankfurter Allgemeine Zeitung* (FAZ). The tone of these articles could be guessed from their headlines, such as "Whoever Occupies Another Country Must Not Wonder if the People Fight Back," "All Palestine is a Prison," and "The Problem is Called Israel." Pro-Israel groups in Germany protested. Some 200 people—including Alexander Brenner; journalist Ralph Giordano; and Lala Süsskind, president of the Women's International Zionist Organization—signed a petition circulated by Prof. Karl E. Grözinger of the University of Potsdam that said the FAZ articles were reminiscent of the "sinister days of anti-Semitism. . . ." The FAZ responded that the charges of anti-Semitism were absurd and that the articles in question did not necessarily reflect the opinion of the paper's editors.

Certain intellectual circles also reflected the anti-Israel trend. Author Günter Grass, the same man who condemned the U.S. for attacking Afghanistan, told *Der Spiegel* (Oct. 10) that "Israel must not only get out of the occupied areas. Its occupation of Palestinian land, and its settlements, are all criminal acts. This must not only stop, but it has to be retroactive. Otherwise, there will be no peace." Grass said that he meant this not as an attack on the Jewish state, but as helpful advice from a friend. But CCJG president Paul Spiegel did not see it that way, and placed Grass "on a level with radical enemies of Israel." Spiegel declared it unacceptable to deny that "Israel is the victim and not the perpetrator in this bloody war of terrorism," and concluded that Grass had allied himself with "other non-Jewish intellectuals in Germany who, directly or indirectly, for years have been questioning Israel's right to exist," a charge that Grass denied. Speaking in support of Grass, Jürgen Koppelin, a Bundestag member of the Free German Party, told the German news agency DPA that "Paul Spiegel just has to accept that criticism of Israel's politics is not the same as criticism of the existence of Israel."

The Israeli embassy worked hard to combat Israel's negative treatment in the press, and the American Jewish Committee's Berlin office commissioned a study of German media coverage of the Middle East that was due to be released, in German, in 2002.

Anti-Semitism and Extremism

Old-style right-wing extremism and anti-Semitism continued to plague the generally healthy democracy of Germany.

A survey released by the University of Leipzig in December 2001 indicated that about 12 percent of Germans had extreme right-wing views. Sampling the views of 4,005 Germans in the western part of the country and 1,020 in the east, it found that 10 percent agreed that "the influence of the Jews is still too big today," and that foreigners should leave the country. Nine percent said they preferred dictatorship to democracy. Though many observers of the far-right scene worried about recruitment of youth to extremist parties, most of the extremists in the survey were elderly and not well educated, and many were unemployed.

Since the federal government changed the criteria for defining right-wing hate crimes in May 2001—including politically motivated crimes under that category for the first time—it was impossible to compare the 2001 figures to previous years. In all, the government registered 10,113 such crimes for 2001, a disproportionate number of them in Germany's eastern states. The great majority of the total—6,823—were "propaganda" crimes, involving public expression of racism, or verbal or written threats; 579 were attacks on property; and 508 were physical attacks in which 385 people were wounded. There were seven charges of attempted murder. The postcommunist party, PDS, expressed great skepticism about the statistics and charged the government with leaving out certain crimes to make the situation appear rosier than it really was. The PDS pointed out that the state of Brandenburg reported about 1,000 more right-wing extremist crimes within its boundaries than did the federal government for the same region.

As for anti-Semitic crimes, the federal government reported 989 incidents in 2001, down from 1,084 in 2000. However, 108 cases were reported in the fourth quarter of the year alone, including six physical attacks with four injuries and at least 41 instances of public expression or display of illegal material (such as swastikas, the raised arm of the "Hitler greeting," the singing of SS songs, and Holocaust denial).

At the end of November, Paul Spiegel, president of the CCJG, told the annual SPD party conference in Nuremberg that right-wing extremism was taking on an extremely troubling, "virulent" direction, including an increase in vandalism against Jewish cemeteries and synagogues. Noting that a swastika had been drawn on Dresden's new synagogue only a day after it opened on November 9, Spiegel said criminal acts that used to be hidden were increasingly taking place in "open daylight." He called on the government to act more forcefully against such crimes, and warned of links between Germany's far right and Islamic extremists.

The Palestinian cause had indeed became a more prominent part of the far right's anti-Jewish, anti-American platform, and the ties intensified after September 11. In the days immediately following the attacks in the U.S., the memorial at the Dachau concentration camp was vandalized with anti-Semitic, anti-Israel, and anti-American graffiti. On October 3, the 11th anniversary of German unification, some 1,000 supporters of the far-right National Democratic Party demonstrated in Berlin, with one of the rally leaders reportedly calling for "the death of the United States as a world power." Observers of the far-right scene noted that extremists had taken to wearing traditional Palestinian headscarves during public demonstrations, so that both in rhetoric and in dress it was difficult to distinguish between the far right and the far left. However, connections between Islamic extremists and German right-wingers remained tentative, limited to Holocaust denial and anti-Jewish, anti-Israel sentiments. Except for a small number of converts to Islam, right-wing racism toward Arabs appeared to limit the possibilities for cooperation.

Unlike 2000, when a spate of violent crimes, including the murders of several immigrants and homeless people, as well as an unexplained explosion injuring Jewish immigrants in Düsseldorf and an arson attack on the Düsseldorf synagogue, led to a crisis of conscience, public interest in the crimes of right-wing extremists was far more reserved in 2001. Several initiatives begun in 2000 against extremism continued though 2001, with the federal government spending tens of millions of dollars on educational programs fostering tolerance, such as "Show Your Face," a cooperative effort by the government and the CCJG.

Right-wing extremism on the Internet remained difficult to combat, since much of the German-language right-wing extremist and neo-Nazi material outlawed in Germany came in online from U.S. providers. In the fall of 2001, at the request of the German Foreign Ministry, the American Jewish Committee intervened with an Internet provider to prevent American neo-Nazi agitator Gary Lauck from hacking his own propaganda onto the sites of the German Interior Ministry and the Federal Office for the Protection of the Constitution.

Lawmakers sought to mobilize support for a ban on the far-right National Democratic Party (NPD), which the Schröder government had compared to the Nazis of the 1920s. Only two parties had ever been banned in postwar Germany, one communist and the other neo-Nazi, both in the 1950s. Though the NPD had had no electoral success, the 7,000-member party attracted many disaffected young Germans through ethnocentrism, xenophobia, anti-Semitism, and hatred of America. After overcoming free-speech concerns, both houses of Parliament and the federal government approved the ban. On October 1, the German Supreme Court, or Bundesverfassungsgericht, said it would grant a hearing to the NPD, which protested the move. The hearing was scheduled for early February 2002.

The NPD used the campaign to ban it to attract sympathy, and held numerous demonstrations in 2001 on the theme that their democratic right to free speech and assembly was under threat. In the largest NPD demonstration ever in Berlin, on December 1, nearly 4,000 members marched. The demonstration brought right-wingers within a few blocks of two synagogues—this was on Saturday, the Jewish Sabbath—and other Jewish communal buildings, and drew an angry response from counter-demonstrators. Members of the Jewish community, who would not officially demonstrate on the Sabbath, moved their afternoon prayer service outside, in front of the New Synagogue, as helicopters hovered overhead and thousands of protesters milled in the street. Paul Spiegel called the NPD rally a "provocation of huge dimensions," a view reflected by the mainstream political parties and ordinary citizens.

There were legal steps taken during 2001 relating to extremist outrages. New, harsher sentences were handed down on October 10 to the two young men convicted in the October 2000 arson attack on the Düsseldorf Synagogue, following an outcry over the initial punishments. One year was added to the sentence of Khalid Z., a 21-year-old Moroccan-born German citizen, bringing his term to two-and-a-half years in prison. Belal T., a 20-year-old Palestinian, received 22 months on probation, up from 18 months. His sentence was lighter because he had apologized to the Jewish community of Düsseldorf after his initial release from investigative custody. Now, Khalid Z. said in court that he wanted a similar meeting with local Jewish leaders. The two had told the court they committed the act out of anger after seeing TV images of a Palestinian child shot by Israeli soldiers. Judge Werner Arendes said he could understand their emotions, having seen those images himself. But this was no excuse for the crime, said the judge, who added that German Jews had been deeply upset by the attack on the synagogue. "You have lived long enough in Germany to become familiar with the history of the Jews," he told the two men.

In another case, in November, four defendants were convicted in the

1986 bombing of the West Berlin disco in which two U.S. soldiers and a Turkish woman were killed. Only one defendant, Verena Chanaa, who placed the bomb, was found guilty of murder and given the highest possible sentence, 14 years in prison.

Michel Friedman, the CCJG vice president, sued Hermann Reichertz, who had called him a *Zigeunerjuden,* or "Gypsy-Jew," for defamation. In August, Friedman lost his case, the court ruling that neither "Gypsy" nor "Jew" was a defamatory term. Friedman appealed the decision.

Holocaust-Related Matters

In September, it was announced that the new "Topography of Terror" exhibit and archive on the Gestapo would open in Berlin in May 2005, 60 years after the end of World War II. Some 37 million euros in federal and state funds were pledged to build a permanent museum on the site of the former Nazi secret police headquarters.

In October, work began on the national Holocaust memorial in Berlin, whose design, by American architect Peter Eisenman, was approved in 1999 by Parliament after more than ten years of debate and discussion. Construction of the memorial, to consist of 2,700 concrete slabs on a 204,500 square foot site near the Brandenburg Gate and the future U.S. embassy, was expected to be completed by January 27, 2004, the 59th anniversary of the liberation of Auschwitz. It was expected to cost some $22 million.

In the summer, Lea Rosh, the non-Jewish writer and TV personality who initiated the idea for the project back in 1988, launched a controversial fund-raising campaign for the memorial. It featured giant posters with the slogan, There Was Never a Holocaust, printed over an image of snow-topped mountains and a pristine blue lake. In small letters the ad continued, "there are still many who believe that's true, and in 20 years there may be even more," followed by a plea for donations to the memorial. Holocaust survivors and German Jewish leaders joined in condemning the ad campaign—one survivor even filed a lawsuit—on the grounds that the large headline, which was all that most viewers would read, could be interpreted as Holocaust denial. Paul Spiegel of the CCJG commented, "the subject of the Holocaust is not suitable for advertising campaigns." The campaign was dropped.

The Hamburg Institute for Social Research reopened its "Crimes of the Wehrmacht" traveling exhibit in December, in Berlin, after a two-year hiatus. The original exhibit was withdrawn in 1999 because of the misidentification of nine photos. The revelation of mistakes in the exhibit had greatly pleased its detractors, including neo-Nazi groups that claimed all the photos were faked, reflecting decades of general public consumption of the myth that only the SS, not the regular army, committed war crimes during World War II (see AJYB 2000, pp. 348–49). Now the errors had been corrected, and the revised exhibit, stressing text rather than photos, drew positive reviews. But neo-Nazis groups protested the new exhibit just as loudly as they had the original, not just in Berlin, where the exhibit opened, but in Bielefeld as well, its next stop.

In December, Paul Latussek, head of the Thuringen branch of the Organization for Refugees, resigned his post in disgrace after publicly expressing doubts about the number of victims murdered at Auschwitz. The organization represented Germans expelled from Nazi-occupied lands after the end of World War II. Because it was illegal to deny the Holocaust in Germany, state prosecutors were reportedly looking into the possibility of filing charges against Latussek.

In October, another dark secret of former East Germany was revealed. Papers discovered by Berlin historian Andreas Weigelt showed that in the 1970s East German secret police exhumed some 600 bodies of Jewish victims of the Nazis from a mass grave in Lieberose at a satellite camp of the Sachsenhausen concentration camp; security officials ordered examinations of the corpses and the removal of gold teeth. The gold, totaling more than 2 pounds in all, was most likely melted down by the finance department of the Ministry for State Security.

The "Finkelstein Debate" came to Germany when Norman Finkelstein arrived in Berlin on February 8. This American writer was the author of *The Holocaust Industry: Reflections on the Exploitation of Jewish Suffering,* a damning indictment of Jewish leaders who, he claimed, cynically exploited what happened to Jews in the Holocaust in order to revive American Jewish identity, squeeze money out of European governments for the benefit of Jewish organizations, and support the policies of Israel. While U.S. critics generally panned the book and the American reading public ignored it, Finkelstein found an interested public in Germany, and the translation into German became a best seller in 2000 (see "The Assault on Holocaust Memory," AJYB 2001, pp. 3–20).

Many German historians and political scientists considered the book unscientific and even irrational, but Finkelstein attracted large crowds to his presentation in Berlin. A sizable group of neo-Nazis who showed up were ultimately expelled. Also present were protesters who chanted that the term "Holocaust Industry" should be applied to those German companies that built the machinery of death and/or used slave laborers, not to the Jewish organizations that have sought compensation and restitution of property to Jewish and non-Jewish survivors.

Although the impact of Finkelstein's visit faded later in the year, many worried that right-wing extremists were not the only Germans who appreciated his biting criticism of the Jewish establishment. There was considerable resentment among conservative Germans about the ongoing issue of reparations for survivors, and Finkelstein's charges could very well help begin breaking old taboos against anti-Semitic stereotypes of avaricious Jews.

In August, a controversy arose about wartime writings by Rabbi Leo Baeck, the leader of Reform Judaism in Germany, who headed the Reichsvertretung, or Union of Jews in Germany, during the Nazi period, and hence represented the Jews in their dealings with the regime. Baeck was long considered a saintly figure, refusing to leave the Jewish community of Germany even when offered asylum abroad. When he was deported to Theresientstadt in 1943, Baeck, then almost 70 years old, was appointed head of the Jewish council in the concentration camp. He survived the war and settled in England where he died in 1956.

Material unearthed by Hermann Simon, director of Berlin's Centrum Judaicum, raised questions about the extent to which Baeck—who, in 1933, said that "the thousand-years of history of Jews in Germany has come to an end"—had actually kowtowed to the SS in writing his 1,600-page wartime report, "The Development of the Legal Position of Jews in Europe, Chiefly in Germany." Baeck himself said after the war that he did the report for members of the conservative resistance, who planned to use it after the expected downfall of Nazism to argue for Jewish rights in a new Germany.

However Simon revealed that in the early 1980s he had found papers in the attic of the Jewish Community House in East Berlin indicating that Baeck had done the work under contract to, and the control of, the Gestapo. Among these papers were notes apparently dictated to Baeck by SS-Sturmbannführer Friedrich Suhr, head of the SS Jewish department, between September 1941 and October 1942. Simon said he hid the material so it would not come into the hands of the German communist government, and even after the downfall of the communist regime he debated with himself for years whether to publicize these notes, since they seemed to cast a negative light on Baeck. Even now, after going public, Simon made it clear that he had no desire to cast doubt on the "great service that Leo Baeck rendered to German Jewry." German historian Götz

Aly suggested that Suhr, charged with handling diplomatic activities related to the "solving of the Jewish question in Europe," may have wanted better to understand the process of Jewish emancipation in other lands in order to prepare the ground for the liquidation of Jewish populations outside Germany, or, more innocently, may have planned to use Baeck's study as the basis for his own doctoral dissertation.

Compensation

After years of negotiations, held up by German industry's demands for immunity from future litigation, the Remembrance and Future Fund, created by the German government and industry in 1999, finally reached agreement with Jewish organizations in the spring of 2001. This set the wheels in motion for payment of compensation to Nazi-era slave and forced laborers. The fund totaled about 5 billion euros, with equal contributions from German industry and government. In the summer, the Bundestag voted to extend the deadline for applications from August 11 to the end of 2001.

A board member of the fund announced that an estimated 1.5 million applications for funds had been received—only about 10 percent of them from Jews—30,000 more than had been expected. Paul Spiegel, president of the CCJG, called on claimants' lawyers to give up a portion of their fees so that all survivors might receive compensation. Some 51 attorneys were sharing a total of DM 118 million, divided according to the number of clients they represented in class-action suits. Munich attorney Michael Witti said he received only about $95 for each of his approximately 30,000 clients.

In June, the first payments, amounting to about $7,000, went out from the Remembrance and Future Fund to former slave laborers in the Czech Republic—2,500 concentration camp survivors and the 7,500 oldest forced laborers—and in Frankfurt am Main in Germany. In Frankfurt, Karl Brozik, the German representative of the Claims Conference, the international organization that negotiated for survivors, himself handed DM 10,000 to the victims. By October, more than 500,000 euros had been paid to more than 300,000 former slave and forced laborers. The German industry foundation announced in October that it had collected its entire assigned contribution from some 6,500 firms. A new director of the foundation was chosen, Hildgund Jehle, an ethnologist who had worked for the Volkswagen Foundation. By the end of 2001, the foundation was drawing up guidelines for grants to cultural, educational, and social programs to keep the memory of the Holocaust alive for future generations.

In October, Germany rejected Polish claims of unfair treatment in the payment of compensation to Polish Nazi-era forced laborers. A half-million Polish survivors were to receive almost a quarter of the money from the Remembrance and Future Fund, but Poland said Germany had used an unfavorable exchange rate in calculating compensation. The German government responded that the Finance Ministry had checked its numbers and found no improprieties.

Religious bodies that had benefited from forced and slave labor also announced compensation programs. The Catholic Church said that it would set up its own fund, and not participate in the German government and industry fund. The Protestant umbrella organization in a section of Berlin declared that it would pay about $500 each to 74 Nazi-era forced laborers who were made to work in cemeteries in Berlin between 1942 and 1945. The church, which had also contributed about $170,000 to the government and industry fund, said it would also pay widows of the cemetery workers.

In other news, in March, a Berlin court rejected a lawsuit brought by leaders of the Slovakian Jewish community claiming compensation for Slovak victims of the Holocaust. Their case was based on the fact that the pro-Nazi Slovak government had given more than $60 million in confiscated Jewish assets to the Germans to pay for the deportation of more than 57,000 Slovak Jews to death camps. In rejecting the suit, the German court said the problem could only be resolved through international agreement.

JEWISH COMMUNITY

Demography and the Immigration Debate

Germany had one of the fastest growing Jewish communities in the world, thanks to the arrival of tens of thousands of Jews from the former Soviet Union. Since 1990, the federal government had received more than 203,000 immigration applications from Jews in the FSU, and 125,000 actually arrived (many subsequently leaving), and the number of people officially registered as Jews more than tripled, from 30,000 to over 90,000 in 2001.

According to a 1991 agreement between the government and the Jewish community, Russian-speaking immigrants who could prove their Jewish heritage would be given the right to remain in Germany and to receive social assistance and help with integration, whether or not their Jewish heritage was maternal or paternal. They did not get automatic German citizenship, retaining refugee status for six years under the Geneva Convention, after which they could apply for citizenship. Most of the ex-Soviet Jews were well-educated professionals and had difficulty finding jobs in Germany. To the great annoyance of many Jewish old-timers, the newcomers seemed eager to associate with the community in order to reap the benefits of language education and job training provided to new Jewish immigrants, but said they could not afford to pay the dues that supported these programs and showed little interest in learning about their Jewish identity.

Paul Spiegel, head of the CCJG, made headlines when he suggested that the immigration law that Germany was considering (see above, p. 405) should include regulations limiting Jewish immigration to those who could prove Jewish lineage through the maternal line, or who had converted to Judaism according to rabbinical law. He suggested that experts be hired to check the validity of immigrants' claims to be Jewish, since, he went on, it was well known that there was a black market for Jewish identity papers in the former Soviet Union. Up to 30 percent of people entering Germany by claiming Jewish heritage, charged Spiegel, were non-Jews who used this opportunity as their big break, and then disappeared once inside Germany.

Spiegel's support for tougher immigration requirements for Jews drew harsh criticism from Andreas Nachama, former president of the Berlin Jewish Community, who said that anyone who was persecuted as a Jew should be allowed into Germany. He quoted the late Ignatz Bubis, Spiegel's predecessor at the helm of the CCJG, who had said that Germany's commitment to help the persecuted precluded asking someone if he had a Jewish mother.

Communal Affairs

The 83 local Jewish communities in Germany operated under the umbrella of the Einheitsgemeinde, or "united community," which oversaw funding for communal needs. While officially Orthodox, the community was slowly moving toward acceptance of the liberal streams of Judaism. The expanding Jewish population created a need for more synagogues, schools, and community centers. This was especially evident in the smaller cities, such as Krefeld, which had 130 Jews in 1989–1990 and 901 in 2001, and was still without a rabbi or cantor.

The Jewish community of the large city of Dresden, in eastern Germany, replaced its communist-era synagogue, which had room for just 90 worshipers, with a new structure to accommodate its 350 members. The new cube-shaped building was dedicated November 9, the 63rd anniversary of Kristallnacht, the night in 1938 when the original synagogue on that site was one of hundreds destroyed during the pogrom against Jewish property in both Germany and Austria. The project cost more than $10 million and was supported by the city of Dresden and the state of Sachsen, as well as by $2 million in private donations collected by the ecumenical Foundation for the Rebuilding of the Dresden Synagogue. Some 6,000 people showed up for the opening ceremonies, far more than the 1,200 who were expected. Many waited in line to have what they said was their first look inside a synagogue. Among the guests were U.S. ambassador Coats; German political figures; and Jewish and Christian leaders. The ceremony was broadcast live across the country. Paul Spiegel, president of the CCJG, called the structure "a miracle" that he never could have imagined ten years earlier. The next night, the building was defaced with Nazi graffiti (see above, pp. 414–15).

Similar expansion occurred elsewhere in eastern Germany. In December, a new Jewish community center and synagogue were dedicated in Frankfurt an der Oder, near the Polish border. About $50,000 was spent to renovate an old villa in the center of the city, previously used as a kindergarten. The city also planned to create a museum about the 700-year history of its Jewish community. When Hitler came to power in 1933, there were 586 Jews in the city; in 2001 there were about 220, most of them from the former Soviet Union.

In Würzburg, in the southwestern part of the country, Jakov Ebert was named rabbi in December. A native of Tel Aviv, Ebert became the first rabbi to serve this Jewish community since its destruction by the Nazis. Some 1,000 Jews lived in Würzberg in 2001.

In June, the Union of Progressive Jews in Germany, Austria, and Switzerland (UPJGAS) held a conference on "Renewal of Jewish Life: 200 Years of Reform Judaism in Germany," in the city of Halberstadt. Cosponsored by the Moses Mendelssohn Academy of Halberstadt, which was founded in 1995, the conference included lectures, workshops, religious services, and the awarding of the Israel Jacobson Prize to Rabbi Walter Homolka.

Another milestone in modern German Jewish life came in December, with Tarbut, touted as the first "Jewish Cultural Congress in German-speaking Regions." The event was held in the picturesque Bavarian Alpine setting of Schloss Elmau. The goal of Tarbut was to bring controversial issues to the table, including stereotypes of Jews, mixed marriage, the effects of the new Russian-speaking immigrants on Jewish life in Germany, and the overall health of European Jewry. The brainchild of Rachel Salamander, award-winning Jewish cultural activist and Jewish bookstore owner, and Michael Brenner, chairman of the Department of Jewish History and Culture at the University of Munich, the conference included some of the most prominent communal, religious, and academic figures in German Jewry, such as Paul Spiegel, head of the CCJG; Dr. Salomon Korn, head of the Frankfurt Jewish Community; Rabbi Paul Eisenberg of Vienna; Julius Schoeps, director of the Moses Mendelssohn Center in Potsdam; Charlotte Knobloch, head of the Munich Jewish Community; Rabbi Walter Rothschild of Berlin and Munich; Anetta Kahane of the Berlin Jewish Community; German Jewish journalist Josef Joffe; and Diana Pinto, Jewish representative to the European Union.

Berlin

The Jewish community in the capital city of Berlin had increased from about 6,000 people to about 12,000 over the previous decade, largely due to immigration from the FSU. In early May, Dr. Alexander Brenner was elected president of the Berlin Jewish Community, replacing incumbent Andreas Nachama, who returned to his work as director of the Topography of Terror Foundation, the archive and memorial exhibit on the history of the Gestapo in Berlin. Among Nachama's accomplishments was securing official support for an egalitarian congregation in the city, as well as securing contracts for Berlin's first two female cantors. Brenner, 71, was born in a Polish village near the Ukrainian border, son of a shopkeeper. When he was 11, he, his parents, and a sister were forced to resettle in Siberia. After World War II, the family was sent back to Poland. While the rest of the family emigrated to Israel, he went to Berlin, where he studied chemistry and physics. Brenner, who spoke English, German, Hebrew, Polish, Russian, and Yiddish fluently, began his career as a research scientist and then worked for the Federal Board of Health. He had since held German diplomatic posts in the former Soviet Union and in Israel. Brenner said he intended to do more to integrate the recent immigrants, who, both young and old, came with little knowledge of Jewish tradition, history, and religion.

In other Berlin communal news, the British-born Rabbi Walter Rothschild, who in 2000 had lost his job as the Liberal rabbi in Berlin, was hired as rabbi in Munich. Rabbi Chaim Rozwaski became an official rabbi of Berlin, in charge of the liberal-traditional synagogue on Pestalozzistrasse. The egalitarian congregation worshipping at Berlin's Oranienburgerstrasse Synagogue continued to flourish, and a new Liberal group began meeting regularly at the location of the former American army chapel.

The second Bet Debora conference, for female rabbis, cantors, scholars, and community activists, took place in May in Berlin, on the theme of "The Jewish Family—Myth and Reality." The program was organized by Berliners Lara Daemmig and Elisa Klapheck, who planned to publish a volume based on the presentations. The conference discussed both traditional and alternative definitions of family. Most participants were Reform Jewish women, though there were also many Conservative Jews and some from an Orthodox background. As was the case with the original conference, held in May 1999, this Bet Debora event was sponsored in part by the Jewish Community of Berlin, a fact that organizers said reflected the community's readiness to attend to the concerns of its non-Orthodox members.

Education

Three new Jewish educational programs for adults opened in Germany in the fall. Two provided rabbinical training—Germany's first since World War II—and the third offered German women their first organized opportunity for higher Jewish education. Though the number of students in all three was small, many viewed the programs as signs that postwar German Jewry was coming of age.

Three rabbinical candidates began study in October at the new, multidenominational rabbinical program of the Institute of Judaic Studies in Heidelberg. It operated in coordination with Yeshiva University (Orthodox) and the Jewish Theological Seminary (Conservative) in New York, the Leo Baeck College (Liberal) in London, and the Schechter Seminary (Conservative) and Beit Morasha (Modern Orthodox) in Israel. At the same time, five candidates began their studies at a new Liberal seminary, the Abraham Geiger College in Potsdam, affiliated with the Moses Mendelssohn Center at the University of Potsdam. Many Reform Jews in America responded generously to appeals for financial support for the Geiger program, which was billed as a return of Reform Judaism to the land of its birth.

In Frankfurt, meanwhile, seven German Jewish women began an Orthodox Jewish educational program at the new Ronald S. Lauder Midrasha for Women, a sister school to the two-year-old Lauder Jüdisches Lehrhaus for men in Berlin. Rabbi Binyamin Krauss was director of the program, which offered training in Hebrew, Bible, Jewish law and tradition, and Jewish philosophy.

Interfaith Relations

The Protestant Church of Friedrichstadt announced plans in 2001 to use its building, opposite the new Jewish Museum in Berlin, as a meeting place for dialogue between Jews and Christians.

In December, the Bavarian administrative court began discussions on a complaint by teacher Konrad Riggenmann that the requirement that there be a cross in every Bavarian classroom infringed upon his religious freedom. It was the first time that a teacher, and not parents, had complained against the Bavarian "school-cross" law. Riggenmann said the cross was not only a symbol of the execution of Jesus, but of the murder of 13 million Jews in the name of Christianity since the Crusades. The Bavarian cultural ministry countered that teachers knew they would have contact with this symbol when they entered their profession, and that the cross symbolized "the culture and the history that stand behind the educational system of Bavaria."

Culture

MUSEUMS AND EXHIBITS

Pride in German Jewish history was the story of 2001, symbolized by the long-awaited opening of the Jewish Museum in Berlin. The museum was federally funded, with a budget of about $10 million.

It was officially inaugurated at a gala event on Sunday, September 9. Inside the zinc-covered, angular building designed by architect Daniel Libeskind were depictions of nearly two millennia of Jewish life in Germany. Some 850 invited guests—including Chancellor Schröder, President Rau, and the German-born former U.S. secretary of state Henry Kissinger—had a preview of the exhibit and a lavish dinner. The museum was scheduled to open to the public on September 12, but security concerns after the terrorist attacks on the U.S. forced a postponement.

The exhibit's aim was to connect a rich history with a hopeful future, ever mindful of the break in civilization that was the Holocaust. "The National Socialists wanted not only to destroy European Jewry physically, but to have control over how Jewish culture and German-Jewish relationships would be portrayed," said President Rau at the dinner, referring to the museum about an "extinct" people that Hitler planned to build. "That is why it is so important that in this museum we find images and witness of almost 2,000 years of the German-Jewish relationship." Schröder, after visiting the museum, said he always found it "miraculous that there are Jews living in Germany today, and that we meet together as friends." Paul Spiegel called the museum "long overdue." Noting the increase in xenophobic crime in Germany, Spiegel noted: "If one does not know Jewry, one can continue to see Jews as foreign."

The exhibit, designed by the project director, Ken Gorbey of New Zealand, received a number of negative comments from the press, museum critics, and some in the Jewish community, who called it superficial and questioned its emphasis on the assimilation of Jews into German culture. But there was a general consensus that the museum provided a good introduction to Jewish traditions and the history of German Jewry. It included artworks, books, Judaica, and household items. Displays were both high-tech and down-to-earth, with computer consoles and children's corners. The museum sought to deal with stereotypes, such as the notion that Jews were greedy: a display explained how, during certain periods, Jews were not permitted to work at any jobs aside from moneylending. The meaning of Jewish religious rituals were explained in direct terms—circumcision tools, for example, were on display.

German Jewish history was a key theme. The oldest item in the exhibit was a 10th-century book on loan from the Vatican, which referred to a Jewish community in Germany. In a space devoted to accomplishments of Jews in the 20th century, there was a page from Albert Einstein's notebook, with the famous equation $E=MC^2$. One of the few rooms left unadorned was the Holocaust Tower, a dark concrete chamber, a place for contemplation. Its door, when shut, would disappear in darkness. The museum also had an annex about a mile away, in a former Jewish quarter, the former brush-making workshop of Otto Weidt, who saved about 30 Berlin Jews from deportation to concentration camps by employing them. The small exhibit created in these rooms by Berlin students had become a part of the new museum. In addition, the New York-based Leo Baeck Institute established a branch of its archive at the Berlin Jewish Museum. For its inaugural event, the Institute planned a conference in Berlin for April 2002.

The museum quickly became a popular destination for Berliners and tourists. By late November 2001, the museum had recorded more than 217,000 visitors since its September 9 opening, making it one of the most visited museums of Germany.

This was by no means the only exhibit focusing on Jewish themes in Germany. One in Emsland about Jews under the Nazis, under the title "Everyday Jewish Life: Between Hope and Fear," was on display in October and November. Two related exhibits there covered "Jews in Germany Today" and "Jewish Holidays and Practices," featuring photographs by American photojournalist Edward Serotta.

In November, an exhibit about the "aryanization" of Jewish property during the Nazi era opened in the Koblenz Archives. Michel Friedman, vice president of the CCJG, spoke at the opening ceremony on November 23, saying that the confiscation of Jewish property was one step on the way to the Holocaust, and that it was important to recognize and respond to the earliest signs of discrimination.

The Maximilian Museum in Augsburg announced in December that it had received a valuable document related to the 19th-century history of German Jewry. The document, bound in silver, came from a family named Kaula that made its name in lending gold.

In December, the traveling exhibit "Milestones for Peace" opened in Aachen, its first German stop. The exhibit, already seen in New York and in Venice, consisted of Jerusalem stones collected and sent to artists and writers around the world, who were asked to create works related to themes of peace. The prototype was created by Peruvian artist Ivan Macha, together with Polish artist Ryszard Wasko and Israeli artist Iris Elhanani.

Also in December, a new memorial exhibit about former slave laborers was dedicated in the eastern German city of Leipzig. It recounted the exploitation of 90,000 forced laborers and concentration camp prisoners who had to work in armaments factories in Leipzig during World War II. Its location was Permoserstrasse 15, where at one time the largest Nazi tank manufacturing center stood. The exhibit included everyday objects, letters, lists of the names of forced laborers, and videotaped testimony.

Hartmut Topf, a descendent of the family that manufactured ovens used in concentration camps, said he wanted to create a memorial to Holocaust victims at the location of his family's former factory in Erfurt. It remained to be seen whether the city administration would support it.

Films and Performances

The 51st Berlinale International Film Festival was kicked off in February with a ceremony honoring film star Kirk Douglas, 84. Douglas, whose parents were Russian Jews, and who spoke Yiddish at home, told the audience that this helped him during various filmings in Germany.

Among the most important, if not best received films at the festival was Jean-Jacques Annaud's epic about the devastating World War II battle of Stalingrad, *Duel—Enemy at the Gates.* Annaud recreated the campaign fought in 1942–43 in which more than a million Soviet soldiers and 800,000 German soldiers were killed before the Nazis withdrew. The Israeli-American film *Trembling Before God,* about homosexuality in Orthodox communities, won the Teddy for best documentary film on a gay-lesbian topic. Another film with a Jewish theme, *I Am Josh Polonski's Brother,* by American director Raphaël Nadjari, told the story of three brothers, Abe, Ben, and Josh, with a textile business in Brooklyn. *Reshimat Ahava* (Love Inventory), by Israeli documentary filmmaker David Fisher, related the story of a young woman's search for a sister who disappeared as an infant. A documentary that warmed the hearts of many was *The Sweetest Sound* by American Jewish filmmaker Alan Berliner, who decided to look for other people who share the name "Berliner," and brought them all together. This film was shown later at the Berlin Jewish Film Festival as well.

Other films screened at the 2001 Jewish Film Festival included *Fighter,* a documentary by American filmmaker Amir Bar-Lev about two friends and Holocaust survivors from Prague who lived through National Socialism and communism; *Waiting for Messiah,* a romantic comedy about Jews in Buenos Aires, by Argentinean director Daniel Burman; and *Timbrels and Torahs* by American directors Miriam Chaya and Judith Montell, about the search for new and old Jewish rituals for women.

The annual two-week Jewish cultural festival in Berlin was dedicated in 2001 to the Israeli city of Tel Aviv. Some 40 programs of theater, music, exhibits, readings, and films were included, as well as, for the first time, a fashion show, featuring Berlin star models wearing designs by Kedem Sasson and Avivid Izher and parading down the runway to the beat of music provided by Israeli deejay Shimrit Maron. The Tel Aviv Kammer-Theater performed an adaptation of Chekov's *Requiem,* the last work of the late Israeli writer and director Hanoch Levi. The final concert was a solo performance by Israeli pop singer Yehudit Ravitz, together with the Israel Philharmonic.

Several other German cities also held their annual Jewish festivals, including Munich and Erfurt.

In June, the Munich-based Elysium Academy of Continuing Education in the Arts held a series of musical and literary events in Bernreid, Berlin, and Leipzig under the title, "Point of Escape: Exile," focusing on artists who fled Nazi Germany.

Among the remarkable concerts held in 2001 in Berlin were two sold-out outdoor performances in June by Israeli singer Chava Alberstein, the American avant-garde klezmer group the Klezmatics, and American pop star Peter Yarrow, formerly of Peter, Paul, and Mary. Held in the area behind the New Synagogue/Centrum Judaicum on Oranienburgerstrasse, the concerts were filmed by German and Israeli TV, as well as by the American nonprofit station PBS.

In July, a controversy arose in Israel when Daniel Barenboim, conductor of the Berlin Staatskapelle and musical director of the Chicago Symphony Orchestra, chose to play a piece by Richard Wagner at the Israel Festival. This broke the festival's taboo against including pieces by the known anti-Semite and favorite composer of Adolf Hitler. Reportedly, Barenboim had originally agreed not to play Wagner's opera *Die Walküre* after Holocaust survivors, politicians, and officials of the Simon Wiesenthal Center protested, but he then conducted Wagner's overture to the opera *Tristan und Isolde* as an encore to the July 7 concert. A Knesset committee decided that Barenboim, a Jew, should be boycotted until he asked for forgiveness. In what might have been an act of defiance against the call for a boycott, Barenboim was the featured conductor in a Mahler concert marking the opening of the new Jewish Museum in Berlin on September 9. He received unrestrained applause from the full house at the Berlin Philharmonic.

A new Jewish theater, Bamah, opened in Berlin on May 26, 2001, with a medley of works by Jewish artists. During the year, the theater, founded by Israeli-born director Dan Lahav, presented a broad international repertoire of works by Jewish authors, readings, and musical evenings, as well as staged celebrations of Jewish holidays and the Sabbath (not performed on Friday nights) planned especially for non-Jews interested in learning more about Jewish celebrations. Lahav, who had German-Jewish roots, had been living in the country since 1981.

Germany continues to provide fertile ground for Jewish popular culture, consumed mostly by non-Jewish Germans. Bagels, no longer relegated to bagel shops, were on many quality restaurant menus. Jewish museums, walking tours, and cultural events drew enthusiastic crowds.

Klezmer music, performed by Jews and non-Jews, was celebrated by some and deplored by others, the latter dismissing this and other "faux" Jewish culture as "Jewish Disneyland." Nevertheless, non-Jewish thirst for knowledge about Jewish culture and religion and life was quite real.

Publications

The memoirs of Paul Spiegel, president of the CCJG, were published in 2001 by Ullstein Verlag under the title *Wieder zu Hause? Erinnerungen* (At Home Again? Recollections). The book received much public attention and favorable reviews. Toward the end of the year Spiegel gave numerous readings from the book to audiences across Germany. Born in 1937 in Warendorf, Spiegel survived the Holocaust in hiding with a Belgian foster family. His parents survived as well, but his sister was murdered in Auschwitz. In the book, Spiegel described his flight from Germany as a child, his return, and his hopes for the future of Jews in Germany.

A new book on Hitler, *Hitler's Secret—The Double Life of a Dictator,* by Bremen historian Lothar Machtan, caused a stir by stating unequivocally that Hitler had numerous gay friends in the 1920s and that his "homosexual nature" affected his politics. Machtan said it was time to break the taboo on examining Hitler's private life.

The second edition of *Golem—Europäisch-jüdisches Magazin* (Golem—European-Jewish Magazine), was published in November by Philo Verlag in Berlin. The magazine, in which all contributions are published in three languages, English, German, and French, was a nonprofit venture by a group of Berlin-based writers, editors, and artists.

In December, Bear Family Records released *Vorbei . . . Beyond Recall,* a 500-plus page book and 11-CD package (14 hours) of rare German-Jewish recordings from the 1933–1938 period, likely the last such recordings made in Nazi Germany. They included classical music, Yiddish comedians, German cabaret, Palestinian folk songs, and cantorial singing. Some were rescued and restored from single copies or test pressings. The accompanying text had contributions from numerous historians, with an introduction by Rabbi Andreas Nachama, whose late father was a cantor in Berlin from the postwar years until his death in 2000.

In December, a new book in German about the 900-year history of the Jews in the Gelderlands was published. The 412-page volume, 12 years in the making, was based on research by Bernhard Kück, city archivist, and Gerd Halmanns, and was sponsored by the Workshop of the Jewish

House of Prayer of Issum and the Historical Foundation of Geldern and Environs.

Personalia

In September, Paul Spiegel, head of the CCJG, was named an "honorary citizen" of the city of Warendorf on the Ems. Spiegel's father had been arrested and badly beaten in that city during Kristallnacht on November 9, 1938.

The annual Leo Baeck Prize was awarded in October to Hans-Jochen Vogel, former head of the SPD. Vogel now headed an organization called Against Forgetting—For Democracy.

New York's Leo Baeck Institute gave its Leo Baeck Medal to German president Johannes Rau, in recognition of his work toward reconciliation between Jews and Christians. The award was presented in November during Rau's visit to the United States.

In November, B'nai B'rith in Berlin honored schoolteacher Rüdiger Röttger of Hochneukirch for his Holocaust education project. Since 1996, Röttger had worked with students on the history of Jewish life in the town during the Nazi era and afterwards, and restored the local Jewish cemetery. Röttger was the first non-Jew to receive the prize.

Also in November, a memorial tablet honoring the late Rabbi Menachem Mendel Schneerson, the leader of Chabad, was installed in Berlin. Schneerson was born in Ukraine and studied mathematics and physics in Berlin from 1928 to 1933 before leaving for Paris and later fleeing to the United States.

The annual Obermayer German Jewish History Award, given by Arthur Obermayer, honored non-Jewish Germans who contributed toward recording or preserving the Jewish history of their communities. Winners of the 2001 prizes were: Josef Motschmann, a theology teacher and marriage counselor who researched Jewish history in Staffelstein, where he was born; Monica Kingreen, a historian and teacher who, since 1983, conducted research on the Jewish history of her town, Windecken, and published several books and articles on the subject; Olaf Ditzel, a bookstore owner who, with his colleagues, restored a *mikveh* in Vacha in Thuringia; Günter Boll, a schoolteacher and researcher who began scholarly work on the Jewish communities of Alsace in 1981, after he rescued rare Jewish documents and objects from a burning trash site; and Heinrich Schreiner, retired state bank president from Mainz, who organized the reconstruction and restoration of the Mainz-Weisenau synagogue, and directed its use for cultural and religious events.

One remarkable honoree was not able to attend the ceremony: Gisele Bunge, an 82-year-old widow in Gardelegen, had for decades defied the communist authorities in her town to document the history and fate of Jews there. She made contact with Jewish families with roots in Gardelegen, and wrote a history of the Jewish community.

Stefan Heym, the German Jewish writer and politician who chose to live in former East Germany, died on December 16, while on a visit to Israel, at the age of 88. The Berlin resident fled Nazi Germany and later became a prominent critic of the communist government from within. He served as honorary president of the German branch of the PEN writers' association and had been a guest speaker at a conference in Jerusalem on the German poet of Jewish heritage, Heinrich Heine, just three days before he died.

TOBY AXELROD

Austria

National Affairs

Despite its shaky start, the governing coalition, made up of the People's Party (ÖVP) and its junior partner, the Freedom Party (FPÖ), attained apparent stability. The government, which came to power in February 2000 (see AJYB, 2001, p. 397), pursued a conservative policy in domestic matters. Despite a buoyant economy and low unemployment, there was a large budget deficit, and the government responded by cutting social services and pensions. In foreign policy, the coalition hewed closely to the lines laid down by the European Union on such matters as the Middle East conflict and, after September 11, the war in Afghanistan.

On the political front, several public opinion polls showed the conservative People's Party maintaining the level of support it had garnered in the October 1999 national election, and the opposition Social Democratic Party (SPÖ) rebounding a bit from its lackluster 1999 performance. The extreme right-wing Freedom Party, however, was losing popularity—a decline that had begun almost as soon as its leader, Jörg Haider, led the party into coalition with the People's Party. (Although Haider resigned the party leadership in 2000 and was replaced by the vice chancellor, Susanne Riess-Passer, he still dominated the Freedom Party and sat on the coalition committee that set government policy.) Disappointing showings in the Styria and Burgenland provincial elections in late 2000 provided concrete evidence of the FPÖ's problems.

The party's downward spiral continued in the Vienna election, held on March 25, 2001. The big winners were the Social Democrats, who got 46.8 percent, as compared to 39.2 percent five years earlier. The People's Party, the socialists' coalition partner in city hall over the previous five years, increased its share of the vote from 15.3 to 16.4 percent, and the Greens surged from 7.9 to 12.5 percent. The Freedom Party's share of the vote, however, plunged from 27.9 percent in 1996 to 20.3 in 2001. Although the party remained the second largest in the province that was home to a fifth of the country's population, the result was a setback for the FPÖ and a blow to the personal prestige of Haider, long seen as a skilled politician, who had campaigned actively in the capital.

In addition to his usual attacks against foreigners, Haider had launched an unprecedented offensive against Ariel Muzicant, president of the Israelitische Kultusgemeinde (IKG), the community organization of Austria's Jews, which was widely denounced both at home and abroad as anti-Semitic. Haider accused Muzicant of being "unpatriotic" for allegedly spreading lies abroad about threats to the Austrian Jewish community that, Haider charged, had been used by the World Jewish Congress to blacken Austria's reputation. In one speech, Haider also made a punning reference to Muzicant's first name, Ariel, the name of a brand of detergent. Haider said that Muzicant had *Dreck am Stecken,* which literally meant dirt sticking to someone, but was generally understood to mean having skeletons in one's closet, or a shady criminal past. The FPÖ leader insisted his remarks were not anti-Semitic but a legitimate attack against a political opponent. Muzicant, who had already sued Haider for libel for previous remarks that he considered anti-Semitic, denied that the Austrian Jewish community had any part in the World Jewish Congress's statement about Austria, and announced that he intended to sue Haider for defamation of character. In April the federal prosecutor ruled, without explanation, that he would not bring criminal charges against Haider.

Haider's tactics marked a departure from his past political practice of steering clear of attacks against Jews. It was widely assumed that playing the anti-Semitic card was a gamble on his part to stem the party's declining fortunes, especially since the recent approval of a large financial settlement for Jewish and other victims of Nazi atrocities had caused some grumbling in the country. There was even speculation that Haider wanted his remarks to draw international condemnation of Austria, in the hope that this would set off a nationalist Austrian backlash helpful to the FPÖ. If this was his intention, he failed.

Despite the decline in the Freedom Party's fortunes, it remained Europe's most successful far-right political party; it and Italy's National Alliance were the only two such parties in Western or Central Europe to enter a national governing coalition. Furthermore, a political analyst at Vienna's Center for Applied Political Research, Franz Sommer, argued that even the election result in Vienna was something of a victory for the Freedom Party, demonstrating its ability to stabilize its electoral support at a high level, over 20 percent.

Quite aside from Haider's Jew-baiting, the Freedom Party, in the Vienna election, continued to offer the racist and xenophobic slogans that were its stock-in-trade. Thus one of the placards of the party's top candidate, Helene Partik-Pabl, read: "FOREIGNERS: I understand the worries of the Viennese." Other campaign material linked foreigners, especially blacks, to crime, particularly drug-dealing. Damien Agbogbe, a 32-year-old professor of religion born in Togo, and the first black candidate to run for office in Vienna, was the frequent object of verbal abuse and threatening phone calls. Human rights groups, notably the International Helsinki Federation, accused the Freedom Party of playing on people's fears in a manner reminiscent of the Nazis. The Vienna election seemed to confirm information about Austria contained in a report issued in April by the Council of Europe's European Commission Against Racism and Intolerance (ECRI), covering events only up to June 2000. "The widespread use of racist and xenophobic propaganda in politics is of deep concern," it said of Austria, and not only within the Freedom Party. The report pointed to numerous instances of discrimination, and even some police violence against blacks. It stated also that gypsies and Jews were often targeted by racists, and blamed the Austrian media for contributing to "an atmosphere of hostility and rejection towards members of minority groups," including Jews. The ECRI recommended changes in the law to fight racism and xenophobia, and a crackdown on racism within police ranks.

Israel and the Middle East

Following the swearing-in of the new government in February 2000 that included the Freedom Party, Israel withdrew its ambassador and only maintained a lower-ranking official, accredited as a chargé d'affaires. Apart from the FPÖ's xenophobic policies, its leader, Jörg Haider, had, at various times in the past, praised certain policies of Hitler's Germany, though he subsequently apologized. Despite the withdrawal of the Israeli ambassador from Vienna, Austria retained its ambassador, Wolfgang Paul, in Tel Aviv. In July, Israel upgraded its level of representation in Vienna by sending a senior diplomat, Avraham Toledo, who held the rank of ambassador even though he served only as chargé d'affaires. Israel's refusal to return its ambassador even after the European Union countries restored normal diplomatic ties with Vienna in September 2000 (see AJYB 2001, pp. 397–98) came in for criticism from some quarters in Israel. The head of the organization of Austrian immigrants in Israel, Gideon Eckhaus, wrote a letter in the name of the organization's central committee to Foreign Minister Shimon Peres in May, calling on him to reconsider Israel's policy and return its ambassador to Vienna. Eckhaus, and others who sought this change, argued that the current Austrian government had been quite forthcoming in awarding compensation to Jews for the wrongs suffered during the National Socialist era, and therefore merited full diplomatic contact with Israel.

As a result of the disruption of regular relations between the two countries, there was no exchange of visits by high-ranking officials or political figures during the year, with the exception of Austrian vice chancellor Susanne Riess-Passer's visit to Israel in October. Riess-Passer, who also served as minister of sports and was the highest-ranking minister of the Freedom Party in the government, came for the stated purpose of attending the October 7 World Cup qualifying soccer match between Austria and Israel in Tel Aviv. (The game ended in a 0-0 tie.) She was not invited to Israel, nor did any government official receive her. Some speculated that she came in order to reassure members of the Austrian soccer team, some of whom had announced they would not travel to Israel because of the security situation. Others believed she made the trip on the mistaken advice of Freedom Party general secretary Peter Sichrovsky that he could arrange some meetings for her with Israeli officials. This, despite the clear warning by the Israeli chargé d'affaires that there could be "no official appointments."

The ban on meeting with leaders of the government did not extend to members of the Austrian political opposition. In October, the leader of the Social Democratic Party, Alfred Gusenbauer, and the head of the Greens, Alexander Van der Bellen, paid an official visit to Israel and met with Foreign Minister Peres.

At the UN, Austria joined with other European Union countries in voting against Israel on issues relating to the Palestine question. There were reports, however, that Austrian diplomats worked to soften the more hard-line stance toward Israel favored by certain of these countries. At the UN World Conference Against Racism that met in September in Durban, South Africa, the Austrian delegation opposed resolutions that sought to equate Zionism with racism. In addition, unlike the sharply critical tone of media reportage in other EU countries about Israeli policy toward the Palestinian Authority and the new intifada, news reports in Austria were generally factual and largely devoid of condemnation.

Yasir Arafat, president of the Palestinian Authority, made an impromptu visit to Vienna in February to win support for the faltering Middle East peace talks, holding meetings with Chancellor Wolfgang Schüssel and Foreign Minister Benita Ferrero-Waldner. Arafat told reporters that the peace process "needs a push" from the European Union, in particular Austria, and from the international community as a whole. Arafat, whose friendly relations with Austria began in the 1970s when Bruno Kreisky was chancellor, also met with President Thomas Klestil.

While political relations between Austria and Israel remained strained, educational and cultural exchanges continued. As part of a continuing effort to educate the Austrian public about the Shoah, the Israeli government hosted 25 Austrian teachers at the Yad Vashem Holocaust memorial center. In October, the Israeli chargé d'affaires addressed 50 teachers in the city of Linz on the influence of the Holocaust on Israeli society. A film conference involving a number of Austrian film directors took place in June at Ben-Gurion University in Beersheba. An exhibition titled "I Had a Dream: The Zionist Youth Movement in Austria," was held in Jerusalem from July though September. Another exhibition, "Austrian Presence in the Holy Land," hosted by the Jewish National Library in Jerusalem September 2–25, featured pictures and accounts of Austro-Hungarian activities in the Holy Land when the latter was part of the Ottoman Empire. Twelve Israeli youths visited Austria as guests of the government under its "back to the roots" program. The Ashkenazi chief rabbi of Israel, Rabbi Israel Meir Lau, paid a brief visit to Austria, where he met with President Klestil and Mayor Michael Häupl of Vienna.

The formal opening of the Center for Austrian Studies at the Hebrew University in Jerusalem took place in May. Jointly financed by the Austrian government and several Austrian citizens, with Prof. Robert S. Wistrich as academic chairman, the center was intended to deepen cultural and scholarly cooperation between Austria and Israel.

Holocaust Restitution and Compensation

In Washington, D.C., on January 17—just three days before the Clinton administration left office—President Clinton's special envoy on Holocaust claims, Deputy Treasury Secretary Stuart Eizenstat, achieved a deal with the Austrians. "Today's agreement," Ambassador Ernst Sucharipa, Austria's chief negotiator, said, "constitutes on our side a major contribution to completing our response to the terrible fact of Nazi persecution," though, he went on, "I know that no amount of money can undo the tremendous suffering and losses that have been inflicted on our Jewish citizens."

Under the arrangement, $150 million would be distributed in an expedited manner. Each claimant was to receive $7,000 for losses of apartment and small-business leases, household property, and personal valuables and effects. In the event that an eligible person died after October 24, 2000, his or her heirs could apply for the money. Responsibility for administering payments was lodged with the Nationalfond, established in 1995 (see AJYB, 2001, p. 402). This fund had already compiled a list of survivors who were eligible to receive payments under previous legislation, and the new disbursements began immediately. In June, President Bush praised Austria's prompt fulfillment of its obligations. In a letter to Chancellor Schüssel, Bush wrote: "I would like to congratulate your government, the Austrian people, and the Austrian business community for these highly responsible actions and applaud your leadership on this important issue." As of December 31, 2001, payments had been made to 11,000 persons living in many different countries.

In addition, the agreement provided that the Austrian government establish a General Settlement Fund (GSF) in the amount of $210 million, also to be administered by the Nationalfond. Its purpose was to acknowledge, through voluntary payments, the moral responsibility for losses and damages inflicted upon Jewish citizens and other victims of National Socialism. Persons or associations persecuted by the Nazi regime, or forced to leave the country to escape such persecution and who/which suffered property losses or damages, were eligible to apply for compensation. Heirs of such persons and legal successors of defunct associations might also apply. The categories of property for which compensation could be sought were liquidated businesses, real property, bank accounts and stocks, bonds and mortgages, insurance policies, and occupational or educational losses. In addition, applications would be accepted for actual restitution of real estate (land) and buildings (in the case of Jewish organizations, also tangible movable property) which were owned by the federal government or the city of Vienna as of January 17, 2001. Two international panels, created under the terms setting up the new fund, were to rule on the validity of claims. The deadline for filing applications was set for May 27, 2003.

A key stipulation of the agreement was that no money would be paid out of the GSF until the achievement of legal closure, that is, the dismissal of all U.S. class-action suits against Austria and/or Austrian companies relating to the National Socialist era. As of the end of 2001, the fund had made no payments because two such suits were still pending in U.S. federal courts.

An additional $112 million was to be paid out in the form of social benefits to survivors living outside of Austria, including those who were under six years of age in 1938, when Hitler took over the country. These monies were to be available for nursing allowances, the right to retroactively purchase pension rights, and similar purposes. Responsibility for paying out this money was assigned to the Ministry of Social Affairs and the administrative authorities of the Austrian pension system. Once again, as was the case with the GSF, no disbursements would be made in the absence of legal closure, which was still not attained at year's end.

The government also pledged more money to restore and maintain Jewish cemeteries, expedite the restitution of looted artwork, reestablish the Hakoah soccer field that was leased by Austrian Jews in Vienna in the 1930s, and provide a subvention of $8 million to build a new Hakoah facility. In addition, $25 million would be made available to settle insurance claims from survivors who bought policies during the Nazi years. These sums were on top of $382 million previously allocated for the estimated 150,000 survivors of forced and slave labor in Austria, of which the first payment, totaling $36 million, was made in July to 20,000 people who worked as slave laborers for Nazi Germany.

Although they could not keep the agreement from going into effect, there were those who criticized it. Ariel Muzicant, president of the IKG and the leader of the Austrian Jewish community's delegation to the negotiations, refused to sign the deal on the grounds that it did not go far enough in compensating for the loss of property. Toward the end of the year Muzicant met with representatives of the federal government and Austria's nine provincial governments to resolve outstanding issues that had not been addressed by the accord of January 17. Negotiations with the federal authorities centered not only on Holocaust compensation, but also on strengthening the IKG's social infrastructure, such as services to the Jewish elderly and new immigrants, meeting rising security costs, improving Jewish schools, and reconstructing synagogues. The sum involved was on the order of $22.5 million. The talks with the provincial officials dealt with the return of looted ritual artifacts and artworks, upkeep of Jewish cemeteries, and help for social institutions. Under an agreement hammered out in December but not yet signed by the parties at the end of the year, the provinces committed themselves to compensate the Federation of Jewish Communities of Austria $16 million over five years.

Jörg Haider, on the other hand, criticized the Washington agreement for going too far. He said it was a "treacherous hope" for Chancellor Schüssel to agree to the deal in the hope that it would earn him "overwhelming applause from the East Coast"—an allusion to American Jews—since the demands would only escalate. Haider said that his party acknowledged the need to resolve the problem of Holocaust compensation, but added that *"einmal muss Schluss sein"* (at some point there must be an end). On several other occasions during the course of the year Haider kept coming back to the theme that Austria must leave the past behind and concentrate on the future.

The Holocaust Victims' Information and Support Center (HVISC, or "Anlaufstelle"), which was established in July 1999, had expanded its work to promote the interests of Jewish Holocaust victims in and from Austria (see AJYB, 2001, p. 403). Since its establishment, the HVISC staff had held 2,300 individual consultations, placed 13,000 telephone calls, and drafted 17,000 letters to Austrian Jewish victims of the Holocaust in Austria and abroad. On the basis of archival research and some 5,000 completed questionnaires concerning seized assets, the HVISC prepared background documentation for the restitution negotiations with the federal and provincial governments.

The HVISC was also active in securing the restitution of artworks. Two of its representatives sat on the Austrian Commission for the Investigation of the Provenance of Art Objects. Since the 1998 Austrian federal law concerning "Return of Works of Art from Austrian Federal Museums and Collections" did not provide for a search for heirs, the HVISC sometimes did its own investigations. In 2001 the Austrian government restituted 74 artworks that had been taken from ten collections once owned by Jews. For the 1999–2001 period, the number of works restituted was 619 from 42 different collections. Of these, the HVISC had identified heirs of 14 of the collections.

Another HVISC function, delegated to it by the IKG, was the creation of a data bank with documentation on the dissolution of Jewish social institutions, associations, and foundations, the destruction of synagogues and Jewish cemeteries, and the theft of capital assets and movable properties during the National Socialist era. As part of this effort, it published a detailed report in October, *The Vienna Jewish Community: The Robbing and Liquidation,* complete with documents, pictures, and full analysis. IKG president Muzicant used this documentation in his negotiations with provincial governments on compensation. The HVISC also reorganized much of the Vienna Jewish community's archival material dealing with the seizure of assets during the Nazi years and the acts of restitution after 1945, and made it available both to historians and to Jewish and government agencies involved in restitution issues.

In January, Austria was admitted to the Task Force for International Cooperation on Holocaust Education, Remembrance and Research. Created in the spring of 1998 at the initiative of Swedish prime minister

Goran Persson, the task force was originally made up of representatives from France, Germany, Israel, the Netherlands, Poland, Sweden, the United Kingdom, and the United States, though membership was open to all countries. Its purpose was to mobilize political support worldwide for perpetuating the memory of the Holocaust.

JEWISH COMMUNITY

Demography

The Jewish population registered with the IKG numbered about 6,600, around the same as the previous year. Knowledgeable observers, however, estimated the actual number of Jews living in the country to be at least twice that. The overwhelming majority of Jews continued to be concentrated in Vienna. Only about 500–600 made their homes elsewhere, primarily in the large provincial cities of Salzburg, Innsbruck, Graz, and Linz.

The Jewish community worried about its numbers—there was a small but steady emigration, and virtually no new immigrants. It was estimated that several hundred Jews, many of whom had come from the former Soviet republic of Georgia, had emigrated in search of better economic opportunities, mainly in Eastern Europe. To offset this outflow, the IKG had requested the government in 2000 to waive certain provisions of the country's highly restrictive immigration laws so as to allow in the same number of Jews who had left. Receiving no response, the IKG had, at least for now, decided not to pursue the matter. An IKG campaign offering incentives to new members induced 120 people to join the official Jewish community.

Communal Affairs

In July, the Jewish community of Vienna celebrated the 175th anniversary of the dedication of the Stadttempel synagogue, which opened its doors for religious services in 1826. Among those addressing the assemblage of political and religious dignitaries and members of the Jewish community were Austria's president, Thomas Klestil, Chaim Eisenberg, the chief rabbi of the country, and IKG president Ariel Muzicant. A similar event took place in Salzburg that month to commemorate the centenary of that city's synagogue. President Klestil also spoke on that occasion, lauding the continued Jewish presence in Salzburg. Also in attendance were the mayor of the city, the governor of the province, Eisenberg, Muzicant, and dignitaries from the Salzburg Jewish community.

A religious milestone was reached with the installation in April of Vienna's first woman rabbi. Vienna-born Eveline Goodman-Thau was named rabbi of the liberal congregation Or Chadash. Founded in 1991 and emphasizing worship, social action, and help for the needy based on the principles of equality and inclusiveness, Or Chadash was affiliated with the World Union for Progressive Judaism.

Plans proceeded for the establishment of a Shoah research center in Vienna. In talks with IKG president Muzicant, Mayor Michael Häupl indicated that the city would provide financial support for the project. The proposed center would work in close cooperation with the Documentation Archives—a foundation headed by Prof. Wolfgang Neugebauer—the Jewish Documentation Center run by Simon Wiesenthal, and the University of Vienna's Department of Contemporary History and other units of the university.

The Jewish Cultural Weeks Festival, in November, provided a wide array of events: dance, featuring the Noa Dar and Bat Sheva troupes from Israel; plays, such as a performance by the Yidishpil company at Vienna's Atzmon theater; and films, including a number of French productions dealing with Jewish themes.

Among the exhibitions mounted by the Vienna Jewish Museum in 2001 was one of selected works of Ludwig Meidner (1884–1966), which ran from October 5 through January 20, 2002. A painter and graphic artist who was little known in Austria during his lifetime, Meidner was an important representative of German Expressionism. After World War I, Jewish identity became an increasingly important aspect of his life and work. Meidner was forced to emigrate when the Nazis came to power. After a bitter exile in England, he returned to Germany, and died in Darmstadt. Another exhibition, entitled "Displaced," which ran from November 14, 2001 through February 24, 2002, dealt with Paul Celan's six-month sojourn in Vienna in late 1947 and early 1948. Photos, books, and other rare collectors' items told the cultural and political story of a strife-torn city that was unable to offer the homeless poet a permanent abode.

The St. Polten-based Institute for the History of Jews in Austria continued to publish research studies and hold its annual congress on diverse topics relating to Austrian Jewry in the past and present. Established in 1987, in 2001 it published, among other works, *The 18th-Century Toler-*

ance Policies of Joseph II and Their Effect on the Austrian Economy by Prof. Klaus Lohrmann, director of the institute, and *The Role of Jewish Women in Austria, Germany and Central Europe* by Dr. Marta Keil. The institute's annual congress, held in July, focused on Contemporary Issues Facing Jewish Communities in Central Europe. Approximately 200 people from many countries attended.

In the presence of military attachés from a number of countries, a monument was dedicated in Vienna's Jewish cemetery on June 24 to honor Jewish soldiers from allied armies and partisans who gave their lives in World War II.

MURRAY GORDON SILBERMAN

East-Central Europe

POSTCOMMUNIST COUNTRIES CONTINUED the process of development and integration into Europe at different rates, largely determined by economic progress. The Czech Republic and Hungary remained front-runners to join the European Union in 2004, but Poland's economic slump threatened to delay that country's bid to enter. An EU report in November attributed Poland's slowdown to a "poorly coordinated policy mix, combined with . . . political domestic uncertainty." Most EU officials and observers, however, felt that EU enlargement would be impossible without the inclusion, in the first wave, of Poland, which had the largest economy in the area.

There was continuing concern over the persistence of racism—directed primarily against Roma (Gypsies)—and anti-Semitism in the region. These were becoming increasingly cross-border activities as skinheads held international gatherings (including concerts featuring hate music), and the Internet created easy links. *Mein Kampf* and other anti-Semitic tracts were published in several countries, and anti-Semitic articles appeared in the media.

Jewish communities, institutions, and individuals continued—also, at various rates of speed—the process of integration and community building. Many set up or enlarged Web sites and Internet links. Countries in the region took part in the European Day of Jewish Culture, on September 2, a continent-wide initiative that saw hundreds of Jewish heritage sites in 23 countries opened to the public. Jewish communities also sent representatives to various international Jewish meetings, including a get-together with the Conference of Presidents of Major American Jewish Organizations in Berlin in February, a gathering of the general assembly of the European Council of Jewish Communities in Spain at the end of May, and the World Jewish Congress annual meeting in Jerusalem in November.

Internally, questions revolving around conversion to Judaism and criteria for membership in the Jewish community remained pressing issues, and several communities opened the door to a greater non-Orthodox Jewish religious presence. Throughout the year there was deep concern about the situation in Israel. While homegrown anti-Semitism had by no means abated, these Jewish communities appeared to feel less alarmed than did large Jewish communities in the West about the possible repercussions of the Palestinian intifada and the attacks of September 11.

Bosnia-Herzegovina

About 1,000 Jews lived in Bosnia-Herzegovina, more than two-thirds of them in the capital, Sarajevo, about 200 in the Muslim-Croat controlled sector of the country, and about 125 in the Serbian-controlled Republika Srpska. As Bosnia slowly recovered from its 1992–1995 war, Jews continued to depend heavily on international humanitarian aid, much of it channeled through the American Jewish Joint Distribution Committee (JDC). In Sarajevo, the community operated a Sunday school for about 30 Jewish and non-Jewish children, a nonsectarian home-care program for the elderly, and well-attended Israeli folk-dance classes.

The tiny Jewish community symbolized the ideal of interethnic coexistence in Bosnia, and for that reason enjoyed a political importance out of proportion to its numbers. This was why senior officials made a point of attending special Passover seders in Sarajevo.

Jewish leaders were active in interfaith and interethnic dialogue. Jakob Finci, president of the Jewish community, was appointed chairman of the Federal Constitutional Commission and was also involved in efforts to establish a "truth commission," modeled on the one in South Africa, to deal with the perpetrators of wartime atrocities.

In April, Bosnian Jews were joined by local Muslim, Croat, and Serb religious leaders and by foreign dignitaries in a ceremony formally laying the cornerstone for a new synagogue and Jewish cultural center in the southern city of Mostar. The complex was being built just 100 meters from the site of the famous 16th-century stone bridge that was destroyed by Croat mortar fire in November 1993 and was to be rebuilt under the auspices of UNESCO. Construction of the synagogue and center would be financed by Mostar municipal authorities, and they pledged to have the building completed in 2002. Although only about 45 Jews lived in Mostar, Jewish community leader Zoran Mandlbaum had become a local hero during the Bosnian war for his nonsectarian humanitarian work, and his efforts were crucial in getting the synagogue project started.

This ceremony marked the first time in several months that leaders of Bosnia's three main religions had joined together. Mostar's Croat mayor and Muslim deputy mayor also attended, along with a number of foreign ambassadors and other senior diplomats. No American representatives were there, however, because the U.S. banned travel to Mostar and surrounding areas for its citizens after violent riots there earlier in the month by Croat extremists—the worst violence in Bosnia since the Dayton accords of 1995 ended the Bosnian war. The travel ban also prevented a ten-member delegation of the JDC board from attending the ceremony, but the group did manage to meet in Sarajevo with Karlo Filipovic, president of the Federation of Bosnia-Herzegovina, who had taken up his post just six weeks earlier.

In June, representatives of the Catholics, Orthodox Christians, Jews, and Muslims of Bosnia met in Rome under the auspices of the Roman Catholic Sant' Egidio community, a charity involved in relief work and interfaith dialogue. They appealed to the world's major powers to take steps to reconstruct religious buildings damaged or destroyed in the Bosnian war, and to sponsor "education for peace and faith."

Bulgaria

Bulgaria's economy expanded by 4.9 percent in 2001, but conditions remained difficult. The country had one of the lowest GDP-per capita among countries aspiring to join the European Union. Bulgarian Jews suffered economic woes together with other Bulgarians, with the elderly and others on fixed incomes hardest hit.

Bulgaria went through startling political changes. In April, former King Simeon II registered his own new political party, the Simeon II National Movement, to run in the June 17 parliamentary elections. Simeon had reigned as a child from 1943 to 1946, and returned to Bulgaria in 1996 after living most of his life in exile. His party pledged to eliminate corruption in politics and attract foreign investment. The party swept to victory, and Simeon, 64, became prime minister.

His foreign policy adviser, Solomon Passy, a Jew, became foreign minister. Over the previous decade Passy, 44, had been a key proponent of Bulgaria's membership in NATO and the EU. He had ties with the American Jewish Committee and other international Jewish organizations and favored close relations with Israel. Georgi Parvanov, the leader of the Bulgarian Socialist Party, was elected president in November, defeating incumbent Petar Stoyanov.

There were several neo-Nazi incidents during the year, though these were rare in comparison to other postcommunist states. During New Year's Eve celebrations in downtown Sofia, some people in the crowd waved a flag with a swastika on it, drawing a denunciation from President Stoyanov who said that the Bulgarian people "will never accept individuals or groups with a Nazi ideology." Bulgaria, he went on, "must on no account allow a handful of people to stain its image, which has been created not only in the last ten years, but also during World War II, when Bulgarian citizens served as an example to many European nations by showing solidarity with, and tolerance toward, persecuted Jews."

Toward the end of the year, a translation of *Mein Kampf* was published legally for the first time in Bulgaria and was said to be selling well. The edition included a preface by a historian saying it was a racist and anti-Semitic book. An aggressive advertising campaign accompanied publication, with hundreds of posters showing Hitler pasted up on Sofia walls. The publisher, however, denied putting up the posters. Jewish leaders slammed the poster campaign as "fascist propaganda." In 2000, Bulgarian police had barred the sale of a translation of *Mein Kampf* that was published illegally because the imprint did not identify the publisher.

The story of how Bulgaria saved its 50,000 Jews during World War II gained wide publicity during the year. A new documentary film about it by Israeli director Nitzan Aviram premiered in Sofia in January based on a 1998 book by Michael Bar-Zohar, *Beyond Hitler's Grasp.* Bar-Zohar was one of the Bulgarian Jews who had been saved, as was Emanuel Siessmann, the current Israeli ambassador to Bulgaria. Later in the year *The Optimists,* another film on the subject, by Jacky and Lisa Comforty, opened in the United States.

In April, Sir Sigmund Sternberg of the International Council of Christians and Jews visited Bulgaria at the invitation of the government. His organization founded an interfaith trialogue group with the participation of the Bulgarian Orthodox Church, the papal nuncio, the Islamic mufti, and the Jewish community. President Stoyanov lent his support.

Relations with Israel were good, with considerable Israeli investment in the Bulgarian economy. But a crisis flared between the government and the Israeli owner of Bulgaria's flag carrier, Balkan Airlines. That Israeli owner was the Zeevi Holding Company, which had bought 75 percent of Balkan Airlines in 1999 for $150,000 and a pledge to pay off the airline's $120-million debt while also investing $100 million in it over a five-year period. But in February 2001 all flights were grounded and the airline's executive director fled the country. Zeevi Holding demanded that the Bulgarian government pay it $230 million for breaches in the acquisition agreement and $6 million in compensation for assets missing from the company after its purchase. The airline was placed into receivership little more than a week later. Zeevi Holding sold its stake in it, but the finance minister said the sale was invalid. On May 5, the government revoked Balkan Airlines' aviation license and a court later declared the airline bankrupt, though some flights were resumed while administrators sought new investors.

In December, the Ministry of Foreign Affairs awarded the Gold Laurel Branch decoration to Daniel S. Mariaschin, executive vice president of B'nai B'rith International.

Jewish Community

In April, Jews from Kansas City, whose local federation had a partnership arrangement with Bulgarian Jewry, brought a Torah scroll to Sofia to take the place of 11 priceless scrolls that had been stolen in February. The Torah was installed during a ceremony coinciding with Holocaust Memorial Day commemorations. With the help of JDC representatives, the Torah had been flown to Bucharest and taken overland by car to Sofia—a journey of about eight hours.

Hanukkah ceremonies under the rubric "eight days of Jewish renewal in Bulgaria" served to symbolize the revival of Jewish communal life for Bulgaria's approximately 5,000 Jews. Top Bulgarian officials took part, the prime minister lighting the first candle in the synagogue, where some 300 people were gathered. Candles were lit on subsequent nights at events organized for different age groups and held at several Jewish locations besides the synagogue, including the Beit Haam JCC, the Jewish school, and the old-age home. The ceremonies were followed by lectures and study sessions about Hanukkah.

On the final weekend of Hanukkah, about 120 young Jewish adults from all over Bulgaria came to Sofia for a Hanukkah seminar designed to enhance Jewish identification among this age group and reach out to the unaffiliated. The participants learned about the holiday, engaged in discussions, and socialized. A separate group of about 90 university students held their own party to light the seventh candle. On the eighth and final day of Hanukkah, children attended a workshop program at the JCC and then had a party.

Croatia

Croatia continued to consolidate the democratic reforms put into motion after the death, in 1999, of nationalist strongman Franjo Tudjman. The government was cooperating with the Hague Tribunal for War Crimes in the former Yugoslavia, and reduced its support for hard-line

Croatian nationalists in Bosnia. President Stipe Mesic said the government would promote Holocaust education in Croatian schools.

In the spring, when Israel's new ambassador, David Granit, presented his credentials, Mesic condemned anti-Semitism and said his nation had left behind a period when it was "flirting with Nazi-fascist ideas." He also vowed not to forget Croatia's World War II history as a Nazi puppet state.

In October, Mesic made the first visit ever to Israel by a Croatian president. He told the Knesset: "As the president of the Republic of Croatia, I sincerely condemn with all my heart the crimes that were carried out against Jews during World War II by the government that collaborated [with the Nazis] and unfortunately bore the name Croatia. . . . I take every opportunity to ask forgiveness from all those who were hurt by Croatians anytime, first of all the Jews." In an interview with *Ha'aretz,* Mesic said he wanted to see Israeli investment in Croatia. For its part, Israel hoped to sell security-related products to the Croatian military. In January, Croatia had to cancel a $100-million agreement with Israel to modernize its MiG-21 jets because of a lack of funds.

In December, archives, tapes, documents, and other material telling the story of the Jasenovac concentration camp were reinstalled in the Jasenovac Museum. They had been removed for safekeeping during the Yugoslav wars of the 1990s, and in 2000 were sent to the Holocaust Memorial Museum in Washington where they were catalogued and restored at a cost of $150,000. The museum at Jasenovac, dismantled in 1991, was rebuilt to house the relics, which were due to go on display in 2002.

In the summer, the Jewish communities in Zagreb and Osijek received hate mail calling on Jews to leave the country or be "cleansed."

Jewish Community

About 2,000 Jews were registered in Croatia's nine Jewish communities, three-quarters of them in the capital of Zagreb. Jews were an officially recognized national minority and thus qualified for state aid, including money for a kindergarten, old-age home, newspaper, and a variety of Jewish cultural projects. The community was moving to refurbish the Jewish summer camp at Pirovac on the Adriatic coast, to which it had regained title. The community also maintained a recently established Documentation Center for Research on the Holocaust. In October, historian Ivo Goldstein, a prominent member of the community, published a detailed book on the Holocaust in Croatia.

The rate of intermarriage was high, with some 80 percent of Zagreb's

Jewish community members either born to intermarried couples or married to non-Jews. However unlike the situation in many Western countries, it was typical for the non-Jewish spouse to identify with the Jewish community, so that most of the younger community members had only one Jewish parent, or even just one Jewish grandparent. Jewish leaders, fearing the community could lose its national-minority status if its numbers dipped too low, urged members to declare their nationality as "Jewish" during the national census of 2002.

Rabbi Kotel Dadon, based in Zagreb since 1999, was Modern Orthodox, and he influenced a growing number of younger Jews to attend synagogue. Shabbat dinners for families at the Jewish community center were also popular. Nonetheless, most community members were not religiously observant and regarded Jewish identity in terms of tradition and secular culture.

In April, Zagreb hosted a youth seminar that drew nearly three dozen young Jews from Croatia, Slovenia, Serbia, and Bosnia. In addition to study sessions, cultural events, and opportunities for socializing, they joined Holocaust survivors at ceremonies commemorating the victims of the Jasenovac prison and death camp, where 17,000 Jews and scores of thousands of Serbs, Roma, and others were killed by Croatian fascists. Interviews with the young Jews indicated that many still felt they were "Yugoslav Jews," despite the bloody breakup of the former Yugoslavia. A large number said they wanted to marry a Jewish spouse, but saw little possibility of finding a Jewish mate in their home countries. In October, the Croatian Jewish community hosted a meeting at a resort complex on the Adriatic island of Brac for adult Jews who came from all over the former Yugoslavia.

Czech Republic

Racist attacks—primarily on Roma (Gypsies)—skinhead activity, and other evidence of right-wing extremism caused concern throughout the year and prompted calls for action. The Interior Ministry released figures showing that the number of crimes committed by the far right in the Czech Republic had risen in 2000 by more than 15.2 percent to 384. At the beginning of April, the Board of Romany Regional Representatives set up a crisis committee to monitor the situation. Increasing numbers of Roma sought asylum in Britain and other western countries.

The growing popularity of rock concerts by racist bands was a specific concern. Interior Ministry figures showed that more than 80 such concerts took place in 2000. One concert, on April 6 near Prague, sparked an outcry. It was attended by about 400 skinheads from the Czech Republic, Germany, Slovakia, and Poland. One of the bands was a Slovak group called Juden Mord—"Death to Jews"—whose CD cover featured a picture of the Auschwitz gates. Police monitored the concert but made no arrests, saying it was a "private party." But their failure to act drew sharp criticism. President Václav Havel said he was shocked by the apparent police indifference. Interior Minister Stanislav Gross vowed to crack down on such extremism.

Jewish organizations pressured the government to take action. In a letter to Gross, the Czech Federation of Jewish Communities said that the name Juden Mord "is in our opinion so self-explanatory that to have allowed the concert to take place cannot be considered anything other than indirect support of anti-Semitism." Police did intervene at a similar concert in another town near Prague on April 14. They detained but later released ten of the 150 skinheads in attendance and deported a Slovak skinhead who had attended the April 6 concert.

In May, Czech Jewish leaders issued a statement expressing concern about the racist rock concerts and other neo-Nazi activities, and appealed directly to the Czech public for support in combating the threat. The Czech Catholic Bishops' Conference supported the Jewish statement, and other Christian leaders also condemned as alarming the "indifference on the part of a large segment of the public, including those who are in responsible positions, toward the expression of neo-Nazi postures and the ever-growing cult of violence."

That month, five policemen in Karlovy Vary attacked and beat a Roma man. They were later charged with "racially motivated behavior." In July Prague's Jewish leadership sharply condemned the murder of a Roma by a skinhead in the town of Svitavy, saying it underscored the urgency of their earlier appeal.

These calls apparently had an effect. In early August police intervened at a concert organized by skinheads. They detained one participant wearing a shirt with Nazi symbols and said he would be prosecuted for supporting a movement aimed at repressing the rights and freedoms of citizens. About 40 right-wing extremists staged a protest in Prague against the police intervention, accusing Interior Minister Gross of hindering free speech. They said skinheads were fired from jobs because of their opinions. On August 25, police stopped a rock concert in Plzen (Pilsen) when the audience began chanting Nazi leader Rudolf Hess's name. They detained more than 20 participants and charged three of them with supporting a movement aimed at suppressing the rights and freedoms of others. On August 11, skinheads attacked a gay club in the town of Liberec. Police detained two people and charged them with disturbing the peace.

In the late summer, a range of state and nongovernmental agencies, backed by a division of the European Union, launched an ad campaign on prime-time Czech television and billboards around the country that ridiculed neo-Nazis. Czech Jewish representatives applauded the campaign, but some critics suggested that by making light of the extremists the ads failed to address their true danger. The Czech far-right Republican Party filed a criminal complaint, accusing the campaign organizers of scaremongering.

Publication of *Mein Kampf* in the Czech Republic continued to make waves. In March, Vit Varak, who sold Czech translations of the book over the Internet, was convicted of supporting a movement suppressing the rights of Czech citizens and fined nearly $3,000. In February, citing "serious judicial mistakes," the Prague City Court overturned a December 2000 sentence against Michal Zitko, the publisher of another Czech-language translation, and sent the case back to the district court for reexamination. In November, the district court upheld the three-year suspended jail sentence against Zitko and ordered him to pay a fine amounting to around $54,000. He again lodged an appeal.

As in previous years, there were reports of vandalism of Jewish cemeteries, most of which were abandoned or rarely visited.

Tension developed between Czech Jews and the local Muslim community in October over anti-Jewish statements published in a booklet and on a Web site run by the Islamic Foundation in Prague. Official Muslim representatives defused the situation by disassociating themselves from the texts.

In the fall, Arthur Avnon replaced Erelly Hadar as Israel's ambassador to the Czech Republic.

Jewish Community

There were approximately 3,000 registered members of Jewish communities in the Czech Republic, about half of them living in Prague, but Jewish leaders estimated that there were many more unaffiliated Jews in the country. Ten officially mandated Jewish communities and a number of secular Jewish institutions came under the aegis of the Federation of Jewish Communities.

In April, Prague's Jewish community elected 32-year-old Tomas Jelinek as chairman, a post considered the most powerful Jewish position in the country. Jelinek, who also represented the Czech Republic on the International Commission on Holocaust Era Insurance Claims and was chairman of the board of the Czech Endowment Fund for Holocaust Victims, worked as an economic adviser to President Havel. But he had to leave his job in Havel's office in the fall after being told that his position as chairman of the Jewish community, tantamount to heading a business, made him ineligible to hold a government post.

The organized Jewish community was officially Orthodox even though most Jews were non-Orthodox or secular. This had caused friction for some time, and there were those who wanted to introduce pluralism in the Jewish community. Soon after his election, Jelinek said he wanted all streams of Judaism to be equal. In the spring, the Czech Federation of Jewish Communities revealed results of an opinion poll that found 80 percent of respondents wanting the federation to include non-Orthodox streams. In response, the federation took up for consideration the creation of a partnership arrangement with the Reform movement's World Union for Progressive Judaism.

There were many signs of new vitality within the Jewish community. About 400 people attended the annual Jewish charity ball in March, which raised around $8,000 for the Prague Jewish Community Foundation. In the summer, Rabbi Samuel Abramson became the first rabbi in 60 years in the spa town of Karlovy Vary. Though the 90-member community wanted a Reform rabbi, Abramson, 34, was Modern Orthodox and a trained veterinarian, and was charged with overseeing kashrut standards throughout the country.

In early September, the chief rabbi, Karol Sidon, officiated at the first wedding in more than 30 years to be held at Prague's ornate Jubilee Synagogue. The groom was David Stecher, chairman of the Prague Jewish community's supervisory board, who, 19 years earlier in the same synagogue, had become the only Prague Jew of his generation to celebrate a bar mitzvah. Community members hailed his wedding to Jitka Sobotkova as a sign of a renaissance of Jewish life in the city.

The controversy over a 13th-century Jewish cemetery discovered under the construction site for an insurance company in downtown Prague in 1999 (see AJYB 2000, pp. 379–80) appeared to have been resolved. In 2000, the remains of 160 bodies were removed from the site and ritually reburied. In the fall of 2001, a tombstone and memorial for those deceased were dedicated at Prague's New Jewish Cemetery. The monument ceremony also honored hundreds of graves being encased in concrete at the building site under a compromise arrangement with the Czech state that enabled construction to proceed. The inscription on the memorial thanked the Czech state, Prague's Jewish community, and "foreign Jewish institutions" for preserving the remains. Plans were also under way to erect a memorial at the original burial site.

There were a number of Holocaust commemorations. In January, a ceremony in Brno marked the mass deportations to Auschwitz of Czechoslovak Roma in March 1943. A new plaque, at what had been the Nazi Protectorate police headquarters there, also commemorated the deportations. Of about 5,000 deported Roma, only 500 survived. On March 25, the annual ceremony in Poprad commemorating the victims of the first mass deportation of Jewish girls and women to Nazi death camps was disrupted by an explosion apparently caused by a percussion bomb. No one was injured. In the spring, a record 80 schools from 26 Czech cities and towns took part in the eighth annual "man is not a number" competition aimed at educating teenagers about the Holocaust. Pupils submitted 300 paintings and 150 essays on Holocaust themes. In October, a group of Czech Holocaust survivors traveled to Poland to mark the 60th anniversary of the first Czech transports to the Lodz Ghetto. In September, Israeli ambassador Hadar presented "Righteous among the Nations" certificates, most of them posthumously, to 15 citizens of the Czech Republic and Slovakia. Jewish representatives from nine countries—Britain, Croatia, the Czech Republic, Germany, Hungary, Italy, the Netherlands, Poland, and Slovakia—met in Prague in the fall to plan a new European Association of Jewish Child Survivors of the Holocaust.

The Prague-based Endowment Fund for Victims of the Holocaust, a $2.5-million fund operated by the Czech Federation of Jewish Communities, set a December 31 deadline for individuals from all nationalities to apply for Holocaust compensation for property seized during World War II. Czech legislators had, in 2000, voted to provide the money as a humanitarian gesture.

The Prague Jewish Museum expanded its facilities and featured numerous exhibitions and cultural activities. In February, the museum relocated its headquarters to a new state-of-the-art complex next to the city's recently restored Spanish Synagogue. The new center included art restoration workshops, a library, archives, a café, and an exhibition hall, as well as offices. In the fall, a new display of priceless silver Judaica was installed in the synagogue as a permanent exhibition, "Synagogue Silver from Bohemia and Moravia."

Numerous concerts, exhibitions, publications, performances, and other

Jewish-themed cultural events took place throughout the year. Among them: a combination of music, readings, and performance called Purim Reflections, held in March in Prague's Spanish Synagogue; in the spring, a discussion at the 11th Prague Writers Festival, attended by British author Salman Rushdie, about the life and works of the late Italian Jewish writer Primo Levi; and in the fall, the creation of a new monthly magazine about Jewish identity in a changing world, *Hamaskil,* by Sylvia Wittman, a longtime Jewish activist in Prague.

Several films on Jewish themes made news. The American ABC network filmed a miniseries about Anne Frank in Prague. *Divided We Fall* by director Jan Hrebejk, about a Czech couple who hid a Jew during the Shoah, was nominated for an Academy Award for best foreign-language film. *The Power of Humanity,* a film about Nicholas Winton, an Englishman who saved the lives of hundreds of young Czech Jewish refugees during World War II, premiered in the fall. The documentary *Fighter* by Amir Bar-Lev followed two Czech Holocaust survivors in their 70s—Jan Wiener and author Arnost Lustig, both of whom moved to the United States after the war—as they revisited the sites of Wiener's wartime odyssey of escape through Czechoslovakia, Slovenia, Yugoslavia, and Italy. New York-based Czech native Zuzana Justman's new film, *A Trial in Prague,* which opened in the fall, was a documentary about the anti-Semitic trial of Rudolf Slansky and other top communist leaders in Czechoslovakia in 1952. Of the 14 officials tried on trumped-up charges of treason and espionage, 11 were Jews.

Hungary

Eager to progress on the road toward joining the European Union, Hungary, by the end of the year, had successfully brought its domestic laws into line with EU standards in 23 of the 31 stipulated policy areas for aspiring member states. Early in the year, the National Assembly overwhelmingly passed a "status law" to take effect at the beginning of 2002 that granted ethnic Hungarians living in Romania, Ukraine, the former Yugoslavia, and Slovakia, countries bordering Hungary, access to state-funded jobs, education, and health care in Hungary. The affected countries at first denounced the law, but at the end of 2001, Hungary managed to reach an agreement on it with Romania.

Throughout the year, Prime Minister Viktor Orban's ruling rightist FIDESZ party denied that it might make a political deal with the notorious far-right Hungarian Justice and Life Party (MIEP). Nonetheless Jews worried about the influence MIEP seemed to be getting in the government and about a creeping if ambiguous form of political anti-Semitism expressed in the mass media. Racism, particularly against Roma, also seemed to be on the rise: a number of Roma sought asylum in France and other countries, prompting Canada to impose visa requirements on Hungarian citizens in December. The Canadian ambassador to Hungary said that some 8,000 Hungarians had applied to Canada for asylum since 1998, of whom only 8–15 percent had been accepted. Most of the asylum seekers were believed to be Roma.

A committee of the Council of Europe issued a report in the spring accusing Hungarian police of brutality against people in their custody, primarily foreigners, juvenile offenders, and Roma. A survey released in November showed that 14 percent of students in their final year of teacher-training college expressed racist views or harbored prejudices. Only 7.4 percent held open and tolerant views, while 36.5 percent could be described as "mildly affected by prejudice." After September 11, MIEP's outspoken chairman, Istvan Csurka, broke ranks with other Hungarian political forces and said the terrorist attacks were a consequence of U.S. policies and globalization.

Hungarian Jews protested both the general climate and individual episodes of anti-Semitism. In January, the Jewish leadership protested an attempt by MIEP to obtain a retrial of World War II prime minister Laszlo Bardossy. Bardossy, implicated in the deaths of hundreds of thousands of Jews, had been executed in 1946 for war crimes. In the summer, a small street in the village of Paty was named after Admiral Miklós Horthy, Hungary's head of state from 1920 till 1944. This was first time since the war that a street in Hungary had been named after him. In the spring, Hungary's justice minister rejected a request filed in 1999 by the Jewish community for a law that would make Holocaust denial illegal. In the fall, a Hungarian representative to the World Jewish Congress conference in Jerusalem said there was a "new wave of political anti-Semitism in the country, formally and informally supported by the government."

Several incidents received particular attention. In July, there was a sharp anti-Semitic reaction when a company owned by a Jewish businessman bought the popular Ferencvaros soccer club. MIEP deputy chairman Laszlo Bognar called the purchase "antinational," since the team "was sacrificed to a group of dirty, greedy, unscrupulous businessmen without morals, who have nothing to do with Ferencvaros or the

Hungarian people." Six Jewish organizations sued Bognar, accusing him of "incitement against a community." But the Prosecutor General's Office decided not to prosecute.

A furor arose in September over an anti-Semitic article published by MIEP parliament member and deputy chairman Lorant Hegedus, Jr., in a MIEP magazine in Budapest. Hegedus, a Calvinist pastor, wrote that a Christian Hungarian state would have avoided devastation by the Tartars and Turks as well as rule by the Habsburgs if "a hoard of vagabonds from Galicia had not entered the country. . . ." Clearly referring to Jews, Hegedus called on Hungarians to "exclude them, otherwise they will do the same with you."

Opposition politicians called the article "fascist" and "hate speech." In November, the Hungarian Calvinist church synod said the article was against the Gospels and incompatible with the Calvinist faith. In December, the Calvinist church and the Federation of Hungarian Jewish Religious Communities agreed that both would refrain from taking political positions and from supporting or accepting support from political parties. Also in December, parliament suspended Hegedus's parliamentary immunity, opening the door to possible indictment for inciting hatred against a community.

As demonstrated by the Hegedus case, racism and anti-Semitism in the mass media were problems. In the fall, the B'nai B'rith chapter in Budapest published a book documenting recent anti-Semitic discourse in the Hungarian media and other public forums. It was based on research carried out throughout 2000 by its Jewish Documentation Center, founded in 1999 to monitor and document Hungarian Jewish life as well as racist and anti-Semitic acts in the country.

Broadcasts on Pannon Radio—often described as a mouthpiece for MIEP—were particularly worrying. In November, the National Radio and Television Board described the station as "solely committed to the dissemination of an extremist ideology" bearing the mark of "far-right nationalism and of conspiracy theories." Its programs, according to the board, promoted anti-Semitism, xenophobia, and hatred against Roma and homosexuals, thus violating the media law and the constitution. Soon after this report was published, the new U.S. ambassador to Hungary, Nancy Goodman Brinker, ruffled feathers by expressing concern at the rise in anti-Semitism and xenophobia in the country. Goodman, a Jew, told a meeting at the Hungarian Academy of Science that such forms of intolerance "are the only unpleasant features" that she had encountered in her first two months in Budapest. She said she has not experienced "anything like it anywhere else."

There were also episodes of vandalism against Jewish sites, including the cemeteries in Jaszkarajeno and Siofok.

Not all the news was bad. There were many initiatives to teach Hungarians about the Holocaust, commemorate its victims, and to combat racism. Hungary instituted its first official Holocaust Memorial Day on April 16, the date the first ghetto in Hungary was set up in 1944. The National Assembly, Hungary's parliament, officially marked the occasion with a ceremony the next day, and on that occasion Jewish leaders asked it to bar all racist and anti-Semitic manifestations in its chambers and renewed their call for outlawing Holocaust denial and incitement against ethnic minorities. MIEP's 12 members boycotted the ceremony.

Ahead of Holocaust Memorial Day, the Hannah Arendt Association, a Holocaust education organization, joined with the Goethe Institute in Budapest in sponsoring a three-day seminar to help prepare teachers for the observances, since this was the first time that Hungarian schools had ever held a Holocaust commemoration. On March 28, the minister of education said the observances indicated "that the Holocaust is part of our national history," adding, "Our aim is not to arouse a guilty conscience, but a sense of responsibility in today's children." As part of the ceremonies, which coincided with Israel's Holocaust Remembrance Day, the Israeli embassy unveiled a plaque to Hannah Senesh, a Hungarian Jewish fighter with the Haganah in Palestine who was tortured and killed by Hungarian fascists after parachuting into Nazi Europe in 1944. A group of private citizens began work in the spring on establishing a Holocaust museum in Budapest.

In May, the Supreme Court jailed right-wing extremist Kemal Ekrem for conspiring to topple the constitutional order. In 1996, Ekrem had founded a group dedicated to carrying on the legacy of Hungary's World War II fascist Arrow Cross movement. In November, the Budapest Prosecutor-General's Office charged seven people with offenses connected with the publication of the *Protocols of the Elders of Zion*. Aron Monus, one of the accused, printed more than 3,000 copies in 1999. He also published a Hungarian translation of *Mein Kampf*. In December, Budapest mayor Gabor Demszky banned a planned skinhead concert and rally that was to have taken place in a popular rock-music venue. Demszky said that the concert, expected to draw skinheads from several countries, would have turned into a racist rally.

On a one-day visit to Hungary in August, Israeli foreign minister Shimon Peres met with Hungarian leaders and Jewish community representatives and laid a wreath at the Holocaust memorial next to Budapest's main synagogue. Asked about rising anti-Semitism, he said it was Hungary's problem to tackle. In October, the Austrian embassy unveiled a memorial plaque to Raoul Wallenberg, bringing to five the number of plaques or memorials in Budapest to the Swedish diplomat who saved Jews during the Shoah. In December, Israel's ambassador to Hungary, Judith Varnai Shorer, awarded the "Righteous among the Nations" citation to 31 Hungarians who helped save Jews during World War II. That brought to nearly 500 the number of Hungarians receiving the award since Hungary and Israel reestablished diplomatic relations in 1989.

Jewish Community

Estimates of the number of Jews in Hungary ranged from 54,000 to 130,000 or more. About 90 percent lived in Budapest, the vast majority of them nonobservant, secular or totally unaffiliated. Only 6,000 or so were formally registered with the Jewish community, and about 20,000 had some affiliation with Jewish organizations or institutions. The dominant religious affiliation was Neolog, similar to America's Conservative Judaism. There was a very small Orthodox community made up of both Modern Orthodox and Hassidim. Neolog communities were grouped in the Alliance of Jewish Communities in Hungary, while the Orthodox operated as the Autonomous Orthodox Community. Sim Shalom, a small Reform congregation established in Budapest in 1992 that functioned outside these official umbrella structures, was associated with the World Union of Progressive Judaism and led by a female rabbi. There was also an active Chabad-Lubavitch presence. At Passover, Budapest underwent a matzo shortage; the local matzo bakery had closed down and the Jewish community had failed to import enough.

There were three Jewish day schools and several kindergartens operating in Budapest, as well as a Jewish University incorporating a rabbinical seminary and a teachers college. Total enrollment in all of these institutions was about 1,800. Budapest's Balint Jewish Community Center had an active program of lectures, clubs, courses, and public events. In February, about 20 representatives of Hungarian Jewish organizations began a four-month course in basic fund-raising techniques. The first such training program implemented for Hungarian Jews, it was conducted by the staff of a professional development foundation. In October, some 80 JDC staffers working in or dealing with the former Soviet Union (FSU) held their regular semiannual retreat in Budapest, the first time it had ever taken place outside Israel or the FSU itself. The purpose of the retreat was to examine models of community development in countries where Jewish communal life had persisted, if weakly, under communism, to weigh their pluses and minuses, and to consider whether they could be applied in, or adapted to, the FSU.

The Lauder/JDC international Jewish summer camp at Szarvas in southern Hungary drew about 2,000 Jewish children from all over eastern and central Europe. Young Jews from the United States and other western countries also attended. The camp was used for seminars throughout the year.

Hungarian Jews expressed deep concern about Israel, some making solidarity trips there. For the first time, young Hungarian Jews registered to go on Birthright Israel trips in the winter of 2001/2002.

In the spring, Jewish communities in the Czech Republic, Slovakia, Hungary, and Poland joined together to establish the Central and Eastern European Jewish Communities Jewish Studies Support Research Grant, a scholarship fund for students of Jewish studies at the Central European University (CEU) in Budapest. CEU also ran a popular public lecture series on Jewish topics. In July, it cosponsored a three-day international conference on Jewish identities in the postcommunist era.

In June, 130 women from 20 countries came to Budapest for the European conference of the International Council of Jewish Women.

Throughout 2001 there were numerous Jewish cultural and social events. Early in the year, Italian filmmaker Alberto Negrin finished shooting a miniseries for Italian TV about Giorgio Perlasca, an Italian businessman who worked alongside Wallenberg to save Jews in Budapest. In March, some 500 Jewish singles from around the world converged on Budapest for a singles weekend culminating in a "Jewish European Ball" held in the Museum of Fine Arts. Also in March, the third annual Israeli film week drew large crowds. Theaterfest, sponsored by the Federation to Maintain Jewish Culture in Hungary in April, featured three short Jewish-themed plays. This was part of a larger "day of Jewish culture," which also included an auction of Jewish art. Another Judaica auction in November drew local, foreign, and Internet bidders, and included items from two private collections. The highlight was a 19th-century megillah that sold for about $5,000. In the summer, a major exhibition of works by Marc Chagall opened at the Jewish Museum, including seven paintings on international display for the first time. The fourth annual Jewish culture week took place in Budapest in August. The artist Laszlo Feher had a major exhibit in December.

There was considerable Jewish dissatisfaction with delays in compensation to the relatives of Holocaust victims. A 1999 law had granted about $140 per person, far less than the sum for relatives of victims of communist terror, and in December 2000 the Constitutional Court, agreeing that this was unfair, had canceled the law. But no new compensation legislation was forthcoming. In July 2001, Peter Tordai, head of the Federation of Jewish Communities in Hungary, appealed to Prime Minister Orban to speed up the process, and went so far as to threaten street demonstrations.

In February, President Ferenc Madl awarded the commander's Cross of the Order of Merit to Israel Singer, secretary general of the World Jewish Congress. U.S. physicist Edward Teller, the father of the hydrogen bomb, became the first person to receive a newly revived award that had been granted to artists and scientists in prewar Hungary. A delegation from Budapest presented the Corvin chain to Teller, 93, at his home near San Francisco. Teller, who is Jewish, fled Hungary before the Shoah. In December, Germany's ambassador to Hungary awarded Erno Lazarovits, foreign affairs director of the Federation of Jewish Communities in Hungary, the German Order of Merit, Grand Cross, for his work promoting Jewish-Christian relations and a positive image of Germany. Also in December, 50 of the 52 sports writers affiliated with the International Chess Writers Association voted Hungarian Jewish chess star Judit Polgár the best female chess player of the last century.

Macedonia

Fighting between Macedonian troops and ethnic Albanian rebels erupted in February, and a number of times during the year threatened to escalate into full-scale Balkan warfare. In May, a broad-based coalition government of national unity took power in the country. It signed a Western-brokered peace accord with the rebels in August and legislated guarantees of equal rights for Albanians in November, but tensions lingered nevertheless.

Macedonia's 200-member Jewish community spoke out for peace, sometimes in joint statements with other religious groups. In June, Macedonian Orthodox, Catholic, Jewish, Muslim, and Methodist leaders issued a statement expressing their "commitment to the One God for peace for our common country" and urging international support for concrete peace initiatives. It said, "Our churches and religious communities are not involved in the conflict, and we strongly reject any effort to allow ourselves to be involved and to be manipulated, as well as any misuse of religious symbols and language for the purposes of violence." It also condemned "the use of sacred places and buildings for military purposes, and their desecration and destruction [as well as] incidents of harassment of religious people." The statement—months in the making—was released at the close of a three-day meeting of Macedonian religious leaders organized in Switzerland by the World Congress of Churches.

In August, Macedonia's five official religious communities again expressed "joint concern" about the tense situation in their country despite cease fire initiatives, and "about the continuous threatening, damage and pillage of religious buildings—churches, monasteries and mosques."

Poland

Poland's economic growth, slowing nearly to a standstill, was estimated at just 1 percent for the year. More than three million people—a record high in postcommunist Poland—were out of work in November, reflecting a jobless rate of 16.8 percent.

A dominant theme through much of the year was a lacerating debate, carried out in the media, churches, public meetings, conferences, and other forums, over the Polish role in the Holocaust. The furor was sparked by the publication in 2000 of a book, *Neighbors,* by New York-based sociologist Jan T. Gross, which described the massacre of 1,600 Jews in the village of Jedwabne by local Polish Catholics in 1941 (see AJYB 2001, pp. 424–25). The exchanges were the freest, most open, and deepest exploration of Poland's responsibility in the Holocaust ever to take place, and they polarized the country. Several Web sites were devoted to the issue, including www.pogranicze.sejny.pl/english/jedwabne, which included a list of dozens of articles, in English, on the affair. A documentary about the massacre aired on Polish television in March.

In May, at a special prayer service at All Saints' Church in Warsaw, some 100 Roman Catholic bishops, led by the primate, Cardinal Jozef Glemp, apologized for the Jedwabne massacre and for all wrongs committed by Poles and Catholics against Jews. Rabbi Michael Schudrich of Warsaw was invited to the ceremony but did not attend as it coincided with the holiday of Shavuot.

"We want, as pastors of the Church in Poland, to stand in truth before God and people, but mainly before our Jewish brothers and sisters, referring with regret and repentance to the crime that in July 1941 took place in Jedwabne and in other places," said Bishop Stanislaw Gadecki, chair of the Polish church's council for dialogue with other religions. "Among the perpetrators [at Jedwabne] were also Poles and Catholics, baptized people," he went on. "We are in deep sorrow over the actions of those who over history, but particularly in Jedwabne and in other places, have inflicted suffering on Jews, and even death. We condemn all signs of intolerance, racism and anti-Semitism, which are sinful." Jews welcomed the unprecedented move, but rejected suggestions by Cardinal Glemp that Jews should apologize for the actions of Jewish communists who, Glemp charged, had persecuted Polish patriots after the war.

On July 10, 60 years to the day after the Jedwabne massacre, President Aleksander Kwasniewski and other top Polish leaders were joined by local officials, Jewish leaders, and relatives and descendants of the murdered Jews for a ceremony to unveil a new monument at the site of the slaughter. A smaller monument attributing the massacre to German Nazis was removed in March. Jews were unhappy with the inscription on the new monument: although it did remove reference to the perpetrators as having been German Nazis, it did not say who actually did the killing. In a speech at the July 10 ceremony, Kwasniewski apologized for the massacre and begged forgiveness from the victims and their families "in my own name, and in the name of those Poles whose conscience is shattered by that crime." The ceremony was preceded by a commemoration in the Warsaw synagogue on July 6, the 15th day of the Jewish month Tammuz, the *yahrzeit* (anniversary according to the Jewish calendar) of the slaughter. Jewish leaders said the synagogue ceremony was a "complement not a competition" to the official event.

Many people came to the July 10 ceremony from around Poland, but the local Jedwabne priest and other Roman Catholic officials were absent. Also, many Jedwabne villagers felt they had been unfairly stigmatized by the massacre revelations and stayed home. Opinion polls showed that about half of Poles refused to accept Polish responsibility for the killings. Jedwabne's mayor resigned in August because town councilors failed to support efforts to memorialize the massacre. In December, investigators from the Institute of National Remembrance looking into the Jedwabne massacre said they had uncovered evidence that local people perpetrated the killing without the active involvement of Nazi forces.

Another embarrassing revelation, albeit minor in comparison, occurred in March, when President Kwasniewski's top foreign-policy aide, Andrzej Majkowski, admitted he had taken part in the communist anti-

Semitic campaign of 1968. He apologized for his actions but rejected calls to quit his government post.

Poland held general elections in September. Voters frustrated with the country's poor economic performance ousted the rightist Solidarity bloc and restored the former communists to power, with Leszek Miller as prime minister. Miller's postcommunist Democratic Left Alliance (SLD) got about 41 percent of the vote. The liberal Civic Platform, founded earlier in the year, came in a distant second with about 12 percent. Neither the Solidarity bloc, which had headed the government for the previous four years, nor the Freedom Union, a liberal party friendly to Jewish interests, got enough votes even to get into the parliament. Three radical fringe groups, however, did do well enough to enter the parliament, picking up, together, more than a quarter of the votes. Self-Defense, the radical farmers' union, became the third force in parliament with more than 10 percent of the vote; the rightist Law and Justice party got 9 percent; and the extreme right and pro-Catholic League of Polish Families got 7.3 percent. The latter included individuals who had openly expressed anti-Semitism and were closely tied to the anti-Semitic Radio Maryja.

On the popular level, the sale and dissemination of anti-Semitic pamphlets and books aroused concern. In June, Jews in Warsaw complained about an anti-Semitic bookstore in the basement of All Saints' Church called Antyk—The Conservative Bookstore. Ironically, this was the same church where the Polish bishops had hosted the unprecedented service for contrition for sins against the Jews in May, and several of the anti-Semitic books on sale were sharp attacks on Jan T. Gross.

Gdansk priest Henryk Jankowski continued to demonstrate anti-Semitism. At Easter, he displayed a model of the barn in Jedwabne in which the local Jews were killed, along with the inscription: "The Jews killed Jesus and they are in the process of crucifying Poland." Senior church officials ordered him to remove the display and religious and civic leaders condemned Jankowski. In December, a court in the southwest city of Opole found former university professor Dariusz Ratajczak guilty of spreading Holocaust denial in a book, but the court waived punishment because of what it called "the negligible damage"—only 350 copies of the book were printed in 1999, and just five copies were now to be found on sale in bookshops. Ratajczak had already been suspended from teaching because of his publication.

In April Polish authorities ordered the closure of a controversial discotheque located near the Auschwitz camp on the site of a former tannery where slave laborers worked and died. Also in April, more than

1,000 teenagers from around the world came to Poland for the annual March of the Living Holocaust commemoration. During the trip, a group of 200 high school students from Florida and New Jersey took part in a new project aimed at fostering dialogue between Jewish and Polish teens. "The Next Generation: Strengthening Ties between Polish Society and the American Jewish Community" was devised by the American Jewish Committee in cooperation with the Polish embassy in Washington and the International March of the Living. It entailed face-to-face dialogue with Polish high school students and young leaders, based on a special curriculum about the Holocaust, anti-Semitism, contemporary Poland, and the ways in which Jews and Catholic Poles thought about each other. Its goal was to open contacts, break down stereotypes, and enable young Jews and Poles to commemorate the Shoah together and move forward with mutual understanding and respect.

In July, a Polish court sentenced Henryk Mania, 78, to eight years in prison for helping the Nazis kill Jews at Chelmno camp. In November, Polish researchers announced the discovery of mass graves at the Sobibor death camp, which was razed by the Nazis in 1943 after inmates staged an uprising. Some 250,000 people, most of them Jews, were believed to have died in the camp. About 50 people escaped and survived.

The International Auschwitz Council decided in September against a former Jewish prisoner's claim to a series of seven watercolor portraits of Roma (Gypsy) inmates she painted there, saying the portraits should remain in the Auschwitz museum. Dina Gottliebova painted the portraits on the orders of Josef Mengele in 1943 and 1944. All the people she painted were subsequently killed.

As every year, there were episodes of desecration of Jewish sites. In May, vandals wrecked about 30 tombstones at the Jewish cemetery at Oświęcim, the town were the Auschwitz camp was located. Among the vandalized tombs was that of Shimshon Klueger, the last Jew to live in the town, who died in 2000. Also in May, arsonists set a fire that caused minor damage to the museum at the former Majdanek camp near Lublin. In June anti-Semitic slogans were sprayed and axes stuck in a picture of Jesus Christ in the building next to the Auschwitz camp that at one time housed a controversial convent.

Jewish Community

Estimates of the number of Jews in Poland ranged widely, from the 7,000–8,000 officially registered with the community, belonging to Jewish organizations, or receiving aid from the JDC, to the 10,000–15,000 people of Jewish ancestry who showed interest in rediscovering their heritage, to as many as 30,000–40,000 people with some Jewish ancestry. The Lauder Foundation ran the country's most extensive Jewish educational programs, including a K–12 day school with more than 160 pupils. At a joyful ceremony in May, the school received a 120-year-old Torah scroll, originally from Poland, from the Ezra Academy of Woodbridge, Connecticut. The Joint Distribution Committee, which provided extensive social welfare aid, continued also to refocus activities on education and leadership training through the Pedagogical Center it ran in Warsaw. The Polish Jewish community expanded and upgraded its Web site, www.jewish.org.pl, to provide information about the community and news about cultural, religious, and other activities.

In the spring, a shipment of matzo and other Passover supplies was delayed for weeks because of the outbreak of foot-and-mouth disease in Europe, and only direct intervention by the offices of the president and the veterinary general of Poland enabled the goods to arrive in time for the holiday. Passover was celebrated with numerous communal seders in Poland that were run by local Jewish communities and the Lauder Foundation, which published a new guide to celebrating Passover, complete with recipes. In addition, the liberal Jewish group Bejt Warszawa brought American rabbi Cynthia Culpeper to lead a seder in Warsaw. During her ten-day stay, she led a discussion about her experiences as a woman rabbi and conducted a naming ceremony for the newborn daughter of Bejt Warszawa members. Culpeper returned in the fall for the High Holidays.

In the summer, Rabbi Josef Kanofsky took up the post of director of the Lauder Foundation in Poland, replacing Jonah Bookstein, who moved to the United States to continue his studies. Bookstein's wife, Rachel Steiner Bookstein, had also worked for the Lauder Foundation, in particular teaching about the role of women and the family in Judaism. In the fall, Ivan Caine, a Conservative rabbi, took up the post of rabbi in Wroclaw, where a nondenominational *havurah* had functioned since the early 1990s with equal participation by men and women. In September, Caine took part in the "march of silence" organized by Wroclaw officials to show solidarity with the American people after September 11.

The arrival of Caine meant that there were now four full-time rabbis in Poland, all Americans or American-trained. In addition to Kanofsky and Caine, Michael Schudrich served as rabbi of Warsaw and Lodz, and Rabbi Sacha Pecaric was the director of the Lauder Foundation's Kraków branch.

In December, at Hanukkah, Jerzy Kichler from Wroclaw was elected to a second term as president of the Union of Jewish Religious Communities in Poland at a meeting in Warsaw of 74 delegates representing eight organized Jewish communities around the country—Warsaw, Kraków, Lodz, Wroclaw, Katowice, Szczecin, Bielsko-Biala, and Legnica—and several smaller local branches. The delegates later took part in the opening of an exhibition on Warsaw's Jews, "Remembrance: Jewish Monuments in Warsaw," that was held in the city's Nozyk Synagogue as part of celebrations marking the synagogue's centennial year. Funded primarily by the Warsaw city government with additional funding from the JDC and private sources, the exhibit included contemporary images of Jewish sites as well as historic photographs of prewar Warsaw.

Nozyk was the only Warsaw synagogue that survived World War II. It was now used for services and formed part of a larger complex serving the Jewish community. It and another prewar building next door housed Jewish clubs, offices, meeting rooms, educational and welfare services, the Pedagogical Center, and kosher eating facilities. Another nearby building housed the Yiddish theater and a secular Yiddish cultural society.

Efforts at obtaining restitution of Jewish property seized during World War II inched forward. In July—mindful of the looming deadline of May 7, 2002, for filing restitution claims for Jewish communal property confiscated by the Nazis and nationalized by the postwar communist regime—Poland's Jews and the World Jewish Restitution Organization (WJRO) put aside their previous differences and resumed cooperation. At a meeting in Warsaw, the two agreed on a modified version of an agreement reached in June 2000 that had collapsed earlier in the year before it could be implemented. Claims for only a fraction of the estimated 4,000 communal sites had been filed, due to infighting between the two groups (see above, p. 59).

In March, the Sejm, the Polish parliament, approved a bill allowing partial compensation to people whose property had been seized by the communist regime from 1944 to 1962. Claimants had to have held Polish citizenship until the end of 1999, a requirement that disqualified some 40,000 people, mostly Holocaust survivors and their heirs who had left the country before that date. President Kwasniewski vetoed the bill, saying it was too expensive.

In June, Jewish leaders asked a state company in Bialystok to halt construction of an office building near the site of a 19th-century Jewish cemetery after about 250 bones and ten skulls were found. The cemetery, where cholera victims were buried in the 1830s, was razed under communist rule in the 1960s.

There were numerous Jewish cultural events, exhibits, educational and spiritual seminars, and conferences during the year. Poland was one of four countries with small Jewish populations chosen by the London-based Institute for Jewish Policy Research (JPR) for a "mapping of Jewish culture" survey. This was an attempt to chart all Jewish cultural events in Italy, Sweden, Belgium, and Poland during the twelve-month period from May 2000 through April 2001. Preliminary results, made public in July, indicated a total of more than 700 events in the four countries, including 196 individual events and seven Jewish culture festivals in Poland. The ratio of cultural events to Jewish population clearly showed that most of the target audience was not Jewish.

Warsaw hosted its first Jewish culture festival in June. It featured concerts, exhibitions, performances, films, lectures, workshops, and guided tours of Jewish historic sites, including the Warsaw Ghetto and the historic Jewish cemetery. The Lauder Foundation sponsored it, in cooperation with other organizations. In late June a Yiddish culture festival and music workshop took place in Sejny, northern Poland. The 11th Festival of Jewish Culture took place in early July in Kraków, and President Kwasniewski wrote the foreword to the souvenir program. An exhibit documenting Nazi persecution of Gypsies opened at Auschwitz in August. The fourth annual Jewish Book Days took place in Warsaw in September. Also in September, a Center for Jewish Studies was established at Maria Curie-Sklodowska University in Lublin. In Warsaw, the Lauder Foundation opened its Moses Schorr Interdisciplinary Center for Jewish Studies. In October, 40 Polish teachers and 40 Lithuanian teachers met for three days in Kraków to study the Holocaust, through an initiative of the London Jewish Cultural Center. Polish television aired a film in November on Polish-Jewish relations, telling the story of a rabid anti-Semite who found out that he was himself Jewish. In December, the Jewish Historical Institute in Warsaw organized a seminar for Polish teachers on the fate of Polish Jews during and after the Shoah.

During the year, Roman Polanski shot his new film, *The Pianist,* in Warsaw. Based on the book by Wladyslaw Szpilman, it recounts the author's survival in wartime Poland. *From Kristallnacht to Crystal Day: A Synagogue in Wroclaw Glows Again,* a documentary film by Ellen Friedland and Curt Fissel about the renewal of Jewish life in Poland, aired on

PBS nationwide in April. During the year, preparations continued for the establishment of a Museum of Polish Jewish History in Warsaw.

In February, the YIVO Institute for Jewish Research in New York awarded the Jan Karski and Pola Nirenska Prize to Maria and Kazimierz Piechotka, non-Jewish Polish architects renowned for their work in documenting Polish synagogues. In March, the Polish Council of Christians and Jews presented its annual "figure of reconciliation" award to the Israeli poet and author Halina Birenbaum, a child survivor of the Warsaw Ghetto, Majdanek, and Auschwitz, who lost all her family in the Shoah. Zygmunt Nissenbaum, a survivor of the Warsaw Ghetto who, in the 1980s, established a foundation to protect Jewish monuments in Poland, died in August at his home in Germany, aged 75.

Romania

The Romanian economy remained precarious, and at the end of May Prime Minister Adrian Nastase reported that nearly half of Romanians "live on the edge of poverty." He said that in the previous four years the number of people living below the poverty line had increased by 20 percent, and that the percentage of poor people in Romania was surpassed in Europe only by Albania, Russia, and Moldova.

In January, President Ion Iliescu joined Romanian Jews in a memorial ceremony at Bucharest's Choral Synagogue to mark the 60th anniversary of the torture and slaughter of Jews by the Romanian fascist Iron Guard during a failed coup against Romania's pro-Nazi military ruler Marshal Ion Antonescu that took place January 21–23, 1941. Antonescu crushed the rebels and then outlawed the Iron Guard. Iliescu said "one must not forget" what "delirium of intolerance and anti-Semitism" signifies for Romanian history. But other than that, he added, Romania had not contributed to the "long European history" of persecution of the Jews. He also called it "unjustified to attribute to Romania an artificially inflated number of [Jewish] victims for the sake of media impact." In a speech in April, Iliescu said Romanian society had "developed an immunity system against interethnic hatred, intolerance, xenophobia, extremism, anti-Semitism, and racism," and that Romanians were now "firmly convinced" that the existence of national minorities on their territory "is an advantage contributing to the enrichment and diversification of the national cultural and scientific heritage."

Nonetheless, there was concern throughout the year over right-wing nationalist extremism, manifestations of racism and anti-Semitism, and nostalgia for Antonescu's pro-Nazi World War II Romanian government. Romania was under particular scrutiny, since the Greater Romania Party (GRP), which considered Antonescu a hero, became the country's second-largest party in the 2000 elections, winning one-fourth of the seats in the chamber of deputies, the lower house of Parliament. GRP leader Corneliu Vadim Tudor, known for his anti-Jewish views, was defeated by Iliescu in a runoff presidential election in December 2000. Romania's quest for membership in NATO, many believed, could be hurt by the influence of political extremists on the government.

In January, a newspaper published a document from the communist Securitate secret police purporting to show that Teoctist, the Orthodox patriarch, had been a member of the fascist Iron Guard, participated in its attempted coup against Antonescu in January 1941, and helped burn down a synagogue in Iasi. The patriarchate described the document as "pure invention." The Securitate were known to falsify material in their files. Officials later called the accusations a "smear campaign."

Since the fall of communism, several pro-Antonescu groups and other organizations claiming to be successors of the Iron Guard had emerged. In the spring, two such groups, the Marshal Ion Antonescu League and the Marshal Antonescu Foundation, merged into a single body whose leadership included a former Iron Guard member and several fiercely anti-Semitic Holocaust deniers.

On several occasions, statues or plaques were planned or actually erected to honor Antonescu. In February, three American Jewish organizations—the American Jewish Committee, the Anti-Defamation League (ADL), and B'nai B'rith—wrote to President Iliescu protesting such efforts, specifically mentioning a decision by the Bacau municipality to erect a statue. They said they would like to support Romania's aspirations for membership in NATO but "for this to occur . . . Romania needs to make a clear break with the Antonescu legacy." The letter said that statues of Antonescu "as well as plaques and street-naming in his honor" were tantamount to "paying homage to one of the darkest periods in Romania's past." The ADL made another protest in the summer, after a bust of Antonescu was unveiled in a church courtyard in Bucharest.

In November, Romanian Jewish leaders praised Prime Minister Nastase for telling prefects around the country to drop any plans for statues honoring Antonescu and for releasing evidence that Antonescu had ordered the mass slaughter of Jews in occupied Odessa. During a visit to the United States in October, Nastase also pledged to curb the Antonescu cult—and was criticized for this in his country by right-wing media and politicians.

Anti-Semitic publications had been on the rise since the 2000 electoral success of the GRP. In May, the Supreme Court asked prosecutors to investigate the availability of Nazi and other anti-Semitic propaganda, including the *Protocols of the Elders of Zion*, at an international book fair in Bucharest. Also in May, the Hyperion publishing house in Cluj apologized for issuing a book containing jokes that belittled the Holocaust, and ordered any remaining copies to be withdrawn from sale, though most of the more-than 22,000 copies had already been sold. The book was written by a Cluj city councilor representing the GRP. The prosecutor general's office launched a criminal investigation against him for inciting racial hatred after Israel's ambassador to Romania, Avi Millo, complained about the book. Vadim Tudor, the GRP leader who himself had voiced anti-Semitic sentiments, issued a statement apologizing for the "macabre and inadmissible" publication.

In August, another book by a GRP lawmaker caused controversy. Following protests by Jewish, Roma, and ethnic Hungarian leaders, the prosecutor general's office launched an investigation into *The Nationalist* by parliament member Vlad Hogea. A statement by the Federation of Jewish Communities said the book constituted "a grave incitement to interethnic and racial hatred" in violation of the Romanian constitution's ban on anti-Semitic and racist material. Most of the essays in the book had been previously published in other anti-Semitic publications. *Greater Romania,* Tudor's magazine, violently attacked the Jewish community, saying its protests against Hogea's book were an attempt to stifle free speech.

Romania maintained close relations with Israel on various levels. There were thousands of Romanian guest workers in Israel. In May, two of them were killed and one injured in a Palestinian bomb attack. Israeli foreign minister, Shimon Peres, met with President Iliescu on December 4 in Bucharest. Peres, who also received an honorary doctorate from Bucharest University, called Iliescu "a great friend of the Jewish state" and said Romania had long played an important role in the search for peace in the Middle East. The day before he met with Peres, Iliescu released a statement condemning the terrorist attacks in Jerusalem and Haifa of December 2 and 3. But he also warned that Yasir Arafat must not be forced from the political scene.

During the year, Iliescu discussed the Middle East situation with other leaders from the region, including Egyptian president Hosni Mubarak who visited Romania in April. Prime Minister Nastase made an official visit to Israel in July.

JEWISH COMMUNITY

Between 11,000 and 16,000 Jews were believed to live in Romania, about half of them in Bucharest, the capital. Most Romanian Jews were elderly. Educational, religious, and welfare programs were carried out by the Federation of Romanian Jewish Communities (FEDROM), funded by the JDC. The Lauder Foundation ran the Lauder Reut Kindergarten and Lower School in Bucharest. The Jewish publishing house HaSefer issued books on Jewish themes, and a biweekly Jewish newspaper, *Realitatea Evreiasca,* included pages in Hebrew and English as well as Romanian.

The Israel-based Rabbi Menachem Hacohen commuted every few weeks to serve as Romania's senior rabbi. He was aided in Bucharest by Rabbi Eliezer Glantz, who served as the ritual slaughterer. Rabbi Ernst Neumann was based in Timisoara. During the year, FEDROM continued the groundbreaking youth, community development, and leadership-training programs it initiated in 2000. There were a number of seminars, including one in Bucharest in April to train 30 young people who showed leadership potential. Seven Romanian Jewish representatives attended the European Council of Jewish Communities general assembly in Spain at the end of May.

Research carried out in 2000 by Jodi Guralnick, the JDC's Ralph I. Goldman Fellow, set the stage for targeting programs to the "missing" middle generation of adults aged 30–60. These included clubs and cultural events, leadership-training and educational seminars, and the collection of names and addresses for a database. Paul Schwartz, appointed coordinator of middle-generation programs, personally visited 14 Jewish communities around the country, and contacted by phone and sent questionnaires to 45 communities in an effort to obtain necessary information for the database. Schwartz estimated that there were about 2,500 people in the middle generation. While most were formally affiliated with the community, few participated in Jewish activities. The first middle-generation clubs were set up in the summer in Bucharest, Timisoara, Cluj, and Oradea, with the help of the OTER network of youth clubs established little more than a year before.

As part of the community's youth educational programs, a pedagogical center in Bucharest was expanded, and educational materials were translated into Romanian and disseminated. About 150 households received their Jewish education through correspondence courses. There were also Jewish computer clubs in about a dozen communities, and several organizations set up new Web sites.

Despite these advances, it was evident that the communist-era mentality still lingered. In some communities, elderly communal leaders feared being displaced by younger activists. FEDROM's still highly centralized structure caused some provincial Jewish communities to demand more say in decision-making. Also, despite the new youth programs, most young Romanian Jews still appeared to want to leave the country, not only for economic reasons but also because of the upsurge in anti-Semitism and political extremism.

Numerous commemorative and cultural events took place during the year. In August, ceremonies were held to mark the centenary of the synagogue in Brasov, designed by the prolific Budapest architect Lipot Baumhorn, who designed more synagogues than any other architect in modern Europe. The centennial of the synagogue in Ploiesti was celebrated not long after; Israel's new ambassador, Sandu Mazor, who was born in Ploiesti, attended.

Zigu Ornea, a Jewish intellectual and the most prominent contemporary cultural historian of Romania, died on November 15 at the age of 71. The author of many books on 19th- and 20th-century Romanian political history and its impact on the country's cultural life, he was director of the HaSefer publishing house.

Slovakia

There was continuing concern throughout the year about racist violence and xenophobia, particularly against Roma.

In January, the publisher of the first Slovak translation of *Mein Kampf* was charged with support of a movement suppressing citizens' rights and freedoms. In April, police seized neo-Nazi CDs and memorabilia at a rock concert attended by more than 300 skinheads in western Slovakia. In September, People against Racism, a volunteer civic group, set up a telephone antiracism hot line that the victims of racially motivated attacks could call for legal and other advice. People against Racism marked the Day of Human Rights, December 10, by launching a campaign for tolerance.

There were episodes of vandalism against Jewish cemeteries, including that in Levice, where more than 50 tombstones were damaged. In July, vandals damaged or destroyed historic tombstones in Zvolen just two years after a major renovation of the cemetery. The attacks prompted Jewish leaders to call on local authorities for increased security.

Slovakia marked its first Holocaust remembrance day on September 9, the anniversary of the date in 1941 when the parliament of the pro-Nazi Slovak puppet state imposed the harsh anti-Semitic laws that preceded the deportation of Slovak Jews to death camps that began in March 1942. The fascist Slovak leadership paid the Nazis DM 500 in exchange for each expelled Jew and a promise that the deportees would never return to Slovakia. Some 57,000 were sent to their deaths.

A series of commemorative events took place around the country, attended by senior officials and a high-level Israeli delegation. Beginning September 6, there were memorial ceremonies, exhibits, publications, and a symposium on racist hatred in the past and the present. Avraham Burg, speaker of the Israeli Knesset, was guest of honor at a ceremony at the Museum of the National Uprising in Banska Bystrica, and in Bratislava Burg chaired an award ceremony for people who made a special contribution to the struggle against anti-Semitism. At another ceremony in Kremnica, at the site of a Jewish mass grave, President Rudolf Schuster said "the genocide of the Jewish people during World War II must be constantly remembered, because many people have started to underestimate" its extent and its lessons. He called for educational efforts to explain the Holocaust to young people and for tougher penalties for Holocaust denial and racial or religious bigotry. On November 8, the Slovak penal code was amended to make the denial of the Holocaust and belittling its crimes a punishable offense.

Slovak Jews were disappointed at the Slovak Catholic church's proposal to the Vatican that Bishop Jan Vojtassak be beatified. The Jews argued that the bishop, who served on the Slovak State Council during World War II and knew about plans to deport the Jews, had kept silent. A spokesman for the Confederation of Slovak Bishops rejected this, saying that Vojtassak had saved many Jews during the war and that testimonies of those rescued were attached to the beatification proposal. After World War II, the communist regime jailed Vojtassak for 12 years.

Filming began in the spring in Slovakia for an American miniseries on the Warsaw Ghetto uprising, starring Donald Sutherland and David Schwimmer.

Jewish Community

Fewer than 4,000 Jews were believed to live in Slovakia. The main communities were Bratislava and Kosice, in eastern Slovakia, each with about 500 Jews.

Work began in May on construction of a memorial to the 19th-century sage Chatam Sofer and 23 other important rabbis who were buried in an underground mausoleum in Bratislava. Bratislava city hall, the local Jewish community, and a U.S.-based cemetery restoration committee consisting of descendants and admirers of Chatam Sofer signed an agreement in 1999 to build the monument, and it was scheduled to open to the public in early December 2001. But disputes over money and planning delayed progress of the $1.5 million project, and construction, already behind schedule, was halted at the end of November.

On August 5 the Los Angeles-born scholar Shawn Landres married Zuzana Riemer in Kosice in an Orthodox ceremony that was the first full-scale, traditional Jewish wedding of a Kosice Jewish community member in decades. The congregation was bolstered by a visiting group of Hassidim from New York, and they took active part in the celebrations. London-based Rabbi Hershel Gluck, who for more than 20 years has traveled widely in Europe to promote Jewish revival, performed the ceremony, aided by Prof. Jonathan Webber, Landres's doctoral adviser at Oxford. (There was no resident rabbi in Kosice.) Webber explained each step of the ceremony to the congregation, as many members had little knowledge of traditional Jewish ritual.

Slovak Jews inched toward arrangements for Holocaust compensation. In March, a Berlin court rejected a multimillion-dollar lawsuit filed against Germany by Slovakia's Central Union of Jewish Religious Communities. Slovak Jews were seeking money the wartime Slovak government paid to Nazi Germany to deport Slovak Jews. In August, after two years of pressure from the Jewish community, the government of Slovakia agreed to set up a joint commission, consisting of ten government officials and ten Jewish representatives, to consider compensation for property confiscated by the Nazis. The Central Union said proceeds would be used for Jewish charities, social projects, and the maintenance of Jewish monuments. In December, the commission reached agreement on its agenda: resolving outstanding ownership questions, preparing a list of properties that could qualify for compensation, establishing a foundation to help maintain Jewish cultural heritage sites, compensating individuals, and financing projects to strengthen existing Jewish communities in Slovakia.

Slovenia

Slovenia's tiny Jewish community made great strides in 2001. The Jewish organization based in the capital, Ljubljana, had been weak and carried out practically no social, cultural or religious functions until the late

1990s, when a new, active leadership took over. With support from the JDC, the community obtained a meeting room in 1997 and ran programs, including a youth group, a women's group, and courses in Hebrew.

By 2001 membership in the community had doubled—to about 150. Jewish leaders were looking for bigger premises and hoped to found a real synagogue. Rabbi Ariel Haddad, an adherent of Chabad and director of the Jewish museum in Trieste, Italy—on the border with Slovenia about an hour's drive from Ljubljana—took up the position of Slovenia's chief rabbi in 1999. He went to Ljubljana about once a month to meet with local Jews, hold classes, and sometimes officiate at services.

The first organized community seder in Ljubljana took place in 2000, and Haddad brought all the kosher food with him from Trieste, already cooked. In 2001 about 100 people attended the seder in the downtown Hotel Union, which loaned the premises and kitchen for free. Haddad came a few days early and koshered the kitchen, so that all the cooking was done on site.

During the year, work began on a Slovenian translation of the Passover Haggadah.

Yugoslavia

Yugoslavia continued its difficult journey into the post-Milosevic era. President and strongman Slobodan Milosevic was ousted in October 2000, opening the door to democratic reforms and Yugoslavia's reentry into mainstream European life. On April 1, authorities arrested Milosevic after commandos stormed his compound, and at the end of June he was transferred to the UN War Crimes Tribunal in The Hague, where he was charged with crimes against humanity and violations of the laws and customs of war.

Yugoslavia's 3,000 Jews, about half of whom lived in Belgrade, were highly integrated, mostly secular, and often intermarried. They generally praised the policy of the new president, Vojislav Kostunica, on Jewish issues. He delighted the Jewish community in April by taking part in ceremonies in Belgrade's synagogue marking Holocaust Memorial Day. Other leading government figures also participated, along with the Israeli ambassador and representatives of Jewish communities. It was the first time a Yugoslav president attended such a ceremony.

Nonetheless, Jews reported an upsurge of anti-Semitic episodes after Kostunica took office. These included several offensive slogans and swastikas scrawled on city walls, and the vandalizing of Jewish memorial plaques in the towns of Kikinda and Zrenjanin. Gravestones in several Jewish cemeteries, including those of Zrenjanin, Belgrade, and Zemun, were also vandalized. A Belgrade theater that once housed a synagogue was defaced with swastika posters and Nazi graffiti in February, as was a building on the grounds of the Jewish cemetery and a culture center hosting an exhibit on Roma art. Among the many protests against those incidents, President Kostunica issued a public apology to the Jews and Roma in Yugoslavia. He blamed the vandalism on people who "wish to turn the wheels of history back to the dark ages."

Jews also reported receiving hate mail. Offensive propaganda and slogans appeared in books, pamphlets, and on the Internet, and some movements and individuals publicly accused Jews of being the enemies of the Serbian people. Despite this, there was some indication by the latter part of the year that anti-Semitic incidents were waning. A public-opinion poll at the end of the summer showed that 42 percent of respondents had a positive attitude toward Jews, 12 percent had a negative attitude, and 44 percent were undecided. Comparison with earlier surveys showed 21 percent with negative attitudes in 1994, 15 percent in 1996, and 10 percent in 2000.

Jewish leaders also slammed an attempt by far-right nationalist leader Vojislav Seselj and his extremist Radical Party to compare their position to that of Jews during the Holocaust. Aca Singer, president of the Federation of Yugoslav Jewish communities, protested an incident early in the year during which Seselj and other Radicals in the Serbian Parliament donned yellow armbands and claimed that they were "modern Jews" who were being threatened by the new post-Milosevic government.

In May, Klara Mandic, who founded the Serbian-Jewish Friendship Society in the 1980s, was murdered in her apartment. Besides being a prominent Jew, Mandic was politically close to both Milosevic and Bosnian Serb leader Radovan Karadzic, and there was speculation that politics or anti-Semitism had been behind her murder. Robbery, however, appeared to be the cause. Motives for an attack in May on another prominent Jewish woman, Mira Poljakovic, were less clear. Poljakovic, vice president of the Jewish community in Subotica, was beaten up on the street. Besides her position in the Jewish community, Poljakovic, a lawyer, was outspoken in her opposition to Milosevic and defended members of the anti-Milosevic youth movement, Otpor.

A war-damaged mosque in the Kosovo village of Shqiponje was repaired and rebuilt with funding from Jews, Catholics, and Muslims. Representatives of the JDC, which spearheaded the project, attended an ecumenical dedication ceremony in September together with the Muslim grand mufti and the Roman Catholic bishop. The restoration fell under the $2-million nonsectarian relief program in Kosovo that the JDC initiated in 1999 to aid the hundreds of thousands of refugees who returned to Kosovo after the end of hostilities. Funding came from individual donations to the special "mailbox for Kosovo" set up by JDC, through which it renovated 40 schools and established a psychology department at the University of Pristina, and, working together with ORT, sponsored numerous vocational-training courses.

In October, a foundation was established aimed at restoring and revitalizing the century-old synagogue in the town of Subotica in northern Yugoslavia. Called SOS Synagogue, the foundation included Jewish representatives and local political figures. It was headed by former Subotica mayor Jozsef Kasza, currently serving as deputy prime minister of Serbia. Though owned by the city, the synagogue was part of a complex of Jewish buildings that otherwise were still owned and used by the small but active local Jewish community. In Belgrade, the synagogue was restored during the summer and work progressed on organizing a kosher kitchen and restaurant. Five of Yugoslavia's nine Jewish communities offered Hebrew classes, there were many Jewish cultural activities, and major restoration and reorganization work was completed at the Jewish Historical Museum.

At the annual assembly in December of the Federation of Jewish Communities in Yugoslavia, several major challenges for Yugoslav Jews were discussed. These included the lack of funds that made "existential survival" problematic, the special hardships endured by the elderly—particularly Holocaust survivors on tiny fixed incomes—and the issue of property restitution. There were also calls for a reorganization of the federation. The welfare of the community was thought to depend largely on pending legislation, including proposed new laws governing national minorities, religious communities, and property restitution.

RUTH ELLEN GRUBER

Former Soviet Union

National Affairs

IN RUSSIA, PRESIDENT VLADIMIR PUTIN continued to consolidate his power by restoring Russia's role as an important actor in world affairs, appointing people loyal to him to key positions, and projecting an image of confidence, vigor, and honesty. In contrast, Ukrainian president Leonid Kuchma came under severe domestic criticism for ordering the arrest and, allegedly, even the murder of political rivals and investigative journalists, and for suppressing dissent—though both Russia and the United States shied away from criticizing Kuchma or modifying their relationships with Ukraine. Both presidents, Putin and Kuchma, continued to maintain cordial relations with their respective Jewish communities, paying careful attention, as well, to world Jewish organizations.

Russia benefited from OPEC's cut in oil production. While OPEC was cutting its production by 13 percent, Russia, the world's second largest oil producer, increased production by 7 percent, faster than any non-OPEC oil-producing country. Since oil and gas account for half of Russia's export earnings, the increase in sales had a direct and positive impact on the Russian economy. The resulting reduction in inflation and rise in the standard of living redounded to the political benefit of President Putin and his government. Nevertheless, some regions within Russia lagged far behind others in economic development. Ironically, despite the increased oil production, there were severe fuel shortages in Siberia and the Russian Far East. During one of the coldest winters in years, with temperatures dropping to as low as –58 degrees, many residents in those parts of the country were without heat, causing illness and death.

Despite the upturn, Russia faced serious economic challenges. The entire Russian budget for 2001 was $42 billion, and the nation owed $48 billion to Western creditor nations (the "Club of Paris"). But with a growth rate estimated at about 4 percent and with huge earnings from energy exports, Russia, for the first time in many years, was able to make payments on both principal and interest to her Western creditors. On the other hand, Ukraine, Georgia, and other former Soviet republics, as well as countries in Asia and Africa, owed Russia enormous amounts of money, primarily in payment for energy supplies.

President Putin, expressing satisfaction with the improving economy, nevertheless noted with regret that Russia's main source of income was still resource extraction, similar to the economies of the underdeveloped former colonies of Western countries and unlike the income sources of developed countries. Total stock market capitalization in Russia was about $50 billion, less than half of that of Nokia, the telecommunications manufacturer in neighboring Finland.

Putin continued to win political battles against his critics, particularly the "oligarchs" who had been favored by his predecessor, Boris Yeltsin. Vladimir Gusinsky, a media magnate who also served as president of the Russian Jewish Congress, lost control of NTV television, the network that had been the most critical and independent of the government. He also lost control of other media, including the magazine *Itogi* and the daily newspaper *Sevodnya*. Gazprom, Russia's largest company and the major producer of natural gas, controlled 46 percent of NTV. In May, Putin managed to replace 66-year-old Rem Vyakhirev as head of Gazprom. His successor, Aleksei Miller, 39, had worked as a deputy to Putin for five years in St. Petersburg and Moscow. The government secured a bare majority of the 11 seats on the board of Gazprom, effectively bringing this economic giant under its control.

In March, Putin replaced the defense and interior ministers. Military spending for 2001 was put at $8 billion out of a $42-billion national budget. Putin aimed to reduce this proportion and cut Russia's armed forces from about 1.2 million men and women to about 850,000, while at the same time improving conditions for them. It was well known that the Russian military was plagued by draft evasion, desertion, hazing, suicides, low morale, and even hunger, to the point where soldiers were stealing or begging for food.

The war in Chechnya continued. At least 40,000 regular army troops and a large contingent of internal-security forces were stationed there, but they still could not decisively defeat the Chechen forces. The Russian government admitted to about 3,000 dead and 8,000 wounded since the war had been renewed in the summer of 1999.

There were several Russian-American confrontations over spying, despite an overall cordial and even friendly relationship between the two countries. Edmond Pope, just the second American in 40 years to be convicted of espionage in Russia—U-2 spy-plane pilot Francis Gary Powers was the other—was released in December 2000. However, an American graduate student on the Fulbright Program, John Edward Tobin, was arrested on a minor drug charge in January and charged with espionage a month later. Tobin claimed that the Federal Security Bureau (FSB), successor to the Soviet-era KGB, had tried to recruit him as a spy, and when he refused he was accused of spying for the United States. After six months in jail and many representations by American officials, Tobin was released. But in March, the United States and Russia each expelled 50 of the other's diplomats on the grounds that they had engaged in activities incompatible with their official roles. Some speculated that the FSB was trying to slow or halt Russia's movement toward closer relations with the United States.

The Russian Orthodox Church continued its opposition to other Christian denominations, battling Catholic, Protestant, and Jehovah's Witnesses groups. The head of the Orthodox Church, Patriarch Aleksei II, protested against Pope John Paul's visit to Ukraine and instructed his followers to protest actively against it. Indeed, when the pope arrived in Ukraine in late June, followers of the Moscow-based Orthodox Church followed their leader's instruction and demonstrated. However, a breakaway Ukrainian Orthodox church, headed by Patriarch Filaret, enthusiastically greeted the pope, as did Greek Catholics and Roman Catholics, though the Kiev-based main Ukrainian Orthodox Church did not. While in Kiev, the pope visited Babi Yar, site of the murder of over 33,000 Jews by the Nazis in September 1941. He was accompanied by Ukraine's chief rabbi, the American-born Yaakov Bleich.

Journalist Georgy Gongadze, who had been investigating corruption in Ukraine, had disappeared in September 2000, and his headless body was discovered that November. A member of Ukrainian president Kuchma's bodyguard, Mykola Melnichenko, fled the country and was hiding in Western Europe when he released tapes implicating Kuchma in ordering political killings, including that of Gongadze. In January 2001, there were mass demonstrations, for and against Kuchma, in Kiev. On February 11, some 5,000 marchers there demanded Kuchma's resignation. The president denied the authenticity of the tapes and refused to resign. Instead, he dismissed two top intelligence officials. At the same time, Yulia Timoshenko, who had made a fortune in the gas business but had pledged, as deputy prime minister, to eliminate corruption in the energy sector, was arrested some time after her dismissal from her government post. Ironically, she was charged with corruption. Her former superior, Prime Minister Viktor Yushchenko, who had a reputation as an economic reformer and battler against corruption, was forced to resign on April 26, the 15th anniversary of the nuclear-power-station disaster at Chernobyl.

A coalition of communists, Kuchma supporters, and parties led by

Ukraine's business oligarchs voted to bring down the government. Anatoly Kinakh, a close ally of Kuchma and leader of the Union of Industrialists and Entrepreneurs, was appointed the new prime minister. It was widely noted that the presidential administration had become much larger than that of the prime minister and the cabinet, and that the president's office controlled a larger budget and supervised more of the law-enforcement functions.

Putin and Kuchma, meeting in February, agreed that Ukraine and Russia would reconnect their power grids and work on joint development of the Antonov-70 airliner. A mine explosion in Donetsk, eastern Ukraine, killed at least 36 miners, one of many accidents that continued to plague Ukraine's antiquated mining industry.

In Moldova, one of the smallest and poorest of the Soviet successor states, the Communist Party swept to an impressive victory in parliamentary elections, winning more than half the vote and 70 percent of the seats. It succeeded a Western-oriented government.

Israel and the Middle East

Russian government spokesmen consistently deplored the violence that had broken out in Israel and the territories, calling on both sides to show restraint. On January 23, President Putin hosted Israeli president Moshe Katzav at a state dinner in the Kremlin, having created a new kosher kitchen for the occasion that was supervised by the Chabad-Lubavitch rabbinate. President Katzav also visited Georgia, where he praised Georgian president Eduard Shevardnadze for facilitating Jewish emigration in the waning years of the USSR, when Shevardnadze was Soviet foreign minister, and for nurturing close ties between Georgia and Israel, where tens of thousands of Georgian Jews resided.

Israeli infrastructure minister Avigdor Lieberman, a native of Moldova, visited the Central Asian states of Kazakhstan and Kyrgyzstan in July to promote economic ties. The volume of Israel's trade with Kazakhstan, a very large country well endowed with natural resources, had doubled in 2000 to about $17 million.

About 1,500 young Jews from the states of the former Soviet Union participated in the Birthright Israel program that heavily subsidized two-week trips to Israel for those who had never been there before. This was double the number of FSU participants the previous year, and the jump was in sharp contrast to the diminished number of travelers from Western countries.

On October 4, a missile shot down a Sibir Airlines Tu-154 plane that was on its way from Israel to Siberia, carrying mostly Israelis who were former Soviet citizens. All 78 passengers died (66 of them were Israelis) as the plane crashed into the Black Sea. Ukrainian authorities at first denied any responsibility, but under Russian pressure, on October 13, the commander of the Ukrainian air-defense forces, Col. Gen. Vladimir Tkachov, admitted that the crash had been caused by an errant missile fired in a Ukrainian training exercise. The Ukrainian government issued an apology to Israel. (See below, pp. 594–95).

Anti-Semitism

On April 26, the Russian Duma—the lower house of the parliament—failed to pass a resolution appealing to President Putin to work against "all manifestations of anti-Semitism," since the proposal did not get a majority of all members. The resolution received 129 votes in favor, 17 against, and 303 deputies did not vote.

In June, 43 Jewish gravestones were desecrated in Velikie Luki, Pskov region. At the same time, a local Jewish community center there was vandalized. A similar incident occurred in August in the Siberian city of Krasnoyarsk, where 50 Jewish graves were daubed with swastikas. Swastikas were also painted on Moscow's Choral Synagogue in September. A fire destroyed the synagogue in Riazan on August 16, and arson was suspected. A Jewish school was destroyed by fire in Kazan, capital of Tatarstan, on July 13.

Holocaust-Related Developments

Kazys Gimzauskas, accused of participation in the killing of Jews in Vilnius during World War II, was convicted by a Lithuanian court on February 15, but was judged too ill to be imprisoned. The 93-year-old Gimzauskas had fled the United States for Lithuania in 1993, where no formal investigation was launched for the first three years of his residence in the country.

A Lithuanian state commission to commemorate the 60th anniversary of the Holocaust in Lithuania was formed. It planned to mark Holocaust Remembrance Day on September 23. Parliament passed a resolution condemning genocide and highlighting "the duty of the Lithuanian State to remind the country of its painful historical moments in order to avert the recurrence of the bloodshed of Holocaust victims." On March 26, Lithuania asked Great Britain to extradite Anton Gecas, an 85-year-old former commander of Lithuanian auxiliary police during World War II. On September 13, however, before any action was taken, Gecas died in Edinburgh, Scotland.

On May 29, a court in Melbourne, Australia, ruled that Konrad Kalejs, 88, could be extradited to Latvia to face charges of war crimes and genocide for his role in the persecution of Jews. Latvia had, up to then, never yet tried anyone suspected of war crimes. Kalejs, however, died before extradition could take place (see below, p. 497).

In June, officials of Russia's Fund for Mutual Understanding and Reconciliation began to distribute compensation to those who had been forced laborers under the Nazis and to about 16,000 survivors of concentration and extermination camps.

A scandal erupted in Ukraine in May, when workers from the Yad Vashem Institute in Jerusalem chiseled fragments from wall paintings by the Polish-Jewish writer and artist Bruno Schulz and spirited them out of the country to Israel. The paintings were on the walls of an apartment in Drohobych, where Schulz had been at first protected by a Nazi officer and then shot on a Drohobych street by a rival of that officer. These were the last known works by Schulz. Spokesmen for the local Jewish community and for the Ukrainian government both condemned Yad Vashem's actions. A furious debate followed, in the newspapers of Ukraine, Israel, Poland, and the United States, over who was the proper heir and custodian of artistic works created by Jews murdered in the Holocaust. Yad Vashem planned to exhibit the paintings in its projected new historical museum (see above, pp. 71–74).

JEWISH COMMUNITY

Emigration

Emigration from the FSU slowed in 2001 because of the deteriorating political and economic situation in Israel, the improving Russian economy, and the near shutdown of immigration to the United States after the September 11 attacks by Islamic terrorists on New York's World Trade Center and the Pentagon in Washington. In 2000, 50,859 immigrants from the FSU had come to Israel, but, from January through August 2001, only 21,015 made the move. Immigration to the United States declined from 4,862 in 2000 to 4,010 in 2001. After September 11, the American embassy in Moscow closed down its immigration service and the U.S. government made drastic cuts in government assistance to refugees. In October, not a single FSU immigrant arrived in the United States, and only 22 did so over the next two months. As a consequence of declining immigration in recent years, HIAS, the main Jewish immigration agency in the United States, had already cut its staff by nearly 40 percent, and Germany had replaced the U.S. as the second most popular destination, trailing only Israel, for those emigrating from the FSU.

It was noted that in the first five months of 2001, only 221 Jews had left the Jewish Autonomous Oblast (Birobidzhan) for Israel, compared with about 3,000 who had left in 1999 and 1,106 in 2000. This probably reflected both the depleted pool of potential emigrants as well as the perceived deterioration of Israel's economic and security situation.

The age structure of FSU immigrants to Israel remained quite stable. Slightly over 20 percent of them were under the age of 18, and about 13 percent were 65 or older. A quarter of the immigrants were between the ages of 18 and 32. The largest occupational category continued to be "engineers" (about 10 percent), and the next largest category (5 percent) were teachers.

Communal Affairs

Two changes occurred in rapid succession in the leadership of the Russian Jewish Congress (RJC), the largest national Jewish organization. On March 1, Vladimir Gusinsky, who had been the founding president of the RJC, resigned; he could no longer perform his duties since he was then living outside Russia. Leonid Nevzlin, 41, who was deputy chief of the Yukos Oil Company, replaced Gusinsky as interim president, and, in May, was elected president. In an interview with an Israeli Russian-language newspaper, Nevzlin stated that the RJC had spent more than $25 million since 1996, $7.5 million in the year 2000 alone. Nevzlin related that his first wife had been Jewish and his daughter by that marriage had attended a Moscow Jewish school, but that his present wife was a practicing member of the Russian Orthodox faith, and their daughter had been baptized (*Vesti,* June 7, 2001).

When, in December, Nevzlin was elected to the Russian Federation Council, the upper house of the Russian parliament, he resigned as RJC president since, he said, he could not devote sufficient time to the latter. He was succeeded by a businessman and long-time Jewish activist, Evgenyi Satanovsky, 47. Satanovsky was head of a business conglomerate called Ariel and had participated in the Va'ad, the first national Jewish organization established in the postcommunist USSR, in 1989. He had sponsored research and study about Israel and Jewish affairs in several institutions.

Since the FSU Jewish population was disproportionately elderly, the work of local welfare organizations, usually supported by the American Jewish Joint Distribution Committee (JDC), played a central role in communal life. A network of such organizations, usually called *hasadim* (plural of the Hebrew word *hesed,* meaning an act of kindness), had developed, with the local units providing medical and social services to Jews. In Simferopol in the Crimean region of Ukraine, for example, some 3,000 people benefited from "meals on wheels" delivered to the infirm and housebound; medical advice and care and physical rehabilitation; and "warm homes" in which holidays were celebrated and social gatherings held. The Hesed Shimon Society, named for Shimon Korotko, one of the founders, in 1989, of the Crimean Jewish Cultural Society, included several clubs, such as one for veterans and another for women—the latter linked to Kesher, an international Jewish women's organization. Hesed Shimon provided "warm homes" in the small towns of Armiansk, Dzhankoe (once the site of a Jewish collective farm), and Krasnogvardeiskii village. Larger towns and cities had more comprehensive and diversified *hasadim.*

In Moscow, work was said to have begun in February on a $5-million project to renovate the Choral Synagogue, built in 1886, and to renovate nearby buildings, in order to create a "Jewish campus" or "Jewish quarter" that would include a community center, Jewish schools, a Jewish bookstore, and a kosher restaurant. Indeed, by March, the synagogue dome and Magen David (Star of David) that had been removed in the late-19th century had been restored.

In Riga, Latvia, a Jewish community library was opened on June 4 in conjunction with the third reunion of Jews born in, or formerly residents of, Latvia, but now living elsewhere. The president of Latvia, Vaira Vike-Fraiberga, spoke to the gathering and assured these Jews that "Latvia is your homeland."

It was reported that the Jewish population of Bukhara, Uzbekistan, was now some 1,000–1,500, sharply down from about 20,000 in 1989, reflecting a general massive out-migration of Central Asian Jews. Many of them resettled in Israel and others in New York, where they created their own communities and associated institutions. The Chabad-Lubavitch Hassidic group, whose activities in Central Asia were funded in large part by Lev Leviev, a native of the area, was replacing traditional communal organizations in several cities. Critics of Chabad charged that it was using financial inducements to gain adherents and was replacing local traditions with Chabad practices, while others praised it for its willingness to serve a rapidly diminishing population.

President Putin sent greetings to Russia's Jews on the eve of Rosh Hashanah and mentioned what he saw as a religious revival among them, saying: "Many Jews [have] discovered the unique wealth of their national culture and religion." He pledged to fight anti-Semitism and assist in the further development of Jewish communities in the country.

A small statue commemorating the great Yiddish writer Sholem Aleichem was put up in Moscow at the corner of Bol'shaya Bronnaya and Mala Bronnaya streets. This location in the center of the city was where the State Yiddish Theater had stood from the 1920s until its forcible liquidation in 1948. It was also close to one of Moscow's few synagogues, a building constructed by Samuel Poliakov, one of Russia's richest Jews before the 1917 revolution.

Religion

The Reform (Progressive) movement claimed 15,000 members in its 40 FSU congregations, united under the organizational banner of the Religious Union for Progressive Jewish Congregations. There was, however, only one resident Reform rabbi in Ukraine, Alex Dukhovny, grandson of a Hassidic rebbe and a native of Ukraine, who trained for the rabbinate at the Leo Baeck College in London. A spokesman for the American Reform movement, Rabbi Ammiel Hirsch, announced that the movement would commit $1 million to the Reform congregations in the FSU, nearly half of which were in Ukraine. In Kiev, there were two Reform kindergartens with 100 children.

The Conservative movement sponsored six Sunday schools and one all-day school in Ukraine, but had no affiliated congregations or schools elsewhere in the FSU. Its school in Chernivtsi had an enrollment of 260 children, not all of whom were Jewish, in 11 grades. In February, the first Conservative congregation was registered in Ukraine, in the city of Uzhgorod in the Transcarpathian region. About 30 families were affiliated with the new congregation, and 45 children attended its Sunday school.

Chabad-Lubavitch, which enjoyed a high profile in most of the FSU, claimed 198 congregations and 54 rabbis, most of whom were citizens of the United States or Israel. It planned to spend $27 million on its activities during 2001. In an interview with an Israeli Russian-language newspaper, Rabbi Berel Lazar (Chabad), one of two "chief rabbis" of Russia, criticized the other, Adolf Shaevich, for having been too accommodating to the Soviet government in the 1980s. Lazar defended his own election as chief rabbi in 2000 on the grounds that Shaevich was too closely tied to Vladimir Gusinsky and that he had refused an invitation to meet with Jewish congregational leaders, who then elected Lazar as chief rabbi. Rabbi Lazar claimed there were 70 rabbis and ten yeshivahs in the FSU, the latter graduating 30 rabbis a year, but that most of them left the country, especially for New York, "where a million Russian Jews live" (*Luch,* Jan. 31, 2001). According to HIAS figures, however, in all of the United States there were only about 335,000 Jews who had immigrated from the FSU. In March, the Russian government dropped Rabbi Shaevich from the Presidential Council on Relations with Religious Organizations, and two months later Rabbi Lazar resigned from the board of the Russian Jewish Congress, on which Shaevich served.

In November, the Chabad-dominated Federation of Jewish Communities of Russia held its second national congress. According to the newspaper *Kommersant* (Nov. 20), 200 delegates from 135 communities attended (Chabad sources cited 400 delegates from 143 communities). The Russian minister of culture, Mikhail Shvidkoy, represented the government; Israeli ambassador Natan Meron also brought greetings; and the executive vice president of the Russian Jewish Congress attended and praised the federation's leadership.

There were reported to be 70 "messianic Jewish" congregations in Ukraine, with memberships ranging from ten to a thousand. Aleksander Lokshin, who had immigrated to the United States from Russia in 1992, headed an organization called Magen (shield), dedicated to combating missionary activity.

ZVI GITELMAN

Australia

National Affairs

AUSTRALIA ENTERED THE OFFICIAL BEGINNING of the 21st century amid anxiety about a predicted economic downturn and anticipation of an end-of-year election that threatened the continuation of the Liberal-National coalition government of Prime Minister John Howard, which had held power since 1996. The signs were not good for the prime minister early in the year, as the combination of an unpopular consumption tax, high fuel prices, and a record low value for the Australian dollar contributed to the government's shocking by-election loss in one of its safest seats. Looking every inch the prime-minister-in-waiting, opposition leader Kim Beazley of the Australian Labor Party (ALP) steered a cautious path, making his major policy initiative an ambitious educational program called "Knowledge Nation."

As time passed, the government seemed to regain some support when the consumption tax was simplified and the economy stabilized. Then came two unforeseen events: the *Tampa,* and September 11.

In July, the growing problem of illegal immigration was dramatically illustrated when a boatload of mainly Afghan refugees rescued by the Norwegian-registered cargo vessel MV *Tampa* was denied permission to seek asylum at the nearest Australian territory, Christmas Island. Australian navy personnel boarded the boat, and, after several days of standoff, the asylum-seekers were directed to a hastily improvised processing camp in Nauru, an independent country, with the expenses paid for by Australia. The government's firm stand caused consternation in some quarters, including Indonesia, from where the refugees had boarded their dilapidated vessel. But the great majority of Australians supported the decision to insist on an orderly refugee and asylum policy, and the government enjoyed a surge in popularity.

On September 11, Prime Minister Howard was in Washington, D.C. for a series of meetings when the hijacked planes hit the World Trade Center and the Pentagon killing thousands, several Australians among them.

Howard immediately voiced his full support for concerted international action to confront terrorism, and later, invoking the ANZUS Treaty (a 1952 mutual-security pact between Australia, New Zealand, and the U.S.), committed a substantial number of Australian troops to assist the U.S.-led operation in Afghanistan. Australia also continued to play a significant role in the naval blockade of Iraq. This tough stand solidified support for the government, and even though the opposition also supported the asylum-seeker and post-September-11 policies, on November 10 John Howard was comfortably reelected to a third term.

The election also capped a disastrous year for the far-right populist Pauline Hanson and her controversy-riddled party, One Nation. With Hanson outside Parliament, her party was beset by a lack of direction. It won three seats in the Queensland state election in February, a significant reduction from the 11 members elected in 1998. Legal action launched by the Australian Electoral Commission against Hanson and former One Nation director David Ettridge for fraud distracted the party in its preparations for the federal election in the fall. Amid the sense of crisis generated by September 11, the party was correctly perceived as irrelevant. Hanson and new recruit Graeme Campbell, a former Australian Labor Party MP and sympathizer with the far-right League of Rights, were high-profile Senate candidates in Queensland and Western Australia, respectively, but both fell well short of their goal. This left Senator Len Harris, elected in 1998, the party's sole representative in the Federal Parliament. Hanson subsequently resigned as leader of One Nation.

Australian army personnel continued their participation in the international peacekeeping force in East Timor as the fledgling state advanced towards independence, scheduled for May 2002. Relations with Indonesia improved marginally, although tensions arose with the new administration of Megawati Sukarnoputri over the issue of illegal asylum-seekers. Just as the government negotiated for the *Tampa* refugees to be taken for processing to a third country, Nauru, similar agreements were negotiated with other Pacific governments to house refugees on a temporary basis—a policy soon dubbed "the Pacific solution."

The Australian policy of mandatory detention in special centers of those arriving in the country illegally came under increasing fire from some quarters for excessive harshness. The government countered that maintaining the integrity of Australian borders necessitated a thorough and lengthy scrutiny of applicants both from a security standpoint and in terms of health, especially as many unauthorized arrivals had no documents. Riots and incidents of self-harm continued to bedevil the immigration-detention centers. Conditions at the Woomera facility in remote South Australia were the most heavily criticized.

Australia and Israel

Both the government and the opposition were largely supportive of Israel. Leading figures from both sides of the political divide decried the use of violence to achieve political goals, condemned Palestinian terror attacks, acknowledged the right of Israelis to live in peace and security, and bemoaned the opportunities passed up by Yasir Arafat and his repeated breaches of cease-fires. Prime Minister Howard described himself in Parliament in February as "a long-standing friend of Israel," adding, "I know there are many in the House who would be happy to carry that label." There was a successful delegation to Israel of five MPs from the opposition ALP in April, including four shadow ministers, led by Simon Crean (deputy ALP leader at the time, who became leader after the November election), as well as other political visits. Parliamentary Friends of Israel groups, federally and in Victoria and New South Wales, continued to flourish.

On the debit side, a solid core of backbenchers, as well as minor-party legislators, consistently condemned Israel. A report issued in September by the Joint Standing Committee on Foreign Affairs, Defense, and Trade on "Australia's Relations with the Middle East" gave cause for concern. The multiparty committee, whose membership included three shadow ministers, recommended "that all Australian political and official public statements condemning terrorism and violence in the context of the Middle East conflict continue to be framed in terms which clearly apply to *all* parties in the conflict." There were also many findings of "fact" in the main body of the report that upset supporters of Israel, and eight Liberal members of the committee released a dissenting minority report to correct them.

In the UN, Australia generally showed its sympathy for Israel, usually by abstaining on resolutions hostile to the Jewish state. At the August–September UN Durban Conference Against Racism, the Australian delegation conducted itself with distinction. After the early departure of the United States and Israel, it was generally the Australian delegation that spoke out in opposition to the anti-Israel and anti-Semitic resolutions that were advanced. John Dauth, Australia's ambassador to the UN, used a right of reply to point out that the declaration passed by the parallel NGO (nongovernmental organization) forum was unacceptable and a discredit to all those identified with it, as several sections were "deplorable" (see above, pp. 100–04). Australia boycotted the conference held in Geneva in December, where the contracting parties to the Fourth Geneva Convention met for the purpose of condemning Israel.

Media Bias

Significant elements of the Australian media continued to demonstrate bias against Israel, portraying it as the prime aggressor in the conflict with the Palestinians, or, at best, as being equally at fault. Often, these media neglected to provide the context necessary for a full understanding of events. The major electronic media used a preponderance of commentators and academics whose hostility to Israel was evident. A serious imbalance was evident in interviews, as pro-Israel interviewees were often subjected to a hostile pattern of questioning and badgering, while Palestinian representatives and their supporters were given considerably friendlier treatment.

There were many examples of such bias in the government-owned Australian Broadcasting Corporation (ABC). Its news program, covering the Israeli bombing of a building in August, said ". . . an Israeli attack on a Palestinian building left eight dead including two children," without mentioning that the building was a Hamas headquarters. Israel's targeted killings were generally described as "assassinations" (on one day, three separate ABC Radio reports referred to one instance as "murder"), while Palestinian terrorists were termed "militants," "extremists," "activists," or even "officials," but very rarely "terrorists." ABC's Middle East correspondent, Tim Palmer, had a way of repeatedly "spinning" the news to cast criticism on Israeli behavior.

Similarly, the Special Broadcasting Service (SBS), the multicultural network, in its television news and current-affairs programming, highlighted Israeli reactions to violence rather than the Palestinian attacks that caused them—at times not even mentioning the initial provocation. Longer in-depth pieces on the Middle East shown on both ABC and SBS almost invariably focused disproportionately on Palestinian suffering and one-sided attribution of blame to Israel. Philip Adams on ABC Radio responded to a comment by Professor Gerald Steinberg of Bar-Ilan University about "the language of hate" coming from mosques by angrily saying: "We also hear the language of hate from synagogues as well."

The Channel 9 Australian public-affairs program "Sixty Minutes" also caused concern. Reporter Richard Carleton, who had done something similar in reporting on the onset of the intifada in 2000, made inaccurate and provocative statements in a story about Israel and the territories, such as describing the West Bank as "Palestinian territory Israel has illegally occupied now for 34 years." In what was to have been an interview with Israeli foreign minister Shimon Peres, Carleton instead argued with Peres, telling him that Israel would regain the moral high ground if it "no longer occupied this country."

In the print media, one of the worst offenders continued to be the leading daily newspaper in the national capital, the *Canberra Times,* whose editorials and opinion pieces were overwhelmingly anti-Israel. There were problems with most of the other major newspapers as well. Two journalists who stood out for their informative and balanced work were Greg Sheridan, foreign editor of the *Australian Financial Review,* and Ross Dunn, Middle East correspondent for the Fairfax newspapers.

Anti-Semitism and Extremism

For all of 2001, the database of anti-Semitic incidents compiled by the Executive Council of Australian Jewry (ECAJ) recorded more than 30 reports per month of violence, vandalism, intimidation or harassment directed at Jewish community members and communal institutions, with synagogues being targeted more than in previous years. Incidents of assault, arson, and vandalism were up over 60 percent as compared to the average in recent years, and more than 10 percent above the previous record year, 1991, the year of the Gulf War. Threats by telephone, mail, leaflets, posters, or e-mail were more than 65 percent above average, and were at the second highest level since records began being collected.

Among the most disturbing incidents reported were:

- A series of firebomb attacks at a synagogue and community center, including one while people were inside;
- Assaults on young Jewish men, including one which resulted in the victim requiring serious surgery;
- Petrol bombs thrown into private homes of Jewish religious leaders;
- The smashing of windows at synagogues and other communal institutions through the use of heavy implements;
- Vandalizing of private Jewish homes and communal offices in three Australian states;

- Assaults on Jews on their way to or from synagogue, with eggs, rocks, bottles, or firecrackers being thrown;
- Jews in private vehicles being harassed, intimidated, and threatened by occupants of other vehicles with extreme anti-Semitic invective;
- Direct threats made by youths to Jewish schoolchildren and officials of communal organizations; and
- Harassment of Jewish participants in public forums.

Extremist Groups

Extremist and anti-Semitic groups in Australia varied greatly in their memberships, activities, and target audiences. Most of the better-known Australian groups maintained links with foreign extremists such as militia movements in the U.S., Christian Identity churches, the Lyndon LaRouche organization, various groups of conspiracy theorists, the Australian League of Rights, and others.

In 1996, the ECAJ had lodged a complaint with the Human Rights and Equal Opportunity Commission about the content of the Internet site of the Adelaide Institute—a small organization devoted to Holocaust denial run by Dr. Frederick Toben. More complaints about the site from other Jewish organizations continued to accumulate, and, in October 2001, the hearing commissioner released her findings. She concluded that material on the Web site contained insulting expressions in relation to Jews and the Holocaust that were clearly intended to be offensive and intimidating, and that caused offence and anxiety. Furthermore, she noted, none of the material on the Adelaide Institute site was historically, intellectually, or scientifically persuasive.

The commission found that Fredrick Toben had engaged in unlawful conduct and ordered him to "remove the contents of the Adelaide Institute Web site from the World Wide Web and not republish the content of that Web site in public elsewhere." Toben was also required to make a public apology and publish it on the World Wide Web, and to undertake not to "publish any such material in the future."

The Australian League of Rights, described by the Human Rights and Equal Opportunity Commission as "undoubtedly the most influential and effective, as well as the best organized and most substantially financed, racist organization in Australia," continued to hold meetings, conduct action campaigns, and seek publicity for its anti-Semitic perspective on domestic and international affairs. With founder Eric Butler now retired and in failing health, the league, under director Betty Luks, published its weekly newsletters, monthly magazines, and a quarterly journal, and maintained its Web site.

As in years past, the Citizens Electoral Councils (CEC) distributed large quantities of literature reflecting the views of their mentor, Lyndon LaRouche. These included bizarre and offensive anti-Semitic conspiracy theories targeting Jewish and other antiracist organizations in Australia. Beside mass mailings, another common tactic was handing out pamphlets and magazines to unsuspecting citizens in shopping areas commonly frequented by Jews. CEC was particularly active in campaigning (unsuccessfully) against legislation passed by the state of Victoria outlawing the incitement and perpetration of racially motivated violence. Throughout the year, Jewish leaders in Victoria, Western Australia, and New South Wales complained about CEC activities. The CEC also established a new political party, the Curtin Labor Alliance, in an attempt to attract votes away from the Labor Party in the 2001 federal election. Leading Labor figures condemned the move, using the opportunity to highlight the dangers of the LaRouche cult.

Small neo-Nazi groups, such as the Sydney-based Southern Cross Hammer Skinheads and their Melbourne counterpart, Blood and Honour, made their presence felt primarily through the Internet. The largest neo-Nazi group was the Adelaide-based National Action. Its leader, Michael Brander, claimed on his Web site that he was being persecuted "because he states that he does not think that the plan to exterminate Europe's Jews in the Second World War is proven." Brander sued a journalist who called him a racist for defamation, but the Adelaide magistrate threw out his case, noting that "denial of the Holocaust and failure to condemn the principles espoused by Adolf Hitler and the Nazi party" were proof of his racism.

The deceptively named Australian Civil Liberties Union (ACLU) continued to advocate Holocaust denial, with most of the group's public announcements aimed at protecting the "rights" of Holocaust deniers and other extremists. *Your Rights 2001* was the 27th annual edition of the ACLU's handbook. Various editions of the book had attacked multiculturalism and Asian immigration, promoted the likes of Pauline Hanson and Fredrick Toben, and strongly criticized a range of behaviors that the ACLU attributed to the Jewish community.

Nazi War Criminals

The major war-crimes case in Australia in 2001 was that of Konrad Kalejs. A Latvian-born Australian citizen, Kalejs had been deported from the U.S. and Canada for his involvement in Nazi crimes, fled to Great Britain, and, after being exposed by the media there, arrived back in Australia in December 1999. Australian authorities arrested Kalejs in December 2000 following an extradition request from the government of Latvia. At the initial hearing of the request in May 2001, a magistrate found that Kalejs should be extradited, as all the formalities had been observed and the request was genuinely for the stated purpose. In the course of her judgment, the magistrate said, "It seems to me that the lapse of time means little given the offences for which extradition is sought." Kalejs appealed both against the magistrate's decision and against the initial decision of the minister for justice to allow extradition proceedings. The appeal against the minister for justice was heard in September, with the judge reserving decision. Kalejs, however, died on November 8.

Another prominent suspect living in Australia, Antanas Gudelis, had been under investigation by Lithuanian authorities since 1999, but he died in August, though the fact was not revealed until September 12.

JEWISH COMMUNITY

Demography

The Australian Jewish community continued to grow through immigration, particularly from South Africa and the former Soviet Union (FSU). The total number of Jews was between 110,000 and 125,000 out of a total population of some 19 million. There were probably hundreds of thousands of other Australians who had some ancestral relationship with the Jewish community, largely due to the predominantly male Jewish immigration in the first century of European colonization. Of Jews born overseas, South African Jews were the largest group, followed by natives of Poland, Russia, Hungary, and Germany. Losses attributable to aliyah and a low birthrate were more than compensated for by immigration. The Jewish community was still heavily concentrated in Melbourne and Sydney, with the Brisbane-Gold Coast area growing steadily.

Census figures—which were approximate, since answering questions on religion was not compulsory—indicated that 15–20 percent of married Jewish men and women had non-Jewish spouses in 2001, though anecdotal evidence suggested a considerably higher figure. Compared to members of other religions, Jewish Australians were more likely to marry and to do so at a later age, and they were less likely to cohabit without marriage. The Jewish community included a disproportionately high percentage of elderly people.

There were 14,000–20,000 Jews from the former Soviet Union in Australia, most of them living in Sydney and Melbourne. Australia's Jewish community had received, per capita, more immigrants from the FSU than even Israel, at least double the proportion received by the U.S., and seven times the number that went to Canada. Despite the assistance provided by local communities, particularly on the arrival of these Jews in the country, communal leadership remained concerned that, while these newcomers were integrating well into Australian society, they were not similarly integrating into the Jewish community.

Communal Affairs

Jeremy Jones was elected executive vice president of the Executive Council of Australian Jewry (ECAJ), the most important Jewish representative body in the country, succeeding Nina Bassat. Ron Weiser continued as president of the Zionist Federation of Australia, and Stanley Roth became federal president of the United Israel Appeal. Mark Leibler remained national chairman of the Australia/Israel and Jewish Affairs Council (AIJAC), which continued its close association with the American Jewish Committee, and Dr. Colin Rubenstein continued as its executive director.

Education

More than half of all Jewish children aged 4–18—including almost 70 percent of those aged 4–12—received full-time Jewish education in the 19 Jewish day schools in Australia. Spanning the religious spectrum, these schools continued to rank at the highest level for academic achievement. This reflected the community's major investment in the schools as a means of preserving Jewish continuity. Day-school enrollments continued to grow, despite ongoing concerns over high costs and the challenge to the community to find new sources of funding.

There was an increased emphasis on adult education, largely under the influence of the Melton Program, which had nearly 500 students in Sydney and Melbourne. Short-term courses utilizing guest lecturers also proved popular. Top priorities for the future, according to Australian Jewish educators, were expanded Jewish studies on the university level and teacher education to provide quality faculty for the day schools.

Interfaith Dialogue

The Australian Jewish community maintained interfaith dialogue on a number of levels. During 2001, the ECAJ participated in two national dialogues, one with representatives of the Uniting Church in Australia, and the other its annual dialogue with the Australian Catholic Bishops' Conference. The ECAJ, its affiliates, and a number of senior rabbis participated in the activities of the World Conference on Religion and Peace, and members of the Jewish community around Australia participated in local councils of Christians and Jews.

Jeremy Jones continued as chair of the Advisory Group of Faith Communities on Aboriginal Reconciliation, a body that brings together leaders of a number of Christian denominations, Buddhists, Muslims, Jews, Hindus, and Baha'is on a regular basis to coordinate activities against racism and on behalf of indigenous Australians.

While there was no formal dialogue program with Muslim bodies during 2001, after September 11, the ECAJ, the National Council of Churches of Australia, and the Australian Federation of Islamic Councils issued a joint statement. Also, there were a number of public activities in which Jews, Muslims, and others worked together.

Culture

Australian Jews played a significant role in the artistic and cultural life of the country. An example was the one-act multimedia production, *And Then They Came for Me—Remembering the World of Anne Frank.* Directed by Ira Hal Seidenstein, it related the story of Anne Frank and her family through the reminiscences of two survivors who knew Anne during the Nazi occupation of Holland. Two important books by Jewish Australians were Arnold Zable's highly acclaimed *Café Scheherazade,* and Diane Armstrong's *The Voyage of Their Life: The Story of the SS Derna and Its Passengers,* which charted the journey of a ship that carried Jewish Holocaust-survivor emigrés from Marseilles to Australia. An acclaimed contribution to literature on the Holocaust was Ruth Wajnryb's

The Silence: How Tragedy Speaks, an examination of the linguistic practices of victims of trauma, based upon the experiences of the children of Holocaust survivors.

The Sydney Jewish Museum continued its tradition of providing valuable contributions to Jewish cultural life and to the wider community with its exhibition, Crossroads: Shanghai and the Jews in China. The city of Shanghai provided a safe haven for 18,000 Jews fleeing Nazi Germany and Austria in November 1938. A decade later, 2,500 of these Jews made it to Australia, and the exhibition documented their experiences. The Melbourne Jewish Museum similarly maintained its high standards of exhibition, and also organized guided tours of areas of significance to the history of Jews in the city.

Personalia

Several members of the Jewish community received commendations on the Queen's Birthday Honor Roll in 2001. David Baffsky, industry leader and philanthropist, Jeffrey Mahemoff, a former Bialik College president, and Dr. Paul Zimmet, a specialist in the treatment of diabetes, were all inducted into the Officers of the Order of Australia. Other honors went to Prof. Michael Besser (AM), for service to medicine as a clinician, teacher, and administrator; Prof. Fred Ehrlich, for work on rehabilitation and care for the aged and people with disabilities, and for community service; Rabbi David Rogut of North Shore Synagogue, for his service to the Jewish community and education; Estelle Gold, for 51 years of work with meals-on-wheels and the National Council of Jewish Women; Cecile Herman, for 34 years of service to the community through meals-on-wheels and her association with the Benevolent Society; Dr. Peter Sheridan for his service to the community through providing access to information resources for those stricken with multiple sclerosis; and Steven Rich, for services provided to the development of Papua New Guinea and as deputy chairman of the Salvation Army for 25 years.

The following were made Members of the Order of Australia: Israel Herzog, for his service to the Jews of Victoria; Dr. Geoffrey Metz for his involvement with the Royal Australasian College of Physicians; Leon Mow for his support for the International Diabetes Institute and other research institutes; Jacob Kronhill, awarded posthumously, for outreach for cancer patients as well as his work in human rights and aboriginal reconciliation; and Harvey Shaw, the former president of the Federation of Jewish Ex-Servicemen and Women.

Dr. Bryan Gaensler, 27 years old, became the youngest person ever called upon to deliver the national Australia Day address. He used the opportunity publicly to embrace his dual heritage—Jewish and Australian.

Australia and the wider Jewish community mourned the death of longtime Jewish community activist and businessman Paul Alexander Morawetz; ophthalmologist Dr. Reuben Hertzberg; anti-Hitler resistance fighter and academic Dr. Ruth Blatt; art lover Adrian Rawlins; philanthropist Ernest Lunzer; food-technology pioneer Fritz Reuter; and Holocaust survivor and Yiddish intellectual Wolf Besser.

COLIN L. RUBENSTEIN

South Africa

National Affairs

NOTWITHSTANDING A DECREASING budget deficit, growing exports, and progress in housing, schooling, health clinics, and other social programs, the government, led by the African National Congress (ANC), faced growing criticism. Complaints focused on its handling of the crisis in Zimbabwe, its floundering HIV/AIDS policy, apparent irregularities in arms dealings, and the slow pace of economic privatization.

Taking into consideration the global economic slowdown and the effects of the terrorist attacks in the U.S., the economy performed well, growing at nearly 2 percent. However, the value of the currency declined precipitously in the last three months of the year, with the rand falling by 25 percent against the U.S. dollar, ending the year 37 percent down, as inflation increased to 10 percent. The sudden, massive decline in the value of the rand sparked accusations of "sinister practices" from the head of the South African Chamber of Business, Kevin Wakeford. A Commission of Inquiry into the Rapid Depreciation of the Exchange Rate of the Rand and Related Matters, under John Myburgh, was established in December to determine what caused the free fall.

President Thabo Mbeki devoted considerable energy to regional problems, including ongoing instability in the Democratic Republic of the Congo (DRC), Burundi, and Zimbabwe. Within the framework of the African Renaissance—a high-priority project of President Mbeki—the New Partnership for African Development (NEPAD) was established, its executive headquarters to be located in South Africa. NEPAD was to make the international community aware of world poverty and of the need to reform multilateral institutions so as to deal with it.

Rampant crime, the need for job creation, and extensive corruption in official circles remained important issues on the government agenda. The ANC chief whip in the National Assembly, Tony Yengeni, was charged with accepting a special deal on a vehicle for his own use from a company that was bidding on contracts to provide arms to South Africa. A special report drawn up by the South African Medical Research Council (MRC) described the scourge of HIV/AIDS in the country as a "plague of biblical proportions." HIV infections had increased from 1 percent of the population in 1990 to almost 25 percent a decade later, and the pandemic was expected to kill an estimated five-to-seven million people by 2010. MRC president William Makgoba said that there was "no greater threat to the African Renaissance than the spectre of HIV/AIDS in South Africa." Professor Barry Schoub, an epidemiologist, told the 41st National Congress of the South African Jewish Board of Deputies (SAJBOD) in Johannesburg in August: "Until recently it was perceived that HIV/AIDS did not effect the Jewish community. Gradually and progressively, the Jewish community has been touched more by this pandemic."

The New National Party (NNP) withdrew from the opposition Democratic Alliance (DA) in October, resulting in the DA losing political control of the Western Cape province. NNP leader Martinus van Schalkwyk announced that his party would be working with the ANC in the interest of nation-building and reconciliation.

Issues of race and the legacy of apartheid remained. Over 30 percent of the labor force was unemployed and the distribution of wealth was hardly changed, despite the emergence of a black middle class in the cities.

At the end of August, the South African government hosted the United Nations World Conference Against Racism, Racial Discrimination, Xenophobia and Related Intolerance (WCAR) in Durban (see above, pp. 85–111). As predicted by Helen Suzman, the liberal veteran of South African politics, the anti-Israel lobby hijacked the occasion, turning it into an anti-Zionist fiasco and a "waste of time."

The South African government, which did its best to keep the meeting on track, made no public expression of empathy with the Jews' sense of vulnerability at the conference. Nonetheless, shortly afterwards President Mbeki delivered his message of goodwill on the occasion of the Jewish New Year, praising the SAJBOD for having adopted the theme "South Africa—Ikhaya—Our Home" at their national conference in August. "Clearly," he went on, "Jewish South Africans have taken their place in the South African nation, secure in their religious and cultural practices" (*SA Jewish Report,* Sept. 28).

South Africans on the whole shared in the trauma of Americans in the wake of the September 11 attacks. President Mbeki responded unequivocally, acknowledging the right of the United States to act in self-defense under Article 51 of the UN Charter. South Africa offered nonmilitary cooperation, a decision praised by the chairman of the Muslim Judicial Council (MJC), Sheikh Ebrahim Gabriels. However the U.S.-led military operations in Afghanistan provoked substantial anti-American feeling, including marches against the American embassies in Pretoria and Cape Town. There was sympathy for Osama bin Laden in certain Muslim circles as well as reports of young Muslims planning to join the Taliban resistance. Achmat Cassiem, leader of the radical Muslim movement Qibla, called on Muslims to respond to the call of jihad (*Sunday Times,* Oct. 14).

Israel-Related Activity

In January, Tova Herzl took up her position as Israeli ambassador to South Africa. Ms. Herzl spent her formative years in South Africa where her father was director of the board of Jewish education and spiritual leader of the Rondebosch Hebrew Congregation, both in Cape Town. Tova Herzl attended Herzlia High School and obtained a B.A. from the University of Cape Town. Discussing her new position, Herzl said she would concentrate on areas of mutual interest between South Africa and Israel, "what we have in common rather than what divides us." In particular she wanted to bring tolerance and understanding to the Middle East conflict. "The big challenge for me and for you," she told a Zionist welcoming function in Cape Town, "is to show that Israel has a viewpoint, that in the Middle East there are two sides to the story."

Speaking at the annual meeting of the South Africa-Israel Chamber of Commerce, Tito Mboweni, governor of the South African Reserve Bank, expressed hope that trade between the two countries would continue to grow. South Africa's exports to Israel rose by 4.2 percent in 2000. Coal, diamonds, base metals, and agricultural products made up the bulk of the exports. South Africa, in turn, imported mainly machinery and electrical equipment from Israel. The acquisition of high-tech equipment from Israel grew by 21 percent from 1999 to 2000. South Africa, according to the governor, was running a trade surplus with Israel of about 19 percent. Israeli companies continued to invest in South Africa, mainly in telecommunications, chemicals, and agricultural equipment. A report in November from the Israel Trade Center claimed that trade between South Africa and Israel was worth $500 billion.

In February, after the election of Ariel Sharon as Israel's prime minister, the *SA Jewish Report* (Feb. 9) noted editorially that his success was "largely a consequence of Palestinian violence and rejectionism." In the newspaper's view, "Israelis should not be demonized because they chose

Sharon in response to the aggressive war they have been subjected to over the past few months. . . . South African President Thabo Mbeki and the ANC—with their longstanding close links to the Palestinian leadership—will have to decide how to respond to Israel's new political leadership. By displaying the appropriate understanding of Israel's position, and not only that of the Palestinians, they could potentially play a constructive role in the search for peace."

South African Jews maintained ongoing contacts with Israel. The community introduced the Na'aleh program, which allowed children to complete the final two or three years of high school in Israel. Fourteen teenagers signed up. The program, initiated in the former Soviet Union, was based on the idea that parents will follow their children to settle in Israel. A solidarity mission of Jewish leaders visited Israel in April. Three months later the Southern African Rabbinical Association held its annual conference in Israel as another mark of solidarity with the Jewish state. To bring rural South African Jews in touch with events in Israel, the SAJBOD and the South African Zionist Federation (SAZF) brought speakers to visit small towns. The South African Union of Jewish Students (SAUJS), together with the international organization Birthright Israel, gave 100 students the opportunity to visit Israel at no personal cost. In June, an Israel Action Committee (IAC) was established in Johannesburg under the auspices of Rabbi Raphael Katz. This was a project of the Tzeirei Tzion Shul of Yeshivah College Johannesburg, and the SAZF.

Yossi Beilin, the former Israeli cabinet minister, visited South Africa as a guest of the labor Zionist group Habonim Dror, which celebrated its 70th anniversary. Beilin told the gathering that peace would require the dismantling of the settlements, and he called their construction Israel's biggest mistake since 1967.

Although 5,000 Jews attended Israel Independence Day events in Johannesburg and 4,000 gathered to celebrate in Cape Town, the *SA Jewish Report* wrote of declining Zionist passion among South African Jews. In an article commenting on Israeli prime minister Sharon's observation that Argentina and South Africa were ideal sources for a new wave of immigration, the paper, in its May 5 edition, lamented the weakening of Zionism in South Africa:

> Anyone who remembers the powerful role that Zionism played in this community 30 years ago, and the enormous influence of Zionist youth movements like Habonim and Betar on young people's lives, can hardly fail to be saddened at how things have changed.
>
> A significant percentage of SA Jews still pay lip-service to support

> for Israel, notwithstanding the fact that another significant proportion of the community refuses to support the Jewish state for religious reasons.
>
> But the truth is that aside from a trickle, Jews who are emigrating from South Africa are not going to Israel, but to Australia, Canada and other Western countries.

David Saks, senior researcher at the SAJBOD, disagreed, noting the successful Independence Day celebrations and a slight uptick in South African aliyah during 2000. However, Rabbi Ben Isaacson, speaking in Johannesburg in June, noted a decline in Zionist commitment within South African Jewry, evident in the second-fiddle role that the South African Zionist Federation (SAZF) played in communal affairs. Isaacson pointed to the seeming paradox of a huge increase in Torah observance among South African Jews at the same time that identification with Israel was decreasing.

In May, Yasir Arafat attended the meeting of the Nonaligned Movement (NAM) held in Pretoria. He told the gathering that the Palestinian people had decided "not to walk away from the peace process under any circumstances" and that he accepted Egyptian-Jordanian peace proposals. In turn, President Mbeki called for the logjam between the Israelis and Palestinians to be broken. The situation, he noted, was "very grave." NAM remained committed to an independent Palestinian state, and Aziz Pahad, the deputy foreign minister, said that South Africa supported the peace effort. In a separate arrangement, South African and Palestinian representatives signed an agreement to train Palestinian doctors. "The agreement will also assist in developing technical assistance and build institutional capacity of the ministries of health from both countries," was the way a South African spokesman explained the initiative.

Jewish reaction to Arafat's comments at the NAM conference was mixed. According to Tova Herzl, Arafat's actions would be more important than his words. She contended that South Africa, with its moral authority, could play a constructive role and was, indeed, already doing so: "South Africa has been making an active effort to tone down the rhetoric and we really do appreciate it," she said. In contrast, Kenny Katz, chairman of the SAZF, argued that Arafat was only going through the motions of peace. He believed Sharon was handling the situation correctly and expressed disappointment with Mbeki.

Durban Conference

Well before the World Conference Against Racism was to convene in Durban, leaders of the South African Jewish community warned that it would be—in the words of the *SA Jewish Report*—"A Jamboree of Hypocrisy." Shortly before the conference, the SAJBOD lodged a strongly worded complaint with the South African Nongovernmental Organization Coalition, the official coordinating body of South African NGOs, after several of its representatives visited the Palestinian territories in early July on a "fact-finding mission" as guests of a pro-Palestinian group. These visitors, who declined to meet with Israeli officials, afterward publicly attacked Israel, despite lacking the legal right to make political statements on behalf of all South African NGOs.

The week before the opening of the conference, South African Jewry got a taste of what to expect as some 15,000 Muslims marched through Cape Town to the Parliament, bringing the city to a halt. They were protesting what they termed atrocities that Israel committed against the Palestinians. The marchers carried banners proclaiming Zionism a form of racism, condemning Sharon as a war criminal, and lauding Hamas. Sheik Achmat Sedick, secretary general of the Muslim Judicial Council (MJC), appealed to the government to "take immediate action against Israel by breaking off all diplomatic and trade relations."

The biennial general meeting of the Israel United Appeal-United Communal Fund (IUA-UCF) was in session at the time, and Judge Richard Goldstone sought to calm the delegates. Noting that the demonstrators were "only a very small percentage of our population," he remarked that "Islam has not become attractive in southern Africa—there's no mosque in any township that I'm aware of. Our constitution outlaws hate speech, the government doesn't tolerate racism and I don't believe it to be a serious threat to the integrity and security of the Jewish community" (*SA Jewish Report,* Aug. 24).

Predictably, the NGO Forum of the conference lambasted Israel in an ugly display of venom and anti-Zionism (see above, pp. 96–104). Attempts to present a positive view of Zionism were drowned out by Palestinians and their allies, who pushed the equation of Zionism with racism and Israel as an apartheid state. This was "anti-Semitism in the guise of anti-Zionism," exclaimed Marlene Bethlehem, national president of the SAJBOD. "The onslaught on Israel and the Jewish people is an absolute scandal and it is racism and anti-Semitism of the worst kind," said

Mervyn Smith, former national president of the SAJBOD. Particularly galling was the Muslims' use, for propaganda purposes, of a few ultra-Orthodox Jewish opponents of Zionism and of Uri Davis, a secular Jewish anti-Zionist from Israel. Davis, in fact, participated in a lively meeting in Cape Town, under Jewish auspices. Not surprisingly, the *SA Jewish Report* applauded the withdrawal of the United States and Israel from the conference, which South Africa's President Mbeki, in contrast, deeply regretted.

"Radical Islam is on the march," noted the *SA Jewish Report* three weeks after the conference ended, "and Israel has been identified as the 'little Satan' and lumped together with America, the 'big Satan.' Both are seen as enemies to be destroyed at all costs in a holy war." One-time anti-apartheid activist and founder of the New Zionist Organization, Rabbi Ben Isaacson, drew an ominous lesson for South African Jews, warning that there was "no long-term future for Jewry in the country we have contributed so much to and the country that we love" (*SA Jewish Report,* Sept. 28).

On September 23, Jews in Cape Town, Durban, and Johannesburg joined other Jewish communities around the world in public demonstrations of solidarity with the State of Israel.

In the wake of the Durban conference, South African Jewish leaders increasingly questioned the government's self-declared policy of evenhandedness in the Middle East. Toward the end of the year, a delegation of the SAZF met with Deputy Foreign Minister Pahad and the director of the Middle East desk, Malcolm Ferguson, to discuss the matter. The delegation expressed concern at the blatantly pro-Palestinian posture of the ANC—the leading party in the government—and of the Congress of South African Trade Unions (COSATU). Pahad reiterated the government's policy of evenhandedness and distinguished it from the positions of the ANC and COSATU. He said that the government strongly backed the existence and security of Israel, and stressed the urgent need for interaction between Jews and Muslims in South Africa. In December, when it was reported that the ANC and the South African government were seeking to play a role in negotiations between Israelis and Palestinians, the *SA Jewish Report* (Dec. 7) urged: "one message the South Africans should hammer home to the Palestinians is that terrorism cannot be justified by any ideological cause. . . ."

About 2,500 Muslims marched in Cape Town on al Quds Day in mid-December, many wearing kaffiyehs. Three children dressed up as suicide bombers held wooden machine guns that had "Hezballah" written on them. Achmat Cassiem, leader of the radical Muslim organization Qibla, said that what "was seen as the final solution for the Jews in the diaspora, that is the creation of the Zionist Terrorist State of Israel, has become its worst nightmare and possibly its final nightmare."

The Kasrils/Ozinsky Declaration

In October, Ronnie Kasrils, the minister of water affairs and forestry, launched a powerful attack on Israel during a special Middle East debate in the National Assembly. The session was held against the backdrop of a report by the Parliament's "fact-finding mission" that had visited the Middle East in July. Despite dissent from a number of DA parliamentarians, the report noted parallels between "the oppression experienced by Palestinians under the hand of Israel and the oppression experienced under apartheid."

Kasrils chose the occasion to read a statement he had coauthored with an ANC member of the Western Cape provincial legislature, Max Ozinsky. Drawing comparisons with apartheid South Africa, the statement identified the fundamental cause of the conflict in "the suppression of the Palestinians' struggle for national self-determination." Quoting former Israeli foreign minister Shlomo Ben-Ami, the statement developed the notion that a people under occupation could not be expected to honor its agreements with its "occupier." Kasrils argued:

> The establishment of the state of Israel in 1948 inflicted a great injustice on the Palestinian people, compounded by the subsequent Israeli rule of the occupied territories and denial of the legitimate rights of the Palestinian refugees.
>
> A recognition of the fundamental causes of the ongoing violence does not—and I say this as a South African of Jewish descent—constitute anti-Semitism nor does it amount to a denial of Israel's right to exist. Rather it constitutes an urgent call on the Israeli government to redress and satisfy legitimate claims, without which—and this is the point—peace negotiations will fail.

Kasrils went on to explain how the Holocaust informed his moral outlook. After the enormous suffering of European Jewry, he was "utterly appalled at the ruthless security methods employed by the Israeli government against Palestinians, much of which smack of the way fascism in Europe dealt with people that they considered to be non-people." In his view, the security of Israelis and Palestinians were "inseparably intertwined" and there was no alternative to a negotiated settlement that recognized both Palestine and Israel "as fully independent sovereign states" living in peaceful coexistence and cooperation. Kasrils went on to argue that if Israel wished to become a "respected society" it would have to "grant full, equal rights to all who dwell within its borders." He called on South Africans of Jewish descent, and Jews everywhere, to support justice for Palestine and peace and security for all in the "Holy Land."

The SAJBOD, perhaps anticipating the thrust of his remarks, had provided "information packets" to all parliamentarians prior to the debate, hoping to counter the expected flood of anti-Israeli invective that might induce the government to veer away from its policy of even-handedness in the Middle East. The speech drew a harsh response from Jews. Russell Gaddin, national chairman of the SAJBOD, described Kasrils as uninformed about the Israel-Palestinian conflict and suggested that the minister was using his Jewish background to gain credibility for the ANC's pro-Palestinian stance. All Jews, added Gaddin, sought a peaceful solution to the conflict (*Cape Argus,* Oct. 25).

The *SA Jewish Report* (Nov. 2) noted Kasrils's particular timing: "Coming a few months after the UN conference against racism in Durban, where the Arab and Muslim bloc was so successful in convincing South Africans that Israel is an apartheid-like state, Kasrils's statement pours salt into a wound an anxious Jewish community is already feeling." Some Jewish critics, including leading rabbis, charged that not only was his analysis of the Middle East situation mistaken, but that he had no right to comment on the matter because of his position in the cabinet and/or the fact that he was a nonpracticing Jew.

A vicious public debate ensued that received intense media coverage. It featured a "Declaration of Conscience on the Israeli-Palestinian Conflict" in support of Kasrils, launched with 284 signatures of Jews in Cape Town and Johannesburg in November. Among the signatories were a number of veteran anti-apartheid activists including Nobel Laureate Nadine Gordimer. Helen Suzman and a number of other well-known Jewish liberals refused to sign.

Anti-Semitism

There was a substantial increase in anti-Semitic sentiment during 2001. Evidence of this could be found in reports of harassment of individuals, vandalism of Jewish property, offensive comments on radio talk shows and on television, tasteless editorial comment and newspaper cartoons in the mainstream press as well as some outright anti-Semitic letters-to-the-editor, and the sale of books denying the Holocaust and alleging Jewish conspiracies.

While the far-right newspaper, *Die Afrikaner,* occasionally carried offensive articles, the anti-Zionist rhetoric that developed in connection with the Durban conference dominated, and it increasingly blurred with classic anti-Semitic motifs. Hostile rhetoric was driven by the Muslim population, which numbered about 650,000, far outstripping the 80,000 South African Jews. Over half the Muslims resided in greater Cape Town. An Islamist group, the Media Review Network (MRN), linked to the Free Palestine Campaign and the Palestinian Solidarity Committee and in contact with radical Muslim groups internationally, consistently engaged the media over the Israeli-Palestinian question, and a local Muslim Web site carried vicious anti-Jewish material.

People Against Gangsterism and Drugs (PAGAD), an essentially Muslim group, was declared a foreign terrorist organization by the U.S. State Department following the attacks of September 11. PAGAD had been associated with urban terror in the late 1990s, but the arrest and conviction of many of its members had ended its terror campaign.

The SAJBOD maintained a vigilant posture and took action against anti-Semitism whenever possible. At the SAJBOD's 41st annual conference in Johannesburg in August, speakers called on the community to speak out assertively. Delivering the keynote address, Mendel Kaplan, former chairman of the World Jewish Congress, maintained that it was time Jews stopped being timid and defensive. "We should speak up for our rights as South African citizens. . . . What do we have to apologize for?" asked Kaplan. Similar sentiments were heard at the annual conference of the Cape Council of the SAJBOD in November. Michael Bagraim, the chairman, called for a more proactive policy against anti-Semitism: "No longer can we say as we did in the 60s, 70s and 80s that 'we must not rock the boat,' and no longer can we say as we did in the 90s that we are doing things 'behind the scenes.' It is now necessary for us to be in your face." His words were greeted with loud applause (*SA Jewish Report*, Aug. 24, Nov. 16).

Holocaust-Related Matters

In May 1998, Radio 786, a Cape Town Muslim community station run by the Islamic Unity Convention (IUC), had broadcast an anti-Semitic interview with Yaqub Zaki on Zionism and Israel. Zaki, a Scottish convert to Islam, spoke of world Jewish conspiracies and denied the Holocaust. At the time, the SAJBOD complained to the Independent Broadcasting Authority (IBA) that the interview violated the code of conduct for broadcasting services. This code outlawed anything offensive to the religious convictions or feelings of any section of the population, or likely to prejudice the safety of the state, the public order, or relations between sections of the population. The IUC, for its part, claimed that the legislation establishing the code was unconstitutional since it infringed on civil rights and freedom of speech.

In April 2001, the Johannesburg High Court ruled in favour of the IUC on technical and procedural grounds. The decision did not deal with the substance of the matter. Justice D. Marais was highly critical of the IBA and its complaints department, finding that its officials had been grossly incompetent in dealing with the SAJBOD complaint (*SA Jewish Report,* Apr. 27). The SAJBOD appealed the case, and it was heard by the Constitutional Court in November. The issue, again, was not the substance of the SAJBOD complaint, but whether the broadcasting regulations under which Radio 786 was granted its licence contravened freedom of expression. No decision had been reached at year's end.

In March, the SAJBOD wrote to the Lebanese ambassador to South Africa, requesting a meeting to convey strong objections to a planned conference in Beirut promoting Holocaust denial. The SAJBOD also wrote to Aziz Pahad, South Africa's deputy minister of foreign affairs, asking the government to protest the event. In the end, the conference was not held.

The Cape Town Holocaust Centre (CTHC) maintained its prominent role in human-rights education. In May, it hosted a special reception to honor its patron, Nobel Laureate and Archbishop Emeritus Desmond Tutu. Speaking on the occasion, Tutu noted how much blacks in South Africa owed to Jews, "who were in fact some of the very few white people who thought that we were human" (*Cape Jewish Chronicle,* July). Prof. Michael Marrus, eminent historian and dean of the Graduate School at the University of Toronto, gave the second anniversary lecture at the CTHC. His topic was the Vatican and the Jews of Rome.

JEWISH COMMUNITY

Demography

A national census was undertaken in October, and preliminary results would not be known till 2003. Though religion was an optional category, communal leaders urged Jews to indicate their Jewish identity in the 2001 census.

Even in the absence of hard data, the major demographic fact was clearly emigration. Delivering the keynote address at the 61st annual meeting of the United Herzlia Schools, Chief Rabbi Cyril Harris spoke of the "awesome responsibility" of schools to guide their pupils on controversial issues such as emigration. "I don't think it is our job to create wonderful South African expatriates, but wonderful South Africans to stay. We're hemorrhaging in the immediate postgraduate age group and, in 20 to 30 years time, the Jewish community in this country will be old and poor." While recognizing that it was a basic human right to live where one chose, Rabbi Harris said the country was going to be "in great trouble" if the present trend were not reversed. "A personal decision may be a selfish one when viewed from the point of view of the country's needs," he said (*SA Jewish Report,* June 8).

Communal Affairs

A SAJBOD investigation revealed that almost every Jewish organization in Johannesburg—many of which were responsible for national projects—was experiencing financial difficulty. According to Russell Gaddin, the SAJBOD chairman, the problem was not emigration, too much money going to Israel, or the impoverishment of the community. Rather, he claimed, it was the changing nature of religious life in Johannesburg where insular, "right-wing" Orthodoxy had grown, and the result was unnecessary duplication. "Can Johannesburg afford 50 synagogues and temples? And can the northern suburbs afford 17 *shtieblach* [small prayer houses]?" asked Gaddin. There were 12 Jewish day schools, including four new "Torah" schools, in Johannesburg, the latter combined accommodating fewer than 80 pupils. There were three systems of kashrut in operation. "The end result," complained Gaddin, "is that everyone of these little groups is funding its own and not contributing to the mainstream organizations of the community. And when these fringe organizations run into financial difficulty, they turn to the mainstream community for their funding" (*SA Jewish Report,* Mar. 23).

Consolidation was clearly necessary. The Johannesburg Jewish Helping Hand and Burial Society (Hevrah Kadisha), the largest Jewish welfare organization on the African continent, took over the activities of Our Parents' Home. This move followed the society's successful takeovers of Jewish Community Services in 1999 and Sandringham Gardens Jewish

Aged Home in 2000, as well as the subsequent move of the society's administrative offices from Houghton to Sandringham. "Consolidated resources such as accommodation, services, finances and medical care will undoubtedly lead to a more enhanced and effective technique," explained Colin Datnow, the chairman. In another move toward integration of community services, Arcadia Jewish Children's Home moved from Parktown to Raedene, Johannesburg.

Johannesburg was not the only community facing difficulties. According to the incoming chairman of the Cape Council, Philip Krawitz, Cape Town Jewry was undergoing a transition. It was no longer wealthy, did not have the ear of the government, and faced a difficult job market against the backdrop of affirmative action for blacks. He believed the situation was ripe for a religious revival.

In April, Israeli ambassador Tova Herzl officially opened Beyachad, the building in Johannesburg that would house all the major South African Jewish organizations, including the three key bodies: the SAJBOD, SAZF, and IUA-UCF. Collectively, the work of the organizations was built around the concept of four "pillars": education, religion, welfare, and society. Beyachad ran the joint services of the organizations and also took responsibility for the societal pillar.

Crime continued to be a major source of concern. At a joint forum of the Gauteng Council of the SAJBOD and 12 Jewish members of the Johannesburg city council and Gauteng provincial legislature (all members of the DA) held in February, general pessimism was expressed at the ANC's handling of crime. Concern also surfaced about Jewish youth being supplied with alcohol by parents. According to Lionel Stern, chairman of the Johannesburg Community Policing Area, some of the robberies in Jewish homes were the work of "children who stole from their parents' belongings to get money to buy drugs and alcohol." He advocated an educational program for the parents to make them aware of the dangers of alcohol.

A number of prominent individuals visited South Africa during the year. Among them were talk-show host and educator Esther Jungreis, who was the guest of the Union of Jewish Women (UJW); Shlomo Grawitz, co-world chairman of the Jewish National Fund; and Judge Hadassah Ben-Itto of Israel, guest of the Cape Town chapter of the International Association of Jewish Lawyers and Jurists.

In January, 64 underprivileged Jewish children attended the annual Bikkur Cholim camp at Lakeside, Cape Town.

Community Relations

There were a number of outreach initiatives during 2001. Jewish leaders joined in a march in Cape Town against violence towards women and children. The Hebrew Order of David in the Gauteng area participated in several charitable endeavours.

The UJW opened a "comfort zone" at a police station in Atlantis, outside Cape Town, to provide help to traumatized victims of sex crimes, and a "comfort room" at the Somerset Hospital in Cape Town. For its efforts, the UJW was presented with a "white ribbon award" by Woman Demand Dignity, an organization founded to protect women from abuse. In October, the UJW held a seminar on dealing with prejudice and stereotyping, where a number of speakers from different ethnic and religious groups shared their understandings and experiences.

Tikkun, a Jewish program to help the underprivileged, substantially increased its programs. It established a community center that included a library in the poverty-stricken area of Delft outside Cape Town, and partly funded a joint initiative on farming education for some 4,000 schools nationwide. Tikkun also distributed 1,000-rands worth of blankets at two of its projects. Tikkun held a museum day in Cape Town on September 11 linking students from the Herzlia Middle School with those from Luhlaza Senior Secondary School, a disadvantaged "black" school. "It was quite bizarre," said Tikkun's Cape director, Barbara Miller, "because the event took place on the same day as the terrorist attacks in New York. On the one side of the world there was a hugely bridge-building process happening, while on the other side there was this totally destructive act (*SA Jewish Report,* Oct. 26).

The seventh He'atid leadership group left for Israel in March. He'atid focused on preparing leaders for South Africa, particularly among the black population, and imparting entrepreneurial skills. There was an active alumni organization of 114 members with centers operating in Bloemfontein, Port Elizabeth, East London, Cape Town, and Durban. Alumni had already established 70 community and business projects and secured the participation of 34 companies and organizations.

Religion

Demographic changes resulted in the opening and closing of a number of synagogues. The Pretoria Hebrew Congregation opened a new synagogue complex, including the new Adath Synagogue. Ohr Samayach, an outreach movement founded in 1987 by Rabbis Larry Shain and Shmuel Mofson, moved into expanded premises in Glenhazel, Johannesburg. Ohr Samayach, which now ran the Shaarei Torah Primary School, also opened a synagogue in Sea Point, Cape Town, attracting a large number of newly Orthodox Jews. The movement organized a four-day educational retreat program, outside Johannesburg, for secular Jews.

The Schoonder Street Synagogue in Cape Town closed down and services moved to the Herzlia High School campus under a new name, Kehillat Shira Chadasha. The Jeppestown Hebrew Congregation in Johannesburg closed. The historic Kimberley synagogue held its centenary commemoration. Rabbi Ephraim Buchwald, founder and director of the National Jewish Outreach Program in the U.S., spent six days in Cape Town in March as a guest of the United Orthodox Synagogue.

In Cape Town, the Bnei Akiva minyan merged with the Arthur's Road Synagogue. The combined congregation became a center of Torah learning with more than 20 classes each week, in addition to the activities of the Yeshivah of Cape Town, which was housed in the same premises.

Sixty-two people participated in a special Shabbat held on Robben Island, the prison where former president Nelson Mandela had been incarcerated. The event was organized by the Yeshivah of Cape Town in cooperation with the Cape Council of the United Orthodox Synagogue. Torah study sessions dealt with the relation of religious values to political issues. This was the first time a Jewish prayer service had ever been held on the island. The *SA Jewish Report* (Nov. 30) noted the contrast between this affirmation of South African national values in a Jewish symbolic context and the "increasingly insular attitude of many South African Jews, who are seeking sustenance in self-imposed ghettos—physically or of the mind or spirit—or who are quietly packing their bags and leaving for distant shores where they believe the grass is greener."

Education

Financial problems continued to plague the King David schools in Johannesburg. For the first time in 50 years, children whose parents could not afford tuition were turned away at the start of 2001. "We have always lived up to our credo that no Jewish child will be deprived of a Jewish education through inability to pay fees—but we no longer have money for the provision of subsidies," said a distraught Glynn Ismay, chairman of the South African Board of Jewish Education (SABJE). Ismay called on the community "to save the situation" (*SA Jewish Report,* Jan. 26). Enrollments dropped from 3,850 to 3,600. Ismay said the crisis had been caused by the withdrawal of government subsidies (from 7.7 million rands in 1995, to 6.7 million in 1999, to zero in 2000), emigration of full-paying families, abnormally high outstanding debts and past school fees, demographic changes, and a large overdraft of 24 million rands ($2.1 million). According to the SABJE financial director, Tony Roth, the fee structure was in line with other private schools.

An editorial in the *SA Jewish Report* (Mar. 3) commenting on the crisis echoed Russell Gaddin's criticism of the Johannesburg community:

> While there has been a large degree of rationalization, there are still organizations, small and large, intent on doing their own thing. This ranges from fringe communities, who have built their own ghetto, with their own private sources of income, to smaller bodies, which essentially undertake the same work as recognized community-funded institutions. This includes the plethora of smaller Jewish schools, which could well find a home in the mainstream Jewish day schools of King David, Yeshivah College and Torah Academy.

In February, a Pretoria-based trust responded generously to the financial crisis, and by June an innovative plan to solve the King David schools' financial crisis had been put into place. Allan Zulberg, a senior executive with proven business skills and an understanding of the Jewish community and its educational needs, was appointed to manage a reorganization.

The Jewish community faced a considerable challenge from Jews for Jesus, which worked in conjunction with the Olive Tree Foundation, a Christian organization. A major campaign took place in Johannesburg, where the missionary group targeted shopping centers and the University of the Witwatersrand, and held weekly Friday night prayer services. In response, a "Jews for Judaism" actively countered Christian missionizing. Its director, Rabbi Graeme Finkelstein, said that Jewish education was the best answer.

The Johannesburg College of Adult Jewish Education was launched in February under the auspices of the Sydenham/Highlands North Synagogue. Rabbi Yossy Goldman, spiritual leader of the synagogue and prime mover of the educational project, said the "grassroots out there are interested in learning about their heritage" (*SA Jewish Report,* Feb. 2). An internationally renowned author and speaker, Rabbi Maurice Friedman, gave the opening lecture at the launch.

In November, a group of Jewish educators from Jerusalem visited South African Jewish day schools on behalf of the Jewish Agency.

Culture

An exhibition of children's art from the Terezin concentration camp opened in Johannesburg, a joint project of the embassy of the Czech Republic and the SAJBOD.

Saul Reichlin performed *Sholem Aleichem in the Shtetl* at the South African Jewish Museum, Cape Town, and at the Chief Rabbi Harris Communal Centre in Johannesburg.

The *SA Jewish Report* celebrated its third anniversary. The Jewish weekly prided itself "for allocating space for opinion from all streams of Jewish thought and activity" and for its "independence unprecedented in Jewish publications in South Africa." In August, Anton Harber, the highly respected former editor of the *Mail & Guardian,* was elected chairman of the board of the *SA Jewish Report*. "I accepted the position because I think it's important," he explained. "I think it's run by an excellent and dedicated group of people and it deserves to succeed, but it will not succeed if elements of the community try to hijack it for their sectional interests."

Publications

Some noteworthy publications of Jewish interest were *The Jews of South Africa—An Illustrated History to 1953,* edited by Naomi Musiker (based on an unpublished manuscript by Gus Saron); *E-mail for a Jewish Mother* by Mona Berman; *Pictures of a Strange Town: A Story of the Terezin Shtetl* by Sandra Lee Braude; *Hearing Grasshopper Jump: The Story of Raymond Ackerman as told to Denise Prichard; Contemporary Jewish Writing in South Africa: An Anthology,* edited by Claudia Bathsheba Braude; and a photographic history, *Looking Back: Jews in the Struggle for Democracy and Human Rights in South Africa,* compiled by Milton Shain, Adrienne Folb, Albie Sachs, Jon Berndt, Jon Weinberg, Barry Feinberg, and André Odendaal.

Personalia

Tony Leon, leader of the opposition DA, married an Israeli, Michal Even-Zahav; Ali Bacher, appointed executive director of the 2003 Cricket World Cup Policy Committee; Rachel Shapiro, appointed executive of the West Province Zionist Council (WPZC); Jeanne Futeran, elected president of the Maccabi World Union; Myra and Elliot Osrin, presented the

Lexus Lifetime Achiever Award for 40 years of communal work; renowned paleontologist Professor Phillip Tobias and philanthropist Helen Lieberman received the SAJBOD Human Rights Award; Rabbi Abraham Tanzer, head of Yeshivah College and spiritual leader of the Glenhazel Yeshivah Congregation, Johannesburg, received the Distinguished Rabbinical Services Award from the Rabbi Aloy Foundation; veteran communal leader Solly Yellin awarded an honorary doctorate from Ben Gurion University of the Negev; and Shea Albert appointed director of the South African Jewish Museum.

Dayan Gross, executive director of the Cape Council of the SAJBOD, took up a position with the Jewish federation in Cleveland, Ohio, in the United States. He was replaced by Suzanne Belling.

Among prominent South African Jews who died during 2001 were former Johannesburg mayor and member of Parliament Alec Gorshel; communal leader Ian Sachs; Zionist stalwart Dr. Allen Berman; Dr. Moses Cyrus Weiler, the first rabbi to serve the Progressive community in South Africa; entrepreneur and philanthropist Jack Goldin; historian Phyllis Lewsen; Josephine Freeman, founder of the Zionist Luncheon Club; Gus Levy, cofounder of the Johannesburg Jewish Male Choir; distinguished lawyer Victor Mansell; communal leader Rubi Chaitman; Zalman Levy, doyen of Yiddish culture in South Africa; former mayor of Johannesburg Max Neppe; distinguished jurist Alec Oshry; cricket benefactor Wilfred Isaacs; and distinguished communal leader Hanns Saenger.

MILTON SHAIN

Israel

FUTILE ATTEMPTS TO ESCAPE from an escalating cycle of violence marked the year 2001, which many believed to be the most difficult year for the Jewish state since 1948, when it fought its War of Independence. What the Palestinians called the Al-Aqsa intifada began in late September 2000, continued on into early 2001 even while peace negotiations were in progress, and for all intents and purposes amounted to the seventh war in Israel's 53-year history—after the War of Independence, the 1956 campaign in Sinai, the 1967 Six-Day War, the 1969–71 war of attrition, the 1973 Yom Kippur War, and the 1982 war in Lebanon. But this latest war was the first since 1948 to be fought, by and large, on Israeli-controlled territory, and the first in which military casualties were matched by civilian dead and wounded. During a year of bloodshed and violence, 208 Israelis lost their lives and over 1,500 were wounded.

In diplomatic terms, the year began with Israelis and Palestinians engaged in talks at Taba, Egypt, in a last-ditch effort to close a deal that had seemed close to realization half a year earlier, at Camp David. It ended with diplomatic dialogue severed and contacts limited to futile attempts, not to achieve lasting peace, but just to get a cease-fire.

In the interim, Israel got a new prime minister. But the tough policies of the Likud's Ariel Sharon, who won the February 6 election on the slogan "Only Sharon Can Bring Peace," seemed to produce even more violence: greater terror, almost daily attacks, and a growing feeling of insecurity on the streets and highways of Israel.

DIPLOMACY AND POLITICS

Negotiations on the Road to Elections

Attorney General Elyakim Rubinstein, who two weeks previously had affirmed that the government had full power to negotiate with the Palestinians even though elections were due in slightly more than a month, raises eyebrows on January 2 by writing to Prime Minister Ehud Barak questioning the morality of taking fateful decisions so close to election day, even though Barak was pledged to bring any proposed deal to the Knesset for approval. Conceding that "carrying out negotiations indeed seems to fall under the prime minister's area of responsibility," Rubinstein said that, in continuing talks with the Palestinians, Barak should avoid making major moves "unless there is no other choice, such as directing the army or defending the country in time of war." Political figures on the left accused Rubinstein of yielding to pressure from the right, which, throughout the run-up to the elections, had argued that Barak had no right to negotiate with the Palestinians since any deal reached could well be a desperate attempt to swing votes in his favor and away from the Likud candidate, Ariel Sharon.

Though the actual campaign had not yet officially opened, there was already some jockeying for position. Sharon, acting on the advice of his advisers to run a low-key campaign, nevertheless appeared at a January 1 press conference with former prime minister Benjamin (Bibi) Netanyahu. Afterwards, Sharon aides accused Netanyahu of "sabotage" for saying only that voters should support Sharon "because Barak's policies endanger the State of Israel," which they considered a mere half-hearted endorsement of the Likud candidate.

With Barak trailing in all the polls by double-digit margins, former president Ezer Weizman said that he would support the Likud candidate "because the country needs some order," adding: "I am thinking about what is good for the state." Weizman's endorsement came despite the former president's strong backing for the peace process in the past. Another damaging-to-Barak endorsement came from the Center Party's Dan Meridor, a partner in Barak's coalition, who explained: "There is no way that I can support the policy of the government, and so I will support the opposite line."

On January 2, with only 18 more days left in his term, President Bill Clinton entertained Palestinian Authority president Yasir Arafat at the White House. Despite the visit and Clinton's continuing efforts to attain an Israeli-Palestinian deal while he was still in office, U.S. officials expressed pessimism, saying that they did not think there was "sufficient understanding" between the sides to reach any kind of deal. Meanwhile, the Palestinians circulated a document containing a point-by-point critique of the Clinton proposals, saying they would continue negotiations only if they were satisfied by the clarifications they had asked from Clinton on four key issues—Jerusalem, borders, settlements, and the Palestinians' "right of return" into Israel proper. The White House, for its part, was under the impression that it had extracted a pledge from Arafat to cooperate in antiterror measures, intensify efforts to stop the violence, and arrest at least some terrorists.

Also that day, Barak formally opened his campaign at Labor headquarters in Tel Aviv's Hatikva Quarter. The atmosphere of the meeting was glum, with several key Labor figures, including Jerusalem Affairs Minister Haim Ramon, conspicuously absent. A *Ha'aretz* reporter on the scene said that "Barak was the only one who tried to smile. . . . A heavy scent of defeat hung in the air."

On January 7, as U.S. peace envoy Ambassador Dennis Ross was about to visit the region for a last-ditch effort to arrive at a deal before the end of the Clinton administration, the president himself appeared before the Israel Policy Forum in Washington and outlined the parameters of his proposals (see above, pp. 198–99). The next night, however, hundreds of thousands of Israelis attend a mass rally in Jerusalem to express opposition to Clinton's plan to transfer part of the capital city to the Palestinian Authority. Police estimated the crowd at 250,000, while organizers claimed 400,000—either way, one of the largest assemblies ever held in the city. Thousands formed a human chain around most of the Old City, a giant picture of the capture of the Temple Mount during the Six-Day War was projected on the walls of the Old City, and loudspeakers blared out, "the Temple Mount is in our hands," the famous statement of the late general Mordechai (Motta) Gur, at the time commander of the paratroop brigade. Speakers include former Supreme Court president Moshe Landau, who recalled the thick retaining walls that divided pre-1967 Jerusalem, Chairman Ronald Lauder of the Conference of Presidents of Major American Jewish Organizations, who claimed to represent "tens of millions of Jews throughout the world" opposed to ceding any part of Jerusalem, and Avital Sharansky, wife of former interior minister Natan Sharansky, who said that the liberation of Jerusalem in 1967 had triggered the renaissance of Jewish awareness in the former Soviet Union.

Sharon raised the low profile he has been maintaining during the campaign in an interview with *Kfar Chabad,* an ultra-Orthodox weekly. Asked why he publicly rejected the understandings reached in 2000 at Camp David but did not explicitly repudiate the 1993 Oslo agreement with the Palestinian Authority, Sharon responded: "The Oslo accord is an agreement which no longer exists. Period." Sharon went on to explain earlier statements about his possible flexibility toward Palestinian demands. "When I talk about painful concessions, I mean we are not going to reconquer Nablus and Jericho. That's a painful concession, because these are the cradle of the Jewish people. I don't know of any people in the world that has surrendered national historic assets, unless defeated in a war—and we were not vanquished in a war." Launching his campaign on January 10 in a festive rally at Jerusalem's main convention center, Sharon spoke of "unity" and "peace." He said that "no real peace can be achieved without concessions, and we will reach a peace based on a compromise." Nevertheless, he pledged, "under any agreement we will protect Israel's security interests."

Barak continued to trail badly in the polls, and pressure mounted on him to withdraw from the prime ministerial race in favor of elder statesman Shimon Peres, who was running almost even with, or only slightly behind, Sharon in many of the surveys. Peres, for his part, did nothing to discourage such sentiments.

Barak's prospects, very poor among Jewish Israelis, were made even worse by the certainty that he would not get anywhere near the 90-percent level of support from Israeli Arabs that he received in the 1999 victory over Netanyahu. Indeed, Israeli Arab groups openly advocated a boycott of the February 6 vote, blaming Barak and his adminstration for the killing of 13 Israeli Arabs in clashes with police during demonstrations in early October 2000, soon after the intifada started. Under the slogan "We will never forget or forgive," one group said in a statement: "Boycotting elections is a national obligation . . . for the purpose of changing the current political formula, expressed in the view that Labor takes the Arab vote as a predetermined, guaranteed preserve." A Labor loss caused, at least in part, by the failure of Arab support, the statement suggested, might "lay the foundations for a new relationship" between Israel's center-left party and the million-plus-strong Arab sector, the nation's largest minority.

On January 11, President Moshe Katzav, whose office was supposed to be nonpartisan, stated his personal opinion in a public forum. Katzav told residents of the Jordan Valley area of the West Bank that he was disappointed with the decline of public opposition to certain concessions to the Palestinians. "Seven years ago," he said, "no one would have dared to speak aloud of recognizing the PLO. Three years ago, most Israelis did not support the establishment of a Palestinian state. Half a year ago, most Israelis spoke of a united Jerusalem firmly, resolutely. And I feel that this too has diminished." Katzav argued that any future agreement would have to take into account the possibility that Palestinians were insincere when speaking of a desire for peace, and he supported Attorney General Rubinstein's "moral" argument against the present government's striking a peace deal with the Palestinians, even though it had the full legal right to do so.

Efforts to achieve an Israeli-Palestinian deal before the end of the Clinton administration effectively ended on January 12, when the outgoing U.S. president announced that it would be up to the incoming George W. Bush administration to continue peace efforts. Clinton added the obvious—that Bush would not be obligated by the Clinton administration's positions. (On January 19, the day before Clinton left office, Israel and the United States signed an agreement reducing U.S. economic aid by $120 million a year while adding $60 million to military aid. The economic aid had been given to Israel over the years to service loans for the purchase of arms in the 1970s, when the United States gave loans rather than grants of military aid. The gradual phase-out of the economic aid was due to be completed in 2008.)

After the murder of an Israeli, Roni Tzalah, in Gaza on January 14, Barak slowed the pace of peace contacts with the Palestinians. He also rejected a proposal from Peres for a paper stating the points of agreement and disagreement that had been reached in talks so far.

In the official opening of TV advertising for the campaign (in Israel, there are no media spots other than blocs of time designated by the Central Elections Committee during a specified period of time before the election), Barak and Sharon traded charges on a variety of subjects. In a special segment for Arab voters, Barak expressed regret for the killing of 13 Israeli Arabs the previous October. In his broadcast to the wider public, Barak said he was sorry for so often going it alone, and promised that, if reelected, he would consult more closely with senior members of his own cabinet. The Barak broadcasts also attacked Sharon for getting Israel embroiled in a war in Lebanon in 1982, and featured a series of simulated "news bulletins" purporting to show a just-elected Sharon gradually leading Israel into another war.

Likud politicians said they would not respond to such negative tactics, which, they said, were aimed at frightening the public. Sharon's television campaign, however, did highlight episodes of terror during the Barak years, and claimed that only the Likud candidate could bring peace and unity. In one spot, Jerusalem mayor Ehud Olmert—who himself had been a candidate for the Likud leadership after the June 1999 resignation of Netanyahu—charged Barak with making excessive concessions over Jerusalem. (Barak, striking back, claimed that the Jerusalem mayor had met with him just before the Camp David meetings in the summer of 2000 to discuss practical solutions for the capital, and that "Olmert opened up maps and aerial photographs, proposing positions I might take at Camp David, ones whose consequence would be the division of Jerusalem.")

Barak's shaky position was not enhanced when tens of thousands of government and municipal workers went out on strike. The strike was settled after nine days, at the end of January, when the Histadrut labor union backed down from its demand for a 16-percent across-the-board wage increase, accepting instead a raise of 3.6 percent and a one-time payment of 1,250 shekels (about $300 at the time). Total cost to the economy of the pay package: 3.5 billion shekels, over $650 million.

On January 21, marathon talks began at Taba, in Egyptian Sinai just south of Eilat. Leading the Israeli delegation was Shlomo Ben-Ami, the acting foreign minister. Binyamin (Fuad) Ben-Eliezer, the transport minister in Barak's government, opposed the talks, saying they represented "a loaded gun" against Israel, and that the PA "will use the timing to squeeze more concessions out of Israel." Ben-Eliezer was joined in his oppposition by two other Labor ministers, Dalia Itzik and Haim Ramon. Sharon, for his part, accused Barak of trying to score a last-minute diplomatic coup to change the outcome of the election.

The following day, Tourism Minister Amnon Lipkin-Shahak, the leader of the Center Party and a member of the Israeli team at Taba, commented: "There are serious discussions as well as signs that indicate a change, and a serious approach." Still, Shahak cautioned, "There are no new positions on either side. It is a discussion on how to bridge the gaps between positions." The talks were interruped briefly after the killing of two Israeli restauranteurs in Tul Karm on January 23, when Barak temporarily recalled the Israeli negotiators (see below, p. 548).

Contacts with the committee headed by former U.S. senator George Mitchell, which was investigating the causes of the violence and ways to lower it, were suspended on January 21, in protest over the visit of Larry Pope, the committee's technical chief, to the Temple Mount without an Israeli escort. A few days later Israel said it would not resume cooperation with the committee unless Pope were removed, saying that his unescorted visit to the mount clearly indicated his lack to sensitivity to the religious and political complexities of the site. Indeed, that same day Israel also ordered the police to stop the Wakf, the Muslim religious trust, from work it was doing on the mount (see below, pp. 585–86).

The Taba talks ended on January 27. The heads of the two delegations, Shlomo Ben-Ami and Ahmed Qurei (Abu Ala), speaker of the Palestinian National Assembly, jointly declared that the sides "have never been so close to attaining an agreement." They expressed the belief that it "will be possible to bridge remaining gaps when the talks are resumed after elections in Israel." The daily *Ha'aretz,* citing Israeli sources, reported that the discussions at Taba addressed the size of the blocs of settlements to be incorporated into Israel and the borders of a Palestinian state (both sides exchanging maps), security (the establishment of a joint panel to discuss Israeli overflights of Palestinian airspace, even while the PA maintained its opposition to the presence of any Israeli troops in the Jordan Valley), and the Palestinian refugees. On this last issue, Yossi Beilin, Israel's justice minister and a member of the Israeli team, said that a "menu of solutions" was formulated to address the explosively controversial issue of a Palestinian "right of return" and Israel's historic "responsibility" for the plight of the refugees, and that one idea was the formation of an international body to handle compensation and resettlement. According to the *Ha'aretz* report, Beilin was optimistic.

On the Palestinian side, Abu Ala spoke positively of "six days of serious activity," but the PA's information minister, Yasir Abd Rabbo, a member of the delegation, was more cautious in his assessment. "It's not that simple," he told a radio interviewer. "There are many questions that require answers from the Israeli side. Yes, one could say there was development on some questions . . . and there was a readiness for drawing closer on some questions. But I would not want to say that the questions are approaching solution. And from another point of view, one must assert that there was no firm [Israeli] policy of progress during six months or during the last year. When playing and zigzagging with positions ends, then we will realize progress."

The Likud, predictably, called the joint statement by Ben-Ami and Abu Ala a campaign gimmick to help Barak. A party statement proclaimed: "Making a secret agreement, Barak has conceded everything and gained nothing. Barak has promised peace before, but brought war. Once again he is selling lies." Michael Kleiner, a Knesset member of the far-right National Union, said the joint statement was "an effort to defraud the public."

Israeli and Palestinian officials involved in the Taba negotiations tried to arrange a Barak-Arafat meeting in Sweden to finalize a deal. But the Palestinian leader, in a speech to the annual World Economic Forum on January 28 in Davos, Switzerland, accused Israel of making "barbaric war" by using shells and bullets with depleted uranium—a forbidden substance—against Palestinian women and children. A furious Barak called off the Swedish summit. Over the next few days attempts were made to revive the idea, but on February 4, two days before the election, Barak informed UN secretary general Kofi Annan and Swedish prime minister Goran Persson to abandon efforts to arrange a meeting.

In a January 29 interview on Israel TV's Channel 2, Arafat rejected the claim made by Yasir Abd Rabbo, his own information minister, that the agreement reached at Taba was *harta-barta*—slang for meaningless talk. "Taba was not *harta-barta,* he said. We accept that what we achieved there was not all that we are looking for, not all that you are looking for, but it was a step forward, and the most important thing is that we agreed to continue." Channel 2 also interviewed President Hosni Mubarak of Egypt, who said he had not heard from candidate Sharon, but would meet him for the sake of regional peace. The Egyptian leader played down talk of a possible war. "Who is talking about war?" he asked. "We aren't, it's not in our interest. We are interested in stability, not war."

Landslide

At the end of January, some polls showed Barak trailing by as much as 18 percent. Barak's campaign team desperately began distributing to voters simulated army emergency call-up orders, saying that Israelis would have to choose between such notices, which would surely be distributed for real after Sharon was elected, or a letter informing them of a reduction in their mandatory reserve duty because regional peace had been achieved, which they would get if Barak were reelected. Voters were informed that they had only a few more days to decide which letter would end up in their mailbox. After Likud MK Tzipi Livni protested to the Central Elections Committee that this was an improper use of the IDF for political purposes, Justice Mishael Cheshin, who headed the committee, issued an order barring Labor—or anyone else—from issuing such fake orders.

A memorial march was held a few days before the election to mark the 19th anniversary of a 1982 Peace Now demonstration outside the prime minister's office protesting the invasion of Lebanon, an invasion engineered by Sharon, then the minister of defense. It was at that demonstration that peace activist Emil Grunzweig was killed by a grenade thrown into the crowd. "Emil, We Won't Forget. Arik [Sharon], We Won't Forget," read one of the placards. Raya Harnik, whose son Goni was killed taking the strategic Beaufort heights in South Lebanon during that war, spoke emotionally to the gathering: "We did not forgive and forget that we agreed to sacrifice our children. Now we hear sounds of war from the same political camp."

On the advice of his team of political advisors, which included the American expert Arthur Finkelstein, Sharon ran a low-key campaign, avoided discussing his previous record, and did not reply to Labor charges that he planned to reoccupy the West Bank and possibly start a new war. Though Likud campaigners at major crossroads around the country bore signs warning that Barak "is bringing the [Palestinian] refugees back to Israel," the effort seemed superfluous. Barak, trailing very badly in the polls, was fending off last-minute efforts to have Shimon Peres replace him on the ballot.

In a preelection interview with the mass-circulation daily *Yediot Aharonot,* Sharon said he would create a broad-based government designed to heal the rifts "between right and left, religious and secular, immigrants and veteran Israelis, Jews and Arabs." On February 5, the day before the election, Sharon got the formal support of the ultra-Orthodox parties—United Torah Judaism (UTJ), made up predominantly of Ashkenazi Jews of Eastern European origin, and Shas, whose electorate was mainly Sephardi Jews with roots in Middle Eastern countries. Since most Orthodox voters tended to have right-wing views, this was not surprising. But it nevertheless came as a final blow to Barak: since this election was only for prime minister and not the Knesset, the Labor camp had hoped that the ultra-Orthodox, whose main political interests were economic, might stay home on February 6.

Final polls showed Sharon with an unsurmountable lead—according to Channel 2 TV, it was 58-42, while Labor's own internal figures gave the challenger a 14-percent margin. A last-minute Labor effort to get out the Arab vote was aimed at preserving the party and lessening the humiliation of the impending defeat: Barak issued a public apology for the killing of 13 Israeli Arabs the previous October.

Sharon scored a smashing victory, capturing 62.4 percent of the vote to Barak's 37.6 percent. The nearly 25-point margin was the largest in Israeli history. Only 18 percent of Israel's 500,000 Arab voters turned out on election day. Partly because of this unofficial Arab boycott but also because the result was a foregone conclusion, the overall turnout was just 62 percent of eligible voters, as compared to average turnouts of 80 percent in previous elections. After the returns were counted, Abdulmalik Dehamshe, an MK from the United Arab List, said: "Today we proved that we are not in anyone's pocket." Dehamshe called the boycott "an electoral declaration of independence." About 70 percent of immigrants from the former Soviet Union who were eligible to vote cast ballots, and, according to one exit poll, 62.8 percent supported Sharon. At the previous election, in 1999, about 90 percent of the "Russians" voted, about 58 percent of them supporting Barak.

Although the victorious Sharon had made it clear during the campaign that he wanted to include the vanquished Labor leader in a national unity government, Barak surprised almost everyone by announcing his resignation from the Labor leadership and the Knesset, saying he would step out of politics "for a while." This left the Labor Party in shambles, with a bitter succession fight likely. Barak took the opportunity to defend his peace policies, but he conceded that he might have been ahead of his time: "Perhaps," he noted, "our public is not mature enough to face up to the painful truths that we laid out before it. Perhaps the Palestinians are not mature enough either, and resorted to the barren solution of violence." Barak ended on a hopeful note, saying that eventually "the truth will triumph" among Israelis and Palestinians.

In his victory speech to delighted followers at Jerusalem's main convention center the day after the election, Sharon disclosed that he had just spoken with President George W. Bush, who reminded him, during the phone call, of a helicopter trip the two men had taken several years earlier through the Jordan Valley and parts of the West Bank (Sharon used the term "Samaria"). "And he [Bush] said to me: 'No one believed then that I would be president and you would be prime minister. But as things turned out . . . I have been elected president and you have been elected prime minister.'" Sharon told the crowd that Israel "has embarked on a new path, a path of domestic unity and harmony, of striving for security and genuine peace." He was pledged to achieve "genuine peace and stability," and added: "I know that peace requires painful compromise on the part of both sides. Any diplomatic accord will be founded on security for all people of the region." His goal was "realistic political accords . . . based on mutual respect and the reciprocal fulfillment of obligations."

Reacting to Sharon's election, Arafat tried to sound optimistic, saying that the result did not necessarily mean the end of the peace process. "We respect the choice of the Israeli people," he commented. But Nabil Shaath, a member of various negotiating teams and the PA's planning minister, took a more pessimistic view, telling Israel's Channel 2: "Judging from Sharon's past, there is no way we can make any progress."

Keeping his preelection pledge to create a broad-based government, Sharon immediately entered into negotiations with all political parties.

On February 26, after Barak announced his withdrawal from politics, the central committee of Labor—which, with 26 seats, was the largest single bloc in the 120-member Knesset—agreed to join Sharon's national unity government. There was, however, strong opposition to the move from Laborites fearful that their party would lose its identity by entering the coalition.

The Knesset approved the new government on March 7, by 72 to 21. Eight political parties were included in the cabinet. Labor got the key defense (Binyamin Ben-Eliezer) and foreign-affairs (Shimon Peres) portfolios. Finance went to Silvan Shalom, a Likud politician married to Judy Nir Moses, a member of the family that owned the mass-circulation *Yediot Aharonot* Hebrew daily. Shas increased its hold on power with five ministries, and Salah Tarif, a Druse member of the Labor Party, became the first non-Jew ever in an Israeli cabinet, being given the post of minister-without-portfolio.

Government Ministers

Prime Minister and Acting Absorption Minister: Ariel Sharon, Likud
Defense Minister: Binyamin Ben-Eliezer, Labor
Foreign Minister and Deputy Prime Minister: Shimon Peres, Labor
Finance Minister and Deputy Prime Minister: Silvan Shalom, Likud
Interior Minister and Deputy Prime Minister: Eli Yishai, Shas
Internal Security Minister: Uzi Landau, Likud
Justice Minister: Meir Sheetreet, Likud
Housing Minister and Deputy Prime Minister: Natan Sharansky, Yisrael ba'Aliya
Minister of Industry and Trade: Dalia Itzik, Labor
Culture, Science, and Sports Minister: Matan Vilna'i, Labor
Transport Minister: Ephraim Sneh, Labor
Agriculture Minister: Shalom Simhon, Labor
Communications Minister: Reuven (Ruby) Rivlin, Likud
Education Minister: Limor Livnat, Likud
Environment Minister: Tzachi Hanegbi, Likud
Regional Cooperation Minister: Tzipi Livni, Likud
Religious Affairs Minister: Asher Ohana, Shas
Labor and Social Welfare Minister: Shlomo Benizri, Shas
Health Minister: Nissim Dahan, Shas
Tourism Minister: Rehavam Ze'evi, National Union-Yisrael Beitenu

Infrastructure Minister: Avigdor Lieberman, National Union-Yisrael Beitenu

Minister for Jerusalem Affairs: Eliyahu Suissa, Shas

Minister without portfolio in charge of liaison with Knesset: Danny Naveh, Likud

Minister without portfolio and social-affairs coordinator: Shmuel Avital, One Nation

Minister without portfolio: Ra'anan Cohen, Labor

Minister without portfolio: Salah Tarif, Labor

New Government, Old Problems

On February 8, Barak wrote President George W. Bush noting that the ideas brought up at Camp David and Taba were not binding on the new government of Israel. Barak recalled that President Clinton, when presenting his ideas, had insisted that they would become null and void at the end of his term. President Bush, for his part, issued a statement distancing his administration from the ideas and parameters of the Clinton administration in regard to the Israel-Palestinian peace process.

In early February, Bush appeared to take a first step toward opening his own dialogue with the parties by dispatching Secretary of State Colin Powell—who was visiting the region anyway to gain suport for the policy of containment of Iraq—to separate meetings with Sharon and Arafat. In addition to seeking a halt to the violence, Powell called on Sharon to end enforced closures of the West Bank and Gaza, saying that it was "necessary to lift the siege as soon as possible so that economic activity can begin again in the region." Sharon responded that the blockade would end only after a complete cessation of Palestinian hostilities. In his meeting with the U.S. secretary of state, Arafat pushed his often-advanced idea of an international force—a plan that was anathema to Israel—and asked for U.S. pressure to get Israel to halt the building of Jewish settlements on occupied land in the West Bank and Gaza.

On February 26, the European Union announced a 60-million-euro (about $60 million) package of economic measures to prevent the collapse of the Palestinian Authority. However the EU conditioned the emergency aid on the PA's adoption of an austerity budget. Without the aid and the new budget, it explained, "there is a very real risk of loss of legitimacy and public disillusionment with the Authority which could lead to anarchy, the atomization of power, and increased lawnessness."

Sharon's campaign had emphasized that only the ex-general knew how to deal with terror, but Sharon revealed little about his plans for doing so, even after forming his new government. In a March 11 interview with CNN's Wolf Blitzer, who, in the 1970s and 1980s, had been the Washington correspondent of the *Jerusalem Post,* the new prime minister said that "the mistake of the former government was that it agreed to negotiate under fire and under terror." The effect, he contended, was to increase Palestinian demands and extract concessions that made Israel weaker. "This government has another policy. We will not negotiate under pressure," he insisted. Arafat, for his part, made a speech to the Palestinian National Council, the PA's parliament, attacking Israel's policy "of military escalation, siege, and starvation." Meanwhile, Israel, in response to continued terror attacks and firing on the Jerusalem suburb of Gilo, tightened its control around Bethlehem, south of the capital, and Ramallah to the north.

On March 13, the Foreign Ministry publishes a list of guidelines on the positions of the new government, which, it said, were issued by Foreign Minister Peres in coordination with Sharon. The document stressed Israel's determination to reach peace, said that "restoring security and calm" was at the top of the government's priorities, emphasized that "the conduct of peace negotiations calls for tranquility," made it clear that Israel was willing to lift restrictions in Palestinian areas where there was calm, and in fact announced that it was lifting the close on Tul Karm, Qalqilya, Bethlehem, and Hebron.

Sharon paid his first visit to Washington as prime minister on March 19–20, meeting President Bush, Secretary Powell, and other top officials. According to a Reuters report, Bush expressed surprise at the PA's use of a film clip hailing Muhammad al-Dura, the 12-year-old Gaza boy killed in a crossfire during the early days of the intifada, and other child "martyrs." The president said he "had trouble understanding why Palestinians would place their children in harm's way, rather than trying to protect them."

Meeting with the Council of Europe's Middle East subcommitee on March 20, Foreign Minister Peres said that progress must be based on an end to the violence, use of the language of peace rather than of confrontation ("The two peoples are extremely angry at each other and have lost their capacity for dialogue"), a return to the negotiating table, and easing living conditions in the territories. Unlike Sharon, who demanded a full cessation of hostile acts before any other steps could be taken, Peres argued that all four conditions could be implemented simultaneously.

Peres then met with PA's planning minister, Nabil Sha'ath, and its chief negotiator, Sa'eb Erakat, in Athens on April 4. This was the first high-level Israeli-PA encounter since the February elections. Though Peres announced after the meeting that security officials from the two sides, together with U.S. representatives, would meet at the Erez checkpoint to discuss ways of ending the violence, there were more terror attacks and more Israeli responses.

The U.S. stepped up its efforts to quell the violence in mid-May. Secretary Powell designated William Burns, a veteran diplomat who had served as U.S. ambassador to Jordan, as his point man in the region. On May 21, the committee headed by former U.S. senator George Mitchell formally issued its long-awaited report on the causes of the violence, together with recommendations to bring it to a halt. (Other members of the Mitchell Committee, following the mandate issued at the Sharm al-Sheikh summit in November 2000, were former Turkish president Süleyman Demirel, Norwegian foreign minister Thorbjörn Jagland, former U.S. senator Warren Rudman, and Javier Solana, the European Union's security chief.)

The committee, in a letter dated April 30 and released three weeks later, recommended that the parties reaffirm their commitments to previous agreements and resume security cooperation, while working together to establish a meaninful cooling-off period and to implement additional confidence-building measures. The committee called on the PA to "make a 100-percent effort to prevent terrorist operations and to punish perpetrators . . . [including] immediate steps to apprehend and incarcerate terrorists" operating within the PA's jurisdiction. At the same time, it said the PA should prevent gunmen from firing from its territory on Israeli populated areas or IDF forces, which, it said, "places civilians on both sides at unnecessary risk." The report called on Israel to freeze all settlement, including the "thickening" or "natural growth" of existing settmements. It also said Israel should lift closures, transfer tax monies that it collected for the PA, allow Palestinians to return to jobs in Israel, and prevent settler violence against Palestinians and their property.

The report rejected the allegations of both sides as to what triggered the outbreak of the Al-Aqsa intifada. It stated flatly that Ariel Sharon's visit to the Temple Mount on September 28 "did not cause the Al-Aqsa intifada. But it was poorly timed and the provocative effect should have been foreseen; indeed it was foreseen by those who urged that the visit be prohibited." The committee further criticized the decision of the police to "use lethal means" when Palestinians rioted on the Temple Mount the next day, September 29. On the other hand, the panel had "no basis on which to conclude that there was a deliberate plan by the PA to initiate a campaign of violence at the first opportunity." Nevertheless, there was also no evidence that the PA tried to contain the violence once it began. "Amid rising anger, fear and mistrust," it said, "each side assumed the worst about the other and acted accordingly."

Tensions in the region remained high. An Israeli army spokesman termed "a terribly tragic event" the killing of a four-month-old girl, Iman Hijo, by Israeli fire directed against targets in the Khan Yunis refugee camp in the southern Gaza Strip. An Israeli strike against a crew firing mortar shells from PA territory in the northern Gaza Strip on May 9 killed Abd al-Karim Maname, a Hezballah activist who once served as a bodyguard of the Islamic Resistance Movement's spiritual leader, Sheikh Ahmed Yassin. And on May 15, Syrian president Bashar al-Assad cut off a state visit to Egypt and rushed back to Damascus after Israeli defense minister Ben-Eliezer, visiting the Golan Heights, suggested that the Syrians were responsible for a rocket attack on Israeli forces at Har Dov (known in Arabic as Jebel Rus) on the foothills of Mt. Hermon. In his "message" to Assad, Ben-Eliezer said, "I suggest that you tell Hezballah, clearly, not to escalate the situation on your back. I am telling you that violence will not help."

In early May, the Israeli navy announced the capture of the *San Tornini,* a Lebanese fishing vessel loaded with arms that was headed for Gaza to deliver them to the PA. According to the army, the deadly cargo—intercepted off Haifa—included 50 Katyusha rockets, four SA-7 shoulder-held antiaircraft missiles, 20 RPG rocket-propelled grenade launchers, two 60-mm. mortars with 98 rounds of 60-mm. ammunition for them, 62 land mines, 30 Kalashnikov AK-47 assault rifles, and 13,000 rounds of Kalashnikov ammunition. The army described the weapons as infinitely more sophisticated than what the PA had been using previously, adding that the 107-mm. Katyushas, if fired from Gaza, could hit the southern Israeli city of Ashkelon.

On May 23, Sharon announced a unilateral cease-fire, telling the army to fire at Palestinians only in self-defense. In a televised speech, he called on the Palestinians to stop the violence. "Peace will be achieved only through talks. Stop the violence and accept us as a serious and responsible partner for reaching peace," he said. Though Sharon remarked that he considered the Mitchell recommendations "a positive basis that can enable both sides to end the cycle of violence and return to the negotiating table," he insisted that a substantial cooling-off period would be necessary between the end of violence and the resumption of talks.

Even after a Hamas suicide bomb at a busy discotheque at the Tel Aviv Dolphinarium on June 1 killed 21 Israelis, Sharon vowed to maintain the cease-fire. Under increasing domestic pressure to act in response to the worst terror act since the start of the new intifada, Sharon told members of the Likud that "the government stance requires that we act responsibly. We need to see the whole of the problem, the security problems and the very complicated political problems." German foreign minister Joschka Fischer, who was at his hotel across the street from the Dolphinarium at the time of the suicide attack, sought to defuse the potentially explosive situation by meeting with Israeli leaders and with Arafat. Acting out of what Israelis believed was fear of heavy retaliation, Arafat himself announced a cease-fire on June 2, saying: "We will exert now our utmost efforts to stop the bloodshed of our people, and of the Israeli people, and to do all that is needed to achieve an immediate and unconditional, real, and effective cease-fire."

Both CIA director George Tenet and EU security chief Javier Solana arrived in the area, hoping to prevent the violence from escalating. On June 13, Tenet finalized a cease-fire plan under which the PA agreed to halt acts of violence and incitement against Israel, and Israel promised to loosen the blockade around Palestinian areas and pull its security forces back to the positions they occupied before the start of the intifada the previous September.

Sharon headed for the United States in late June, stopping on the way in London to confer with British prime minister Tony Blair. At a joint press conference before their private meeting on June 26, it was clear that Bush and Sharon differed. While Bush said there had been enough progress to send Secretary of State Powell to the region to start paving the way for the next steps as envisioned by the Mitchell Report, Sharon stuck to his demand that there could be no progress so long as hostilities and incitement continued. Sharon emphasized the need for an "absolute end" to the violence, while Bush insisted that "progress is being made," adding: "Is it as fast as we'd like? No, it's not. But the fundamental question my administration asks is, are we making progress? Is peace closer today than it was yesterday? We believe that the answer is yes—the cycle of violence must be broken." Sharon, on the other hand, said that Israel "will not negotiate under fire and terror . . . last week, we had five people killed by terror, that's like 250 people, maybe 300 people, in the United States. There can be no compromise with terror, and if we stick to our positions that demand an absolute end to terror before the next stage, our neighbors will understand that we have to do it." Bush praises Sharon for showing patience in the face of casualties. "But," he added, "we also believe that progress has been made, and it is important it doesn't fall apart." He expressed the hope that the cease-fire would hold so that the Mitchell process could move forward.

Sharon met with Powell two days later, on June 28, and afterward the two men announced details for the consolidation of the cease-fire. There would be a seven-day period of complete quiet, then a six-week cooling-off period, in turn followed by the implementation of the confidence-building measures envisioned in the Mitchell Report. Palestinians, however, objected to allowing Sharon to determine when and whether there had been seven days of complete quiet. Arguing that Israel was stalling, they demanded a limited three-week cooling-off period, followed by implementation of Mitchell, leading to renewed negotiations.

In the interim, settlement activity continued. On June 27, the Israeli army reported that 60 of the 66 outposts set up by settlers outside their larger communities on the West Bank were, to one extent or another, illegal; 24 of them had been established, the report said, since the start of the intifada at the end of September 2000. According to the army, of the 60 illegal outposts 21 were absolutely illegal, 29 had irregularites in the planning process, and the status of the others was questionable. It added that 19 of these outpost were protected by the army, 12 by armed civilians, and 35 had no formal protection at all.

In mid-August, Sharon strengthened his base of support—and fulfilled a long-held goal—by bringing the Center Party, which had stayed out of the coalition when it was formed in March, into the government. The key figure was Dan Meridor, the former Likud leader who had left that party during the Netanyahu administration. Meridor, formerly chairman of the Knesset's key Foreign Affairs and Defense Committee, now became minister-without-portfolio, responsible for strategic planning and national security—including the Mossad and the Shin Bet security services, the Atomic Energy Commission, and the National Security Council. Roni Milo, the former Tel Aviv mayor and another ex-Likudnik, replaced Tzipi Livni as minister for regional cooperation, while David Magen, a third former Likud MK, took over as chairman of the Knesset Foreign Affairs and Defense Committee.

9/11 and After

The September 11 terror attacks on the World Trade Center in New York and the Pentagon in Washington had a palpable effect on Israelis and Palestinians. The very next day, September 12, about 100 Israelis—

and many more Arabs—living in the U.S. were among the foreign nationals picked up by the FBI, which combed the country for anyone who might not be in the country legally, and whose actions might indicate terrorist connections. In many cases, they were kept in solitary confinement and not released for several months.

After suffering severe embarrassment when TV showed rejoicing on the streets of East Jerusalem and Ramallah, the PA acted quickly to stifle demonstrations in support of Osama bin Laden and his Al Qaeda terror network. Some Palestinian officials went so far as to suggest that the scenes may have been staged by TV crews, and there were reports of threats against TV journalists. Arafat and other PA officials denounced the attacks on the U.S. on September 12, expressing fear that Israel might take advantage of the tough new U.S. stance against terror to rachet up its military operations against the PA.

But it was domestic terror, not what happened in the U.S., that motivated Israel to move into Jenin, in the northern West Bank, the "nest of terrorism" from which a series of deadly operations, including a suicide bombing at the Nahariya train station in which three Israelis died, had been launched. About 14 Palestinians were killed in Jenin. Israeli troops also moved briefly into the edge of the Gaza Strip in another attempt to clean out positions used to fire upon Israeli territory.

Sharon, calling Arafat Israel's bin Laden, resisted U.S. efforts to obtain a pullout from PA areas, and vetoed a meeting between Peres and Arafat that had been scheduled for September 16. The prime minister said that any future meeting between the two could only follow 48 hours of complete quiet. That quiet did not come; after a shooting attack in Jerusalem, Israel sent its troops into the outskirts of Ramallah. After another ostensible Arafat call for a cease-fire, as well as increased U.S. and European pressure, Sharon announced on September 18 that the military action against the Palestinians would be halted: Israeli forces would only fire in self-defense, or in immediate response to a Palestinian attack. Hamas and Islamic Jihad, however, declared a continuation of offensive operations against Israel.

The Peres-Arafat meeting, rescheduled for September 23, was delayed once again by renewed violence, but the two men finally met on September 26. They agreed to reactivate the Tenet-brokered cease-fire deal, but violence broke out again almost immediately, with new terror attacks and Israeli retaliation. Israeli sources said that Arafat had not issued the directives necessary to slow down violence, although Peres did concede that the Israeli army overreacted. In the five days following the Peres-

Arafat meeting, news agencies reported that some 17 Palestinians had been killed and 150 wounded, and 11 Israelis wounded.

British foreign secretary Jack Straw's late-September visit to Israel was marred by comments Straw made in Tehran, on an earlier stop in his Middle East tour. Speaking in the Iranian capital, Straw issued a statement saying: "I understand that one of the factors that helps breed terrorism is the anger many people in this region feel at events over the years in Palestine." Prime Minister Sharon's office called Straw's remarks "one-sided" and "sympathetic to Palestinian terrorism," and canceled a planned meeting between Straw and the Israeli prime minister. Sharon, however, reinstituted the meeting after a phone conversation with British prime minister Tony Blair. Blair's office said that no apologies were made for Straw; Sharon's office quoted Blair as telling the prime minister that Straw's statement did not reflect his own position, and urging Sharon to go ahead with the meeting.

During this period the Americans were building their antiterror coalition. Sharon and other Israeli leaders were disturbed that Israel had been tacitly excluded from the alliance, while Syria and Iran were apparently not being held accountable for their role in sponsoring terror in general, and terror attacks against Israel in particular. At a press conference in Tel Aviv on October 4, Sharon openly expressed his fear that Israel was being abandoned, raising eyebrows abroad and arousing some criticism at home. He called on the Western democracies "not to repeat the horrible error of 1938. The enlightened democracies of Europe decided to sacrifice Czechoslovakia in favor of a convenient temporary solution. Do not try to appease the Arabs on our backs. We are unable to accept that. Israel will not be Czechoslovakia. Israel will fight terrorism."

The comment brought a rare rebuke from the White House. Presidential spokesman Ari Fleischer called Sharon's remarks "unacceptable" and emphasized that President Bush "is an especially close friend of Israel." Furthermore, asserted Fleischer, "the United States would not do anything that would appease the Arabs at Israel's expense." Sharon backed down two days later. In a statement issued by his office, the prime minister expressed his "appreciation of the deep friendship and special relations between the United States and Israel, and especially George W. Bush." Sharon, the statement continued, "requested to forward his appreciation of the bold and courageous decision of the president to fight terrorism. Israel fully supports this position and cooperates with it." Secretary Powell proclaimed an end to the mini-crisis. "It's over," he said. "From time to time we'll have these little cloudbursts, but that does not affect the strength of our relationship . . . Israel has no better friend than the United States, and they know that we know that."

On October 16, the prime minister said he would accept Palestinian statehood, but only under certain circumstances—which he said he would not disclose, lest that plan become the starting-point for future negotiations. Sharon's office denied a report that his plan envisioned a staged process leading to a Palestinian state in several years and complete Israeli evacuation of the Gaza Strip. The office emphasized, again, that there would be no negotiations until the Mitchell recommendations were fully implemented.

The diplomatic process, at this point, appeared to be tilting in Arafat's favor. The PA leader toured European capitals, garnering support for the establishment of a Palestinian state, according to the daily *Ha'aretz,* from prime ministers Tony Blair of Britain, Bertie Aherne of Ireland, and Wim Kok of the Netherlands. At the same time, 28 former top U.S. diplomats and foreign-policy officials who had expertise and experience in the Middle East—including former U.S. envoys to Israel Samuel Lewis, Thomas Pickering, and Edward Walker—wrote to Bush, urging him to act to resolve the Israeli-Palestinian conflict "for a range of reasons, one of which is to prevent our enemies from using the conflict to continue their acts of horror against us."

Israel came in for wide criticism after it moved soldiers into the outskirts of West Bank cities, in reaction to the October 18 assassination in Jerusalem of Tourism Minister Rehavam Ze'evi. After the troops moved in, Arafat met with the U.S. consul general in Jerusalem, Ronald Schlicher (whose post, because of its wide responsibilities in the West Bank and Gaza, was called by some Israelis "ambassador to the Palestinians"), UN special envoy Terje Larsen, and European Union Mideast envoy Miguel Moratinos. Arafat wanted U.S. help in getting Israel to stop its military operation in the territories, and Schlicher and Larsen told him to take "immediate steps" against terror.

On October 22, State Department spokesman Philip Reeker said that the "Israel Defense Force should be withdrawn immediately from all Palestinian-controlled areas, and no further such incursions should be made." Reeker also called on the PA to "do all in its power to halt violence, and to bring to justice the terrorists whose actions are betraying Palestinian interests." The Americans also conveyed a message to Israel, via U.S. ambassador Dan Kurtzer, acknowledging that Israel has informed them that it did not intend to stay indefinitely in the West Bank positions it had recently taken. Sharon, for his part, indicated that the troops would stay until the operation's objectives were achieved. A senior Israeli defense source told *Ha'aretz* that there is "no intention to withdraw from the Area A territories, because there are serious alerts about planned terrorist attacks from those Palestinian areas."

EU leaders visited Israel and the PA in mid-November in an attempt to get the Tenet-Mitchell process started. They were disappointed by Sharon, who stuck to his guns and resisted efforts to lift his demand for seven days of quiet before the start of a formal cease-fire. "In my meeting with the Americans," Sharon told a press conference following his talks, "it was agreed that seven days were needed to see whether Arafat implements the cease-fire. . . . We are firm on what we agreed on with the Americans, that is our position and it is going to be our position in the future." Sharon added that diplomatic negotiations, as envisaged by Mitchell, should only take place after an absolute cessation of terror and incitement; a seven-day trial period for the cease-fire; a six-week cooling-off period; and, finally, confidence-building measures. (Peres, it was well known, was willing to dispense with the seven days of quiet provided that Arafat took credible action against terrorism.) The Europeans were not persuaded by Sharon; according to the usually reliable *Ha'aretz,* EU security chief Javier Solana, speaking to reporters after meeting with Sharon, called the insistence on seven days of quiet "stupidity."

Meanwhile, there were reports of internal difficulties on the Palestinian side. Continuing economic uncertainty brought on by the intifada, some feared, could cause the collapse of the PA, and the Israeli army was worried that this would trigger a wide-scale uprising along the lines of the first intifada of 1987—but with the use of arms. This was hardly the first time that stories about the PA's imminent demise had circulated. As early as February, PA officials had taken pains to divert blame for its problems, pointing out that many of its administrative and financial difficulties, were the direct result of Israeli policy, including the lack of freedom of movement and delays in Israel's transfer of tax revenues collected from Palestinians working in Israel. "Every day of siege costs the PA $10 million," the PA declared. "Israel must remove the siege immediately if it does not want to choke off the Palestinian Authority's economy."

Sharon, in November, spoke more and more openly against Arafat, contending that the PA head was no longer a partner for anything, not even a cease-fire, and charging that Arafat continually and consistently violated agreements. Though never suggesting that Israel would go so far as to eliminate Arafat, Sharon was reported to believe that Israel would be better off if the PA came under the control of security officials such as Jibril Rajoub, the head of West Bank Preventive Security. Such men, in Sharon's opinion, were less tied to ideology, and their pragmatism would possibly enable them to strike a deal based on limited territorial compromise, while postponing, for now, the potentially deal-breaking issues of Jerusalem and the Palestinian refugees' "right of return."

On November 26, the daily *Ha'aretz* reported that senior intelligence sources had told Sharon that Arafat did not appear to be part of a possible solution to the Israeli-Palestinian conflict, for a number of reasons. First, many people in the Palestinian political system were talking about a post-Arafat era. These intelligence sources, said the newspaper, recommended that Israel devote its attention to building contacts with the "next generation" of PA leaders. According to the report, senior Palestinian leadership, feeling that Arafat was leading them down a dead end after registering no political gains after more than a year of violence, complained openly to foreign diplomats and, indeed, to Arafat himself. A second threat to Arafat, Israeli intelligence believed, was the Palestinian "street," which was giving more support to Hamas and Islamic Jihad. Third, Israeli military pressure had seriously damaged Arafat's ability to rule. And fourth, Europe was becoming disenchanted with Arafat, EU officials having discovered that the PA leader had lied to them.

Secretary Powell outlined U.S. Middle East policy in a long-awaited speech at the University of Louisville on November 19. He outlined a two-state solution for the Israeli-Palestinian conflict, while emphasizing the United States' "enduring and ironclad commitment to Israel's security." He called on the Palestinans to "end violence and prepare people for hard compromises ahead," and to make a "100-percent effort to end the violence and terror," including the arrest, prosecution, and punishment of those responsible. The secretary of state—who noted that he was speaking on the 24th anniversary of Egyptian president Anwar Sadat's historic November 1977 visit to Jerusalem, the precursor to the 1978 Camp David agreements and the 1979 Israeli-Egyptian peace treaty—made the U.S. view on settlements in the territories equally clear, saying that they preempted peace efforts. Powell, therefore, called on Israel to end the occupation and allow the Palestinians to establish a "viable" state in which they might control their own lives.

Zinni Mission

Powell also announced that William Burns and retired U.S. Marine general Anthony Zinni would travel to the Middle East on a mediation mission. The U.S. administration's hopes for Zinni were based largely on his reputation for toughness. But in Israel, there were misgivings about the general's lack of strategic vision about the Middle East and about his extensive past contacts with Arab countries. But, after a meeting with Edward Walker, former U.S. ambassador to Israel and assistant secretary of state for Near Eastern affairs in the Clinton administration, the Israeli embassy in Washington sent back an optimistic report, according to *Ha'aretz.* The paper quoted the report as saying: "The fact that Zinni is close to Arab countries could help with a solution. His lack of information could be an opportunity for Israel to present its case." It also suggested that Zinni's inexperience in the conflict could be an advantage. Walker had reportedly said: "We had 15 years of people who knew every detail but they didn't lead anywhere. Maybe someone who comes from somewhere else can refresh the thinking and help reach a solution."

The difficulty of Zinni's task was accentuated a few hours before his arrival in Israel, when Sharon reiterated his insistence on seven days of quiet as a condition for the start of the six-week cooling-off period stipulated in the Mitchell Report. "Israel places great importance on reaching a cease-fire and will do everything it can in order to achieve this aim," said Sharon. "Israel is committed to the Tenet and Mitchell agreements. I hope that the [arrival] of General Zinni will further the process and hasten the start of the seven days of quiet that has been decided upon."

Sharon greeted Zinni personally, taking the envoy on a helicopter tour of the country, including—in addition to the West Bank and Gaza, Jerusalem, and the "seam" areas in the Sharon plain north of Tel Aviv—a visit to his wife Lily's grave at the family farm in the Negev. However Zinni's arrival was also greeted by a new wave of violence. In Gaza, a mortar attack killed an Israeli soldier, five Palestinian boys were killed by an Israeli booby-trap meant for Palestinians firing mortars, and a suicide bomber blew himself up; in the West Bank, meanwhile, the Israelis assassinated Muhammad Abu Hanud, the top Hamas military man there, also killing two of his deputies. Palestinians insisted that the targeting of Abu Hanud was a deliberate Israeli attempt to sabotage the Zinni mission even before it started. "I cannot forecast whether these [U.S.] efforts will succeed because Sharon is trying to drown these efforts in a sea of blood," Palestinian information minister Yasir Abd Rabbo told the Voice of Palestine radio. Other Palestinians suggested that Sharon ordered the hit on Abu Hanud to provoke Hamas into a revenge attack, placing Hamas in a quandary: a violent response would damage Arafat in the Zinni-Burns talks, but failure to respond would damage the organization's prestige. On the Israeli side, Defense Minister Ben-Eliezer justified killing Abu Hanud. Since the Hamas leader had been planning further attacks, explained Ben-Eliezer, refraining from the assassination was "inconceivable," even on the eve of the U.S. peace mission.

Just before his own meetings with Zinni, Arafat told a press conference that he would expend "100-percent effort" to effect a cease-fire. Still, he told Zinni that he rejected Israel's demand for seven days of quiet before implementing the Tenet and Mitchell recommendations. According to senior PA officials, the Israelis were setting a trap for the Americans, since the demand for seven days of quiet—hardly realistic, in the eyes of the Palestinians—would surely sabotage the Zinni initiative. After meeting with Arafat in Ramallah, Zinni said that "both sides have suffered far too much in the last months."

Zinni was as horrified as the rest of the world by the double suicide bombing that took place December 1 on the Ben Yehuda pedestrian mall in central Jerusalem, in which 11 Israelis lost their lives. He stayed on in the region nonetheless, continuing to press for implementation of some kind of cease-fire. In mid-December, after Israel pledged not to take offensive action against Palestinians and only to open fire in self-defense, Zinni attended a joint security meeting in Jerusalem, where he asked Israel to hold off on punitive actions and demanded that the PA take a series of steps to thwart terrorism and round up suspects. Back in the U.S., meanwhile, President Bush expressed his disappointment with Arafat's record in fighting terror. During a meeting with officials of the Conference of Presidents of Major American Jewish Organizations, Bush said, "The U.S. has incontrovertible information showing that Arafat has not arrested Hamas military leaders."

Zinni announced he would stay in the region for another 48 hours and meet with top security officials on both sides. Israel pledged to "act responsibly, and prevent escalation. We have absolutely no intention of acting in an unbridled way. We want Zinni to succeed, and it would be wrong for him to come across as being partisan. We won't provide the Palestinians with excuses not to act." But Israel reserved the right to act in immediate response to gunfire or other attacks on Israel targets, and to neutralize "human time bombs" who were on the way to carry out attacks against Israel. Jibril Rajoub, head of PA Preventive Security on the West Bank, accused Israel of breaking its promise already by attempting to assassinate Mohammed Sidr of the Islamic Jihad in Hebron, even though Sidr did not appear on the list of top terror suspects Israel had submitted to the PA.

In response, Israeli security officials compained that the PA had yet to demonstrate resolve in clamping down on terror. Most leading terror suspects, the Israelis noted, continued to roam freely in the territories, and even those suspects who were ostensibly arrested or detained were not being interrogated by the PA's security officers. While conceding a drop in the number of attacks in the territories and inside Israel proper, Israel insisted that this was due to PA political pressure on Hamas and Islamic Jihad to hold off while Zinni was in the region, and not to a crackdown on terror groups.

On December 3, Sharon delivered a speech to the nation blaming the wave of terror on Arafat. "He is directly responsible for everything that is happening—and he is the greatest obstacle to peace in the Middle East," Sharon said. The terror acts, he added, were designed to "expel us from here. Their aim is to bring us to total despair, a loss of hope and a loss of the national vision which directs us. That won't happen."

On December 9, Israelis get a moral boost from the city that was victim to the world's largest terror attack. Rudy Giuliani, still the mayor of New York, visited Israel together with his successor, Michael Bloomberg, and Governor George Pataki of New York State. The highlight of the trip was a stop at the impromptu memorial to the 11 victims of the December 1 Ben Yehuda mall double suicide bombing.

Whatever progress Zinni might have made came crashing down on December 12, when Palestinian gunmen attacked a bus at the entrance to the largely ultra-Orthodox town of Immanuel on the West Bank, killing ten Israelis. The killers first set a roadside bomb, and then fired with automatic weapons on rescue efforts. Israel responded by breaking off all ties with the PA, sending troops and tanks to lay siege to Palestinian towns, declaring Arafat "irrelevant" to peace efforts, destroying his personal helicopters at their hangar in Gaza, and denying him freedom of movement by moving troops close to Arafat's headquarters in Ramallah.

Washington refrained from issuing its usual call for Israeli restraint, and Israel interpreted this as support for its position. According to U.S. press reports, Powell asked his European counterparts not to invite Arafat for state visits. Washington vetoed a pro-Palestinian resolution at the UN Security Council. The Americans also recalled Zinni to Washington for consultations, State Department spokesman Richard Boucher saying that Zinni would remain in contact with both sides, and eventually return. White House spokesman Ari Fleischer added that Zinni was never meant to stay in the region "forever."

As Zinni left, Arafat, under intense international pressure, addressed his people on Palestinian TV in Arabic, to mark the Muslim holiday of Id al-Fitr, the end of the holy month of Ramadan. He called on them to observe a cease-fire. "Today, I am reiterating my call for a comprehensive cessation to all the armed activities," Arafat declared from his office in Ramallah. "I call for a complete halt to all activities, especially the suicide attacks that we always condemn." Arafat also accused Sharon of declaring war on the Palestinian Authority. Appealing directly to the Israeli public, he said that the only way out of the crisis was to resume peace talks immediately and move toward a Palestinian state on the West Bank and Gaza, with Jerusalem as its capital.

Israel greeted the statement with skepticism. Sources in Sharon's office said that Israel "is sick and tired of talk and false promises and will do what it must to protect its citizens and its existence." Foreign Minister Peres commented: "If the PA wants to exist, it must get out of the cycle of terror." Defense Minister Ben-Eliezer added: "It's nice to talk but the test is action. We've never seen Arafat really fight terror. The test will be real activity against terror."

Violence dropped off significantly thereafter, and Islamic groups pledged to refrain from suicide attacks inside Israel. But Israel continued to insist that such restraint was merely cosmetic, and that the PA had no intention of eschewing violence in the long run. The cease-fire call, according to Israeli sources, was merely a tactical move to reduce pressure on Arafat, as indicated by the sham nature of the PA's arrests—the detainees were allowed freedom of movement—and by the absence of any serious investigation or interrogation of master terrorists.

A YEAR OF BLOODSHED

Killings Continue

The first day of 2001 set the tone for what would be a bloody year. On January 1, Dr. Thabet Thabet, a pediatrician and leader of Yasir Arafat's Fatah movement, was killed by unidentifed—but presumably Israeli—assassins near his home in Tul Karm. Local residents said that an Israeli helicopter hovered overhead as the killers pumped 14 bullets into the body of Thabet, who had been known in the past as an active supporter of the Oslo peace process. Members of Israel's Peace Now movement, who had met with Thabet on numerous occasions, expressed shock that Israel had targeted the physician for a selective killing.

A few days later, Prime Minister Barak justified the policy of assassinations—without reference to the Thabet killing—before the Knesset Foreign Affairs and Defense Committee, saying that Israel had to fight terror by any means at its disposal. But committee chairman Dan Meridor, the former Likud finance and justice minister who helped form the Center Party before the 1999 elections, declared his opposition to such killings, arguing that the law did not allow harming anyone without due process and trial unless the person was in the process of carrying out a terror attack.

Also on January 1, a car bomb went off at about 7 p.m. at a busy intersection in downtown Netanyah. Thirty-four Israelis were injured in the blast, which did serious damage to stores along the busy shopping street. Earlier in the day, two Palestinian gunmen were killed in a battle with Israeli forces near Tul Karm.

Meanwhile, the daily *Ha'aretz* reported that the families of 13 Israeli Arabs killed in clashes with police in early-October 2000 had each received $10,000 from Iraq, on orders of President Saddam Hussein. Earlier, the same familes had gotten 20,000 shekels (about $5,000 at the time) from the Israeli Islamic movement.

On January 5, the army, responding to the Netanya car-bombing a few days earlier, tightened security in the Gaza Strip, effectively dividing the area into three sectors. Palestinians from the Gaza City area were not allowed to pass into the central area, and residents of the central area were blocked from passage either to Gaza City in the north, or to the Rafiah/Khan Yunis area at the southern end of PA territory. Security was also tightened in the West Bank.

Movement was somewhat eased a week later, in tandem with efforts to revive the peace talks. The army lifted its encirclement of Jenin, Qalqilya, and the western exit to Nablus, and ended its division of the Gaza Strip into three sectors. It also allowed the international crossings at the Allenby Bridge, near Jericho, and at Rafiah, at the southern end of the Gaza Strip, facing Sinai, to be reopened, and once again permitted the passage of Palestinian cargo through the Karni checkpoint at the northern end of the Gaza Strip. It also reinstated passes to Palestinian VIPs, allowing their holders to travel freely in the territories without the restrictions to which ordinary Palestinians were routinely subjected. Security contacts between the two sides resumed, but, according to Palestinian reports, not all Israeli troops were pulled back from positions they had taken since the outbreak of violence.

Though the atmosphere seemed somewhat improved, Israelis—and the world—were horrified by the TV pictures of the public execution of two Palestinians convicted of collaboration with Israel. The men executed, over the weekend of January 12–13, were Alam Bani Odeh, in Nablus, and Majdi Mahawi, in Gaza. A firing squad wearing ski masks shot Bani Odeh to death at a square in central Nablus, as an estimated 5,000 spectators call out "*Allahu akhbar*" (God is great). Odeh was conviced of complicity in the fatal explosion of the car of his cousin, Hamas activist Ibrahim Bani Odeh, on November 23, 2000. According to the Palestinians, Alam Bani Odeh took his cousin's car for a few hours just prior to the blast, and turned it over to Israeli agents who planted the explosive in it. Mahawi was executed for allegedly setting a trap near Rafiah on December 22, 2000, for his cousin, Jamal Abd al-Razak of Hamas. In an Israeli attack on the taxi in which Abd al-Razak was riding, the Hamas man and three others were killed. The executions, and especially the public manner in which they were carried out, raised protests in Israel and other places; human-rights groups pointed out that the executions happened within days of the men's convictions, effectively denying them any right of appeal.

On January 14, Roni Tzalah, an Israeli, was kidnapped and murdered in the southern Gaza Strip. Shortly afterward, other Israelis living in Gaza rampaged through several nearby villages, burning cars and shops, uprooting trees, and destroying Palestinian greenhouses and irrigation equipment. Fatah Tanzim took responsibility for the Tzalah killing, as it did for the January 17 murder of Hisham Miki, 54, the head of Palestinian TV. Miki, a close associate of Yasir Arafat, was shot to death by masked gunmen as he sat over lunch in a Gaza seaside restaurant; his killers said the assassination was a blow against PA corruption.

Israel, suffering from conventional forms of terror, was horrified on the morning of January 18, when Palestinian security forces turned over the body of 16-year-old Ophir Rahum to Israel. Rahum had been lured to Jerusalem by a woman he met on the Internet who identified herself as "Sally" and promised to have sex with him. They arranged a meeting at the Jerusalem central bus station; from there she drove him to Ramallah and took him to two senior Fatah operatives, Hassan al-Kadi and Abdu Fatah Doleh, from the village of Beituniya, near Ramallah. The boy was shot to death in the car, with an AK-47 assault rifle. His body was temporarily buried, then turned over to Palestinian officials by local residents. Within a few days the Shin Bet, using records from the boy's computer and an Internet chat room, located Amana Muna, 25, who admitted her role, but first said that she and the others had planned only to kidnap the boy. Brought before a court later, she declared herself proud of what she had done.

Ha'aretz quoted two of Ophir's friends as saying that their pal had already met the woman once in Jerusalem, at the home of one of her friends. "Ophir was certain that she was a tourist. He had no idea she was an Arab. He described her as having black hair and being good looking, and was very excited that a woman in her 20s was interested in him. I am sure he was not aware of any danger. He trusted her because he had been with her in the past," one told the newspaper after Ophir's funeral.

On January 23, Israel was shocked again by the brutal, execution-style murder of two Israeli restarateurs, Motti Dayan, 27, and Etgar Zeituni, 34, who had gone to Tul Karm to buy flower pots for their Yuppies sushi bar on Tel Aviv's trendy Sheinkin Street. Accompanied by an Israeli Arab (who was later cleared of any involvement in the killings), they stopped to eat at the Abu Nidal restaurant in the PA-controlled town, and were grabbed by a group of masked men who drove them to a road near the Nur Shams refugee camp where they pushed the men out of the car and shot them in the head. The killers reportedly filmed the murder.

Tensions remained high throughout the period of the Israeli elections, with rioting and more violence after Sharon's victory. Israel continued its policy of targeted killings. On February 13, Mosoud Ayad, who, Israel said, was linked to Hezballah and was responsible for a number of mortar attacks on Gaza Strip settlements, was killed by Israeli helicopters. And on February 19, Hamas operative Mahmoud Madani, who, Israel claimed, was responsible for two February 8 car bombs in Jerusalem's Me'ah She'arim ultra-Orthodox neighborhood, was shot by Israeli security units inside Nablus.

Terror took a new form on February 14, when Khalil Abu Qibeh, a Palestinian who worked legally ferrying laborers from Gaza to Israel, drove his bus into a crowd of soldiers and civilians at a bus stop near Holon. Eight people were killed.

Another potential kidnap-murder episode was avoided on March 25, when Arafat intervened to obtain the freedom of four Israelis, three of them Arabs and one of them a Jew, who were taken into custody by members of Arafat's Fatah movement in Tul Karm. The men were spotted as Israelis in the Tarboosh restaurant, and arrested. Arafat, informed of the incident, sent out Palestinian security forces to find the Israelis and make sure they were unharmed. They were returned to Israel several hours later. Israeli police said that "dozens" of criminal files had been opened in the preceding months against Israelis, Jewish and Arab, who violated the ban against entering PA-controlled Area A.

But, on March 26, another horrifying killing took place. Shalhevet Pas, ten months old, was shot to death by a Palestinian sniper. At the time of the shooting, the baby was being held by her mother near their home in Hebron's Jewish Quarter, and the shots were fired from PA-controlled Abu Sneina, a hilltop neighborhood overlooking the Jewish Quarter. Settlers demanded that Israel move into Abu Sneina and "win the war against terrorism." The Pas family delayed their daughter's funeral beyond the traditional one day between death and burial, vowing that she would be put to rest only after the army conquered Abu Sneina. The hilltop was not taken, and Shalhevet was finally buried a week later, in Hebron's ancient Jewish cemetery. Hebron settlers took out their anger by going on a rampage against Palestinian shops in the city, triggering gas-balloon explosions in several of them.

In response to mortar attacks on Israeli settlements in the Gaza Strip, Israel sent tanks and bulldozers into the Khan Yunis refugee camp, at the southern end of the strip, on April 11. And on April 16, after mortar shells hit the outskirts of the Israeli development town of Sderot, east of the northern end of the strip, Israel temporarily took over PA land in the village of Beit Hanun. Israel withdrew its troops the next day, insisting that the operation was over—although Palestinians suggested that the pullback came only after pressure from the United States, whose secretary of state, Colin Powell, called the action "excessive and disproportionate." A few days later, another similar raid took place in southern Gaza, where Israeli tanks moved in to destroy a Palestinian police post and then withdrew after a few hours.

On April 16, Israeli planes—responding to the April 14 killing of soldier Ehud Litvak by a Hezballah rocket on the Lebanese border—bombed a Syrian radar station near Beirut. Three Syrian soldiers were killed in the attack, Israel's first strike against Syrian forces in five years. Despite rising tensions, Jordanian foreign minister Abdul Illa al-Khatib came to Jerusalem for talks with Shimon Peres, his counterpart; Khatib was the first top Arab diplomat to visit Israel since Sharon took office.

The attack on the Syrian radar station reflected the Sharon government's view that, despite the relatively lengthy pauses between Hezballah actions against Israeli troops along the northern border, Sheikh Hassan Nasrallah and others in the leadership of the Shi'ite Muslim organization had been operating on the assumption that Israel would not respond. The strike against Syrian targets was intended as a signal to Damascus, which was in de-facto control of Lebanon.

In response to Palestinian mortar fire on the Jerusalem neighborhood of Gilo, Israeli forces moved briefly into neighboring Beit Jalla on May

6. Israeli sources said that radical Palestinians, including the Tanzim militia of Arafat's Fatah movement, had been attacking from the mainly Christian town partly because of the impact an Israeli attack there would have on world opinion. Israel said it had planned the operation to take only a few hours, but Palestinians claimed that the area was a major battlefield, and they had lost one dead and 20 wounded in the fighting. There were no Israeli casualties. But exchanges of fire continued, and on May 14 seven Palestinians died and four Israelis were injured in shooting between Beit Jalla and Gilo.

A day later, in response to a mortar attack, Israel shelled southern Gaza, killing a four-month-old baby; Sharon said that Israel "will make every effort to try and avoid tragic cases" in the future.

Violence continued through much of May. Two Israeli teenagers were brutally stoned to death just outside the settlement of Tekoa, near the historic Herodion fortress east of Bethlehem, on May 9. An Israeli raid near Ramallah on May 14 killed five Palestinian police officers; Palestinians said that four of the men were asleep when the Israeli attack took place, and Arafat accused Israel of "a dirty immoral operation." Yasir Abd Rabbo, the PA's information minister, said the killing was "well-calculated . . . and consistent with the policy of the Israeli army, to carry out assassinations and mass executions of Palestinian security forces and officials." Israel explained that until just before the attack, the post had been used by Force 17, Arafat's presidential guard, which had been involved in numerous terror attacks in the area, although Lt. Gen. Shaul Mofaz, Israel's chief of staff, admitted that the results of the operation were "not as intended."

On May 15, Palestinians marked the 53rd anniversary of Israeli independence—or in their terms "al-Nakba" (the Disaster). In a day of rioting throughout the territories, Palestinians counted their casualties at four dead and over 2,000 injured.

After a Palestinian suicide bomb at a Netanya shopping center killed five Israelis on May 18, Israel struck back hard. The same day, it sent F-16 warplanes to drop heavy bombs on PA targets—most of them police posts already abandoned by the Palestinians, in anticipation of the imminent attacks. Twelve Palestinians, however, were killed.

The U.S. was far from pleased by Israel's use of American-made warplanes in this operation. On May 21, Powell called for an immediate, unconditional end to violence, and launched a more active role for the U.S. in efforts to bring about a cease-fire. Sharon announced that he had ordered Israeli troops to stop initiating actions against the Palestinians, but the terror organizations did not cooperate. The following week saw a rash of bombings: a car bomb in Hadera injured 65, another car bomb just missed an army convoy in the Gaza Strip, four people were hurt when two car bombs went off in central Jerusalem, and yet another car bomb exploded in Netanya, injuring four. Not even Palestinian VIPs were spared the effects of tightened security—an army shell hit the home of Jibril Rajoub, head of PA Preventive Security in the West Bank. Rajoub, who was in the house at the time, was not injured, but five of his aides suffered slight wounds. Defense Minister Ben-Eliezer said categorically, "I cannot imagine that any IDF commander would think of firing at Jibril Rajoub and his home." The army explained that it was returing fire from the building; it knew that the house belonged to Rajoub, but he was not a target.

Tel Aviv Dolphinarium

On June 1, 21 people—most of them teenage immigrants from the former Soviet Union—were killed in a suicide bombing outside a disco at the Dolphinarium on the Tel Aviv seafront. Israel immediately sealed off the West Bank and Gaza, and Sharon convened an emergency cabinet meeting, but Israel did nothing. Responding to criticism of the army's inaction, Sharon declared that restraint was also a display of strength. In the weeks after the Dolphinarium attack, security forces said they suspected that the nuts, bolts, and nails that were part of the bomber's "package" might have been treated with bacteria in order to magnify the lethal effect, noting that infections from the Tel Aviv atrocity were 25 percent greater than what was normal in such cases. A 22nd person later died of his wounds.

On June 22, two Israeli soldiers were killed by a car bomb in the Gaza Strip. The men, Avi Izhak and Ofer Kit, had gone to help a Palestinian woman calling for help, and approached a jeep parked by the side of the road. The Hamas suicide bomber inside the vehicle then blew himself up.

Palestinian terror was not Israel's only worry. On June 24, the daily *Ha'aretz,* quoting Mossad intelligence reports, suggested that the Al Qaeda organization of Osama bin Laden "may try to carry out a major attack on an Israeli embassy." Security was tightened around Israeli legations in East Africa, where bin Laden forces bombed U.S. embassies in Kenya and Zambia in 1998; at the same time, Washington put its troops in the Persian Gulf on Delta-stage alert.

Israel continued its policy of targeted elimination of terror leaders. Osama Jawabreh, 29, of Fatah, nicknamed "Nanny," was killed by an explosion at a public phone in Nablus. This killing was almost identical to the elimination, in April, of Islamic Jihad military chief Iyad Hardan. The Shin Bet described Jawabreh as an explosives expert, and said he was building car bombs to be sent into Israeli cities. Because of the rash of attacks on the road, the army ordered settlers to travel in convoys on certain highways in the West Bank, or in cars protected against gunfire. Such a level of armor-plating for an ordinary automobile, according to *Ha'aretz,* cost 350,000 shekels (over $80,000).

In mid-June, Israeli Arab journalist Yusuf Samir, in his 60s, returned to Israeli territory after spending more than two months in PA custody. The Egyptian-born Samir—the father of popular Israeli singer Haya Samir—had vanished in Bethlehem on April 4, after a run-in with members of Yasir Arafat's presidential guard. For the two months that Samir was missing, the PA had denied any knowledge of his whereabouts. But Samir now charged he had been held by PA security forces, who interrogated him and accused him of spying for Israel. He said that he had escaped from the place where he was held, in Bethlehem's Duha neighborhood, when a guard fell asleep at his post, and managed to reach the Israeli army's checkpoint at Rachel's Tomb, on the outskirts of the city. Israeli sources, however, suggested that Samir's escape had been staged by the PA, which had become embarrassed by the affair.

Attempted bombings continued intermittently. In late July, a car bomb went off prematurely, injuring no one, in a car park under an apartment building in Jerusalem's Pisgat Ze'ev neighborhood, and another 7-kg. explosive device, hidden in a watermelon, was found in a bus near the city's Malha shopping mall, and defused. Egged bus driver Menashe Nuriel pushed a potential suicide bomber out of his bus in the Jordan Valley on August 2. The next day, an alert security guard spotted a bomb planted in a detergent box at the Tel Aviv central bus station.

Eight soldiers and two civilians were lightly wounded on August 5, when Ali Ibrahim Joulani of East Jerusalem fired an automatic rifle at pedestrians outside the offices of the Defense Ministry, near the Azrieli Tower office complex in central Tel Aviv. After spraying the area with bullets, Joulani—who had a history of working with Israelis, no known terror links, and no criminal record—got into his car and apparently tried to escape. He was shot to death by a police officer on the scene.

Sbarro

On August 9, a Hamas suicide bomber blew himself up in the Sbarro pizza restaurant at the corner of King George Street and Jaffa Road in downtown Jerusalem. Fifteen Israelis—including five members of one family—were killed in the blast. (In September, the Palestinian Authority closed down an exhibition by students at a-Najah University in Nablus, commemorating the month that had past since the Sbarro bombing. The "Sbarro Café Exhibition" included "body parts" from mannequins, and red paint, to indicate blood, was splashed on the walls. Another part of the exhibit paid tribute to the *shaheed,* or martyrs, who carried out suicide-bomb operations, including a depiction of one, as shown in videotapes taken by Hamas and Islamic Jihad, with a Koran in one hand and a AK-47 Kalashnikov assault rifle in the other. According to one account, the display also showed a Palestinian crouched behind a rock, getting ready to pounce on a mannequin in the garb of an ultra-Orthodox Jew, as a taped recording, playing on the loudspeakers, called out: "Oh Believer. There is a Jewish man behind me. Come and kill him.")

Despite heightened security precautions that had the police and the army on a constant state of high alert, suicide bombings continued. An Islamic Jihad attacker exploded his bomb on August 12 just outside the Wall Street coffee shop in the Haifa suburb of Kiryat Bialik, wounding 20 people. Had he triggered the explosive device inside the store, the toll would have undoubtedly been much higher. Israel responded by closing down a number of Palestinian institutions in East Jerusalem—including Orient House, the PA headquarters in the city—and deployed F-16s to bomb the police headquarters in Ramallah. The Orient House closing drew wide criticism from the United States and Europe, and Palestinians described it as an escalation that would bring the intifada to the capital.

On August 16, a Palestinian cabdriver was killed north of Ramallah. As his cab was hit by stones, the cabbie lost control, and died in the crash. Police suspected that the taxi was hit by a rock thrown from an Israeli vehicle headed in the opposite direction, which was seen by passengers inside the taxi.

Israeli security forces remained on a high state of alert, and numerous terror acts were stopped before the perpetrators could reach their intended targets. On August 16–17, for example, a police dragnet was set into motion after warnings of planned suicide bombings in the north of the country, perhaps in Haifa, Hadera, or Afula. Police stopped a suspicious car with two Palestinians in it outside the Israeli Arab village of Baka al-Garbiyeh and arrested two suspects. The car contained a 10-kg. explosive device, and the suspects said that one of them, who had worked in the Haifa area and knew Hebrew well, had planned to carry out a suicide terror attack at the City Hall nightclub on Shabtai Levy Street in

Haifa, which was hosting a large party for teenagers that night. Police and Shin Bet officials noted that Hamas and other radical Palestinian organizations had increasingly been targeting places of entertainment, particularly those frequented by young people.

Israel continued to respond to Palestinian attacks by moving into PA-controlled areas briefly in order to make arrests and destroy key firing positions. It began such an occupation of the Abu Sneina hill, overlooking the Jewish Quarter of Hebron, on August 22, and destroyed two positions used by snipers. Two days later, the Israeli forces withdrew.

The policy of "selective eliminations" netted its most important target yet on August 27, when two rockets fired from a helicopter hit the second-floor office of Abu Ali Mustafa, 63, the leader of the Popular Front for the Liberation of Palestine (PFLP). The office was very close to the Ramallah headquarters of Yasir Arafat. Mustafa, the highest-ranking Palestinian killed in the current intifada, was sitting at his desk, and died instantly. While the Palestinians claimed that he was only a political leader, Israel believed he was personally responsible for the planning and execution of several terrorist attacks against Israel, including the dispatch of two car bombs (a PFLP specialty) to Jerusalem. Abu Ali Mustafa was actually the nom de guerre of Mustafa Zibri, who succeeded the Marxist-leaning PFLP's founder, George Habash, as secretary general of the group. He had returned to the West Bank in 1999, after 32 years in exile.

About a month after the Mustafa killing, the PFLP, the second-largest PLO faction after Arafat's Fatah, selected Ahmed Saadat as its new leader. Saadat, 48, a teacher of mathematics, had spent ten years in Israeli jails. He was considered a representative of the PFLP's "radical" wing, and in some quarters his selection was seen as pushing the PFLP toward more aggressive anti-Israeli actions.

In early September, the PFLP "responded" to the Mustafa assassination by setting off four car bombs in downtown Jerusalem; there were no serious injuries. Another attack in the same area of the capital by a Hamas suicide bomber dressed as an ultra-Orthodox Jew, on September 4, resulted in the wounding of 13 Israelis and a grisly scene, as the bomber's body parts were scattered over a wide area on Nevi'im Street near the Bikur Holim Hospital. The man appeared to be headed towards the main Jaffa Road-King George Street intersection (scene of the Sbarro pizzeria bombing less than a month earlier) when he was spotted by two border policemen, and when they approached him he blew himself up. One of the four people seriously wounded in the attack was one of the policemen, an Ethiopian immigrant.

Violence continued intermittently over the next month, with more terror attacks—including a suicide bombing at the Nahariya train station on September 9 carried out by an Israeli Arab from the Abu Snaan village near Acre, and a drive-by shooting on the West Bank. In response, Israel dispatched tanks and troops into Jenin, on the northern West Bank, and sent forces briefly into Ramallah and areas of the Gaza Strip.

On October 4, Palestinian gunmen firing from the hilltop Abu Sneina quarter (the same area from which the shots that killed baby Shalhevet Pas were fired) hit Sukkot holiday worshipers at Hebron's Machpela Cave (Cave of the Patriarchs). The following day, Israeli troops moved into Abu Sneina and held the area for ten days before withdrawing. Seven Palestinians were reportedly killed in the fighting.

Ze'evi Assassination

On October 18, Tourism Minister Rehavam Ze'evi, a controversial figure from the far-right party National Union-Yisrael Beitenu, was shot to death by gunmen from the Popular Front for the Liberation of Palestine. The shooting took place just outside the room on the eighth floor of the Jerusalem Hyatt Hotel where Ze'evi had spent his weekdays in Jerusalem for years. The minister had gone back to his room after an early breakfast to be interviewed on the phone; the gunmen were waiting for him in the corridor. Ze'evi's body was discovered by his wife and constant companion, Ya'el. His funeral the following day was a show of strength by the right wing, with calls for stronger action against the PA. Two of the four men suspected of involvement in the killing were soon picked up by the Israelis. (About a month later, a Shin Bet report indicated that some of the responsibility for Ze'evi's death rested on the minister himself, because he refused to accept security guards, maintained a regular schedule, and insisted on living in the Hyatt, although it was adjacent to Arab neighborhoods in East Jerusalem. The report recommended adoption of a law requiring VIPs who have been assigned Shin Bet bodyguards to obey those security people, as was the case in other countries.)

Israel responded to the killing by moving its troops into six Palestinian towns. On the same day, Atef Abayat, a Fatah Tanzim leader whom Israel held responsible for several drive-by murders in the Bethlehem area, was killed by an explosion in his car. A week later, Abayat's cousin and two other Palestinians accused of involvement in terror were killed in a similar blast. Israel continued its policy of targeted killings—the most prominent victim was Jamil Jadallah of Hamas in Hebron.

Israel pulled its forces out of Bethlehem on October 29. According to Palestinian claims, about 50 Palestinians were killed in intermittent fighting during the two-week incursion into PA-controlled Area A. Troops remained in place around other cities. Terror continued, however, virtually unabated in late November and early December—a shooting attack at the Afula market on November 27, a suicide bombing and a drive-by shooting on November 29, and two large-scale attacks: the December 1 double suicide bombing in Jerusalem's Ben Yehuda downtown pedestrian mall in which 11 Israelis died, and a December 2 suicide bus bomb in Haifa with 15 fatalities. Israel's response was surprisingly restrained, despite mounting pressure on Sharon.

On November 22, five Palestinian boys in Khan Yunis were killed when an Israeli boobytrap went off as they were on their way to school. The army at first denied there were any munitions in the area, and only on December 19 did it admit responsibility, adding that a series of operational errors were involved.

On November 23, Israel's policy of targeted killing netted Hamas master-terrorist Muhammad Abu Hanud, 34, of Asira al-Shamalieh, near Nablus. Two other top Hamas terror operatives were killed in the operation. Abu Hanud had been personally involved in a lengthy series of bombings directed against Israeli civilians, had taken part in the overall planning of Hamas operations in the West Bank, and, in the summer of 1997, had personally dispatched five suicide bombers. According to Israel, Abu Hanud had been a senior player in the planning of the August 9 Sbarro bombing in Jerusalem and the June 1 Dolphinarium attack in Tel Aviv, and the controller of a number of suicide bombers based in Tul Karm who were intercepted by Israeli security forces before reaching their targets. In August 2000, before the start of the intifada, three soldiers of Israel's elite Duvdevan antiterror unit were killed by friendly fire in a botched attempt to capture Abu Hanud at his home village (see AJYB 2001, p. 485).

In early December, the sheikh of the Al-Azhar mosque in Cairo—who, by virtue of his post, was one of the most influental religious authorities in the Muslim world—ruled that Islamic law did not authorize suicide attacks against innocent victims. That quickly drew a response from the mufti of Jerusalem, Sheikh Arameh Sabri, who charged that the sheikh's religious ruling was brought about by outside pressure. "Those who do not have the courage to speak the truth should remain quiet," said Sabri, an appointee of PA head Arafat. "Resistance is legitimate and those who give their lives do not require permission from anyone." Sabri declared that Muslims "must stand at the side and encourage" those who engage in jihad, holy war. And, in an interview with the international Arabic-language *Al-Hayat* newspaper, he responded to a question about attacking innocent Israeli civilians: "Who is civilian and who is military? There have been many more Palestinian civilians than fighters killed in the intifada. School children whose bodies were torn to pieces. Pregnant women who were prevented from reaching hospitals, where many times the mother and the child both died."

Israel reacted strongly to a December 12 Hamas attack at the entrance to the West Bank ultra-Orthodox town of Immanuel, where attackers planted a roadside bomb that crippled a bus and then fired on rescue efforts, killing ten people in all. Israel then launched heavy attacks on West Bank and Gaza targets and tightened its siege on West Bank cities—including moving tanks very close to Arafat's headquarters in Ramallah and restricting the PA boss's movements. Amid reports that Israel was seeking to push Arafat out, the cabinet declared the PA leader "irrelevant." Arafat, seeking to relieve growing military pressure from Israel and political pressure from the EU and the U.S., delivered a speech on December 16 on PA TV in Arabic, in which he called for an end to "armed activities" against Israel (see above, p. 545).

The call got a tepid response from Palestinians. Hamas indicated that it would hold off, for the time being, on attacks inside Israel; Islamic Jihad made no such commitment. Violence did seem to taper off—though Israel pointed out that it was still continuing at a lower level. There were more attacks in the territories. On December 24, for example, Vitaly Binus, 47, was driving along a road between Nablus and Tul Karm when he was attacked by three Fatah gunmen. Binus fought them off, but was seriously wounded. Before losing consciousness, though, he managed to shoot one of the attackers to death. Meanwhile, efforts to root out terrorists responsible for earlier murderous attacks continued. On December 24, the Shin Bet security service announced it had cracked the Hamas cell that carried out the December 2 Haifa bus bombing; the key suspects were two bomb-making brothers from Jenin.

Israel prevented Yasir Arafat from making his traditional Christmas Eve visit to Bethlehem, saying that it would allow the PA leader to make the trip of a few miles from Ramallah, north of Jerusalem, to Bethlehem, south of the city, only if the PA turned over the two PFLP killers of Tourism Minister Ze'evi who were still at large.

In a survey of its activity against Palestinian targets during 2001, the Israeli air force reported that its assault helicopters had fired 500 missiles of various types, and that F-16 warplanes had dropped 80 bombs, the largest of which weighed one ton. The air force indicated that civilian casualties of its attacks had been relatively few (it did not give a number), but noted that despite the use of precision weapons, even the most minor mishap could lead to injuries and death for innocent civilians.

Police registered 1,794 terror acts on Israelis in 2001, compared to 410 in 2000. For the year, 208 people were killed and 1,523 injured. Police sappers defused 27 bombs in 2001, and nine terrorists were killed by police during terror strikes. Jerusalem suffered 90 attacks, the most of any city; these included 35 bombings and 28 incidents of gunfire.

Israeli Victims of Terror Attacks, 2001

January 14—The bullet-ridden body of Roni Tzalah, 32, of Kfar Yam in Gush Katif, is found near the Kfar Yam hothouses. Tzalah was apparently killed by Palestinians who worked on his farm.

January 17—The bullet-riddled body of Ophir Rahum, 16, of Ashkelon, is handed over to Israeli authorities. On the previous day, Rahum traveled to Jerusalem to meet a young woman with whom he had conducted a relationship over the Internet. She then drove him toward Ramallah. At a prearranged location, another vehicle drove up and three Palestinian gunmen inside shot Rahum more than 15 times. One terrorist drove off with Rahum's body and dumped it, while the others fled in the second vehicle.

January 23—Motti Dayan, 27, and Etgar Zeituny, 34, cousins from Tel Aviv, are abducted from a restaurant in Tul Karm by masked Palestinian gunmen and executed.

January 25—Akiva Pashkos, 45, of Jerusalem, is shot dead in a terror attack near the Atarot industrial zone north of Jerusalem.

January 29—Arye Hershkowitz, 55, of Ofra, north of Ramallah in the West Bank, is killed by shots fired from a passing car near the Rama junction.

February 1—Dr. Shmuel Gillis, 42, a father of five from the settlement of Karmei Tzur, is killed by Palestinian gunmen who fire at his car near the Aroub refugee camp on the Jerusalem-Hebron highway. Lior Attiah, 23, of Afula is shot to death by terrorists while traveling near Jenin.

February 5—Sgt. Rujayah Salameh, 23, is killed by sniper fire near Rafiah at the southern end of the Gaza Strip.

February 11—Tzachi Sasson, 35, of Kibbutz Rosh Tzurim in Gush Etzion, is shot and killed by Palestinian gunmen while driving home from Jerusalem.

February 14—Simcha Shitrit, 30, of Rishon Lezion; Staff-Sgt. Ofir Magidish, 20, of Kiryat Malachi; Sgt. David Iluz, 21, of Kiryat Malachi; Sgt. Julie Weiner, 21, of Jerusalem; Sgt. Rachel Levi, 19, of Ashkelon; Sgt. Kochava Polanski, 19, of Ashkelon; Cpl. Alexander Manevich, 18, of Ashkelon; and Cpl. Yasmin Karisi, 18, of Ashkelon are killed when a bus driven by a Palestinian plows into a group of soldiers and civilians waiting at a bus stop near Holon, south of Tel Aviv. Another 25 people are injured in the attack.

February 26—The body of Mordechai Shefer, 55, of Kfar Sava, is found in an olive grove near Moshav Hagor. Investigators suspect terrorism.

March 1—Claude Knap, 29, of Tiberias is killed and nine people injured when a terrorist detonates a bomb in a Tel Aviv-to-Tiberias shared *sherut* (service) taxi at the Mei Ami junction in Wadi Ara, north of Tel Aviv.

March 4—Naftali Dean, 85, of Tel Mond; his niece, Shlomit Ziv, 58, of Netanya; and Yevgenya Malchin, 70, of Netanya are killed in a suicide bombing in downtown Netanya; 60 people are injured. Hamas claims responsibility.

March 19—Baruch Cohen, 59, of Efrat, dies when shots are fired at his car while he is driving to work in Jerusalem from his home in the Gush Etzion area. After being hit by bullets, he loses control of the car and collides with an oncoming truck.

March 26—Shalhevet Pas, ten months old, is killed by sniper fire, while being held by her mother, at the entrance to the Jewish Quarter in Hebron.

March 28—Eliran Rosenberg-Zayat, 15, of Givat Shmuel and Naftali Lanzkorn, 13, of Petah Tikva die in a suicide bombing at the Mifgash Hashalom ("Peace Stop") gas station several hundred meters from an IDF roadblock near the entrance to Qalqilya, east of Kfar Sava. The boys are on their way to a religious school in the West Bank. Four others are wounded in the attack, for which Hamas claims responsibility.

April 1—Reserve Staff Sgt. Ya'akov Krenschel, 23, of Nahariya, dies of wounds suffered in a firefight between army and Palestinian forces southeast of Nablus. Dina Guetta, 42, of Haifa, is stabbed to death on Ha'atzmaut Street; her murder turns out to be an initiation ceremony into a terrorist cell, which is apprehended in July.

April 2—Sgt. Danny Darai, 20, of Arad, is killed by a Palestinian sniper after completing guard duty at Rachel's Tomb at the entrance to Bethlehem.

April 21—The mutilated body of Stanislav Sandomirsky, 38, of Beit Shemesh, is found in the trunk of his car near a village north of Ramallah. Sandomirsky vanished on his way home from Jerusalem to Beit Shemesh the previous night.

April 22—Dr. Mario Goldin, 53, of Kfar Sava, dies when a Hamas terrorist detonates a powerful bomb at a bus stop on the corner of Weizman and Tchernichovsky streets in the city, north of Tel Aviv. About 60 people are injured.

April 28—Shlomo Elmakias, 20, of Netanya, an off-duty soldier, dies, and four women passengers are wounded in a drive-by terrorist shooting attack on the Wadi Ara highway in the Galilee.

April 28—Simcha Ron, 60, of Nahariya, is found stabbed to death in Kfar Ba'aneh, near Carmiel in the Galilee. The terrorists responsible are apprehended in July.

May 1—Assaf Hershkowitz, 30, of Ofra, is killed when his vehicle overturns after being fired upon at a junction between Ofra and Beit El. The victim's father, Arye, was killed not far from the same place in January.

May 8—Terrorists kill Arnaldo Agranionic, 48, at the Binyamin Farm, a lonely outpost where he lived, on an isolated hilltop east of Itamar in Samaria.

May 9—Yossi Ish-Ran, 14, and Kobi Mandell, 14, both of Tekoa, are found stoned to death in a cave about 200 meters from the small settlement near Herodion, south of Jerusalem, where they lived.

May 10—Constantin Straturula, 52, and Virgil Martinesc, 29, two Romanian citizens employed by an Israeli contractor, are killed in a bomb attack while repairing a vandalized fence at the Kissufim Crossing into the Gaza District.

May 15—Idit Mizrahi, 20, of Rimonim, is fatally shot in an ambush as she, her father, and brother drive along the Alon Road in the West Bank on their way to a wedding. Terrorists fire 30 bullets, 19 of which hit the family's car.

May 18—Tirza Polonsky, 66, of Moshav Kfar Haim; Miriam Waxman, 51, of Hadera; David Yarkoni, 53, of Netanya; Yulia Tratiakova, 21, of Netanya; and Vladislav Sorokin, 34, of Netanya die in a suicide bombing at Hasharon Mall in the seaside city of Netanya. Over 100 others are wounded. Hamas claims responsibility.

May 18—Lt. Yair Nebenzahl, 22, of Neve Tzuf is killed and his mother seriously wounded in a Palestinian roadside ambush north of Jerusalem.

May 23—Asher Iluz, 33, of Modi'in dies in an ambush outside Ariel, where he was heading to supervise road paving.

May 25—The burnt body of Yosef Alfasi, 50, of Rishon Lezion, is discovered near the West Bank city of Tul Karm.

May 29—Gilad Zar, 41, of Itamar, dies in a terrorist ambush while driving in the West Bank between Kedumim and Yizhar. The Fatah Tanzim claim responsibility. Sarah Blaustein, 53, and Esther Alvan, 20, of Efrat, are killed in a drive-by shooting near Neve Daniel in the Etzion bloc south of Jerusalem.

May 31—Zvi Shelef, 63, of Mevo Dotan, is the victim of a drive-by shooting attack north of Tul Karm. Shot in the head, he dies en route to the hospital.

June 1—Marina Berkovizki, 17, of Tel Aviv; Roman Dezanshvili, 21, of Bat Yam; Ilya Gutman, 19, of Bat Yam; Anya Kazachkov, 16, of Holon; Katherine Kastaniyada-Talkir, 15, of Ramat Gan; Aleksei Lupalu, 16, of Ukraine; Mariana Medvedenko, 16, of Tel Aviv; Irina Nepomneschi, 16, of Bat Yam; Yelena Nelimov, 18, of Tel Aviv; Yulia Nelimov, 16, of Tel Aviv; Raisa Nimrovsky, 15, of Netanya; Pvt. Diez (Dani) Normanov, 21, of Tel Aviv; Simona Rodin, 18, of Holon; Ori Shahar, 32, of Ramat Gan; Liana Sakiyan, 16, of Tel Aviv; Maria Tagilchev, 14, of Netanya; and Irena Usdachi, 18, of Holon die in a suicide bombing outside a disco near Tel Aviv's Dolphinarium along the seafront promenade just before midnight on Friday night. Sergei Pancheskov, 20, of Ukraine; Yael-Yulia Sklianik, 15, of Holon; Jan Bloom, 25, of Ramat Gan; and Yevgenia Dorfman, 15, of Bat Yam later die from their injuries. The explosion also wounds 120 people.

June 11—Yehuda Shoham, aged 5 months, of Shilo in the West Bank, dies of injuries incurred on June 5, when he was critically injured by a rock thrown at the family's car near the settlement, north of Jerusalem.

June 12—Father Georgios Tsibouktzakis, 34, a Greek Orthodox monk from the St. George Monastery in Wadi Kelt in the Judean desert, is shot and killed while driving on the Jerusalem-Ma'ale Adumim road, east of the capital. A week later, the Shin Bet security service arrests two members of Force 17, Arafat's presidential guard, who, it says, confess to the murder. According to the report, the killers—who mistook the monk for an Israeli because he was driving a car with yellow Israeli license plates—said they had obtained the weapons they used, two AK-47 Kalashnikov assault rifles, from an aide to Tanzim militia head Marwan Barghouti.

June 14—Lt. Col. Yehuda Edri, 45, of Ma'ale Adumim near Jerusalem is killed by a Palestinian informant for Israeli intelligence in a shooting attack on the Bethlehem bypass tunnel road connecting the Gush Etzion bloc with Jerusalem. One of his security guards is seriously injured.

June 18—Dan Yehuda, 35, of Homesh dies in a drive-by shooting between Homesh and Shavei Shomron, near Nablus. Doron Zisserman, 38, of Einav, is shot and killed in his car by sniper fire near the entrance to Einav, east of Tul Karm.

June 20—Ilya Krivitz, 62, of Homesh in Samaria, is shot to death at close range in an ambush in the Palestinian town of Silat a-Dahar, near his home.

June 22—Sgt. Aviv Iszak, 19, of Kfar Saba, and Sgt. Ofir Kit, 19, of Jerusalem, are killed in a suicide bombing near Dugit in the Gaza Strip, when a jeep with yellow Israeli license plates, supposedly stuck in the sand, blew up as they approached.

June 28—Ykaterina (Katya) Weintraub, 27, of Ganim in northern Samaria is killed and another woman injured by shots fired at the two-car convoy on the Jenin bypass road.

July 2—Aharon Obadyan, 41, of Zichron Ya'akov is shot to death near Baka al-Sharkia, north of the West Bank city of Tul Karm and close to the 1967 Green Line border, after shopping at the local market, which borders on the Israeli Arab town of Baka al-Gharbiyia.

July 2—The body of Yair Har-Sinai, 51, of Susiya in the Hebron hills, is found. He had been killed by shots to the head and chest.

July 4—Eliahu Na'aman, 32, of Petah Tikva, is shot at point-blank range just inside the Green Line frontier between Israel proper and the West Bank, at Sueika, near Tul Karm.

July 9—Capt. Shai Shalom Cohen, 22, of Pardes Hanna, is killed and another soldier is wounded when an explosive charge detonates beneath their jeep after they leave the Aduraim IDF base south of Hebron.

July 13—Yehezkel (Hezi) Mualem, 49, father of four from Kiryat Arba, is shot and killed between Kiryat Arba and Hebron. Mualem was at the spot to protest a shooting attack the previous day.

July 14—David Cohen, 28, of Betar Illit, dies of injuries sustained in a drive-by shooting in Kiryat Arba on July 12.

July 16—Cpl. Hanit Arami, 19, and Sgt. Avi Ben Harush, 20, both of Zichron Yaakov, are killed and 11 wounded, three seriously, when an Islamic Jihad suicide bomber explodes at a bus stop near the train station in Binyamina, halfway between Netanya and Haifa.

July 24—The body of Yuri Guschkin, 18, of Jerusalem, brutally murdered, bearing stab and gunfire wounds, is found in Ramallah. Guschkin, son of a family of new immigrants who lived in the northern Pisgat Ze'ev neighborhood, was lured to the area by Palestinians he met at a nightspot in downtown Jerusalem. In mid-August,

Nassar Abu Zeidah, the main suspect in the killing, is tracked down by a police unit and shot to death attempting to escape. He and three other Palestinians, according to the police account, got Guschkin drunk before kidnapping him.

July 26—Ronen Landau, 17, of Givat Ze'ev, northeast of Jerusalem, is shot and killed by Palestinian terrorists. The young man and a friend with whom he had gone to see a movie were being driven home by his father when the car was ambushed on the main road near Givon, just outside the capital.

August 5—Tehiya Bloomberg, 40, of Karnei Shomron, mother of five and five-months pregnant, dies when Palestinian gunmen open fire on the family vehicle between Alfei Menashe and Karnei Shomron in the West Bank, not far from Kfar Sava. Three people are seriously wounded, including her husband, Shimon, and daughter, Tzipi, 14.

August 6—Yitzhak Snir, 51, of Ra'anana, an Israeli diamond merchant, is shot dead in Amman, in the yard of the building where he kept a flat. His body is found the following morning. Jordanian authorties insist that Snir, who visited Jordan often, was killed for criminal motives.

August 7—Wael Ghanem, 32, an Israeli Arab from Taibeh, is shot and killed by Palestinian assailants on the road near the West Bank town of Qalqilya. Police believe the motive is suspected collaboration with Israeli authorities. Zohar Shurgi, 40, of Moshav Yafit in the Jordan Valley, is shot and killed by terrorists while driving home that evening on the Trans-Samaria Highway.

August 9—Giora Balash, 60, of Brazil; Zvika Golombek, 26, of Carmiel; Shoshana Yehudit Greenbaum, 31, of the U.S.; Tehila Maoz, 18, of Jerusalem; Frieda Mendelsohn, 62, of Jerusalem; Michal Raziel, 16, of Jerusalem; Malka Roth, 15, of Jerusalem; Mordechai Schijveschuurder, 43, of Neria; Tzira Schijveschuurder, 41, of Neria; Ra'aya Schijveschuurder, 14, of Neria; Avraham Yitzhak Schijveschuurder, 4, of Neria; Hemda Schijveschuurder, 2, of Neria; Lily Shimashvili, 33, of Jerusalem; Tamara Shimashvili, 8, of Jerusalem; and Yocheved Shoshan, 10, of Jerusalem are killed and about 130 injured in a suicide bombing at the Sbarro pizzeria on the corner of King George Street and Jaffa Road in the center of Jerusalem. Hamas and Islamic Jihad claim responsibility. On the same day, Aliza Malka, 17, a boarding student at Kibbutz Merav, is killed by terrorists in a drive-by shooting at the entrance to the kibbutz in the Gilboa region, west of Beit She'an. Three teenage girls who are with her in the car are injured, one seriously.

August 25—Maj. Gil Oz, 30, of Kfar Sava; St.-Sgt. Kobi Nir, 21, of Kfar Sava; and Sgt. Tzachi Grabli, 19, of Holon are killed and seven soldiers wounded when two Palestinian terrorists infiltrate a stronghold base in Gush Katif in the Gaza Strip at about 3:00 a.m. The attackers, members of the PLO Fatah faction and of the Palestinian security forces, are killed by IDF soldiers. That evening a married couple, Sharon Ben-Shalom, 26, and Yaniv Ben-Shalom, 27, of Ofarim, are killed when Palestinian gunmen open fire on their car as they return home on the Jerusalem-Modi'in highway. Their children, aged one and two, are lightly wounded. Sharon's brother, Doron Sviri, 20, of Jerusalem, also wounded in the attack, dies the following day.

August 26—Dov Rosman, 58, of Netanya, is killed in a shooting attack shortly before 5 p.m. near the village of Zaita, on the Green Line between Israel and the West Bank not far from Kibbutz Magal. Rosman, a merchant, had gone to the spot to rendezvous with a Palestinian customer.

August 27—Meir Lixenberg, 38, of Itamar, father of five, is shot and killed by Palestinian terrorists from a roadside ambush while traveling between Har Bracha and Itamar, south of Nablus.

August 29—Oleg Sotnikov, 35, of Ashdod, a truck driver employed by Dor Energy, is killed in a shooting attack outside the Palestinian village of Kutchin, west of Nablus. Sotnikov drove his tanker truck into the area alone, after an escort failed to show up.

August 30—Amos Tajouri, 60, of Modi'in, is shot in the head at point-blank range by a masked gunman in the Arab village of Na'alin, while dining at a restaurant owned by close friends. According to Mursi Amira, owner of the restaurant, Tajouri had lent him money to open the establishment.

September 6—Lt. Erez Merhavi, 23, of Moshav Tarum, dies in an ambush shooting near Kibbutz Bahan, east of Hadera, while driving to a wedding. A female officer with him is seriously injured.

September 9—Ya'akov Hatzav, 42, of Hamra in the Jordan Valley, Sima Franko, 24, of Beit She'an, a kindergarten teacher, and their driver are killed in a shooting attack 300 meters south of the Adam Junction in the Jordan Valley. They were in a minibus transporting teachers to the regional school when it was attacked by Palestinian terrorists. Later that day Dr. Yigal Goldstein, 47, of Jerusalem; Morel Derfler, 45, of Mevasseret Zion; and Sgt. Daniel Yifrah, 19, of Jerusalem are killed and some 90 injured, most of them lightly, in a suicide bombing near the Nahariya train station in northern Israel. The bomber is identifed as coming from the nearby Israeli Arab village of Abu Snan.

September 11—Border Policemen Sgt. Tzachi David, 19, of Tel Aviv, and St.-Sgt. Andrei Zledkin, 26, of Carmiel, are killed when

Palestinian gunmen opened fire on the Ivtan Border Police base near Kibbutz Bachan in central Israel.

September 12—Ruth Shu'i, 46, of Alfei Menashe, is shot from a passing vehicle while on her way home at about 7:30 p.m., near the village of Habla near Qalqilya. Injured in the head and abdomen, she dies en route to Meir Hospital in Kfar Saba.

September 15—Meir Weisshaus, 23, of Jerusalem, is fatally shot late Saturday night in a drive-by shooting near the Ramat Shlomo ultra-Orthodox neighborhood on the Ramot-French Hill road in northern Jerusalem.

September 16—Sgt. David Gordukal, 23, of Upper Nazareth, dies in an exchange of fire south of Ramallah, during which five senior Palestinian terrorists are arrested and a number of Palestinian positions and a camp of Force 17, Yasir Arafat's presidential guard, are attacked.

September 20—Sarit Amrani, 26, of Nokdim, is killed and her husband Shai seriously wounded in a shooting attack near Tekoa, south of Bethlehem. The couple's three children, also traveling in the vehicle, are not injured.

September 24—Salit Sheetrit, 28, of Kibbutz Sde Eliyahu in the Jordan Valley, is killed in a drive-by shooting at Shadmot Mehola on the road throught the Biq'a, the part of the Jordan Valley that is in the West Bank.

October 2—Cpl. Liron Harpaz, 19, of Alei Sinai, and Assaf Yitzhaki, 20, of Lod, are killed when Palestinian terrorists infiltrated the northern Gaza community of Alei Sinai, opening fire on residents and hurling grenades into homes. Fifteen others are wounded in the attack. Yitzhaki had come to the settlement to visit Harpaz, his girl friend.

October 4—Sgt. Tali Ben-Armon, 19, an off-duty woman soldier from Pardesia, Haim Ben-Ezra, 76, of Givat Hamoreh, and Sergei Freidin, 20, of Afula, die when a Palestinian terrorist in the uniform of an Israeli paratrooper opens fire on civilians at the central bus station in Afula. Thirteen other Israelis are wounded.

October 5—Hananya Ben-Avraham, 46, of Elad, is killed in a machine-gun ambush near Avnei Hefetz in central Israel.

October 7—Yair Mordechai, 43, of Kibbutz Sheluhot, is killed when a suicide terrorist detonates a large bomb strapped to his body near the entrance to the kibbutz in the Beit She'an Valley.

October 17—Tourism Minister Rehavam Ze'evi, 75, is assassinated by two shots to the head outside his room at the Jerusalem Hyatt

Hotel. The Popular Front for the Liberation of Palestine claims responsibility.

October 18—Lior Kaufman, 30, of Ramat Hasharon, is killed and two others are injured, one seriously, by shots fired at their jeep in the Judean desert, near the Mar Saba monastery.

October 28—St.-Sgt. Yaniv Levy, 22, of Zichron Yaakov, is killed by Palestinian terrorists in a drive-by machine-gun ambush near Kibbutz Metzer in northern Israel. The Tanzim wing of Arafat's Fatah faction claims responsibility.

October 28—Ayala Levy, 39, of Elyachin; Smadar Levy, 23, of Hadera; Lydia Marko, 63, of Givat Ada; and Sima Menachem, 30, of Zichron Yaakov, are killed when two terrorists armed with assault rifles and expanding bullets open fire, from a vehicle, on Israeli pedestrians at a crowded bus stop in downtown Hadera. About 40 are wounded, three critically.

November 2—St.-Sgt. Raz Mintz, 19, of Kiryat Motzkin, is shot to death at an IDF roadblock near Ofra, north of Ramallah.

November 4—Shoshana Ben-Yishai, 16, of Betar Illit, and Menashe (Meni) Regev, 14, of Jerusalem, are killed when a Palestinian terrorist opens fire with a submachine gun at the Egged 25 bus at the French Hill junction in northern Jerusalem. An additional 45 people are injured. The terrorist is killed by border police and uniformed officers stationed at the busy intersection.

November 6—Capt. (Res.) Eyal Sela, 39, of Moshav Nir Banim, is shot dead by three Palestinian terrorists on the southern Nablus bypass road.

November 9—Hadas Abutbul, 39, of Mevo Dotan in northern Samaria, is shot and killed by Palestinian terrorists as she drives home from work in nearby Shaked.

November 11—Aharon Ussishkin, 50, head of security at Moshav Kfar Hess, east of Netanya, is summoned to the entrance of the moshav to investigate a suspicious person. The man, a Palestinian, pulls a pistol and shoots Ussishkin to death.

November 24—Sgt. Barak Madmon, 26, of Holon, an IDF reservist, is killed by a mortar shell that lands in the soccer field of Kfar Darom in Gush Katif, while on his way to take up guard duty.

November 27—Noam Gozovsky, 23, of Moshav Ramat Zvi, and Michal Mor, 25, of Afula, are killed when two terrorists from the Jenin area open fire with AK-47 Kalashnikov assault rifles on a crowd of people near the central bus station in Afula. Police officers and a reserve soldier kill the terrorists in the ensuing firefight. Another 50 people are injured, ten of them moderately to seriously.

November 27—Etti Fahima, 45, of Netzer Hazani in the Gaza Strip, is killed and three others are injured when a Palestinian terrorist throws grenades and opens fire at a convoy on the road between the Kissufim crossing and Gush Katif in the Gaza Strip.

November 29—Sgt. Yaron Pikholtz, 20, of Ramat Gan, is killed and a second soldier injured in a drive-by shooting on the Green Line, near the West Bank village of Baka el-Sharkiya. On the same day, Inbal Weiss, 22, of Zichron Ya'akov; Yehiav Elshad, 28, of Tel-Aviv; and Samuel Milshevsky, 45, of Kfar Sava, are killed and nine others wounded in a suicide bombing on an Egged 823 bus near the city of Hadera, en route from Nazereth to Tel Aviv.

December 1—Assaf Avitan, 15, Michael Moshe Dahan, 21, Israel Ya'akov Danino, 17, Yosef El-Ezra, 18, Sgt. Nir Haftzadi, 19, Golan Turgeman, 15, Guy Vaknin, 19, and Moshe Yedid-Levy, all of Jerusalem, Yuri (Yoni) Korganov, 20, of Ma'alei Adumim, and Adam Weinstein, 14, of Givon Hahadasha, are killed and about 180 others injured—17 seriously—in a double suicide bombing on the Ben-Yehuda mall in central Jerusalem. A car bomb designed to hamper rescue efforts explodes on nearby Rabbi Kook Street 20 minutes later. Ido Cohen, 17, of Jerusalem, fatally injured in the attack, dies of his wounds on December 8.

December 2—Prof. Baruch Singer, 51, of Gedera, is killed when Palestinian gunmen open fire on his car near the northern Gaza settlement of Alei Sinai.

December 2—Tatiana Borovik, 23, Mara Fishman, 51, Ina Frenkel, 60, Ronen Kahalon, 30, Samion Kalik, 64, Mark Khotimliansky, 75, Cecilia Kozamin, 76, Yelena Lomakin, 62, Yitzhak Ringel, 41, Rassim Safulin, 78, Leah Strick, 73, Faina Zabiogailu, 64, Mikhail Zaraisky, 71, Riki Hadad, 30, of Yokne'am, and Rosaria Reyes, 42, of the Philippines, are killed and 40 others injured in a suicide bombing on an Egged 16 bus in Haifa.

December 12—Border Police chief warrant officer Yoel Bienenfeld, 35, of Moshav Tel Shahar, Avraham Nahman Nitzani, 17, of Betar Illit, Yair Amar, 13, Esther Avraham, 42, Moshe Gutman, 40, Yirmiyahu Salem, 48, Israel Sternberg, 46, all of Emmanuel, David Tzarfati, 38, of Ginot Shomron, and Hananya Tzarfati, 32, and Ya'akov Tzarfati, 64, of Kfar Saba, are killed when three terrorists attack a Dan 189 bus and several passenger cars with a roadside bomb, antitank grenades, and light arms fire near the entrance to Emmanuel in Samaria at 6 p.m. About 30 others are injured. Both Fatah and Hamas claim responsibility.

December 25—Sgt. Michael Sitbon, 23, of Beit Shemesh, an IDF reserve soldier, is killed, and four other soldiers are injured in a shooting attack near the Jordanian border north of Beit She'an.

Unfinished Business

On The Trail of the Lynchers

The army and the Shin Bet security services announced on June 25 that they had recently arrested two Ramallah-area residents suspected of being among the ringleaders of the October 12, 2000, lynching of Israeli army reservists Vadim Nozich and Yossi Avrahami at the Ramallah police station (see AJYB 2001, p. 497). One of the detainees was Aziz Salha, 20, from the village of Dir Jarir, who was photographed waving his bloody hands from the second floor of the police station during the lynching. According to Israeli security sources, Salha said that, after rumors spread about two Israeli soldiers being held in the police station, a mob broke into the building. Salha and others had gone into the room where the soldiers were being held, and beat and choked one of them. When he saw that his hands were covered with blood, he went to the window to show the crowd below. The second key suspect, according to the army, was Muhammad Nuara, 18, a Fatah Tanzim activist from a village near Ramallah. Nuara said he had stabbed one of the soldiers. These arrests brought to 15 the number of suspects taken into custody in the lynching case. Israel said it would continue to hunt down all those who participated in the crime.

On April 15, Irina Nozich gave birth to a son in Netanya. The boy was named Vadim, after his father.

Har Dov Kidnap Victims

On October 7, 2000, three soldiers—Adi Avitan, Benny Avraham, and Omar Sueid—were kidnapped by Hezballah at Har Dov on the northern border (see AJYB 2001, p. 484). On January 10, 2001, the special committee set up by the army to investigate the kidnapping exposed serious failures in the Northern Command leading up to the Hezballah operation. The committee, headed by retired major general Yossi Peled, said that senior officers had correctly identified the Har Dov area as a potential trouble spot, but that operational changes, including movement in convoys of two vehicles, had never been identified. The report added that Hezballah observers on the other side of the border fence had probably been able to determine that the kidnap spot was on the "seam" between the sectors controlled by two different IDF units, the Galilee

Brigade of paratroops and the Hermon Brigade of the Engineering Corps, in which the kidnapped soldiers served. In fact, the report added, the Hermon Brigade had actually simulated a kidnap attempt in an exercise during September 2000, but had never implemented the operational conclusions of that simulation. It also criticized the reaction time of IDF units, and said that the first rescue group arrived at the site fully 17 minutes after the detonation of the explosive device that Hezballah used to injure the three soldiers at the start of the kidnap operation.

Over the course of the year, rumors circulated about a possible exchange of the boys for a group of Hezballah prisoners in Israel, including long-time captives Sheikh Abdul Karam Obeid and Mustafa Dirani, who were being held by Israel as "bargaining cards" for a potential deal for the remains of three soldiers missing since the Lebanese war and for captured airman Ron Arad. In late January, in fact, reports in the Lebanese and Israeli press indicated that talks on a prisoner swap via a German intermediary were in a "decisive stage." The newspaper owned by Lebanese prime minister Rafiq Hariri said that the key was a "more receptive" attitude on the part of Israel, but Hezballah denied a deal was in the making.

During the summer, Israel sought to view videotapes, taken by UN soldiers in the sector, that were said to shed light on some aspects of the kidnapping. However the UN refused to hand over the tapes, arguing that to do so would, in effect, constitute taking sides in the conflict. In the end, Israel was allowed to send experts to view the tapes, one of which was said to include pictures of UN troops laughing in the aftermath of the kidnapping.

On November 11, Israeli army chief chaplain Rabbi Yisrael Weiss ruled that the kidnapped men were to be considered soldiers killed in action, whose place of burial was unknown. The chaplain announced his finding based on information provided by the defense establishment, and only after consulting with a number of prominent rabbis, including Chief Rabbis Yisrael Meir Lau and Eliyahu Bakshi-Doron, and Shas spiritual leader Rabbi Ovadia Yosef. The familes of the three soldiers initially accepted the ruling. Shortly after the announcement, however, Sheikh Hassan Nasrallah, the Hezballah leader, continued to cast doubt on the fate of the soldiers. He said that Israel was to blame for the suffering of the Avitan, Avraham, and Sueid familes for not acceding to his organization's demands, and termed the Israeli announcement that the three men were dead "a game we refuse to play. Let them say what they want, it's their business."

A few days after the chief chaplain's statement, Defense Minister Ben-Eliezer, in an interview with Army Radio, cast some light on the kind of evidence the army had received, though he was not specific: "We received information, and the information was very tough. It left no doubt that the three boys were killed." Later in the interview, Ben-Eliezer said that "someone saw," but refused to add additional details when pressed by the interviewer.

Or Commission Hearings

Former prime minister Ehud Barak stayed clear of the controversy that erupted between top police officers and the cabinet minister responsible for them at hearings of the commission of inquiry formed to look into the death of 13 Israeli Arab citizens during rioting in early October 2000 (see AJYB 2001, pp. 504–05). The hearings of the commission, headed by Supreme Court Justice Theodor Or, continued intermittently throughout the year, and they were marred by violent attacks by relatives of some of those killed on some police officers involved in the killings. Because of the threat of violence, special security measures were taken to keep spectators and witnesses apart.

Barak, who testified in November, praised the police and refrained from placing blame on the top command. In his one day of testimony, Barak was not prepared to go into details about the riots. Instead, he focused on his government's policy and on an analysis of the events and the way they were handled. When asked to comment on the behavior of senior police officers, Barak avoided giving a direct answer, saying he preferred not to make definitive judgments regarding past events about which he had insufficient information.

The former prime minister denied suggestions that his government had not done enough to help Israel's one million Arab citizens. He also categorically rejected the idea that he should not have allowed Ariel Sharon, then leader of the opposition, to visit the Temple Mount on the eve of Rosh Hashanah 2000—the event generally considered to have triggered the new Palestinian intifada. Barak said intelligence reports had indicated that the visit would pass peacefully. Barak also did not feel that police had used excessive force in dispersing Muslim rioters on the Temple Mount on September 29, the day after the Sharon visit. "The rioters," he said, "are responsible for the riots as are those who incited them."

In his testimony, Shlomo Ben-Ami, who was internal security minister in October 2000, struck back at senior police commanders who had accused him of inaction and of failure to support them. He also criticized the police for not reporting to their superiors. Ben-Ami attempted to explain away his own failure to launch a comprehensive investigation into the causes of the 13 deaths by saying that he had devoted all of his energies to bringing a halt to the deadly fire against Israeli citizens.

Ben-Ami blamed former national police chief Yehuda Wilk for failing to provide him, as the minister in charge, with vital reports during the course of the early-October 2000 disturbances, and said that Alik Ron, at the time the commander of the police in the Northern District, had disobeyed explicit orders from the political echelon. He said that Ron, Wilk, and others did not report to him on the deployment of marksmen from the special antiterror squad, and charged that Wilk had even denied that the sharpshooters had been called out. He added that, at Umm al-Fahm on October 2, Ron's actions against demonstrators armed with slingshots was in direct contravention of a directive from the political echelon, which Wilk was supposed to have delivered to Ron.

Ben-Ami said that, when he had taken over as internal security minister, he had ordered the police to show restraint and sensitivity toward the Arab sector, and not to use either real or rubber bullets unless lives were actually in danger. Responding to criticism that he could not properly have handled the internal security job at the time because he was also serving as acting foreign minister and was thus deeply involved in negotiations with the Palestinians, Ben-Ami said that the jobs were interrelated, since foreign affairs actually helped him carry out his duties in the internal-security area.

Earlier, Ron had claimed that the police were unprepared for the rioting in the Israeli Arab sector, which broke out a few days after the first violence, involving Palestinians, on the Temple Mount. Ron admitted that "it was possible to foresee that the riots would take place," but that "it fell upon us [the police] like a bolt out of the blue" because of lack of clarity in intelligence reports. The former Northern District police commander responded to accusations that his men had used excessive force by saying that over the past few years there had been a "horrible rise in the violence against policemen" due to a lack of police manpower. He charged that Israeli Arab MKs had inflamed citizens against the police, and that, in many mosques in the north, Muslim clerics had referred to slain Jews as "monkeys and pigs."

Mayor Ramez Jerayssi of Nazareth, who testified in June, gave a different version of the police's relations with Israeli Arabs. He said Arab citizens saw the police presence in Nazareth and elsewhere as a provocation, an embodiment of Israeli authority, and that this raised tensions. "Every contact between police and [Arab] young people is like lighting a fire beside a barrel of explosives," Jerayssi said. After Justice Or's comment that "perhaps an educational effort is needed to explain that police are there to maintain order," Jerayssi said: "Maybe the police should change their method of operating in the field first."

Much of the testimony at the hearing was extremely damaging to the police. Snipers from the special antiterror squad told the commission that senior commanders who were not on the scene authorized them to shoot live ammunition at youths armed with slingshots who were 40–70 meters away, during riots in Nazareth. At that range, police regulations only permitted the firing of rubber-coated projectiles. Members of the antiterror unit testified to the commission from behind a curtain, and were introduced to the panel by their initials rather than their first names, for their own protection. Other witnesses testified with a glass shield separating them from the audience. These procedures were instituted after the father of one of the Israeli Arab victims physically attacked Chief Superintendent Guy Reif, after the latter claimed that he had not fired directly at rioters, but had only shot into the ground, resulting in the wounding of one demonstrator. (Two youths had been killed in clashes at the Israeli Arab town of Sakhnin, where Reif was commanding the force at the time.) Reif got a bloody nose in the altercation, while other members of the audience hurled objects toward Reif, calling him a murderer. One woman fainted, and others began weeping hysterically.

Camp David Retrospective

While serving as acting foreign minister in 2000, Shlomo Ben-Ami had been a key Israeli participant in the American-brokered Camp David peace talks (see AJYB 2001, pp. 490–94), which ended in failure and were followed by the new Palestinian intifada. In the summer of 2001, around the first anniversary of Camp David, Ben-Ami was one of a number of Israelis who spoke out publicly about the reasons for the failure. In a lengthy interview with *Ha'aretz,* Ben-Ami insisted that the talks collapsed "because Arafat failed to put forward proposals of his own, and succeed in conveying to us that at some point his demands would have an end." Ben-Ami contended that, at Camp David, Israel, unlike the

Palestinians, defined its vital interests concisely. "We didn't expect to meet the Palestinians half way, and not even two-thirds of the way," but, he said, Israel did expect there would be, at some point, a meeting of minds and a compromise. "The feeling was that they were constantly trying to drag us into some sort of black hole with more and more concessions, without it being at all clear where all the concessions were leading, what the finish line was."

Ben-Ami noted that the method of negotiation, involving both top leaders—Barak and Arafat—all the time, was probably a mistake; it might have been better, he felt, to have the leaders just set the guidelines, and allow lower-level negotiators to do the work. But he denied that Prime Minister Barak was to blame for insisting on a "comprehensive" settlement—what some critics called an "all-or-nothing" or "take-it-or-leave-it" approach—in his dealings with Arafat. Ben-Ami recalled that on the final night at Camp David, before the meeting broke up, Israel offered a partial deal, and it was Arafat who refused: Ben-Ami said he suggested to Arafat that the discussions on Jerusalem be delayed for two years. "'Not even two hours,' Arafat said, waving two of his fingers." "On the one hand," Ben-Ami told *Ha'aretz,* "they weren't ready to compromise on the core issues, certainly not on Jerusalem, but, on the other, they didn't agree on a partial settlement either."

Responding to allegations that Barak had humiliated the Palestinians and failed to show them respect, Ben-Ami conceded that Barak had a closed and introverted personality, was hard to like, and did not make emotional contact with others. To reinforce the point, Ben-Ami recalled one "warming-up" dinner hosted by Madeleine Albright, the U.S. secretary of state at the time, at which Barak sat "like a pillar of salt." "But," asked Ben-Ami, "does anyone really think that if Ehud Barak had been nicer to Arafat, that Arafat would have given up on the right of return? Or on the Temple Mount?"

There was no chemistry whatsoever between the two leaders, said Ben-Ami, and the personal coincided with the political—the summit was "an encounter between a person who was looking for a rational settlement and another person who talks and embodies myths. That encounter didn't work, in retrospect I understand that it never could have worked." In Ben-Ami's view, no "rational Israeli leader" could have reached a settlement with Arafat at Camp David. "The man," he said, speaking of the PA leader, "is simply not built that way."

Palestinian Textbooks

The Civilian Administration in the West Bank and Gaza released a study, in November, on the new Palestinian textbooks that had been introduced in the territories over the past year. It found that the books, although somewhat more moderate than the Jordanian and Egyptian texts previously used, still taught hatred of Israel.

The textbooks used in PA schools, from elementary through high school, not only denied Israel's right to exist and praised the struggle against it, but also contained anti-Semitic stereotypes. The books described Israel as "a country of gangs, born in crime," called Zionism a racist movement and a "germ," and explained that the 1993 Oslo Accords were not a move towards peace, but intended "to get the Palestine Liberation Army into the territories." One text charged that Israel set fire to the Al-Aksa mosque in 1969 (this was actually done by a deranged Australian non-Jew, Dennis Michael Rohan) as part of the Zionist plan to take control of Haram al-Sharif (the Temple Mount), destroy the Muslim buildings there, and rebuild the Jewish Temple. Another text said that Zionism aspired to Judaize Palestine by expelling its Arab residents.

Indeed, the PA textbooks did not even discuss Israel as a state, but only in the context of issues such as the settlements, the use of natural resources, wars, and investigations. The books' maps had no place called "Israel," only a "Palestine" whose borders included present-day Israel. Some of the maps contained the Arab names of towns as they were called before the establishment of Israel. According to the textbooks, the Palestinian refugee camps were temporary quarters, until the residents could return to the places they were forced to abandon in 1948 and 1967.

Human Rights Abuses

The annual U.S. State Department report on human rights for 2000, issued in late-February 2001, accused both Israel and the Palestinian Authority of abuses. The report said that Israeli security bodies often used excessive force, in violation of their own rules, and condemned Israel's "targeted killings" of those Palestinians that Israel said were planning attacks. The same report noted that PA forces frequently failed to prevent other armed Palestinians from firing on Israelis, in their presence, and had themselves been involved in attacks on, and clashes with, Israelis. In all, the report said, the record of the entire Middle East on human rights was poor, and it singled out Iraq for some of its harshest criticism.

Al Qaeda in Israel?

On February 22, Israeli authorites announced that they were holding Jihad Latif Shuman, 31, a British-Lebanese citizen also known as Gerard Shuman, in administrative detention. Shuman, according to an official government statement, had entered Israel, using his British passport, on December 31, 2000, and had stayed in two Jerusalem hotels. When he was arrested on January 5, his possessions included a yarmulke, a timer, a large amount of cash, and several cellphones. Shuman—a computer-science graduate of the American University in Beirut—told interrogators that his Hezballah controllers had sent him from Lebanon to Britain, and had ordered him to leave his Lebanese passport at a "drop" there. He was told to rent an apartment and a voice-mailbox in London, obtain a cellphone, and use a travel agency that would take cash for a ticket to Israel. In Israel, he was told to speak only English and to dig up a dead drop in the Wadi Joz area of East Jerusalem, where he would also pick up other items. Shuman admitted that he had called his controllers in Lebanon with information about his stay in Israel. At his remand hearing before a judge, Shuman complained about mistreatment during his interrogation.

Shuman's mission was strikingly similar to that of Richard Reid, the "shoe bomber" apprehended aboard a Paris-to-Miami flight early in 2002. Reid, it would turn out, was in Israel during the summer of 2001, reportedly conducting reconnaissance on possible Al Qaeda targets, and also visited Egypt.

ECONOMIC DEVELOPMENTS

Slowdown Continues

The downward trend of the Israeli economy, brought on primarily by the outbreak of large-scale violence beginning in late-September 2000, accelerated during all of 2001. The economy was also a victim of the global slowdown that had been felt for more than a year, but was exacerbated by the terrorist attacks on the World Trade Center in New York and the Pentagon on September 11.

The result was the worst year for the country's economy since 1953, when the then-young State of Israel was preoccupied with the absorption of hundreds of thousands of Jewish immigrants from around the world. The Gross Domestic Product (GDP) for 2001 was negative, at –0.5-percent, in striking contrast to the increase of 6.4 percent registered in 2000. Economists, though, were quick to point out that 2000's GDP figure was deceptive, representing a brief period of rapid growth for the first nine months of the year; in fact, they noted, the general trend of the five years from 1996 to 2001 was recessionary.

But in fact the –0.5-percent figure for 2001 was deceptively positive. Since population during the year increased by 2.4 percent, per-capita GDP—the real test of an economy's performance—actually declined by a cumulative 2.9 percent for the year, after rising by 3.6 percent in 2000. The business sector figure was even worse, declining by 2.1 percent after rising by a robust 8.5 percent the previous year.

If the year as a whole was bad, the fourth quarter was even worse. GDP fell by an annualized 7.2 percent in the fourth quarter of 2001, following drops of 4 percent in the third quarter and 3.5 percent in the second. Business product plummeted 11.8 percent in the fourth quarter, after falling 4.5 percent in the third quarter and 6.8 percent in the second. Business product fell steadily in all of the five quarters since the start of the violence in September 2000. Per-capita figures showed the same trend: GDP per capita fell an annualized 9.5 percent in the fourth quarter.

Another clear indicator of the state of the economy was the government's deficit for 2001, which reached a record 21.3 billion shekels, 12.9 billion shekels more than the planned deficit of 8.4 billion and a stunning 4.6 percent of GDP. Accountant General Nir Gilad noted that 2.3 billion shekels of the deficit was illusory, the result of delay in the transfer of U.S. aid, which would later be incorporated into the 2001 figure. But even with the aid, the 19-billion shekel deficit was three times higher than planned, and 19 times the 1-billion shekel deficit recorded in 2000.

The 4.6-percent-of-GDP deficit should be compared with the government's official target of 1.75 percent of GDP. Even with the U.S. aid added to the government's 2001 revenues, the budget deficit still amounted to 4.1 percent of GDP, 2.3 times the target. The worsening of the deficit occurred mainly in the final quarter of 2001. It was due to a considerable fall in tax revenues and to excess government spending, partly because of the security situation.

Negative figures continued across the board. Investments were down 8.9 percent, after rising by 1.1 percent in 2000; exports, which had risen 23.9 percent in 2000 on the back of the high-tech industry, fell by 13.1 percent, as world markets for Israeli goods, particularly technology goods, were weak before the shocks of September 11, and got much weaker still in the period of insecurity that followed. As domestic demand contracted, imports, which had risen by 1.2 percent in 2000, also declined, by 6.4 percent. Housing construction, another engine for economic growth in better times, declined by 15.8 percent.

Private consumption, which accounted for 64 percent of Israel's GDP, also slowed. In 2001 it grew by only 3.1 percent, compared to 6.6 percent in the preceding year. Public consumption, which constituted 30 percent of the GDP, grew at a similar rate, 3.2 percent. Both these factors, plus the relatively sharp decrease in imports, helped to moderate somewhat the recessionary pressures.

As an export-based economy with a small domestic market of just over 6 million souls, Israel inevitably suffered from the recession that affected the rest of the world. The global GDP growth figure of 0.8 percent, down from 2000's 4.7 percent, was one key indicator of the way the wind was blowing. Similar declines were felt in Israel's two key foreign markets: GDP growth in the United States, which had increased by 4.1 percent in 2000—the last of ten very fat years for the world's largest and most important economy—rose by only 1 percent, while European growth declined more moderately, from 3.5 percent in 2000 to 1.5 percent in 2001. Even Japan, which had been stuck in the depths of economic crisis for a decade, was affected, with GDP growth declining from a modest 1.5 percent in 2000 to only 0.6 percent in 2001.

As a consequence, exports of Israeli goods, which had grown in 2000 at a rate of 24 percent and were the key engine in that year's rapid growth, operated in the opposite direction in 2001, declining by 13 percent in real terms. The main factor, of course, was the slowdown around the world, and particularly in the United States. Technology exports, which accounted for 53 percent of all exports in 2000, declined by 10 percent. And yet, even despite the decline, exports were still 19 percent higher than they had been in 1999. Exports of services also fell by 23 percent in real terms, a result of the slowdown in sales of start-up companies, revenues from which fell by about half.

Revenues of the national Mifal Hapayis lottery rose by 6.38 percent to 2.97 billion shekels in 2001, but lottery officials had predicted an increase of 8 percent. Lottery sales slowed significantly in the second half of 2001, probably because of the worsening security situation, the slowing economy, and fear of terror attacks in crowded shopping malls and city centers, where many Mifal Hapayis stands were located.

Growing Deficit, Low Inflation

Israel's trade deficit grew 2.6 percent in 2001, from $6.9 billion in 2000 to $7.1 billion in 2001. Exports in 2001 were $25.7 billion as compared to $28.3 billion in 2000, a decline of $2.6 billion. Imports in 2001 totaled $32.7 billion, a decline of $2.5 billion from the figure of $35.2 billion in 2000. High-tech exports—77 percent of industrial exports—declined by $1.1 billion, while imports of raw materials (excluding diamonds and fuel) fell by $1.5 billion. Two-thirds of the decline in raw-material imports were in high-tech industries. The downward trend, evident during the entire year, was particularly evident in December, when the gap between imports and exports totaled $597 million, up 57 percent from November and 63 percent more than December 2000.

The high-tech slowdown was reflected in sharp staff cuts by dozens of companies—including some that had been industry leaders—and the closing of other firms. The most striking victim was Chromatis, a maker of digital data-transmission equipment, which closed down in August, a little more than a year after it had been purchased for a record price of $4.8 billion by Lucent, the U.S. telecommunications infrastructure firm. The main reason for the closing, according to Lucent, was the lack of customer demand for Chromatis-Lucent products.

The continuing contraction of the economy brought with it an unusually low rate of inflation. For the year, the Consumer Price Index (CPI), compiled by the Central Bureau of Statistics in Jerusalem, increased by only 1.4 percent, far below the "target" of 2.5–3.5 percent envisaged in the 2001 budget. In fact, 2001 was the third consecutive year in which the CPI fell below government expectations: in 1999 it rose by 1.3 percent (compared to a target of 4 percent), and in 2000, when the government built its budget on the expectation of a 3–4 percent inflation rate, it was unchanged.

The continuing gap between inflationary planning and actual inflation increased the pressure on the Bank of Israel and its governor, David Klein, to lower the interest rate. Through most of the year, Klein sought to cut the rate the central bank charged commercial banks in small increments, reducing it from 8.2 percent at the end of December 2000 to 5.8 percent in December 2001, while resisting pressure from manufacturers and some public figures for a major cut. (The gradual lowering of interest had actually been in progress since late 1998, when it stood at 13.5 percent. It was started by Prof. Jacob Frenkel, a World Bank economist who was Klein's predecessor as governor of the central bank.)

But on December 21, as part of a package deal in which the government promised to trim its unpassed budget for 2002 by 6.15 billion shekels (about $1.5 billion), set a deficit target of 3 percent of GDP, and make certain adjustments in exchange-rate calculations, Klein agreed to trim a whopping 2 percent off interest, bringing the basic rate down to 3.8 percent from its previous 5.8 percent. The immediate reaction to the rate cut was predictable: a quick depreciation of the shekel, which reached about 6 percent before year's end and continued into January 2002, upward moves in the prices of local shares (these became more attractive investments as compared to the lower rates of interest on shekel deposits), and a decline in yields on the bond market, especially in short-term bonds linked to the CPI. At year's end, some economists were predicting a continuing rise in the shekel-dollar rate to levels of as much as 4.7 shekels to the U.S. dollar, representing a 10–12 percent depreciation in the Israeli currency. Such depreciation would, inevitably, raise the shekel prices of imported goods such as automobiles and consumer appliances, and increase the price of homes and housing rentals, which were traditionally calculated in dollars. On the other hand, the lowering of the value of the Israeli currency was a great boon to export-oriented industries, whose locally incurred costs, including infrastructure and labor, were sharply lower dollarwise, while their sales brought in a larger number of shekels.

Uneasy Investors

The lack of confidence of investors was reflected in figures released by the Ministry of Industry and Trade's Investment Center, which said that the grants it issued fell by 12 percent in 2001 to $1 billion, excluding a $239-million investment in a new factory built by Tower Semiconductor in Migdal Ha'emek. The number of requests for support, 658, was similar to the 2000 number, but 29.6 percent lower than the 1999 figure. The number of approved requests fell 10.6 percent, to 440, for investments totaling $1.2 billion, including the entrepreneur's matching portion.

Some 86 percent of the projects approved and 80 percent of the money handed out by the ministry's investment center went to companies in the electronics, electricity, software, machinery, chemicals, and plastics sectors, while the remainder went to traditional industries. Investments in "priority" enterprises, such as development towns in outlying areas and on Israel's borders, totaled $781 million, up from $638 million in 2000. The drop in investments, and even more in requested investments, signaled a wide-scale cutback in investors' plans to open new factories, and reflected pessimism about the future of the economy.

One of the few areas where there was substantial investment was in companies dealing with mobile Internet technology, a field in which Israel was a world leader. During the year, $160 million was invested in 80 such companies, many of them start-ups.

At the same time, Israelis invested $5 billion overseas in 2001, compared with $9.9 billion in 2000. Since 1998, total direct foreign investment totaled $6.2 billion. Foreign investments by Israelis in shares traded on foreign stock exchanges totaled $3.5 billion over the same period.

But if investment provided some glimmer of optimism, most of the news was less hopeful. Industrial production, for example, which had grown by 10 percent in 2000, fell by 5.7 percent in 2001—the worst performance by Israeli industry since the first intifada in 1988–93. About 17,000 industrial workers were laid off in 2001. Trend figures showed that industrial production had been falling for 18 months, since the start of the global high-tech crisis, and that the political and security unrest locally merely exacerbated an existing trend.

Tourism in the Doldrums

The number of tourists to Israel fell dramatically, by 54 percent in 2001, as compared with 2000. The total number of tourists—1.218 million—was only 100,000 higher than the number that visited Israel in 1991, the year of the Gulf War, and was similar to the situation during the 1970s.

As in previous years, the United States provided the largest number of tourists, 266,000 entries, more than one-fifth of the total. However, the number of tourists from the United States was down 45 percent. Britain contributed 140,000 tourists, 12 percent of the total number and a drop of 30 percent from 2000. Other countries: France—129,000, down 36 percent; Germany—65,000, down 63 percent; and Russia—56,000, down 25 percent. Declines from some other countries were particular sharp, mainly from states where large numbers of people had accompanied Pope John Paul II on his visit to Israel in March 2000. Those included Italy, down 85 percent to 25,000, and Poland, down 69 percent to 13,000.

Tourist overnights in Israeli hotels dropped by 60 percent in 2001, the Hotel Association said. There were only 3.8 million tourist overnights during they year—the smallest number since 1970. And that figure meant that there were many more vacancies in 2001 than 30 years before, since Israel now had 46,000 hotel rooms as compared to 15,000 in the 1970s.

The hard-hit tourism industry took some solace in the fact that Israeli overnights for the year rose by 14 percent, to 11.3 million. But total overnights fell by 23 percent, compared to 2000. According to the Hotel

Association, occupancy rates were at a low ebb—only 43 percent of capacity nationwide. Even in 1991, the year of the Gulf War, occupancy for the year amounted to 53 percent of capacity. The situation was, of course, exacerbated by the creation of new hotel rooms over the past decade, in advance of the tourism boom that had been expected in the Millennium Year of 2000. Jerusalem hotels were particularly hard hit, with only a 23-percent occupancy rate in 2001.

Outbound tourism by Israelis, which had grown exponentially throughout the 1990s and into 2000, took a turn in the opposite direction in 2001, as per capita overseas travel fell by 1.3 percent. Though the number of excursions abroad, 3.56 million, represented a slight increase, 0.9 percent, over 2000, with the population growth of over 2 percent factored in, the average rate of foreign travel per Israeli declined. This was another effect of accelerating economic weakness, since the figure included not only Israelis traveling abroad for pleasure, but also Israelis on foreign business trips. Other figures confirmed the trend. The average overseas stay, 11 days, was shorter than in previous years: In 1997, traveling Israelis spent 12.5 days abroad, and in 1993 the figure was 17 days. Tourist exits to Egypt, including Taba, just across the border from Eilat, fell by 76 percent; total tourist exits to neighboring countries plummeted by 32 percent, from 576,000 in 2000 to 393,000 in 2001.

Bright Spots

Although 2001 was a very bad year for high-tech investment, two Israeli companies did manage to buck the negative trend. Indeed, those two firms, Versity and GIven Imaging, were the only Israeli companies to conduct Initial Public Offerings (IPOs) on Wall Street in 2001. Versity, a developer of integrated circuits, raised $23 million in March 2001, but GIven's task was much more difficult. The company, which had developed a miniaturized pill-sized camera and transmitter that is swallowed, and sends out pictures of the entire gastrointestinal tract, was due to offer its shares on the NASDAQ exchange in New York in mid-September; the offering, naturally, was delayed after the terror attacks. GIven—whose adapted technology was developed at Rafael, Israel's government-owned arms-development authority, was the first company from anywhere to hold its IPO on Wall Street after 9/11. It raised $60 million.

Israel Aircraft Industries (IAI), the government-owned aerospace firm, was another of the few companies that did well in 2001. In fact, IAI met its 2001 sales target, despite Israel's security situation and the slowdown in global aviation that worsened following September 11. During the year, IAI signed $2.9 billion worth of new contracts—26 percent higher than company forecasts of $2.3 billion. IAI sales in 2000 totaled $2.2 billion. The cancellation of the sale to China of Phalcon early-warning airborne command-and-control posts in 2000, under heavy U.S. pressure, did not affect sales, IAI officials said—although the damages to be paid for calling off the $240-million sale had still to be determined at year's end. IAI reported increased sales of information-gathering systems and night-vision equipment, offsetting a decline in some other areas of operation such as maintenance of foreign aircraft. This diversification was a key part of IAI's long-term strategy to switch the balance of its sales more heavily towards the civilian sector and away from defense, IAI officials said.

During the year, Galaxy Aerospace, the maker of executive jets jointly owned by IAI and the Pritzker family of Chicago—owners of the Hyatt hotel chain—was sold to General Dynamics for $600 million.

Israel's defense exports totaled almost $2.6 billion in 2001, rising from $2.49 billion in 2000. The 2001 figure represented a record, since the only year with a higher defense export figure, 1997, included in its calculations the proceeds of the later-canceled sale of the Phalcon early-warning aircraft to China. In all, these exports represented more than two-thirds of the production of Israel's defense industries, which amounted to about $3.6 million, according to the Defense Ministry's sales division, known by its Hebrew acronym Sibat. According to Sibat's figures, Israel accounted for about 10 percent of the world's total defense exports of $25–$30 million.

Sales of electrical appliances in Israel rose sharply in 2001—refrigerators by 25 percent, video (or DVD) recorders by 32 percent, dishwashers by 16.5 percent, washing machines and air conditioners by 9 percent, and television sets by 4.5 percent. This happened despite the economic slowdown and security fears—or perhaps because of them. Some observers suggested that people were spending more time at home because they were afraid of going outside, and therefore needed more appliances. Another statistic supporting this hypothesis was that the sale of new cars dropped by 8.5 percent.

OTHER DOMESTIC MATTERS

Israel by the Numbers

Israel's population reached 6.4 million, 5.2 million of them—81 percent—Jews. This brought the Israeli share of the world Jewish population (of 13.25 million) to 38 percent (see below, pp. 000–00). The total population of Israel grew by 152,000 over the year, a growth rate of 2.4 percent—the Arab sector growing at a much higher rate of 4.6 percent.

Only 43,000 new immigrants arrived in Israel in 2001, the lowest figure since the start of the immigration from the former Soviet Union (FSU) in 1990, the Central Bureau of Statistics (CBS) reported. The 2000 figure had been 63,000, and the annual average in the late 1990s had been around 70,000. The drop was attributed not so much to the intifada violence, but more to the shrinking size of the Jewish community in the FSU, which was still the main source of newcomers—34,000 in 2001, 77 percent of the total. Since 1990, according to the CBS figures, 1.06 million people had immigrated to Israel, mostly from the FSU. That amounted to 37 percent of the total of 2.9 million people who immigrated to Israel since the founding of the state.

Of the states of the FSU, Ukraine supplied the most immigrants to Israel during the year, 14,000, as compared to 20,000 in 2000. Russia accounted for 11,000, down from 2000's 19,000. There were 3,300 from Ethiopia, 1,400 from Argentina (up from 1,100 in 2000), 1,200 from the United States (unchanged from 2000), and 1,000 from France (also unchanged). Twenty percent of immigrants were 14 years old and younger, 9 percent were 65 and older. Though the overall immigration figure was the lowest in a decade, the CBS offered a note of consolation: 2001's immigration was larger than the 15,000-a-year average for the 1980s, before the collapse of the Soviet Union and the massive inflow of immigrants from Russia, Ukraine, and the other ex-Soviet republics. In the 1980s, about 15 percent of the smaller overall total of immigrants came from Africa, principally Ethiopia, 29 percent from the Americas and Oceania, and only 19 percent originated in the Soviet Union.

Immigration had, in fact, declined steadily after a major spurt in 1990, when almost 200,000 newcomers came to Israel, and 1991, when the figure was 176,000. From 1992 onward, between 70,000 and 80,000 immigrants a year came to Israel in most years, the only exceptions being 1997, when there were 66,000, 1998, when the figure dropped to 56,000, and 2000.

A total of 9,419 Israeli couples divorced in 2001 as compared to 9,210 in 2000, an increase of 2.3 percent, according to Rabbi Eli Ben-Dahan, director of the rabbinic courts. This marked a reversal of the steady decline in divorce that had set in after the rate reached a high of 5 percent in the mid-1990s. Over that period there had been a drastic drop in the divorce rate on the West Bank—45 percent—but a rise in divorce in the country's development towns.

Israelis appeared to be traveling on the roads less in 2001 because of the security situation, and the number of all traffic accidents declined by 12 percent for the year. However, the number of traffic fatalities rose by 8.3 percent, from 518 in 467 serious accidents in 2000, to 561 in 494 serious accidents in 2001. The number of people killed in traffic accidents now exceeded the number killed in Israel's wars, according to police figures: Since 1948, there had been 21,586 traffic deaths and 20,729 military fatalities.

Crime increased in 2001, reversing the downward trend of 2000 and 1999. Murder was up 28 percent—from 135 cases in 2000 to 173 in 2001—and armed robbery rose 10.66 percent. Drug-related crimes rose by 4.7 percent. Increases were also recorded in car theft and home break-ins. But sexual offenses declined slightly. A total of 3,554 sex-offense files were opened, as compared to 4,057 in 2000, and the number of rape files opened dropped from 682 in 2000 to 658 in 2001—a decrease of 3.5 percent. Israel's rate of stolen cars, 15 per 1,000, was the highest in the world, according to the National Insurance Union.

Absence without leave from the army increased by 30 percent in 2001, according to a report presented to the Knesset Foreign Affairs and Defense Committee by Brig. Gen. Uzi Lev-Tzur, the army's ombudsman. Lev-Tzur said that most of the violators attributed their unauthorized absences to the financial situation of their families. At the same time, the ombudsman said that the number of complaints filed by soldiers about alleged humiliating treatment in the army had fallen by 15 percent, and complaints about improper medical treatment by 25 percent. There were, however, a high number of complaints about sleep deprivation, Lev-Tzur said, without providing figures.

Fuad Wins Labor Race

Binyamin Ben-Eliezer, 65, the minister of defense known universally as "Fuad," was elected to the leadership of the Labor Party after a bitter four-month battle against Avraham Burg, 46, speaker of the Knesset, who was thought to be way ahead before the party primaries on September 4. However Burg showed only a tiny lead after the primary votes were counted, and, after extensive bickering and an exchange of charges, a revote was called in 51 polling stations where the result was disputed. Ben-Eliezer won most of the ballots cast in the December 26 revote, and that gave him a 2,000-vote victory (50.8 percent). Burg had termed the revote a "farce," and Labor members from the Druze and Arab communities announced that they would not participate. The Knesset speaker did not bother to campaign during the last week before the second vote, saying that he preferred devoting his time to his parliamentary duties. After the revote sealed his defeat, Burg commented, "For weeks we knew that the results were determined in advance."

With his election, Ben-Eliezer assumed the role of senior Labor minister in the government of national unity. "I intend to maintain Shimon Peres's place in the party and will not do anything to detract from his stature," he said. "But let me make it clear, from now on I am the senior minister in the party," he added. Baghdad-born Ben-Eliezer, who immigrated to Israel with his family at the age of 13, thus became the first Sephardi leader in the history of Labor, the party which, in its previous incarnation as Mapai, stretched back to the beginning of the State of Israel. "Until they told me yesterday, I thought I was an Israeli in every way," the new party leader said. "You can't take from me the fact that I was born in Iraq, or that my given name is Fuad."

The victory of Ben-Eliezer—an ex-general who once was military governor of the West Bank—meant that Labor was more likely to stay in the government than would have been the case under the dovish Burg. Still, there were those in the party who pressed for an early exit from the governing coalition, including Haim Ramon and Yossi Beilin, both of whom were widely viewed as strong candidates to succeed to the leadership of Labor. Ramon congratulated Ben-Eliezer in an Army Radio interview. "You have to admire him," Ramon said, "for starting a race in which he had almost no chance of winning and ending up as the Labor party chairman." Beilin, however, criticizing Ben-Eliezer for "overtaking Sharon from the right," called him only the "legal" but not the "legitimate" leader of Labor, and expressed the hope that someone else would be the party's candidate for prime minister in the next election.

Temple Mount Excavations

On January 21, Prime Minister Barak ordered police to stop excavation work on the Temple Mount (Haram al-Sharif) by the Wakf, the Muslim religious trust in charge of adminstration of the Al-Aqsa Mosque and the Dome of the Rock. Complaints about unauthorized digging there had been circulating for months, with Attorney General Elyakim Rubinstein, the Antiquities Authority, and the Archeology Council all lodging protests. Right-wing groups and prominent archeologists charged that the digging had destroyed artifacts dating back to antiquity, and said that some significant pieces had been found amid the debris from the digging that was dumped by the Wakf in the Kidron Valley. The Wakf had not allowed any Jewish archeologists on the site since September 28, 2000, the day before the start of the new intifada.

Barak, who at first was reluctant to involve himself in this religiously and politically volatile matter, finally acted after the Council for the Prevention of the Destruction of Antiquities on the Temple Mount charged that the state was not doing enough to supervise activities on the site. Dr. Gabi Barkai, an archeologist, said, "Large-scale work—some of which was authorized, and most of which was not—has been carried out over the past months on the eastern section of the Temple Mount, along the eastern wall, between King Solomon's Stables and the Rahamim Gate, together with underground work in various other areas of the mount."

Press reports indicated that about 1,500 tons of earth, which may have contained unexamined archeological remnants, had been removed from the mount between the start of the new intifada in late September and Barak's order in January. In addition, the Shin Bet security service reportedly told Barak about the Wakf's long-term plans to start using several parts of the mount, including the refurbished underground area known as King Solomon's Stables, as mosques. The Shin Bet also noted that paving and construction work had been performed at the area around the Mercy Gate. A few days after Barak's order, Israel Radio reported that the Wakf had dug a tunnel between King Solomon's Stables and the underground remains of the ancient Al-Aqsa, equipped with electric lighting and an observation point at the Al-Aqsa end.

Yatom Disqualified

The Supreme Court, on December 27, disqualified Ehud Yatom, a former high official in the Shin Bet security service, from serving as the prime minister's chief adviser on terror. The ruling came after two Meretz MKs, opposition leader Yossi Sarid and Mossi Raz, former head of the Peace Now movement, challenged Yatom's appointment because of his involvement in the 1984 Bus 300 scandal, in which two Palestinian terrorists who had been captured alive were killed by the security agency. The Shin Bet later tried to cover up the killings and cast the blame on

Yitzhak Mordechai, then a high-ranking army officer. Yatom—who was pardoned by then-president Chaim Herzog before he could be indicted—admitted killing the two Palestinians, describing, in a 1996 interview, how he had crushed their heads with a rock.

After the Supreme Court ruling, Likud politician and Deputy Internal Security Minister Gideon Ezra, a former second-in-command of the Shin Bet, said the failure to appoint Yatom would have grave implications in the fight against terror. Yatom himself called it "a sad day for all the security services." Yatom—whose ex-general brother Danny Yatom had been a key aide to former prime minister Ehud Barak—had been disqualified from other high-level jobs because of his role in the Bus 300 scandal. In 1998, for example, when Dan Tichon, then speaker of the Knesset, wanted to make Yatom the chief of Knesset security, a legal opinion by Attorney General Elyakim Rubinstein predicted that such an appointment would probably "meet with substantial legal obstacles if it is brought to judicial scrutiny."

Legacies of Violence

A law passed by the Knesset on December 19 barred the president from ever granting a pardon to anyone convicted of assassinating a prime minister. The vote was 63-5, with eight abstentions. The new statute meant that Yigal Amir, serving a life sentence for the 1995 assassination of Prime Minister Yitzhak Rabin, could never be pardoned for his crime. "I hope we have managed to put political assassinations behind us, and that the murder of a prime minister was a one-time happening," said Avshalom Vilan, MK from the left-wing Meretz Party, who sponsored the bill. Deputy Defense Minister Dalia Rabin-Pelosof, Rabin's daughter, said she hoped the law would help prevent other such murders. During the debate on the bill, several Labor MKs noted that President Moshe Katzav had made it clear that he did not favor the bill, on the grounds that it would limit presidential power. Katzav, though, said that his skeptical view of the bill had nothing to do with the Rabin case, and that he would never pardon Amir.

However, President Katzav triggered considerable controversy by deciding to free Margalit Har-Shefi, who, in 1999, was sentenced to nine months in prison for failing to tell the police that Yigal Amir had told her of his plan to assassinate Yitzhak Rabin. Katzav said that Har-Shefi, who, after going through a series of appeals, had entered prison on March 21, "has paid her debt to society and has been punished." Critics of the president's move included Rabin's daughter, Deputy Defense Minister

Rabin-Pelosof, and Justice Minister Meir Sheetrit—who nevertheless signed the pardon papers out of what he said was respect for the presidency. Har-Shefi, released from the Neve Tirza women's prison on August 10, had served less than half of her sentence. Three weeks earlier, the parole board had denied her request for an early release, saying she had expressed no remorse. Har-Shefi had constantly maintained that she never believed Yigal Amir when he told her that he planned to kill Rabin, and that was why she had not gone to the police.

Before Har-Shefi went to jail, she had worked as a substitute teacher in the settlement of Psagot, not far from Ramallah. But on February 1, then-prime minister Barak, in his capacity as acting education minister, ordered her fired. Barak said he would not allow the education of Israeli children "to be placed in the hands of one implicated in the murder of Yitzhak Rabin."

In 1993, Yoram Shkolnik fired shots from his Uzi into a Palestinian who had been captured and tied up after an incident in which the prisoner was said to have stabbed another settler at Ma'aleh Hever, a settlement in the South Hebron Hills. He was sentenced to life imprisonment. On February 18, 2001, Shkolnik, now 32 years old, was released after serving seven-and-a-half years, the Supreme Court upholding a decision of the parole board. A month earlier, the high court had stopped Shkolnik's release hours before he was to be freed in order to hear an appeal from the state. Shkolnik's sentence had previously been commuted to 11 years by former president Ezer Weizman.

Human-rights organizations protested Shkolnik's release, as they had the light sentence meted out to another settler, Nahum Korman, a month earlier. Korman got six months of community service and a fine of 70,000 shekels ($17,000 at the time) for killing an 11-year-old Palestinian boy, Hilmi Shusha, in 1996, after a car was stoned.

Nazareth Mosque

In 1999, the Muslim majority in Nazareth—the city venerated by Christians as the birthplace of Jesus—began work on a new mosque adjacent to the Basilica of the Annunciation, where, Christian tradition had it, the Angel Gabriel visited Mary. Christian leaders, including the pope and the Vatican hierarchy, were upset, and Israel found itself in the unenviable position of having to offend either Muslims or Christians (see AJYB 2000, p. 474).

Excavation for the new mosque began on November 12, 2001, and the

Christian world exerted considerable pressure on Israel to bring it to a halt. On November 28, the leaders of all the Christian communities in Israel issued a statement warning "our Jewish friends" that construction of the mosque would have "destructive effects" on the Christian-Jewish dialogue. Undoubtedly acting under the direction of the Israeli government, the Regional Commission for Planning Regulation asked a Nazareth court to halt the excavation, and it did so on December 19, though few believed that this would put the controversy to rest.

Charges, Investigations, Convictions

Campaign Laws

In October, State Comptroller Eliezer Goldberg issued a report of his investigation into the financing of Ariel Sharon's succesful contest for the leadership of Likud in September 1999, when Benjamin Netanyahu resigned as leader after losing the election for prime minister, that summer, to Ehud Barak. Goldberg reported that Sharon, together with his son, Omri, had violated campaign laws by funneling some 5.9-million shekels through a dummy corporation, Anaex Research, established by Dov Weisglass, Ariel Sharon's lawyer, and run by Omri Sharon. The funds were used for polling and to provide other services for the Sharon campaign.

In a letter to the comptroller on August 27, Ariel Sharon said that he had heard of Anaex "for the first time" in a preliminary draft of Goldberg's report. However, according to a report on Israel's Channel 2 TV in late September, during Goldberg's questioning of the prime minister, Sharon was shown a 100,000-shekel check he had written and signed. Sharon admitted that he had signed the check, but told Goldberg that his son Omri handled all financial matters. Goldberg's report said that Omri Sharon and Gavriel Manor, the figurehead CEO of Anaex, had declined to answer questions, "because they were concerned about self-incrimination," with Omri Sharon adding that his refusal to answer was also "to avoid hurting others." According to Goldberg, Omri Sharon's lawyer, Dan Sheinman, insisted that the money had been spent to improve Ariel Sharon's personal image and was therefore not covered by the law on campaign finance.

Ariel Sharon announced: "Since the comptroller's report determined that these were illegal contributions, I intend to return the money to Anaex so it can be returned to its donors." By mid-November he had returned 4.7 million shekels—$1.1 million at the time.

AZMI BISHARA

Speaking at a June 11 memorial marking a year since the death of Syrian president Hafez al-Assad, in Assad's birthplace of Kardaha, northern Syria, Israeli MK Azmi Bishara of the (Arab) Balad Party called on Arab countries to promote "resistance" against Israel. "After the Hezballah victory," he said, referring to Israel's withdrawal the previous year from South Lebanon, "and after the failure of the Camp David Summit, Israel started to reduce this sphere of influence. Today, Israel puts forward a choice—either accept Israel's dictates, or full-scale war. There is no possibility of carrying on with a third alternative." Bishara attacked the Sharon government for bringing the Middle East to the point where "either Israel's program is accepted or the whole region goes to the brink of war."

Bishara was one of ten speakers at the memorial. Others included Hezballah leader Sheikh Hassan Nasrallah, Lebanese president Émile Lahoud, Iranian vice president Hassan Habibi, and leaders of other militant and pro-Iranian groups. In his speech, Nasrallah vowed to return to the disputed Shebba farms area on the foothills of Mt. Hermon—which he still claimed as Lebanese, though the UN had determined it to have been part of Syria before its conquest in 1967 by Israel, and therefore not returnable to Lebanon—with "blood, jihad, and resistance." Ten days earlier, before going to Syria, Bishara was questioned by police about his role in facilitating the visits of Israeli citizens to Syria, an enemy country. Bishara called this investigation into his reported practice of helping Israeli Arabs visit Palestinians who had been living in Syria since 1948 "political persecution."

Reaction to Bishara's words was predictably intense. Likud MK Ze'ev Boim called on Internal Security Minister Uzi Landau to arrest Bishara on his return to Israel. Effi Oshaya, chairman of the Labor faction in the Knesset, urged Bishara to ask Syria to pay half his salary, explaining that even though the MK was an Israeli citizen and parliamentarian, he actually served Damascus. "Bishara's appearance with Nasrallah," Oshaya said, "shames the State of Israel and deepens the divide between Jews and Arabs in Israel," adding that Bishara "is spitting in the faces" of the families of three Israeli soldiers who were kidnapped by Hezballah, "with Syrian support," in October 2000.

After the Knesset lifted Bishara's parliamentary immunity, the State Attorney's Office filed an indictment against him on November 11. The charge sheet, in Jerusalem District Court, alleged that he supported a terrorist organization, and the office noted that it would, at some later time, also charge Bishara and his two parliamentary aides, Mussa Diab and Ashraf Kursham, with abetting illegal trips to Syria.

Yitzhak Mordechai

On March 21, a magistrate's court in Jerusalem convicted Yitzhak Mordechai, a former defense and transport minister, of indecent assault on two women, and acquitted him of a similar charge against a third. Mordechai was found guilty of harassing a female army officer who worked for him when he headed the IDF's Northern Command in 1992, and of harassing a Likud party activist at his home in Mevasseret Yerushalayim, outside Jerusalem, while he was defense minister in 1996. The evidence in the third case, in which the complainant was a clerk in the Tel Aviv office of the Transport Ministry, was not sufficient to warrant a conviction, the judges said. The court rejected Mordechai's contention that the police investigation was flawed, adding that the defendant's evasive behavior during the course of the investigation had damaged his credibilty. In late November, the Jerusalem district court upheld Mordechai's conviction. The former minister said, however, that he would carry his appeal to the Supreme Court. "I will do everything in my power to prove my innocence at the highest levels," he said.

Ofer Nimrodi

Ofer Nimrodi, publisher of the daily *Ma'ariv* Hebrew newspaper, was convicted of fraud, obstruction of justice, falsifying corporate documents, and witness harassment by a Tel Aviv district court on October 24, and sentenced to 25 months in jail. Nimrodi was also fined 349,000 shekels (about $75,000) in a plea-bargain agreement. The jail term included ten months of a suspended sentence on his 1998 conviction for wiretapping, and 15 months on the later charges, which stemmed from Nimrodi's behavior during the investigation of the earlier offense, when he ordered wiretaps of his newspaper competitors. The 15 months that Nimrodi had already been in police custody under a court remand order in the obstruction-of-justice case were to be counted against his sentence, so that—with the usual time off for good behavior—Nimrodi would serve only a few additional weeks in jail.

Avigdor Kahalani

Avigdor Kahalani, the former internal-security minister, was cleared of three charges of obstructing justice, breach of trust, and breach of confidence by a Tel Aviv magistrate's court on March 20. Kahalani was accused of trying to find out if police were investigating Ofer Nimrodi, the *Ma'ariv* publisher, on charges of obstructing justice in a wiretap case (see above). Kahalani's former chief of operations at the ministry, Yossi Levy, had already been convicted of negligence in the case, and, in a plea bargain, had been fined 30,000 shekels (about $7,500). Levy and Kahalani were said to have attempted, on Nimrodi's request, to find out about the then-secret investigation. The judge in the case, Oded Elyagon, called the entire case "a trial balloon" that ended up with nothing more than "hot air." The prosecution appealed Elyagon's decision, but the Supreme Court turned it down later in the year.

Avigdor Lieberman

Infrastructure Minister Avigdor Lieberman was ordered to pay fines totaling 17,500 shekels ($4,000 at the time), in a plea-bargain aggreement accepted in Jerusalem magistrate's court on September 25. Lieberman admitted striking one 12-year-old boy and threatening another after the two fought with Lieberman's son in 1999, on the West Bank settlement where the Russian-born leader of the Yisrael Beitenu party lived.

Salah Tarif

Police recommended in mid-July that Minister for Arab Affairs Salah Tarif, the first non-Jew ever to serve in an Israeli cabinet, be indicted for involvement in the bribery of an Interior Ministry official by a Palestinian man seeking Israeli citizenship. Police passed the file on to the State Attorney's Office, saying there was sufficient evidence to charge Tarif, a Druse, with acting as an intermediary for Hosni Badran in contacts with Rafi Cohen, the former head of the Interior Ministry's Population Registry Department. After meeting with Cohen in 1999, police said, Badran engaged in a fictitious marriage with a 22-year-old new immigrant.

"Deri Law"

A bill permitting the parole of convicts who had served half their sentences, instead of the previous requirement that the criminal serve two-thirds of the sentence, was approved in a 48-47 Knesset vote on February 13. An amendment sponsored by Shas made the law applicable to prisoners already serving their time in jail, so that it would apply to former party leader Arye Deri, serving a four-year sentence for bribery and other offenses (see AJYB 2000, pp. 476–77).

Yemenite Children

In the early years of the state, an unknown number of children were taken from Yemenite families living in *ma'abarot* (immigrant transit camps). The parents were told that the children were in hospitals, and, later, that they had died. For decades, however, rumors circulated that the children had actually been adopted by by Ashkenazi families, and activists from the Yemenite community demanded to know the truth. Two official investigative commissions, one in the late 1960s and the other in the early 1990s, had found no evidence to support the allegation.

In 1995, yet a third commission was established after violent protests by the Mishkan Ohalim movement, led by Rabbi Uzi Meshulam. The Cohen-Kedmi Commission, over the course of almost seven years, heard testimony from 900 relatives of Yemenite children who disappeared from 1948 to 1954, in addition to 150 other witnesses, and unequivocally rejected claims of a plot by the "establishment" to turn the children over to Ashkenazi familes. The commission report, published on November 4, said that there was adequate documentation for the deaths of 972 of 1,033 missing babies, five had been found to be alive, and the fate of the other 56 was unknown.

Yemenite activists, including families of some of the children who, the commission said, had died, denounced the decision and said that the real facts were still being covered up.

1997 Maccabiah

A Tel Aviv district court rejected the appeal of five men convicted of involvement in the 1997 Maccabiah Games bridge collapse, in which four members of the Australian delegation to the "Jewish Olympics" lost their lives and 70 more were injured (see AJYB 1998, pp. 462–64). In its October 10 decision, the court said: "It was one of the worst civil disasters in Israel's history. The negligence of the appellants is so great, so unmistakable, and so obvious. How did they have the gall to appeal their convictions and raise such infuriating contentions?"

The court added that the appellants—engineer Micha Bar-Ilan, sentenced to 21 months in prison; Yehoshua Ben-Ezra and Baruch Karagula, partners and managers of the Ben-Ezra–Karagula steel plant, sentenced to 15 months; Adam Mishori, general manager of Irgunit, which built the bridge, sentenced to nine months; and Maccabiah Games chairman Yoram Eyal, who got six months of community service—"behaved with gross negligence, abused the public's trust, and were careless with the lives of thousands of Maccabiah participants, who marched on an unsafe bridge, several of them to their deaths. The appellants abandoned the Maccabiah participants and their families to disaster, and they should ask their grieving and injured brothers' pardon and forgiveness for their criminal negligence, arrogance, and lack of attention."

Earlier in the year, on February 11, Israel agreed to pay Australian Jewish athlete Sasha Elterman $4 million for injuries sustained in the bridge collapse. Elterman underwent nearly 40 operations after being hurt when the bridge, just outside the Ramat Gan Naational Stadium, collapsed into the polluted Yarkon River.

Judaica Ring

On April 3, police announced they had broken an international ring that had been stealing Judaica in Israel and selling it around the world. The investigation began in March, when some of the ten suspects in the case tried to sell Torah *rimonim* (ornaments) at an auction. Organizers of the auction suspected that the objects were stolen, and, later, police found hundreds of similar objects, worth millions of dollars, in the Jerusalem home of one of the suspects.

Disasters

Air Sibir

Air Sibir Flight 1812, on a routine weekly flight from Ben-Gurion International Airport to Novisibirsk on October 4, blew up about 185 kilometers from the Black Sea resort city of Sochi, roughly an hour after it took off. All those aboard—78 people, including 66 Israelis—were killed. Most of the passengers were new immigrants to Israel from Russia, who were going to visit relatives in the Siberian city; many of the others were Russians returning from paying similar visits to Israeli kin.

At first, a terror attack was suspected—Russian president Vladimir Putin publicly suggested as much—but there was also talk that the ten-year-old Tupolev plane had not been maintained properly. Taking no chances, authorities at Ben-Gurion put the airport on high alert, halting all outgoing flights for several hours as security teams rechecked all baggage. But within hours, U.S. Department of Defense sources, apparently basing their conclusions on U.S. satellites monitoring missile launches around the world, indicated that the midair explosion had been caused by a missile fired during joint Russian-Ukrainian military exercises near the Crimean peninsula, west of the crash site. However, the Ukrainians insisted that they had tracked every missile fired during their exercise and all were accounted for, adding that no missiles had been aimed in the direction of the airline.

The joint Russian-Ukrainian maneuvers were being conducted about 250 kilometers from the crash scene. After the initial denials, Ukrainian president Leonid Kuchma fired Defense Minister Oleksandr Kuzmuk and his aides. Kuchma ordered a check of all Ukrainian missiles, banned new missile launches until the investigation was over, and promised that his country would pay compensation if it indeed were responsible. He said that Ukraine "will do everything necessary to soften the pain and suffering of the families." On October 13, Ukrainian officials confirmed that one of their country's S-200 missiles had struck the place. Kuchma denied suggestions that his country had attempted to avoid responsibility for the tragedy. "We have tried to be as transparent as possible from the very beginning," he said, "and have taken all steps to ensure an efficient investigation."

Relatives of many of the Israeli citizens killed in the crash were flown to Sochi to witness the search. But few bodies were recovered. Housing Minister Natan Sharansky, himself an immigrant from the former Soviet Union, noted that the crash was the second harsh blow suffered by Israel's million former Soviet citizens, after the June 1 Dolphinarium disco bombing, in which most of the 21 victims were of Russian origin. "It's really difficult to describe. It's a harsh blow to people who have been Israeli for just a few years . . . and finally started to get absorbed in society, finally started to get accustomed to their new life," he said.

Wedding Hall

At least 23 people were killed on May 24, when the Versailles banquet hall, on the top floor of a three-story building in Jerusalem, collapsed.

Over 100 others were injured, many of them trapped in the rubble for hours until they could be rescued. Amid public outrage at the evident laxity in enforcing construction codes, the government established a formal commission of inquiry into building practices, and police interrogated ten people—including the architect who developed Pal-Kal, the system of ceiling support that was thought to be responsible for the collapse. Since the building had only minimal insurance, survivors and injured victims demanded that the government declare the collapse an official disaster, making them eligible for compensation.

Religious and Secular

The Tel Aviv city administration caused an uproar in late July when it decided that the law designed to force the closing of places of entertainment on Tisha B'Av (the fast day commemorating the destruction of the First and Second Temples in Jerusalem) applied only to "entertainment halls," not cafés, restaurants, or bars. As a consequence, Tel Aviv mayor Ron Hulda'i instructed municipal inspectors not to issue fines to the proprietors of establishments which remained open on the day. Still, the mayor said he was not trying to make an ideological statement or to undermine the solemnity of the day, but was merely conforming to the legal realities as laid out by city's legal counselor.

The decision had little actual impact on Tel Aviv, where eating places and bars had generally been open on this day of fasting and mourning. But it did trigger consternation and angry protests from Orthodox political circles. Rabbi Natan Elnatan of Shas, deputy mayor of Tel Aviv, threatened to cause a national coalition crisis if Prime Minister Sharon did not force Hulda'i to rescind his decision, and Interior Minister Eli Yishai of Shas ordered his ministry's lawyers to check if the Tel Aviv action was really legal. Moderate Orthodox politicians chimed in as well. Deputy Foreign Minister Michael Melchior of the left-leaning Meimad Party (Modern Orthodox), said: "Apparently the Tel Aviv municipality does not think that the residents of the city need to know about the destruction of the Temple, about the Diaspora, and about the uprising. In its attitude, it is separating the city from the rest of the country." On the other hand, MK Yossi Paritzky of the anticlerical Shinui Party praised the Tel Aviv mayor, who, he said, had proved "that Tel Aviv-Jaffa is a city that never sleeps, and is devoid of religious coercion." He expressed hope that other mayors would follow Hulda'i's example.

Sports

The Maccabi Tel Aviv basketball team won the championship of the European Suproleague on May 13, defeating Panatanaikos of Athens by 81-67 in the final. Almost 8,000 Israelis went to Paris to see the game, and tens of thousands of Israelis celebrated the victory in Tel Aviv's Rabin Square.

Ariel Ze'evi won the 100-kg. gold medal at the European Judo Championships, on May 20. Ze'evi won the title by scoring an "ippon" (knockout) over Ghislain Lemeire of France in the final, which he reached by beating opponents from Ukraine, the Netherlands, and Georgia. Ze'evi had been Israel's best hope for a medal at the 2000 Olympics in Sydney, but finished fifth.

Alexandr Averbukh won a silver medal in the men's pole vault at the World Track and Field Championships held in Edmonton, Canada, in early August. Averbukh also won gold at the Russian winter track championships in February.

Other Israeli victories: Emil Sutovski, the Azerbaijan-born Israeli chess champ, the European individual chess championship in Macedonia in June; 470-class sailors Yogeg Yosef and Shafa Amir, the silver medal in the world junior yachting championships, held in Turkey in September; Gal Friedman, a bronze medal in the European windsurfing championships in Marseilles in September; Galit Chait and Sergei Sakhnovsky, silver medals in the Skate Canada competition in Saskatchewan; Matti Mazor, 12 years old, and Hod Dahari, 11, gold medals in swimming, yachting, and track, at the world championships for disabled children in Miami; Shahar Pe'er, 14 years old, the prestigious Orange Bowl junior girls title in the Key Biscayne, Florida, youth tennis tournament.

The 16th Maccabiah Games—known popularly as the Jewish Olympics, where Jewish athletes from all over the world compete—ended nine days of competition on July 23 with a ceremony at Sultan's Pool in Jerusalem. The games themselves had appeared in danger, because of the security situation, until shortly before their opening on July 14 in Jerusalem's Teddy Stadium. In the end, however, organizers said that 5,281 sportsmen and sportswomen from 43 countries took part in the competitions, including 1,300 from Israel. The largest foreign delegations came from the United States (387), Canada (300), Argentina (160), Brazil (115), and Russia (110). Although the level of competition may have been lower than anticipated because some outstanding athletes canceled their participation, organizers emphasized that holding the games under such circumstances was an emphatic affirmation of Jewish unity.

Addressing the closing ceremony, Prime Minister Sharon thanked the participants, saying, "You have shown great solidarity and great courage during hard days for Israel. There are hard days ahead, but no doubt we will win. I am sure you will be our best ambassadors around the world, and I hope that when you come back next time to participate, you will decide to settle here."

Personalia

Honors and Awards

The 2001 Israel Prizes went to Prof. Aviezer Ravitzky of the Hebrew University (Jewish Thought); Prof. Gavriel Solomon of Haifa University and Prof. Ya'akov Rand of Bar-Ilan University (Education); Prof. Ruth Ben-Israel of Tel Aviv University and Prof. Yehoshua Weisman of the Hebrew University (Jurisprudence); Prof. Marcel Elyakim of the Hadassah-Hebrew University School of Medicine, Prof. Ruth Arnon of the Weizmann Institute, and Prof. Bracha Ramot of Tel Aviv University (Medicine); Profs. Yosef Imri and Shmuel Strieman of the Weizmann Institute (Physics); noted composer Zvi Avni, and Profs. Yehezkel Braun and Herzl Shmueli of Tel Aviv University (Music); wheelchair basketball star Baruch Hagai (Sport); and Abba Eban, Mordechai Ben-Porat, and Yitzhak Shamir (life's work and special contribution to the society and the state). The Truman Peace Prize, awarded by the Hebrew University's Truman Research Institute for the Advancement of Peace, went to Richard Holbrooke, former U.S. ambassador to the UN.

Appointments

Shlomo Aharonishky became Israel's police commissioner, replacing Yehuda Wilk; Brig.-Gen. Suzy Yogev, previously the commander of Chen, the Women's Army Corps, which had been disbanded as part of the army's new recognition of women's role in the military, was named adviser to the chief of staff on women's issues; Majali Wahabe became the first member of the Druse sect to be director general of a government ministry when he assumed that role for the Ministry of Regional Cooperation in May; two judges, Edmond Levy, who presided at the murder trial of Rabin assassin Yigal Amir, and Ayala Procaccia, were elevated to the Supreme Court; Benny Elon, MK of the right-wing Moledet (National Union), was named tourism minister replacing the assassinated Rehavam Ze'evi, his party colleague; Bishop Irineos was chosen Greek Orthodox patriarch of Jerusalem, succeeding the deceased Diodoros I; Avi Beker became the first Israeli to get an executive-level position at a major world Jewish organization when he was named secretary general of the World Jewish Congress; journalist and TV personality Amnon Dankner succeeded Ya'akov Erez as editor of *Ma'ariv,* Israel's second-largest Hebrew daily, despite controversy over Dankner's public support for his publisher, Ofer Nimrodi, during latter's trials for wiretapping and other offenses; Yafet Alemu, who came to Israel from Ethiopia via Sudan in the 1983 Operation Moses, became the first non-Orthodox Ethiopian rabbi when he was ordained by the (Conservative) Jewish Theological Seminary's branch in Jerusalem.

Deaths

Diodoros I, 77, for two decades the Greek Orthodox patriarch of Jerusalem, in January; Michael Elkins, 84, long-time Israel correspondent for the BBC and *Newsweek* and for the last decade ombudsman of the *Jerusalem Report,* who was the first to report Israel's stunning victory in the 1967 Six-Day War, in March; Doron Ashkenazi, 45, widower of the late pop singer Ofra Haza, of a cocaine overdose, in April; Yoram Bronowski, 52, translator, critic, and journalist at the *Ha'aretz* Hebrew-language daily, in April; Yossi Yadin, 81, veteran actor and founder of Tel Aviv's Cameri Theater, and brother of the late archeologist and deputy prime minister Yigael Yadin, in May; Walter Eytan, 90, veteran diplomat and the first director general of Israel's Foreign Ministry, in May; Faisal al-Husseini, 60, scion of a prominent Jerusalem Arab family and the PLO official responsible for Jerusalem affairs, in Kuwait, where he was representing the PA at a conference of Gulf States in May, buried on June 1 at Jerusalem's Al-Aqsa Mosque where thousands of Palestinians from the territories, waving PLO and PA flags, attended the funeral, without interference from Israeli security forces; Justice Dov Levin of the Supreme Court, 76, head of the Israeli council on traffic accidents, in June; Levi Ben-Avishai Ben-Pinhas, 82, high priest of the 700-strong Samaritan community, in June; Yehiel Dinur, 84, novelist who wrote in Hebrew about the Holocaust under the name K. Zetnik (pronounced Ka-Tzetnik), in August—when called as a witness at the 1961 trial of Adolf

Eichmann in Jerusalem, Dinur collapsed on the stand; Dudu Dotan, 53, popular Israeli comedian, actor, and author of children's books, while on a September vacation in Turkey; Gideon Lev-Ari, 65, noted radio newscaster and former head of the government-owned station, in October; Binyamin Ziegel, 79, founder of the Israel Police National Fraud Unit in 1974 and dogged investigator of several prominent white-collar criminals, in October; Alec Israel, 59, literary editor of the *Jerusalem Post,* in October; Rabbi Eliezer Menachem Schach, 103, head of the Ponevezh Yeshivah in Bnai Brak and acknowledged leader of the "Lithuanian," non-Hassidic ultra-Orthodox community, spiritual father of both the Sephardi Shas and Ashkenazi Degel Hatorah political parties, in November; Yigal Lev, 68, *Ma'ariv* journalist and former head of the National Journalists' Union, in November; Prof. Ya'akov Matzner, 54, dean of the Hebrew University Medical School, Prof. Amiram Eldor, 59, hematologist at Tel Aviv's Ichilov Hospital, and Avishai Berkman, 50, senior Tel Aviv municipal official, all in a November plane crash near Zurich; Reuven (Robbie) Shapira, 52, former African fishing magnate and owner of the Hapoel Haifa soccer club, by his own hand in Nigeria, over his failing business and heavy debts for the soccer club, in December.

HANAN SHER

World Jewish Population, 2002

THE WORLD'S JEWISH POPULATION was estimated at 13.3 million at the beginning of 2002—an increase of about 40,000 over the previous year's revised estimate.[1]

Figures on population size, characteristics, and trends are a primary tool in the assessment of Jewish community needs and prospects at the local level and worldwide. The estimates for major regions and individual countries reported in this article reflect a prolonged and ongoing effort to study scientifically the demography of contemporary world Jewry.[2] Data collection and comparative research have benefited from the collaboration of scholars and institutions in many countries, including replies to direct inquiries regarding current estimates. It should be emphasized, however, that the elaboration of a worldwide set of estimates for the Jewish populations of the various countries is beset with difficulties and uncertainties.[3] Users of Jewish population estimates should be aware of these difficulties and of the inherent limitations of our estimates.

Major geopolitical and socioeconomic changes have affected the world scene since the end of the 1980s, particularly the political breakup of the Soviet Union, Germany's reunion, South Africa's political transition, problems with Latin American economies, and the volatile situation in Israel and the Middle East. Jewish population trends were most sensitive to these developments, large-scale emigration from the former USSR

[1]The previous estimates, as of January 1, 2001, were published in AJYB 2001, vol. 101, pp. 532–569. See also Sergio DellaPergola, Uzi Rebhun, and Mark Tolts, "Prospecting the Jewish Future: Population Projections 2000–2080," ibid., pp. 103–146; and previous AJYB volumes for further details on earlier estimates.

[2]Many of these activities are carried out by, or in coordination with, the Division of Jewish Demography and Statistics at the A. Harman Institute of Contemporary Jewry (ICJ), the Hebrew University of Jerusalem. The collaboration of the many institutions and individuals in the different countries who have supplied information for this update is acknowledged with thanks.

[3]For overviews of the subject matter and technical issues see Paul Ritterband, Barry A. Kosmin, and Jeffrey Scheckner, "Counting Jewish Populations: Methods and Problems," AJYB 1988, vol. 88, pp. 204–21; Sergio DellaPergola, "Modern Jewish Demography," in Jack Wertheimer, ed., *The Modern Jewish Experience* (New York, 1993), pp. 275–90.

(FSU) and rapid population growth in Israel being the most visible effects. Geographical mobility and the increased fragmentation of the global system of nations notwithstanding, over 80 percent of world Jewry live in two countries, the United States and Israel, and 95 percent are concentrated in ten countries. The aggregate of these major Jewish population centers virtually determines world Jewry's total size.

Main Problems in Jewish Population Research

Determinants of Jewish Population Change

One fundamental aspect of population in general and of Jewish population in particular is its perpetual change. Population size and composition continuously change reflecting a well-known array of determinants. Two of these are shared by all populations: (a) the balance of vital events (births and deaths); (b) the balance of international migration (immigration and emigration). Both of these factors affect increases or decreases in the physical presence of individuals in a given place. The third determinant consists of identificational changes (accessions and secessions) and only applies to populations defined by some cultural or symbolic peculiarity, as is the case with Jews. The latter type of change does not affect people's physical presence but rather their willingness to identify themselves with a specific religious, ethnic or otherwise culturally defined group.

The country figures presented here for 2002 were updated from those for 2001 in accordance with the known or estimated changes in the interval — vital events, migrations, and identificational changes. In our updating procedure, whether or not exact data on intervening changes are available, we consistently apply the known or assumed direction of change, and accordingly add to or subtract from previous Jewish population estimates. If there is evidence that intervening changes balanced each other off, Jewish population remains unchanged. This procedure proved highly efficient in the past. Whenever improved Jewish population figures became available reflecting a new census or survey, our annually updated estimates generally proved on target.

The more recent findings basically confirm the estimates we had reported in previous AJYB volumes and, perhaps more importantly, our interpretation of the trends now prevailing in the demography of world

Jewry.[4] Concisely stated, these involve a positive balance of vital events among Jews in Israel and a negative one in nearly all other Jewish communities; a positive migration balance for Israel, the United States, Germany, and a few other Western countries, and a negative one in Latin America, Eastern Europe, Muslim countries, and some Western countries as well; a positive balance of accessions and secessions in Israel, and an often negative, or, in any event, rather uncertain one elsewhere. While allowing for improvements and corrections, the 2002 population estimates highlight the increasing complexity of the sociodemographic and identificational processes underlying the definition of Jewish populations, and hence the estimates of their sizes. This complexity is magnified at a time of enhanced international migration, often implying double counts of people on the move. Consequently, as will be clarified below, the analyst has to come to terms with the paradox of the *permanently provisional* character of Jewish population estimates.

Sources of Data

In general, the amount and quality of documentation on Jewish population size and characteristics is far from satisfactory. In recent years, however, important new data and estimates became available for several countries through official population censuses and Jewish-sponsored sociodemographic surveys. National censuses yielded results on Jewish populations in the Soviet Union (1989), Switzerland (1990), Canada, South Africa, Australia, and New Zealand (both 1991 and 1996), Brazil, Ireland, the Czech Republic, and India (1991), Romania and Bulgaria (1992), the Russian Republic and Macedonia (1994), Israel (1995), Belarus, Azerbaijan, Kazakhstan, and Kyrgyzstan (1999), and Estonia, Latvia, and Tajikistan (2000). The U.K. 2001 census included a new optional question on religion. Permanent national population registers, including information on the Jewish religious or national group, exist in several European countries (Switzerland, Norway, Finland, Estonia, Latvia, and Lithuania), and in Israel.

---

[4]See Roberto Bachi, *Population Trends of World Jewry* (Jerusalem, 1976); U.O. Schmelz, "Jewish Survival: The Demographic Factors," AJYB 1981, vol. 81, pp. 61–117; U.O. Schmelz, *Aging of World Jewry* (Jerusalem, 1984); Sergio DellaPergola, "Changing Cores and Peripheries: Fifty Years in Socio-demographic Perspective," in Robert S. Wistrich, ed., *Terms of Survival: The Jewish World since 1945* (London, 1995) pp. 13–43; Sergio DellaPergola, *World Jewry beyond 2000: Demographic Prospects* (Oxford, 1999).

Where official sources on Jewish population are not available, independent sociodemographic studies have provided most valuable information on Jewish demography and socioeconomic stratification, as well as on Jewish identification. The largest of such studies so far have been the National Jewish Population Survey (NJPS) in the United States (1970–71 and 1990). Similar surveys were conducted over the last decade in South Africa (1991 and 1998), Mexico (1991), Lithuania (1993), the United Kingdom and Chile (1995), Venezuela (1998–99), Hungary, the Netherlands and Guatemala (1999), and Moldova and Sweden (2000). Several further Jewish population studies were separately conducted in major cities in the United States and in other countries. Additional evidence on Jewish population trends can be obtained from the systematic monitoring of membership registers, vital statistics, and migration records available from Jewish communities and other Jewish organizations in many countries or cities, notably in the United Kingdom, Germany, and Buenos Aires. Detailed data on Jewish immigration routinely collected in Israel help to assess changing Jewish population sizes in other countries. Some of this ongoing research is part of a coordinated effort constantly to update the profile of world Jewry.[5]

A new round of official censuses and Jewish surveys is expected to highlight the demographic profile of large Jewish communities at the dawn of the new millennium, primarily the U.S. National Jewish Population Survey (2000–01), the 2001 censuses of Canada, the Ukraine, and Australia, and the 2002 census of the Russian Republic. These new findings will allow for a significant revision and improvement of the currently available database on Jewish population.

Definitions

A major problem in Jewish population estimates periodically circulated by individual scholars or Jewish organizations is a lack of coherence and uniformity in the definition criteria followed—when the issue of defining the Jewish population is addressed at all. Three operative concepts

[5]Following the International Conference on Jewish Population Problems held in Jerusalem in 1987, initiated by the late Dr. Roberto Bachi of the Hebrew University and sponsored by major Jewish organizations worldwide, an International Scientific Advisory Committee (ISAC) was established. Currently chaired by Dr. Sidney Goldstein of Brown University, ISAC aims to coordinate and monitor Jewish population data collection internationally. See Sergio DellaPergola and Leah Cohen, eds., *World Jewish Population: Trends and Policies* (Jerusalem, 1992).

should be considered in order to put the study of Jewish demography on serious comparative ground.

The *core Jewish population*[6] includes all those who, when asked, identify themselves as Jews; or, if the respondent is a different person in the same household, are identified by him/her as Jews. This is an intentionally comprehensive and pragmatic approach reflecting the nature of most available sources of data on Jewish population. In countries other than Israel, such data often derive from population censuses or social surveys where the interviewees decide how to answer to relevant questions on religious or ethnic preferences. Such definitions of a person as a Jew, reflecting *subjective* feelings, broadly overlap but do not necessarily coincide with Halakhah (rabbinic law) or other normatively binding definitions. They do *not* depend on any measure of that person's Jewish commitment or behavior—in terms of religiosity, beliefs, knowledge, communal affiliation, or otherwise. The *core* Jewish population includes all converts to Judaism by any procedure, as well other people who declare themselves to be Jewish. Also included are persons of Jewish parentage who claim no current religious or ethnic belonging. Persons of Jewish parentage who adopted another religion are excluded, as are other individuals who did not convert out but explicitly identify with a non-Jewish group. In Israel, personal status is subject to the rulings of the Ministry of the Interior, which relies on rabbinical authorities. Therefore the *core* Jewish population in Israel does not simply express subjective identification but reflects definite legal rules, namely Halakhah.

The *enlarged Jewish population*[7] includes the sum of (a) the *core* Jewish population; (b) all other persons of Jewish parentage who are *not* Jews currently (or at the time of investigation); and (c) all of the respective further non-Jewish household members (spouses, children, etc.). Non-Jews with Jewish background, as far as they can be ascertained, include: (a) persons who have themselves adopted another religion, even though they may claim still to be Jews by ethnicity or religion; (b) other persons with Jewish parentage who disclaim being Jews. It is customary in sociodemographic surveys to consider the religio-ethnic identification of parents.

[6]The term *core Jewish population* was initially suggested by Barry A. Kosmin, Sidney Goldstein, Joseph Waksberg, Nava Lerer, Ariela Keysar, and Jeffrey Scheckner, *Highlights of the CJF 1990 National Jewish Population Survey* (New York, 1991).

[7]The term *enlarged Jewish population* was initially suggested by Sergio DellaPergola, "The Italian Jewish Population Study: Demographic Characteristics and Trends," in U.O. Schmelz, P. Glikson, and S.J. Gould, eds., *Studies in Jewish Demography: Survey for 1969–1971* (Jerusalem-London, 1975), pp. 60–97.

Some censuses, however, do ask about more distant ancestry. For both conceptual and practical reasons, this enlarged definition does not include other non-Jewish relatives who lack a Jewish background and live in exclusively non-Jewish households.

The *Law of Return,* Israel's distinctive legal framework for the acceptance and absorption of new immigrants, awards Jewish new immigrants immediate citizenship and other civil rights. According to the current, amended version of the Law of Return, a Jew is any person born to a Jewish mother, or converted to Judaism (regardless of denomination—Orthodox, Conservative, or Reform), who does not have another religious identity. By ruling of Israel's Supreme Court, conversion from Judaism, as in the case of some ethnic Jews who currently identify with another religion, entails loss of eligibility for Law of Return purposes. The law per se does not affect a person's Jewish status, which, as noted, is adjudicated by Israel's Ministry of Interior and rabbinical authorities. The law extends its provisions to all current Jews and to their Jewish or non-Jewish spouses, children, and grandchildren, as well as to the spouses of such children and grandchildren. As a result of its three-generation and lateral extension, the Law of Return applies to a large population, one of significantly wider scope than *core* and *enlarged* Jewish populations defined above.[8] It is actually quite difficult to estimate what the total size of the *Law of Return* population could be. These higher estimates are not discussed below systematically, but some notion of their possible extent is given for the major countries.

The following estimates of Jewish population distribution in each continent (table 1 below), country (tables 2–9), and metropolitan area (table 10) consistently aim at the concept of *core* Jewish population.

Presentation of Data

Until 1999, Jewish population estimates presented in the *American Jewish Year Book* referred to December 31 of the year preceding by two the date of publication. Since 2000 our estimates refer to January 1 of the current year of publication. The effort to provide the most recent possible picture entails a shorter span of time for evaluation and correction

---

[8]For a concise review of the rules of attribution of Jewish personal status in rabbinic and Israeli law, including reference to Jewish sects, isolated communities, and apostates, see Michael Corinaldi, "Jewish Identity," chap. 2 in his *Jewish Identity: The Case of Ethiopian Jewry* (Jerusalem, 1998).

of available information, hence a somewhat greater margin of inaccuracy. Indeed, where appropriate, we revised our previous estimates in the light of newly accrued information on Jewish populations (see tables 1 and 2). Corrections were also applied retrospectively to the 2001 figures for major geographical regions so as to ensure a better base for comparisons with the 2002 estimates. Corrections of the latest estimates, if needed, will be presented in future volumes of the AJYB.

Accuracy Rating

We provide separate figures for each country with approximately 100 or more resident *core* Jews. Residual estimates of Jews living in other smaller communities supplement some of the continental totals. For each of the reported countries, the four columns in tables 3–7 provide an estimate of midyear 2000 total population,[9] the estimated 1/1/2002 Jewish population, the proportion of Jews per 1,000 of total population, and a rating of the accuracy of the Jewish population estimate.

There is wide variation in the quality of the Jewish population estimates for different countries. For many Diaspora countries it would be best to indicate a range (minimum-maximum) rather than a definite figure for the number of Jews. It would be confusing, however, for the reader to be confronted with a long list of ranges; this would also complicate the regional and world totals. The figures actually indicated for most of the Diaspora communities should be understood as the central value of the plausible range of the respective core Jewish populations. The relative magnitude of this range varies inversely to the accuracy of the estimate.

The three main elements that affect the accuracy of each estimate are the nature and quality of the base data, how recent the base data are, and the method of updating. A simple code combining these elements is used to provide a general evaluation of the reliability of the Jewish population figures reported in the detailed tables below. The code indicates different quality levels of the reported estimates: (A) Base figure derived from countrywide census or relatively reliable Jewish population survey; updated on the basis of full or partial information on Jewish population movements in the respective country during the intervening period. (B) Base figure derived from less accurate but recent countrywide Jewish

---

[9]Data and estimates derived from the United Nations Population Division, *Population, Resources, Environment and Development Databank* (New York, 2002).

population data; partial information on population movements in the intervening period. (C) Base figure derived from less recent sources, and/or unsatisfactory or partial coverage of a country's Jewish population; updated according to demographic information illustrative of regional demographic trends. (D) Base figure essentially speculative; no reliable updating procedure. In categories (A), (B), and (C), the year in which the country's base figure or important partial updates were obtained is also stated. For countries whose Jewish population estimate for 2002 was not only updated but also revised in the light of improved information, the sign "X" is appended to the accuracy rating.

One additional tool for updating Jewish population estimates is provided by a new set of demographic projections developed at the Hebrew University of Jerusalem.[10] Such projections extrapolate the most likely observed or expected trends out of a Jewish population baseline assessed by detailed age-sex groups as of end-year 1995. Even where reliable information on the dynamics of Jewish population change is not immediately available, the powerful connection that generally exists between age composition of a population and the respective vital and migration movements helps to provide plausible scenarios of the developments bound to occur in the short term. Where better data were lacking, we used indications from these projections to refine the 2002 estimates as against previous years. On the other hand, projections are clearly shaped by a definite and comparatively limited set of assumptions, and need to be periodically updated in the light of actual demographic developments.

Global Overview

World Jewish Population Size

The size of world Jewry at the beginning of 2002 is assessed at 13,296,100. World Jewry constituted about 2.19 per 1,000 of the world's total population. One in about 457 people in the world is a Jew. According to the revised figures, between 2001 and 2002 the Jewish population grew by an estimated 44,000 people, or about 0.3 percent. This compares with a total world population growth rate of 1.4 percent (0.1 percent in more developed countries, 1.7 percent in less developed countries). De-

[10]See DellaPergola, Rebhun, and Tolts, "Prospecting the Jewish Future."

spite all the imperfections in the estimates, world Jewry continued to be close to "zero population growth," with increase in Israel (1.5 percent) slightly overcoming decline in the Diaspora (–0.3 percent).

Table 1 gives an overall picture of Jewish population for the beginning of 2002 as compared to 2001. For 2001 the originally published estimates are presented along with somewhat revised figures that take into account, retrospectively, the corrections made in certain country estimates in the light of improved information. These corrections resulted in a net decrease of the 2001 world Jewry's estimated size by 2,000. This change resulted from upward corrections for Azerbaijan (+500), and downward corrections for Turkey (–2,000) and Tajikistan (–500). Explanations are given below of the reasons for these corrections.

The number of Jews in Israel rose from 4,952,200 in 2001 to 5,025,000 at the beginning of 2002, an increase of 72,800 people, or 1.5 percent. In contrast, the estimated Jewish population in the Diaspora declined from 8,299,900 (according to the revised figures) to 8,271,100—a decrease of 28,800 people, or –0.3 percent. These changes primarily reflect the continuing Jewish emigration from the FSU. In 2001, the estimated Israel-Diaspora net migratory balance amounted to a gain of about 15,000 Jews for Israel.[11] Internal demographic evolution (including vital events and conversions) produced a further growth of about 58,000 among the Jewish population in Israel, and a further loss of about 14,000 in the Diaspora. Recently, instances of accession or "return" to Judaism can be observed in connection with the emigration process from Eastern Europe and Ethiopia, and the comprehensive provisions of the Israeli Law of Return (see above). The return or first-time access to Judaism of some of such previously unincluded or unidentified individuals has contributed to slowing down the pace of decline of the relevant Diaspora Jewish populations and some further gains for the Jewish population in Israel.

As noted, corrections should be introduced in previously published Jewish population estimates in the light of improved information that became available at a later date. Table 2 provides a synopsis of the world Jewish population estimates relating to the period 1945–2002, as first published each year in the *American Jewish Year Book* and as corrected retroactively, incorporating all subsequent revisions. These revised data

---

[11]Israel, Central Bureau of Statistics, *Population and Vital Statistics 1997* (Jerusalem, 1998), pp. 2–8.

TABLE 1. ESTIMATED JEWISH POPULATION, BY CONTINENTS AND MAJOR GEOGRAPHICAL REGIONS, 2001 AND 2002[a]

Region	2001 Original Abs. N.	2001 Revised Abs. N.	2001 Revised Percent[b]	2002 Abs. N.	2002 Percent[b]	Yearly % Change 2001–2002
World	13,254,100	13,252,100	100.0	13,296,100	100.0	0.3
Diaspora	8,301,900	8,299,900	62.6	8,271,100	62.2	–0.3
Israel	4,952,200	4,952,200	37.4	5,025,000	37.8	1.5
America, Total	6,479,300	6,479,300	48.9	6,476,300	48.7	–0.0
North[c]	6,064,000	6,064,000	45.8	6,064,000	45.6	0.0
Central	52,600	52,600	0.4	52,500	0.4	–0.2
South	362,700	362,700	2.7	359,800	2.7	–0.8
Europe, Total	1,582,800	1,580,800	11.9	1,558,500	11.7	–1.4
European Union	1,032,100	1,032,100	7.8	1,034,400	7.8	0.2
Other West	19,700	19,700	0.1	19,600	0.1	–0.5
Former USSR[d]	434,000	434,000	3.3	410,000	3.1	–5.5
Other East and Balkans[d]	97,000	95,000	0.7	94,500	0.7	–0.5
Asia, Total	5,000,500	5,000,500	37.7	5,069,900	38.1	1.4
Israel	4,952,200	4,952,200	37.4	5,025,000	37.8	1.5
Former USSR[d]	28,000	28,000	0.2	25,000	0.2	–10.7
Other	20,300	20,300	0.2	19,900	0.1	–2.0
Africa, Total	88,300	88,300	0.7	87,200	0.7	–1.2
North[e]	7,500	7,500	0.1	7,400	0.1	–1.3
South[f]	80,800	80,800	0.6	79,800	0.6	–1.2
Oceania[g]	103,200	103,200	0.8	104,200	0.8	1.0

[a]January 1.
[b]Minor discrepancies due to rounding.
[c]U.S.A. and Canada.
[d]The Asian parts of Russia and Turkey are included in Europe.
[e]Including Ethiopia.
[f]South Africa, Zimbabwe, and other sub-Saharan countries.
[g]Australia, New Zealand.

correct, sometimes significantly, the figures published until 1980 by other authors, and since 1981 by ourselves. Thanks to the development over the years of an improved database, these new revisions are not necessarily the same revised estimates that we published year by year in the AJYB based on the information that was available at each date. It is expected that further retrospective revisions will be necessary as a product of ongoing and future research.

The revised figures in table 2 clearly portray the slowing down of Jewish population growth globally since World War II. Based on a post-Holocaust world Jewish population estimate of 11,000,000, a growth of 1,079,000 occurred between 1945 and 1960, followed by growths of 506,000 in the 1960s, 234,000 in the 1970s, 49,000 in the 1980s, and 344,000 in the 1990s. While it took 13 years to add one million to world Jewry's postwar size, it took 38 years to add another million. The modest recovery of the 1990s mostly reflects the already noted cases of individuals first entering or returning to Judaism, especially from Eastern Europe, as well as a short-lived "echo effect" of the postwar baby-boom (see below).

TABLE 2. WORLD JEWISH POPULATION ESTIMATES: ORIGINAL AND CORRECTED, 1945–2002

Year	Original Estimate[a]	Corrected Estimate[b]	Yearly % Change[c]
1945, May 1	11,000,000	11,000,000	
1950, Jan. 1	11,303,400	11,297,000	0.57
1960, Jan. 1	12,792,800	12,079,000	0.67
1970, Jan. 1	13,950,900	12,585,000	0.41
1980, Jan. 1	14,527,100	12,819,000	0.18
1990, Jan. 1	12,810,300	12,868,000	0.04
2000, Jan. 1	13,191,500	13,212,500	0.26
2001, Jan. 1	13,254,100	13,252,100	0.30
2002, Jan. 1	13,296,100		0.33

[a]As published in AJYB, various years. Estimates reported here as of Jan. 1 were originally published as of end of previous year.
[b]Based on updated, revised, or otherwise improved information. Original estimates for 1990 and after, and all corrected estimates: The A. Harman Institute of Contemporary Jewry, The Hebrew University of Jerusalem.
[c]Based on corrected estimates, besides latest year.

DISTRIBUTION BY MAJOR REGIONS

Just about half of the world's Jews reside in the Americas, with about 46 percent in North America. Over 38 percent live in Asia, including the Asian republics of the former USSR (but not the Asian parts of the Russian Republic and Turkey)—most of them in Israel. Europe, including the Asian territories of the Russian Republic and Turkey, accounts for about 12 percent of the total. Fewer than 2 percent of the world's Jews live in Africa and Oceania. Among the major geographical regions listed in table 1, the number of Jews in Israel—and, consequently, in total Asia—increased in 2001. Moderate Jewish population gains were also estimated for the European Union (including 15 member countries), and Oceania. Central and South America, other regions in Europe, Asian countries outside of Israel, and Africa sustained decreases in Jewish population size.

Individual Countries

THE AMERICAS

In 2002 the total number of Jews in the American continents was estimated at close to 6.5 million. The overwhelming majority (94 percent) resided in the United States and Canada, less than 1 percent lived in Central America including Mexico, and about 6 percent lived in South America—with Argentina and Brazil the largest Jewish communities there (see table 3).

United States. Field work for the 2000–01 National Jewish Population Survey (NJPS), sponsored by United Jewish Communities (UJC), was completed but final results were not yet available at the time of this writing. The 1989–90 National Jewish Population Survey (NJPS) provided the current benchmark information about the size and characteristics of U.S. Jewry and the basis for subsequent updates.[12] In the summer of 1990 the core Jewish population in the United States comprised 5,515,000 per-

---

[12]The 1989–1990 National Jewish Population Survey was conducted under the auspices of the Council of Jewish Federations with the supervision of a National Technical Advisory Committee chaired by Dr. Sidney Goldstein of Brown University. Dr. Barry Kosmin of the North American Jewish Data Bank and City University of New York Graduate School directed the study. See Kosmin et al., *Highlights;* and Sidney Goldstein, "Profile of American Jewry: Insights from the 1990 National Jewish Population Survey," AJYB 1992, vol. 92, pp. 77–173.

TABLE 3. ESTIMATED JEWISH POPULATION DISTRIBUTION IN THE AMERICAS, 1/1/2002

Country	Total Population	Jewish Population	Jews per 1,000 Population	Accuracy Rating
Canada	30,757,000	364,000	11.8	B 1996
United States	283,230,000	5,700,000	20.1	B 1990
Total North America[a]	314,114,000	6,064,000	19.3	
Bahamas	304,000	300	1.0	D
Costa Rica	4,024,000	2,500	0.6	C 1993
Cuba	11,199,000	600	0.1	C 1990
Dominican Republic	8,373,000	100	0.0	D
El Salvador	6,278,000	100	0.0	C 1993
Guatemala	11,385,000	900	0.1	A 1999
Jamaica	2,576,000	300	0.1	A 1995
Mexico	98,872,000	40,400	0.4	B 1991
Netherlands Antilles	215,000	200	0.9	B 1998
Panama	2,856,000	5,000	1.8	C 1990
Puerto Rico	3,915,000	1,500	0.4	C 1990
Virgin Islands	114,000	300	2.6	C 1986
Other	23,051,000	300	0.0	D
Total Central America	173,162,000	52,500	0.3	
Argentina	37,032,000	195,000	5.3	C 1990
Bolivia	8,239,000	500	0.1	C 1999
Brazil	170,406,000	97,300	0.6	B 1991
Chile	15,211,000	20,900	1.4	B 1995
Colombia	42,105,000	3,400	0.1	C 1996
Ecuador	12,646,000	900	0.1	C 1985
Paraguay	5,496,000	900	0.2	B 1997
Peru	25,662,000	2,600	0.1	C 1993
Suriname	417,000	200	0.5	B 1986
Uruguay	3,337,000	22,300	6.7	C 1993
Venezuela	24,170,000	15,800	0.7	A 1999
Total South America[a]	345,647,000	359,800	1.0	
Total	832,923,000	6,476,300	7.8	

[a]Including countries not listed separately.

sons. Of these, 185,000 were not born or raised as Jews but currently identified with Judaism. An estimated 210,000 persons, not included in the previous figures, were born or raised as Jews, but in 1990 identified with another religion. A further 1,115,000 people—415,000 of them adults and 700,000 children below age 18—had a Jewish parent but had not themselves been raised as Jews, and declared a religion other than Judaism at the time of the survey. Altogether, these various groups formed an extended Jewish population of 6,840,000. NJPS also covered 1,350,000 non-Jewish-born members of eligible (Jewish or mixed) households. The study's enlarged Jewish population thus reached about 8.2 million. The 1990 Jewish population estimates are within the range of a sampling error of plus or minus 3.5 percent.[13] This means a 5.3–5.7-million range for the core Jewish population in 1990.

Since 1990, the international migration balance of U.S. Jewry should have generated Jewish population increase. According to HIAS (Hebrew Immigrant Aid Society), the main agency involved in assisting Jewish migration from the FSU to the United States, over 250,000 migrants were assisted over the period 1991–2000.[14] These figures refer to the *enlarged* Jewish population concept, thus incorporating the non-Jewish members of mixed households. The actual number of FSU Jews settling in the U.S. was therefore somewhat smaller, still quite substantial though steadily declining since 1992. More migrants arrived from Israel, Latin America, South Africa, Iran, and other countries. At the same time Israeli statistics continue to show moderate but steady numbers of immigrants from the United States. Between 1990 and 2000, a total of about 20,000 American Jews went on aliyah, and larger numbers of Israelis left the United States after a prolonged stay and returned to Israel, bringing with them their U.S.-born children.[15]

The 1990 NJPS provided evidence of a variety of factors contributing to slowing down Jewish population growth in the U.S.: low levels of "effectively Jewish" fertility, aging of the Jewish population, increasing rates of outmarriage, declining rates of conversion to Judaism (or "choosing" Judaism), rather low proportions of children of mixed marriages being identified as Jewish, and a growing tendency to adopt non-Jewish ritu-

---

[13] See Kosmin et al., *Highlights,* p. 39.

[14] See HIAS, *Annual Report* (New York) for these years.

[15] *Statistical Abstract of Israel*, vol. 49, 1998, pp. *4*-3, *4*-5, *5*-7; Yinon Cohen and Yitzchak Haberfeld, "The Number of Israeli Immigrants in the United States in 1990," *Demography* 34, no. 2, 1997, pp. 199–212.

als.[16] As a consequence, a surplus of Jewish deaths over Jewish births probably prevailed among U.S. Jewry. From the NJPS benchmark core Jewish population of 5,515,000, accounting for a positive balance of immigration net of emigration and assuming some quantitative erosion in the light of recent marriage, fertility, and age-composition trends, we estimated the current Jewish population at 5,700,000—the world's largest.

Another study completed in 2001 based on a countrywide sample, the American Jewish Identification Survey (AJIS), estimated a core Jewish population of 5,340,000 and an enlarged total of 10 million, including non-Jewish members of Jewish households and households of Jewish descent without any core member.[17] AJIS aimed at replicating the 1990 NJPS methodology, whereas the 2000–01 NJPS introduced several conceptual and technical changes intended to improve its effectiveness in portraying American Jewry. AJIS findings imply a decline of 175,000 in the core Jewish population and an increase of 1,975,000 in the non-core total since 1990. The latter figure comprises 845,000 adults of Jewish parentage with other religions, 173,000 children with Jewish parentage and other religion, and 957,000 other non-Jews. The AJIS would indicate that the processes of demographic and identificational erosion shown by the 1990 NJPS significantly strengthened during the 1990s. Our revision of the U.S. Jewish population estimate will be determined once the 2000–01 NJPS becomes available.

The North American Jewish Data Bank (NAJDB) continued its yearly compilation of local Jewish population estimates. These are reported elsewhere in this volume.[18] The NAJDB estimates were updated to 6,136,000 in 2000, including an unknown percent of non-Jewish members of Jewish households. Besides a significant downward revision in 1991, following NJPS, changes in NAJDB estimates reflected corrections and adaptations made in the figures for several local communities—some of them in the light of new local community studies. Clearly, compilations

---

[16]See Goldstein, "Profile"; U.O. Schmelz and Sergio DellaPergola, *Basic Trends in U.S. Jewish Demography* (New York, 1988); Sergio DellaPergola, "New Data on Demography and Identification among Jews in the U.S.: Trends, Inconsistencies and Disagreements," *Contemporary Jewry* 12, 1991, pp. 67–97.

[17]Egon Mayer, Barry Kosmin, and Ariela Keysar, *American Jewish Identity Survey 2001* (New York, 2001).

[18]The first in a new series of yearly compilations of local U.S. Jewish population estimates appeared in Barry A. Kosmin, Paul Ritterband, and Jeffrey Scheckner, "Jewish Population in the United States, 1986," AJYB 1987, vol. 87, pp. 164–91. For 2000 see Jim Schwartz and Jeffrey Scheckner, "Jewish Population in the United States, 2000," AJYB 2001, vol. 101, pp. 253–280. The 2001 update appears above, pp. 247–74, in this volume.

of local estimates, even if done as painstakingly as those of the NAJDB, are subject to a great many local biases, and tend to fall behind the actual pace of national trends. This is especially true in a context of vigorous internal migrations, as in the United States.[19] In our view, and in spite of sampling biases, national surveys such as NJPS offer a more reliable Jewish population baseline at the countrywide level than the sum of local estimates.[20]

Canada. As customary in Canada, the mid-decade 1996 census provided information on ethnic origins, whereas the 1991 census included questions on both religion and ethnic origin, plus information on year of immigration of the foreign-born, and languages. In 1996, 351,705 Canadians reported a Jewish ethnic origin, 195,810 of them as a single response and 155,900 as one selection in a multiple response with up to four options.[21] To interpret these data it is necessary to refer to the 1991 Canadian census, which enumerated 318,070 Jews according to religion.[22] Of these, 281,680 also reported to be Jewish by ethnicity (as one of up to four options to the latter question), while 36,390 reported one or more other ethnic origins. Another 38,245 persons reported no religion and a Jewish ethnic origin, again as one of up to four options. With due allowance for the latter group, a total core Jewish population of 356,315 obtains for 1991. A further 49,640 Canadians who reported being Jewish by ethnic origin but identified with another religion (such as Catholic, Anglican, etc.), were not included in the 1991 core estimate. Including them would produce an extended Jewish population of 405,955 in 1991.

The 1991 census equivalent of the 1996 census figure of 351,705 ethnic Jews (including those not Jewish by religion, but excluding those Jews who did not report a Jewish ethnic origin), was 349,565. Based on a sim-

---

[19]See Uzi Rebhun, "Changing Patterns of Internal Migration 1970–1990: A Comparative Analysis of Jews and Whites in the United States," *Demography* 34, no. 2, 1997, pp. 213–223.

[20]The NAJDB estimate for total U.S. Jewry in 2000 exceeds ours by 436,000 (a difference of 7.6 percent). Since 1990 we have estimated a Jewish population increase of 185,000 as against 621,000 according to NAJDB, and a decline of 175,000 according to AJIS.

[21]The sum inconsistency appears in the original report: Statistics Canada, *Top 25 Ethnic Origins in Canada, Showing Single and Multiple Responses, for Canada, 1996 Census (20% Sample Data)* (Ottawa, 1998).

[22]Statistics Canada, *Religions in Canada—1991 Census* (Ottawa, 1993); Jim L. Torczyner, Shari L. Brotman, Kathy Viragh, and Gustave J. Goldmann, *Demographic Challenges Facing Canadian Jewry; Initial Findings from the 1991 Census* (Montreal, 1993); Jim L. Torczyner and Shari L. Brotman, "The Jews of Canada: A Profile from the Census," AJYB 1995, vol. 95, pp. 227–260. See also Leo Davids, "The Jewish Population of Canada, 1991," in Sergio DellaPergola and Judith Even, eds., *Papers in Jewish Demography 1993 in Memory of U. O. Schmelz* (Jerusalem, 1997), pp. 311–23.

ilar criterion of ethnic origin, Canadian Jewry thus increased by 2,140 people over the 1991–1996 period. Though it should be stressed that the ethnic-origin definition is not consistent with our concept of a core Jewish population, the evidence was of very slow Jewish population increase—notwithstanding continuing immigration. Taking into account the increasingly aged Jewish population structure, we suggest that in the years following the 1991 census the continuing migratory surplus would have generated a modest surplus over the probably negative balance of internal evolution. For the beginning of 2002, we updated the 1991 baseline of 356,300 to 364,000, making the Canadian Jewish population the world's fourth largest. The 2001 census will provide a better baseline.

Central America. The 1991 population survey of the Jews in the Mexico City metropolitan area[23] pointed to a community less affected than others in the Diaspora by the common trends of low fertility, intermarriage, and aging. Some comparatively more traditional sectors in the Jewish community still contributed a surplus of births over deaths, and overall—thanks also to some immigration—the Jewish population was quite stable or moderately increasing. The new medium Jewish population estimate for 1991 was put at 37,500 in the Mexico City metropolitan area, and at 40,000 nationally. Official Mexican censuses over the years provided rather erratic and unreliable Jewish population figures. This was the case with the 1990 census, which came up with a national total of 57,918 (aged five and over). As in the past, most of the problem derived from unacceptably high figures for peripheral states. The new census figures for the Mexico City metropolitan area (33,932 Jews aged five and over in the Federal District and State of Mexico) came quite close—in fact were slightly below—our survey's estimates. Taking into account a modest residual potential for natural increase, as shown by the 1991 survey, but also some emigration, we estimated the Jewish population at 40,400.

The Jewish population was estimated at about 5,000 in Panama, 2,500 in Costa Rica, 1,500 in Puerto Rico, and 900 in Guatemala.[24]

---

[23]Sergio DellaPergola and Susana Lerner, *La población judía de México: Perfil demográfico, social y cultural* (México-Jerusalén, 1995). The project, conducted in cooperation between the Centro de Estudios Urbanos y de Desarrollo Urbano (CEDDU), El Colegio de Mexico, and the Division of Jewish Demography and Statistics of the A. Harman Institute of Contemporary Jewry, The Hebrew University, was sponsored by the Asociación Mexicana de Amigos de la Universidad Hebrea de Jerusalén.

[24]Carlos Tapiero, The Jewish Community of Guatemala: Sociodemographic Profile and Cultural and Religious Identity (Hebrew and Spanish), unpublished M.A. thesis, Jerusalem, 2001.

South America.[25] Argentinean Jewry, the largest in Latin America and seventh largest in the world, was marked by a negative population balance. Various surveys conducted in some central sections of Buenos Aires at the initiative of the Asociación Mutualista Israelita Argentina (AMIA), as well as in several provincial cities, pointed to increased aging and intermarriage.[26] Short of a major new survey in the Greater Buenos Aires area, quality of national estimates remained inadequate. Since the early 1960s, when the Jewish population was estimated at 310,000, the pace of emigration and return migration was significantly affected by the variable nature of economic and political trends in the country, generating a negative balance of external migrations. Most Jews lived in the Greater Buenos Aires area, with about 25–30,000 left in provincial cities and minor centers. The predominantly middle class Jewish community suffered from Argentina's national economic crisis, to the point of an emerging problem of "new Jewish poverty."[27] The Jewish institutional network was negatively affected, including Jewish education. Between 1990 and 2000, over 10,000 persons migrated to Israel and numbers were significantly rising in 2001–02, while unspecified numbers moved to other countries. Diminishing numbers of burials performed by Jewish funeral societies were also symptoms of population decline, though the high cost of Jewish funerals might have induced some Jewish families to prefer a non-Jewish ceremony. Accordingly, the estimate for Argentinean Jewry was reduced to 195,000 in 2002.

In Brazil, the population census of 1991 indicated a Jewish population of 86,816, a decline of 4,979 against the previous 1980 census. In 1991, 42,871 Jews lived in the state of São Paulo (44,569 in 1980), 26,190 in the state of Rio de Janeiro (29,157), 8,091 in Rio Grande do Sul (8,330), and 9,264 in other states (9,739).[28] Since some otherwise identifying Jews

---

[25]For a more detailed discussion of the region's Jewish population trends, see U.O. Schmelz and Sergio DellaPergola, "The Demography of Latin American Jewry," AJYB 1985, vol. 85, pp. 51–102; Sergio DellaPergola, "Demographic Trends of Latin American Jewry," in J. Laikin Elkin and G.W. Merks, eds., *The Jewish Presence in Latin America* (Boston, 1987), pp. 85–133.

[26]Rosa N. Geldstein, *Censo de la Población Judía de la ciudad de Salta, 1986; Informe final* (Buenos Aires, 1988); Yacov Rubel, *Los Judios de Villa Crespo y Almagro: Perfil Sociodemográfico* (Buenos Aires, 1989); Yacov Rubel and Mario Toer, *Censo de la Población Judía de Rosario, 1990* (Buenos Aires, 1992); Centro Union Israelita de Cordoba, *First Sociodemographic Study of Jewish Population; Cordoba 1993* (Cordoba, 1995).

[27]See a brief overview of the problems in Laura Golbert, Norma Lew, and Alejandro Rofman, *La nueva pobreza judía* (Buenos Aires, 1997).

[28]IBGE, *Censo demográfico do Brazil* (Rio de Janeiro, 1997).

might have failed to declare themselves as such in that census, we had adopted a corrected estimate of 100,000 since 1980, assuming that the overall balance of Jewish vital events, identificational changes, and external migrations was close to zero. The 1991 census figures pointed to Jewish population decline countrywide, most of it in Rio de Janeiro where Jewish population had been decreasing since 1960. In São Paulo—Brazil's major Jewish community—all previous census returns since 1940 and various other Jewish survey and register data supported the perception of a growing community, but the 1991 census figure contradicted that assumption.[29] A 1992 study in the state of Rio Grande do Sul and its capital, Porto Alegre—Brazil's third largest community—unveiled an enlarged Jewish population of about 11,000.[30] The corresponding core Jewish population could be estimated at about 9,000, some 10 percent above the 1991 census figure and quite consistent with it. In the light of this and other evidence of a substantially stable Jewish population, though one confronting high rates of intermarriage and a definite erosion in the younger age groups,[31] we estimated Brazil's Jewish population at 97,300 in 2002, the 11th largest Jewish community in the world.

In Chile, a sociodemographic survey conducted in the Santiago metropolitan area in 1995 indicated an enlarged Jewish population of 21,450, of which 19,700 were Jews and 1,750 non-Jewish relatives, including persons not affiliated with any Jewish organization.[32] Assuming another 1,300 Jews living in smaller provincial communities, a new countrywide estimate of 21,000 Jews was obtained. Previous lower estimates, reflecting results of the 1970 population census and a 1982–83 community survey, possibly overestimated the net effects of Jewish emigration. The new survey portrayed a rather stable community, with incipient signs of aging and assimilation.

In Venezuela, a new sociodemographic survey was carried out in

---

[29]Henrique Rattner, "Recenseamento e pesquisa sociológica da comunidad judaica de São Paulo, 1968," in Henrique Rattner, ed., *Nos caminhos da diáspora* (São Paulo, 1972); Claudia Milnitzky, ed., *Apendice estatistico da comunidade judaica do estado de São Paulo* (São Paulo, 1980); Egon and Frieda Wolff, *Documentos V; Os recenseamentos demográficos oficiais do seculo XX* (Rio de Janeiro, 1993–1994).

[30]Anita Brumer, *Identidade em mudança; Pesquisa sociológica sobre os judeus do Rio Grande do Sul* (Porto Alegre, 1994).

[31]Rene D. Decol "Imigrações urbanas para o Brasil: o caso dos Judeus," unpublished Ph.D. diss., University of Campinas, 1999; Daniel Sasson, *A comunidade judaica do Rio de Janeiro; Metodologia da pesquisa* (Rio de Janeiro, 1997).

[32]Gabriel Berger et al., *Estudio Socio-Demográfico de la Comunidad Judía de Chile* (Santiago-Buenos Aires, 1995).

1998–99.[33] Based on a comprehensive list of affiliated households and an indicative sample of the unaffiliated, and supplemented by a compilation of Jewish death records, the survey and subsequent emigration trends suggested a Jewish population estimate of 15,800 in 2002.

On the strength of fragmentary information available, our estimates for Uruguay, Colombia, and Peru[34] were slightly reduced to 22,300, 3,400, and 2,600 respectively.

Europe

Over 1.5 million Jews lived in Europe at the beginning of 2002, two-thirds in Western Europe and one-third in Eastern Europe and the Balkan countries—including the Asian territories of the Russian Republic and Turkey (see table 4). In 2001 Europe lost 1.4 percent of its Jewish population, mainly through continuing emigration from the European republics of the FSU.

European Union. Incorporating 15 countries since the 1995 accession of Austria, Finland, and Sweden, the European Union (EU) had an estimated combined Jewish population of 1,034,400—an increase of 0.2 percent over the previous year. Different trends affected the Jewish populations in each member country.[35]

With the breakup of the USSR, France had the third largest Jewish population in the world, after the United States and Israel. The estimated size of French Jewry, assessed at 530,000 in the 1970s,[36] was rather stable over the following 20 years.[37] The Jewish community of France continued to absorb a small inflow of Jews from North Africa, its age composition being younger than in other European countries. Migration to Israel amounted to 7,500 in 1980–1989 and over 15,000 in 1990–2000.

---

[33]Sergio DellaPergola, Salomon Benzaquen, and Tony Beker de Weinraub, *Perfil sociodemográfico y cutural de la comunidad judía de Caracas* (Caracas, 2000). The survey was sponsored by the two main local Jewish community organizations, the Asociación Israelita de Venezuela and the Union Israelita de Caracas, and by the Asociación de Amigos de la Universidad Hebrea de Jerusalén.

[34]Local observers had expected quicker reduction of Jewish population size. See Leon Trahtemberg Siederer, *Demografia judía del Peru* (Lima, 1988).

[35]See Sergio DellaPergola, "Jews in the European Community: Sociodemographic Trends and Challenges," AJYB 1993, vol. 93, pp. 25–82.

[36]Doris Bensimon and Sergio DellaPergola, *La population juive de France: socio-démographie et identité* (Jerusalem-Paris, 1984).

[37]Erik H. Cohen, *L'Etude et l'éducation juive en France ou l'avenir d'une communauté* (Paris, 1991).

Since the 1990s, aging tended to bring a moderate surplus of deaths over births, while intermarriage was steadily growing. In view of these trends, our French Jewish population estimate was revised to 525,000 in 1995 and 519,000 at the beginning of 2002. A new survey completed in 2002 will soon provide fresh insights on French Jewry.

A significant downward revision of the size of Jewish population in the United Kingdom was released in 1998 by the Community Research Unit (CRU) of the Board of Deputies of British Jews.[38] Current compilation of Jewish birth and death records showed an excess of deaths over births in the range of about 1,000–1,500 a year.[39] A survey of British Jews conducted in 1995 indicated a significant rise in intermarriage (38 percent of all married men, and 50 percent among Jewish men less than 30 years old), implying increasing assimilatory losses.[40] Further attrition derived from emigration (over 7,000 emigrants to Israel in 1980–1989 and about 6,000 in 1990–2000). Allowing for a further continuation of these well-established trends, we adopted an estimate of 273,500 for 2002 (fifth largest worldwide).

In 1990 Germany was politically reunited. In the pre-unification West German Federal Republic, the 1987 population census reported 32,319 Jews.[41] Immigration compensated for the surplus of deaths over births in this aging Jewish population. Estimates of the small Jewish population in the former (East) German Democratic Republic then ranged between 500 and 2,000. According to available reports, over 150,000 immigrants from the FSU settled in united Germany since the end of 1989, including non-Jewish family members.[42] Detailed records of Jews affiliated with

---

[38]Marlena Schmool and Frances Cohen, *A Profile of British Jewry: Patterns and Trends at the Turn of the Century* (London, 1998)

[39]Steven Haberman, Barry A. Kosmin, and Caren Levy, "Mortality Patterns of British Jews 1975–79: Insights and Applications for the Size and Structure of British Jewry," *Journal of the Royal Statistical Society*, A, 146, pt. 3, 1983, pp. 294–310; Steven Haberman and Marlena Schmool, "Estimates of British Jewish Population 1984–88," *Journal of the Royal Statistical Society*, A, 158, pt. 3, 1995, pp. 547–562; Stanley Waterman and Barry Kosmin, *British Jewry in the Eighties: A Statistical and Geographical Guide* (London, 1986); Marlena Schmool, *Report on Community Statistics* (London, yearly publication).

[40]Marlena Schmool and Frances Cohen, *British Synagogue Membership in 1990* (London, 1991); Stephen Miller, Marlena Schmool, and Antony Lerman, *Social and Political Attitudes of British Jews: Some Key Findings of the JPR Survey* (London, 1996).

[41]Statistisches Bundesamt, *Bevölkerung und Erwerbstätigkeit, Volkszählung vom 25 Mai 1987*, Heft 6 (Stuttgart, 1990).

[42]See Madeleine Tress, "Welfare State Type, Labour Markets and Refugees: A Comparison of Jews from the Former Soviet Union in the United States and the Federal Republic of Germany," *Ethnic and Racial Studies* 21, no.1, 1998, pp. 116–37.

the Zentralwohlfahrtsstelle der Juden in Deutschland (ZDJ)[43] show an increase from 27,711 at the beginning of 1990 to 93,326 at the beginning of 2002. By the same community registers, were it not for steady immigration from the FSU, the number of Jews would have declined from about 28,000 in 1990 to less than 18,000 in 2002, due to the continuing excess of Jewish deaths over Jewish births. We assume that there are enough incentives for most newcomers to be willing to affiliate with the Jewish community, but allow for some time lag between immigration and registration with the organized Jewish community, and take into account a certain amount of permanent nonaffiliation. Assuming the latter at about 10,000, an estimate of 103,000 core Jews (not including non-Jewish members of households) obtained for 2002, making Germany the eighth largest Jewish community worldwide.

Belgium, Italy, and the Netherlands each had Jewish populations ranging around 30,000. The tendency toward internal shrinkage of all these Jewries was partially offset by immigration. In Belgium, the size of the Jewish population, estimated at 31,400, was probably quite stable owing to the comparatively strong Orthodox section in that community. In Italy, compulsory membership in Jewish communities became voluntary in 1987. Although most Jews reaffiliated, the new, looser legal framework facilitated the ongoing attrition of the Jewish population. Recent Jewish community records for Milan indicated an affiliated Jewish population of 6,500, in contrast to over 8,000 in the 1960s, despite substantial immigration from other countries in the intervening period. These and other data on declining birthrates in most other cities prompted a reduction in our national estimate for Italy to 29,400.[44] In the Netherlands, a recent study indicated a growing number of residents of Israeli origin, substantially offsetting the declining trends among veteran Jews.[45] In the light of a new Jewish population survey that covered an enlarged Jewish population of 43,000–45,000,[46] includ-

---

[43]Zentralwohlfartsstelle der Juden in Deutschland, *Mitgliederstatistik; Der Einzelnen Jüdischen Gemeinden und Landesverbände in Deutschland* (Frankfurt, yearly).

[44]For an overview see Sergio DellaPergola, "La popolazione ebraica in Italia nel contesto ebraico globale," in Corrado Vivanti, ed., *Storia d'Italia, Ebrei in Italia* (Torino, 1997), vol.2, pp. 895–936.

[45]C. Kooyman and J. Almagor, *Israelis in Holland: A Sociodemographic Study of Israelis and Former Israelis in Holland* (Amsterdam, 1996); Philip van Praag, "Between Speculation and Reality," *Studia Rosenthaliana*, special issue published together with vol. 23, no. 2, 1989, pp. 175–79.

[46]Personal communication by Dr. Chris Kooyman, Stichting Joods Maatschappelijk Werk, Amsterdam.

ing Israeli and Russian new immigrants, we revised the core Jewish population estimate to 28,000.

Other EU member countries had smaller and, overall, slowly declining Jewish populations. Possible exceptions are Sweden and Spain, whose Jewish populations were very tentatively estimated at 15,000 and 12,000, respectively, based on figures on affiliation in the major cities. Austria's permanent Jewish population was estimated at 9,000. While a negative balance of births and deaths has long prevailed, connected with great aging and frequent outmarriage, immigration from the FSU tended to offset internal losses. The small Jewish populations in other Nordic countries were, on the whole, numerically stable. In Ireland, the 1991 census indicated 1,581 Jews. Since 1961 the Jewish population has regularly declined by 500–600 every ten years, leading to a 2002 estimate of 1,000.

Other West Europe. Few countries remain in Western Europe which have not joined the EU. In 2002 they accounted for a combined Jewish population of 19,700. The estimate of Switzerland's Jewish population was based on the results of the 1990 census. The official count indicated 17,577 Jews as against 18,330 in 1980—a decline of 4 percent.[47] Allowing for undeclared Jews and for about 1,000 emigrants to Israel during the 1990s, we put the 2002 estimate at 17,700.

Former USSR (European parts). Since 1989, the demographic situation of East European Jewry was radically transformed by the dramatic geopolitical changes in the region.[48] Official governmental sources provide the fundamental basis of information on the number of Jews in the FSU.[49] The Soviet Union's censuses and subsequent data distinguish the Jews as one recognized "nationality" (ethnic group). In a society that, until recently, left little or no space for religions, the ethnic definition criterion could be considered comprehensive and valid. Data from the last

[47]Bundesamt für Statistik, *Wohnbevölkerung nach Konfession und Geschlecht,1980 und 1990* (Bern, 1993).

[48]For the historical demographic background see U.O. Schmelz, "New Evidence on Basic Issues in the Demography of Soviet Jews," *Jewish Journal of Sociology* 16, no. 2, 1974, pp. 209–23; Mordechai Altshuler, *Soviet Jewry since the Second World War: Population and Social Structure* (Westport, Conn., 1987); Mordechai Altshuler, *Soviet Jewry on the Eve of the Holocaust: A Social and Demographic Profile* (Jerusalem, 1998).

[49]Dr. Mark Tolts of the A. Harman Institute of Contemporary Jewry at the Hebrew University actively contributed to the preparation of FSU Jewish population estimates. See two studies by Tolts, *Main Demographic Trends of the Jews in Russia and the FSU* (Jerusalem, 2001), and *Statistical Analysis of Aliyah and Jewish Emigration from Russia* (Jerusalem, 2002).

TABLE 4. ESTIMATED JEWISH POPULATION DISTRIBUTION IN EUROPE, 1/1/2002

Country	Total Population	Jewish Population	Jews per 1,000 Population	Accuracy Rating
Austria	8,080,000	9,000	1.1	C 1995
Belgium	10,249,000	31,400	3.1	C 1987
Denmark	5,320,000	6,400	1.2	C 1990
Finland	5,172,000	1,100	0.2	B 1999
France[a]	59,268,000	519,000	8.8	C 1990
Germany	82,017,000	103,000	1.3	B 2001
Greece	10,610,000	4,500	0.4	B 1995
Ireland	3,803,000	1,000	0.3	B 1993
Italy	57,530,000	29,400	0.5	B 1995
Luxembourg	437,000	600	1.4	B 2000
Netherlands	15,864,000	28,000	1.8	B 1999
Portugal	10,016,000	500	0.0	C 1999
Spain	39,910,000	12,000	0.3	D
Sweden	8,842,000	15,000	1.7	C 1990
United Kingdom	59,415,000	273,500	4.6	B 1995
Total European Union	376,533,000	1,034,400	2.7	
Gibraltar	25,000	600	24.0	B 1991
Norway	4,469,000	1,200	0.3	B 1995
Switzerland	7,170,000	17,700	2.5	B 1990
Other	829,000	100	0.1	D
Total other West Europe	12,493,000	19,600	1.6	
Belarus	10,187,000	24,300	2.4	B 1999
Estonia	1,393,000	1,900	1.4	B 2001
Latvia	2,421,000	9,600	4.0	B 2001
Lithuania	3,696,000	3,700	1.0	B 2001
Moldova	4,295,000	5,500	1.3	B 2000
Russia[b]	145,491,000	265,000	1.8	B 2000
Ukraine	49,568,000	100,000	2.0	C 1997
Total former USSR in Europe	217,051,000	410,000	1.9	

TABLE 4.—*(Continued)*

Country	Total Population	Jewish Population	Jews per 1,000 Population	Accuracy Rating
Bosnia-Herzegovina	3,977,000	300	0.1	C 1996
Bulgaria	7,949,000	2,300	0.3	B 1992
Croatia	4,654,000	1,300	0.3	C 1996
Czech Republic	10,272,000	2,800	0.3	B 1998
Hungary	9,968,000	51,300	5.1	C 1999
Macedonia	2,034,000	100	0.0	C 1996
Poland	38,605,000	3,500	0.1	D
Romania	22,438,000	10,800	0.5	B 1997
Serbia and Montenegro	10,552,000	1,700	0.2	C 1996
Slovakia	5,399,000	3,300	0.6	D
Slovenia	1,988,000	100	0.1	C 1996
Turkey[b]	66,668,000	17,000	0.3	B 2001 X
Total other East Europe and Balkans[c]	187,638,000	94,500	0.5	
Total	793,715,000	1,558,500	2.0	

[a]Including Monaco.
[b]Including Asian regions.
[c]Including Albania

all-Soviet population census, carried out in January 1989, revealed a total of 1,450,500 Jews,[50] confirming the declining trend shown by the previous three USSR censuses: 2,267,800 in 1959, 2,150,700 in 1970, and 1,810,900 in 1979.

Our reservation about USSR Jewish census figures in previous AJYB volumes bears repeating—some underreporting is not impossible, but it cannot be easily quantified and should not be exaggerated. The prolonged existence of a totalitarian regime produced conflicting effects on census declarations: on the one hand, it stimulated a preference for other

[50]Goskomstat SSSR, *Vestnik Statistiki* 10, 1990, pp. 69–71. This figure does not include about 30,000 Tats who were in fact Mountain Jews—a group mostly concentrated in the Caucasus area that enjoys fully Jewish status and the prerogatives granted by Israel's Law of Return.

than Jewish nationalities in the various parts of the FSU, especially in connection with mixed marriages; on the other hand, it preserved a formal Jewish identification by coercion, through the mandatory registration of nationality on official documents such as internal passports. Viewed conceptually, the census figures represent the core Jewish population in the USSR. They actually constitute a good example of a large and empirically measured core Jewish population in the Diaspora, consisting of the aggregate of self-identifying Jews. The figures of successive censuses were remarkably consistent with one another, and with the known patterns of emigration and internal demographic evolution of the Jewish population in recent decades. Our estimates reflect for each FSU republic separately all available data and estimates concerning Jewish emigration, births, deaths, and geographical mobility between the different republics.

Jewish emigration played the major role among demographic changes intervening since 1989.[51] The economic and political crisis that culminated in the disintegration of the Soviet Union as a state in 1991 generated a major emigration upsurge in 1990 and 1991. Emigration continued at lower but significant levels throughout 2001. Over the whole 1990–2000 period, over 1.4 million people defined as Jews by the enlarged Law of Return criteria, emigrated from the FSU. Of these, nearly 900,000 went to Israel, about 300,000 to the United States, and over 200,000 chose other countries, mainly Germany. Out of the total number of migrants, about 980,000 were Jewish by the core definition. Periodic declines in the volume of emigration should not be misconstrued: when compared to the fast declining Jewish population figures in the FSU, the emigration trend remained remarkably stable.

While mass emigration was an obvious factor in Jewish population decrease, a heavy deficit of internal population dynamics developed and

[51]Yearly migration estimates can be compiled according to (ex-)Soviet, Israeli, American, German, and other sources, especially Israel Central Bureau of Statistics and HIAS yearly reports. See also Mark Tolts, "Jewish Demography in the Former Soviet Union," in Sergio DellaPergola and Judith Even, eds., *Papers in Jewish Demography 1997* (Jerusalem, 2001), pp. 109–139; Yoel Florsheim, "Emigration of Jews from the Soviet Union in 1989," in *Jews and Jewish Topics in the Soviet Union and Eastern Europe* 2, no. 12, 1990, pp. 22–31; Sidney Heitman, "Soviet Emigration in 1990," *Berichte des Bundesinstitut fur Ostwissenschaftliche und internationale studien* 33, 1991; Barbara Dietz, Uwe Lebok, and Pavel Polian, "The Jewish Emigration from the Former Soviet Union to Germany," *International Migration* 40, no. 2, 2002, pp. 29–48; and Zentralwohlfahrtsstelle. . . .

even intensified due to the great aging that prevailed for many decades among FSU Jewry. For example, in 1993–1994 the balance of recorded vital events in Russia included 2.8 Jewish births versus 30.0 deaths per 1,000 Jewish population; in Ukraine, the respective figures were 4.2 and 35.9 per 1,000; in Belarus, 5.2 and 32.6 per 1,000; in Latvia, 3.1 and 24.5 per 1,000; in Moldova 5.9 and 34.6 per 1,000.[52] These figures imply yearly losses of many thousands to the respective Jewish populations. Frequencies of outmarriage approached 80 percent among Jews who married in Russia in the late 1980s, and in Ukraine and Latvia in 1996. Outmarried parents generally preferred a non-Jewish nationality for their children.[53] The significantly younger age composition of Jewish emigrants exacerbated aging in the countries of origin.[54] As a result, Jewish population rapidly shrank.[55]

---

[52]Mark Tolts, "The Jewish Population of Russia, 1989–1995," *Jews in Eastern Europe* 3, no. 31, 1996, pp. 15–19; Tolts, "Jewish Demography in the Former Soviet Union."

[53]Mark Tolts, "Some Basic Trends in Soviet Jewish Demography," in U. O. Schmelz and Sergio DellaPergola, eds., *Papers in Jewish Demography 1989* (Jerusalem, 1993), pp. 237–243; Viacheslav Konstantinov, "Jewish Population of the USSR on the Eve of the Great Exodus," *Jews and Jewish Topics in the Soviet Union and Eastern Europe* 3, no. 16, 1991, pp. 5–23; Mordechai Altshuler, "Socio-demographic Profile of Moscow Jews," ibid., pp. 24–40; Mark Tolts, "The Balance of Births and Deaths Among Soviet Jewry," *Jews and Jewish Topics in the Soviet Union and Eastern Europe* 2, no. 18, 1992, pp. 13–26; Leonid E. Darsky, "Fertility in the USSR: Basic Trends," unpublished paper presented at the European Population Conference, Paris, 1991; Mark Tolts, "Jewish Marriages in the USSR: A Demographic Analysis," *East European Jewish Affairs* 22, no. 2, 1992, pp. 3–19; Sidney and Alice Goldstein, *Lithuanian Jewry 1993: A Demographic and Sociocultural Profile* (Jerusalem, 1997).

[54]Age structures of the Jewish population in the Russian Federal Republic were reported in: Goskomstat SSSR, *Itogi vsesoiuznoi perepisi naseleniia 1970 goda,* Vol. 4, Tab. 33 (Moscow, 1973); Goskomstat SSSR, *Itogi vsesoiuznoi perepisi naseleniia 1979 goda*, Vol. 4, Part 2, Tab. 2 (Moscow, 1989); Goskomstat SSSR, *Itogi vsesoiuznoi perepisi naseleniia 1989 goda* (Moscow, 1991). Age structures of recent Jewish migrants from the USSR to the United States and to Israel appear, respectively, in HIAS, *Statistical Report* (New York, yearly publication) and unpublished annual data kindly communicated to the author; Israel, Central Bureau of Statistics, *Immigration to Israel*, Special Series, (Jerusalem, yearly publication); Yoel Florsheim, "Immigration to Israel and the United States from the former Soviet Union, 1992," *Jews in Eastern Europe* 3, no. 22, 1993, pp. 31–39; Mark Tolts, "Trends in Soviet Jewish Demography since the Second World War," in Ya'acov Ro'i, ed., *Jews and Jewish Life in Russia and the Soviet Union* (London, 1995) pp. 365–82; and Tolts, "Jewish Demography in the Former Soviet Union."

[55]Mark Tolts, "Demographic Trends of the Jews in the Three Slavic Republics of the Former USSR: A Comparative Analysis," in DellaPergola and Even, eds., *Papers in Jewish Demography 1993,* pp. 147–175; Mark Tolts, "The Interrelationship between Emigration and the Sociodemographic Trends of Russian Jewry," in Noah Levin-Epstein, Yaakov Ro'i, and Paul Ritterband, eds., *Russian Jews on Three Continents* (London, 1997), pp. 147–176.

On the strength of these considerations, our estimate of the core Jewish population in the FSU (including the Asian regions) was reduced from the census figure of 1,480,000 at the beginning of 1989 (including Tats) to 890,000 in 1993, and 435,000 at the beginning of 2002. Of these, 410,000 lived in the European republics and 25,000 in the Asian republics (see below). Tentative estimates of the enlarged Jewish population, including non-Jewish members of Jewish households, would probably be twice as high, and higher estimates would obtain for the total number eligible for the Law of Return.

Russia kept the largest Jewish population among the FSU republics—currently the fifth largest in the world. As against a 1989 census-based estimate of 570,000, including Tats, the February 1994 national Microcensus of the Russian Republic based on a 5-percent sample revealed a Jewish population of about 400,000, plus approximately 8,000 Tats.[56] This amounts to a total of 408,000, with a range of variation between 401,000 and 415,000 allowing for sampling errors. In 2002, on the eve of a new national census, our estimate for Russia was 265,000. In spite of decline, Russia's share of the total Jewish population of the FSU significantly increased over time due to lower emigration frequencies. Waiting for the results of the 2001 national census, we estimated Jews in the Ukraine at 100,000 in 2002 versus 487,300 in 1989, reflecting continuing large-scale emigration—currently the ninth largest community worldwide. In Belarus, the 1999 census[57] indicated a Jewish population of 27,798 (112,000 in 1989). For 2002 we estimated 24,300 Jews there. In Moldova, a survey conducted in 2000 at the request of the JDC-FSU Division and the local Jewish community confirmed the patterns of a declining and very elderly population.[58] We estimated the core total at 5,500 for 2002 (65,800 in 1989). Based on updated figures from the local national population registers, a combined total of 15,200 was estimated for the three Baltic states of Latvia, Lithuania, and Estonia (versus 39,900

---

[56]See V. Aleksandrova, "Mikroperepisis' naseleniia Rossiiskoi Federatsii," *Voprosy Statistiki*, 1994 (1), p. 37 (Moscow, 1994). See also Tolts, "The Interrelationship between Emigration and the Sociodemographic Trends."

[57]Ministry of Statistics and Analysis of the Republic of Belarus, *Population of the Republic of Belarus: Results of the 1999 Population Census Conducted in the Republic of Belarus* (Minsk, 2000).

[58]Malka Korazim, Ester Katz, and Vladimir Bruter, *Survey of the Jewish Population in Moldova* (Jerusalem, 2002).

in 1989). The figure for Latvia includes a 1,800 upward correction based on the 2000 census.[59]

The new population censuses conducted in parts of the FSU produced figures only barely higher than our estimates based on a yearly accountancy of known or expected vital events and international migration. Some of these inconsistencies can be explained by any combination of the following five factors: (a) migration of several thousands of Jews between the various FSU republics since 1991, especially to the Russian Republic; (b) a higher proportion of non-Jews than previously assumed among the enlarged pool of Jewish emigrants from the FSU, resulting in excessively lowered estimates of the number of core Jews remaining there; (c) a Jewish identification in the most recent sources by people who declared a different national (ethnic) identification in previous censuses; (d) counting, in the republics' national censuses and population registers, some people as residents—according to the legal criteria of the country of origin—who have actually emigrated to Israel or other countries; (e) and some returns to Russia and other republics from Israel[60] and other countries by migrants who are still registered as residents of the latter. While it is difficult to establish the respective weight of each of these factors, their overall impact has so far been secondary in the assessment of Jewish population changes. Factors (d) and (e) above point to likely double counts of FSU Jews in the respective countries of origin and of emigration. Consequently our world synopsis of core Jewish populations may be overestimated by several thousands.

The respective figures for the enlarged Jewish population—including all current Jews as well as other persons of Jewish parentage and their non-Jewish household members—are substantially higher in the FSU, where high intermarriage rates have prevailed for several decades. While a definitive estimate for the total USSR cannot be provided for lack of appropriate data, evidence for Russia and the other Slavic republics indicated a high ratio of non-Jews to Jews in the enlarged Jewish population. In 1989, 570,000 Jews in Russia together with 340,000 non-Jewish household members formed an enlarged Jewish population of 910,000; in 2001, the 275,000

[59]Goldstein, *Lithuanian Jewry 1993*; Lithuanian Department of Statistics, *Demographic Yearbook 1996* (Vilnius, 1997); Central Statistical Bureau of Latvia, *Demographic Yearbook of Latvia 2001* (Riga, 2001).

[60]Council of Europe, *Recent Demographic Developments in Europe, 2000* (Strasbourg, 2000).

core Jews and their 245,000 non-Jewish household members produced an enlarged population of 520,000.[61] The ratio of enlarged to core therefore increased from 1.6 in 1989 to 1.9 in 2001. Due to the highly self-selective character of aliyah, non-Jews constituted a relatively smaller share of all new immigrants from the FSU than their share among the Jewish population in the countries of origin, but such share was rapidly increasing.[62]

The wide provisions of Israel's Law of Return apply to virtually the maximum emigration pool of self-declared Jews and close non-Jewish relatives. Any of the large figures attributed in recent years to the size of Soviet Jewry, insofar as they were based on demographic reasoning, did not relate to the core but to various (unspecified) measures of an enlarged Jewish population. The evidence also suggests that in the FSU core Jews constitute a smaller share (and the non-Jewish fringe a larger share) of the enlarged Jewish population than in some Western countries, such as the United States. Just as the number of declared Jews evolved consistently between censuses, the number of persons of Jewish descent who preferred not to be identified as Jews was consistent too. However, recent political developments, and especially the current emigration urge, probably led to greater readiness to acknowledge a Jewish self-identification by persons who did not describe themselves as such in past censuses. These "returnees" imply an actual net increment to the core Jewish population of the FSU, Israel, and world Jewry.

Other East Europe and Balkans. A survey of Hungarian Jewry provided evidence on the size and characteristics of the largest community in Eastern Europe outside the FSU.[63] As against an overall membership

---

[61]Mark Tolts, "Russian Jewish Migration in the Post-Soviet Era," *Revue Européenne des Migrations Internationales* 16, no. 3, 2001, pp. 183–99; Evgeni Andreev, "Jews in Russia's Households (based on the 1994 Microcensus)," in DellaPergola and Even, eds., *Papers in Jewish Demography 1997,* pp. 141–59; Tolts, "Jewish Demography in the Former Soviet Union."

[62]Israel's Ministry of Interior records the religion-nationality of each person, including new immigrants. Such attribution is made on the basis of documentary evidence supplied by the immigrants themselves, and checked by competent authorities in Israel. According to data available from the Interior Ministry's Central Population Register, 90.3 percent of all new immigrants from the USSR during the period Oct. 1989–Aug. 1992 were recorded as Jewish. In 1994, the percent had declined to 71.6, in 1998 it was less than 60 percent, and in 2000 less than 50 percent. See Israel Central Bureau of Statistics, *Immigration to Israel 1998* (Jerusalem, 2000), and unpublished data. See also Sergio DellaPergola, "The Demographic Context of the Soviet Aliya," *Jews and Jewish Topics in the Soviet Union and Eastern Europe* 3, no. 16, 1991, pp. 41–56.

[63]The survey was directed by Prof. Andras Kovács of the Central European University in Budapest. Publication is forthcoming.

in local Jewish organizations estimated at about 20,000–25,000, the new data revealed a wide gap between core and enlarged Jewish population figures. The broader definition including all persons of Jewish ancestry encompassed 150,000–200,000 persons. On the other hand, a detailed reconstruction of Jewish international migration and vital statistics based on the World Jewish Congress end-1945 estimate of about 144,000 Holocaust survivors, and the 1948 Hungarian census figure of 134,000[64] produced a total of 50,000–55,000 for end-2000. The number of applicants for compensation (about 20,000 persons born before May 9, 1945, and defined according to the "enlarged" criteria) seems consistent with these calculations. Our admittedly minimal estimate of a core Jewish population of 51,300 for 2002 reflects the clear excess of deaths over births that prevails in Hungary in general, and among Jews particularly.

The January 1992 census of Romania reported a Jewish population of 9,107. Based on the detailed Jewish community records available with the Federatia Comunitatilor Evreiesi, our estimate for the 2002 was 10,800. The Czech census of 1991 reported 1,292 Jews, but according to the Federation of Jewish Communities there were at least twice as many, and that is reflected in our estimate of 2,800. The number of Jews in Poland and Slovakia was very tentatively estimated at 3,500 and 3,300 respectively. In Bulgaria, the census of December 4, 1992, reported 3,461 Jews;[65] our 2002 estimate, reflecting emigration, was 2,300. Crisis in the former Yugoslavia encouraged Jewish population decline. The core Jewish population for the total of five successor republics was assessed at about 3,500 at the beginning of 2002. Of these, fewer than 2,000 lived in Serbia and Montenegro, and 1,300 in Croatia.[66] The Jewish population of Turkey, where a significant surplus of deaths over births has been reported for several years, was reestimated at about 17,000.[67]

---

[64]Tamás Stark, "Hungarian Jewry during the Holocaust and after Liberation," in DellaPergola and Even, eds., *Papers in Jewish Demography 1993,* pp. 139–145.

[65]*Statistical Yearbook* (Sofia, 1992).

[66]For an overview see Melita Svob, *Jews in Croatia: Migration and Changes in Jewish Population* (Zagreb, 1997).

[67]Shaul Tuval, "The Jewish Community of Istanbul, 1948–1992: A Study in Cultural, Economic and Social Processes," unpublished Ph. D. diss., Jerusalem, 1999, and personal communication.

ASIA

Israel. At the beginning of 2002, Israel's Jewish population was 5,025,000[68]—second largest in the world and 565,000 more than the number enumerated in the November 1995 census. Crossing the line of 5 million Jews in Israel during 2001 was a significant landmark in Jewish population history. Adding over 250,000 non-Jewish members of immigrant families, mostly from the FSU but also from Ethiopia and other countries, an enlarged Jewish population of 5,278,700 obtained,[69] out of Israel's total population of 6,508,400 (not including the Palestinian population of the territories).

Israel accounted for 99 percent of the over-5 million Jews in Asia, including the Asian republics of the former USSR but excluding the Asian territories of the Russian Republic and Turkey (see table 5). At the beginning of 2002, Israeli Jews constituted 37.8 percent of total world Jewry.[70] Israel's Jewish population grew in 2001 by 72,800, or 1.5 percent. The pace of growth was slowing down after reaching growth rates of 6.2 percent in 1990, 5 percent in 1991, and 2–2.5 percent between 1992 and 1996. The number of new immigrants in 2001 (43,443) declined by 28 percent versus 2000 (60,130), which in turn represented a 22-percent decline as compared to 1999 (76,766). About 25 percent of Jewish population growth in 2001 derived from the net migration balance, against 32 percent in 2000; most Jewish population growth derived from natural increase. Moreover, 4,000 persons underwent Orthodox conversion in Israel in 1999, and 3,500 did in 2001—most of them immigrants from Ethiopia and the FSU and their children who were previously listed as non-Jews.[71] More than half of all new candidates for conversion to Judaism attended the Institute for Judaism Studies that the Orthodox, Conservative, and Reform movements run jointly in Israel.

---

[68]Israel Central Bureau of Statistics, *Population and Vital Statistics* (Jerusalem, 2002); *Monthly Bulletin of Statistics* (Jerusalem, 2002).

[69]The Israel Central Bureau of Statistics refers to such enlarged population as "Jews and others."

[70]We thank the staff of Israel's Central Bureau of Statistics for facilitating compilation of published and unpublished data. For a comprehensive review of sociodemographic changes in Israel, see U.O. Schmelz, Sergio DellaPergola, and Uri Avner, "Ethnic Differences among Israeli Jews: A New Look," AJYB 1990, vol. 90, pp. 3–204. See also Sergio DellaPergola, "Demographic Changes in Israel in the Early 1990s," in Y. Kop, ed., *Israel's Social Services 1992–93* (Jerusalem, 1993), pp. 57–115.

[71]Data released by rabbinical courts and special conversion courts. See *Ha'aretz*, Dec. 24, 2000.

TABLE 5. ESTIMATED JEWISH POPULATION DISTRIBUTION IN ASIA, 1/1/2002

Country	Total Population	Jewish Population	Jews per 1,000 Population	Accuracy Rating
Israel[a]	6,508,800	5,025,000	772.0	A 2001
Azerbaijan	8,041,000	7,900	1.0	C 1999 X
Georgia	5,262,000	5,000	1.0	C 2000
Kazakhstan	16,172,000	4,500	0.3	B 1999
Kyrgyzstan	4,921,000	900	0.2	B 1999
Tajikistan	6,087,000	100	0.0	C 1999 X
Turkmenistan	4,737,000	600	0.1	C 1999
Uzbekistan	24,881,000	6,000	0.2	C 1999
Total former USSR in Asia[b]	73,888,000	25,000	0.3	
China[c]	1,282,437,000	1,000	0.0	D
India	1,008,937,000	5,300	0.0	B 1996
Iran	70,330,000	11,200	0.2	C 1986
Iraq	22,946,000	100	0.0	C 1997
Japan	127,096,000	1,000	0.0	C 1993
Korea, South	46,740,000	100	0.0	C 1998
Philippines	75,653,000	100	0.0	D
Singapore	4,018,000	300	0.1	B 1990
Syria	16,189,000	100	0.0	C 1995
Thailand	62,806,000	200	0.0	C 1988
Yemen	18,349,000	200	0.0	B 1995
Other	789,434,200	300	0.0	D
Total other Asia	3,524,935,200[d]	19,900	0.0	
Total	3,605,332,000	5,069,900	1.4	

[a]Total population of Israel 1/1/2002. Jewish population includes 207,700 residents of Palestinian Territories.
[b]Including Armenia. Not including Asian regions of Russian Republic.
[c]Including Hong Kong.
[d]Including an estimated 3,200,000 in Palestinian Territories.

At the beginning of 2001, Israel's enlarged Jewish population (including non-Jewish household members) amounted to 5,180,600. Of these, 4,794,600 lived on land included in Israel before the 1967 war, 172,000 lived in Jerusalem neighborhoods incorporated since 1967, 191,500 in the West Bank, 6,700 in the Gaza strip, and 15,800 on the Golan Heights.[72]

Former USSR (Asian parts). The total Jewish population in the Asian republics of the former USSR was estimated at 25,000 at the beginning of 2002. Ethnic conflicts in the Caucasus area and the fear of Muslim fundamentalism in Central Asia continued to cause concern, stimulating Jewish emigration.[73] At the beginning of the 1990s, minimal rates of natural increase still existed among the more traditional sectors of these Jewish communities, but conditions were rapidly eroding this residual surplus.[74] Reflecting these trends, the largest community remained in Azerbaijan (8,900 according to the 1999 census and 7,900 in 2002,[75] versus 30,800 in 1989), followed by Uzbekistan (6,000 in 2002 vs. 94,900), Georgia (5,000 vs. 24,800), Kazakhstan (6,800 according to the 1999 census[76] and 4,500 in 2002, vs. 19,900 in 1989), and the remaining republics (1,600 overall—900 of them in Kyrgyzstan—vs. 24,000 in 1989).

Other countries. It is difficult to estimate the Jewish population of Iran, last counted in the 1986 national census.[77] Based on evidence of continuing decline, the 2002 estimate was reduced to 11,200. In other Asian countries with veteran communities the Jewish population tended toward disappearance. The recent reduction was more notable in Syria and Yemen after Jews were officially allowed to emigrate.

In India, the 1991 census provided a figure of 5,271 Jews, 63 percent of whom lived in the state of Maharashtra, including the main community of Mumbai.[78] Another 1,067 persons belonging to such religious

---

[72]Sergio DellaPergola, "Demography in Israel/Palestine: Trends, Prospects, Policy Implications," unpublished paper presented at IUSSP XXIV General Population Conference, Salvador de Bahia, 2001.

[73]Israel Central Bureau of Statistics, *Immigration to Israel 1998* (Jerusalem, 2000); Ministry of Immigrants Absorption, Division of Data Systems, *Selected Data on Aliyah, 2000* (Jerusalem, 2001); Jewish Agency for Israel, Division of Aliyah and Absorption, *Data on Aliyah by Continents and Selected Countries* (Jerusalem, 2001).

[74]Tolts, "The Balance of Births and Deaths."

[75]Not including the Jewish portion of the Tat group.

[76]Statistical Agency of the Republic of Kazakhstan, *Natsionaln'nyi sostav naseleniia Respubliki Kazakhstan: Itogi perepisi naseleniia 1999 goda v Respublike Kazakhstan*, vol. 1 (Almaty, 2000).

[77]Data kindly provided by Dr. Mehdi Bozorgmehr, Von Grunebaum Center for Near Eastern Studies, University of California-UCLA, Los Angeles.

[78]Asha A. Bhende, Ralphy E. Jhirad, and Prakash Fulpagare, *Demographic and Socio-Economic Characteristics of the Jews in India* (Mumbai, 1997).

groups as Messianic Judaism and Enoka Israel, all from Mizoram, were also counted. A survey conducted in 1995–96 by ORT India covered 3,330 individuals, fairly well educated and experiencing the customary patterns of postponed marriage, declining fertility, and aging. Our 2002 estimate was 5,300.

Very small Jewish communities, partially of a transient character, exist in several countries of Southeast Asia. After the reunion in 1997 of Hong Kong with the mainland, China's permanent Jewish population was estimated at roughly 1,000, the same as Japan's.

Africa

About 87,000 Jews were estimated to remain in Africa at the beginning of 2002, of which about 90 percent lived in the Republic of South Africa (see table 6). The 1980 national census counted about 118,000 Jews among South Africa's white population.[79] Substantial Jewish emigration since then was partially compensated for by Jewish immigration and return migration of former emigrants, but an incipient negative balance of internal changes produced some further attrition. The 1991 population census did not provide a reliable new national figure on Jewish population size, since the question on religion was optional and only 65,406 white people declared themselves to be Jewish. The results of a Jewish-sponsored survey of the Jewish population in the five major South African urban centers, completed—like the census—in 1991, confirmed ongoing demographic decline.[80] Based on that evidence, the most likely range of Jewish population size was estimated at 92,000 to 106,000 for 1991, with a central value of 100,000. According to the 1996 census there were 55,734 white Jews, 10,449 black Jews, 1,058 "coloured" (mixed-race) Jews, and 359 Indian Jews. Continuing Jewish emigration from South Africa to Israel and other countries in the West (especially Australia), stimulated by personal insecurity and other fears about the future, was reflected in a survey carried out in 1998.[81] A new estimate was suggested of 80,000 for 2000, lowered to 78,000 in 2002, making South Africa the 12th largest Jewish population worldwide.

---

[79]Sergio DellaPergola and Allie A. Dubb, "South African Jewry: A Sociodemographic Profile," AJYB 1988, vol. 88, pp. 59–140.

[80]The study was directed by Dr. Allie A. Dubb and supported by the Kaplan Centre for Jewish Studies, University of Cape Town. See Allie A. Dubb, *The Jewish Population of South Africa: The 1991 Sociodemographic Survey* (Cape Town, 1994).

[81]Barry A. Kosmin, Jaqueline Goldberg, Milton Shain, and Shirley Bruk, *Jews of the New South Africa: Highlights of the 1998 National Survey of South African Jews* (London, 1999).

TABLE 6. ESTIMATED JEWISH POPULATION DISTRIBUTION IN AFRICA, 1/1/2002

Country	Total Population	Jewish Population	Jews per 1,000 Population	Accuracy Rating
Egypt	67,884,000	100	0.0	C 1993
Ethiopia	62,908,000	100	0.0	C 1998
Morocco	29,878,000	5,600	0.2	B 1995
Tunisia	9,459,000	1,500	0.2	B 1995
Other	69,593,000	100	0.0	D
Total North Africa	239,722,000	7,400	0.0	
Botswana	1,541,000	100	0.1	B 1993
Congo D.R.	50,948,000	100	0.0	B 1993
Kenya	30,669,000	400	0.0	B 1990
Namibia	1,757,000	100	0.1	B 1993
Nigeria	113,862,000	100	0.0	D
South Africa	43,309,000	78,000	1.8	B 1999
Zimbabwe	12,627,000	700	0.1	B 1993
Other	299,565,000	300	0.0	D
Total other Africa	554,278,000	79,800	0.1	
Total	794,000,000	87,200	0.1	

In recent years, the Jewish community of Ethiopia was at the center of an international effort of rescue. In 1991, the overwhelming majority of Ethiopian Jews—about 20,000 people—were brought to Israel, most of them in a one-day dramatic airlift. Some of these migrants were non-Jewish members of mixed households. It was assumed that only few Jews had remained in Ethiopia, but in subsequent years the small remaining core Jewish population appeared to be larger than previously estimated. Between 1992 and 2001, nearly 20,000 immigrants from Ethiopia arrived in Israel—mostly non-Jewish relatives seeking reunification with their Jewish families. Although possibly more Jews may appear asking to emigrate to Israel, and more Christian relatives of Jews already in Israel may press for emigration before Israel terminates its current family reunification program, a conservative figure of 100 Jews was tentatively suggested for 2002. Small Jewish populations remained in various African countries south of the Sahara.

The remnant of Moroccan and Tunisian Jewry tended to shrink slowly through emigration, mostly to Israel, France, and Canada. The 2002 estimate was 5,600 for Morocco and 1,500 for Tunisia.[82] As some Jews had a foothold both in Morocco or Tunisia and also in France or other Western countries, their geographical attribution was uncertain.

Oceania

The major country of Jewish residence in Oceania (Australasia) is Australia, where 95 percent of the estimated total of 104,000 Jews live (see table 7). A total of 79,805 people in Australia described their religion as Jewish in the 1996 national census.[83] This represented an increase of 5,419 (7.3 percent) over the 1991 census figure of 74,186 declared Jews.[84] In Australia, the question on religion is optional. In 1996, over 25 percent (and in 1991, over 23 percent) of the country's whole population either did not specify their religion or stated explicitly that they had none. This large group must be assumed to contain persons who identify in other ways as Jews, although it is not certain whether Jews in Australia state their religion more or less often that other Australians. In a 1991 survey in Melbourne, where roughly half of all Australia's Jews live, less than 7 percent of the Jewish respondents stated they had not identified as Jews in the census.[85] The Melbourne survey actually depicted a very stable community combining growing acculturation with moderate levels of intermarriage. Australian Jewry received migratory reinforcements during the last decade, especially from South Africa, the FSU, and Israel. At the same time, there were demographic patterns with negative effects on Jewish population size, such as declining birth cohorts and strong aging.[86] Taking into account these factors, our 2002 estimate was 99,000—sub-

---

[82]See George E. Gruen, "Jews in the Middle East and North Africa," AJYB 1994, vol. 94, pp. 438–464; and data communicated by Jewish organizations.

[83]William D. Rubinstein, "Jews in the 1996 Australian Census," *Australian Jewish Historical Society Journal* 14, no. 3, 1998, pp. 495–507.

[84]Bill Rubinstein, "Census Total for Jews Up by 7.7 Percent; Big Gains in Smaller States," unpublished report (Geelong, Victoria, 1993).

[85]John Goldlust, *The Jews of Melbourne; A Report of the Findings of the Jewish Community Survey, 1991* (Melbourne, 1993).

[86]Sol Encel and Nathan Moss, *Sydney Jewish Community; Demographic Profile* (Sydney, 1995).

TABLE 7. ESTIMATED JEWISH POPULATION DISTRIBUTION IN OCEANIA, 1/1/2002

Country	Total Population	Jewish Population	Jews per 1,000 Population	Accuracy Rating
Australia	19,138,000	99,000	5.2	B 1996
New Zealand	3,778,000	5,100	1.3	B 1996
Other	7,645,000	100	0.0	D
Total	30,561,000	104,200	3.4	

stantially more than official census returns, but less than would obtain by adding the full proportion of those who did not report any religion in the census. Thus Australian Jewry was the tenth largest worldwide. The 2001 census will provide an improved population baseline.

In New Zealand, according to the 1996 census, 4,821 people indicated a Jewish religious affiliation; a total of 1,545 indicated an Israeli/Jewish/Hebrew ethnicity, of which 633 were also Jewish by religion, 609 had another religion, and 303 reported no religion. Adding the latter to those who reported a Jewish religion, a core Jewish population estimate of 5,124 obtained.[87]

Dispersion and Concentration

Country Patterns

While Jews are widely dispersed throughout the world, they are also concentrated to a large extent (see table 8). In 2002, over 97 percent of world Jewry lived in the 15 countries with the largest Jewish populations; and over 80 percent lived in the two largest communities—the United States and Israel. Similarly, ten leading Diaspora countries together comprised over 92 percent of the Diaspora Jewish population; three countries (United States, France, and Canada) accounted for nearly 80 percent, and the United States alone for nearly 69 percent of total Diaspora Jewry.

[87]Statistics New Zealand, *1996 Census of Population and Dwellings, Ethnic Groups* (Wellington, 1997).

TABLE 8. COUNTRIES WITH LARGEST JEWISH POPULATIONS, 1/1/2002

Rank	Country	Jewish Population	% of Total Jewish Population: In the World %	In the World Cumulative %	In the Diaspora %	In the Diaspora Cumulative %
1	United States	5,700,000	42.9	42.9	68.9	68.9
2	Israel	5,025,000	37.8	80.7	=	=
3	France	519,000	3.9	84.6	6.3	75.2
4	Canada	364,000	2.7	87.3	4.4	79.6
5	United Kingdom	273,500	2.1	89.4	3.3	82.9
6	Russia	265,000	2.0	91.4	3.2	86.1
7	Argentina	195,000	1.5	92.8	2.4	88.5
8	Germany	103,000	0.8	93.6	1.2	89.7
9	Ukraine	100,000	0.8	94.3	1.2	90.9
10	Australia	99,000	0.7	95.1	1.2	92.1
11	Brazil	97,300	0.7	95.8	1.2	93.3
12	South Africa	78,000	0.6	96.4	0.9	94.2
13	Hungary	51,300	0.4	96.8	0.6	94.8
14	Mexico	40,400	0.3	97.1	0.5	95.3
15	Belgium	31,400	0.2	97.3	0.4	95.7

Table 9 demonstrates the magnitude of Jewish dispersion. The 94 individual countries listed above as each having at least 100 Jews are scattered over six continents. In 2002, nine countries had a Jewish population of 100,000 or more; another 4 countries had 50,000 or more; 14 countries had 10,000–50,000; 11 countries had 5,000–10,000; and 56 countries had fewer than 5,000 Jews each. In relative terms, too, the Jews were thinly scattered nearly everywhere in the Diaspora. There is not a single Diaspora country where Jews amounted to 25 per 1,000 (2.5 percent) of the total population. In most countries they constituted a far smaller fraction. Only three Diaspora countries had more than 10 per 1,000 (1 percent) Jews in their total population; and another five countries had more than 5 Jews per 1,000 (0.5 percent) of population. The respective eight countries were, in descending order of the proportion but regardless of the absolute number of their Jews: Gibraltar (24.0 per 1,000), United States (20.1), Canada (11.8), France (8.8), Uruguay (6.7), Argentina (5.3), Australia (5.2), and Hungary (5.1). Other major Diaspora communities having lower proportions of Jews per 1,000 of total

TABLE 9. DISTRIBUTION OF THE WORLD'S JEWS, BY NUMBER, AND PROPORTION (PER 1,000 POPULATION) IN EACH COUNTRY, 1/1/2002

Number of Jews in Country	Total	Jews per 1,000 Population 0.0-0.9	1.0-4.9	5.0-9.9	10.0-24.9	25.0+
		Number of Countries				
Total[a]	94	62	23	5	3	1
100–900	34	30	3	-	1	-
1,000–4,900	22	20	2	-	-	-
5,000–9,900	11	4	7	-	-	-
10,000–49,900	14	7	6	1	-	-
50,000–99,900	4	1	1	2	-	-
100,000–999,900	7	-	4	2	1	-
1,000,000 or more	2	-	-	-	1	1
		Jewish Population Distribution (Absolute Numbers)				
Total	13,296,100	309,500	1,009,200	886,600	6,064,600	5,025,000
100–900	10,900	9,100	1,200	0	600	0
1,000–4,900	47,300	41,700	5,600	0	0	0
5,000–9,900	70,400	24,800	45,600	0	0	0
10,000–49,900	296,200	136,600	137,300	22,300	0	0
50,000–99,900	325,600	97,300	78,000	150,300	0	0
100,000–999,900	1,819,500	0	741,500	714,000	364,000	0
1,000,000 or more	10,725,000	0	0	0	5,700,000	5,025,200
		Jewish Population Distribution (Percent of World's Jews)[c]				
Total	100.0	2.3	7.6	6.7	45.6	37.8
100–900	0.1	0.1	0.0	0.0	0.0	0.0
1,000–4,900	0.4	0.3	0.0	0.0	0.0	0.0
5,000–9,900	0.5	0.2	0.3	0.0	0.0	0.0
10,000–49,900	2.2	1.0	1.0	0.2	0.0	0.0
50,000–99,900	2.4	0.7	0.6	1.1	0.0	0.0
100,000–999,900	13.7	0.0	5.6	5.4	2.7	0.0
1,000,000 or more	80.7	0.0	0.0	0.0	42.9	37.8

[a]Excluding countries with fewer than 100 Jews, with a total of 1,200 Jews. Minor discrepancies due to rounding.

population were the United Kingdom (4.6 per 1,000), Russia (1.8), Germany (1.3), Ukraine (2.0), Brazil (0.6), South Africa (1.8), Mexico (0.4), and Belgium (3.1).

TABLE 10. METROPOLITAN AREAS WITH LARGEST JEWISH POPULATIONS, 1/1/2002

Rank	Metro Area[a]	Country	Jewish Population	Share of World's Jews %	Cumulative %
1	Tel Aviv[b,c]	Israel	2,575,000	19.4	19.4
2	New York[d]	U.S.	2,051,000	15.4	34.8
3	Los Angeles[d]	U.S.	668,000	5.0	39.8
4	Haifa[e]	Israel	597,000	4.5	44.3
5	Jerusalem[f]	Israel	575,000	4.3	48.6
6	Southeast Florida[d, g]	U.S.	498,000	3.7	52.4
7	Paris[h]	France	310,000	2.3	54.7
7	Be'er Sheva[e]	Israel	310,000	2.3	57.0
9	Philadelphia[d]	U.S.	285,000	2.1	59.2
10	Chicago[d]	U.S.	265,000	2.0	61.2
11	Boston[d]	U.S.	254,000	1.9	63.1
12	San Francisco[d]	U.S.	218,000	1.6	64.7
13	London[i]	United Kingdom	195,000	1.5	66.2
14	Buenos Aires[j]	Argentina	175,000	1.3	67.5
15	Toronto[k]	Canada	175,000	1.3	68.8
16	Washington[k]	U.S.	166,000	1.2	70.1
17	Moscow[l]	Russia	108,000	0.8	70.9
18	Baltimore[k]	U.S.	106,000	0.8	71.7
19	Detroit[d]	U.S.	103,000	0.8	72.5
20	Montreal[k]	Canada	95,000	0.7	73.2

[a]Most metropolitan areas include extended inhabited territory and several municipal authorities around central city. Definitions vary by country.
[b]As newly defined in the 1995 Census.
[c]Includes Ramat Gan, Bene Beraq, Petach Tikwa, Bat Yam, Holon, Rishon LeZiyon, Netanya and Ashdod, all with a Jewish population above 100,000.
[d]Consolidated Metropolitan Statistical Area (CMSA).
[e]New definition, 2001.
[f]Adapted from data supplied by Jerusalem Municipality, Division of Strategic Planning and Research.
[g]Miami-Ft. Lauderdale and West Palm Beach-Boca Raton.
[h]Departments 75, 77, 78, 91, 92, 93, 94, 95.
[i]Greater London and contiguous postcode areas.
[j]Capital Federal and Partidos del Gran Buenos Aires.
[k]Metropolitan Statistical Area (MSA).
[l]Territory administered by city council.

In the State of Israel, by contrast, the Jewish majority amounted to 772 per 1,000 (77.2 percent) in 2002—including the 207,700 Jews but not the Arab population of the Palestinian National Authority and other administered areas. Excluding both Jews and non-Jews in the West Bank and Gaza, the proportion of Jews in Israel (with East Jerusalem and the Golan Heights) was 76.5 percent. Jews represented 8.5 percent of the total population in the West Bank and 0.6 percent in the Gaza Strip.

Concentration in Major Cities

Intensive international and internal migrations led to the concentration of an overwhelming majority of the Jews into large urban areas. Table 10 ranks the cities where the largest Jewish populations were found in 2002.[88] These 20 central places and their suburban and satellite areas altogether comprised over 73 percent of the whole world Jewish population. Ten of these cities were in the U.S., four in Israel, two in Canada, and one each in France, the United Kingdom, Argentina, and Russia. The ten metropolitan areas in the United States included 78 percent of total U.S. Jewry, and the four Israeli major urban areas included 80 percent of Israel's Jewish population.

Even more striking evidence of the extraordinary urbanization of the Jews is the fact that over one-third of all world Jewry live in the metropolitan areas of Tel Aviv and New York, and 52 percent live in only six large metropolitan areas: in and around New York (including areas in New Jersey and Connecticut), Los Angeles (including neighboring counties), and Southeastern Florida in the U.S.; and in the Tel Aviv, Haifa, and Jerusalem conurbations in Israel.

SERGIO DELLAPERGOLA

---

[88]Definitions of metropolitan statistical areas vary across countries. Estimates reported here reflect the criteria and updates adopted in each place. For U.S. estimates, see above, pp. 257–58; for Canadian estimates see Torczyner and Brotman, "Jews of Canada"; for other Diaspora estimates, A. Harman Institute of Contemporary Jewry; for Israeli estimates, Israel Central Bureau of Statistics, *Population and Vital Statistics 1999* and *Monthly Bulletin*. Following the 1995 population census in Israel, major metropolitan urban areas were redefined. Netanya and Ashdod, each with a Jewish population exceeding 100,000, were included in the outer ring of the Greater Tel Aviv area. A metropolitan area for Beer Sheva was newly established in 2001, covering a Jewish population nearly double that of the central city.

Directories
Lists
Obituaries

National Jewish Organizations*

UNITED STATES

Organizations are listed according to functions as follows:

Note also cross-references under these headings:

COMMUNITY RELATIONS

American Council for Judaism (1943). PO Box 9009, Alexandria, VA 22304. (703)836-2546. Pres. Stephen L. Naman; Exec. Dir. Allan C. Brownfeld. Seeks to advance the universal principles of a Judaism free of nationalism, and the national, civic, cultural, and social integration into American institutions of Americans of Jewish faith. *Issues of the American Council for Judaism; Special Interest Report.* (www.acjna.org)

American Jewish Committee (1906). The Jacob Blaustein Building, 165 E. 56 St., NYC 10022. (212)751-4000. FAX: (212) 750-0326. Pres. Harold Tanner; Exec. Dir. David A. Harris. Protects the rights and freedoms of Jews the world over; combats bigotry and anti-Semitism and promotes democracy and human rights for all; works for the security of Israel and deepened understanding between Americans and Israelis; advocates public-policy positions rooted in American democratic values and the perspectives of Jewish her-

*The information in this directory is based on replies to questionnaires circulated by the editors. Web site addresses, where provided, appear at end of entries.

itage; and enhances the creative vitality of the Jewish people. Includes Jacob and Hilda Blaustein Center for Human Relations, Project Interchange, William Petschek National Jewish Family Center, Jacob Blaustein Institute for the Advancement of Human Rights, Institute on American Jewish-Israeli Relations. *American Jewish Year Book; Commentary; AJC Journal.* (WWW.AJC.ORG)

AMERICAN JEWISH CONGRESS (1918). Stephen Wise Congress House, 15 E. 84 St., NYC 10028. (212)879-4500. FAX: (212)249-3672. E-mail: pr@ajcongress.org. Pres. Jack Rosen; Exec. Dir. Neil B. Goldstein. Works to foster the creative survival of the Jewish people; to help Israel develop in peace, freedom, and security; to eliminate all forms of racial and religious bigotry; to advance civil rights, protect civil liberties, defend religious freedom, and safeguard the separation of church and state; "The Attorney General for the Jewish Community." *Congress Monthly; Judaism; Inside Israel; Radical Islamic Fundamentalism Update.* (WWW.AJCONGRESS.ORG)

AMERICAN JEWISH PUBLIC RELATIONS SOCIETY (1957). 575 Lexington Ave., Suite 600, NYC 10022. (212)644-2663. FAX: (212)644-3887. Pres. Diane J. Ehrlich; V-Pres., membership, Lauren R. Marcus. Advances professional status of public-relations practitioners employed by Jewish organizations and institutions or who represent Jewish-related clients, services, or products; upholds a professional code of ethics and standards; provides continuing education and networking opportunities at monthly meetings; serves as a clearinghouse for employment opportunities. *AJPRS Reporter; AJPRS Membership Directory.*

AMOS: THE NATIONAL JEWISH PARTNERSHIP FOR SOCIAL JUSTICE (2001). 443 Park Avenue South, 11th Floor, New York, NY 10016. (212)424-9010. FAX: (212)686-1353. Chair Lynn Lyss; Exec. Dir. Jeremy Burton. Names for a biblical prophet who taught social justice., Amos was established to promote and increase the centrality of social justice values in Jewish communal life and provide practical, capacity-building skills training to help Jewish institutions and leadership engage effectively in this work. (WWW.AMOSPARTNERSHIP.ORG)

ANTI-DEFAMATION LEAGUE OF B'NAI B'RITH (1913). 823 United Nations Plaza, NYC 10017. (212)885-7700. FAX: (212) 867-0779. E-mail: webmaster@adl.org. Natl. Chmn. Glen A. Tobias; Natl. Dir. Abraham H. Foxman. Seeks to combat anti-Semitism and to secure justice and fair treatment for all citizens through law, education, and community relations. *ADL on the Frontline; Law Enforcement Bulletin; Dimensions: A Journal of Holocaust Studies; Hidden Child Newsletter; International Reports; Civil Rights Reports.* (WWW.ADL.ORG)

ASSOCIATION OF JEWISH COMMUNITY RELATIONS WORKERS (1950). 7800 Northaven Road, Dallas, TX 75230. (214) 615-5229. FAX: (214)373-3186. Pres. Marlene Gorin. Aims to stimulate higher standards of professional practice in Jewish community relations; encourages research and training toward that end; conducts educational programs and seminars; aims to encourage cooperation between community-relations workers and those working in other areas of Jewish communal service.

CENTER FOR JEWISH COMMUNITY STUDIES (1970). 1515 Locust St., Suite 703, Philadelphia, PA 19102. (215)772-0564. FAX: (215)772-0566. E-mail:jcpa@netvision.net.il or cjcs@worldnet.att.net. Jerusalem office:Jerusalem Center for Public Affairs. Pres. Amb. Dore Gold; Dir. Gen. Zvi Marom; Chmn. Bd. of Overseers Michael Rukin. Worldwide policy-studies institute devoted to the study of Jewish community organization, political thought, and public affairs, past and present, in Israel and throughout the world. Publishes original articles, essays, and monographs; maintains library, archives, and reprint series. *Jerusalem Letter/Viewpoints; Jewish Political Studies Review.* (WWW.JCPA.ORG).

CENTER FOR RUSSIAN JEWRY WITH STUDENT STRUGGLE FOR SOVIET JEWRY/SSSJ (1964). 240 Cabrini Blvd., #5B, NYC 10033. (212)928-7451. FAX: (212)795-8867. Dir./Founder Jacob Birnbaum; Chmn. Dr. Ernest Bloch. Campaigns for the human rights of the Jews of the former USSR, with emphasis on emigration and Jewish identity; supports programs for needy Jews there and for newcomers in Israel and USA, stressing employment and Jewish education. As the originator of the grassroots movement for Soviet Jewry in the early 1960s, possesses unique archives.

COALITION ON THE ENVIRONMENT & JEWISH LIFE (1993). 443 Park Ave. S., 11th fl., NYC 10016-7322. (212)684-6950, ext. 210. FAX: (212)686-1353. E-mail: info@coejl.org. Dir. Mark X. Jacobs. Promotes environmental education, advocacy, and action in the American Jewish community. Sponsored by a broad coalition of Jewish organizations; member of the National Religious Partnership for the Environment. *Bi-annual newsletter.* (WWW.COEJL.ORG)

COMMISSION ON SOCIAL ACTION OF REFORM JUDAISM (1953, joint instrumentality of the Union of American Hebrew Congregations and the Central Conference of American Rabbis). 633 Third Ave., 7th fl., NYC 10017. (212)650-4160. FAX: (212)650-4229. E-mail: csarj@uahc.org. Wash. Office:2027 Massachusetts Ave., NW, Washington, DC 20036. Chmn. Robert Heller; Dir. Rabbi Daniel Polish; Dir. Religious Action Center of Reform Judaism, Rabbi David Saperstein. Policy-making body that relates ethical and spiritual principles of Judaism to social-justice issues; implements resolutions through the Religious Action Center in Washington, DC, via advocacy, development of educational materials, and congregational programs. *Tzedek V'Shalom (social action newsletter); Chai Impact (legislative update).*

CONFERENCE OF PRESIDENTS OF MAJOR AMERICAN JEWISH ORGANIZATIONS (1955). 633 Third Ave., NYC 10017. (212)318-6111. FAX: (212)644-4135. Chmn. Mortimer B. Zuckerman; Exec. V.-Chmn. Malcolm Hoenlein. Seeks to strengthen the U.S.-Israel alliance and to protect and enhance the security and dignity of Jews abroad. Toward this end, the Conference of Presidents speaks and acts on the basis of consensus of its 54 member agencies on issues of national and international Jewish concern.

CONSULTATIVE COUNCIL OF JEWISH ORGANIZATIONS-CCJO (1946). 420 Lexington Ave., Suite 1731, NYC 10170. (212)808-5437. Chmn. Ady Steg & Clemens N. Nathan. A nongovernmental organization in consultative status with the UN, UNESCO, ILO, UNICEF, and the Council of Europe; cooperates and consults with, advises, and renders assistance to the Economic and Social Council of the UN on all problems relating to human rights and economic, social, cultural, educational, and related matters pertaining to Jews.

COORDINATING BOARD OF JEWISH ORGANIZATIONS (1947). 823 United Nations Plaza, NYC 10017. (212)557-9008. FAX: (212)687-3429. Ch. Cheryl Halpern; Exec. Dir. Dr. Harris O. Schoenberg. To promote the purposes and principles for which the UN was created.

COUNCIL OF JEWISH ORGANIZATIONS IN CIVIL SERVICE, INC. (1948). 45 E. 33 St., Rm. 601, NYC 10016. (212)689-2015. FAX: (212)447-1633. Pres. Louis Weiser; 1st V.-Pres. Melvyn Birnbaum. Supports merit system; encourages recruitment of Jewish youth to government service; member of Coalition to Free Soviet Jews, NY Jewish Community Relations Council, NY Metropolitan Coordinating Council on Jewish Poverty, Jewish Labor Committee, America-Israel Friendship League. *Council Digest.*

INSTITUTE FOR PUBLIC AFFAIRS (*see* UNION OF ORTHODOX JEWISH CONGREGATIONS OF AMERICA)

INTERNATIONAL LEAGUE FOR THE REPATRIATION OF RUSSIAN JEWS, INC. (1963). 2 Fountain Lane, Suite 2J, Scarsdale, NY 10583. (914)683-3225. FAX: (914)683-3221. Pres. Morris Brafman; Chmn. James H. Rapp. Helped to bring the situation of Soviet Jews to world attention; catalyst for advocacy efforts, educational projects, and programs on behalf of Russian Jews in the former USSR, Israel, and U.S. Provides funds to help Russian Jewry in Israel and the former Soviet Union.

JEWISH COUNCIL FOR PUBLIC AFFAIRS (formerly NATIONAL JEWISH COMMUNITY RELATIONS ADVISORY COUNCIL) (1944). 443 Park Ave. S., 11th fl., NYC 10016-7322. (212)684-6950. FAX: (212)686-1353. E-mail: jcpainfo@thejcpa.org. Chmn. Michael Bohnen;; Exec. Dir. Dr. Hannah Rosenthal. National coordinating body for the field of Jewish community relations, comprising 13 national and 122 local Jewish community-relations agencies. Promotes understanding of Israel and the Middle East; supports Jewish communities around the world; advocates for equality and pluralism, and against discrimination, in American society. Through the Council's work, its constituent organizations seek agreement on policies, strategies, and programs for effective utilization of their resources for common ends. *Insider (Weekly)*. (www.JEWISHPUBLICAFFAIRS.ORG)

JEWISH LABOR COMMITTEE (1934). Atran Center for Jewish Culture, 25 E. 21 St., NYC 10010. (212)477-0707. FAX: (212) 477-1918. Pres. Stuart Appelbaum; Exec. Dir. Avram B. Lyon. Serves as liaison between the Jewish community and the trade union movement; works with the U.S. and international labor movement to combat anti-Semitism, promote intergroup relations, and engender support for the State of Israel and Jews in and from the former Soviet Union; promotes teaching in public schools about the Holocaust and Jewish resistance; strengthens support within the Jewish community for the social goals and programs of the labor movement; supports Yiddish-language and cultural institutions. *Jewish Labor Committee Review; Issues Alert; Alumni Newsletter.*

———, NATIONAL TRADE UNION COUNCIL FOR HUMAN RIGHTS (1956). Atran Center for Jewish Culture, 25 E. 21 St., NYC 10010. (212)477-0707. FAX: (212)477-1918. Exec. Dir. Avram Lyon. Works with the American labor movement in advancing the struggle for social justice and equal opportunity, and assists unions in every issue affecting human rights. Fights discrimination on all levels and helps to promote labor's broad social and economic goals.

JEWISH PEACE FELLOWSHIP (1941). Box 271, Nyack, NY 10960. (914)358-4601. FAX: (914)358-4924. E-mail: jpf@forusa.org. Hon. Pres. Rabbi Philip Bentley; Ch. Murray Polner. Unites those who believe that Jewish ideals and experience provide inspiration for a nonviolent philosophy and way of life; offers draft counseling, especially for conscientious objection based on Jewish "religious training and belief"; encourages Jewish community to become more knowledgeable, concerned, and active in regard to the war/peace problem. *Shalom/Jewish Peace Letter.* (WWW.JEWISHPEACEFELLOWSHIP.ORG)

JEWISH WAR VETERANS OF THE UNITED STATES OF AMERICA (1896). 1811 R St., NW, Washington, DC 20009. (202)265-6280. FAX: (202)234-5662. E-mail: jwv@jwv.org. Natl. Exec. Dir. Herb Rosenbleeth; Natl. Commander Bernard Becker. Seeks to foster true allegiance to the United States; to combat bigotry and prevent defamation of Jews; to encourage the doctrine of universal liberty, equal rights, and full justice for all; to cooperate with and support existing educational institutions and establish new ones; to foster the education of ex-servicemen, ex-servicewomen, and members in the ideals and principles of Americanism. *Jewish Veteran.*

———, NATIONAL MUSEUM OF AMERICAN JEWISH MILITARY HISTORY (1958). 1811 R St., NW, Washington, DC 20009. E-mail: nmajmh@nmajmh.org. (202)265-6280. FAX:(202)234-5662. Pres. Neil Goldman; Asst. Dir./Archivist Sandor B. Cohen; Curator, Ramela Feltus. Documents and preserves the contributions of Jewish Americans to the peace and freedom of the United States; educates the public concerning the courage, heroism, and sacrifices made by Jewish Americans who served in the armed forces; and works to combat anti-Semitism. *The Jewish War Veterans).*

NATIONAL ASSOCIATION OF JEWISH LEGISLATORS (1976). 65 Oakwood St., Albany, NY 12208. (518)527-3353. FAX: (518) 458-8512. E-mail: najl01@aol.com. Exec. Dir. Marc Hiller; Pres. Sen. Richard Cohen, Minn. state senator. A nonpartisan Jewish state legislative network focusing on domestic issues and publishing newsletters. Maintains close ties with the Knesset and Israeli leaders.

NCSJ: ADVOCATES ON BEHALF OF JEWS IN RUSSIA, UKRAINE, THE BALTIC STATES AND EURASIA (formerly AMERICAN JEWISH CONFERENCE ON SOVIET JEWRY) (1964; reorg. 1971). 2020 K St., NW, Suite 7800, Washington, DC 20036-1835. (202)898-2500. FAX: (202)898-0822. E-mail: ncsj@ncsj.org. N.Y. office:823 United Nations Plaza, NYC 10017. (212)808-0295. Chmn. Harold Paulluks; Pres. Dr. Robert J. Meth; Exec. Dir. Mark B. Levin. Coordinating agency for major national Jewish organizations and local community groups in the U.S., acting on behalf of Jews in the former Soviet Union (FSU); provides information about Jews in the FSU through public education and social action; reports and special pamphlets, special programs and projects, public meetings and forums. *Newswatch; annual report; action and program kits; Tekuma.* (WWW.NCSJ.ORG)

———, SOVIET JEWRY RESEARCH BUREAU. Chmn. Denis C. Braham; Pres. Howard E. Sachs. Organized by NCSJ to monitor emigration trends. Primary task is the accumulation, evaluation, and processing of information regarding Jews in the FSU, especially those who apply for emigration.

NATIONAL JEWISH COMMUNITY RELATIONS ADVISORY COUNCIL (*see* JEWISH COUNCIL FOR PUBLIC AFFAIRS)

NATIONAL JEWISH DEMOCRATIC COUNCIL (1990). 777 N. Capital St., NE, Suite 305, Washington, DC 20002. (202)216-9060. FAX: (202)216-9061. E-mail: info@njdc.org. Chmn. Monte Friedkin; Founding Chmn. Morton Mandel; Exec. Dir. Ira N. Forman. An independent organization committed to strengthening Jewish participation in the Democratic party primarily through grassroots activism. The national voice of Jewish Democrats, NJDC is dedicated to fighting the radical right and promoting Jewish values and interests in the Democratic party. *Capital Communiqué; Extremist Watch.* (WWW.NJDC.ORG)

REPUBLICAN JEWISH COALITION (1985). 415 2nd St., NE, Suite 100, Washington, DC 20002. (202)547-7701. FAX: (202)544-2434. E-mail: rjc@rjchq.org. Natl. Chmn. Cheryl Halpern; Hon. Chmn. Max M. Fisher, Richard J. Fox, Sam Fox, Lawrence Kadish, George Klein, and Amb. Mel Sembler; Exec. Dir. Matt Brooks. Promotes involvement in Republican politics among its members; sensitizes Republican leaders to the concerns of the American Jewish community; promotes principles of free enterprise, a strong national defense, and an internationalist foreign policy. *RJC Bulletin.* (WWW.RJCHQ.ORG)

SHALEM CENTER (1994). 5505 Connecticut Avenue, NW, No. 1140, Washington, DC 20015. (877)298-7300. FAX: (888)766-1506. E-mail: shalem@shalem.org.il. Pres. Yoram Hazony (Israel); Academic Director, Daniel Polisar (Israel). The purposes and activities of the Shalem Center are to increase public understanding and conduct educational and research activities on the improvement of Jewish national public life, and to develop a community of intellectual leaders to shape the state of Israel into a secure, free, and prosperous society. *Azure.* (WWW.SHALEMCENTER.ORG)

SHALOM CENTER (1983). 6711 Lincoln Dr., Philadelphia, PA 19119. (215)844-8494. E-mail: shalomctr@aol.com. (Part of Aleph Alliance for Jewish Renewal.) Exec. Dir. Rabbi Arthur Waskow. National resource and organizing center for Jewish perspectives on dealing with overwork in American society, environmental dangers, unrestrained technology, and corporate irresponsibility. Initiated A.J. Heschel 25th Yahrzeit observance. Trains next generation of *tikkun olam* activists. Holds colloquia on issues like environmental causes of cancer. *New Menorah.* (WWW.SHALOMCTR.ORG)

STUDENT STRUGGLE FOR SOVIET JEWRY (*see* CENTER FOR RUSSIAN JEWRY)

UN WATCH (1993). 1, rue de Varembé, PO Box 191, 1211 Geneva 20, Switzerland. (41-22)734.14.72. FAX: (41-22)734.16.13. E-mail: unwatch@unwatch.org. Exec. Dir. Andrew M. Srulevitch; Chm. Amb. Alfred H. Moses. An affiliate of the AJC, UN Watch measures UN performance by the yardstick of the UN's Charter; advocates the non-discriminatory application of the Charter; opposes the use of UN fora to attack Israel and promote anti-Semitism; and seeks to institutionalize at the UN the fight against worldwide anti-Semitism. *The Wednesday Watch.* (WWW.UNWATCH.ORG)

UNION OF COUNCILS (formerly UNION OF COUNCILS FOR SOVIET JEWS) (1970). 1819 H St., NW, Suite 230, Washington, DC 20005. (202)775-9770. FAX: (202)775-9776. E-mail: ucsj@ucsj.com. Pres. Yosef I. Abramowitz; Natl. Dir. Micah H. Naftalin. Devoted to promoting religious liberty, freedom of emigration, and security for Jews in the FSU (former Soviet Union) through advocacy and monitoring of anti-Semitism, neo-facism, human rights, rule of law, and democracy. Offers educational, cultural, medical, and humanitarian aid through the Yad L'Yad partnership program pairing Jewish communities in the US and the FSU; advocates for refuseniks and political prisoner. (WWW.FSUMONITOR.COM)

WORLD CONGRESS OF GAY, LESBIAN, BISEXUAL & TRANSGENDER JEWS (1980). 8 Letitia St., Philadelphia, PA 19106-3050. (609)396-1972. FAX: (215)873-0108. E-mail: president@wcgljo.org. Pres. Scott R. Gansl (Philadelphia, PA); V.-Pres. Francois Spiero (Paris, France). Supports, strengthens, and represents over 67 Jewish gay and lesbian organizations across the globe and the needs of gay and lesbian Jews generally. Challenges homophobia and sexism within the Jewish community and responds to anti-Semitism at large. Sponsors regional and international conferences. *The Digest.* (WWW.WCGLJO.ORG/WCGLJO/)

WORLD JEWISH CONGRESS (1936; org. in U.S. 1939). 501 Madison Ave., 17th fl., NYC 10022. (212)755-5770. FAX: (212) 755-5883. Pres. Edgar M. Bronfman; Co-Chmn. N. Amer. Branch Prof. Irwin Cotler (Montreal) & Evelyn Sommer; Dr. Avi Beker, Secretary General. Seeks to intensify bonds of world Jewry with Israel; to strengthen solidarity among Jews everywhere and secure their rights, status, and interests as individuals and communities; to encourage Jewish social, religious, and cultural life throughout the world and coordinate efforts by Jewish communities and organizations to cope with any Jewish problem; to work for human rights generally. Represents its affiliated organizations-most representative bodies of Jewish communities in more than 80 countries and 35 national organizations in American section-at UN, OAS, UNESCO, Council of Europe, ILO, UNICEF, and other governmental, intergovernmental, and international authorities. *WJC Report; Bolet'n Informativo OJI; Christian-Jewish Relations; Dateline: World Jewry; Coloquio; Batfutsot; Gesher.*

CULTURAL

AMERICAN ACADEMY FOR JEWISH RESEARCH (1929). 420 Walnut Street, Philadelphia, PA 19106. (215)238-1290. FAX: (215)238-1540. Pres. Robert Chazan. Encourages Jewish learning and research; holds annual or semiannual meeting; awards grants for the publication of scholarly works. *Proceedings of the American Academy for Jewish Research; Texts and Studies; Monograph Series.*

AMERICAN GATHERING OF JEWISH HOLOCAUST SURVIVORS. 122 W. 30 St., #205. NYC 10001. (212)239-4230. FAX: (212)279-2926. E-mail: mail@americangathering.org. Pres. Benjamin Meed. Dedicated to documenting the past and passing on a legacy of remembrance. Compiles the National Registry of Jewish Holocaust Survivors-to date, the records of more than 165,000 survivors and their families-housed at the U.S. Holocaust Memorial Museum in Washington, DC; holds an annual Yom Hashoah commemoration and occasional international gatherings; sponsors an intensive summer program for U.S. teachers in Poland and Israel to prepare them to teach about the Holocaust. *Together (newspaper).*

AMERICAN GUILD OF JUDAIC ART (1991). 15 Greenspring Valley Rd., Owings Mills, MD 21117. (410)902-0411. FAX: (410) 581-0108. E-mail: lbarch@erols.com. Pres. Mark D. Levin; 1st V.-Pres. Richard McBee. A not-for-profit membership organization for those with interests in the Judaic arts, including artists, galleries, collectors & retailers of Judaica, writers, educators, appraisers, museum curators, conservators, lecturers, and others personally or professionally involved in the field. Helps to promote members' art. *Hiddur (quarterly); Update (members' networking newsletter).*

AMERICAN JEWISH HISTORICAL SOCIETY (1892). 15 W. 16 St., NYC 10011. (212) 294-6160. FAX: (212)294-6161. E-mail: ajhs@ajhs.cjh.org. Pres. Kenneth J. Bialkin; Dir. Dr. Michael Feldberg. Collects, catalogues, publishes, and displays material on the history of the Jews in America; serves as an information center for inquiries on American Jewish history; maintains archives of original source material on American Jewish history; sponsors lectures and exhibitions; makes available audiovisual material. *American Jewish History; Heritage.* (WWW.AJHS.ORG)

AMERICAN JEWISH PRESS ASSOCIATION (1944). Natl. Admin. Off.: 1828 L St. NW, Suite 720, Washington, DC 20036. (202)

785-2282. FAX: (202)785-2307. E-mail: toby@dershowitz.com. Pres. Marc Klein; Exec. Dir. Toby Dershowitz. Seeks the advancement of Jewish journalism and the maintenance of a strong Jewish press in the U.S. and Canada; encourages the attainment of the highest editorial and business standards; sponsors workshops, services for members; sponsors annual competition for Simon Rockower Awards for excellence in Jewish journalism. *Membership bulletin newsletter.*

AMERICAN SEPHARDI FEDERATION (1973). 15 W. 16 St., 6th Floor, NYC 10011. (212)294-8350. FAX: (212)294-8348. E-mail: asf@asf.cjh.org. Hon. Pres. Leon Levy; Exec. Dir. Vivienne Roumani-Denn. The central voice of the American Sephardic community, representing a broad spectrum of Sephardic organizations, congregations, and educational institutions. Seeks to strengthen and unify the community through education, communication, advocacy, and leadership development, creating greater awareness and appreciation of its rich and unique history and culture. *Sephardic Today.* (WWW.AMSEPHFED.ORG)

AMERICAN SOCIETY FOR JEWISH MUSIC (1974). c/o The Center for Jewish History, 15 W. 16 St., NYC 10011. (212)294-8328. FAX: (212)294-6161. Pres. Michael Leavitt; V.-Pres. Judith Tischler & Martha Novick; Sec. Fortuna Calvo Roth; Bd. Chmn. Rabbi Henry D. Michelman; Treas. Cantor Nathaniel Benjamin. Promotes the knowledge, appreciation, and development of Jewish music, past and present, for professional and lay audiences; seeks to raise the standards of composition and performance in Jewish music, to encourage research, and to sponsor performances of new and rarely heard works. *Musica Judaica Journal.*

ASSOCIATION OF JEWISH BOOK PUBLISHERS (1962). c/o Jewish Book Council, 15 East 26th Street, 10th Floor, New York, NY 10010. (212)532-4949. FAX: (212)481-4174. Email: arjhill@jewishbooks.com. Pres. Ellen Frankel. As a nonprofit group, provides a forum for discussion of mutual areas of interest among Jewish publishers, and promotes cooperative exhibits and promotional opportunities for members. Membership fee is $85 annually per publishing house.

ASSOCIATION OF JEWISH LIBRARIES (1965). 15 E. 26 St.,10th fl, NYC 10010. (212)725-5359. FAX: (212)481-4174. E-mail: ajl@jewishbooks.org. Pres. David T. Gilner; V.-Pres. Toby Rossner. Seeks to promote and improve services and professional standards in Jewish libraries; disseminates Jewish library information and guidance; promotes publication of literature in the field; encourages the establishment of Jewish libraries and collections of Judaica and the choice of Judaica librarianship as a profession; cocertifies Jewish libraries (with Jewish Book Council). *AJL Newsletter; Judaica Librarianship.*

B'NAI B'RITH KLUTZNICK NATIONAL JEWISH MUSEUM (1957). 1640 Rhode Island Ave., NW, Washington, DC 20036. (202) 857-6583. FAX: (202)857-1099. A center of Jewish art and history in the nation's capital, maintains temporary and permanent exhibition galleries, permanent collection of Jewish ceremonial objects, folk art, and contemporary fine art, outdoor sculpture garden and museum shop, as well as the American Jewish Sports Hall of Fame. Provides exhibitions, tours, educational programs, research assistance, and tourist information.; *Permanent collection catalogue; temporary exhibit catalogues.*

CENTRAL YIDDISH CULTURE ORGANIZATION (CYCO), INC. (1943). 25 E. 21 St., 3rd fl., NYC 10010. (212)505-8305. FAX: (212) 505-8044. Mng. David Kirszencwejg. Promotes, publishes, and distributes Yiddish books; publishes catalogues.

CONFERENCE ON JEWISH SOCIAL STUDIES, INC. (formerly CONFERENCE ON JEWISH RELATIONS, INC.) (1939). Bldg. 240, Rm. 103. Program in Jewish Studies, Stanford University, Stanford, CA 94305-2190. (650)725-0829. FAX:(650)725-2920. E-mail: jss@leland.stanford.edu. Pres. Steven J. Zipperstein; V.-Pres. Aron Rodrigue. *Jewish Social Studies.*

CONGREGATION BINA (1981). 600 W. End Ave., Suite 1-C, NYC 10024. (212)873-4261. E-mail: samueldivekar@hotmail.com. Pres. Joseph Moses; Exec. V.-Pres. Moses Samson; Hon. Pres. Samuel M. Daniel; Sec. Gen. Elijah E. Jhirad. Serves the religious, cultural, charitable, and philanthropic needs of the Children of Israel who originated in India and now reside in the U.S. Works to foster and preserve the ancient traditions, customs, liturgy, music, and folklore of Indian Jewry and to maintain needed institutions. *Kol Bina.*

CONGRESS FOR JEWISH CULTURE (1948). 25 E. 21 St., NYC 10010. (212)505-8040. FAX: (212)505-8044. Co-Pres. Prof. Yonia Fain & Dr. Barnett Zumoff. Congress for Jewish Culture administers the book store CYCO and publishes the world's oldest Yiddish journal, *The Zukunft*. Currently producing a two volume anthology of Yiddish literature in America. Activities include yearly memorials for the Warsaw ghetto uprising and the murdered Soviet Yiddish writers, also readings and literary afternoons. *The Zukunft; Bulletin: In the World of Yiddish.*

ELAINE KAUFMAN CULTURAL CENTER (1952). 129 W. 67 St., NYC 10023. (212)501-3303. FAX: (212)874-7865. Email: lhard@ekcc.org. Hon. Chmn. Leonard Goodman; Chmn. Elaine Kaufman; Pres. Phyllis Feder; Exec. Dir. Lydia Kontos. Offers instruction in its Lucy Moses School for Music and Dance in music, dance, art, and theater to children and adults, in Western culture and Jewish traditions. Presents frequent performances of Jewish and general music by leading artists and ensembles in its Merkin Concert Hall and Ann Goodman Recital Hall. The Birnbaum Music Library houses Jewish music scores and reference books. *In Harmony (quarterly newsletter); EKCC Events (bimonthly calendar); Bimonthly concert calendars; catalogues and brochures.* (WWW.EKCC.ORG)

HISTADRUTH IVRITH OF AMERICA (1916; reorg. 1922). 426 W. 58 St., NYC 10019. (212)957-6658/9. Fax: (212)957-5811. E-mail: HebrewUSA@aol.com. Pres. Miriam Ostow; Exec. V.P. Moshe Margolin. Emphasizes the primacy of Hebrew in Jewish life, culture, and education; aims to disseminate knowledge of written and spoken Hebrew in N. America, thus building a cultural bridge between the State of Israel and Jewish communities throughout N. America. *Hadoar; Lamishpacha; Tov Lichtov; Sulam Yaakov; Hebrew Week; Ulpan.* (WWW.HEBREWUSA.ORG)

HOLOCAUST CENTER OF THE UNITED JEWISH FEDERATION OF GREATER PITTSBURGH (1980). 5738 Darlington Rd., Pittsburgh, PA 15217. (412)421-1500. FAX: (412)422-1996. E-mail: lhurwitz@ujf.net. Pres. Holocaust Comm. Chair Dr. Barbara Burstin; UJF. Ch. James A. Rudolph; Dir. Linda F. Hurwitz. Develops programs and provides resources to further understanding of the Holocaust and its impact on civilization. Maintains a library, archive; provides speakers, educational materials; organizes community programs. Published collection of survivor and liberator stories. (WWW.UJFHC.NET)

HOLOCAUST MEMORIAL CENTER (1984). 6602 West Maple Rd., West Bloomfield, MI 48322. (248)661-0840. FAX: (248)661-4204. E-mail: info@holocaustcenter.org. Founder & Exec. V.-Pres. Rabbi Charles Rosenzveig. America's first freestanding Holocaust center comprising a museum, library-archive, oral history collection, garden of the righteous, research institute and academic advisory committee. Provides tours, lecture series, teacher training, Yom Hashoah commemorations, exhibits, educational outreach programs, speakers' bureau, computer database on 1,200 destroyed Jewish communities, guided travel tours to concentration camps and Israel, and museum shop. Published *World Reacts to the Holocaust; Newsletter.*

HOLOCAUST MEMORIAL RESOURCE & EDUCATION CENTER OF CENTRAL FLORIDA (1982). 851 N. Maitland Ave., Maitland, FL 32751. (407)628-0555. FAX: (407)628-1079. E-mail: execdir@holocaustedu.org. Pres. Stan Sujka, MD; Bd. Chmn. Tess Wise. An interfaith educational center devoted to teaching the lessons of the Holocaust. Houses permanent multimedia educational exhibit; maintains library of books, videotapes, films, and other visuals to serve the entire educational establishment; offers lectures, teacher training, and other activities. *Newsletter; Bibliography; "Holocaust-Lessons for Tomorrow"; elementary and middle school curriculum.*

THE HOLOCAUST MUSEUM AND LEARNING CENTER IN MEMORY OF GLORIA GOLDSTEIN (1995) (formerly St. Louis Center for Holocaust Studies) (1977). 12 Millstone Campus Dr., St. Louis, MO 63146. (314)432-0020. FAX: (314)432-1277. E-mail: dreich@jfedstl.org. Chmn. Richard W. Stein; Dir. Dan A. Reich; Asst. Dir. Brian Bray. Develops programs and provides resources and educational materials to further an understanding of the Holocaust and its impact on civilization; has a 5,000 sq. ft. museum containing photographs, artifacts, and audiovisual displays. *Newsletter.*

INTERNATIONAL ASSOCIATION OF JEWISH GENEALOGICAL SOCIETIES (1988). 4430 Mt. Paran Pkwy NW, Atlanta, GA 30327-3747. (404)261-8662. Fax: (404) 228-7125. E-mail: homargol@aol.com. Pres. Howard Margol. Umbrella organization of more than 70 Jewish Genealogical Societies (JGS) worldwide. Represents organized Jewish genealogy, encourages Jews to research their family history, promotes new JGSs, supports existing societies, implements projects of interest to individuals researching their Jewish family histories. Holds annual conference where members learn and exchange ideas. (WWW.IAJGS.ORG)

INTERNATIONAL JEWISH MEDIA ASSOCIATION (1987). U.S.: c/o St. Louis Jewish Light, 12 Millstone Campus Dr., St. Louis, MO 63146. (314)432-3353. FAX: (314)432-0515. E-mail: stlouislgt@aol.com and ajpamr@aol.com. Israel:PO Box 92, Jerusalem 91920. 02-202-222. FAX: 02-513-642. Pres. Robert A. Cohn (c/o St. Louis Jewish Light); Exec. Dir. Toby Dershowitz. 1828 L St. NW, Suite 402, Washington, DC 20036. (202)785-2282. FAX: (202)785-2307. E-mail: toby@dershowitz.com. Israel Liaisons Jacob Gispan & Lifsha Ben-Shach, WZO Dept. of Info. A worldwide network of Jewish journalists, publications and other media in the Jewish and general media, which seeks to provide a forum for the exchange of materials and ideas and to enhance the status of Jewish media and journalists throughout the world. *IJMA Newsletter; Proceedings of the International Conference on Jewish Media.*

INTERNATIONAL NETWORK OF CHILDREN OF JEWISH HOLOCAUST SURVIVORS, INC. (1981). 13899 Biscayne Blvd. Suite 404, N. Miami, FL 33181. (305)919-5690. FAX: (305)919-5691. E-mail: info@hdec.org. Pres. Rositta E. Kenigsberg; Founding Chmn. Menachem Z. Rosensaft. Links Second Generation groups and individuals throughout the world. Represents the shared interests of children of Holocaust survivors; aims to perpetuate the authentic memory of the Holocaust and prevent its recurrence, to strengthen and preserve the Jewish spiritual, ideological, and cultural heritage, to fight anti-Semitism and all forms of discrimination, persecution, and oppression anywhere in the world.

THE JACOB RADER MARCUS CENTER OF THE AMERICAN JEWISH ARCHIVES (1947). 3101 Clifton Ave., Cincinnati, OH 45220. (513)221-1875 ext. 403. FAX: (513)221-7812. E-mail: aja@cn.huc.edu. Exec. Dir. Dr. Gary P. Zola. Promotes the study and preservation of the Western Hemisphere Jewish experience through research, publications, collection of important source materials, and a vigorous public-outreach program. *American Jewish Archives Journal, Monographs, Pamphlets, booklets, educational materials and posters.*

JEWISH BOOK COUNCIL (1946; reorg. 1993). 15 E. 26 St., NYC 10010. (212)532-4949, ext. 297. E-mail: jbc@jewishbooks.org. Pres. Rabbi Maurice S. Corson; Bd. Chmn. Henry Everett; Exec. Dir. Carolyn Starman Hessel. Serves as literary arm of the American Jewish community and clearinghouse for Jewish-content literature; assists readers, writers, publishers, and those who market and sell products. Provides bibliographies, list of publishers, bookstores, book fairs. Sponsors National Jewish Book Awards, Jewish Book Month, Jewish Book Fair Network. *Jewish Book Annual; Jewish Book World.* (WWW.JEWISHBOOKCOUNCIL.ORG)

THE JEWISH FEDERATION'S LOS ANGELES MUSEUM OF THE HOLOCAUST (MARTYRS MEMORIAL) (org. mid-1960s; opened 1978). 6006 Wilshire Blvd., Los Angeles, CA 90036. (323)761-8170. FAX: (323) 761-8174. E-mail: museumgroup@jewishla.org. Chmn. Gary John Schiller, M.D.; Dir./Curator Marcia Reines Josephy. A photo-narrative museum and resource center dedicated to Holocaust history, issues of genocide and prejudice, curriculum development, teacher training, research and exhibitions. *PAGES, a newslettr; Those Who Dared; Rescuers and Rescued; Guide to Schindler's List; Anne Frank: A Teaching.*

JEWISH HERITAGE PROJECT (1981). 150 Franklin St., #1W, NYC 10013. (212)925-9067. E-mail: jhpffh@jps.net. Exec. Dir. Alan Adelson. Strives to bring to the broadest possible audience authentic works of literary and historical value relating to Jewish history and culture. With funding from the National Endowment of the Arts, Jewish Heritage runs the National Initiative in the Literature of the Holocaust. Not a grant giving organization. Distributor of the film *Lodz Ghetto,* which it developed, as well as its companion volume *Lodz Ghetto:Inside a Community Under Siege; Better Than Gold: An Immigrant Family's First Years in Brooklyn.*

JEWISH MUSEUM (1904, under auspices of Jewish Theological Seminary). 1109 Fifth Ave., NYC 10128. (212)423-3200. FAX: (212)423-3232. Dir. Joan H. Rosenbaum; Bd. Chmn. Robert J. Hurst. Expanded museum features permanent exhibition on the Jewish experience. Repository of the largest collection of Jewish related paintings, prints, photographs, sculpture, coins, medals, antiquities, textiles, and other decorative arts-in the Western Hemisphere. Includes the National Jewish Archive of Broadcasting. Tours, lectures, film showings, and concerts; special programs for children; cafe; shop. *Special exhibition catalogues; annual report.* (WWW.THEJEWISHMUSEUM.ORG)

JEWISH PUBLICATION SOCIETY (1888). 2100 Arch St., 2nd fl., Philadelphia, PA 19103. (215)832-0600. FAX: (215)568-2017. E-mail: jewishbook@jewishpub.org. Pres. Allan R. Frank; CEO/Ed.-in-Chief Dr. Ellen Frankel. Publishes and disseminates books of Jewish interest for adults and children; titles include TANAKH, religious studies and practices, life cycle, folklore, classics, art, history. *Booklink JPS Catalogue.* (WWW.JEWISHPUB.ORG)

JUDAH L. MAGNES MUSEUM-JEWISH MUSEUM OF THE WEST (1962). 2911 Russell St., Berkeley, CA 94705. (510)549-6950. FAX: (510)849-3673. E-mail: pfpr@magnesmuseum.org. Pres. Fred Weiss; Dir. Susan Morris. Collects, preserves, and makes available Jewish art, culture, history, and literature from throughout the world. Permanent collections of fine and ceremonial art; rare Judaica library, Western Jewish History Center (archives), Jewish-American Hall of Fame. Changing exhibits, traveling exhibits, docent tours, lectures, numismatics series, poetry and video awards, museum shop. *Magnes News; special exhibition catalogues; scholarly books.*

JUDAICA CAPTIONED FILM CENTER, INC. (1983). PO Box 21439, Baltimore, MD 21208-0439. Voice Relay Service (1-800) 735-2258; TDD (410)655-6767. E-mail: lweiner@jhucep.org. Pres. Lois Lilienfeld Weiner. Developing a comprehensive library of captioned and subtitled films and tapes on Jewish subjects; distributes them to organizations serving the hearing-impaired, including mainstream classes and senior adult groups, on a free-loan, handling/shipping-charge-only basis. *Newsletter.*

LEAGUE FOR YIDDISH, INC. (1979). 200 W. 72 St., Suite 40, NYC 10023. (212)787-6675. E-mail: mschaecht@aol.com. Pres. Dr. Zuni Zelitch; Exec. Dir. Dr. Mordkhe Schaechter. Encourages the development and use of Yiddish as a living language; promotes its modernization and standardization; publisher of Yiddish textbooks and English-Yiddish dictionaries; most recent book *The Standardized Yiddish Orthography (New York, 200); Afn Shvel (quarterly).* (WWW.METALAB.UNC.EDU/YIDDISH/YIDLEAGUE)

LEO BAECK INSTITUTE, INC. (1955). 15 W. 16 St., NYC 10011-6301. (212)744-6400. FAX: (212)988-1305. E-mail: lbi1@lbi.com. Pres. Ismar Schorsch; Exec. Dir. Carol Kahn Strauss. A research, study, and lecture center, museum, library, and archive relating to the history of German-speaking Jewry. Offers lectures, exhibits, faculty seminars; publishes a series of monographs, yearbooks, and journals. *LBI News; LBI Yearbook; LBI Memorial Lecture; occasional papers.*

LIVING TRADITIONS (1994), (c/o WORKMAN'S CIRCLE) 45 East 33rd Street, New York, NY 10016. (212)532-8202. E-mail: henry@livingtraditions.org. Pres. Henry Sapoznik; V.-Pres. Sherry Mayrent. Nonprofit membership organization dedicated to the study, preservation, and innovative continuity of traditional folk and popular culture through workshops, concerts, recordings, radio and film documentaries; clearinghouse for research in klezmer and other traditional music; sponsors yearly weeklong international cultural event, "Yiddish Folk Arts Program/'KlezKamp.'" *Living Traditions (newsletter).* (WWW.LIVINGTRADITIONS.ORG)

THE MARTIN BUBER FORUM (1990), PMB #22112 101 W. 23 St., NYC (10011). (212)242-5637. Hon. Chmn. Prof. Maurice Friedman; Pres. Martin Warmbrand.

Conducts discussion groups on the life and thought of Buber. *Martin Buber Review (annual).*

MEMORIAL FOUNDATION FOR JEWISH CULTURE, INC. (1964). 15 E. 26 St., Suite 1703, NYC 10010. (212)679-4074. FAX: (212)889-9080. Acting Pres. Prof. Anita Shapira; Exec. V.-Pres. Jerry Hochbaum. Through the grants that it awards, encourages Jewish scholarship, culture, and education; supports communities that are struggling to maintain Jewish life; assists professional training for careers in communal service in Jewishly deprived communities; and stimulates the documentation, commemoration, and teaching of the Holocaust. (WWW.MFJC.ORG)

MUSEUM OF JEWISH HERITAGE—A LIVING MEMORIAL TO THE HOLOCAUST (1984). One Battery Park Plaza, NYC 10004-1484. (212)968-1800. FAX: (212)968-1368. Bd. Chmn. Robert M. Morgenthau; Museum Pres. Dr. Alfred Gottschalk; Museum Dir. David Marwell. New York tri-state's principal institution for educating people of all ages and backgrounds about 20th-century Jewish history and the Holocaust. Repository of Steven Spielberg's Survivors of the Shoah Visual History Foundation videotaped testimonies. Core and special exhibitions. *18 First Place (newsletter); Holocaust bibliography; educational materials.* (WWW.MJH-NYC.ORG)

MUSEUM OF TOLERANCE OF THE SIMON WIESENTHAL CENTER (1993). 9786 W. Pico Blvd., Los Angeles, CA 90035-4792. (310)553-8403. FAX: (310)553-4521. E-mail: avra@wiesenthal.com. Dean-Founder Rabbi Marvin Hier; Assoc. Dean Rabbi Abraham Cooper; Exec. Dir. Rabbi Meyer May. A unique experiential museum focusing on personal prejudice, group intolerance, struggle for civil rights, and 20th-century genocides, culminating in a major exhibition on the Holocaust. Archives, Multimedia Learning Center designed for individualized research, 6,700-square-foot temporary exhibit space, 324-seat theater, 150-seat auditorium, and outdoor memorial plaza. (WWW.WIESENTHAL.COM)

NATIONAL CENTER FOR THE HEBREW LANGUAGE (1996). 633 Third Ave., 21st Fl., NYC 10017. (212)339-6023. FAX: (212)318-6193. E-mail: ivritnow@aol.com. Pres. Dr. Alvin I. Schiff; Exec. Dir. Dr. Joseph Lowin. The NCHL advocates for Hebrew language and culture; serves as a Hebrew resource center; and is a catalyst for networking in Hebrew language and culture. It coordinates a Mini-Ulpan at the GA, publishes "Directory of Hebrew Classes," organizes "Lunch & Hebrew Lit" nationwide, and runs a Conference of Hebrew Teacher Trainers. *IvritNow/IvritAkhshav.* (WWW.IVRIT.ORG)

NATIONAL FOUNDATION FOR JEWISH CULTURE (1960). 330 Seventh Ave., 21st fl., NYC 10001. (212)629-0500. FAX: (212) 629-0508. E-mail: nfjc@jewishculture.org. Pres. Lynn Korda Kroll; Exec. Dir. Richard A. Siegel. The leading Jewish organization devoted to promoting Jewish culture in the U.S. Manages the Jewish Endowment for the Arts and Humanities; administers the Council of American Jewish Museums and Council of Archives and Research Libraries in Jewish Studies; offers doctoral dissertation fellowships, new play commissions, and grants for documentary films, recording of Jewish music, contemporary choreography, fiction and non-fiction writing, and cultural preservation; coordinates community cultural residencies, local cultural councils, and national cultural consortia; sponsors conferences, symposia, and festivals in the arts and humanities. *Jewish Culture News; Culture Currents (electronic).*

NATIONAL MUSEUM OF AMERICAN JEWISH HISTORY. Independence Mall E. 55 N. Fifth St. Philadelphia, PA 19106-2197. (215)923-3811. FAX: (215)923-0763. E-mail: nmajh@nmajh.org. Exec. Dir. Wesley A. Fisher. The only museum in the nation to offer education, exhibits, and programs dedicated to preserving the history and culture of the Jewish people in America; located across from the Liberty Bell. (WWW.NMAJH.ORG)

NATIONAL MUSEUM OF AMERICAN JEWISH MILITARY HISTORY (*see* JEWISH WAR VETERANS OF THE U.S.A.)

NATIONAL YIDDISH BOOK CENTER (1980). 1021 West St., Amherst, MA 01002. (413)256-4900. FAX: (413)256-4700. E-mail: yiddish@bikher.org. Pres. Aaron Lansky; V.-Pres. Nancy Sherman. Since 1980 the center has collected 1.5 million Yiddish books for distribution to libraries and readers worldwide; offers innovative English-language programs and produces a magazine. New permanent home in Amherst, open to the public, features a book repository, exhibits, a bookstore, and a theater. *The Pakn Treger (English language magazine).*

ORTHODOX JEWISH ARCHIVES (1978). 42 Broadway, New York, NY 10004. (212) 797-9000, ext. 73. FAX: (212)269-2843. Exec. V-Pres. Rabbi Shmuel Bloom & Shlomo Gertzullin; Dir. Rabbi Moshe Kolodny. Founded by Agudath Israel of America; houses historical documents, photographs, periodicals, and other publications relating to the growth of Orthodox Jewry in the U.S. and related communities in Europe, Israel, and elsewhere. Particularly noteworthy are its holdings relating to rescue activities organized during the Holocaust and its traveling exhibits available to schools and other institutions.

RESEARCH FOUNDATION FOR JEWISH IMMIGRATION, INC. (1971). 570 Seventh Ave., NYC 10018. (212)921-3871. FAX: (212) 575-1918. Pres. Curt C. Silberman; Sec./Coord. of Research Herbert A. Strauss; Archivist Dennis E. Rohrbaugh. Studies and records the history of the migration and acculturation of Central European German-speaking Jewish and non-Jewish Nazi persecutees in various resettlement countries worldwide, with special emphasis on the American experience. *International Biographical Dictionary of Central European Emigrés, 1933-1945; Jewish Immigrants of the Nazi Period in the USA.*

SEPHARDIC EDUCATIONAL CENTER (1979). 10808 Santa Monica Blvd., Los Angeles, CA 90025. (310)441-9361. FAX: (310) 441-9561. E-mail: secforever@aol.com. Founder & Chmn. Jose A. Nessim, M.D. Has chapters in the U.S., North, Central, and South America, Europe, and Asia, a spiritual and educational center in the Old City of Jerusalem, and executive office in Los Angeles. Serves as a meeting ground for Sephardim from many nations; sponsors the first worldwide movement for Sephardic youth and young adults. Disseminates information about Sephardic Jewry in the form of motion pictures, pamphlets, and books, which it produces. *Hamerkaz (quarterly bulletin in English).* (WWW.SECWORLDWIDE.ORG)

SEPHARDIC HOUSE (1978). 15 West 16th Street, NYC 10011. (212)294-6170. FAX: (212)294-6149. E-mail: sephardichouse@cjh.org. Pres. Morrie R. Yohai; Exec. Dir. Dr. Janice E. Ovadiah. A cultural organization dedicated to fostering Sephardic history and culture; sponsors a wide variety of classes and public programs, film festivals, including summer program in France for high-school students; publication program disseminates materials of Sephardic value; outreach program to communities outside of the New York area; program bureau provides program ideas, speakers, and entertainers; International Sephardic Film Festival every two years. *Sephardic House Newsletter; Publication Catalogue.* (WWW. SEPHARDICHOUSE.ORG)

SIMON WIESENTHAL CENTER (1977). 1399 South Roxbury Drive., Los Angeles, CA 90035-4701. (310)553-9036. FAX: (310) 553-4521. Email: avra@wiesenthal.com. Dean-Founder Rabbi Marvin Hier; Assoc. Dean Rabbi Abraham Cooper; Exec. Dir. Rabbi Meyer May. Regional offices in New York, Miami, Baltimore, Toronto, Paris, Jerusalem, Buenos Aires. The largest institution of its kind in N. America dedicated to the study of the Holocaust, its contemporary implications, and related human-rights issues through education and awareness. Incorporates 185,000-sq.-ft. Museum of Tolerance, library, media department, archives, "Testimony to the Truth" oral histories, educational outreach, research department, international social action. *Response Magazine.* (WWW.WIESENTHAL.COM)

SKIRBALL CULTURAL CENTER (1996), an affiliate of Hebrew Union College. 2701 N. Sepulveda Blvd., Los Angeles, CA 90049. (310)440-4500. FAX: (310)440-4595. Pres. & CEO Uri D. Herscher; Bd. Chmn. Howard Friedman. Seeks to interpret the Jewish experience and to strengthen American society through a range of cultural programs, including museum exhibitions, children's Discovery Center, concerts, lectures, performances, readings, symposia, film, and educational offerings for adults and children of all ages and backgrounds, through interpretive museum exhibits and programming; museum shop and café. *Oasis magazine; catalogues of exhibits and collections.* (WWW.SKIRBALL.ORG)

SOCIETY FOR THE HISTORY OF CZECHOSLOVAK JEWS, INC. (1961). 760 Pompton Ave., Cedar Grove, NJ 07009. (973)239-2333. FAX: (973)239-7935. Pres. Rabbi Norman Patz; V.-Pres. Prof. Fred Hahn; Sec. Anita Grosz. Studies the history of Czechoslovak Jews; collects material and disseminates information through the publication of books and pamphlets; conducts annual memorial service for Czech Holocaust victims. *The Jews of Czechoslovakia (3 vols.); Review I-VI.*

THE SOCIETY OF FRIENDS OF TOURO SYNAGOGUE NATIONAL HISTORIC SITE, INC. (1948). 85 Touro St., Newport, RI 02840. (401)847-4794. FAX: (401)845-6790. E-mail: sof@tourosynagogue.org. Pres. Andrew M. Teitz; Exec. Dir. Jane S. Sprague. Helps maintain Touro Synagogue as a national historic site, opening and interpreting it for visitors; promotes public awareness of its preeminent role in the tradition of American religious liberty; annually commemorates George Washington's letter of 1790 to the Hebrew Congregation of Newport. *Society Update.*

———, TOURO NATIONAL HERITAGE TRUST (1984). 85 Touro St., Newport, RI 02840. (401)847-0810. FAX (401)847-8121. Pres. Bernard Bell; Chmn. Benjamin D. Holloway. Works to establish national education center within Touro compound; sponsors Touro Fellow through John Carter Brown Library; presents seminars and other educational programs; promotes knowledge of the early Jewish experience in this country.

SPERTUS MUSEUM, SPERTUS INSTITUTE OF JEWISH STUDIES (1968). 618 S. Michigan Ave., Chicago, IL 60605. (312)322-1747. FAX: (312)922-6406. Pres. Spertus Institute of Jewish Studies, Dr. Howard A. Sulkin. The largest, most comprehensive Judaic museum in the Midwest with 12,000 square feet of exhibit space and a permanent collection of some 10,000 works reflecting 5,000 years of Jewish history and culture. Also includes the redesigned Zell Holocaust Memorial, permanent collection, changing visual arts and special exhibits, and the children's ARTIFACT Center for a hands-on archaeological adventure. Plus, traveling exhibits for Jewish educators, life-cycle workshops, ADA accessible. *Exhibition catalogues; educational pamphlets.*

———, ASHER LIBRARY, SPERTUS INSTITUTE OF JEWISH STUDIES, (approx. 1930), 618 S. Michigan Ave., Chicago, IL 60605. (312)322-1749, FAX (312)922-6406. Pres. Spertus Institute of Jewish Studeis, Dr. Howard A. Sulkin; Director, Asher Library, Glenn Ferdman. Asher Library is the largest public Jewish Library in the Midwest, with over 100, 000 books and 550 periodicals; extensive collections of music, art, rare books, maps and electronic resources; nearly 1,000 feature and documentary films available on video cassette. Online catalogue access available. Also, the Chicago Jewish Archives collects historical material of Chicago individuals, families, synagogues and organizations. *ADA accessible.*

SURVIVORS OF THE SHOAH VISUAL HISTORY FOUNDATION (1994). PO Box 3168, Los Angeles, CA 90078-3168. (818)777-7802. FAX: (818)866-0312. Exec. Dir. Ari C. Zev. A nonprofit organization, founded and chaired by Steven Spielberg, dedicated to videotaping and preserving interviews with Holocaust survivors throughout the world. The archive of testimonies will be used as a tool for global education about the Holocaust and to teach racial, ethnic, and cultural tolerance.

UNITED STATES HOLOCAUST MEMORIAL MUSEUM (1980; opened Apr. 1993). 100 Raoul Wallenberg Place, SW, Washington, DC 20024. (202)488-0400. FAX: (202)488-2690. Chmn. Fred. Zeidman. ; Dir. Sara J. Bloomfeld. Federally chartered and privately built, its mission is to teach about the Nazi persecution and murder of six million Jews and millions of others from 1933 to 1945 and to inspire visitors to contemplate their moral responsibilities as citizens of a democratic nation. Opened in April 1993 near the national Mall in Washington, DC, the museum's permanent exhibition tells the story of the Holocaust through authentic artifacts, videotaped oral testimonies, documentary film, and historical photographs. Offers educational programs for students and adults, an interactive computerized learning center, and special exhibitions and community programs. *United States Holocaust Memorial Museum Update (bimonthly); Directory of Holocaust Institutions; Journal of Holocaust and Genocide Studies (quarterly).* (WWW.USHMM.ORG)

THE WILSTEIN (SUSAN & DAVID) INSTITUTE OF JEWISH POLICY STUDIES (1998). 160 Herrick Road, Newton Centre, MA 02459. (617)559-8790. FAX: (617)559-8791. E-mail: wilstein@hebrewcollege.edu. Dir. Dr. David M. Gordis; Assoc. Dir. Rabbi Zachary I. Heller; Chmn. Howard I. Friedman. The Wilstein Institute's West Coast Center in Los Angeles and East Coast Center at Hebrew College in Boston provide a bridge between academics, community leaders, professionals, and the organizations and institutions of Jewish life. The institute serves as an international research and development resource for American Jewry. *Bulletins, various newsletters, monographs, research reports, and books.*

YESHIVA UNIVERSITY MUSEUM (1973). Center for Jewish History, 15 W. 16 St., NYC 10011-6301. (212)294-8335. E-mail: rglickberg@yum.cjh.org. Dir. Sylvia A. Herskowitz; Chmn. Erica Jesselson. Collects, preserves, and interprets Jewish life and culture through changing exhibitions of ceremonial objects, paintings, rare books and documents, synagogue architecture, textiles, contemporary art, and photographs. Oral history archive. Special events, holiday workshops, live performances, lectures, etc. for adults and children. Guided tours and workshops are offered. Exhibitions and children's art education programs also at branch galleries on Yeshiva University's Main Campus, 2520 Amsterdam Ave., NYC 10033-3201. *Seasonal calendars; special exhibition catalogues; newsletters.*

YIDDISHER KULTUR FARBAND-YKUF (1937). 1133 Broadway, Rm. 820, NYC 10010. (212)243-1304. FAX: (212) 243-1305. E-mail: mahosu@amc.one. Pres./Ed. Itche Goldberg. Publishes a bimonthly magazine and books by contemporary and classical Jewish writers; conducts cultural forums; exhibits works by contemporary Jewish artists and materials of Jewish historical value; organizes reading circles. *Yiddishe Kultur.*

YIVO INSTITUTE FOR JEWISH RESEARCH (1925). 15 W. 16 St., NYC 10011. (212)246-6080. FAX: (212)292-1892. E-mail: yivomail@yivo.cjh.org. Chmn. Bruce Slovin; Exec. Dir. Dr. Carl J. Rheins. Engages in historical research and education pertaining to East European Jewish life; maintains library and archives which provide a major international, national and New York resource used by institutions, individual scholars, and the public; provides graduate fellowships in East European and American Jewish studies; offers Yiddish language classes at all levels, exhibits, conferences, public programs; publishes books. *Yedies-YIVO News; YIVO Bleter.*

———, MAX WEINREICH CENTER FOR ADVANCED JEWISH STUDIES/YIVO INSTITUTE (1968). 15 W. 16 St., NYC 10011. (212)246-6080. FAX: (212)292-1892. E-mail: mweinreich@yivo.cjh.org. Provides advanced-level training in Yiddish language and literature, ethnography, folklore, linguistics, and history; offers guidance on dissertation or independent research; post-doctoral fellowships available.

YUGNTRUF-YOUTH FOR YIDDISH (1964). 200 W. 72 St., Suite 40, NYC 10023. (212)787-6675. FAX: (212)799-1517. E-mail: ruvn@aol.com. Chmn. Dr. Paul Glasser; V.-Chmn. Marc Caplan; Coord. Brukhe Lang Caplan. A worldwide, nonpolitical organization for young people with a knowledge of, or interest in, Yiddish; fosters Yiddish as a living language and culture. Sponsors all activities in Yiddish:reading, conversation, and creative writing groups; annual weeklong retreat in Berkshires; children's Yiddish play group; sale of shirts. *Yugntruf Journal.*

ISRAEL-RELATED

THE ABRAHAM FUND (1989). 477 Madison Ave., 4th fl., NYC 10022. (212)303-9421. FAX: (212)935-1834. E-mail: info@AbrahamFund.org. Chmn. & Vice Pres. Barbara Merson, Exec. V.P. Dan Pattir. Seeks to enhance coexistence between Israel's Jewish and Arab citizens. Since 1993, has granted $6 million to grassroots coexistence projects in a wide array of fields, including education, social services, economic development, and arts and culture. Publishes *The Handbook of Interethnic*

Coexistence. *Coexistence Newsletter*. (WWW.COEXISTENCE.ORG)

AMERICA-ISRAEL CULTURAL FOUNDATION, INC. (1939). 51 E. 42nd St., Suite 400, NYC 10017. (212)557-1600. FAX: (212)557-1611. E-mail: USA AICF@aol.com. Chmn. Emer. Isaac Stern (in memoriam); Pres. Vera Stern. Supports and encourages the growth of cultural excellence in Israel through grants to cultural institutions; scholarships to gifted young artists and musicians. *Newsletter*. (WWW.AICF.ORG)

AMERICA-ISRAEL FRIENDSHIP LEAGUE, INC. (1971). 134 E. 39 St., NYC 10016. (212)213-8630. FAX: (212)683-3475. E-mail: aifl@nyworld.com. Hon. Chmn. Mortimer B. Zuckerman; Bd. Chmn. Kenneth J. Bialkin; Exec.V.-Pres. Ilana Artman. A nonsectarian, nonpartisan organization which seeks to broaden the base of support for Israel among Americans of all faiths and backgrounds. Activities include educational exchanges, tours of Israel for American leadership groups, symposia and public-education activities, and the dissemination of printed information. *Newsletter*.

AMERICAN ASSOCIATES, BEN-GURION UNIVERSITY OF THE NEGEV (1973). 342 Madison Ave., Suite 1224, NYC 10173. (212)687-7721. FAX: (212)370-0686. E-mail: info@aabgu.org. Pres. Zvi Alov; Exec. V-Pres. Seth Moscovitz. Since 1972, the American Associates, Ben—Gurion University of the Negev has played a vital role in building a world-class center for research and education in the desert. A nonprofit cooperation with nine regional offices throughout the United States, AABGU prides itself on its efficiency and effectiveness in raising funds to help Ben-Gurion University bring knowledge to the Negev and to the world. AABGU plays a vital role in helping BGU fulfill its unique responsibility to develop Negev, the focus of the future of Israel.(WWW.AABGU.ORG)

AMERICAN COMMITTEE FOR SHAARE ZEDEK JERUSALEM MEDICAL CENTER (1949). 49 W. 45 St., Suite 1100, NYC 10036. (212)354-8801. FAX: (212)391-2674. E-mail: pr@szmc.org.il. Natl. Pres. & Chmn. Intl. Bd. of Gov. Menno Ratzker; Chair Erica Jesselson. Increases awareness and raises funds for the various needs of this 100-year old hospital, including new medical centers of excellence, equipment, medical supplies, school of nursing and research; supports exchange program between Shaare Zedek Jerusalem Medical Center and Albert Einstein College of Medicine, NY. *Heartbeat Magazine*.

AMERICAN COMMITTEE FOR SHENKAR COLLEGE IN ISRAEL, INC. (1971). 855 Ave. of the Americas, #531, NYC 10001. (212) 947-1597. FAX: (212)643-9887. E-mail: acfsc@worldnet.att.net. Pres. Nahum G. (Sonny) Shar; Exec. Dir. Charlotte A. Fainblatt. Raises funds and coordinates projects and research with Shenkar College of Engineering and Design, Israel. A unique government academic institute in Israel dedicated to education and research in areas impacting Israel's industries and its artistic and scientific development. Textile, Fashion, Interior and Product design courses are offered with Scientific courses:Plastics, Chemistry, Software and Industrial Management and Marketing. Certified by Israel's Council of Higher Education, it offers continuing education and complete testing facilities for the textile/apparel industry and plastics engineering. *Shenkar News*.

AMERICAN COMMITTEE FOR THE BEER-SHEVA FOUNDATION (1988). PO Box 179, NYC 10028. (212)534-3715. FAX: (973) 992-8651. Pres. Ronald Slevin; Sr. V.-Pres. Joanna Slevin; Bd. Chmn. Sidney Cooperman. U.S. fundraising arm of the Beer-Sheva Foundation, which funds vital projects to improve the quality of life in the city of Beer-Sheva: nursery schools for pre-K toddlers, residential and day centers for needy seniors, educational programs, facilities and scholarships (especially for new olim, the physically and mentally challenged), parks, playgrounds, and other important projects. Also offers special services for immigrants—such as heaters, blankets, clothing, school supplies, etc. *Brochures*.

AMERICAN COMMITTEE FOR THE WEIZMANN INSTITUTE OF SCIENCE (1944). 130 E. 59 St., NYC 10022. (212)895-7900. FAX: (212)895-7999. E-mail: info@acwis.org. Chmn. Robert Asher; Pres. Albert Willner, M.D.; Exec. V.-Pres. Martin Kraar. Through 13 regional offices in the U.S. raises funds, disseminates information, and does American purchasing for the Weizmann Institute in Rehovot, Israel, a world-renowned center of scientific research and graduate study. The institute conducts research in disease, energy, the environment, and other areas; runs an international summer science program for gifted high-school students. *Interface; Weizmann Now; annual report.* (WWW.WEIZMANN-USA.ORG)

AMERICAN FRIENDS OF ALYN HOSPITAL (1932). 19 W. 44 St., Suite 1418, NYC 10036. (212)869-8085. FAX: (212)768-0979. E-mail: friendsofalyn@mindspring.com. Pres. Minette Halpern Brown; Exec. Dir. Cathy M Lanyard. Supports the Alyn-Woldenberg Family Hospital/Pediatric and Adolescent Rehabilitation Center in Jerusalem. Treats children suffering from birth defects (such as muscular dystrophy and spina bifida) and traumas (car accidents, cancer, and fire), enables patients and their families to achieve independence and a better quality of life. (WWW.ALYN.ORG)

AMERICAN FRIENDS OF ASSAF HAROFEH MEDICAL CENTER (1975). PO Box 21051, NYC 10129. (212)481-5653. FAX: (212) 481-5672. Chmn. Kenneth Kronen; Exec. Dir. Rhoda Levental; Treas. Robert Kastin. Support group for Assaf Harofeh, Israel's third-largest government hospital, serving a poor population of over 400,000 in the area between Tel Aviv and Jerusalem. Raises funds for medical equipment, medical training for immigrants, hospital expansion, school of nursing, and school of physiotherapy. *Newsletter.*

AMERICAN FRIENDS OF BAR-ILAN UNIVERSITY (1955). 235 Park Ave. So., NYC 10003. (212)673-3460. FAX: (212)673-4856. Email: nationaladmin@biuny.com, beverlyf@biuny.com. Chancellor Rabbi Emanuel Rackman; Chmn. Global Bd. Aharon Dahan; Pres. Amer. Bd. Melvin Stein; Exec. V.-Pres. Gen. Yehuda Halevy. Supports Bar-Ilan University, an institution that integrates the highest standards of contemporary scholarship in liberal arts and sciences with a Judaic studies program as a requirement. Located in Ramat-Gan, Israel, and chartered by the Board of Regents of the State of NY. *Bar-Ilan News; Bar-Ilan University Scholar; Heritage Newsletter.*

AMERICAN FRIENDS OF BETH HATEFUTSOTH (1976). 633 Third Ave., 21st fl., NYC 10017. (212)339-6034. FAX: (212)318-6176. E-mail: afbhusa@aol.com. Pres. Stephen Greenberg; Chmn. Sam E. Bloch; Exec. Dir. Gloria Golan. Supports the maintenance and development of Beth Hatefutsoth, the Nahum Goldmann Museum of the Jewish Diaspora in Tel Aviv, and its cultural and educational programs for youth and adults. Circulates its traveling exhibitions and provides various cultural programs to local Jewish communities. Includes Jewish genealogy center (DOROT), the center for Jewish music, and photodocumentation center. *Beth Hatefutsoth (quarterly newsletter).*

AMERICAN FRIENDS OF HAIFA UNIVERSITY (*see* AMERICAN SOCIETY OF THE UNIVERSITY OF HAIFA)

AMERICAN FRIENDS OF HERZOG HOSPITAL/EZRATH NASHIM-JERUSALEM (1895). 800 Second Ave., 8th fl., NYC 10017. (212)499-9092. FAX:(212)499-9085. E-mail: herzogpr@hotmail.com. Co-Pres. Dr. Joy Zagoren , Amir Sternhell; Exec. Dir. Stephen Schwartz. Herzog Hospital is the foremost geriatric and psychiatric health care facility in Israel, and a leading research center in genetics, Alzheimer's and schizophrenia, with expertise in neurogeriatrics, physical rehabilitation, and long-term respiratory care. Its Israel Center for the Treatment of Psychotrauma provides therapy and seminars to help Israelis cope with the ongoing violence. (WWW.HERZOGHOSPITAL.ORG)

AMERICAN FRIENDS OF LIKUD. P.O.Box 8711, JAF Station, NYC 10116. (212)308-5595. FAX: (212)688-1327. E-mail: Thelikud@aol.com. Natl. Chmn. J. Phillip Rosen, Esq; Pres. Julio Messer,M.D; Natl. V. Pres. Jacques Torczyner; Natl. Treasurer Milton S. Shapiro, Esq.; Exec. Dir. Salomon L. Vaz Dias. promotes public education on the situation in the Middle East, particularly in Israel, as well as advancing a general awareness of Zionism; provides a solid partnership of public support for the State of Israel, its citizens and its democratically-elected governments. American Friends of Likud is an active member of:Conference of Presidents of Major American Jewish Organizations; American Zionist Movement; World Zionist Organization; Jewish

Agency for Israel; Jewish National Fund/Keren Kayemet Leyisraeel.

AMERICAN FRIENDS OF NEVE SHALOM/WAHAT AL-SALAM (1988). 4201 Church Road, Suite 4, NYC 10013. (856)235-3667. FAX: (856)235-4674. E-mail: afnswas@oasisofpeace.com. Pres. Deborah First; V.-Pres. Adeeb Fadil; Exec. Dir. Deanna Armbruster. Supports and publicizes the projects of the community of Neve Shalom/Wahat Al-Salam, the "Oasis of Peace." For more than twenty years, Jewish and Palestinian citizens of Israel have lived and worked together as equals. The community teaches tolerance, understanding and mutual respect well beyond its own borders by being a model for peace and reaching out through its educational institutions. A bilingual, bicultural Primary School serves the village and the surrounding communities. Encounter workshops conducted by the School for Peace, both in the community and beyond, have reached tens of thousands of Jewish and Palestinian youth and adults.

AMERICAN FRIENDS OF RABIN MEDICAL CENTER (1994). 220 Fifth Avenue, Suite 1301, NYC 10001-2121. (212)279-2522. Fax: (212)279-0179. E-mail: afrmc826@aol.com. Pres. Woody Goldberg; Exec. Dir. Burton Lazarow. Supports the maintenance and development of this medical, research, and teaching institution in central Israel, which unites the Golda and Beilinson hospitals, providing 12% of all hospitalization in Israel. Department of Organ Transplantation performs 80% of all kidney and 60% of all liver transplants in Israel. Affiliated with Tel Aviv University's Sackler School of Medicine. *New Directions Quarterly.*

AMERICAN FRIENDS OF RAMBAM MEDICAL CENTER (1969). 226 West 26th Street, NYC 10001. (212)644-1049. FAX: (775)562-5399. E-mail: michaelstoler@princetoncommercial.com. Pres/CEO. Michael R. Stoler. Represents and raises funds for Rambam Medical Center (Haifa), an 887-bed hospital serving approx. one-third of Israel's population, incl. the entire population of northern Israel (and south Lebanon), the U.S. Sixth Fleet, and the UN Peacekeeping Forces in the region. Rambam is the teaching hospital for the Technion's medical school.

AMERICAN FRIENDS OF TEL AVIV UNIVERSITY, INC. (1955). 39 Broadway, 15th Floor., NYC 10006. (212)742-9070. FAX: (212)742-9071. Email: info@aftau.org. Bd. Chmn. Alan L. Aufzien; Pres. Robert J. Topchik; Exec. V.-Pres. Sam Witkin. Promotes higher education at Tel Aviv University, Israel's largest and most comprehensive institution of higher learning. Included in its nine faculties are the Sackler School of Medicine with its fully accredited NY State English-language program, the Rubin Academy of Music, and 70 research institutes, including the Moshe Dayan Center for Middle East & African Studies and the Jaffe Center for Strategic Studies. *Tel Aviv University News; FAX Flash.*

AMERICAN FRIENDS OF THE HEBREW UNIVERSITY (1925; inc. 1931). 11 E. 69 St., NYC 10021. (212)472-9800. FAX: (212)744-2324. E-mail: info@afhu.org. Pres. Ira Lee Sorkin; Bd. Chmn. Keith L. Sachs; Exec. V.-Pres. Adam Kahan. Fosters the growth, development, and maintenance of the Hebrew University of Jerusalem; collects funds and conducts informational programs throughout the U.S., highlighting the university's achievements and its significance. *Wisdom; Scopus Magazine.* (WWW.AFHU.ORG)

AMERICAN FRIENDS OF THE ISRAEL MUSEUM (1972). 500 Fifth Ave., Suite 2540, NYC 10110. (212)997-5611. FAX: (212) 997-5536. Pres. Barbara Lane; Exec. Dir. Carolyn Cohen. Raises funds for special projects of the Israel Museum in Jerusalem; solicits works of art for permanent collection, exhibitions, and educational purposes. *Newsletter.*

AMERICAN FRIENDS OF THE ISRAEL PHILHARMONIC ORCHESTRA (AFIPO) (1972). 122 E. 42 St., Suite 4507, NYC 10168. (212)697-2949. FAX: (212)697-2943. Interim Co-Pres. Albert Schussler & Elaine Wolfenshon; Exec. Dir. Suzanne K. Ponsot. Works to secure the financial future of the orchestra so that it may continue to travel throughout the world bringing its message of peace and cultural understanding through music. Supports the orchestra's international touring program, educational projects, and a wide array of musical activities in Israel. *Passport to Music (newsletter).*

AMERICAN FRIENDS OF THE OPEN UNIVERSITY OF ISRAEL. 180 W. 80 St., NYC 10024. (212)712-1800. FAX: (212)496-3296. E-mail: afoui@aol.com. Natl. Chmn. Irving M. Rosenbaum; Exec.V.-Pres. Eric G. Heffler. *Open Letter*. (WWW.OPENU.AC.IL)

AMERICAN FRIENDS OF THE SHALOM HARTMAN INSTITUTE (1976). 42 E. 69 St., Suite 401, NYC 10021. (212)772-9711. FAX: (212)772-9720. E-mail: afshi@akula.com. Pres. Richard F. Kaufman; Admin. Dorothy Minchin. Supports the Shalom Hartman Institute in Jerusalem, an international center for pluralist Jewish education and research, serving Israel and world Jewry. Founded in 1976 by David Hartman, the Institute includes:the Institute for Advanced Judaic Studies, with research centers for contemporary halakha, religious pluralism, political thought and peace and reconciliation; the Institute for Teacher and Leadership Training, educating Israeli principals, teachers, graduate students and leaders; and the Institute for Diaspora Education, which offers seminars and sabbaticals to rabbis, educators and lay leaders of diverse ideological commitments. (WWW.HARTMANINSTITUTE.COM)

AMERICAN FRIENDS OF THE TEL AVIV MUSEUM OF ART (1974). 545 Madison Ave. (55 St.), NYC 10022. (212)319-0555. FAX: (212)754-2987. Email: dnaftam@aol.com. Chmn. Stanley I. Batkin; Exec. Dir. Dorey Neilinger. Raises funds for the Tel Aviv Museum of Art for special projects, art acquisitions, and exhibitions; seeks contributions of art to expand the museum's collection; encourages art loans and traveling exhibitions; creates an awareness of the museum in the USA; makes available exhibition catalogues, monthly calendars, and posters published by the museum.

AMERICAN-ISRAEL ENVIRONMENTAL COUNCIL (formerly COUNCIL FOR A BEAUTIFUL ISRAEL ENVIRONMENTAL EDUCATION FOUNDATION) (1973). c/o Perry Davis Assoc., 25 W. 45 St., Suite 1405, NYC 10036. (212)840-1166. Fax: (212)840-1514. Pres. Alan Silberstein. A support group for the Israeli body, whose activities include education, town planning, lobbying for legislation to protect and enhance the environment, preservation of historical sites, the improvement and beautification of industrial and commercial areas, and sponsoring the CBI Center for Environmental Studies located in Yarkon Park, Tel Aviv. *Yearly newsletter; yearly theme oriented calendars in color.*

AMERICAN ISRAEL PUBLIC AFFAIRS COMMITTEE (AIPAC) (1954). 440 First St., NW, Washington, DC 20001. (202)639-5200. FAX: (202)347-4889. Pres. Lonny Kaplan; Exec. Dir. Howard A. Kohr. Registered to lobby on behalf of legislation affecting U.S.-Israel relations; represents Americans who believe support for a secure Israel is in U.S. interest. Works for a strong U.S.-Israel relationship. *Near East Report.* (WWW.AIPAC.ORG)

AMERICAN-ISRAELI LIGHTHOUSE, INC. (1928; reorg. 1955). 276 Fifth Ave., Suite 713, NYC 10001. (212)686-7110. Pres. Mrs. Leonard F. Dank; Sec. Mrs. Ida Rhein. Provides a vast network for blind and physically handicapped persons throughout Israel, to effect their social and vocational integration into the mainstream of their communities. Center of Services for the blind; built and maintains Rehabilitation Center for blind and handicapped persons (Migdal Or) in Haifa.

AMERICAN JEWISH LEAGUE FOR ISRAEL (1957). 130 E. 59 St., NYC 10022. (212)371-1583. FAX: (212)371-3265. E-mail: AJLImlk@aol.com. Pres. Dr. Martin L. Kalmanson. Seeks to unite all those who, notwithstanding differing philosophies of Jewish life, are committed to the historical ideals of Zionism; works independently of class, party, or religious affiliation for the welfare of Israel as a whole. Not identified with any political parties in Israel. Member of World Jewish Congress, World Zionist Organization, American Zionist Movement. *Newsletter.*

AMERICAN PHYSICIANS FELLOWSHIP FOR MEDICINE IN ISRAEL (1950). 2001 Beacon St., Suite 210, Boston, MA 02135-7771. (617)232-5382. FAX: (617)739-2616. E-mail: apf@apfmed.org. Pres. Sherwood L. Gorbach, M.D.; Exec. Dir. Ellen-Ann Lacey. Supports projects that advance medical education, research, and care in Israel and builds links between the medical communities of Israel and N. Amer.; provides fellowships for Israeli physicians training in N. Amer. and arranges lectureships in Israel by prominent N. Amer. physicians; sponsors CME seminars in Israel and N. Amer.; coordinates U.S./ Canadian medical emergency volunteers for Israel. *APF News.*

AMERICAN RED MAGEN DAVID FOR ISRAEL, INC. (1940) (a/k/a ARMDI & Red Magen David). 888 Seventh Ave., Suite 403, NYC 10106. (212)757-1627. FAX: (212)757-4662. E-mail: armdi@att.net. Natl. Pres. Robert L. Sadoff, M.D.; Exec. V.-Pres. Benjamin Saxe. An authorized tax-exempt organization; the sole support arm in the U.S. of Magen David Adom (MDA), Israel's equivalent to a Red Cross Society; raises funds for the MDA emergency medical, ambulance, blood, and disaster services which help Israel's defense forces and civilian population. Helps to supply and equip ambulances, bloodmobiles, and cardiac rescue ambulances as well as 45 pre-hospital MDA Emergency Medical Clinics and the MDA National Blood Service Center and MDA Fractionation Institute in Ramat Gan, Israel. *Lifeline.*

AMERICAN SOCIETY FOR TECHNION-ISRAEL INSTITUTE OF TECHNOLOGY (1940). 810 Seventh Ave., 24th fl., NYC 10019. (212) 262-6200. FAX: (212)262-6155. Pres. Evelyn Berger; Chmn. Larry Jackier; Exec. V.-Pres. Melvyn H. Bloom. The American Technion Society (ATS) is the Technion-Israel Institute of Technology's liaison organization in the United States. Based in New York City, it is the leading American organization with more than 20,000 supporters and 19 satellite offices around the country, the ATS is driven by the belief that the economic future of Israel is in high technology and the future of high technology in Israel is at the Technion. *Technion USA.*

AMERICAN SOCIETY FOR THE PROTECTION OF NATURE IN ISRAEL, INC. (1986). 28 Arrandale Ave., Great Neck, NY 11024. (212)398-6750. FAX: (212)398-1665. E-mail: aspni@aol.com. Co-Chmn. Edward I. Geffner & Russell Rothman. A nonprofit organization supporting the work of SPNI, an Israeli organization devoted to environmental protection and nature education. SPNI runs 26 Field Study Centers and has 45 municipal offices throughout Israel; offers education programs, organized hikes, and other activities; seeks ways to address the needs of an expanding society while preserving precious natural resources. *SPNI News.*

AMERICAN SOCIETY FOR YAD VASHEM (1981). 500 Fifth Ave., 42nd fl., NYC 10110-1699. (212)220-4304. FAX: (212)220-4308. E-mail: yadvashem@aol.com. Chmn. Eli Zborowski; Dev. Dir. Shraga Y. Mekel; Ed. Dir. Marlene Warshawski Yahalom, Ph.D. Development arm of Yad Vashem, Jerusalem, the central international authority created by the Knesset in 1953 for the purposes of commemoration and education in connection with the Holocaust. *Martyrdom and Resistance (newsletter).* (WWW.YADVASHEM.ORG)

AMERICAN SOCIETY OF THE UNIVERSITY OF HAIFA (formerly AMERICAN FRIENDS OF HAIFA UNIVERSITY) (1972). 220 Fifth Ave., Suite 1301, NYC 10001. (212)685-7880. FAX: (212)267-5916. Pres.Paul Amir; Sec./Treas. Robert Jay Benowitz. Promotes, encourages, and aids higher and secondary education, research, and training in all branches of knowledge in Israel and elsewhere; aids in the maintenance and development of Haifa University; raises and allocates funds for the above purposes; provides scholarships; promotes exchanges of teachers and students.

AMERICAN ZIONIST MOVEMENT (formerly AMERICAN ZIONIST FEDERATION) (1939; reorg. 1949, 1970, 1993). 110 E. 59 St., NYC 10022. (212)318-6100. FAX: (212)935-3578. E-mail: info@azm.com. Pres. Melvin Salberg; Exec. Dir. Karen J. Rubinstein. Umbrella organization for 20 American Zionist organizations and the voice of unified Zionism in the U.S. Conducts advocacy for Israel; strengthens Jewish identity; promotes the Israel experience; prepares the next generation of Zionist leadership. Regional offices in Chicago and Dallas. Groups in Detroit, Pittsburgh, Washington, DC. *The Zionist Advocate.* (WWW.AZM.ORG)

AMERICANS FOR A SAFE ISRAEL (AFSI) (1971). 1623 Third Ave., Suite 205, NYC 10128. (212)828-2424. FAX: (212)828-1717. E-mail: afsi@rcn.com. Chmn. Herbert Zweibon; Exec. Dir. Helen Freedman. Seeks to educate Americans in Congress, the media, and the public about Israel's role as a strategic asset for the West; through meetings with legislators and the media, in press releases and publications AFSI promotes Jewish rights to Judea and Samaria, the Golan, Gaza, an indivisible Jerusalem, and to all of Israel. AFSI believes in the concept of "peace for peace" and rejects the concept of "territory for peace." *The Outpost (monthly)*. (WWW.AFSI.ORG.AFSI)

AMERICANS FOR PEACE NOW (1984). 1815 H St., NW, 9th fl., Washington, DC 20006. (202)728-1893. FAX: (202)728-1895. E-mail: apndc@peacenow.org. Pres. & CEO Debra DeLee; Chmn. Pat Barr. Conducts educational programs and raises funds to support the Israeli peace movement, Shalom Achshav (Peace Now), and coordinates U.S. advocacy efforts through APN's Washington-based Center for Israeli Peace and Security. *Jerusalem Watch; Peace Now News; Settlement Watch; Fax Facts; Middle East Update (on-line); Benefits of Peace.* (WWW.PEACENOW.ORG)

AMIT (1925). 817 Broadway, NYC 10003. (212)477-4720. FAX: (212)353-2312. E-mail: info@amitchildren.org. Pres. Sondra Sokal; Exec. Dir. Marvin Leff. The State of Israel's official reshet (network) for religious secondary technological education; maintains innovative children's homes and youth villages in Israel in an environment of traditional Judaism; promotes cultural activities for the purpose of disseminating Zionist ideals and strengthening traditional Judaism in America. *AMIT Magazine.*

AMPAL-AMERICAN ISRAEL CORPORATION (1942). 1177 Avenue of the Americas, NYC 10036. (212)782-2100. FAX: (212) 782-2114. E-mail: ampal@aol.com. Bd. Chmn. Daniel Steinmetz; CEO Shuki Gleitman. Acquires interests in businesses located in the State of Israel or that are Israel-related. Interests include leisure-time, real estate, finance, energy distribution, basic industry, high technology, and communications. *Annual report; quarterly reports.*

ARZA/WORLD UNION, NORTH AMERICA (1977). 633 Third Ave., 6th fl., NYC 10017-6778. (212)650-4280. FAX: (212) 650-4289. E-mail: arza/wupjna@uahc.org. Pres. Philip Meltzer; Exec. Dir. Rabbi Ammiel Hirsch. Membership organization dedicated to furthering the development of Progressive Judaism in Israel, the FSU, and throughout the world. Encourages Jewish solidarity, promoting religious pluralism and furthering Zionism. Works to strengthen the relationship of N. American Reform Jews with Progressive Jewish communities worldwide and to educate and inform them on relevant issues. *Quarterly newsletter*. (WWW.RJ.ORG/ARZAWUNA)

BETAR EDUCATIONAL YOUTH ORGANIZATION (1935). 4 East 34th Street, NYC, 10016. (646)742-9364. FAX: (646)742-9366. E-mail: betarorg@idt.net. Pres. Shav Rubinstein; Bd. Member Morris Berkower. Betar is a Zionist active college students' movement, which dedicates itself to promoting Israeli issues in the American media. Betar was founded in 1923 by Zeev Jabotinsky, among its' famous alumni are Nenachem Begin and Itzhak Shamir. Betar's goal is the gathering of all Jewish people in their ancient land.

BOYS TOWN JERUSALEM FOUNDATION OF AMERICA INC. (1948). 12 W. 31 St., Suite 300, NYC 10001. (212)244-2766. (800) 469-2697. FAX: (212)244-2052. E-mail: btjny@compuserve.com. Raphael Benaroya, Pres. Michael J. Scharf; Hon. Chmn. Josh S. Weston; Chmn. Raphael Benaroya; Exec. V.-Pres. Rabbi Ronald L. Gray. Raises funds for Boys Town Jerusalem, which was established in 1948 to offer a comprehensive academic, religious, and technological education to disadvantaged Israeli and immigrant boys from over 45 different countries, including Ethiopia, the former Soviet Union, and Iran. Enrollment:over 1,000 students in jr. high school, academic and technical high school, and a college of applied engineering. Boys Town was recently designated as the "CISCO Regional Academy," the first center in Jerusalem for the instruction of the CISCO Networking Management Program. *BTJ Newsbrief.*

CAMERA-COMMITTEE FOR ACCURACY IN MIDDLE EAST REPORTING IN AMERICA (1983). PO Box 35040, Boston, MA 02135. (617)789-3672. FAX: (617)787-7853. E-mail: media@camera.org. Pres./Exec. Dir. Andrea Levin; Chmn. Leonard Wisse. CAMERA monitors media coverage of Israel, responds to error, omissions, and distortion, promotes factual information and works to educate the media and public about key issues related to conflict in the Middle East. CAMERA encourages members to participate in fostering full and fair coverage through communication with the media. *CAMERA Media Report (quarterly); CAMERA on Campus; CAMERA Media Directory, CAMERA Monographs, Action Alerts, Backgrounders.* (WWW.CAMERA.ORG)

COUNCIL FOR A BEAUTIFUL ISRAEL ENVIRONMENTAL EDUCATION FOUNDATION (*see* AMERICAN-ISRAEL ENVIRONMENTAL COUNCIL)

EMUNAH OF AMERICA (formerly HAPOEL HAMIZRACHI WOMEN'S ORGANIZATION) (1948). 7 Penn Plaza, NYC 10001. (212) 564-9045, (800)368-6440. FAX: (212)643-9731. E-mail: info@emunah.org. Natl. Pres. Dr. Marcia Genuth; Exec. V.-Pres. Carol Sufian. Maintains and supports 200 educational and social-welfare institutions in Israel within a religious framework, including day-care centers, kindergartens, children's residential homes, vocational schools for the underprivileged, senior-citizen centers, a college complex, and Holocaust study center. Also involved in absorption of Soviet and Ethiopian immigrants (recognized by Israeli government as an official absorption agency). *Emunah Magazine; Lest We Forget.* (WWW.EMUNAH.ORG)

FEDERATED COUNCIL OF ISRAEL INSTITUTIONS—FCII (1940). 4702 15th Ave., Brooklyn, NY 11219. (718)972-5530. Bd. Chmn. Z. Shapiro; Exec. V.-Pres. Rabbi Julius Novack. Central fund-raising organization for over 100 affiliated institutions; handles and executes estates, wills, and bequests for the traditional institutions in Israel; clearinghouse for information on budget, size, functions, etc. of traditional educational, welfare, and philanthropic institutions in Israel, working cooperatively with the Israeli government and the overseas department of the Council of Jewish Federations. *Annual financial reports and statistics on affiliates.*

FRIENDS OF THE ISRAEL DEFENSE FORCES (1981). 298 5th Avenue, NYC 10001. (212) 244-3118. FAX: (212)244-3119. E-mail: fidf@fidf.com. Chmn. Marvin Josephson; Pres. Jay Zises; Natl. Dir. Brig. Gen. Eliezer Hemeli. Supports the Agudah Lema'an Hahayal, Israel's Assoc. for the Well-Being of Soldiers, founded in the early 1940s, which provides social, recreational, and educational programs for soldiers, special services for the sick and wounded, and summer programs for widows and children of fallen soldiers. (WWW.FIDF.COM)

GESHER FOUNDATION (1969). 25 W. 45 St. Suite 1405, NYC 10036. (212)840-1166. FAX: (212)840-1514. E-mail: gesherfoundation@aol.com. Pres./Founder Daniel Tropper; Chmn. Philip Schatten. Seeks to bridge the gap between Jews of various backgrounds in Israel by stressing the interdependence of all Jews. Runs encounter seminars for Israeli youth; distributes curricular materials in public schools; offers Jewish identity classes for Russian youth, and a video series in Russian and English on famous Jewish personalities.

GIVAT HAVIVA EDUCATIONAL FOUNDATION, INC. (1966). 114 W. 26 St., Suite 1001, NYC 10001. (212)989-9272. FAX: (212)989-9840. E-mail: mail@givathaviva.org. Chmn. Yvonne Baum Silverman. Supports programs at the Givat Haviva Institute, Israel's leading organization dedicated to promoting coexistence between Arabs and Jews, with 40,000 people participating each year in programs teaching conflict resolution, Middle East studies and languages, and Holocaust studies. Publishes research papers on Arab-Jewish relations, Holocaust studies, kibbutz life. In the U.S., GHEF sponsors public-education programs and lectures by Israeli speakers. *Givat Haviva News; special reports.* (WWW.DIALOGATE.ORG.IL)

HABONIM-DROR NORTH AMERICA (1935). 114 W. 26 St., Suite 1004, NYC 10001-6812. (212)255-1796. FAX: (212)929-3459. E-mail: programs@habonimdror.org. (Mazkir Tnua) Jamie Levin; Shliach Onri Welmer. Fosters identification with progressive, cooperative living in Israel; stimulates study of Jewish and Zionist culture, history, and contemporary society. Sponsors summer and year programs in Israel and on kibbutz, 7 summer camps in N. America modeled after kibbutzim, and *aliyah* frameworks. *B'Tnua (on-line and print newsletter).* (WWW.HABONIMDROR.ORG)

HADASSAH, THE WOMEN'S ZIONIST ORGANIZATION OF AMERICA, INC. (1912). 50 W. 58 St., NYC 10019. (212)355-7900. FAX: (212)303-8282. Pres. Bonnie Lipton; Exec. Dir. Dr. Ellen Marson. Largest women's, largest Jewish, and largest Zionist membership organization in U.S. In Israel: Founded and funds Hadassah Medical Organization, Hadassah College of Technology, Hadassah Career Counseling Institute, Young Judea summer and year-course programs, as well as providing support for Youth Aliyah and JNF. U.S. programs: Jewish and women's health education; advocacy on Israel, Zionism and women's issues; Young Judaea youth movement, including six camps; Hadassah Leadership Academy; Hadassah Research Institute on Jewish Women; Hadassah Foundation. *Hadassah Magazine; Update; Hadassah International Newsletter; Medical Update; American Scene.* (WWW.HADASSAH.ORG)

———, YOUNG JUDAEA (1909; reorg. 1967). 50 W. 58 St., NYC 10019. (212)303-8014. FAX: (212)303-4572. E-mail: info@youngjudaea.org. Natl. Dir. Doron Krakow. Religiously pluralistic, politically nonpartisan Zionist youth movement sponsored by Hadassah; seeks to educate Jewish youth aged 8–25 toward Jewish and Zionist values, active commitment to and participation in the American and Israeli Jewish communities; maintains six summer camps in the U.S.; runs both summer and year programs in Israel, and a jr. year program in connection with both Hebrew University in Jerusalem and Ben Gurion University of the Negev. College-age arm, Hamagshimim, supports Zionist activity on campuses. *Kol Hat'nua; The Young Judaean; Ad Kahn.* (WWW.YOUNGJUDAEA.ORG)

HASHOMER HATZAIR, SOCIALIST ZIONIST YOUTH MOVEMENT (1923). 114 W. 26 St., Suite 1001, NYC 10001. (212)627-2830. FAX: (212)989-9840. E-mail: mail@hashomerhatzair.org. Dir. Giora Salz; Natl. Sec. Moran Banai. Seeks to educate Jewish youth to an understanding of Zionism as the national liberation movement of the Jewish people. Promotes aliyah to kibbutzim. Affiliated with Kibbutz Artzi Federation. Espouses socialist-Zionist ideals of peace, justice, democracy, and intergroup harmony. *Young Guard.* (WWW.HASHOMERHAZAIR.ORG)

INTERNS FOR PEACE INTERNATIONAL (1976). 475 Riverside Dr., Room 204., NYC 10115. (212)870-2226. FAX: (212)870-2119. Intl. Dir. Rabbi Bruce M. Cohen; Intl. Coord. Karen Wald Cohen. An independent, nonprofit, nonpolitical educational program training professional community peace workers. In Israel, initiated and operated jointly by Jews and Arabs; over 190 interns trained in 35 cities; over 80,000 Israeli citizens participating in joint programs in education, sports, culture, business, women's affairs, and community development; since the peace accord, Palestinians from West Bank and Gaza training as interns. Martin Luther King Project for Black/Jewish relations. *IFP Reports Quarterly; Guidebooks for Ethnic Conflict Resolution.* (WWW.INTERNSFORPEACE.ORG)

ISRAEL CANCER RESEARCH FUND (1975). 1290 Avenue of the Americas, NYC 10104. (212)969-9800. FAX: (212)969-9822. E-mail: mail@icrfny.org. Pres. Yashar Hirshaut, M.D.; Chmn. Leah Susskind; Exec. V.P. Donald Adelman. The largest single source of private funds for cancer research in Israel. Has a threefold mission:To encourage innovative cancer research by Israeli scientists; to harness Israel's vast intellectual and creative resources to establish a world-class center for cancer study; to broaden research opportunities within Israel to stop the exodus of talented Israeli cancer researchers. *Annual Report; Research Awards; ICRF Brochure; Newsletter.*

ISRAEL HISTADRUT FOUNDATION (*see* ISRAEL HUMANITARIAN FOUNDATION)

ISRAEL HUMANITARIAN FOUNDATION (IHF) (1960). 276 Fifth Ave., Suite 901, NYC 10001. (212)683-5676, (800)434-5IHF. FAX: (212)213-9233. E-mail: info@ihf.net. Pres. Marvin M. Sirota; Exec.V.-Pres. Stanley J. Abrams. Nonprofit American philanthropic organization that supports humanitarian needs in Israel; strives to improve the standard of living of Israel's population in need through its support of education, general health and neonatal care, medical and cancer research, the elderly, disabled and youth-in-need. *Impact.*

ISRAEL POLICY FORUM (1993). 165 East 56th Street, 2nd Floor, NYC 10022. (212)245-4227. FAX: (212)245-0517. E-mail: ipf@ipforum.org. 1030 15 St., NW, Suite 850, Washington, DC 20005. (202)842-1700. FAX:(202)842-1722. E-mail: ipf@ipforum.org. Chmn. Jack Bendheim;

Pres. Judy Stern Peck; Exec. Dir. Debra Wasserman. An independent leadership institution whose mission is to encourage an active U.S. role in resolving the Arab-Israeli conflict. IPF generates this support by involving leaders from the business, political, entertainment, academic, and philanthropic communitites in the peace effort, and by fostering a deeper understanding of the peace process among the American public. *Forum Fax, Washington Bulletin, Security Watch.* (WWW.IPFORUM.ORG)

THE JERUSALEM FOUNDATION, INC. (1966). 60 E. 42 St., Suite 1936, NYC 10165. (212)697-4188. FAX: (212)697-4022. E-mail: info@jfoundation.com. Chmn. William Ackman; Exec. Dir. Sandra Rubin. A nonprofit organization devoted to improving the quality of life for all Jerusalemites, regardless of ethnic, religious, or socioeconomic background; has initiated and implemented more than 1,500 projects that span education, culture, community services, beautification, and preservation of the city's historic heritage and religious sites.

JEWISH INSTITUTE FOR NATIONAL SECURITY AFFAIRS (JINSA) (1976). 1717 K St., NW, Suite 800, Washington, DC 20006. (202)833-0020. FAX: (202)296-6452. E-mail: info@jinsa.org. Pres. Norman Hascoe; Exec. Dir. Tom Neumann. A nonprofit, nonpartisan educational organization working within the American Jewish community to explain the link between American defense policy and the security of the State of Israel; and within the national security establishment to explain the key role Israel plays in bolstering American interests. (WWW.JINSA.ORG)

JEWISH INSTITUTE FOR THE BLIND-JERUSALEM, INC. (1902, Jerusalem). 15 E. 26 St., NYC 10010. (212)532-4155. FAX: (212)447-7683. Pres. Rabbi David E. Lapp; Admin. Eric L. Loeb. Supports a dormitory and school for the Israeli blind and handicapped in Jerusalem. *INsight.*

JEWISH NATIONAL FUND OF AMERICA (1901). 42 E. 69 St., NYC 10021. (212) 879-9300. (1-800-542-TREE). FAX: (212) 570-1673. E-mail: communications@jnf.org. Pres. Ronald S. Lauder; Exec. V.-Pres. Russell F. Robinson. Jewish National Fund is the American fund-raising arm of Keren Kayemeth LeIsrael, the official land agency in Israel and is celebrating its 100th Anniversary this year. JNF works in the following areas:water resource development, afforestation and ecology, eduction, tourism and recreation, community development and research. (WWW.JNF.ORG)

JEWISH PEACE LOBBY (1989). 8604 Second Avnue, PMB 317, Silver Spring, MD 20910. (301)589-8764. FAX: (301)589-2722. Email: peacelobby@msn.com. Pres. Jerome M. Segal. A legally registered lobby promoting changes in U.S. policy vis-a-vis the Israeli-Palestinian conflict. Supports Israel's right to peace within secure borders; a political settlement based on mutual recognition of the right of self-determination of both peoples; a two-state solution as the most likely means to a stable peace. *Annual Report.*

KEREN OR, INC. JERUSALEM CENTER FOR MULTI-HANDICAPPED BLIND CHILDREN (1956). 350 Seventh Ave., Suite 200, NYC 10001. (212)279-4070. FAX: (212)279-4043. E-mail: kerenorinc@aol.com. Chmn. Dr. Edward L. Steinberg; Pres. Dr. Albert Hornblass; Exec. Dir. Rochelle B. Silberman. Funds the Keren-Or Center for Multi-Handicapped Blind Children at 3 Abba Hillel Silver St., Ramot, Jerusalem, housing and caring for over 70 resident and day students who in addition to blindness or very low vision suffer from other severe physical and/or mental disabilities. Students range in age from 1 1/2 through young adulthood. Provides training in daily living skills, as well as therapy, rehabilitation, and education to the optimum level of the individual. *Insights Newsletter.*

LABOR ZIONIST ALLIANCE (formerly FARBAND LABOR ZIONIST ORDER) (1913). 275 Seventh Ave., NYC 10001. (212)366-1194. FAX: (212)675-7685. E-mail: labzionA@aol.com. Pres. Jeffry Mallow; Exec. Dir. Ari M. Chester. Seeks to enhance Jewish life, culture, and education in U.S.; aids in building State of Israel as a cooperative commonwealth and its Labor movement organized in the Histadrut; supports efforts toward a more democratic society throughout the world; furthers the democratization of the Jewish community in America and the welfare of Jews everywhere; works with labor and liberal forces in America; sponsors Habonim-Dror labor Zionist youth movement. *Jewish*

Frontier; Yiddisher Kempfer. (WWW.JEWISH FRONTIER.ORG)

MACCABI USA/SPORTS FOR ISRAEL (formerly UNITED STATES COMMITTEE SPORTS FOR ISRAEL) (1948). 1926 Arch St., 4R, Philadelphia, PA 19103. (215)561-6900. Fax: (215)561-5470. E-mail: maccabi@maccabiusa.com. Pres. Toni Worhman. Sponsors U.S. team for World Maccabiah Games in Israel every four years; seeks to enrich the lives of Jewish youth in the U.S., Israel, and the Diaspora through athletic, cultural, and educational programs; develops, promotes, and supports international, national, and regional athletic-based activities and facilities. *Sportscene Newsletter; Commemorative Maccabiah Games Journal; financial report.* (WWW.MACCABIUSA.COM)

MERCAZ USA (1979). 155 Fifth Ave., NYC 10010. (212)533-7800, ext. 2016. FAX: (212)533-2601. E-mail: info@mercazusa.org. Pres. Evelyn Seelig; Exec. Dir. Rabbi Robert R. Golub. The U.S. Zionist organization for Conservative/Masorti Judaism; works for religious pluralism in Israel, defending and promoting Conservative/Masorti institutions and individuals; fosters Zionist education and *aliyah* and develops young leadership. *Mercaz USA Quarterly Newsletter.* (WWW.MERCAZ USA.ORG)

MERETZ USA FOR ISRAELI CIVIL RIGHTS AND PEACE (1991). 114 W. 26 St., Suite 1002, NYC 10001. (212)242-4500. FAX: (212)242-5718. E-mail: meretzusa@aol.com. Pres. Harold M. Shapiro; Exec. Dir. Charney V. Bromberg. A forum for addressing the issues of social justice and peace in Israel. Educates about issues related to democracy, human and civil rights, religious pluralism, and equality for women and ethnic minorities; promotes the resolution of Israel's conflict with the Palestinians on the basis of mutual recognition, self-determination, and peaceful coexistence. *Israel Horizons.*

NA'AMAT USA, THE WOMEN'S LABOR ZIONIST ORGANIZATION OF AMERICA, INC. (formerly PIONEER WOMEN/NA'AMAT) (1925). 350 Fifth Ave., Suite 4700, NYC 10118-4799. (212)563-5222. FAX: (212) 563-5710. E-mail: naamat@naamat.org. Natl. Pres. Lynn Wax. Part of the World Movement of Na'amat (Movement of Working Women and Volunteers), the largest Jewish women's organization in the world, Na'amat USA helps provide social, educational, and legal services for women, teenagers, and children in Israel. It also advocates legislation for women's rights and child welfare in Israel and the U.S., furthers Jewish education, and supports Habonim Dror, the Labor Zionist youth movement. *Na'amat Woman magazine.* (WWW.NAAMAT.ORG)

NATIONAL COMMITTEE FOR LABOR ISRAEL (1923). 275 Seventh Ave., NYC 10001. (212)647-0300. FAX: (212)647-0308. E-mail: ncli@laborisrael.org. Pres. Jay Mazur; Exec. Dir. Jerry Goodman; Chmn. Trade Union Council Morton Bahr. Serves as a bridge among Israel's labor sector, including its General Federation of Labor, Histadrut, the American labor movement, the Jewish community and the general public. Brings together Jews and non-Jews to build support for Israel and advance closer Israel-Arab ties. Cooperates with Israels labor sector. National in scope, it conducts education in the Jewish community and among labor groups to promote better relations with labor Israel. Raises funds for youth, educational, health, social and cultural projects in Israel from a constituency which includes labor unions, foundations, government agencies and individual donors and supporters. *Occasional background papers* (WWW.LABORISRAEL.ORG)

NEW ISRAEL FUND (1979). 1101 14th St., NW, 6th fl., Washington, DC 20005-5639. (202)842-0900. FAX: (202)842-0991. E-mail: info@nif.org. New York office:165 E. 56 St., NYC 10022. (212)750-2333. FAX: (212)750-8043. Pres. Yoram Peri; Exec. Dir. Norman S. Rosenberg. A partnership of Israelis and North Americans dedicated to promoting social justice, coexistence, and pluralism in Israel, the New Israel Fund helps strengthen Israeli democracy by providing grants and technical assistance to the public-interest sector, cultivating a new generation of social activists, and educating citizens in Israel and the Diaspora about the challenges to Israeli democracy. *Quarterly newsletter; annual report; other reports.* (WWW.NIF.ORG)

PEF ISRAEL ENDOWMENT FUNDS, INC. (1922). 317 Madison Ave., Suite 607, NYC 10017. (212)599-1260. Chmn. Sidney A. Luria; Pres. B. Harrison Frankel;

Sec. Mark Bane. A totally volunteer organization that makes grants to educational, scientific, social, religious, health, and other philanthropic institutions in Israel. *Annual report.*

PIONEER WOMEN/NA'AMAT (*see* NA'AMAT USA)

POALE AGUDATH ISRAEL OF AMERICA, INC. (1948). 2920 Avenue J, Brooklyn, NY 11210. (718)258-2228. FAX: (718)258-2288. Pres. Rabbi Fabian Schonfeld. Aims to educate American Jews to the values of Orthodoxy and aliyah; supports kibbutzim, trade schools, yeshivot, moshavim, kollelim, research centers, and children's homes in Israel. *PAI News; She'arim; Hamayan.*

———, WOMEN'S DIVISION OF (1948). Pres. Miriam Lubling; Presidium: Sarah Ivanisky, Tili Stark, Peppi Petzenbaum. Assists Poale Agudath Israel to build and support children's homes, kindergartens, and trade schools in Israel. *Yediot PAI.*

PRO ISRAEL (1990). 1328 Broadway, Suite 435, NYC. (212)594-8996. FAX: (212)594-8986. E-mail: proisrael@aol.com. Pres. Dr. Ernest Bloch; Exec. Dir. Rabbi Julian M. White. Educates the public about Israel and the Middle East; provides support for community development throughout the Land of Israel, particularly in Judea, Samaria, Gaza, and the Golan Heights. Projects include the Ariel Center for Policy Research and Professors for a Strong Israel.

PROJECT NISHMA (*see* ISRAEL POLICY FORUM)

RELIGIOUS ZIONISTS OF AMERICA. 25 W. 26 ST., NYC 10010. (212)689-1414. FAX: (212)779-3043.

———, BNEI AKIVA OF THE U.S. & CANADA (1934). 25 W. 26 St., NYC 10010. (212)889-5260. FAX: (212)213-3053. Exec. Dir. Judi Srebro; Natl. Dir. Steve Frankel. The only religious Zionist youth movement in North America, serving over 10,000 young people from grade school through graduate school in 16 active regions across the United States and Canada, six summer camps, seven established summer, winter, and year programs in Israel. Stresses communal involvement, social activism, leadership training, and substantive programming to educate young people toward a commitment to Judaism and Israel. *Akivon; Pinkas Lamadrich; Daf Rayonot; Me'Ohalai Torah; Zraim.* (WWW.BNEIAKIVA.ORG)

———, MIZRACHI-HAPOEL HAMIZRACHI (1909; merged 1957). 25 W. 26 St., NYC 10010. (212)689-1414. FAX: (212)779-3043. Pres.Rabbi Simcha Krauss; Exec. V.-Pres. Dr. Mandell I. Ganchrow. Disseminates ideals of religious Zionism; conducts cultural work, educational program, public relations; raises funds for religious educational institutions in Israel, including yeshivot hesder and Bnei Akiva. *Newsletters; Kolenu.*

———, NATIONAL COUNCIL FOR TORAH EDUCATION OF MIZRACHI-HAPOEL HAMIZRACHI (1939). 25 W. 26 St., NYC 10010. Pres. Rabbi Israel Schorr. Organizes and supervises yeshivot and Talmud Torahs; prepares and trains teachers; publishes textbooks and educational materials; organizes summer seminars for Hebrew educators in cooperation with Torah Department of Jewish Agency; conducts ulpan. *Hazarkor; Chemed.*

SCHNEIDER CHILDREN'S MEDICAL CENTER OF ISRAEL (1982). 130 E. 59 St., Suite 1203, NYC 10022. (212)759-3370. FAX: (212)759-0120. E-mail: mdiscmci@aol.com. Bd. Chmn. H. Irwin Levy; Exec. Dir. Shlomit Manson. Its primary goal is to provide the best medical care to children in the Middle East. *UPDATE Newsletter*

SOCIETY OF ISRAEL PHILATELISTS (1949). 24355 Tunbridge Lane, Beachwood, OH 44122. (216)292-3843. Pres Henry B. Stern; Exec. Secry. Howard S. Chapman; Journal Ed. Dr. Oscar Stadtler. Promotes interest in, and knowledge of, all phases of Israel philately through sponsorship of chapters and research groups, maintenance of a philatelic library, and support of public and private exhibitions. *The Israel Philatelist; monographs; books.*

STATE OF ISRAEL BONDS (1951). 575 Lexington Ave., Suite 600, NYC 10022. (212) 644-2663; (800)229-9650. FAX: (212)644-3887. E-mail: raphael.rothstein@israelbonds.com. Bd. Chmn. Burton P. Resnick; Pres./CEO Gideon Patt. An international organization offering securities issued by the government of Israel. Since its inception in 1951 has secured $25 billion in investment capital for the development of every aspect of Israel's economic infrastructure, including agriculture, commerce, and industry, and for absorption of immigrants. *Israel "Hadashot-News"*. (WWW.ISRAELBONDS.COM)

THEODOR HERZL FOUNDATION (1954). 633 Third Ave., 21st fl., NYC 10017. (212)339-6040. FAX: (212)318-6176. Email: info@midstream.org. Chmn. Kalman Sultanik; Sec. Sam E. Bloch. Offers cultural activities, lectures, conferences, courses in modern Hebrew and Jewish subjects, Israel, Zionism, and Jewish history. *Midstream.*

———, HERZL PRESS. Chmn. Kalman Sultanik; Dir. of Pub. Sam E. Bloch. Serves as "the Zionist Press of record," publishing books that are important for the light they shed on Zionist philosophy, Israeli history, contemporary Israel and the Diaspora and the relationship between them. They are important as contributions to Zionist letters and history. *Midstream.*

TSOMET-TECHIYA USA (1978). 185 Montague St., 3rd fl., Brooklyn, NY 11201. (718)596-2119. FAX: (718)858-4074. E-mail: eliahu@aol.com. Chmn. Howard B. Weber. Supports the activities of the Israeli Tsomet party, which advocates Israeli control over the entire Land of Israel.

UNITED CHARITY INSTITUTIONS OF JERUSALEM, INC. (1903). 1467 48 St., Brooklyn, NY 11219. (718)633-8469. FAX: (718)633-8478. Chmn. Rabbi Charlop; Exec. Dir. Rabbi Pollak. Raises funds for the maintenance of schools, kitchens, clinics, and dispensaries in Israel; free loan foundations in Israel.

UNITED ISRAEL APPEAL, INC. (1925). 111 Eighth Ave., Suite 11E, NYC 10011. (212)284-6900. FAX: (212)284-6988. Chmn. Bennett L. Aaron; Exec. V.-Chmn. Daniel R. Allen. Provides funds raised by UJA/Federation campaigns in the U.S. to aid the people of Israel through the programs of the Jewish Agency for Israel, UIA's operating agent. Serves as link between American Jewish community and Jewish Agency for Israel; assists in resettlement and absorption of refugees in Israel, and supervises flow and expenditure of funds for this purpose. *Annual report; newsletters; brochures.*

UNITED STATES COMMITTEE SPORTS FOR ISRAEL (*see* MACCABI USA/SPORTS FOR ISRAEL)

US/ISRAEL WOMEN TO WOMEN (1979). 45 West 36th Street, 10th Floor, NYC 10018. (917)351-0920. FAX: (917)351-0921. E-mail: info@usisraelwomen.org. Ch. Nina Kaufman, esq.; Exec. Dir. Joan Gordon. Provides critical seed money for grassroots efforts advocating equal status and fair treatment for women in all spheres of Israeli life; targets small, innovative, Israeli-run programs that seek to bring about social change in health, education, civil rights, domestic violence, family planning, and other spheres of Israeli life. *Newsletters. (WWW.USISRAELWOMEN.ORG)*

VOLUNTEERS FOR ISRAEL (1982). 330 W. 42 St., Suite 1618, NYC 10036-6902. (212)643-4848. FAX: (212)643-4855. E-mail: vol4israel@aol.com. Pres. Jeanne Schater; Vice Pres. Cora Schilowitz. Provides aid to Israel through volunteer work, building lasting relationships between Israelis and Americans. Affords persons aged 18 and over the opportunity to participate in various duties currently performed by overburdened Israelis on IDF bases and in other settings, enabling them to meet and work closely with Israelis and to gain an inside view of Israeli life and culture.

WOMEN'S LEAGUE FOR ISRAEL, INC. (1928). 160 E. 56 St., NYC 10022. (212)838-1997. FAX: (212)888-5972. Pres. Harriet Lainer; Exec. Dir. Dorothy Leffler. Maintains centers in Haifa, Tel Aviv, Jerusalem, Natanya. Projects include Family Therapy and Training, Centers for the Prevention of Domestic Violence, Meeting Places (supervised centers for noncustodial parents and their children), DROR (supporting families at risk), Yachdav-"Together" (long-term therapy for parents and children), Central School for Training Social Service Counselors, the National Library for Social Work, and the Hebrew University Blind Students' Unit.

WORLD CONFEDERATION OF UNITED ZIONISTS (1946; reorg.1958). 130 E. 59 St., NYC 10022. (212)371-1452. FAX: (212) 371-3265. Co-Pres. Marlene Post & Kalman Sultanik. Promotes Zionist education, sponsors nonparty youth movements in the Diaspora, and strives for an

Israel-oriented creative Jewish survival in the Diaspora. *Zionist Information Views (in English and Spanish).*

WORLD ZIONIST ORGANIZATION-AMERICAN SECTION (1971). 633 Third Ave., 21st fl., NYC 10017. (212)688-3197. Chmn. Kalman Sultanik. As the American section of the overall Zionist body throughout the world, it operates primarily in the field of aliyah from the free countries, education in the Diaspora, youth and Hechalutz, organization and information, cultural institutions, publications; conducts a worldwide Hebrew cultural program including special seminars and pedagogic manuals; disperses information and assists in research projects concerning Israel; promotes, publishes, and distributes books, periodicals, and pamphlets concerning developments in Israel, Zionism, and Jewish history. *Midstream.*

———, DEPARTMENT OF EDUCATION AND CULTURE (1948). 633 Third Ave., 21st fl., NYC 10017. (212)339-6001. FAX: (212) 826-8959. Renders educational services to boards and schools: study programs, books, AV aids, instruction, teacher-in-training service. Judaic and Hebrew subjects. Annual National Bible Contest; Israel summer and winter programs for teachers and students.

———, ISRAEL ALIYAH CENTER (1993). 633 Third Ave., 21st fl., NYC 10017. (212)339-6060. FAX: (212)832-2597. Exec. Dir. N. Amer. Aliyah Delegation, Kalman Grossman. Through 26 offices throughout N. Amer., staffed by *shlichim* (emissaries), works with potential immigrants to plan their future in Israel and processes immigration documents. Through Israel Aliyah Program Center provides support, information, and programming for olim and their families; promotes long-term programs and fact-finding trips to Israel. Cooperates with Tnuat Aliyah in Jerusalem and serves as American contact with Association of Americans and Canadians in Israel.

YOUTH RENEWAL FUND. 488 Madison Ave., 10th fl., NYC 10022. (212)207-3195. FAX: (212)207-8379. E-mail: info@youthrenewalfund.org. Pres. Samuel L. Katz; Comm. & Dev. Mgr. Renatt Brodsky. Provides underprivileged Israeli youth with supplemental educational programs in core subjects including math, science, English, Hebrew, and computers. Since 1989, YRF has raised over $6 million, which has benefited more than 12,500 Israeli children. *YRF Review.* (WWW.YOUTHRENEWALFUND.ORG)

ZIONA. 641 Lexington Avenu, 24th Floor, New York, NY 10022. (212)688-2890. FAX: (212)688-1327. Email: thezionist@aol.com. Pres. Arnie T. Goldfarb; Ex. Vice Pres. Rev. Salomon L. Vaz Dias. ZIONA is a volunteer organization, whose members are motivated and inspired to strengthen their partnership with Israel, ensure Jewish continuity, and realize their potential as a dynamic force in American society. In Israel, ZIONA initiates and supports pace-setting health care, education and youth institutions, and land development to meet the country's changing needs; helps to restore the ancient cemetery on the Mount of Olives in Jerusalem. ZIONA's Medical Organization (H.M.O.), is dedicated to quality and excellence in care and service. Patients from all over Israel and beyond its borders are treated annually, without distinction as to race, religion or nationality. *The Zionist Update* (WWW.ZIONA.ORG)

ZIONIST ORGANIZATION OF AMERICA (1897). ZOA House, 4 E. 34 St., NYC 10016. (212)481-1500. FAX: (212)481-1515. E-mail: email@zoa.com. Natl. Pres. Morton A. Klein; Exec. Dir. Dr. Janice J. Sokolovsky. Strengthens the relationship between Israel and the U.S. through Zionist educational activities that explain Israel's importance to the U.S. and the dangers that Israel faces. Works on behalf of pro-Israel legislation; combats anti-Israel bias in the media, textbooks, travel guides, and on campuses; promotes *aliyah*. Maintains the ZOA House in Tel Aviv, a cultural center, and the Kfar Silver Agricultural and Technical High School in Ashkelon, which provides vocational training for new immigrants. *ZOA Report; Israel and the Middle East:Behind the Headlines.*(WWW.ZOA.ORG)

OVERSEAS AID

AMERICAN FRIENDS OF THE ALLIANCE ISRAÉLITE UNIVERSELLE, INC. (1946). 420 Lexington Ave., Suite 1731, NYC 10170. (212)808-5437. FAX: (212)983-0094. E-mail: afaiu@onsiteaccess.com. Pres. Albert Sibony; Exec. Dir. Warren Green.

Participates in educational and human-rights activities of the AIU and supports the Alliance system of Jewish schools, teachers' colleges, and remedial programs in Israel, North Africa, the Middle East, Europe, and Canada. *Alliance Review.*

AMERICAN JEWISH JOINT DISTRIBUTION COMMITTEE, INC.—JDC (1914). 711 Third Ave., NYC 10017-4014. (212)687-6200. FAX: (212)370-5467. E-mail: newyork@jdcny.org. Pres. Eugene J. Ribakoff; Exec. V.-Pres. Steven Schwager. Provides assistance to Jewish communities in Europe, Asia, Africa, and the Mideast, including welfare programs for Jews in need. Current concerns include:Rescuing Jews from areas of distress, facilitating community development in the former Soviet Union; helping to meet Israel's social service needs by developing innovative programs that create new opportunities for the country's most vulnerable populations; youth activities in Eastern Europe and nonsectarian development and disaster assistance. *Annual Report; Snapshots: JDC's Activities in the Former Soviet Union; JDC: One People, One Heart.* (WWW.JDC.ORG).

AMERICAN JEWISH PHILANTHROPIC FUND (1955). 122 E. 42 St., 12th fl., NYC 10168-1289. (212)755-5640. FAX: (212)644-0979. Pres. Charles J. Tanenbaum. Provides college scholarship assistance to Jewish refugees through pilot programs being administered by the Jewish Family Service in Los Angeles and NYANA in New York.

AMERICAN JEWISH WORLD SERVICE (1985). 45 West 36th Street., NYC 10018. (212) 736-2597. FAX: (212)736-3463. E-mail: jws@ajws.org. Chmn. Don Abramson; Pres. Ruth W. Messinger. Provides nonsectarian, humanitarian assistance and emergency relief to people in need in Africa, Asia, Latin America, Russia, Ukraine, and the Middle East; works in partnership with local nongovernmental organizations to support and implement self-sustaining grassroots development projects; serves as a vehicle through which the Jewish community can act as global citizens. *AJWS Reports (newsletter).* (WWW.AJWS.ORG)

AMERICAN ORT, INC. (1922). 817 Broadway, NYC 10003. (212)353-5800/(800)364-9678. FAX: (212)353-5888. E-mail: info@aort.org. Pres. Robert L. Sill; Exec. Dir. Paul B. Firstenburg. American ORT coordinates all ORT operations in the U.S., in cooperation with Women's American ORT; promotes and raises funds for ORT, the world's largest non-governmental education and training organization, with a global network teaching over 300,000 students in more than 60 countries. In Israel, 100,000 students attend 140 schools and training centers; there are 22 ORT schools and centers in the former Soviet Union; and in the U.S., over 15,000 students are served by ORT's Technical Institutes in Chicago, Los Angeles, and New York, and in Jewish day school programs in Atlanta, Chicago, Cleveland, Detroit, Florida, Los Angeles, and the National Capital Area (Washington, D.C.). *American ORT News; American ORT Annual Report; American ORT Planned Giving News.* (WWW.AORT.ORG)

———, WOMEN'S AMERICAN ORT (1927). 315 Park Ave. S., NYC 10010-3677. (212)505-7700; (800)51-WAORT. FAX: (212)674-3057. E-mail: waort@waort.org. Pres. Carol Linch; Exec. V.P. & Dir. Alice Herman. Strengthens the worldwide Jewish community by empowering people to achieve economic self-sufficiency through technological and vocational training; educates 290,000 students in 60 countries including the United States, Israel and the former Soviet Union; supports ORT programs through membership, fundraising and leadership development; domestic agenda promotes quality public education, women's rights and literacy. *Women's American ORT Reporter; Women's American ORT Annual Report.* (WWW.WAORT.ORG)

CONFERENCE ON JEWISH MATERIAL CLAIMS AGAINST GERMANY, INC. (1951). 15 E. 26 St., Rm. 906, NYC 10010. (212)696-4944. FAX: (212)679-2126. E-mail: info@claimscon.org. Pres. Dr. Israel Singer; Exec. V.-Pres. Gideon Taylor. Represents Jewish survivors in negotiations for compensation from the German government and other entities once controlled by the Nazis. Also an operating agency that administers compensation funds, recovers Jewish property and allocates funds to institutions that serve Holocaust survivors. The Claims Conference—made up of the conference on Jewish Material Claims Against Germany and the Committee for

Jewish Claims on Austria—is one of the founders of the World Jewish Restitution Organization, Memorial Foundation for Jewish Culture and the United Restitution Organization. *Newsletter; Annual Report; Guide to Restitution and Compensation; Special Update*. (WWW.CLAIMSCON.ORG)

HIAS, INC. (HEBREW IMMIGRANT AID SOCIETY) (1880; reorg. 1954). 333 Seventh Ave., NYC 10001-5004. (212)967-4100. FAX: (212)967-4483. E-mail:public@hias.org. Chair Neil Greenbaum; Pres. & CEO Leonard Glickman. The oldest international migration and refugee resettlement agency in the United States, dedicated to assisting persecuted and oppressed people worldwide and delivering them to countries of safe haven. As the migration arm of the American Jewish community, it also advocates for fair and just policies affecting refugees and immigrants. Since its founding in 1881, the agency has rescued more than four and a half million people. *Bi-Annual report*.

THE JEWISH FOUNDATION FOR THE RIGHTEOUS (1986). 305 Seventh Ave., 19th fl., NYC 10001. (212)727-9955. FAX: (212) 727-9956. E-mail: jfr@jfr.org. Pres. Paul Goldberger; Exec. V.P. Stanlee J. Stahl. Provides monthly support to 1,700 aged and needy Righteous Gentiles living in 30 countries who risked their lives to save Jews during the Holocaust. The Foundation's education program focuses on educating teachers and their students about the history of the Holocaust and the significance of altruistic behavior for our society. *Newsletter (3 times a year)*. (WWW.JFR.ORG)

NORTH AMERICAN CONFERENCE ON ETHIOPIAN JEWRY (NACOEJ) (1982). 132 Nassau St., Suite 412, NYC 10038. (212)233-5200. FAX: (212)233-5243. E-mail: nacoej@aol.com. Pres. Kenneth Kaiserman; Exec. Dir. Barbara Ribakove Gordon. Provides programming for Ethiopian Jews in Israel in the areas of education (elementary school, high school and college) and cultural preservation. Assists Ethiopian Jews remaining in Ethiopia. National speakers bureau offers programs to synagogues, schools, and Jewish and non-Jewish organizations. Exhibits of Ethiopian Jewish artifacts, photos, handicrafts, etc. available. *Lifeline (newsletter)*. (WWW.CIRCUS.ORG/NACOEJ)

RE'UTH WOMEN'S SOCIAL SERVICE, INC. (1937). 130 E. 59 St., Suite 1200, NYC 10022. (212)836-1570. FAX: (212)836-1114. Chmn. Ursula Merkin; Pres. Rosa Strygler. Maintains, in Israel, subsidized housing for self-reliant elderly; old-age homes for more dependent elderly; Lichtenstadter Hospital for chronically ill and young accident victims not accepted by other hospitals; subsidized meals; Golden Age clubs. Recently opened a wing for chronically ill children. *Annual dinner journal*.

THANKS TO SCANDINAVIA, INC. (1963). The American Jewish Committee, 165 East 56th Street, 8th Fl., NYC 10022. (212)751-4000 ext. 403. FAX: (212)838-2120. Email: tts@ajc.org. Pres. Richard Netter; Exec. Dir. Rebecca Neuwirth. Provides scholarships and fellowships at American universities and medical centers to students and doctors from Denmark, Finland, Norway, and Sweden in appreciation of the rescue of Jews from the Holocaust. Informs Americans and Scandinavians of these singular examples of humanity and bravery. Speakers available on rescue in Scandinavia; also books, videos, and tapes. *Annual report*.

UJA FEDERATION OF NORTH AMERICA. (1939). (*see* UNITED JEWISH COMMUNITIES)

UNITED JEWISH COMMUNITIES (1999). 111 Eighth Ave., 11th fl., NYC 10011-5201. (212)284-6500. FAX: (212)284-6822. Chmn. James Tisch; Pres./CEO Stephen H. Hoffman. Formed from the merger of the United Jewish Appeal, the Council of Jewish Federations and United Israel Appeal, is the dominant fundraising arm for North American Jewry, and represents 189 Jewish Federations and 400 independent communities across the continent. It reflects the values and traditions of education, leadership, advocacy and social justice, and continuity of community that define the Jewish people.

RELIGIOUS AND EDUCATIONAL ORGANIZATIONS

AGUDATH ISRAEL OF AMERICA (1922). 42 Broadway, NYC, 10004. (212)797-9000. FAX: (212)269-2843. Exec. V.-Pres. Rabbi Shmuel Bloom; Exec. Dir. Rabbi Boruch B. Borchardt. Mobilizes Orthodox Jews to cope with Jewish problems in the spirit of the Torah; speaks out on contemporary issues from an Orthodox viewpoint; sponsors a broad range of projects aimed at enhancing religious living, education, children's welfare, protection of Jewish religious rights, outreach to the assimilated and to arrivals from the former Soviet Union, and social services. *Jewish Observer; Dos Yiddishe Vort; Coalition.*

———, AGUDAH WOMEN OF AMERICA-N'SHEI AGUDATH ISRAEL (1940). 42 Broadway, NYC 10004. (212)363-8940. FAX: (212)747-8763. Presidium Aliza Grund & Rose Isbee; Dir. Hannah Kalish, Esq. Organizes Jewish women for philanthropic work in the U.S. and Israel and for intensive Torah education. Its new division, N'shei C.A.R.E.S., (Community, Awareness, Responsibility, Education, & Support), conducts seminars and support groups promoting the health and well-being of Jewish women and their families.

———, BOYS' DIVISION-PIRCHEI AGUDATH ISRAEL (1925) 42 Broadway, NYC 10004 (212)797-9000. Natl. Coord. Rabbi Shimon Grama. Educates Orthodox Jewish children in Torah; encourages sense of communal responsibility. Branches sponsor weekly youth groups and Jewish welfare projects. National Mishnah contests, rallies, and conventions foster unity on a national level. *Leaders Guides.*

———, GIRLS' DIVISION—BNOS AGUDATH ISRAEL (1921). 42 Broadway, NYC 10004. (646)254-1600. Natl. Dir. Leah Zagelbaum. Sponsors regular weekly programs on the local level and unites girls from throughout the Torah world with extensive regional and national activities. *Kol Bnos.*

———, YOUNG MEN'S DIVISION—ZEIREI AGUDATH ISRAEL (1921) . . . 42 Broadway, NYC 10004. (212)797-9000, ext. 57. Dir. Rabbi Labish Becker. Educates youth to see Torah as source of guidance for all issues facing Jews as individuals and as a people. Inculcates a spirit of activism through projects in religious, Torah-educational, and community-welfare fields. *Am Hatorah; Daf Chizuk.*

AGUDATH ISRAEL WORLD ORGANIZATION (1912) 42 Broadway, 14th Floor, NYC 10004. (212)797-9000. FAX: (212)254-1650. Chmn. Rabbi Yehudah Meir Abramowitz; U.N. Rep. Prof. Harry Reicher, Esq. Represents the interests of Orthodox Jewry on the national and international scenes. Sponsors projects to strengthen Torah life worldwide.

ALEPH: ALLIANCE FOR JEWISH RENEWAL (1963; reorg. 1993). 7318 Germantown Ave., Philadelphia, PA 19119-1720. (215) 247-9700. FAX: (215)247-9703. Bd. Chmn. Dr. Martin Kantrowitz; Rabbinic Dir. R. Daniel Siegel. Serving the worldwide grassroots movement for Jewish spiritual renewal, ALEPH organizes and nurtures communities, trains lay and rabbinic leaders, creates new liturgy and adult learning resources, sponsors conferences, retreats and seminars and works for social and environmental justice. *New Menorah/Or Hador combined quarterly journal and newletter of the Network of Jewish Renewal Communities (NJRC).* (WWW.ALEPH.ORG)

AM KOLEL JUDAIC RESOURCE CENTER (1990). 15 W. Montgomery Ave., Rockville, MD 20850. (301)309-2310. FAX: (301)309-2328. E-mail: amkolel@aol.com. Pres. David Shneyer. An independent Jewish resource center, providing a progressive Jewish voice in the community. Activities include:religion, educational and cultural programs; classes, workshops and seminars; interfaith workshops and programs; tikkun olam (social action) opportunities. The staff provides training and resources to emerging and independent communities throughout N. America. Am Kolel sponsors Jews United for Justice, the Center for Inclusiveness in Jewish Life (CIJL) and Yedid DC. *Directory of Independent Jewish Communities and Havurot in Maryland, DC and Virginia; Rock Creek Haggadah.*

AMERICAN ASSOCIATION OF RABBIS (1978). 350 Fifth Ave., Suite 3304, NYC 10118. (212)244-3350, (516)244-7113. FAX: (516)344-0779. E-mail: tefu@aol.com. Pres. Rabbi Jeffrey Wartenberg; Exec. Dir. Rabbi David L. Dunn. An organization of rabbis serving in pulpits, in areas of education, and in social work. *Quarterly bulletin; monthly newsletter.*

AMERICAN STUDENTS TO ACTIVATE PRIDE (ASAP/OU College Affairs) (1993). 11 Broadway, 14th fl., NYC 10004. (212) 563-4000. FAX: (212)564-9058. E-mail: davidfel@ix.netcom.com. Pres. Zelda Goldsmith; Natl. Dir. Rabbi David

Felsenthal; Chmn. Bernard Falk. A spiritual fitness movement of Jewish college students promoting Torah learning and discussion. Supports 100 learning groups at over 65 campuses as well as regional and national seminars and shabbatonim. *Good Shabbos (weekly); Rimon Discussion Guide (monthly); Jewish Student College Survival Guide (yearly).*

ASSOCIATION FOR JEWISH STUDIES (1969). MB 0001, Brandeis University, PO Box 549110, Waltham, MA 02454-9110. (781)736-2981. FAX: (781)736-2982. E-mail: ajs@brandeis.edu. Pres. Lawrence H. Schiffman; Exec. Dir. Aaron L. Katchen. Seeks to promote, maintain, and improve the teaching of Jewish studies in colleges and universities by sponsoring meetings and conferences, publishing a newsletter and other scholarly materials, aiding in the placement of teachers, coordinating research, and cooperating with other scholarly organizations. *AJS Review; AJS Perspectives.* (WWW.BRANDEIS.EDU/AJS)

ASSOCIATION FOR THE SOCIAL SCIENTIFIC STUDY OF JEWRY (1971). c/o Prof. Carmel U. Chiswick, Department of Economics (m/c 144), University of Illinois at Chicago, 601 S. Morgan Street, Chicago, Il 60607-7121 (312)996-2683. FAX: (312) 996-3344. E-mail: cchis@uic.edu, Israel @brandeis.edu. Pres. Sherry Israel; V.-Pres. Riv-Ellen Prell; Sec.-Treas. Carmel Chiswick. Journal Ed. Rela Geffen; Mng. Ed. Egon Mayer; Newsletter Ed. Gail Glicksman. Arranges academic sessions and facilitates communication among social scientists studying Jewry through meetings, journal, newsletter and related materials and activities. *Contemporary Jewry; ASSJ Newsletter.*

ASSOCIATION OF HILLEL/JEWISH CAMPUS PROFESSIONALS (*see* TEKIAH: ASSOCIATION OF HILLEL/JEWISH CAMPUS PROFESSIONALS)

ASSOCIATION OF ORTHODOX JEWISH SCIENTISTS (1948). 25 W. 45th St., Suite 1405, NYC 10036. (212)840-1166. FAX: (212)840-1514. E-mail: aojs@jerusalemail.com. Pres. Allen J. Bennett, M.D.; Bd. Chmn. Rabbi Nachman Cohen. Seeks to contribute to the development of science within the framework of Orthodox Jewish tradition; to obtain and disseminate information relating to the interaction between the Jewish traditional way of life and scientific developments—on both an ideological and practical level; to assist in the solution of problems pertaining to Orthodox Jews engaged in scientific teaching or research. Two main conventions are held each year. *Intercom; Proceedings; Halacha Bulletin; newsletter.*

B'NAI B'RITH HILLEL FOUNDATIONS (*see* HILLEL)

B'NAI B'RITH YOUTH ORGANIZATION (1924). 1640 Rhode Island Ave., NW, Washington, DC 20036. (202)857-6633. FAX: (212)857-6568. Chmn. Youth Comm. Audrey Y. Brooks; Dir. Sam Fisher. Helps Jewish teenagers achieve self-fulfillment and make a maximum contribution to the Jewish community and their country's culture; helps members acquire a greater knowledge and appreciation of Jewish religion and culture. *Shofar; Monday Morning; BBYO Parents' Line; Hakol; Kesher; The Connector.*

CANTORS ASSEMBLY (1947). 3080 Broadway, Suite 613, NYC 10027. (212)678-8834. FAX: (212)662-8989. E-mail: caoffice@aol.com. Pres. Sheldon Levin; Exec. V.-Pres. Stephen J. Stein. Seeks to unite all cantors who adhere to traditional Judaism and who serve as full-time cantors in bona fide congregations to conserve and promote the musical traditions of the Jews and to elevate the status of the cantorial profession. *Annual Proceedings; Journal of Synagogue Music.* (WWW.CANTORS.ORG)

CENTER FOR CHRISTIAN-JEWISH UNDERSTANDING OF SACRED HEART UNIVERSITY (1992). 5151 Park Ave., Fairfield, CT 06432. (203)365-7592. FAX: (203)365-4815. Pres. Dr. Anthony J. Cernera; Exec. Dir. Rabbi Joseph H. Ehrenkranz. An educational and research division of Sacred Heart University; brings together clergy, laity, scholars, theologians, and educators with the purpose of promoting interreligious research, education, and dialogue, with particular focus on current religious thinking within Christianity and Judaism. *CCJU Perspective.*

CENTRAL CONFERENCE OF AMERICAN RABBIS (1889). 355 Lexington Ave., NYC 10017. (212)972-3636. FAX: (212)692-0819. E-mail: info@ccarnet.org. Pres. Rabbi Martin S. Weiner; Exec. V.-Pres. Rabbi Paul J. Menitoff. Seeks to conserve and promote Judaism and to disseminate its teachings in a liberal spirit. The CCAR Press provides liturgy and prayerbooks to the worldwide Reform Jewish community. *CCAR Journal: A Reform Jewish Quarterly; CCAR Yearbook.* (WWW.CCARNET.ORG)

CLAL—NATIONAL JEWISH CENTER FOR LEARNING AND LEADERSHIP (1974). 440 Park Ave. S., 4th fl., NYC 10016-8012. (212)779-3300. FAX: (212)779-1009. E-mail: info@clal.org. Pres. Rabbi Irwin Kula; Chmn. Barbara B. Friedman; Exec. V.-Chmn. Donna M. Rosenthal. Provides leadership training for lay leaders, rabbis, educators, and communal professionals. A faculty of rabbis and scholars representing all the denominations of Judaism make Judaism come alive, applying the wisdom of the Jewish heritage to help shape tomorrow's Jewish communities. Offers seminars and courses, retreats, symposia and conferences, lecture bureau and the latest on-line information through CLAL web site. *Sacred Days calendar; monographs; holiday brochures; CLAL Update.* (WWW.CLAL.ORG)

COALITION FOR THE ADVANCEMENT OF JEWISH EDUCATION (CAJE) (1977). 261 W. 35 St., #12A, NYC 10001. (212)268-4210. FAX: (212)268-4214. E-mail: cajeny@caje.org. Chmn. Alan Wiener; Exec. Dir. Dr. Eliot G. Spack. *Jewish Education News; CAJE Page; timely curricular publications; Hanukat CAJE series.* (WWW.CAJE.ORG)

CONGRESS OF SECULAR JEWISH ORGANIZATIONS (1970). 19657 Villa Dr. N., Southfield, MI 48076. (248)569-8127. FAX: (248)569-5222. E-mail: csjd@csjd.org. Chmn. Alan J. Wiener; V.-Chmn. Karen Knecht; Exec. Dir. Dr. Eliot G. Spack. An umbrella organization of schools and adult clubs; facilitates exchange of curricula and educational programs for children and adults stressing the Jewish historical and cultural heritage and the continuity of the Jewish people. *New Yorkish (Yiddish literature translations); Haggadah; The Hanuka Festival; Mame-Loshn.*

CONVERSION TO JUDAISM RESOURCE CENTER (1997). 74 Hauppauge Rd., Rm. 53, Commack, NY 11725. (631)462-5826. E-mail: inform@convert.org. Pres. Dr. Lawrence J. Epstein; Exec. Dir. Susan Lustig. Provides information and advice for people who wish to convert to Judaism or who have converted. Puts potential converts in touch with rabbis from all branches of Judaism.

COUNCIL FOR JEWISH EDUCATION (1926) 426 W. 58 St., NYC 10019. (845)368-8657, Fax (845)369-6583. E-mail: wjscje@aol.com. Pres. Dr. Morton J. Summer; Editor Rabbi Irwin E. Witty. Fellowship of Jewish education professionals-administrators, supervisors, and teachers in Hebrew high schools and Jewish teachers colleges-of all ideological groupings; conducts national and regional conferences; represents the Jewish education profession before the Jewish community; cooperates with Jewish Agency Department of Education in promoting Hebrew culture and studies. *Journal of Jewish Education.*

EDAH (1996) 47 W. 34 St., Suite 700, NYC 10001. (212)244-7501. FAX: (212)244-7855. Pres. Murray Laulicht; Dir. Rabbi Saul J. Berman. Gives voice to the ideology and values of modern Orthodoxy, valuing open intellectual inquiry and expression in both secular and religious arenas, engagement with the social, political, and technological realities of the modern world, the religious significance of the State of Israel, and the unity of Clal Yisrael. *Monograph series.* (WWW.EDAH.ORG)

FEDERATION OF JEWISH MEN'S CLUBS (1929). 475 Riverside Dr., Suite 450, NYC 10115. (212)749-8100; (800)288-FJMC. FAX: (212)316-4271. E-mail: fjmc@jtsa.edu. Intl. Pres. Leonard Gimb; Exec. Dir. Rabbi Charles E. Simon. Promotes principles of Conservative Judaism; develops family education and leadership training programs; offers the Art of Jewish Living series and Yom HaShoah Home Commemoration; sponsors Hebrew literacy adult-education program; presents awards for service to American Jewry. Latest innovation-"The Ties that Bind," a motivational and instructional video about Tefillin. *Torchlight; Hearing Men's Voices.* (WWW.FJMC.ORG)

FEDERATION OF RECONSTRUCTIONIST CONGREGATIONS AND HAVUROT (*see* JEWISH RECONSTRUCTIONIST FEDERATION)

HILLEL: THE FOUNDATION FOR JEWISH CAMPUS LIFE (formerly B'NAI B'RITH HILLEL FOUNDATIONS) (1923). 1640

Rhode Island Ave., NW, Washington, DC 20036. (202)857-6560. FAX: (202)857-6693. E-mail: info@hillel.org. Chmn. Intl. Bd. Govs. Edgar M. Bronfman; Chmn. Foundation for Jewish Campus Life Chuck Newman; Pres. & Intl. Dir. Richard M. Joel. The largest Jewish campus organization in the world, its network of 500 regional centers, campus-based foundations, and affiliates serves as a catalyst for creating a celebratory community and a rich, diverse Jewish life on the campus. *The Hillel Annual Report; On Campus newsletter; Hillel Now newsletter; The Hillel Guide to Jewish Life on Campus (published with Princeton Review).* (WWW.HILLEL.ORG)

INSTITUTE FOR COMPUTERS IN JEWISH LIFE (1978). 7074 N. Western Ave., Chicago, IL 60645. (773)262-9200. FAX: (773)262-9298. E-mail: rosirv@aol.com. Pres. Thomas Klutznick; Exec. V.-Pres. Dr. Irving J. Rosenbaum. Explores, develops, and disseminates applications of computer technology to appropriate areas of Jewish life, with special emphasis on Jewish education; creates educational software for use in Jewish schools; provides consulting service and assistance for national Jewish organizations, seminaries, and synagogues.

INTERNATIONAL FEDERATION OF SECULAR HUMANISTIC JEWS (1983). 224 West 35th Street, Suite 410, NYC 10024. (212)564-6711. FAX: (212)564-6721. E-mail: info@ifshj.org. Co-Ch. Felix Posen (Europe), Yair Tzaban (Israel) & Sherwin Wine (USA). The International Federation of Secular Humanistic Jews provides a voice for secular Jews worldwide in their common goal to foster Secular Humanistic Judaism as an option for modern Jewish identity. The IFSHJ develops awareness of Secular and Humanistic Judaism by serving as a resource and for general information, and developing literature, conferences, and communications that promote philosophy of Secular and Humanistic Judaism in the world community. *Newsletter (Hofesh); Contemplate: The International Journal of Secular Jewish Thought.*

INTERNATIONAL INSTITUTE FOR SECULAR HUMANISTIC JUDAISM (1985). 28611 West Twelve Mile Rd., Farmington Hills, MI 48334. (248)476-9532. FAX: (248)476-8509. E-mail: iishj@iishj.org. Chmn. Rabbi Sherwin T. Wine. Established in 1985 in Jerusalem to serve the needs of a growing movement, its two primary purposes are to commission and publish educational materials and to train rabbis, leaders, teachers, and spokespersons for the movement. The Institute has two offices-one in Israel (Jerusalem) and one in N. America and offers educational and training programs in Israel, N. America, and the countries of the former Soviet Union. The N. American office, located in a suburb of Detroit, offers the Rabbinic Program, the Leadership Program, and the Adult Education Program. *Brochure, educational papers, and projects.*

JEWISH CHAUTAUQUA SOCIETY, INC. (sponsored by NORTH AMERICAN FEDERATION OF TEMPLE BROTHERHOODS) (1893). 633 Third Ave., NYC 10017. (212)650-4100/(800)765-6200. FAX: (212)650-4189. E-mail: jcs@uahc.org. Pres. Irving B. Shnaider; Chancellor Stuart J. Aaronson; Exec. Dir. Douglas E. Barden. Works to promote interfaith understanding by sponsoring accredited college courses and one-day lectures on Judaic topics, providing book grants to educational institutions, producing educational videotapes on interfaith topics, and convening interfaith institutes. A founding sponsor of the National Black/Jewish Relations Center at Dillard University. *ACHIM Magazine.*

JEWISH EDUCATION IN MEDIA (1978). PO Box 180, Riverdale Sta., NYC 10471. (212)362-7633. FAX: (203)359-1381. Pres. Ken Asher; Exec. Dir. Rabbi Mark S. Golub. Devoted to producing television, film, and video-cassettes for a popular Jewish audience, in order to inform, entertain, and inspire a greater sense of Jewish identity and Jewish commitment. "L'Chayim," JEM's weekly half-hour program, which is seen nationally on NJT/National Jewish Television, features outstanding figures in the Jewish world addressing issues and events of importance to the Jewish community. (WWW.LCHAYIM.COM)

JEWISH EDUCATION SERVICE OF NORTH AMERICA (JESNA) (1981). 111 Eighth Ave., 11th fl., NYC 10011. (212)284-6950. FAX: (212)284-6951. E-mail: info@jesna.org. Pres. Jonathan S. Woocher; Bd. Ch. Joseph Kanfer. The Jewish Federation system's educational coordinating, planning, and development agency. Promotes excellence in Jewish education by initiating exchange of ideas, programs, and materials; providing information, consultation, educational resources, and policy guidance; and collaborating with partners in N. America and Israel to develop educational programs. *Agenda: Jewish Education; planning guides on Jewish Renaissance; research reports; Jewish Educators Electronic Toolkit.* (WWW.JESNA.ORG)

JEWISH RECONSTRUCTIONIST FEDERATION (formerly FEDERATION OF RECONSTRUCTIONIST CONGREGATIONS AND HAVUROT) (1954). 7804 Montgomery Ave., Suite 9, Elkins Park, PA 19027-2649. (215)782-8500. Fax: (215)782-8805. E-mail: info@jrf.org. Pres. Richard Haimowitz; Exec. V.-Pres. Mark Seal. Provides educational and consulting services to affiliated congregations and havurot; fosters the establishment of new Reconstructionist communities. Publishes *Kol Haneshamah*, an innovative series of prayer books, including a new mahzor and haggadah; provides programmatic materials. Regional offices in New York, Los Angeles, Chicago, Philadelphia, and Washington DC. *Reconstructionism Today.* (WWW.JRF.ORG)

———, RECONSTRUCTIONIST RABBINICAL ASSOCIATION (1974). 1299 Church Rd., Wyncote, PA 19095. (215)576-5210. FAX: (215)576-8051. E-mail: info@therra.org. Pres. Rabbi Nancy Fuchs-Kreimer; Exec. Dir. Rabbi Richard Hirsh. Professional organization for graduates of the Reconstructionist Rabbinical College and other rabbis who identify with Reconstructionist Judaism; cooperates with Jewish Reconstructionist Federation in furthering Reconstructionism in the world. *Newsletters; position papers.*

———, RECONSTRUCTIONIST RABBINICAL COLLEGE (*see* p. 692)

JEWISH TEACHERS ASSOCIATION—MORIM (1931). 45 E. 33 St., Suite 310, NYC 10016-5336. (212)684-0556. Pres. Phyllis L. Pullman; V.-Pres. Ronni David; Sec. Helen Parnes; Treas. Mildred Safar. Protects teachers from abuse of seniority rights; fights the encroachment of anti-Semitism in education; offers scholarships to qualified students; encourages teachers to assume active roles in Jewish communal and religious affairs. *Morim JTA Newsletter.*

KULANU, INC. (formerly AMISHAV USA) (1993). 11603 Gilsan St., Silver Spring, MD 20902. (301)681-5679. FAX: (301) 681-1587. Email: jdzeller@umich.edu. Pres. Jack Zeller; Sec. Karen Primack. Engages in outreach to dispersed Jewish communities around the world who wish to return to their Jewish roots. Current projects include the formal conversion of Shinlung-Menashe tribesmen in India currently practicing Judaism, and supplying materials and rabbis for conversos/marranos in Mexico and Brazil. *Newsletter.*

NATIONAL COMMITTEE FOR FURTHERANCE OF JEWISH EDUCATION (1941). 824 Eastern Pkwy., Brooklyn, NY 11213. (718)735-0200; (800)33-NCFJE. FAX: (718)735-4455. Pres. Dr. Steven Rubel; Bd. Chmn. Rabbi Shea Hecht; Chmn. Exec. Com. Rabbi Sholem Ber Hecht. Seeks to disseminate the ideals of Torah-true education among the youth of America; provides education and compassionate care for the poor, sick, and needy in U.S. and Israel; provides aid to Iranian Jewish youth; sponsors camps and educational functions, family and vocational counseling services, family and early intervention, after-school and preschool programs, drug and alcohol education and prevention; maintains schools in Brooklyn and Queens. Every year distributes 25,000 toys/gifts through Toys for Hospitalized children; runs the Release-time program of Greater NY, offers classes FT/PT through Hadar Matorah Rabbinal Seminary. *Panorama; Cultbusters; Intermarriage; Brimstone & Fire; Focus; A Life Full of Giving.*

NATIONAL COUNCIL OF YOUNG ISRAEL (1912). 3 W. 16 St., NYC 10011. (212)929-1525. FAX: (212)727-9526. E-mail: ncyi@youngisrael.org. Pres. Shlomo Mostofsky; Exec. V.-Pres. Rabbi Pesach Lerner. Through its network of member synagogues in N. America and Israel maintains a program of spiritual, cultural, social, and communal activity aimed at the advancement and perpetuation of traditional, Torah-true Judaism; seeks to instill in American youth an understanding and appreciation of the ethical and spiritual values of Judaism. Sponsors rabbinic and lay leadership conferences, synagogue services, rabbinic services, rabbinic and lay leader training, rabbinic placement, women's division, kosher dining clubs, and youth programs. *Viewpoint Magazine; Divrei Torah Bulletin; NCYI Suggestion Box; The Rabbi's Letter.* (WWW.YOUNGISRAEL.ORG)

———, AMERICAN FRIENDS OF YOUNG ISRAEL IN ISRAEL—YISRAEL HATZA'IR (1926). 3 W. 16 ST., NYC 10011. (212)929-1525. FAX: (212)727-9526. E-mail: ncyi@youngisrael.org. Pres. Meir Mishkoff. Promotes Young Israel synagogues and youth work in Israel; works to help absorb Russian and Ethiopian immigrants.

———, YOUNG ISRAEL DEPARTMENT OF YOUTH AND YOUNG ADULTS ACTIVITIES (reorg. 1981). 3 W. 16 St., NYC 10011. (212)929-1525; (800)617-NCYI. FAX: (212)243-1222. Email: youth@yiyouth.org. Dir. Bradley Karasik. Fosters varied program of activities for the advancement and perpetuation of traditional Torah-true Judaism; instills ethical and spiritual values and appreciation for compatibility of ancient faith of Israel with good Americanism. Runs leadership training programs and youth shabbatonim; support programs for synagogue youth programs; annual national conference of youth directors; ACHVA summer programs for teens IN Israel and U.S.; Nachala summer program in Israel for Yeshiva H.S. girls and Natzach summer program for Yeshiva H.S. boys. *Torah Kidbits; Shabbat Youth Manual; Y.I. Can Assist You; Synagogue Youth Director Handbook.* (WWW.YIYOUTH.ORG)

NATIONAL HAVURAH COMMITTEE (1979). 7135 Germantown Ave., Philadelphia, PA 19119-1720. (215)248-1335. FAX: (215) 248-9760. E-mail: institute@havurah.org. Ch. Neil Satz Litt. A center for Jewish renewal devoted to spreading Jewish ideas, ethics, and religious practices through havurot, participatory and inclusive religious mini-communities. Maintains a directory of N. American havurot and sponsors a weeklong summer institute, regional weekend retreats. *Havurah! (newsletter).* (WWW.HAVURAH.ORG)

NATIONAL JEWISH CENTER FOR LEARNING AND LEADERSHIP (*see* CLAL)

NATIONAL JEWISH COMMITTEE ON SCOUTING (Boy Scouts of America) (1926). 1325 West Walnut Hill Lane, PO Box 152079, Irving, TX 75015-2079. (972)580-2000. FAX: (972)580-7870. Chmn. Rabbi Peter Hyman. Assists Jewish institutions in meeting their needs and concerns through use of the resources of scouting. Works through local Jewish committees on scouting to establish Tiger Cub groups (1st grade), Cub Scout packs, Boy Scout troops, and coed venturer crews in synagogues, Jewish community centers, day schools, and other Jewish organizations wishing to draw Jewish youth. Support materials and resources on request.

NATIONAL JEWISH GIRL SCOUT COMMITTEE (1972). 33 Central Dr., Bronxville, NY 10708. (914)738-3986, (718)252-6072. FAX: (914)738-6752. E-mail: njgsc@aol.com. Chmn. Rabbi Herbert W. Bomzer; Field Chmn. Adele Wasko. Serves to further Jewish education by promoting Jewish award programs, encouraging religious services, promoting cultural exchanges with the Israel Boy and Girl Scouts Federation, and extending membership in the Jewish community by assisting councils in organizing Girl Scout troops and local Jewish Girl Scout committees. *Newsletter.*

NATIONAL JEWISH HOSPITALITY COMMITTEE (1973; reorg. 1993). PO Box 53691, Philadelphia, PA 19105. (800)745-0301. Pres. Rabbi Allen S. Maller; Exec. Dir. Steven S. Jacobs. Assists persons interested in Judaism-for intermarriage, conversion, general information, or to respond to missionaries. *Special reports.*

NORTH AMERICAN ALLIANCE FOR JEWISH YOUTH (199650 West 58th Street, NYC, NY, 10019 (212)494-1023. FAX: (212) 906-9371. E-mail: info@naajewishyouth.org. Chmn. Joseph E. Brenan; Dir. Heather Kibel. Serves the cause of informal Jewish and Zionist education in America; provides a forum for the professional leaders of the major N. American youth movements, camps, Israel programs, and university programs to address common issues and concerns, and to represent those issues with a single voice to the wider Jewish and Zionist community. Sponsors annual Conference on Informal Jewish Education for Jewish youth professionals from across the continent.

OZAR HATORAH, INC. (1946). 625 Broadway, 11th Fl. NYC, 10012. (212)253-7245. FAX: (212)437-4773. Email: agutman@ozarhatorah.org. Pres. Henry Shalom; Sec. Sam Sutton; Exec. Dir. Rabbi Jean

Paul Amoyelle. An international educational network which builds Sephardic communities worldwide through Jewish education.

PARDES PROGRESSIVE ASSOCIATION OF REFORM DAY SCHOOLS (1990). 633 Third Ave., NYC 10017-6778. (212)650-4000. FAX: (480)951-0829. E-mail: educate @uahc.org. Pres. Zita Gardner; Chmn. Carol Nemo. An affiliate of the Union of American Hebrew Congregations; brings together day schools and professional and lay leaders committed to advancing the cause of full-time Reform Jewish education; advocates for the continuing development of day schools within the Reform movement as a means to foster Jewish identity, literacy, and continuity; promotes cooperation among our member schools and with other Jewish organizations that share similar goals. *Visions of Excellence (manual).*

P'EYLIM-LEV L'ACHIM (1951). 1034 E. 12 St. Brooklyn, NY 11230. (718)258-7760. FAX: (718)258-4672. E-mail: joskarmel@ aol.com. Natl. Dir. Rabbi Joseph C. Karmel; Exec. V.-Pres. Rabbi Nachum Barnetsky. Seeks to bring irreligious Jews in Israel back to their heritage. Conducts outreach through 12 major divisions consisting of thousands of volunteers and hundreds of professionals across the country; conducts anti-missionary and assimilation programs; operates shelters for abused women and children; recruits children for Torah schools.

RABBINICAL ALLIANCE OF AMERICA (Igud Harabonim) (1942). 3 W. 16 St., 4th fl., NYC 10011. (212)242-6420. FAX: (212) 255-8313. Pres. Rabbi Abraham B. Hecht. Seeks to promulgate the cause of Torah-true Judaism through an organized rabbinate that is consistently Orthodox; seeks to elevate the position of Orthodox rabbis nationally and to defend the welfare of Jews the world over. Also has Beth Din Rabbinical Court for Jewish divorces, litigation, marriage counseling, and family problems. *Perspective; Nahalim; Torah Message of the Week; Registry.*

RABBINICAL ASSEMBLY (1901). 3080 Broadway, NYC 10027. (212)280-6000. FAX: (212)749-9166. Pres. Rabbi Vernon H. Kurtz; Exec. V.-Pres. Rabbi Joel H. Meyers. The international association of Conservative rabbis; actively promotes the cause of Conservative Judaism and works to benefit *klal yisrael*; publishes learned texts, prayer books, and works of Jewish interest; administers the work of the Committee on Jewish Law and Standards for the Conservative movement; serves the professional and personal needs of its members through publications, conferences, and benefit programs and administers the movement's Joint Placement Commission. *Conservative Judaism; Proceedings of the Rabbinical Assembly; Rabbinical Assembly Newsletter.*

RABBINICAL COUNCIL OF AMERICA, INC. (1923; reorg. 1935). 305 Seventh Ave., Suite 1200, NYC 10001. (212)807-7888. FAX: (212)727-8452. Pres. Rabbi Hershel Billet; Exec. V.-Pres. Rabbi Steven M. Dworken. Promotes Orthodox Judaism in the community; supports institutions for study of Torah; stimulates creation of new traditional agencies. *Hadorom; Tradition.* (WWW.RABBIS.ORG)

SOCIETY FOR HUMANISTIC JUDAISM (1969). 28611 W. Twelve Mile Rd., Farmington Hills, MI 48334. (248)478-7610. FAX: (248)478-3159. E-mail: info@shj.org. Pres. Shari Gelber; Pres. Elect Phillip Gould; Exec. Dir. M. Bonnie Cousens. Serves as a voice for Jews who value their Jewish identity and who seek an alternative to conventional Judaism, who reject supernatural authority and affirm the right of individuals to be the masters of their own lives. Publishes educational and ceremonial materials; organizes congregations and groups. *Humanistic Judaism (quarterly journal); Humanorah (quarterly newsletter).* (WWW.SHJ.ORG)

TEKIAH: ASSOCIATION OF HILLEL/JEWISH CAMPUS PROFESSIONALS (1949). c/o Hillel Foundation of New Orleans, 912 Broadway, New Orleans, LA 70118. (504)866-7060. FAX: (504)861-8909. E-mail: president@tekiah.org. Pres. Rabbi Jeffrey Kurtz-Lendner. Seeks to promote professional relationships and exchanges of experience, develop personnel standards and qualifications, safeguard integrity of Hillel profession; represents and advocates before the Foundation for Jewish Campus Life, Council of Jewish Federations. *Handbook for Hillel Professionals; Guide to Hillel Personnel Practices.* (WWW.TEKIAH.ORG)

TEVA LEARNING CENTER/SHOMREI ADAMAH (1988). 307 Seventh Ave., #900, NYC 10001. (212)807-6376. FAX: (212)

924-5112. E-mail: teva@tevacenter.org. Co-Dir. Nili Simhai; Asst. Dir., Noam Dolgin Exists to renew the ecological wisdom inherent in Judaism. Runs Jewish environmental education programs for Jewish day schools, synagogues, community centers, camps, university groups and other organized groups. *Let the Earth Teach You Torah, Ecology and the Jewish Spirit.*

TORAH SCHOOLS FOR ISRAEL—CHINUCH ATZMAI (1953). 40 Exchange Pl., NYC 10005. (212)248-6200. FAX: (212)248-6202. Exec. Dir. Rabbi Henach Cohen. Conducts information programs for the American Jewish community on activities of the independent Torah schools educational network in Israel; coordinates role of American members of international board of governors; funds special programs of Mercaz Hachinuch Ha-Atzmai B'Eretz Yisroel; funds religous education programs in America and abroad.

TORAH UMESORAH—NATIONAL SOCIETY FOR HEBREW DAY SCHOOLS (1944). 160 Broadway, NYC 10038. (212)227-1000. FAX: (212)406-6934. E-mail: umesorah @aol.com. Chmn. David Singer; Pres. Yaakov Rajchenbach; Exec. V.-Pres. Rabbi Joshua Fishman. Establishes Hebrew day schools and Yeshivas in U.S. and Canada and provides a full gamut of services, including placement, curriculum guidance, and teacher training. Parent Enrichment Program provides enhanced educational experience for students from less Jewishly educated and marginally affiliated homes through parent-education programs and Partners in Torah, a one-on-one learning program. Publishes textbooks; runs shabbatonim, extracurricular activities; national PTA groups; national and regional teacher conventions. *Olomeinu-Our World.*

———, NATIONAL ASSOCIATION OF HEBREW DAY SCHOOL PARENT-TEACHER ASSOCIATIONS (1948). 160 Broadway, NYC 10038. (212)227-1000. FAX: (212)406-6934. Natl. PTA Coord. Bernice Brand. Acts as a clearinghouse and service agency to PTAs of Hebrew day schools; organizes parent education courses and sets up programs for individual PTAs. *Fundraising with a Flair; PTA with a Purpose for the Hebrew Day School.*

———, NATIONAL CONFERENCE OF YESHIVA PRINCIPALS (1956). 160 Broadway, NYC 10038. (212)227-1000. FAX: (212)406-6934. E-mail: umesorah@aol. com. Pres. Rabbi Rabbi Schneur Aisenstark; Bd. Chmn. Rabbi Dov Leibenstein; Exec. V.-Pres. Rabbi A. Moshe Possick. Professional organization of elementary and secondary yeshivah/day school principals providing yeshivah/day schools with school evaluation and guidance, teacher and principal conferences-including a Mid-Winter Conference and a National Educators Convention; offers placement service for principals and teachers in yeshivah/day schools. *Directory of Elementary Schools and High Schools.*

———, NATIONAL YESHIVA TEACHERS BOARD OF LICENSE (1953). 160 Broadway, NYC 10038. (212)227-1000. Exec. V.-Pres. Rabbi Joshua Fishman; Dir. Rabbi Yitzchock Merkin. Issues licenses to qualified instructors for all grades of the Hebrew day school and the general field of Torah education.

UNION FOR TRADITIONAL JUDAISM (1984). 241 Cedar Lane, Teaneck, NJ 07666. (201)801-0707. FAX: (201)801-0449. Pres. Burton G. Greenblatt; Exec. V.-Pres. Rabbi Ronald D. Price. Through innovative outreach programs, seeks to bring the greatest possible number of Jews closer to an open-minded observant Jewish lifestyle. Activities include Kashrut Initiative, Operation Pesah, the Panel of Halakhic Inquiry, Speakers Bureau, adult and youth conferences, and congregational services. Includes, since 1992, the Morashah rabbinic fellowship. *Hagahelet (quarterly newsletter); Cornerstone (journal); Tomeikh Kahalakhah (Jewish legal responsa).*

UNION OF AMERICAN HEBREW CONGREGATIONS (1873). 633 Third Ave., NYC 10017-6778. (212)650-4000. FAX: (212) 650-4169. E-mail: uahc@uahc.org. Pres. Rabbi Eric H. Yoffie; V.-Pres. Rabbi Lennard R. Thal; Bd. Chmn. Russell Silverman. Serves as the central congregational body of Reform Judaism in the Western Hemisphere; serves its approximately 900 affiliated temples and membership with religious, educational, cultural, and administrative programs. *Reform Judaism.* (WWW.UAHC.ORG)

———, AMERICAN CONFERENCE OF CANTORS (1953). 5591 Chamblee Dunwoody Rd. Bldg. 1360, Ste. 200, Atlanta, GA

30338. (770)390-0006. FAX: (770)390-0020. E-mail: accantors@aol.com. Pres. Richard Cohen, Exec. V.-Pres. Scott E. Colbert Exec. VP; Dir. of Placement Ida Rae Cohana; Admin. Asst. Deborah Barber. Members are invested or certified by accredited seminars, i.e., Hebrew Union College-Jewish Institute of Religion School of Sacred Music. Through the Joint Cantorial Placement Commission, the ACC serves Reform congregations seeking cantors. Dedicated to creative Judaism, preserving the past, and encouraging new and vital approaches to religious ritual, liturgical music and ceremony. *Koleinu.*

———, COMMISSION ON SOCIAL ACTION OF REFORM JUDAISM (see p. 647)

———, COMMISSION ON SYNAGOGUE MANAGEMENT (UAHC-CCAR) (1962). 633 Third Ave., NYC 10017-6778. (212)650-4040. FAX: (212)650-4239. Chmn. Marshall Krolick; Dir. Dale A. Glasser. Assists congregations in management, finance, building maintenance, design, construction, and art aspects of synagogues; maintains the Synagogue Architectural Library.

———, NATA (NATIONAL ASSOCIATION OF TEMPLE ADMINISTRATORS) (1941). 6114 La Salle Ave., Box 731, Oakland, CA 94611. (800)966-6282. FAX: (925)283-7713. E-mail: nataorg@hotmail.com. FTA Elizabeth L. Hirsh. Professional organization for UAHC synagogue administrators. Sponsors graduate training in synagogue management with Hebrew Union College; offers in-service training, workshops, and conferences leading to certification; provides NATA Consulting Service, NATA Placement Service for synagogues seeking advice or professional administrators; establishes professional standards. *NATA Journal.*

———, NATIONAL ASSOCIATION OF TEMPLE EDUCATORS (NATE) (1955). 633 Third Ave., 7th fl., NYC 10017-6778. (212)452-6510. FAX: (212)452-6512. E-mail: nateoff@aol.com. Pres. Julie A. Vanek; Exec. Dir. Rabbi Stanley T. Schickler. Represents educators within the general body of Reform Judaism; fosters the full-time profession of the Jewish educator; encourages the growth and development of Jewish religious education consistent with the aims of Reform Judaism; stimulates communal interest in and responsibility for Jewish religious education. *NATE NEWS.* (WWW.RJ.ORG/NATE)

———, NORTH AMERICAN FEDERATION OF TEMPLE BROTHERHOODS (1923). 633 Third Ave., NYC 10017. (212)650-4100. FAX: (212)650-4189. E-mail: nftb@uahc.org. Pres.Irving B. Shnaider; JCS Chancellor Stuart J. Aaronson; Exec. Dir. Douglas Barden. Dedicated to enhancing the world through the ideal of brotherhood, NFTB and its 300 affiliated clubs are actively involved in education, social action, youth activities, and other programs that contribute to temple and community life. Supports the Jewish Chautauqua Society, an interfaith educational project. *ACHIM (formerly Brotherhood magazine)* (WWW.RJ.ORG/NFTB)

———, UAHC DEPARTMENT OF JEWISH EDUCATION (1923). 633 Third Ave., 7th fl., NYC 10017. (212)650-4112. FAX: (212)650-4229. E-mail: jkatzew@uahc.org. Chmn. Dr. Rabbi Jan Katzew, Robert Heller; Dir. Dr. Rabbi Jan Katzew. Long-range planning and policy development for congregational programs of lifelong education; materials concerning Reform Jewish Outreach, Teacher Development and Reform Day Schools; activities administered by the UAHC Department of Education. *V'Shinantam; Torah at the Center, Family Shabbat Table Talk, Galilee Diary, Jewish Parent Page.*

———, WOMEN OF REFORM JUDAISM—THE FEDERATION OF TEMPLE SISTERHOODS (1913). 633 Third Ave., NYC 10017. (212)650-4050. FAX: (212)650-4059. E-mail: wrj@uahc.org. Pres. Helene H. Waranch; Exec. Dir. Ellen Y. Rosenberg. Serves more than 600 sisterhoods of Reform Judaism; promotes interreligious understanding and social justice; provides funding for scholarships for rabbinic students; founded the Jewish Braille Institute, which provides braille and large-type Judaic materials for Jewish blind; supports projects for Israel; is the women's agency of Reform Judaism, an affiliate of the UAHC; works in behalf of the Hebrew Union College-Jewish Institute of Religion and the World Union for Progressive Judaism. *Notes for Now; Art Calendar; Windows on WRJ.* (WWW.RJ.ORG/WRJ)

———, YOUTH DIVISION AND NORTH AMERICAN FEDERATION OF TEMPLE YOUTH (1939). 633 Third Ave, NYC

10017-6778. (212)650-4070. FAX: (212) 650-4199. E-mail: youthdivision@uahc.org. Dir. UAHC Youth Div. Rabbi Allan L. Smith; Assoc. Dir. UAHC Youth Div. Rabbi Andrew Davids. Dedicated to Jewishly enhancing the lives of the young people of North America's Reform congregations through a program of informal education carried out in UAHC Camp-Institutes (11 camps for grades 2 and up), UAHC/NFTY Israel Programs (summer and semester), European and domestic teen travel, NFTY/Junior & Senior High School Programs (youth groups), and Kesher/College Education Department (Reform havurot on campuses).

UNION OF ORTHODOX JEWISH CONGREGATIONS OF AMERICA (1898). 11 Broadway, 14th fl., NYC 10004. (212)563-4000. FAX: (212)564-9058. E-mail: ou@ou.org. Pres. Harvey Blitz.; Exec. V.-Pres. Rabbi Dr. Tzvi Hersh Weinreb. Serves as the national central body of Orthodox synagogues; national OU kashrut supervision and certification service; sponsors Institute for Public Affairs; National Conference of Synagogue Youth; National Jewish Council for the Disabled; Israel Center in Jerusalem; Torah Center in the Ukraine; New Young Leadership Division; Pardes; provides educational, religious, and organization programs, events, and guidance to synagogues and groups; represents the Orthodox Jewish community to governmental and civic bodies and the general Jewish community. *Jewish Action magazine; OU Kosher Directory; OU Passover Directory; OU News Reporter; Synagogue Trends; Our Way magazine; Yachad magazine; Luach & Limud Personal Torah Study, Leadership Briefing, Behind the Union Symbol.* (WWW.OU.ORG)

———, INSTITUTE FOR PUBLIC AFFAIRS (1989). 11 Broadway, 14th fl., NYC 10004. (212)613-8124. FAX: (212)613-0724. E-mail: ipa@ou.org. Pres. Harvey Blitz; Chmn. Richard Stone; Dir. Nathan Diament; Dir. Intl. Affairs & Comm. Rel. Betty Ehrenberg. Serves as the policy analysis, advocacy, mobilization, and programming department responsible for representing Orthodox/traditional American Jewry. *IPA Currents (quarterly newsletter).*

———, NATIONAL CONFERENCE OF SYNAGOGUE YOUTH (1954). 11 Broadway, 14th fl., NYC 10004. (212)563-4000. E-mail: ncsy@ou.org. Central body for youth groups of Orthodox congregations; provides educational guidance, Torah study groups, community service, program consultation, Torah library, Torah fund scholarships, Ben Zakkai Honor Society, Friends of NCSY, weeklong seminars, Israel Summer Experience for teens and Camp NCSY East Summer Kollel & Michlelet, Teen Torah Center. Divisions include Senior NCSY, Junior NCSY for preteens, Our Way for the Jewish deaf, Yachad for the developmentally disabled, Israel Center in Jerusalem, and NCSY in Israel. *Keeping Posted with NCSY; Darchei Da'at.*

———, WOMEN'S BRANCH OF THE ORTHODOX UNION (1923). 156 Fifth Ave., NYC 10010. (212)929-8857. Pres. Sophie Ebert. Umbrella organization of Orthodox sisterhoods in U.S. and Canada, educating women in Jewish learning and observance; provides programming, leadership, and organizational guidance, conferences, conventions, Marriage Committee and projects concerning mikvah, Shalom Task Force, and Welcoming Guests. Works with Orthodox Union Commissions and outreach; supports Stern and Touro College scholarships and Jewish braille publications; supplies Shabbat candelabra for hospital patients; NGO representative at UN. *Hachodesh; Hakol.*

UNION OF ORTHODOX RABBIS OF THE UNITED STATES AND CANADA (1902). 235 E. Broadway, NYC 10002. (212)964-6337(8). Dir. Rabbi Hersh M. Ginsberg. Seeks to foster and promote Torah-true Judaism in the U.S. and Canada; assists in the establishment and maintenance of yeshivot in the U.S.; maintains committee on marriage and divorce and aids individuals with marital difficulties; disseminates knowledge of traditional Jewish rites and practices and publishes regulations on synagogal structure; maintains rabbinical court for resolving individual and communal conflicts. *HaPardes.*

UNION OF SEPHARDIC CONGREGATIONS, INC. (1929). 8 W. 70 St., NYC 10023. (212)873-0300. FAX: (212)724-6165. Pres. Rabbi Marc D. Angel; Bd. Chmn. Edward Misrahi. Promotes the religious interests of Sephardic Jews; prints and distributes Sephardic prayer books. *Annual International Directory of Sephardic Congregations.*

UNITED LUBAVITCHER YESHIVOTH (1940). 841-853 Ocean Pkwy., Brooklyn, NY 11230. (718)859-7600. FAX: (718)434-1519. Supports and organizes Jewish day schools and rabbinical seminaries in the U.S. and abroad.

UNITED SYNAGOGUE OF CONSERVATIVE JUDAISM (1913). 155 Fifth Ave., NYC 10010-6802. (212)533-7800. FAX: (212)353-9439. E-mail: info@uscj.org. Pres. Judy Yudof; Exec. V.-Pres. Rabbi Jerome M. Epstein. International organization of 760 Conservative congregations. Maintains 17 departments and 15 regional offices to assist its affiliates with religious, educational, youth, community, and administrative programming and guidance; aims to enhance the cause of Conservative Judaism, further religious observance, encourage establishment of Jewish religious schools, draw youth closer to Jewish tradition. Extensive Israel programs. *United Synagogue Review; Art/Engagement Calendar; Program Suggestions; Directory & Resource Guide; Book Service Catalogue of Publications.* (WWW.USCJ.ORG)

———, COMMISSION ON JEWISH EDUCATION (1930). 155 Fifth Ave., NYC 10010. (212)533-7800. FAX: (212)353-9439. E-mail: education@uscj.org. Chmn. Temma Kingsley; Dir. Rabbi Robert Abramson. Develops educational policy for the United Synagogue of Conservative Judaism and sets the educational direction for Conservative congregations, their schools, and the Solomon Schechter Day Schools. Seeks to enhance the educational effectiveness of congregations through the publication of materials and in-service programs. *Tov L'Horot; Your Child; Shiboley Schechter; Advisories.*

———, COMMISSION ON SOCIAL ACTION AND PUBLIC POLICY (1958). 155 Fifth Ave., NYC 10010. (212)533-7800. FAX: (212)353-9439. Chmn. Hon. Jerry Wagner; Dir. Sarrae G. Crane. Develops and implements positions and programs on issues of social action and public policy for the United Synagogue of Conservative Judaism; represents these positions to other Jewish and civic organizations, the media, and government; and provides guidance, both informational and programmatic, to its affiliated congregations in these areas. *HaMa'aseh.*

———, JEWISH EDUCATORS ASSEMBLY (1951). 426 W. 58 St., NYC 10019. (212)765-3303. FAX: (212)765-3310. Pres. Dr. Mark S. Silk; Exec. Dir. Susan Mitrani Knapp. The Jewish Educators Assembly is the professional organization for the Jewish educators within the Conservative movement. The JEA provides a forum to discuss the trends and challenges within Conservative Jewish education as well as provides professional development and a sense of community for educational directors. Services offered: annual conference, placement service, career services, research grants, personal benefits and *V'Aleh Ha-Chadashot* newsletter.

———, KADIMA (formerly PRE-USY; reorg. 1968). 155 Fifth Ave., NYC 10010-6802. (212)533-7800. FAX: (212)353-9439. E-mail: kadima@uscj.org. Dir. Karen L. Stein; Dir. of Youth Activities Jules A Gutin. Involves Jewish preteens in a meaningful religious, educational, and social environment; fosters a sense of identity and commitment to the Jewish community and the Conservative movement; conducts synagogue-based chapter programs and regional Kadima days and weekends. *Mitzvah of the Month; Kadima Kesher; Chagim; Advisors Aid; Games; quarterly Kol Kadima magazine.*

———, NORTH AMERICAN ASSOCIATION OF SYNAGOGUE EXECUTIVES (1948). 155 Fifth Ave., NYC 10010. (212)533-7800, ext 2609. FAX: (631)732-9461. E-mail: office@naase.org. Pres. Judith Kranz, FSA, ATz; Hon. Pres. Amir Pilch, FSA; Exec. Dir. Harry Hauser. Aids congregations affiliated with the United Synagogue of Conservative Judaism to further the aims of Conservative Judaism through more effective administration (Program for Assistance by Liaisons to Synagogues—PALS); advances professional standards and promotes new methods in administration; cooperates in United Synagogue placement services and administrative surveys. *NAASE Connections Newsletter; NAASE Journal.*

———, UNITED SYNAGOGUE YOUTH (1951). 155 Fifth Ave., NYC 10010. (212)533-7800. FAX: (212)353-9439. E-mail: youth@uscj.org. Pres. Jesse Olitzky; Exec. Dir. Jules A. Gutin. Seeks to strengthen identification with Conservative Judaism, based on the personality, development, needs, and interests of the adolescent, in a mitzvah framework. *Achshav; Tikun Olam; A.J. Heschel Honor Society Newsletter; SATO Newsletter; USY Program Bank; Hakesher Newsletter for Advisors.*

VAAD MISHMERETH STAM (1976). 4907 16th Ave., Brooklyn, NYC 11204. (718) 438-4980. FAX: (718)438-9343. Pres. Rabbi David L. Greenfield. A nonprofit consumer-protection agency dedicated to preserving and protecting the halakhic integrity of Torah scrolls, tefillin, phylacteries, and mezuzoth. Publishes material for laymen and scholars in the field of scribal arts; makes presentations and conducts examination campaigns in schools and synagogues; created an optical software system to detect possible textual errors in stam. Teaching and certifying sofrim worldwide. Offices in Israel, Strasbourg, Chicago, London, Manchester, Montreal, and Zurich. Publishes *Guide to Mezuzah* and *Encyclopedia of the Secret Aleph Beth. The Jewish Quill; and many other publications.*

WASHINGTON INSTITUTE FOR JEWISH LEADERSHIP & VALUES (1988). 6101 Montrose Road, Suite 200, Rockville, MD 20852. (301)770-5070. FAX: (301)770-6365. E-mail: wijlv@wijlv.org. Founder/Pres. Rabbi Sidney Schwarz; Bd. Chmn. Mark Levitt. The Washington Institute for Jewish Leadership and Values is a non-profit educational organization dedicated to the renewal of American Jewish life through the integration of Jewish learning, values and social responsibility. Our flagship program, *Panim el Panim*:High School in Washington, each year brings over 1,000 Jewish teens from across the country to Washington, D.C. to learn about political and social activism in the context of Jewish learning and values. We also sponsor the Jewish Civics Initiative, the largest national Jewish service/learning program for teens. The Institute also sponsors a Synagogue Transformation Project, and conducts leadership training. *Jewish Civics: A Tikkun Olam/World Repair Manual; Jews, Judaism and Civic Responsibility.*

WOMEN'S LEAGUE FOR CONSERVATIVE JUDAISM (1918). 475 Riverside Drive, NYC 10115. (212)870-1260. FAX: (212)772-3507. Email: womensleague@wlcj.org. Pres. Janet Tobin; Exec. Dir. Bernice Balter. Parent body of Conservative (Masorti) women's synagogue groups in U.S., Canada, Puerto Rico, Mexico, and Israel; provides programs and resources in Jewish education, social action, Israel affairs, American and Canadian public affairs, leadership training, community service programs for persons with disabilities, conferences on world affairs, study institutes, publicity techniques; publishes books of Jewish interest; contributes to support of Jewish Theological Seminary of America. *Women's League Outlook magazine; Ba'Olam world affairs newsletter.*

WORLD COUNCIL OF CONSERVATIVE/MASORTI SYNAGOGUES (1957). 155 Fifth Ave., NYC 10010. (212)533-7800, ext. 2014, 2018. FAX: (212)533-9439. E-mail: worldcouncil@compuserve.com. Pres. Rabbi Alan Silverstein; Rabbi of Council, Rabbi Benjamin Z. Kreitman. Organize and support Conservative/Masorti congregations in Latin America, Europe, Australia and South Africa. *World Spectrum.*

WORLD UNION FOR PROGRESSIVE JUDAISM (1926). 633 Third Ave. NYC 10017. (212)650-4280. FAX: (212)650-4289. E-mail: arzawupjna@uahc.org. Pres. Ruth Cohen; Exec. Dir. Rabbi Uri Regev. International umbrella organization of Liberal Judaism; promotes and coordinates efforts of Liberal congregations throughout the world; starts new congregations, recruits rabbis and rabbinical students for all countries; organizes international conferences of Liberal Jews. *World News.*

SCHOOLS, INSTITUTIONS

THE ACADEMY FOR JEWISH RELIGION (1956). 6301 Riverdale Avenue, Riverdale, NY 10471. (718)543-9360. FAX: (718) 5431038. E-mail: admin@ajrsem.org. Acting Pres. Rabbi David Greenstein; Dean Rabbi Dr. Ora Horn Prouser. The pluralistic rabbinic and cantorial seminary uniting teachers and students from all streams of Judaism, passionately committed to their own paths, yet respectful and supportive of the paths of others. Emphasis on integrating learning, practice, and spirt through traditional and contemporary approaches. Training for congregations, chaplaincy, education, community work.

ANNENBERG RESEARCH INSTITUTE (*see* CENTER FOR JUDAIC STUDIES)

BALTIMORE HEBREW UNIVERSITY (1919). 5800 Park Heights Ave., Baltimore, MD 21215. (410)578-6900; (888)248-7420. FAX: (410)578-6940. E-mail: bhu@bhu.edu. Pres. Dr. Robert O. Freedman; Bd. Chmn. Michael Hettleman. Offers PhD, MA, BA, and AA programs in Jewish studies, Jewish education, biblical and Near Eastern archaeology, philosophy, literature, history, Hebrew language, literature, and contemporary Jewish civilization; School of Continuing Education; Joseph Meyerhoff Library; community lectures, film series, seminars. *BHU Today.* (WWW.BHU.EDU)

———, BALTIMORE INSTITUTE FOR JEWISH COMMUNAL SERVICE. (410)578-6932. FAX: (410)578-1803. Dir. Karen S. Bernstein; Co-Dir. Cindy Goldstein. Trains Jewish communal professionals; offers a joint degree program: an MA from BHU and an MAJE from BHU, an MSW from U. of Maryland School of Social Work, or an MPS in policy sciences from UMBC; MA with Meyerhoff Graduate School and Johns Hopkins U. in nonprofit management.

———, BERNARD MANEKIN SCHOOL OF UNDERGRADUATE STUDIES. Dean Dr. George Berlin. BA program; interinstitutional program with Johns Hopkins University; interdisciplinary concentrations: contemporary Middle East, American Jewish culture, and the humanities; Russian/English program for new Americans; assoc. of arts (AA) degree in Jewish studies.

———, LEONARD AND HELEN R. STULMAN SCHOOL OF CONTINUING EDUCATION. Dean Dr. George Berlin. Noncredit program open to the community, offering a variety of courses, trips, and events covering a range of Jewish subjects. *Elderhostel, Ulpan Modern Hebrew Department.*

———, PEGGY MEYERHOFF PEARLSTONE SCHOOL OF GRADUATE STUDIES. Dean Dr. Barry M. Gittlen. PhD and MA programs; MA in Jewish studies; MAJE in Jewish education; PhD in Jewish studies; a double master's degree with an MA from BHU and an MAJE from BHU, an MSW from the University of Maryland School of Social Work, or an MPS in policy sciences from UMBC; MA with Baltimore Institute and Johns Hopkins U. in nonprofit management.

BRAMSON ORT COLLEGE (1977). 69-30 Austin St., Forest Hills, NY 11375. (718)261-5800. Dean of Academic Services Barry Glotzer. A two-year Jewish technical college offering certificates and associate degrees in technology and business fields, including accounting, computer programming, electronics technology, business management, office technology. Additional locations in Brooklyn.

BRANDEIS-BARDIN INSTITUTE (1941). 1101 Peppertree Lane, Brandeis, CA 93064. (805)582-4450. FAX: (805)526-1398. E-mail: info@thebbi.org. Pres. Dr. Lee T. Bycel; Chair, Bd. Of Dir. Helen Zukin. A Jewish pluralistic, nondenominational educational institution providing programs for people of all ages:BCI (Brandeis Collegiate Institute), a summer leadership program for college-age adults from around the world; Camp Alonim, a summer Jewish experience for children 8-16; Gan Alonim Day Camp for children in kindergarten to 6th grade; weekend retreats for adults with leading contemporary Jewish scholars-in-residence; Jewish music concerts; Family Days and Weekends, Grandparents Weekends, Elderhostel, Young Adult programs, dance weekends, institute for newly marrieds. *Monthly Updates; BBI Newsletter.*

BRANDEIS UNIVERSITY (1948). 415 South St., Waltham, MA 02454. (781)736-2000. Pres. Jehuda Reinharz; Provost Irving Epstein; Exec. V.-Pres./CEO Peter B. French; Sr. V.-Pres. of Devel. Nancy Winship. Founded under Jewish sponsorship as a nonsectarian institution offering undergraduate and graduate education. The Lown School is the center for all programs of teaching and research in Judaic studies, ancient Near Eastern studies, and Islamic and modern Middle Eastern studies. The school includes the Department of Near Eastern and Judaic Studies; the Hornstein Program in Jewish Communal Service, a professional training program; the Cohen Center for Modern Jewish Studies, which conducts research and teaching in contemporary Jewish studies, primarily in American Jewish studies; and the Tauber Institute for the study of European Jewry. *Various newsletters, scholarly publications.*

———, NATIONAL WOMEN'S COMMITTEE (1948). MS 132, Waltham, MA 02454-9110. (781)736-4160. FAX: (781)736-

4183. E-mail: bunwc@brandeis.edu. Pres. Marcia F. Levy; Exec. Dir. Joan C. Bowen. Provides support for Brandeis University and its Libraries. It connects Brandeis, a non-sectarian university founded by the American Jewish community, to its members and their communities through programs that reflect the ideals of social justice and academic excellence. In addition to its fundraising activities, NWC offers its members opportunity for intellectual pursuit, continuing education, community service, social interaction, personal enrichment and leadership development. Open to all, regardless of race, religion, nationality or gender. *Connecting.*

CENTER FOR JUDAIC STUDIES, School of Arts and Sciences, University of Pennsylvania. 420 Walnut St., Philadelphia, PA 19106. (215)238-1290. FAX: (215)238-1540. Dir. David B. Ruderman. *Jewish Quarterly Review.*

CLEVELAND COLLEGE OF JEWISH STUDIES (1964). 26500 Shaker Blvd., Beachwood, OH 44122. (216)464-4050. FAX: (216)464-5827. Pres. David S. Ariel; Dir. of Student Services Diane M. Kleinman. Provides courses in all areas of Judaic and Hebrew studies to adults and college-age students; offers continuing education for Jewish educators and administrators; serves as a center for Jewish life and culture; expands the availability of courses in Judaic studies by exchanging faculty, students, and credits with neighboring academic institutions; grants bachelor's and master's degrees.

DROPSIE COLLEGE FOR HEBREW AND COGNATE LEARNING (*see* CENTER FOR JUDAIC STUDIES)

GRATZ COLLEGE (1895). 7605 Old York Rd., Melrose Park, PA 19027. (215)635-7300. FAX: (215)635-7320. Bd. Chmn. Dr. Matti K. Gershenfeld; Pres. Dr. Jonathan Rosenbaum. Offers a wide variety of undergraduate and graduate degrees and continuing education programs in Judaic, Hebraic, and Middle Eastern studies. Grants BA and MA in Jewish studies, MA in Jewish education (joint program in special needs education with La Salle U.), MA in Jewish music, MA in Jewish liberal studies, MA in Jewish communal studies, certificates in Jewish communal studies (joint program with U. of Penna. School of Social Work and Temple U), Jewish education, Israel studies, Judaica librarianship (joint program with Drexel U.), and Jewish music. Joint graduate program with Reconstructionist Rabbinical College in Jewish education and Jewish music. Netzky Division of Continuing Education and Jewish Community High School. *Various newsletters, annual academic bulletin, scholarly publications, centennial volume, Gratz newsletter and occasional papers.*

HEBREW COLLEGE (1921). 160 Herrick Road, Newton Center, MA 02459. (617) 559-8600. FAX: (617)559-8601. Pres. Dr. David M. Gordis; Ch. Bd. Dir. Mickey Cail; Ch. Bd. Trustees Ted Benard-Cutler. Through training in Jewish texts, history, literature, ethics, and Hebrew language, prepares students to become literate participants in the global Jewish community. Offers graduate and undergraduate degrees and certificates in all aspects of Jewish education, Jewish studies, and Jewish music; serves students of all ages through its Prozdor High School, Camp Yavneh, Ulpan Center for Adult Jewish Learning, and *Me'ah*—One Hundred Hours of Adult Jewish Learning. *Hebrew College Today; Likut.* (WWW.HEBREWCOLLEGE.EDU)

HEBREW SEMINARY OF THE DEAF (1992). 4435 W. Oakton, Skokie, IL 60076. (847)677-3330. FAX: (847)677-7945. E-mail: hebrewsemdeaf@juno.com. Pres. Rabbi Douglas Goldhamer; Bd. Chmn. Alan Crane. Trains deaf and hearing men and women to become rabbis and teachers for Jewish deaf communities across America. All classes in the 5-year program are interpreted in Sign Language. Rabbis teaching in the seminary are Reform, Conservative, and Reconstructionist.

HEBREW THEOLOGICAL COLLEGE (1922). 7135 N. Carpenter Rd., Skokie, IL 60077. (847)982-2500. FAX: (847)674-6381. E-mail: htc@htcnet.edu. Chancellor Rabbi Dr. Jerold Isenberg; Rosh Hayeshiva Rabbi Shlomo Morgenstern. Hebrew Theological College, a fully accredited institution, includes the Bet Midrash for Men, Blitstein Institute for Women, Kanter School of Liberal Arts and Sciences, Fasman Yeshiva High School, Community Service Division, Silber Memorial Library, Bellows Kollel, Israel Experience Program and Yeshivas HaKayitz summer camp. *Likutei Pshatim, Shmuel, Academic Journal.* (WWW.HTCNET.EDU)

HEBREW UNION COLLEGE—JEWISH INSTITUTE OF RELIGION (1875). 3101 Clifton Ave., Cincinnati, OH 45220. (513)221-1875. FAX: (513)221-1847. Pres. Rabbi David Ellenson; Chancellor Dr. Alfred Gottschalk; V.-Pres. Admin. & Finance Arthur R. Grant; V.-Pres. Devel. Erica S. Frederick; Chmn. Bd. Govs. Burton Lehman; Provost Dr. Norman J. Cohen. Academic centers: 3101 Clifton Ave., Cincinnati, OH 45220 (1875), Dean Rabbi Kenneth Ehrlich. 1 W. 4 St., NYC 10012 (1922), Dean Rabbi Aaron Panken. FAX: (212)388-1720. 3077 University Ave., Los Angeles, CA 90007 (1954), Dean Rabbi Lewis Barth; FAX: (213)747-6128. 13 King David St., Jerusalem, Israel 94101 (1963), Dean Rabbi Michael Marmur; FAX: (972-2)6251478. Prepares students for Reform rabbinate, cantorate, Jewish education and educational administration, communal service, academic careers; promotes Jewish studies; maintains libraries, archives, and museums; offers master's and doctoral degrees; engages in archaeological excavations; publishes scholarly works through Hebrew Union College Press. *American Jewish Archives; Bibliographica Judaica; HUC-JIR Catalogue; Hebrew Union College Annual; Studies in Bibliography and Booklore; The Chronicle; Kesher.* (WWW.HUC.EDU)

———, AMERICAN JEWISH PERIODICAL CENTER (1957). 3101 Clifton Ave., Cincinnati, OH 45220. (513)221-1875, ext. 396. FAX: (513)221-0519. Dir. Herbert C. Zafren. Maintains microfilms of all American Jewish periodicals 1823-1925, selected periodicals since 1925. *Jewish Periodicals and Newspapers on Microfilm (1957); First Supplement (1960); Augmented Edition (1984).*

———, BLAUSTEIN CENTER FOR PASTORAL COUNSELING. 1 West 4th Street, NYC, 10012. (212)824-2238. FAX: (212)388-1720. Email: nwiener@huc.edu. Dir. Nancy Wiener. In partnership with CCAR, prepares spiritual leaders to sensitively and capably help congregants to deal with the critical issues they face throughout their lives; enables rabbinical students to complete a variety of supervised clinical experiences, including a year of congregational workd as well as pastoral counseling internships, and an academic grounding in psychodynamics and pastoral counseling; and develops new approaches to teaching counseling skills, grounding reflections on practical field work experiences in the teachings of Jewish texts.

———, CENTER FOR HOLOCAUST AND HUMANITY EDUCATION. 3101 Clifton Ave., Cincinnati, OH 45220. (513)221-1875, ext. 355. FAX: (513)221-1842. Email: holocaustandhumanity@huc.edu. Dir. Dr. Racelle R. Weiman. Co-sponsored by Hebrew Union College-Jewish Institute of Religion and Combined Generations of the Holocaust of Greater Cincinnati; offers graduate level courses for educational professionals and clergy; surveys and assesses Holocaust education needs in public and private sectors; innovates curriculum development and evaluation; provides teacher training, pedgogic resources, and programming for general public of all ages and faiths; convenes conferences and symposia; cooperates with university consortium on outreach initiatives; creates traveling exhibits; fosters tolerance education and prejudice reduction in the school system.

———, EDGAR F. MAGNIN SCHOOL OF GRADUATE STUDIES (1956). 3077 University Ave., Los Angeles, CA 90007. (213)749-3424. FAX: (213)747-6128. E-mail: magnin@huc.edu. Dir. Dr. Reuven Firestone. Supervises programs leading to DHS, DHL, and MA degrees; participates in cooperative PhD programs with U. of S. Calif.

———, GRADUATE STUDIES PROGRAM. 1 W. 4 St. NYC 10012. (212)824-2252. FAX: (212)388-1720. E-mail: nysgrad@huc.edu. Dir. Dr. Carol Ochs. Offers the DHL (doctor of Hebrew letters) degree in a variety of fields; the MAJS (master of arts in Judaic studies), a multidisciplinary degree; and is the only Jewish seminary to offer the DMin (doctor of ministry) degree in pastoral care and counseling.

———, HUC-UC CENTER FOR THE STUDY OF ETHICS AND CONTEMPORARY MORAL PROBLEMS (1986). 3101 Clifton Ave., Cincinnati, OH 45220. (513)221-1875, EXT. 367. FAX: (513)221-1842. Email: ethics@huc.edu. Dir. Dr. Jonathan Cohen. Co-sponsored by Hebrew Unon College-Jewish Institute of Religion and the University of Cincinnati; dedicated to the study of contemporary moral problems on the basis of values that are at the heart of Judeo-Christian and secular ethical traditions; provides forum for open discussion and reflection on important moral dilemmas that arise in modern life; promotes the incorporation of ethical values in personal life, professional practice, and community development; launching MA and PhD programs in Jewish and Comparative Law and Applied Ethics; offering development programs for legal, medical, and social work professionals; promoting cooperative research among academic institutions, social service, and not-for-profit organizations in Greater Cincinnati.

———, IRWIN DANIELS SCHOOL OF JEWISH COMMUNAL SERVICE (1968). 3077 University Ave., Los Angeles, CA 90007. (800)899-0925. FAX: (213)747-6128. E-mail: swindmueller@huc.edu. Dir. Dr. Steven F. Windmueller. Offers certificate and master's degree to those employed in Jewish communal services, or preparing for such work; offers joint MA in Jewish education and communal service with Rhea Hirsch School; offers dual degrees with the School of Social Work, the School of Public Administration, the Annenberg School for Communication, Marshall School of Business and the School of Gerontology of the U. of S. Calif. and with other institutions. Single master's degrees can be completed in 15 months and certificates are awarded for the completion of two full-time summer sessions. (WWW.HUC.EDU)

———, JACOB RADER MARCUS CENTER OF THE AMERICAN JEWISH ARCHIVES (*see* p. 653)

———, JEROME H. LOUCHHEIM SCHOOL OF JUDAIC STUDIES (1969). 3077 University Ave., Los Angeles, CA 90007. (213)749-3424. FAX: (213)747-6128. Dir. Dr. Reuven Firestone. Offers programs leading to MA, BS, BA, and AA degrees; offers courses as part of the undergraduate program of the U. of S. Calif.

———, NELSON GLUECK SCHOOL OF BIBLICAL ARCHAEOLOGY (1963). 13 King David St., Jerusalem, Israel 94101. (972)2-6203333. FAX: (972)2-6251478. Dir. Avraham Biran. Offers graduate-level research programs in Bible and archaeology. Summer excavations are carried out by scholars and students. University credit may be earned by participants in excavations. Consortium of colleges, universities, and seminaries is affiliated with the school. Skirball Museum of Biblical Archaeology (artifacts from Tel Dan, Tel Gezer, and Aroer).

———, RHEA HIRSCH SCHOOL OF EDUCATION (1967). 3077 University Ave., Los Angeles, CA 90007. (213)749-3424. FAX: (213)747-6128. Dir. Sara Lee. Offers PhD and MA programs in Jewish and Hebrew education; conducts joint degree programs with U. of S. Calif.; offers courses for Jewish teachers, librarians, and early educators on a nonmatriculating basis; conducts summer institutes for professional Jewish educators.

———, SCHOOL OF EDUCATION (1947). 1 W. 4 St., NYC 10012. (212)824-2213. FAX: (212)388-1720. E-mail: nysed@huc.edu. Dir. Jo Kay. Trains teachers and principals for Reform religious schools; offers MA degree with specialization in religious education.

———, SCHOOL OF GRADUATE STUDIES (1949). 3101 Clifton Ave., Cincinnati, OH 45220. (513)221-1875, ext. 230. FAX: (513)221-0321. E-mail: gradschool@huc.edu. Dir. Dr. Adam Kamesar. Offers programs leading to MA and PhD degrees; offers program leading to DHL degree for rabbinic graduates of the college.

———, SCHOOL OF JEWISH STUDIES (1963). 13 King David St., Jerusalem, Israel 94101. (972)2-6203333. FAX: (972)2-6251478. E-mail: jerusalem@huc.edu. Acting Pres. Dr. Norman J. Cohen; Dean Rabbi Michael Marmur; Assoc. Dean Rabbi Shaul R. Feinberg. Offers first year of graduate rabbinic, cantorial, and Jewish education studies (required) for North American students; graduate program leading to ordination for Israeli rabbinic students; non-degree Beit Midrash/Liberal Yeshivah program of Jewish studies (English language); in-service educational programming for teachers and educators (Hebrew language); Hebrew Ulpan for immigrants and visitors; Abramov Library of Judaica, Hebraica, Ancient Near East and American Jewish Experience; Skirball Museum of Biblical Archaeology; public outreach programs (lectures, courses, concerts, exhibits).

———, SCHOOL OF SACRED MUSIC (1947). 1 W. 4 St., NYC 10012. (212)824-2225. FAX: (212)388-1720. Dir. Cantor Israel

Goldstein. Trains cantors for congregations; offers MSM degree. *Sacred Music Press.*

———, SKIRBALL CULTURAL CENTER (*see* p. 656)

INSTITUTE OF TRADITIONAL JUDAISM (1990). 811 Palisade Ave., Teaneck, NJ 07666. (201)801-0707. FAX: (201)801-0449. Rector (Reish Metivta) Rabbi David Weiss Halivni; Dean Rabbi Ronald D. Price. A nondenominational halakhic rabbinical school dedicated to genuine faith combined with intellectual honesty and the love of Israel. Graduates receive "yoreh yoreh" smikhah.

JEWISH THEOLOGICAL SEMINARY (1886; reorg. 1902). 3080 Broadway, NYC 10027-4649. (212)678-8000. FAX: (212) 678-8947. Chancellor Dr. Ismar Schorsch; Bd. Chmn. Gershon Kekst. Operates undergraduate and graduate programs in Judaic studies; professional schools for training Conservative rabbis, educators and cantors; the JTS Library; the Ratner Center for the Study of Conservative Judaism; Melton Research Center for Jewish Education; the Jewish Museum; Ramah Camps and the Ivry Prozdor high-school honors program. Other outreach activities include the Distance Learning Project, the Finkelstein Institute for Religious and Social Studies, and the Wagner Institute lay leadership program. *Academic Bulletin; JTS Magazine; Gleanings; JTS News.* (WWW.JTSA.EDU)

———, ALBERT A. LIST COLLEGE OF JEWISH STUDIES (formerly SEMINARY COLLEGE OF JEWISH STUDIES—TEACHERS INSTITUTE) (1909). 3080 Broadway, NYC 10027. (212)678-8826. Dean Dr. Shuly Rubin Schwartz. Offers complete undergraduate program in Judaica leading to BA degree; conducts joint programs with Columbia University and Barnard College enabling students to receive two BA degrees.

———, GRADUATE SCHOOL OF JTS (formerly INSTITUTE FOR ADVANCED STUDY IN THE HUMANITIES) (1968). 3080 Broadway, NYC 10027-4649. (212)678-8024. FAX: (212)678-8947. E-mail: gradschool @jtsa.edu. Dean Dr. Stephen P. Garfinkel; Asst. Dean Dr. Bruce E. Nielsen. Programs leading to MA, DHL, and PhD degrees in Judaic studies; specializations include Ancient Judaism, Bible and Ancient Semitic Languages, Interdepartmental Studies, Jewish Art and Material Culture, Jewish Education, Jewish History, Jewish Literature, Jewish Philosophy, Jewish Women's Studies, Liturgy, Medieval Jewish Studies, Midrash, Modern Jewish Studies, Talmud and Rabbinics, and Dual Degree Program with Columbia University School of Social Work.

———, H.L. MILLER CANTORIAL SCHOOL AND COLLEGE OF JEWISH MUSIC (1952). 3080 Broadway, NYC 10027. (212)678-8036. FAX: (212)678-8947. Dean Cantor Henry Rosenblum. Trains cantors, music teachers, and choral directors for congregations. Offers full-time programs in sacred music leading to degree of MSM, and diploma of *Hazzan.*

———, JEWISH MUSEUM (*see* p. 654)

———, LIBRARY OF THE JEWISH THEOLOGICAL SEMINARY. 3080 Broadway, NYC 10027. (212)678-8075. FAX: (212)678-8998. E-mail: library@jtsa.edu. Librarian Dr. Mayer E. Rabinowitz. Contains one of the largest collections of Hebraica and Judaica in the world, including manuscripts, incunabula, rare books, and Cairo Geniza material. The 320,000-item collection includes books, manuscripts, periodicals, sound recordings, prints, broadsides, photographs, postcards, microform, videos and CD-ROM. Exhibition of items from the collection are ongoing. Exhibition catalogs are available for sale. The Library is open to the public for on-site use (photo identification required). *Between the Lines.* (WWW.JTSA.EDU/LIBRARY)

———, LOUIS FINKELSTEIN INSTITUTE FOR RELIGIOUS AND SOCIAL STUDIES (1938). 3080 Broadway, NYC 10027. (212)870-3180. FAX: (212)678-8947. E-mail: finkelstein@jtsa.edu. Dir. Rabbi Gerald Wolpe. Since 1938 has maintained an innovative interfaith and intergroup relations program, pioneering new approaches to dialogue across religious lines. Through scholarly and practical fellowship, highlights the relevance of Judaism and other contemporary religions to current theological, ethical, and scientific issues, including the emerging challenge of bioethics.

———, MELTON RESEARCH CENTER FOR JEWISH EDUCATION (1960). 3080 Broadway, NYC 10027. (212)678-8031. E-mail:

stbrown@jtsa.edu. Dir. Dr. Steven M. Brown; Admin. Lisa Siberstein-Weber. Develops new curricula and materials for Jewish education; prepares educators through seminars and in-service programs; maintains consultant and supervisory relationships with a limited number of pilot schools; develops and implements research initiatives; sponsors "renewal" retreats. *Gleanings; Courtyard: A Journal of Research and Reflection on Jewish Education.*

———, NATIONAL RAMAH COMMISSION (1947). 3080 Broadway, NYC 10027. (212)678-8881. FAX: (212)749-8251. Pres. Alan H. Silberman; Natl. Dir. Sheldon Dorph. Sponsors an international network of 16 summer camps located in the US, Canada, S. America, Russia, and Israel, emphasizing Jewish education, living, and culture; offers opportunities for qualified college students and older to serve as counselors, administrators, specialists, etc., and programs for children with special needs (Tikvah program); offers special programs in U.S. and Israel, including National Ramah Staff Training Institute, Ramah Israel Seminar, Ulpan Ramah Plus, and Tichon Ramah Yerushalayim. Family and synagogue tours to Israel and summer day camp in Israel for Americans.

———, PROJECT JUDAICA (1992). 3080 Broadway, NYC 10027. (212)678-8983. Dir. Dr. David Fishman. Students in this intensive, five year program sponsored with YIVO and the Russian State University for the Humanities in Moscow pursue the university's general curriculum while majoring in Jewish history and culture taught by JTS faculty and advanced students. Graduates receive a diploma (the equivalent of an MA) or a candidate of sciences degree (the equivalent of a PhD) from RSUH.

———, RABBINICAL SCHOOL (1886). 3080 Broadway, NYC 10027. (212)678-8817. Dean Allan Kensky. Offers a program of graduate and professional studies leading to the degree of Master of Arts and ordination; includes one year of study in Jerusalem and an extensive field-work program.

———, RADIO AND TELEVISION (1944). 3080 Broadway, NYC 10027. (212)678-8020. Produces radio and TV programs expressing the Jewish tradition in its broadest sense, including hour-long documentaries on NBC and ABC. Distributes cassettes of programs at minimum charge.

———, REBECCA AND ISRAEL IVRY PROZDOR (1951). 3080 Broadway, NYC 10027. (212)678-8824. E-mail: prozdor@jtsa.edu. Principal Rhonda Rosenheck; Community Advisory Board Chmn. Michael Katz. The Hebrew high school of JTS, offers a program of Jewish studies for day school and congregational school graduates in classical texts, Hebrew, interdisciplinary seminars, training in educational leadership, and classes for college credit. Classes meet one evening a week and on Sundays in Manhattan and at affiliated programs. *High School Curricula.*

———, SAUL LIEBERMAN INSTITUTE FOR TALMUDIC RESEARCH (1985). 3080 Broadway, NYC 10027. (212)678-8994. FAX: (212)678D8947. E-mail: liebinst@jtsa.edu. Dir. Shamma Friedman; Coord. Jonathan Milgram. Engaged in preparing for publication a series of scholarly editions of selected chapters of the Talmud. The following projects support and help disseminate the research:Talmud Text Database; Bibliography of Talmudic Literature; Catalogue of Geniza Fragments.

———, SCHOCKEN INSTITUTE FOR JEWISH RESEARCH (1961). 6 Balfour St., Jerusalem, Israel 92102. (972)2-5631288. FAX: (972)2-5636857. E-mail: sjssg@vms.huji.ac.il. Dir. Dr. Shmuel Glick. Comprises the Schocken collection of rare books and manuscripts and a research institute dedicated to the exploration of Hebrew religious poetry (*piyyut*). *Schocken Institute Yearbook (P'raqim).*

———, WILLIAM DAVIDSON GRADUATE SCHOOL OF JEWISH EDUCATION (1996). 3080 Broadway, NYC 10027. (212)678-8030. E-mail: edschool@jtsa.edu. Dean Dr. Aryeh Davidson. Offers master's and doctoral degrees in Jewish education; continuing education courses for Jewish educators and Jewish communal professionals; and programs that take advantage of the latest technology, including distance learning and interactive video classrooms.

MAALOT—A SEMINARY FOR CANTORS AND JUDAISTS (1987). 15 W. Montgomery Ave., Suite 204, Rockville, MD 20850. (301)309-2310. FAX: (301)309-2328.

Pres./Exec. Off. David Shneyer. An educational program established to train individuals in Jewish music, the liturgical arts, and the use, design, and application of Jewish customs and ceremonies. Offers classes, seminars, and an independent study program.

MESIVTA YESHIVA RABBI CHAIM BERLIN RABBINICAL ACADEMY (1905). 1605 Coney Island Ave., Brooklyn, NY 11230. (718)377-0777. Exec. Dir. Y. Mayer Lasker. Maintains fully accredited elementary and high schools; collegiate and postgraduate school for advanced Jewish studies, both in America and Israel; Camp Morris, a summer study retreat; Prof. Nathan Isaacs Memorial Library; Gur Aryeh Publications.

NATIONAL CENTER FOR THE HEBREW LANGUAGE (*see* p. 655)

NER ISRAEL RABBINICAL COLLEGE (1933). 400 Mt. Wilson Lane, Baltimore, MD 21208. (410)484-7200. FAX: (410)484-3060. Rosh Hayeshiva, Rabbi Aharon Feldman; Pres. Rabbi Herman N. Neuberger. Trains rabbis and educators for Jewish communities in America and worldwide. Offers bachelor's, master's, and doctoral degrees in talmudic law, as well as teacher's diploma. College has four divisions: Israel Henry Beren High School, Rabbinical College, Teachers Training Institute, Graduate School. Maintains an active community-service division. Operates special programs for Iranian and Russian Jewish students. *Ner Israel Update; Alumni Bulletin; Ohr Hanair Talmudic Journal; Iranian B'nei Torah Bulletin.*

RABBINICAL COLLEGE OF TELSHE, INC. (1941). 28400 Euclid Ave., Wickliffe, OH 44092. (216)943-5300. Roshe Hayeshiva and Pres. Rabbi Zalman Gifter and Rabbi Yitzchok Sorotzkin ; V.-Pres. Rabbi Abba Zalka Gewirtz. College for higher Jewish learning specializing in talmudic studies and rabbinics; maintains a preparatory academy including a secular high school, postgraduate department, teacher-training school, and teachers' seminary for women. *Pri Etz Chaim; Peer Mordechai; Alumni Bulletin.*

RECONSTRUCTIONIST RABBINICAL COLLEGE (1968). 1299 Church Rd., Wyncote, PA 19095. (215)576-0800. FAX: (215)576-6143. E-mail: rrcinfo@rrc.edu. Pres. Dan Ehrenkranz; Bd. Chmn. Donald L. Shapiro; Genl. Chmn. Aaron Ziegelman. Coeducational. Trains rabbis and cantors for all areas of Jewish communal life:synagogues, academic and educational positions, Hillel centers, federation agencies, and chaplaincy for hospitals, hospices, and geriatric centers; confers title of rabbi and cantor and grants degrees of Master and Doctor of Hebrew Letters and Master of Arts in Jewish Studies. *RRC Report; Reconstructionist.*(WWW.RRC.EDU)

SPERTUS INSTITUTE OF JEWISH STUDIES (1924). 618 S. Michigan Ave., Chicago, IL 60605. (312)922-9012. FAX: (312)922-6406. Pres. Howard A. Sulkin; Bd. Chmn. Franklin Nitikman; V.-Pres. for Academic Affairs Byron L. Sherwin. An accredited institution of higher learning offering one doctor of Jewish studies degree; master's degree programs in Jewish studies, Jewish education, Jewish communal service, and human-services administration; plus an extensive program of continuing education. Major resources of the college encompass Spertus Museum, Asher Library, Chicago Jewish Archives, and Spertus College of Judaica Press.

——, SPERTUS MUSEUM (*see* p. 657)

TOURO COLLEGE (1970). Executive Offices: 27 West 23rd Street., NYC 10010. (212)643-0400. FAX: (212)627-9049. Pres. Dr. Bernard Lander; Bd. Chmn. Mark Hasten. Non-profit comprehensive college with Judaic Studies, Liberal Arts and professional programs leading to BA, BS, MA, MS and JD degrees at campuses in NYC and Long Island; emphasizes relevance of Jewish heritage to Western civilization. Undergraduate and graduate degree programs in Moscow and Jerusalem. California campuses offer DO degree and distance learning BS, MS, MBA and PhD degrees.

——, COLLEGE OF LIBERAL ARTS AND SCIENCES. 27-33 W. 23 St., NYC 10010. (212)463-0400. FAX: (212)627-9144. Exec. Dean Stanley Boylan. Offers comprehensive Jewish studies along with studies in the arts, sciences, humanities, and preprofessional studies in health sciences, law, accounting, business, computer science, education, and finance. Women's Division, 160 Lexington Ave., NYC 10016. (212)213-2230. FAX: (212)683-3281. Dean Sara E. Freifeld.

———, INSTITUTE OF JEWISH LAW. (631)421-2244, ext. 335. A constituent of Touro College Jacob D. Fuchsberg Law Center, the Institute of Jewish Law provides an intellectual framework for the study and teaching of Jewish law. Coedits *Dinei Israel* (Jewish Law Journal) with Tel Aviv University Law School.

———, JACOB D. FUCHSBERG LAW CENTER (1980). Long Island Campus, 300 Nassau Rd., Huntington, NY 11743. (516)421-2244. Dean Howard A. Glickstein. Offers studies leading to JD degree.

———, MOSCOW BRANCH. Oztozhenka #38, Moscow, Russia 119837. Offers BS program in business and BA program in Jewish studies.

———, SCHOOL OF GENERAL STUDIES. Midtown Main Campus, 27 W. 23 St., NYC 10010. (212)463-0400; Harlem Main Campus, 240 E. 123 St., NYC 10035; Sunset Park extension, 475 53rd St., Brooklyn, NY 11220; Flushing Extension, 133-35 Roosevelt Ave., Queens, NY 11374. Dean Stephen Adolphus. Associate and bachelor degree programs in human services, education N-6, computing, business and liberal arts; special emphasis on service to non-traditional students.

———, TOURO COLLEGE FLATBUSH CENTER (1979). 1602 Ave. J, Brooklyn, NY 11230. (718)252-7800. Dean Robert Goldschmidt. A division of the College of Liberal Arts and Sciences; options offered in accounting and business, education, mathematics, political science, psychology, special education and speech. Classes are given on weeknights and during the day on Sunday.

———, TOURO COLLEGE ISRAEL. 20 Pierre Koenig St., Jerusalem, Israel. (02) 6796666. FAX: (02)6796688. V-Pres., Israel, Matityahu Adler; Dean of Faculty, Israel, Prof. Moshe Lieberman. Touro College Israel offers both undergraduate and graduate degrees in management, marketing, economics, finance, and accounting. Touro College also offers a graduate degree in Jewish Studies. Courses in both these programs are given in Hebrew. In addition undergraduate courses in our one year program are offered in English. (WWW.TOURO.AC.IL)

———, TOURO COLLEGE SCHOOL OF HEALTH SCIENCES (1986). 1700 Union Blvd, Bay Shore, NY 11706. (516)665-1600. FAX: (516)665-6902. E-mail: edwarda@touro.edu. Pres. Dr. Bernard Lander; Dean Dr. Joseph Weisberg. Offers the following programs:MS/MD with Faculty of Medicine, Technion Institute, Israel; BS/MS Occupational Therapy; BS/MS Physical Therapy; MS Public Health; Advanced MS Orthopedic Physical Therapy; MS Forensic Examination; MS Clinical Engineering; MS Early Intervention; MS Gerontology; BS Physician Assistant; AAS Occupational Therapy Assistant; AAS Physical Therapists Assistant.

———, TOURO GRADUATE SCHOOL OF JEWISH STUDIES (1981). 160 Lexington Ave., NYC 10016. (212)213-2230. FAX: (212)683-3281. E-mail: moshesh@touro.edu. Pres. Bernard Lander; Dean Michael A. Shmidman. Offers courses leading to an MA in Jewish studies, with concentrations in Jewish history or Jewish education. Students may complete part of their program in Israel through MA courses offered by Touro faculty at Touro's Jerusalem center.

UNIVERSITY OF JUDAISM (1947). 15600 Mulholland Dr., Los Angeles, CA 90077. (310)476-9777. FAX: (310)476-0347. E-mail: gleuenthal@uj.edu. Pres. Dr. Robert D. Wexler. The College of Arts and Sciences is an accredited liberal arts college for undergraduates offering a core curriculum of Jewish, Western, and non-Western studies, with majors including bioethics (a premedical track in partnership with Cedars-Sinai Medical Center), business, English, Jewish studies, journalism, literature & politics, political science, psychology, and U.S. public policy. Accredited graduate programs in non-profit business administration (MBA), Jewish education, and psychology with an emphasis on developmental disabilities. The Ziegler School of Rabbinic Studies provides an intensive four-year program with Conservative ordination. Home of the Center for Policy Options, conducting public policy research in areas of concern to the Jewish community, and the Whizin Center for the Jewish Future, a research and programming institute. Offers the largest adult Jewish education program in the U.S., cultural-arts programs, and a variety of outreach services for West Coast Jewish communities. *Vision*.

WEST COAST TALMUDICAL SEMINARY (Yeshiva Ohr Elchonon Chabad) (1953).

7215 Waring Ave., Los Angeles, CA 90046. (323)937-3763. FAX: (323)937-9456. Dean Rabbi Ezra Schochet. Provides facilities for intensive Torah education as well as Orthodox rabbinical training on the West Coast; conducts an accredited college preparatory high school combined with a full program of Torah-talmudic training and a graduate talmudical division on the college level. *Torah Quiz; Kovetz Migdal Ohr; Kovetz Ohr HaMigdal.*

YESHIVA TORAH VODAATH AND MESIVTA TORAH VODAATH RABBINICAL SEMINARY (1918). 425 E. 9 St., Brooklyn, NY 11218. (718)941-8000. Bd. Chmn. Chaim Leshkowitz. Offers Hebrew and secular education from elementary level through rabbinical ordination and postgraduate work; maintains a teachers institute and community-service bureau; maintains a dormitory and a nonprofit camp program for boys. *Chronicle; Mesivta Vanguard; Thought of the Week; Torah Vodaath News; Ha'Mesifta.*

———, YESHIVA TORAH VODAATH ALUMNI ASSOCIATION (1941). 425 E. 9 St., Brooklyn, NY 11218. (718)941-8000. Pres. George Weinberger. Promotes social and cultural ties between the alumni and the schools through classes and lectures and fund-raising; offers vocational guidance to students; operates Camp Ohr Shraga; sponsors research fellowship program for boys. *Annual Journal; Hamesivta Torah periodical.*

YESHIVA UNIVERSITY (1886). Wilf Campus, 500 W. 185 St., NYC 10033-3201. (212)960-5400. FAX: (212)960-0055. Pres. Dr. Norman Lamm; Chmn. Bd. of Trustees Robert M. Beren. The nation's oldest and most comprehensive independent university founded under Jewish auspices, with 18 undergraduate and graduate schools, divisions, and affiliates; widespread programs of research and community outreach; publications; and a museum. A broad range of curricula lead to bachelor's, master's, doctoral, and professional degrees. Undergraduate schools provide general studies curricula supplemented by courses in Jewish learning; graduate schools prepare for careers in medicine, law, social work, Jewish education, psychology, Jewish studies, and other fields. It has seven undergraduate schools, seven graduate and professional schools, and four affiliates. *Yeshiva University Review; Yeshiva University Today.* (WWW.YU.EDU)

Yeshiva University has four campuses in Manhattan and the Bronx: Wilf Campus, 500 W. 185 St., NYC 10033-3201; Midtown Campus, 245 Lexington Ave., NYC 10016-4699; Brookdale Center, 55 Fifth Ave., NYC 10003-4391; Jack and Pearl Resnick Campus, Eastchester Rd. & Morris Pk. Ave., Bronx, NY 10461-1602.

Undergraduate schools for men at Wilf Campus (212)960-5400: Yeshiva College (Bd. Chmn. Jay Schottenstein; Dean Dr. Norman T. Adler) provides liberal arts and sciences curricula; grants BA degree. Isaac Breuer College of Hebraic Studies (Dean Dr. Michael D. Shmidman) awards Hebrew teacher's diploma, AA, BA, and BS. James Striar School of General Jewish Studies (Dean Dr. Michael D. Shmidman) grants AA degree. Yeshiva Program/Mazer School of Talmudic Studies (Max and Marion Grill Dean Rabbi Zevulun Charlop) offers advanced course of study in Talmudic texts and commentaries. Irving I. Stone Beit Midrash Program (Dean Dr. Michael D. Shmidman) offers diversified curriculum combining Talmud with Jewish studies.

Undergraduate school for women at Midtown Campus (212)340-7700: Stern College for Women (Bd. Chmn. Marjorie Diener Blenden; Dr. Monique C. Katz; Dean Dr. Karen Bacon) offers liberal arts and sciences curricula supplemented by Jewish studies programs; awards BA, AA, and Hebrew teacher's diploma.

Sy Syms School of Business at Wilf Campus and Midtown Campus (Bd. Chmn. Bernard L. Madoff; Dean Dr. Charles Snow) offers undergraduate business curricula in conjunction with study at Yeshiva College or Stern College; grants BS degree.

Universitywide programs serving the community and the nation include the S. Daniel Abraham Israel Program; Joseph Alexander Foundation Program for Enhancemant of Science Education; Samuel H. and Rachel Golding Center for Judaic Studies; Samuel H. and Rachel Golding Institute for Biomedical Education; Carl C. Icahn Foundation Institutes for Child Protection; Irving and Hanni Rosenbaum Aliyah Incentive Fund; Holocaust Studies Program; Yeshiva University Press; Yeshiva University Museum.

———, ALBERT EINSTEIN COLLEGE OF MEDICINE (1955). Eastchester Rd. & Morris Pk. Ave., Bronx, NY 10461-1602. (718)430-2000. Pres. Dr. Norman Lamm; Chpers. Bd. of Overseers Robert A. Belfer; Marilyn and Stanley M. Katz Dean Dr. Dominick P. Purpura. Prepares physicians and conducts research in the health sciences; awards MD degree; includes Sue Golding Graduate Division of Medical Sciences (Dir. Dr. Anne M. Etgen), which grants PhD degree. Einstein's clinical facilities and affiliates encompass Jack D. Weiler Hospital of Albert Einstein College of Medicine, Jacobi Medical Center, Montefiore Medical Center, Long Island Jewish Medical Center, Beth Israel Medical Center, Bronx-Lebanon Hospital Center, and Rose F. Kennedy Center for Research in Mental Retardation and Developmental Disabilities. *Einstein; Einstein Today; Einstein Quarterly Journal of Biology and Medicine.*

———, ALUMNI OFFICE, 500 W. 185 St., NYC 10033-3201. (212)960-5373. FAX: (212)960-5336. E-mail: alumdesk@ymail.yu.edu. University Dir. Alumni Affairs Robert R. Saltzman. Seeks to foster a close allegiance of alumni to their alma mater by maintaining ties with all alumni and servicing the following associations:Yeshiva College Alumni; Stern College for Women Alumnae; Sy Syms School of Business Alumni; Albert Einstein College of Medicine Alumni; Ferkauf Graduate School of Psychology Alumni; Wurzweiler School of Social Work Alumni; Rabbinic Alumni; Benjamin N. Cardozo School of Law Alumni. *Yeshiva University Review; AECOM Alumni News; Ferkauf Progress Notes; Wurzweiler Update; Jewish Social Work Forum.*

———, AZRIELI GRADUATE SCHOOL OF JEWISH EDUCATION AND ADMINISTRATION (1945). 245 Lexington Ave., NYC 10016-4699. (212)340-7705. FAX: (212) 340-7787. Pres. Dr. Norman Lamm; Chmn. Bd. Of Dirs. Moshael J. Straus; Dean Dr. David J. Schnall. Offers MS degree in Jewish elementary and secondary education; specialist's certificate and EdD in administration and supervision of Jewish education. Block Education Program, subsidized by a grant from the Jewish Agency's Joint Program for Jewish Education, provides summer course work to complement year-round field instruction in local communities.

———, BELFER INSTITUTE FOR ADVANCED BIOMEDICAL STUDIES (1978). Eastchester Rd. & Morris Pk. Ave., Bronx, NY 10461-1602. (718)430-2801. Dir. Dr. Dennis Shields. Integrates and coordinates the Albert Einstein College of Medicine's postdoctoral research and training-grant programs in the basic and clinical biomedical sciences. Awards certificate as research fellow or research associate on completion of training.

———, BENJAMIN N. CARDOZO SCHOOL OF LAW (1976). 55 Fifth Ave., NYC 10003-4391. (212)790-0200. E-mail:lawinfo@ymail.yu.edu. Pres. Dr. Norman Lamm; Chmn. Bd. Of Directors Earle I. Mack; Dean David Rudenstine. Offers a rigorous and enriched legal education leading to juris doctor (JD) degree and two LLM programs—in intellectual property and in general law. Programs and services include Jacob Burns Institute for Advanced Legal Studies; Jacob Burns Center for Ethics in the Practice of Law; Bet Tzedek Legal Services Clinic, including the Herman J. Stich Program for the Aged and Disabled; Cardozo International Institute/Uri and Caroline Bauer Israel Program; Leonard and Bea Diener Institute of Jewish Law; Floersheimer Center for Constitutional Democracy; Ford Foundation Program in International Law and Human Rights; Samuel and Ronnie Heyman Center on Corporate Governance; Kukin Program for Conflict Resolution; Romie Shapiro Program in International Law and Human Rights; Stephen B. Siegel Program in Real Estate Law; Sol S. Singer Research Program in Real Property Law; Howard M. Squadron Program in Law, Media, and Society; Center for Professional Development. *Cardozo Life; Cardozo Law Review; Cardozo Arts and Entertainment Law Journal; Cardozo Women's Law Journal; Cardozo Journal of International and Comparative Law; Cardozo Studies in Law and Literature; Post-Soviet Media Law and Policy Newsletter; New York Real Estate Reporter.*

———, BERNARD REVEL GRADUATE SCHOOL OF JEWISH STUDIES (1935). 500 W. 185 St., NYC 10033-3201. (212)960-5253. Pres. Dr. Norman Lamm; Chmn. Bd. Of Directors Mordecai D. Katz;

Dean Dr. Arthur Hyman. Offers graduate programs in Bible, Talmudic studies, Jewish history, and Jewish philosophy; confers MA and PhD degrees. Harry Fischel Summer Program offers the Revel program during the summer.

———, FERKAUF GRADUATE SCHOOL OF PSYCHOLOGY (1957). Eastchester Rd. & Morris Pk. Ave., Bronx, NY 10461-1602. (718)430-3941. FAX: (718)430-3960. E-mail: gill@aecom.yu.edu. Pres. Dr. Norman Lamm; Chair Bd. of Governors. Dr. Jayne G. Beker; Dean Dr. Lawrence J. Siegel. Offers MA in applied psychology; PsyD in clinical and school-clinical child psychology; and PhD in developmental and clinical health psychology. Programs and services include the Leonard and Muriel Marcus Family Project for the Study of the Disturbed Adolescent; Max and Celia Parnes Family Psychological and Psychoeducational Services Clinic.

———, (affiliate) PHILIP AND SARAH BELZ SCHOOL OF JEWISH MUSIC (1954). 560 W. 185 St., NYC 10033-3201. (212)960-5353. FAX: (212)960-5359. Dir. Cantor Bernard Beer. Provides professional training of cantors and courses in Jewish liturgical music; conducts outreach; publishes *Journal of Jewish Music and Literature;* awards associate cantor's certificate and cantorial diploma.

———, (affiliate) RABBI ISAAC ELCHANAN THEOLOGICAL SEMINARY (1896). 2540 Amsterdam Ave., NYC 10033-9986. (212)960-5344. FAX: (212)960-0061. Chmn. Bd. of Trustees Julius Berman; Max and Marion Grill Dean Rabbi Zevulun Charlop. Leading center in the Western Hemisphere for Torah study and rabbinic training. RIETS complex encompasses 15 educational entities and a major service and outreach center with some 20 programs. Grants semikhah (ordination) and the degrees of master of religious education, master of Hebrew literature, doctor of religious education, and doctor of Hebrew literature. Includes Rabbi Joseph B. Soloveitchik Center of Rabbinic Studies; Gabriel Levine Post-Graduate School for Rabbinic Studies; Morris and Nellie L. Kawaler Rabbinic Training Program; Irving I. Stone Rabbinic Internship Program; Aaron, Martha, Isidore N., and Blanche Rosansky Foundation Contemporary Halakhah Program.

Kollelim include Marcos and Adina Katz Kollel (Institute for Advanced Research in Rabbinics); Kollel l'Horaah (Yadin Yadin) and External Yadin Yadin; Israel Henry Beren Institute for Higher Talmudic Studies (HaMachon HaGavohah L'Talmud); Bella and Harry Wexner Kollel Elyon and Semikhah Honors Program; Ludwig Jesselson Kollel Chaverim; Caroline and Joseph S. Gruss Institute in Jerusalem.

Riets sponsors one high school for boys (Manhattan) and one for girls (Queens).

The Max Stern Division of Communal Services (Acting Dir. Rabbi David A. Israel), provides personal and professional service to the rabbinate and related fields, as well as educational, consultative, organizational, and placement services to congregations, schools, and communal organizations around the world; coordinates a broad spectrum of outreach programs, including Association of Modern Orthodox Day Schools and Yeshiva High Schools, Stone-Sapirstein Center for Jewish Education, Gertrude and Morris Bienenfeld Department of Rabbinic Services, Gindi Program for the Enhancement of Professional Rabbinics, Continuing Rabbinic Education Initiatives, Leadership Education and Development Program (LEAD), Kiruv College Outreach Program, Community Kollel and Beit Midrash and Boardroom Learning Programs, Project Kehillah, Myer and Pauline Senders Off-Campus Lecture Series, Jewish Medical Ethics Consultation Service, National Commission on Torah Education.The Torah U-Madda Project, supported by the Joseph J. and Bertha K. Green Memorial Fund, includes the Orthodox Forum and publishes the *The Torah U-Madda Journal and Ten Da'at*.

Sephardic components are Jacob E. Safra Institute of Sephardic Studies and the Institute of Yemenite Studies; Sephardic Community Program; Dr. Joseph and Rachel Ades Sephardic Outreach Program; Maybaum Sephardic Fellowship Program.

———, SIMON WIESENTHAL CENTER (see p. 656)

———, WOMEN'S ORGANIZATION (1928). 500 W. 185 St., NYC 10033-3201. (212) 960-0855. Chmn. Natl. Bd. Dinah Pinczower. Supports Yeshiva University's national scholarship program for students training in education, community service, law, medicine, and other professions. Its Torah Chesed Fund provides monthly stipends to needy undergraduate students.

———, WURZWEILER SCHOOL OF SOCIAL WORK (1957). 500 W. 185 St., NYC 10033-3201. (212)960-0800. FAX: (212) 960-0822. Pres. Dr. Norman Lamm; Chair Bd. of Governors David I. Schachne; Dorothy and David I. Schachne Dean Dr. Sheldon R. Gelman. Offers graduate programs in social work and Jewish communal service; grants MSW and PhD degrees and certificate in Jewish communal service. MSW programs are: Concurrent Plan, 2-year, full-time track, combining classroom study and supervised field instruction; Plan for Employed Persons (PEP), for people working in social agencies; Block Education Plan (Dir. Dr. Adele Weiner), which combines summer course work with regular-year field placement in local agencies; Clergy Plan, training in counseling for clergy of all denominations; Silvia and Irwin Leiferman Center for Professional Training in the Care of the Elderly. *Jewish Social Work Forum.*

———, (affiliate) YESHIVA OF LOS ANGELES (1977). 9760 W. Pico Blvd., Los Angeles, CA 90035-4701. (310)772-2424. FAX: (310)772-7661. E-mail: mhmay@wiesenthal.com. Dean Rabbi Marvin Hier; Bd. Chmn. Samuel Belzberg; Dir. Academic Programs Rabbi Sholom Tendler. Affiliates are Yeshiva University High Schools of Los Angeles, Jewish Studies Institute and Kollel Torah MiTzion.

———, YESHIVA UNIVERSITY MUSEUM (see p. 658)

SOCIAL, MUTUAL BENEFIT

ALPHA EPSILON PI FRATERNITY (1913). 8815 Wesleyan Rd., Indianapolis, IN 46268-1171. (317)876-1913. FAX: (317) 876-1057. E-mail: office@aepi.org. Internatl. Pres. Andrew P. Fradkin; Exec. V.-Pres. Sidney N. Dunn. International Jewish fraternity active on over 100 campuses in the U.S. and Canada; encourages Jewish students to remain loyal to their heritage and to assume leadership roles in the community; active in behalf of Soviet Jewry, the State of Israel, the United States Holocaust Memorial Museum, Tay Sachs Disease, Mazon:A Jewish Response to Hunger, and other causes. *The Lion of Alpha Epsilon Pi (quarterly magazine).*

AMERICAN ASSOCIATION OF JEWS FROM THE FORMER USSR, INC. (AAJFSU) (1989). 119 Fulton St., 5th fl., rm.3, NYC 10038. (212)964-1946. FAX: (212)964-1946. E-mail: AAJFSU@yahoo.com. Pres. Stephen H. Hoffman; Bd. Chmn. James S. Tisch. National not-for-profit, grassroots mutual assistance and refugee advocacy organization, which unites and represents interests of over 600,000 Russian speaking Jewish refugees and legal immigrants from the former Soviet Union. Has chapters and independent associations in 7 states, including New York, Ohio, Colorado, New Jersey, Massachusetts, Wisconsin and Maryland. The national organization is a member of the National Immigration Forum and it is affiliated with the United Jewish Communities, Washington Action Office. New York Chapter is a member of the Jewish Community Relations Council of New York and the New York Immigration Coalition. Local Chapters work in cooperation with Jewish Federation of New York. The AAJFSU assists newcomers in their resettlement and vocational and cultural adjustment, fosters their Jewish identity and involvement in civic and social affairs, fights anti-Semitism and violation of human rights in the FSU and the U.S. through cooperation with other human rights organizations and advocacy, supports struggle of Israeli Jews for sustainable peace, provides advocacy in cases of political asylum for victims of anti-Semitism in the FSU and naturalization, provides assistance in social safety net and naturalization of the elderly and disabled. *Chronicles of Anti-Semitism and Nationalism in Republics of the Former USSR (in English, annually); Information Bulletin (in Russian, bimonthly).*

AMERICAN FEDERATION OF JEWS FROM CENTRAL EUROPE, INC. (1938). 570 Seventh Ave., NYC 10018. (212)921-3871. FAX: (212)575-1918. Pres. Fritz Weinschenk; Bd. Chmn. Curt C. Silberman; Exec. Asst. Dennis E. Rohrbaugh. Seeks to safeguard the rights and interests of American Jews of German-speaking Central European descent, especially in reference to restitution and indemnification; through its affiliate Research Foundation for Jewish Immigration sponsors research and publications on the history, immigration, and acculturation of Central European émigrés in the U.S. and worldwide; through its affiliate Jewish Philanthropic Fund of 1933 supports social programs for needy Nazi victims in the U.S.; undertakes cultural activities, annual conferences, publications; member, Council of Jews from Germany, London.

AMERICAN VETERANS OF ISRAEL (1951). 136 E. 39 St., NYC 10016. E-mail: spielgelsi @aol.com. Pres. Samuel Z. Klausner; V-Pres. David Kaplan. Maintains contact with American and Canadian volunteers who served in Aliyah Bet and/or Israel's War of Independence; promotes Israel's welfare; holds memorial services at grave of Col. David Marcus; is affiliated with World Mahal. *Newsletter.*

ASSOCIATION OF YUGOSLAV JEWS IN THE UNITED STATES, INC. (1941). 130 E. 59 St., Suite 1202, NYC 10022. (212)371-6891. V.-Pres. & Chmn. Emanuel Salom; Sec. Dr. Joseph Stock. Assistance to all Jews originally from Yugoslavia—Bosnia, Serbia, Croatia—and new settlers in Israel. *Bulletins.*

BNAI ZION—THE AMERICAN FRATERNAL ZIONIST ORGANIZATION (1908). 136 E. 39 St., NYC 10016. (212)725-1211. FAX: (212)684-6327. Pres. Michael J. Lazar; Exec. V.-Pres. Mel Parness. Fosters principles of Americanism, fraternalism, and Zionism. The Bnai Zion Foundation supports various humanitarian projects in Israel and the USA, chiefly the Bnai Zion Medical Center in Haifa and homes for retarded children-Maon Bnai Zion in Rosh Ha'ayin and the Herman Z. Quittman Center in Jerusalem Ahava Project. Also supports building of new central library in Ma'aleh Adumim. In U.S. sponsors program of awards for excellence in Hebrew for high school and college students. Chapters all over U.S. *Bnai Zion Voice (quarterly).* (WWW.BNAIZION.ORG)

BRITH ABRAHAM (1859; reorg. 1887). 136 E. 39 St., NYC 10016. (212)725-1211. FAX: (212)684-6327. Grand Master Robert Freeman. Protects Jewish rights and combats anti-Semitism; supports Soviet and Ethiopian emigration and the safety and dignity of Jews worldwide; helps to support Bnai Zion Medical Center in Haifa and other Israeli institutions; aids and supports various programs and projects in the U.S.: Hebrew Excellence Program-Gold Medal presentation in high schools and colleges; Camp Loyaltown; Brith Abraham and Bnai Zion Foundations. *Voice.*

BRITH SHOLOM (1905). 3939 Conshohocken Ave., Philadelphia, PA 19131. (215)878-5696. FAX: (215)878-5699. Pres. Seymour Rose; Exec. Dir. Roy Shenberg; Exec. V. P., Jerome Verlin. Fraternal organization devoted to community welfare, protection of rights of Jewish people, and activities that foster Jewish identity and provide support for Israel. Through its philanthropic arm, the Brith Sholom Foundation (1962), sponsors Brith Sholom House in Philadelphia, nonprofit senior-citizen apartments; and Brith Sholom Beit Halochem in Haifa, Israel, rehabilitation, social, and sports center for disabled Israeli veterans, operated by Zahal. Chmn. Martin Winit; Exec. Dir. Saundra Laub. *Brith Sholom Digest; monthly news bulletin.*

FREE SONS OF ISRAEL (1849). 250 Fifth Ave., Suite 201, NYC 10001. (212)725-3690. FAX: (212)725-5874. Grand Master Arlene Hoberman Kyler; Grand Sec. Ronald J. Laszlo. Oldest Jewish fraternal-benefit society in U.S. Affordable membership men & women (18+). Supports Israel, UJA projects, non-sectarian toy drives/philanthropies. Social Action fights anti-Semitism, supports human rights. Member benefits-IBM Metro Credit Union, scholarships, cemetery, discounted Long Term Care Insurance, educational and social functions, Free Model Seder. *Free Sons Reporter.* (WWW.FREESONS.ORG)

JEWISH LABOR BUND (Directed by WORLD COORDINATING COMMITTEE OF THE BUND) (1897; reorg. 1947). 25 E. 21 St., NYC 10010. (212)475-0059. FAX: (212) 473-5102. Acting Pres. Motl Zelmanowics; Sec. Gen. Benjamin Nades. Coordinates activities of Bund organizations throughout the world and represents them in the Socialist International; spreads the ideas of socialism as formulated by the Jewish Labor Bund; publishes books and periodicals on world problems, Jewish life, socialist theory and policy, and on the history, activities, and ideology of the Jewish Labor Bund. *Unser Tsait* (U.S.); *Lebns-Fragn* (Israel); *Unser Gedank* (Australia).

SEPHARDIC JEWISH BROTHERHOOD OF AMERICA, INC. (1915). 97-45 Queens Blvd., Rm. 610, Rego Park, NY 11374. (718)459-1600. Pres. Bernard Ouziel; Sec. Irving Barocas. A benevolent fraternal organization seeking to promote the industrial, social, educational, and religious welfare of its members. *Sephardic Brother.*

THE WORKMEN'S CIRCLE/ARBETER RING (1900). 45 E. 33 St., NYC 10016. (212) 889-6800. FAX: (212)532-7518. E-mail: member@circle.org. Pres. Martin Krupnick; Exec. Dir. Robert Kestenbaum. Fosters Jewish identity and participation in Jewish life through Jewish, especially Yiddish, culture and education, friendship, mutual aid, and the pursuit of social and economic justice. Offices are located throughout the U.S. and Canada. Member services include:Jewish cultural seminars, concerts, theater, Jewish schools, children's camp and adult resort, fraternal and singles activities, a Jewish Book Center, public affairs/social action, health insurance plans, medical/dental/legal services, life insurance plans, cemetery/funeral benefits, social services, geriatric homes and centers, and travel services. *The Call.* (WWW.CIRCLE.ORG)

ZETA BETA TAU FRATERNITY (1898). 3905 Vincennes Rd., Suite 101, Indianapolis, IN 46268. (317)334-1898. FAX: (317)334-1899. E-mail: zbt@zbtnational.org. Pres. Ronald J. Taylor, M.D.; Exec. Dir. Jonathan I. Yulish. Oldest and historically Jewish fraternity; promotes intellectual awareness, social responsibility, integrity, and brotherhood among over 5,000 undergrads and 110,000 alumni in the U.S. and Canada. Encourages leadership and diversity through mutual respect of all heritages; nonsectarian since 1954. A brotherhood of Kappa Nu, Phi Alpha, Phi Epsilon Pi, Phi Sigma Delta, Zeta Beta Tau. *The Deltan (quarterly).* (WWW.ZBT.ORG)

SOCIAL WELFARE

AMC CANCER RESEARCH CENTER (formerly JEWISH CONSUMPTIVES' RELIEF SOCIETY, 1904; incorporated as American Medical Center at Denver, 1954). 1600 Pierce St., Denver, CO 80214. (303)233-6501. FAX: (303)239-3400. E-mail: edelmanj@amc.org. Pres./CEO Bob R. Baker; Exec. V-Pres. Research Dr. Tom Slaga. A nationally recognized leader in the fight against cancer; employs a three-pronged, interdisciplinary approach that combines laboratory, clinical, and community cancer-control research to advance the prevention, early detection, diagnosis, and treatment of the disease. The exclusive scientific focus of our work is the prevention and control of cancer and other major diseases. *The Quest for Answers; Annual Report.* (WWW.AMC.ORG)

AMCHA FOR TSEDAKAH (1990). 9800 Cherry Hill Rd., College Park, MD 20740. (301)937-2600. Pres. Rabbi Bruce E. Kahn. Solicits and distributes contributions to Jewish charitable organizations in the U.S. and Israel; accredits organizations which serve an important tsedakah purpose, demonstrate efficiency and fiscal integrity, and also support pluralism. Contributors are encouraged to earmark contributions for specific organizations; all contributions to General Fund are forwarded to the charitable institutions, as operating expenses are covered by a separate fund. *Newspaper supplement.*

AMERICAN JEWISH CORRECTIONAL CHAPLAINS ASSOCIATION, INC. (formerly NATIONAL COUNCIL OF JEWISH PRISON CHAPLAINS) (1937). 10 E. 73 St., NYC 10021-4194. (212)879-8415. FAX: (212) 772-3977. (Cooperates with the New York Board of Rabbis.) Supports spiritual, moral, and social services for Jewish men and women in corrections; stimulates support of correctional chaplaincy; provides spiritual and professional fellowship for Jewish correctional chaplains; promotes sound standards for correctional chaplaincy; schedules workshops and research to aid chaplains in counseling and with religious services for Jewish inmates. Constituent, American Correctional Chaplains Association. *Chaplains Manual.*

AMERICAN JEWISH SOCIETY FOR SERVICE, INC. (1950). 15 E. 26 St., Rm. 1029, NYC 10010. (212)683-6178. Email: aud1750@aol.com. Founder/Chmn. Henry Kohn; Pres. Lawrence G. Green; Exec. Dirs. Carl & Audrey Brenner. Conducts voluntary work-service camps each summer to enable high school juniors and seniors to perform humanitarian service.

ASSOCIATION OF JEWISH AGING SERVICES (formerly NORTH AMERICAN ASSOCIATION OF JEWISH HOMES AND HOUSING FOR THE AGING) (1960). 316 Pennsylvania Ave., SE, Suite 402, Washington, DC 20003. (202)543-7500. FAX: (202)543-4090. E-mail: ajas@ajas.org. Pres. Jodi L. Lyons; Chmn. Michael Ellentuck. Represents nearly all the not-for-profit charitable homes and housing for the Jewish aging; promotes excellence in performance and quality of service through fostering communication and education and encouraging advocacy for the aging; conducts annual conferences and institutes. *Directory; The Scribe (quarterly newsletter).*

ASSOCIATION OF JEWISH CENTER PROFESSIONALS (1918). 15 E. 26 St., NYC 10010-1579. (212)532-4949. FAX: (212)481-4174. E-mail: ajcp@jcca.org. Pres. Susan Bender; Exec. Dir. Joe Harris. Seeks to enhance the standards, techniques, practices, scope, and public understanding of Jewish community center professionals and kindred agency work. *Kesher.*

ASSOCIATION OF JEWISH COMMUNITY ORGANIZATION PERSONNEL (AJCOP) (1969). 14619 Horseshoe Trace, Wellington, FL 33414. (561)795-4853. FAX: (561)798-0358. E-mail: marlene@ajcop.org. Pres. Mitch Orlik; Exec. Dir. Louis B. Solomon. An organization of professionals engaged in areas of fund-raising, endowments, budgeting, social planning, financing, administration, and coordination of services. Objectives are to develop and enhance professional practices in Jewish communal work; to maintain and improve standards, practices, scope, and public understanding of the field of community organization, as practiced through local federations, national agencies, other organizations, settings, and private practitioners. *Prolog (quarterly newspaper); Proceedings (annual record of papers and speeches).* (WWW.AJCOP.ORG)

ASSOCIATION OF JEWISH FAMILY AND CHILDREN'S AGENCIES (1972). 557 Cranbury Rd., Suite 2, E. Brunswick, NJ 08816-5419. (800)634-7346. FAX: (732)432-7127. E-mail: ajfca@ajfca.org. Pres./CEO Bert J. Goldberg; Bd. Chair. Lawrence Abramson. The national service organization for Jewish family and children's agencies in the U.S. and Canada. Reinforces member agencies in their efforts to sustain and enhance the quality of Jewish family and communal life. Operates the Elder Support Network for the national Jewish community. *Tachlis (quarterly); Professional Opportunities Bulletin; Executive Digest (monthly).* (WWW.AJFCA.ORG)

BARON DE HIRSCH FUND (1891). 130 E. 59 St., 12th fl., NYC 10022. (212)836-1358. FAX: (212)453-6512. Pres. Jenny Morgenthal; Mng. Dir. Lauren Katzowitz. Aids Jewish immigrants in the U.S. and Israel by giving grants to agencies active in educational, community, and vocational fields.

B'NAI B'RITH (1843). 1640 Rhode Island Ave., NW, Washington, DC 20036. (202) 857-6600. FAX: (202)857-1099. Pres. Richard D. Heideman; Exec. V.-Pres. Daniel S. Manaschin. International Jewish organization, with affiliates in 58countries. Offers programs designed to ensure the preservation of Jewry and Judaism: Jewish education, community volunteer service, expansion of human rights, assistance to Israel, housing for the elderly, leadership training, rights of Jews in all countries to study their heritage. *International Jewish Monthly; B'nai B'rith Today.*

———, ANTI-DEFAMATION LEAGUE OF (see p. 646)

———, HILLEL (see p. 676)

———, KLUTZNICK MUSEUM (see p. 651)

———, YOUTH ORGANIZATION (see p. 675)

CITY OF HOPE NATIONAL MEDICAL CENTER AND BECKMAN RESEARCH INSTITUTE (1913). 1500 E. Duarte Rd., Duarte, CA 91010. (626)359-8111. FAX: (626)301-8115. E-mail: dhalper@coh.org. Pres./CEO Gil N. Schwartzberg. Offers care to those with cancer and other catastrophic diseases, medical consultation service for second opinions, and research programs in genetics, immunology, and the basic life process. *City of Hope Cancer Research Center Report.*

CONFERENCE OF JEWISH COMMUNAL SERVICE (*see* JEWISH COMMUNAL SERVICE ASSOCIATION OF N. AMERICA)

COUNCIL OF JEWISH FEDERATIONS (*see* UNITED JEWISH COMMUNITIES)

INTERNATIONAL ASSOCIATION OF JEWISH VOCATIONAL SERVICES (formerly JEWISH OCCUPATIONAL COUNCIL) (1939). 1845

Walnut St., Suite 640, Philadelphia, PA 19103. (215)854-0233. FAX: (215)854-0212. E-mail: coheng@iajus.org. Exec. Dir. Genie Cohen; Vivian Seigel, President. Not-for-profit membership association of Jewish-sponsored social service agencies in the U.S., Canada, and Israel. Provides member agencies with technical, informational, and communications support; researches funding opportunities, develops collaborative program models, and represents Jewish vocational network nationally and internationally. Sponsors annual conference for members. Member agencies provide a wide range of educational, vocational, and rehabilitation services to both the Jewish and non-Jewish communities. *Executive quarterly newsletter*. (WWW.IAJVS.ORG)

INTERNATIONAL COUNCIL ON JEWISH SOCIAL AND WELFARE SERVICES (1961). c/o American Jewish Joint Distribution Committee, 711 Third Ave., NYC 10017. (NY liaison office with UN headquarters.) (212)687-6200. FAX: (212)370-5467. E-mail: steve@jdcny.org. Chmn. David Cope-Thompson; Exec. Sec. Eli Benson. Provides for exchange of views and information among member agencies on problems of Jewish social and welfare services, including medical care, old age, welfare, child care, rehabilitation, technical assistance, vocational training, agricultural and other resettlement, economic assistance, refugees, migration, integration, and related problems; representation of views to governments and international organizations. Members:six national and international organizations.

JEWISH BRAILLE INSTITUTE OF AMERICA, INC. (1931). 110 E. 30 St., NYC 10016. (212)889-2525. FAX: (212)689-3692. E-mail: dbarbara@jbilibrary.org. Pres. Barbara B. Friedman; Exec. V.-Pres. Dr. Ellen Isler. Provides Judaic materials in braille, talking books, and large print for blind, visually impaired, and reading-disabled; offers counseling for full integration into the life of the Jewish community. International program serves clients in more than 50 countries; sponsors special programs in Israel and Eastern Europe to assist the elderly as well as students. *Jewish Braille Review; JBI Voice; Likutim, Hebrew-language magazine on blindness issues.* (WWW.JEWISH BRAILLE.ORG)

JEWISH CHILDREN'S ADOPTION NETWORK (1990). PO Box 16544, Denver, CO 80216-0544. (303)573-8113. FAX: (303)893-1447. E-mail: jcan@qwest.net. Pres. Stephen Krausz; Exec. Dir. Vicki Krausz. An adoption exchange founded for the primary purpose of locating adoptive families for Jewish infants and children. Works with some 200 children a year, throughout N. Amer., 85-90% of whom have special needs. No fees charged for services, which include birth-parent and adoptive-parent counseling. *Quarterly newsletter.* (WWW.USERS.QWEST.NET/~JCAN)

JEWISH COMMUNAL SERVICE ASSOCIATION OF N. AMERICA (1899; formerly CONFERENCE OF JEWISH COMMUNAL SERVICE). 3084 State Hwy. 27, Suite 9, Kendall Park, NJ 08824-1657. (732)821-1871. FAX: (732)821-5335. E-mail: jcsana@aol.com. Pres. Dr. Ron B. Meier; Exec. Dir. Joel Ollander. Serves as forum for all professional philosophies in community service, for testing new experiences, proposing new ideas, and questioning or reaffirming old concepts; umbrella organization for 7 major Jewish communal service groups. Concerned with advancement of professional personnel practices and standards. *Journal of Jewish Communal Service; Concurrents.*

JEWISH COMMUNITY CENTERS ASSOCIATION OF NORTH AMERICA (formerly JWB) (1917). 15 E. 26 St., NYC 10010-1579. (212)532-4949. FAX: (212)481-4174. E-mail: info@jcca.org. Chair Jerome B. Makowsky; Pres. Allan Finkelstein. The leadership network of, and central agency for, the Jewish Community Center movement, comprising more than 275 JCCs, YM-YWHAs, and camps in the U.S. and Canada, which annually serve more than one million members and an additional million non-member users. The JCC Association offers a wide range of services and resources to strengthen the capacity of its affiliates to provide educational, cultural, social, Jewish identity-building, and recreational programs to enhance the lives of North American Jews of all ages and backgrounds. Additionally, the movement fosters and strengthens connections between North American Jews and Israel as well as with world Jewry. JCC Association is also the U.S. government-accredited agency for serving the religious and social needs of Jewish military personnel, their families, and patients in VA hospitals through JWB Chaplains Council. *JCC Circle; Chaplines; other newsletters for JCC professionals.* (WWW.JCCA.ORG)

———, JEWISH WELFARE BOARD JEWISH CHAPLAINS COUNCIL (formerly COMMISSION ON JEWISH CHAPLAINCY) (1940). 15 E. 26 St., NYC 10010-1579. (212)532-4949. FAX: (212)481-4174. E-mail: nathanlandman@jcca.com. Chmn. Rabbi David S. Goldstein; Dir. Rabbi David Lapp; Dep. Dir. Rabbi Nathan M. Landman. Recruits, endorses, and serves Jewish military and Veterans Administration chaplains on behalf of the American Jewish community and the major rabbinic bodies; trains and assists Jewish lay leaders where there are no chaplains, for service to Jewish military personnel, their families, and hospitalized veterans. *CHAPLINES newsletter.*

JEWISH FAMILY AND CHILDREN'S PROFESSIONALS ASSOCIATION (*see* JEWISH SOCIAL SERVICES PROFESSIONALS ASSOCIATION)

JEWISH FUND FOR JUSTICE (1984). 260 Fifth Ave., Suite 701, NYC 10001. (212)213-2113. FAX: (212)213-2233. E-mail: jfjustice@jfjustice.org. Bd. Chmn. John Levy; Exec. Dir. Marlene Provizer. A national, publicly-supported foundation committed to fighting poverty in America as an affirmation of Jewish identity and values. Funds community-based organizations generating positive changes in the lives of low-income people and their communities; provides educational programs teaching Jewish youth the importance of social justice through text and first-hand experiences; and promotes Jewish awareness of poverty and involvement in advancing social justice. Giving opportunities include general support, family, wedding, and youth endowment funds and planned giving. *Annual report, newsletter.* (WWW.JFJUSTICE.ORG)

JEWISH FUNDERS NETWORK (1990). 15 E. 26 St., Suite 1038, NYC 10010. (212)726-0177. FAX: (212)726-0195. E-mail: jfn@jfunders.org. Exec. Dir. Evan Mendelson. A national membership organization dedicated to advancing the growth and quality of Jewish philanthropy through more effective grant making to Jewish and secular causes. Individual philanthropists, foundation trustees, and foundation staff discuss emerging issues, gain expertise in operational aspects of grant making, explore intergenerational/family dynamics of family foundations, and exchange information among peers. *Quarterly Newsletter; Special Reports on Philanthropy.* (WWW.JFUNDERS.ORG)

JEWISH SOCIAL SERVICES PROFESSIONALS ASSOCIATION (JSSPA) (1965). c/o AJFCA, 557 Cranbury Rd., Suite 2, E. Brunswick, NJ 08816-0549. (800)634-7346. FAX: (732)432-7127. E-mail: ajfca@ajfca.org. Chmn. Seymour Friedland, Ph.D; Chair Elect Jaclynn Faffer, Ph.D. Brings together executives, supervisors, managers, caseworkers, and related professionals in Jewish Family Service and related agencies. Seeks to enhance professional skills, improve personnel standards, further Jewish continuity and identity, and strengthen Jewish family life. Provides a national and regional forum for professional discussion and learning; functions under the auspices of the Association of Jewish Family and Children's Agencies. *Newsletter.* (WWW.AJFCA.ORG)

JEWISH WOMEN INTERNATIONAL (1897). 1828 L St., NW, Suite 250, Washington, DC 20036. (202)857-1300. FAX: (202) 857-1380. E-mail: jwi@jwi.org. Pres. Barbara Rabkin; Exec. Dir. Gail Rubinson. Jewish Women International breaks the cycle of violence by developing emotionally healthy adults, empowering women and strengthening families. Jewish Women International accomplishes its goals through direct service programs, education, advocacy and the promotion of "best practice" models. Offers programs in the United States, Canada, and Israel. *Jewish Woman Magazine (quarterly).* (WWW.JEWISHWOMEN.ORG)

JWB (*see* JEWISH COMMUNITY CENTERS ASSOCIATION OF NORTH AMERICA)

LEVI HOSPITAL (1914). 300 Prospect Ave., Hot Springs, AR 71901. (501)624-1281. FAX: (501)622-3500. E-mail: levihospital@hsnp.com. Pres. Philip M. Clay; Admin. Patrick G. McCabe. Offers outpatient rehab, including therapy sessions in large thermal heated pool. Other programs: adult/geriatric inpatient and outpatient psychiatric program, child/adolescent psychiatric clinic, hospice care, home health care, osteoporosis clinic, Levi Rehabilitation Unit, a cooperative effort of Levi and St. Joseph's hospitals (inpatient rehab). *The Progress Chart; The Legacy.*

MAZON: A JEWISH RESPONSE TO HUNGER (1985). 1990 S. Bondy Drive, Suite 260, Los Angeles, CA 90025. (310)442-0020. FAX: (310)442-0030. E-mail: mazonmail@mason.org. Exec. Dir. Eric Schockman, PhD. A grant-making and fundraising organization that raises funds in the Jewish community and provides grants to nonprofit 501(c)(3) organizations which aim to prevent and alleviate hunger in the United States and abroad. Grantees include food pantries, food banks, multi-service organizations, advocacy, education and research projects, and international relief and development organizations. *Annual Report, 2 newsletters each year.*

NATIONAL ASSOCIATION OF JEWISH CHAPLAINS (1988). 901 Route 10, Whippany, NJ 07981. (973)884-4800 ext. 287. FAX: (973)736-9193. E-mail: cecille3@juno.com. Pres. Rabbi Stephen Roberts; Natl. Coord. Cecille Allman Asekoff. A professional organization for people functioning as Jewish chaplains in hospitals, nursing homes, geriatric, psychiatric, correctional, and military facilities. Provides collegial support, continuing education, professional certification, and resources for the Jewish community on issues of pastoral and spiritual care. *The Jewish Chaplain.*

NATIONAL COUNCIL OF JEWISH PRISON CHAPLAINS, INC. (*see* AMERICAN JEWISH CORRECTIONAL CHAPLAINS ASSOCIATION, INC.)

NATIONAL COUNCIL OF JEWISH WOMEN (1893). 53 W. 23 St., NYC 10010. (212) 645-4048. FAX: (212)645-7466. E-mail: actionline@ncjw.org. Pres. Jan Schneiderman; Exec. Dir. Susan Katz. Works to improve the lives of women, children, and families in the United States and Israel; strives to insure individual rights and freedoms for all. NCJW volunteers deliver vital services in 500 U.S. communities and carry out NCJW's advocacy agenda through a powerful grassroots network. *NCJW Journal; Washington Newsletter.* (WWW.NCJW.ORG)

NATIONAL INSTITUTE FOR JEWISH HOSPICE (1985). PO Box 48025, Los Angeles, CA 90048. (800)446-4448. 330 Broad Ave., Englewood, NJ 07631. (201)816-7324. FAX: (201)816-7321. Pres. Rabbi Maurice Lamm; Exec. Dir. Shirley Lamm. Serves as a national Jewish hospice resource center. Through conferences, research, publications, referrals, and counseling services offers guidance, training, and information to patients, family members, clergy of all faiths, professional caregivers, and volunteers who work with the Jewish terminally ill. *Jewish Hospice Times.*

NATIONAL JEWISH CHILDREN'S LEUKEMIA FOUNDATION (1990). 172 Madison Avenue, NYC 10016. (212)686-2722. FAX: (212)686-2750. E-mail: leukemia@erols.com. Pres./Founder Zvi Shor. Dedicated to saving the lives of children. Programs:Bone Marrow Donor Search, Stem Cell Banking-freezing cells from babies' umbilical cords for long-term storage, in case of need for bone marrow; Make-A-Dream-Come True-granting wishes for terminally ill children; Referral Service; Patient Advocacy. (WWW.LEUKEMIAFOUNDATION.ORG)

NATIONAL JEWISH MEDICAL AND RESEARCH CENTER (formerly NATIONAL JEWISH HOSPITAL/NATIONAL ASTHMA CENTER) (1899). 1400 Jackson St., Denver, CO 80206. (800)222-LUNG. E-mail: lungline@njc.org. Pres./CEO Lynn M. Taussig, MD; Bd. Chmn. Lawrence Gelfond. The only medical and research center in the United States devoted entirely to respiratory, allergic, and immune system diseases, including asthma, tuberculosis, emphysema, severe allergies, AIDS, and cancer, and autoimmune diseases such as lupus. Dedicated to enhancing prevention, treatment, and cures through research, and to developing and providing innovative clinical programs for treating patients regardless of age, religion, race, or ability to pay. *New Directions*; *Medical Scientific Update.* (WWW.NATIONALJEWISH.ORG)

NORTH AMERICAN ASSOCIATION OF JEWISH HOMES AND HOUSING FOR THE AGING (*see* ASSOCIATION OF JEWISH AGING SERVICES)

UNITED JEWISH COMMUNITIES (*see* p. 673)

UNITED ORDER TRUE SISTERS, INC. (UOTS) (1846). 100 State St., Suite 1020, Albany, NY 12207. (518)436-1670, Fax (518)436-1573. Pres. Mirian S. Cohen; Fin. Sec.

Betty Peyser; Treas. Rose Goldberg. Charitable, community service, especially home supplies, etc., for indigent cancer victims; supports camps for children with cancer. *Inside UotS.* (www.uots.org)

WORLD COUNCIL OF JEWISH COMMUNAL SERVICE (1966; reorg. 1994). 711 Third Ave., 10th fl., NYC 10017. (212)687-6200. FAX: (212)370-5467. Pres. Howard Charish; Assoc. Pres. Dr. Jack Habib; Exec. V.-Pres. Theodore Comet. Seeks to build Jewish community worldwide by enhancing professional-to-professional connections, improving professional practice through interchange of experience and sharing of expertise, fostering professional training programs, and stimulating research. Conducts quadrennial conferences in Jerusalem and periodic regional meetings. *Proceedings of international conferences; newsletters.*

PROFESSIONAL ASSOCIATIONS*

AMERICAN ASSOCIATION OF RABBIS (Religious, Educational)

AMERICAN CONFERENCE OF CANTORS, UNION OF AMERICAN HEBREW CONGREGATIONS (Religious, Educational)

AMERICAN JEWISH CORRECTIONAL CHAPLAINS ASSOCIATION, INC. (Social Welfare)

AMERICAN JEWISH PRESS ASSOCIATION (Cultural)

AMERICAN JEWISH PUBLIC RELATIONS SOCIETY (Community Relations)

ASSOCIATION OF HILLEL/JEWISH CAMPUS PROFESSIONALS (Religious, Educational)

ASSOCIATION OF JEWISH CENTER PROFESSIONALS (Social Welfare)

ASSOCIATION OF JEWISH COMMUNITY ORGANIZATION PERSONNEL (Social Welfare)

ASSOCIATION OF JEWISH COMMUNITY RELATIONS WORKERS (Community Relations)

CANTORS ASSEMBLY (Religious, Educational)

CENTRAL CONFERENCE OF AMERICAN RABBIS (Religious, Educational)

COUNCIL OF JEWISH ORGANIZATIONS IN CIVIL SERVICE (Community Relations)

INTERNATIONAL JEWISH MEDIA ASSOCIATION (Cultural)

JEWISH CHAPLAINS COUNCIL, JWB (Social Welfare)

JEWISH COMMUNAL SERVICE ASSOCIATION OF N. AMERICA (Social Welfare)

JEWISH EDUCATORS ASSEMBLY, UNITED SYNAGOGUE OF CONSERVATIVE JUDAISM (Religious, Educational)

JEWISH SOCIAL SERVICES PROFESSIONALS ASSOCIATION (Social Welfare)

JEWISH TEACHERS ASSOCIATION—MORIM (Religious, Educational)

NATIONAL ASSOCIATION OF HEBREW DAY SCHOOL ADMINISTRATORS, TORAH UMESORAH (Religious, Educational)

NATIONAL ASSOCIATION OF JEWISH CHAPLAINS (Social Welfare)

NATIONAL ASSOCIATION OF TEMPLE ADMINISTRATORS, UNION OF AMERICAN HEBREW CONGREGATIONS (Religious, Educational)

NATIONAL ASSOCIATION OF TEMPLE EDUCATORS, UNION OF AMERICAN HEBREW CONGREGATIONS (Religious, Educational)

NATIONAL CONFERENCE OF YESHIVA PRINCIPALS, TORAH UMESORAH (Religious, Educational)

NORTH AMERICAN ASSOCIATION OF SYNAGOGUE EXECUTIVES, UNITED SYNAGOGUE OF CONSERVATIVE JUDAISM (Religious, Educational)

RABBINICAL ALLIANCE OF AMERICA (Religious, Educational)

RABBINICAL ASSEMBLY (Religious, Educational)

RABBINICAL COUNCIL OF AMERICA (Religious, Educational)

RECONSTRUCTIONIST RABBINICAL ASSOCIATION (Religious, Educational)

UNION OF ORTHODOX RABBIS OF THE U.S. AND CANADA (Religious, Educational)

WORLD CONFERENCE OF JEWISH COMMUNAL SERVICE (Community Relations)

---

*For fuller listings see under categories in parentheses.

WOMEN'S ORGANIZATIONS*

AMIT WOMEN (Israel-Related)

BRANDEIS UNIVERSITY NATIONAL WOMEN'S COMMITTEE (Educational)

EMUNAH WOMEN OF AMERICA (Israel-Related)

HADASSAH, THE WOMEN'S ZIONIST ORGANIZATION OF AMERICA (Israel-Related)

JEWISH WOMEN INTERNATIONAL (Social Welfare)

NA'AMAT USA, THE WOMEN'S LABOR ZIONIST ORGANIZATION OF AMERICA (Israel-Related)

NATIONAL COUNCIL OF JEWISH WOMEN (Social Welfare)

UOTS (Social Welfare)

WOMEN OF REFORM JUDAISM—FEDERATION OF TEMPLE SISTERHOODS, UNION OF AMERICAN HEBREW CONGREGATIONS (Religious, Educational)

WOMEN'S AMERICAN ORT, AMERICAN ORT FEDERATION (Overseas Aid)

WOMEN'S BRANCH OF THE UNION OF ORTHODOX JEWISH CONGREGATIONS OF AMERICA (Religious, Educational)

WOMEN'S DIVISION OF POALE AGUDATH ISRAEL OF AMERICA (Israel-Related)

WOMEN'S LEAGUE FOR CONSERVATIVE JUDAISM (Religious, Educational)

WOMEN'S LEAGUE FOR ISRAEL, INC. (Israel-Related)

WOMEN'S ORGANIZATION, YESHIVA UNIVERSITY (Religious, Educational)

YOUTH AND STUDENT ORGANIZATIONS*

AGUDATH ISRAEL OF AMERICA (Religious, Educational)

B'NAI B'RITH YOUTH ORGANIZATION (Religious, Educational)

BNEI AKIVA OF NORTH AMERICA, RELIGIOUS ZIONISTS OF AMERICA (Israel-Related)

HABONIM—DROR NORTH AMERICA (Israel-Related)

HASHOMER HATZAIR, SOCIALIST ZIONIST YOUTH MOVEMENT (Israel-Related)

HILLEL (Religious, Educational)

KADIMA, UNITED SYNAGOGUE OF CONSERVATIVE JUDAISM (Religious, Educational)

NATIONAL CONFERENCE OF SYNAGOGUE YOUTH, UNION OF ORTHODOX JEWISH CONGREGATIONS OF AMERICA (Religious, Educational)

NATIONAL JEWISH COMMITTEE ON SCOUTING (Religious, Educational)

NATIONAL JEWISH GIRL SCOUT COMMITTEE (Religious, Educational)

NORTH AMERICAN ALLIANCE FOR JEWISH YOUTH (Religious, Educational)

NORTH AMERICAN FEDERATION OF TEMPLE YOUTH, UNION OF AMERICAN HEBREW CONGREGATIONS (Religious, Educational)

STUDENT STRUGGLE FOR SOVIET JEWRY—*SEE* CENTER FOR RUSSIAN JEWRY (Community Relations)

YOUNG JUDAEA/HASHACHAR, HADASSAH (-Israel-Related)

YUGNTRUF—YOUTH FOR YIDDISH (Cultural)

CANADA

AISH HATORAH (1981). 949 Clark Ave., W., Thornhill, ONT L4J8G6. (905)764-1818. FAX: (905)764-1606. E-mail: www.Aish.com. Edu. Dir. Rabbi Ahron Hoch; Dr. Allan Seidenfeld. An educational center, a community center, and a network of synagogues throughout Toronto; seeks to reawaken Jewish values, ignite Jewish pride and promote Jewish unity through education; reaches out to Jews from all backgrounds in a friendly, warm and non-judgmental environment. *Shabbat Shalom Fax, Monthly newsletter-Village Shul, Winter, Sping, Summer, Fall Calendars.* (WWW.AISH.EDU)

B'NAI BRITH CANADA (1875). 15 Hove St., Downsview, ONT M3H 4Y8. (416) 633-6224. FAX: (416)630-2159. E-mail: faimant@bnaibrith.ca. Pres. Rochelle Wilner; Exec. V.-Pres. Frank Dimant. Canadian Jewry's major advocacy and

*For fuller listings see under categories in parentheses.

service organization; maintains an office of Government Relations in Ottawa and co-sponsors the Canada Israel Committee; makes representations to all levels of government on matters of Jewish concern; promotes humanitarian causes and educational programs, community projects, adult Jewish education, and leadership development; dedicated to the preservation and unity of the Jewish community in Canada and to human rights. *The Jewish Tribune.*

———, INSTITUTE FOR INTERNATIONAL AFFAIRS (1987). E-mail: institute@bnaibrith.ca. Ch. Rochelle Wilner; Natl. Dir. Ruth Klein. Identifies and protests the abuse of human rights worldwide. Advocates on behalf of Israel and Jewish communities in distress. Monitors national and international legislation dealing with war crimes. Activities include briefs and consultations with governmental and non-governmental organizations, research and public education, advocacy and community mobilization, media monitoring, and international conferences and fact-finding missions. *Ad hoc publications on human rights issues.*

———, LEAGUE FOR HUMAN RIGHTS (1964). Co-Chmn. Marvin Kurz & Dr Harriet Morris. National volunteer association dedicated to combating racism, bigotry, and anti-Semitism. Educational programs include multicultural antiracist workshops, public speakers, Holocaust education, Media Human Rights Awards; legal and legislative activity includes government submissions, court interventions, monitoring hate-group activity, responding to incidents of racism and anti-Semitism; community liaison includes intergroup dialogue and support for aggrieved vulnerable communities and groups. Canadian distributor of ADL material. *Heritage Front Report: 1994; Anti-Semitism on Campus; Skinheads in Canada; Annual Audit of Anti-Semitic Incidents; Holocaust and Hope Educators' Newsletter; Combatting Hate: Guidelines for Community Action.*

———, NATIONAL FIELD SERVICES DEPARTMENT. Natl. Dir. Pearl Gladman. Services community affordable housing projects, sports leagues, food baskets for the needy; coordinates hands-on national volunteer programming, Tel-Aide Distress Line; responsible for lodge membership; direct-mail campaigns, annual convention and foundation dinners.

CANADIAN FRIENDS OF CALI & AMAL (1944). 7005 Kildare Rd., Suite 14, Côte St. Luc, Quebec, H4W 1C1. (514)484-9430. FAX: (514)484-0968. Pres. Harry J.F. Bloomfield, QC; Exec. Dir. Fran Kula. Incorporates Canadian Association for Labour Israel (Histadrut) and Canadian Friends of Amal; supports comprehensive health care and education in Israel. Helps to provide modern medical and surgical facilities and the finest vocational, technical education to the Israeli people of all ages.

CANADIAN FRIENDS OF THE HEBREW UNIVERSITY OF JERUSALEM (1944). 3080 Yonge St., Suite 5024, Toronto, ONT M4N 3N1. (416)485-8000. FAX: (416) 485-8565. E-mail: inquiry@cfhu.org. Pres. Dr. Charles C. Gold; Natl. Dir. Charles S. Diamond. Represents the Hebrew University of Jerusalem in Canada; serves as fund-raising arm for the university in Canada; recruits Canadian students and promotes study programs for foreign students at the university; sponsors social and educational events across Canada.

CANADIAN JEWISH CONGRESS (1919; reorg. 1934). 100 Sparks Street, Ottawa, Ontario K1P 5B7. (613)233-8703. FAX: (613)233-8748. E-mail: canadianjewishcongress@cjc.ca. Pres. Moshe Ronen; Exec. V. Pres. Jack Silverstone; Natl. Exec. Dir./Genl. Counsel Jack Silverstone. The community's national voice on public affairs, Canadian Jewish Congress works with governments, community organizations and other partners to fight antisemitism and racism, to promote positive links to Israel and to other Jewish communities, and to support humanitarian and human rights efforts. *National Small Communities Newsletter; DAIS; National Archives Newsletter; regional newsletters.*

CANADIAN YOUNG JUDAEA (1917). 788 Marlee Ave., Suite 205, Toronto, ONT M6B 3K1. (416)781-5156. FAX: (416) 787-3100. E-mail: cyj@idirect.com Natl. Shaliach Ryan Hass; Eastern Region Shaliach Yossi Cadan; Natl. Exec. Dir. Risa Epstein. Strives to attract Jewish youth to Zionism, with goal of aliyah; educates youth about Jewish history and Zionism; prepares them to provide leadership in Young Judaea camps in Canada and Israel and to be concerned Jews. *Judaean L'Madrich; Young Judaean.*

CANADIAN ZIONIST FEDERATION (1967). 5151 Côte St. Catherine Rd., #206, Montreal, PQ H3W 1M6. (514)739-7300. FAX: (514)739-9412. Pres. Kurt Rothschild; Natl. Sec. Florence Simon. Umbrella organization of distinct constituent member Zionist organizations in Canada; carries on major activities in all areas of Jewish life through its departments of education and culture, aliyah, youth and students, public affairs, and small Jewish communities, for the purpose of strengthening the State of Israel and the Canadian Jewish community. *Canadian Zionist.*

———, BUREAU OF EDUCATION AND CULTURE (1972). Pres. Kurt Rothschild. Provides counseling by pedagogic experts, in-service teacher-training courses and seminars in Canada and Israel; national pedagogic council and research center; distributes educational material and teaching aids; supports annual Bible contest and Hebrew-language courses for adults; awards scholarships to Canadian high-school graduates studying for one year in Israel.

HADASSAH—WIZO ORGANIZATION OF CANADA (1917). 1310 Greene Ave., Suite 900, Montreal, PQ H3Z 2B8. (514)937-9431. FAX: (514)933-6483. E-mail: natoff@canadian-hadassah-wizo.org. Natl. Pres. Marion Mayman; Natl. Exec. V.-Pres. Lily Frank. Largest women's volunteer Zionist organization in Canada, located in 43 Canadian cities; dedicated to advancing the quality of life of the women and children in Israel through financial assistance and support of its many projects, day-care centers, schools, institutions, and hospitals. In Canada, the organization promotes Canadian ideals of democracy and is a stalwart advocate of women's issues. *Orah Magazine.*

HASHOMER HATZAIR (1913). 1111 Finch Ave. W., #456, Downsview, ONT M3J 2E5. (416)736-1339. FAX: (416)736-1405. E-mail: mail@givathaviva.ca. Shlicha-Ora Merin; Pres. Sheryl Neshel; Sec. Lipa Roth. A Zionist youth movement established over 80 years ago with centers all over the world. In Toronto, there are weekly meetings during the school year where children get a strong sense of their Jewish identity and connection to Israel, celebrate Jewish holidays together and learn to be contributing members of the community. Hashomer Hatzair runs a 6-day residential winter camp and a 6-week summer camp for youth ranging from 7-16 on Otty Lake.

INTERNATIONAL JEWISH CORRESPONDENCE (IJC) (1978). c/o Canadian Jewish Congress, 1590 Dr. Penfield Ave., Montreal, PQ H3G 1C5.9 (514)931-7531. FAX: (514)931-0548. E-mail: barrys@cjc.ca. Founder/Dir. Barry Simon. Aims to encourage contact between Jews of all ages and backgrounds, in all countries, through pen-pal correspondence. Send autobiographical data and stamped self-addressed envelope or its equivalent (to cover cost of Canadian postage) to receive addresses.

JEWISH IMMIGRANT AID SERVICES OF MONTREAL (JIAS) (1922). 5500 Westbury, 2nd Floor, Montreal, Quebec H3W-2W8. (514)342-9351. FAX: (514)342-0287. E-mail: jiasmail@aol.com. Pres. Joe Kislowicz; Exec. Dir. Shellie Ettinger. JIAS is a national organization assisting the lawful entry of Jews into Canada, as well as their settlement and integration. *JIAS News for Clients.*

JEWISH NATIONAL FUND OF CANADA (Keren Kayemeth Le'Israel, Inc.) (1901). 1980 Sherbrooke St. W., Suite 500, Montreal, PQ H3H 1E8. (514)934-0313. FAX: (514)934-0382. E-mail: mtl@jnf.canada.org. Natl. Pres. Sandra Posluns; Exec. V.-Pres. Joe Rabinovitch. Fund-raising organization affiliated with the World Zionist Organization; involved in afforestation, soil reclamation, and development of the land of Israel, including the construction of roads and preparation of sites for new settlements; provides educational materials and programs to Jewish schools across Canada.

LABOUR ZIONIST ALLIANCE OF CANADA (1909). 272 Codsell Ave., Downsview, ONT M3H 3X2. (416)630-9444. FAX: (416)630-9451. Pres. Josef Krystal; City Committee Chmn. Montreal-Harry Froimovitch. Associated with the World Labor Zionist movement and allied with the Israel Labor party. Provides recreational and cultural programs, mutual aid, and fraternal care to enhance the social welfare of its membership; actively promotes Zionist education, cultural projects, and forums on aspects of Jewish and Canadian concern.

MERETZ CANADA (1950s). 1111 Finch Ave. W., Suite 456, Downsview, ONT M3J 2E5. (416)736-1339. FAX: (416)736-1405. Pres. Joseph Podemski., Vice Pres. Lipa Roth. Acts as a voice of Socialist-Democratic and Zionist points of view within the Jewish community and a focal point for progressive Zionist elements in Canada; affiliated with Hashomer Hatzair and the Givat Haviva Educational Center.

MIZRACHI ORGANIZATION OF CANADA (1941). 296 Wilson Ave., North York, ONT M3H 1S8. (416)630-9266. FAX: (416)630-2305. Pres. Jack Kahn. Promotes religious Zionism, aimed at making Israel a state based on Torah; maintains Bnei Akiva, a summer camp, adult education program, and touring department; supports Mizrachi-Hapoel Hamizrachi and other religious Zionist institutions in Israel which strengthen traditional Judaism. *Mizrachi Newsletter*.

NATIONAL COMMUNITY RELATIONS COMMITTEE OF CANADIAN JEWISH CONGRESS (1936). 4600 Bathurst St., Willowdale, Toronto, ONT M2R 3V2. (416)631-5673. FAX: (416)635-1408. E-mail: mprutschi @ujafed.org. Chmn. Mark S. Weintraub; Pres. Moshe Ronen; Dir. Manuel Prutschi. Seeks to safeguard the status, rights, and welfare of Jews in Canada; to combat anti-Semitism, and promote understanding and goodwill among all ethnic and religious groups.

NATIONAL COUNCIL OF JEWISH WOMEN OF CANADA (1897). 118-1588 Main St., Winnipeg, MAN R2V 1Y3. (204)339-9700. FAX: (204)334-3779. E-mail: info@ ncjwc.org. Chmn. Carol Slater; Natl. V.-Pres. Roz Fine & Brenlee Gurvey Gales. Dedicated to furthering human welfare in the Jewish and general communities, locally, nationally, and internationally; through an integrated program of education, service, and social action seeks to fulfill unmet needs and to serve the individual and the community. *National By-Lines.*

ORT CANADA (1948). 3101 Bathurst St., Suite 604, Toronto, ONT M6A 2A6. (416)787-0339. FAX: (416)787-9420. E-mail: ortcan@pathcom.com. Pres. Dr. Roger Korman; Exec. Dir. Joel Shapiro; Admin. Beverley Schneider. Chapters in 11 Canadian cities raise funds for ORT's nonprofit global network of schools where Jewish students learn a wide range of marketable skills, including the most advanced high-tech professions. *Focus Magazine.*

STATE OF ISRAEL BONDS (CANADA-ISRAEL SECURITIES, LTD.) (1953). 970 Lawrence Ave. W., Suite 502, Toronto, ONT M6A 3B6. (416)789-3351. FAX: (416)789-9436. Pres. Norman Spector; Bd. Chmn. George A. Cohon. An international securities organization offering interest-bearing instruments issued by the government of Israel. Invests in every aspect of Israel's economy, including agriculture, commerce, and industry. Israel Bonds are RRSP-approved.

Jewish Federations, Welfare Funds, Community Councils

UNITED STATES

ALABAMA

BIRMINGHAM

THE BIRMINGHAM JEWISH FEDERATION (1936; reorg. 1971); Box 130219 (35213-0219); (205)879-0416. FAX: (205)803-1526. E-mail: federation@bjf.org.

MOBILE

MOBILE JEWISH WELFARE FUND, INC. (inc. 1966); One Office Park, Suite 219 (36609); (334)343-7197. FAX: (334)343-7197. E-mail: mjwf123@aol.com. Pres. Eileen Susman.

MONTGOMERY

JEWISH FEDERATION OF MONTGOMERY, INC. (1930); 2820 Fairlane Dr. (36120-0058); (334)277-5820. FAX: (334)277-8383. E-mail: jfedmgm@aol.com. Pres. Alan Weil; Admin. Dir. Susan Mayer Bruchis.

ARIZONA

PHOENIX

JEWISH FEDERATION OF GREATER PHOENIX (1940); 32 W. Coolidge, Suite 200 (85013); (602)274-1800. FAX: (602)266-7875. E-mail: info@jewishphoenix.org. Pres. Neil Hiller; Exec. Dir. Arthur Paikowsky. (www.jewishphoenix.org)

TUCSON

JEWISH FEDERATION OF SOUTHERN ARIZONA (1946); 3822 East River Rd., Suite 100 (85718); (520)577-9393. FAX: (520)577-0734. E-mail: jfink@jfsa.org. Pres. Linda Tumarkin; Exec. Dir. Stuart Mellan. (www.jfsa.org)

ARKANSAS

LITTLE ROCK

JEWISH FEDERATION OF ARKANSAS (1911); 425 N. University (72205); (501)663-3571. FAX: (501)663-7286. E-mail: jflar@aristotle.net. Pres. Doris Krain; Exec. Dir. Ziva Starr.

CALIFORNIA

EAST BAY

JEWISH FEDERATION OF THE GREATER EAST BAY (INCLUDING ALAMEDA & CONTRA COSTA COUNTIES) (1917); 401 Grand Ave., Oakland (94610-5022); (510)839-2900. FAX: (510)839-3996. E-mail: admin@jfed.org. Pres. Jerry Yanowitz; Exec. V.-Pres. Ami Nahshon. (www.jfed.org)

FRESNO

JEWISH FEDERATION OF FRESNO; 295 W. CROMWELL AVE., SUITE 111 (93711-6161); (559)432-2162. FAX: (559)432-0425.

LONG BEACH

JEWISH FEDERATION OF GREATER LONG BEACH AND W. ORANGE COUNTY (1937; inc. 1946); 3801 E. Willow St. (90815); (562)426-7601. FAX: (562)424-3915. E-mail: kgibbs@jewishlongbeach.org. Pres. Richard Lipeles; Exec. Dir. Michael S. Rassler. (www.jewishlongbeach.org)

LOS ANGELES

Jewish Federation Council of Greater Los Angeles (1912; reorg. 1959); 6505 Wilshire Blvd., 8th fl. (90048); (323)761-8000. FAX: (323)761-8235. E-mail: webcoordinator@jewishla.org. Pres. Lionel Bell; Exec. V.-Pres. John Fishel. (www.jewishla.org)

ORANGE COUNTY

Jewish Federation of Orange County (1964; inc. 1965); 250 E. Baker St., Suite A, Costa Mesa (92626); (714)755-5555. FAX: (714)755-0307. E-mail: info@jfoc.org. Pres. Charles Karp; Exec. Dir. Bunnie Mauldin. (www.jfoc.org)

PALM SPRINGS

Jewish Federation of Palm Springs and Desert Area (1971); 255 N. El Cielo, Suite 430 (92262-6990); (760)325-7281. FAX: (760)325-2188. E-mail: msjfedps@gte.net. Pres. Larry Pitts; Exec. Dir. Mitzi Schafer. (www.jewishpalmsprings.org)

SACRAMENTO

Jewish Federation of the Sacramento Region (1948); 2351 Wyda Way (95825); (916)486-0906. FAX: (916)486-0816. E-mail: jfed2@juno.com. Pres. Skip Rosenbloom; Exec. Dir. Phillis Helene Cohen. (www.jewishsac.org)

SAN DIEGO

United Jewish Federation of San Diego County (1936); 4797 Mercury St. (92111-2102); (858)571-3444. FAX: (858)571-0701. E-mail: fedujf@ujfsd.org. Pres. Mary Ann Scher; Exec. V.-Pres. Stephen M. Abramson. (www.jewishinsandiego.org)

SAN FRANCISCO

Jewish Community Federation of San Francisco, the Peninsula, Marin, and Sonoma Counties (1910; reorg. 1955); 121 Steuart St. (94105); (415)777-0411. FAX: (415)495-6635. E-mail: info@sfjcf.org. Pres. John Goldman; Exec. V.-Pres. Phyllis Cook. (www.sfjcf.org)

SAN GABRIEL AND POMONA VALLEY

Jewish Federation of the Greater San Gabriel and Pomona Valleys; 258 W. Badillo St. (91723-1906); (626)967-3656. FAX: (626)967-5135. E-mail: sgpvfed@aol.com.

SAN JOSE

Jewish Federation of Greater San Jose (incl. Santa Clara County except Palo Alto and Los Altos) (1930; reorg. 1950); 14855 Oka Rd., Suite 2, Los Gatos (95030); (408)358-3033. FAX: (408)356-0733. E-mail: federation@jfgsj.org. Pres. Howard May; Exec. Dir. Jon Friedenberg. (www.jfgsj.org)

SANTA BARBARA

Santa Barbara Jewish Federation (1974); 524 Chapala St. (93190); (805)957-1115. FAX: (805)957-9230. E-mail: sbjfed@silcom.com. Pres. Jeri Eigner; Exec. Dir. Shelly Katz.

VENTURA COUNTY

Jewish Federation of Ventura County; 7620 Foothill Rd. (93004); (805)647-7800. FAX: (805)647-0482. E-mail: ujavtacty@worldnet.att.net.

COLORADO

DENVER/BOULDER

Allied Jewish Federation of Colorado (1936); 300 S. Dahlia St., Denver (80222); (303)321-3399. FAX: (303)322-8328. E-mail: ajfcolo@aol.com. Chmn. Edward A. Robinson; Pres. & CEO:Steve Gelfand. (www.jewishcolorado.org)

CONNECTICUT

BRIDGEPORT

Jewish Federation Of Eastern Fairfield County. (1936; reorg. 1981); 4200 Park Ave. (06604-1092); (203)372-6567. FAX: (203)374-0770. E-mail: jccs@snet.net. Chmn. Stanley Strouch; Pres. & CEO Daniel P. Baker. (www.jccs.org)

DANBURY

The Jewish Federation of Greater Danbury, Inc. (1945); 105 Newton Rd. (06810); (203)792-6353. FAX: (203)748-5099. E-mail: info@thejf.org. Pres. Daniel Wolinsky; Exec. Dir. Judy Prager. (www.thejf.org)

EASTERN CONNECTICUT

Jewish Federation of Eastern Connecticut, Inc. (1950; inc. 1970); 28 Channing St., New London (06320); (860)442-8062. FAX: (860)443-4175. E-mail: jfec@worldnet.att.net. Pres. Myron Hendel; Exec. Dir. Jerome E. Fischer.

GREENWICH

GREENWICH JEWISH FEDERATION (1956); One Holly Hill Lane (06830-6080); (203)622-1434. FAX: (203)622-1237. E-mail: pezmom3@aol.com. Pres. Jonathan Nelson; Exec. Dir. Pam Zur.

HARTFORD

JEWISH FEDERATION OF GREATER HARTFORD (1945); 333 Bloomfield Ave., W. Hartford (06117); (860)232-4483. FAX: (860) 232-5221. E-mail: aperrault@jewishhartford.org. Pres. Henry M. Zachs; Acting Exec. Dir. Steven Bayer.

NEW HAVEN

JEWISH FEDERATION OF GREATER NEW HAVEN (1928); 360 Amity Rd., Woodbridge (06525); (203)387-2424. FAX: (203)387-1818. E-mail: marinak@megahits.com Pres. David Schaefer; Exec. Dir. Neil Berro. (WWW.JEWISHNEWHAVEN.ORG)

NORWALK

(See Westport)

STAMFORD

UNITED JEWISH FEDERATION (inc. 1973); 1035 Newfield Ave., PO Box 3038 (06905); (203)321-1373. FAX: (203)322-3277. E-mail: office@ujf.org. Pres. Corrine Lotstein; Dir. of Dev. Edith Samers. (WWW.UJF.ORG)

WATERBURY

JEWISH FEDERATION OF WESTERN CONNECTICUT (1938); 73 Main St. S., Box F, Woodbury (06798-3404); (203)263-5121. FAX: (203)263-5143. E-mail: jfedwtby@aol.com. Pres. Dan Goodman; Exec. Dir. Rob Zwang.

WESTPORT-WESTON-WILTON-NORWALK

UJA/FEDERATION OF WESTPORT—WESTON—WILTON—NORWALK (inc. 1980); 431 Post Road E., Suite 22, Westport (06880); (203)226-8197. FAX: (203)226-5051. E-mail: rkessler@optonline.net. Pres. Sandra Lefkowitz; Exec. Dir. Robert Kessler. (WWW.UJAFEDERATION.ORG)

DELAWARE

WILMINGTON

JEWISH FEDERATION OF DELAWARE, INC. (1934); 100 W. 10th St., Suite 301 (19801-1628); (302)427-2100. FAX: (302)427-2438. E-mail: delawarejfd@jon.cjfny.org. Pres. Barbara H. Schoenberg; Exec. V. Pres. Judy Wortman. (WWW.SHALOMDEL.ORG)

DISTRICT OF COLUMBIA

WASHINGTON

THE JEWISH FEDERATION OF GREATER WASHINGTON, INC. (1935); 6101 Montrose Rd., Rockville, MD (20852); (301)230-7200. FAX: (301)230-7265. E-mail: info@jewishfedwash.org. Pres. Dede Feinberg; Exec. V.-Pres. Misha Galperin. (WWW.JEWISHFEDWASH.ORG)

FLORIDA

BREVARD COUNTY

JEWISH FEDERATION OF BREVARD (1974); 108-A Barton Ave., Rockledge (32955); (407)636-1824. FAX: (407)636-0614. E-mail: jfbrevard@aol.com. Pres. Gary Singer; Exec. Dir. Joanne Bishins.

BROWARD COUNTY

JEWISH FEDERATION OF BROWARD COUNTY (1943; 1968); 5890 S. Pine Island Rd., Davie (33351-7319); (954)748-8400. FAX: (954)748-6332. E-mail: info@jewishfedbroward.org. Pres. David B. Schulman; Exec. Dir. Gary N. Rubin. (WWW.JEWISHFEDBROWARD.ORG)

COLLIER COUNTY

JEWISH FEDERATION OF COLLIER COUNTY (1974); 1250 Tamiami Trail N., Suite 202, Naples (33940); (941) 263-4205. FAX: (941)263-3813. E-mail: jfccfl@aol.com. Pres. Ann Jacobson.

DAYTONA BEACH

(See Volusia & Flagler Counties)

FT. LAUDERDALE

(See Broward County)

GAINESVILLE

JEWISH COUNCIL OF NORTH CENTRAL FLORIDA; P.O. Box 14937, Gainesville (32604); (352)371-3846. E-mail: oberger@gnv.fdt.net.

JACKSONVILLE

JACKSONVILLE JEWISH FEDERATION, INC. (1935); 8505 San Jose Blvd. (32217); (904)448-5000. FAX: (904)448-5715. E-mail: jaxjewishfed@jon.cjfny.org. Pres. Dr. Kenneth Sekine; Exec. V.-Pres. Alan Margolies.c (WWW.JAXJEWISH.ORG)

LEE COUNTY

JEWISH FEDERATION OF LEE AND CHARLOTTE COUNTIES (1974); 6237-E Presidential Court, Ft. Myers (33919-3568); (941)481-4449. FAX: (941)481-0139. E-mail: jfedswfl@aol.com. Pres. Rozzi Osterman; Exec. Dir. Annette Goodman. (WWW.JEWISHFEDERATIONSWFL.ORG)

MIAMI

GREATER MIAMI JEWISH FEDERATION, INC. (1938); 4200 Biscayne Blvd. (33137); (305)576-4000. FAX: (305)573-4584. E-mail: info@gmjf.or. Pres. Michael Scheck; Exec. V.-Pres. Jacob Solomon. (WWW.JEWISHMIAMI.ORG)

ORLANDO

JEWISH FEDERATION OF GREATER ORLANDO (1949); 851 N. Maitland Ave.; PO Box 941508, Maitland (32794-1508); (407)645-5933. FAX: (407)645-1172. Pres. James S. Grodin; Exec. Dir. Eric Geboff.

PALM BEACH COUNTY

JEWISH FEDERATION OF PALM BEACH COUNTY, INC. (1962); 4601 Community Dr., W. Palm Beach (33417-2760); (561)478-0700. FAX: (561)478-9696. E-mail: info@jfedpbco.org. Pres. Eugene J. Ribakoff; Exec. V.-Pres. Jeffrey L. Klein. (WWW.JEWISHPALMBEACH.ORG)

JEWISH FEDERATION OF SOUTH PALM BEACH COUNTY, INC. (1979); 9901 Donna Klein Blvd. Boca Raton (33428-1788); (561)852-3100. FAX: (561)852-3136. E-mail: dstern@jewishboca.org. (WWW.JEWISHBOCA.ORG)

PENSACOLA

PENSACOLA JEWISH FEDERATION; 800 No. Palafox (32501); (850)434-7992.

PINELLAS COUNTY

JEWISH FEDERATION OF PINELLAS COUNTY, INC. (incl. Clearwater and St. Petersburg) (1950; reincorp. 1974); 13191 Starkey Rd., #8, Largo (33773-1438); (727) 530-3223. FAX: (727)531-0221. E-mail: pinellas@jfedpinellas.org. Pres. David Abelson; Interim Exec. Dir. Bonnie Friedman. (WWW.JFEDPINELLAS.ORG)

SARASOTA-MANATEE

SARASOTA-MANATEE JEWISH FEDERATION (1959); 580 S. McIntosh Rd. (34232-1959); (941)371-4546. FAX: (941)378-2947. E-mail: jlederman@smjf.org. Pres. Scott Gordon; Exec. Dir. Jan C. Lederman. (WWW.SMJF.ORG)

TALLAHASSEE

APALACHEE FEDERATION OF JEWISH CHARITIES; PO Box 14825 (32317-4825); (850)877-3989; FAX: (850)877-7989. E-mail: mdlevy@pol.net.

TAMPA

TAMPA JEWISH FEDERATION (1941); 13009 Community Campus Dr. (33625-4000); (813)264-9000. FAX: (813)265-8450. E-mail: tjfjcc@aol.com. Pres. Lili Kaufman; Exec. V.-Pres. Howard Borer.

VOLUSIA & FLAGLER COUNTIES

JEWISH FEDERATION OF VOLUSIA & FLAGLER COUNTIES, INC. (1980); 733 S. Nova Rd., Ormond Beach (32174); (904)672-0294. FAX: (904)673-1316. Pres. Steven I. Unatin; Exec. Dir. Gloria Max.

GEORGIA

ATLANTA

JEWISH FEDERATION OF GREATER ATLANTA, INC. (1905; reorg. 1967); 1440 Spring St., NW (30309-2837); (404)873-1661. FAX: (404)874-7043/881-4027. E-mail: kkaplan@jfga.org. Pres. Dr. Arnold Rubenstein; Exec. Dir. David I. Sarnat.

AUGUSTA

AUGUSTA JEWISH FEDERATION (1937); 898 Weinberger Way, Evans (30809-3636); (706)228-3636. FAX: (706)868-1660/823-3960. E-mail: mpousman@hotmail.com. Pres. Dr. Louis Scharff; Exec. Dir. Michael Pousman.

COLUMBUS

JEWISH FEDERATION OF COLUMBUS, INC. (1944); PO Box 6313 (31906); (706)568-6668. Pres. Murray Solomon; Sec. Irene Rainbow.

SAVANNAH

SAVANNAH JEWISH FEDERATION (1943); 5111 Abercorn St. (31403); (912)355-8111. FAX: (912)355-8116. E-mail: jrgreen4@juno.com. Pres. Dr. Paul Kulbersh; Exec. Dir. Sharon Gal.

ILLINOIS

CHAMPAIGN-URBANA

CHAMPAIGN-URBANA JEWISH FEDERATION (1929); 503 E. John St., Champaign (61820); (217)367-9872. FAX: (217)367-0077. E-mail: cujf@shalomcu.org. Pres. Anthony E. Novak; Exec. Dir. (Ms.) L. Lee Melhado. (WWW.SHALOMCU.ORG)

CHICAGO

JEWISH FEDERATION OF METROPOLITAN CHICAGO/JEWISH UNITED FUND OF METROPOLITAN CHICAGO (1900); Ben Gurion Way, 1 S. Franklin St. (60606-4694); (312)346-6700. FAX: (312)444-2086. E-mail: webinfo@juf.org. Chmn. Fred Bondy; Pres. Steven B. Nasatir. (WWW.JUF.ORG)

JOLIET

JOLIET JEWISH WELFARE CHEST (1938); 250 N. Midland Ave. at Campbell St. (60435); (815)741-4600.

PEORIA

JEWISH FEDERATION OF PEORIA (1933; inc. 1947); 2000 W. Pioneer Pwky., Suite 10B (61615-1835); (309)689-0063. FAX: (309) 689-0575. Pres. Jennifer Dolin; Exec. Dir. Eunice Galsky.

QUAD CITIES

JEWISH FEDERATION OF QUAD CITIES (1938; comb. 1973); 1705 2nd Ave., Suite 405, Rock Island (61201); (309)793-1300. FAX: (309)793-1345. E-mail: qcfederation@juno.com. Pres. Paul Light; Exec. Dir. Ida Kramer.

ROCKFORD

JEWISH FEDERATION OF GREATER ROCKFORD (1937); 1500 Parkview Ave. (61107); (815)399-5497. FAX: (815)399-9835. E-mail: rockfordfederation@juno.com. Pres. Sterne Roufa; Exec. Dir. Marilyn Youman.

SOUTHERN ILLINOIS

JEWISH FEDERATION OF SOUTHERN ILLINOIS, SOUTHEASTERN MISSOURI, AND WESTERN KENTUCKY (1941); 6464 W. Main, Suite 7A, Belleville (62223); (618)398-6100. FAX: (618)398-0539. E-mail: silfed@aol.com. Co-Pres. Harvey Cohen & Carol Rudman; Exec. Dir. Steven C. Low.

SPRINGFIELD

SPRINGFIELD JEWISH FEDERATION (1941); 2815 Old Jacksonville Rd., Ste 103A (62704); (217)787-7223. FAX: (217)787-7470. E-mail: sjf@springnet1.com. Pres. Rita Victor; Exec. Dir. Gloria Schwartz.

INDIANA

FORT WAYNE

FORT WAYNE JEWISH FEDERATION (1921); 227 E. Washington Blvd. (46802-3121); (219)422-8566. FAX: (219)422-8567. E-mail: fwjewfed@aol.com. Pres. Scott Salon; Exec. Dir. Jeff Gubitz.

INDIANAPOLIS

JEWISH FEDERATION OF GREATER INDIANAPOLIS, INC. (1905); 6705 Hoover Rd. (46260-4120); (317)726-5450. FAX: (317) 205-0307. E-mail controljfg@aol.com. Pres. Claudette Einhorn; Exec. V.-Pres. Harry Nadler. (WWW.JEWISHININDY.ORG)

LAFAYETTE

JEWISH FEDERATION OF GREATER LAFAYETTE (1924); PO Box 3802, W. Lafayette (47906); (765)426-4724. E-mail: jfgl1@aol.com. Pres.Earl Prohofsky; Finan. Sec. Laura Starr; Admin. Judy Upton.

NORTHWEST INDIANA

JEWISH FEDERATION OF NORTHWEST INDIANA (1941; reorg. 1959); 2939 Jewett St., Highland (46322); (219)972-2250. FAX: (219)972-4779. E-mail: defwej@aol.com. Pres. Carol Karol; Exec. Dir. David Tein.

ST. JOSEPH VALLEY

JEWISH FEDERATION OF ST. JOSEPH VALLEY (1946); 3202 Shalom Way, South Bend (46615); (219)233-1164. FAX: (219)288-4103. E-mail: mgardner@fedsjv.org. Pres. Dr. Douglas H. Barton; Exec. V.-Pres. Marilyn Gardner. (WWW.JFEDSJV.ORG)

IOWA

DES MOINES

JEWISH FEDERATION OF GREATER DES MOINES (1914); 910 Polk Blvd. (50312); (515)277-6321. FAX: (515)277-4069. E-mail: jcrcia@aol.com. Pres. Robert M. Pomerantz; Exec. Dir. Elaine Steinger.

SIOUX CITY

JEWISH FEDERATION OF SIOUX CITY (1921); 815 38th St. (51104-1417); (712)258-0618. FAX: (712)258-0619. Pres. Michele Ivener; Admin. Dir. Doris Rosenthal.

KANSAS

KANSAS CITY

See listing under Missouri

WICHITA

MID-KANSAS JEWISH FEDERATION, INC. (serving South Central Kansas) (1935); 400 N. Woodlawn, Suite 8 (67208); (316)686-4741. FAX: (316)686-6008. Pres. Marie Levy; Exec. Dir. Judy Press.

KENTUCKY

CENTRAL KENTUCKY

CENTRAL KENTUCKY JEWISH FEDERATION (1976); 340 Romany Rd., Lexington (40502-2400); (606)268-0672. FAX: (606)268-0775. Pres.Martin Barr; Exec. Dir. Daniel Chejfec. (WWW.JEWISHLEXINGTON.ORG)

LOUISVILLE

JEWISH COMMUNITY FEDERATION OF LOUISVILLE, INC. (1934); 3630 Dutchmans Lane (40205); (502)451-8840. FAX: (502) 458-0702. E-mail: jfed@iglou.com. Pres. Gerald D. Temes MD; Exec. Dir. Alan S. Engel. (WWW.JEWISHLOUISVILLE.ORG)

LOUISIANA

BATON ROUGE

JEWISH FEDERATION OF GREATER BATON ROUGE (1971); 3354 Kleinert Ave. (70806); (504) 387-9744. FAX: (504)387-9487. E-mail: jfedofbr@postoffice.att.net. Pres. Harvey Hoffman.

NEW ORLEANS

JEWISH FEDERATION OF GREATER NEW ORLEANS (1913; reorg. 1977); 3500 N. Causeway Blvd., Suite 1240, Metairie (70002-3524); (504)828-2125. FAX: (504)828-2827. E-mail: jewishnews@jewishnola.com. Pres. Hugo Kahn; Exec. Dir. Eric Stillman. (WWW.JEWISHNEWORLEANS.ORG)

SHREVEPORT

NORTHERN LOUISIANA JEWISH FEDERATION (1941; inc. 1967); 4700 Line Ave., Suite 117 (71106-1533); (318)868-1200. FAX: (318) 868-1272. E-mail: sjfed@juno.com. Pres. Rick Murov; Exec. Dir. Howard L. Ross. (WWW.NLJFED.ORG)

MAINE

LEWISTON-AUBURN

LEWISTON-AUBURN JEWISH FEDERATION (1947); 74 Bradman St., Auburn (04210); (207)786-4201. FAX: (207)783-1000. Pres. Scott Nussinow.

PORTLAND

JEWISH COMMUNITY ALLIANCE OF SOUTHERN MAINE (1942); 57 Ashmont St. (04103); (207)773-7254. FAX: (207)772-2234. E-mail: info@mainejewish.org. Pres. Michael Peisner; Exec. Dir. David Unger. (WWW.MAINEJEWISH.ORG)

MARYLAND

BALTIMORE

THE ASSOCIATED: JEWISH COMMUNITY FEDERATION OF BALTIMORE (1920; reorg. 1969); 101 W. Mt. Royal Ave. (21201-5728); (410) 727-4828. FAX: (410)752-1327. E-mail: information@associated.org. Chmn. Barbara L. Himmelrich; Pres. Darrell D. Friedman. (WWW.ASSOCIATED.ORG)

COLUMBIA

JEWISH FEDERATION OF HOWARD COUNTY; 8950 Rte. 108, Suite 115, Columbia (21045); (410)730-4976; FAX: (410)730-9393. E-mail: jfohc@starpower.net. Pres. Toby Knopf; Exec. Dir. Roberta Greenstein. (WWW.EROLS.COM/JFOHC)

MASSACHUSETTS

BERKSHIRE COUNTY

JEWISH FEDERATION OF THE BERKSHIRES (1940); 235 East St., Pittsfield (01201); (413)442-4360. FAX: (413)443-6070. E-mail: jreichbaum@berkshire.net. Pres. Stephen Rudin; Exec. Dir. Jaquelynne Reichbaum. (WWW.BERKSHIREWEB.COM/JEWISHFEDER)

BOSTON

COMBINED JEWISH PHILANTHROPIES OF GREATER BOSTON, INC. (1895; inc. 1961); 126 High St. (02110-2700); (617)457-8500. FAX: (617)988-6262. E-mail: info@cjp.org. Chmn. Cynthia B. Shulman; Pres. Barry Shrage. (WWW.CJP.ORG)

MERRIMACK VALLEY

MERRIMACK VALLEY JEWISH FEDERATION (Serves Andover, Haverhill, Lawrence, Lowell, Newburyport, and 22 surrounding communities) (1988); PO Box 937, Andover (01810-0016); (978)688-0466. FAX: (978) 688-1097. E-mail: jan@mvjf.org. Pres. James H. Shainker; Exec. Dir. Jan Steven Brodie. (WWW.MVJF.ORG)

NEW BEDFORD

JEWISH FEDERATION OF GREATER NEW BEDFORD, INC. (1938; inc. 1954); 467 Hawthorn St., N. Dartmouth (02747); (508)997-7471. FAX: (508)997-7730. Co-Pres. Harriet Philips, Patricia Rosenfield; Exec. Dir. Wil Herrup.

NORTH SHORE

JEWISH FEDERATION OF THE NORTH SHORE, INC. (1938); 21 Front St., Salem (01970-

3707); (978)598-1810. FAX: (978)741-7507. E-mail: mail@jfns.org. Pres. Shepard M. Remis; Exec. Dir. Neil A. Cooper. (WWW.JFNS.ORG)

SPRINGFIELD

JEWISH FEDERATION OF GREATER SPRINGFIELD, INC. (1925); 1160 Dickinson St. (01108); (413)737-4313. FAX: (413)737-4348. E-mail: cfschwartz@jewishspringfield.org. Pres. Jeffrey Mandell; Exec. Dir. Joel Weiss. (WWW.JEWISH SPRINGFIELD.ORG)

WORCESTER

JEWISH FEDERATION OF CENTRAL MASSACHUSETTS (1947; inc. 1957); 633 Salisbury St. (01609); (508)756-1543. FAX: (508) 798-0962. E-mail: meyerb@aol.com. Pres. Dr. Robert Honig; Exec. Dir. Meyer L. Bodoff.

MICHIGAN

ANN ARBOR

JEWISH FEDERATION OF WASHTENAW COUNTY/UJA (1986); 2939 Birch Hollow Dr. (48108); (734)677-0100. FAX: (734)677-0109. E-mail: jccfed@aol.com. Pres. Morley Witus; Exec. Dir. Nancy N. Margolis.

DETROIT

JEWISH FEDERATION OF METROPOLITAN DETROIT (1899); 6735 Telegraph Rd., Suite 30, PO Box 2030, Bloomfield Hills (48301-2030); (248)642-4260. FAX: (248)642-4985. E-mail: jfmd@jfmd.org. Pres. Penny Blumenstein; Exec. V.-Pres. Robert P. Aronson. (WWW.THISISFEDERATION.ORG)

FLINT

FLINT JEWISH FEDERATION (1936); 619 Wallenberg St. (48502); (810)767-5922. FAX: (810)767-9024. E-mail: fjf@tm.net. Pres. Dr. Steve Burton; Exec. Dir. Joel B. Kaplan. (http://users.tmnet/flint)

GRAND RAPIDS

JEWISH COMMUNITY FUND OF GRAND RAPIDS (1930); 330 Fuller NE (49503); (616)456-5553. FAX: (616)456-5780. E-mail: jcfgr@iserv.net. Pres. Richard Stevens; Admin. Dir. Rosalie Stein; V.P. Maxine Shapiro.

MINNESOTA

DULUTH-SUPERIOR

NORTHLAND JEWISH FUND (1937); 1602 E. Second St., Duluth (55812); (218)724-8857. FAX: (218)724-2560. E-mail: sstevens@computerpro.com. Pres. Neil Glazman.

MINNEAPOLIS

MINNEAPOLIS JEWISH FEDERATION (1929; inc. 1930); 13100 Wayzota Blvd. (55305); (612)593-2600. FAX: (612)593-2544. E-mail: sfreeman@mplsfed.org. Pres. Michael Horovitz; Exec. Dir. Joshua Fogelson. (WWW.JEWISHMINNESOTA.ORG)

ST. PAUL

UNITED JEWISH FUND AND COUNCIL (1935); 790 S. Cleveland, Suite 201 (55116); (651) 690-1707. FAX: (651)690-0228. Pres. James Stein; Exec. Dir. Samuel Asher. (WWW.JEWISHMINNESOTA.ORG)

MISSOURI

KANSAS CITY

JEWISH FEDERATION OF GREATER KANSAS CITY MO/KS (1933); 5801 W. 115 St., Overland Park, KS (66211-1824); (913)327-8100. FAX: (913)327-8110. E-mail: cherylm@jewishkc.org. Pres. John Uhlmann; Exec. Dir. Todd Stettner. (WWW.JEWISHKC.ORG)

ST. JOSEPH

UNITED JEWISH FUND OF ST. JOSEPH (1915); 1816 Walnut (64503); (816)233-1186. FAX: (816)233-9399. Elliot Zidell; Exec. Sec. Sherri Ott.

ST. LOUIS

JEWISH FEDERATION OF ST. LOUIS (incl. St. Louis County) (1901); 12 Millstone Campus Dr. (63146-9812); (314)432-0020. FAX: (314)432-1277. E-mail: jfedstl@jfedstl.org. Pres. Mont S. Levy; Exec. V.-Pres. Barry Rosenberg. (WWW.JEWISHSTLOUIS.ORG)

NEBRASKA

LINCOLN

JEWISH FEDERATION OF LINCOLN, INC. (1931; inc. 1961); PO Box 67218 (68506); (402)489-1015. FAX: (402)476-8364. Pres. Herb Friedman; Exec. Dir. Karen Sommer.

OMAHA

JEWISH FEDERATION OF OMAHA (1903); 333 S. 132nd St. (68154-2198); (402)334-8200. FAX: (402)334-1330. E-mail: pmonsk@top.net. Pres. Howard Kooper; Exec. Dir. Jan Perelman. (WWW.JEWISHOMAHA.ORG)

NEVADA

LAS VEGAS

Jewish Federation of Las Vegas (1973); 3909 S. Maryland Pkwy. # 400 (89119-7520); (702)732-0556. FAX: (702)732-3228. Pres. David Dahan; Exec. Dir. Ronni Epstein. (www.jewishlasvegas.com)

NEW HAMPSHIRE

MANCHESTER

Jewish Federation of Greater Manchester (1974); 698 Beech St. (03104-3626); (603)627-7679. FAX: (603) 627-7963.

NEW JERSEY

ATLANTIC AND CAPE MAY COUNTIES

Jewish Federation of Atlantic and Cape May Counties (1924); 3393 Bargaintown Rd., Box 617, Northfield (08225-0196); (609)653-3030. FAX: (609)653-8881. E-mail: jfedacm@cyberenet.net. Pres. Joseph Rodgers; Exec. V.-Pres. Bernard Cohen.

BERGEN COUNTY

UJA Federation of Bergen County and North Hudson (inc. 1978); 111 Kinderkamack Rd., River Edge (07661); (201)488-6800. FAX: (201)488-1507. E-mail: contact@jewishbergen.org. Pres. Edward Dauber; Exec. V.-Pres. Ron B. Meier. (www.jewishbergen.org)

CENTRAL NEW JERSEY

Jewish Federation of Central New Jersey (1940; merged 1973); 1391 Martine Ave., Scotch Plains (07076); (908)889-5335. FAX: (908)889-5370. E-mail: community@jfedcnj.org. Pres. Alfred A. Gelfand; Exec. V.-Pres. Stanley Stone. (www.jfedcnj.org)

CLIFTON-PASSAIC

Jewish Federation of Greater Clifton-Passaic (1933); 199 Scoles Ave., Clifton (07012-1125). (973)777-7031. FAX: (973) 777-6701. E-mail: yymuskin@jfedclifton-passaic.com. Pres. George Kramer; Exec. V.-Pres. Yosef Y. Muskin.

CUMBERLAND COUNTY

Jewish Federation of Cumberland County (inc. 1971); 1063 E. Landis Ave. Suite B, Vineland (08360-3752); (609)696-4445. FAX: (609)696-3428. E-mail: jfedcc@aol.com. Pres. James Potter; Exec. Dir. Ann Lynn Lipton.

METROWEST NEW JERSEY

United Jewish Federation of MetroWest (1923); 901 Route 10, Whippany (07981-1156); (973)884-4800. FAX: (973)884-7361. E-mail: webmail@ujfmetrowest.org. Pres. Steven Klinghoffer; Exec. V.-Pres. Max L. Kleinman. (www.ujfmetrowest.org)

MIDDLESEX COUNTY

Jewish Federation of Greater Middlesex County (org. 1948; reorg. 1985); 230 Old Bridge Tpk., S. River (08882-2000); (732)432-7711. FAX: (732)432-0292. E-mail: jfednj@aol.com. Pres. Roy Tanzman; Exec. Dir. Gerrie Bamira. (www.jfgmc.org)

MONMOUTH COUNTY

Jewish Federation of Greater Monmouth County (1971); 100 Grant Ave., PO Box 210, Deal (07723-0210); (732)531-6200-1. FAX: (732)531-9518. E-mail: pfdnuss@msn.com. Pres. David Portman; Chmn. William A. Schwartz; Exec. Dir. David A. Nussbaum.

NORTH JERSEY

Jewish Federation of North Jersey (1933); One Pike Dr., Wayne (07470-2498); (973)595-0555. FAX: (973)595-1532. Branch Office: 17-10 River Rd., Fair Lawn (07410-1250); (973)794-1111. E-mail: jfnj@aol.com. Pres. George Liss; Exec. Dir. Martin Greenberg.

OCEAN COUNTY

Ocean County Jewish Federation (1977); 301 Madison Ave., Lakewood (08701); (732)363-0530. FAX: (732)363-2097. Pres. David Rosen; Exec. Dir. Alan Nydick.

PRINCETON MERCER BUCKS

United Jewish Federation of Princeton Mercer Bucks (merged 1996); 3131 Princeton Pike, Bldg. 2A, Lawrenceville (08648-2207); (609)219-0555. FAX: (609)219-9040. E-mail: ujfpmb@bellatlantic.net. Pres. Eliot Freeman; Exec. Dir. Andrew Frank. (www.ujfpmb.org)

SOMERSET COUNTY

Jewish Federation of Somerset, Hunterdon & Warren Counties (1960); 775 Talamini Rd., Bridgewater (08807); (908)725-6994. FAX: (908)725-9753. E-mail: dnaar@jfedshaw.org. Pres. Martin Siegal; Exec. Dir. Daniel A. Nadelman.

SOUTHERN NEW JERSEY

JEWISH FEDERATION OF SOUTHERN NEW JERSEY (incl. Camden, Burlington, and Gloucester counties) (1922); 1301 Springdale Rd., Suite 200, Cherry Hill (08003-2769); (856)751-9500. FAX: (856)751-1697. Pres. Dr. Robert Belafsky; Exec. V.-Pres. Stuart Alperin.

NEW MEXICO

ALBUQUERQUE

JEWISH FEDERATION OF GREATER ALBUQUERQUE (1938); 5520 Wyoming Blvd., NE (87109-3167); (505)821-3214. FAX: (505) 821-3351. E-mail: nmjfga@nmjfga.org. Pres. Dr. Larry Lubar; Exec. Dir. Andrew Lipman. (WWW.NMJFGA.ORG)

NEW YORK

ALBANY

(See Northeastern New York)

BROOME COUNTY

JEWISH FEDERATION OF BROOME COUNTY; 500 Clubhouse Rd., Vestal (13850); (607)724-2332; FAX: (607)724-2311.

BUFFALO (INCL. NIAGARA FALLS)

JEWISH FEDERATION OF GREATER BUFFALO, INC. (1903); 787 Delaware Ave. (14209); (716)886-7750. FAX: (716)886-1367. Pres. Irving M. Shuman; Exec. Dir. James M. Lodge.

DUTCHESS COUNTY

JEWISH FEDERATION OF DUTCHESS COUNTY; 110 Grand Ave., Poughkeepsie (12603); (914)471-9811. FAX: (914) 471-0659. E-mail: jfeddutchess@mindspring.com. Pres. Tomasina Schneider; Exec. Dir. Bonnie Meadow.

ELMIRA-CORNING

JEWISH CENTER AND FEDERATION OF THE TWIN TIERS (1942); Grandview Ave. Extension, Elmira (14905-0087); (607)734-8122. FAX: (607)734-8123. Pres. John Spiegler; Admin. Diane Huglies.

NEW YORK

UJA-FEDERATION OF JEWISH PHILANTHROPIES OF NEW YORK, INC. (incl. Greater NY, Westchester, Nassau, and Suffolk counties) (Fed. org. 1917; UJA 1939; merged 1986); 130 E. 59 St. (10022-1302); (212)980-1000. FAX: (212)888-7538. E-mail: contact@ujafedny.org. Pres. Larry Zicklin; Exec. V.-Pres. & CEO John Ruskay. (WWW.UJAFEDNY.ORG)

NORTHEASTERN NEW YORK

UNITED JEWISH FEDERATION OF NORTHEASTERN NEW YORK (1986); Latham Circle Mall, 800 New Loudon Rd., Latham (12110); (518)783-7800. FAX: (518)783-1557. E-mail: info@jewishfedny.org. Pres. Dr. Lewis Morrison; Exec. Dir. Jerry S. Neimand. (WWW.JEWISHFEDNY.ORG)

ORANGE COUNTY

JEWISH FEDERATION OF GREATER ORANGE COUNTY (1977); 68 Stewart Ave., Newburgh (12550); (845)562-7860. FAX: (914)562-5114. E-mail: jfogoc@aol.com. Pres. Mona Rieger; Admin. Dir. Joyce Waschitz.

ROCHESTER

JEWISH COMMUNITY FEDERATION OF GREATER ROCHESTER, NY, INC. (1939); 441 East Ave. (14607-1932); (716)461-0490. FAX: (716)461-0912. E-mail: info@jewishrochester.org. Pres. Jay Birnbaum; Exec. Dir. Lawrence W. Fine.

ROCKLAND COUNTY

JEWISH FEDERATION OF ROCKLAND COUNTY (1985); 900 Route 45, Suite 1, New City (10956-1140); (914)362-4200. Fax: (914)362-4282.

SCHENECTADY

(See Northeastern New York)

SYRACUSE

SYRACUSE JEWISH FEDERATION, INC. (1918); 5655 Thompson Rd. So., DeWitt (13214-0511); (315)445-2040. FAX: (315)445-1559. Pres. Linda Alexander; Exec. V.-Pres. Richard Friedman. (WWW.JEWISHROCHESTER.ORG)

TROY

(See Northeastern New York)

ULSTER COUNTY

JEWISH FEDERATION OF ULSTER COUNTY (1951); 159 Green St., Kingston (12401); (845)338-8131. FAX: (845)338-8131. E-mail: ucjf@ulster.net. Pres. Michelle Tuchman; Exec. Dir. Joan Plotsky. (WWW.ULSTER.NET/UCJF)

UTICA

JEWISH COMMUNITY FEDERATION AND CENTER OF UTICA (1950; reorg. 1994); 2310 Oneida St. (13501-6009); (315)733-2343.

FAX: (315)733-2346. Pres. Ann Siegel; Exec. Dir. Barbara Ratner-Gantshar.

NORTH CAROLINA

ASHEVILLE

WESTERN NORTH CAROLINA JEWISH FEDERATION (1935); 236 Charlotte St. (28801-1434); (828)253-0701. FAX: (828)254-7666. Pres. Stan Greenberg; Exec. Dir. Marlene Berger-Joyce.

CHARLOTTE

THE JEWISH FEDERATION OF GREATER CHARLOTTE (1938); 5007 Providence Rd. (28226-5849); (704)366-5007. FAX: (704) 944-6766. E-mail: jfgc@shalomcharlotte.org. Pres. Sarah Schreibman; Exec. Dir. Marvin Goldberg. (WWW.JFGC.ORG)

DURHAM-CHAPEL HILL

DURHAM-CHAPEL HILL JEWISH FEDERATION & COMMUNITY COUNCIL (1979); 3700 Lyckan Pkwy., Suite B, Durham (27707-2541); (919)489-5335. FAX: (919)489-5788. E-mail: federation@shalomdch.org. Pres. Elaine Marcus; Exec. Dir. Lew Borman. (http://shalomdch.org)

GREENSBORO

GREENSBORO JEWISH FEDERATION (1940); 5509C W. Friendly Ave. (27410-4211); (336)852-5433. FAX: (336)852-4346. E-mail: mchandler@shalomgreensboro.org. Pres. Ronald Green; Exec. Dir. Marilyn Forman-Chandler. (WWW.SHALOMGREENSBORO.ORG)

RALEIGH

RALEIGH-CARY JEWISH FEDERATION (1987); 8210 Creedmoor Rd., Suite 104 (27613); (919)676-2200. FAX: (919)676-2122. E-mail: info@rcjf.org. Pres. Jim Maass; Exec. Dir. Judah Segal. (WWW.RCJF.ORG)

OHIO

AKRON

AKRON JEWISH COMMUNITY FEDERATION (1935); 750 White Pond Dr. (44320-1128); (330)869-CHAI (2424). FAX: (330)867-8498. Pres. David Kock; Exec. Dir. Michael Wise. (WWW.JEWISHAKRON.ORG)

CANTON

CANTON JEWISH COMMUNITY FEDERATION (1935; reorg. 1955); 2631 Harvard Ave., NW (44709-3147); (330)452-6444. FAX: (330) 452-4487. E-mail: cantonjcf@aol.com. Pres. Edward Buxbaum.

CINCINNATI

JEWISH FEDERATION OF CINCINNATI (1896; reorg. 1967); 4380 Malsbary Rd., Suite 200 (45242-5644); (513) 985-1500. FAX: (513)985-1503. E-mail: jfed@jfedcin.org. Pres. Kim M. Heiman; Chief Exec. Officer Rabbi Michael R. Zedek. (WWW.SHALOMCINCY.ORG)

CLEVELAND

JEWISH COMMUNITY FEDERATION OF CLEVELAND (1903); 1750 Euclid Ave. (44115-2106); (216)566-9200. FAX: (216)861-1230. E-mail: info@jcfcleve.org. Exec. V.-Pres. & CEO Joel Fox. (WWW.JEWISHCLEVELAND.ORG)

COLUMBUS

COLUMBUS JEWISH FEDERATION (1926); 1175 College Ave. (43209); (614)237-7686. FAX: (614)237-2221. E-mail: cjf@tcjf.org. Pres. Gordon Zacks; Exec. Dir. Mitchel Orlik. (WWW.TCJG.ORG)

DAYTON

JEWISH FEDERATION OF GREATER DAYTON (1910); 4501 Denlinger Rd. (45426-2395); (937)854-4150. FAX: (937)854-2850. Pres. Joseph Bettman; Exec. V.-Pres. Peter H. Wells.

STEUBENVILLE

JEWISH COMMUNITY COUNCIL (1938); 300 Lovers Lane (43952); (614)264-5514. FAX: (740)264-7190. Pres. Curtis L. Greenberg; Exec. Sec. Jennie Bernstein.

TOLEDO

JEWISH FEDERATION OF GREATER TOLEDO (1907; reorg. 1960); 6505 Sylvania Ave., Sylvania (43560-3918); (419)885-4461. FAX: (419)885-3207. E-mail: jftoledo@cjfny.org. Pres. Joel Beren; Exec. Dir. Alix Greenblatt.

YOUNGSTOWN

YOUNGSTOWN AREA JEWISH FEDERATION (1935); 505 Gypsy Lane (44504-1314); (330)746-3251. FAX: (330)746-7926. E-mail: samkoopl@juno.com. Pres. Dr. Ronald Roth; Exec. V.-Pres. Sam Kooperman.

OKLAHOMA

OKLAHOMA CITY

JEWISH FEDERATION OF GREATER OKLAHOMA CITY (1941); 710 W. Wilshire, Suite C (73116-7736). (405)848-3132. FAX: (405)848-3180. E-mail: okcfed@flash.net. Pres. Harriet Carson; Exec. Dir. Edie S. Roodman.

TULSA

Jewish Federation of Tulsa (1938); 2021 E. 71 St. (74136); (918)495-1100. FAX: (918)495-1220. Pres. Andrew M. Wolov; Exec. Dir. David Bernstein.

OREGON

PORTLAND

Jewish Federation of Portland (incl. Northwest Oregon and Southwest Washington communities) (1920; reorg. 1956); 6651 SW Capitol Hwy. (97219); (503)245-6219. FAX: (503)245-6603. E-mail: charlie@jewishportland.org. Pres. Priscilla Kostiner; Exec. Dir. Charles Schiffman. (www.jewishportland.org)

PENNSYLVANIA

BUCKS COUNTY

(See Jewish Federation of Greater Philadelphia)

ERIE

Jewish Community Council of Erie (1946); 1611 Peach St., Suite 405 (16501-2123); (814)455-4474. FAX: (814)455-4475. E-mail: jcceri@erie.net. Pres. Robert Cohen; Admin. Dir. Cynthia Penman; Dir. of Soc. Srvcs. Barbara Singer.

HARRISBURG

United Jewish Community of Greater Harrisburg (1941); 3301 N. Front St. (17110-1436); (717)236-9555. FAX: (717)236-8104. E-mail: communityreview @desupernet.net. Pres. Raphael Aronson; Exec. Dir. David Weisberg. (www.hbgjewishcommunity.com)

LEHIGH VALLEY

Jewish Federation of the Lehigh Valley (1948); 702 N. 22nd St., Allentown (18104); (610)821-5500. FAX: (610)821-8946. E-mail: ivfed@enter.net.

PHILADELPHIA

Jewish Federation of Greater Philadelphia (incl. Bucks, Chester, Delaware, Montgomery, and Philadelphia counties) (1901; reorg. 1956); 2100 Arch St. (19103); (215)832-0500. FAX: (215)832-1510. E-mail: lyouman@philjnet.org. Pres. Michael R. Belman; Exec. V.-Pres. Howard E. Charish. (www.jewishphilly.org)

PITTSBURGH

United Jewish Federation of Greater Pittsburgh (1912; reorg. 1955); 234 McKee Pl. (15213-3916); (412)681-8000. FAX: (412) 681-3980. E-mail: information@ujf.net. Chmn. David Burstin; Pres. Howard M. Rieger. (www.ujf.net)

READING

Jewish Federation of Reading, Pa., Inc. (1935; reorg. 1972); 1700 City Line St. (19604); (610)921-2766. FAX: (610)929-0886. E-mail: stanr@epix.net. Pres. Sheila Lattin; Exec. Dir. Stanley Ramati. (www.readingjewishcommunity.com)

SCRANTON

Jewish Federation of Northeastern Pennsylvania (1945); 601 Jefferson Ave. (18510); (570)961-2300. FAX: (570)346-6147. E-mail: jfednepa@epix.net. Pres. Louis Nivert; Exec. Dir. Seymour Brotman. (www.jfednepa.org)

WILKES-BARRE

Jewish Federation of Greater Wilkes-Barre (1950); 60 S. River St. (18702-2493); (717)822-4146. FAX: (717)824-5966. E-mail: wbreport@aol.com. Pres. Murray Ufberg; Exec. Dir. Don Cooper.

RHODE ISLAND

PROVIDENCE

Jewish Federation of Rhode Island (1945); 130 Sessions St. (02906); (401)421-4111. FAX: (401)331-7961. E-mail: shalom @jfri.org. Pres. Edward D. Feldstein; Exec. Dir. Steven A. Rakitt. (www.jfri.org)

SOUTH CAROLINA

CHARLESTON

Charleston Jewish Federation (1949); 1645 Raoul Wallenberg Blvd., PO Box 31298 (29407); (843)571-6565. FAX: (843)852-3547. E-mail: ejkatzman@aol.com. Pres. Anita Zucker; Exec. Dir. Ellen J. Katzman.

COLUMBIA

Columbia Jewish Federation (1960); 4540 Trenholm Rd., PO Box 6968 (29206-4462); (803)787-2023. FAX: (803)787-0475. E-mail: ternercjf@hotmail.com. Pres. Stephen Serbin; Exec. Dir. Steven Terner.

SOUTH DAKOTA

SIOUX FALLS

Jewish Welfare Fund (1938); 510 S. First Ave. (57102-1003); (605)332-3335. FAX: (605)334-2298. E-mail: asnh94@prodigy

.com. Pres. Laurence Bierman; Exec. Sec. Stephen Rosenthal.

TENNESSEE

CHATTANOOGA

JEWISH COMMUNITY FEDERATION OF GREATER CHATTANOOGA (1931); 3601 Ringgold Rd. (37412); PO Box 8947 (37412); (423)493-0270. FAX: (423)493-9997. E-mail: dlevine@jcfgc.com. Pres. Claire Binder; Exec. Dir. Debra Levine.

KNOXVILLE

KNOXVILLE JEWISH FEDERATION, INC. (1939); 7800 Deane Hill Dr. (37919); (423)693-5837. FAX: (423)694-4861. E-mail: ajcckjf@aol.com. Pres. Pace Robinson; Exec. Dir. Dr. Bernard Rosenblatt. (WWW.JEWISHKNOXVILLE.ORG)

MEMPHIS

MEMPHIS JEWISH FEDERATION (incl. Shelby County) (1935); 6560 Poplar Ave. (38138-3614); (901)767-7100. FAX: (901)767-7128. E-mail: jfeld@memjfed.org. Pres. Louise Sklar; Exec. Dir. Jeffrey Feld.

NASHVILLE

NASHVILLE JEWISH FEDERATION (1936); 801 Percy Warner Blvd. (37205-4009); (615)356-3242. FAX: (615)352-0056. E-mail: jnash jfed@aol.com. Pres. Peter Haas.

TEXAS

AUSTIN

JEWISH COMMUNITY ASSOCIATION OF AUSTIN (1939; reorg. 1956); 7300 Hart Lane (78731); (512)735-8000. FAX: (512)735-8001. E-mail: austinjfed@jfaustin.org. Pres. Linda Millstone; Exec. Dir. Sandy Sack. (WWW.JFAUSTIN.ORG)

BEAUMONT

BEAUMONT JEWISH FEDERATION; PO Box 1891 (77704-1981); (409)832-2881.

CORPUS CHRISTI

COMBINED JEWISH APPEAL OF CORPUS CHRISTI; 750 Everhart Rd. (78411-1906); (512)855-6239. FAX: (512)853-9040.

DALLAS

JEWISH FEDERATION OF GREATER DALLAS (1911); 7800 Northaven Rd. (75230-3226); (214)369-3313. FAX: (214)369-8943. E-mail: jharburger@jfgd.org. Pres. Donald Schaffer; Exec. Dir. Gary Weinstein. (WWW.JEWISHDALLAS.ORG)

EL PASO

JEWISH FEDERATION OF EL PASO, INC. (1937); 405 Wallenberg Dr. (79912-5605); (915)584-4437. FAX: (915)584-0243. Pres. Gary Weiser; Exec. Dir. Larry Harris. (WWW.JEWISHFED.HUNTLEIGH.NET)

FORT WORTH

JEWISH FEDERATION OF FORT WORTH AND TARRANT COUNTY (1936); 4801-B Briarhaven Rd. (76109); (817)569-0892. FAX: (817)569-0896. E-mail: jfedfwtc@aol.com. Pres. Harold Gernsbacher; Exec. Dir. Naomi Rosenfield.

HOUSTON

JEWISH FEDERATION OF GREATER HOUSTON (1936); 5603 S. Braeswood Blvd. (77096-3907); (713)729-7000. FAX: (713)721-6232. E-mail: lwunsch@houstonjewish.org. Pres. Marvin Woskow; Exec. V.-Pres. Lee Wunsch. (WWW.HOUSTONJEWISH.ORG)

SAN ANTONIO

JEWISH FEDERATION OF SAN ANTONIO (incl. Bexar County) (1922); 12500 NW Military Hwy., Suite 200 (78231); (210)302-6960. FAX: (210)408-2332. E-mail: freedm@jfsatx. Pres. Elaine Cohen; Exec. Dir. Mark Freedman. (WWW.JFSATX)

WACO

JEWISH FEDERATION OF WACO & CENTRAL TEXAS (1949); PO Box 8031 (76714-8031); (817)776-3740. FAX: (817)776-4424. E-mail: debhersh@aol.com. Pres. Abbye M. Silver; Exec. Sec. Debbie Hersh-Levy.

UTAH

SALT LAKE CITY

UNITED JEWISH FEDERATION OF UTAH (1936); 2416 E. 1700 South (84108); (801)581-0102. FAX: (801) 581-1334. Pres. Robert Wolff; Exec. Dir. Donald Gartman.

VIRGINIA

RICHMOND

JEWISH COMMUNITY FEDERATION OF RICHMOND (1935); 5403 Monument Ave., PO Box 17128 (23226-7128); (804)288-0045. FAX: (804)282-7507. E-mail: executivedirector@jewishrich.com. Pres. Stewart Kasen; Exec. Dir. Marsha F. Hurwitz. (WWW.JEWISHRICHMOND.COM)

TIDEWATER

UNITED JEWISH FEDERATION OF TIDEWATER (incl. Norfolk, Portsmouth, and Virginia

Beach) (1937); 5029 Corporate Woods Dr., Suite 225, Virginia Beach (23462-4370); (757)671-1600. FAX: (757)671-7613. E-mail: ujft@ujft.org. Pres. David Brand; Exec. V.-Pres. Mark L. Goldstein.

VIRGINIA PENINSULA

United Jewish Community of the Virginia Peninsula, Inc. (1942); 2700 Spring Rd., Newport News (23606); (757)930-1422. FAX: (757)930-3762. E-mail: unitedjc @erols.com. Pres. Roy H. Lasris; Exec. Dir. Rodney J. Margolis. (www.ujcvp.org)

WASHINGTON

SEATTLE

Jewish Federation of Greater Seattle (incl. King County, Everett, and Bremerton) (1926); 2031 Third Ave. (98121); (206)443-5400. FAX: (206)443-0306. E-mail: wnedyj@jewishinseattle.org. Pres. Dr. Michael Spektor; Exec. V.-Pres. Barry M. Goren. (www.jewishinseattle.org)

WEST VIRGINIA

CHARLESTON

Federated Jewish Charities of Charleston, Inc. (1937); PO Box 1613 (25326); (304)345-2320. FAX: (304)345-2325. E-mail: mzltov@aol.com. Pres. Stuart May; Exec. Sec. Lee Diznoff.

WISCONSIN

MADISON

Madison Jewish Community Council, Inc. (1940); 6434 Enterprise Lane (53719-1117); (608)278-1808. FAX:(608)278-7814. E-mail: morrison@mjcc.net. Pres. Joel Minkoff; Exec. Dir. Steven H. Morrison. (www.jewishmadison.org)

MILWAUKEE

Milwaukee Jewish Federation, Inc. (1902); 1360 N. Prospect Ave. (53202); (414)390-5700. FAX: (414)390-5782. E-mail: info@milwaukeejewish.org. Pres. Stephen L. Chernof; Exec. V.-Pres. Richard H. Meyer. (www.milwaukeejewish.org)

CANADA

ALBERTA

CALGARY

Calgary Jewish Community Council (1962); 1607 90th Ave. SW (T2V 4V7); (403)253-8600. FAX: (403)253-7915. E-mail: cjcc@jewish-calgary.com. Pres. Nate Feldman; Exec. Dir. Myrna Linder. (www.jewishcalgary.com)

EDMONTON

Jewish Federation of Edmonton (1954; reorg. 1982); 7200 156th St. (T5R 1X3); (780)487-5120. FAX: (780)481-1854. E-mail: edjfed@net.com.ca. Pres. Stephen Mandel; Exec. Dir. Lesley A. Jacobson.

BRITISH COLUMBIA

VANCOUVER

Jewish Federation of Greater Vancouver (1932; reorg. 1987); 950 W. 41st Ave., Suite 200 (V5Z 2N7); (604)257-5100. FAX: (604)257-5110. E-mail: jfed@jfgv.com. Pres. Sondra Ritter. (www.jfgv.com)

MANITOBA

WINNIPEG

Jewish Federation of Winnipeg/Combined Jewish Appeal (1938; reorg. 1973); 123 Doncaster St., Suite C300 (R3N 2B2); (204)477-7400. FAX: (204)477-7405. E-mail: bfreedman@aspercampus.mb.ca. Pres. Howard Morry; Exec. V.-Pres. Robert Freedman. (www.jewishwinnipeg.org)

ONTARIO

HAMILTON

UJA/Jewish Federation of Hamilton/Wentworth & Area (1932; merged 1971); PO Box 7258, 1030 Lower Lions Club Rd., Ancaster (L9G 3N6); (905)648-0605 #305. FAX: (905)648-8350. E-mail: hamujajf@interlynx.net. Pres. Cheryl Greenbaum; Exec. Dir. Patricia Tolkin Eppel.

LONDON

London Jewish Federation (1932); 536 Huron St. (N5Y 4J5); (519)673-3310. FAX:

(519)673-1161. Pres. Ron Wolf; Off. Mgr. Debra Chatterley.

OTTAWA

UNITED JEWISH APPEAL OF OTTAWA (1934); 21 Nadolny Sachs Private (K2A 1R9); (613)798-4696. FAX: (613)798-4695. E-mail: uja@jccottawa.com. Pres. Barbara Farber; Exec. Dir. Mitchell Bellman. (WWW.UJAOTTOWA.COM)

TORONTO

UJA FEDERATION OF GREATER TORONTO (1917); 4600 Bathurst St. (M2R 3V2); (416)635-2883. FAX: (416)631-5715. E-mail: webmaven@feduja.org. Pres. Joseph Steiner; Exec. V.-Pres. Allan Reitzes. (WWW.FEDUJA.ORG)

UIA FEDERATIONS OF CANADA (1998); 4600 Bathurst St. (M2R 3V2); (416)636-7655. FAX: (416)636-9897. E-mail: mfinkelstein@uiafed.org. Exec. V-Pres. Maxyne Finkelstein.

WINDSOR

JEWISH COMMUNITY FEDERATION (1938); 1641 Ouellette Ave. (N8X 1K9); (519)973-1772. FAX: (519)973-1774. Pres. Dr. Michael Malowitz; Exec. Dir. Steven Brownstein. (WWW.WJCC.ORG)

QUEBEC

MONTREAL

FEDERATION CJA (formerly Allied Jewish Community Services) (1965); 1 Carrie Cummings Square (H3W 1M6); (514)735-3541. FAX: (514)735-8972. E-mail: dcantor@federationcja.org. Pres. Stanley Plotnick; Exec. V.-Pres. Danyael Cantor. (WWW.FEDERATIONCJA.ORG)

Jewish Periodicals*

UNITED STATES

ALABAMA

DEEP SOUTH JEWISH VOICE (1990) (formerly THE SOUTHERN SHOFAR). PO Box 130052, Birmingham, 35213. (205)595-9255. FAX: (205)595-9256. E-mail: dsjvoice@aol.com. Lawrence M. Brook. Monthly. (WWW.DEEPSOUTHJEWISHVOICE.COM)

ARIZONA

ARIZONA JEWISH POST (1946). 2601 N. Campbell Ave., #205, Tucson, 85719. (520)319-1112. FAX: (520)319-1118. E-mail: posteds@aol.com. Sandra R. Heiman. Fortnightly. Jewish Federation of Southern Arizona.

JEWISH NEWS OF GREATER PHOENIX (1948). 1625 E. Northern Ave., Suite 106, Phoenix, 85020. (602)870-9470. FAX: (602)870-0426. E-mail: editor@jewishaz.com. Pub. Rabbi Barry Cohen. Weekly. (WWW.JEWISHAZ.COM)

CALIFORNIA

THE AMERICAN RABBI (1968). 22711 Cass Ave., Woodland Hills, 91364. (818)225-9631. FAX: (818)225-8354. E-mail: david@inpubco.com. Ed.-in-Ch./Pub. David Epstein; Ed. Harry Essrig. Quarterly.

CENTRAL CALIFORNIA JEWISH HERITAGE (1914). 20201 Sherman Way, Winnetka, 91306. (818)576-9000. FAX: (818)576-9910. E-mail: heritagepub@earthlink.net. Dan Brin. Six times a year. Heritage Group.

HERITAGE-SOUTHWEST JEWISH PRESS (1914). 20201 Sherman Way, Suite 204, Winnetka, 91306. (818)576-9000. FAX: (818)576-9910. E-mail: heritagepub@earthlink.net. Dan Brin. Weekly. Heritage Group.

JEWISH BULLETIN OF NORTHERN CALIFORNIA (1946). 225 Bush St., Suite 1480, San Francisco, 94104-4281. (415)263-7200. FAX: (415)263-7223. E-mail: info@jbnc.com. Marc S. Klein. Weekly. San Francisco Jewish Community Publications, Inc.

JEWISH COMMUNITY CHRONICLE (1947). 3801 E. Willow St., Long Beach, 90815. (562)426-7601, ext. 1021. FAX: (562)595-5543. E-mail: jchron@surfside.net. Harriette Ellis. Fortnightly except July & August/ once per month 22 issues a year. Jewish Federation of Greater Long Beach & West Orange County.

JEWISH COMMUNITY NEWS (1976). 14855 Oka Rd., Suite 2, Los Gatos, 95030. (408)358-3033, ext. 31. FAX: (408)356-0733. E-mail: jcn@jfgsj.org. Eileen Goss; Adv. Lindsay Greensweig (408)286-6669. Monthly. Jewish Federation of Greater San Jose.

JEWISH JOURNAL OF GREATER LOS ANGELES (1986). 3660 Wilshire Blvd., Suite 204, Los Angeles, 90010. (213)368-1661. FAX: (213)368-1684. E-mail: jjla@aol.com. Gene Lichtenstein. Weekly.

JEWISH NEWS (1973). 15060 Ventura Blvd., Suite 210, Sherman Oaks, CA 91403.

*The information in this directory is based on replies to questionnaires circulated by the editors. For organization bulletins, see the directory of Jewish organizations.

(818)786-4000. FAX: (818)380-9232. Phil Blazer. Monthly. (Also weekly Sunday TV and radio broadcasts in LA, NY, and Miami.)

JEWISH SOCIAL STUDIES: HISTORY, CULTURE, AND SOCIETY (1939). c/o Program in Jewish Studies, Bldg. 240, Rm. 103, Stanford University, Stanford, 94305-2190. (650)725-0829. FAX: (650)725-2920. E-mail: jss@stanford.edu. Steven J. Zipperstein, Aron Rodrigue. Three times a year. Conference on Jewish Social Studies, Inc.

JEWISH SPORTS REVIEW. 1800 S. Robertson Blvd., #174, Los Angeles, 90035. (800)510-9003. E-mail: shel@jewish sportsreview.com. Shel Wallman/ Ephraim Moxson. Bimonthly. (WWW.JEWISHSPORTSREVIEW.COM)

LOS ANGELES JEWISH TIMES (formerly B'NAI B'RITH MESSENGER) (1897). 5455 Wilshire Blvd., Suite 903, Los Angeles, 90036. (323)933-0131. FAX: (323)933-7928. E-mail: lajtart@aol.com. Ed.-in-Chief Joe Bobker; Mng. Ed. Jane Fried. Weekly.

ORANGE COUNTY JEWISH HERITAGE. 24331 Muirlands Blvd., Suite D-347, Lake Forest, 92630. Phone/FAX: (949)362-4446. E-mail: ocnews@hotmail.com. Stan Brin. Bi-weekly.

SAN DIEGO JEWISH PRESS HERITAGE (1914). 3615 Kearny Villa Rd., #111, San Diego, 92123. (619)265-0808. FAX: (619)265-0850. E-mail: sdheritage@home.com. Donald H. Harrison. Weekly.

SAN DIEGO JEWISH TIMES (1979). 4731 Palm Ave., La Mesa, 91941. (619)463-5515. FAX: (619)463-1309. E-mail: jewish times@msn.com. Colleen Silea. Fortnightly.

SHALOM L.A. (1988). 16027 Ventura Blvd., #400, Encino, 91436. (818)783-3090. FAX: (818)783-1104. Gal Shor. Weekly. Hebrew.

TIKKUN MAGAZINE (1986). 2107 Van Ness Ave., Suite 302, San Francisco, 94109. (415)575-1200. FAX: (415)575-1434. E-mail: magazine@tikkun.org. Michael Lerner. Bimonthly. Institute for Labor & Mental Health. (WWW.TIKKUN.ORG)

WESTERN STATES JEWISH HISTORY (1968). 22711 Cass Ave., Woodland Hills, 91364. (818)225-9631. FAX: (818)225-8354. E-mail: david@inpubco.com. Ed.-in-Ch. Gladys Sturman; Ed. David Epstein. Quarterly. Western States Jewish History Association.

COLORADO

INTERMOUNTAIN JEWISH NEWS (1913). 1275 Sherman St., Suite 214, Denver, 80203-2299. (303)861-2234. FAX: (303)832-6942. E-mail: ijn@rmii.com. Exec. Ed. Rabbi Hillel Goldberg; Pub. Miriam Goldberg. Weekly.

CONNECTICUT

CONNECTICUT JEWISH LEDGER (1929). 740 N. Main St., W. Hartford, 06117. (860)231-2424. FAX: (860)231-2428. E-mail: editorial@jewishledger.com. Lisa Lenkiewicz. Weekly.

JEWISH LEADER (1974). 28 Channing St., PO Box 1468, New London, 06320. (860)442-7395. FAX: (860)443-4175. E-mailjfecmim@aol.com. Ed. Mimi Perl. Biweekly. Jewish Federation of Eastern Connecticut.

DELAWARE

JEWISH VOICE. 100 W. 10th St., Suite 301, Wilmington, 19801. (302)427-2100. FAX: (302)427-2438. E-mail: jewishvoic @aol.com. Lynn Edelman. 22 times per year. Jewish Federation of Delaware.

DISTRICT OF COLUMBIA

AZURE (1996). 5505 Connecticut Ave., NW, Suite 1140, Washington, 20015. (877)298-7300. FAX: (888)766-1506. E-mail: patrick@shalemcenter.org. Dan Polisar. Quarterly. Hebrew/English. The Shalem Center. (WWW.AZURE.ORG.IL)

B'NAI B'RITH INTERNATIONAL JEWISH MONTHLY (1886, under the name Menorah). 1640 Rhode Island Ave., NW, Washington, 20036. (202)857-6646. FAX: (202)296-1092. E-mail: erozenman@ bnaibrith.org. Eric Rozenman. Quarterly. B'nai B'rith International.

CAPITAL COMMUNIQUÉ (1991). 777 N. Capital St., NE, Suite 305, Washington, 20002. (202)216-9060. FAX: (202)216-9061. Jason Silberberg. Bi-annually. National Jewish Democratic Council.

THE JEWISH VETERAN (1896). 1811 R St., NW, Washington, 20009-1659. (202)265-6280. FAX: (202)234-5662. E-mail:

jwv@jwv.org. Seymour Brody. 5 times per year. Jewish War Veterans of the U.S.A.

MOMENT (1975). 4710 41 St., NW, Washington, 20016. (202)364-3300. FAX: (202)364-2636. E-mail: editor@momentmag.com. Hershel Shanks. Bimonthly. Jewish Educational Ventures, Inc.

FSU MONITOR (1990). 1819 H Street, NW, Suite 230, Washington, 20006. (202)775-9770. FAX: (202)775-9776. E-mail: ucsj@ucsj.com. Nickolai Butkevich. Quarterly. Union of Councils for Soviet Jews.

NEAR EAST REPORT (1957). 440 First St., NW, Suite 607, Washington, 20001. (202)639-5254. FAX: (202)347-4916. Dr. Raphael Danziger. Fortnightly. Near East Research, Inc.

SECURITY AFFAIRS (1976). 1717 K St., NW, Suite 800, Washington, 20006. (202)833-0020. FAX: (202)296-6452. E-mail: info@jinsa.org. Jim Colbert. Quarterly. Jewish Institute for National Security Affairs.

WASHINGTON JEWISH WEEK. *See under* MARYLAND

FLORIDA

THE CHRONICLE (1971). 580 S. McIntosh Rd., Sarasota, 34232. (941)371-4546. FAX: (941)378-2947. Barry Millman. Fortnightly. Sarasota-Manatee Jewish Federation.

HERITAGE FLORIDA JEWISH NEWS (1976). PO Box 300742, Fern Park, 32730. (407)834-8787. FAX: (407)831-0507. E-mail: heritagefl@aol.com. Pub. Jeffrey Gaeser; Asst. Ed. Shari Lee Beymon. Weekly.

JACKSONVILLE JEWISH NEWS (1988). 8505 San Jose Blvd., Jacksonville, 32217. (904)448-5000, (904)262-1971. FAX: (904)448-5715. E-mail: srgnews@aol.com. Susan R. Goetz. Monthly. Jacksonville Jewish Federation.

JEWISH JOURNAL (PALM BEACH-BROWARD-DADE) (1977). 601 Fairway Dr., Deerfield Beach, 33441. (954)698-6397. FAX: (954)429-1207. Alan Gosh. Weekly. South Florida Newspaper Network.

JEWISH PRESS OF PINELLAS COUNTY (Clearwater-St.Petersburg) (1985). PO Box 6970, Clearwater, 33758-6970; 13191 Starkey Rd., Crownpointe #8, Largo, 33773-1438. (727)535-4400. FAX:(727) 530-3039. E-mail: jptb@aol.com. Karen Wolfson Dawkins. Biweekly. Jewish Press Group of Tampa Bay (FL), Inc. in cooperation with the Jewish Federation of Pinellas County.

JEWISH PRESS OF TAMPA (1987). PO Box 6970, Clearwater 33758-6970; 13191 Starkey Rd., Crownpointe #8, Largo 33773-1438. (727)535-4400. FAX: (727) 530-3039. E-mail: jptb@aol.com. Karen Wolfson Dawkins. Biweekly. Jewish Press Group of Tampa Bay (FL), Inc.

SHALOM TODAY (1994) Jewish Federation of Broward County, 5890 S. Pine Island Road, Davie, FL 33328. (954)352-6900. FAX: (954)252-6893. Editor Ray Levi. Weekly. Jewish Federation of Broward County.

GEORGIA

ATLANTA JEWISH TIMES (1925). 6065 Roswell Rd., Suite 700, Atlanta 30328. (404)252-1600. FAX: (404)252-1172. E-mail: bmenaker@atlantajewishtimes.com. Bob Menaker. Weekly.

ILLINOIS

CHICAGO JEWISH NEWS (1994). 5301 W. Dempster, Skokie, Ill 60077. (847)966-0606. FAX: (847)966-1656. E-mail: info@chicagojewishnews.com. Joseph Aaron. Weekly.

CHICAGO JEWISH STAR (1991). PO Box 268, Skokie, 60076-0268. (847)674-7827. FAX: (847)674-0014. E-mail: chicago-jewish-star@mcimail.com. Ed. Douglas Wertheimer; Assoc. Ed. Gila Wertheimer. Fortnightly.

JEWISH COMMUNITY NEWS (1941). 6464 W. Main, Suite 7A, Belleville, 62223. (618) 398-6100/ (877)714-6103. FAX: (618)398-0539. E-mail: silfed@aol.com Steve Low. Quarterly. Jewish Federation of Southern Illinois. (WWW.SIMOKYFED.COM)

JUF NEWS & GUIDE TO JEWISH LIVING IN CHICAGO (1972). One S. Franklin St., Rm. 701G, Chicago, 60606. (312)357-4848. FAX: (312)855-2470. E-mail: jufnews@juf.org. Aaron B. Cohen. Monthly (Guide, annually). Jewish United Fund/ Jewish Federation of Metropolitan Chicago.

INDIANA

ILLIANA NEWS (1976). 2939 Jewett St., Highland, 46322. (219)972-2250. FAX:

(219)972-4779. E-mail: jfedofnwi@aol.com. Monthly (except July/Aug.). Jewish Federation of Northwest Indiana, Inc.

INDIANA JEWISH POST AND OPINION (1935). 238 S. Meridian St., #502, Indianapolis, 46225. (317)972-7800. FAX: (317)972-7807. E-mail: jpost@surf-ici.com. Ed Stattmann. Weekly.

NATIONAL JEWISH POST AND OPINION (1932). 238 S. Meridian St., Indianapolis, 46225. (317)972-7800. FAX: (317)972-7807. E-mail: jpost@surf.ici.com. Gabriel Cohen. Weekly.

PROOFTEXTS: A JOURNAL OF JEWISH LITERARY HISTORY (1980). Indiana University Press, 601 N. Morton St., Bloomington, 47404. (812)855-9449. FAX: (812)855-8507. E-mail: journals@indiana.edu. Editorial address (for contributors):NEJS Dept., Brandeis U., Waltham, MA 02254. Alan Mintz, David G. Roskies. Three times a year.

KANSAS

KANSAS CITY JEWISH CHRONICLE (1920). 7373 W. 107 St., Overland Park, 66212. (913)648-4620. FAX: (913)381-1402. E-mail: chronicle@sunpublications.com. Rick Hellman. Weekly. Sun Publications.

KENTUCKY

COMMUNITY (1975). 3630 Dutchmans Lane, Louisville, 40205-3200. (502)451-8840. FAX: (502)458-0702. E-mail: jfed@iglou.com. Shiela Steinman Wallace. Biweekly. Jewish Community Federation of Louisville.

KENTUCKY JEWISH POST AND OPINION (1931). 1701 Bardstown Rd., Louisville, 40205. (502)459-1914. Ed Stattman. Weekly.

LOUISIANA

JEWISH CIVIC PRESS (1965). 804 Main Street, Suite A-2, Forest Park, GA 30297. (404)231-2194. E-mail: jewishcivicpress@yahoo.com. Claire & Abner Tritt, eds. and pubs. Monthly.

JEWISH NEWS (1995). 3500 N. Causeway Blvd., Suite 1240, Metairie, 70002. (504)828-2125. FAX: (504)828-2827. E-mail: jewishnews@jewishnola.com. Gail Naron Chalew. Fortnightly. Jewish Federation of Greater New Orleans.

MARYLAND

BALTIMORE JEWISH TIMES (1919). 2104 N. Charles St., Baltimore, 21218. (410)752-3504. FAX: (410)752-2375. Phil Jacobs. Weekly.

WASHINGTON JEWISH WEEK (1930, as the National Jewish Ledger). 1500 East Jefferson St., Rockville, 20852. (301)230-2222. FAX: (301)881-6362. E-mail: wjweek@aol.com. Debra Rubin. Weekly.

MASSACHUSETTS

AMERICAN JEWISH HISTORY (1893). Two Thornton Rd., Waltham, 02453. (781)891-8110. FAX: (781)899-9208. E-mail: ajhs@ajhs.org. Marc Lee Raphael. Quarterly. American Jewish Historical Society.

JEWISH ADVOCATE (1902). 15 School St., Boston, 02108. (617)367-9100. FAX: (617)367-9310. E-mail: thejewadv@aol.com. Steven Rosenberg. Weekly.

THE JEWISH CHRONICLE (1927). 131 Lincoln St., Worcester, 01605. (508)752-2512. E-mail: jchronicle@aol.com. Pub. Sondra Shapiro; Ed. Ellen Weingart. Bimonthly.

JEWISH GUIDE TO BOSTON & NEW ENGLAND (1972). 15 School St., Boston, 02108. (617)367-9100. FAX: (617)367-9310. Rosie Rosenzweig. Irregularly. The Jewish Advocate.

THE JEWISH JOURNAL/NORTH OF BOSTON (1976). 201 Washington St., PO Box 555, Salem, 01970. (978)745-4111. FAX: (978) 745-5333. E-mail: editorial@jewishjournal.org. Judith Klein. Biweekly. Russian section. North Shore Jewish Press Ltd.

THE JEWISH NEWS OF WESTERN MASSACHUSETTS (*see* Jewish Advocate)

METROWEST JEWISH REPORTER (1970). 76 Salem End Rd., Framingham, 01702. (508)872-4808. FAX: (508)879-5856. Marcia T. Rivin. Monthly. Combined Jewish Philanthropies of Greater Boston.

PAKN-TREGER (1980). 1021 West St., Amherst, 01002. (413)256-4900. FAX: (413)256-4700. E-mail: pt@bikher.org. Nancy Sherman. Three times a year. National Yiddish Book Center.

SH'MA (1970). 90 Oak Street, 4th Floor, Newton MA 02459. (781)449-9894. FAX: (781)449-9825. E-mail: susanb@jflmedia.

com. Susan Berrin. Monthly. Jewish Family & Life.

MICHIGAN

DETROIT JEWISH NEWS (1942). 27676 Franklin Rd., Southfield, 48034. (248) 354-6060. FAX: (248)354-6069. E-mail: rsklar@thejewishnews.com. Robert Sklar. Weekly.

HUMANISTIC JUDAISM (1968). 28611 W. Twelve Mile Rd., Farmington Hills, 48334. (248)478-7610. FAX: (248)478-3159. E-mail: info@shj.org. M. Bonnie Cousens, Ruth D. Feldman. Quarterly. Society for Humanistic Judaism.

WASHTENAW JEWISH NEWS (1978). 2935 Birch Hollow Dr., Ann Arbor, 48108. (734)971-1800. FAX: (734)971-1801. E-mail: wjna2@aol.com. Susan Kravitz Ayer. Monthly.

MINNESOTA

AMERICAN JEWISH WORLD (1912). 4509 Minnetonka Blvd., Minneapolis, MN 55416. (952)259-5280. FAX: (952)920-6205. E-mail: amjewish@isd.net. Mordecai Specktor. Weekly.

MISSISSIPPI

DEEP SOUTH JEWISH VOICE (*see* Alabama)

MISSOURI

KANSAS CITY JEWISH CHRONICLE. *See under* KANSAS

ST. LOUIS JEWISH LIGHT (1947; reorg. 1963). 12 Millstone Campus Dr., St. Louis, 63146. (314)432-3353. FAX: (314)432-0515. E-mail: stlouislgt@aol.com. Robert A. Cohn. Weekly. St. Louis Jewish Light.

NEBRASKA

JEWISH PRESS (1920). 333 S. 132 St., Omaha, 68154. (402)334-6450. FAX: (402)334-5422. E-mail: ckatzman@jewishomaha.org. Carol Katzman. Weekly. Jewish Federation of Omaha.

NEVADA

JEWISH REPORTER (1976). 3909 S. Maryland Pkwy., Suite 400, Las Vegas, 89119-7520. (702)948-5129. FAX: (702)967-1082. E-mail: lvjewishreporter@aol.com. Terri Herman. Bimonthly. Jewish Federation of Las Vegas.

LAS VEGAS ISRAELITE (1965). PO Box 14096, Las Vegas, 89114. (702)876-1255. FAX: (702)364-1009. Michael Tell. Bimonthly.

NEW HAMPSHIRE

JEWISH SPECTATOR (1935). P.O. Box 267, New London, 03257. (603)526-2513. FAX: (603)526-2514. E-mail: jsisrael@netmedia.net.il. Rabbi Mark Bleiweiss. Quarterly. Friends of Jewish Spectator, Inc.

NEW JERSEY

AVOTAYNU (1985). 155 N. Washington Ave., Bergenfield, 07621. (201)387-7200. FAX: (201)387-2855. E-mail: info@avotaynu.com. Sallyann Amdur Sack. Quarterly.

JEWISH CHRONICLE (1982). 1063 East Landis Ave.,Suite B, Vineland, 08360. (856)696-4445. FAX: (856)696-3428. E-mail: jfedcc@aol.com. Ann Lynn Lipton. Bimonthly. The Jewish Federation of Cumberland County.

JEWISH COMMUNITY NEWS. 1086 Teaneck Rd., Teaneck, 07666. (201)837-8818. FAX: (201)833-4959. E-mail: jewishstd2@aol.com. Rebecca Kaplan Boroson. Fortnightly. Jewish Federation of North Jersey and Jewish Federation of Greater Clifton-Passaic.

JEWISH COMMUNITY VOICE (1941). 1301 Springdale Rd., Suite 250, Cherry Hill, 08003-2762. (856)751-9500, ext. 217. FAX: (856)489-8253. E-mail: jvceditor@aol.com. Harriet Kessler. Biweekly. Jewish Federation of Southern NJ.

THE JEWISH JOURNAL (1999). 320 Raritan Ave., Suite 203, Highland Park, 08904. (732)393-0023. FAX: (732)393-0026. E-mail: jewish@castle.net. Ron Ostroff. Monthly. Published in cooperation with the Ocean County Jewish Federation.

JEWISH STANDARD (1931). 1086 Teaneck Rd., Teaneck, 07666. (201)837-8818. FAX: (201)833-4959. Rebecca Kaplan Boroson. Weekly.

JEWISH STAR (1985). 230 Old Bridge Turnpike, South River, 08882-2000. (732)432-7711. FAX: (732)432-0292. E-mail: jfgmc@aol.com. Marlene A. Heller. Fortnightly. Jewish Federation of Greater Middlesex County.

THE JEWISH STATE (1996). 320 Raritan Ave., Suite 203, Highland Park, 08904. (732) 393-0023. FAX: (732)393-0026. E-mail: jewish@castle.net. Ron Ostroff. Weekly.

JEWISH VOICE & OPINION (1987). 73 Dana Place, Englewood, 07631. (201)569-2845. FAX: (201)569-1739. Susan L. Rosenbluth. Monthly.

JEWISH VOICE OF GREATER MONMOUTH COUNTY (1971). 100 Grant Ave., Deal Park, 07723. (732)531-6200. FAX: (732)531-9518. E-mail: pfdnuss@msn.com. Lauren Silver. Monthly. Jewish Federation of Greater Monmouth County and Ocean County Jewish Federation.

JOURNAL OF JEWISH COMMUNAL SERVICE (1899). 3084 State Hwy. 27, Suite 9, Kendall Pk., 08824-1657. (732)821-1871. FAX: (732)821-5335. E-mail: jcsana@aol.com. Gail Naron Chalew. Quarterly. Jewish Communal Service Association of North America.

NEW JERSEY JEWISH NEWS (1947). 901 Route 10, Whippany, 07981-1157. (973) 887-3900. FAX: (973)887-5999. E-mail: 6853202@mcimail.com. David Twersky. Weekly. United Jewish Federation of MetroWest.

THE SPEAKER (1999). 320 Raritan Ave., Suite 203, Highland Park, 08904. (732) 393-0023. FAX: (732)393-0026. E-mail: jewish@castle.net. Ron Ostroff. Monthly. Published in cooperation with the Jewish Federation of Somerset, Hunterdon & Warren Counties.

NEW MEXICO

NEW MEXICO JEWISH LINK (1971). 5520 Wyoming NE, Albuquerque, 87109. (505)821-3214. FAX: (505)821-3351. E-mail: nmjlink@aol.com. Tema Milstein. Monthly. Jewish Federation of Greater Albuquerque.

NEW YORK

AFN SHVEL (1941). 200 W. 72 St., Suite 40, NYC, 10023. (212)787-6675. E-mail: yidleague@aol.com. Mordkhe Schaechter. Quarterly. Yiddish. League for Yiddish, Inc.

AGENDA: JEWISH EDUCATION (1949; formerly PEDAGOGIC REPORTER). JESNA, 111 Eighth Ave., Suite 11E, NYC, 10011-5201. (212)284-6950. FAX: (212)284-6951. E-mail: info@jesna.org. Amy Stein. Twice a year. Jewish Education Service of North America, Inc.

ALGEMEINER JOURNAL (1972). 225 E. Broadway, NYC, 10002. (212)267-5561. FAX: (212)267-5624. E-mail: Algemeiner@aol.com. Gershon Jacobson. Weekly. Yiddish-English.

AMERICAN JEWISH YEAR BOOK (1899). 165 E. 56 St., NYC, 10022. (212)751-4000. FAX: (212)751-4017. E-mail: research@ajc.org. David Singer, Lawrence Grossman. Annually. American Jewish Committee.

AMIT (1925). 817 Broadway, NYC, 10003. (212)477-4720. FAX: (212)353-2312. E-mail: amitmag@aol.com. Rita Schwalb. Quarterly. AMIT (formerly American Mizrachi Women).

AUFBAU (1934). 2121 Broadway, NYC, 10023. (212)873-7400. Voice mail: (212)579-6578. FAX: (212)496-5736. E-mail: aufbau2000@aol.com. Monika Ziegler/Andreas Mink/Irene Armbruster. Fortnightly. German-English. New World Club, Inc.

BUFFALO JEWISH REVIEW (1918). 15 E. Mohawk St., Buffalo, 14203. (716)854-2192. FAX: (716)854-2198. E-mail: buffjewrev@aoc.com. Harlan C. Abbey. Weekly. Kahaal Nahalot Israel.

THE CALL (1933). 45 E. 33 St., NYC, 10016. (212)889-6800, ext. 225. FAX: (212)532-7518. E-mail: socolove@circle.org. Emily Socolov. Three times a year. The Workmen's Circle/Arbeter Ring.

CCAR JOURNAL: A REFORM JEWISH QUARTERLY (formerly JOURNAL OF REFORM JUDAISM) (1953). 355 Lexington Ave., NYC, 10017. (212)972-3636. FAX: (212)692-0819. Ed. Stephen Pearce. Mng. Ed. Elliot Stevens. Quarterly. Central Conference of American Rabbis.

CIRCLE (1943). 15 E. 26 St., NYC, 10010-1579. (212)532-4949. FAX: (212)481-4174. E-mail: info@jcca.org. Miriam Rinn. Quarterly. Jewish Community Centers Association of North America (formerly JWB).

COMMENTARY (1945). 165 E. 56 St., NYC, 10022. (212)751-4000. FAX: (212)751-1174. E-mail: mail@commentarymagazine.com. Ed. Neal Kozodoy; Ed.-at-Large Norman Podhoretz. Monthly. American Jewish Committee.

CONGRESS MONTHLY (1933). 15 E. 84 St., NYC, 10028. (212)879-4500. Jack Fischel. Six times a year. American Jewish Congress.

CONSERVATIVE JUDAISM (1945). 3080 Broadway, NYC, 10027. (212)280-6065. FAX: (212)749-9166. E-mail: rapubs@jtsa.edu. Rabbi Martin S. Cohen. Quarterly. Rabbinical Assembly and Jewish Theological Seminary of America.

FORVERTS (Yiddish Forward) (1897). 45 E. 33 St., NYC, 10016. (212)889-8200. FAX: (212)684-3949. Boris Sandler. Weekly. Yiddish. Forward Association, Inc.

FORWARD (1897). 45 E. 33 St., NYC, 10016. (212)889-8200. FAX: (212)447-6406. E-mail: newsdesk@forward.com. J. J. Goldberg. Weekly. Forward Newspaper, L.L.C.

HADAROM (1957). 305 Seventh Ave., NYC, 10001. (212)807-7888. FAX: (212)727-8452. Rabbi Gedalia Dov Schwartz. Annual. Hebrew. Rabbinical Council of America.

HADASSAH MAGAZINE (1914). 50 W. 58 St., NYC, 10019. (212)688-0227. FAX: (212)446-9521. Alan M. Tigay. Monthly (except for combined issues of June-July and Aug.-Sept.). Hadassah, the Women's Zionist Organization of America.

HADOAR (1921). 426 W. 58 St., NYC, 10019. (212)957-6658/9/8662-HEBREW. FAX: (212)957-5811. E-mail: HebrewUSA@aol.com. Ed. Shlomo Shamir; Lit. Ed. Dr. Yael Feldman. Biweekly. Hebrew. Hadoar Association, Inc., Organ of the Histadruth of America. (WWW.HEBREWUSA.ORG)

I.A.J.E. NEWSLETTER (1999). (718)339-0337. E-mail: sanuav@stjohns.edu. Victor D. Sanua. International Association of Jews from Egypt.

JBI VOICE (1978). 110 E. 30 St., NYC, 10016. (212)889-2525, (800)433-1531, FAX (212)689-3692. Email: dbarbara@jbilibrary.org. Dena Barbara. Ten times a year in U.S. (audiocassettes). English. Jewish Braille Institute of America.

JEWISH ACTION (1950). 11 Broadway, NYC, 10004. (212)613-8146. FAX: (212)613-0646. E-mail: ja@ou.org. Nechama Carmel. Quarterly. Orthodox Union.

JEWISH BOOK ANNUAL (1942). 15 E. 26 St., 10th fl., NYC, 10010. (212)532-4949, ext. 297. E-mail: jbc@jewishbooks.org. Dr.Stephen H. Garrin. Hebrew & English with bibliography in Yiddish. Jewish Book Council.

JEWISH BOOK WORLD (1945). 15 E. 26 St., NYC, 10010. (212)532-4949, ext. 297. FAX: (212)481-4174. E-mail: jbc@jewishbooks.org. Esther Nussbaum. Three times annually. Jewish Book Council.

JEWISH BRAILLE REVIEW (1931). 110 E. 30 St., NYC, 10016. E-mail: dbarbara@jbilibrary.org. (212)889-2525, (800)433-1531. Dena Barbara. 10 times a year in U.S. (braille). English. Jewish Braille Institute of America.

JEWISH CURRENTS (1946). 22 E. 17 St., Suite 601, NYC, 10003-1919. (212)924-5740. FAX: (212)414-2227. Bi-Montly. Association for Promotion of Jewish Secularism, Inc.

JEWISH EDUCATION NEWS (1980). 261 W. 35 St., Fl. 12A, NYC 10001. (212)268-4210. FAX: (212)268-4214. E-mail: publications@caje.org. Mng. Ed. Judi Resnick. Tri-annually. Coalition for the Advancement of Jewish Education.

THE JEWISH FRONTIER (1934). P.O. Box 4013, Amity Station, New Haven, CT 06525. (203)397-4903. FAX: (212)675-7685. E-mail: jewish-frontier@yahoo.com. Nahum Guttman-Graff. Bimonthly. Labor Zionist Letters, Inc. Managing Editor Bennett Lovett-Graff

JEWISH HERALD (1984). 1689 46 St., Brooklyn, 11204. (718)972-4000. E-mail: jewishherald@aol.com. Leon J. Sternheim. Weekly.

JEWISH JOURNAL (1969). 11 Sunrise Plaza, Valley Stream, 11580. (516)561-6900. FAX: (516)561-6971. Ed. Paul Rubens; Pub. Harold Singer. Weekly.

JEWISH LEDGER (1924). 2535 Brighton-Henrietta Town Line Rd., Rochester, 14623. (716)427-2434. FAX: (716)427-8521. Barbara Morgenstern. Weekly.

THE JEWISH OBSERVER (1963). 42 Broadway, NYC, 10004. (212)797-9000. FAX: (646)254-1600. E-mail: aiamail@aol.com. Rabbi Nisson Wolpin. Monthly (except July and Aug.). Agudath Israel of America.

JEWISH OBSERVER OF CENTRAL NEW YORK (1978). 5655 Thompson Road, DeWitt, NY 13214. (315)445-2040 ext. 116 FAX: (315)445-1559. E-mail: jocny@aol.com. Bette Siegel. Biweekly. Syracuse Jewish Federation, Inc.

JEWISH POST OF NY (1993). 262 West 38th St., NYC, 10018. (212)398-7313. FAX: (212)398-3933. E-mail: jpost@nais.com. Ed. Gad Nahshon. Monthly. Link Marketing & Promotion, Inc.

JEWISH PRESS (1950). 338 Third Ave., Brooklyn, 11215. (718)330-1100. FAX: (718)935-1215. E-mail: jpeditor@aol.com. Jerry Greenwald. Weekly.

JEWISH TELEGRAPHIC AGENCY COMMUNITY NEWS REPORTER (1962). 330 Seventh Ave., 11th fl., NYC, 10001-5010. (212)643-1890. FAX: (212)643-8498. E-mail: www.jta.org/info@jta.org. Lisa Hostein. Monthly. (WWW.JTA.ORG)

JEWISH TELEGRAPHIC AGENCY DAILY NEWS BULLETIN (1917). 330 Seventh Ave., 11th fl., NYC, 10001-5010. (212)643-1890. FAX: (212)643-8498. E-mail: www.jta.org/info@jta.org. Exec. Ed. Mark Joffe; Ed. Lisa Hostein. Daily. (WWW.JTA.ORG)

JEWISH TELEGRAPHIC AGENCY WEEKLY NEWS DIGEST (1933). 330 Seventh Ave., 11th fl., NYC, 10001-5010. (212)643-1890. FAX: (212)643-8498. E-mail: www.jta.org/info@jta.org. Exec. Ed. Mark Joffe; Ed. Lisa Hostein. Weekly. (WWW.JTA.ORG)

JEWISH TRIBUNE. PMB #372, 169 South Main St., New City, 10956; Exec. off. (mailing address): 115 Middle Neck Rd., Great Neck, 11021. (845)352-5151. FAX: (516)829-4776. E-mail: lijeworld@aol.com. Jerome W. Lippman. Weekly. Jewish Tribune; Long Island Jewish World; Manhattan Jewish Sentinel.

JEWISH WEEK (1876; reorg. 1970). 1501 Broadway, NYC, 10036-5503. (212)921-7822. FAX: (212)921-8420. E-mail: editor@thejewishweek.org. Gary Rosenblatt. Weekly.

JEWISH WORLD (1965). 3 Vatrano Road, Albany, 12205. (518)459-8455. FAX: (518) 459-5289. E-mail: 6859675@mcimail.com. Sam S. Clevenson. Weekly.

JOURNAL OF JEWISH EDUCATION-CJE (formerly JEWISH EDUCATION) (1929). 426 W. 58 St., Suite 329, NYC, 10019. (914)368-8657. FAX: (212)284-6951. Dr. Bernard Ducoff. Three times a year. Council for Jewish Education.

JOURNAL OF REFORM JUDAISM. *See* CCAR Journal

JTS MAGAZINE (formerly MASORET) (1991). 3080 Broadway, NYC, 10027. (212)678-8950. FAX: (212)864-0109. E-mail: ekustonowitz@jtsa.edu. Three times a year. Jewish Theological Seminary. Editor Esther Kustanowitz.

JUDAISM (1952). 15 E. 84 St., NYC, 10028. (212)360-1500. FAX: (212)249-3672. Editor's address: Kresge Col., U. of California, Santa Cruz, CA, 95064. (831)459-2566. FAX: (831)459-4872. Subscription address: 15 E. 84 St., NYC 10028. (212)360-1500. E-mail: judaism@cats.ucsc.edu. Prof. Murray Baumgarten. Quarterly. American Jewish Congress.

KASHRUS MONTHLY-YOUR UPDATE ON KOSHER (1990). PO Box 204, Brooklyn, 11204. (718)336-8544. Rabbi Yosef Wikler. Monthly. Kashrus Institute. E-mail: editorial@kashrusmagazine.com.

KASHRUS MAGAZINE-THE PERIODICAL FOR THE KOSHER CONSUMER (1980). PO Box 204, Brooklyn, 11204. (718)336-8544. E-mail: editorial@kashrusmagazine.com. Rabbi Yosef Wikler. Five times per year (February, April, June, September, December). Kashrus Institute. (WWW.KOSHERMAGAZINE.COM)

KOL HAT'NUA (Voice of the Movement) (1975). c/o Young Judaea, 50 W. 58 St., NYC, 10019. (212)303-4576. FAX: (212)303-4572. E-mail: meat345@aol.com. Dov Wilker. Quarterly. Hadassah Zionist Youth Commission-Young Judaea.

KULTUR UN LEBN-CULTURE AND LIFE (1960). 45 E. 33 St., NYC, 10016. (212)889-6800. FAX: (212)532-7518. E-mail: wcfriends@aol.com. Joseph Mlotek. Quarterly. Yiddish. The Workmen's Circle.

LAMISHPAHA (1963). 426 W. 58 St., NYC, 10019. (212)957-6658/9/8862-HEBREW. FAX: (212)957-5811. E-mail: general@hist-ivrit.org. Dr. Vered Cohen-Raphaeli. Illustrated. Monthly (except July and Aug.). Hebrew. Histadruth Ivrith of America. (WWW.HEBREWUSA.ORG)

LIKUTIM (1981). 110 E. 30 St., NYC, 10016. (212)889-2525. Joanne Jahr. Two times a year in Israel (print and audiocassettes). Hebrew. Jewish Braille Institute of America.

LILITH-THE INDEPENDENT JEWISH WOMEN'S MAGAZINE (1976). 250 W. 57 St., #2432,

NYC, 10107. (212)757-0818. FAX: (212)757-5705. E-mail: lilithmag@aol.com. Susan Weidman Schneider. Quarterly. (WWW.LILITHMAG.COM)

LONG ISLAND JEWISH WORLD (1971). 115 Middle Neck Rd., Great Neck, 11021. (516)829-4000. FAX: (516)829-4776. E-mail: lijeworld@aol.com. Jerome W. Lippman. Weekly.

MANHATTAN JEWISH SENTINEL (1993). 115 Middle Neck Rd., Great Neck, 11021. (212)244-4949. FAX: (212)244-2257. E-mail: lijeworld@aol.com. Jerome W. Lippman. Weekly.

MARTYRDOM AND RESISTANCE (1974). 500 Fifth Ave., 42nd Floor, NYC, 10110-1699. (212)220-4304. FAX: (212)220-4308. E-mail: yadvashem@aol.com. Ed. Dr. Harvey Rosenfeld; Ed.-in-Chief Eli Zborowski. Bimonthly. International Society for Yad Vashem.

MIDSTREAM (1954). 633 Third Ave., 21st fl., NYC, 10017. (212)339-6020. FAX: (212)318-6176. E-mail: info@midstream.org. Leo Haber. Eight times a year. Theodor Herzl Foundation, Inc.

NA'AMAT WOMAN (1925). 350 Fifth Ave., Suite 4700, NYC, 10118-4799. (212)563-5222. FAX: (212)563-5710. Judith A. Sokoloff. Quarterly. English-Yiddish-Hebrew. NA'AMAT USA, the Women's Labor Zionist Organization of America.

OLOMEINU-OUR WORLD (1945). 5723 18th Ave., Brooklyn, 11204. (718)259-1223. FAX: (718)259-1795. E-mail: torahumesorah@torahworld.net. Rabbi Yaakov Fruchter. Monthly. English-Hebrew. Torah Umesorah-National Society for Hebrew Day Schools.

PASSOVER DIRECTORY (1923). 11 Broadway, NYC, 10004. (212)613-8135. FAX: (212) 613-0772. E-mail: lieberd@ou.org Deborah Lieber. Annually. Union of Orthodox Jewish Congregations of America.

PROCEEDINGS OF THE AMERICAN ACADEMY FOR JEWISH RESEARCH (1920). 51 Washington Sq. South, NYC, 10012-1075. (212)998-3550. FAX: (212)995-4178. Dr. Nahum Sarna. Annually. English-Hebrew-French-Arabic-Persian-Greek. American Academy for Jewish Research.

RCA RECORD (1953). 305 Seventh Ave. NYC, 10001. (212)807-7888. FAX: (212) 727-8452. Rabbi Mark Dratch. Quarterly. Rabbinical Council of America.

REFORM JUDAISM (1972; formerly DIMENSIONS IN AMERICAN JUDAISM). 633 Third Ave., 6th fl., NYC, 10017. (212)650-4240. Aron Hirt-Manheimer. Quarterly. Union of American Hebrew Congregations. (www.uahc.org)

THE REPORTER (1971). 500 Clubhouse Rd., Vestal, 13850. (607)724-2360. FAX: (607)724-2311. E-mail: TReporter@aol.com. Judith S. Huober. Weekly. Jewish Federation of Broome County, Inc.

THE REPORTER (1966). 315 Park Ave. S., NYC 10010. (212)505-7700. FAX: (212)674-3057. E-mail; editor@waort.org. Marlene A. Heller. Semi-Annual. Women's American ORT, Inc.

RESPONSE: A CONTEMPORARY JEWISH REVIEWC (1967). Columbia University Post Office, PO Box 250892, NYC, 10025. E-mail: response@panix.com. Chanita Baumhaft. Annual.

RUSSIAN FORWARD (1995). 45 E. 33 St., NYC, 10016. (212)889-8200. FAX: (212)448-9124. E-mail: rforward99@yahoo.com. Leonid Shkolnik. Weekly. Russian.

SYNAGOGUE LIGHT AND KOSHER LIFE (1933). 47 Beekman St., NYC, 10038. (212)227-7800. Rabbi Meyer Hager. Quarterly. The Kosher Food Institute.

TRADITION (1958). 305 Seventh Ave., NYC, 10001. (212)807-7888. FAX: (212)727-8452. Rabbi Michael Shmidman. Quarterly. Rabbinical Council of America.

UNITED SYNAGOGUE REVIEW (1943). 155 Fifth Ave., NYC, 10010. (212)533-7800. FAX: (212)353-9439. E-mail: info@uscj.org. Lois Goldrich. Semiannually. United Synagogue of Conservative Judaism.

UNSER TSAIT (1941). 25 E. 21 St., 3rd fl., NYC, 10010. (212)475-0059. Bimonthly. Yiddish. Jewish Labor Bund.

VIEWPOINT MAGAZINE (1952). 3 W. 16 St., NYC, 10011. (212)929-1525, ext. 131. E-mail:ncyi@youngisrael.org. Esther Altmann. Quarterly. National Council of Young Israel.

VOICE OF THE DUTCHESS JEWISH COMMUNITY (1989). 110 Grand Ave., Poughkeepsie, 12603. (845)471-9811. FAX: (845)471-0659. E-mail: jfeddutchess@

mindspring.com. Business off.:500 Clubhouse Rd., Vestal, 13850. (607)724-2360. FAX: (607)724-2311. Sandy Gardner and Judith Huober. Monthly. Jewish Federation of Dutchess County, Inc.

WOMEN'S LEAGUE OUTLOOK MAGAZINE (1930). 48 E. 74 St., New York, 10021. (212)628-1600. FAX: (212)772-3507. E-mail: wleague74@aol.com. Marjorie Saulson. Quarterly. Women's League for Conservative Judaism.

WORKMEN'S CIRCLE CALL. *See* The Call

WYOMING VALLEY JEWISH REPORTER (formerly WE ARE ONE) (1995). 500 Clubhouse Rd., Vestal, 13850. (607)724-2360. FAX: (607)724-2311. E-mail: TReporter@aol.com. Judith S. Huober. Every other week. Wilkes-Barre Jewish Community Board.

YEARBOOK OF THE CENTRAL CONFERENCE OF AMERICAN RABBIS (1890). 355 Lexington Ave., NYC, 10017. (212)972-3636. FAX: (212)692-0819. Rabbi Elliot L. Stevens. Annually. Central Conference of American Rabbis.

YIDDISH (1973). Queens College, NSF 350, 65-30 Kissena Blvd., Flushing, 11367. (718)997-3622. Joseph C. Landis. Quarterly. Queens College Press.

DI YIDDISHE HEIM (1958). 770 Eastern Pkwy., Brooklyn, 11213. (718)735-0458. Rachel Altein, Tema Gurary. Twice a year. English-Yiddish. Neshei Ub'nos Chabad-Lubavitch Women's Organization.

YIDDISHE KULTUR (1938). 1133 Broadway, Rm. 820, NYC, 10010. (212)243-1304. FAX: (212)243-1305. E-mail: mahosu@aol.com. Itche Goldberg. Bimonthly. Yiddish. Yiddisher Kultur Farband, Inc.—YKUF.

DOS YIDDISHE VORT (1953). 84 William St., NYC, 10038. (212)797-9000. Joseph Friedenson. Bimonthly, (November-December monthly). Yiddish. Agudath Israel of America.

YIDDISHER KEMFER (1900). 275 Seventh Ave., NYC, 10001. (212)675-7808. FAX: (212)675-7685. Dr. Jacob Weitzney. Bimonthly. Yiddish. Labor Zionist Alliance.

YIDISHE SHPRAKH (1941). 15 W. 16 St., NYC, 10011. (212)246-6080, ext. 6139. FAX: (212)292-1892. Dr. Mordkhe Schaechter. Irregularly. Yiddish. YIVO Institute for Jewish Research.

YIVO BLETER (1931). 15 W. 16 St., NYC, 10011. (212)246-6080. FAX: (212)292-1892. E-mail: yivomail@yivo.cjh.org. Dr. David E. Fishman. Biannually. Yiddish. YIVO Institute for Jewish Research.

THE YOUNG JUDAEAN (1909). 50 W. 58 St., NYC, 10019. (212)303-4588. FAX: (212)303-4572. E-mail: ugoldflam@youngjudaea.org. Uri Goldflam. Quarterly. Young Judaea Zionist Youth Movement/Hadassah.

YUGNTRUF: YIDDISH YOUTH MAGAZINE (1964). 200 W. 72 St., Suite 40, NYC, 10023. (212)787-6675. FAX: (212)799-1517. E-mail: yugntruf@yugntruf.org. Elinor Robinson. Two to four times a year. Yiddish. Yugntruf Youth for Yiddish.

ZUKUNFT (The Future) (1892). 25 E. 21 St., NYC, 10010. (212)505-8040. FAX: (212) 505-8044. Chaim Beider & Yonia Fain. Quarterly. Yiddish. Congress for Jewish Culture.

NORTH CAROLINA

CHARLOTTE JEWISH NEWS (1978). 5007 Providence Rd., Charlotte, 28226. (704) 944-6765. FAX: (704)365-4507. E-mail: amontoni@shalomcharlotte.org. Amy Krakovitz. Monthly (except July). Jewish Federation of Greater Charlotte.

JEWISH FEDERATION NEWS (1986). 8210 Creedmoor Rd., Suite 104, Raleigh, 27613. (919)676-2200. FAX: (919)676-2122. Sarah Falk. Monthly. Wake County Jewish Federation.

MODERN JUDAISM (1980). Oxford University Press, 2001 Evans Rd., Cary, 27513. (919)677-0977. FAX: (919)677-1714. E-mail: jnlorders@oup-usa.org. (Editorial address:Center for Judaic Studies, Boston University, 745 Commonwealth Ave., Boston, 02215. (617)353-8096. FAX: (617)353-5441. Steven T. Katz. Three times a year.

OHIO

AKRON JEWISH NEWS (1929). 750 White Pond Drive, Akron, 44320. (330)869-2424. FAX: (330)867-8498. E-mail: TobyLiberman@jewishakron.org. Toby Liberman. Fortnightly. Jewish Community Board of Akron.

American Israelite (1854). 906 Main St., Rm. 508, Cincinnati, 45202-1371. (513) 621-3145. FAX: (513)621-3744. E-mail: amisralite@aol.com. Stanley H. Bard. Weekly.

American Jewish Archives Journal (1948). 3101 Clifton Ave., Cincinnati, 45220-2488. (513)221-1875. FAX: (513)221-7812. E-mail: aja@cn.huc.edu. Ed. Dr. Gary P. Zola; Mng. Ed. Dr. Frederic Krome. Twice a year. Jacob Rader Marcus Center, American Jewish Archives, HUC-JIR.

Cleveland Jewish News (1964). 3645 Warrensville Center Rd., Suite 230, Cleveland, 44122. (216)991-8300. FAX: (216)991-2088. E-mail: editorial@cjn.org. Cynthia Dettelbach. Weekly. Cleveland Jewish News Publication Co.

Index to Jewish Periodicals (1963). PO Box 18525, Cleveland Hts., 44118. (216)381-4846. FAX: (216)381-4321. E-mail: index@jewishperiodicals.com. Lenore Pfeffer Koppel. Annually. Available in book and CD-ROM form. (www.jewishperiodicals.com)

Jewish Journal (1987). 505 Gypsy Lane, Youngstown, 44504-1314. (330)744-7902. FAX: (330)746-7926. Email: yojjournal@aol.com Sherry Weinblatt. Biweekly (except July/Aug.). Youngstown Area Jewish Federation. (www.jewishjournalplus.com)

Ohio Jewish Chronicle (1922). 2862 Johnstown Rd., Columbus, 43219. (614)337-2055. FAX: (614)337-2059. Email: ojc@iwaynet.net. Judy Franklin. Weekly.

Stark Jewish News (1920). 2631 Harvard Ave. NW, Canton, 44709. (330)452-6444. FAX: (330)452-4487. E-mail: canton jcf@aol.com. Linda Sirak. Monthly. Canton Jewish Community Federation; United Jewish Council of Greater Toledo.

Studies in Bibliography and Booklore (1953). 3101 Clifton Ave., Cincinnati, 45220. (513)221-1875. FAX: (513)221-0519. E-mail: lwolfson@huc.edu. Herbert C. Zafren. Irregularly. English-Hebrew-etc. Library of Hebrew Union College-Jewish Institute of Religion.

Toledo Jewish News (1951). 6505 Sylvania Ave., Sylvania, 43560. (419)885-4461. FAX: (419)724-0423. E-mail: Toljewnew@aol.com. Laurie Cohen. Monthly. Jewish Federation of Greater Toledo.

OKLAHOMA

Tulsa Jewish Review (1930). 2021 E. 71 St., Tulsa, 74136. (918)495-1100. FAX: (918)495-1220. Ed Ulrich. Monthly. Jewish Federation of Tulsa.

OREGON

Bridges: A Journal for Jewish Feminists and Our Friends (1990). PO Box 24839, Eugene, 97402. (541)343-7617. FAX: (541)343-7617. E-mail: clare@bridgesjournal.org. Mng. Ed. Clare Kinberg.

Jewish Review (1959). 6680 SW Capitol Highway, Portland, OR 97219. Edit.:(503)245-4340. FAX: (503)245-4342. Adv.: 503)670-2883. FAX: (503) 620-3433. E-mail: news@jewishreview.org. Paul Haist. Regular column in Russian. Fortnightly. Jewish Federation of Portland. (www.jewishreview.org)

PENNSYLVANIA

Community Review (1925). 3301 N. Front St. Annex, Harrisburg, 17110. (717)236-9555, ext.3402. FAX:(717)236-2552. E-mail: communityreview@desupernet.net. Carol L. Cohen. Fortnightly. United Jewish Community of Greater Harrisburg.

Contemporary Jewry (1974, under the name Jewish Sociology and Social Research). Baltimore Hebrew University, 5800 Park Heights Avenue, Baltimore, MD 21215. (410)578-6915. FAX:(410) 635-7320. E-mail: rmg@bhu.edu. Ed. Rela Mintz Geffen; Mng. Ed. Egon Mayer. Annually. Association for the Social Scientific Study of Jewry.

Jerusalem Letter/Viewpoints (1978). 1515 Locust St., Suite 703, Philadelphia, 19102. (215)772-0564. FAX: (215)772-0566. Zvi R. Marom. Fortnightly. Jerusalem Center for Public Affairs.

Jewish Chronicle of Pittsburgh (1962). 5600 Baum Blvd., Pittsburgh, 15206. (412)687-1000. FAX: (412)687-5119. E-mail: pittjewchr@aol.com. Joel Roteman. Weekly. Pittsburgh Jewish Publication and Education Foundation.

Jewish Exponent (1887). 2100 Arch St., Philadelphia, 19103. (215)832-0740. FAX: (215)569-3389. E-mail: jexponent@

aol.com. Jonathan S. Tobin. Weekly. Jewish Federation of Greater Philadelphia.

JEWISH POLITICAL STUDIES REVIEW (1989). 1515 Locust St., Suite 703, Philadelphia, 19102. (215)772-0564. FAX: (215)772-0566. Mark Ami-El. Twice a year. Jerusalem Center for Public Affairs.

JEWISH QUARTERLY REVIEW (1910). 420 Walnut St., Philadelphia, 19106. (215) 238-1290. FAX: (215)238-1540. E-mail: jqroffice@sas.upenn.edu. Ed. David M. Goldenberg; Mng. Ed. Bonnie L. Blankenship. Quarterly. Center for Advanced Jewish Studies, University of Pennsylvania.

NEW MENORAH (1978). 7318 Germantown Ave., Philadelphia, 19119-1793. (215)247-9700. FAX: (215)247-9703. Rabbi Arthur Waskow, PhD. Quarterly. Aleph: Alliance for Jewish Renewal.

RECONSTRUCTIONISM TODAY (1993). Beit Devora, 7804 Montgomery Ave., Suite 9, Elkins Park, 19027-2649. (215)782-8500. FAX: (215)782-8805. E-mail: jrfnatl@aol.com. Lawrence Bush. Quarterly. Jewish Reconstructionist Federation.

THE RECONSTRUCTIONIST (1935). 1299 Church Rd., Wyncote, 19095-1898. (215)576-5210. FAX: (215)576-8051. E-mail: rhirsh@therra.org. Rabbi Richard Hirsh. Semiannually. Reconstructionist Rabbinical College.

RHODE ISLAND

JEWISH VOICE OF RHODE ISLAND (1973). 130 Sessions St., Providence, 02906. (401)421-4111. FAX: (401)331-7961. E-mail: jvoice @aol.com. Jane S. Sprague. Monthly. Jewish Federation of Rhode Island.

RHODE ISLAND JEWISH HERALD (1930). 99 Webster St., Pawtucket, 02860. (401)724-0200. FAX: (401)726-5820. Luke O'Neill. Weekly. Herald Press Publishing Company.

RHODE ISLAND JEWISH HISTORICAL NOTES (1951). 130 Sessions St., Providence, 02906. (401)331-1360. FAX: (401)272-6729. E-mail: rjhist@aol.com. Leonard Moss. Annually. Rhode Island Jewish Historical Association.

SOUTH CAROLINA

CHARLESTON JEWISH JOURNAL. 1645 Wallenberg Blvd., Charleston, 29407. (843)571-6565. FAX: (843)556-6206. Ellen Katman. Monthly. Charleston Jewish Federation.

TENNESSEE

HEBREW WATCHMAN (1925). 4646 Poplar Ave., Suite 232, Memphis, 38117. (901)763-2215. FAX: (901)763-2216. Herman I. Goldberger. Weekly.

OBSERVER (1934). 801 Percy Warner Blvd., Suite 102, Nashville, 37205. (615)354-1637, ext. 237. FAX: (615)352-0056. E-mail: judy@jewishnashville.org. Judith A. Saks. Biweekly (except July). Jewish Federation of Nashville.

SHOFAR. PO Box 8947, Chattanooga, 37414. (423)493-0270, Ext. 12. FAX: (423)493-9997. E-mail: shofar@jcfgc.com. Rachel Schulson. Ten times a year. Jewish Federation of Greater Chattanooga.

TEXAS

JEWISH HERALD-VOICE (1908). 3403 Audley Street, Houston, 77098-1923. (713)630-0391. FAX: (713)630-0404. E-mail: joexhk@aol.com. Jeanne Samuels. Weekly. Four special issues:Rosh Hashanah; Passover; Wedding Planner; Bar/Bat Mitzvah Planner.

JEWISH JOURNAL OF SAN ANTONIO (1973). 8434 Ahern, San Antonio, 78213. (210)828-9511. FAX: (210)342-8098. Barbara Richmond. Monthly (11 issues). Jewish Federation of San Antonio.

TEXAS JEWISH POST (1947). 3120 S. Freeway, Fort Worth, 76110. (817)927-2831. FAX: (817)429-0840. 11333 N. Central Expressway, Suite 213, Dallas, 75243. (214)692-7283. FAX: (214)692-7285. Weekly.

VIRGINIA

RENEWAL MAGAZINE (1984). 5029 Corporate World Dr., Suite 225, Virginia Beach, 23462. (757)671-1600. FAX: (757)671-7613. E-mail: news@ujft.org. Reba Karp. Quarterly. United Jewish Federation of Tidewater.

SOUTHEASTERN VIRGINIA JEWISH NEWS (1959). 5029 Corporate World Dr., Suite 225, Virginia Beach, 23462. (757)671-1600. FAX: (757)671-7613. E-mail: news @ujft.org. Reba Karp. 22 issues yearly. United Jewish Federation of Tidewater.

WASHINGTON

JEWISH TRANSCRIPT (1924). 2041 Third Ave., Seattle, 98121. (206)441-4553. FAX: (206)441-2736. E-mail: jewishtran@aol.com. Donna Gordon Blankinship. Fortnightly. Jewish Federation of Greater Seattle. (WWW.JEWISHTRANSCRIPT.COM)

WISCONSIN

WISCONSIN JEWISH CHRONICLE (1921). 1360 N. Prospect Ave., Milwaukee, 53202. (414)390-5888. FAX: (414)271-0487. E-mail: milwaukeej@aol.com. Vivian M. Rothschild. Weekly. Milwaukee Jewish Federation.

INDEXES

INDEX TO JEWISH PERIODICALS (1963). PO Box 18525, Cleveland Hts., OH 44118. (216)381-4846. FAX: (216)381-4321. E-mail: index@jewishperiodicals.com. Lenore Pfeffer Koppel. Annually. Available in book and CD-ROM form. (WWW.JEWISHPERIODICALS.COM)

NEWS SYNDICATES

JEWISH TELEGRAPHIC AGENCY, INC. (1917). 330 Seventh Ave., 11th fl., NYC., 10001-5010. (212)643-1890. FAX: (212)643-8498. Mark J. Joffe, Lisa Hostein. Daily. (WWW.JTA.ORG)

CANADA

CANADIAN JEWISH HERALD (1977). 17 Anselme Lavigne, Dollard des Ormeaux, PQ H9A 1N3. (514)684-7667. FAX: (514)684-7667. Ed./Pub. Dan Nimrod. Irregularly. Dawn Publishing Co., Ltd.

THE CANADIAN JEWISH NEWS (1971). 1500 Don Mills Rd., Suite 205, North York, ONT M3B 3K4. (416)391-1836. FAX: (416)391-0829 (Adv.); (416)391-1836. FAX: (416)391-0829. Mordechai Ben-Dat. 50 issues a year. Some French.

CANADIAN JEWISH OUTLOOK (1963). #3-6184 Ash St., Vancouver, BC V5Z 3G9. (604)324-5101. FAX: (604)325-2470. E-mail: outlook@vcn.bc.ca. Carl Rosenberg. Six times per year. Canadian Jewish Outlook Society.

DAIS (1985) (formerly INTERCOM). 100 Sparks St., #650, Ottawa, ONT KIP 5B7. (613)233-8703. FAX: (613)233-8748. E-mail: canadianjewishcongress@cjc.ca. Jack Silverstone. Three times a year. Canadian Jewish Congress.

DIRECTIONS (1998) (formerly DIALOGUE (1988)). 1 Carré Cummings, Suite 202, Montreal, Quebec H3W 1M6. (514)345-64111. FAX: (514)345-6412. E-mail: etay@cjc.ca. Eta Yudin. Quarterly. French-English. Canadian Jewish Congress, Quebec Region.

JEWISH FREE PRESS (1990). 8411 Elbow Dr., SW Calgary, AB. T2V 1K8. (403) 252-9423. FAX: (403)255-5640. E-mail: jewishfp@cadvision.com. Judy Shapiro. Fortnightly.

JEWISH POST & NEWS (1987). 113 Hutchings St., Winnipeg, MAN R2X 2V4. (204) 694-3332. FAX: (204)694-3916. E-mail: jewishp@mts.net. Matt Bellan. Weekly.

JEWISH STANDARD (1928). 1912A Avenue Road, Suite E5, Toronto, ONT M5M 4A1. (416)537-2696. FAX: (416)789-3872. Email: thejewishstandardasympatico.ca. Ed./Pub. Michael Hayman. Fortnightly.

THE JEWISH TRIBUNE (1950). 15 Hove St., Toronto, ONT M3H 4Y8. (416)633-6224. FAX: (416)633-6299. E-mail: editor@istar.ca. B'nai Brith Canada, forthnightly.

JEWISH WESTERN BULLETIN (1930). 301, 68 E. Second Ave., Vancouver, BC V5T 1B1. (604)689-1520. FAX: (604)689-1525. E-mail: jbeditor@istar.ca. Baila Lazarus. Weekly. 57786 BC Ltd.

JOURNAL OF PSYCHOLOGY AND JUDAISM (1976). 1747 Featherston Dr., Ottawa, ONT K1H 6P4. (613)731-9119. Reuven P. Bulka. Quarterly. Center for the Study of Psychology and Judaism.

OTTAWA JEWISH BULLETIN (1954). 21 Nadolny Sachs Private., Ottawa, ONT K2A 1R9. (613)798-4696. FAX: (613) 798-4730. E-mail: bulletin@jccottawa.com. Barry Fishman. Nineteen times a year. Ottawa Jewish Bulletin Publishing Co. Ltd.

SHALOM (1975). 5670 Spring Garden Rd., Suite 508, Halifax, NS, B3J 1H1.

(902)422-7491. FAX: (902)425-3722. E-mail: jgoldberg@theajc.ns.ca. Jon M. Goldberg. Quarterly. Atlantic Jewish Council.

LA VOIX SÉPHARADE (1966). 1 Carré Cummings, Montreal, PQ H3W 1M6. (514)733-4998, (514)733-8696. FAX: (514)733-3158. E-mail: csq@csq.qc.ca. Ed. James Dahan; Pub. Elie Benchitrit. Bimonthly (five times a year). French and occasional Spanish and English. Communauté Sépharade du Québec.

NEWS AND VIEWS (1942) (formerly WINDSOR JEWISH FEDERATION). 1641 Ouellette Ave., Windsor, ONT N8X 1K9. (519)973-1772. FAX: (519)973-1774. Exec. Dir. Harvey Kessler. Quarterly. Windsor Jewish Federation.

THE WORLD OF LUBAVITCH (1980). 770 Chabad Gate, Thornhill, ONT L4J 3V9. (905)731-7000. FAX: (905)731-7005. Rabbi Moshe Spalter. Bimonthly. English-Hebrew. Chabad Lubavitch of Southern Ont.

Obituaries: United States*

ABEL, LIONEL, playwright, essayist; b. NYC (Brooklyn), Nov. 28, 1918; d. NYC, Apr. 20, 2001. Educ.: high school. Prof., English, State U. of N.Y. Buffalo, 1967–1979, prof. emer., 1979–. Au: four well-received plays, including *Absalom,* chosen as best off-Broadway play of 1956, and several books, including *Metatheatre: A New View of Dramatic Form* (1963); *Moderns on Tragedy* (1967); *The Intellectual Follies: A Memoir of the Literary Venture in New York and Paris* (1984); *Important Nonsense* (1987). Authorized translator of the works of Jean-Paul Sartre.

ADLER, LARRY, harmonica virtuoso; b. Baltimore, Md., Feb. 10, 1914; d. London, England, Aug. 7, 2001. Educ.: Baltimore City Coll. After teaching himself to play the instrument, won Baltimore harmonica championship, 1927, played in N.Y. with nightclub bands and in musical theater, and subsequently attained great popularity in England. Appeared in several films beginning in 1934; composed music for film and TV scores, commercials, children's recordings; soloist with major orchestras; performed for Allied troops, WWII, for concentration camp survivors, and for Israeli troops in 1967 war. Under pressure for his political views, left U.S. permanently for England, 1952. Au.: *How I Play* (1937); *Larry Adler's Own Arrangements* (1960).

ARKOFF, SAMUEL Z., movie producer; b. Fort Dodge, Iowa, June 12, 1918; d. Burbank, Cal., Sept. 16, 2001. Educ.: U. Iowa; Loyola U. (JD). Cryptographer, U.S. Army Air Force, WWII. Co-founder, Amer. Releasing, 1954; pres., chmn. bd., Amer. Internat'l. Pictures, Inc., 1956–1979; pres., chmn., Samuel Z. Arkoff Co., 1980–; pres., Arkoff Internat'l. Pictures, 1981–. Made more than 500 movies that were very popular with teenage audiences, including *I Was a Teenage Werewolf* (1957); *Beach Party* (1963); *The Wild Angels* (1966); *What's Up Tiger Lily?* (film debut of Woody Allen, 1973); *Heavy Traffic* (1973); *Love at First Bite* (1979); and *Amityville Horror* (1979). The Museum of Modern Art honored his films with a retrospective, 1979. Recipient: Allied States Assn. Motion Picture Owners Producer of Year; Theatre Owners of Amer. Master Showman of Decade.

BEAME, ABRAHAM D., political leader; b. London, England, Mar. 20, 1906; d. NYC, Feb. 10, 2001. Educ.: CCNY (BBA). Partner, Beame-Greidinger C.P.A.s, 1925–45; high school teacher, 1929–45; instr., accounting and auditing, Rutgers U., 1944–45; asst. budget dir., NYC, 1946–52; dir., 1952–61; comptroller, 1962–65, 1970–73; unsuccessful Democratic candidate for mayor, 1965, los-

*Including American Jews who died between January 1 and December 31, 2001.

ing to John V. Lindsay; private financial consultant, 1966–69; mayor of NYC (first Jew to hold that office), 1974–77; member of numerous civic and business advisory bds, 1978–. As mayor, presided over severe NYC fiscal crisis, citywide blackout, celebration of U.S. bicentennial.

BERGREEN, MORRIS H., businessman, philanthropist; b. Passaic, N.J., Sept. 28, 1917; d. NYC, July 9, 2001. Educ.: NYU (BA); Fordham U. (LLB). Served U.S. Army Air Force, WWII. Sr. partner, Bergreen & Bergreen, 1953–86, 1995–; of counsel, Milbank, Tweed, Hadley & McCloy, 1986–95; pres., Croyden Co., Westminster Broadcasting Corp., Claridge Broadcasting Corp.; genl. mgr., Grosvenor Investment Co., Skirball Investment Co.; prin. owner, Gaylord Brothers; pres., Skirball Found., 1986–; founding mem. bd. trustees, Skirball Museum and Cultural Center; hon. v.-pres., Amer. Jewish Com.; adv. bd., Amer. Jewish Com. Skirball Inst. for Amer. Values; chmn. publs. com., *Commentary* magazine; trustee, Bronfman Center for Jewish Student Life/NYU, NYU Medical Center, Jewish Home and Hosp. for Aged; bd. govs., Hebrew Union Coll., Oxford Center for Hebrew and Jewish Studies Oxford U. Recipient: Albert Gallatin Medal, NYU; Distinguished Leadership Award, Amer. Jewish Com.

BLOCK, HERBERT L. (HERBLOCK), editorial cartoonist; b. Chicago, Ill., Oct. 13, 1909; d. Washington, D.C., Oct. 7, 2001. Educ.: Lake Forest Coll.; Art Inst. of Chicago. Served U.S. Army Information and Educ. Div., WWII. Editorial cartoonist, *Chicago Daily News,* 1929–33, Newspaper Enterprise Assn., 1933–43, *Washington Post,* 1946–. Designed U.S. postage stamp commemorating 175th anniversary of Bill of Rights, 1966. Au.: 12 books of political and social commentary. Recipient: Pulitzer Prize (three times); Presidential Medal of Freedom; American Newspaper Guild Award; Heywood Broun Award; numerous other awards in recognition of contributions to journalism, civil liberties, civil rights.

BURSTEIN, BEATRICE S., jurist; b. NYC (Brooklyn), May 18, 1915; d. Lawrence, N.Y., Jan. 6, 2001. Educ.: NYU (BA); St. Johns U. (LLB). Attorney, private practice, 1937–62; founding partner, Burstein & Agata, 1958; mem., N.Y. State Comm. of Corrections, 1955–61 (first woman ever appointed), U.S. Comm. on Juvenile Delinquency, 1961; judge, Nassau County District Court, 1962–68, family court, 1968–72, N.Y. State Supreme Court, 1972–91; judicial hearing officer, N.Y. State Appellate Div., 1991–2000. Ended solitary confinement of children, pioneered schools in jails and outpatient drug treatment centers.

CAHAN, WILLIAM G., surgeon; b. NYC, Aug. 2, 1914; d. NYC, Oct. 7, 2001. Educ.: Harvard U. (BS); Columbia U. (MD). Served U.S. Army Air Force, WWII. Surgeon, N.Y. Presbyterian Hosp., 1939, Hosp. for Joint Diseases, 1940–41; fellow, cancer surgery, Memorial Hosp., 1942–48; surgeon, Memorial Sloan-Kettering Cancer Center, 1949–90, sr. attending surgeon, 1990–; faculty, Cornell U. Medical Coll., 1950–84, emeritus, 1984–. Developed innovations in use of radiation, removal of lymph nodes in cancer patients; as chmn., People for a Smoke-Free Indoors, played key role in NYC laws restricting smoking. Au.: *No Stranger to Tears* (1992). Recipient: Amer. Cancer Soc. Distinguished Service Award.

DAVIS, LEONARD, insurer, philanthropist; b. NYC, Jan. 28, 1924; d. on cruise to South Amer., Jan. 15, 2001. Educ.: CCNY (BA). Founder and pres., Colonial Penn Insurance Co., 1963–84, making it one of the largest insurance underwriters in the country. Major contributor to CCNY (over $10 million) for Aaron Davis Hall performing-arts center, Leonard Davis Center for the Arts, Sophie Davis School of Biomedical Educ.; to U. of Pa. for Leonard Davis Inst. of Health Economics; to U. of Southern Cal. for nation's first school of gerontology; to Hebrew U. for Leonard Davis Inst. for the Study of Internat'l. Relations. Founding mem., U.S. Holocaust Memorial Museum.

FRIEDMAN, MEYER, physician; b. Kansas City, Kans., July 13, 1910; d. San Francisco, Cal., Apr. 27, 2001. Educ.: Yale U. (AB); Johns Hopkins U. (MD). Served U.S. Marine Corps, WWII. Medical resident, Michael Reese Hosp., 1936–38, U. Wis. Genl. Hosp., 1938–39; dir., Harold Brunn Inst., Mt. Zion Medical Center U. Cal. at San Francisco, 1939–75, where Meyer Friedman Inst. was named for him, 1984; pioneer in linking heart attacks to emotional states, coining "Type A" and "Type B" personalities. Au.: *Functional Cardiovascular Disease* (1947); *Pathogenesis of Coronary Artery Disease* (1969); *Type A Behavior and Your Heart* (with Ray Rosenman, 1974). Recipient: Heart Research Found. Award; Upjohn Distinguished Scientist Award.

GLICKMAN, MARTY, sports announcer; b. NYC, Aug. 14, 1917; d. NYC, Jan. 3, 2001. Educ.: Syracuse U. (BA). Mem., U.S. track team at 1936 Olympics in Berlin, but kept out of competition, allegedly due to anti-Semitism. Began sports announcing, radio station WHN, 1939; radio announcer for New York Knickerbockers NBA basketball team, 1946–67, N.Y. Giants (23 years) and N.Y Jets (11 years) NFL football teams, Yonkers Raceway (12 years), numerous pre- and post-game shows for Major League Baseball. Au.: *The Fastest Kid on the Block* (1996). Mem., Basketball Hall of Fame; N.Y. Sports Hall of Fame; N.Y. Jewish Sports Hall of Fame. Recipient: U.S. Olympic Com. Gen. Douglas MacArthur Award.

GORDON, CYRUS H., orientalist, educator; b. Philadelphia, Pa., June 29, 1908; d. Brookline, Mass., Mar. 30, 2001. Educ.: U. Pa. (AB, MA, PhD). Served U.S. Army, WWII. Instr., semitics, U. Pa., 1930–31; field archaeologist, Amer. Schools for Oriental Research, 1931–35; teaching fellow, Johns Hopkins U., 1935–38; mem., Inst. of Advanced Study, Princeton, N.J., 1939–40, 1941–42; prof., Assyriology and Egyptology, Dropsie U., 1946–56; prof., Near Eastern studies, Brandeis U., 1956–73, emeritus, 1973–; Gottesman prof., Hebrew studies, NYU, 1973–89, emeritus, 1989–. Au.: *Ugaritic Grammar* (1940); *Ugaritic Handbook* (1947); *Ugaritic Literature* (1949); *Introduction to Old Testament Times* (1953); *Ugaritic Manual* (1955); *Hammurabi's Code* (1957); *The Common Background of Greek and Hebrew Civilizations* (1965); *Evidence for the Minoan Language* (1966); *Before Columbus* (1971). Honored with two Festschriften.

GREENBERG, JOSEPH H., anthropologist; b. NYC (Brooklyn), May 28, 1915; d. Stanford, Cal., May 7, 2001. Educ.: Columbia U. (AB); Northwestern U. (PhD). Served U.S. Army Signal Intelligence Service, WWII. Faculty, U. Minn., 1946–48; asst. prof., anthropology, Columbia U., 1948–53, assoc. prof., 1953–57, prof., 1957–62; prof., Stanford U., 1962–85; coord., Stanford Project on Language Universals. Au.: *Languages of Africa* (1963); *Anthropological Linguistics* (1968); *Language Typology* (1974); *Universals of Human Language*, 4 vols. (1978); *Language in the Americas* (1987); *Indo-European and Its Closest Relatives* (2000). Recipient: Guggenheim Award (twice); Haile Selassie Award for African Research.

HAMBURGER, VIKTOR, embryologist; b. Landeshut, Germany (now Poland), July 9, 1900; d. St. Louis, Mo., June 12, 2001; in U.S. since 1932, when he was Rockefeller Fellow at U. Chicago and stayed after Nazis came to power. Educ.: U. Freiburg, Germany (PhD). Prof., zoology, Washington U. (St. Louis), 1941–68, chmn., biology dept., 1941–66, distinguished prof. emer., 1968–. Au.: *The Heritage of Experimental Embryology* (1988); *Selected Papers* (1990), including several path-breaking studies of early development of the nervous system and origins of behavior. Recipient: F.O. Schmitt Medal in neuroscience; Louis Gross Horwitz Prize; Karl Lashly Award.

HORWICH, FRANCES R., educator; b. Ottawa, Ohio, July 16, 1908; d. Chicago, Ill., July 25, 2001. Educ.: U. Chicago (BA); Northwestern U. (EdD). After teaching elementary school, serving as principal, and teaching education at universities, initiated "Ding Dong School," broadcast live on WNBQ TV in Chicago, 1952, picked up that same year by NBC, moving to WNET, 1959. At its peak, the show—considered the pioneer educational program on TV—was seen in almost 40 cities by an estimated 3 million preschoolers each weekday morning. Recipient: George Foster Peabody Award.

KRAMER, STANLEY, filmmaker; b. NYC, Sept. 29, 1913; d. Los Angeles, Cal., Feb. 19, 2001. Educ.: NYU (BS). Served U.S. Army making training films, WWII. Founder and pres., Stanley Kramer Prods., 1949, Stanley Kramer Co., 1950, Stanley Kramer Pictures Corp., 1954. Produced and directed such classics as *Not As a Stranger* (1954); *The Defiant Ones* (1958); *On the Beach* (1959); *Inherit the Wind* (1960); *Judgement at Nuremberg* (1961); *It's a Mad, Mad, Mad, Mad World*

(1963); *Ship of Fools* (1965); *Guess Who's Coming to Dinner* (1967). Produced *High Noon* (4 Academy Awards, 1952); *Caine Mutiny* (1953). Recipient: Irving G. Thalberg Award; NY Film Critics Award.

LAPIDUS, MORRIS, architect; b. Odessa, Russia, Nov. 25, 1902; d. Miami Beach, Fla., Jan. 18, 2001; in U.S. since 1903. Educ.: NYU; Columbia U. (bachelor of architecture). Architect, Alan H. Warren & Wetmore, 1926–28; Arthur Weisner, 1928–30; Ross-Frankel Inc., 1930–42; prin., Morris Lapidus Assoc., 1942–84. Constructed more than 500 stores, designed numerous apartment buildings and synagogues, the first mall in America (Lincoln Rd. Mall), and some 200 hotels, most notably the Fountainebleau and Eden Roc in Miami Beach and the Americana in Bal Harbour, derided as "faux French" kitsch but later praised as "postmodern." Au.: *A Quest for Emotion in Architecture* (1961); *The Future by Design* (1962); *Architecture: A Profession and a Business* (1967); *An Architecture of Joy* (1979); *Too Much Is Never Enough,* an autobiography (1994). Recipient: numerous awards from architectural and civic groups.

LEROY, WARNER, restauranteur; b. Hollywood, Cal., Mar. 5, 1935; d. NYC, Feb. 22, 2001. Educ.: Stanford U. (BA). After working as producer, director, and theater manager in NYC, opened Maxwell's Plum restaurant, 1966, attracting the "jetset" crowd; took over and reopened Tavern on the Green, 1976, the Russian Tea Room, 1999. Created Great Adventure amusement park-safari experience, Jackson Township, N.J.

LEUCHTER, BEN ZION, journalist; b. Philadelphia, Pa., Dec. 11, 1926; d. Key Biscayne, Fla., Jan 14, 2001. Educ.: Haverford Coll. (AB). Served U.S. Merchant Marine, WWII. Editor, asst. publisher, Vineland (N.J.) *Times-Journal,* 1949–73, editorial chmn., 1973–77; pres., Minuteman Publications, 1978–80; v.-pres., Beacon Communications, 1981–; v.-pres., Jewish Telegraphic Agcy., 1980–; founding chmn., Natl. Jewish Resource Center (now CLAL), 1974–76; pres., HIAS, 1988–92; mem., UJA natl. young leadership cabinet, 1962–69, natl. v. chmn., 1978–84; cochmn., AIPAC natl. governing council, 1976–82; founding pres., Vineland Jewish Community Council, 1970. Au.: *How a Small-Town Editor Saw the World* (2000). Recipient: Golden Quill Award, Atlantic City Press Club; Best Story of the Year, Philadelphia Press Club.

MANDEL, LEONARD, physicist; b. Berlin, Germany, May 9, 1927; d. Pittsford, N.Y., Feb. 9, 2001; in U.S. since 1964. Educ.: U. London (BSc, PhD). Technical Officer, Imperial Chemical Industries, 1951–54; lect., sr. lect., Imperial Coll. U. of London, 1954–64; prof., physics, U. Rochester, 1964–, prof., optics, 1977–80. Au.: almost 300 articles, including seminal papers on quantum mechanics, demonstrating that the act of observation changes behavior of light particles. Recipient: Marconi Medal, Italian Natl. Research Council; Thomas Young Medal, Great Britain Inst. of Physics; Max Born Medal (first recipient).

MILSTEIN, SEYMOUR, businessman, philanthropist; b. NYC, July 21, 1920; d. NYC, Oct. 2, 2001. Educ.: NYU (BA). Worked for Mastic Tile Co., building contracting firm founded by his father, named pres., 1955; after business sold to Rubberoid, named dir., v.-pres., 1959; with brother Paul took over United Brands, Starrett Housing Corp., 1970, Emigrant Savings Bank, 1986. Before recent breakup of partnership with Paul, the brothers owned Manhattan real estate worth billions of dollars, including office buildings, apartment houses, and hotels. Chmn., N.Y. Presbyterian Hosp., 1989–96, his family's $25-million gift making possible its Milstein Hosp. Building; chmn., Bronx Lebanon Hosp. Center, 1964–73; founding mem., U.S. Holocaust Memorial Museum.

OAKES, JOHN B. journalist; b. Elkins Park, Pa., Apr. 23, 1913; d. NYC, Apr. 5, 2001. Educ.: Princeton U. (AB); Oxford U. (Rhodes scholar, AB, AM). Served U.S. Army and OSS, WWII, with numerous decorations. Reporter, Trenton (N.J.) *Times,* 1936–37; *Washington Post,* 1937–41; editor, *N.Y. Times* Week in Review, 1946–49, named to editorial bd., 1949, wrote monthly column on environment, 1951–61, editorial page editor, 1961–76 (originated op-ed page, 1970), sr. editor, 1977–78, contributing columnist, 1977–90. Member, Interior Dept. adv. bd. on national parks; involved in numerous environmental, journalistic, and human-right orgs.; trustee, Temple Emanu-El, NYC. Au.: *The Edge of Freedom* (1961); *Tomorrow's American* (1977); *On the Vineyard* (1980); *The March to War* (1991). Recipient: George Polk Memorial Award; Silurian Soc. Award; John Muir Award (Sierra Club).

PAM, AVROHOM, rabbi, educator; b. Vidz, Russia, July 9, 1913; d. NYC (Brooklyn), Aug. 17, 2001; in U.S. since 1927. Educ.: Yeshiva Torah Vodaath, Brooklyn, N.Y. (ordination). Teacher of Talmud, Yeshiva Torah Vodaath, 1937–, dean, 1970–. Mem., Council of Torah Sages of Agudath Israel of Amer.; active in providing Jewish education for immigrants from former Soviet Union, promoting ethical behavior among Orthodox.

PELAVIN, MICHAEL, communal leader; b. Flint, Mich., Sept. 5, 1936; d. Delray Beach, Fla., Jan 19, 2001. Educ.: U. Mich.; Wayne State U.; Detroit Coll. of Law (JD). V.-pres., Pelavin, Pelavin and Powers; dir., numerous privately held corps. Chmn., UJA young leadership cabinet, 1973; pres., Flint Jewish Fed., 1973–76; chmn., Natl. Jewish Comm. Relations Adv. Bd. (NJCRAC, now JCPA), 1986–89, where he advocated loan guarantees for Israel and promoted Jewish emigration from USSR. Pres., Flint Jewish Community Center; gen. chmn., UJA campaign; bd. mem., Council of Jewish Feds., United Israel Appeal, AIPAC, ACLU; founding mem., MIPAC multi-issue Jewish political action com.

RABKIN, BARBARA A., communal leader; b. Long Beach, N.Y., Dec. 30, 1949; d. Gaithersburg, Md., Aug. 29, 2001. Educ.: Syracuse U. (BA); Catholic U. (MSW). Joined Jewish Women Internat'l. (then B'nai B'rith Women), 1960s; pres., local chapter; pres., Mid-Atlantic region, natl. pres., 2000–, focusing on ending domestic violence, organizing shelters for battered women; dir. of volunteers, Visiting Nurse Assn. of Northern Va.; bereavement coord., Montgomery Hospice.

ROSENBERG, ROY, rabbi; b. Baltimore, Md., Dec. 22, 1930; d. Lock Haven, Pa., Aug. 11, 2001. Educ.: U. Pa. (BA); Hebrew Union Coll. (ordination, MHL, DHL). Served as chaplain U.S. Army, 1956–58. Rabbi, Temple Emanu-El, Rochester, N.Y., 1953–56, Temple Emanu-El, Honolulu, 1958–66, Temple Sinai, New Orleans, 1966–70; faculty, Loyola U., New Orleans, 1970–72; rabbi, Beth Sholom People's Temple, Brooklyn, 1972–75; founding rabbi, Temple of Universal Judaism, NYC, 1975–97. Known for performing intermarriages, often together with clergy of other faiths. Au.: *The Anatomy of God: The Book of Concealment* (1973); *Who Was Jesus?* (1986); *Happily Intermarried: Authoritative Advice for a Joyous Jewish-Christian Marriage* (with Peter Meehan and John Wade Payne, 1988).

RUDIN, LEWIS, businessman, civic leader; b. NYC, Apr. 4, 1927; d. NYC, Sept. 20, 2001. Educ.: NYU. Served U.S. Army, WWII. Joined father's business, Rudin Management, 1945, building NYC apartment houses and, beginning 1955, office towers, value of holdings eventually estimated at $2 billion. Together with other large real-estate owners founded Assn. for a Better N.Y., 1971, to promote the city (originating "I Love N.Y." slogan); aided in weathering NYC fiscal crisis, keeping U.S. Tennis Assn. in city. Major contrib: Hebrew Home for the Aged; Hebrew U.; Columbia U.; Schneider Children's Hospital; Lincoln Center; Central Park Conservancy; Metropolitan Museum of Art; and many other causes.

SCHOR, NAOMI, literary critic; b. NYC, Oct. 10, 1943; d. New Haven, Conn., Dec. 2, 2001. Educ.: Barnard Coll. (BA); Yale U. (PhD). After teaching at Brown U., Duke U., and Harvard U., named Benjamin F. Barge Prof., Yale U., 1999–. Au.: *Breaking the Chain* (1985); *Reading in Detail* (1987); *George Sand and Idealism* (1993); *Bad Objects* (1995); *One Hundred Years of Melancholy* (1997). Ed.: *Essential Difference* (1994); *Feminism Meets Queer Theory* (1997). Founding ed., *Differences: A Journal of Feminist Cultural Studies.* Known for use of psychoanalytic theory and deconstruction in French studies.

SHAPIRO, IRVING S., lawyer, business exec.; b. Minneapolis, Minn., July 15, 1916; d. Greenville, Del., Sept. 13, 2001. Educ.: U. Minn. (BS, LLB). Attorney, private practice, 1941–42; Office of Price Admin., 1942–43; U.S. Justice Dept. criminal div., 1943–51; E.I. DuPont de Nemours & Co., 1951–70, sr. v.-pres., 1970–73, chmn./ceo, 1974–81 (first lawyer to head DuPont, one of first Jews to head a major Amer. corp.); partner, Skadden, Arps, Slate.

Meagher & Flom, 1981–89, of counsel, 1989–. As chmn. of Business Roundtable, 1976, secured business support for federal legislation outlawing compliance with Arab boycott of Israel. Trustee, Ford Found., U. Minn., U. Pa.; pres., Jewish Fed. Del., 1968–70. Recipient of numerous awards from business, civic, and Jewish groups.

SOLOVEICHIK, AHRON, rabbi, educator; b. Pruzhany, Russia, May 11, 1917; d. Chicago, Ill., Oct. 5, 2001; in U.S. since 1929. Educ.: Yeshiva U. (BA), NYU (LLB). Teacher of Talmud, Yeshiva Rabbi Chaim Berlin, Brooklyn, N.Y., 1950s–1962; Yeshiva U., 1962–66, 1983–; dean, Hebrew Theol. Coll., Skokie, Ill., 1966–74; founder and dean, Yeshiva Brisk, Chicago, 1974–. Au.: *Logic of the Heart, Logic of the Mind* (1991); *The Warmth and the Light* (1992).

SQUADRON, HOWARD M., lawyer, communal leader; b. NYC, Sept. 5, 1926; d. NYC, Dec. 26, 2001. Educ.: CCNY (AB), Columbia U. (LLB). Attorney, Stroock, Stroock & Lavan, 1948–50; Amer. Jewish Cong., 1950–52; Phillips, Nizer, Benjamin & Krim, 1952–54; ptnr., Squadron, Elenoff, Plesent and Lehrer, 1954–, where he handled many high-profile cases, representing major corporations and also defending individuals in civil-rights and civil-liberties litigation. Active in Amer. Jewish Cong. from 1961, sr. v.-pres., 1974–78, pres., 1978–84; chmn. Conf. of Pres. of Major Jewish Orgs., 1980–82. Founder, Internat'l. Center of Photography; Squadron Program in Law, Media, and Society, Cardozo School of Law, Yeshiva U.; Abraham Fund.

STERN, ISAAC, violinist; b. Kremenetz, Ukraine, July 21, 1920; d. NYC, Sept. 23, 2001; in U.S. since 1921. Educ.: San Francisco Conservatory. Recital debut, 1934; orchestral debut with San Francisco Symphony Orchestra, 1936; Carnegie Hall debut 1943 (first of more than 200 performances there); N.Y. Philharmonic debut, 1944 (first of more than 100 performances with it); performed for Allied troops, WWII; European debut, Lucerne Festival, 1948; first U.S. violinist to tour USSR, 1956; performed in China at invitation of govt., 1979; played with numerous major orchestras worldwide, made over 100 recordings, soundtracks for films. After organizing campaign to save Carnegie Hall from being torn down, served as pres., 1960–. Devoted Zionist; chair, America-Israel Cultural Found.; played with Israel Philharmonic on Mt. Scopus immediately after 1967 war; founded Jerusalem Music Center, 1973; performed in Israel during 1973 war, organized musicians' boycott of UNESCO events after that body suspended programs in Israel, 1974; played while wearing gas mask in Israel during Gulf War missile attack, 1991; would not play in Germany. Recipient: numerous Grammy Awards; French Legion of Honor; Nat. Medal of Honor; Presidential Medal of Honor; and many others.

STERN, WILLIAM A., communal professional; b. Yoslo, Austria, July 7, 1910; d. Tamarac, Fla., Jan 18, 2001; in U.S. since 1911. Educ.: Long Island U. (BA); NYU (MA). Served U.S. Army, WWII. Branch dir., Workmen's Circle, 1938–43; nat. dir. English-speaking branches, 1946–63; nat. admin. dir., 1963–70; exec. dir., 1970–79; ed., Workmen's Center *Call,* 1946–79. Pres., Forward Assn., 1989–94; chmn. admn. com., Jewish Labor Com., 1972–; chmn. exec. com., Workers Defense League, 1974–; cochmn., Lower Eastside Neighborhood Assn.

YOLLES, STANLEY F., public health official; b. NYC, Apr. 19, 1919; d. Stony Brook, N.Y., Jan. 12, 2001. Educ.: Brooklyn Coll. (BA); Harvard U. (MA); NYU (MD); Johns Hopkins U. (MPH). Served U.S. Army, WWII. Nat. Inst. of Mental Health staff psychiatrist, 1954; assoc. dir. community services, 1955–57; dir., 1957–60; assoc. dir. extramural programs, 1960–63; deputy dir. NIMH, 1963–64; acting dir., 1964; dir., 1964–70; founder and chmn., dept. of psychiatry, State U. of N.Y. Stony Brook Medical School, 1971–81; dir., Long Island Research Inst., 1974–81. Influential voice against mandatory sentences for drug use, opening of community mental health centers. Led first official U.S. delegation to study mental health in USSR, 1967.

Calendars

SUMMARY JEWISH CALENDAR, 5762–5766 (Sept. 2001–Aug. 2006)

HOLIDAY	5762			5763			5764			5765			5766		
		2001			2002			2003							
Rosh Ha-shanah, 1st day	T	Sept.	18	Sa	Sept.	7	Sa	Sept.	27	Th	Sept.	16	T	Oct.	4
Rosh Ha-shanah, 2nd day	W	Sept.	19	S	Sept.	8	S	Sept.	28	F	Sept.	17	W	Oct.	5
Fast of Gedaliah	Th	Sept.	20	M	Sept.	9	M	Sept.	29	S	Sept.	19	Th	Oct.	6
Yom Kippur	Th	Sept.	27	M	Sept.	16	M	Oct.	6	Sa	Sept.	25	Th	Oct.	13
Sukkot, 1st day	T	Oct.	2	Sa	Sept.	21	Sa	Oct.	11	Th	Sept.	30	T	Oct.	18
Sukkot, 2nd day	W	Oct.	3	S	Sept.	22	S	Oct.	12	F	Oct.	1	W	Oct.	19
Hosha'na' Rabbah	M	Oct.	8	F	Sept.	27	F	Oct.	17	W	Oct.	6	M	Oct.	24
Shemini 'Aẓeret	T	Oct.	9	Sa	Sept.	28	Sa	Oct.	18	Th	Oct.	7	T	Oct.	25
Simḥat Torah	W	Oct.	10	S	Sept.	29	S	Oct.	19	F	Oct.	8	W	Oct.	26
New Moon, Ḥeshwan, 1st day . .	W	Oct.	17	S	Oct.	6	S	Oct.	26	F	Oct.	15	W	Nov.	2
New Moon, Ḥeshwan, 2nd day .	Th	Oct.	18	M	Oct.	7	M	Oct.	27	Sa	Oct.	16	Th	Nov.	3
New Moon, Kislew, 1st day . . .	F	Nov.	16	T	Nov.	5	T	Nov.	25	S	Nov.	14	F	Dec.	2
New Moon, Kislew, 2nd day . . .				W	Nov.	6	W	Nov.	26						
Ḥanukkah, 1st day	M	Dec.	10	S	Nov.	30	Sa	Dec.	20	W	Dec.	8	M	Dec.	26
New Moon, Ṭevet, 1st day	Sa	Dec.	15	Th	Dec.	5	Th	Dec.	25	M	Dec.	13	Sa	Dec.	31
New Moon, Ṭevet, 2nd day . . .	S	Dec.	16	F	Dec.	6	F	Dec.	26				S	Jan.	1
								2004						2006	
Fast of 10th of Ṭevet	T	Dec.	25	S	Dec.	15	S	Jan.	4	W	Dec.	22	T	Jan.	10

	2002			2003			2004			2005			2006		
New Moon, Shevaṭ	M	Jan.	14	Sa	Jan.	4	Sa	Jan.	24	T	Jan.	11	M	Jan.	30
Ḥamishshah-ʻasar bi-Shevaṭ	M	Jan.	28	Sa	Jan.	18	Sa	Feb.	7	T	Jan.	25	M	Feb.	13
New Moon, Adar I, 1st day	T	Feb.	12	S	Feb.	2	S	Feb.	22	W	Feb.	9	T	Feb.	28
New Moon, Adar I, 2nd day	W	Feb.	13	M	Feb.	3	M	Feb.	23	Th	Feb.	10	W	Mar.	1
New Moon, Adar II, 1st day				T	Mar.	4				F	Mar.	11			
New Moon, Adar II, 2nd day				W	Mar.	5				Sa	Mar.	12			
Fast of Esther	M	Feb.	25	M	Mar.	17	Th	Mar.	4	Th	Mar.	24	M	Mar.	13
Purim	T	Feb.	26	T	Mar.	18	S	Mar.	7	F	Mar.	25	T	Mar.	14
Shushan Purim	W	Feb.	27	W	Mar.	19	M	Mar.	8	Sa	Mar.	26	W	Mar.	15
New Moon, Nisan	Th	Mar.	14	Th	Apr.	3	T	Mar.	23	S	Apr.	10	Th	Mar.	30
Passover, 1st day	Th	Mar.	28	Th	Apr.	17	T	Apr.	6	S	Apr.	24	Th	Apr.	13
Passover, 2nd day	F	Mar.	29	F	Apr.	18	W	Apr.	7	M	Apr.	25	F	Apr.	14
Passover, 7th day	W	Apr.	3	W	Apr.	23	M	Apr.	12	Sa	Apr.	30	W	Apr.	19
Passover, 8th day	Th	Apr.	4	Th	Apr.	24	T	Apr.	13	S	May	1	Th	Apr.	20
Holocaust Memorial Day	T	Apr.	9	Tu	Apr.	29	S	Apr.	18	F	May	6*	T	Apr.	25
New Moon, Iyar, 1st day	F	Apr.	12	F	May	2	W	Apr.	21	M	May	9	F	Apr.	28
New Moon, Iyar, 2nd day	Sa	Apr.	13	Sa	May	3	Th	Apr.	22	T	May	10	Sa	Apr.	29
Israel Independence Day	W	Apr.	17	W	May	7	M	Apr.	26	S	May	14†	W	May	3
Lag Ba-ʻomer	T	Apr.	30	T	May	20	S	May	9	F	May	27	T	May	16
Jerusalem Day	F	May	10*	F	May	30*	W	May	19	M	June	6	F	May	26*
New Moon, Siwan	S	May	12	S	June	1	F	May	21	W	June	8	S	May	28
Shavuʻot, 1st day	F	May	17	F	June	6	W	May	26	M	June	13	F	June	2
Shavuʻot, 2nd day	Sa	May	18	Sa	June	7	Th	May	27	T	June	14	Sa	June	3
New Moon, Tammuz, 1st day	M	June	10	M	June	30	Sa	June	19	Th	July	7	M	June	26
New Moon, Tammuz, 2nd day	T	June	11	T	July	1	S	June	20	F	July	8	T	June	27
Fast of 17th of Tammuz	Th	June	27	Th	July	17	T	July	6	S	July	24	Th	July	13
New Moon, Av	W	July	10	W	July	30	M	July	19	Sa	Aug.	6	W	July	26
Fast of 9th of Av	Th	July	18	Th	Aug.	7	T	July	27	S	Aug.	14	Th	Aug.	3
New Moon, Elul, 1st day	Th	Aug.	8	Th	Aug.	28	T	Aug.	17	S	Sept.	4	Th	Aug.	24
New Moon, Elul, 2nd day	F	Aug.	9	F	Aug.	29	W	Aug.	18	M	Sept.	5	F	Aug.	25

*Observed Thursday, a day earlier, to avoid conflict with the Sabbath.

†Observed Thursday, two days earlier, to avoid conflict with the Sabbath.

CONDENSED MONTHLY CALENDAR (2001–2004)

2001, Jan. 25–Feb. 23] SHEVAṬ (30 DAYS) [5761

Civil Date	Day of the Week	Jewish Date	SABBATHS, FESTIVALS, FASTS	PENTATEUCHAL READING	PROPHETICAL READING
Jan. 25	Th	Shevaṭ 1	New Moon	Num. 28: 1–15	
27	Sa	3	Wa-'era'	Exod. 6:2–9:35	Ezekiel 28:25–29:21
Feb. 3	Sa	10	Bo'	Exod. 10:1–13:16	Jeremiah 46:13–28
8	Th	15	Ḥamishah 'asar Bi-Shevaṭ		
10	Sa	17	Be-shallaḥ (Shabbat Shirah)	Exod. 13:17–17:16	Judges 4:4–5:31 *Judges 5:1–31*
17	Sa	24	Yitro	Exod. 18:1–20:23	Isaiah 6:1–7:6; 9:5–6 *Isaiah 6:1–13*
23	F	30	New Moon, first day	Num. 28:1–15	

Italics are for Sephardi Minhag.

2001, Feb. 24–Mar. 24] ADAR (29 DAYS) [5761

Civil Date	Day of the Week	Jewish Date	SABBATHS, FESTIVALS, FASTS	PENTATEUCHAL READING	PROPHETICAL READING
Feb. 24	Sa	Adar 1	Mishpaṭim, New Moon, second day (Shabbat Sheḳalim)	Exod. 21:1–24:18 Num. 28:9–15 Exod. 30:11–16	II Kings 12:1–17 *II Kings 11:17–12:17*
Mar. 3	Sa	8	Terumah (Shabbat Zakhor)	Exod. 25:1–27:19 Deut. 25:17–19	I Samuel 15:2–34 *I Samuel 15:1–34*
8	Th	13	Fast of Esther	Exod. 32:11–14 Exod. 34:1–10 (morning and afternoon)	Isaiah 55:6–56:8 (afternoon only)
9	F	14	Purim	Exod. 17:8–16	Book of Esther (night before and in the morning)
10	Sa	15	Teẓawweh Shushan Purim	Exod. 27:20–30:10	Ezekiel 43:10–27
17	Sa	22	Ki tissa' (Shabbat Parah)	Exod. 30:11–34:35 Num. 19:1–22	Ezekiel 36:16–38 *Ezekiel 36:16–36*
24	Sa	29	Wa-yaḳhel-Peḳude (Shabbat Ha-ḥodesh)	Exod. 35:1–40:38 Exod. 12:1–20	Ezekiel 45:16–46:18 *Ezekiel 45:18–46:15*

Italics are for Sephardi Minhag.

2001, Mar. 25–Apr. 23] NISAN (30 DAYS) [5761

Civil Date	Day of the Week	Jewish Date	SABBATHS, FESTIVALS, FASTS	PENTATEUCHAL READING	PROPHETICAL READING
Mar. 25	S	Nisan 1	New Moon	Num. 28:1–15	
31	Sa	7	Wa-yiḳra'	Levit. 1:1–5:26	Isaiah 43:21–44:24
Apr. 5	Th	12	Fast of Firstborn		
7	Sa	14	Ẓaw (Shabbat Ha-gadol)	Levit. 6:1–8:36	Malachi 3:4–24
8	S	15	Passover, first day	Exod. 12:21–51 Num. 28:16–25	Joshua 5:2–6:1,27
9	M	16	Passover, second day	Levit. 22:26–23:44 Num. 28:16–25	II Kings 23:1–9, 21–25
10	T	17	Ḥol Ha-mo 'ed, first day	Exod. 13:1–16 Num. 28:19–25	
11	W	18	Ḥol Ha-mo'ed second day	Exod. 22:24–23:19, Num. 28:19–25	
12	Th	19	Ḥol Ha-mo'ed, third day	Exod. 34:1–26 Num. 28:19–25	
13	F	20	Ḥol Ha-mo'ed, fourth day	Num. 9:1–14 Num. 28:19–25	
14	Sa	21	Passover, seventh day	Exod. 13:17–15:26 Num. 28:19–25	II Samuel 22:1–51
15	S	22	Passover, eighth day	Deut. 15:19–16:17 Num. 28:19–25	Isaiah 10:32–12:6
20	F	27*	Holocaust Memorial Day		
21	Sa	28	Shemini	Levit. 9:1–11:47	II Samuel 6:1–7:17 *II Samuel 6:1–19*
23	M	30	New Moon, first day	Num. 28:1–15	

*Observed April 19, to avoid conflict with the Sabbath.

Italics are for Sephardi Minhag.

2001, Apr. 24–May 22] IYAR (29 DAYS) [5761

Civil Date	Day of the Week	Jewish Date	SABBATHS, FESTIVALS, FASTS	PENTATEUCHAL READING	PROPHETICAL READING
Apr. 24	T	Iyar 1	New Moon, second day	Num. 28:1–15	
28	Sa	5**	Tazria', Mezora'	Levit. 12:1–15:33	II Kings 7:3–20
May 5	Sa	12	Aḥare mot, Ḳedoshim	Levit.16:1–20:27	Amos 9:7–15 *Ezekiel 20:2–20*
11	F	18	Lag Ba-'omer		
12	Sa	19	Emor	Levit. 21:1–24:23	Ezekiel 44:15–31
19	Sa	26	Be-har, Be-ḥuḳḳotai	Levit. 25:1–27:34	Jeremiah 16:19–17:14
21	M	28	Jerusalem Day		

** Also Israel Independence Day, observed April 26 to avoid conflict with the Sabbath.

Italics are for Sephardi Minhag.

2001 May 23–Jun. 21] SIWAN (30 DAYS) [5761

Civil Date	Day of the Week	Jewish Date	SABBATHS, FESTIVALS, FASTS	PENTATEUCHAL READING	PROPHETICAL READING
May 23	W	Siwan 1	New Moon	Num. 28:1–15	
26	Sa	4	Be-midbar	Num. 1:1–4:20	Hosea 2:1–22
28	M	6	Shavu'ot, first day	Exod. 19:1–20:23 Num. 28:26–31	Ezekiel 1:1–28; 3:12
29	T	7	Shavu'ot, second day	Deut. 15:19–16:17 Num. 28:26–31	Habbakuk 3:1–19 *Habbakuk 2:20–3:19*
June 2	Sa	11	Naso'	Num. 4:21–7:89	Judges 13:2–25
9	Sa	18	Be-ha'alotekha	Num. 8:1–12:16	Zechariah 2:14–4:7
16	Sa	25	Shelaḥ lekha	Num. 13:1–15:41	Joshua 2:1–24
21	Th	30	New Moon, first day	Num. 28:1–15	

Italics are for Sephardi Minhag.

2001, June 22–July 20] TAMMUZ (29 Days) [5761

Civil Date	Day of the Week	Jewish Date	SABBATHS, FESTIVALS, FASTS	PENTATEUCHAL READING	PROPHETICAL READING
June 22	F	Tammuz 1	New Moon, second day	Num. 28:1–15	
23	Sa	2	Ḳoraḥ	Num. 16:1–18:32	I Samuel 11:14–12:22
30	Sa	9	Ḥuḳḳat	Num. 19:1–22:1	Judges 11:1–33
July 7	Sa	16	Balaḳ	Num. 22:2–25:9	Micah 5:6–6:8
8	S	17	Fast of 17th of Tammuz	Exod. 32:11–14 Exod. 34:1–10 (morning and afternoon)	Isaiah 55:6–56:8 (afternoon only)
14	Sa	23	Pineḥas	Num. 25:10–30:1	Jeremiah 1:1–2:3

Italics are for Sephardi Minhag.

2001, July 21–Aug. 19] AV (30 DAYS) [5761

Civil Date	Day of the Week	Jewish Date	SABBATHS, FESTIVALS, FASTS	PENTATEUCHAL READING	PROPHETICAL READING
July 21	Sa	Av 1	Maṭṭot, Mas'e New Moon	Num. 30:2–36:13 Num. 28:9–15	Jeremiah 2:4–28; 3:4 *Jeremiah 2:4–28; 4:1–2*
28	Sa	8	Devarim (Shabbat Hazon)	Deut. 1:1–3:22	Isaiah 1:1–27
29	S	9	Fast of 9th of Av	Morning: Deut. 4:25–40 Afternoon: Exod. 32:11–14 34:1–10	(Lamentations is read the night before) Jeremiah 8:13–9:23 (morning) Isaiah 55:6–56:8 (afternoon)
Aug. 4	Sa	15	Wa-ethannan (Shabbat Naḥamu)	Deut. 3:23–7:11	Isaiah 40:1–26
11	Sa	22	'Eḳev	Deut. 7:12–11:25	Isaiah 49:14–51:3
18	Sa	29	Re'eh	Deut. 11:26–16:17	I Samuel 20:18–42
19	S	30	New Moon, first day	Num. 28:1–15	

Italics are for Sephardi Minhag.

2001, Aug. 20–Sept. 17] ELUL (29 DAYS) [5761

Civil Date	Day of the Week	Jewish Date	SABBATHS, FESTIVALS, FASTS	PENTATEUCHAL READING	PROPHETICAL READING
Aug 20	M	Elul 1	New Moon, second day	Num. 28:1–15	
25	Sa	6	Shofeṭim	Deut. 16:18–21:9	Isaiah 51:12–52:12
Sept 1	Sa	13	Ki Teẓe’	Deut. 21:10–25:19	Isaiah 54:1–55:5
8	Sa	20	Ki Tavo’	Deut. 26:1–29:8	Isaiah 60:1–22
15	Sa	27	Niẓẓavim	Deut. 29:9–30:20	Isaiah 61:10–63:9

Italics are for Sephardi Minhag.

2001, Sept. 18–Oct. 17] TISHRI (30 DAYS) [5762

Civil Date	Day of the Week	Jewish Date	SABBATHS, FESTIVALS, FASTS	PENTATEUCHAL READING	PROPHETICAL READING
Sept. 18	T	Tishri 1	Rosh Ha-shanah, first day	Gen. 21:1–34 Num. 29:1–6	1 Sam. 1:1–2:10
19	W	2	Rosh Ha-shanah second day	Gen. 22:1–24 Num. 29:1–6	Jeremiah 3:2–20
20	Th	3	Fast of Gedaliah	Exod. 32:11–14 34:1–10 (morning & afternoon)	Isaiah 55:6–56:8 (afternoon only)
22	Sa	5	Wa-yelekh (Shabbat Shuvah)	Deut. 31:1–30	Hosea 14:2–10 Micah 7:18–20 Joel 2:15–27 *Hosea 14:2–10* *Micah 7:18–20*
27	Th	10	Yom Kippur	Morning: Levit. 16:1–34 Num. 29:7–11 Afternoon: Levit. 18:1–30	Isaiah 57:14–58:14 Jonah 1:1–4:11 Micah 7:18–20
29	Sa	12	Ha'azinu	Deut. 32:1–52	II Samuel 22:1–51
Oct 2	T	15	Sukkot, first day	Levit. 22:26–23:44 Num. 29:12–16	Zechariah 14:1–21
3	W	16	Sukkot, second day	Levit. 22:26–23:44 Num. 29:12–16	I Kings 8:2–21
4–7	Th–S	17–20	Ḥol Ha-mo'ed	Th Num. 29:17–25 F Num. 29: 20–28 Sa Exod. 33:12–34:26, Num. 29:26–34 S Num. 29:26–34	 Ezekiel 38:18–39:16
8	M	21	Hosha'na' Rabbah	Num. 29:26–34	
9	T	22	Shemini 'Aẓeret	Deut. 14:22–16:17 Num. 29:35–30:1	I Kings 8:54–66
10	W	23	Simḥat Torah	Deut. 33:1–34:12 Gen. 1:1–2:3 Num. 29:35–30:1	Joshua 1:1–18 *Joshua 1:1–9*
13	Sa	26	Be-re'shit	Gen. 1:1–6:8	Isaiah 42:5–43:10 *Isaiah 42:5–21*
17	W	30	New Moon first day	Num. 28:1–15	

Italics are for Sephardi Minhag.

2001, Oct. 18–Nov. 15] ḤESHWAN (29 DAYS) [5762

Civil Date	Day of the Week	Jewish Date	SABBATHS, FESTIVALS, FASTS	PENTATEUCHAL READING	PROPHETICAL READING
Oct. 18	Th	Ḥeshwan 1	New Moon, second day	Num. 28:1–15	
20	Sa	3	Noaḥ	Gen. 6:9–11:32	Isaiah 54:1–55:5 *Isaiah 54:1–10*
27	Sa	10	Lekh lekha	Gen. 12:1–17:27	Isaiah 40:27–41:16
Nov. 3	Sa	17	Wa-yera'	Gen. 18:1–22:24	II Kings 4:1–37 *II Kings 4:1–23*
10	Sa	24	Ḥayye Sarah	Gen. 23:1–25:18	I Kings 1:1–31

Italics are for Sephardi Minhag.

2001, Nov. 16–Dec. 15] KISLEW (30 DAYS) [5762

Civil Date	Day of the Week	Jewish Date	SABBATHS, FESTIVALS, FASTS	PENTATEUCHAL READING	PROPHETICAL READING
Nov. 16	F	Kislew 1	New Moon	Num. 28:1–15	
17	Sa	2	Toledot	Gen. 25:19–28:9	Malachi 1:1–2:7
24	Sa	9	Wa-yeẓe'	Gen. 28:10–32:3	Hosea 12:13–14:10 *Hosea 11:7–12:12*
Dec. 1	Sa	16	Wa-yishlah	Gen. 32:4–36:43	Hosea 11:7–12:12 *Obadiah 1:1–21*
8	Sa	23	Wa-yeshev	Gen. 37:1–40:23	Amos 2:6–3:8
10–14	M–F	25–29	Ḥanukkah, first to fifth days	M Num. 7:1–17 T Num. 7:18–29 W Num. 7:24–35 Th Num. 7:30–41 F Num. 7:36–47	
15	Sa	30	Miḳeẓ; New Moon, first day; Ḥanukkah, sixth day	Gen. 41:1–44:17 Num. 28:9–15 Num. 7:42–47	Zechariah 2:14–4:7 *Zechariah 2:14–4:7* *Isaiah 66:1, 24* *Isaiah 20:18,42*

Italics are for Sephardi Minhag.

2001, Dec. 16–Jan. 13, 2002] ṬEVET (29 DAYS) [5762

Civil Date	Day of the Week	Jewish Date	SABBATHS, FESTIVALS, FASTS	PENTATEUCHAL READING	PROPHETICAL READING
Dec. 16	S	Ṭevet 1	New Moon, second day; Ḥanukkah, seventh day	Num. 28:1–15 Num. 7:48–53	
17	M	2	Ḥanukkah, eighth day	Num. 7:54–8:4	
22	Sa	7	Wa-yiggash	Gen. 44:18–47:27	Ezekiel 37:15–28
25	T	10	Fast of 10th of Ṭevet	Exod. 32:11–14; 34:1–10 (morning and afternoon)	Isaiah 55:6–56:8 (afternoon only)
29	Sa	14	Wa-yeḥi	Gen. 47:28–50:26	I Kings 2:1–12
2002 Jan. 5	Sa	21	Shemot	Exod. 1:1–6:1	Isaiah 27:6–28:13; 29:22–23 *Jeremiah 1:1–2:3*
12	Sa	28	Wa-'era'	Exod. 6:2–9:35	Ezekiel 28:25–29:21

Italics are for Sephardi Minhag.

2002, Jan. 14–Feb. 12] SHEVAṬ (30 DAYS) [5762

Civil Date	Day of the Week	Jewish Date	SABBATHS, FESTIVALS, FASTS	PENTATEUCHAL READING	PROPHETICAL READING
Jan. 14	M	Shevaṭ 1	New Moon	Num. 28:1–15	
19	Sa	6	Bo'	Exod. 10:1–13:16	Jeremiah 46:13–28
26	Sa	13	Be-shallaḥ (Shabbat Shirah)	Exod. 13:17–17:16	Judges 4:4–5:31 *Judges 5:1–31*
28	M	15	Ḥamishah 'asar bi-Shevaṭ		
Feb. 2	Sa	20	Yitro	Exod. 18:1–20:23	Isaiah 6:1–7:6; 9:5–6 Isaiah 6: 1–13
9	Sa	27	Mishpaṭim (Shabbat Sheḳalim)	Exod. 21:1–24:18 Exod. 30:11–16	II Kings 12:1–17 *II Kings 11:17–12:17*
12	T	30	New Moon, first day	Num. 28: 1–15	

Italics are for Sephardi Minhag.

2002, Feb. 13–Mar. 13] ADAR (29 DAYS) [5762

Civil Date	Day of the Week	Jewish Date	SABBATHS, FESTIVALS, FASTS	PENTATEUCHAL READING	PROPHETICAL READING
Feb. 13	W	Adar 1	New Moon, second day	Num. 28:1–15	
16	Sa	4	Terumah	Exod. 25:1–27:19	I Kings 5:26–6:13
23	Sa	11	Teẓawweh (Shabbat Zakhor)	Exod. 27:20–30:10 Deut. 25:17–19	I Samuel 15:2–34 *I Samuel 15:1–34*
25	M	13	Fast of Esther	Exod. 32:11–14 Exod. 34:1–10 (morning and afternoon)	Isaiah 55:6–56:8 (afternoon only)
26	T	14	Purim	Exod. 17:8–16	Book of Esther (night before and in the morning)
27	W	15	Shushan Purim		
Mar. 2	Sa	18	Ki tissa' (Shabbat Parah)	Exod. 30:11–34:35 Num. 19: 1–22	Ezekiel 36:16–38 *Ezekiel 36:16–36*
9	Sa	25	Wa-yaḳhel, Peḳude (Shabbat Ha-ḥodesh)	Exod. 35:1–40:38 Exod. 12:1–20	Ezekiel 45:16–46:18 *Ezekiel 45:18–46:15*

Italics are for Sephardi Minhag.

2002, Mar. 14–Apr. 12] NISAN (30 DAYS) [5762

Civil Date	Day of the Week	Jewish Date	SABBATHS, FESTIVALS, FASTS	PENTATEUCHAL READING	PROPHETICAL READING
Mar. 14	Th	Nisan 1	New Moon	Num. 28:1–15	
16	Sa	3	Wa—yiḳra'	Levit. 1:1–5: 26	Isaiah 43:21–44:24
23	Sa	10	Ẓaw (Shabbat Ha-gadol)	Levit. 6:1–8: 36	Malachi 3:4–24
27	W	14	Fast of Firstborn		
28	Th	15	Passover, first day	Exod. 12:21–51 Num. 28:16–25	Joshua 5:2–6:1, 27
29	F	16	Passover, second day	Levit. 22:26–23:44 Num. 28:16–25	II Kings 23:1–9, 21–25
30	Sa	17	Ḥol Ha-mo'ed, first day	Exod. 33:12–34:26 Num. 28:16–25	Ezekiel 37:1–14
31	S	18	Ḥol Ha-mo'ed, second day	Exod. 33:12–34:26 Num. 28:19–25	
Apr. 1	M	19	Ḥol Ha-mo'ed, third day	Exod. 22:24–23:19 Num. 28:19–25	
2	T	20	Ḥol Ha-mo'ed, fourth day	Num. 28: 19–25	
3	W	21	Passover, seventh day	Exod. 13:17–15:26 Num. 28:19–25	II Samuel 22:1—51
4	Th	22	Passover, eight day	Deut. 15:1–16:17 Num. 28:19 –25	Isaiah 10:32–12:6
6	Sa	24	Shemini	Levit. 9:1–11:47	II Samuel 6:1 –7:17 *II Samuel 6:1–19*
9	T	27	Holocaust Memorial Day		
12	F	30	New Moon, first day	Num. 28:1–15	

Italics are for Sephardi Minhag.

2002, Apr. 13–May 11] IYAR (29 DAYS) [5762

Civil Date	Day of the Week	Jewish Date	SABBATHS, FESTIVALS, FASTS	PENTATEUCHAL READING	PROPHETICAL READING
Apr. 13	Sa	Iyar 1	Tazria', Meẓora'; New Moon, second day	Levit. 12:1–15:33 Num. 28:9–15	Isaiah 66:1–24
17	W	5	Israel Independence Day		
20	Sa	8	Aḥare mot, Ḳedoshim	Levit. 16:1–20:27	Amos 9:7–15 *Ezekiel 20:2–20*
27	Sa	15	Emor	Levit. 21:1–24:23	Ezekiel 44:15–31
30	T	18	Lag Ba-'omer		
May 4	Sa	22	Be-har, Be-ḥuḳḳotai	Levit. 25:1–27:34	Jeremiah 16:19–17:14
10	F	28	Jerusalem Day*		
11	Sa	29	Be-midbar	Num 1:1–4:20	I Samuel 20:18–42

*Observed May 9, to avoid conflict with the Sabbath.

Italics are for Sephardi Minhag.

2002, May 12–June 10] SIWAN (30 DAYS) [5762

Civil Date	Day of the Week	Jewish Date	SABBATHS, FESTIVALS, FASTS	PENTATEUCHAL READING	PROPHETICAL READING
May 12	S	Siwan 1	New Moon	Num. 28:1–15	
17	F	6	Shavu'ot, first day	Exod. 19:1–20:23 Num. 28:26–31	Ezekiel 1:1–28, Ezekiel 3:12
18	Sa	7	Shavu'ot, second day	Deut. 15:19–16: 17 Num. 28:26–31	Habbakuk 3:1–19 *Habbakuk 2:20–3:19*
25	Sa	14	Naso'	Num. 4:21–7:89	Judges 13:2–25
June 1	Sa	21	Be-ha'alotekha	Num. 8:1–12:16	Zechariah 2:14–4: 7
8	Sa	28	Shelaḥ lekha	Num. 13:1–15:41	Joshua 2:1–24
10	M	30	New Moon, first day	Num. 28:1–15	

Italics are for Sephardi Minhag.

2002, June 11–July 9] TAMMUZ (29 DAYS) [5762

Civil Date	Day of the Week	Jewish Date	SABBATHS, FESTIVALS, FASTS	PENTATEUCHAL READING	PROPHETICAL READING
Jun 11	T	Tammuz 1	New Moon, second day	Num. 28:1–15	
15	Sa	5	Ḳoraḥ	Num. 16:1–18:32	I Samuel 11:14–12:22
22	Sa	12	Ḥuḳḳat, Balaḳ	Num. 19:1–25:9	Micah 5:6–6:8
27	Th	17	Fast of 17th of Tammuz	Exod. 32:11–14 Exod. 34: 1–10 (morning and afternoon)	Isaiah 55:6–56:8 (afternoon only)
29	Sa	19	Pineḥas	Num. 25:10–30:1	Jeremiah 1:1–2:3
July 6	Sa	26	Maṭṭot Mas‘e	Num. 30:2–36:13	Jeremiah 2:4–28 Jeremiah 3:4 *Jeremiah 2:4–28* *Jeremiah 4:1–2*

Italics are for Sephardi Minhag.

2002, July 10–Aug. 8] AV (30 DAYS) [5762

Civil Date	Day of the Week	Jewish Date	SABBATHS, FESTIVALS, FASTS	PENTATEUCHAL READING	PROPHETICAL READING
July 10	W	Av 1	New Moon	Num. 28:1–15	
13	Sa	4	Devarim (Shabbat Ḥazon)	Deut. 1:1–3:22	Isaiah 1:1–27
18	Th	9	Fast of 9th of Av	Morning: Deut. 4:25–40 Afternoon: Exod. 32:1–14 Exod. 34:1–10	(Lamentations is read the night before) Jeremiah 8:13–9:23 (morning) Isaiah 55:6–56:8 (afternoon)
20	Sa	11	Wa-ethḥannan (Shabbat Nahamu)	Deut. 3:23–7:11	Isaiah 40:1–26
27	Sa	18	'Eḳev	Deut. 7:12–11:25	Isaiah 49:14–51:3
Aug. 3	Sa	25	Re'eh	Deut. 11:26–16:17	Isaiah 54:11–55:5
8	Th	30	New Moon, first day	Numbers 28:1– 15	

Italics are for Sephardi Minhag.

2002, Aug. 9–Sept. 6] ELUL (29 DAYS) [5762

Civil Date	Day of the Week	Jewish Date	SABBATHS, FESTIVALS, FASTS	PENTATEUCHAL READING	PROPHETICAL READING
Aug. 9	F	Elul 1	New Moon, second day	Num. 28:1–15	
10	Sa	2	Shofeṭim	Deut. 16:18–21:9	Isaiah 51:12–52:12
17	Sa	9	Ki teẓe'	Deut. 21:10–25:19	Isaiah 54:1–10
24	Sa	16	Ki tavo'	Deut. 26: 1–29:8	Isaiah 60:1–22
31	Sa	23	Niẓẓavim, Wa-yelekh	Deut. 29:9–31:30	Isaiah 61:10–63:9

Italics are for Sephardi Minhag.

2002, Sept. 7–Oct. 6] TISHRI (30 DAYS) [5763

Civil Date	Day of the Week	Jewish Date	SABBATHS, FESTIVALS, FASTS	PENTATEUCHAL READING	PROPHETICAL READING
Sept. 7	Sa	Tishri 1	Rosh Ha-shanah, first day	Gen. 21:1–34 Num. 29:1–6	I Samuel 1:1–2:10
8	S	2	Rosh Ha-shana, second day	Gen. 22:1–24 Num. 29:1–6	Jeremiah 31:2–20
9	M	3	Fast of Gedaliah	Exod. 32:11–14 Exod. 34:1–10 (morning and afternoon)	Isaiah 55: 6–56:8 (afternoon only)
14	Sa	8	Ha'azinu (Shabbat Shuvah)	Deut. 32:1–52	Hosea 14:2–10 Micah 7:18–20 Joel 2:15–27 *Hosea 14:2–10* *Micah 7:18–20*
16	M	10	Yom Kippur	Morning: Levit. 16:1–34 Num. 29:7–11 Afternoon: Levit. 18:1–30	Isaiah 57:14–58:14 Jonah 1:1–4:11 Micah 7:18–20
21	Sa	15	Sukkot, first day	Levit. 22:26–23:44 Num. 29:12–16	Zechariah 14:1–21
22	S	16	Sukkot, second day	Levit. 22:26–23:44 Num. 29:12 –16	I Kings 8:2–21
23-26	M-Th	17-20	Ḥol Ha'mo'ed	M: Num. 29:17–25 T: Num. 29:20–28 W: Num. 29:23–31 Th: Num. 29:26–34	
27	F	21	Hosha'na' Rabbah	Num. 29:26–34	
28	Sa	22	Shemini 'Aẓeret	Deut. 14:22–16:17 Num. 29:35–30:1	I Kings 8:54–66
29	S	23	Simḥat Torah	Deut. 33:1–34:12 Gen. 1:1–2:3 Num. 29:35–30:1	Joshua 1:1–18 *Joshua 1:1–9*
Oct. 5	Sa	29	Be-re'shit	Gen. 1:1–6:8	I Samuel 20:18–42
6	S	30	New Moon, first day	Num. 28: 1–15	

Italics are for Sephardi Minhag.

2002, Oct. 7–Nov. 5] ḤESHWAN (30 DAYS) [5763

Civil Date	Day of the Week	Jewish Date	SABBATHS, FESTIVALS, FASTS	PENTATEUCHAL READING	PROPHETICAL READING
Oct. 7	M	Ḥeshwan 1	New Moon, second day	Num. 28:1–15	
12	Sa	6	Noaḥ	Gen. 6:9–11:32	Isaiah 54:1–55:5 *Isaiah 54:1–10*
19	Sa	13	Lekh lekha	Gen. 12:1–17:27	Isaiah 40:27–41:16
26	Sa	20	Wa-yera'	Gen. 18:11–22:24	II Kings 4:1–37 *II Kings 4:1–23*
Nov. 2	Sa	27	Ḥayye Sarah	Gen. 23:1–25:18	I Kings 1:1–31
5	T	30	New Moon, first day	Num. 28:1–15	

Italics are for Sephardi Minhag.

2002, Nov. 6–Dec. 5] KISLEW (30 DAYS) [5763

Civil Date	Day of the Week	Jewish Date	SABBATHS, FESTIVALS, FASTS	PENTATEUCHAL READING	PROPHETICAL READING
Nov. 6	W	Kislew 1	New Moon, second day	Num. 28:1–15	
9	Sa	4	Toledot	Gen. 25:19–28:9	Malachi 1:1–2:7
16	Sa	11	Wa-yeẓe'	Gen. 28:10–32:3	Hosea 12:13–14:10 *Hosea 11:7–12:12*
23	Sa	18	Wa-yishlaḥ	Gen. 32:4–36:43	Hosea 11:7–12:12 *Obadiah 1:1–21*
30	Sa	25	Wa-yeshev; Ḥanukkaḥ, first day	Gen. 37:1–40:23 Num. 7:1–17	Zechariah 2:14–4:7
Dec. 1-4	S–W	26–29	Hanukkah, second to fifth days	S Num. 7:18–29 M Num. 7:24–35 T Num. 7:30–41 W Num. 7:36–41	
5	Th	30	New Moon, first day; Ḥanukkah, sixth day	Num. 28:1–15 Num. 7:42–47	

Italics are for Sephardi Minhag.

2002, Dec. 6–Jan. 3, 2003] ṬEVET (29 DAYS) [5763

Civil Date	Day of the Week	Jewish Date	SABBATHS, FESTIVALS, FASTS	PENTATEUCHAL READING	PROPHETICAL READING
Dec. 6	F	Ṭevet 1	New Moon, second day; Ḥanukkah, seventh day	Num. 28:1–15 Num. 7:48–59	
7	Sa	2	Mi-ḳeẓ; Ḥanukkah, eight day	Gen. 41:1–44:17 Num. 7:54–8:4	I Kings 7:40–50
14	Sa	9	Wa-yiggash	Gen. 44:18–47:27	Ezekiel 37:15–28
15	S	10	Fast of 10th of Ṭevet	Exod. 32:11–14 Exod. 34:1–10 (morning and afternoon)	Isaiah 55:6–56:8 (afternoon only)
21	Sa	16	Wa-yeḥi	Gen. 47:28–50:26	I Kings 2:1–12
28	Sa	23	Shemot	Exod. 1:1–6:1	Isaiah 27:6–28:13 Isaiah 29:22–23 *Jeremiah 1:1–2:3*

Italics are for Sephardi Minhag.

2003, Jan. 4–Feb. 2] SHEVAṬ (30 DAYS) [5763

Civil Date	Day of the Week	Jewish Date	SABBATHS, FESTIVALS, FASTS	PENTATEUCHAL READING	PROPHETICAL READING
Jan. 4	Sa	Shevaṭ 1	Wa-'era'; New Moon	Exod. 6:2–9:35 Num. 28:9–15	Isaiah 66: 1–24
11	Sa	8	Bo'	Exod. 10:1–13:16	Jeremiah 46:13–28
18	Sa	15	Be-shallaḥ (Shabbat Shirah) Ḥamishar 'asar bi-Shevaṭ	Exod. 13:17–17:16	Judges 4:4–5:31 *Judges 5:1–31*
25	Sa	22	Yitro	Exod. 18:1–20:23	Isaiah 6:1–7:6; 9:5–6 *Isaiah 6: 1–13*
Feb. 1	Sa	29	Mishpaṭim	Exod. 21:1–24:18	1 Samuel 20: 18–42
2	S	30	New Moon, first day	Num. 28: 1–15	

Italics are for Sephardi Minhag.

2003, Feb. 3–Mar. 4] ADAR I (30 DAYS) [5763

Civil Date	Day of the Week	Jewish Date	SABBATHS, FESTIVALS, FASTS	PENTATEUCHAL READING	PROPHETICAL READING
Feb. 3	M	Adar I 1	New Moon, second day	Num. 28:1–15	
8	Sa	6	Terumah	Exod. 25:1–27:19	I Kings 5:26–6:13
15	Sa	13	Tezawweh	Exod. 27:20–30:10	Ezekiel 43:10–27
22	Sa	20	Ki tissa'	Exod. 30:11–34:35	I Kings 18:1–39 *I Kings 18:20–39*
Mar. 1	Sa	27	Wa-yakhel (Shabbat Shekalim)	Exod. 35:1–38:20 Exod. 30:11–16	II Kings 12:1–17 *II Kings 11:17–12:17*
4	T	30	New Moon first day	Num. 28:1–15	

Italics are for Sephardi Minhag.

2002, Feb. 5–Apr. 2] ADAR II (29 DAYS) [5763

Civil Date	Day of the Week	Jewish Date	SABBATHS, FESTIVALS, FASTS	PENTATEUCHAL READING	PROPHETICAL READING
Mar. 5	W	Adar II 1	New Moon, second day	Num. 28:1–15	
8	Sa	4	Pekude	Exod. 38:21–40:38	I Kings 7:51–8:21 *I Kings 7:40–50*
15	Sa	11	Wa-yikra' (Shabbat Zakhor)	Levit. 1:1–5:26 Deut. 25:17–19	I Samuel 15:2–34 *I Samuel 15:1–34*
17	M	13	Fast of Esther	Exod. 32:11–14 Exod. 34:1–10 (morning and afternoon)	Isaiah 55:6–56:8 (afternoon only)
18	T	14	Purim	Exod. 17:8–16	Book of Esther (night before and in the morning)
19	W	15	Shushan Purim		
22	Sa	18	Zaw (Shabbat Parah)	Levit. 6:1–8:36 Num. 19: 1–22	Ezekiel 36:16–38 *Ezekiel 36:16–36*
29	Sa	25	Shemini (Shabbat Ha-hodesh)	Levit. 9:1–11:47 Exod. 12:1–20	Ezekiel 45:16–46:18 *Ezekiel 45:18–46:15*

Italics are for Sephardi Minhag.

2003, Apr. 3–May 2] NISAN (30 DAYS) [5763

Civil Date	Day of the Week	Jewish Date	SABBATHS, FESTIVALS, FASTS	PENTATEUCHAL READING	PROPHETICAL READING
Apr. 3	Th	Nisan 1	New Moon	Num. 28:1–15	
5	Sa	3	Tazria'	Levit. 12:1–13:59	II Kings 4:42–5:19
12	Sa	10	Meẓora' (Shabbat Ha-gadol)	Levit. 14:1–15:33	Malachi 3:4–24
16	W	14	Fast of Firstborn		
17	Th	15	Passover, first day	Exod. 12:21–51 Num. 28:16–25	Joshua 5:2–6:1, 27
18	F	16	Passover, second day	Levit. 22:26–23:44 Num. 28:16–25	II Kings 23:1–9, 21–25
19	Sa	17	Ḥol Ha-mo'ed, first day	Exod. 33:12–34:26 Num. 28:19–25	Ezekiel 37:1–14
20	S	18	Ḥol Ha-mo'ed, second day	Exod. 13:1–16 Num. 28:19–25	
21	M	19	Ḥol Ha-mo'ed, third day	Exod. 22:24–23:19 Num. 28:19–25	
22	T	20	Ḥol Ha-mo'ed, fourth day	Num. 9: 1–14 Num. 28:19–25	
23	W	21	Passover, seventh day	Exod. 13:17–15:26 Num. 28:19–25	II Samuel 22:1—51
24	Th	22	Passover, eight day	Deut. 15:19–16:17 Num. 28:19–25	Isaiah 10:32–12:6
26	Sa	24	Aḥarei mot	Levit. 16:1–18:30	Amos 9:7–15 *Ezekiel 20:2–20*
29	T	27	Holocaust Memorial Day		
May 2	F	30	New Moon, first day	Num. 28:1–15	

Italics are for Sephardi Minhag.

2003, May 3–May 31] IYAR (29 DAYS) [5763

Civil Date	Day of the Week	Jewish Date	SABBATHS, FESTIVALS, FASTS	PENTATEUCHAL READING	PROPHETICAL READING
May 3	Sa	Iyar 1	Ḳedoshim; New Moon, second day	Levit. 19:1–20:27 Num. 28:9–15	Isaiah 66:1–24
7	W	5	Israel Independence Day		
10	Sa	8	Emor	Levit. 21:1–24:23	Ezekiel 44:15–31
17	Sa	15	Be-har	Levit. 21:1–26:2	Jeremiah 32:6–27
20	T	18	Lag Ba-'omer		
24	Sa	22	Be-ḥuḳḳotai	Levit. 26:3–27:34	Jeremiah 16:19–17:14
30	F	28	Jerusalem Day*		
31	Sa	29	Be-midbar	Num 1:1–4:20	I Samuel 20:18–42

*Observed May 29, to avoid conflict with the Sabbath.

Italics are for Sephardi Minhag.

2003, June 1–30] SIWAN (30 DAYS) [5763

Civil Date	Day of the Week	Jewish Date	SABBATHS, FESTIVALS, FASTS	PENTATEUCHAL READING	PROPHETICAL READING
June 1	S	Siwan 1	New Moon	Num. 28:1–15	
6	F	6	Shavu'ot, first day	Exod. 19:1–20:23 Num. 28:26–31	Ezekiel 1:1–28, 3:12
7	Sa	7	Shavu'ot, second day	Deut. 15:19–16: 17 Num. 28:26–31	Habbakuk 3:1–19 *Habbakuk 2:20–3:19*
14	Sa	14	Naso'	Num. 4:21–7:89	Judges 13:2–25
21	Sa	21	Be-ha'alotekha	Num. 8:1–12:16	Zechariah 2:14–4:7
28	Sa	28	Shelaḥ lekha	Num. 13:1–15:41	Joshua 2:1–24
30	M	30	New Moon, first day	Num. 28:1–15	

Italics are for Sephardi Minhag.

2003, July 1–29] TAMMUZ (29 DAYS) [5763

Civil Date	Day of the Week	Jewish Date	SABBATHS, FESTIVALS, FASTS	PENTATEUCHAL READING	PROPHETICAL READING
July 1	T	Tammuz 1	New Moon, second day	Num. 28:1–15	
5	Sa	5	Ḳoraḥ	Num. 16:1–18:32	I Samuel 11:14–12:22
12	Sa	12	Ḥuḳḳat, Balaḳ	Num. 19:1–25:9	Micah 5:6–6:8
17	Th	17	Fast of 17th of Tammuz	Exod. 32:11–14 Exod. 34: 1–10 (morning and afternoon)	Isaiah 55:6–56:8 (afternoon only)
19	Sa	19	Pineḥas	Num. 25:10–30:1	Jeremiah 1:1–2:3
26	Sa	26	Maṭṭot Mas'e	Num. 30:2–36:13	Jeremiah 2:4–28 Jeremiah 3:4 *Jeremiah 2:4–28* *Jeremiah 4:1–2*

Italics are for Sephardi Minhag.

2003, July 30–Aug. 29] AV (30 DAYS) [5763

Civil Date	Day of the Week	Jewish Date	SABBATHS, FESTIVALS, FASTS	PENTATEUCHAL READING	PROPHETICAL READING
July 30	W	Av 1	New Moon	Num. 28:1–15	
Aug. 2	Sa	4	Devarim (Shabbat Ḥazon)	Deut. 1:1–3:22	Isaiah 1:1–27
7	Th	9	Fast of 9th of Av	Morning: Deut. 4:25–40 Afternoon: Exod. 32:11–14 Exod. 34:1–10	(Lamentations is read the night before) Jeremiah 8:13–9:23 (morning) Isaiah 55:6–56:8 (afternoon)
9	Sa	11	Wa-etḥannan (Shabbat Nahamu)	Deut. 3:23–7:11	Isaiah 40:1–26
16	Sa	18	‘Eḳev	Deut. 7:12–11:25	Isaiah 49:14–51:3
23	Sa	25	Re’eh	Deut. 11:26–16:17	Isaiah 54:11–55:5
28	Th	30	New Moon, first day	Numbers 28:1– 15	

Italics are for Sephardi Minhag.

2003, Aug. 30–Sept. 26] ELUL (29 DAYS) [5763

Civil Date	Day of the Week	Jewish Date	SABBATHS, FESTIVALS, FASTS	PENTATEUCHAL READING	PROPHETICAL READING
Aug. 30	F	Elul 1	New Moon, second day	Num. 28:1–15	
31	Sa	2	Shofeṭim	Deut. 16:18–21:9	Isaiah 51:12–52:12
Sept. 6	Sa	9	Ki teẓe'	Deut. 21:10–25:19	Isaiah 54:1–10
13	Sa	16	Ki tavo'	Deut. 26: 1–29:8	Isaiah 60:1–22
20	Sa	23	Niẓẓavim, Wa-yelekh	Deut. 29:9–31:30	Isaiah 61:10–63:9

Italics are for Sephardi Minhag.

2003, Sept. 27–Oct. 26] TISHRI (30 DAYS) [5764

Civil Date	Day of the Week	Jewish Date	SABBATHS, FESTIVALS, FASTS	PENTATEUCHAL READING	PROPHETICAL READING
Sept. 27	Sa	Tishri 1	Rosh Ha-shanah, first day	Gen. 21:1–34 Num. 29:1–6	I Samuel 1:1–2:10
28	S	2	Rosh Ha-shana, second day	Gen. 22:1–24 Num. 29:1–6	Jeremiah 31:2–20
29	M	3	Fast of Gedaliah	Exod. 32:11–14 Exod. 34:1–10 (morning and afternoon)	Isaiah 55:6–56:8 (afternoon only)
Oct. 4	Sa	8	Ha'azinu (Shabbat Shuvah)	Deut. 32:1–52	Hosea 14:2–10 Micah 7:18–20 Joel 2:15–27 *Hosea 14:2–10* *Micah 7:18–20*
6	M	10	Yom Kippur	Morning: Levit. 16:1–34 Num. 29:7–11 Afternoon: Levit. 18:1–30	Isaiah 57:14–58:14 Jonah 1:1–4:11 Micah 7:18–20
11	Sa	15	Sukkot, first day	Levit. 22:26–23:44 Num. 29:12–16	Zechariah 14:1–21
12	S	16	Sukkot, second day	Levit. 22:26–23:44 Num. 29:12–16	I Kings 8:2–21
13-16	M-Th	17-20	Ḥol Ha'mo'ed	M: Num. 29:17–25 T: Num. 29:20–28 W: Num. 29:23–31 Th: Num. 29:26–34	
17	F	21	Hosha'na' Rabbah	Num. 29:26–34	
18	Sa	22	Shemini 'Aẓeret	Deut. 14:22–16:17 Num. 29:35–30:1	I Kings 8:54–66
19	S	23	Simḥat Torah	Deut. 33:1–34:12 Gen. 1:1–2:3 Num. 29:35–30:1	Joshua 1:1–18 *Joshua 1:1–9*
25	Sa	29	Be-re'shit	Gen. 1:1–6:8	I Samuel 20:18–42
26	S	30	New Moon, first day	Num. 28: 1–15	

Italics are for Sephardi Minhag.

2003, Oct. 27–Nov. 25] ḤESHWAN (30 DAYS) [5764

Civil Date	Day of the Week	Jewish Date	SABBATHS, FESTIVALS, FASTS	PENTATEUCHAL READING	PROPHETICAL READING
Oct. 27	M	Ḥeshwan 1	New Moon, second day	Num. 28:1–15	
Nov. 1	Sa	6	Noaḥ	Gen. 6:9–11:32	Isaiah 54:1–55:5 *Isaiah 54:1–10*
8	Sa	13	Lekh lekha	Gen. 12:1–17:27	Isaiah 40:27–41:16
15	Sa	20	Wa-yera'	Gen. 18:11–22:24	II Kings 4:1–37 *II Kings 4:1–23*
22	Sa	27	Ḥayye Sarah	Gen. 23:1–25:18	I Kings 1:1–31
25	T	30	New Moon, first day	Num. 28:1–15	

Italics are for Sephardi Minhag.

2003, Nov. 26–Dec. 25] KISLEW (30 DAYS) [5764

Civil Date	Day of the Week	Jewish Date	SABBATHS, FESTIVALS, FASTS	PENTATEUCHAL READING	PROPHETICAL READING
Nov. 26	W	Kislew 1	New Moon, second day	Num. 28:1–15	
29	Sa	4	Toledot	Gen. 25:19–28:9	Malachi 1:1–2:7
Dec. 6	Sa	11	Wa-yeẓe’	Gen. 28:10–32:3	Hosea 12:13–14:10 *Hosea 11:7–12:12*
13	Sa	18	Wa-yishlaḥ	Gen. 32:4–36:43	Hosea 11:7–12:12 *Obadiah 1:1–21*
20	Sa	25	Wa-yeshev; Ḥanukkaḥ, first day	Gen. 37:1–40:23 Num. 7:1–17	Zechariah 2:14–4:7
21-24	S–W	26–29	Ḥanukkah, second to fifth days	S Num. 7:18–29 M Num. 7:24–35 T Num. 7:30–41 W Num. 7:36–41	
25	Th	30	New Moon, first day; Ḥanukkah, sixth day	Num. 28:1–15 Num. 7:42–47	

Italics are for Sephardi Minhag.

2003, Dec. 26–Jan. 3, 2004] ṬEVET (29 DAYS) [5764

Civil Date	Day of the Week	Jewish Date	SABBATHS, FESTIVALS, FASTS	PENTATEUCHAL READING	PROPHETICAL READING
Dec. 26	F	Ṭevet 1	New Moon, second day; Ḥanukkah, seventh day	Num. 28:1–15 Num. 7:48–53	
27	Sa	2	Mi-ḳeẓ; Ḥanukkah, eight day	Gen. 41:1–44:17 Num. 7:54–8:4	I Kings 7:40–50
2004 Jan. 3	Sa	9	Wa-yiggash	Gen. 44:18–47:27	Ezekiel 37:15–28
4	S	10	Fast of 10th of Ṭevet	Exod. 32:11–14 Exod. 34:1–10 (morning and afternoon)	Isaiah 55:6–56:8 (afternoon only)
10	Sa	16	Wa-yeḥi	Gen. 47:28–50:26	I Kings 2:1–12
17	Sa	23	Shemot	Exod. 1:1–6:1	Isaiah 27:6–28:13 Isaiah 29:22–23 *Jeremiah 1:1–2:3*

Italics are for Sephardi Minhag.

Index